THE INTERNATIONAL ENCYCLOPEDIA OF EDUCATION

SECOND EDITION

THE

INTERNATIONAL ENCYCLOPEDIA OF EDUCATION

SECOND EDITION

Volume 10

Editors-in-Chief

TORSTEN HUSÉN

University of Stockholm, Sweden

T. NEVILLE POSTLETHWAITE

University of Hamburg, Germany

PERGAMON

UK	Elsevier Science Ltd, The Boulevard, Langford Lane, Kidlington, Oxford OX5 1GB, England
USA	Elsevier Science Inc, 660 White Plains Road, Tarrytown, New York 10591-5153,USA
JAPAN	Elsevier Science Japan, Tsunashima Building Annex, 3-20-12 Yushima, Bunkyoku, Tokyo 113, Japan

---

Copyright © 1994 Elsevier Science Ltd

All rights reserved. No part of this publication may be reproduced, stored in any retrieval system or transmitted in any form or by any means: electronic, electrostatic, magnetic tape, mechanical, photocopying, recording or otherwise, without permission in writing from the publishers.

REF. LB 15 I569 1994

Second edition 1994

Library of Congress Cataloging in Publication Data
International encyclopedia of education (2nd ed.)
The international encyclopedia of education / editors-in-chief Torsten Husén, T. Neville Postlethwaite. — 2nd ed.
p. cm.
1. Education—Dictionaries. 2. Education—Research—Dictionaries. I. Husén, Torsten, 1916– II. Postlethwaite, T. Neville.
LB15.I569 1994
370'.3—dc20 94–3059

British Library Cataloguing in Publication Data
A catalogue record for this book is available from the British Library.

ISBN 0–08–041046–4 (cloth : set : alk. paper)

∞™ The paper used in this publication meets the minimum requirements of the American National Standard for Information Sciences—Permanence of Paper for Printed Library Materials, ANSI Z39.48–1984.

Printed in Great Britain by BPC Wheatons Ltd, Exeter

CONTENTS

HONORARY EDITORIAL ADVISORY BOARD

MALCOLM S ADISESHIAH
Madras Institute of Development Studies, Madras, India

BURTON R CLARK
University of California, Los Angeles, California, USA

GILBERT DE LANDSHEERE
University of Liège, Liège, Belgium

RICARDO DIEZ HOCHLEITNER
Fundación Santillana, Madrid, Spain

MICHAEL J DUNKIN
University of New South Wales, Oatley, New South Wales, Australia

ROBERT GLASER
University of Pittsburgh, Pittsburgh, Pennsylvania, USA

HEITOR GURGULINO DE SOUZA
United Nations University, Tokyo, Japan

ANN LIEBERMAN
Teachers College, Columbia University, New York, USA

NIKOLAI D NIKANDROV
Russian Academy of Education, Moscow, Russia

A HARRY PASSOW
Teachers College, Columbia University, New York, USA

GEORGE PSACHAROPOULOS
World Bank, Washington, DC, USA

LEE SHULMAN
Stanford University, Stanford, California, USA

COLIN TITMUS
University of Leeds, Leeds, UK

E A YOLOYE
University of Ibadan, Ibadan, Nigeria

EDITORIAL BOARD

DON ADAMS
University of Pittsburgh, Pittsburgh, Pennsylvania, USA

LORIN W ANDERSON
University of South Carolina, Columbia, South Carolina, USA

WILLIAM L BOYD
Pennsylvania State University, University Park, Pennsylvania, USA

MARTIN CARNOY
Stanford University, Stanford, California, USA

ERIK DE CORTE
University of Leuven, Leuven, Belgium

DONALD P ELY
Syracuse University, New York, USA

JOSEPH P FARRELL
Ontario Institute for Studies in Education, Toronto, Ontario, Canada

LILIAN G KATZ
ERIC/EECE, Urbana, Illinois, USA

JOHN P KEEVES
The Flinders University of South Australia, Bedford Park, South Australia, Australia

KENNETH KING
University of Edinburgh, Edinburgh, UK

GABRIELE LAKOMSKI
University of Melbourne, Parkville, Victoria, Australia

HENRY LEVIN
Stanford University, Stanford, California, USA

ARIEH LEWY
Tel Aviv University, Tel Aviv, Israel

SIXTEN MARKLUND
University of Stockholm, Stockholm, Sweden

JOHN U OGBU
University of California, Berkeley, California, USA

DENIS C PHILLIPS
Stanford University, Stanford, California, USA

TJEERD PLOMP
University of Twente, Enschede, The Netherlands

T NEVILLE POSTLETHWAITE
University of Hamburg, Hamburg, Germany

LAWRENCE J SAHA
The Australian National University, Canberra, ACT, Australia

ALBERT TUIJNMAN
University of Twente, Enschede, The Netherlands

HERBERT J WALBERG
University of Illinois at Chicago, Chicago, Illinois, USA

MARGARET C WANG
Temple University, Philadelphia, Pennsylvania, USA

FRANZ E WEINERT
Max Planck Institut für Psychologische Forschung, Munich, Germany

Social Studies Teacher Education

Many of the issues in the education of social studies teachers are those of teacher education generally. However, to the extent that beliefs and assumptions about the nature of social studies influence beliefs about how teachers ought to be prepared, teacher educators in social studies confront some unique problems as well. This entry begins with an overview of the debate about the meaning, scope, and purpose of social studies and then proceeds to an examination of the issues in social studies teacher education.

1. Unique Characteristics of Social Studies

One of the distinguishing characteristics of social studies has been the ongoing debate about the definition, scope, and nature of the field. Although history and geography have long been a part of the core elementary and secondary curricula of many countries, the term "social studies" did not appear until early in the twentieth century. It has been a source of controversy ever since.

One of the earliest references to social studies appeared in the 1916 report of the Committee on Social Studies of the Commission on the Reorganization of Secondary Education in the United States (see Saxe 1991). In that report, the term referred collectively to history and the social sciences. The report also emphasized the role of social studies in preparing young people to be participating citizens in a democratic society. Since that time, educators in the United States, and increasingly in other countries, have debated whether students ought to study history and the social sciences, particularly geography and civics, as separate disciplines primarily for the purpose of gaining academic knowledge, or whether the emphasis should be on interdisciplinary study drawing from history, the social sciences, and the humanities, with its focus on the understanding and solution of social problems.

This debate about the meaning of social studies is about how young people are to be socialized to the political and social systems of their countries. Advocates of an interdisciplinary approach are generally reformers seeking to find ways to involve citizens in political decisions. The underlying assumption is that such citizen involvement will help shape a society that is more just and equitable. Those who advocate the study of separate disciplines tend to be more concerned with socializing youth to society as it is. In this approach, the emphasis is on appreciation of the country's heritage and its existing political system, not on changing that system. While these two approaches are not mutually exclusive, advocates of both positions have very clear and fixed conceptions of the country's needs and of what it means to be a citizen. Practitioners, however, tend to find this debate irrelevant to their concerns and to teach as they have been taught, thus making reform and change in the teaching of social studies a slow process.

In the United Kingdom, this debate emerged in the early 1970s. With the lowering of the voting age, the raising of the school-leaving age, and increasing immigration from Commonwealth nations, there was pressure for a rethinking of political and social education. The Programme for Political Education (PPE), launched in 1974, emphasized an issues-based approach to social education, a major departure from the traditional academic study of the disciplines. The PPE promoted activity-based teaching and learning, and the acquisition and development of skills needed for political participation (Lister 1991).

In many African nations, the concern with shaping an appropriate social education developed as countries gained their independence in the 1960s (Merryfield and Muyanda-Mutebi 1991). Eleven countries meeting in Mombasa, Kenya in 1968 agreed to a form of social studies which stresses an interdisciplinary problem-solving approach. The goals which emerged from the Mombasa Conference included an emphasis on understanding the environment and the effects of human interaction with the environment. These goals continue to be advocated by the African Social and Environmental Studies Programme (ASESP), formerly the African Social Studies Programme, of which 17 nations are members.

On the other hand, education in Saudi Arabia is based on the assumption that Islam, rather than a secular democracy, is the guiding force (Al-Jabr 1991). This set of unifying values means that there is little debate about whether social education should be based on the disciplines, or adopt a problem-solving approach. The goals of the National Council for the Social Studies of Saudi Arabia emphasize the study of the traditional subjects of history, geography, and political and economic institutions. Mention is also made of the study of social problems, suggesting that the debate in other countries has influenced goals in Saudi Arabia.

2. Issues in Social Studies Teacher Preparation

In some countries, such as the United States and the member states of ASESP, the national and international social studies organizations advocate an interdisciplinary approach that concentrates on social issues. These organizations have a good deal of influence over curriculum developers and teacher educators who are likely to see the major task of social studies teacher education as preparing teachers to teach in ways consistent with this emphasis on social issues. Few teachers in any country have experienced the interdisciplinary problem-solving approach at the precollege level. In addition, their university experience has almost always been in the study of the separate disciplines for the sake of gaining academic knowledge. The main problem of social studies teacher education is how to enable teachers to teach differently from the ways in which they have been taught.

This problem is magnified by the conflicting messages received by novice teachers enrolled in teacher education programs with a social studies emphasis. These teacher education programs likely present an activity-oriented, problem-solving, interdisciplinary approach to the teaching of social studies. However, this approach is probably not reflected at school sites at which they are subsequently employed. Research has repeatedly demonstrated that the experience of student teaching and the attitudes and behavior of cooperating teachers have far more influence on beginning teachers than do university teacher preparation programs. Unless cooperating teachers use the interdisciplinary approach to the teaching of social studies, it is unlikely that the beginning teacher will adopt that approach.

In African nations, teacher educators, as well as teachers, often feel threatened by the relatively new problems-based approach advocated by ASESP (Obebe 1983, Nziramasanga 1989). The conflict is less between teacher education and classroom realities than it is between goals subscribed to at the national level and the teacher preparation that students are likely to experience.

The debate about the nature of social studies in teacher education is one aspect of a broader debate about the relationship between subject-matter knowledge and teaching effectiveness. While this is not a problem unique to the preparation of social studies teachers, it has special implications for teachers of social studies who must master multiple disciplines whether or not they are likely to teach from an interdisciplinary perspective. Calls for teacher education reform in the United States and the United Kingdom, as well as in other countries, focus on the need for greater academic knowledge among teachers. In social studies, this is supported by traditionalists who advocate the teaching of separate academic disciplines. Research has not, however, demonstrated a link between subject-matter knowledge and effective teaching.

3. *Models and Programs*

Various efforts at inservice teacher education have sought to change the way classroom teachers teach social studies. Following the development of the PPE in the United Kingdom in 1974, inservice programs and publications were created to help teachers teach for political literacy and develop in their students a commitment to procedural values and a critical stance toward education. Similar inservice projects have been undertaken in the United States, although these programs are not directed nationally but are the result of efforts at the school district level.

While these programs appear to have had some modest effect, the swing of both countries toward conservatism in the 1980s slowed, and even called into question, these inservice efforts. The emphasis promoted by policymakers in the United States and the United Kingdom has shifted away from the teaching of social studies toward the teaching of the academic disciplines. Concerns for social cohesion have led policymakers to advocate a cultural literary approach to social education.

Similar inservice efforts have been made in various African nations under the auspices of ASESP. Again, the results are modest—not surprising given the conservative nature of teaching and schooling. As noted above, teachers tend to teach as they have been taught. While change is slow, however, classroom teachers have the potential to be the best advocates of new teaching methods and new conceptions of curriculum. Experienced classroom teachers can provide the training ground for novice teachers who are informed about new approaches, but have not experienced them.

4. *Developments in the 1990s*

In the 1990s, the reflective inquiry approach to teacher education began to have an increasing influence on thinking about teacher education (Adler 1991). Based on the work of Schon (1987), Zeichner and Liston (1987), and others, this approach to teacher education is intended to help prospective teachers become better decision makers in schools and classrooms. Reflective inquiry, however, means different things to different proponents (Adler 1991). The term "critical inquiry" has been used by those who advocate helping teachers to develop a critical awareness of power relationships in education and the cultural and political implications of particular teaching practices.

This approach to teacher education is compatible with the social studies approach to the preparation of teachers of history and the social sciences. Both social studies and critical inquiry are based upon assumptions of participatory democracy and images of a more just and equitable society.

There is little evidence, however, that a critical inquiry approach to teacher education has had an impact on the classroom practice of the teachers who were schooled in this approach. Unless schools encourage and nurture critical inquiry among their staff, there is little reason to expect this approach to teacher education to have a widespread impact. Critical inquiry is nonetheless consistent with reform recommendations that teachers be treated as autonomous professionals, capable of contributing to important decisions about curriculum and about issues that have impact upon the classroom. If teacher education as critical inquiry and respect for teachers as professionals are seen as guiding principles for the way schools are managed, and not mere empty slogans, both curriculum and pedagogy may change in ways that are consistent with the goals of social studies.

Another promising aspect of teacher education has been the increased collaboration between university education programs and schools. In the United States, teacher education reform recommendations have encouraged the development of such partnerships. These partnerships are intended not only to socialize novice teachers more effectively into existing school settings, but also to develop collaborative arrangements to improve both the preparation and the ongoing work of teachers. Experienced teachers are given the opportunity to work with colleagues and university professors.

Such collaborations involve teachers co-teaching a methods course with university faculty. This opportunity enables preservice teachers to work at the university site with practicing teachers. It also gives practicing teachers an opportunity to think and share ideas about social studies curriculum and pedagogy.

Partnerships between classroom practitioners and university researchers are another aspect of this movement. Efforts to engage teachers as researchers are being made in several countries. Pioneering work in the United Kingdom and Australia (Lister 1991), as well as other countries, shows promise in breaking down the barriers between researchers and practitioners.

It is this sort of linking which can make possible the development of teacher preparation which has a real impact on the way teachers teach. By influencing the contexts in which practitioners work and to which beginning teachers are socialized, and by working directly with practitioners in making changes in teaching practices, both beginning and experienced teachers can actually participate in the sort of curriculum and pedagogy they are learning about at the university. This approach opens up the possibility of a social studies which puts into practice the goals of participatory and critical citizenship envisioned by the social studies reformers of the early twentieth century.

5. *Issues in the Field*

Social studies educators still face the major issue which emerged in the twentieth century, that of defining the field and reaching some consensus on its aims and scope. This overriding curriculum concern influences conceptions of how to educate social studies teachers. The issue is further confounded by the need to establish consensus not merely among teacher educators and curriculum developers, but practitioners as well. Efforts to work closely with partnership schools in the preparation of teachers form one important aspect of this move toward coherence.

Social studies educators and teacher educators must respond to international movements and issues. The aim of social studies is to prepare young people to be effective, informed citizens. In the light of both growing global interdependence and national fragmentation, this purpose must be kept under constant review. Furthermore, the questions of what it means to be a citizen and to what institutions loyalties are owed should be reassessed. In a changing world these are difficult questions. Moreover, one should query whether the Western ideals of participatory democracy are to be taken as guiding principles for non-Western nations. In short, the fundamental question confronting social studies teachers and teacher educators is, what do students need to know to live in a rapidly changing world, and how can teachers best be prepared to meet those needs?

References

Adler S A 1991a The reflective practitioner and the curriculum of teacher education. *J. Educ. for Teaching* 17(2): 139–50

Al-Jabr S M 1990 Social education in Saudi Arabia. *Soc. Educ.* 54(2): 109–10

Lister I 1991 Research on social studies and citizenship education in England. In: Shaver J (ed.) 1991

Merryfield M, Muyanda-Mutebi P 1991 Research on social studies in Africa. In: Shaver J (ed.) 1991

Nziramasanga C T 1989 Social studies curriculum development in Zimbabwe. *Int. J. Soc. Educ.* 4(2): 44–52

Obebe B 1983 Social studies in the secondary school curriculum in Nigeria. *Indiana Soc. Stud. Q.* 36(2): 26–32

Saxe D W 1991 *Social Studies in Schools: A History of the Early Years*. State University of New York Press, Albany, New York

Schon D A 1987 *Educating the Reflective Practitioner: Toward a New Design for Teaching and Learning in the Professions*. Jossey-Bass, San Francisco, California

Zeichner K M, Liston D P 1987 Teaching student teachers to reflect. *Harv. Educ. Rev.* 57(1): 23–48

Further Reading

Adler S A 1991b The education of social studies teachers. In: Shaver J (ed.) 1991

Banks J A, Parker W C 1990 Social studies teacher education. In: Houston W R (ed.) 1990 *Handbook of Research on Teacher Education*. Macmillan, New York

Shaver J (ed.) *Handbook of Research on Social Studies Teaching and Learning*. Macmillan, New York

Torney-Purta J 1991 Cross-national research in social studies. In: Shaver J (ed.) 1991

S. A. Adler

Socialization

Socialization, in its broadest sense, is the process whereby individuals become members of society or members of sectors of society. It is concerned with how individuals adopt, or do not adopt, the values, customs, and perspectives of the surrounding culture or subcultures.

The interactive nature of socialization, that is, the interaction of values, customs, and perspectives on individuals as well as the adaptation of those values, customs, and perspectives as a result of negotiation among members of groups, has made it fertile ground for the social sciences, but especially for psychologists and sociologists either working alone or in combination as social psychologists. Each discipline, however, has tended to approach the subject from a different angle. Psychologists have focused on how individuals learn and, in particular, on stages of development, whereas sociologists have focused on the relationships into which individuals move.

The first section in this entry elaborates on the brief definition of socialization provided in this introduction. This is followed by a review of the antecedents to current theories of socialization and how they relate to more general sociological theory, a review of current theory and research on socialization, and an overview of the issues raised by research into the different contexts in which socialization takes place. Section 5 is an examination of the application to the field of education of studies into socialization, both in the sense of schooling as a socializing context and as regards the effects on schooling of other contexts such as the family.

While the discussion of the antecedents to current theory embraces psychological, anthropological, and sociological theory, most of the discussion of current theory and its application to education draws upon the sociological tradition.

1. An Elaboration of the Concept of Socialization

Bush and Simmons (1981) comment that distinctions between the concepts of maturation, development, and socialization are stressed in sociological work on socialization. Research into maturation processes and developmental stages has, however, contributed to research and theory on socialization.

Bush and Simmons also comment that maturation is depicted as entailing a more or less automatic unfolding of biological potential in a predictable sequence, while development is viewed as a set of sequential changes from simple to more complex structures within the boundaries set by both biological and social structures. Both the concepts of development and socialization stress an interaction between individual behavior and the environment, but socialization does not necessarily entail sequential change from simple to complex structures.

Wentworth (1980 p. 83) has defined socialization as: "the activity that confronts and lends structure to the entry of nonmembers into an already existing world or a sector of that world."

As described by Musgrave (1987), embodied in this definition of the concept of socialization are the implications that it is a crucial link between the existing culture of a group and its members, that it can refer to processes at many levels, and that there is no assumption that the norms learned are believed or must be obeyed, that is, the norms are not necessarily internalized and change is therefore possible. This final implication allows for resistance to socializing forces, acknowledges that individuals may construct their own norms and, consequently, makes central to the study of socialization the issue of deviance, that is, behavior which does not meet existing norms.

Socialization is therefore interactive: the values, customs, and perspectives of cultures and subcultures influence how individuals behave but do not necessarily determine that behavior. Cultural influences and individual patterns of development both require consideration.

Related to this, Gecas (1981) notes that the concept of socialization has two fairly distinct meanings in sociology, both of which are valid and necessary for an adequate conceptualization. One stresses the individual's adaptation and conformity to societal requirements, and the other emphasizes the individual's development into a self-assertive, distinct human being. Gecas comments that the changes that individuals undergo become sociologically relevant in the context of organized social relationships and, in this sense, there is a "membership" component to socialization:

> This component of socialization is most evident in the concept of identification, one of the key processes in socialization. Two aspects of socialization are relevant here: identification *of* and identification *with* . . . Identification *of* deals with the establishment of identities, that is, the determination of who one is and who the others are in the situation. Identification *with* refers to the emotional and psychological attachment that one has with some person or group. (Gecas 1981 p. 166)

Musgrave (1987 p. 3) has also referred to socialization as forward looking and to the effects of prior socializing experiences:

> The outcomes are important to those involved, both to those responsible for the continuity of groups, that is those with some power, and to those being socialised, whether unconsciously or because they hope to become members of some group. Sociologists often speak of anticipatory socialisation to highlight this forward-looking aspect. What has, however, to be noted is that prior socialisation may prepare potential members of groups well or less well for further experiences.

Individuals, during the course of their lives, do not experience one process of socialization but are subjected to many. Agents of socialization include wider cultural influences, families, and the formal organizations in which individuals work or learn (schools, military academies, prisons, public service bureaucracies, and the like). Sieber and Gordon (1981) categorize these socializing organizations into "total institutions," such as prisons, military academies, and boarding schools, and organizations that are less total in their regimes such as schools, summer camps, and the like. Goffman (1961) discusses the pervasive socializing influences of institutions with long duration and high intensity compared with other less pervasive or intensive institutions, of which schools are one example. Focusing on the contexts in which socialization takes place requires that special attention be given to the social structural features of these situations, such as patterns of interaction, group composition, and other group features like size and boundary permeability (see Gecas 1981).

Gecas comments that contexts of socialization vary in scope and duration. After Wheeler (1966), a distinction can be made between "developmental socialization systems" whose purpose is the training, education, or further socialization of individuals, and "re-socialization systems" whose purpose is to correct some deficiency in earlier socialization. A distinction has also been made (see Brim and Wheeler 1966) between "primary" and "secondary" socialization: the former refers to roles learned earlier in life and the latter to those that occur later. While the temporal distinction has some usefulness, Musgrave (1987) warns against the belief that primary socialization is necessarily more permanent than secondary and has warned that these distinctions can lead to a deterministic view, in that actors are seen to be socialized and cannot create patterns of behavior to meet needs.

2. Antecedents to Current Theories of Socialization

Bush and Simmons (1981) have traced the historical antecedents to current theory on socialization and have referred to the classical works of Freud, Piaget, Cooley, George Herbert Mead, Margaret Mead, Benedict, Erikson, and Mannheim.

Freud's (1961, originally published in 1930) psychosexual stage theory, and in particular his theory of the three inborn structures of the mind or personality (the id, the ego, and the superego), provided one of the most influential interpretations of the socialization process. The development of the ego and the superego are seen as the basic tasks of socialization, and identification, that is, the act of becoming like something or someone is the key process. Each psychosexual stage identified by Freud is defined by where and upon whom an individual's libidinal energy is cathected at a given time.

Piaget's (1970) theory of development, which is concerned with the progressive construction and reconstruction of cognitive structures as the child develops, has also been influential in the field of socialization. According to Piaget, the child actively assimilates and organizes new information according to existing cognitive structures, and this produces the cognitive reorganization that constitutes the various stages of development outlined in his theory.

The work of Cooley (1964) and Mead (1934) on the emergence of the self through social interaction, and in particular their distinction of the "I" and "me," is also central to socialization, as is the work of Mead (1928) and Benedict (1938) on the ways in which the culture of a society can affect the character and outcomes of life transitions.

Erikson (1950), who conceived of eight ages of man, with each stage having its specific development task that must be accomplished for individuals to progress to the next stage, provides one of the most influential frameworks to deal specifically with the issue of socialization over the whole life span. Mannheim (1952) focuses on the effects of generations as a source of social change and as a potential influence on the socialization process.

Bush and Simmons (1981) argue that these very diverse classical theories have shaped the themes or raised points of contention that continue to pervade the study of socialization. In particular, they refer to the issues of continuity or discontinuity of processes of socialization and the universality of socialization processes over time and space.

Musgrave (1987), from a sociological perspective, has also reviewed past theories of socialization. He has argued that sociological theory, as applied to socialization, has followed two main paths. The first is the "organic" approach, which sees society as a network of interrelated positions filled by individuals who are in agreement about how they should interact. The key concept in this approach is structure, which is analyzed in terms of roles and statuses within institutions. The second is the "conflict" approach, which analyzes society in terms of groups whose interests conflict. The key concepts are logically conflict and interests, but power is also important. Both of these approaches have been used to analyze social behavior and, in particular, socialization at the societal and interpersonal levels.

Musgrave comments that until the 1960s the major tradition in considering socialization was the organic approach at the societal level. Sociologists examined how individuals became social beings by learning the different roles attached to positions they were expected to move through. As examples of this approach, Musgrave refers to the classical work of Margaret Mead, Durkheim, and Parsons. As Musgrave has reported, this approach has been criticized on the grounds that the logic tends to be teleological (a particular effect implies a particular cause), there is scant attention paid to issues of conflict and change, and, mainly because of this, the approach, knowingly or not, supports a conservative ideology.

Musgrave notes that since the 1960s some sociologists have worked at the societal level but from a conflict approach. The main emphasis of these writers has been on the way social groups with different interests come into conflict and on the results of that conflict. Musgrave refers to the work of sociologists both within the Marxist tradition and outside that tradition. Musgrave comments that there have been difficulties with both arms of this approach. He notes the internecine squabbles of the Marxist sociologists about what is true doctrine and the fact that Marxist predictions have not come to pass, and he notes theoretical and methodological problems with the approach of the non-Marxist sociologists.

Musgrave argues that it was also in the 1960s that greater emphasis was placed on interpersonal interaction, and he refers to the pioneering works of Goffman, Weber, Husserl, Schutz, and Berger and Luckman. Like societal theories, the interpersonal approach developed in both the organic and conflict traditions. Musgrave notes in fact that the work on symbolic interactionism, which focuses on the ways actors construct meanings in interaction, work usually associated with George Herbert Mead, has been applied to both organic and conflict theories

Examples of work in the organic tradition alone include the culture and personality theorists such as Margaret Mead, whose work examined the links between societal structure and personality, and the ethnomethodologists such as Garfinkel, who studied the ways in which people come to perceive and produce everyday interaction (see, e.g., Garfinkel 1967). Examples of work at the interpersonal level described by Musgrave and conducted within the conflict tradition include the work of Blau (1964) and Homans (1961) on exchange theory. In the view of these theorists, society is a network of transactions or exchanges carried out by explicit or implicit bargaining.

Musgrave comments that work at the interpersonal level has also been subjected to criticism at the theoretical and methodological level.

Musgrave concludes that each of the four approaches has helped the gradual clarification of ideas about social interaction but each has theoretical weaknesses. He argues therefore that there is a need for a unifying approach:

> In it emphasis is put upon the actor as a potentially creative subject who, depending upon how power is structured within his career, constructs rather than reconstructs sometimes cognitive, but particularly moral knowledge, as this is communicated to him both through language and other cues. (Musgrave 1987 p. 23)

3. Current Theory and Research into Socialization

Bush and Simmons (1981) have reviewed current theory and research into socialization and have argued that underlying virtually all of the contemporary sociological views is the assumption that socialization is a continuing, lifelong process, although some writers would argue that change over time is anomalous, while others see it as a logical extension of values, norms, and the like that are formed in childhood and adolescence.

Bush and Simmons refer to the contemporary work that has revolved around the processes of role acquisition, role conflict, and role transitions, including role loss. Among the issues that have been addressed in this research have been an investigation of the stressful effects of role discontinuity, the effects on stress reduction of anticipatory socialization, the effects of the nature of role changes (do role changes that involve gains have the same effects as those involving losses?), the effects on role transition of rites of passage and being "off-time," the effects of lack of clarity on role consensus, and the effects on individuals of role conflict.

Bush and Simmons also refer to three general perspectives to socialization throughout the lifetime that have emerged: life-stage theories, lifespan developmental psychology, and life-course orientation.

4. Contexts of Socialization

Gecas (1981), while acknowledging that the number of contexts of socialization in a complex society is almost limitless, examines in some detail five contexts: the family, school, peer group, occupational setting, and radical resocialization settings. Zimmer and Witnov (1985) referred to a number of agents of socialization: culture, nations, family, formal organization, technology (television and computers), literature, and leaders. They examined in some detail three of these agents: culture, the family, and formal organization.

In Sect. 4 below a brief reference is made to the major themes that are present in theory and research with respect to three of these contexts: the family, peer groups, and occupational organizations. Section 5 deals separately with issues concerned with education and socialization.

4.1 The Family Context

Both Gecas and Zimmer and Witnov comment that the family is the context most closely associated with the topic of socialization because as an institution its major function is the socialization and care of children, both for membership of the family group and membership of the larger society. They argue that, because relationships within a family are usually intimate, intensive, and relatively enduring, socialization which takes place there is usually the most pervasive and consequential.

The issues raised in research and theory concerning socialization in the family have referred both to relationships within families and to the place of the family in society. Among the issues raised in the former are: the effects of the social organization of the family and in particular of the distribution of power within it; the processes of socialization, such as modeling, role-playing, and reinforcement, and the outcomes of these processes; the development in children of sex role identity, aggression, morality, and achievement; and the effects on socialization of different parental styles, family size and configuration, and single-parent families. With regard to the place of the family in the larger system of social institutions, one of the most common issues addressed in research and theory is the location of the family in the social class system.

4.2 The Childhood Peer Group Context

Gecas (1981) notes that the most important feature of the peer group is that it is a voluntary association, which means that boundaries of such groups are fluid. The peer group is also relatively independent of parental control, and consequently can be the context for the development of deviant or delinquent behavior. Gecas notes that association in peer groups is between status equals, and interaction is therefore more likely to be based on egalitarian norms, although informal status hierarchies, typically based on achievement in activities valued by the group, do develop. A third feature of such groups, noted by Gecas, is that they are typically segregated by sex.

Gecas argues that socialization in peer groups is characterized by its effect on three broad areas of the child's development: the development and validation of the self, the development of competence through role taking, and the acquisition of knowledge not gained in the family. The key to the importance of the peer group in these areas lies in the friendship bonds that are formed.

4.3 The Occupational Context

While the primary role of occupational organizations is not socialization, the structure of occupational settings can affect individual attitudes and values. Moreover, most large organizations have processes of induction and orientation which are designed to socialize new recruits into that organization.

Robbins et al. (1986) have described the process of occupational socialization as one of adaptation which takes place when an individual passes from outside the organization to the role of an inside member. Organizational socialization attempts to adapt the new employee to the organization's culture by conveying how things are done. From the perspective of the organization, acceptance by the employee of the organization's pivotal standards is imperative for individual performance and organizational stability. Nevertheless individuals vary in the degree to which they conform totally to the traditions and customs of the organization.

Gecas (1981) notes that occupational settings vary considerably with regard to a wide range of features such as power and authority relationships, worker participation, bureaucratization, and work complexity. One important distinction which tends to emerge in large organizations is between labor and management: workers in management are more likely to identify with the organization and nonmanagerial workers are more likely to identify with each other and may come into conflict with those in management.

It has been suggested that the conditions experienced in work can affect attitudes and values of workers. Kohn and his associates argue that certain structural features of work, such as the amount of autonomy or complexity, can give rise to values of autonomy or conformity (see, for example, Kohn and Schooler 1978). Kanter (1977) argues that the adaptation of individuals to their work situation and their degree of commitment to work is a function of their location on three structural dimensions: the opportunity structure, the power structure, and the social composition of peer clusters.

As Gecas (1981) comments, work settings, like other socialization contexts, are affected by the larger society within which they exist. He notes that much of the sociological literature has dealt with the alienating effects of capitalism and he draws attention to the pioneering work of Marx and the research of Bowles and Gintis (1976).

5. Socialization and the School Context

The school, like the family, has an explicit socialization function. The extent of this function in the context of schooling is, however, more controversial and touches on the very nature of schooling. While it is accepted that schools have responsibilities in the affective domain as well as the academic domain, the extent of the former responsibilities are unclear and in constant flux. These responsibilities are not only controversial in the sense that they overlap with the responsibilities of the other agencies, particularly the family, but it is often argued that society loads schools with a range of responsibilities that go well beyond their academic mandate and ultimately detract from that mandate. The delicacy of these issues is not new. For example, the place of religious education in schools proved one of the most controversial issues in the development of schooling in many countries, and in the late twentieth century the teaching of sex education in schools has evoked mixed responses. There are parents who hold that this is an area of responsibility for the family, not the school.

5.1 Schooling and Other Socialization Contexts

While schooling is viewed as the major educational context for children, a great deal of education takes place outside school, and in particular in the family.

In fact, the publication of the Coleman Report in the United States (Coleman et al. 1966) and subsequent confirmatory reports or reviews (see Averch et al. 1972, Jencks et al. 1972) led to the belief that schools make little difference in educational achievement, and it is the social status of the students' families that account for most of the difference in achievement levels. Subsequently, these findings have been challenged both on methodological and theoretical grounds and it is generally accepted that schooling has a greater effect on student achievement than was originally acknowledged. Research into the characteristics of effective schools has been one of the growth areas of educational research in the late 1980s and the 1990s.

Nonetheless, by the time children go to school they will have learned a great deal that will affect their schooling experience. Kerckhoff (1986) notes, for example, that families contribute greatly to the motivational and cognitive skill levels exhibited by their children, and they continue to influence those qualities throughout schooling. Important aspects of the family that contribute to these influences include parental expectations, cultural differences, social status differences, and parent–child interactions.

The cultural differences are evident both from within-nation studies and cross-nation studies. For example, research in Australia (see Sturman 1986) has consistently shown the higher educational aspirations of students whose backgrounds are from non-English-speaking countries. Similarly, Fuller et al. (1986) have argued that some of the differences between educational achievement levels in Japan and the United States can be attributed to the fact that elements of socialization in the Japanese family are more deeply agreed upon, less variable across parents, and more tightly coupled with the educational system.

Kerckhoff also draws attention to the important influence of peer groups on schooling, in particular because the organization of schooling ensures that students spend a great deal of time with their peers. He notes that friendship relations in school can affect educational aspirations and other aspects of the schooling process. (see *Student Friendships and Conflict in School*).

5.2 The Socializing Processes of Schooling

The socializing processes of schools can be overt or hidden. For example, teachers, because they tend to come from a similar social background, may unknowingly pass on to students certain attitudes and values. Other aspects of schooling may be more open.

Gecas (1981) argues that the most conspicuous socialization process in the classroom is social reinforcement such as praise, blame, privileges, and particularly the allocation of grades. From a review of the research, Gecas suggests that teachers reward students who conform to the social order of the school with higher grades. Thus, personality characteristics such as drive to achieve, citizenship, dependability, perseverance, and punctuality may be rewarded more highly than actual achievement. Gecas also refers to the research which suggests that teacher expectations of students can become important predictors of student achievement.

Gecas commented that students are, however, not necessarily passive recipients of the pressures they experience. They may engage in activities that alter these experiences to make them more favorable to their interests, such as the avoidance of failure by nonparticipation in certain activities, or participating but using the minimum of effort.

5.3 Schooling and the Larger Social Setting

One of the more influential theories that has been applied to education and which touches on the socialization effects of schooling is the idea that the educational system reproduces a system of knowledge based on the class relations which exist outside schools (Bourdieu and Passeron 1977). However, as Musgrave (1987) reports, critics argue that the theory does not explain how the process occurs at the interpersonal level and that, in fact, reproduction does not always take place. Musgrave comments that one way of conceptualizing this failure has been to examine resistance in education: both teachers and students can become alienated from a system where they are asked to do what they may not wish to do and the result of the alienation can be resistance.

Analysis of the links between education and the economy has tended to argue a structural correspondence, that is, that the educational system perpetuates the economic order (see Bowles and Gintis 1976). However, Musgrave (1987) notes that the critics of the correspondence theory point, to the difficulty in establishing the direction of causation and hence to the failure of the theory to address the mechanism of influence (see *Contemporary Sociological Theories of Education*).

6. Conclusion

Research and theory on socialization covers a very wide area, ranging from micro studies of interpersonal relationships to macro studies of societal structures and cultural influences. The contexts of socialization range from the wider culture to the family, peer group, and occupational settings. This entry has attempted to map the area and draw attention to the complexity of the subject matter.

References

Averch H S, Carroll J, Donaldson T S, Kiesling H J, Pincus J 1972 *How Effective is Schooling*? Rand Corporation, Santa Monica, California

Benedict R 1938 Continuities and discontinuities in cultural conditioning. *Psychiatry* 1: 161–67

Blau P 1964 *Exchange and Power in Social Life*. Wiley, New York
Bourdieu P, Passeron J C 1977 *Reproduction in Education, Society and Culture*. Sage, London
Bowles S, Gintis H 1976 *Schooling in Capitalist America*. Routledge and Kegan Paul, London
Brim O G, Wheeler S (eds.) 1966 *Socialization After Childhood: Two Essays*. Wiley, New York
Bush D M, Simmons R G 1981 Socialization processes over the life course. In: Rosenberg M, Turner R H(eds.) 1981 *Social Psychology: Sociological Perspectives*. Basic Books, New York
Coleman J S et al. 1966 *Equality of Educational Opportunity*. US Government Printing Office, Washington, DC
Cooley C H 1964 [1902] *Human Nature and the Social Order*. Scribner's, New York
Erikson E H 1950 *Childhood and Society*. Norton, New York
Freud S 1961 [1930] *Civilization and Its Discontents*. Dorsey, New York
Fuller B, Holloway S D, Azuma H, Hess R D, Kashiwagi K 1986 Contrasting achievement rules: Socialization of Japanese children at home and in school. In: Kerckhoff A C(ed.) 1986 *Research in Sociology of Education and Socialization: A Research Annual*, Vol. 6. JAI Press, Greenwich, Connecticut
Garfinkel H 1967 *Studies in Ethnomethodology*. Prentice-Hall, Englewood Cliffs, New Jersey
Gecas V 1981 Contexts of socialization. In: Rosenberg M, Turner R H (eds.) 1981 *Social Psychology: Sociological Perspectives*. Basic Books, New York
Goffman E 1961 *Asylums: Essays on the Social Situation of Mental Patients and Other Inmates*. Doubleday/Anchor, New York
Homans G C 1961 *Social Behavior: Its Elementary Forms*. Harcourt, Brace and World, New York
Jencks C et al. 1972 *Inequality: A Reassessment of the Effect of Family and Schooling in America*. Basic Books, New York
Kanter R M 1977 *Men and Women of the Corporation*. Basic Books, New York
Kerckhoff A C 1986 Family position, peer influences, and schooling. In: Richardson J G (ed.) 1986 *Handbook of Theory and Research for the Sociology of Education*. Greenwood Press, New York
Kohn M L, Schooler C 1978 The reciprocal effects of the substantive complexity of work and intellectual flexibility: A longitudinal assessment. *Am. J. Sociol.* 84: 24–52
Mannheim K 1952 The problem of generations. In: Mannheim K (ed.) 1952 *Essays in the Sociology of Knowledge*. Routledge and Kegan Paul, London
Mead G H 1934 *Mind, Self, and Society*, University of Chicago Press, Chicago, Illinois
Mead M 1928 *Coming of Age in Samoa*. Morrow, New York
Musgrave P W 1987 *Socialising Contexts: The Subject in Society*. Allen and Unwin, Sydney
Piaget J 1970 *Structuralism*. Basic Books, New York
Robbins S P, Low P S, Mourell M P1986 *Managing Human Resources*. Prentice-Hall, Sydney
Sieber R T, Gordon A J (eds.) 1981 *Children and Their Organizations: Investigations in American Culture*. Hall, Boston, Massachusetts
Sturman A 1986 *Immigrant Australians and Education*, Australian Education Review No. 22. ACER, Hawthorn
Wentworth W M 1980 *Context and Understanding: An Inquiry into Socialization Theory*. Elsevier, New York
Wheeler S 1966 The structure of formally organized socialization settings. In: Brim O G, Wheeler S (eds.) 1966
Zimmer J M, Witnov S J 1985 Socialization. In: Husén T, Postlethwaite T N (eds.) 1985 *The International Encyclopedia of Education*, 1st edn. Pergamon Press, Oxford

Further Reading

Goslin D A (ed.) 1973 *Handbook of Socialization Theory and Research*. Rand McNally, Chicago, Illinois
Kerckhoff A C (ed.) 1983 *Research in Sociology of Education and Socialization: A Research Annual*, Vol. 4. JAI Press, Greenwich, Connecticut

A. Sturman

Sociology of Adult Education

While the sociology of school education is a well-developed study, sociological studies of adult education are much more infrequent. This entry seeks to demonstrate the complexities of the concept of adult education and, thereafter, to examine ways by which it might be analyzed and in the process will refer to some well-known works in studies of children's education.

There are many ways in which adult education differs from school education, but perhaps the most obvious sociological difference is that whereas school education occurs almost entirely in that sector of society called "education," this is not the case for adult education: adults are educated in college, in their work, in their leisure, at home, in and by a variety of different organizations, and so on. Educators of children are schoolteachers, but educators of adults might be adult educators, university teachers, human resource developers, vocational educators, trainers, or even political activists seeking to educate the general public about specific political concerns. Hence, it may be seen that there are many fields of practice in which the teaching and learning process occurs among adults, but many of them are not within the education sector of society.

Adult education is operationally defined here as the institutionalized processes of teaching and learning that exist for those individuals who are regarded as adults, irrespective of the sector of society in which it occurs. Such a broad and imprecise definition suggests that the boundaries of the concept are blurred, which reflects the social reality. Indeed, as societies have become more complex through the growth in technological knowledge, the division of labor, and the subsequent creation of pluralism, so the education of adults has expanded to perform educative functions in each of the different social institutions.

Following Coombs and Ahmed (1974) (see also LaBelle 1982), the education of adults may be broadly divided into three categories: (a) formal, where the education occurs in educational institutions, for example, schools, vocational schools, colleges, and universities; (b) nonformal, where the education takes place outside of such organizations, for example, in the community, or popular education; and (c) informal, where the education occurs through personal interaction or participation. While this distinction does not adequately categorize adult education, it does provide a framework for the first three sections of the following discussion, although it is recognized that some forms may be located in more than one division, for example, adult basic education, or study circles. In Sect. 4 the emergence of distance education is taken as an example of a form of education for adults which reflects late modernity. In Sect. 5 some of the dominant theoretical areas of study that have been addressed by adult education scholars will be discussed, and in the final section the professionalization of adult education will be examined.

1. Formal Adult Education

Formal education for adults is conducted within an organizational context, with there being a variety of providers. Obviously the state is a major provider of formal adult education, which may be either vocational or nonvocational, but there are others, such as employers, professional organizations, trades unions, private and voluntary educational agencies, and voluntary agencies such as the churches. By definition, educational providers organize and run educational programs for adults, although they do not necessarily have to be the funding agency—often the providers act as agents of the state, although others are independent, financially and otherwise.

While it is possible to find similarities between the sociological analyses of formal adult education and school education, it would be simplistic to suggest that the two were the same, as the following example demonstrates. Governments with right-wing political ideologies have influenced the curriculum of schools so that they include a greater emphasis on science and technology, but this change in curriculum has not had a great effect upon the structures of schooling. However, in some instances the implementation of the same policies in the education of adults has resulted in continuing professional education and liberal adult education being almost totally separated from each other and regarded as different forms of education, with the former being treated as important and centrally funded, while the latter is regarded as a leisure-time pursuit to be followed at the learners' own expense in their own free time. Such a division is rather artificial: all forms of education can assist learners to develop self-confidence which may have effects on both work and leisure, and some people may learn a subject, such as a foreign language, as a leisure-time pursuit, but then use it in the course of employment. However, the fact that this separation has occurred illustrates that formal education funded by the state, whether it be for children or adults, is controlled and functions to produce the outcomes desired by government. Such conclusions allow for Marxist analyses of adult education, of which there have been a limited number (e.g., Youngman 1986).

It could be argued that all technological societies need a highly skilled and knowledgeable work force and that one of the functions of formal adult education is to produce this. By contrast, it would be possible to argue, following Althusser (1971), that the elite ruling capitalist class controls the apparatus of state and that it uses the formal education of adults to ensure that there is a highly skilled work force that will perpetuate the capitalist system. Hence the emphasis on vocational education to this end, rather than the liberal adult education which might produce articulate adults who might question the whole system.

All organizations operate systems of control, so that the education provided by the churches, and some other similar organizations, is designed either to initiate or socialize the participants into the culture and beliefs of the organization, or else to prepare the workers in the organization to be more efficient in what they do. This form of education is thus an agency of cultural, or subcultural, hegemony in the sense Gramsci used the concept, since it does not involve physical coercion (Entwistle 1979 p. 12). This interpretation is applicable to a great deal of adult educational activity. Consequently, it can be argued that formal education for adults serves as a mechanism of cultural reproduction (Bourdieu and Passeron 1977), whether it occurs at the level of the state or the organization.

In the United Kingdom there are only a few voluntary organizations, such as the Workers' Educational Association and the Women's Institute, which seek to offer education for personal and social development, much of which is a leisure-time pursuit, and it is significant that the right-wing government of the 1980s restricted the funding of both liberal adult education and the Workers' Educational Association, and their future was immediately placed in jeopardy.

Personal and social development is also the theme of much adult education for women (Thompson 1983) and ethnic minorities (Cassara 1990). In these instances, adult education can be viewed as an instrument of empowerment, providing a sense of identity and purpose for those who are underprivileged and oppressed.

Some forms of education may, therefore, be viewed as dysfunctional, and in these instances those who exercise power seek to control or to curtail these activities. It may thus be concluded that the formal education of adults is recognized by those who exercise power as a potentially significant political phenomenon, which is precisely the argument put forward by Freire (1972a), who claimed that education could be both oppressive and liberating. There are two distinct sociological paradigms, the functionalist and the conflict, which have been used by scholars analyzing formal adult education, and when contrasted in this way it is easy to place value judgments upon it, from whatever ideological persuasion it is analyzed.

One of the common criticisms of functionalism is that it implies an unchanging society, whereas conflict is trying to generate change. However, it is also possible to argue that, although there is a tendency to inertia in bureaucratic organizations, including the state, one of the aims of the formal education of adults is to produce change and through the implementation of the government policy of supporting vocational education, this is being achieved. Adult educators, who tend to adopt a more individualistic and psychological approach to education, often claim that education produces change agents, but clearly the education of adults is being used by government as an agent of social change (moreover in accord with its own ideological predispositions) rather than individual change. There are similar examples, such as the use of formal adult education to acculturate immigrants to their new country, for example, in the United States, where Carlson (1987) called it "Americanization education" (see also Thomas 1991). Therefore, the education of adults in its formal sense is often an instrument in governmental policy. Griffin (1987) has provided the most complete analysis of adult education and social policy.

Since formal adult education is organizational it is hardly surprising that a great number of studies have been conducted about enrollment and participation. Many of these have tended to adopt a psychological approach because this has been the dominant perspective in United States adult education. Even so, there has been a general acceptance that adult education tends to be a middle-class pursuit, since it is middle-class people who have sufficient cultural capital to benefit from it (Bourdieu 1973). Courtney (1992), however, began to analyze participation in sociological terms and noted that some of the functions of participation included social mobility and the reinforcement of the cultural values acquired during the mobility process. In Sweden, in a continuation of the Malmö longitudinal study which was commenced in 1938, Tuijnman (1989) has shown that male attendance at adult education classes throughout the life span influences career prospects, job satisfaction, well-being, and, indirectly, earnings.

A great deal of the formal education of adults which has been discussed in this section may also be categorized as "education from above" (Jarvis 1985a); the same could not be claimed for the nonformal education of adults, which is much more a form of "education of equals."

2. *Nonformal Education of Adults*

Nonformal education for adults occurs outside of the formal educational institution and may be discovered in a variety of different forms, such as adult literacy, study circles, personal development training, health education, community development, and even social action campaigns. They are not all regarded as educational, but all have an educative function which may be intended or unintended. Many of these activities are fully institutionalized, even to the extent of there being departments and units of government for nonformal education in some countries, and in most societies in the world adult literacy is at least partially government funded. Nonformal education, therefore, is a recognized type of education occurring outside of the formal structures of the educational system. It need not take place in a classroom or even in a building, and it often involves a teacher and a small group of students.

Each of these types of nonformal education for adults is different and has varying social functions, some of which are discussed here. While the individual benefits of literacy may be self-evident, the social functions are less obvious. Its social significance, for instance, is acknowledged by the term "functional literacy," which tends to mean that individuals should acquire the necessary literacy skills to play their part in society, including its occupational and economic life. At this level, literacy programs can help individuals play a full part in society, but such programs serve other functions, for example, the modern state is bureaucratic and its language is writing, so it is important for the smooth operations of the state that its citizens can read and write. Indeed, illiterate citizens cannot read instructions, census returns, or even their tax returns, so that surveillance cannot be effective nor can these matters be recorded or controlled easily. Thus literacy education has a number of less frequently acknowledged functions. Perhaps the term "computer literacy" indicates how the concept is relative and changing as society becomes increasingly technological. This is more fully discussed by Levine (1986).

In certain democracies in the world, the state also provides financial support for nonformal liberal adult education in the form of study circles. The support of the state for such activities demonstrates something of the democratic nature of society, although the control of the funding indicates that there are limits placed on the democratic process. Where the support is enshrined within a legal framework, as it is for the study circles in Scandinavia, then liberal adult education may serve a democratic political function in society.

Nonformal adult education also occurs through the educative function of certain movements and pressure groups. The fact that these groups, however radical, see themselves as having an educative function indicates that they have not moved to a revolutionary position—for education is a prerevolutionary activity and, in this sense, while appearing to be radical, it acts as a focus for discontent and dissatisfaction within society. Hence the twofold nature of this educative exercise: (a) to focus and manage discontent, and (b) to perform a democratic function of educating people to be more active in changing their society. Many of these movements and groups are discussed in the adult education literature under the rubric of radical adult education (Lovett 1988). Occasionally, however, there is the recognition that community education must spill over into social, even revolutionary, action (Freire 1972b). There are many similar nonformal radical adult education groups performing the same functions and having aims in society, however, working primarily and peacefully for community development. These are generally classified as forms of community education (see Fletcher and Thompson 1980).

Additionally, nonformal education has been institutionalized in some professions through the use of trained mentors or teacher–practitioners whose work function is to train new recruits to occupations and professions in the workplace. In these instances, skilled practitioners receive some training in teaching techniques so that they can mentor new recruits. Naturally, this serves to ensure that practical knowledge and skills are transmitted to new recruits, but it also has a socializing function—new recruits are socialized into the current practices of the workplace without disrupting the work situation and so cultural reproduction is facilitated.

3. *Informal Education*

Some scholars might question the extent to which informal education is actually education, since it is individualistic, noninstitutionalized, and experiential. In this sense they seek to distinguish clearly between education and learning in a way that some adult education literature fails to do. However, there are institutionalized processes of teaching and learning that are more informal. For instance, there have been a number of studies of learning in the workplace (Marsick 1987), where the institutionalized supervisory role is educative.

The growth of the affective adult education movement, often regarding itself as experiential education and going under a number of names from encounter groups to human potential development, is certainly one major development in informal education, although it might also legitimately be categorized as nonformal education. This movement combines both educational and therapeutic functions of group dynamics. One of its major exponents has been Rogers (1983), and this movement has provided therapy, a sense of belonging, and even a sense of religious purpose to its participants. In this context, it is a form of sedative, and yet it also helps prevent the growth of alienation, which is a feature of contemporary society.

LaBelle (1982 p. 162) actually suggests that peer group participation and daily experience provide informal education situations. Certainly they provide the basis of informal learning, but the extent to which this is education is debatable. Certainly it is sometimes claimed that the mass media provide another form of ideological control and so there have been a number of papers advocating that critical reflection is an important part of the learning process (Jarvis 1985b, Brookfield 1987).

However, this does also indicate that as society has become more individuated there has been a corresponding emphasis upon individual and experiential learning. Indeed, there have been sociological studies of adult learning (Jarvis 1987) in which it has been recognized that learning is itself a social phenomenon. One of the major influences underlying this approach is the work of Mead (Strauss 1964). However, one other factor which has played a significant part in this emphasis on learning has been the work on reflection by Freire (1972a) and Habermas (1972), among others. Habermas, for instance, was instrumental in Mezirow's (1981) discussion of levels of reflective learning. This approach to adult learning has become central to much discussion and thinking about adult learning, and it also mirrors Giddens's (1979) emphasis on reflexivity as a crucial element in understanding human action in contemporary society. While some adult educators tend to relate their thinking about reflective learning and individual criticality to critical theory, it would be true to claim that there have been very few studies of adult education from this perspective, the exceptions being Collins (1991) and Hart (1992).

4. *Distance Education: An Educational Structure for Late Modernity*

Distance education has its beginnings at the end of the nineteenth century but it was in the mid twentieth century that this approach to education really developed. Although distance education has been utilized in school education, its expansion has taken place in the field of adult education. It may be regarded as a production of industrial capitalism. Peters (1988) has argued for many years that distance education is rationalistic, entrepreneurial, and involves the division of labor and the technological production and transmission of teaching materials. This argument can be extended to demonstrate that the teaching materials are now an educational commodity and sold in a market-place which is becoming increasingly international. Since the law of the market is operating, there is a danger that the weak will suffer—hence the possibility exists that a new form of cultural imperialism could reassert itself.

However, it is not only the production of teaching materials and the market-place that is significant about the distance-teaching universities for adults: they manifest the structural symbols of modernity. Giddens (1990) has suggested that late modernity is characterized by three elements: the separation of time and space; the development of disembedding mechanisms; and the reflexive appropriation of knowledge. It is suggested here that distance education epitomizes all three of these symbols: there is space–time distancing in teaching and learning, a disembedded structure, and reflective learning.

5. *Dominant Theoretical Perspectives*

Having analyzed four specific forms of adult education, this section is designed to examine from a sociological perspective some of the major adult educational theories that have arisen in literature, such as andragogy, self-directed learning, empowerment, and liberation.

Theoretical perspectives on adult education were emerging in the earlier part of the twentieth century—the first doctorate in the study of adult education being given by the University of London in the early 1920s on a topic, "Adult Education and Spiritual Values," which reflects many of its origins. However, it was not until graduate programs were commenced in the United States that theoretical perspectives really developed and since this was at Teachers College, University of Columbia, it is hardly surprising that Dewey's influence can be detected. The dominant theories of the later part of the century have also been influenced by the culture of the time when they emerged—the 1960s— which embraced the values of humanism, individualism, and self-achievement.

Two American scholars, Cyril Houle and Malcolm Knowles, have been the key figures in this development. Houle (1961) wrote a small book which stimulated a great deal of research on self-directed learning. Malcolm Knowles, a doctoral student of Houle, introduced the concept of andragogy to United States adult education in a number of books and articles. In a sense, self-directed learning reflects the American culture of individualism and self-achievement, so that research in this area has become central to much United States thinking. Knowles learned the term "andragogy" from a Yugoslav adult educator, as andragogy has been prominent there for many years. Unfortunately Knowles did not use the term in the same way as the Yugoslavian adult educators, but it is the United States version which has become well-known in the English-speaking world. Knowles (1970, 1980) originally postulated four assumptions about andragogy: (a) adult learners are self-directed, (b) they have experience which is a reservoir for future learning, (c) they are ready to learn, and (d) they will learn more readily the things relevant to their lives. Immediately it may be seen that Knowles was reflecting some of the same aspects of the 1960s United States culture as Houle, but he also emphasized the humanistic element. There is a sense in which the term "andragogy" itself was as important as its content. United States adult education was growing in the 1960s, many new university departments were being established, and adult education needed an identity which made it distinct from school education; the term "andragogy" provided it. Andragogy, as a concept, emerged when the time was ripe for it, and while Knowles has changed and developed his ideas and heavily criticized the concept itself (Jarvis 1984), andragogy provided adult education with an identity, and its content reflected the culture of the time during the growth period of adult education in the United States.

Radical adult educators, working with the underprivileged and with oppressed groups, have adopted the dominant theme of empowerment to describe a great deal of their work. Clearly, adult education does act to change people, helping them to see themselves as more significant in society.

6. *Professionalization of Adult Education*

There have been attempts by the Commission of Professors of Adult Education in the United States to professionalize adult education, but such a move is fraught with difficulties because of the nature of the occupation. Unlike more traditional occupations, adult education has neither a single structure nor a controlling body. As was pointed out at the beginning of this entry, adult education occurs in many different sectors of society, each sector being able to control its own educators. Hence, nursing education, for instance, can recruit, train, and license its own educators without reference to any other branch of adult education. Indeed, in the higher status professions the educators are much more likely to identify with their profession than they are with a lower status occupation like adult education. Thus the education of adults might be conceptualized as a functional occupation or profession which will not professionalize along any of the paths that students of the professions have, at various times, suggested (e.g., Wilensky 1964). Different sectors may professionalize within their own profession, but this will not directly affect any other branch of adult education.

7. Conclusion

As the population ages, so adult education assumes new forms, but performs similar functions with different age groups. For instance, as people leave their work on retirement and enter what will be for many a prolonged period of leisure, many employers are introducing preretirement education to prepare their workers for the future. Indeed, educational gerontology is a rapidly developing field of adult education, with its own journals and research interests, as it is performing a leisure-time function for the elderly (see, e.g., Glendenning and Percy 1990).

It may be seen, therefore, that the forms and structures of adult education are related to the structures and the levels of development of the societies in which they occur. This is leading to the development of comparative studies in the education of adults (see Lichtner 1989). At the same time, the functions that it performs are similar throughout but, naturally, there is a greater concentration upon leisure-time pursuits among the elderly, compared with those who are still in employment.

See also: Sociology of Education: Overview

References

Althusser L 1971 (trans. Brewster B) *Lenin and Philosophy and Other Essays*. New Left Books, London
Bourdieu P 1973 Cultural reproduction and social reproduction. In: Brown R (ed.) 1973 *Knowledge, Education, and Cultural Change*. Tavistock, London
Bourdieu P, Passeron J-C 1977 (trans. Nice R) *Reproduction in Education, Society and Culture*. Sage Publications, London
Brookfield S D 1987 *Developing Critical Thinkers*. Jossey-Bass, San Francisco, California
Carlson R A 1987 *The Americanization Syndrome: A Quest for Conformity*, rev. edn. Croom Helm, London
Cassara B (ed.) 1990 *Adult Education in a Multicultural Society*. Routledge, London
Collins M 1991 *Adult Education as Vocation*. Routledge, London
Coombs P H, Ahmed M 1974 *Attacking Rural Poverty: How Non-Formal Education Can Help*. Johns Hopkins University Press, Baltimore, Maryland
Courtney S 1992 *Why Adults Learn: Towards a Theory of Participation in Adult Education*. Routledge, London
Entwistle H 1979 *Antonio Gramsci: Conservative Schooling for Radical Politics*. Routledge and Kegan Paul, London
Fletcher C, Thompson N (eds.) 1980 *Issues in Community Education*. Falmer Press, Lewes
Freire P 1972a (trans. Ramos B) *Pedagogy of the Oppressed*. Penguin, Harmondsworth
Giddens A 1979 *Central Problems in Social Theory: Action, Structure and Contradiction in Social Analysis*. Macmillan, London
Giddens A (1990) *The Consequences of Modernity*. Polity Press, Cambridge
Glendenning F, Percy K (eds.) 1990 *Ageing, Education and Society*. Association for Educational Gerontology, University of Keele, Keele
Griffin C 1987 *Adult Education as Social Policy*. Croom Helm, London
Habermas J 1972 (trans. Shapiro J J) *Knowledge and Human Interests*. Heinemann Educational, London
Hart M U 1992 *Working and Educating for Life*. Routledge, London
Houle C O 1961 *The Inquiring Mind*. University of Wisconsin Press, Madison, Wisconsin
Jarvis P 1984 Andragogy—a sign of the times. *Studies in the Education of Adults* 16: 32–38
Jarvis P 1985a *The Sociology of Adult and Continuing Education*. Croom Helm, London
Jarvis P 1985b Thinking critically in an information society: A sociological analysis. *Lifelong Learning: An Omnibus of Practice and Research* 8(6): 11–14
Jarvis P 1987 *Adult Learning in the Social Context*. Croom Helm, London
Knowles M S 1970 *The Modern Practice of Adult Education: Andragogy versus Pedagogy*. Association Press, Chicago, Illinois
Knowles M S 1980 *The Modern Practice of Adult Education: From Pedagogy to Andragogy*, rev. edn. Follett, Chicago, Illinois
LaBelle T J 1982 Formal, non-formal and informal education: A holistic perspective on lifelong learning. *Int. Rev. Educ.* 28(2): 159–75
Levine K 1986 *The Social Context of Literacy*. Routledge and Kegan Paul, London
Lichtner M (ed.) 1989 *Comparative Research in Adult Education*. Centro Europeo dell'Educazione, Frascati
Lovett T (ed.) 1988 *Radical Approaches to Adult Education: A Reader*. Routledge, London
Marsick V J (ed.) 1987 *Learning in the Workplace*. Croom Helm, London
Mezirow J A 1981 Critical Theory of Adult Learning and Education. *Adult Educ.* 32(1): 3–24
Peters O 1988 Distance teaching and industrial production: A comparative interpretation in outline. In Sewart D, Keegan D, Holmberg B (eds.) *Distance Education: International Perspectives*, 2nd edn. Routledge, London
Rogers C 1983 *Freedom to Learn for the 80's*. Merrill, Columbus, Ohio
Strauss A (ed.) 1964 *George Herbert Mead on Social Psychology*. University of Chicago Press, Chicago, Illinois
Thomas A M 1991 *Beyond Education: A New Perspective on Society's Management of Learning*. Jossey-Bass, San Francisco, California
Thompson J L 1983 *Learning Liberation: Women's Response to Men's Education*. Croom Helm, London
Tuijnman A 1989 *Recurrent Education, Earnings and Well-being*. Almqvist and Wiksell International, Stockholm
Wilensky H A L 1964 The professionalization of everyone? *Am. J. Sociol.* 70: 137–58
Youngman F 1986 *Adult Education and Socialist Pedagogy*. Croom Helm, London

P. Jarvis

Sociology of Education: Overview

By the late nineteenth and early twentieth centuries, the precursors of modern sociology had established the foundation for a sociological analysis of education. This was especially true of the three major founding fathers of sociology, Emile Durkheim, Karl Marx, and Max Weber.

The sociology of education, with its origins embedded in the early development of sociology, has become a major subfield in the discipline. No survey of educational research can ignore the contribution of the sociology of education, both in terms of its contribution to the sociology discipline, as well as its contribution to educational theory, research, and policy. Much of sociological theory and research takes into account the importance of education, either as cause or consequence. Education, in all of its levels and structures, is a key variable in sociological research. The study of education is as important to sociology as the sociological study of education is important for understanding education and the formulation of educational policy.

The aims of this entry are: (a) to discuss the basic characteristics of a sociological perspective of education, (b) to present an overview of the sociology of education in the context of the development of the sociology discipline, (c) to point to trends in modern sociology of education, and (d) to discuss the contribution of the sociology of education to educational change, policy, and planning. Specialized entries in the *Encyclopedia* discuss in depth many other topical fields in the sociology of education.

1. The Sociological Perspective in the Study of Education

It is difficult to give a single, comprehensive definition of the sociology of education as practiced in the discipline. Marjoribanks (1985) traced the first definition of the field, called "educational sociology" at the time, to Suzallo's (1913) definition in the *Cyclopedia of Education*, which focused on methodology, that is, "one of the four special approaches utilized in that scientific study of education which founds its philosophy or inclusive theory upon detailed observation and analysis" (cited in Marjoribanks 1985 p. 4680).

Seventy-five years later an attempt to define the field emphasized its eclectic and broad scope. According to Bidwell and Friedkin (1988), the most central focus of the sociology of education is "the analysis of educational activities—their form and content, their embeddedness in broader social structures, and their outcomes for individuals and collectivities" (p. 449). From this latter perspective, the field includes the study of virtually every aspect connected with all levels of the educational structures and processes in society, and includes family background, socialization, teacher and classroom processes, educational organizations and hierarchies, and short- and long-term educational outcomes.

In this respect, Durkheim was correct when he argued that education was "an eminently social matter," and that no aspect of education can be understood without taking into account the social forces and consequences which characterize it.

1.1 Sociology of Education as the Study of Social Control

Bidwell and Friedkin (1988) contend that underlying the variety of topics and perspectives addressed by sociologists of education is the theme of social control. This theme was the dominant concern of the European sociologists of the nineteenth century. For example, Durkheim saw education primarily as a mechanism through which the "ideal adult" would be produced for society. He believed that education, as an instrument of moral integration, is the means whereby the norms and values of society are transmitted from one generation to the next.

Marx believed that education was a way of imposing a dominant ideology on members of society, particularly the working classes, so that they would accept, and not question, their position in society. Althusser (1972), a French Marxist of the late twentieth century, referred to this process as one of symbolic violence, particularly as compared to the physical and repressive violence exercised by the military and the police, for example.

Weber too, among the classical sociological thinkers, saw education largely in control terms. Thus, even though Weber focused his analysis of society on bureaucracy and rationality, for him education served as a credential whereby an appropriate way of life would be prepared for.

Much of the research in modern sociology of education continues to focus on the control aspect of education, although not necessarily in an exclusive manner. Socialization in schools, studies of the classroom, and social aspects of the curriculum are examples of areas which focus on the extent to which education serves as an integrative or control mechanism in society.

1.2 Sociology of Education as the Study of Opportunity

Views other than that of education as social control have become commonplace. A major focus of much research is the extent to which education serves as an agent of opportunity or, conversely, as an agent which reproduces the inequalities in society.

Included in this context are studies of education and various aspects of social stratification. Topics such as education and social mobility, status attainment, empowerment skills, and education and national development are examples of education seen as an agent of opportunity in society.

Insofar as sociology is the study of patterns of human relationships, particularly as they emerge from the tensions and conflicts of group life and contradictions in social structures, the sociology of education applies this perspective to the study of education.

The often heated debates about these two processes—education as opportunity and education as social reproduction—have thrust the sociology of education into the forefront of sociological enquiry generally, particularly with respect to questions of social inequality. Many writers have seen the oppositional forces in the sociology of education as a virtual battleground for theoretical development and research effort, and even for the adoption of educational policies about inequality and educational reform (Collins 1977a, 1977b, Halsey et al. 1980).

Thus, from a sociological point of view, there is little social life that is untouched by the experience of formal education. In most contemporary societies, virtually everyone has experienced at least primary and some secondary schooling. Thus education not only forms individuals, but through individuals has an impact on the very fabric of society. In like manner, the nature of education in any society is affected by the culture and structure of each society's institutions. This interactive relationship between individuals, educational institutions, and society means that education is one of the most relevant of the social institutions, and it penetrates virtually all aspects of society which are sociological (see *Classical Sociological Theories of Education; Contemporary Sociological Theories of Education*).

2. The Sociology of Education: From Margin to Mainstream

2.1 Origins

Virtually all social thinkers, since the time of Plato and Aristotle, have considered the education of the young as part of their theory of society. From a social point of view, the process of education has always been linked with other social processes, either as a source of social stability or a source of social conflict. However, given that the discipline of sociology itself did not emerge until the early nineteenth century with the writings of Auguste Compte (1798–1857), what could be called a sociology of education did not emerge until Emile Durkheim (1858–1917) began to teach, and write about, education and educational institutions to students at the Sorbonne, where he was made Professor of Pedagogy and Sociology in 1913. Durkheim quite rightly can be called the father of the sociology of education. The other major nineteenth-century sociologists, in particular Max Weber (1864–1920) and Karl Marx (1818–83), did not write directly about education, either as a process, or social institution, or formal organization. Nevertheless all three have had considerable influence on the development of schools of thought within contemporary sociology of education. Thus functionalism, Marxist conflict theory, Weberian conflict theory, phenomenology and the sociology of knowledge, and critical theory have their origins in these early writers, and can be found in the orientations and perspectives used in contemporary educational research.

Just as the sociology of education was marginal to most of the founding fathers of sociology, so too were its origins in the discipline of sociology, as well as in educational theory and research. In its early stages, that is, from the 1920s to the 1940s, the ambivalence of educational sociology, as it was then called, was reflected in the presumption by sociologists that the study of schools and of education was of little importance and therefore of low status in the sociology discipline, and in the presumption by educators that research into education by sociologists was "ivory-tower nonsense" and had little to say about the day-to-day functioning of teaching and learning (Hansen 1967).

This was particularly true regarding the development of the sociology of education in the United States and the United Kingdom. Banks (1971) points out that between 1910 and 1926 the number of courses in United States colleges and universities increased from 40 to 194, and between 1916 and 1936, 25 textbooks were published. However, the number of courses had declined by 1940, partially because most of the teaching took place outside of departments of sociology and thus outside of the mainstream of sociology. Furthermore, the subject was often taught with emphasis on prescriptions about proper pedagogical methods, that is, in teaching teachers how and what to teach and why. Courses were therefore steeped in practical ideology, and directly counter to the scientific and positivist spirit which prevailed in United States sociology during these decades. The normative and descriptive orientation of what was then called educational sociology conflicted with the notion of value-freedom and scientific analysis which dominated the other fields of sociology.

Even the journal *Educational Sociology*, founded in 1927, reflected these two approaches, and the contrast between the orientation of its contents before and after 1963, when it came under the jurisdiction of the American Sociological Association, is obvious to even the most casual observer. Also significant is the fact that after 1963 the journal was called *Sociology of Education*, and the retiring editor confessed to being concerned about the direction the new journal might take. Of the original orientation of the journal, he observed that it was conceived "as a magazine of theory and practice which would 'bridge the gap' between sociology as a science and education as an art" (Dodson 1963 p. 407). It was feared, however, that the journal might be taken over by sociologist theoreticians who spin out theory "with no responsibility for testing it—to say nothing about the extent of its applicability" (p. 408). Furthermore, concern was expressed that the journal should report research conducted on schools and not on university captive populations. Dodson hoped that the new journal would encourage academic sociologists out of their "cloistered environs and aid them in getting their hands dirty with the 'raw meat' of education in its broader spectrum" (p. 409). Clearly at this time there was a mistrust as to what might happen to the journal if taken over by academic sociologists.

Also the field was considered to be theoretically impoverished. In 1963 James Conant, the United States educator, commented: "As to whether the present group of professors who consider themselves educational sociologists, should perpetuate themselves, I have the greatest doubts" (cited in Banks 1971 p. 2). Likewise, Corwin, in his assessment of the field, observed that "the early limitations of the sociology of education do not lie so much in the inadequacy of its conclusions as in the sterility of the questions that it asked" (Corwin 1965 p. 65).

Even in the United Kingdom, where sociological research into education played a central role in the reform of schooling through the studies of Halsey, Douglas, and others, it had little impact on the preparation of teachers or the better understanding of classroom processes (Banks 1971). Archer (1972) lamented that the sociology of education was among the "least adventurous specialisms" in sociology, and remained "tightly shackled to its subject matter, reflecting the priorities and preoccupations of educators rather than the theoretical concerns of sociologists" (p. v). Her complaint was that sociologists had been too preoccupied with analyses of "the classroom, the school and social differentials in achievement and interaction, and thus shown a complementary neglect of research about educational systems." In other words, there was no macrosociology of education. She partly remedied this criticism by her study of the origins of educational systems in the United Kingdom, Denmark, France, and Russia, in which she combined a micro and macro approach (Archer 1979), and also in her edited volume containing analyses of the expansion of educational systems (Archer 1982).

The ambivalence about the sociology of education prevailed elsewhere in the English-speaking world. In Australia and New Zealand in 1980 it was noted that the sociology of education held a "distinctly minor place" in educational research generally (Bates 1980). Furthermore, it was argued that Australian sociologists of education were noncritical, atheoretical, and practical in their teaching and research orientations, being dominated by a "paucity of criticism" and a research orientation described as "political arithmetic" (Musgrave 1980). These views existed at a time when the sociology of education dominated the interests of Australian and New Zealand sociologists, with 25 percent giving sociology of education as one of their three main areas of interest (Saha 1990). Also, the study of education was ranked second in popularity among United Kingdom sociologists but was not mentioned among the top 10 areas of interest among United States sociologists (Simon 1969).

However, by the mid-1980s, the sociology of education was one of the most popular and productive areas within sociology. There are three dedicated journals in the English language: *Sociology of Education* (Vol. 1: 1927), the *British Journal of Sociology of Education* (Vol. 1: 1980), and *International Studies in Sociology of Education* (Vol. 1: 1991). *The Sociology of Education Abstracts* (Vol. 1: 1965) annually abstracts 600 journal articles and books, and draws upon over 370 journals from a large number of countries and in at least nine languages. The reasons for the increasing popularity, productivity, and vitality of sociology of education from the 1960s onward lay in a number of theoretical and methodological developments which, while sometimes in conflict with each other, nevertheless contributed to the increasing importance of the field and its move into the mainstream of sociology generally.

2.2 Theoretical and Methodological Developments

During the 1950s and 1960s, when most advanced societies regarded schools as strategic institutions for implementing change, the central concern for research in the sociology of education was with school reform, equality, and social mobility. The methodology and absence of theory in these early studies, which were characteristic in both the United States and the United Kingdom, were labeled "political arithmetic" (Karabel and Halsey 1977, Marjoribanks 1985). It was only after the mid-1960s and early 1970s that developments emerged which were to have a considerable effect on the rejuvenation of the sociology of education.

2.2.1 The "new" sociology of education. During the above period a new strand of the sociology of education was developing, but with a focus on micro phenomena. During this period Bernstein was conducting research on language codes and learning, and pointed to the hitherto ignored symbols and meanings in the classroom situation as a possible locus of inequality in educational processes. Bernstein's research gradually led him to focus on the ways knowledge is valued, classified, and controlled in various kinds of pedagogic processes (Bernstein 1971, 1975).

However, the actual watershed of what became known as the "new" sociology of education occurred at the 1970 British Sociological Association Conference, where the papers in the sociology of education "reflected the very interesting fact that the definition of this whole field of sociological enquiry was changing in important ways" (Brown 1973 p. 2). In the minds of some, this "new" approach, which combined other antipositivist sociological movements such as symbolic interactionism, phenomenology, ethnomethodology, Marxist sociology, and the sociology of knowledge, constituted a paradigm shift in the sociology of education comparable to a scientific revolution in the Kuhnian sense (Saha 1978). Perhaps the most important aspect of the "new" sociology of education was that it directed attention to the study, using mainly qualitative methods, of classroom interaction, classroom language, and the curriculum, the last having been a hitherto neglected field for sociological research (Young 1971). Knowledge itself became the main focus of study: how knowledge was defined, controlled, and transmitted to students. (See *Reproduction Theory; Resistance Theory*.)

2.2.2 Education and status attainment. A second direction in the sociology of education emerged in the United States at about the same time that the "new" sociology of education was developing in the United Kingdom: the use of causal models to investigate the multiple determinants of educational outcomes, and subsequently, the effect of educational attainments on occupational and career attainments. Although the use of highly quantifiable data and statistical techniques was not new in the sociological study of education on either side of the Atlantic, the development of status attainment models added social–psychological variables to the educational and occupational attainment process (Haller 1982). The use of causal (path) models dominated one aspect of sociology of education research from the 1970s to the early 1990s in many countries, including the United States (Sewell and Hauser 1980), the United Kingdom (Halsey et al. 1980), the Netherlands (Bakker et al. 1989), Sweden (Tuijnman 1989), Australia (Saha 1985), and Canada (Boyd et al. 1985). (See *Social Mobility, Social Stratification, and Education; Stratification in Educational Systems; Measurement of Social Background; Aspirations and Expectations of Students*.)

2.2.3 Critical theory. A movement which emerged in the sociology of education during the late 1970s was critical theory, with a focus on the study of education as a form of oppression by dominant groups. Writers such as Freire (1985), Giroux (1992), and Apple (1982) are well-known to educationists and educational researchers. However, critical theory as a sociological theory of society is probably less known, and its implications for educational policy and planning are less apparent. Nevertheless, this theoretical development has become important and deserves attention as a useful framework for formulating and identifying educational planning objectives and strategies.

Critical theory emerged out of the Frankfurt School which was established in Frankfurt, Germany, in 1923. During the ensuing years, including a period of dispersion during the Second World War, members of the Frankfurt School, particularly Horkheimer, Adorno, Fromm, Marcuse, and Habermas, developed a range of theoretical approaches which, on the one hand, are a reaction to the scientism of positivist sociology and, on the other, are an attempt to develop a general theoretical approach which combines theory and practice (Bottomore 1984). Although the focal points and precise details of writers vary, the general perspective and its implications for education are coherent and relevant.

Critical theory is based on the assumption that the power of capitalism has come to dominate all aspects of both social life and the mechanisms of social control in society. Concepts such as "the totally administered society," "one-dimensional man," and "communicative competence" typify the portrayal of social life in modern capitalism. The purpose of critical theory is not to explain and analyze, but to help emancipate and transform society through the process of education (see *Critical Theory and Education*).

2.2.4 Education as an institution. An approach to the sociological study of education which focuses on cultural rules, otherwise known as institutions, has been developed by Meyer and his colleagues (Meyer et al. 1987). This approach assumes that observed patterns of activity are manifestations of the institutionalization of rules which give meaning and value to particular entities and activities. Thus even structural characteristics which constrain behavior, such as organizational structures, are seen as themselves constrained by wider institutionalized rules. Phenomena such as educational expansion (Meyer et al. 1992), the growing power of the state (Boli 1989), or the increase of female enrollments, can be understood as manifestations of the emergence of rules according to which these phenomena occur.

Research using this perspective has focused on education and citizenship (Boli 1989), the curriculum, and the increasing participation of women.

By the late 1970s, as a result of these many developments, the sociology of education had moved into the mainstream of sociological debate generally. One writer called it "one of the most vibrant and respected areas of sociological research" (Karabel 1979 p. 85). During this period, sociologists of education focused much of their research on questions of equality of opportunity for education and career, and also on the role of education for social mobility and social reproduction (Saha 1987). These debates became so important that some writers suggested that the sociology of education had become a battleground for theories and policies about inequality and social reform (Tepperman 1979, Halsey et al. 1980). By the mid-1980s the sociology of education had become very much a mainstream area in the discipline of sociology generally.

2.3 Sociology of Education as an International Discipline

The sociology of education has changed considerably since its early development in various Western societies. Insofar as schooling has now become a universal experience, its place in social processes is crucial. The sociological study of education contributes to the location of this social institution and process in a wider societal context.

There is some documentation about the development of the sociology of education in other Western countries. Surveys of research in the sociology of education, for example, in the former Federal Republic of Germany (Goldschmidt and Jenne 1969) and in the United Kingdom (Swift and Acland 1969) presented a picture of a growing field, although somewhat conservative in orientation. Likewise in France the work of Boudon (1974) most closely approximated traditional sociology of education, but it was also in France that Marxist approaches were developed.

In many other countries the sociology of education was developing at about the same time. In India, for example, the earliest identifiable studies in the sociology of education were conducted in 1953 and 1967 (Chitnis 1982). In 1974, 89 studies were identified and reviewed, but by 1980 the number had more than doubled. The themes addressed by these studies were: (a) the backgrounds, attitudes, and values of students and teachers, (b) the socializing functions of schooling, (c) the expansion and growth of education in India, (d) equality and social mobility, (e) the organization and structure of education, and (f) the role of teachers and students (Chitnis 1982). Chitnis considered the future of the sociology of education in India to have promising potential.

The sociology of education in Spain, like many countries outside the United States and the United Kingdom, has a relatively short history. Early studies occurred in the 1960s and were typified by an emphasis on human capital theory, particularly in relation to economic development in Spain (Subirats 1990). After 1970 and the Education Act, the sociology of education began to develop more radical topics. Much influenced by French sociology, the sociology of education since the mid-1970s has been dominated by neo-Marxist interests, with research being conducted on schooling and social reproduction, into the effectiveness (or ineffectiveness) of schools, on the link between school and work, and particularly on the role of universities in social reform. Empirical research has since followed themes common to other Western countries, for example, the sexist character of education, socialization, democracy in education, and classroom interaction. As Spanish sociology entered the 1990s, Subirats (1990) argued that the two requirements for the continued relevance of Spanish sociology of education was more communication between researchers, and more dialogue between academics, educators, and politicians to discuss educational problems.

The international character and importance of the sociology of education is reflected in the strength of the field in the International Sociological Association. The Research Committee on Sociology of Education in the early 1990s was one of the largest and most active of 34 research committees. The vitality of the field is further indicated by the number of texts produced in various countries which summarize research, for example in the United States (Bennett and LeCompte 1990, Ballentine 1993), Canada (Mifflen and Mifflen 1982), France (Cherkaoui 1989), Australia (Saha and Keeves 1990, Foster and Harman 1992), and Africa (Datta 1984). An international survey of the teaching of the sociology of education found that the five most popular topics were: (a) theory in the sociology of education, (b) the school as organization and system, (c) the functions of education, (d) the social foundations of education, and (e) stratification and education (Ballentine et al. 1984). Clearly, these priorities in the field vary between countries, and they change over time as research and theoretical developments occur within particular cultural and political systems.

3. Themes and Developments in the Sociology of Education

Although the sociology of education has branched out into a number of identifiable subfields, such as the sociology of the curriculum and the sociology of teaching, there are a number of themes and developments which have dominated both theory and research across all subfields. In this section a number of these themes are described in terms of their relevance for educational knowledge and research.

3.1 Structure and Agency

For over 20 years, one of the major issues in sociology has been the dualism between macro and micro approaches to the study of human behavior. Macro approaches typically focus upon aspects of social structures as explanatory variables, and thus tend to adopt deterministic and constraining theories about human behavior, with little or no acknowledgment of individual autonomy or freedom. Typical variables for the macro-oriented sociologists are those of social class, gender, ethnicity, capitalism, and organizational hierarchies. Conversely, micro-oriented sociologists tend to focus upon individual actors, regarding them as autonomous with few or no constraints by the outside social and structural environment. Typical variables for the microsociologists are the subjective meanings of human interaction, resistance, aspects of action, and voluntaristic behavior.

Each of these approaches has been linked, in a simplistic manner, to quantitative and qualitative methodologies. Thus those who tend to take a macro approach also tend to use survey data or similar types of quantitative data. Conversely, those who take a micro-oriented approach tend to use ethnographic methods and focus on subjective interpretations or articulations of social situations. Although there have been attempts to combine macro and micro approaches, the dualism has been difficult to overcome.

In the study of education this has meant an almost irreconcilable gulf between those who have produced studies of classroom interaction, peer group interaction, and similar behaviors, and those adopting a macro-perspective, who have tended to study the statistical relationships between variables, largely measuring structural characteristics such as socioeconomic status, social class, gender, ethnicity, and the like. The impasse between the two approaches has prompted some researchers to observe that the only solution is to continue to develop both macro- and microsociology (Archer 1979).

Related to the macro/micro controversy, and perhaps an obstacle to solving it, has been the question of structure and agency. The conceptualization of these two dimensions of social action also represents a dualism in the sociological study of education. This dualism focuses on alternative explanations of social action: large-scale structural forces or individual voluntaristic forces. In other words, social action is seen as existing on two distinct levels (Shilling 1992). Examples of the former in the sociology of education are structuralist neo-Marxists, such as Althusser (1972) and Bowles and Gintis (1976), who explain social reproduction in schools in terms of the contradictions of the capitalist economic system. Regarding the agency frame of reference, those who adopt an interpretive perspective tend to see the source of action in the individual at the micro level.

Although Shilling (1992) identifies three attempts to overcome this impasse, the most successful and best-known is that put forward by Giddens in his structuration theory. According to Giddens (1984) it is necessary to distinguish between systems and structures. Most sociologists confuse the two and refer to social systems when they mean structures. Giddens contends that social structures are both a cause and an outcome of social interaction. In the production of social action, structures are reproduced. Thus the structures are the rules and resources of social action which both influence and are reproduced by action. Giddens therefore preserves both the notion of constraints on human behavior by outside forces, as well as the agency of human actors in that same behavior.

The solution of the structure/agency dualism is important for the future of the sociology of education, for otherwise there will remain the division, the compartmentalization, of studies of macro educational processes and micro-level aspects of behavior in classrooms, on playgrounds, or in families (see *Contemporary Sociological Theories of Education*).

3.2 Critical Pedagogy and Postmodernism

It would be difficult to assume that the sociological study of education would be unaffected by the intellectual movements of the late twentieth century, such as postmodernism, deconstructionism, and critical pedagogy. Although not generally considered to be part of mainstream sociology of education, these intellectual movements approach the study of education from a critical, oppositional, and sometimes neo-Marxist perspective.

Critical pedagogy, derived from the critical theory perspective, advocates that the classroom should become the arena for "intellectual resistance towards the ways in which our roles, our lives, and our subjectivities are defined and constituted" (Shapiro 1991). Ultimately, those who espouse critical pedagogy in classrooms aspire to the emergence of a truly democratic culture through a form of education which is empowering and liberating from the dominant ideology. An early application of critical theory to educational practice was described in Shor (1980), and more theoretically elaborated in Giroux (1992). Those who espouse a critical pedagogy regard educational processes as social and political, and thus any analysis of the deception inherent in capitalist schooling is inherently sociological, though far from the sociology of education that dominates the mainstream of the discipline.

Postmodernism, as a social theory and intellectual movement, differs from critical pedagogy and critical theory in that the notion of an underlying reality is denied. The notion of a postmodernist break or rupture with modernity has occurred through the penetration of the media, advertising, and television. The surface signs (language) take on a meaning of their own without an underlying meaning. It has been argued that postmodernist social theory makes the notion of intellectual resistance and liberation meaningless (Shapiro 1991) and thus devoid of educational relevance.

As developing theoretical movements, it remains to be seen how critical pedagogy and postmodernism will influence the understanding of educational processes and educational policy and practice (see *Postmodernism and Education*).

3.3 Equality and Efficiency

In most Western societies, the concepts of equality and inequality have been central to much of the planning for and expectations from educational systems. Generally speaking, inequality is defined as a social problem, and education is usually seen as a way of resolving social inequality. Furthermore, most modern democracies espouse the principles of meritocracy for opportunity, rewards, and self-betterment. In this context, education plays a double role, for not only is it expected to provide a major mechanism for bringing about greater equality, but it also serves as a mechanism for self-betterment, and therefore for social mobility.

Clearly then, since education is linked to equality and inequality, it is essential to clarify what is meant by the term. Oxenham (1985) argues that two seemingly contradictory dimensions underlie notions of equality with respect to education. The first of these includes the notions of fairness and equity, and generally means that "random inequalities of nature" should be acknowledged and taken into account in the educative process. Thus naturally bright children should be treated in ways which will allow that brightness to be developed to its full potential. Not to do so would be unequal and inefficient.

However, in contrast to the first is a second dimension, that education should help to rectify (mitigate) the "random inequities of nature." In other words, insofar as is possible, every person should have an equal opportunity to excel in ways that are not constrained by natural differences.

Sociological research in education has addressed the origins of inequality in education, the consequences of inequality, and policies which may make educational access and outcomes more equitable but also more efficient. Much of the research into the importance of family background and schooling in educational and occupational attainments has the question of inequality underlying it. The extent to which education either creates or reinforces inequalities means that ultimately it operates in an inequitable and possibly inefficient manner. Thus the subfields of adult education, the curriculum, learning, special education, and teaching are all concerned, in one form or another, with equality and efficiency in the educational system (see *Equality of Educational Opportunity: Philosophical Issues*).

3.4 Gender and Education

The process of differentiation by sex in education occurs early in schooling and continues throughout the education process. In most countries, the attainments and achievement of males and females at different education levels, and in different subject areas, differs considerably. In a study of science achievement in 9 countries (Australia, the United Kingdom, Finland, Hungary, Italy, the Netherlands, Sweden, Thailand, and the United States) between 1970 and 1984, Keeves and Kotte (1992) found that not only had the social roles of women changed in all countries (with respect to participation in the labor force and the declining fertility rate), but that the participation of women at the secondary and tertiary levels had also increased, and in some countries, female students had passed the males.

Keeves and Kotte (1992) found that in all countries boys outperformed girls in science, even when other variables were taken into account, such as home background, aptitude of student, values and motivation to do science, and attitudes toward science. The authors concluded, however, that their model left much unanswered in explaining why it is that boys do better in science than girls: "it is not firmly established exactly how the effects of being male or female operate to influence achievement outcomes in science" (p. 163).

Although it can be argued that sex differentiation has its origins in the family during infancy and childhood, the school remains a key institution which accounts for unequal educational outcomes. Connell et al. (1982) have argued that the school both constructs and reconstructs gender relations such that the subordinate status of females is continually confirmed. The fact that females are staying in school longer in many countries does not mean that gender differences are being eradicated.

Continued research into the processes which maintain or break down the sexual division of labor will remain high on the agenda of sociologists of education. Furthermore, social policies to eradicate gender inequalities in schooling can only become effective when they are based on sound research evidence, which is scanty (see *Sex Differences and Educational Outcomes*).

3.5 Cultural Pluralism and Multicultural Education

The increasing movement of peoples across and between national boundaries continues to pose important research issues for sociologists of education. While the schooling of minority groups within countries has been a long-standing item on the sociology research agenda, particularly in countries such as the United States, the United Kingdom, Canada, and Australia, the emergence of heterogeneous populations through voluntary and nonvoluntary migration has called into question again whether education serves as an assimilationist mechanism or a protector of unique cultural systems and identities. In reality the debate over the notion of a core curriculum and a multicultural curriculum has yet to be resolved, particularly with respect to learning among members of racial and ethnic minorities (Ogbu 1992).

Considerable research has been conducted on the factors which contribute to the academic achievement of minority groups in various countries, but these studies have often assumed homogeneity within minority groups themselves, and have also assumed that members of minority groups share with the dominant group similar values regarding education and its outcomes. Ogbu (1992) has argued that those who advocate a strong core curriculum (as in Germany, Japan, South Korea, and Taiwan) and those who support a more pluralistic multicultural curriculum overlook the wider societal and dominant cultural impact on the learning processes of minority students.

A further dimension of plural societies is that of

religion. The issues surrounding the existence of private schools, in particular issues of funding, school choice, and efficiency and effectiveness of educational systems, have highlighted the impact of dual or plural structures. Sociologists of education have directed considerable attention to the study of public and private schools and have yet to reach a consensus as to the impact of the private sector on the public sector. While it is not clear whether private schools themselves are responsible for the higher attainments of their students, it is clear that the social and cultural environments of these schools do impart cultural and social capital which may be socially advantageous (see Coleman and Hoffer 1987).

Future sociologists of education will focus more on the educational processes related to the education of refugees, the consequences of new international economic and social alliances, such as the European Community, and improved knowledge about the determinants of academic achievement across and within minority groups of all types. (See *Multicultural Education; Public and Private Schools: Sociological Perspectives; Race and Ethnicity in Education; School Choice, Foundations of.*)

3.6 Dropouts and Burnouts: Alienation in Schools

School retention rates have steadily risen since the 1960s in almost all countries of the world. Nevertheless there remains considerable concern over those students in the 1990s who do not complete secondary school. There are numerous reasons for this concern. Rumberger (1987) gives five: (a) the short-term increase in dropouts since 1968, at least in the United States, (b) the participation of minority group students with high dropout rates is increasing, (c) as academic standards rise, dropout rates will also rise, (d) the standard of educational credentials required for virtually all jobs can be expected to rise, and (e) completion rates will increasingly be used as an indicator of performance for secondary schools.

Most of the research on school dropouts has regarded the phenomenon as pathological, and as representing a loss to the individual as well as to society. Lee and Burkam (1992) group the causes of dropping out into three categories: (a) the personal and psychological characteristics of dropouts, (b) the academic and psychological behaviors of dropouts, and (c) schools as contributors to dropping out. Thus they argue that dropouts (or "at risk" students) tend to come from low-status, minority backgrounds and from single parent or stepparent households, have high levels of alienation, have higher rates of truancy, and do not attend schools (such as Catholic schools) which have lower dropout rates (pp. 422–23).

LeCompte and Dworkin (1991) confirm these findings, but draw attention to the equivalent phenomenon among teachers, namely burnout. They argue that teachers also experience alienation and often leave the profession because of burnout. However, they also observe that many teachers who experience burnout and lose their commitment do not leave the profession, a process they call role entrapment. This phenomenon poses two problems for the quality of teaching in schools: first, new programs are difficult to implement with unenthusiastic teachers, and, second, staffing becomes a problem when teachers who should leave do not. The authors suggest that school reforms fail because of inappropriate measures of school success or failure, mismatched reforms, quick-fix reforms, or reforms which leave the alienating structure unchanged.

In short, alienation in schools, both from individual and structural causes, results in problems which are only beginning to be researched. Sociologists of education in most countries will continue to research these processes as long as there are school dropouts and burned-out teachers. (See *School and Classroom Dynamics; School Dropouts; Teacher Burnout.*)

3.7 Democracy and Education

Citizenship education has become a key objective among educators, politicians, and sociologists in many countries. The advent of plural societies in Europe and elsewhere and the radical critiques of education in capitalist societies have caused citizenship as an educational objective to become an issue since the 1980s. Citizenship education not only concerns the development of an appropriate curriculum, but also the democratic process of the classroom itself.

There is wide variation between countries in the extent to which political education is explicit in the curriculum, whether it is a required subject and centrally controlled (e.g., in Germany), or whether it is left up to local state or school district levels (e.g., in the United States). In many countries, political education of any kind is not a requirement for school students, in spite of the fact that as adults the students will be expected to participate actively in the political life of the country (e.g., Australia), or not to participate at all (e.g., Hong Kong). However, even in the latter two countries, the issue of the introduction of political education is controversial.

The issue of citizenship education focuses attention on noncognitive outcomes of schooling and is concerned with democratic curricula and the acquisition of empowerment skills. Although not yet studied in great depth by sociologists, this form of noncognitive outcome, sometimes considered a part of moral or values education, will be higher on the research agenda by the beginning of the twenty-first century. (See *Empowerment Skills, Acquisition of; Political Socialization and Education; Student Political Activism and Student Movements.*)

4. Sociology of Education and Educational Policy and Planning

Educational planning is generally understood to be the identification, development, and implementation of strategies designed to attain, efficiently and effectively, the educational needs and goals of students and society (Coombs 1970). The practice of educational planning is not a new phenomenon, and according to some, can be traced to the writings of Plato, to Renaissance scholars, and, more recently, to post-Second World War experts.

What characterizes current planning activities is that planners have tended to rely upon nonsocial assumptions in formulating their planning models. Demographic projections, workforce models, rate-of-return approaches, and school mapping all approach the task of educational planning as though the social aspects of educational behavior are irrelevant. Each of these techniques has at its base an implicit theory which assumes that the needs of society can be clearly specified and measured in economic terms, and that the social behavior of individuals in response to these needs is unproblematic. It is for this reason that Windham (1980) and Lenhardt (1985) argue that educational planning needs a social theory of society which includes both structure and process, and both macro and micro dimensions.

4.1 Sociological Theories and Educational Planning

What has sociology of education research contributed toward a better understanding of the "social" aspects of education? To begin with, research from the functionalist perspective has demonstrated that education is related to other social institutions and cannot be manipulated without affecting and being affected by them. Any attempt to change education without taking into account family structures, the economy, the labor market, and other institutions runs the risk of resistance on the part of individuals and the failure of the reform program.

Also from within this framework, it is clear that education does serve as an agent (although sometimes moderate) in the selection and allocation process of individuals into the marketplace, and that generally the more education a person acquires, the better his or her life chances. As indicated earlier, there is a large body of literature documenting the positive relationship between education and social mobility, and the role of education in the status attainment process. In spite of some reservations about this research, it is difficult to deny that education plays a major role in expanding the opportunities and choices of individuals, and research findings have been used to support programs aimed at the disadvantaged, and at expanding equality in society generally.

Research from within the conflict perspective, especially from the Marxist-oriented sociologists, has documented the bias in the educational process in favor of the already advantaged, who seem to get the better opportunities. From this research it is also apparent that education can sometimes be used by those in power to achieve goals favorable to themselves. Although some social reproduction does occur through the educational system, so does the expansion of opportunity and social mobility.

Research from the interactionist perspective has documented the importance of classroom interaction in the educational process. The expectations of teachers have been found to exert considerable influence on the attitudes and performance of students (the "self-fulfilling prophecy" effect). Furthermore, it is from this kind of research that one can understand how well-planned curriculum reforms can fail to change what goes on in the classroom. Teachers, parents, and peer groups must be included in any program designed to change educational processes within schools, and ultimately within classrooms.

4.2 The Social Process of Planning

Research from these sociological perspectives has documented that the actors in the planning process—the politicians, bureaucrats, and planners—are part of the very system they want to change. The functionalists can explain how it is that these persons act largely to preserve the status quo, even though the planning programs may appear very radical. The Marxists can explain in whose interests planning decisions are made, while the interactionists can explain at the micro level how and why the actors in the planning process come to define planning objectives in particular ways, and how competing views are "defined away."

Finally, sociological research has helped explain the importance of consultation with all interested parties in the educational planning process. Coleman (1976) has argued that the compensatory education and desegregation programs in the United States during the 1960s and early 1970s were flawed by lack of adequate information about objectives and methods. Resistance to any social reform can indicate conflicting interests which could have been avoided had adequate information been obtained beforehand. It is only by understanding these social forces that means can be taken to ensure that the objectives and strategies of educational planning are appropriately, efficiently, and effectively formulated and implemented.

5. Sociology of Education in the Twenty-first Century

The rapid development of the sociology of education during the late nineteenth century and the twentieth century has resulted in considerable accumulated knowledge about educational systems and how they work in different cultural and organizational settings. The discipline has become increasingly relevant for policy-making, as well as for theoretical development and methodological application. It is also a field of study which is increasingly comparative, as knowledge about educational systems across national and cultural boundaries adds to both the knowledge of consistencies in educational processes, and the idiosyncratic properties of education in different structural and cultural settings.

Although it would be erroneous to assume that the sociology of education will develop in all societies according to the directions indicated here, the development of the field will continue to reflect the preoccupation of countries in the performance of schools and the educational needs of society. In this respect, Durkheim was correct in arguing that education was eminently social. It will continue to be so, and will continue to attract the vigorous attention of sociologists.

See also: Sociology of Adult Education; Curriculum: Sociological Perspectives; Special Education, Sociology of; Sociology of Teaching

References

Althusser L 1972 Ideology and ideological state apparatuses. In: Cosin B R (ed.) 1972 *Education, Structure and Society*. Penguin, Harmondsworth

Apple M W 1982 *Education and Power*. Routledge and Kegan Paul, Boston, Massachusetts

Archer M S 1972 Foreword. In: Archer M S (ed.) 1972 *Students, University and Society: A Comparative Sociological Review*. Heinemann Educational Books, London

Archer M S 1979 *Social Origins of Educational Systems*. Sage, London

Archer M S 1982 Introduction: Theorizing about the expansion of educational systems. In: Archer M S (ed.) 1982 *The Sociology of Educational Expansion: Take-Off, Growth and Inflation in Educational Systems*. Sage Publications, Beverly Hills, California

Bakker B F M, Dronkers J, Meijnen G W 1989 *Educational Opportunities in the Welfare State. Longitudinal Studies in Educational and Occupational Attainment in the Netherlands*. Instituut Voor Toegepaste Sociale Wetenschappen, Nijmegen

Ballentine J H 1993 *The Sociology of Education: A Systematic Analysis*, 2nd edn. Prentice-Hall, Englewood Cliffs, New Jersey

Ballentine J, Wagenaar T, King E 1984 Teaching about the sociology of education: Cross cultural variations in content and style. Paper presented to the International Sociological Association Interim Conf. of the Research Committee on Sociology of Education, Paris

Banks O 1971 *The Sociology of Education*, 2nd edn. Batsford, London

Bates R J 1980 Problems and prospects for a sociology of New Zealand education. *The Australian and New Zealand Journal of Sociology* 16(2): 4–8

Bennett K P, LeCompte M D 1990 *How Schools Work: A Sociological Analysis of Education*. Longman, New York

Bernstein B B 1971 *Class, Codes and Control. Vol. 1: Theoretical Studies Towards a Sociology of Language*. Routledge and Kegan Paul, London

Bernstein B B 1975 *Class, Codes and Control. Vol. 3: Towards a Theory of Educational Transmissions*. Routledge and Kegan Paul, London

Bidwell C E, Friedkin N E 1988 The sociology of education. In: Smelser N J (ed.) 1988 *Handbook of Sociology*, Sage Publications, Newbury Park, California

Boli J 1989 *New Citizens for a New Society: The Institutional Origins of Mass Schooling in Sweden*. Pergamon Press, Oxford

Bottomore T 1982 *The Frankfurt School*. Tavistock, London

Boudon R 1974 *Education, Opportunity, and Social Inequality. Changing Prospects in Western Society*. John Wiley-Interscience, New York

Bowles S, Gintis H 1976 *Schooling in Capitalist America*. Routledge and Kegan Paul, London

Boyd M et al. (eds.) 1985 *Ascription and Achievement: Studies in Mobility and Status Attainment in Canada*. Carleton University Press, Ottawa

Brown R 1973 Introduction. In: Brown R (ed.) 1973 *Knowledge, Education and Cultural Change: Papers in the Sociology of Education* Tavistock, London

Cherkaoui M 1989 *Sociologie de l'éducation*. Presses Universitaires de France, Paris

Chitnis S 1982 Sociology of education in India: Emerging trends and needed research. In: Nayar P K B (ed.) 1982 *Sociology in India: Retrospect and Prospect*. B R Publishing, New Delhi

Coleman J S 1976 Policy decisions, social science information, and education. *Sociol. Educ.* 49(4): 304–12

Coleman J S, Hoffer T 1987 *Public and Private High Schools: The Impact of Communities*. Basic Books, New York

Collins R 1977a Functional and conflict theories of educational stratification. In: Karabel J, Halsey A H (eds.) 1977 *Power and Ideology in Education*. Oxford University Press, New York

Collins R 1977b Some comparative principles of educational stratification. *Harv. Educ. Rev.* 47(1): 1–27

Connell R W, Ashenden D J, Kessler S, Dowsett G W 1982 *Making the Difference: Schools, Families and Social Division*. Allen and Unwin, London

Coombs P H 1970 *What Is Educational Planning?* International Institute of Educational Planning, UNESCO, Paris

Corwin R G 1965 *A Sociology of Education*. Appleton-Century Crofts, New York

Datta A 1984 *Education and Society: A Sociology of African Education*. Macmillan, London

Dodson D W 1963 Valedictory. *The Journal of Educational Sociology* 36(9): 407–09

Foster L, Harman K 1992 *Australian Education: A Sociological Perspective*, 3rd edn. Prentice-Hall, Sydney

Freire P 1985 *The Politics of Education*. Macmillan, London

Giroux H 1992 *Border Crossings: Cultural Workers and the Politics of Education*. Routledge, New York

Goldschmidt D, Jenne M 1969 Educational sociology in the Federal Republic of Germany. *Social Science Information* 8(4): 19–29

Haller A O 1982 Reflections on the social psychology of status attainment. In: Hauser R M, Mechanic D, Haller

A O, Hauser T S (eds.) 1982 *Social Structure and Behavior*. Academic Press, New York
Halsey A H, Heath, A F, Ridge J M 1980 *Origins and Destinations: Family, Class and Education and Modern Britain*. Clarendon Press, Oxford
Hansen D A 1967 The uncomfortable relation of sociology and education. In: Hansen D A, Gerstle J E (eds.) 1967 *On Education: Sociological Perspectives*. Wiley, New York
Karabel J 1979 The sociology of education: Perils and possibilities. *Am. Sociol.* 14(2): 85–91
Karabel J, Halsey A H 1977 Educational research: A review and an interpretation. In: Karabel J, Halsey A H (eds.) 1977 *Power and Ideology in Education*. Oxford University Press, New York
Keeves J P, Kotte D 1992 Disparities between the sexes in science education: 1970–1984. In: Keeves J P (ed.) 1992 *The IEA Study of Science III: Changes in Science Education and Achievement: 1970 to 1984*. Pergamon Press, Oxford
LeCompte M D, Dworkin A G 1991 *Giving Up on School: Student Dropouts and Teacher Burnouts*. Corwin Press, Newbury Park, California
Lee V E, Burkam D T 1992 Transferring high schools: An alternative to dropping out? *Am. J. Educ.* 100(4): 420–53
Lenhardt G 1985 Ideology in educational planning. In: Husen T, Postlethwaite T N (eds.) 1985 *The International Encyclopedia of Education*. Pergamon Press, Oxford
Marjoribanks K 1985 Sociology of education. In: Husén T, Postlethwaite T N (eds.) 1985 *International Encyclopedia of Education*. Pergamon Press, Oxford
Meyer J W, Boli J, Thomas G M 1987 Ontology and rationalization in the Western cultural account. In: Thomas G M, Meyer J W, Ramirez F O, Boli J (eds.) 1987 *Institutional Structure: Constituting the State, Society, and the Individual*. Sage Publications, Newbury Park, California
Meyer J W, Ramirez F O, Soysal Y N 1992 World expansion of mass education, 1870–1980. *Sociol. Educ.* 65(2): 128–49
Mifflen F J, Mifflen S C 1982 *The Sociology of Education: Canada and Beyond*. Detselig Enterprises, Calgary
Musgrave P W 1980 The sociology of the Australian curriculum: A case study in the diffusion of theory. *The Australian and New Zealand Journal of Sociology* 16(2): 15–19
Ogbu J U 1992 Understanding cultural diversity and learning. *Educ. Researcher* 21(8): 5–14
Oxenham J 1985 Equality, policies for educational. In: Husén T, Postlethwaite T N (eds.) 1985 *The International Encyclopedia of Education*. Pergamon Press, Oxford
Rumberger R W 1987 High school dropouts: A review of issues and evidence. *Rev. Educ. Res.* 57(2): 101–21
Saha L J 1978 The "new" sociology of education and the study of learning environments: Prospects and problems. *Acta Sociol.* 21(1): 47–63
Saha L J 1985 The legitimacy of early school leaving: Occupational orientations, vocational training plans, and educational achievement among urban Australian youth. *Sociol. Educ.* 58(4): 228–40
Saha L J 1987 Social mobility versus social reproduction: Paradigms and politics in the sociology of education. *New Educ.* 9(1, 2): 14–28
Saha L J 1990 Towards an Australian sociology of education. In: Saha L J, Keeves J P (eds.) 1990
Saha L J, Keeves J P (eds.) 1990 *Schooling and Society in Australia: Sociological Perspectives*. Australian National University Press, Sydney
Sewell W H, Hauser R M 1980 The Wisconsin longitudinal study of social and psychological factors in aspirations and achievements. In: Kerckhoff (ed.) 1980 *Research in the Sociology of Education and Socialization*, Vol. 1. JAI Press, Greenwich, Connecticut
Shapiro S 1991 The end of radical hope? Postmodernism and the challenge to critical pedagogy. *Educ. Soc.* 9(2): 112–22
Shilling C 1992 Reconceptualising structure and agency in the sociology of education: Structuration theory and schooling. *Br. J. Sociol. Educ.* 13(1): 69–87
Shor I 1987 *Critical Teaching and Everyday Life*. University of Chicago Press, Chicago, Illinois
Simon R J 1969 A Comment on sociological research and interest in Britain and the United States. *Sociol. Rev.* 17: 5–9
Subirats M 1990 Sociology of education in Spain. In: Giner S, Moreno L (eds.) 1990 *Sociology in Spain*. Consejo Superior de Investigaciones Cientificas, Madrid
Suzallo H 1913 Sociology, educational. In: Moore P (ed.) 1913 *A Cyclopedia of Education*, Vol. 5. Macmillan, New York
Swift D F, Acland H 1969 The sociology of education in Britain, 1960–1968: A bibliographical review. *Social Science Information* 8(4): 31–64
Tepperman L 1979 Editor's introduction. In: Murphy R 1979 *Sociological Theories of Education*. McGraw-Hill Ryerson, Toronto
Tuijnman A 1989 *Recurrent Education, Earnings and Well-being*. Almqvist and Wiksell, Stockholm
Windham D M 1980 Micro-educational decisions as a basis for macro-educational planning. In: Weiler H N (ed.) 1980 *Educational Planning and Social Change*. International Institute for Educational Planning, UNESCO, Paris
Young M F D 1971 An approach to the study of curricula as socially organized knowledge. In: Young M F D (ed.) 1971 *Knowledge and Control: New Directions for the Sociology of Education*. Collier-Macmillan, London

L. J. Saha

Sociology of Teaching

The sociology of teaching and the role of teachers in society comprises one area of interest to sociologists of education. This area includes the examination of teachers' work in sociohistorical contexts, the description of teachers' social characteristics, and the process of socialization in teaching.

1. The Role of Teachers in Society: Sociological Perspectives

Three major theoretical perspectives have dominated sociology as analytic frameworks for understanding social structure and process: structural-functionalism, conflict theory, and interpretive theories.

These theories point to the central role of teachers and educational institutions, whether in the transmission of cultural knowledge, values, and beliefs, in the reproduction of economic structures and stratification of the work force, or in the socialization process. A brief overview of their assumptions is presented as a backdrop to understanding sociologists' views on the role of education and teachers in society.

Structural-functionalism, a macro-sociological or large-scale approach, looks at societies and the interrelationship of their structures or institutions (such as education) and the functions they serve in preserving the status quo or well-being of a society. Societies are seen as systems of functionally interrelated and interdependent parts, held together and stabilized through adherence to basic values.

Emile Durkheim first wrote about education as the institution through which values are transmitted and internalized by societal members, and, in this sense, is moral in nature and intent. Moral education is thought to be the task of teachers, so their commitment to the mainstream values and beliefs of a society is crucial. Durkheim found teachers' roles quite powerful because, subject to little external supervision, they ensure cultural transmission of values from generation to generation. Thus they are instrumental in preserving the ongoing social order. While the functionalist perspective has been criticized for its conservative or even static view of society, sociologists continue to use its terminology in examining the functions of schooling in society, and teachers' roles in the transmission of ideas, values, and beliefs to students.

Conflict theorists, including Marxist and neo-Marxists, have found structural functionalism inadequate in explaining the dynamic nature of societies. Instead, they view society as a system characterized by social inequality, which generates social conflict and results in social change. The source of inequality in a society is determined by its economic organization and the unequal distribution of property or resources. Schools are seen as a crucial link between the economy and individuals' economic opportunities within the existing class structure. Furthermore, schools serve to reinforce inequality because they are controlled by powerful elites whose interests are served and whose children benefit most.

From this perspective, the work of Bowles and Gintis (1976) has been particularly influential in demonstrating how the rise of capitalism paralleled the growth of public education in the United States. They assert that schools served the capitalist class by supplying them with a ready, willing, and able supply of workers through the transmission of values which encouraged such traits as obedience to authority, punctuality, and responsibility for work. They believe a myth was (and is) created which leads the public to believe that equal educational opportunity is available to people of all social classes but that, in reality, schools reward students differentially according to their social class origins. This reproduces the social division of labor in society.

Teachers are instrumental in this reproduction process, and to the extent that they base judgments of students on their social class, they perpetuate inequality. Good examples of this process in schools in the United States are found in the work of Anyon (1980) and Page (1987), who look at teachers' judgments of students based on how students have been tracked in schools by their social class. The work of Metz (1990) examines the ways teachers' own social class origins affect their perceptions and treatment of students in the United States, as does that of Connell et al. (1982) among Australian teachers. Apple has written on the proletarianization of teaching as an occupation, and on teachers' roles within the social class structure (1985).

Interpretive theories, microlevel in analysis, are based on the meanings or interpretations of social situations that people construct through their interactions with others. Individuals coordinate their actions with others through shared symbol systems, the most important of which is language. Interpretive sociologists, and particularly symbolic interactionists, are interested in the development of the self-concept, the socialization process, and the ability of individuals to take the role of others in planning their own actions. Application of these theories in the sociology of education has relied on qualitative research methods to gain an understanding of day-to-day school life from the perspective of those who are a part of school organizations.

United Kingdom sociologists of education, particularly, have made significant contributions to an understanding of teacher–pupil relationships and classroom interaction patterns from an interactionist perspective (see Stubbs and Delamont 1976). A focus on teachers is found in Woods (1983), who examined the ideological basis of different teacher subcultures depending on their position within the school system. An example of the reciprocal effects of teachers' and students' behaviors on the others' actions and perceptions is found in Spencer's (1981) study of students' use of impression management in elementary school classrooms.

1.1 Characteristics of Teaching in Sociohistorical Context

Dramatic changes in social, cultural, and material patterns in the late nineteenth century and the early twentieth century provided the context in which to understand growth and changes in education systems and their effects on the professionalization of teaching. Along with rapid increases in industrialization, there were periods of significant population growth and demographic shifts from rural to urban settings.

Taken together, these political, economic, and demographic transformations created changes in the labor force, which directly affected the social organization of educational systems and schools.

Throughout this period, teaching was regarded as temporary work for basically untrained people. In the United States, schools and teachers moved to where the children were located, or taught several sessions in one location. On a yearly basis, they taught only a few months (Parelius and Parelius 1987, Warren 1989). In a history of education in the United Kingdom, Musgrave (1968) has described teachers through the turn of the nineteenth century as similar to those of the United States. They basically were untrained or "sweated labour." Teachers in rural areas tended to have the lowest levels of training, while teachers in urban areas had the highest.

The adoption of compulsory school attendance policies and the growth of mass public education created a critical shortage of trained teachers and a need for more efficient mechanisms for training teachers and measuring their effectiveness in standardized ways. The development of normal schools as teacher-training institutions has served in most countries in the world to fulfill this need for a certified labor force in schools (Herbst 1989). Despite the expansion of teacher training, however, shortages of qualified teachers continued to be a serious problem. In the United States this problem was exacerbated by the shift to local control by school districts which often fell short of funds. To deal with the problem these districts looked for less expensive teachers. Male teachers began leaving schools in large numbers as the broader job market opened up, and, because most job markets were closed to women, they were hired as teachers and worked for lower wages. By the first decades of the twentieth century, teaching was seen as a revolving-door career (Rury 1989). For men who stayed in teaching, most went on to administrative positions, and turnover rates for women teachers were extremely high because of sanctions against their being married and teaching. The feminization of teaching did not occur because school districts hired only women because they were cheaper, nor because women willingly accepted low wages. Instead, "cash poor," largely rural school districts hired women because they were an available labor source, and women accepted low wages because their options in the work force were seriously limited (Warren 1985, Strober and Lanford 1986).

The feminization of teaching is a phenomenon found in all countries. Clifford (1989) found that in France between 1900 and 1936 the proportion of male teachers in elementary schools decreased from one-half to one-third, and in Germany in 1900, 85 percent of teachers were male, with significant decreases shown during the same time period. By the turn of the nineteenth century in the United States, three-fourths of all teachers were women, and by 1920, they comprised 86 percent of all teachers. From data collected around the 1930s, out of 26 nations, 41.5 percent of teachers were male. At the secondary level, however, there were higher proportions of men worldwide (71.8 percent), except for the United States and Ireland where men represented less than half of secondary-school teachers. Since that time, however, in the United States secondary teachers have become increasingly male.

Around the time of the Second World War, both because males were in short supply, and later because of the postwar baby boom's creation of rapid growth in school enrollment, teacher shortages became particularly acute. To meet these demands, sanctions against women teachers marrying were eliminated, although women continued to leave teaching to have children. High teacher turnover rates were reflected in Musgrave's (1968) description of United Kingdom teachers in the early 1960s; 19,000 teachers per year came into schools, but 18,000 left.

Although schools in all countries have depended on women as their labor pool, women teachers have been strikingly absent from the history of teaching until work in the 1980s and 1990s by feminist scholars. Historical overviews are provided by Hoffman (1981), Kaufman (1984), and Althenbaugh (1992), who examine women's personal accounts of their teaching in the United States at the turn of the century, whereas Spencer (1986) looks at accounts of contemporary women teachers. Also, a collection edited by Prentice and Theobald (1991) on women teachers in the United Kingdom, Australia, Canada, and the United States, as well as DeLyon and Migniudo's (1989) and Acker's (1989) volumes on United Kingdom teachers, add to a much more complex view of women teachers' roles in the history of schooling.

1.2 Social Characteristics of Teachers

Among the ways that sociologists have described teachers and assessed their homogeneity and heterogeneity is by their social characteristics. Overall, the teaching force comprises a significant proportion of the labor force throughout the world. A report on teachers in OECD (Organisation for Economic Co-operation and Development) countries shows that despite alarmist views the size of the teaching force has not declined over recent years (OECD 1990). Instead, a significant drop in birthrates in all countries, except Australia and Sweden, has created a shrinking student population rather than a shrinking teaching force.

As was seen in Sect. 1.1, the most distinctive social characteristic of schoolteachers is that they have been predominantly female since the early stages of industrialization. The picture in the early 1990s, however, shows considerable diversity between countries and within countries at different levels of the education system (OECD 1990). Women are predominant at preprimary and primary or elementary levels, while secondary levels show a more mixed picture. With some exceptions, women make up less than half of secondary teachers in most countries.

The most striking gender difference is found in the significant underrepresentation of women in administrative positions. This is true for all OECD countries, and in some countries, such as Canada, Australia, and the Netherlands, there has even been a reduction of women in leadership positions. In Australia, for example, between 1971 and 1983 in Victoria, the number of female secondary heads was reduced by half (Burke 1989, cited in OECD 1990). The fact that men manage most schools means they also typically earn significantly higher salaries than women teachers. Thus the gender gap creates and perpetuates a parallel wage gap within teaching.

Another social characteristic of teachers is their age. Historically, during periods of teacher shortages and low levels of teacher training, teachers entered teaching at 15 or 16 years of age. As requirements for training increased, the age of entrance to teaching also increased. Rury (1989) points out that the influence of changing roles for women in this century is reflected in a bimodal age distribution of teachers. This is created by entrance into teaching at a young age, and re-entry after marriage and raising children.

The report of teachers of OECD countries concludes that aging as a factor affecting the teaching force may be exaggerated (OECD 1990). For example, in the United States the median age of teachers was the same in 1961 as in 1986: 41 years. Rather than aging, teachers are now at a historical norm. In general, to say teachers are an"aging" population reflects shifts in credentialing requirements rather than the lack of new entrants in the profession. The report acknowledges that although the long-term effects of an aging teaching population can result in such problems as teacher shortages and more teachers at higher salary levels, there is no evidence to support the notion that younger teachers are better than older teachers. In fact, the opposite would seem to be the case because older teachers are also more experienced.

1.3 Social Mobility of Teachers

An important indicator of a person's position in the social structure is his or her occupation. For many sociologists, occupational mobility is considered the most important measure of social mobility. However, social mobility, or the movement from one position to another in a social system, is too complex a factor on which to base international comparisons of teachers. Such comparisons are particularly difficult, given the vast differences in economic systems and their effects on the classification and characteristics of social classes within countries.

In the United States, there has been a shift in teachers' social class background since the turn of the nineteenth century from farm and blue-collar backgrounds to middle- and upper-middle-class backgrounds. Havighurst and Levine (1979) found that by 1939 teachers were mostly from the lower middle class, and in the decades after that time, teachers came increasingly from more heterogeneous backgrounds. By 1986 teachers' fathers' occupations were as follows: farmers, 13.1 percent; unskilled workers, 8.7 percent; skilled or semiskilled workers, 29.9 percent; clerical or sales workers, 5.0 percent; managerial or self-employed, 21.5 percent; professional or semiprofessionals, 21.9 percent (NEA 1987). As teachers' backgrounds have become more similar to those of their parents, the extent to which they show intergenerational mobility, has reduced.

A study of Polish teachers showed their level of satisfaction with teaching and pay was correlated to their qualifications, to the location of their job, and to their social class background—primarily farming or manual work (Górowska-Fells 1991). The explanation for greater dissatisfaction among teachers from higher social class backgrounds is that they see the discrepancy between their current position and that of their families. Dissatisfaction among teachers with blue-collar backgrounds may be due to discrepancies between their positions within the country's intelligentsia and their low pay when compared to other white-collar workers, between their salary and the many duties they must perform, and between their low salaries and the high prestige level afforded teachers in Polish society.

The occupational prestige (that is, societal judgments or social approval accorded to an occupation) of teachers has been low. For example, the findings of a rating system of occupational prestige developed in the United States in 1947 by the National Opinion Research Center (NORC) show that since that time teachers have ranked below professions such as medicine and law and above other public service semiprofessions. In Poland, where social prestige is solely dependent on one's occupation, teachers, with other professions requiring high levels of education, have ranked high on surveys of occupational prestige (Górowska-Fells 1991).

A factor in ranking occupational prestige is teachers' salaries, which are used as indicators of the value a society places on teachers' work. International comparisons of teachers' salaries are extremely difficult given differences in currencies, as well as geographical location and types of school within countries (rural to urban, public and private schools), responsibilities in and out of the classroom, length of working day, years of teaching experience, and level of teacher qualifications. However, in the European Community several organizations have compared teachers' salaries both within and between countries. Peck (1992) has summarized their findings and found that teachers' pay in the mid- to late-1980s was less than industrial workers in Italy (58 percent of industrial workers' pay), Austria (66 percent),

England and Wales (75 percent), and Norway (95 percent). The best teachers' pay was found in Switzerland (128 to 312 percent of industrial workers' pay), the Netherlands, West Germany, and Denmark. Comparisons between countries showed the highest paid teachers were in Luxembourg, West Germany, and Denmark, and the lowest paid in Scotland, Belgium, France, and Italy. These data assume teachers are a homogeneous group, but gender differences in pay are found across all OECD countries; teachers' salaries have been high for women compared to other women workers, but low for men (OECD 1990).

Salmon (1987) has concluded that in the United States, not only are teachers' salaries lower than other professions, but during the 10-year period between 1976–77 and 1986–87, teachers lost gains in salary in relation to inflation rates. Anthony (1987) takes this pattern a step further and found that, not only are teachers' salaries less then other professions which require a four-year college education, but teachers are also no better off than people in occupations that do not require a college degree. Lawton (1987) estimates it would require a 25 percent increase in pay to place teachers at international norms for the position of teachers in the overall occupational structure.

Despite teachers' low pay in the United States, in a study conducted by the International Consortium for Cross-cultural Research in Education of nearly 4,000 teachers in the United States, the United Kingdom, West Germany, Japan, Singapore, and Poland, the least frustration with working conditions was reported among teachers in the United States (Wiśniewski 1991). In fact, 40 percent of teachers in the United States reported high levels of satisfaction with their work, while only about 20 percent of teachers in Singapore and the United Kingdom, 14 percent of those in West Germany and Poland, and 9 percent of those in Japan reported high levels of satisfaction. At the same time West German teachers reported the most satisfaction with their pay (50 percent), while only one-third of the teachers in Singapore, 30 percent of those in the United States, 7 percent of those in the United Kingdom, and 2 percent in Japan and Poland reported satisfaction.

In the United States about one-half of all teachers have second jobs. This varies by gender, with 72 percent of the males having second jobs, and 33 percent of the females. Peck (1992) reports that Greek teachers, among the lowest paid in Europe, also frequently hold second jobs. The effect of teachers taking second jobs which are not necessarily commensurate with their education is that it diminishes the status of teachers in the eyes of the public (Anthony 1987).

In summary, teachers have suffered from low pay and low prestige in most societies throughout the history of teaching (Herbst 1989). As the overall level of education of societies increases, and teachers come from higher social classes, both their intergenerational and intragenerational mobility becomes more limited. Within teaching, social mobility continues to be mostly horizontal, particularly for women, just as Becker (1952) described it in the 1950s.

2. *Teaching as a Profession*

Whether or not an occupation is considered a profession has been measured by different, yet arbitrary, sets of standards. Sociologists characterize a profession as having a specialized body of knowledge based on systematic theories and transmitted through a formalized educational process, a clearly defined code of ethics which serves as a basis for monitoring by others in the profession, an orientation to serving the public, authority over clients, and autonomy and control over the work environment.

Through the 1970s, sociologists of education examined teaching from this definition and deemed it short of fulfilling these characteristics (Etzioni 1969, Lortie 1975). Some, but not all, of the characteristics of a profession are found; teaching has no specialized body of knowledge, teachers have less training than the traditional professions, and they work in isolated environments with little autonomy over working conditions. These problems, as well as teachers' presumed lack of commitment to their work and unstructured work patterns, were attributed to the fact that most teachers are women. Therefore, teaching was labeled a "semiprofession" and grouped with other female-dominated occupations, including nursing and social work.

It has been suggested that attempts to evaluate whether teaching is a profession are of use only to sociologists for the sake of comparisons with other work, but are of "limited practical value" (OECD 1990, Griffin 1992). Among the suggestions for reexamination of professionalism among teachers are that the concept should not be used as a dichotomous categorization, but instead should describe points along a continuum or that the term "open professionalism" be used to indicated blurred distinctions in categorization (OECD 1990). It has also been suggested that because commitment to teaching has been assessed through the use of arbitrary standards, it does not reflect the balance of women's commitments to their families and to their work (Grant 1989, Spencer 1985). Rather than lack of commitment to their work, women show nontraditional career patterns. And last, there is a need for the reconceptualization of teachers' careers, which typically do not follow a linear path and should be considered in relation to changing labor markets for women. Teachers' careers are in a state of constant change as teachers adapt to new situations and organizational contexts (Goodson and Walker 1991).

Careers, then, should be regarded as "a series of experiences in coming to terms with situations and making choices subject to constraints" (Acker 1989 p. 9).

2.1 Teacher Recruitment

The single most powerful recruiter of teachers is the schools themselves. People who have had positive experiences in school can prolong that experience by becoming teachers. Their many years of observation of teachers serves as a basis for their career decision and a model for their own behavior in the classroom.

In view of teachers' low salaries in most countries it is not surprising that they are attracted to teaching for its intrinsic rewards. In the United States teachers' altruism is seen as one of the most common reasons given for entering teaching in annual surveys administered to teachers in the latter half of the twentieth century (Lortie 1975). The results of the 1987 poll reflect this continuity in attractors to teaching: a desire to work with young people (65.6 percent), belief in the value of education in society (37.2 percent), and interest in a particular subject (37.1 percent) (NEA 1987).

While interpersonal and service themes have been prevalent over time, other factors which have influenced recruitment to teaching have been crosscut by gender issues. The restriction of occupational choices for women in the work force has served as an attractor to teaching, as well as the flexibility of work schedule which women find more compatible with family life.

2.2 Teacher Training and Socialization

Teacher socialization, or the process through which teachers learn and internalize accepted patterns of behavior in schools, has remained remarkably similar across time, beginning with Waller's (1984) seminal work, first published in 1932, through Lortie's (1975) highly influential work, to studies by Spencer (1985) and Johnson (1990). Griffin (1992) divides this process into three stages: the prospective teacher stage, the new teacher stage, and the experienced teacher stage.

The prospective teacher stage includes teacher education, plus what Lortie calls the period of "mini-apprenticeship" and others call practicum or student teaching experience. An examination of the social characteristics of teacher education students shows that teachers are much more highly educated than in the past. However, standardized test scores among students in the United States show they do much less well when compared to others who earn college degrees. Parelius and Parelius (1987) report that teachers have always scored poorly on standardized tests of academic ability and achievement. They claim that standards for becoming a teacher have never been high as a result of historical periods when demand for teachers was high and schools of education lowered standards to meet the demand. Standards were also lowered during periods when students have been attracted to other fields. Kerr (1983) explains that the talent pool for teaching has diminished, or a "brain drain" has occurred. This has created dual problems in which those with the best teaching credentials do not enter teaching at all, and of those who are hired, the best teachers leave because of the loss in teacher salary buying power and changes in job opportunities for women. In response to these criticisms of teacher education students, it should be borne in mind that about 11 percent of them are drawn from the highest quintile of the Scholastic Aptitude Test (SAT), which is a much higher proportion than one would expect for an occupation which is characterized by low pay and low status (Schlechty and Vance 1983).

Sykes (1983) characterizes this stage of teacher socialization by its "ease of entry" into teaching through minimal expenditures of time, money, and effort, and goes on to say that, "In fact, the current limitations of teacher education represent a nicely calibrated adaptation to the economic status of teachers. As constituted, teacher education continues to be a recruitment incentive by virtue of its very *lack* of rigor" (p. 581).

An ongoing debate across countries focuses on whether more emphasis should be placed on the extension of teacher training in subject matter or on pedagogical methods (OECD 1990). There are marked differences between countries in terms of the quality and relevance of teacher education courses, as well as the length of teacher training. Countries which have extended the length of teacher preparation are the Republic of Ireland, France, Austria, Finland, Switzerland, and Portugal. Counter to the trend in the United States to require secondary-level teachers to complete more rigorous training in their subject area, in the Netherlands there has been a reduction of training in an academic area from six to four years and more emphasis on teaching practice.

The final phase of the prospective teacher stage is student teaching or practicum, which serves as a transitional phase of anticipatory socialization which aids adaptation to the first teaching experience (Hoy 1968). Mickelson (1990) cites a study at the University of Victoria, British Columbia, Canada, in which 86 percent of education students placed much higher value on their practicum than on their university course work.

The new teacher stage includes the first year of teaching. This stage has been described as a survival stage in which teachers resort to trial-and-error methods for solving classroom problems. Their problems are exacerbated by the lack of collegial support networks for new teachers in schools and the inhibitions teachers have of asking other teachers for help. It is at this stage that teachers are socialized into the school culture and to the norms and expectations for their behaviors.

The experienced teacher stage is an ongoing phase of socialization. As their experience increases, teachers learn strategies for coping and learn to live with the isolated structure of classrooms within schools. Their attitudes toward their work, students, and work environment are shaped through experience as well as through interactions with other teachers. Comments of other teachers in informal settings, such as teachers' workrooms and lounges, are particularly powerful forums for the transmission of expectations for students and for the school as a workplace.

3. Conclusion

Teaching as an occupation and the social characteristics of teachers have been and will continue to be affected by social conditions and societal expectations for schools and for teachers' roles. Sociologists of education will chart those changes as they pay increasing attention to micro-level analyses which focus on the perspectives of teachers about their work.

See also: Teaching: Implicit Theories

References

Acker S (ed.) 1989 *Teachers, Gender and Careers*. Falmer Press, London

Altenbaugh R J (ed.) 1992 *The Teacher's Voice*. Falmer Press, London

Anthony P 1987 Teachers in the economic system. In: Alexander K, Monk D (eds.) 1987 *Attracting and Compensating America's Teachers*. Ballinger, Cambridge, Massachusetts

Anyon J 1980 Social class and the hidden curriculum of work. *J. Educ.* 162(1): 67–92

Apple M W 1985 Teaching and "women's work": A comparative historical and ideological analysis. *Teach. Coll. Rec.* 86(3): 455–73

Becker H S 1952 The career of the Chicago public school teachers. *Am. J. Sociol.* 57: 470–77

Bowles S, Gintis H 1976 *Schooling in Capitalist America*. Basic Books, New York

Burke G 1989 Teachers in Australia: Teacher supply and teacher quality: Social and economic aspects. OECD Working Document, Paris

Clifford G J 1989 Man/woman/teacher: Gender, family and career in American educational history. In: Warren D (ed.) 1989

Connell R W, Ashenden D J, Kessler S, Dowsett G W 1982 *Making the Difference: Schools, Families and Social Division*. George Allen and Unwin, Sydney

DeLyon H, Migniudo F W (eds.) 1989 *Women Teachers: Issues and Experiences*. Open University Press, Milton Keynes

Etzioni A (ed.) 1969 *The Semi-Professions and Their Organization: Teachers, Nurses, Social Workers*. The Free Press, New York

Goodson I F, Walker R 1991 *Biography, Identity and Schooling: Episodes in Educational Research*. Falmer Press, London

Górowska-Fells M 1991 The financial position of the Polish teachers in the mid nineteen-eighties. Zeszyt 49, University of Warsaw, Warsaw

Grant R 1989 Women teachers' career pathways: Towards an alternative model of "career." In: Acker S (ed.) 1989

Griffin G 1992 Teacher education. In: Alkin M (ed.) 1992 *Encyclopedia of Educational Research*, 6th edn. Macmillan, New York

Havighurst R J, Levine D U 1979 *Society and Education*, 5th edn. Allyn and Bacon, Boston, Massachusetts

Herbst J 1989 *And Sadly Teach: Teacher Education and Professionalization in American Culture*. University of Wisconsin Press, Madison, Wisconsin

Hoffman N (ed.) 1981 *Woman's "True" Profession: Voices from the History of Teaching*. The Feminist Press, Old Westbury, New York

Hoy W K 1968 The influence of experience on the beginning teacher. *Sch. Rev.* 76(3): 312–23

Johnson S M 1990 *Teachers at Work: Achieving Excellence in Our Schools*. Basic Books, New York

Kaufman P W 1984 *Women Teachers on the Frontier*. Yale University Press, New Haven, Connecticut

Kerr D 1983 Teaching competence and teacher education in the United States. In: Shulman L S, Sykes G (eds.) 1983 *Handbook of Teaching and Policy*. Longman, New York

Lawton S 1987 Teachers' salaries: An international perspective. In: Alexander K, Monk D (eds.) 1987 *Attracting and Compensating America's Teachers*. Ballinger, Cambridge, Massachusetts

Lortie D C 1975 *Schoolteacher: A Sociological Study*. University of Chicago Press, Chicago, Illinois

Metz M 1990 How social class differences shape teachers' work. In: McLaughlin M W, Talbert J E, Bascia N (eds.) 1990 *The Contexts of Teaching in Secondary Schools: Teachers' Realities*. Teachers College Press, New York

Mickelson N I 1990 The role of the practicum in the preparation of teachers. In: Orteza y, Miranda E, Magsino R F (eds.) 1990 *Teaching, Schools, and Society*. Falmer Press, London

Musgrave P W 1968 *Society and Education in England Since 1800*. Methuen, London

NEA (National Education Association) 1987 *Status of the American Public School Teacher, 1985–86*. NEA, Westhaven, Connecticut

OECD 1990 *The Teacher Today: Tasks, Conditions, Policies*. Organisation for Economic Co-operation and Development, Paris

Page R 1987 Teachers' perceptions of students: A link between classrooms, school cultures, and the social order. *Anthropol. Educ. Q.* 18(2): 77–99

Parelius R J, Parelius A P 1987 *The Sociology of Education*. Prentice-Hall, Englewood Cliffs, New Jersey

Peck B T 1992 Perspectives on teachers' pay. *Phi Del. Kap.* 73(9): 734–35

Prentice A, Theobald M R (eds.) 1991 *Women Who Taught: Perspectives on the History of Women and Teaching*. University of Toronto Press, Toronto

Rury J L 1989 Who became teachers? The social characteristics of teachers in American history. In: Warren D (ed.) 1989

Salmon R G 1987 Teacher salaries: Progress over the decade. In: Alexander K, Monk D (eds.) 1987

Schlechty P C, Vance V S 1983 Recruitment, selection,

and retention: The shape of the teaching force. *Elem. Sch. J.* 83(4): 469–87
Spencer D A 1981 Looking behind the teacher's back. *Elem. Sch. J.* 81(5): 281–89
Spencer D A 1986 *Contemporary Women Teachers: Balancing School and Home*. Longman, New York
Strober M H, Lanford A G 1986 The feminization of public school teaching: Cross-sectional analysis 1850–1880. *Signs* 11(2): 212–35
Stubbs M, Delamont D (eds.) 1976 *Explorations in Classroom Observation*. Wiley, London
Sykes G 1983 Caring about teachers. Response to Donna Kerr. *Teach. Coll. Rec.* 84(3): 579–92
Waller W 1984 What teaching does to teachers: Determinants of the occupational type. In: Hargreaves A, Woods P (eds.) 1984 *Classrooms and Staffrooms: The Sociology of Teachers and Teaching*. Open University Press, Milton Keynes
Warren D 1985 Learning from experience: History and teacher education. *Educ. Researcher* 14(10): 5–12
Warren D (ed.) 1989 *American Teachers: Histories of a Profession at Work*. Macmillan, New York
Wiśniewski W 1991 Job satisfaction of secondary school teachers in six countries: the USA, England, West Germany, Japan, Singapore, and Poland. Zeszyt 49, University of Warsaw, Warsaw
Woods P 1983 *Sociology and the School: An Interactionist Viewpoint*. Routledge and Kegan Paul, London

Further Reading

Dreeben R 1970 *The Nature of Teaching*. Scott Foresman, Glenview, Illinois
Popkewitz T S 1991 *A Political Sociology of Educational Reform: Power/Knowledge in Teaching, Teacher Education and Research*. Teachers College Press, New York

D. A. Spencer

Sociometric Methods

Sociometry and sociometric methods are concerned with the study of the ways people interact with one another. Knowledge about how people in groups choose one another for friendship, work, and other activities tells us much about group structures and the ways they change. This knowledge also tells us about the ways that individuals in groups behave, and why.

The origins and development of sociometry are inextricably linked with educational research. Moreno, the originator of sociometry and the sociometric method, based many of his early observations on studies of student classroom structure and the evolution of groups (Moreno 1934). He clearly documented the structures of groups from kindergarten to the eighth grade. The analysis of group properties is facilitated by the sociometric test which requires an individual to choose his associates for any group of which he is or might become a member. The individual is expected to make the choices without restraints and is not limited to members of his or her own group. In order to be sociometric, the test must determine, according to specified criteria (e.g., sitting or working together), the feelings of individuals toward each other (attraction or rejection). The representation of these choices in two-dimensional space is known as a "sociogram," which portrays in graphic form the sociometric "stars," the "isolates," the "cliques," and other patterns of group structure.

Virtually no aspect of the educational process has been unexplored by sociometric research, including cognitive development, creativity and innovativeness, school success, and teacher effectiveness.

1. Early and Recent Uses of Sociometric Methods

Both the techniques of designing a sociometric test, as well as the statistical procedures for analyzing the results, have undergone considerable change over the years.

In its original form, the sociometric test was deceptively simple. Northway (1967) suggests that in any test, three or four criteria should be used as the basis for choices, the choices should be limited in number, and the choice questions should be stated in the conditional mood. Hence, the appropriate question is not "With whom do you associate," but "If all things were possible and you could associate with anyone you liked, with whom would you choose to associate?" Although Northway argued that three criteria and three choices for each individual were desirable, others have contended that an unspecified number of choices is necessary to locate the full range of choice patterns (Lindzey and Byrne 1968).

There have been many variations on the standard sociometric question. One has been the "self-rating method" whereby the subject predicts by whom he or she will be chosen and how all members of the group will relate to each other through their choices. Other methods include "scaling instruments" which are designed to elicit ratings of members of groups in terms of their capacity to meet certain needs, such as affiliation and recognition. More complex approaches have combined sociometric data with other information to portray the group structure more accurately, while the time spent with individuals on certain tasks and interpersonal attractiveness have also found their way into sociometric tests.

In fact, it has been found that different approaches can produce different sociometric results. Schwarzwald et al. (1986) found that "nomination" and "rating" methods resulted in different patterns of sex and ethnic group cleavages in the classroom. In terms of willingness to participate in activities of low, medium, or high intimacy, junior high school students were asked to identify three classmates most desired as partners for each activity (the nomination approach), and also to rate students in terms of a positive desire for each classmate (the rating approach). The researchers found that the nomination technique produced a heightened picture of sex and ethnic cleavage relative to the rating approach, and also that the former was insensitive to the level of intimacy of the sociometric content.

1.1 Quantitative Methods in Sociometric Analysis

The earliest approach to the quantification and organization of sociometric data was the matrix whereby all choices are recorded and then summed. The names of individuals are listed along the vertical and horizontal axes and the choices are recorded in the cells for each criterion which is being tested. According to Northway (1967) the total number of choices for all criteria provides a social acceptance score or an indication of sociometric status. The actual number of persons choosing the subject gives a social receptiveness score, while the number of individuals chosen by the subject gives a social expansion score. It is also possible to identify groups of individuals for whom choices are or are not reciprocated, as well as the social isolates who neither choose nor are chosen.

Other methods have been applied to sociometric data. Of considerable use has been the probability model which identifies individuals who receive greater or fewer choices than they would ordinarily receive by chance. More complex matrix approaches consist of reordering rows and columns, by trial and error, until the clique structure of the group is located. Likewise, factor analysis has been used to identify and isolate underlying dimensions of group structure (Proctor and Loomis 1951, Lindzey and Byrne 1968, Hallinan 1974).

1.2 Graphic Presentation of Sociometric Data

The sociogram provides a graphic portrayal of sociometric information. It is constructed on the principle that choices between individuals may be symmetric (reciprocated), asymmetric (not reciprocated), or nonexistent. The major limitation of the sociogram is that it cannot deal adequately with large groups. Some researchers have argued, for example, that 20 persons is the ideal size for sociometric analysis, although more have been used.

In its original form, group members were designated by symbols with lines and arrows to indicate the direction of choice (Moreno 1934 pp. 33–44). Northway (1967) introduced the notion of the "target sociogram" which contained four concentric circles similar to an archery target. Each circle represented four quartiles or the four levels of probability: significantly above chance, above chance, below chance, and significantly below chance—from the center outward. The "stars" were placed in the center circle and the "isolates" in the outside circle. A vertical line through the center of the diagram was used to separate males and females, and the choice levels for each circle were usually indicated below each circle line (Northway 1967, Gronlund 1959).

Recent usage of the sociogram has tended to focus on cliques rather than individuals. An early example of this clique-oriented structure is found in Coleman's (1961) analysis of adolescent friendship groups and their value systems. Hargreaves (1967) focused his attention on the clique structure of groups rather than individual "stars" or "isolates." Figure 1 reproduces a sociogram from Hargreaves's analysis of Form 4A boys in Lumley Secondary Modern School for Boys in England. Here it can be seen that Clique A dominates the group structure but with Cliques B and C also prevalent. The "star" of Clique A is Adrian (No. 29) who is also school captain.

The sociogram can display some of the main features of group sociometric structure, and also some of the variations in structure within different organizational environments. For example, Ford (1969) studied friendship choice in three English secondary schools (grammar, comprehensive, and modern secondary) to test the hypothesis that the comprehensive school students would manifest more sociometric mixing than students in the other two types of schools because of its more heterogeneous student population. In the event, she found that sex differentiation in sociometric choices prevailed in all schools and in all streams. Furthermore she found that differentiation by social class in all schools and streams also prevailed, except for the top three streams in the elite grammar school. Students in the comprehensive school, although in heterogeneous social environments, tended to choose friends from their own social class and from within their stream. These patterns are clearly visible in the sociograms which Ford constructed (see Ford 1969 pp. 86–99).

Ford concluded that the exceptional case of the upper streams in the grammar school could be explained in terms of the dominance of the high aspirations of all students in these streams, irrespective of class background, and thus indicates the greater importance of "class of aspiration" over "class of origin" in sociometric choices.

1.3 Limitations of Sociometric Data

The sociogram can sometimes be misused or misinterpreted. Gronlund (1959) has identified four common errors: (a) the sociogram usually depicts a graphic picture of desired associations, not actual associations; (b) the sociogram depicts the internal structure of the group, and therefore provides an incomplete depiction of group structure; (c) the choice patterns are sometimes seen as representing a fixed group structure rather than a changing social process; and (d) the sociometric structure will appear different when constructed by different individuals.

There is a further problem related to that previously noted by Schwarzwald et al. (1986) above. The findings of sociometric research sometimes

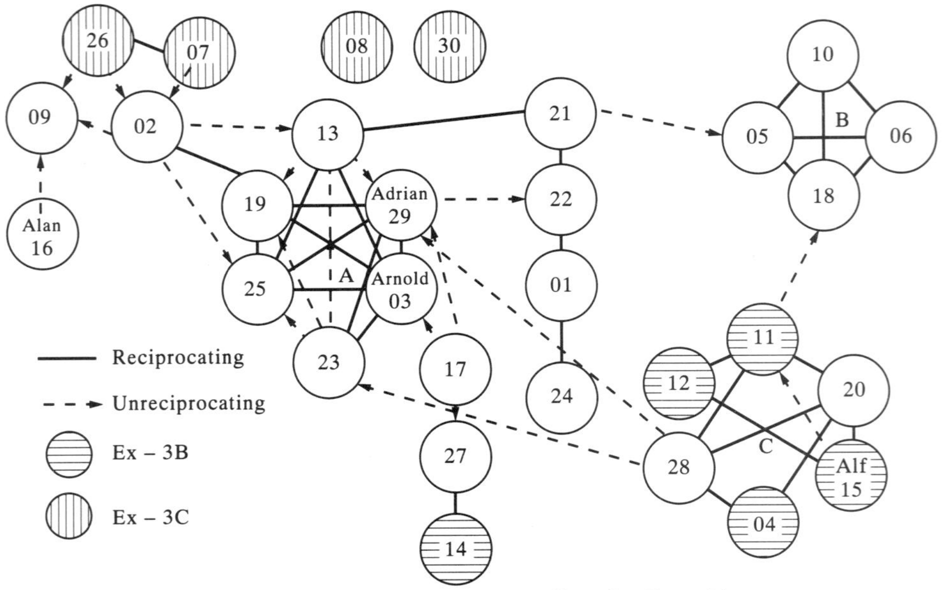

Figure 1
Sociogram depicting group structure of Form 4A (hatched circles represent students not in form 3A the previous year)

appear to contradict findings using other methods. This was the case with Denscombe et al. (1986) who found that the ethnic bias resulting from a sociometric study of British primary school students did not agree with the perceptions of teachers, who reported a high level of student integration and interracial mixing. A study using fieldwork observations of the same students supported the teachers' perceptions rather than that resulting from the sociometric research. It would appear that the sociometric research design produces a particular description, and sometimes explanation, of social reality using a specific measurement, but that other designs and measurements may result in other descriptions or explanations. Thus interpretations and generalizations based on sociometric methods must be made with care.

2. *Sociometrics and Educational Research*

The importance of sociometry for educational research rests on the recognition that individual behavior is profoundly influenced by the group of which the individual is a member. Within the classroom, motivation, achievement, conduct, pupil–pupil and pupil–teacher relations are affected by group social composition and particularly informal group structure. A selective discussion of the findings of educational research using sociometric techniques points to some patterns of classroom behavior resulting from the sociometric context.

2.1 Intelligence and Achievement

There are distinct sociometric differences between students with extremely high or low intelligence (Gronlund 1959). Low intelligence may interfere with social acceptance by a person's peers, but high intelligence is not sufficient for high sociometric status. Pupils tend to choose those who are similar in intelligence, and a high deviation from group norms results in low peer acceptance. Gronlund (1959) identifies many studies which suggest that high levels of achievement are related to high social acceptance, but the direction of causality is not clear. However, the relationship is strongest where achievement is most highly valued by the group. The same pattern seems to hold for other skills which are highly valued, for example, in sport, playing a musical instrument, or social skills.

2.2 Social Factors

Social factors influence sociometric choice. Hollingshead's (1949) study pointed to high class homophily with regard to adolescent friendship patterns: two-thirds of all girls' clique relations and more than half the boys' were between members of the same social class. A reanalysis of recent data from Elmtown showed less choice between class equals, which suggests that over time the class structure in Elmtown had become more open and flexible, and hence less a criterion for sociometric choice (Cohen 1979).

Similar patterns have been found regarding other social factors, such as family status, residential proximity and even child-rearing strategies. Hart et al. (1990) report a study of mothers and their first-to-fourth grade children, using home interviews with the mothers before the beginning of the school year, and subsequent studies of the pupils after the school year began. They found that children of power assertive mothers also practiced assertive techniques, and they expected successful outcomes for these assertive methods. However, these assertive pupils were less accepted by their peers in terms of sociometric choice.

2.3 Classroom Interaction

It is generally recognized that greater involvement in group activity and satisfactory social relationships leads to less emotional tension and thus provides a better environment for classroom learning. Shared group activities tend to promote greater affective ties, and teachers can manipulate the classroom situation to promote greater interaction and thus more interpersonal relationships. Classroom organization, both controlled and uncontrolled by the teacher, has a pronounced effect on the social development of students.

3. Applicability of Sociometrics to the Improvement of Social and Cognitive Development

The knowledge derived from sociometric research is directly applicable to the improvement of social and cognitive development. Sociometric grouping whereby each individual is best placed for his or her own social and cognitive development is fundamental. Sociodrama and the use of roleplaying have also received attention for promoting beneficial classroom structures. Finally, a recognition of the importance of power and influence, leadership and headship, both between students and between teacher and student, facilitates the utilization of group structures already present in the classroom setting (see *Group Processes in the Classroom*).

4. Future Directions in Sociometric Research

New developments in sociogram construction include three-dimensional models based on a number of variables. Klovdahl (1982) has used computer programs to create and manipulate visual, including stereoscopic, representations of sociometric data and has suggested that the increasing availability of sophisticated interactive computer graphics promises to stimulate the development of theory about complex relational data. Many of these developments are taking place in the broader field of social network research, which includes the study of communities and organizations, as well as schools and other educational institutions.

Hallinan (1974) finds the traditional quantitative techniques of sociometric analysis too weak for an adequate analysis of the complexity of group sentiment and structure, and argues that there is more promise in the use of powerful mathematical theories and methods, such as Markov chains, matrix algebra, abstract algebra, game theory, and differential equations. With respect to schooling, greater attention to the process of group formation, its development and decline, is required to understand better the dynamics of classroom interaction and their consequences. Finally, there is need to utilize what is now known about sociometrics in educational practice, particularly classroom pedagogy, to improve further classroom learning and general school effectiveness.

See also: Ability Grouping and Tracking in Schools; Peer Relations and Development; Peer Relations and Learning; School and Classroom Dynamics; School Organizational Effects on Student Outcomes; Social Interaction and Learning; Student Friendships and Conflict in School

References

Cohen J 1979 Socioeconomic status and high school friendship choice: Elmtown's youth revisited. *Social Networks* 2(1): 65–74

Coleman J S 1961 *The Adolescent Society: The Social Life of the Teenager and its Impact on Education*. Free Press, New York

Denscombe M, Szulc H, Patrick C, Wood A 1986 Ethnicity and friendship: The contrast between sociometric research and fieldwork observation in primary school classrooms. *Brit. Educ. Res. J.* 12(3): 221–35

Ford J B 1969 *Social Class and the Comprehensive School*. Routledge and Kegan Paul, London

Gronlund N E 1959 *Sociometry in the Classroom*. Harper and Row, New York

Hallinan M T 1974 *The Structure of Positive Sentiment*. Elsevier, New York

Hargreaves D H 1967 *Social Relations in a Secondary School*. Routledge and Kegan Paul, London

Hart C H, Ladd G W, Burleson B R 1990 Children's expectations of the outcomes of social strategies: Relations with sociometric status and maternal disciplinary styles. *Child Dev.* 61(1): 127–37

Hollingshead A B 1949 *Elmtown's Youth: The Impact of Social Classes on Adolescents*. Wiley, New York

Klovdahl A S 1982 A note on images of networks. *Social Networks* 3(3): 197–214

Lindzey G, Byrne D 1968 Measurement of social choice and interpersonal attractiveness. In: Lindzey G, Aronson E (eds.) 1968 *The Handbook of Social Psychology. Vol. 2: Research Methods*, 2nd edn. Addison-Wesley, Reading, Massachusetts

Moreno J L 1934 *Who Shall Survive? A New Approach to the Problem of Human Interrelations*. Nervous and Mental Disease, Washington, DC

Northway M L 1967 *A Primer of Sociometry*. University of Toronto Press, Toronto

Proctor C H, Loomis C P 1951 Analysis of sociometric data. In: Jahoda M, Deutsch M, Cook S W (eds.) 1951 *Research Methods in Social Relations: With Special Ref-*

erence to Prejudice, Part. 2: Selected Techniques. Dryden, New York

Schwarzwald J, Laor T, Hoffman M 1986 Impact of sociometric method and activity content on assessment of intergroup relations in the classroom. *Brit. J. Educ. Psychol.* 56(1): 24–31

Sociometry: A Journal of Interpersonal Relations 1937–78 (since 1978 known as *Social Psychology*)

L. J. Saha

Software Publishing

Since the early 1980s, a new industry has emerged, namely that of educational software publishing. It is a curious industry insofar as it originated in the days of mainframe computer usage by schools, often via terminals connected by telephone to a remote location. The software that was available to schools was generally given freely and the schools were encouraged in the belief that it had no intrinsic value, that is, it did not have to be purchased. The emergence of the stand-alone microcomputer created a demand for educational software, which in the first phase of development was often less powerful than that used on the remote mainframes. The development of the microcomputer in terms of color, memory size, speed, screen control, user interface, sound, screen dynamics, and portability has been accelerating since 1977 without any sign of slowing down. The problems encountered by the software developers and publishers have been significant in terms of exploiting new technologies and at the same time, maintaining economic viability. Another development is that software specifically written for the business and commercial markets has begun to be used by teachers, more because of its power and reliability than its suitability for use in the classroom. Some publishers have extended their activities to include curriculum materials that help teachers use the business software in an educational context.

1. The Software Developers

The first educational software used in schools was, in the great majority of cases, developed by "enthusiasts" rather than professional writers. Often these enthusiasts were teachers who had written a program for their own students and made it available to other teachers, sometimes at little or no cost. The software was rarely documented and never had any associated curriculum materials. Although many of these programs circulated in the late 1970s and early 1980s, the quality was low and very few have survived.

1.1 Government Initiatives

The customers, that is, the teachers, began to demand quality rather than quantity in the mid-1980s, and as a result a number of initiatives were instigated to raise standards and produce software more appropriate to teachers' needs. Prominent amongst these initiatives were the United Kingdom's Microelectronics Education Project, the French *Lycée Nanoreseau* initiative, the Dutch Nivo Project, the Spanish Atenea Project, the Portuguese Project Minerva, the Minnesota Educational Computing Corporation in the United States, PACES in Pakistan and the Indian CLASS Project. The majority were national government initiatives in which software production featured as an activity within the wider domains of teacher training, development of the information technology curriculum, and computer awareness. Often university and other higher education institutional teams were established to design, write, and test software as part of the government initiative. King's College, London, and the universities of Nottingham in the United Kingdom, Coimbra in Portugal, Twente in the Netherlands, Uppsala in Sweden, and Leuven in Belgium all played their part, along with many others, in raising standards, researching innovative designs, and improving "user friendliness."

1.2 Development Teams

Unlike the production of a traditional textbook, which often relied on a single author, an educational software package may well be developed by a highly specialized team comprising a curriculum expert, programmer, graphic designer, and possibly even an educational psychologist. In the 1990s, the powerful packages for learning are more likely to emanate from such a team, with both educational and technical expertise well represented in the development. The role of the teachers in this development phase should not be forgotten. Often a piece of software will go through a number of refinements before publishing. Field trails by teachers, using the software with students, help to find "bugs," and evaluate curriculum and learning intentions, together with suitability for the current curricula. Styles of software design have changed significantly since the early 1980s, moving from a rigid tutorial or didactic approach to a more heuristic environment. Control has shifted considerably, from the software designer to the learner. Users of educational software in the early 1990s feel much more in command of their own learning strategy.

1.3 Standards

Some standards have emerged, partly as a result of the influence of hardware manufacturers and commercial software producers, and partly through the demands of a maturing clientele. These standards include the use of icons to describe an activity; command menus, either pull-down or on screen; the use of the mouse or tracker ball to move around the screen; and the concept of one or more windows within the screen within which activities can take place. Conventions within standard tools such as word processors, spreadsheets, database interrogators, and so on are now commonplace and users find it relatively easy to convert from one brand of tool to another.

2. The Publishers

The publishers of educational software fall into a number of categories. Some are long-established traditional book publishers who have, in some cases, added the new medium to their portfolio, even extending their activities to publishing CD-ROMs and interactive media using optical disks. The software that they publish may come from governmental development projects, private authors, or be developed in-house. Companies such as Comet Verlag (Germany), Otava (Finland), Hatier (France), Scholastic and Sunburst (USA) and Longman (UK) are in this category. The figure varies from country to country, but the traditional book publishers have only a small proportion of the total market.

Both central and local government agencies in some countries publish software, usually through a governmental project. Examples of these are Atenea (Spain), Minerva (Portugal), the *Catalunya Programa d'Informatica Educativa* (northeast Spain), the Royal Ministry of Education, Research, and Church Affairs Computing Initiative in Norway, Orfeus in Denmark, PACES in Pakistan and MEU Cymru in Wales. Perhaps the most successful educational software publishers are those that specialize in the field. These may be entirely private such as Edicinco in Spain, Visiria in the Netherlands, 4Mation and Sherston in the United Kingdom, Softmill in Finland, Almanac in Russia, Interprint in India or Softcat in the United States.

The last category can be described as institutional. A significant number of colleges and universities publish their own software, sometimes quite professionally. Examples are Newman College in the United Kingdom, the universities of Helsinki, Athens, Leuven, Genoa, Wroclaw, and the Ship Building Institute of St Petersburg together with the Siberian Academy of Sciences in Novosibirsk. The total number of educational software publishers in the United Kingdom alone numbered over 400 in the early 1990s and worldwide the figure is estimated as between 2,000 and 3,000. In the United Kingdom, the more significant publishers have formed a trade association known as the Educational Software Publishers Association (ESPA) to protect both the purchaser and publisher in terms of quality and to develop standards on issues such as licensing and copyright.

3. Production

A number of different elements make up an educational software package. In its simplest form, the purchaser would expect to find at least one disk and a booklet encased in either a folder or small box. Publishers may well provide the disk or set of disks in more than one size or machine version. For the majority of microcomputers used in schools, disks come in two sizes, namely 5.25 in. (13 cm) or 3.5 in. (8.9 cm) diameter, with the former being more vulnerable to damage and capable of carrying less data. Colloquially they are often referred to as "floppies" and "stiffies" respectively. The 3.5 in. disks can be regular double density (DD) or high density (HD). A 3.5 in. HD disk can store 1.44 megabytes (MB), or about 1.5 million characters. For some machines, for example the Amstrad PCW, the disks are less than 5.25 in. and encased in a rectangular sleeve, as opposed to the square sleeve of the 5.25 in. floppy.

Publishers are thus faced with the decision of which machine type and disk drive size to cater for. A study of the potential market will help narrow the field. Purchasers need to define precisely what system they are buying software for. The disk should carry the name of the program, the publisher, a version number, for example v4.0g, a dated copyright notice and the machine type. This latter information could be a microcomputer name such as Apple Macintosh or an operating system/environment such as Microsoft Disk Operating System (MS-DOS). The booklets accompanying the software might include a reference (technical) manual, a tutorial guide, a teacher's guide, curriculum applications, or a student's guide. Some packs may have maps, charts, activity cards, and a video or audiotape to extend the learning experience. With such rapid advances taking place in the technology, one can soon expect CD-ROMs and various forms of optical media to carry the interactive software and data, gradually to supplant the floppy disk.

3.1 Packaging and Distribution

Publishers still think in terms of books when it comes to packaging. Most software packs are either A4 or A5 or the standard United States equivalents and are designed to display the name on the spine when the package is on a shelf. Several publishers provide their packages with International Standard Book Numbers (ISBNs), so ensuring that they are listed systematically in bibliographic databases such as Bookbank.

The normal method of purchase is by mail order. Very few educational software packages ever find their way into the shops. Publishers generally have to mail schools frequently to advise them of new software on the market, or advertise in national educational magazines and journals.

4. Licensing

The demand for multiple copies of software to use

on a number of stand-alone microcomputers in a school or college has resulted in the publishers offering a variety of licensing schemes. In the simplest case, a computer software license may only permit the use of the software on one machine at any one time. In effect, if a school wishes to "bulk buy" multiple copies of a particular package to run on a fixed number of microcomputers, stand-alone or networked, a price will be quoted by the publisher usually in bands up to a maximum of a stated number of machines. Often a price for unlimited site licenses will be quoted, allowing the educational institution the flexibility to use the software anywhere within a defined location. The multiplying factor on a single-user price can range one to ten, but will normally be around five. Sometimes the licensing price will be hidden in the overall price of a network system containing a number of workstations and a portfolio of bundled or included software available to use across the complete network. Adding more stations to the network may revoke the original licensing agreement. Purchasers of software are usually required to sign two copies of a licensing agreement, one being kept by the publisher, the other by the "site" administrator.

4.1 Software Protection

Publishers use a number of methods to protect their software. A procedure to install the software on an internal hard disk may allow the user to perform the operation only a limited number of times, say twice. Networked software can be "tuned" to work only on a specified network. A dongle, a small device containing a software key on a chip, may have to be plugged into the back of the microcomputer before a program will work or, most commonly, the disk will be "locked" in some way, thus preventing a copy from being made. Having listed these various methods in use, it must be noted that many publishers trust educational institutions to obey the rules of the license and often encourage teachers to make one back-up copy of each disk purchased, for their own security.

5. Copyright Issues

Copyright and the publishing of electronically held material, be it text, graphics, or video images is an area of considerable confusion both for the publisher and for the user. Copyright exists to protect the intellectual property of authors. Responsible publishers make clear the copyright position on both the electronic media and accompanying documentation. Unfortunately many other publishers do not. Sometimes, a copyright notice will appear as, for example, "(c) 1993 ABC Software Publishing. These programs may be freely copied for use in educational establishments in a stated territory." This implies that a national or regional license has been negotiated for schools in a particular region or that national or local government funding has been invested in the development of the programs and free use has been negotiated between government and publisher. The possible variations on this theme are endless. The fact that a copyright notice is not printed in some way on material does not imply that copyright does not exist. In fact, the mere publication of material in any form by any person or company automatically activates the existence of copyright adhering to that material.

5.1 Illegal Copying

Not all countries are signatories to the Berne Convention on Copyright. Where clear national copyright laws exist, illegal copying constitutes theft and is punishable under law. Where there are no copyright laws, it is the duty of teachers and others concerned with education to demonstrate moral responsibility, even in the face of adverse trends in the commercial software marketplace. The industry concerned with producing educational software is a fragile one. The widespread illegal copying or, worse still, the pirating of software (i.e., copying and selling for gain) will discourage creativity and responsible publishing worldwide.

6. Networks

Exploitation of the advantages afforded by the use of local area networks (LANs) in education is very much on the increase. Many publishers of software distinguish between stand-alone and network versions in their product range. The user would expect to pay significantly more for a network license, but a number of savings can be made. If a class of 30 students share 15 stand-alone machines, all using the same software package, then loading programs and associated files of data, waiting for hard copy at the printer station, and saving individual work on a floppy disk can all amount to a considerable loss of valuable time for both teachers and learners. In some cases, publishers prefer to publish for a network environment where their software is protected by software than for the stand-alone machine which can be copied and distributed without any safeguards.

7. Versioning

Quality educational software is an expensive resource to develop and publish. Typically, a significant package will take in excess of two years to develop. The educational purchaser will almost always be buying within a restricted budget and as a result the publishers will be looking for the widest possible markets for their products. This can be done by versioning the same software package for a number of machine platforms and operating systems or by translating the programs and documentation from the original language into another.

7.1 Programming Languages

Versioning can involve a considerable amount of work. It might mean rewriting a program written in BASIC to the language 'C', and unless a software emulator is used, the coding is time-consuming and tedious. Software emulators are very rarely totally effective, particularly when it comes to speed and screen graphics representation. Different machine platforms and operating systems usually have features difficult to exploit fully in an alternative environment. For example, the sounds obtainable on an Acorn Archimedes 5000 are impossible to recreate on a standard IBM PC. In spite of all the difficulties, publishers have quite frequently produced a number of versions of the same package and this detail is reflected in their catalogs. The versioning of multimedia packages on CD-ROM and optical disk media is an area of research in the early 1990s and will depend on a number of factors, including that of international standards for the software interface.

7.2 Translation

Translation from one written language to another on the same machine platform has become increasingly easy to perform, as standards for writing the original software emerge. Essentially, if the text that appears on screen is not buried in the source code but accessed from a well-defined file, the work of translation can be achieved in a few days. The most difficult problem stems from fitting the new language translation into the screen framework or window and finding appropriate expressions to signify a command or action in the second language. Within the European Community, there is a network of publishers and developers concerned with this particular activity known as EPES (European Pool for Educational Software). Outside the pool, software has already been successfully translated from English to such languages as Finnish and Russian. It is worth noting here that the translation of the documentation can be a very expensive task. The rewriting of curriculum materials to suit the local curricula and culture might prove a barrier to the importing country.

8. *Telesoftware*

Telesoftware means software at a distance. There have been a number of experiments in delivering educational software by television and radio broadcasting and distribution via telecommunications systems, for example the telephone. The economics of broadcasting software mean that the publisher rarely gains a profit from the product, and all experiments have been short-lived. Ultimately, someone has to pay for such a service and the end user has neither the means nor the willingness to do so. Delivery of software via the public telephone network has been a little more successful: given that the end user in this case has the appropriate hardware and telecommunications software, it is possible for the delivery to be monitored and charged for, with the publisher receiving some income from the "sale." Where this has been reasonably successful, for instance on the French Minitel system and on British Prestel, further problems have arisen with delivery speeds and the lack of any documentation. The result has been that most of the software has been of a trivial nature. Serious publishers of educational software have tended to ignore telesoftware as a mechanism for distributing their products.

9. *The Future of Software Publishing*

There are likely to be fewer publishers working in this field worldwide as the industry stabilizes. International industry standards recognized by the business and commercial sectors will influence hardware design and the predominant software environments. The leisure industry will dictate standards for multimedia, just as it did for film and video. Publishers will specialize increasingly and there will be a significant growth in the range of CD-ROMs useful in the educational field. By the year 2000 the portable laptop computer will probably be as widespread as the calculator and, in relative terms, will cost very little. The distinction between education and entertainment will blur and publishers will seek to satisfy the demands of the world of "edutainment."

See also: Software Tools in Courseware Design

Bibliography

Aston M H 1981 Towards an integrated approach to distribution of educational software. In: *Computers in Education*. (Proceedings of the Third World Conference on Computers in Education [WCCE 81], Lausanne) North-Holland, Amsterdam

Aston M H, Rantanen J 1986 Towards a set of European standards for the development of educational software tools for 16/32-bit micros. (Proceedings of EURIT 86) University of Twente, Enschede

Aston M H, Dolden R 1993 *Logiciel sans Frontières*. Proceedings of CAL 93, University of York. Pergamon Press, Oxford

British Council 1990 *The British Educational Software Publishers Handbook*. The Advisory Unit, Computers in Education, Hatfield

Commission of the European Communities 1990 *Versioning of Educational Software: Final Report*. CPI, Copenhagen

Crabb G 1988 *The Production of Software for Distribution in EEC Countries: Copyright and Contract Issues*. CET, London

Hall W S 1991 Adapt your program for world-wide use with Windows internationalization support. *Microsoft Systems Journal* 6(6): 29–59

Hojsholt-Poulson L 1992 *European Pool for Software (EPES) Strategy Paper*. Orfeus, Århus
International Publishers Association 1992 *Rights: Copyright and Related Rights in the Service of Creativity*, Vol. 6, No. 2. IPA, Paris
Leiblum M D 1990 Cataloguing CAL courseware: An exposé. *Comp. Educ.* 15(1–3): 7–12
National Council for Educational Technology 1992 *Educational Software: A Directory of Currently Available Software for Schools and Colleges*. Whitaker, London
National Educational Resources Information Service (NERIS) On-line and CD-ROM subscription (published 3 times annually). NERIS, Woburn
Scottish Council for Educational Technology 1990 *Portability of Educational Software in Relation to the Creation of a Viable European Market*. Office for Official Publications of the European Communities, Luxembourg
Tagg W et al. 1990 *Advice to Schools on Software Licences and Copyright*. NAACE, St Albans

M. H. Aston

Software Tools in Courseware Design

The development of educational courseware is a complex process requiring a variety of skills and a considerable amount of time. Software tools are computing environments that carry out, facilitate, or speed up any of the tasks involved in the process of designing and producing courseware.

Many software tools for use in courseware design are developed in-house for particular purposes. Many more are adopted or adapted from commercially available packages; word processors, paint and draw programs, character definition software, graphics editors, ideas processors, and modeling programs are some examples.

Some courseware development, particularly in areas of skills training and vocational education, follows recognized and well-documented methods of instructional design. Other courseware development activity—often projects concerned with materials for schools use—have shown a greater variety in development approaches. In all cases development of courseware has been affected by the availability of software tools to aid the development process, making it more efficient and cost-effective. This entry surveys the types of software tool used in courseware design, both within the instructional design paradigm and for the less structured approaches. It looks briefly at some of the problems associated with the use of software tools, and considers areas for future development.

1. Use of Software Tools in Courseware Design

There is considerable variation from country to country, and somewhat less within countries, in the extent of use of software tools for courseware development and in the types of tool used. Tool use depends on several factors. These include patterns of funding for courseware development and, associated with this, who is developing the courseware, the nature of the balance between training or vocational goals and broader educational goals for the courseware, and the kinds of individual packages being developed.

Sources of funding for courseware development determine to a great extent the purpose of new courseware and the environment and methodology for its development. In situations where there is government funding or significant private sector sponsorship of courseware development (e.g., the government-funded projects for development of software for schools in the United Kingdom and several continental European countries, or in training environments in industries of many kinds), development teams or projects of some size are set up, and issues of productivity and of compatibility of work between development team members are particularly important. Software tools are used to address many of these issues. These tools might be commercially available packages, such as authoring languages or shells of various kinds, or they might be tools developed as part of the projects, such as libraries of useful subroutines, or screen display shells in house style.

Without major funding, courseware, often for school use, is developed on a smaller scale. Individuals or small groups based, for example, in schools or tertiary institutions, develop packages of a particular type or for specific educational purposes. During the early 1990s, these might use a file management package or an environment such as HyperCard, but previously developers used few tools beyond the programming languages available on the machines on which they worked.

Courseware developed for purposes such as skills training can often be written using repetitive patterns and structures. In these situations tools such as authoring languages, software shells of various kinds, and a variety of other tools can be used quite extensively to increase author productivity while creating materials well-suited to the purpose. Other courseware may be less skills oriented. It might, for example, attempt to provide a computer-based microworld in which learners can explore an idea or concept in a relatively open-ended way, perhaps initiating and structuring many of the learning activities themselves. Development of such software is not easily supported by the most common courseware development tools. However, some modeling programs of this type have been written using shells developed for modeling, and some of the newer programming languages and software environments may well assist this type of courseware development as well (Squires and Millwood 1988).

An Australian project (Wills 1991) explored interactions between industrial training and the more general educational approaches taken by schools.

The project runs courses in courseware development for teachers and practitioners from the computer-based training industry together, aiming to expose industry trainers to the educational philosophies behind school-level courseware, while taking advantage of new authoring tools and multimedia facilities to increase teachers' courseware productivity.

The extent to which software tools are used in courseware design also depends on the specific types of courseware packages being developed. Tutorial and drill types of courseware are particularly suitable for development using available software tools. Courseware which makes extensive use of graphics can be well-supported, as good graphics and animation tools exist. Databases, some types of games, and some simulation and modeling packages can also be developed using tools to facilitate the work.

2. Software Tools for Instructional Design Paradigms

The first stage in the instructional design approach to courseware development involves analysis procedures such as needs assessment, problem definition, goal setting, and the specification of learner characteristics. One or more tools might support each of these activities; such tools are usually developed specifically for the purpose, often in-house for a particular project.

The design stage involves activities such as the specification and sequencing of objectives, and determination of instructional and assessment strategies. Prototyping tools enable generation of mock-ups of final screens so that the developer and the user can quickly make changes without having to go through a lengthy specification stage on paper. Prototyping of this sort can be particularly important to improve communication between members of a development team, and between team and client when that situation exists (see *Prototyping as a Design Activity*). These tools may be developed in-house, but commercially available packages can also be used. For example Chandra (1988) describes the use of a graphics editor and sequencer to enable formulation of ideas directly onto the computer, without programming. Intended screens are drawn with the graphics editor and saved as separate files, and the sequencer is used to "run" these, giving the designer feedback on the flow and execution of the program and providing an environment for interactive design of the program specification.

The development stage includes the actual preparation of the courseware programs. Software tools are available to support many aspects of this phase. These include page specification tools, tools to create and edit text and graphics, tools to allow specification of help material, and tools which prompt and validate learner input. Third-generation programming languages with libraries (see, e.g., Watson 1987), and fourth-generation programming languages are used. User interface management systems have been developed to handle the user interface independently of the application being developed; WIMP environments are one example. Wilson et al. (1988) provide a review of existing dialogue design tools, and describe a toolkit for the creation, modification, and maintenance of menu-based interfaces. Database management systems can be used to handle the data for an application independently of the application itself, and multimedia versions of these are available. Debugging tools to search systematically for errors in code are also widely used at this stage. Documentation support tools are used to assist in the preparation and modification of documentation and print materials which might accompany the courseware programs.

Evaluation can also be supported by software tools. For example, "tracker" software can follow users' paths through a program and provide information for the developers. Chandra (1988) describes the adaptation of a generally available spreadsheet program to provide evaluation questionnaires on the computer, the results from which can be processed statistically and displayed graphically by the spreadsheet facility as needed.

3. Author Languages, Authoring Systems, and Hypertext

Much of this type of courseware design work uses one of the many available author languages or authoring systems developed for the purpose, and in the early 1990s hypertext systems are being used in this context as well.

Author languages are designed to facilitate creation of instructional sequences, though the designer does need some knowledge of programming. These languages usually offer sound and graphics manipulation commands, and include facilities for displaying information, accepting and processing user input, identifying locations in the program and controlling sequencing, and recording user data for later analysis.

Authoring systems are typically menu- or icon-driven computing environments, prompting and guiding users throughout the development process, and enabling authors with no knowledge of programming to create courseware. Authoring systems can incorporate graphics, music, sound, animation, and input from external sources such as videodisks and CD-ROMs. In contrast to author languages, authoring systems provide course management, including definition or selection of a particular instructional strategy (e.g., drill, tutorial, quiz), specification of response data to be collected, ability to try out a lesson just created, and documentation capability. The major advantage of using these systems is speed. However, there are limitations on the style of courseware that can be developed in this way, as it must reflect the instructional model or models contained within the authoring system.

Radev (1988) and Colpaert et al. (1988) describe use of database software to enhance authoring systems. This facilitates development of courseware for tasks such as the learning of foreign languages for special purposes, enabling selection of language structures and vocabulary to suit individual needs. It is also possible to write software tools and courseware shells or models in authoring languages, for further increases in productivity.

Hypertext is a nonlinear body of information with links between documents or different parts of a document (see *Hypertext, Educational Applications of*). Hypermedia refers to software that can link text, graphics, animation, sound, and video, in a nonlinear web of information. The most widely known tool of this kind is HyperCard with its HyperTalk programming language for the Macintosh computer, but products of this kind are also available for other computers. Hypertext systems are generally easy to use for developing text screens, creating or importing graphic images, controlling other hardware, and linking all available resources flexibly and nonsequentially, so they offer greater versatility than most authoring systems. One survey indicated that HyperCard enabled production of computer-based training frames in half to two-thirds the time taken otherwise (Lewis and Mace 1988), and this environment is being used increasingly for prototyping as well.

4. Other Uses for Software Tools in Courseware Design

Squires and Millwood (1988) introduced the notion of prototyping computer-assisted learning software in an educational sense through educational programming languages such as LOGO, Smalltalk or Prolog, focusing particularly on the use of LOGO for this purpose. The programming language acts as an environment for the designer to try out educational ideas, and the cognitive model inherent in the language can affect the style and content of the courseware that is developed, producing programs that are more open-ended in character. Squires and Millwood (1988) describe two examples, one concerned with the development of foreign language courseware, and the other a general purpose modeling system. They contend that as hardware develops, the availability of such software environments is likely to become commonplace, making educational prototyping through programming easily available to courseware developers.

Designing courseware for international use raises the issue of the need to make modifications to programs to suit the country of use. Kearsley (1990) suggests the provision of built-in editing tools to facilitate local modification by users.

Courseware developers sometimes need to transfer electronically the code of a program resident in one brand of machine to another. Some projects have developed software tools in-house to enable such transfers to be done between particular pairs of machines, but commercially developed transfer tools have become available for most needs in this area.

Content-free special purpose software tools have been developed for writing particular types of courseware packages. These include adventure game shells, simulation and modeling toolkits, and data base shells. The courseware developer simply inserts data concerning the specific application into an already extant structure or shell. (See *Educational Computer Software, Production of*.)

5. Problems with Software Tools for Courseware Design

The use of software tools in courseware design is good computer science practice, and can considerably increase the efficiency with which courseware can be produced. However, there may be some associated problems. Many of the authoring tools are not general, but specific for certain types of educational software, and they generally do not support portability. When a commercially produced system or shell is used for development of new courseware, issues of copyright and ownership can arise and must be resolved. The time taken to develop new software tools in-house can take up a major part of total time allocated for a courseware development project. This is only justifiable if these tools provide sufficient overall increase in productivity. Generally such tools would need to be used many times, though this raises the problem of the tools becoming dated quickly as hardware develops and software techniques change.

6. Needs, Trends, and Future Developments

In 1988 a seminar for courseware developers and researchers from several European countries addressed the question of new tools needed to improve current practice in courseware design (Lewis and Mace 1988). Suggestions included better tools to support the design phase of the process, particularly for initial knowledge structuring, task analysis, and course logic layout. Other needs were tools for analysis of training needs, tools to support refinement or modification of designs, tools for rapid prototyping, and cost-effective tools for user modeling.

Lewis and Mace (1989) outline requirements for authoring tools for simulation courseware for computer-based training. They describe a project to develop, evaluate, and produce a set of advanced software tools, particularly for prototyping and model building, to enable more effective provision of courseware involving extensive use of simulations.

Scanlon and Smith (1988) describe work using the Alternate Reality Kit, a graphical animated environment implemented in the Smalltalk-80 language for creating interactive simulations, under development at the Xerox Palo Alto Research Center. Using the Alternate Reality Kit, Scanlon and Smith rewrote a bubble chamber simulation program in a very much shorter time than that taken for the original development in UCSD Pascal. They needed only a few minutes to extend the program to include some new very powerful features.

Courseware designers seek better integration between tools, with special-purpose tools existing and working together in one development environment. One example under development aims to produce a single environment that makes readily available to courseware designers a complete range of tools and information necessary for performing all the tasks related to the development process (Gustafson and Reeves 1990). With networking, multiple designers will be able to share information, drafts, and final products, and track the progress of projects. The long-range goal is to create a complete course development system including a capacity to train instructional developers and to guide, monitor, and assist them with an overlay of expert systems.

See also: Courseware Design; Software Publishing; Instructional Design Models

References

Chandra P 1988 Adaptable interactive CBL design tools for education. In: Lovis F, Tagg E D (eds.) 1988 *Computers in Education*. Elsevier, Amsterdam

Colpaert J, Decoo W, Van Elsen E 1988 Courseware for LSP (Languages for Special Purposes): Creating units at will in a selection system. In: Lovis F, Tagg E D (eds.) 1988 *Computers in Education*. Elsevier, Amsterdam

Gustafson K, Reeves T 1990 IDioM: A platform for a course development expert system. *Educ. Technol.* 30(3): 19–25

Kearsley G 1990 Designing educational software for international use. *Journal of Research on Computing in Education* 23(2): 242–50

Lewis R, Mace T 1988 Support tools for authoring - A seminar report. Occasional Paper InTER/7/88, Department of Psychology, University of Lancaster

Lewis R, Mace T 1989 Authoring tools for simulation-based CBT: An interim report. Occasional Paper InTER/13/89, Department of Psychology, University of Lancaster

Radev R 1988 Using database systems for producing courseware. In: Lovis F, Tagg E D (eds.) 1988 *Computers in Education*. Elsevier, Amsterdam

Scanlon E, Smith R 1988 A rational reconstruction of a bubble chamber simulation using the alternate reality kit. *Computer Education* 12: 199–207

Squires D, Millwood R 1988 The influence of new software environments on CAL development. *Computer Education* 12: 67–71

Watson D 1987 *Developing CAL: Computers in the Curriculum*. Harper and Row, London

Wills S 1991 Teachers as educational software designers: Industry/university cooperation. *Education and Computing* 7: 267–72

Wilson N, McAlpin A, McChesney I 1988 A software toolkit for human–computer dialogue design and development. In: Lovis F, Tagg E D (eds.) 1988 *Computers in Education*. Elsevier, Amsterdam

A. McDougall

South Africa: System of Education

1. General Background

South African society is in the process of extensive political and economic change. This process is moving at a rapid pace toward a nonracial democratic society. Structures and institutions are changing in terms of form, content, and functions in order to be able to reflect a new democratic value system. Constitutional negotiations are taking place at different levels and between the whole spectrum of participants. Education is on the agenda. The government's Educational Renewal Strategy document (Department of National Education 1991b), as well as, among others, the proposals of the African National Congress (1991), make it clear that fundamental changes in education are an important part of societal changes. This new, yet to be created education system must be generally acceptable, adaptable, and affordable. Within the framework of limited resources, and a growing demand for equal educational opportunities, it is evident that this description of the South African educational system could well become outdated by the mid-1990s.

The Republic of South Africa is located south of the Limpopo River at the southernmost tip of Africa. It has a surface area of 1,123,226 square kilometers. This excludes the landlocked, politically independent countries of Lesotho and Swaziland, as well as the so-called four TBVC states (the Transkei, Bophuthatswana, Venda, and Ciskei) which are not internationally acknowledged as independent. These four states, as well as six self-governing territories within South Africa (Lebowa, Kwazulu, Qwaqwa, Gazankulu, KwaNdebele, and KaNgwane), have the responsibility for providing their own education, but receive financial aid from South Africa.

The country is characterized by ethnic and cultural diversity. This is reflected in the number of languages spoken by the 30.8 million inhabitants (1990). The mother tongue of the majority of Whites is either Afrikaans (56%) or English (36%). Zulu-speaking peoples number some 7.6 million, the Xhosa-speaking some 3 million, the Sotho (including the North Sotho, South Sotho, and Tswana-speaking tribes) approximately 7.6 million, the Tsonga a little over 1.5 million, and the Venda about 200,000. The variety of ethnic and language groups forms one of the main problems for educational provision, and the medium of instruction is a hotly debated issue.

Much of the character of the South African education system has resulted from the philosophy of separate provision of education for the different ethnic groups ("apartheid"). This formally commenced after the Second World War with the creation of a separate department of education (that of Bantu Education) for Blacks. South Africa has largely separate schools for each of the four main population groups (Asians, Blacks, Coloreds, and Whites). The principle of separate schooling for the various race groups will be removed from the statute books. This is indicated by the annulment of several acts of parliament that formalized "apartheid," such as the Population Registration Act, the Land Act, and the Group Areas Act.

In 1990 South Africa had 30.8 million inhabitants, 956,000 of whom were Asian, 21 million Black, 3.2 million Colored, and 5 million White. The total population is growing at a rate of 2.07 percent per annum and is expected to reach 53.9 million (or between 64 and 65 million if the TBVC states are included) by the year 2010. The implication for education becomes clear when it is recognized that 49 percent of the population is under the age of 18.

In 1990, 55.9 percent of the population lived in urban centers. The recent abolition of influx control is placing additional demands on the provision of education. Some urban areas recorded a 100 percent growth rate in little more than 6 months, causing excessive growth in the number of students attending available schools.

South Africa's Gross National Product (GNP) in real terms (with 1985 as basic year) increased from R75 billion in 1970 to R119 billion in 1990. The contribution of agriculture and mining to the GNP decreased from 35 percent in 1946 to 15.8 percent in 1990. In 1990 net gold exports comprised R18 billion of the total exports of R72 billion, while imports amounted to R67 billion. Economically active South Africans increased from 4.6 million in 1951 to 10.9 million in 1989. During the same period the workforce in the agricultural sector decreased from 33 to 13.6 percent of the economically active population. The relative employment in the mining sector decreased from 16 to 8.5 percent of the total workforce. The remainder of the workforce is employed in sectors and industries such as manufacturing (15.9%); electricity, water, and gasworks (1.1%); construction (6.4%); transport and communication (4.8%); commercial (10.8%); financial (3.9%); and community, social, and personal services (22.6%). Approximately 11.1 percent of economically active inhabitants are employed in a professional, semiprofessional, technical, managerial, administrative, and executive capacity; and 21 percent of these are Blacks. The economic development reflected by these changes is creating an increasing demand for more varied, specialized, and vocationally orientated education.

In 1985, 9.2 percent of the economically active population held a postschool educational qualification (degree, diploma, certificate, or trade qualification), while 17.7 percent had no formal education. Those with incomplete primary and secondary education constitute 23.8 and 30.5 percent respectively of the economically active population, while those with complete primary and secondary education constitute 8.5 and 10.5 percent respectively.

Estimates of the total number of unemployed persons are close to 6 million. It is therefore expected that by the year 2000 some 10 million persons will be jobless. The stimulation of economic growth which will lead to the creation of more jobs features high on the priority list of the government which subscribes to a market-orientated philosophy. A number of economists and politicians, however, favor a more socialist philosophy and affirmative action to promote economic growth and to correct the existing inequalities. Pressure is consequently brought to bear on the education system to help effect a solution to these problems.

2. *Politics and the Goals of the Education System*

Since 1948 the political scene has been dominated by the ruling National Party of the White electorate. However, in 1990, the unbanning of organizations such as the African National Congress and the South African Communist Party, and the scrapping of discriminatory legislation such as the Separate Amenities Acts and the Population Registration Act to name but a few, has paved the way for negotiations and a more democratic society.

In 1980 the Human Sciences Research Council conducted at the request of the South African government an in-depth investigation into all facets of education in South Africa. This investigation resulted, among other things, in the formulation of 11 guiding principles of educational provision. Despite the fact that these principles are interpreted differently by various interest groups, they are still generally accepted as a common basis for the formulation of educational objectives and policies. The 11 principles are listed below:

(a) equal educational opportunities;

(b) a balance of commonality and diversity;

(c) freedom of choice;

(d) relevance;

(e) linkage between formal and nonformal education;

(f) state and parental responsibility for formal education;

(g) state and private sector responsibility for nonformal education;

(h) state support for private education;

(i) balance between administrative centralization and decentralization;

(j) professional status of educators;

(k) continuing research.

The implementation of these principles is limited by the present constitutional framework, government policies, and legislation. The basis on which the proposed positive recognition of diversity (principle b) was to be afforded, was racial, instead of educationally relevant, such as language, culture, or religion. The removal (lifting) of these constraints is essential as the implementation of the true spirit of the principles is dependent on the acceptance and involvement of all the participants—parents, teachers, and organized society—of the education system.

The broad objectives of the educational sectors are outlined by legislation. The emphasis is on providing relevant education for all, according to the needs of the individual (aptitude and interest), and those of the community (labor force demands).

In general it can be stated that during the primary phases of schooling, the emphasis is on the promotion of literacy, numeracy, and the general development and socialization of the child. As in other countries, broader economic and social objectives tend to become more significant at the upper-secondary and tertiary levels of the education system.

3. *The Formal System of Education*

3.1 *Primary, Secondary, and Tertiary Education*

Figure 1 presents an outline of the structure of the formal education system. Key statistics on enrollments and resources in the major education sectors can be observed in Table 1.

With the exception of Black children, school attendance is compulsory for children between the ages of 7 and 16. This includes the junior primary, senior primary, junior secondary (3 years each), and in most cases one year of the senior secondary phase. By way of 11 state departments of education, schooling is in general provided on a separate basis for the various population or ethnic groupings. Reform policy will, however, ensure that the legal separation in schools according to race is phased out (e.g., by means of a Bill of Human Rights and the annulment of the Population Registration Act). It was estimated that in 1988 about 22 percent of Black children between the ages of 6 and 14 were not attending school.

The formal education system provides for preprimary, primary, secondary, and tertiary institutions and is characterized by differentiation in terms of language and culture. The medium of instruction varies, but is usually mother tongue education. All children are taught the two official languages: Afrikaans and English. Both are compulsory for matriculation, with the exception of Blacks who can substitute an African language for either English or Afrikaans during the last three school years. In most Black schools the initial period of four years of instruction in the child's mother tongue is followed by instruction in English. Teachers in many cases, however, continue instruction in the relevant mother tongue.

Primary education usually commences at the age of 6 and lasts for 6 years. Apart from reading, writing, and arithmetic in the basis years, subjects such as health education, mathematics, environmental studies (or geography), science, music, arts and crafts, religious studies, physical training, and languages (mother tongue and English) are offered.

The secondary school phase provides for differentiation but in comprehensive units, mainly focusing on broadening the general knowledge of the various academic subjects to prepare pupils for their choice of career or for further study. From Standard 7 onwards students choose, in addition to the compulsory official languages, four subjects from the following main streams: general, commercial, natural science, social science, technical, art, agricultural and domestic science. Most students, however, follow the general curriculum (more than 50% in 1984). In 1990 only about 1 percent of the school population attended technical colleges.

A new curriculum model for primary and secondary education was recommended in December 1991 that provides for earlier tracking into vocational training.

In 1985 approximately 600,000 (6.4%) Black pupils attended farm schools, each of which had, on average, less than 100 pupils. This requires teachers to teach simultaneously at different grade levels. These children therefore often experience problems in continuing with secondary education. The attrition rate for Black students is in general much higher than that for pupils of other groups. This is generally ascribed to the existing inequalities in educational provision. Approximately 30 percent of the teachers in Black education are suitably qualified (i.e., having had 12 years of schooling followed by 3 years of teacher training). Pupil–teacher ratios are 41:1 (compared to 20:1 for those of White schools), and often overcrowded classrooms reflect this. During the 1980s Black schools have become increasingly politicized. Participation in strikes and other forms of disruptive behavior by pupils affect education.

The school year commences in January, usually consists of four quarters, and ends in early December. School hours, for 5 days per week, average 5.5

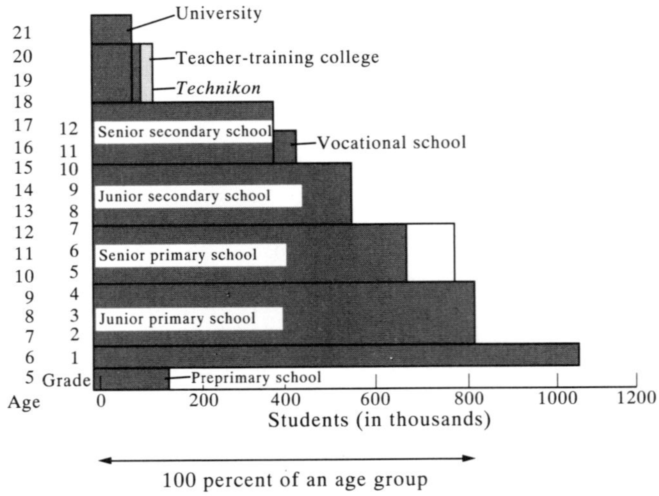

Figure 1
South Africa: Structure of the formal education system

Table 1
Enrollments and Resources in Formal Education, South Africa 1990

	Comprehensive schools		Tertiary education	
	Primary section	Secondary section	Teacher-training *technikons*	Universities
Number of students[a]	5,263,129	2,254,927	133,508	286,910
Percentage of age group enrolled[b]				
Age 15–16	67.4%		—	—
17–18	42.9%		—	—
20–24	—		—	—
Number of institutions[c]	20,207		85	17
Average number of students per institution	372		1,570	1,687
Student–teacher ratio[d]	25.0		9.2	9.2
Expenditure per student[e]	R1,480[f]		R5,172	R7,890

a The school data include students enrolled in private schools and technical colleges. It includes teacher-training, *technikon*, and post-Standard 10 level technical college students. About 35 percent of university students are enrolled at distance learning centers (e.g., UNISA [120,000], Vista) b Statistics for universities not available c Excludes special school education, but includes technical colleges and private schools d Excludes special school personnel, but includes permanent personnel and/or full-time equivalent personnel e The school data refer to the 1991–92 financial year and comprise estimates of government expenditure as supplied by Department of National Education. Amount of R5,172 is for *technikon* education only f Figures are for the 1991–92 financial year

hours per day. The average number of school days per year is 200.

Tertiary education mainly takes place at *technikons*, teacher-training institutions (discussed in Sect. 6 below), and universities. By far the largest number of tertiary students attend universities. In 1990 the ratio of university to *technikon* students was 7:2. Although the natural sciences (including medicine and engineering) are offered at universities, most students enroll for courses in the social sciences. A gradual process of rationalization, which was introduced in the 1980s, has become imperative as a result of a decrease in state subsidies for universities. In some cases this has forced the amalgamation of disciplines offered by the 17 universities. The University of South Africa (with over 110,000 students) and Vista University offer higher education by means of correspondence courses. Labor shortages in certain job categories suggest that an imbalance exists between the number of universities and the more vocationally oriented *technikons*. The ratio of White to Black students enrolled at universities for 1990 was 10:1. The number of students enrolled at universities and *technikons* between 1970 and 1990 respectively increased from 82,909 to 286,910, and from 36,253 to 83,424. The minimum admission requirement for attending university is a matriculation exemption certificate. However, with regard to certain disciplines or fields, additional requirements exist at most universities. During 1991 more White male than female students attended universities (88,696 against 68,736). However, more Black female than male students (59,195 against 50,935) were enrolled at universities.

3.2 Preschool Education

The predominant aim of preschool education is to offer an enriched learning environment in order to prepare children for school. Although this kind of education is provided on a limited scale only, it has been recommended as a measure to ameliorate the present high attrition rate in Black education.

3.3 Special Education

Approximately 34,000 children attended 222 special schools in 1990, constituting about 0.01 percent of the total student population. A variety of institutions cater for the special needs of the physically and mentally handicapped such as those for autistic, deaf, hard of hearing, blind, partially sighted, epileptic, cerebral palsied, physically handicapped, and those for children with special learning disabilities. Mainstreaming has not yet been attempted. These institutions are mostly state-aided and have to make use of sponsors to generate sufficient or additional funding. They increasingly focus on vocational training. Advisory bodies exist to coordinate the transition or transfer from an institution to a suitable type of work.

3.4 Vocational, Technical, and Business Education

The low and occasionally negative economic growth rate since the late 1970s and the shortage of technically trained workers has resulted in an increasing interest in vocational and technical training, as well as in business-oriented courses. The *Raad vir Geesteswetenskaplike Navorsing* (1989) and *Departement van Onderwys en Kultuur* (1990) undertook important studies in this area. The 1991 Education Reform documents focused on labor force development, and there are indications that secondary education will be diversified to provide for more career-oriented training and education (see Sect. 10 below). Financial limitations imposed by general economic conditions hamper the availability of funds for education, and the involvement to a much larger extent of the private sector seems unavoidable.

Apart from the *technikons* which more than doubled their enrollments in the 1980s, special "training boards" (accredited by the Registrar of Manpower Training) were established to oversee the development and provision of inservice and other special training courses for the different industries such as mining, building, printing, and so forth. A large variety of training programs, such as apprentice training and other training schemes, is made available in the many private, industrial, and other training centers. In 1990 these centers trained approximately 514,598 persons. The state provides a variety of financial incentive schemes for the training of workers.

3.5 Adult and Nonformal Education

Adult and nonformal education is provided by the government as well as by private organizations. The main objectives for government involvement are related to economic development needs—addressing the high number of unemployed and the high population growth rate, and eradicating illiteracy. It is, however, difficult to indicate the extent of these programs as formal data are not available. A special project was launched in 1988 to train the unemployed. According to the Department of Manpower, more than 610,000 people attended training courses under this initiative up to 1990.

Under the auspices of the Department of Health and Welfare, a population development program covering the essentials of birth control, health, and nutrition, is offered. Literacy programs for adults have also been developed. These are offered by the Department of Education and Training, among others, which is responsible for the education of Blacks.

A large number of parastatal and private organizations are involved in the development of human potential. Organizations such as the Development Bank of Southern Africa are increasingly becoming involved in the funding and development of human resources. The private sector established a council (the PRISEC) for the development of education and training programs. The Independent Development Trust, which received a grant of R500 million from the government for educational purposes, also develops and offers some educational programs.

Formal training institutions such as technical colleges are increasingly becoming involved in nonformal education, offering more flexible and adaptable training courses. These courses aim at satisfying short-term needs in specific areas.

4. Administrative and Supervisory Structure and Operation

In terms of the 1983 amendments to the South African Constitution, the education of each of the four population groups was described as "own affairs," and has subsequently become, in terms of its cultural and value framework, the responsibility of each relevant group. "Own affairs" administrations were made responsible for the provision of education, including responsibility for "their" respective universities and *technikons*. The Constitution provides for three departments of education and culture, which are responsible to the House of Assembly (Whites), the House of Representatives (Coloreds), and the House of Delegates (Asians). Separate departments of education exist for the self-governing Black states (KwaZulu, Lebowa, Gazankulu, Qwaqua, KwaNdebele, and KaNgwane). The central government provides for and controls education for all other Blacks living in South Africa through the Department of Education and Training.

The National Policy for General Education Affairs Act (Act 76 of 1984) defines the spheres and determines certain limits within which education must be provided by the various "own affairs" education departments. These include norms (criteria, rules, or prescriptions according to which action should be taken, and/or something/someone could be judged or compared), and standards for the financing of running costs and capital expenditure, salaries and conditions of employment for staff; the professional registration of teachers; norms and standards for syllabuses and examination, as well as those for certification of qualifications. The general education policy is determined by the Minister of National Education in consultation with all the ministers of education of the departments of state for education. In developing such policy, a number of statutory councils and committees assist the Minister in an advisory capacity.

Parliament approves the budget for education, for redistribution by the Minister of National Education. The budget allocated by Parliament for financial aid to the four TBVC states is the responsibility of the Minister of Foreign Affairs.

For administrative purposes, South Africa is divided into a number of regions. Sub-state departments were established to administer these regions. Figure 2 presents a schematic overview of the present educational administrative system.

The educational departments of the various population groups are responsible for matters such as the recruitment and appointment of teachers for public schools, the supply of buildings and land, the provision of equipment and materials, and within the bounds of general policy have responsibility for the curriculum. In the case of White schools, the four provinces of South Africa have considerable say in all matters pertaining to schooling. The functions of the former inspectorates have been changed, and are mainly advisory in nature, although the inspectorates still exert considerable influence.

Schools for Whites generally have elected management boards comprising parents, the school principal, and his deputy. Besides these, parent and parent–teacher associations exist to promote involvement of the community in school affairs. These associations assist schools in generating additional funds for the purpose of maintenance and the purchase of additional equipment and facilities, but have little or no effective decision-making authority. Such boards are becoming increasingly prevalent in schools catering for education to the other population groups.

In 1990 additional models for the administration of schools were developed by the Department of Education and Culture: House of Assembly. Schools have a choice to vote for three models: Model A, B, or C. The Model A school constitutes a private, but government subsidized school; Model B empowers a school to lay down rules in regard to school entrance; while Model C is a state-aided school. More than 200 schools have already opted for Model B and have opened their doors to students of other race groups.

Furthermore, in 1991, the government announced arrangements by which unutilized or underutilized schools for Whites could be used to provide education mainly for Blacks. These arrangements revolve around educational services rendered on an agency basis to other departments by the Department of Education and Culture: House of Assembly.

5. Educational Finance

The education budget as a proportion of the state budget increased from 16.2 percent in 1985–86 to 20.3 percent in 1990–91. The Department of National Education distributes funds according to set formulas to the other education departments. Of the 1989–90 education budget, 32 percent was allocated to the Department of Education and Culture: House of Assembly; 6 percent to the Department of Education and Culture: House of Delegates; 15 percent to the Department of Education and Culture: House of Representatives; and 34 percent to the Department of Education and Training and the self-governing states combined. Education in the TBVC states is financed through the Department of Foreign Affairs and is not included in the figures mentioned above. Although the education budget increased by 57 percent in nominal terms between 1987–88 and 1990–91, in real terms it represented a decrease of 6 percent. This was due mainly to an annual increase in pupils and students of about 4.4 percent during

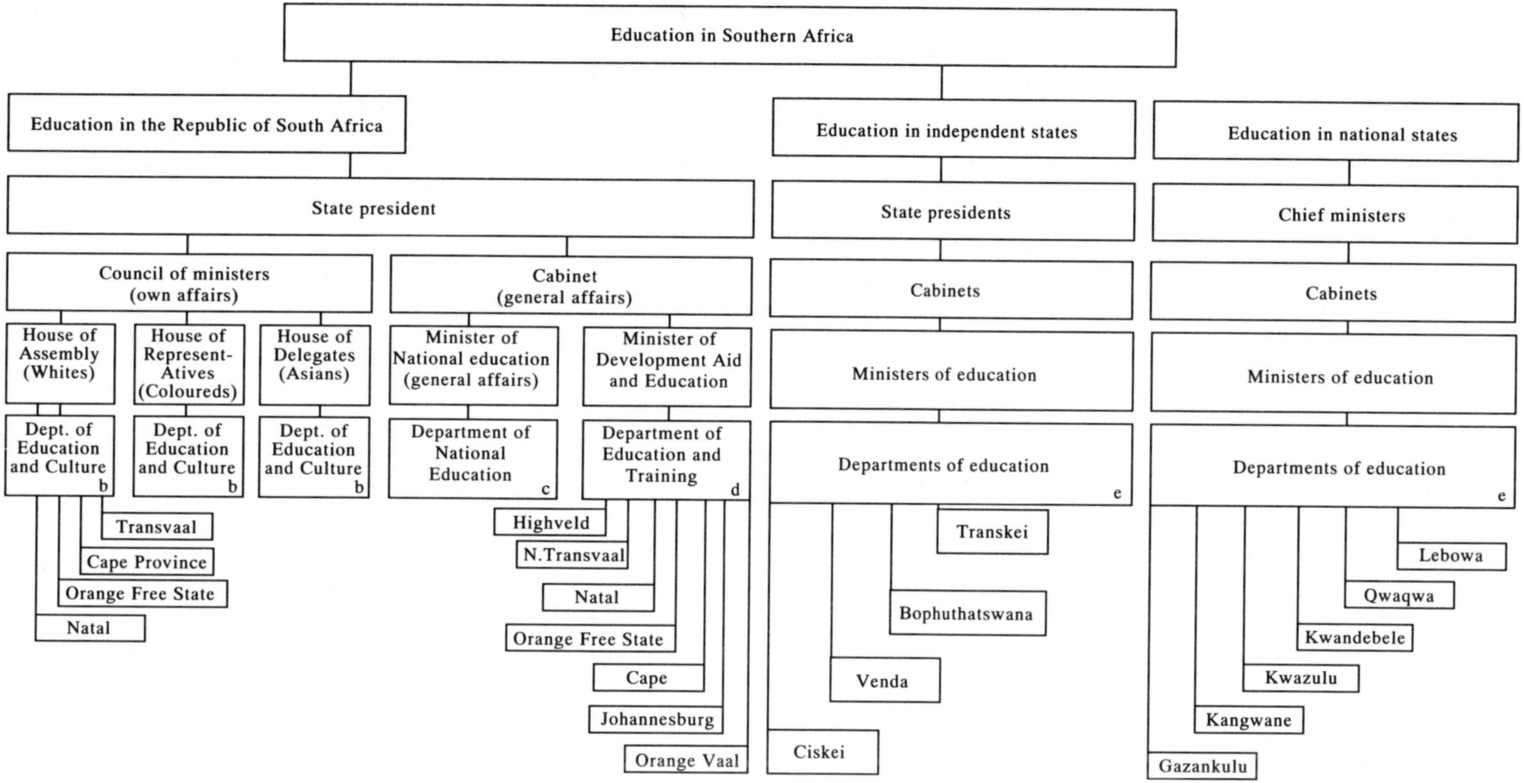

Figure 2
The decentralized educational administrative structure in South Africa[a]

source: Du Pisani et al. 1991

a Uniform educational standards: except for the National States, as well as Bophuthatswana, Ciskei, and Venda, where pupils write the examinations set by the Department of Education and Training, all other departments have their own examining bodies. In order to provide for control over norms and standards of subject matter and examination, as well as awarding of certificates at the various exit points in school, technical college, and nonformal education, the South African Certification Council was founded according to Act 85 of 1986. The mission of the Council is to ensure that all certificates awarded by the Council at a specific exit point represent the same standard of education and examination. b The administration of education for Whites, Coloreds, and Asians is considered to be an own affair and rests with separate departments of education for each of these population groups c The Department of National Education is responsible for the formulation of educational policy in South Africa d The Department of Education and Training administers the education of Blacks outside the National and Independent States e Ten separate departments of education administer education for Blacks of the different ethnic groups in the independent (TBVC) and National States.

this period. In 1990–91 education expenditure amounted to approximately 5.5% of GNP.

Of the 1990–91 education budget 11.3 percent was allocated to universities, 2.7 percent to *technikons*, 0.5 percent to private ordinary schools, and 85.5 percent to the rest of the education sector. Approximately 70 percent of the total education expenditure is spent on the remuneration of teachers and lecturers, implying that in 1991 a 1 percent salary increase would cost the state about R15 million. There are inequalities in per capita expenditure for public ordinary schools between the various population groups. In 1989 the per capita expenditure for college and school education amounted to R3,572 in the case of the Department of Education and Culture: House of Assembly; R927 for the Department of Education and Training; and R647 for the self-governing states. Calculations indicate that equalizing expenditure on the basis of the expenditure for White education will absorb more or less 48 percent of the total state budget for primary and secondary education alone. This will be a major problem for the development of the education system.

The Department of National Education recommends at least 0.5 percent of total expenditure should be used for adult and nonformal education. The 1980s has seen the growth of foreign financial assistance for education purposes, especially for Blacks, but the full extent of assistance is impossible to calculate. Private and parastatal organizations are increasing their support for specific educational projects.

In 1990, there were 384 private fee-paying schools. Since the early 1980s these schools have children from all population groups. In an effort to accommodate Black students in schools catering exclusively for White pupils, and possibly to ameliorate financial problems, the three additional models proposed by the Department of Education and Culture: House of Assembly provide for degrees of privatization.

Bursaries which are as a rule based on educational merits and type of study, as well as loans from banks and other institutions at moderate interest rates, are available to students.

6. *Supplying Personnel for the Education System*

In 1991 more than 256,000 (full-time equivalent) comprehensive school educators were employed in schools. A further 29,000 noneducators occupied administrative positions, and more than 35,000 employees worked as service workers. Nonteaching personnel thus totaled more than 63,000. Some 61 percent of school teachers are female. Although gender parity exists in all respects in education, men are still more likely than women to occupy senior administrative positions in schools.

Teacher shortages in especially the disadvantaged communities are common, and scholarships are offered for teacher training. The enrollment figures for Black pupils predict an increase of about 400,000 per year at the start of the 1990s, and this will increase to almost 700,000 per year by the turn of the century. It is estimated that the total pupil enrollment in South Africa (including the independent states) will be a staggering 9.9 million in 1991, and 14.7 million in 2001. This will require exceptional measures to ensure teacher supply. The shortages in subjects such as mathematics, biology, and the physical sciences are more acute in rural than in urban areas.

Education departments undertake annual studies to decide on the number of teacher trainees and practicing teachers required. The education departments recruit trainees by direct liaison with schools, and by offering financial assistance for teacher education purposes. In exceptional circumstances, departments may recruit from commerce and industry by offering special incentives. Practicing teachers and newly qualified teachers are invited to apply for vacancies which are published in official gazettes. Where there are special conditions (such as severe shortages), departments may try to recruit from society at large by, for instance, advertising in newspapers.

Normally, persons desiring to be appointed to teaching posts register with education departments. An education department may (sometimes after consulting the school concerned) place a person in a post. Posts are normally advertised, allowing aspirants to apply for posts which are filled by the department concerned at the recommendation of the school community concerned. Departments may transfer or second teachers already employed by them.

Government school teachers usually serve a one- or two-year probationary period during which teachers are assessed before receiving permanent employment. Private-school teachers are directly employed by the board of the school, and the requirements for permanent employment vary.

Teacher training occurs in universities, teacher-training colleges, and *technikons*. The various education departments are responsible for determining the standard of teacher qualifications. The normal length for the initial training of secondary teachers is four years, although some departments recognize three years. The course generally comprises either a three-year degree, during which a student majors in two subjects, followed by a one-year diploma in education, or an integrated four-year degree or diploma.

The primary-education teacher normally completes a three- or four-year diploma course. At some universities a four-year degree course for primary teachers and even a four-year degree course for preprimary education are offered. Many primary teachers with three-year diplomas later upgrade their qualifications by undertaking a one-year diploma course in areas such as remedial teaching, counseling, or education management.

The qualification level of teachers differs substantially and so does the interpretation of what could be regarded as a professionally qualified teacher. If the completion of 12 years of pretertiary training and 3 years of professional tertiary training is regarded as the minimum for qualified status, in 1991 47.2 percent of practicing teachers were unqualified and 52.8 percent qualified (Department of National Education 1991a).

Evidence of limited promotion opportunities, relatively low salaries, and unattractive and, in some areas, unsafe working conditions have contributed to the fact that the teaching profession has become unattractive as a career. Teachers' salaries are approximately 2 percent lower than those of persons occupying comparable posts in the public service. Salaries in the education sector are approximately 30 percent lower than those in the private sector. This poses problems for the recruitment and retention of staff.

There are attempts to improve working conditions and promotion opportunities. For promotion, demonstrated competence and qualifications are usually emphasized, and not seniority. Improving the situation is difficult because the growing education budget already taxes limited revenues.

Considerable effort is also being directed toward improving and adapting initial teacher as well as inservice training to meet the demands of a drastically changing, nonracial, multicultural society.

Retraining of inservice staff usually takes place when new subjects are added to the school curriculum, when the curriculum is substantively altered, or when subjects are removed from the curriculum. Such training takes the form of formal studies, leading to the awarding of degrees or diplomas or of inhouse training sessions offered by departments such as seminars, orientation courses, or workshops. Continuing professional development by means of inservice training and distance education is encouraged. However, a comprehensive and coordinated program is needed to meet the growing and changing demands.

7. *Curriculum Development and Teaching Methodology*

The National Policy for General Education Affairs Act (Act 76 of 1984) accorded the Minister of National Education with the responsibility for determining general policy for formal, informal, and nonformal education in consultation with all the ministers of departments of state responsible for education. This includes norms and standards for syllabuses, examinations, and the certification of qualifications.

Framework committees under the auspices of the Committee of Heads of Education Departments were established to develop curricula. These committees consist of representatives of all the departments of education and, where necessary, subject experts from universities and relevant private-sector groups. These committees develop and design national curricula frameworks. These core curricula, comprising of aims, content, and evaluation guidelines, form the basis for the further development of syllabuses by the various departments and the management boards of private schools.

The need for a new national curriculum arose because of the diversity of what was taught in different schools and departments, as well as the demand for relevant curricula, especially in terms of vocational orientation.

Curricula for schools administered by the various education departments differ because the syllabuses used are developed by the department administering the schools. Teachers have considerable autonomy in deciding their own teaching methodology. Most teachers, however, feel more comfortable when they closely follow the contents of the textbooks supplied. They are generally more inclined to disseminate information than to utilize new experimental methods.

The curricula used in practically all primary schools expose students to reading and writing, as well as to mathematics, science (health education), social studies (history), expressive and performing arts, religion, physical education, and one additional language. Up to the fourth grade such subjects are taught by general classroom teachers. Thereafter specialists are employed.

Secondary schools provide for differentiation in subject areas, such as the natural or social sciences, commerce, business, home economics, agriculture, and technical subjects. These subjects can usually be taken at one of three levels of difficulty: lower, standard, or higher. University entrance requirements still tend to dominate the choice of subjects. A matter for concern is that relatively few Black pupils take courses in natural sciences and mathematics. In 1988, only 15, 32, and 0.3 percent of all Black pupils in Standard 10 respectively took physical science, mathematics, and technical drawing.

A key issue in curriculum development is the quest for relevant education, and the standardization of the large variety of curricula used by the various education departments with sufficient room being left for the accommodation of cultural diversity. A new curriculum model has been developed by the Committee of Heads of Education Departments which proposes earlier vocational training.

8. *The System of Examinations, Promotions, and Certifications*

Internal examinations determine the annual promotion of pupils from one school level to the next. At the end of the Standard 10, a public examination is taken. This examination is set by any one of nine examining bodies. The standards of the examining bodies have been coordinated and moderated by the Joint Matriculation Board in order to assure the equivalence of the various certificates. This role arose from the traditional function of the Joint Matriculation Board, a body established to regulate university entrance requirements.

In 1986 parliament established the South African Certification Council. This council was given the authority to establish national norms and standards for certification, and to appoint examining bodies. It is the curriculum determined by the Minister of National Education that will form the basis for the establishment of norms and standards for certification. Thus in future, all school-leaving certificates will be issued by the Council. The Committee of University Principals will establish minimum requirements for university entrance from the Matriculation Board. The examining function of the Joint Matriculation Board, which functions mainly for pupils from private schools, will most probably be taken over by the Independent Examination Board.

The most important problem facing the Certification Council will be the establishment of equivalence of standards for the various examining bodies. Research has already commenced. Research and assessment are undertaken by the Human Sciences Research Council as well as by special research units attached to the education departments.

9. Educational Assessment, Evaluation, and Research

During the 1980s many changes in educational evaluation and research took place, but no national assessment of educational achievement has yet been undertaken. In 1985 the Department of National Education assumed responsibility for the collection of data and the dissemination of information on the education system. This led to the development of an extensive data bank on the education system. Evaluation systems, especially in regard to the financial aspects of education, were developed.

The most prominent indicators on which data are published on a regular basis are: per capita expenditure, teacher–student ratios, the percentage of qualified (Standard 10 or N3 plus 3 years or more professional training) teaching personnel, the number of students aged 6 to 16 years attending school, Grade 1–Standard 10 ratios, population growth rate, and student–classroom ratios.

The Human Sciences Research Council, in conjunction with the various education authorities, also often undertakes and sponsors research projects on education. A question bank with standardized items for objective testing has been developed, and extensive research on cross-cultural assessment of achievement is regularly undertaken.

10. Major Reforms in the 1980s and 1990s

Since 1970, education in South Africa has been characterized by strife, protest, extensive inquiry, and several major reform proposals. Against the political fluidity of the late 1980s, several research projects resulting in reform proposals were undertaken. This process was initiated in 1981 by the Human Sciences Research Council's proposals for educational reform. Extensive proposals for reform were also published in June 1991 in the form of an Education Renewal Strategy, and in November 1991 in the form of a Curriculum Model by the Committee of Education Heads. These reform proposals followed a functionalist approach based on identified major problem areas and after extensive consultation with expert and representative bodies reform strategies were proposed. The core of the problems were found to be: (a) backlogs in respect of teachers, classrooms, and other educational services, particularly for the schooling of Black pupils, owing to rapid population growth, recent large-scale population migration, and poor economic conditions; (b) the politically contentious nature of the education system as a result of its racial basis, which has inter alia led to conflict and resistance and even to the collapse of discipline and order in certain geographical areas; and (c) the exceptional problems associated with the provision of schooling in a society which is deeply divided on ethnic, cultural, and economic lines.

In a policy statement by the state president on February 1, 1991 a clear indication was given of the need for the educational system to change. The guidelines for a new education system must:

(a) be nondiscriminatory,

(b) offer equal educational opportunities,

(c) enjoy the acceptance and support of the majority of the people, and

(d) leave room for community-based education for those who desire it.

A study of the reform proposals and those of other organizations leaves no doubt about the seriousness and complexity of the challenge to reform the education system in such a way as to contribute toward the future development of a prosperous, just, and democratic society in South Africa.

References

African National Congress (ANC) 1991 *Discussion Paper for the ANC on Education Policy*. (mimeo)

Department of National Education 1991a *Education Realities in South Africa, 1990* (NATED 02–300 [91/06]). Government Printer, Pretoria

Department of National Education 1991b *Education—Renewal Strategy: Discussion Document*. University of South Africa, Pretoria

Departement van Onderwys en Kultuur: Administrasie Volksraad 1990 *Die evaluering en bevordering van loopbaanonderwys*. Hoofverslag van die Komitee insake die evaluering en bevordering van loopbaanonderwys in die Departement van Onderwys en Kultuur, Administrasie Volksraad. Walters-verslag, Pretoria

Human Sciences Research Council 1981 *Provision of Education in the RSA*. Human Sciences Research Council, Pretoria

Raad vir Geesteswetenskaplike Navorsing 1989 *Die RGN/NOR Ondersoek na Vaardigheidsopleiding in die RSA*. Raad vir Geesteswetenskaplike Navorsing. Pittendrich-verslag, Pretoria

Further Reading

Behr A L 1988 *Education in South Africa. Origins, Issues and Trends: 1652–1988*. Academica, Cape Town

Central Statistical Service 1986 *Population Census: Report No. 02.85.07. Economic Characteristics: Statistics According to Occupation Industry and Identity of Employer* (DI D10). Government Printer, Pretoria

Christie P 1988 *The Right to Learn. The Struggle for Education in South Africa*, 4th edn. Sached Trust/Ravan Press Pty. Ltd., Braamfontein

Davenport T R H 1991 *South Africa: A Modern History*, 4th edn. Macmillan SA, Johannesburg

Department of National Education 1990 *Preliminary Education Statistics for 1990* (NATED 02–214 [90/08]). Government Printer, Pretoria

Du Pisani T, Plekker S J, Dennis C R, Straus J P 1991 *Education and Manpower Development 1990, No. 11*. RIEP, University of the Orange Free State, Bloemfontein

Heese C 1990 *Aspekte van die onderwys in Suid-Afrika*. Kernaantekeninge vir Vergelykende Opvoedkunde, Universiteit van Stellenbosch

Malherbe E G 1925 *Education in South Africa. Vol. 1: 1652–922*. (Repr. 1975) Juta and Co. Ltd., Johannesburg

Malherbe E G 1977 *Education in South Africa. Vol. 2: 1923–75*. Juta and Co. Ltd., Johannesburg

Republic of South Africa 1990 *South African Statistics 1990*. (Compiled by the Central Statistical Service). Government Printer, Pretoria

Republic of South Africa 1991 *South African Labour Statistics 1991* (D1,D6). Central Statistical Service, Pretoria

Republic of South Africa 1991–92 *South Africa 1991–92. Official Yearbook*. South African Communication Service, Pretoria

South African Reserve Bank 1991 *Quarterly Bulletin* (June) No. 180. South African Reserve Bank, Pretoria

M. J. Bondesio; S. J. Berkhout

Southern and Western Europe: Adult Education

Adult education has gained in importance in many European countries. This is evident from growing participation rates, growing public and private expenditures, and an increasing policy interest.

The importance of adult education stems mainly from economic considerations. Knowledge is a production factor, and the economic continuity and success of firms, regions, and even of nations depend on a well-skilled labor force. Economic competition, to an increasing extent, becomes competition among workforces and their human capital.

However, other functions of adult education gain in importance as well. The training of the unemployed must ensure their re-entry into the labor market. The teaching of basic skills like literacy and numeracy serves the social integration of groups that are in danger of being marginalized. Moreover, the value of these functions is also to an extent judged by economic criteria. The sociocultural dimension of adult education, with its emphasis upon personal development and cultural orientation, has to a certain extent moved to second stage, although it is still vital. It is in these forms of adult education that regional and national identities manifest themselves most strongly (see *Adult Education and Training Markets*).

This entry describes and compares the systems of adult education in several European countries. Not all the European countries are covered. The Nordic countries are covered in another entry, although Sweden is included here as well, for comparative reasons (see *Nordic Countries: Adult Education*). However, the entry makes no claim to be a comparative study in the true sense (Knoll 1989). For such a purpose, basic statistics on adult education are often too defective; especially insofar as data concerning the private sector are often lacking. The data from the southern European countries tend to be less detailed than those from northern and western Europe and consequently their description is more global. One also gets the impression that the problems facing these countries are of a qualitatively different nature (see *Measurement of Adult Education; Adult and Nonformal Education: Statistics*).

Some of these defects may also apply to the figures presented in this entry. Part of the problem is that national definitions are often difficult to compare. As a pragmatic solution, "adult education" is considered to be the sum total of all the forms of adult and continuing training and education for people who have finished their initial education. Boundary problems of course remain. Adult students in higher education, for example, are included. Forms of education for young people, combining school and practical work, as in the German dual system, are excluded. The same applies to the huge territory of informal learning and on-the-job training.

Finally, systems of adult education are part of the larger social and political context and they change with the changes in that context. The unification of Germany, for example, will have far-reaching consequences for the system of adult education, but at this stage it is impossible to predict or even describe these consequences. With these sobering remarks, the European situation with respect to adult education will be examined.

1. France

The French system of adult education can roughly be divided into three subsystems: the system of vocational adult education, which is partly controlled by the social partners and partly by the private institutions; the system of second chance education, leading to nationally recognized diplomas and linked with the regular educational system; and the system of sociocultural adult education, which is dominated by private, nonprofit institutions.

In France, there is a strong emphasis on the vocational aspects of adult education, which is divided into the public sector (financed by national and regional authorities and mainly aimed at the unemployed) and the firm-based sector (financed by enterprises with more than 10 employees, that have been responsible by law for the training of their employees since 1971) (see *Legislation in Adult Education*).

The law of 1971 is one of the most prominent characteristics of French adult education. According to the Law, all but the smallest firms are obliged to reserve a percentage of the payroll for the training of their employees. In 1992, the legal obligation was 1.2 percent of the payroll, but enterprises spent a lot more in reality. In 1987, the obligation was 2.5 percent on average (in some of the bigger enterprises this could amount to 7% of the payroll) (Centre INFFO 1989). From the fund thus formed, obligatory contributions must be made to paid educational leave and training efforts aimed at combating youth unemployment. The bulk of the fund is used for the training of employees. This can be done by means of in-company training or through buying the training from private, for-profit institutions and providers associated with the branches of industry or from public agencies. The latter, however, play a modest role in this market. The trade unions have a strong influence on the organization of the training efforts within the scope of the Law on adult education and enterprise training.

The training efforts of enterprises have grown considerably since the introduction of the Law. In 1987, the participation rate was 31 percent of the total workforce (*Actualité de la Formation Permanente* 1988). The law also regulates paid educational leave, which may be used for professional as well as general educational purposes (see *Paid Educational Leave and Collective Bargaining*).

Public vocational adult education is mostly aimed at those who fall outside the scope of the training laws—for example, because they are employed in small-sized businesses or because they lack paid employment. In 1987, the central government trained 2.8 million people and regional governments another 400,000 (Centre INFO 1989). The main target group comprises the young and unemployed, but the training of government employees is also important. The actual training takes place in public training centers for the unemployed or is bought from other public institutions for adult education.

The possibilities for granting diplomas at secondary general school level (*baccalauréat*) are restricted to public daytime and evening schools (GRETAs) and distance education (CNED). These institutions offer a variety of courses ranging from diploma courses to training programs for the unemployed and other vocational courses.

The higher education system is rather closed to adults, at least for those who lack the necessary entry qualifications. Universities organize preparatory courses, often in collaboration with institutions for adult education. In exceptional cases, work experience may give exemption from entry requirements. Although there is a tendency for universities to offer special courses—for example, to those who study under the Law of 1971—the number of adult students in regular university education is relatively modest.

The pattern of provision by the adult education associations is multifaceted. According to French law, every group of at least seven persons may form an association and is eligible for a grant, mostly from local government or public organizations. The content is mostly socioculturally oriented, but vocational adult education courses are also offered.

2. Federal Republic of Germany (FRG)

The consequences of the unification of the two Germanies for the system of adult education are as yet unclear. Another complication is the federal structure of the FRG. Adult education is a responsibility of the separate states (*Länder*), while federal legislation is not developed.

During the 1980s there has been much growth in adult education participation in Germany. In 1987, one-fourth of the adult population participated, with equal shares for vocational and general adult education (Bundesminister für Bildung und Wissenschaft 1987). Compared with most other European countries, this is a high participation rate which, however, strongly covariates with the level of education previously obtained, socioeconomic position, and age. The proportion of women in adult education, even of vocational types, has increased during the late 1980s.

More than half of the total provision of vocational adult education is offered by enterprises. Private for-profit institutions account for 6 percent of the market for vocational adult education. In general, these courses do not lead to qualifications that are certified by the state or by professional associations.

The *Volkshochschulen* (see *Folk High Schools*) are major providers. Although vocational adult education is not their main strength, the sheer number of participants makes them an important provider. A typical German phenomenon is the important role of the employers' organizations for the different professions and branches of industry (*Kammern*) in vocational education. They offer high quality courses that often build upon the dual system of vocational youth education. These courses lead to publicly recognized qualifications, such as the title of *Meister* (master) in the manufacturing industry.

Institutes for vocational higher education (*Hochschulen*) may offer graduate vocational courses, but their zest for engaging in these activities is not great (Krais 1990).

A great variety of organizations offer general adult education. As far as the number of participants is concerned, *Volkshochschulen* and church institutions are the major providers, drawing 8.6 and 10 million participants in 1987 (Krais 1990). Taking into account the length and quality of the courses, the *Volkshochschulen* rank as the most important provider. Major subjects are (foreign) languages, economics, mathematics, science, and health. On a modest scale, trade unions and party organizations also offer general adult education.

Volkshochschulen and other institutions (like evening schools) offer courses leading to diplomas on the secondary general school level. The *Volkshochschulen* have developed a modular system in which the diploma can be reached in stages.

Higher education institutions play a very modest role in the provision of adult education. To be eligible for higher education, a formal entry qualification (*Abitur*) is needed, and there are few facilities for adult students to achieve it, such as part-time courses and study loans. There is one university entirely based on distance education, while other institutions for higher education also have facilities for offering distance education.

In 1987, the state budget for adult education (federal and *Länder*) was about DM 12 billion, of which three-fourths were devoted to training activities for the unemployed and other groups with a weak position on the labor market. Income maintenance for those attending public training programs takes a major part of this expense. The remaining fourth of the state budget is used to subsidize the different institutions. In practice, the *Volkshochschulen* and the institutions managed by the churches or the trade unions receive a major part of the budget. The state grant ranges from 30 percent to 100 percent. Public expenditure on adult education rose from 4.6 percent of total education expenditure in 1970 to 10.5 percent in 1988. This is a clear indication of the increased significance of the adult education sector in Germany.

A yearly budget of DM 10 billion is mentioned for enterprise training. However, when earnings forgone are included, this figure rises to DM 34 billion (Krais 1990).

Some *Länder*—like Berlin, Lower Saxony, Hamburg, and Hessen—have an arrangement for paid educational leave, allowing workers to attend vocational courses or citizenship courses for a few days per year.

3. Sweden

The Nordic region is treated separately (see *Nordic Countries: Adult Education*), but because of the exemplary nature of some characteristics of its adult education system, Sweden is also included in this European overview.

Sweden has an elaborate system of adult education provision. Characteristic are training as an integral part of labor market policy, a relatively open system of higher education, and an ample system of opportunities for educational leave. Participation is high; about half of the population in the age group 18–64 years participates in organized adult education, which is one of the highest figures in Europe. Sweden also has a leading position in terms of public expenditure as a share of total public spending. About 15 percent of the educational budget is spent on adult education, and total public and private expenditures on adult education amount to 3 percent of the Gross National Product (GNP). Most other European countries spend between 1 and 2 percent of the GNP (Boot 1989). The approach to labor market training in the context of "the Swedish model" has drawn attention internationally. This model is based on an active labor market policy. Instead of spending a large share of the funds required for income maintenance of the unemployed on social security benefits, Sweden spends it on employment exchange, training, and temporary job creation. Social security benefits are seen as a last resort. Training is a crucial instrument and, in 1987, Sweden (with Denmark) spent more money on labor market training (0.49% of GNP) than any other European country (OECD 1989).

Labor market policy is the responsibility of the National Labor Market Board (*Arbetsmarknadsstyrelsen*, AMS), whereas labor market training is implemented by the Labor Market Training Agency (*Arbetsmarknadsutbildningen*, AMU). Both have a tripartite board and are largely decentralized. The local employment agencies of the AMS define the demand for training, while the local AMU training centers offer the relevant courses. Although the training demand of the employment agencies is largely covered by the AMU training centers, they can also put out a tender to other providers. On the other hand, AMU centers are free to sell courses to municipal educational authorities and enterprises. For the unemployed, participation is free and the courses have a high success rate in terms of post-program employment (see *Evaluation of Public Training: Industrial Countries*). As usual, public and private enterprises also run their own training programs. It is estimated that about 10 percent of all workers annually attend an in-company training course.

Vocational and general adult education, leading to "recognized" diplomas and certificates, is organized mostly by the municipal adult education authorities (KOMVUX). There are no formal entrance requirements and the organization of the courses is adapted to the learning needs of adults (modular, full-time, and part-time courses). There are special courses for target groups like immigrants. In the early 1990s, there is a tendency to intensify the role of labor market training in KOMVUX.

In 1977, a separate provision for adult basic education (GRUNDVUX) was begun in Sweden. This is also a municipal responsibility. Originally the target group was (functional) illiterates, but to an increasing extent, GRUNDVUX is used by immigrants to learn Swedish. They now comprise half of the participants (see *Adult Basic Education*).

Sociocultural adult education has a rich tradition in Sweden. The first folk high schools were established in the middle of the nineteenth century in rural areas. They now attract participants from all walks of life and offer a great variety of courses. They are administered by local authorities, but also by trade unions, churches, and voluntary associations (see *Folk High Schools*).

The study circles are typical Scandinavian phenomena. In 1986, Sweden had 300,000 study circles with 2.6 million participants. Participants choose their own themes and method of working, but social and artistic subjects are dominant. When the study circles fulfill certain conditions, they can receive a public subsidy (see *Study Circles; Providers of Adult Education*).

With the introduction of the Higher Education Law of 1977, recurrent education was taken as the point of departure for higher education policy (see *Recurrent and Alternation Education; University Adult Education*). The accessibility of higher education was increased through the 25/4 arrangement. This implies that adults older than 24 years, with at least four years of work experience (including taking care of the family) are entitled to enter higher education without a formal qualification, although there are often supplementary requirements for certain courses. As a consequence, the share of adult students in higher education seems to be higher than in other European countries. A modular organization, full-time and part-time courses, and distance education also cater to the needs of adult students (Tuijnman 1990).

Most forms of adult education are free, and participants in adult education are, in principle, entitled to some form of financial assistance, although this can take the form of a loan. This applies especially to people attending labor market training and adult education leading to formal qualifications. Educational leave is governed by law. All forms of adult education can be attended, there is no formal time limit and employees keep their position while they are on leave (see *Time Policies and Lifelong Education*).

4. United Kingdom

The data offered here refer mostly to England and Wales. Scotland and Northern Ireland have a somewhat different system. The system of adult education in England and Wales is very complex and in a state of constant flux. Still, some salient features can be mentioned—for example, that the system is mostly decentralized. Local education authorities (LEAs) are in principle responsible for adult education. Central government covers a large part of the costs of adult education, although there is a tendency for participants to pay high fees, possibly with the exception of certain disadvantaged clientele groups. Central government has recently taken the initiative in the field of vocational adult education.

There is an elaborate system of publicly subsidized providers, often catering for young as well as adult participants. Independent examination boards offer the possibility to sit for examinations, irrespective of the educational route one has taken.

These characteristics make the British system of adult education highly flexible, although some commentators would prefer the term "fragmented." Annually, about 16 percent of the adult population participates in some form of organized adult education.

Three major sectors can be distinguished:

(a) the public sector, which is mainly financed by means of transfers to the local education authorities (LEAs) who manage the bulk of adult education;

(b) the public sector, which is directly financed by the Ministry of Education;

(c) continuing vocational training, which is financed by firms and the public Training Agency.

Local education authorities are principally responsible for the education of the young and the adults within their region. Adult education is only a marginal part of their mandate. Financial sources are users' fees, local taxes, and government grants. The situation of economic austerity in the United Kingdom has especially affected the adult education sector.

Local education authorities organize general as well as vocational education for adults. For the most part, the general courses are provided by schools that also offer vocational courses for adults. A clear case in point are the polytechnics, the institutions of higher education, and the colleges of further education. They offer vocational programs at secondary and tertiary level, as well as a variety of continuing nondegree courses. Adults can also take part in these courses. An estimate puts the number of participants at 1 million (Jennings 1985). Since the introduction of the Education Act of 1988, the polytechnics and some colleges of higher education have come under the direct authority of the Ministry of Education. The consequences of this for the provision of education for adults are not clear. (see *Polytechnical Education*).

General adult education under the authority of the LEAs attracts many participants. The estimates vary from 2–3 million adults. The provision is offered by adult education centers and can be characterized as leisure oriented, although formal diplomas can also be obtained. The leisure courses especially have suffered from budget cuts. The colleges of further education also offer general adult education. Adult basic education has not been affected by budget cuts. Stimulated by the literacy campaigns of the British Broadcasting Corporation (BBC), adult basic education has become a policy priority.

A number of institutions offering courses for adults are directly financed by the Ministry of Education—for example, the universities and their extramural departments, the Open University, the Workers' Educational Association (WEA), and the long-term residential colleges. Below, the focus is on the institutions for higher education.

Traditionally, universities in the United Kingdom have played an important role in adult education. Most conspicious is the tradition of liberal academic adult education. Universities offer a wide range of nondegree courses for a general audience interested in academic subjects. For that purpose, a number of universities received a specific grant and established extramural departments for adult education extension. Since 1988, however, the grant has been abolished and universities must pay for these activities from their overall budget. In 1988, about half a million adults were recruited.

Because of diminishing resources, universities try to expand their market with vocational "post-experience" and "postgraduate" courses, often at the expense of liberal adult education. As the intake of young students diminishes, universities also try to attract new adult constituencies. One way is to recognize alternative educational routes—for example, as in the Open College. Another way is the organization of access studies preparing people for university admission. There has been a proliferation of such programs. The third way is that of pursuing an open access policy as has been the case with the Open University. The Open University, a unique experiment in open access education, has been followed in a number of other European countries. In 1985, there were 100,000 participants, of which 60 percent took a degree course. The percentage of students without formal entry qualifications has risen to 44 percent. (see *Open University; University Adult Education*).

Up to this point, established institutions have been discussed. In recent policy, emphasis has been laid on projects, which—after a starter subsidy—must be able to operate cost-effectively. The established institutions can participate in these projects. An example is the Open College project, in which the colleges for further education and the polytechnics participate. This tendency has been particularly strong in those parts of vocational education and labor market training for which the Department of Employment is responsible.

Because the educational system in the United Kingdom is highly decentralized and lacks an efficient tradition of vocational education, the central government has taken a strong initiative in the field of vocational adult education and training. There has been a steep increase in funds and a host of measures to implement policy. The Training Agency, the successor to the Manpower Services Commission, was established in 1988 under the direct responsibility of the Department of Employment. The implementation of these national programs is highly decentralized. Local training and enterprise councils (TECs) must establish the local training needs of the employed and unemployed and negotiate with the different providers of continuing vocational education and training. Employers have a majority in the TECs. Although there are some public training centers, the majority of the desired training is bought from public and private institutions. Due to their purchasing power, the Training Agency (and the TECs) have a major influence on the system of adult education.

Despite the training efforts of the Training Agency, most training takes place within the enterprises. According to a rough estimate, spending on in-company training is three times as high (£9 billion in 1987) as the expenditures of the Training Agency (Het Verenigd Koninkrijk, Ministerie van Economische Zaken 1989).

There is no law on (paid) educational leave in the United Kingdom, but there can be arrangements in the context of collective agreements (see *Paid Educational Leave and Collective Bargaining*).

5. The Netherlands

The system of adult education in the Netherlands is undergoing a process of change. There are efforts to create coherence in a fragmented system; money and authority are transfered to local authorities and the social partners, and the system is being adapted to the demands of the labor market.

About 1.5 percent of the GNP is spent on adult education by both public and private actors. During the late 1980s, 2 million adults participated annually, which amounted to 20 percent of the adult population. Expenditures and participation also continued to increase during the early 1990s. There is a strong relationship between socioeconomic position and participation level. The majority of the participants are employed and a vocational orientation dominates in participation (Houtkoop and Felix 1990).

Private, vocational adult education is dominated by firm-based training. In 1986, 20 percent of the workforce was involved, and the costs amounted to roughly 1.5 percent of the wage bill. In 60 percent of the cases, the programs are organized by the firms concerned; in 15 percent, the programs are organized by institutions working for a branch of industry; and the remaining 25 percent of cases are programs bought from private providers (CBS 1988). There is no legal arrangement for educational leave, but in-company training and educational leave are increasingly a part of collective labor agreements.

A sizable amount of company training is bought from private providers, which have a relatively strong position on the adult education market, especially in the vocational sector. There is a law on the recognition of private institutions, which guarantees quality standards and protects consumers. Although participation is often fully or partly subsidized by the employer, there is also a sizable amount of individual investment. The private institutions are also involved in public training efforts.

Public vocational education can be divided into programs leading to formal qualifications which are often provided by schools, and labor market training for the unemployed and other disadvantaged groups. The former consists of part-time secondary vocational education and part-time higher vocational education. The apprentice system is aimed at young students, but has been made more accessible for adult students as well. For that purpose, the age limit of 27 years has been abolished.

Labor market training for the unemployed is the (financial) responsibility of the Ministry of Labor. There is a tripartite national body that sets financial and policy guidelines. Actual implementation takes place in regional tripartite boards who define training needs and select training facilities. Training takes place in public training centers or can be bought from private and public institutions. To guarantee fair competition between the different institutions, experiments have started with a tender procedure. Participation had increased to 155,000 in 1990 (see *Evaluation of Public Training: Industrial Countries*).

General adult education is the responsibility of the Ministry of Education, which offers programs at different levels. Adult basic education started in 1987. It is covered by a special law, stipulating that provision must be by specialized institutions and by professional teachers. The municipal authorities are responsible for the realization of adult basic education. Participation had increased considerably to 115,000 participants in 1990. Adult basic education has been particularly successful in attracting minority groups and has been given new tasks for the integration of immigrants. Language courses are the programs most chosen. There is some political pressure to give adult basic education a more explicit function as a preparation for low-level vocational programs.

Secondary general adult education leads to formal diplomas, but participants can also obtain separate credits. This type of education used to be very popular among elder women, but participation has slowly decreased to about 100,000. Under a new law, secondary general adult education will also have to offer special transfer programs for people who want to move on to vocational education. Higher education offers part-time degree courses. Special programs for adults, such as the liberal adult education programs in the United Kingdom, are few in the Netherlands. Since 1984, there has been an Open University with open access. Most students only take one or two modules; students embarking on a full degree program are in the minority.

Sociocultural adult education is offered by a large variety of institutions, either subsidized by local authorities or—to an increasing extent—dependent on participants' fees. Some institutions are involved in local projects aimed at combating persistent social disadvantages. Other institutions orient themselves toward the "education for leisure" market (see *Leisure: Adult Education*).

6. Portugal

In Portugal, policy interest in adult education as it is understood in other European countries only started with the revolution of 1974. Since then it has been given a high priority, in view of the comparatively low level of formal educational attainment of the adult population. The development of a coherent system of adult education is hampered by a lack of financial resources, institutional infrastructure, and qualified personnel. Because of a lack of tradition and the low educational level of certain groups, it is difficult to attract certain disadvantaged groups to adult education.

There are three main domains of provision which can be distinguished:

(a) general adult education and sociocultural education provided at the regional and local levels by a great variety of private and public organizations;

(b) continuing vocational training;

(c) general adult education, vocational training, and sociocultural education provided by the Ministry of Education.

The first domain is formed by a wide range of activities addressed to the local community or to specific target groups. They are organized by local public authorities (agricultural and health services, for example) and private organizations (cooperatives, associations, trade unions, and churches), mostly with little public funding.

Vocational training has developed rapidly during the 1980s, to no small extent due to funding by the EEC. It is mainly provided by the Ministry of Labor and Social Welfare either in its own training centers, or in collaboration with enterprises, trade unions, and private training centers. The Ministry of Agriculture also plays an important part in vocational training.

The Ministry of Education is the main provider of adult education. Since 1986, a policy has been established to promote second chance education for adults who have received little formal initial education, and to those who need an educational opportunity to achieve career improvement or cultural advancement. In practice, this has meant, first of all, the growth of literacy programs and adult basic education. Literacy is a major policy objective. Courses are given in regional centers for adult basic education in close cooperation with local authorities. Secondary general adult education leads to formal school diplomas, but the programs are adapted to adult needs (e.g., by introducing vocational elements). Vocational training under the responsibility of the Ministry of Education functions as a preparation for more advanced programs. It always includes elements of adult basic education or general education. Finally, the Ministry of Education promotes social and cultural activities for participants in literacy and other courses, and also for the local communities.

There is no special training for teachers in adult education. Activities are mostly carried out by elementary and secondary school teachers and by volunteers.

7. *Greece*

Adult education provision in Greece has expanded rapidly since the early 1980s. A major reason is that the country obtained full membership of the EC in 1981. Because of this, considerable changes have occurred in the production sector, with new technologies playing an increasingly dominant role, making training and retraining a necessity. Furthermore, financial aid has been provided for adult education and training by the European Social Fund (ESF) and other EC funds. Both developments have been a major stimulus for the adult education system, but have also put it under pressure. The infrastructure has had to be expanded and there has been an increasing demand for adult educators.

Programs are mainly vocationally oriented and targeted at (semi) urban areas, with a strong concentration in the capital. This leaves certain groups in Greece, who are faced with skills shortages and difficulties of basic education and training, underserved. For these groups, an expansion of adult basic education and retraining programs is needed. Small- and medium-sized firms are also underserved, while the consequences of global economic competition are expected to necessitate upgrading and retraining on a large scale.

Description of the providers of adult education in Greece is restricted to the public sector, as hardly any data are available about the private sector. The main providers are the public administration and private corporate bodies operating under the responsibility of government ministries. Most state providers are subsidized by the ESF and other EC funds.

Vocational education is a priority. New legislation on continuing vocational education and training has introduced a new network of further education institutions (Institutions of Vocational Training, IEK) which is designed to increase the opportunities for adult participation in vocational education and training. The institutions are part of the formal education system and, in the early stages, will function on the premises of the technical schools. Some adult education centers operated by the private sector may be incorporated into the system as well. They will provide continuing vocational education and training in accordance with market demands, made more pertinent by European integration. The IEK is financed by the central government, mainly through subsidies granted by the EC.

Training activities for public servants are organized by the Institute for Permanent Education. European integration has led to major changes in regulations concerning the management and operation of public institutions, which in turn has given rise to a large increase in training activities. Specialized bodies are responsible for the training of small industries and crafts, as well as for the workforce in the private sector.

The Ministry of Agriculture is responsible for agricultural extension services, particularly the further training of farmers, and, with 80,000 participants annually, is one of the larger providers.

General adult education is the responsibility of the General Secretariat of Popular Education (GGLE). It has an extensive regional network, especially in rural areas, and, with 97,000 participants, it is the largest provider. The GGLE programs cover a wide range of subjects, including functional literacy and adult basic skills.

8. Italy

Adult education in Italy has been, since 1977, largely decentralized, giving the regions a possibility of formulating and implementing their own regulations on permanent or adult education. Central government determines the total budget, while planning, programming, and budget allocation are a regional responsibility. However, efforts are being made to introduce a National Law on Adult Education to create more coherence in the system and to raise the reputation of this field.

A salient feature of Italian adult education is the "150 hours" arrangement, giving workers the right to 150 hours of study leave on an annual basis. Programs were designed so as to offer people a second chance to obtain secondary school diplomas, but other programs can be attended as well. In the early stages, specific courses with a special didactic approach were set up, but to an increasing extent the courses have taken on the character of regular school programs. Originally only intended for workers, in the early 1990s almost anyone can attend these adult education programs.

Vocational education and training has also become a regional responsibility since 1978. In the law concerned, it is underlined that activities must be dedicated to adults, especially the unemployed. There is a variety of courses offered by schools, organizations of employers, and private organizations. The Ministry of Labor supervises the quality level of diplomas and certificates.

Adults can attend primary and secondary general education. Provision is regionally coordinated, and the Regional Council for Adult Education is ultimately responsible for the provision and the budget. Courses in the context of the "150 hours" arrangement are mostly of a general nature.

9. Conclusion

Adult education is a growth sector in Europe. The number of participants and the level of both public and private expenditures have increased during the 1970s and 1980s. By the 1990s, the focus has come to be on vocational adult education as a means to strengthen the relationship between education and work, to integrate the unemployed, and to maintain and improve the skills of the workforce. The position of general and social–cultural education has declined somewhat—with the exception of literacy and adult basic education programs, which, however, are at least partly also promoted for economic reasons.

The administration of adult education is often highly decentralized, leaving the responsibility for actual planning and implementation in the hands of local authorities or social partners.

As far as participation, expenditure, and policy interests are concerned, adult vocational education assumes a central position. The training of the workforce is, in general, the responsibility of the enterprises. The influence of employees and the government is restricted, with France as a clear exception. However, to an increasing extent, in-company training is becoming part and parcel of collective labor agreements.

Public responsibility for adult vocational education takes two main forms. In the first, the provision of broad vocational education leading to formal diplomas and programs for obtaining more specific qualifications are offered, in many cases developed in close collaboration with enterprises. In Germany, this system is highly formalized. A second form of public responsibility is labor market training for the unemployed and other groups with a weak position in the labor market. The main constituency groups in this case are often the early school-leavers and unemployed youth, but activities aimed at adults have intensified. Planning and control of labor market training is often shared with the social partners and is regionally implemented.

In some countries, like Sweden, the programs are mainly executed in special training centers; in other countries, like France or the United Kingdom, employment training is bought from public or private institutions. Because of the size of the funds being allocated to employment training, public authorities often have a decisive influence on the adult education market (see *Adult Education and Training Markets*).

In southern European countries, there has been a rapid development of adult vocational education. Membership of the EC and integration into the European market have made training and retraining a necessity. Funding by the European Social Fund and other EC funds have been a stimulus, but parts of the systems of adult education and training in these countries have been stretched to their limits as a result, since the infrastructure and the staff have only a limited capacity.

The attention given to vocational education has, in some cases, been at the expense of general adult education. In some countries, expenditures have dropped and fees have risen. The exception is adult basic education, which is a state responsibility in most European countries. Sweden and the Netherlands have a separate provision with a legal basis; in most other countries it is provided by other institutions, often with the help of volunteers. There is a need for literacy courses, especially in the southern European countries, but with the present resources certain regions and groups are underserved.

An important function of adult education is to give people a second chance to obtain formal diplomas, mostly at the secondary level. This is, in most European countries, a public responsibility. Sometimes the programs are offered by the regular school system; sometimes there are separate adult provisions. Several European countries also have distance education facilities. In some countries, the private institutions are allowed to offer diploma courses at the secondary level. The details differ across countries and they are also in a state of constant flux. A common trend is that the public institutions offering these courses are, to an increasing extent, becoming more market oriented (or are forced to do so), offering courses that are in demand and cost-effective.

In many European countries higher education is still not easily accessible for adults lacking the necessary qualifications. There are, however, opportunities to study part-time or by means of distance education. Countries like France or the United Kingdom organize special access courses to prepare people for entrance examinations. In Sweden, adults with work experience can enter higher education without the necessary entry qualifications, although this policy has come under review. Really open access is offered by institutions such as the United Kingdom and the Dutch open universities, which are in sharp contrast with similar university institutions operating in Germany and Spain. Higher education institutions often also offer a variety of other courses, ranging from short vocational programs to graduate programs. A stronger market orientation can also be discerned in higher education. The United Kingdom's tradition of liberal academic adult education for a wide audience is not widespread in other European countries.

Sociocultural adult education still features prominently in many European countries, attracting large audiences. Often popular movements, churches, political parties, or trade unions organize these activities, which reflects the fact that social–cultural adult education is rooted in broader social movements. It is largely a voluntary enterprise, however, and existing state support has come under pressure in a number of European countries. In the Nordic countries, the tradition of "popular enlightment" is particularly strong, and community groups or study circles engaging in educational activities are, under certain conditions, entitled by law to receive grants from local authorities.

Educational leave, whether paid or unpaid, plays a modest role in Europe. The United Kingdom and the Netherlands have arrangements for specific groups, like members of work councils, while several German *Länder* have arrangements for paid educational leave, but only for a short period. In France, every worker is entitled to paid educational leave for a program of his or her own choice. Arrangements in Sweden are ample. Educational leave is not paid for, but this is compensated for by the arrangements for study assistance. Educational leave can be used for different forms of adult education and the duration is not restricted. The "150 hours" arrangement in Italy is open to almost anyone and participants are free to take general or vocational programs. To an increasing extent, educational leave forms part of collective labor agreements.

See also: Adult Education: Concepts, Purposes, and Principles; Providers of Adult Education; Populations and Special Clienteles: Adult Education; Adult Education and Training Markets; Training Concepts and Statistics; Sweden: System of Education; United Kingdom: System of Education; France: System of Education; Netherlands, The: System of Education; Spain: System of Education

References

Actualité de la Formation Permanente 1988 Vol. 93: March/April

Boot P A 1989 Further education and training of adults: Provision, participation, economic impact, and policy options (draft version). Ministry of Social Affairs, The Hague

Bundesminister für Building und Wissenschaft 1987 Berichtssystem Weiterbildungsverhalten 1985. *Bildung-Wissenschaft-Aktuell* 7(87)

CBS 1988 *Bedrijfsopleidingen in Nederland 1986*. CBS, The Hague

Centre INFFO 1989 *La formation professionelle en chiffres*. Centre INFFO, Paris

Het Verenigd Koninkrijk Ministerie van Economische Zaken 1989 *Internationale beleidsvergelijking op het gebied van onderwijs en scholing*. Ministerie van Economische Zaken, Direktie Algemeen Technologiebeleid, The Hague

Houtkoop W, Felix C 1990 *Volwasseneneducatie in Europa*. RVE, Utrecht

Jennings 1985 *The Education of Adults in Britain: A Study of Organisation, Finance and Policy*. Newland Papers No. 10. University of Hull, Department of Adult and Continuing Education, Hull

Knoll J 1989 Adult education from Nordborg (1972) until today. *Int. J. Lifelong Learning* 8(2)

Krais B 1990 Weiterbildung, hoofdstuk 13. In: Max Planck Institut für Bildungsforschung 1990 *Das Bildungswesen in der Bundesrepublik Deutschland*. Rowohlt, Reinbek

OECD 1989 *Economic Surveys: Netherlands 1988/1989*. OECD, Paris

Tuijnman A C 1990 Dilemmas of open admissions policy: Quality and efficiency in Swedish higher education. *High. Educ.* 20: 443–57

Further Reading

European Bureau of Adult Education (EBAE) 1985 *Survey of Adult Education*. EBAE, Amersfoort

Florander J 1988 Denmark. In: Postlethwaite T N (ed.) 1988 *The Encyclopedia of Comparative Education and National Systems of Education*. Pergamon Press, Oxford

Peterson R E (ed.) 1982 *Adult Education and Training in Industrialized Countries*. Praeger, New York

Schütze H G (ed.) 1987 *Adults in Higher Education, Policies and Practice in Great Britain and North America*. Almqvist and Wiksell, Stockholm

Schütze H G, Istance D (eds.) 1987 *Recurrent Education*

Revisited: Modes of Participation and Financing. Almqvist and Wiksell, Stockholm
Werner H, König I 1989 *Arbeitsmarktpolitische Masnahmen in* EG-*Ländern und Sweden*. Nuremberg

W. Houtkoop

Soviet Union: Vocational Education and Training

The formation of the Commonwealth of Independent States and the dissolution of the Soviet Union in December 1991 was formal recognition of a process that had been under way for some time: the breakup of a vast centralized political and economic system and an attempt to integrate it into the world economy. Inevitably, this process has consequences for vocational education and training, presenting it with new tasks. The detailed nature of these tasks has not yet fully emerged—that will depend mainly on developments in the economy—but the movement from a clearly defined and centralized provision to one which is more fluid and responsive has been under way since at least 1988.

1. Soviet Vocational Education

The last truly Soviet initiative in vocational education—Soviet in the sense that it was committed to a centralized planned economy and communist ideology—was the 1984 Reform of the General Education and Vocational School. The reform recognized the serious problems facing the Soviet economy—the need to modernize technology, increase productivity, and improve quality—and that their solution would require a well-trained and educated workforce capable of a creative approach to work. Its weakness was that it sought to achieve its aims within the existing economic and ideological framework which by then was losing its credibility.

One of the reform's main aims was to add, over a period of 10 years or so, universal compulsory vocational education to existing universal compulsory secondary general education, thus reducing the difference in the forms of upper secondary education. Before the reform the 15-year old Soviet student, after eight years of school, had the following options:

(a) remaining in the general education school for two more years to complete general education;

(b) entering a vocational school (PTU) to acquire a skill qualification, completing general education in an evening or shift school;

(c) entering a secondary vocational school (secondary PTU) for a three-year course providing a skill qualification and complete secondary general education; or

(d) entering a specialized secondary school (SSUZ or *tekhnikum*), acquiring a technician level qualification and complete secondary education in a four-year course.

At this time roughly 60 percent of the cohort stayed on at general education school, 30 percent went to PTU or secondary PTU and 10 percent to specialized secondary school. A small number of pupils left school at 15 for work and continued their general education in evening or shift school.

The reform proposed that the number of pupils entering PTUs should be doubled, which would have had the effect of reversing the proportions of pupils entering vocational and general education schools. All PTUs were to be converted to secondary PTUs since the provision of general education in evening and shift schools was far from ideal. In the general education schools, existing labor training was to take on a more vocational character with general orientation courses for 14- and 15-year olds followed by courses leading to specific vocational qualifications in the upper secondary stage. All of these were trends already under way. A start was made on the reforms, and by 1987 over 150 vocational courses suitable for the general education school had been prepared, though the resource and staffing implications for this and for the conversion of PTUs to secondary PTUs were formidable, and the forces released by Gorbachov's policy of *perestroika* and *glasnost*, introduced in 1985, were undermining the principles of compulsion and uniformity on which the reform was based.

1.1 Characteristics of Soviet VET

The nature of Soviet vocational education and training provision was naturally very much shaped by the nature of the Soviet economy; that is to say, it was highly centralized, based largely on obsolescent technology, and closely integrated with local industry and agriculture. Among its main features were:

(a) The levels of training were clearly demarcated; skilled workers trained in schools, in PTUs and in on-the-job training; technicians and para-professionals trained in *tekhnikums* and SSUZ; and professional engineers and technologists trained in higher education.

(b) Institutions were mainly monotechnical, training workers for one branch of industry, for instance SPTU-43 in Leningrad (now St Petersburg) trained turners, lathe operators, borers, fitters, service electricians, pattern makers, and welders for a mechanical engineering factory. The same kind of division of labor applied at the other levels as well.

(c) The training, especially at skilled worker level, was predominantly for narrow skills. This problem had been talked about for many years but little had been done to overcome the inertia of the system.

(d) Institutions were usually attached to a factory, collective farm, or other type of state enterprise, which provided the opportunity for work practice and was supposed to employ the trainees when they had qualified.

(e) Most institutions provided a hostel and a substantial social, cultural, and welfare provision.

The model institution of Soviet vocational education was the secondary PTU. Introduced in 1969, its combination of industrial training and complete secondary education was a response to both the economic demand for well-educated skilled labor and the ideological requirement of social equality. It was an important part of the realization of the aim of universal compulsory secondary education, a contribution to the overcoming of prejudice against vocational education schools, and a strengthening of the bonds between education and industry. Inevitably, a large proportion of its intake were less able and socially disadvantaged pupils for whom it claimed to provide a more congenial atmosphere and more material benefits than the general education school. In practice it often fell short of requirements, failing to produce the broadly skilled workforce which was held to be necessary for the new technology, and achieving its intake targets by what amounted in some cases almost to conscription.

2. *Beginnings of Fundamental Change*

As the Russian Minister of Education, E Dneprov, has pointed out, real education reform did not begin until 1988. The 1984 Reform had been, in his view, a pseudo-reform (Dneprov 1990). The initial direction, toward more democracy and devolution in education, was set by the Communist Party of the Soviet Union (CPSU) at the Central Committee Plenum in February 1988 in the traditional manner but the Party was now less united and had less authority than previously. The existing ministries of education and the State Committee for Vocational Education were abolished and replaced by a single State Committee for Education, including vocational education. Work began on new provisional regulations for all levels of education which were to serve until a fundamental revision of the law relating to education could be made; and a Congress of Education Workers, with representatives from all levels of the system, was held in December to discuss policy in education. The Congress agreed the policy set out by the President of the USSR State Committee for Education, Gennady Yagodin.

However, there was no unanimity on the details of the policy and there were those who felt that it did not depart far enough from previous Soviet practice, as well as those who thought it departed to much too great an extent. The new regulations which came into effect in 1989 allowed for a measure of devolution of decision making to republic and local level along with innovation in institutional organization and curriculum and this, coupled with the declining authority of the Party and the Soviet government, the rise in nationalism, and the new entrepreneurial spirit abroad in some quarters, guaranteed that the changes would not be smooth or controlled from the center.

The struggle for power between the republics, particularly Russia, and the Union affected education too, and in late 1991 full control over education was taken by the republican ministries not long before the dissolution of the Soviet Union. An interrepublican committee, under the chairmanship of Yagodin, was set up to coordinate educational policy and plan strategy and there was also an interrepublican council for vocational education. While these bodies have no authority to enforce decisions they seem to retain residual powers of monitoring and setting standards.

2.1 *Consequences for Vocational Education and Training in the General Education School*

Centrally imposed compulsory vocational education was in principle incompatible with the democratization of the general education school which had to take into account the wishes of the pupils and their parents who were not universally convinced of the value of a trade training as part of school education. The February 1988 Party Plenum envisaged the postponement of vocational training until after the completion of general education at age 17 or so; and the vocationalization of the general education school proposed by the 1984 Reform was widely seen as a mistake. A first attempt to revise the policy on labor training in schools, by a working group set up by the State Committee on Education, which appeared in early 1989, failed to gain approval because of its lack of new ideas and because it was out of step with the concept of general education accepted by the Congress of Education Workers. A revised version put forward later in the same year rejected the idea that labor upbringing in schools was to prepare young people for a particular occupation while continuing to stress the importance of educational labor, "directed to the cognition of the world and one's place in it, as well as to modes of the transformation of reality," and productive labor, "the production of material and spiritual culture." Pupils' interests and inclinations were to be taken into account, a combination of thinking, activity, and reflection on results was to be emphasized and an individualized approach to the child was advocated (Akhalkin 1989).

Vocational courses introduced under the 1984

Reform and the earlier reforms of the Khrushchov period are no doubt still available in schools in many parts of what used to be the Soviet Union but both the principle and the practice have been seriously undermined by curricular devolution and the appearance of a significant number of private schools.

Meanwhile, productive labor in schools was taking a new form, stimulated by the pupil cooperatives then being encouraged by the Soviet government. The best-known and the largest of these was the *Otsy i Deti* (fathers and children) cooperative in Balashikha, near Moscow. In 1989 it involved 15,000 children and 500 adults, had a turnover of 300,000 rubles, and 40 schools had concluded agreements with it. The children were paid for their work and took part in decisions about the use of profits. A legal problem arose because the law on cooperatives did not permit children under 14 to work in them or children under 16 to be members. In spite of this, and in spite of the questionable working conditions for some of the children, it was allowed to operate. "It is labour, economic and vocational education of the schoolchild, the cultivation of an active life position," claimed one of the organizers of the collective (Khlebnikova 1989).

Other pupil collectives are more modest in size. In rural areas they rent land and sell their produce to local farms, and in the towns they produce parts for local factories and make items for sale to the public. More recently the emphasis has shifted to commercial and business education with the introduction of minifirms in some of the more sophisticated metropolitan schools. Economic education is seen as very important for a country moving to a market system. Schools have a great deal of freedom of action in this field at present but the development of a market economy may well eventually bring pressure from trade unions and small entrepreneurs to limit this commercial activity.

2.2 Consequences for the Vocational Schools

If the attempt to introduce vocational education into secondary schools had failed, matters were no better with the efforts to make all PTUs into secondary PTUs and double the intake. There had always been a problem in recruiting young people into the PTUs, which were seen as low status institutions catering for the academically less able. Once the coercive measures of the Soviet system were abandoned the possibility of realizing these aims disappeared. The experiment, as the Deputy Chairman of the USSR State Committee on Education responsible for vocational education put it in 1990, "did not survive the first experience of democratic freedom." Young people were insisting on their right not to have complete secondary education or, for that matter, a skill qualification. Already in 1989, 224,000 15-year olds had gone directly into work, by-passing the PTUs, three times as many as in 1985. In addition, the number of those with only eight years or less of education entering PTUs was also increasing, representing "a new twist in the spiral of dumping ballast from the secondary school into the PTU," while the number of graduates without secondary education turned out by the PTU system actually increased by 120,000 in 1989.

The situation was not helped by a decision in April 1988, presumably a response to the policy of post-compulsory vocational training announced at the February Plenum, to transfer 3,000 of the PTUs from the jurisdiction of the State Committee for Education to the base enterprises. It should be mentioned here that PTUs under the control of the education authorities had never provided anything like all the training required by agriculture and industry, and each branch, ministry, or department provided training within industry in its own field, through its own PTUs, training workshops, and courses, together with individual and brigade (group) on-the-job training. Opposition to the transfer was considerable both from education and industry. The resistance from industry was stiffened by the announcement that state funding for the transfered schools would cease on 1st January 1989. Because many of the enterprises concerned were on a self-accounting footing, what happened when the PTUs were transferred was that the facilities of the PTU became part of the general facilities of the factory, training workshops were used for production, and training itself became more specific and narrow. The social consequences of the transfer were emphasized by some educational opponents who saw a threat to the access of young people from poorer sections of the community to a secondary education, a trade, food and clothing, sport, and cultural facilities.

In the end, just over 400 PTUs were actually transferred. In the Russian republic an agreement was reached to postpone transfer of the agricultural PTUs, enterprises in Tomsk and Armenia refused to accept them, in Estonia and Belorussia the republican governments passed legislation preventing transfer, and the local authorities in Leningrad did likewise. In the face of this opposition the government gave way and the transfers were stopped. Schools that had already been transferred, however, were not returned to the education system. This whole episode illustrates the confusion about policy, the growing conflicts of interests, and the development of local centers of power so characteristic of the period.

The deteriorating economic situation did not help the PTUs either. There had always been a gap between the directives from the center and their realization in practice but by January 1990, as a survey of 7,000 PTUs conducted then showed, only 26 percent were properly resourced, 6.3 percent were likely to be closed, 21 percent had outdated metal working tools and there were only three computers for every 1,000 students.

Clearly the secondary PTU was no longer the model form of vocational school. The changing economic situation, uncertainty about a strategy for vocational education and training, lack of resources, low popular regard for vocational schools coupled with growing freedom of choice, decentralization of decision-making, not to mention society's preoccupation with other seemingly more pressing problems, all contributed to its decline.

3. *New Types of Vocational Education Establishment*

The 1989 Provisional Regulations for the Vocational Education School, like those for the General Education School, allowed greater freedom to institutions to organize themselves in different ways, and here too there were innovations. The State Committee for Education promoted experiments to develop a more flexible structure suitable to the emerging market conditions. The traditional Soviet demarcation between levels of vocational education was tackled by the introduction of Higher Vocational Schools (*Vysshie Professional'nye Uchilishcha*—VPU) including technical lycées and colleges. The technical lycées were based on outstanding secondary PTUs and the colleges on the best *tekhnikums*. Links with higher education institutions were to be established. One of the first examples was created on the basis of PTU 24 in the Siberian town of Barnaul. Its base enterprise was Sibenergomash which produces electrical generators and it cooperated with the Altai Polytechnical Institute in compiling syllabuses and in the use of laboratories.

Technical lycées train workers at three levels of skill: for the traditional narrow skill occupations, for occupations requiring more complex skills, and for technician level jobs. The colleges also train workers for the second two of these levels as well as junior engineers. However, the levels of training provided were also to take into account the demands of industry.

The other demarcation (by industrial branch) was also to be broken down by the introduction of new groups of skills to be taught, including commercial and entrepreneurial know-how in order to take into account actual and likely changes in technology. Great emphasis was placed on science-related industries and occupations and the scope of the VPUs was also extended as compared with the PTUs by the widening of their remit to include not merely initial training of young people, but retraining and upgrading of adult workers as well.

There were 28 VPUs set up in 1989. By 1991 the figure had topped 200 and an Association of Directors of Technical Lycées had been formed under the leadership of N Kononets, the director of a PTU in Rostov-on-Don. One of the first acts of the Association was to call for lycées to be the responsibility of ministries of education and for their financing to be 1.7 of the norm for similar PTUs in the same branch of industry, demonstrating concern about the consequences if the fate of these organizations were to be left to industry or the local authorities.

Old habits die hard and it was soon clear that some places were reponding to the experiment in the way that, in Soviet times, they would have responded to a directive from the Party. PTUs were designated VPUs in spite of the fact that they were lacking in material resources and appropriately trained staff. In some places the skill level and education of the staff was below that of the proposed graduates, while in others the selected PTUs specialized in occupations (such as painter, plasterer, and cable layer) not requiring the kind of skill levels envisaged in the project. Still other VPUs concentrated too much on theoretical and academic knowledge suitable for higher education, a result of the link with Institutes (Yakuba 1991).

Elsewhere, training combines made up of PTUs and other establishments have been put together to provide training crossing branch industry boundaries and there is a general movement away from centralized planning of training toward contracts between vocational training establishments and enterprises. These contracts may be for initial training, retraining, or skill upgrading, as envisaged in the Draft Law on Vocational Education presented by the USSR State Committee in July 1991.

Most of the now independent states that made up the former Soviet Union look set to follow this kind of policy. Certainly, in Russia the policy for vocational education and training draws on this experience and a three-level structure for the provision is envisaged. The first level is intended to provide short, narrow skill initial training courses in training centers, without a general education element. The second level is training for complex trades, to be provided in a variety of vocational education establishments (probably mainly PTUs), while the third level—higher or upper vocational education—for more complex and science-based occupations is to take place in lycées, colleges, and industrial-pedagogical *tekhnikumy*. Things are not so far advanced in the less industralized republics such as Uzbekistan, where only one VPU had been set up in 1991, but a policy document advocates increased flexibility in provision, the establishment of a retraining program, the privatization of some PTUs and a reorientation toward training for small enterprise development (Djuraev et al. 1991).

As yet the number of VPUs and other new types of institution is relatively small and it may be that other forms will develop. Meanwhile the PTUs, *tekhnikumy*, and specialized secondary schools will continue to play an important part in the preparation of young people for work.

4. *Labor Market*

The labor market in the Commonwealth of Independent States is in a deep confusion caused by the disintegration of the unified Soviet economy. In the Soviet system there was, or there had at least seemed to be, a shortage of skilled labor. This was due mainly to overstaffing and attempts to increase production by "extensive means," that is, by building new factories, rather than by increasing productivity. The fact that the limits of the extensive approach had been reached was an important factor in the Soviet economic crisis. An effect of the drive toward increased efficiency in industry was therefore a hitherto unknown, or unacknowledged, phenomenon in the Soviet Union: unemployment. During 1989 one million workers were "released" from employment and the numbers have been increasing rapidly since. A 1991 estimate of the labor surplus in the Soviet Union was 20–25 percent. Coupled with this are skill shortages in some areas, particularly in information technology and commerce, the demand for which is increasing.

The response of vocational education and training to the new labor market is sluggish. The PTUs have continued, for social and political reasons, to produce trainees for occupations where the demand is falling, and failed to produce them for the new businesses. Annually around 1.6 to 1.7 million graduates from PTUs arrive on the labor market, for the most part without practical experience and with knowledge and skills that do not meet the needs of the economy. They are, therefore, in a very weak position to compete with labor that has been shed as a result of rationalization of production. In Uzbekistan, for example, 20 percent of all school leavers (including those from vocational schools) cannot find work.

Technological progress has meant that the number of skilled jobs officially recognized as requiring an increased level of education and training has gone up. Occupations not classified as technician but thought to require the equivalent of a technician level training, for example, have increased from 40 to 411. Added to this is the relative shortage of technicians. The ratio of technicians to professional engineers is roughly one to one, much lower than in the West, and while this may partly be the result of an overproduction of engineers in the Soviet Union, there is a need to come into line with world practices if industry is to be competitive. With the number of *tekhnikumy* remaining static, the requirement for something like the VPUs is indisputable.

The new situation in the labor market makes improved vocational guidance an urgent requirement. Soviet schoolchildren traditionally had high aspirations and there is no sign that their successors are any less ambitious. A survey in 1991 of 15,300 schoolchildren in Moscow and the Moscow region showed that higher education was the aspiration of the overwhelming majority, 88 percent. Only 8 percent aimed at entry to SSUZ or PTU and an even smaller percentage (4%) planned to enter work directly. In fact 46 percent went into work, 14 percent to SSUZ or PTU and 38 percent succeeded in entering higher education. Only 20 percent had plans involving a specific occupation. The survey also noted a negative attitude to traditional occupations like engineering, textiles, and construction and a more positive one to the service sector and information technology. Moscow, of course, is not truly representative: a 1981 survey showed that 60 percent of Moscow school leavers went on to higher education compared with 18.9 percent for Russia as a whole, and this must have a bearing on perceptions of the possibilities. Nevertheless, surveys in other parts of Russia have shown career aspirations to be on a similarly high level. Clearly there is a long way to go before the aspirations and the real possibilities are matched and improved vocational guidance will have an important part to play in this.

5. *Vocational Education and Training for Agriculture*

Agriculture was one of the least efficient sectors of the Soviet economy and there had been many attempts to improve its productivity. Under Gorbachov the rights to an allotment of land for personal use were extended and the Russian government has introduced a measure to bring about rapid privatization in agricultural land. The organs of agricultural training, however, were organized to service the large state farms (*sovkhozy*) and collective farms (*kolkhozy*) which were the result of the collectivization of agriculture in the 1920s and 1930s. Rural PTUs were organized on the same general principles as their urban counterparts and suffered from the same shortcomings. They are now faced with the important task of introducing elements of economic education into their training to prepare their graduates for the new order.

One of the main problems facing rural vocational education and training is the erosion of their resources. The legislation on private allotments often resulted in local authorities allocating land from the rural PTUs for this purpose and the general economic crisis hit the agricultural schools hard, making it virtually impossible for them to obtain usable farm machinery, or sufficient fuel and lubricants. Although the Russian government stepped in to stop the removal of the PTU land more than 100 had none, and the survival of the system in the harsh conditions of transition to a market is threatened (Kiselev 1991). In Uzbekistan many rural vocational schools were meeting social rather than economic needs, providing food and clothing for the children of the poorer sections of the rural community and equipping them with skills for which there was little demand or the supply of which was already more than adequate (Djuraev et al. 1991). Radical changes in the nature of agricultural education and training seem inevitable.

6. Financing of Vocational Education and Training

The growing development of market relations has led to the formation of a market for educational and training services and discussion of the question of who is to pay for vocational education and training. In Russia, which is probably the most advanced of the former Soviet republics in this respect, the role of the state has been confirmed but a private sector is envisaged and at least partial self-financing by state training establishments is to be encouraged. The Russian policy that responsibility for education funding should be devolved to local authorities, who were very short of money, was delayed to provide stability in the transition to full market relations. This is in line with the practices which had been emerging in the last days of the Soviet government and with the draft Soviet legislation on vocational education of 1991.

As far as State institutions are concerned, the idea is that they should obtain part of their income from contracts to supply the training, retraining, and skill upgrading requirements of local enterprises and from the sale of the goods and services produced in work practice to local factories or farms and the community. An example of the contract system in operation is Moscow secondary PTU-106 which trains workers for the Trekhgornaya Manufaktura combine. The combine pays for each worker trained. In the event of a worker not going to Trekhgornaya Manufaktura after training, and in the absence of any extenuating circumstances, the PTU refunds the cost of training. Only student grants and food costs are met by the state. While there is obvious pressure for industry to fund its own training, the awareness of the need for state intervention is widespread, especially among directors of vocational training establishments and others closely involved in the training provision. The competition for resources in all the independent states of the former Soviet Union is so great that there is bound to be a danger everywhere of vocational education and training suffering due to a lack of proper funding.

Some foreign help is available through the EC's know-how fund and it has been agreed that German firms will provide the finance and resources to retrain Soviet soldiers and their families returning from the former East Germany. This German contribution is quite significant, involving 10 centers in Russia, the Ukraine, and Belorussia. Five of these are being provided with German equipment and the staff are going to Germany for training. The skill areas include motor vehicle repairs, agriculture, engineering, construction, and computing. Enterprise and commercial training also figure in the program. It is expected that the five centers will become models for further development, first for the other five and then more widely.

8. Conclusion

Economic change will inevitably be slower than political and ideological change and vocational education is closely bound up with the economy. The question is whether vocational education and training will have a part to play in promoting the transition to a market economy in the newly independent states or whether it will merely follow behind. A crucial factor will be government policies. In Russia there seems to be a commitment to keeping central control to ensure that vocational education and training are an effective element, at least during the transition period, but the desperate economic situation could force the government into cutting back severely on funding. Elsewhere matters are mostly less advanced, but the general picture is similar. It seems very unlikely that there will be formal agreement on a detailed common policy for vocational education among the Commonwealth states but the logic of the situation—existing economic ties, the need to integrate into the world economy, the need to harmonize qualifications and, not least, their common inheritance from the Soviet Union—suggests that they may follow similar paths.

It may well be in St Petersburg, which the Russian government has declared a free economic zone, that new institutional patterns are developed. As Leningrad, the city was at the forefront of developments in Soviet vocational education and is now taking the lead in establishing the new, more flexible, forms of education and training appropriate to a free market.

See also: Vocational Education and Training in Germany: National and International Dimensions; China, People's Republic of: Vocationalizing Education; Vocational Education and Training: Eastern and Central Europe; Technician Training; Vocational Education and Training and the Macroeconomic Environment; Education and Productive Work

References

Akhalkin S 1989 Trudovoe nachalo shkoly. *Uchitel' skaya gazeta* 10 October: 2

Djuraev R, Inagamov T, Cherednikov M 1991 *Training Policies in Uzbekistan: Transition to a Market Economy, Training Policies*, ILO, Geneva

Dneprov E 1990 Chetvertaya reforma. *Uchitel' skaya gazeta* 25: 3, 26: 3

Khlebnikova A 1989 Otsy goroda i deti podzemel' ya. *Uchitel' skaya gazeta* 11 February: 2

Kiselev N V 1991 PTO na sele—uchebnoproizvodstvennaya otrasl' *Professional* 10: 12–14

Yakuba Yu 1991 Vysshee professional'nye shkoly: segodnya i zavtra. *Professional* 10: 50–55

Further Reading

Avis G (ed.) 1987 *Soviet Higher and Vocational Education*, Bradford Occasional Papers No. 8. The Modern Languages Center, University of Bradford, Bradford
Dunstan J (ed.) 1987 *Soviet Education under Scrutiny*. Jordanhill College Publications, Glasgow
Marsh D T 1984 *Vocational Training in the USSR*. Further Education Staff College Information Bank, Blagdon

J. Sams

Spain: System of Education

1. General Background

Spain is situated on the Iberian Peninsula in the southwest of the European continent. It essentially forms part of European history and culture, though its closeness to the African continent has facilitated contact with other cultures which established themselves in North Africa. Its geographical position and historical events have made Spain a crossroads at which many cultures have met. Its varied traditions and languages—Catalonian, Galician, Valencian, Basque, and Castilian which has traditionally been the official national language—have resulted from the mixture, integration, and coexistence of cultures. Furthermore, the historical part which Spain played in the discovery and colonization of America has conferred upon it a special role in liaison between European and American countries.

The country covers 504,782 square kilometers, the Balearic and Canary Islands accounting for 15 percent of this territory. It had a population of nearly 39 million inhabitants in 1990, and a population density of 77 inhabitants per square kilometer. Coastal areas are more populated than the interior regions, with the exception of the capital Madrid. Some 77 percent of all inhabitants lived in urban areas in 1988.

In the period 1980–88, the annual population growth rate was 0.5 percent, with birth and death rates of 12 and 9 people per every 1,000 inhabitants, respectively. The birthrate has fallen gradually since the 1960s; 15 births for every 1,000 inhabitants in 1980 and around 10 in 1989.

A period of modernization and reintegration into the developed Western world was begun in the mid-1960s, a process which ended with the establishment of a democratic system similar to other Western countries in the mid-1970s and the incorporation of Spain into the European Community in the mid-1980s.

In the 1960s, there was major economic development in Spain, accompanied by large-scale internal migration and industrialization. The 1970s were marked by an economic crisis and a change in the political system, a new Constitution being passed in 1978 which established a democratic political system structured as a parliamentary monarchy with political parties. The 1980s were devoted to the strengthening of the political system and the accomplishment of sustained economic growth. The objective of all the policies was centered on Spain's integration into the European Community. For the 1990s, the major political objectives are to achieve more and better integration into Europe and the final implementation of the decentralized state system of autonomous communities.

The economic situation has not been very favorable since the crisis at the beginning of the 1970s, but the Spanish economy did grow at a faster rate than the average for the OECD countries in the 1980s, with investments in production increasing and the process of economic transformation speeding up. In 1988, the per capita Gross National Product (GNP) was US$7,740, but at the beginning of the 1990s there were the problems of inflation (around 6%), unemployment (approximately 15%), and a large foreign trade deficit.

The process of rapid economic development which the country has undergone since the 1960s has led to major social changes—in the kinds of work undertaken, living standards, lifestyle (due to the gradual and large-scale incorporation of women into the labor market), and increased urbanization of the population. Changes in the occupational structure of the Spanish population, as presented in Table 1 show a constant and significant fall in the proportion of people working in the primary sector, while the proportion of people employed in the tertiary sector has increased very markedly.

Table 1
Evolution of the occupational structure of the Spanish population by sectors from 1950 to 1990

Sectors	1950	1960	1970	1980	1990
Primary (agriculture)	51	43	26	18	12
Secondary (industry)	23	28	36	35	33
Tertiary (services)	26	29	38	47	55

2. Politics and the Goals of the Education System

The socioeconomic and political changes that have taken place since the 1960s have had a significant impact on the educational system. The process of modernization in the 1960s led to the reform of the education system, the centerpiece of which was the 1970 General Education Act (LGE). This reform's major objective was to extend education to the whole population, based on the principle of equal opportunities. This law was in force until 1983 for higher education and 1990 for nonuniversity educational levels. Its structure and provisions will continue in operation until the new structure and regulations promulgated by the General Arrangement of Education System Act of October 1990 (LOGSE) have been gradually introduced, a process which, it is estimated, will take 10 years. The main purpose of this new law is to attain higher quality teaching levels, once the objective of providing at least eight-year schooling for the whole population has been achieved.

The 1978 Constitution defined the principles governing the management of education and established citizens' rights to education. Furthermore, it altered the regional organization of the state, starting a process of decentralization of a large number of its duties, at the end of which it is expected to have devolved a large number of governmental powers onto the 17 autonomous communities into which state territory has been divided, including the majority of the powers relating to education.

The general principles of educational policy are centered, first, on the basic right of all citizens to education (basic education being established as compulsory and free), to which end the public authorities are responsible for the general programming of education with the participation of all sectors of society, as well as for the inspection and approval of the educational system. Second, they focus on the objective of education being the full development of the human personality with respect for the democratic principles of coexistence and basic rights and freedom. Third, educational freedom, the freedom to set up private schools and assistance for those that meet the requirements established by law, as well as the right of parents to have their children receive the religious and moral education they wish, are recognized. Fourth, the participation of teachers, parents, and pupils in the control and running of state-funded schools is established; and finally, universities are granted self-government. Other major constitutional rights related to education are: ideological and religious freedom; children's and human rights in general, as laid down in international agreements; and especially the rights of the physically and mentally handicapped and people with sensory impairments. The 1983 University Reform Act (LRU), the 1985 Right to Education Act (LODE), and the 1990 General Arrangement of Education System Act (LOGSE) are the laws which have implemented the constitutional principles.

3. *The Formal System of Education*

The nonuniversity education system legally in force in Spain is the one established by the LOGSE in 1990, although this is still in the process of being introduced. This means that the system really existing

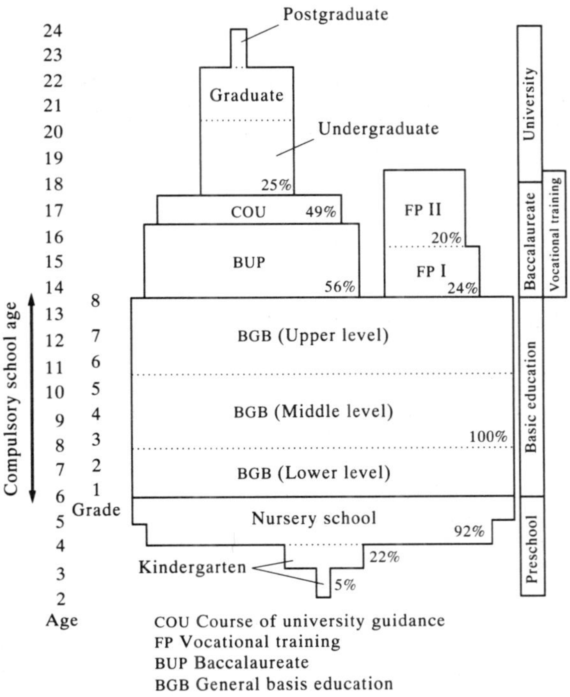

Figure 1
Spain: Structure of the formal education system 1991–92[a]

a Based on the 1970 General Education Act (LGE)

in 1991, and on which data are available, is the one based on the old 1970 General Education Act (LGE).

3.1 *The LGE System*

Figure 1 presents an outline of the Spanish system of education as it was in 1991–92.

The LGE system has four educational levels: preschool education, general basic education (EGB), baccalaureate (BUP), and higher education. Despite its essential difference, vocational training also constitutes an integral part of the system and, together with the baccalaureate, makes up the stage which in Spain is referred to as *Enseñanzas Medias* (secondary education).

There are no admission requirements for preschool education and general basic education (EGB). Preschool education is divided into two stages: kindergarten (2 and 3 years) and infant school (4 and 5 years). Its main purpose is to develop the child's personality. General basic education (EGB) is comprehensive and equal for all pupils. It lasts eight years and is divided into three cycles (2+3+3): lower, intermediate, and higher. The first two cycles are general and comprehensive education. Orientation toward separate subject matter teaching is begun in the last cycle. In sparsely populated rural areas, there are unitary (often one classroom) schools in which just one teacher teaches all of the pupils in different grades. The recommended timetable for the EGB is 25 hours per week and the academic year stretches from 15 September to 20 June.

The third level, the Unified Polyvalent Baccalaureate (BUP) lasts for three years. The Course of University Guidance (COU) consists of a transitional year, mainly aimed at preparation for higher education. Instruction is provided by teachers who have graduated from university.

Vocational training (FP) is divided into two levels (2+2 or 2+3) and constitutes a bridge between the general education system and the world of work. Part of the training is carried out in companies by means of periods of practice, especially at the FP II level. Instruction is provided by university licentiates and master craftsmen. The timetables for BUP and COU are 29 and 26 hours per week, whereas FP I consists of 32 (1st grade) and 34 (2nd grade) hours, plus 9 practical hours per week. The academic year begins on 1 October and ends on 30 June.

Higher education is structured on the basis of departments and can be completed in three kinds of institution: university schools, faculties, and higher technical schools. University schools offer one-cycle courses (3 years) and the faculties and higher technical schools offer courses of at least two cycles (normally 5 years). The third cycle provides for the completion of a doctorate (normally 2 years), with a basic orientation towards research. A doctoral thesis must be presented. In 1992, there were 31 public universities and 4 private universities.

The 1970 Education Act also regulated other types and kinds of education, such as continuing adult education (EPA), special education, distance education, night school courses, or specialized education not integrated into regular system levels. EPA can be completed in institutions set up especially for this purpose or in regular schools and, though the Act included a wide range of possibilities, only basic adult education has been implemented in practice. Distance education, whose courses are nationwide, is organized around the National Center of Basic Distance Education (CENEBAD), the National Institute of Distance Baccalaureate (INBAD), and the Distance University (UNED).

The development of enrollments in the different levels of education for the period 1963 to 1988 is presented in Figure 2. The trends in enrollment show the expansion of schooling during the 1970s up to 1968–87, the increase in postcompulsory education during the 1980s and a decrease in enrollment in preschool education and in general basic education from the mid-1980s onwards. This was due to the fall in the birthrate.

There are private as well as state schools, and the former may be denominational or otherwise, and may receive financial assistance from the state or

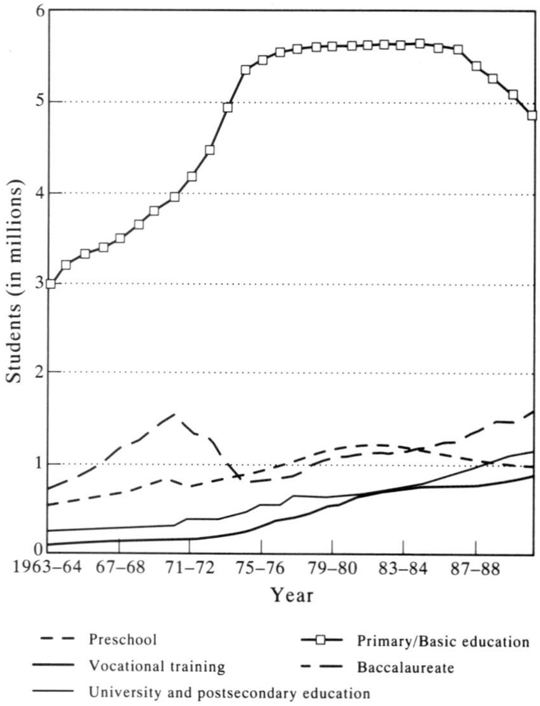

Figure 2
Evolution of the size of the educational system (number of students in the core structure of the system)

other sources. The contribution of the Catholic Church is very important in the private education sector. In primary and secondary education, some 30 to 40 percent of students are enrolled in private schools.

The pupil–teacher ratio is 28:1 in EGB, 17:1 in BUP and COU and 15:1 in FP. In higher education, it is 21:1 in faculties, 19:1 in university schools, and 11:1 in higher technical schools.

3.1.1 Special education. Special Education caters for students with special needs. The overall aim is to have students with special educational needs be able to achieve the general objectives established for all students within the regular education system. In other words, students are only schooled in separate special education classes or schools if their needs cannot be catered for in a regular school. In 1988–89, 40,000 pupils were schooled in separate special education schools (54% in private schools) and some 60,000 under the school integration scheme in regular schools (90% of these attending state schools). In special schools, education is adapted to the abilities of these pupils and is oriented towards vocational training to enable them to be integrated into society and the labor market.

3.1.2 Adult and nonformal education. Adult education is organized around three kinds of instruction: academic, occupational, and sociocultural. The main objective of academic education is literacy and basic adult education. In 1987–88, some 200,000 students took such courses by attending classes and 13,000 were enrolled in distance education schemes. A further 22,000 students took the distance baccalaureate. Occupational training is employment-based and, in addition to funding from state institutions, also receives funding from the European Social Fund. Some 275,000 adults received basic occupational training courses and another 200,000 participated in elite courses, especially in the fields of computer science and business administration and management. Sociocultural training is oriented towards the personal development of adults. On the whole, adult education is organized and funded in the public sector by six ministries (Education; Culture; Social Affairs; Justice; Defense; and Agriculture, Fisheries, and Food); and, in the private sector, by people's universities, people's adult schools, and the Catholic Church.

3.2 A New System of Education

At the end of the 1980s, a series of legal, social, political, and educational issues resulted in a proposed overall reform of the education system in terms of both structure and content. From the legal point of view, it was necessary to adapt both the content and formulation of educational legislation to the new Constitution and to the new political and administrative structure of the state, whereby the legal powers in educational management were divided between the central government and the autonomous community governments. From the social point of view, the demand for education had increased in terms of quantity, variety of disciplines, content, and methods. Furthermore, the widespread incorporation of women into the labor market had generated the need for schooling to start earlier, and economic development had led to a demand for more and higher social, technological, and vocational qualifications, which meant that the time spent in the education system, both before and after compulsory education, were becoming increasingly longer.

The process of integration into the European Community has broadened the future horizons of Spanish society and established new challenges for economic development and social welfare. These require an increase in the level of competitiveness associated with an improvement in the quality of the education system. In a similar way, the right of citizens to move within the framework of a united Europe requires international equivalence to be established for educational and vocational training qualifications. Finally, from the educational point of view, it was necessary to rectify malfunctions and shortcomings in the system established in 1970. The most blatant of these were streaming within the education system at too early an age leading to two certificates, the failure to regulate infant education, curriculum rigidity, little school self-government, and the structural inadequacy of the university transition course. In addition, both grade repetition rates and dropout rates were too high.

The 1990 Education Act (LOGSE) established a new structure for the education system, dividing education into two groups: general-system education (infant education, primary education, compulsory secondary education, postcompulsory secondary education or baccalaureate, higher-grade vocational training, and higher education) and special-system education (arts education—music and dancing, dramatic art, and "3-D" arts and design—and languages). In Figure 3, the new structure of the general education system is shown.

Infant Education will encompass children aged 0 to 6 years and will be divided into two cycles (from 0 to 3 and 3 to 6 years). It will not be compulsory, even though 100 percent of 5-year olds and 92 percent of 4-year olds were already in school in the 1989–90 academic year. The purpose of infant education is to provide children with a set of enriching experiences which encourage their physical and personal development, with the objective of making them mature enough for learning. Teachers will be specialized and there will also be qualified specialists in the first cycle.

Primary education—from 6 to 12 years—and compulsory secondary education (ESO)— from 12 to 16 years—will constitute the ten years of compulsory, comprehensive basic education. Primary education will be made up of three 2-year cycles. Its purpose is to promote children's integration into Spanish culture and provide them with basic communication and cognitive skills. Subjects to be covered include language and literature, mathematics, knowledge of the social and natural environments, arts education (music and "3-D" art), a foreign language (starting at 8 years of age), and physical education. Primary teachers will take charge of a group of pupils throughout each cycle, but may be helped by specialized teachers in the areas of physical education, foreign languages, and music.

Compulsory secondary education (ESO) will also be divided into two cycles, each lasting two years. Optional subjects will gradually be added to core subjects for all pupils. Options will amount to 10 percent of the total curriculum in the first year and 35 percent in the last year. Teachers will be university graduates. Subjects will include natural sciences, physical education, "2-D" and "3-D" expression, geography, history and social sciences, foreign languages, language and literature, mathematics, music, and technology.

There are four types of baccalaureate: arts, natural sciences and health, humanities and social sciences, and technology. The specific purpose of the baccalaureate is to build on pupils' cultural, scientific,

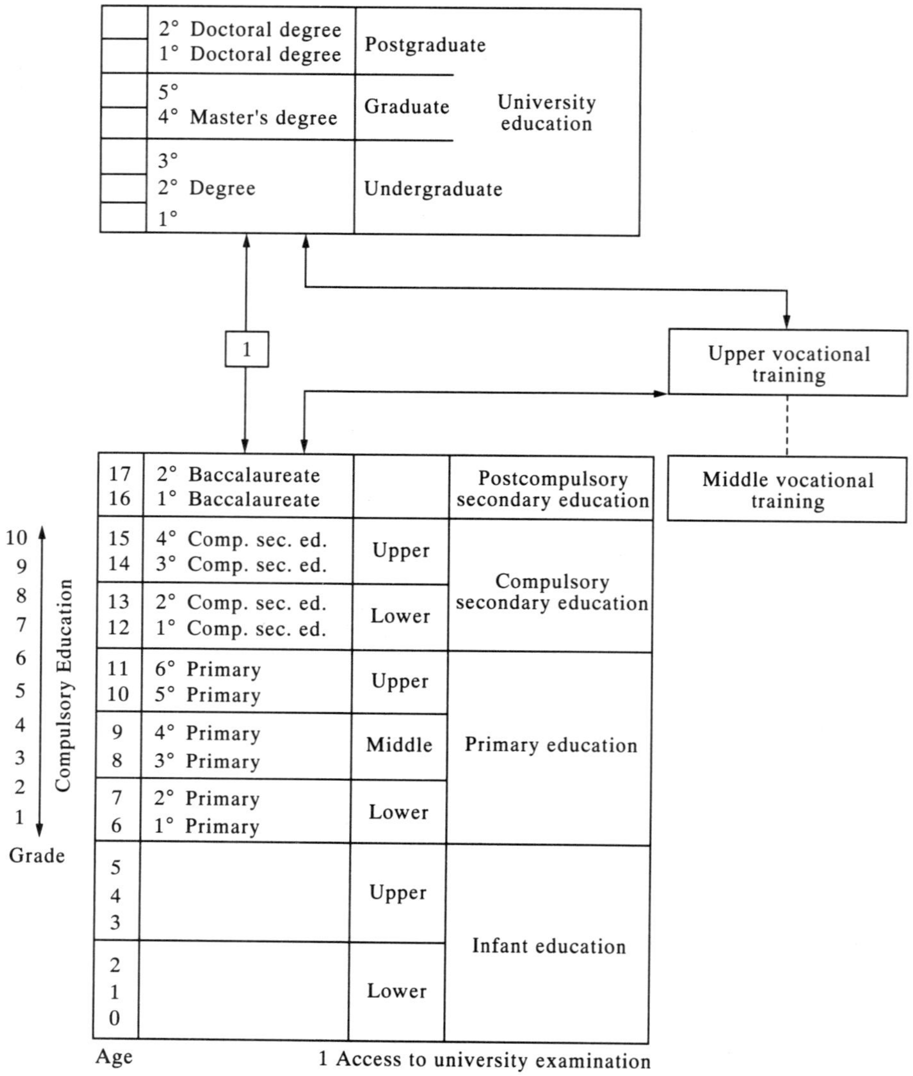

Figure 3
New structure of the general education system[a]

a Based on the 1990 General Arrangement of Education System Act (LOGSE) To be implemented by the year 2000

and social education, and prepare them for higher education or higher vocational training. Baccalaureate teachers will be university graduates. The subjects will be divided into three categories: core subjects, subjects related to the particular kind of baccalaureate, and optional unrelated subjects.

Vocational training will be directed toward practical training in an occupation, constituting a mechanism for linking schools and the work system. It will be made up of the intermediate and higher grades, divided into specific vocational modules of varying lengths. These modules will also serve continuing education and in the training of adult workers.

4. *Administrative and Supervisory Structure and Operation*

The process of state decentralization for educational administration operates at three levels. At the first level, the essential duties for ensuring the basic unity of the national education system fall to the central administration (the Ministry of Education and Science). This includes the overall arrangement of the regular education system for the whole nation, regulation of academic awards and vocational certificates, establishment of school and teaching staff requirements, regulation of Castilian teaching as the common official language, general inspection of the system, student grants and allowances policy, distance education, and international relations. In addition, the ministries of Defense, Labor, Agriculture, Fisheries and Food, Transport, Justice, and Health administer, supervise, and fund their own programs of education.

At the second level, the autonomous communities are responsible for the regulation and administration of all educational matters in their areas within the limits defined by the state. In particular, they are responsible for encouraging local culture, research, and where applicable, teaching of the autonomous community's own language. By 1992, seven autonomous communities (Andalusia, the Canary Islands, Catalonia, Galicia, the Basque Country, Valencia, and Navarre) had assumed full powers in education, constituting their own organizational structure and institutions (education departments) which vary from community to community. The remaining ten communities are in the process of assuming these powers, the Ministry of Education and Science provisionally taking charge of the major part of their management through the provincial head offices of education.

At the third level, the local administrations (town councils) have a priority role in providing land for and maintaining/building state schools, as well as for collaborating in school life through participatory bodies and through the organization of complementary educational activities.

For the supervision of the system, both the central and the autonomous community administrations have implemented their respective technical inspection systems, the duties of which are to advise on and support the educational process, ensure that legislation is complied with, evaluate the operation of the system, and establish communication between schools and the educational authorities and administrations.

The process of decentralizing state powers in matters of education also involves encouraging society to participate. The participatory bodies at the state level are the State Schools Board, the General Vocational Training Board, and the Universities Board. At the higher education level, the social council; the university staff meeting; the governing board; and the boards of faculties, higher technical schools, and university schools are the basic bodies of participation. The participatory bodies at publicly funded, nonuniversity institutions are the school board (made up of representatives of teachers, parents, pupils, auxiliary school staff, and the local community) and the staff meeting.

5. *Educational Finance*

Educational funding comes from public and private sources. Public funding is supplied by the central educational administration (mainly the Ministry of Education and Science and, to a lesser extent, by other ministries), the autonomous community, and local administrations. Public funds are earmarked both for the maintenance of state schools and the subsidization of private schools, as well as for student grants and allowances. Similarly, some private funds go to funding state education.

Table 2
Breakdown of public spending on education, 1989

Categories	%
Educational activities	89.7
Preschool/EGB	38.1
BUP–COU–FP	22.1
Higher education	14.3
Special education	2.1
Other education	4.3
Occupational training	8.8
Additional activities	10.3
Administration	2.6
Grants and allowances	2.9
Complementary services	2.0
Teacher training	0.7
Other activities	2.1
Total public spending	100.0

In state schools, education is completely free for the EGB, baccalaureate, and vocational training levels. Private schools may receive state subsidies mainly for the compulsory levels (EGB) and, in some special cases, for vocational training or may be funded exclusively by family contributions. At state universities, students have to pay for part of the costs of education, while at private universities the students cover all expenses. At all educational levels, families pay for school books and materials, as well as the cost of school meals, transport, and extracurricular activities in both state and private schools.

Total expenditure on education in Spain was 2,717,817 million pesetas in 1990, which amounted to 5.4 percent of the Gross Domestic Product (GDP). In 1991, 4.95 percent of the national budget was earmarked for education. Of this amount, 80 percent came from the public purse (40% from the central administration, 35% from the autonomous communities, and 5% from local administrations) and the remaining 20 percent from families. The breakdown of expenditure by educational activities is shown in Table 2.

The state uses public funds to finance compulsory education in private schools which meet given requirements, such as free education; the establishment of a school board; voluntary religious practice; and the use of set criteria for pupil admission, teacher selection, pupil–teacher ratio, and also meeting given minimum requirements to guarantee teaching quality. This funding covers expenditure on teaching staff, administration and services, maintenance and upkeep of facilities, and investment.

The state also provides grants to students who have the aptitude but not the financial means to complete courses at the noncompulsory levels. Around 700,000 pupils benefited from such allowances in 1991, which amounted to around 60,000 million pesetas. At the compulsory levels, the state provides allowances toward covering the complementary costs of school meals and transport.

The funds allocated by families to education represent almost 2 percent of total private consumption. About 80 percent of this expenditure is for strictly educational activities and 20 percent for complementary activities and school materials.

6. *Supplying Personnel for the Education System*

In the 1989–90 academic year, there were more than 475,000 teachers in the education system: 38,864 in preschool; 228,174 in general basic education (EGB); 92,014 in baccalaureate (BUP) and university guidance course (COU); 59,598 in vocational training (FP); and 57,008 in higher education. Furthermore, 5,511 teachers are charged with special education and 8,560 are assigned to other kinds of education. The proportion of female teachers is 85 percent in preschool, 61 in EGB, 54 in BUP and COU, 41 in FP, and 29 percent in higher education.

In order to be able to work as a teacher at any educational level, one must have a university degree (three years for EGB and five years for the others) as well as teacher training. An important change introduced by the 1990 Education Act is that teachers in preschool education must be qualified. Since 1990, primary school teacher training has been divided into seven specialization categories (infant, primary, foreign language, physical education, music, special, and hearing and language) and lasts three years. A state examination must be passed in order to teach in state schools. The admission procedure in private education is based on employment contracts.

Inservice teacher training is carried out by means of specialized courses or training at the workplace. A large part of inservice training is completed in teachers' centers (CEP) in the area administered by the Ministry of Education and Science, and in similar centers in the autonomous communities with devolved powers in education. During the 1990–91 academic year, 91,744 teachers participated in such training courses and 10,608 took part in training activities at the schools where they work. Since the mid-1980s, emphasis has been placed on the areas of foreign language teaching, new technologies, health education, environmental education, adult, and compensatory education.

7. *Curriculum Development and Teaching Methodology*

One characteristic of the system introduced by the 1970 Education Act is that there is a core curriculum for the whole country defined by the central administration. The 1990 Act establishes the creation of a basic curriculum design which consists of a nationwide core curriculum in which the general objectives of each educational stage, the curriculum areas to be taught, the blocks of subject content, and the didactic and assessment guidelines are specified.

At the first level, the Ministry of Education and Science establishes an initial general curriculum (syllabus) which is the criterion of nationwide unity and to which the provisions of the autonomous communities are added for purposes of cultural pluralism. At the second level, schools develop a more specific curriculum, adapted to make it relevant with regard to the environment and suitable for the school's pupils. This school curriculum plan is drawn up by teams of teachers as a plan of didactic methods adapted to a particular background. At the third level, the teacher translates the school curriculum into particular programs for each class, and where applicable for each student, breaking down the content, activities, and assessment procedures into didactic units suited to the students. The curriculum allows for different kinds of adaptation and diversification to cater for the needs of students with different aptitudes and interests in different sociocultural circumstances and surroundings.

As already stated, the study of a foreign language must begin at the age of eight years, with a second foreign language being offered at the beginning of secondary school as an option.

8. *The System of Examinations, Promotions, and Certifications*

Assessment of the learning process in preschool and general basic education (EGB) is continuous, and upgrading is automatic at the preschool level. A maximum of only one year per cycle may be repeated in EGB until students reach 16 years of age. At the end of the compulsory stage, there are two certificates: the *Graduado Escolar* for pupils who complete this stage successfully (giving access to both the baccalaureate and to vocational training) and the *Certificado de Escolaridad* (which gives access only to vocational training).

Students who pass the all three years of the baccalaureate course receive the baccalaureate certificate without any final examination and, after having completed the course of university guidance (COU), can take the university entrance examination to go on to higher education.

In vocational training, students who pass the first grade (FPI) receive the Auxiliary Technician Certificate for their particular occupation. After completing further courses they can enter second-grade vocational training (FPII) (as can those who have taken the baccalaureate), at the end of which they receive the Specialist Technician Certificate.

In higher education, university schools award the degrees of Diplomate, Architectural Technician, and Engineering Technician. The faculties and higher technical schools award the degrees of Graduate, Architect, or Engineer. Students who complete the first two cycles may enter the third cycle (Doctorate). After a course of adaptation, university school Diplomates, Architectural Technicians, and Engineering Technicians may enter the second cycle at some faculties or higher technical schools.

Under the new 1990 Education Act, preschool assessment will still be continuous and upgrading automatic. There will be continuous assessment throughout primary and secondary education to gather knowledge on each student's development. The main methods of assessment will be monitoring pupils' activities; systematic observation; the analysis of work; and oral, written, or practical tests. Students will proceed to the next cycle upon the achievement of the objectives of the previous cycle. Students may repeat an additional year in a cycle if they have not achieved its objectives, although they may repeat no more than two years throughout compulsory education. Those who achieve all the objectives at the end of secondary school will be awarded the certificate of *Graduado en Educación Secundaria*, which will give them the right to enter baccalaureate or intermediate-grade vocational education. Students not receiving the certificate of *Graduado en Educación Secundaria* will receive a document from the school certifying the number of years completed and their marks.

Students with a positive assessment in all of the baccalaureate subjects will receive the Baccalaureate Certificate which allows them to enter the higher-grade vocational school or take the university entrance examination.

At the end of the vocational education stages, vocational training certificates will be awarded. Upon completion of the intermediate and higher-grade vocational schools, vocational certificates equivalent to Levels 2 and 3 of the European Community qualification will be awarded.

9. Educational Assessment, Evaluation, and Research

Educational research in Spain is mainly carried out at universities and at the Ministry of Education and Science's Center of Research, Documentation, and Evaluation (CIDE). CIDE is the main body funding research, earmarking around 400 million pesetas (US$2.85 million) per year for some 100 research projects to be maintained annually. At the end of the 1980s, the most popular research themes were academic achievement and teaching methods, but with an increasing interest being shown in educational psychology and curriculum matters.

Evaluation studies of the operation of the education system are the responsibility of CIDE and the Technical Education Inspectorate. They usually assess reforms and partial aspects of the education system and also carry out international evaluation studies in cooperation with international bodies such as the International Association for the Evaluation of Educational Achievement, the International Assessment of Educational Progress, and the Organisation for Economic Co-operation and Development. The 1990 Education Act provides for general and nationwide evaluation studies of the system, schools, teachers, and pupils. An Institute of Quality and Evaluation will be established and charged with nationwide evaluation studies on the state and evolution of the quality of the system.

At the beginning of the 1990s, there was insufficient funding for research and a shortage of effective mechanisms for passing on general information to those responsible for formulating policies. In addition, the division of powers between the central administration and the autonomous community administrations as regards research and evaluation was notable. However, the continued improvement in the quality and relevance of research, the trend towards the internationalization of research and evaluation, and the increase in international cooperation in this area are positive features.

10. Major Reforms in the 1980s and 1990s

Any outline of the Spanish education system is necessarily a description of the many reform processes which have been undertaken—the whole Spanish education system having been completely reformed since the 1970s.

It is important to stress that the 1985 Education Act (LODE) established an integrated network of schools (state and private) that guaranteed the right to education and stated that the state would cater to the demand for schooling thus enabling a free choice of school for all on an equal footing. It also set up mechanisms for the community to participate in school life. The 1990 Education Act (LOGSE) reformed the legal structure for the educational system and, in particular, for curriculum renewal. It also created special regulations on the integration of students with special needs into regular primary schools; continuous teacher training, especially as regards the establishment of teacher centers (CEP); and the encouragement of psychopedagogical guidance in schools. All of these reforms have substantially changed nonuniversity education.

The 1983 University Reform Act (LRU) defined the division of governmental and administrative powers between the state administration, the autonomous communities, and the universities themselves. The Act reformed the organization and operation of the universities, strengthened the departmental structure, reshaped the structure of university teaching staff, and established new university curricula for a large number of degrees. All of this drastically changed the face of higher education.

11. Major Problems for the Year 2000

There are several challenges facing the education system up to the year 2000. The first is the implementation of the new system in terms of structure, content, and teaching methodologies. A lack of sufficient financial resources will be the main problem for this implementation. The increase in the quality of all levels of education will be the second most important goal. Another challenge is to improve the retraining and continuous training systems for practicing teachers. Yet a further problem will be the structuring and introduction of an effective vocational training system that provides real occupational skills, closely linked with company production systems, and that satisfactorily plays its role in the transition from education to work.

In higher education, there is a need to increase the quality and relevance of research work, improve relations with the international scientific community, and to rationalize entry to the university teaching profession in order to ensure the quality of university lecturers' teaching and research work.

Finally, the achievement of a suitable balance between the process of decentralization of state powers in education to autonomous community governments, and the simultaneous process of conferring qualifications in education in accord with the European Community requirements are the two main political challenges facing Spanish educational policy.

Bibliography

CIDE 1992 *El Sistema Educativo Español. Informe Nacional para la Red Eurydice*. Ministerio de Educación y Ciencia, Madrid

El País 1991 *Anuario 1991*. El País, Madrid

McNair J 1984 *Education for a Changing Spain*. Manchester University Press, Manchester

McNair J, Beattie N (eds.) 1991 Education for the New Spain. *International Monographs in Community and Educational Policy Studies* 3 (entire issue)

Ministerio de Educación y Ciencia 1973 *Ley General de Educación y Disposiciones Complementarias*. Ministerio de Educación y Ciencia, Madrid

Ministerio de Educación y Ciencia 1989a *Libro Blanco para la Reforma del Sistema Educativo*. Ministerio de Educación y Ciencia, Madrid

Ministerio de Educación y Ciencia 1989b *Plan de Investigación Educativa y de Formación del Profesorado*. Ministerio de Educación y Ciencia, Madrid

Ministerio de Educación y Ciencia 1990 *España. Informe Nacional de Educación. Conferencia Internacional de Educación, 42ª reunión, Ginebra, 1990*. Ministerio de Educación y Ciencia, Madrid

Múñoz-Repiso M et al. 1992 *El Sistema Educativo Español. 1991*. Ministerio de Educación y Ciencia, Madrid

Múñoz-Repiso M et al. 1992 *Las Desigualdades en la Educación en España*. Ministerio de Educación y Ciencia, Madrid

OECD 1986 *Spain: Reviews of National Policies for Education*. OECD, Paris

Riviere A et al. 1988 *El Sistema Educativo Español*. Ministerio de Educación y Ciencia, Madrid

G. A. Gil

Special Education, History of

The development of special education has followed a similar pattern throughout the world. It has its roots in the care-taking activities of philanthropic institutions, and as a rule has expanded alongside the rise of mass education in any country. Historically, two main aims for special education measures can be recognized. First, there is the aim of giving help and support to students with learning and other difficulties caused by impairments and other problematic conditions. Second, there is the intention to free regular teaching in school from problems of handicapped and/or disturbing students, by taking care of them in more or less segregated groups. This entry will outline the main international trends and especially how special education, its organization and preconditions for development, has been dependent on compulsory education in different countries.

1. Special Education Before the Introduction of Compulsory Schooling

The roots of special education are found in the sixteenth century. In the middle of the 1550s the Spanish monk Pedro Ponce de Leon started to teach some deaf children to read, write, and master academic subjects. Another Spaniard, Juan Pablo Bonet wrote the first book about special education of the deaf, describing methods which probably originated from Ponce de Leon. He also introduced a manual alphabet, which can be seen as the basis for sign language methods still in use in the 1990s. The first book in English was published in 1644, and it was soon followed, in 1680, by perhaps the most significant of the earliest books in special education *Didasopholus; or, the Deaf and Dumb Man's Tutor*, written by George Dalgarno, who asserted startlingly that deaf people have the same capacity to learn as hearing people do. This was very revolutionary at that time, as deaf people as a rule had been regarded as "idiots."

Most well-known among the special education pioneers is perhaps the French physician Jean Marc Gaspard Itard (1775–1838), whose book about training and teaching the 12-year old boy Victor, who had been found living like an animal in the forest, is a recognized classic in the field. The wild child's behavior was changed drastically through patient and systematic educative procedures. During the second half of the eighteenth century, the first permanent schools for the deaf were established in England by Thomas Braidwood and his nephew, Joseph Watson.

In Germany an oral method for language teaching for the deaf was developed by Samuel Heinicke (1727–90) and was further developed by Friedrich Moritz Hill some decades later. In France, on the other hand, Pereire, De l'Epée, and Sicard developed a sign language for communication. They also stressed the importance of training the other senses like sight and touch. These two main approaches for training communicative competence among the deaf have since then been continuously disputed. Thomas Hopkins Gallaudet, trained by Sicard, established the first school for the deaf in the United States in 1817, which can be said to be the start of special education there.

It was, thus, physicians who were the first special educators. This is also valid for education for the blind and visually impaired, the second area within the field of special education to emerge. In France, Valentin Haüy founded a national institution for the young blind in 1784, and this was rapidly followed by seven similar schools in Europe. Even sighted students were allowed to attend these philanthropic institutes in an attempt to avoid isolating blind from sighted people. Schools of that kind were also established in the United States, the first one by Samuel Gridley Howe in Massachusetts in 1829. This was the start of a rapid development of residential schools for the blind. The most important subjects of the educational program of these schools were reading and writing. Haüy developed a system of embossed letters, which could be read by touching with the fingers. This was improved upon by the introduction of the braille system, developed by one of Haüy's blind students Louis Braille (1809–52). This use of raised dots in different combinations representing the alphabet, became even more useful and widespread after the inventions of the braille typewriter and a printing system during the 1890s (Irvine 1987).

A third early kind of special education was that for the mentally retarded. The first attempts in this field were made by Itard, mentioned above. His methods and procedures, documented in a book first published in 1801, were of the utmost importance in the education of mentally retarded individuals for more than a century. During the late eighteenth century and at the beginning of the 1800s, ideas and values following the French and American Revolutions inspired many attempts to educate "idiotic" and "insane" children (Hallahan and Kauffman 1988). One of Itard's students, Edouard Seguin, became very influential, not only in France but even more so in the United States. In 1866 he published his book, *Idiocy and Its Treatment by the Psychological Method*, where he described and further developed Itard's methodology. Both Itard and Seguin were of great importance for Maria Montessori (see *Montessori and Education*) in Italy (Montessori 1912, 1917). Many ideas from this early period have persisted until the late twentieth century in special education, for example: education of the whole child, individualization of instruction, beginning instruction at the child's current level of functioning, and the importance of rapport between teacher and pupil (Irvine 1987 p 786).

According to Hallahan and Kauffman (1988) the earliest period of special education in the United States showed remarkable results inspired by the idealism, excitement, and optimism of its leaders. But they also say that during the last part of the nineteenth century special education lost its momentum, with much ineffective institutionalization. Many factors contributed to this decline, such as expectations of miraculous cures, and unwillingness of the public to pay the costs when it was realized how many handicapped children were in need of special education, as well as influences of Charles Darwin's theory of evolution along with ideas that the handicapped were inherently inferior.

The same pattern of decline can also be seen in Europe. But it is interesting to note that this happened during the period when compulsory schooling was being introduced in many Western countries.

2. The Establishment of Compulsory Schooling

The second half of the nineteenth century was an era when compulsory schooling was established, at least in principle, for all children in many countries in Europe and North America. This became of great importance for the further development of special education, particularly during the first decades of the twentieth century. The reasons for this were twofold. Greater proportions of children with different kinds of impairments and handicapping injuries were found or tracked down. This stressed the need for organizing special education help and support, both by extending the already existing institutions or special schools, but even more so by establishing special education in the ordinary schools. Special education was in this sense rooted in the same kind of humanistic thinking as that characteristic for the earlier, more or less philanthropic work.

However, many of these children not only faced difficulties in the schools they were obliged to attend, they also caused problems in the classes and for the teachers. They impeded and disrupted classroom learning and therefore threatened to lower the standard of education for nonhandicapped students. Special education, preferably in special classes or schools, became identified as a need, particularly in terms of getting rid of classroom problems which "threatened" the "normal" students. Both these kinds of motives for special education were explicit at the beginning of the 1900s.

The increased need for special education resulted in a continuing expansion, at least quantitatively. This trend was evident in European countries as well as in North America (see, e.g., Irvine 1987, Bleidick 1983). Most common in Europe in the late 1800s and the first decades of the twentieth century were special classes for slow ability students or slow learners after a German pattern called "Help-classes" (*Hilfsklassen* and *Hilfsschulen*). The first special class of that kind in a public school was established in Germany in 1859, but the rapid growth of help-classes occurred in most countries later, and above all during the first three decades of the twentieth century. In these classes the teaching was adjusted to the preconditions of low ability students by using special education methods. As far as possible the subject matter content was meant to correspond to what was taught in the regular classes, but often comprised shorter courses. The aim was that as many of the special education students as possible should be able to come back to the regular classes after a period of special education and/or to be able to live a normal life in society after school. The aim of replacing the students in regular classes, however, was most often hard or impossible to fulfill.

The invention and introduction of intelligence testing by Alfred Binet in 1905 was for a long time thereafter of immense significance for selecting children for placement in special classes and schools. Especially later on, from the 1930s to the 1950s, certain border and interval IQ values more or less automatically justified such placements. Binet regarded mental ability as a process rather than a quality, but later researchers defined IQ as a fixed and largely inherited constant and unchangeable quality of an individual's personality. It was also regarded as a sound base for special education classification and measurement. The child's learning difficulties were understood mainly as caused by his or her low intelligence. Severely retarded persons were seen not only as a threat for normal schoolchildren but also, especially during the 1930s, under the influence of eugenics, for the population and its offspring. They were therefore segregated, and debates about measures like sterilization, marriage regulations, and birth control were common. Under the Scottish Mental Lunacy and Deficiency Act (1913), four groups of mentally handicapped were recognized. Idiots and imbeciles were regarded as definitely ineducable, whereas feeble-minded and moral imbeciles could be labeled as ineducable after trial (Gabbay and Webster 1983). This classification of ineducables was used in most countries, and not questioned until the 1940s or later.

Low mental ability was not the only reason for school difficulties though. Therefore the help-classes or classes for slow learners included students with a mixture of disabilities and difficulties. A need for more specialized special education developed. Irvine (1987) mentions two classes provided for children exhibiting unmanageable behavior and for unruly boys in the 1870s as the first public school special classes to be established in the United States. It was not until in the 1930s however, that the number of special classes for different handicaps and difficulties started to grow in European countries and in the United States. This was also the pattern for special education for children with severe emotional problems. Psychiatry developed as a discipline and also the psychological testing of individual differences which were used as diagnostic tools in the selection of students.

During the first three decades of the twentieth century, the first special classes for children with orthopedic handicaps were established in Chicago public schools. Such classes were also started in Europe during that period.

The development of special education in Japan followed a later but similar pattern to that in Europe and America. The charitable institutions for the blind and the deaf were established in Kyoto in 1878 and in Tokyo in 1880 (Miron and Katoda 1991). There had been some special classes for intellectually handicapped children already from the 1890s, but it was generally thought that children with intellectual handicaps should be exempted from compulsory education. It was not until the late 1930s that special classes for students with those kinds of handicaps were established in a broader sense. In 1932 the first schools for children with physical handicaps commenced. The special school and special class were first included into the Japanese public school system in the School Education Law (1947), but as students were not obligated to attend special schools or classes, special education was not systematically applied until 1956.

3. 1940–70—A Period of Rapid Growth and Extension

After the Second World War special education services expanded rapidly. This was true both for the numbers of children served and the types of difficulties and/or handicaps dealt with. Irvine (1987) talks about an explosion of new special classes and special schools in North America and very much the same can be said about many countries in Europe, as well as in Australia and Japan. In the Scandinavian countries there was a rapid increase of special classes and also special education clinics (resource rooms) for students with reading and writing difficulties. In Scandinavia, where compulsory schooling starts rather late—at the age of seven—a certain kind of special class for late maturing children, so called "school readiness classes," were established widely.

Special education for extended groups of mentally retarded children, often labeled "ineducable," were established in institutions or special schools. There was also a growing interest in special education for gifted or talented pupils. This latter kind of special education never became common, though. The main reason for this was lack of strong support from most educators.

In North America, but later also in many European countries, special education was also started for pre-school deaf children, and in the late 1960s even for children with such disorders as cerebral palsy and other categories of handicaps. An important reason for this was the findings of special education research, corroborating commonly held beliefs that the development of young children could be changed through early educational intervention.

During this period special education was also established and developed as an academic discipline, with doctoral programs and research, although it was still closely related to other scientific disciplines. Studies of learning in psychology, and most of all predictions of school failures or success by means of tests, focused attention on children with special needs. Also, the development of the education professions themselves resulted in a widespread and growing realization among teachers and school administrators that a large number of children must be given something beyond ordinary classroom training and teaching. Thus, the establishment of special education as a discipline has its roots in several academic disciplines—especially medicine, psychology, sociology, and social work—in addition to professional education (Hallahan and Kauffman 1988). Training programs for special educators developed too. Most of the trainees were teachers from the ordinary schools who were trained to teach children with exceptional learning difficulties.

This very rapid growth and expansion of special education coincided in several Western countries with an extension of compulsory schooling. At the same time as the number of years of schooling increased, the school systems were reformed to be more comprehensive. In principle, all students were kept together in more or less the same school programs instead of being selected and differentiated into either academic or vocationally oriented programs in separate schools. This comprehensiveness became in itself a reason for an increased need for special education. It may seem paradoxical, but increasing comprehensiveness in compulsory education led to increasing segregation and differentiation by means of expanded special education. This was not discussed as a problem, and special education was mostly seen as something good which responded to the needs of students with different kinds of school difficulties.

Concepts like handicap and school difficulties were understood and defined in terms of individual characteristics. Special education was organized and provided according to medical treatment patterns. Research and development were aimed at more precise diagnoses of certain individual impairments and/or injuries causing learning difficulties or other school problems. Such diagnoses formed the bases for the development of more specific teaching methods. After exposure to adequate special education students' difficulties were supposed to be cured and they were expected to go back to their regular classes and be more successful in their school work.

Most of the expansion of special education took place in ordinary public schools. In the United Kingdom and Germany, and a bit later, in Japan, for instance, there were big increases in the number of special classes and schools. In other countries like Sweden, the United States, and Canada, the most profound increase was in the number of different kinds of special education "clinics" or resource rooms. Often the differences between clinics and special classes were quite small, as many students went to clinics for most of their lessons.

Parent and professional organizations began to play an increasingly important role for the development of special education. Special education provision was seen as a democratic civil right for children in need of it. Special education legislations were traditionally "enabling," that is, they stated that schools may provide special education. Later they became mandatory, stating that schools must provide this kind of support for students with special education needs.

4. Special Education Questioned—Demands for Mainstreaming

In 1968 Lloyd Dunn published an article, which sparked off a period of questioning the value and effects of special education. Similar debates had also started elsewhere, for example, in the Scandinavian countries in the late 1960s. One reason for this was results from special education research effect studies. These showed that special education, and especially if given in segregated groups, had not only positive effects but also negative consequences for the students involved. Dunn's and others' arguments were that as special education most often meant segregating handicapped students from their peers in regular classes, the burden of proof of its effectiveness ought to be laid on those organizing special classes.

Many efficacy studies were conducted from 1950–80, as a rule designed to compare the experiences of handicapped children in various types of service delivery configurations, for example, special classes versus general education classrooms and special classes versus resource rooms or clinics. The results of these studies were mixed; they could not be interpreted in a clear-cut way to prove the case either for or against special classes. In general, the studies suggested that special class placement was of little benefit to, or even hampered, academic achievement. There was, however, some evidence that handicapped children felt more comfortable and had more positive peer relations in special groups. Most interesting were results from longitudinal studies extended over several years, which often showed negative consequences of segregated special education in long-term perspectives, often related to self-concept development (e.g., Stangvik 1979).

From the 1960s living conditions for people with handicaps were studied and debated. The claims for a changed understanding of handicap influenced interpretations of results from special education efficacy studies too. The concept of "normalization" was introduced in Scandinavia by Bank-Mikkelsen and Nirje (1969), as a challenge and an aim in policy discussions related to handicap. The argument was that every disabled person should have educational and living standards as close as possible to what was normal for nonhandicapped members of society. The challenge was not to make deviant persons more normal, but to change conditions in wider society in order to increase participatory possibilities for persons with impairments in education as well as in other aspects of social life (Wolfensberger 1972). These ideologically and democratically founded challenges were often called "mainstreaming" and/or "integration." Handicap was understood as a discrepancy between an individual's preconditions and demands characterizing his or her surrounding environment. The severity of handicap was dependent on both individual characteristics and social conditions, for example, ways of teaching in regular educational settings.

Normalization and mainstreaming meant that special education tasks and responsibilities, would need to be broadened in relation to the two aims mentioned above. Results from efficacy studies were interpreted as proving that special education had been more successful in freeing regular classroom teaching from problematic children than in providing better opportunities for children with handicaps to achieve optimal development and participation in social life. Too few students, once transferred to special groups and classes, were able to come back to their regular groups again. Special education knowledge and competence was not questioned as much as the organizational forms in which it came into practice. It should not only be used to give individual help and support, but also to change conditions in regular class teaching in order to increase participation possibilities for disabled children.

The Education for All Handicapped Children Act, PL 94–142, was very influential in the development of special education during the late 1970s and the 1980s, and not only in the United States. Two aspects of the law were of particular importance. First, it was seen as a civil right for every child with a handicap to have his or her special education needs met in the least restrictive environment possible. Second, the education provided should be appropriate for each child's individual need. There should be a written individual educational program (IEP)—in the United Kingdom called a "statement"—which clearly expresses how these special needs could be met. These programs were to set out clearly terms of shared responsibilities between different school personnel, including special educators.

The broadened challenge meant that special educators not only had to give support to individuals with special needs, but also had to initiate changes in regular teaching and thereby, as members of working teams, create better possibilities for successful learning for special needs pupils within regular school groups. These broadened aims for special education have also resulted in reformed teacher-training programs, for example, in Sweden for both special educators and ordinary teachers.

Since the 1970s there has been a fast and promising technical development with great importance for special education, not the least, within information technology. Computers and other kinds of technical aids have helped create revolutionary possibilities for many persons with different kinds of handicap, and have aided special education development.

Until the early 1960s special education was mostly confined to compulsory schooling and to some vocational training programs. Thereafter a growing interest has also been generated for organizing special education support in upper-secondary and higher education, as well as in adult education (Stukát 1990).

In the same period interesting developments in special education in many developing countries have got under way. For many reasons, such as lack of economic resources, these seem to be more mainstreamed compared to early special education in industrialized countries.

See also: Sociology of Teaching; Teacher Education and Special Education Needs

References

Bleidick U 1983 Sonderschule. In: Lenzen D, Schründer A (eds.) 1983 *Enzyklopädie Erziehungswissenschaft*, Vol. 8. Klett-Cotta, Stuttgart

Dunn L M 1968 Special education for the mildly retarded—Is much of it justifiable? *Excep. Child.* 35(1): 5–22

Gabbay J, Webster C 1983 General introduction. Changing educational provision for the mentally handicapped: From the 1890s to the 1980s. *Oxford Rev. Educ.* 9(3): 169–75

Hallahan D P, Kauffman J M (eds.) 1988 *Exceptional Children. Introduction to Special Education*, 4th edn. Prentice-Hall, Englewood Cliffs, New Jersey

Irvine P 1987 History of special education. In: Reynolds C

R, Mann L (eds.) 1987 *Encyclopedia of Special Education*, Vol. 2. Wiley, New York
Miron G, Katoda H 1991 Education for persons with handicaps in Japan, the USA and Sweden. *Scand. J. Educ. Res.* 35(3): 163–78
Montessori M 1912 (transl. George A) *The Montessori Method*. Stokes, New York
Montessori M 1917 *The Advanced Montessori Method: Scientific Pedagogy as Applied to the Education of Children from Seven to Eleven Years*. Heinemann, London
Nirje B 1969 The normalization principle and its human management implications. In: Kugel R, Wolfensberger W (eds.) 1969 *Changing Patterns in Residential Services for the Mentally Retarded*. A President's Committee on Mental Retardation Monograph, Washington, DC
Stangvik G 1979 *Self-Concept and School Segregation*. Acta Universitatis Gothoburgensis: Göteborg Studies in Educational Sciences 28. Gothenburg University, Gothenburg
Stukát K-G 1990 Educational opportunities for adult disabled persons. *Europ. J. Spec. Needs Educ.* 5(3): 165–78
Wolfensberger W 1972 *The Principle of Normalization in Human Services*. National Institute on Mental Retardation, Toronto

Further Reading

Carlberg C, Kavale K 1980 The efficacy of special versus regular class placement for exceptional children: A meta-analysis. *J. Spec. Educ.* 14(3): 295–309
International Journal of Special Education 1988 (Several articles on special education development in some developing countries). *Int. J. Spec. Educ.* 3(1)
Kauffman J M 1976 Nineteenth century views of children's behavior disorders: Historic contributions and continuing issues. *J. Spec. Educ.* 10(4): 335–49
Körgesaar J L 1988 On the development of special and remedial education in the Soviet Union. *Int. J. Spec. Educ.* 3(1): 1–19
Wiederholt J L 1974 Historical perspectives on the education of the learning disabled. In: Mann L, Sabatino D A (eds.) 1974 *The Second Review of Special Education*. JSE, Philadelphia, Pennsylvania

I. Emanuelsson

Special Education, Sociology of

The sociology of special education derives from a contrast between the "medical model" of disability and the social system model. Special education refers to school programs that serve children with physical, cognitive, or emotional disabilities through classes that are separate from those of the regular or mainstream school. Most special education programs are legitimated by the belief that the students suffer personal defects of some kind, whether they be neural lesions associated with learning disabilities or mental retardation, emotional pathologies, or physiological deficits that limit students' abilities to profit from the mainstream school environment.

Sociologists argue that these hypothesized personal defects in students are socially constructed. Research has focused on three ways in which social systems have promoted the creation of special student categories and programs: (a) class, cultural, or political conflicts in society that identify some students as threatening to the school order; (b) social problems that are "medicalized" to hide people's reluctance or inability to address social aspects of those problems; and (c) organizational dynamics from which there emerges a need to control certain students so that they do not disrupt or undermine the regular school program.

1. Special Education and the Broader Society

Since the turn of the twentieth century when Binet invented his individual intelligence scale to identify retarded children in the public schools of Paris (Sarason 1976, Sarason and Doris 1979), special education has had a significance that has transcended the difficulties of teaching children with cognitive disabilities. Explanations of why children fail in school, and why poor school performance tends to be concentrated in the lower socioeconomic classes and in certain ethnic minorities, have directly affected immigration and economic policies throughout the industrialized world.

Arguments that cognitive disabilities have a physiological basis and/or genetic causes were instrumental in the passage of immigration restrictions in the United States during the 1920s (Kamin 1974), and in developing policies of eugenic sterilization. Disbelief in physiological theories led some countries to undertake radical work-training policies for the retarded with surprising results. Labor shortages in postwar Europe led some countries to train retardates for factory work, allowing them to live independent lives in the long term. When Israel inherited a large population of war ophans, believed to be retarded because of deprivation and emotional shock, it developed programs based on the assumption of physiological normality that led to the rehabilitation of some who, in retrospect, were seriously disabled (Feuerstein et al. 1986).

In the wake of the United States civil rights movement, arguments about the heritability of intelligence began anew when some scholars argued that Afro-American children cannot learn as well as Whites because they have inherited mild mental retardation. In contrast, critics argued that intelligence tests are culturally biased. Categorization of minority children as mentally retarded became politically difficult in many United States school districts. A number of states passed laws that imposed administrative controls on the classification process and mandated that children "threatened" with placement in special education classes should be afforded due process.

From this perspective, special education is viewed as a variety of institutional racism. It is a way of controlling or oppressing children from ethnic minorities by placing them in stigmatizing classes with less rigorous curricula and a type of teaching that provides little chance for children to improve their educational fortunes. The notion that special education classes were a dumping ground for undesirable children provided an easy explanation for why, during the 1950s in the United States, so many classes for the mildly retarded contained mostly minority children.

When civil rights attacks were launched, a parallel movement began to expand special education classes to serve severely disabled children and those who were learning disabled. Despite growing restrictions on classes for the mentally retarded, special education generally continued to grow exponentially in many industrialized nations. The students were drawn increasingly from the middle classes and within a decade a dramatically different population was being served as special education became integrated by race and class.

On the surface, this shift undercut the argument that special education programs were serving social control functions in the schools. However, critical theorists (Barton 1986, Carrier 1986, Tomlinson 1982) argue differently. The civil rights conception of social control is a narrow one that focuses only at the level of particular schools. A broader perspective asks how elite classes use schools to control the poor and to reproduce the class structure from generation to generation, and how special education contributes to this societal control.

Critical theorists argue that over time, schools have become increasingly important as instruments of societal social control. Public school systems have become increasingly comprehensive and less disposed to exclude children for low academic achievement. As children are included in schools for more years of their lives, it becomes more difficult for educators to make sharp distinctions among them based on ability.

In this culture of inclusiveness, explanations of failure that focus on the incapacity of individuals become increasingly important as justifications for making educational distinctions. Physiological explanations are a useful expedient to make sense of why low-income children continue to fail in school despite compensatory eduction efforts. This is why the concept of learning disabilities has become so popular despite the lack of solid evidence that these cognitive deficits exist, or that schools can effectively address them in teaching programs (Coles 1987).

In an age when schools are supposed to make equal opportunity available to everyone, learning disabilities provide an explanation for why some children simply cannot profit from school programs. Thus, in the view of critical theory, special education programs represent a form of cultural control. This view explains why there is a loose relationship between the various concepts of educational handicap and what actually happens in school programs.

2. *Labeling and the Medical Model*

Closely parallel to the critical theory view is the application of labeling theory to special education. Mercer (1973) argued that most of the children labeled mentally retarded by public schools were what she called "situationally retarded." That is, they were retarded in the schools and nowhere else. She also claimed that what made them retarded in schools is that they were identified as retarded. This may or may not have much to do with actual behavior, performance, or cognitive ability. There is an organizational logic in schools that makes special education programs useful, and that leads some students to be pulled out of regular programs and put in special classes. The children selected for special classes are not necessarily (or not usually) the ones that a dispassionate screening program would select (McIntyre 1969).

Mercer's complaint is essentially that of the critical theorists. In her view, mental retardation worked primarily to limit the educational opportunity of Afro-American and Mexican-American students in the California school districts she studied. Intelligence tests and the very concept of mental retardation as applied in schools were culturally biased. Retardation is universally and spontaneously identified in human communities, but, she argued, diagnosis must include carefully collected data on a subject's social interaction performance in diverse institutional and community contexts.

This is almost never the case in schools (Milofsky 1986), and so children placed in special education classes represent students who are situationally retarded. They are classified retarded in schools, but they generally are socially normal elsewhere. There is reason to believe that special education students do not represent the most educationally disadvantaged children in their schools, nor the ones who are most clearly cognitively handicapped, nor the students most likely to benefit from intensive, specialized instruction.

There is a capricious or arbitrary nature to the selection process, hence the image of "labeling." Children are labeled like packages for the post office, in that an identifying mark is pasted on the outside of the package, but it has nothing to do with the contents. Unfortunately, being labeled can have long-term, devastating consequences for those affected. This is partly because labels persist as institutional records long after individuals have left programs.

More importantly, people who are labeled as retarded or learning disabled are treated as intellectually compromised people and respond in kind. A disability that might begin as a narrow and specific problem—or that may not exist at all when this interaction sequence or "career" (Goffman 1961) begins—becomes generalized into a role that shapes a child's whole identity. These are the processes of societal reaction and secondary deviation. To observers of school failure, it is the process by which stupidity is socially created (McIntyre 1969).

Mercer recognized that the concept "mental retardation" was itself a cause of difficulty because it was (and continues to be) treated as a physiological attribute of affected children—not unlike a broken leg or color blindness—that is thought to exist in an objectively measurable way. Intelligence quotient test scores are the strongest predictor of which children, among those referred for psychological evaluation and possible special education placement, will actually end up in special classes. The social context of a child's life, and the institutional dynamics that led up to referral, have little meaningful role in identifying the educationally handicapped or, generally, in shaping the management of their cases (Milofsky 1986).

Mercer saw that cognitive disability was treated as a medical problem in the narrowest sense. In the medical model, illness and disability are defined as a disruption to the biological system caused by disease, injuries or lesions, or insufficient development. Disability is contained in the body; it exists objectively in itself and it causes the problems for which someone has sought treatment and therapy. Coles (1987) argues that learning disability theorists continue to follow the medical model, ignoring the complex ways that social contexts and transactional processes shape students' lives in schools and the way that certain children are singled out as problems.

The medical model has long been rejected by social scientists. At a minimum, according to Wright (1960), it is necessary to distinguish between *disabilities* (specific physiological or psychological dysfunctions) and *handicaps* (the expression of a disability in a social role). A specific disability can have widely different social expressions, depending on the barriers to social independence an individual confronts, the social supports available to a person, and an individual's psychological coping resources.

A sensitivity to the social context was central in early writings about learning disabilities. Rather than seeing learning disabilities as severe limitations in cognitive functioning, they were understood to be a product of the restricted teaching environments that prevail in schools as well as of problems "in" children. Classrooms impose a host of specific cognitive demands on children, most of which are irrelevant to learning tasks; for example, receiving instructions aurally, transferring written instructions from vertical to horizontal surfaces, and learning to read and decode texts at 6 years old. Intellectually capable children may fail at these specific tasks, and this incapacity can trigger a sequence of failure experiences that gradually create secondary deviation—school failure or the perception of stupidity. By paying attention to the specifics of a child's cognitive mismatch with the school environment, it might then be possible to change the instructional environment so that a child's idiosyncratic cognitive style does not conflict with the institutional rigidities of the school and set off a career of secondary deviation and failure.

This is a "transactional" way to frame learning disabilities (Sarason and Doris 1979). As the medical model has dominated research on what learning disabilities are and how they may be remediated, however, the sociologically sensitive insights of this approach have mostly been lost. When theory and treatment of educational handicaps eschews careful transactional analysis, then special education ceases to address the ways that idiosyncratic learning styles are given expression in school roles of failure.

3. *Organizational Control*

This omission is devastating if the goal is pragmatically to address student learning problems. The behavior that is observed when any limitation of function occurs is the expression of that disability in a social role or handicap. The disability itself is generally invisible, and if it is not somehow made socially significant it is deemed unimportant. To ignore how a child's failure career evolved creates a devastating gap between theory and educational processes. The effects critical theorists complained about—special education being used to control and oppress low-income children and students from racial minorities—flows from this disconnection. There is a body of arcane theory that justifies the field, but that theory does not shape actual instruction. What goes on in special education classrooms, therefore, is often not very different from what goes on in mainstream classrooms.

The organizational structure of special education also contributes to the "nonspecialness" of special education. A cohesive body of research from the United States (Milofsky 1986), the United Kingdom (Barton 1986, Tomlinson 1982), Canada (Caspo 1984), and Australia (Fulcher 1989) argues that special education is primarily an instrument for social control in schools, and that this accounts for the gap between the manifest purposes of these programs and what they actually do. That is, special education programs exist primarily to help bring orderliness to mainstream or regular school programs. They do this by helping to remove troublesome students from regular classes and also by giving administrative support to teachers in the mainstream.

To call special education social control may sound accusatory to some. As with labeling, however, which in the end turned out to be intrinsic to the original conception of learning disability, the social control framework is a way of focusing on the interactional and strategic context in which special education programs function in schools. It will be shown that the mandate for social control also creates deep ethical and political dilemmas for special education. Recognizing the inherent organizational complexities of special education thus helps in understanding the macrosocial problems these programs raise for educational policy.

The social control perspective rests on several core organizational understandings—or assumptions—about how schools work.

First, the central task of public schooling is to educate "normal" children. "Normal" is a problematic term because integral to sensitivity to learning disability concepts is an awareness of the enormous variability in personal styles, problems, and interests that children bring to classrooms. These diverse styles can in many ways conflict with the operating regime of the schools, spawning failure careers. The main business of schools, however, is to teach children using a model that assumes little variation in the "raw material" (children) and an instructional regime that, controlling for age, varies little from classroom to classroom and school to school. (That is why it is possible to talk easily about a "school system" characteristic of each nation.)

Second, regular classroom teaching is an art, rather than a technology. This is to say that the logic of instruction mandates that teachers have a measure of autonomy in their work, however bureaucratic and controlling their school system supervisors might seek to be.

Third, more important than the personal variations in students, teachers need autonomy because regular classroom teaching requires that instructors forge a group consensus about work in their classrooms. Teachers must become authoritative leaders. Successful instruction depends on the organizational efficiencies that follow when the class accepts the pattern and legitimacy of a teacher's work routines.

To survive, teachers have to establish routines and avoid having individual confrontations with students or group conflicts that make the teacher seem other than an expert adviser to children about how they might best further their own educational programs. Authoritative leadership is an exercise in trust that is fragile, and perhaps not easily achieved in many contemporary public schools.

Fourth, because authority is fragile and also because classroom discipline has become accepted by teachers and supervisors alike as the legitimate measure of effectiveness, disruptiveness is often profoundly threatening to teachers. Much administrative problem solving in schools is directed at identifying sources of disruption, assigning blame (between teachers, principals, families, and student groups), and finding ways to resolve persistent or escalating disruptions.

Fifth, classroom disruption in this way can become a collective distrubance in the informal social fabric of a school. Disruptions have a contagious quality that make them dangerous, both in the sense that schools become physically threatening places, and in the sense that the task goals of schools become difficult to achieve.

Disruptions may involve students who act up and challenge teacher authority. Disruptions may also be quiet, involving students who do not learn well and whose needs are not addressed because teachers conclude they will require more time than they have to give. Thus, to some teachers the passivity associated with mild mental retardation can be as disruptive, in the sense of making a teacher feel inadequate and out of control, as direct confrontation from other students.

Ethnic difference can also make a teacher feel inadequate and out of control. Meanhile, children who feel attacked for their ethnicity may band together in their rejection of schooling. This may become an active program of resistance in schools or a collective rejection of schooling by children from a specific ethnic community.

Sixth, in this context special education programs have to be understood as marginal school programs (Milofsky 1986). This is not to say that they are unimportant or invalid. Rather, they exist on the periphery of the institution, where regular school programs are the core of the institution. This means that for most people, in and out of schools, regular programs have higher priority than special programs.

Despite the various ways that special programs can proclaim their own autonomy, their own access to resources, and their right and obligation to define their own distinctive goals, the structure of special education programs is contingent on the way regular school programs work. In some contexts, enlightened people run the regular program. They understand and respect the needs and goals of the special program and create an organizational environment in which diagnoses and special teaching can proceed as envisioned in the idealistic world of academic research, curricular planning, and policy analysis that has created the legal, administrative, and intellectual superstructure of the field (Fulcher 1989, Weatherley and Lipsky 1992).

More commonly, the content of local special education programs is the product of ongoing, historically shaped negotiations between special and regular program staff at the local level. In some school systems these negotiations happen because a single administrative unit runs both programs. In this sort of arrangement regular educators tend to have more power in the system because they have larger numbers, larger budgets, and more ways to influence the broader political system. The public understands services the regular school program provides, and when there is debate about educational reform it almost always focuses on the success or failure of the regular program. Special education is ignored in these general debates, unless there is a focus on the seemingly unnecessary expenses involved in supporting special education.

Even where special and regular programs are administratively separate, special programs are dependent because the regular program controls the supply of students. Very few special education programs for the mildly handicapped select their students through independent screening programs. Students are generally recruited via a referral process that begins with recommendations from the regular classroom teacher, which are validated by the principal. Students are then passed on to a diagnostic team composed of specialists.

Having to rely on regular program staff for the raw material of special education programs means that special educators must confront and deal with regular educators' ways of defining specialness. Most regular classroom teachers and many school-level administrators (as well as higher-level administrators) have a primitive understanding of the concepts and criteria underlying learning disabilities and other cognitive handicaps. The children referred for special education screening tend to be either those who have severe problems or those whom regular teachers find troublesome and whose problems they think can be blamed on cognitive disabilities.

Referrals by regular teachers are problematic. It is reasonable to think that most of these instructors want to do the right thing for children and, by virtue of having worked with hundreds of children, that many have a finely honed sensitivity to differences in cognitive styles among their students. Most teachers also have an elaborate range of strategies to use on students who do not learn in conventional ways. They are not foolish or casual about how they assess children and many of the students referred for special education are identified by astute teachers.

At the same time, classroom disruption, conflict among school staff, and political chaos at the school system level—resulting in budget shortfalls, staff transfers, arbitrary policies, and the like—are commonplace in public schools in all countries. As conflicts and feelings of insecurity escalate, teachers and principals (and children) look for ways to defend themselves. Special education programs often represent unclaimed resources that regular staff think ought to be used to help make things better in the regular program. Special education staff in schools (teachers and school psychologists primarily) often are willing to help out. Oddly, the professional self-interest of special education staff is often served by their subversion of their own programs.

The transactional character of learning disabilities is one of the main reasons that special educators conspire to undermine the specialness of their own programs. There may be a specific cognitive disability that sets off a chain of events causing a child to assume the role of failure, but if learning disabilities are partly caused by the rigidities of organizational structure, then a sensible special educator is also a social psychologist for the schools. Special educators cannot just treat the child in isolation; they must also deal with the school context from which that child's failure emerged.

This requires that special educators immerse themselves in school politics and build alliances with educators. This is a matter of self-defense—trying to control the original selection of children for special education. It also is an exercise in primary prevention—treating learning problems in classrooms before they become crystallized as careers of failure. Often special educators' involvement includes working with teachers and administrators to address and resolve the complex interactive problems that cause children to be scapegoated by teachers as they justify their own failures.

From a transactional standpoint the only sensible way to do special education is to engage in this sort of aggressive bridge-building to the regular school staff. Definitions of failure are inextricably tied to issues of social control in classrooms and to the dynamic balance of control and autonomy in regular school administrations.

Unfortunately, the cultural politics of school funding does not allow for the allocation of money to pay for freelance specialist consultants or pressure valve programs in schools, which is what the best special education really is. Special education programs are legitimated by the cultural notion that some people are more intelligent than others for genetic and physiological reasons. Society's collective guilt that children from low-income and ethnic minority families do not succeed in schools is assuaged somewhat by these biological explanations. Society is willing to support special programs for these children, as well as for the physically disabled, and at the same time gains some leverage in justifying a high correlation between social class and school outcomes from these programs. The truly handicapped are skimmed out of the school program, it is argued, so that the people left behind have a level playing field. Achievement and failure then can be appropriately rewarded.

Cultural politics are central to the definition of special education because they provide the political legitimacy necessary for a stable funding and program base. Once a policy sponsoring special education exists, a program has to be created, children must be selected, theory must be generated, and workers must be trained. Understandably, there is a gap and some tension between special education as imagined and justified in the political system, and the sort of special education that makes sense in practice. Lip service must be paid to the political justifications for these programs.

There is a deep ethical problem embedded in

special education, however. Although it may be acknowledged that transactionally oriented special educators provide a valuable service in schools and can be important protectors of children, it is also believed that for children to be helped they must be labeled. The legal and administrative meaning of those labels are rooted in the medical model and almost inevitably they distort the real character of students' school problems. Furthermore, to be effective, special educators often must be duplicitous in building their alliances with regular educators and intervening to shape the outcomes of particular cases. By its nature, special education is ethically compromised.

References

Barton L 1986 The politics of special educational needs. *Disability, Handicap and Society* 1(3): 273–90

Carrier J G 1986 *Learning Disability: Social Class and the Construction of Inequality in American Education*. Greenwood Press, New York

Caspo M 1984, Segregation, integration and beyond: A sociological perspective of special education. *British Columbia Journal of Special Education* 8(3): 211–29

Coles G S 1987 *The Learning Mystique. A Critical Look at Learning Disabilities*. Fawcett Columbine, New York

Feuerstein et al. 1986 Learning potential assessment. *Special Services in the Schools* 2(2–3): 85–106

Fulcher G 1989 *Disabling Policies? A Comparative Approach to Education Policy and Disability*. Falmer Press, London

Goffman E 1961 The moral career of a mental patient. In: Goffman E 1961 *Asylums*. Anchor, Garden City, New York

Kamin L 1974 *The Science and Politics of IQ*. Lawrence Erlbaum Assoc., Potomac, Maryland

McIntyre D 1969 Two schools, one psychologist. In: Kaplan F, Sarason S B (eds.) 1969 *The Psycho-Educational Clinic*, Community Mental Health Monograph Series, Vol. 4. Massachusetts Department of Mental Health, Boston, Massachusetts

Mercer J 1973 *Labeling the Mentally Retarded*. University of California Press, Berkeley, California

Milofsky C 1986 Special education and social control. In: Richardson J G (ed.) 1986 *Handbook of Theory and Research for the Sociology of Education*. Greenwood Press, Westport, Connecticut

Sarason S B 1976 The unfortunate fate of Alfred Binet and school psychology. *Teach. Coll. Rec.* 77(4): 579–92

Sarason S B, Doris J 1979 *Educational Handicap, Public Policy, and Social History: A Broadened Perspective on Mental Retardation*. Free Press, New York

Tomlinson S 1982 *A Sociology of Special Education*. Routledge and Kegan Paul, London

Weatherley R, Lipsky M 1992 Street-level bureaucrats and institutional innovation: Implementing special-education reform. In: Hehir T, Latus T (eds.) 1992 *Special Education at the Century's End. Evolution of Theory and Practice Since 1970*. Harvard Educational Review, Reprint Series 23, Cambridge, Massachusetts

Wright B 1960 *Physical Disability—A Psychological Approach*. Harper and Row, New York

C. Milofsky

Special Education, Use of Technology in

Technologies such as microcomputers and laser videodisc systems are used extensively in education. For example, approximately 91 percent of schools in the United States use microcomputers, with about 12 students per computer (Liu et al. 1992). The most comprehensive catalog of instructional videodisc programs shows videodisc programs growing from 425 in 1989 to over 2,000 in 1991 (Pollack 1992). Numerous applications of educational technology have been reported with students of wide-ranging achievement levels; however, the discussion of educational technology use in this entry is limited to children with special needs.

Children with special needs include children identified as having learning or behavioral disabilities, or children identified as "gifted" because they are considerably above average in achievement. The discussion of technology is limited to the application of hardware, software, and a sampling of the instructional design methods used in educating children with special needs.

Two major categories of technology will be discussed: (a) assistive technology—devices and services that will increase, maintain, or improve the functional capabilities of persons with disabilities; and (b) learning technology—hardware or software or design systems used by teachers or by children. Learning technology is further divided into applications for those children who are gifted and those children who have disabilities. Each major section will begin with a general discussion about the technology, followed by examples of technology applications from around the world.

The international scope of the entry is limited to industrialized countries, even though estimates show that 80 percent of all persons with disabilities live in isolated rural areas in developing countries. In many developing countries, persons with disabilities remain in the home, do not receive special services, and are not counted in the census as having a disability (Nathanson 1991). In an extensive review of Third World education, Fuller (1987) found that the use of technology is limited and consists mainly of instructional radio programs. Accordingly, little information is available concerning the use of educational technology in developing countries.

1. Assistive Technology

Assistive technology (AT) includes devices as well as

services. A generally accepted definition of AT in the United States is included in the Individuals with Disabilities Education Act (IDEA):

(a) Assistive technology devices are any item, piece of equipment, or product system, whether acquired commercially or off the shelf, modified, or customized that is used to increase, maintain, or improve the functional capabilities of individuals with disabilities.

(b) The term assistive technology service means any service that directly assists an individual with a disability in the selection, acquisition, or use of an assistive technology device.

Assistive technology is redefining what is possible for a wide range of school children with cognitive and physical disabilities. For example, access to education becomes possible for many children through the use of communication and mobility devices. Without AT, children who cannot communicate verbally are denied many social and learning benefits inherent in a formal education. For many children, AT is the key to receiving an education and may be viewed as the most important form of technology assistance for students with special needs.

1.1 Access to Assistive Technology

Assistive technology devices and services have been used for centuries, but the viability of their use has greatly increased with rapid advances in technology. In the United States attention on assistive technology has grown dramatically with the passage of Public Law 100–407 (the Technology Related Assistance Act of 1988—the "Tech Act"). The development of AT in Canada has been similar to its development in the United States. Close cultural ties, a common language, and geographic proximity make information sharing readily achievable between the two countries.

Funding for AT varies greatly between nations. In the United States funding is provided by a combination of government, private insurance, and the individual. In Canada 75 percent of the cost of AT is provided by the government and in the Netherlands a majority of wheelchairs are provided by the Joint Medical Service. The development of assistive devices in Sweden is strongly linked to a socially based system, and AT devices are free of charge for the customer. In many Third World nations the government provides little or no funding for AT (Nathanson 1991).

1.2 Applications of Assistive Technology

Advances in technology have greatly increased the potential of AT to improve functional capabilities, but not all AT is high-tech. There are simple solutions for accommodating disabilities. AT is often categorized as no-tech, low-tech, or high-tech. This chapter is primarily concerned with high-tech, although a brief description of no-tech and low-tech devices is also included.

1.2.1 No-tech. There are numerous no-tech solutions a teacher may use to reduce barriers encountered by students with disabilities. For instance, important accommodations can be made by simply widening the aisles between student desks, or by making desks and tables accessible, or by tying a rope to a doorknob for a student in a wheelchair to pull the door closed.

1.2.2 Low-tech. Many devices such as power wheelchairs can be controlled by simple digital switches such as a mechanical switch or the "sip and puff" switch. A mechanical, digital switch can be operated by a person who has minimal hand movement. The sip and puff switch can be operated by blowing or sucking on a straw which in turn operates a digital switch. There are also numerous examples of teacher-made materials that can be used to eliminate barriers for students with disabilities, such as page turners, talking clocks, and videotaped textbooks.

1.2.3 High-tech. High-tech devices usually involve computer, optical, and/or video and audio technologies. The rapid improvement and low cost of the microprocessor has been essential in developing many high-tech devices. One high-tech device, the eyegaze system, allows a person with only eye movement to control a computer which in turn can allow communication, control any environmental devices, play games, dial and answer a telephone, and read text. Chapman and Cleveland described the eyegaze system as follows:

> The Eyegaze System uses eye tracking technology to control a computer. The user sits in front of a computer control monitor which displays a variety of control and communication functions. A video camera mounted under the monitor continually observes the user's eye; an image processing software determines the point on the monitor screen where the user is looking. When the user focuses his or her gaze on a desired key for a predetermined time, the computer executes the associated function. (Chapman and Cleveland 1991 p.140).

An alternative method for controlling a computer with eye movement uses cornea–retina potential difference (French et al. 1992). This system uses electrical potential differences produced by vertical eye movement. The electrical potentials are picked up by surface electrodes placed on the skin near the eyes. This system is in development and shows great promise for persons who only have vertical eye movement. Also, it is potentially less complicated than the eyegaze system because it is not dependent on the use of a video camera.

Automatic speech recognition systems are another

group of high-tech devices that have educational implications. One example, the Tangora System, is a speaker-dependent automatic speech-recognition system with a vocabulary of 20,000 words. This system has an average accuracy of 95 percent and can be used to recognize speech over a telephone line. Kanevsky (1991) evaluated the system by performing telephone experiments with 12 students with hearing impairments. The decoding accuracy of the system varied between 75 percent and 98 percent for different speakers. The researchers concluded that persons with hearing impairments are able to achieve good comprehension when the topic of conversation is clear. Speech recognition systems could potentially be used in classrooms, alleviating the need for deaf students to have human signers.

Boonzaier (1992) reported on a project to help blind people which is being developed at the University of Cape Town, South Africa. The system uses large scale integrated circuit (LSI) and analog computer technology to convert three-dimensional visual signals into audio signals. The blind person, with extensive training, could then translate the audio signals into a three-dimensional visual representation. The researchers believe their work constitutes a major breakthrough in real-time data extraction and reduction which has plagued researchers in artificial vision for years.

Brown described a talking newspaper which was developed by the Swedish company TEXTALK for people who have visual impairments. With the TEXTALK System, newspaper print is compressed and stored on a computer hard disk at the newspaper. The compressed information is then sent to an FM receiving/transmitting station which in turn transmits the data to users. The user must have a receiver and a computer to store the text. Readers with vision impairments can then retrieve the text either through speech synthesis, large print, or a braille printer. The TEXTALK System has been used successfully in Sweden, Finland, and the Netherlands.

In Sweden, a computer program called HARMONI is being used on the Compis computer to include blind students in regular computer education classes (Svensson 1988). The HARMONI program produces computer output in synthesized speech, braille, or large print, giving blind students access to the same educational programs as their sighted classmates. A similar project at the University of Karlsruhe in Germany is providing a system to enable optimal integration of blind and visually impaired people into the university (Klaus 1991). They are using a combination of high-level information technology such as the Kurzweil Reading Machine, attaching braillers to students' individual computers, and providing the VISTA enlargement system for students' personal computers. Researchers at the Hospital Ramon y Cajal in Madrid are developing a paperless braille system that utilizes one braille cell to read an 80-character line. Typically reading an 80-character line requires the use of 80 braille cells. The system uses a sliding single cell to read the 80 characters. The system should substantially reduce the cost of paperless Braille systems, since the major expense in these systems is the high cost of each braille cell (Parreño and Magallon 1991).

Van Woerden and Rosier (1992) described a system in the Netherlands designed for the integrated control of mobility, manipulation communication, and the environment. The system allows persons with disabilities access to multiple functions from a single input device. For instance, persons with multiple disabilities can, without help, efficiently switch between wheelchair control, manipulator control, control of their environment, computer access, and communication without help. The development of the integrated control system is sponsored by Technology Initiative for Disabled and Elderly People (TIDE), a European Community program. Similar research is also being conducted on multifunctional control switches by Ferrario and Lodola (1992) in Malano, Italy.

Kwee et al. (1992) described continued development of the Dutch MANUS system. The MANUS system is a wheelchair-mounted manipulator with a modular computer-assisted control structure. It can be configured for a particular user. Configurations are set up and changed on a personal computer (PC) through the use of a patch board which is down loaded into MANUS to define its human interface characteristics. Configurations for the same user can be reprogrammed to accommodate learning and efficiency. In an attempt to improve the cosmetics of wheelchairs while maintaining or improving functionality, Nashihara and Shizukurshi (1992) of the Tohoku Institute of Technology, Sendai, Japan have developed a wooden wheelchair for indoor use. The cosmetically improved wheelchair imparts a "kind smoothness and warmth to physically handicapped people's environment."

2. *Learning Technologies*

Thinking about technology's role in education does not mean thinking about technology; it means thinking about education and incorporating effective instructional strategies into educational software. For example, after reviewing several studies concerned with the effectiveness of using computers to teach mathematics, Gleason et al. (1990) concluded that teachers and students benefit from a careful analysis of instructional content and use of sound instructional design principles to establish programs that successfully teach students with mild disabilities. Hofmeister and Thorkildsen (1989), after reviewing 10 years of their own research, concluded that the videodisc was an effective delivery system, but that the effectiveness of the instruction depended on using established instructional design strategies and capturing the expertise of the best teachers. They also concluded that it was most effective to use the videodisc as a teacher tool and not a teacher replacement. Pogrow (1988), after analyzing the effect of the computer movement, concluded that many of the ineffective applications of computers in education can be attributed to emphasizing hardware rather than working with teachers and integrating computers into their classroom.

The quality of commercial educational software should also be carefully scrutinized. Zane and Frazer (1992) requested effectiveness data from 34 companies that develop and market educational software. None of these companies supplied evidence that their products were empirically tested for effectiveness. The companies were not randomly selected and, therefore, generalization is limited. However, their results support similar findings by Bangert–Drowns and Kozma (1989).

As technology is used more frequently in education, it becomes obvious that a great deal of attention must be placed on evaluating existing software and on using effective instructional design strategies that fully utilize the delivery capabilities of the medium when developing software. Correspondingly, the following sections emphasize instructional design and integration when describing examples of successful use of technology to teach children with special needs.

2.1 Learning Technologies and Students with Disabilities

Lin et al. (1991) used a computer-assisted instruction (CAI) program to teach word recognition to students with mild mental disabilities. They compared the results of the CAI program with a similar paper and pencil program directed by a teacher. They found that posttest accuracy was greater for students in the paper and pencil condition than those who were in the CAI condition. The CAI program allowed the students to monitor their performance and gave them immediate feedback. The researchers concluded that the teacher's moment-by-moment decisions about practicing and the teacher's task-specific verbal instruction which was tailored to the performance of individual learners in the paper and pencil condition led to greater accuracy. Gleason et al. (1990) reported on another study comparing a group using CAI to a group taught by a teacher. Both groups of middle-school students with mild disabilities received instruction in multiplication and division mathematics story problems. The only difference between the two instructional approaches for each group was the medium used to communicate the instruction to the student. Their findings showed no significant differences between the groups; however, both groups showed significant improvement from pretest to posttest. A written posttest showed 93 percent accuracy for the teacher-directed group and 91 percent accuracy for the CAI group. The instructional design for both groups was based on a direct instruction model (Engelmann and Carnine 1982). Teaching focused on linguistic elements in the story problems that could be translated into an equation. This taught students to set up equations for each story problem. Students were required to solve the equation with paper and pencil responses, rather than keyboard responses. The researchers concluded that when CAI is properly designed, the computer can be an effective instructional medium for students with mild learning disabilities. Additionally, when the instruction is properly designed, it is irrelevant whether the medium of instruction is a teacher or a computer.

Using some of the same instructional design principles, Thorkildsen and Lowry (1991) conducted a study involving the use of a videodisc-based program to teach fractions in 17 classrooms, which included students with mild learning disabilities. The instructional design of the program was based on direct instruction principles (Engelmann and Carnine 1982) and a synthesis of the research on effective teaching (Hofmeister and Lubke 1990). The instructional design required close attention to sequencing examples, eliciting oral and written responses from students, extensively using and fading prompts, providing daily assessment of prerequisite skills, insuring that guided practice always preceded independent practice, and providing weekly assessments of mastery. The videodisc program was used in a classroom with a large group of students and was controlled by the teachers. The teacher controlled the videodisc player with a remote control unit that could be used anywhere in the classroom. The findings from this project showed that mainstream students with mild disabilities progressed from an average of 10 percent mastery on a pretest to an average of 65 percent mastery on the posttest. Students in the classroom who were classified as high achievers in mathematics went from an average of 30 percent on the pretest to 90 percent on the posttest. The students with mild disabilities learned at approximately the same rate as the high-achieving students.

A project at Warwick University in the United Kingdom is using CD-ROM technology to increase the rate at which students with physical disabilities can perform educational and vital activities. The project team is developing an intelligent word-processor that will help persons with physical disabilities learn keyboarding skills. The system will predict words during character-by-character input by examining contextual information, word frequency and recency, syntactic rules and knowledge of the domain or subject being written about (Pickering et al. 1988).

Chaudhry and Fakhro (1988) have been implementing computers in a school for children with mental retardation and deafness in Bahrain. They developed a program in Arabic that operates on an

IBM microcomputer and teaches alphabets, counting, money, different shapes, and similar shapes. They noted that the program was well-received by teachers, but they did not present data on the effectiveness of the program. They also noted the difficulty in developing programs in Arabic because the quality of the Arabic fonts was low.

2.2 Gifted Students and Learning Technology

Span (1990) claimed that the use of computers with gifted children is a neglected research area. He suggested that there is a lack of applicable theory and models to guide the needed research. He recommended using the following five principles for gifted education for guiding the needed research: (a) focus on complex study of themes that integrate knowledge; (b) develop productive thinking skills; (c) constantly explore changing knowledge; (d) use specialized resources; and (e) promote self-initiated and self-directed learning.

Information may also be available to guide the application of computers in educating gifted students. For example, Grandgenett, after reviewing the literature on using computers with gifted students, concluded that Taylor's (1980) application categories of tutor, tool, and/or tutee may provide program developers with guidelines for using computers with gifted students. Taylor (1980) proposed using these computer applications categories to help educators think about how the computer can be used in education. Using the principles recommended by Span and Taylor's categories may help educators develop relevant technology-based programs for gifted students.

Little evidence was found that research is being conducted on the effectiveness of using technology

Table 1
Technology applications with students who have been identified as gifted

Author	Date	Curriculum area	Application type	Technology	Country
Lopez	1990	Using LOGO to teach artificial intelligence programming	Tool/tutee	Microcomputers	Brazil
Barnsley	1991	Solving cryptanalysis problems to teach problem solving	Tool	Microcomputers	Australia
Chernyshov	1991	Teaching the basics of quantum mechanics	Tutor	Microcomputer	USSR
Eriksson-Slute	1991	Developing creative thinking through the use of Futuristics and a computer network	Tool	Computer-based network	South Africa
Schaars and Severijnen	1991	Using an intelligent CAI system that adjusts to the talent of the student.	Tutor	Microcomputer	Sweden
Sinclair	1991	Using LOGO to explore math concepts and develop problem solving skills. Produced enhanced abilities in problem solving.	Tutee	Microcomputer	Australia
Maley	1988	Students conducting experiments in a technology-based laboratory. Students developing problem-solving planning, and writing skills.	Tool	Testing equipment	United States
Marcus	1991	Students designing a variety of games, teaching the computer to play, and examining how the computer learns.	Tutee	Micro-1 AI programs	United States
Kotze	1984	Students writing computer programs to develop a structured approach to general problem solving. Developed in a special school for gifted students.	Tutee	Microcomputer	South Africa

with gifted students; however, an extensive literature search revealed numerous articles describing applications. A sample of these applications is contained in Table 1.

A meta-analysis on the effects of computer-assisted instruction on cognitive outcomes showed a moderate effect size (ES = .48) across 32 studies (Liu et al. 1992). All three types of application were included in the studies and tutor applications showed a slightly higher effect size than did problem-solving or simulation programs (tool/tutee applications). This outcome is interesting because many critics of using the computer as a tutor have claimed that tutorials do not use the unique capabilities of the computer, and tutorials can be delivered as effectively by teachers. However, this conclusion is not supported by Liu's (1992) review. Because little research-based information exists on using CAI with gifted students, reviews similar to Liu's are not available for gifted students.

Kozma (1991) conducted a review of the literature on learning with media and contended that using the computer in simulations and problem-solving activities has great potential because computers have the capability of creating dynamic, symbolic representations of nonconcrete, formal constructs that are frequently missing in the middle models of novices. Students can then proceduralize the relationship between constructs and then manipulate the representations within the computer simulation to work out differences between their incomplete, inaccurate mental models and the formal principles represented in the system. This type of learning corresponds more closely to the principles promoted by Passow than does a tutorial type of learning. Obviously, additional research is needed to help determine which types of computer applications may be most effective with gifted students in different areas of the curriculum.

3. Conclusion

Children with special needs can benefit greatly from technology assistance. Assistive technology may be the most important form of technology assistance, because in many cases it provides the critical link to accessible education for children with disabilities. Children with severe mobility, sensory and/or communication impairments may be unable to use educational services without technology assistance. The need for technology is formally recognized in United States law which requires that assistive technology be considered in each student's individualized education plan. Finding funding to pay for AT is a problem in many countries and a major problem in developing countries. Countries such as Canada and Sweden, however, provide funding for AT.

Research findings show that technology-aided instruction can greatly improve the achievement of students with mild learning disabilities. In some studies, however, technology served as little more than a delivery vehicle and did not necessarily contribute to the effectiveness of the technology-based program. Researchers stressed the importance of using empirically based instructional design strategies to develop technology-aided instruction.

Little research was found on the effectiveness of using technology-aided instruction with gifted students. As with students with learning disabilities, research is needed to help determine effective design and application strategies for developing technology-assisted programs for gifted students. Research on design should precede research on the effectiveness of using technology with gifted students and thereby contribute to the success of technology-based programs.

See also: Deaf and Hearing Impaired Youth, Education of; Visually Handicapped Children and Youth, Education of; Integrated Services for Children and Youth with Special Needs; Deaf-Blind Children and Youth, Education of

References

Bangert-Drowns R L, Kozma R B 1989 Assessing the design of instructional software. *Journal of Research on Computing in Education* 21(3): 241–62

Barnsley G 1991 Cryptanalysis: An ideal challenge for the gifted. *Talent for the Future*, Ninth World Conf. on Gifted and Talented Children, The Hague

Boonzaier D A 1992 The earsight project: Mapping of visual space into its 3D audio analogue, a new blind aid. *RESNA Int. Conf.*

Chapman J E, Cleveland N R 1991 Use of an eye-operated EYEGAZE computer system in locked-in syndrome. *Proc. 6th An. RESNA Conf.*

Chaudhry F, Fakhro S Q 1988 Microcomputer integration into a special education institute in Bahrain: A pilot project. *Education Media International* 25(2):

Chernyshov D 1991 Wave structure of the substance: Debroglie waves. *Talent for the Future,* Ninth World Conf. on Gifted and Talented Children, The Hague

Engelmann S, Carnine D 1982 *Theory of Instruction: Principles and Applications*. Irvington, New York

Ferrario M, Lodola M 1992 A multifunctional nape joystick. *RESNA Int. Conf.* 524–26

French J, Siebens A, Tippett D C 1992 Employing the cornea–retinal potential difference to control an ACS. *RESNA Int. Conf.* 441–43

Fuller B 1987 What school factors raise achievement in the Third World? *Rev. Educ. Res.* 57(3): 255–92

Gleason M, Carnine D, Boriero D 1990 Improving CAI effectiveness with attention to instructional design in teaching story problems to mildly handicapped students. *J. Spec. Educ. Technol.* 10(3): 129–36

Hofmeister A, Lubke M 1990 *Research into Practice: Implementing Effective Teaching Strategies*. Allyn and Bacon, Boston, Massachusetts

Hofmeister A, Thorkildsen R J 1989 Videodisc levels: A case study in hardware obsession. *J. Spec. Educ. Technol.* 10(2): 73–79

Kanevsky L 1991 How young high IQ children win the

learning game. *Talent for the Future*, Ninth World Conf. on Gifted and Talented Children, The Hague
Klaus J 1991 Integrating blind and visually handicapped students into university learning and living. *Proc. 6th An. RESNA Conf.* 525–36
Kotze P 1984 Informatics—Preparation for the realities of the future. Paper presented at the International Conference: Education for the Gifted "Ingenium 2000," Stellenbosch.
Kozma R B 1991 Learning with media. *Rev. Educ. Res.* 61: 179–211
Kwee H, Thönnissen M, Cremer G B, Duimel J, Westgeest R 1992 Configuring the MANUS System. *RESNA Int. Conf.* 584–87
Lin A, Podell D M, Rein N 1991 The effects of CAI on word recognition in mildly mentally handicapped and nonhandicapped learners. *J. Spec. Educ. Technol.* 11(1): 16–24
Liu M, Reed M, Phillips P 1992 Teacher education students and computers: Gender, major, prior computer experience, occurrence, and anxiety. *Journal of Research on Computing in Education* 24(4): 457–67
Lopez M A 1990 The use of technology in working with gifted children. *Expanding Awareness of Creative Potentials Worldwide*. Brain Talent-Powers Press, Salt Lake City, Utah
Maley D 1988 Teaching the gifted and talented through technology education. *JN: Technology Teacher* 48(3): 8–13
Marcus S 1991 Technology, the gifted, and the language arts. *Journal of the California Association for the Gifted* 21(1): 15–17
Nashihara H, Shizukurshi K 1992 Development of indoor wheelchair mainly made of wood. *RESNA Int. Conf.* 533
Nathanson J H 1991 The United Nations and people with disabilities. *Issues in International Rehabilitation* 4(2): 20–23
Parreño A, Magallon P 1991 A scanning cell braille line. *Technology and Persons with Disabilities*: 725
Pickering J, Neilson D, Vella C 1988 Information technology and special needs in education. *Education Media International* 25(2):
Pogrow S 1988 The computer movement cover-up. *Electronic Learning* 7(7): 6–7
Pollack R A (ed.)1992 *Videodisc Compendium for Education and Training 1993*. Emerging Technology Consultants Inc., St. Paul, Minnesota
Schaars F, Severijnen 1991 Developing educational software for gifted and talented children: A Dutch example. *Talent for the Future*, Ninth World Conf. on Gifted and Talented Children, The Hague
Sinclair K 1991 Augmenting reasoning abilities in mathematics. *Talent for the Future*, Ninth World Conf. on Gifted and Talented Children, The Hague
Span P 1990 Special benefits of the computer for the education of gifted children. *Expanding Awareness of Creative Potentials Worldwide*: 480–87
Svensson H 1988 The use of new technologies in the education of blind students integrated into ordinary schools. *Using Media for Specialized Education*. Solna
Taylor R (ed.) 1980 *The Computer in the School: Tutor, Tutee, Tool*. Teachers College Press, New York
Thorkildsen R, Lowry W H 1991 Determining the differential effect on math achievement of levels of implementation of a videodisc based program with regular and mildly handicapped students. Paper presented at the American Educational Research Association, Chicago, Illinois
Van Woerden J A, Rosier J C 1992 Integrated control of mobility, manipulation, communication and the environment. *RESNA Int. Conf.* 575–79
Zane T, Frazer C 1992 The extent to which software developers validate their claims. *Journal of Research on Computing in Education* 24(3): 410–19

Further Reading

Church G, Glennen S 1992 *The Handbook of Assistive Technology*. Singular Publishing Group, San Diego, California
Eriksson G 1990 From future shock to futures possibilities for gifted and talented students. *Expanding Awareness of Creative Potentials Worldwide*. Brain Talent-Powers Press, Salt Lake City, Utah
IBM 1991 *Resource Guide for Persons with Learning Impairments*. IBM National Support Center for Persons with Disabilities, P.O. Box 2150, Atlanta, Georgia 30301–2150
LaPlante M P, Hendershot G E, Moss A J 1992 Assistive technology devices and home accessibility features: Prevalence, payment, need, and trends. *Advance Data* 217, Centers for Disease Control
Office of Special Education Programs 1989 *Apple Computer Resources in Special Education and Rehabilitation*. DLM Teaching Resources, Allen, Texas

R. J. Thorkildsen

Specific Language Disorders of Childhood

Language is the most complex cognitive skill of which the human race is capable. It is not surprising, therefore, to find that many children have problems developing this skill. The exact prevalence of language disability is difficult to estimate, due mainly to problems of terminology and types of pathologies included in the various surveys. Studies carried out in the United States, Canada, United Kingdom, and New Zealand estimate a prevalence of approximately 15 percent, with the majority of problems occurring in the preschool years. All surveys show a higher percentage of males with language disability, with an average ratio of 3 males to 1 female.

There are many known factors that cause language disability, including hearing loss, mental retardation, and social and economic deprivation. Difficulties in linguistic development can also occur associated with disorders such as cleft palate, cerebral palsy, and autism.

Specific language disorder (SLD) refers to a small group of children with a deficit in the development of the comprehension and/or expression of spoken language where this is of primary origin and not secondary to disorders such as hearing loss, mental retardation, emotional disturbance, or social deprivation. In the 1988 report of the Invalid Children's Aid Nationwide (ICAN) Association of the United

Kingdom this group was estimated to represent 0.08 percent of the total population. Lahey (1988) proposed a higher incidence of 0.1 and 0.2 percent and pointed out that, while the syndrome is rare, interest in this group has generated more research than might be expected given the numbers involved.

Specific Language Disorder is also termed language impairment, language disorder, or developmental language disorder. In older literature terms such as developmental dysphasia are used but such terms are more appropriate to acquired language disorders.

In addition to linguistic disabilities SLD children may also exhibit such traits as hyper-or hypoactivity, distractibility, or poor physical coordination. This paper will focus on specific language disability and will concentrate on describing subgroups as classified under that general heading.

1. Types of Specific Language Disability

The identification of clinical subtypes is a relatively recent development. Traditionally the problem was categorized at best as receptive, expressive, or of a mixed nature. This simplistic division of language disorder is now considered unsatisfactory and it is accepted that children with SLD do not form a homogeneous group.

Three main approaches have been utilized in the attempt to identify subgroups of SLD: (a) etiological—the traditional medical model in which the disorder is defined by cause; (b) behavioral—a descriptive linguistic approach; (c) process based—a combination of the etiological and behavioral approaches.

The best known classification is possibly that of Rapin and Allen (1983, 1987). These authors used a process-based approach to define language disorder syndromes, thus combining the etiological and behavioral approaches. This classification, in whole or in part, is now used in many English-speaking countries as well as in continental Europe. Clinically based research is ongoing; further changes in the classification of SLD may be expected.

1.1 Subtypes of Specific Language Disorder

Rapin and Allen based their data on a number of sources which included clinical data available for approximately 100 children, referred to a neuropediatric clinic, because of delayed or deviant speech and language. The main subgroups delineated by Rapin and Allen (1987) are as follows:

(a) lexical–syntactic deficit syndrome;

(b) phonological programming deficit syndrome;

(c) phonological–syntactic deficit syndrome;

(d) semantic–pragmatic deficit syndrome;

(e) verbal auditory agnosia or word deafness;

(f) verbal dyspraxia.

Each of these categories will be described, noting prevalence, remediation, and prognosis. It is however important to note that in the early preschool years there can be a shift of patterns over time and therefore diagnosis as a clinical subtype should not take place before approximately 3 years of age.

1.1.1 Lexical–syntactic deficit syndrome. Children with this syndrome generally are late in starting to talk—they tend to be quiet infants but when they start to speak their phonology is normal for their age; thus they are often not identified as having a problem until they commence school. Their main difficulty is a severe word retrieval deficit, even though the required word is available in receptive vocabulary. They may also exhibit difficulty in formulating connected language and often demonstrate problems in recounting an incident or retelling a story (narrative discourse).

Byers-Brown and Edwards (1989) considered that there appear to be two subgroups with lexical–syntactic deficit: (a) children who remain quiet, have limited language ability, and have word-finding difficulty; (b) children who have word-finding difficulties but who tend to use a variety of word fillers in their effort to retrieve words.

This group of children have been studied extensively by German (1989). She stated that investigation into the problems of this group has been limited, with few investigations taking place into the word-finding skills in discourse. Much more detailed investigations on word-finding difficulties are to be found in the adult aphasia literature.

With regard to etiology, Rapin and Allen (1987) stated that there is no information on the anatomic substrate of this disorder. This subgroup represents approximately 20 percent of SLD children. Treatment therapy aims at increasing the child's internal lexicon and building up associated networks to facilitate access. Extensive work is required on word classes, categories, and relationships. Strategies for intervention include word association, phonemic cuing, and gestural or pantomime cues—the child needs to be capable of "self-cued monitoring" and this should be an aim of therapy. Most children in the subgroup eventually acquire serviceable language but continue to use some inappropriate lexical choices and have problems with comprehension of abstract and figurative language.

1.1.2 Phonologic programming deficit syndrome. In their 1983 paper Rapin and Allen included this group in the phonological–syntactic subgroup and only made the further division in their 1987 presentation. Byers-Brown and Edwards (1989) considered that this subgroup forms a bridge between the verbal dyspraxic and the phonological–syntactic syndrome. Children with this syndrome are described by Rapin and Allen (1987) as "much more fluent than those with verbal dyspraxia." The length of utterance is longer than the verbal dyspraxic group, though initially they may be unintelligible. Lees and Urwin (1991) considered the probability of a receptive component to the processing of speech.

Rapin and Allen (1987) held that this group does not have an exact counterpart among the adult aphasias—possibly for this reason no specific etiology is given in the literature. The group constitutes approximately 18 percent of SLD children. This syndrome is in many ways similar to developmental dyspraxia though the need for intensive therapy is unlikely. Most of the subjects in this group will have acquired useful speech by school age and with regular therapy will acquire normal speech.

1.1.3 Phonological–syntactic deficit syndrome. This is the most prevalent group of child language disabilities; it overlaps to some extent with the verbal dyspraxic group. The principal impairments are in the phonological and morphosyntactic systems. A number of studies demonstrate a relationship between phonological disability and measures of syntax, specifically morphological omissions and sentence structure complexity. Phonological complexity and syntactic complexity may interact and produce errors in both domains. These children are also dysfluent and speak in short utterances that may lack "small" words such as articles, prepositions, and pronouns. They may omit word endings that mark tense, number, and possession. Since the 1970s it has become recognized that many of the children earlier referred to as having a "functional articulation disorder" in fact had a breakdown in linguistic ability at the phonological level. It has further been noted that a breakdown at the phonological level is often associated with a deficit in syntactical ability. This is not surprising as both phonology and syntax are concerned with the structural aspects of language. Many of the children have other signs of neurological dysfunction including oromotor dysfunction.

All children with phonological disability do not show syntactical disability. At least two groups of misarticulating children exist: (a) children with multiple phoneme errors; (b) children with residual errors. Syntactic deficits are more commonly found among group (a). This group is also a high-risk group for reading disability.

The etiology of this syndrome is not known, but Rapin and Allen (1987) cited Lou and colleagues in 1984 as reporting "decreased perfusion in the anterior and posterior perisylvian region bilaterally in 4 boys with this syndrome." Approximately 40 percent of SLD children have phonological–syntactic deficit syndrome. It is generally agreed that these children constitute the largest group of the pediatric speech and language therapist's case load. For treatment, the teaching program should be based on the child's individual linguistic profile and will depend upon severity of diagnosed disability. A metalinguistic approach to therapy has been advocated where the child is taught to recognize the features of the language he or she finds difficult to produce. Weekly therapy sessions usually suffice. The prognosis is normally good.

1.1.4 Semantic–pragmatic deficit syndrome. Members of this group are often not recognized as language impaired and are thought of as bizarre. These children display early delayed language development, followed by complex speech with clear articulation. They could be described as verbose, though most of their speech is empty of meaning. At the early stages the receptive aspects are most in evidence, though these may decrease with age. Much of the expressive speech is echolalic; over-learned scripts are used in place of more appropriate greetings or comments; circumlocutions and semantic paraphasias are often used; and there is a lack of semantic specificity—the problem thus is one of language use. They will often respond to one or two words in a sentence rather than to the entire message. Traditionally this group was referred to as having "cocktail party syndrome." While this language profile is often associated with autism, not all children with this syndrome are autistic. The condition may also be associated with hydrocephalus and can be associated with hyperlexia. Rapin and Allen (1987) considered this condition to be similar to acquired transcortical sensory aphasia, which results from damage to the area adjacent to the supramarginal gyrus. Its incidence is rare—approximately 7 percent of SLD children have this syndrome. An intensive treatment program is generally required, involving input from the psychologist, teacher, and speech and language pathologist. Initially the child will need to be encouraged to interact with others. This can prove a difficult process and requires expert handling. Comprehension needs to be developed with no request for expressive language in the early stages. Even in cases of high intellectual ability the prognosis is guarded. Many children will develop useful communicative ability. They will generally remain concrete in their thinking and literal in their language.

1.1.5 Verbal auditory agnosia. This syndrome, also termed "word deafness" or "severe receptive language disability," is characterized by an inability to comprehend language through the auditory modality in the presence of normal auditory acuity (hearing). As a consequence of this decoding problem, encoding is also severely affected. The disorder may be present from birth, as was first described by Worster-Drought and Allen (1930), or be the result of sudden acquired loss of language, sometimes associated with epileptic activity, as was described by Landau and Kleffner (1957). Those in the latter group are often referred to as having Landau-Kleffner syndrome or acquired childhood aphasia. This is the most devastating of all child language disorders. An ability to form good relationships, use eye contact, and so on differentiates this group from children with autistic syndrome. Rapin and Allen (1983) stated the basis for the disorder to be bilateral temporal lobe pathology. It is a rare subtype; none of Rapin and Allen's samples were identified as having this syndrome. For treatment, intensive specialist remediation with placement in a special school is required. Therapy is conducted through the visual mode and is often combined with a sign language. McGinnis (1963) developed a special method for working with these children—the association or, as it came to be termed, the McGinnis Method. Alternative communication—usually a sign system—can play a vital role in the acquisition of communication.

Due to the rarity of the condition, information in the literature about prognosis is generally confined to individual studies. Prognosis is variable and will depend on such factors as intelligence. Some of the affected children may have additional problems of hearing loss or acquired hearing loss over time: in such cases prognosis is not good. In cases without such complications the children may learn to produce and understand some speech, but may continue to require the use of signs.

1.1.6 Verbal dyspraxia (developmental verbal dyspraxia). The use of the term "developmental verbal dyspraxia" has proved controversial and the debate surrounding this disorder is ongoing. For a review of the issue see Stackhouse (1992). The disorder was defined by Byers-Brown and Edwards (1989 p. 125) as "an impairment in the selection, planning and programming of linguistic and of motor schemata for production of language." Rapin and Allen (1987 p. 23) used the phrase "markedly dysfluent or even mute" to describe members of this group who seem to know what they want to say but have problems in doing so. A noticeable trait of these children is the inconsistency of their speech errors—there is generally good comprehension of language. Many of the children have associated motor clumsiness. Members of this group are highly at risk for later written language disability.

Rapin and Allen (1987) considered this syndrome as possibly "a circumscribed lesion that isolates Broca's region from the sensorimotor cortex". Approximately 15 percent of SLD subjects fall into this group. Children who have severe forms of this disorder require placement in language units or schools where they will receive intensive therapy. Most of these children will require to be taught a sign language as a means of communication to allay frustration. Less severe forms of the disorder will benefit from treatment on a once or twice weekly basis. Stress, rhythm, and intonation all require intervention; visual cues prove beneficial; work with a mirror is indicated. Therapy needs to concentrate on the sequence of sounds as opposed to the production of individual sounds. Emphasis is required on slowing the rate of speech and on self-monitoring. The Nuffield Dyspraxia program is specifically designed for remedial work in this area. The prognosis depends on the severity of the condition. The majority of children affected will acquire normal speech, but those with a very severe form of the disorder may always have noticeably slowed speech with obvious errors.

1.2 Summary of subtypes

Clinical subtyping is at an early stage of development, with much further research required before a universally agreed classification system becomes available. It is generally accepted that children with specific language disability do not form a homogeneous group and that specific descriptions are essential to provide relevant management. It is accepted that the majority of children whose language is specifically impaired require a structured environment with much emphasis on developing attention strategies and, when necessary, auditory perceptual skills. As with most disabilities, early intervention is advocated.

The use of six syndromes, within SLD, provides a common basis for the various professionals dealing with language disorder. It also provides a basis for differential diagnosis and a focus for therapeutic intervention. Some children fit well into one of the syndromes while others seem to have more pervasive disorders covering a wider range of symptoms. In some cases the pattern of language impairment changes over time. Research continues into these disorders and their classification.

2. Effects of Language Disorders

2.1 Language Disorders and Reading Difficulties

Since reading and writing are language-based activities, and the comprehension and production of oral language generally precedes involvement with written language, it is reasonable to assume that some of the basic component processes and representations necessary for the comprehension and production of oral and written language are common to both forms. It has even been suggested that reading and writing activities may be considered secondary to the comprehension and production of oral language. Research has shown that reading skill is linked to an incredibly wide range of verbal abilities. Vocabulary, syntactic knowledge, metalinguistic awareness, verbal short-term memory, phonological awareness, speech production, inferential comprehension and semantic fluency, form only a partial list (Stanovich 1991).

2.2 Prevalence of Reading Difficulties

In most developed countries, estimates of the number of children who have reading problems range from 15 to 20 percent. Some of these children have generalized learning deficits, others a specific learning disability related to language learning, and others an even more specific learning disability related to written language alone. There is continual debate about whether they should be considered part of the same continuum, or whether the term "dyslexic" should be applied to the second and third groups. In the strictly literal sense of the term, dyslexia means difficulties with reading and it has been described as "the obvious and hidden speech and language disorder" (Stackhouse and Wells 1991); in practice there is considerable variation in the criteria used to differentiate dyslexics from other learning disabled groups (Whyte 1989).

2.3 Prevalence of Dyslexia

Depending on where one places the cut-off point for a measure of dyslexia a prevalence figure for "true" dyslexia of between 2 and 4 percent was suggested by Miles (1991) with a cohort sample of 12,384 children in England and Wales. This, in fact, is close to the generally accepted prevalence figure, though it has also been proposed that it may vary from place to place. It is generally agreed, however, that when more than about 5 percent are encompassed by the inclusion criteria, deficits of a more general nature are likely to be observed.

3. Language Production and Reading

Children with reading problems have frequently been found to have been delayed in attaining developmental speech milestones and to have more errors in speech production; children referred for speech therapy for certain disorders have been found to have a greater incidence of reading problems than would normally be expected (Supple 1989). Research has so far failed to establish a cause-and-effect relationship between articulation and reading problems. It has been found that children with phonetic speech defects (i.e., cleft palate or other structural abnormalities) are not at risk for reading disability and that while such children have disordered speech production, their underlying representation of phonology is intact. It has also been found in the case of nonspeaking children with cerebral palsy that the development of sound blending skills is not contingent on speech production abilities.

4. Phonological Processing

Since the early 1960s poor phonological processing ability has been identified as a crucial correlate of reading difficulties. Phonological disorders have also been found to be associated with developmental verbal dyspraxia. One view has been that many poor readers are significantly impaired in the auditory discrimination of speech sounds and have difficulty in analyzing the internal structure of printed words. Auditory synthesis has been investigated as a possible underlying factor by Supple (1989), who found significant differences between subjects with normal articulation and those with defective articulation only on this variable and on reading ability. This supported findings by earlier researchers who had investigated both issues separately.

A second conceptualization proposes that some children are not sufficiently aware of the phonetic structure of spoken language and that they have difficulty with phonetic segmentation or mapping alphabetic symbols onto their counterparts.

There has been discussion over whether phonemic awareness and segmentation skills can develop without prior knowledge of the printed word. Since some studies have shown that early, prereading oral language-based training in awareness of these factors may lead to improved reading at a later stage, it is possible that there are underlying cognitive mechanisms that are not yet fully understood and that these abilities have to be integrated in a wider network at perhaps a critical stage if reading skills are to be acquired successfully at the usual age.

4.1 Developmental Lag Hypothesis

According to the developmental lag hypothesis, phonological deficits may occur at earlier age levels, but should have been overcome in older children. Studies by Lundberg and Høien (1989) however, found that older dyslexic groups performed at a substantially lower level than younger normally reading groups on phonological tasks, thus suggesting a biological determination.

4.2 Phonological Difficulties—The Core Problem?

Evidence that it would be premature to define the core deficit solely as a phonological one comes from Scarborough (1990). Her findings suggested that difficulties with syntactic and morphological aspects of language in the earliest preschool years may be more strongly related to later reading disabilities than were expressive phonological deficits. She proposed that the problem may involve broader structural language impairments or even more general symbolic rule learning difficulties, and was also careful to point out that these might just be correlates of some more important unidentified differences between dyslexic and nondyslexic children rather than an indication of an etiological relation between language development, and learning to read. Further evidence on the nonessentiality of phonological abilities for reading comes from the finding by Lundberg and Høien

(1989) that the persistence of phonological difficulties in a small sample of adults was not accompanied by reading problems.

4.3 Underlying Mechanisms?

It is possible that problems with phonology and problems with reading are part of some more general deficit. This is supported by the finding of a significant relationship between stuttering in adults and early articulation disorders, delayed language, and written language problems. The link between problems in oral and written language has been explained in terms of strengths and weaknesses of hemispheric functions by Gordon (1989), who found in a series of studies that verbosequential functions associated with the left hemisphere were performed less well by dyslexic subjects whereas visuospatial functions associated with the right cerebral hemisphere were often performed better by them and, further, that there was a familial concordance for those characteristics.

5. Language and Visual Problems—Chicken or Egg?

Vellutino (1979) among others presented strong evidence to suggest that visual problems in reading disorders were secondary to language-processing difficulties, as shown also by Gordon (1989). For language deficit dyslexics, Rayner (1989) suggested eye movements will reflect the difficulties the reader has with processing the printed word. On the other hand, reading difficulties have been ascribed to deficits in transient channel processing, and to binocular instability due to mildly disordered development of the specialized visuospatial functions of the right hemisphere. It would appear, however, that dyslexia manifests itself in many subtypes since this evidence is contrary to that of Gordon who proposed that dyslexics were particularly strong in visuospatial functioning.

6. Temporal Processing—An Underlying Deficit Common to Language and Reading Disorders?

Tallal and Katz (1989) proposed that the speech production of language impaired children might involve mistiming in the anticipation of coarticulatory gestures and that temporal processing disorders may constrain phonological processing for a large subgroup of dyslexics—just as for language-impaired children. They found a highly significant correlation between the degree of nonverbal acoustic temporal processing deficits and decoding deficits. In addition a number of studies have found that dyslexics manifest slower processing time for both linguistic and nonlinguistic stimuli (Whyte et al. 1985), and they provide evidence to suggest that the nature of the underlying deficit may lie in the inefficiency of neuronal connection, due possibly to differences in posterior brain symmetry. Such a mechanism may interfere with phonological analysis resulting in (a) speech and language disorders in young preschool age children and (b) disorders in reading development in older, school-age children.

7. Etiology of Language and Reading Difficulties—Neurobiological Advances

A number of verified observations have been made regarding the anatomy of the nervous system in reading disorders. Symmetry of the width of the posterior one-third of the cerebral hemisphere, the planum temporale, has been shown by MRI to be a feature of some cases of dyslexia and it has been found to be strongest in those children who also have oral language difficulty. This finding is supported by those of Galaburda et al. (1989) who have studied the postmortem brains of 10 people who were known to have been severely dyslexic. To what extent this symmetry is produced by direct genetic influence is not clear. On the other hand; it is also known that there are individuals with a symmetrical nervous system who show no obvious difficulty in reading. Thus, symmetry is only one feature of the dyslexic nervous system.

Galaburda (1989) has reported further findings of microscopic pathology consisting of first, focal cortical dysgenesis (e.g., ectopias and derangements of the layered pattern below these superficial cell clumps) and, second, fibromyeline plaques. It is suggested that these apparently minor changes in the surface of the brain seen on both sides—maximal left and more frontal than posterior—have a profound influence on the organization of the nervous system; they provoke unusual connections in the same and opposite hemispheres.

Further evidence for idiosyncratic physiological organization of the nervous system in those with reading disorders and in those with different levels of language ability has been found through the use of electroencephalography and its derivatives based on computer-assisted analysis of the power spectrum. Studies of cerebral blood flow and PET scans have suggested a reduction in the left posterior hemisphere during reading tasks among those with reading disabilities. A relationship between specific skills and more general abilities has been suggested, with reports of a relationship between patterns of localization of essential areas for reading or naming in temporal lobe and overall verbal performance as measured by VIQ. Further, there is evidence that the area used for naming is smaller where there is greater facility with language, thus possibly releasing capacity for later acquired language skills such as reading. The later acquisition of reading by language-disordered children could be explained by this model in that the neuronal circuits necessary only become available as earlier language skills are acquired and perfected.

8. Language and Reading Difficulties—Familial Implications

The possibility of familial mechanisms has also been investigated through a number of studies of twins with one member of each pair being reading disabled. Results suggest that there may be genetic factors involved—there is a concordance rate of 71 percent for identical twins against a concordance rate of 49 percent for fraternal twins (deFries and Gillis 1990)—and that these are more important for phonological skills than for orthographic skills. Research is being carried out in the area of linkage analysis using extended family studies which compare a gene's transmission through a family with the transmission of known genetic markers to determine if a gene and any of the markers are linked. Smith et al. (1990) have been able to conclude that there may be a locus on chromosome 6 that has a major effect on dyslexia. The centrometric region of chromosome 15 has also been pinpointed as the possible location of another rarer gene which has a major effect and there are indications that there may be a nondominant gene further down the long arm of chromosome 15.

9. Remediation

It is generally acknowledged that most disabled readers' problems relate to language deficits. Research on remediation has focused on the use of computers with synthetic speech feedback. Controversy still rages about the merits and otherwise of a structured phonic approach versus a more holistic language- and cognitive-based approach in person-to-person remedial teaching. There are no good data (Stanovich 1991) indicating that discrepancy-defined dyslexics respond differently to educational treatments than do "garden variety" poor readers of the same age or than do younger nondyslexic children reading at the same level. The data on differential prognosis for reading are contradictory.

10. Conclusion

While a link between language and reading disorders has been established for many children, there are also children with reading difficulties who seem to have little or no problem in speech perception or speech production. There are still problems in defining dyslexia, as a subset of reading difficulties with a range of subtypes, and its etiology is by no means established. Research is proceeding on all these fronts.

See also: Developmental Disabilities: Severe; Developmental Psychopathology; Language Development; Language in Education, Changing Views of: Anthropological Perspectives; Speech and Language Handicapped: Overview

References

Byers-Brown B, Edwards M 1989 *Developmental Disorders of Language*. Whurr, London

deFries J C, Gillis J J 1990 Etiology of reading deficits in learning disabilities: Quantitative genetic analysis. In: Obrzut J E, Hynd G W (eds.) 1990 *Advances in the Neuropsychology of Learning Disabilities: Methods and Practice*. Academic Press, Orlando, Florida

Galaburda A M, Rosen G F, Sherman G D 1989 The neural origin of developmental dyslexia: Implications for medicine, neurology and cognition. In: Galaburda A M (ed.) 1989 *From Reading to Neurons*. MIT Press, Cambridge, Massachusetts

German D J 1989 A diagnostic model and a test to assess word-finding skills in children. *Br. J. Disord. Commun.* 24(1): 21–39

Gordon H W 1989 The problem of studying specific learning disabilities and the contribution of hemispheric specialization. *Irish Journal of Psychology* 10(4): 479–93

Lahey M 1988 *Language Disorders and Language Development*. Macmillan Inc., New York

Landau W M, Kleffner F R 1957 Syndrome of acquired aphasia with convulsive disorder in children. *Neurology* 7: 523–30

Lees J, Urwin S 1991 *Children with Language Disorders*. Whurr, London

Lundberg I, Høien T 1989 Phonemic deficits: A core symptom of developmental dyslexia? *Irish Journal of Psychology* 10(4): 579–92

McGinnis M 1963 *Aphasic Children: Identification and Education by the Association Method*. Alexander Graham Bell Association for the Deaf, Washington, DC

Miles T 1991 On determining the prevalence of dyslexia. In: Snowling M, Thomson M (eds.) 1991 *Dyslexia: Integrating Theory and Practice*. Blackwell, London

Rapin I, Allen D A 1983 Developmental language disorders: Nosological considerations. In: Kirk U (ed.) 1983 *Neuropsychology of Language, Reading and Spelling*. Academic Press, New York

Rapin I, Allen D A 1987 Developmental dysphasia and autism in preschool children. In: Martin A, Fletcher P, Grunwell P, Hall D (eds.) 1987 *Proceedings of First International Symposium: Specific Speech and Language Disorders in Children*. University of Reading

Rayner K 1989 Eye movements and the perceptual span in beginning and dyslexic readers. In: von Euler C, Lundberg I, Lennerstrand G (eds.) 1989 *Brain and Reading*. Macmillan, London

Scarborough H 1990 Antecedents to reading disability: Preschool language development and literacy experiences of children from dyslexic families. *Reading and Writing*

Smith S D, Pennington B F, Kimberling W J, Ing P S 1990 Familial dyslexia: Use of genetic linkage data to define subtypes. *Journal of the American Academy of Child and Adolescent Psychiatry* 29(2): 204–13

Stackhouse J 1992 Developmental verbal dyspraxia, 1: A review and critique. *European Journal of Disorders of Communication* 27(1): 19–34

Stackhouse J, Wells B 1991 Dyslexia: The obvious and

hidden speech and language disorder. In: Snowling M, Thomson M (eds.) 1991 *Dyslexia: Integrating Theory and Practice*. Whurr, London

Stanovich K E 1991 The theoretical and practical consequences of discrepancy definitions of dyslexia. In: Snowling M, Thomson M (eds.) 1991 *Dyslexia: Integrating Theory and Practice*. Whurr, London

Supple M de M 1989 Phonological disability and reading: What is the link? *Irish Journal of Psychology* 10(4): 568–78

Tallal P, Katz W 1989 Neuropsychological and neuroanatomical studies of developmental language/reading disorders: Recent advances. In: von Euler C, Lundberg I, Lennerstrand G (eds.) 1989 *Brain and Reading*. Macmillan, London

Vellutino F 1979 *Dyslexia: Theory and Research*. MIT Press: Cambridge, Massachusetts

Whyte J 1989 Progress in dyslexia research. *Irish Journal of Psychology* 10(4): 465–78

Whyte J, Curry C, Hale D 1985 Inspection time and intelligence in dyslexic children. *J. Child Psychol. Psychiatry* 26(3): 423–28

Worster-Drought C, Allen I M 1930 Congenital auditory imperception. *J. Neurol. Psychopathol.* 10: 193–236

Further Reading

Kavanagh J F, Truss T J 1988 *Learning Disabilities: Proceedings of the National Conference*. York Press, Maryland

M. Supple; J. Whyte

Specific Learning Disability

1. History and Background

The term "learning disabilities" was proposed by Samuel Kirk in 1963. However, the historical and conceptual roots of learning disabilities may be found in the work of nineteenth- and early twentieth-century physicians in the United Kingdom, France, and Germany. Individuals such as John Bouillaud, Pierre Broca, Carl Wernicke, Henry Head, and James Henchelwood sought to identify brain–behavior relationships particularly focusing on brain pathology and written and/or oral language disorders (Wiederholt 1974).

Broca hypothesized that the left side of the brain was endowed with functions that differed from the right side. He attempted to localize speech disorders to specific areas of the cerebral cortex. Wernicke proposed that aphasia came about from interruptions of neural tracks that connected auditory and speech areas of the brain. Much of the early work on disorders of written language was gathered from the study of adults with acquired brain damage. Henchelwood identified a condition in one of his patients as "word blindness." With this condition, the patient may have normal vision but be no longer able to interpret written or printed language. Subsequent autopsy revealed that the patient with this disorder evidenced rather specific brain pathology. Henchelwood believed that adult cases of word blindness had relevance to school-age children with reading disorders. In fact, he labeled these cases "congenital word blindness." Henchelwood proposed that student difficulties in learning to read may be explained by brain defects that affect the storage of visual memories of words and letters. He suggested a reading instructional program that addressed the remediation of this visual memory deficit. After extensive study of both written and oral language disorders, Samuel Orton (1937) proposed that the location of brain pathology was of greater importance than the amount of brain tissue destroyed; he further believed that one side of the brain was all-important for language function. He argued that normal adults used only one side of the brain for reading. He recommended a reading remediation program that involved the use of multisensory learning, vision, audition, and kinesthetic approaches.

The field of learning disabilities has also been influenced by work on perceptual and motor disorders. A German physician, Kurt Goldstein, engaged in extensive study of brain-injured First World War soldiers. His work provided powerful support for the effects of brain damage on a range of cognitive, perceptual–motor, and affective functions. In turn, his research provided an important conceptual foundation for the work of Alfred Strauss and Heinz Werner with brain-injured mentally retarded children. Working with residentially placed mentally retarded children in the United States, Werner and Strauss distinguished between exogenous and endogenous mental retardation associated with neurological impairments and unspecified familial factors, respectively (Strauss and Lehtinen 1947). They noted similarities in the behavioral characteristics of exogenous children and the characteristics of the brain-injured soldiers described by Goldstein. These characteristics included perceptual disorders, distractibility, uninhibited and less socially acceptable behaviors, and perseveration. Nonretarded children who evidenced this cluster of behaviors were subsequently diagnosed in the 1950s with Strauss' Syndrome. The work of Strauss and his colleagues had a significant influence on the development and implementation of educational programs with an emphasis on perceptual deficits (see Cruickshank et al. 1961, Frostig and Horne 1964, Kephart 1971). Psychiatrists and educators subsequently proposed that the presence of these behavioral, perceptual, and cognitive difficulties may be signs of neurological impairment.

In the spring of 1963 Professor Samuel Kirk, then at the University of Illinois, addressed a meeting of parents and professionals held in Chicago. The purpose of the meeting was to organize an effort to gain educational services for children who were having extensive learning problems in school yet were not retarded, emotionally disturbed, or evidencing sensory handicaps. One of the primary purposes of this meeting was to develop a single, common label to describe children who were identified as having minimal brain damage, perceptual disorders, psychoneurological disorders, Strauss' Syndrome, hyperkinetic disorder, dyslexia, and a host of other terms. Owing to his concern for the potential negative effects of these diagnostic labels on children, Kirk proposed that these various behavioral, cognitive, and perceptual problems be subsumed under a broader behavioral term: "learning disabilities."

The history of learning disabilities reveals a multidisciplinary focus in which medicine played an early and ongoing role in the conceptual development of the field. Much of the understanding of the characteristics of the learning-disabled child grew out of work on adults with diagnosed brain injury and on retarded children. Recognizing the ebb and flow in interest related to brain injury or dysfunction in the history of learning disabilities, there has since been renewed interest by many physicians and neuropsychologists on neurological dysfunctions associated with this disorder. The roots of many of the educational approaches found in the 1990s may be traced to the recommendations physicians made 50 years before, for example, remediation of deficits, multisensory approaches to instruction, and use of students' compensatory abilities. The multidisciplinary nature of the field of learning disabilities and the breadth of characteristics subsumed under the label "learning disabilities," has provided a richness of perspectives and data, but has also suffered from a lack of conceptual focus that has affected both research and practice in the field.

2. *Definition*

In an attempt to define the students whose disorders in language, speech, reading, and associated communication skills he had labeled "learning disabilities," Kirk specifically excluded children who might evidence the previously noted problems but have sensory impairments or mental retardation. One of the first governmental attempts to develop a definition of learning disabilities was initiated in 1967 by the United States National Institute of Neurological Diseases and Blindness (Clements 1966). This definition directly linked learning disabilities to minimal brain dysfunction. A year later the First United States National Advisory Committee on Handicapped Children proposed a definition of learning disabilities which focused on disorders of basic psychological processes and de-emphasized the impact of neurological dysfunctions. This definition was subsequently incorporated into the 1969 Children With Specific Learning Disabilities Act and the Education For All Handicapped Children Act in 1975. Disagreements concerning this definition induced the United States Interagency Committee on Learning Disabilities to modify the definition of learning disabilities in 1987. The definition stresses the heterogeneity of the condition and emphasizes the nature of the problem as intrinsic to the student and although definitional concerns continue to exist, it is this definition which is presented below as it represents one perspective on the issue:

> Learning disabilities is a generic term that refers to a heterogeneous group of disorders manifested by significant difficulties in the acquisition and use of listening, speaking, reading, writing, reasoning, or mathematical abilities, or of social skills. These disorders are intrinsic to the individual and presumed to be due to central nervous system dysfunction. Even though a learning disability may occur concomitantly with other handicapping conditions (e.g., sensory impairment, mental retardation, social and emotional disturbance), with socio-environmental influences (e.g., cultural differences, insufficient or inappropriate instruction, psychogenic factors), and especially with attention deficit disorder, all of which may cause learning problems, a learning disability is not the direct result of those conditions or influences. (Interagency Committee on Learning Disabilities 1987 p. 222)

Despite differences and disagreements among professionals in the United States regarding the nature and definition of learning disabilities, there is some consensual agreement concerning certain premises. The first premise is that learning-disabled students evidence a discrepancy between their ability and their achievement, that is, they do not achieve at a level commensurate with their overall intellectual ability. This concept of discrepancy distinguishes learning-disabled students from individuals with academic difficulties, who are identified as retarded or slow learners. While there appears to be consistent support for this definitional marker, there is a great deal of controversy regarding how much discrepancy is necessary to constitute a learning disability, the technical adequacy of assessment instruments to determine a discrepancy, and the appropriateness of various statistical formulas to derive a discrepancy (Swanson 1991). A second premise is that the problems of a learning-disabled child may have a concomitant relationship with but not be caused by other disabilities. Unfortunately, since students with a variety of disabilities may display similar learning and behavior problems it is frequently difficult to determine which disability is primary. Was a learning disability the cause of an emotional or behavioral problem or was a sensory or emotional disorder the cause of the learning disability? The third premise that provides a common marker for learning-disabled students is that the learning problems are due to factors that are internal to the child and as such do not reflect a teaching failure or an experiential deficit. It is unclear, however, what the critical internal characteristics are, for example, neurological status, information processing deficits, cognitive styles, and so on. Moreover, recognition of the transactional nature of development, which requires consideration of both the child and the caregiving or instructional context, has increased.

The Commission of the European Communities Studies (1980) describes children with learning disabilities as children who evidence spelling retardation, word-blindness, dyslexia, dysgraphy, dyscalculism, retarded perception, and "environmentally conditioned" difficulties. Because of these difficulties the children do not benefit sufficiently from ordinary instruction. In Germany, children with learning disabilities are defined as those children who show marked disturbances or impairments concerning learning abilities and who are in need of educational and therapeutical intervention.

In the United Kingdom, learning-disabled children are called "children with learning difficulties," and are described as students who are not able to progress at the same rate as other children their age (Department of Education and Science 1981). In Belgium, France, and Italy, definitions are found for children with learning problems and language delay which have special characteristics that require a special curriculum and educational help (Commission of the European Communities 1980). In many countries, for instance, Agesia, Barbados, Botswana, China, Egypt, Ethiopia, Malawi, Madagascar, Mali, Panama, Saudi Arabia, Senegal, Syria, Tunisia, Uganda, Yugoslavia, and Zaire (UNESCO 1988) learning disablement is not identified as a category of disability at all.

In Europe it is generally assumed that learning disabilities and learning difficulties may be caused by biological and/or environmental factors. Economic, ecologic, and specific cultural factors of the child's environment may cause learning disabilities. Many learning-disabled children come from disadvantaged social and cultural environments (Montogomery 1990). In many cases it is assumed that the school is responsible for the learning difficulties, because moderate learning disabilities become apparent only after the child enters school (Croll and Moses 1985, Hell 1984, Montgomery 1990).

3. Prevalence

According to the United States Department of Education (1991) *Thirteenth Annual Report to Congress*, children with disabilities between the ages of 6 and 17 comprised approximately 10 percent of the nation's population for the 1989–90 school year. Over 2 million students were identified as learning disabled; this comprises 48.5 percent of the total number of students identified as disabled within the United States. Since 1976–77, the number of students with learning disabilities has grown by 1,256,007 or 160 percent. The relative proportion of these students, as a function of the total number of disabled children served, increased from 24.9 percent in 1976–77 to 48.5 percent in 1989–90. The growth rate in the number of students identified as having learning disabilities has exceeded any other disability. Across the 50 states, there was considerable variation in the percentage of students identified as learning disabled, with some states identifying less than 2 percent of their population aged 6 to 21, while other states had identified almost 6 percent of their population between those ages. Despite the presumption that learning disabilities are due to factors intrinsic to the individual, a variety of systemic factors including levels of school funding, the ethnicity and socioeconomic background of students, and the variation of assessment procedures and instrumentation may play a significant role in influencing the prevalence of learning-disabled children.

Similar rates and variability of prevalence are also found in Europe. For example, in Germany, states have identified between 2 and 6 percent of schoolchildren as learning disabled (Bildung und Wissenschaft 1985). In Bavaria 2.6 percent of the children are considered to have learning disabilities, in Schleswig-Holstein 4.8 percent (Kerkhoff 1980). In England and Wales learning-disabled children account for approximately 3.6 percent of students in regular schools (Department of Education and Science 1978).

4. Diagnosis and Intervention

The multidisciplinary and multitheoretical nature of the field has resulted in the development and implementation of many varied approaches to the diagnosis of and intervention with learning-disabled students. In the United States a general cognitive (IQ test) measure and an achievement measure are two commonly used assessment tools. These measures are selected primarily to rule out the possibility of mental retardation and to insure that there is a significant ability–achievement discrepancy. While IQ and achievement tests are consistently used, there is a great deal of variability in additional measures that have been used to assist in the diagnosis. It has been estimated that over a thousand different measures have been implemented to assist in the identification of learning-disabled students (Keogh et al. 1982). These measures were designed to reflect particular neurological, perceptual–motor, perceptual, or cognitive processing problems within students.

Educational researchers have determined that assessment primarily plays a confirming role in diagnosing these students (Ysseldyke and Thurlow 1984). Regular classroom teachers are the primary referral agents for these students. The diagnostic and placement process for learning-disabled students begins with recognition by a regular classroom teacher that the student is having significant achievement difficulties that may not be due to a general cognitive deficit. Furthermore, the decision by the teacher to refer reflects teachers' recognition that they can not effectively educate that child within their classrooms. Once a student has been referred, there is a high probability that the referred student will be assessed and subsequently diagnosed as learning disabled. In fact, many students may be identified as learning disabled and placed in special education programs even when the psychometric test results fail to document a severe discrepancy. Furthermore, many of the psychometric measures used do not have adequate reliability or validity to determine the presence or absence of an ability–achievement discrepancy.

Many teachers have expressed concern regarding the limited utility of diagnostic psychometric procedures in planning or implementing an intervention program. These concerns have resulted in the increased use of curriculum-based assessment measures which provide a direct indication of the child's performance on tasks that are relevant to classroom instruction (Shinn 1989). Educators are also recommending assessment procedures that provide insight into students' information-processing activities to include consideration of students' metacognitive characteristics, use of cognitive strategies, and attentional characteristics (Swanson 1984).

With remarkable consistency, similar tests (or test types, such as IQ and achievement tests) and/or test procedures are used to diagnose learning disabilities internationally, even when national test norms are not available (Montgomery 1990, UNESCO 1988). In the majority of countries the decision to provide special education services to a student is made by an interdisciplinary team. This team may include a teacher, doctor, psychologists, other education specialists, and school administration officials. Parents may be included as part of the assessment procedure, but are not always asked for their opinion in the placement of their children in special classes; this is the case in most of the developing countries. Parents are rarely included in the child's educational plan (with the exception of Denmark and the US). In some cases the child is included in the decision (as in France, Denmark, and the US).

Paralleling the diagnostic approaches, a variety of treatment recommendations have been proposed to manage the learning-disabled student effectively (Lloyd 1988). These treatment approaches include the use of medication, modified diet, language-based remediation, developmental visual training, sensory integration training, psychotherapy, behavioral modification procedures, direct instruction, content-based intervention programs, and cognitive strategy programs, among others. In Germany, intervention methods attempt to address students' individual needs and are macropedagogic, that is, they take into consideration the whole person (Baier 1980). Macropedagogic measures include therapy, behavioral intervention, and special classes for subject matters. The intervention approaches developed prior to 1970 were primarily derived from work on disabled children; however, many of the more recent instructional innovations have evolved from programs for educationally at-risk, but not disabled, students. For example, programs in the area of direct instruction were derived, in large part, from work with economically disadvantaged children educated in regular classrooms. These programs have been subsequently tested and implemented with learning-disabled students with some considerable success. In the United States there is a growing consensus that specialized intervention programs may work for small numbers of learning-disabled children with unique problems; however, many children may benefit from the same instructional programs that have been implemented effectively with nondisabled students.

5. Educational Directions

Instructional arrangements for learning-disabled students vary tremendously across the international community (UNESCO 1988). For example, during the 1989–90 school year only 1 percent of students identified as learning disabled in the United States were educated in separate schools while 59 percent were taught in resource room settings in regular public schools (see *Resource Room Programs as a Special Education Model*), 20 percent in special-class settings, and 20 percent in regular classroom settings (United States Department of Education 1991). In contrast, special schools are the primary education delivery system used to educate students with learning disabilities in Germany. Other countries in Europe, such as Denmark, educate less than 1 percent of their learning-disabled students in special-school settings. Furthermore, while resource-room settings are the primary special education delivery system in the United States, individual states differ in their preference of educational arrangements. Less than 10 percent of learning-disabled students in Vermont are placed in resource rooms, whereas Alabama uses resource rooms to serve approximately 90 percent of those of their students identified as learning disabled. In Vermont almost 80 percent of such students identified as learning disabled are educated in regular classrooms, yet less than 1 percent of the students in New York state are served in regular classroom settings. Separate-class educational arrangements are used for only 1 percent of learning-disabled students in Idaho, South Dakota, and Vermont, while over 44 percent of learning-disabled students in New Jersey and New York are served in separate-class settings.

UNESCO (1988) summarized the following national preferences in the primary instructional arrangements to instruct children with learning difficulties: special day-schools (e.g., in Jordan, Brazil, Costa

Rica, Czechoslovakia, Ecuador, El Salvador, Guatemala, Indonesia, Iraq, Israel, Malta, Uruguay, and Zambia); special classes in regular schools (in countries including Chile, Cuba, Denmark, Argentina, Costa Rica, Ecuador, Finland, Guatemala, Israel, Nicaragua, Nigeria, Poland, Sri Lanka, Sweden, Thailand, Venezuela, and Zambia); integrated group units (e.g., in Mexico); and/or support teaching in the regular class (in countries including Ecuador, Denmark, Netherlands, Costa Rica, England, Finland, Guatemala, Indonesia, New Zealand, Poland, Rumania, Sri Lanka, Sweden, Uruguay, Venezuela, Zambia, and Thailand). In Norway learning-disabled children are fully integrated into the normal education system. In Belgium, France, and Italy a large number of the learning-disabled children are provided for in private schools. In Ireland, all children with learning difficulties are provided for in private schools. The variation across states within the United States and internationally may reflect differences in educational philosophy and indicate significant variation in the nature of the students that are served.

Two broad areas in which there have been program development efforts internationally are early intervention with preschool-aged children and the transition of learning-disabled individuals from school to work. The countries of the European Community are attempting to integrate learning-disabled children into preschool educational programs. The United States and the European Community are also moving forward in the provision of assistance, guidance, further training, and vocational placement after learning-disabled children leave compulsory school. Some countries (e.g. Denmark, Germany, Ireland, Chile, Finland, Israel, New Zealand, Nicaragua, Nigeria, Norway, and Venezuela) offer education for the learning disabled after compulsory education in the form of vocational education. In Germany, different governmental departments (e.g. the Department of Work, the Department of Vocational Education, and the Department of Special Schools) try to offer work opportunities to these students. The Department of Work provides a list of offices where learning-disabled persons can find a job after vocational education. Students who complete their education in separate schools for the learning disabled but are not employed are provided vocational education programs by the Ministry of Education and Research. Students who continue to have difficulties in the transition from school to employment will be helped through special classes until they are ready to enter the workforce.

In developing countries (e.g., Jordan and Mexico), educational activities focus on more basic areas of educational planning organization, management, financing, legislation enforcement, training of personnel, and the development of culturally appropriate assessment and diagnostic materials. In many developing countries the education of the learning-disabled child was the responsibility of the family. The development of legislation to support the education of disabled students is a high priority. Developing countries share many educational concerns with industrialized countries, particularly in the areas of integration into regular schools, curriculum development, vocational rehabilitation, and job placement. The social, cultural, and economic characteristics of developing nations influence the development of educational provisions for disabled students. Generally, where resources are limited, children with learning difficulties are not educated at all; in many countries they are excluded from the state educational system.

6. *Necessary Research*

To further understanding of learning disabilities, and to support the development of efficacious intervention programs for students affected by them, the following recommended areas for research activity are proposed. First, it is recommended that research activities examine the nature and validity of learning disabilities as an independent disability condition. While most educational researchers agree on the existence of learning disabilities, student heterogeneity, definitional confusion, and diagnostic controversy have frustrated the accumulation of a reliable and valid research base. In turn, controversy continues on basic issues of diagnosis and intervention.

A second area in which research is needed is the interaction of theoretically and empirically based subgroups of learning-disabled students, the nature of instructional tasks, and the design of intervention programs. Information from this program of research may help further define the nature of students' problems within the context of instructional tasks. These research findings would also help in the selection and implementation of instructional activities that are tailored for students.

A third area of research should concern the investigation of contextual variables such as cultural and socioeconomic background variables on students' performance. The majority of the world's children under the age of 5 live in developing countries where infant and preschool mortality rates are similar to those of nineteenth-century Europe. The physical conditions that surround the development of children in these areas clearly reflect the impact of broad cultural factors on at-risk children. Technological advances in Western industrialized societies have led to the survival of many children who would have died at infancy, but have also created additional risk factors for young children, such as lead poisoning. Further, the definition and expression of risk is affected not only by technology in a culture, but also by the demands made on children for education (Werner

1986). While many children in developing countries will leave school after the completion of elementary grades, most children in the United States and Europe are expected to complete high school and possibly receive some additional training to compete for jobs that require an ever-increasing level of mathematical and scientific literacy. There is concern both in the United States and Europe with the impact of broad demographic variables on students' school performance which may subsequently lead to their referral and the identification of learning disability. There is mounting evidence that matching ethnically diverse students on standardized measures of cognitive performance does not indicate cognitive equivalence between ethnic samples (Palmer et al. 1989). Work in this area may provide insight into the possible misidentification of culturally and linguistically diverse children and assist in the development of effective instructional programs for these children.

The fourth area in need of research requires a longitudinal study of learning-disabled students that would focus on the sources of internal and external stresses and support for the learning-disabled student. Such a program of research might increase the understanding of protective factors that may reduce the long-term impact and negative consequences of learning disabilities.

See also: Brain Development and Human Behavior; Learning Characteristics of Students with Special Needs; Learning Theories: Historical Overview and Trends

References

Baier H 1980 *Einführung in die Lernbehindertenpädagogik*. Kohlhammer, Stuttgart

Bildung und Wissenschaft 1985 *Education and Research*, Report Nos. 9–10. Inter Nationes, Bonn

Clements S D 1966 *Minimal Brain Dysfunction in Children*. National Society for Crippled Children/National Institute of Neurological Diseases and Blindness, Washington, DC

Commission of the European Communities Studies 1980 *Special Education in the European Community*, Education Series No. 11. Collection Studies, Brussels

Croll P, Moses D 1985 *One in Five*. Routledge & Kegan Paul, London

Cruickshank W M, Bentzer F-A, Ratzeberu F H, Tannhausser M T 1961 *A Teaching Method for Brain-injured and Hyperactive Children*. Syracuse University Press, Syracuse, New York

Department of Education and Science 1978 *Special Education Needs* (The Warnock Report). HMSO, London

Department of Education and Science 1981 *Education Act*. HMSO, London

Frostig M, Horne D 1964 *The Frostig Program for the Development of Visual Perception*. Follet, Chicago, Illinois

Goldstein, K 1936 The modifications of behavior consequent to cerebral lesions. *Psychiatric Q*. 10: 586–610

Hell P 1984 *Differenzierung oder Integration: Ein Beitrag zur adäquaten Beschulung Lernbehinderter aus schulpädagogischer Sicht*. Peter Lang, Frankfurt

Henchelwood J 1917 *Congenital Word Blindness*. Lewis, London

Interagency Committee on Learning Disabilities 1987 *A Report to the U.S. Congress*. National Institutes of Health, Bethesda, Maryland

Keogh B K, Major-Kingsley S, Omori-Gordon L, Reid H P 1982 *A System of Marker Variables for the Field of Learning Disabilities*. Syracuse University Press, Syracuse, New York

Kephart N C 1971 *The Slow Learner in the Classroom*. Merrill, Columbus, Ohio

Kerkhoff W 1980 Behinderte in Sonderschulen: Ein statistischer Uberblick. *Sonderpädagogik* 10: 20–33

Lloyd J W 1988 Direct academic intervention in learning disabilities. In: Wang M C, Reynolds M C, Walberg H J (eds.) 1988 *Handbook of Special Education: Research and Practice*. Pergamon Press, New York

Montgomery D 1990 *Children with Learning Difficulties: Special Needs in Ordinary Schools*. Cassell, London

Orton S T 1937 *Reading, Writing and Speech Problems in Children*. Norton, New York

Palmer D J, Olivarez A, Willson V L, Fordyce T 1989 Ethnicity and language dominance—Influence on the prediction of achievement based on intelligence test scores in nonreferred and referred samples. *Learn. Disab. Q*. 12(4): 261–74

Shinn M R (ed.) 1989 *Curriculum-based Measurement, Assessing Special Children*. The Guilford Press, New York

Strauss A A, Lehtinen L E 1947 *Psychopathology and Education of the Brain-injured Child*. Grune & Stratton, New York

Swanson H L 1984 Process assessment of intelligence in learning disabled and mentally retarded children: A multidirectional model. *Educ. Psychol*. 19: 149–62

Swanson H L 1991 Operational definitions and learning disabilities: An overview. *Learn. Disab. Q*. 14(4): 242–54

UNESCO 1988 *UNESCO Consultation on Special Education*, Final Report UNESCO Paris

United States Department of Education 1991 *Thirteenth Annual Report to Congress*. US Department of Education, Washington, DC

Werner E E 1986 The concept of risk from a developmental perspective. In: Keogh B K (ed.) *Advances in Special Education*, Vol. 5. JAI Press, Greenwich, Connecticut

Wiederholt J L1974 Historical perspectives on the education of the learning disabled. In: Mann L, Sabatino D A (eds.) 1974 *The Second Review of Special Education*. JSE Press, Philadelphia, Pennsylvania

Ysseldyke J E, Thurlow M L 1984 Assessment practices in special education: Adequacy and appropriateness. *Educ. Psychol*. 9(3): 123–36.

D. J. Palmer; A. Calero-Breckheimer

Speech and Language Disorders and the Hard of Hearing

The topic of speech and language disorders in the hard of hearing population (i.e., those with mild to moderate hearing losses) is a complex issue though it has not been systematically studied. This entry will explore three main areas concerning speech and language disorders in the hard of hearing. First, the speech and language disorders in children with permanent hearing loss will be described. Second, speech and language disorders in children with fluctuating hearing loss will be reviewed. Finally, speech and language disorders in adults will be illustrated.

1. Scope and Nature of the Problem

1.1 Demographic Data

The large numbers of people worldwide with varying degrees of deafness are well-illustrated by the United States. According to the United States National Institute on Deafness and Other Communication Disorders, more than 28 million Americans have a hearing loss; of those 28 million, approximately 2 million are profoundly deaf. Furthermore, more than one-third of the United States population has a significant hearing impairment by age 65 (Davis and Hardick 1986). In children, otitis media is the most common cause of temporary hearing loss, with 70 percent of infants and young children having otitis media by age 3 (Giebink and Daly 1990). Berg and Fletcher (cited in Davis and Hardick 1986) estimated that in the United States there are approximately 1.2 million hearing-impaired children with sensori-neural losses. Of that number, about 600,000 are thought to have a mild loss, 350,000 a moderate loss, and 140,000 a severe loss. They further estimate that 150,000 children need extensive speech-language, communication, academic, and counseling services, while another 950,000 require less extensive but still necessary services. Also, data indicate that there are at least 20 times as many children with mild to moderate losses as those with severe to profound losses (Davis and Hardick 1986). In addition, modern technology has enabled individuals once labeled as "deaf" to function more like a "hard of hearing" person. Also, because of societal opinions, as well as familial influences, many "deaf" individuals (with reference to their audiograms) do not consider themselves deaf or part of the deaf culture. Thus, a problem exists when attempting to classify hearing-impaired individuals beyond the audiogram.

1.2 The Relationship between Hearing Loss and Speech and Language Disorders

Language is the foundation for thinking, learning, and communication in general. Hearing loss affects that foundation for speech and language learning in particular. For children, hearing impairment directly influences speech and language acquisition. For adults, hearing impairment may affect speech production and voice quality. The degree of speech and language impairment from hearing loss is extremely variable. The relationship between hearing loss and speech-language disorders is influenced by age of onset of the hearing loss; age of identification of the hearing loss; fluctuation, permanence, and progression of the loss; intervention, including various (re)habilitation measures (amplification and assistive devices); educational placement; and support systems. Speech–language disorders in hard-of-hearing children (with permanent and fluctuating hearing losses) and adults (with postlingual hearing losses) are presented below.

2. Speech–Language Disorders in Children with Permanent Hearing Loss

The majority of hearing-impaired children show communication delays in the following areas: (a) language comprehension, (b) language production, (c) speech perception, (d) speech production, and (e) classroom discourse. Although hearing-impaired children tend to exhibit speech and language deficits in the domains cited above, the developmental sequence is similar to that of normal-hearing children, albeit delayed (Robbins 1986).

2.1 Language Comprehension

Delays in this area are exhibited in all realms of language comprehension: vocabulary, syntax and morphology, concepts, and connected language (Robbins 1986). Specifically, hearing-impaired children have difficulty in learning abstraction in word meanings and the grammatical rules of the language and in developing object classes. They also confuse grammatical rules (Northern 1986).

Quinn and Tomblin (1985, cited in Robbins 1986) found that many hearing-impaired children rely solely on the "order-of-mention" technique in which the child interprets the utterances in the order in which they are presented. For example, a hearing-impaired child would construe the sentence, "the man was bitten by the dog" as if the man bit the dog. Also, they note that hearing-impaired children are less likely than children with normal hearing to use a "probable event" scheme in which past experience defines the linkage between words. Moreover, hearing-impaired children do not typically comprehend multiple meanings of words in one context without generalizing that meaning to another context.

2.2 Language Production

The majority of information on the language skills of hearing-impaired children deals with production of language. Production of language does not develop in isolation from language comprehension; the two are inextricably linked, although their interaction is not well-defined. In normal-hearing children, many hypotheses have stated that comprehension of a particular language structure precedes production of that structure (Fraser et al. 1963). However, subsequent studies have indicated that this stringent order may not always hold (Bloom 1974 in Robbins 1986). This link of production and comprehension may be even more difficult to discern in hearing-impaired children who are attempting to acquire language through an aural mode. The relationship between production and comprehension is also affected by clinicians who may tend to focus more on production than comprehension, since production is more readily observed than comprehension (Robbins 1986). In other words, language production is more prone to instantaneous feedback and monitoring, while comprehension is addressed more surreptitiously.

Another area of language production affected by hearing loss is vocabulary. Developing children normally exhibit a constant and consistent increase in the number of vocabulary items. Hearing-impaired children show a less systematic increase in their vocabularies. The degree of vocabulary deficit seems to be related to severity of hearing loss (Brannon 1968). In terms of specific word-class usage, hearing-impaired children use all word classes sufficiently with the exception of adverbs, pronouns, and auxiliaries, and tend to overuse nouns and articles (Davis and Hardick 1986).

2.3 Speech Perception

Deficits in language comprehension and production are not the only difficulties that hearing-impaired children exhibit. They show deficits in speech perception as well. One contribution of hearing loss to speech perception is the interruption of the coding of the speech signal in the central nervous system. This interruption may cause some or all of the speech signal to be impeded. Thus, a speech perception deficit occurs.

Both acoustic variables and linguistic variables affect speech perception (van Tasell 1986). Acoustic variables consist of length of the speech unit, its phonetic context, the delivered intensity, and noise level, while linguistic variables can be characterized as the length and complexity of utterances (p. 15). The acoustic and linguistic variables listed above may affect individuals differently in terms of their contribution to perception difficulties. For example, many hearing-impaired individuals will perform with 100 percent accuracy on a test of spondaic words but perform significantly worse on meaningful consonant-vowel-consonant (CVC) words (p. 24). The age and linguistic sophistication of the individual also help to determine the level of accuracy in the process of speech perception. Van Tasell notes, "the reduced amount of speech sound information to which the hearing-impaired listener has access may severely restrict the number of usable acoustic and linguistic cues. To the extent that phonetic information is preserved, the contextual information in speech will be used by hearing-impaired listeners in the same way as it is by normals" (Van Tasell 1986 p. 31). Concomitant language problems may also decrease the ability of hearing-impaired individuals to perceive speech.

2.4 Speech Production

The ability to produce normal speech is directly related to the viability of the auditory system; any impediment in that transmission will likely result in less-than-normal speech. For those children with hearing impairments, the degree of hearing loss bears directly on the ability to produce speech normally. However, it should not be inferred that two people with the same hearing loss will show exactly the same level of speech production skills.

In children with mild to moderate hearing losses, vowel quality is usually similar to that produced by normal-hearing children of the same age (West and Weber 1973). However, children with mild to moderate hearing losses typically exhibit misarticulations similar to those of children with normal hearing but articulation disorders. According to Davis and Hardick (1986), the most common sounds misarticulated by hard of hearing children are:/s/, /z/, ("sh"), /ʃ/, ("th" as in *th* ree), ("th" as in *th* is), /tʃ/ ("ch"), /dz/ ("j" as in judge), and /r/. They also tend to display the following speech patterns: omission of final consonants, infrequent production of voiced fricatives (i.e., /z/, /ð/, /ʒ/ "zh" as in measure), and rare use of voiced back consonants such as /g/, /ʤ/, and /ɔ/ ("ng" as in sing). Despite their misarticulations, hearing-impaired children develop speech sounds in the relative order witnessed in normal-hearing children (Davis and Hardick 1986).

The production of speech sounds is not the only production skill that might be impaired in these children. Depending on the severity of the loss and age of onset, hard-of-hearing children may or may not show suprasegmental errors involving voice inflections, intonational patterns, and stress patterns (Davis and Hardick 1986). They may also show a decline in rhythm, resulting in a speech rate which is slower than normal hearing children, and an increase in pauses related to poor breath control (Dunn and Newton 1986).

2.5 Classroom Discourse

The importance of the ability to use language in the natural environment of the classroom (rather than in such discrete units as receptive and expressive vocabulary or specific syntactic structures) was recognized in the 1980s (Cazden 1988). Davis and Hardick (1986) note that hearing-impaired children with mild to moderate losses are often successfully mainstreamed if they have benefited from early intervention and make optimal use of amplification.

Although there are few studies involving the characteristics of classroom discourse in hearing-impaired children with mild to moderate losses, some conclusions can be drawn. Compared with normal-hearing children, hearing-impaired children produce an equal number of contingent and noncontingent responses, while normal-hearing children produce many more contingent responses (Donnelly and Brackett 1982, cited in Weiss 1986). These authors also noted that the questions asked by hearing-impaired children are more often choice or concrete questions rather than process questions. Moreover, these children typically have good oral communication skills and develop language, reading, and writing skills within one year of their normal hearing peers (Davis and Hardick 1986).

3. *Speech–Language Disorders in Children with Fluctuation Hearing Loss*

Otitis media is the main cause of fluctuating hearing loss in children (Geibenk and Daly 1990). The incidence of otitis media seems to be quite high. Klein (1984, cited in Jenkins 1986) reported that more than two-thirds of the 2,565 children in his study had at least one episode of acute otitis media by the age of 3 years, and more than one-third had at least three episodes by the same age.

By narrowing the scope of investigation even further, researchers have found a number of general characteristics of those with otitis media (summarized in Jenkins 1986): sex differences (males at higher risk than females), race differences (Native Americans and Inuit at greater risk than the White American population, with African-Americans at an even lower risk), familial differences (higher risk if a sibling has had recurrent otitis media), experience differences (breast-fed children are at lower risk than bottle-fed children), individual differences (early onset, prior to 6 months of age, is predictive of later episodes), and clinical differences (children with cleft palate or Down's syndrome have a higher incidence).

Fluctuating hearing loss is often associated with chronic or recurrent otitis media. A child with persistent otitis media may receive a partial or inconsistent auditory signal, miss or confuse important auditory information, and inaccurately encode information (Roberts and Schuele 1990). Persistent otitis media in early childhood may predict later speech, language, learning, and academic difficulties.

Although the detrimental effects of fluctuation hearing loss on speech, language, and academic development have often been mentioned (e.g., Friel-Patti and Finitzo 1990), there are few studies that outline the specific effects of this type of hearing loss. Davis and Hardick (1986) summarized the available studies in this area. Children with hearing loss secondary to otitis media have shown the following characteristics, compared with normal-hearing peers: poorer language and auditory processing skills; delays in reading recognition, mathematical computation, and mathematical problem-solving skills; and reduced abilities in auditory memory and in listening in noise, auditory closure, and sentence repetition tasks. Moreover, even when there are no significant differences between hearing children and those with histories of otitis media, those with middle ear disfunction respond more slowly, appear anxious, seek visual cues, and express a lack of confidence. Kessler (1978, cited in Davis and Hardick 1986) noted that a significantly higher proportion of children described as having early middle ear disease are enrolled in special education to receive such services as reading and academic tutoring and speech-language therapy.

It is obvious that fluctuating hearing losses impact upon speech, language, academic, and reading development. Unfortunately, a fluctuating hearing loss in most children can go undetected for a number of reasons (Davis and Hardick 1986). One is that hearing loss, particularly of a mild nature, is not a tangible impairment. Often, neither the children nor their parents are aware of this level of hearing difficulty. A second reason is that routine and mandatory hearing screening programs do not exist in every school. Even when children are referred for testing, it is often not carried out. If testing is carried out in the school environment, the validity of results may be compromised as testing conditions may not be ideal. Often, in school settings, there is excessive noise and/or outdated and uncalibrated equipment. Finally, no professional group has assumed responsibility and advocacy for children with mild hearing losses.

4. *Speech–Language Disorders in Adults*

Although the speech–language, academic, and learning deficits described above in children with hearing impairment may continue into adulthood, adults who become hard of hearing in adulthood (i.e., postlingually) present a unique set of characteristics and issues. There are three main elements to appraise when describing the characteristics of individuals who became hearing impaired in adulthood (Davis and Hardick 1986): incidence of hearing loss; the major characteristics of hearing loss; and the psychosocial aspects of acquired hearing loss.

Estimates of the incidence of hearing loss in adults range from 13 percent to 25 percent (Spahr 1971). In 1969, the Subcommittee on Human Communication and its Disorders (Davis and Hardick 1986) concluded that in the United States: (a) there were 236,000 deaf individuals of all ages and sexes; (b) approximately 6 million additional Americans had bilateral impairments of a significant degree; (c) there were an additional 2.5 million adults with unilateral hearing impairment; and (d) about 700,000 people had a concomitant handicapping visual deficit. Further, incidence data suggest that no more than 8 percent have pure tone average losses in excess of 77 dB, and that 79 percent have average hearing losses no worse than 56 dB. In addition, the situation is worsened by the fact that approximately 25 percent of American adults over 65 live alone and in poverty, thereby without access to appropriate otological and audiological services.

There is little information on the speech and language characteristics of adults with mild to moderate hearing losses. Common speech and language characteristics of postlingually hearing-impaired adults are affected by etiology, audiometric configuration, type and amount of loss in the two ears, auditory discrimination scores, and age of onset (Davis and Hardick 1986). Adults may exhibit conductive, sensori-neural, or mixed hearing losses. Most common etiologies are presbycusis (hearing loss related to aging) and noise-induced hearing loss. However, other etiologies may be due, though not limited, to ototoxic drugs, head trauma, Ménière's syndrome, labyrinthine otospongeosis, or lesions along the neural pathway (Davis and Hardick 1986).

Individuals with either noise-induced hearing loss or that attributed to presbycusis may show any number of speech and/or language difficulties, including: general reduced hearing sensitivity; general poor speech understanding; poor speech understanding especially in noisy conditions, for those with a noise-induced loss; sensitivity to high-pitched sounds; sensitivity to very loud sounds; and poor performance on difficult listening tasks. They may also exhibit deficits in temporal processing (Humes and Christopherson 1991). The more severe the hearing loss, the more likely it is that changes can be expected in the individual's speech. As is the case with those with severe to profound hearing loss, adults with a mild to moderate hearing loss may exhibit some deterioration in speech production, characterized by imprecise articulation and a change in vocal quality, resulting in increased loudness and a monotone intonational pattern (Davis and Hardick 1986). However, more typical speech production patterns include the omission of sibilant sounds in word final position and the running together of words (Tannahill and Smoski 1985).

Although hearing impairment does not seem to suggest an increased risk for personality changes or mental illness, there are nonetheless adjustments that the hearing-impaired adult must make in order to ensure adaptation to their hearing impairment. According to Davis and Hardick (1986 p. 399):

> the development of hearing loss necessitates adjustments in interpersonal relationships, vocational activities and social participation. The expenditure of extra effort and visual vigilance is required in following the conversation of others; anxiety may be increased as a result of fear of misunderstanding; embarrassment may occur as a result of callous comments by normally hearing people; personal safety of hearing-impaired aging individuals may be jeopardized. In addition, impaired hearing becomes a factor in major decisions of life, such as choosing or changing vocations, marriage, or retirement plans; working-age adults may worry about making costly mistakes, measuring up to job demands, or meeting criteria for advancement; and dependency on others may be increased as a result of difficulty communicating on the telephone and in other situations.

5. Conclusion

It is clear that the speech and language disorders exhibited by hearing-impaired children and adults are varied and multifaceted, and that degree of hearing loss is not the sole factor contributing to level of impairment. The following factors must all be considered to determine appropriately the level of speech and language compromise in these individuals: age of onset; age of identification of hearing loss; fluctuation, permanence, and progression of loss; intervention, including various (re)habilitation measures (amplification and assistive devices); educational placement; and support systems. Not taking the above characteristics into consideration may limit the amount of service that is afforded to children and adults with pre- or postlingual hearing impairment. However, it is essential to emphasize that the level to which individuals are handicapped by hearing impairment varies dramatically from person to person. The future should bring more comprehensive and extensive services to both hearing-impaired children and adults. However, more information must be gathered on the speech and language characteristics of children and adults with mild to moderate hearing losses.

See also: Specific Language Disorders of Childhood; Speech and Language Handicapped: Overview

References

Brannon J 1968 Linguistic word classes in the spoken language of normal, hard of hearing and deaf children. *Journal of Speech and Hearing Research* 11: 279–87

Cazden C 1988 *Classroom Discourse: The Language of Teaching and Learning*. Heinemann Educational, Portsmouth, New Hampshire

Davis J, Hardick E (eds.) 1986 *Rehabilitative Audiology for Children and Adults*. Macmillan Inc., New York

Dunn C, Newton L 1986 A comprehensive model for speech development in hearing-impaired children. *Topics in Language Disorders* 6(3). 25–46

Fraser C, Bellugi U, Brown R 1963 Control of imitation, comprehension, and production. *J. Verbal Learn. Verbal Behav.* 2: 121–35

Friel-Patti S, Finitzo T 1990 Language learning in a prospective study of otitis media with effusion in the first two years of life. *Journal of Speech and Hearing Research* 33(1): 188–94

Geibenk G, Daly K 1990 Epidemiology and management of otitis media in children. *Topics in Language Disorders* 11(1): 1–10

Humes L, Christopherson L 1991 Speech identification difficulties of hearing-impaired elderly persons: The contributions of auditory processing deficits. *Journal of Speech and Hearing Research* 34(3): 686–93

Jenkins J 1986 Cognitive development in children with

recurrent otitis media: Where do we stand? In: Kavanaugh J (ed.) 1986 *Otitis Media and Child Development*. York Press, Parkton, Maryland
Northern J 1986 Hearing and auditory disorders. In: Shames G, Wiig E (eds.) 1986 *Human Communication Disorders*. Merrill, Columbus, Ohio
Robbins A M 1986 Facilitating language comprehension in young hearing-impaired children. *Topics in Language Disorders* 6(3): 12–24
Roberts J, Schuele C 1990 Otitis media and later academic performance: The linkage and implications for intervention. *Topics in Language Disorders* 11(1): 43–62
Spahr F 1971 White House conference on aging. *ASHA* 13: 14–17
Tannahill J, Smoski W 1985 Overview of aural rehabilitation. In: Katz J (ed.) 1985 *Handbook of Clinical Audiology*. Williams and Wilkins, Baltimore, Maryland
Van Tasell D J 1986 Auditory perception of speech. In: Davis J, Hardick E (eds.) 1986
Weiss A 1986 Classroom discourse and the hearing-impaired child. *Topics in Language Disorders* 6(3): 60–70
West J, Weber J 1973 A phonological analysis of the spontaneous language of a four-year-old hard-of-hearing child. *Journal of Speech and Hearing Disorders* 38(1): 25–35

B. Goldstein; A. Iglesias

Speech and Language Handicapped: Overview

Human communication, its acquisition, and development, is essential to most people. Yet there are those who either fail to acquire the ability to communicate or who lose this essential ability through disease or neurological, physiological, or emotional disaster. This entry addresses perspectives drawn from speech and language research since the early 1980s. It highlights new definitions and describes the role of language specialists (frequently called speech therapists, speech–language pathologists, or logopeds) who have completed postsecondary education in the field of human communication sciences and disorders. It also discusses how the very existence of such services varies among countries, the variety of personnel who provide those services, and the various settings within the educational or health system of a specific country where services are offered. In general, emerging Third World countries have few qualified personnel, while postindustrial, technologically oriented countries with national policies that foster services to the handicapped and disabled are at the forefront of research and practice.

1. Defining Speech and Language Disabilities

For many years, language disorders were included within the generic term "speech disorders." To make finer distinctions between them, the two terms were separated into two bodies of research. Not all children and youth with communication problems exhibit both speech and language disabilities concurrently, although there can be co-occurring difficulties. In general, there is too little evidence across languages and cultures to generalize about speech/language disabilities. For example, child language researchers are only now, in the early 1990s, exploring the atypical populations, having previously confined themselves to normal language learners. However, international experience reveals that speech and language disabilities worldwide may be found among those who are autistic, mentally retarded, hearing impaired, severely physically handicapped or emotionally disturbed, or who have cerebral palsy or cleft palate. Limited evidence suggests that children with learning disabilities, dyslexia, attention deficit disorder, and some poor readers, may have exhibited a speech or language difficulty during their preschool years. Both speech and language are utilized in communication, the process by which individuals exchange information and convey ideas. Communication is an interactive process, requiring a speaker who formulates a message and a listener who comprehends it (Bernstein and Tiegerman 1989).

1.1 Speech Disorders

In much of the world, speech disorders are thought to include voice, articulation, and fluency disorders.

> A voice disorder is defined as the absence or abnormal production of vocal quality, pitch, loudness, resonance, and/or duration. An articulation disorder is defined as the abnormal production of speech sounds. A fluency disorder is defined as the abnormal flow of verbal expression, characterized by impaired rate and rhythm which may be be accompanied by struggle behavior. (ASHA 1982 p. 949)

Research in voice disorders is particularly prevalent in Europe, Scandinavia, Japan, and the United States. Fluency disorders (e.g., stuttering and stammering) are also of significant interest in Western Europe, the United Kingdom, Australia, the United States, and Canada. Articulation disorders have long been an object of central interest in most countries since the inability to articulate the sounds of the language can render children unintelligible to their listeners.

1.2 Language Disorders

Called "delayed speech" in the mid-twentieth century, language disabilities have risen in prominence since the 1970s and may be more prevalent than all speech disorders combined. Since the early 1980s, language specialists have gone beyond the sound, word, and sentence level to analyze larger units of language, spoken and written discourse including spoken conversations, oral narratives, and oral and written expository text. With these changes as well as the increased importance of literacy skills has come a change in the perceived role of speech–

language pathologists in many industrialized nations. Researchers and clinicians have come to recognize that the form, content, and function of language is crucial to the communication process. These aspects of language are involved in many language disorders:

(a) Form, that is, *phonology* (the sound system of the language), *morphology* (the structure of words), and *syntax* (combining words to form sentences);

(b) Content, that is, *semantics* (the content of an utterance; the meanings of words and sentences);

(c) Function or use, that is *pragmatics* (i.e., the sociolinguistic system that patterns the use of language).

3. Incidence and Prevalence of some Speech and Language Disorders

The incidence (occurrence) of speech and language disorders and the prevalence (the percentage of the population affected) cannot be estimated worldwide, or even nationwide for most regions of the world. The reasons for this are multiple. Many countries, including the United States, provided special education services by identifying and labeling children by their "primary" disability. Medical diagnoses have rarely included speech and language, but rather focus on known diseases or more clearly observable physiological or neurological disorders including mental retardation, cerebral palsy, cleft palate, brain injury, and so on. Even in the early 1990s, deafness is frequently not identified until the second year of life, and learning disabilities not until the school years. Speech, language, and hearing disorders in the preschool years have often remained unidentified unless they are quite severe. In a significant number of countries social, linguistic, and cultural forces have changed the face of special education and speech, language, and hearing services. These forces have become reflected in state and federal laws and regulations. Learning disabilities became a "handicapping condition" in 1975, and since that time, the numbers of children labeled as mentally retarded or speech/language impaired have dropped dramatically while the number of children identified as learning disabled has risen significantly. "New" disabilities have been identified such as dysphagia, (oral–motor difficulties in swallowing and eating) and attention deficit disorder (ADD, with or without hyperactivity) which is, in the early 1990s, labeled as a handicapping condition in the "other health impaired" category by federal regulations in the United States. As Lesser (1992) reports in her worldwide survey:

> The profession is shaped by diverse political, administrative, and financial influences, which differ from country to country. Its remit also varies from country to country, reflecting an uncertainty as to the nature and numbers of the people it seeks to help . . . Research in this field is therefore seriously prone to misinterpretation of terminology, not only because of differences amongst languages, but because of differences amongst local circumstances. (Lesser 1992 p. 107).

Prevalence estimates, therefore, are best garnered by consulting the national professional associations or responsible governmental agency that exist in most countries which provide services. The American Speech-Language Hearing Association (ASHA) in cooperation with the International Association of Logopedics and Phoniatrics (IALP) publishes a directory of training institutions worldwide, which includes the certifying or supervisory entity (ASHA 1992). The IALP (1992) publishes a yearly directory of its member national societies. These two documents provide information about training programs and professional associations in over 40 countries (Butler and Stewart 1991, IALP 1992).

In North America it is variously estimated that speech and language handicaps account for 10 to 12 percent of children and youth. Figures vary by country and by the fiscal status of those entities providing services. In an increasing number of countries the importance of early prevention and intervention has resulted in ever-increasing numbers of infants, toddlers, and preschoolers at risk or with handicapping conditions being identified, assessed, and served. Of interest to language clinicians are preschoolers with specific language impairment (SLI), a disorder considered to be "primary" by some but not all researchers, since it occurs in the absence of hearing impairment or apparent neurologic damage (Beukelman and Mirenda 1992). Others consider these children as belonging to the heterogeneous group of children known as learning disabled (LD), with the language component being secondary to academic learning disabilities. When LD is accepted as a category, as it is in the United States, it represents the disability with the highest number of identified children (US Department of Education 1988). At the other end of the scale are the nonspeaking, severely language impaired who need augmentative support, and form 0.8 percent of the population in the United States, 0.12 percent in Canada, and 0.12 percent in Australia. While these numbers indicate less than 1 percent of the population worldwide, they also reflect a condition that affects millions.

Articulation and phonology disabilities affect about 7.5 percent of preschool children. This number rapidly decreases in the school-age years (Newman et al. 1985); 1 percent of school-age children exhibit fluency disorders (Andrews et al. 1983) and 6 percent exhibit voice disorders.

Reported incidence of cerebral palsy is 2–2.5:1000, while cleft palate is found in 1 in 750–1,000 Caucasian births, 1 in 500 among Orientals, and 1 in every 2,000–3,000 among African-Americans (McWilliams 1986). Both incidence and prevalence are expected to increase as medical technology and neonatology services expand. Szanton (1988) reports that 2 percent of neonates are identified at birth as disabled. Upon entering school, that number changes to 8–9 percent and increases to 11–12 percent during the school years.

4. The Changing Roles of Speech–Language Pathologists (SLPs) and Logopedists

The Irish Association of Speech and Language Therapists (1992) describes the role of their members as working with developmental speech and language problems, fluency disorders, cleft palate, cerebral palsy, learning disability (mental handicap), stroke, head injury, progressive diseases, ENT conditions, and psychiatric conditions. Services are rendered in hospitals, health centers, schools, clients' homes, child and family centers, and special units. This description also illustrates the multiple roles and contexts in which SLPs and logopedists work in a number of the developed regions of the world (the United Kingdom, Canada, United States, Scandinavia, Western Europe, India, Hong Kong, and Japan). Lesser's (1992) survey found that new training programs beginning in 1991 could be found in Greece, Malta, New Zealand, Taiwan, Jordan, the United Kingdom, and Zimbabwe, although the level and length of training appears to vary widely, perhaps reflecting the resources available to any particular program.

The movement toward the European Economic Community and the European Directive, which assumes equivalence among all training within Europe, fails to reflect the heterogeneity of professional education and is a subject of concern (Lesser 1992 p. 123). Furthermore, there is even more diversity across continents than is represented in Europe. This is further compounded by paradigm shifts occurring in general education and in special education in many of the countries that have instituted special services in the schools. These include increased integration of regular and special education, for example, inclusive education; increased emphasis on early intervention with at-risk and young children and their families; and teaming, the use of multidisciplinary or transdisciplinary teams in assessment and treatment (Bowen et al. 1991, Bullock and Simpson 1991).

5. Changing Paradigms in Research and Practice

The education issues noted above interact with research literature which now strongly supports the interrelated nature of language, learning, and literacy; the changing nature of the populations served, such as the increased number of children for whom the language of the schools or clinic is not their native language; the changing role of assessment and intervention toward evaluation and treatment provided in more naturalistic contexts (e.g., the classroom rather than the clinic); the role of ethnography and other anthropological techniques in describing children's language and learning status; and the whole-language movement from New Zealand and its impact on children whose language is far from "whole." These issues are nested within many nations' perceived commitment to health and education and the escalating costs of those commitments in the 1990s, a time of serious fiscal constraints among many nations (Butler and Stewart 1991).

See also: Language Development; Language Differences versus Language Disorders; Language and Learning in Education

References

American Speech-Language Hearing Association (ASHA) 1982 Definition: Communication disorders and variations. *Asha* 24(11): 949–50

American Speech-Language Hearing Association (ASHA) 1992 *International Directory of Training Programs in Speech-Language Pathology*, rev. edn. ASHA, Rockville, Maryland

Andrews G et al. 1983 Stuttering: Review of research findings and theories circa 1982. *Journal of Speech and Hearing Disorders* 48(3): 232–46

Bernstein D, Tiegerman E 1989 *Language and Communication Disorders in Children*, 2nd edn. Merrill, Columbus, Ohio

Beukelman D, Mirenda P 1992 *Augmentative and Alternative Communication: Management of Severe Communication Disorders in Children and Adults*. Paul H. Brookes, Baltimore, Maryland

Bowen M, Butler K, Jones P, Bresco M, Huang A 1991 Personnel preparation: Some national issues and suggested solutions. In: Bullock M, Simpson R (eds.) 1991

Bullock M, Simpson R 1991 (eds.) *Critical issues in Special Education: Implications for Personnel Preparation*. North Texas State University, Denton, Texas

Butler K, Stewart B 1991 Synonyms, antonyms and acronyms: International perspectives in training. Paper presented before the American Speech–Language Hearing Association, Atlanta, Georgia, November 22

International Association of Logopedics and Phoniatrics (IALP) 1992 *Directory*. ASHA, Rockville, Maryland

Irish Association of Speech and Language Therapists 1992 Role of the speech and language therapist, Unpublished document. IASLT, Dublin

Lesser R 1992 The making of logopedists: An international survey. *Folia Phoniatrica* 44(3–4): 105–26

McWilliams B 1986 Cleft palate. In: Shames G, Wiig E (eds.) 1986 *Human Communication Disorders*, 2nd edn. Merrill, Columbus, Ohio

Newman P, Creaghead N, Secord W 1985 *Assessment and Remediation of Articulation and Phonological Disorders*. Merrill, Columbus, Ohio

Szanton E 1988 Perspective: A new day for infants and children. *Infants and Young Children* 1(1): 5–7

United States Department of Education 1988 *To Assure the Free and Appropriate Public Education of All Handicapped Children. Tenth Annual Report to Congress of the Implementation of the Education of the Handicapped Act*. Government Printing Office, Washington, DC

Further Reading

Butler K 1986 *Language Disorders in Children*. Pro-Ed, Austin, Texas

Crystal D (ed.) 1991 *Child Language Teaching and Therapy* 7(2): 115–237

deMontfort Supple M (ed.) 1982 *Language Disability: Congenital and Acquired*. Boole Press, Dun Laoghaire

Ingram D 1989 *First Language Acquisition: Method, Description and Exploration*. Cambridge University Press, Cambridge

Kamhi A, Catts W (eds.) 1989 *Reading Disabilities: A Developmental Language Perspective*. Little, Brown, Boston, Massachusetts

Kavanagh J (ed.) 1992 *The Language Continuum: From Infancy to Literacy*. York Press, Parkton, Maryland

Kilburg D 1992 *Family Centered Early Intervention for Communication Disorders: Prevention and Treatment of Communication Disorders*. Aspen, Gaithersburg, Maryland

Langdon H 1992 *Hispanic Children and Adults with Communication Disorders. Assessment of Intervention*. Aspen, Gaithersburg, Maryland

Lien I-n 1986 *The Third Sino-American Symposium on Speech–Language Pathology and Communicative Disorders*. The National Taiwan Normal University, Taipei

Silliman E, Wilkinson L 1991 *Communicating for Learning: Classroom Observation and Collaboration*. Aspen, Gaithersburg, Maryland

Snow C, Locke J 1992 *Applied Linguistics: Psychological Studies of Language Processes* 13(2): whole issue

Vaid J (ed.) 1986 *Language Processing in Bilinguals: Psycholinguistic and Neuro-Psychological Perspectives*. Erlbaum, Hillsdale, New Jersey

K. G. Butler

Speech–Sound Disorders: Articulation and Phonology

Phonology is the part of language that encompasses all aspects of the speech–sound system. Articulation, which refers to movements of the tongue and other articulators, is an inextricable part of phonology (Fey 1985). Traditional speech therapy programs, which emphasize articulation and teach one phoneme at a time, require considerably more remediation time for children with severe speech disorders to become intelligible than linguistically based phonological approaches that focus on facilitating the development of broad speech patterns within the framework of language (Hodson and Paden 1991).

1. Speech Sounds: Development and Disorders

Children begin to talk with reduced repertoires of speech sounds, regardless of which language they learn. For example, children across languages leave off word endings when they begin talking ("bow" for "boat"). By the age of 4 years, however, normally developing children demonstrate adult-like speech (Stoel-Gammon and Dunn 1985). This is not to say that their utterances are perfect by this age, but rather that phonologically normal children are generally intelligible before they enter elementary school. Some children, however, experience delayed/disordered speech–sound development.

Children who still evidence severe/profound speech–sound disorders by the time they begin school are at extreme risk for lowered achievement in subjects such as reading and spelling. It is not too surprising that children who say "tea" when they attempt to say a number of other words (e.g., "key," "see," "sheep," and "chief") are going to be at a major disadvantage when they try to specify beginning and ending sounds in words.

2. Phoneme-oriented Articulation Assessment and Therapy

The traditional (Van Riper 1939) phoneme-oriented method of remediating speech–sound disorders, which is usually referred to as "articulation" therapy, as well as the numerous behavioristic programs that were prevalent in the United States in the 1970s and 1980s, involve teaching sounds to perfection, one-by-one. Decisions regarding which sounds to teach and the order of their presentation are typically based on normative data from the 1950s and 1960s. (e.g., Templin 1957). Phoneme acquisition data generally reflect the age at which each of the phonemes was produced perfectly by a high percentage of children tested, without considering syllable-structure aspects or acceptable, readily understandable, allophonic variations.

The traditional method for testing speech–sound errors involves phoneme-oriented articulation tests, which consist of filling in blanks and usually assess only one phoneme per word. Final scores obtained from articulation tests do not reflect differences in types of errors. For example, omissions receive the same weighting in articulation-test final scores as do distortions (e.g., lisps), even though their effects on intelligibility differ markedly.

In traditional articulation therapy, each phoneme is taught first in isolation, then in nonsense syllables, then in initial, final, and medial positions of words, next in phrases and sentences, and finally in conversation. Remediation may require years for children who need to target many sounds. The emphasis in articulation therapy, for the most part, is on phonetic placement and motor drill. Consideration of aspects related to perception and cognitive–linguistic factors is generally lacking in traditional articulation therapy.

Phoneme-oriented procedures are generally adequate for children with two or three speech-sound errors. Highly unintelligible children with extensive deviations, however, progress incredibly slowly via one phoneme at a time methods, often requiring five or six years or even more before they became intelligible. Furthermore, children with severe/profound speech–sound disorders lag behind their peers in developing reading and spelling skills (Clarke-Klein 1991).

3. *Contributions from Linguistics*

The growing interest in language during the 1960s, coupled with phonological research contributions by linguists such as Chomsky and Halle (1968) and Stampe (1969), along with the 1968 translation into English of Jakobson's (1941) seminal work, *Kindersprache, Aphasie und allgemeine Lautgesetze*, provided the impetus for speech–language practitioners to begin looking beyond perfecting singleton phonemes to thinking about broad speech patterns. The initial journey into incorporating linguistically related aspects involved analyzing and teaching distinctive features (McReynolds and Engmann 1975).

Distinctive-feature procedures provided a mechanism for identifying substitution-based deficiencies, such as the lack of stridency in substitutions of /t/, /p/, or /h/ for /s/ and /f/, but omissions, which, in fact, have a more adverse effect on intelligibility, were not scored or identified for remediation within a distinctive-features framework. Remediation based on distinctive features continued to focus on teaching singleton speech sounds according to a specific criterion (e.g., 95 % correct), although efforts were made to select phonemes that would lead to greater generalization to other phonemes containing the same distinctive feature. The publication of Ingram's (1976) landmark book, *Phonological Disability in Children*, paved the way for speech-language practitioners to begin looking at broad simplification patterns, including syllable-structure omissions such as cluster reduction (e.g, "top" for "stop"), and to recognize a system, even in the least intelligible utterances.

4. *Evaluation of Highly Unintelligible Phonologies*

Phonological assessment instruments, which require phonetic transcription of whole words, allow for identification of broad deviation patterns across phoneme classes and syllable structures. The results of phonological analysis give a more accurate representation of children's abilities to produce speech patterns. The first phonologically based assessment instruments appeared in the United States between 1979 and 1981 (Hodson 1980, Ingram 1981, Shriberg and Kwiatkowski 1980, Weiner 1979), followed by a British phonological instrument (Grunwell 1985).

When making clinical decisions (Hodson 1986), the basic requirements for speech–sound assessment are that the results should indicate: (a) whether the individual's speech is disordered, delayed, or within normal limits, and (b) if disordered, and severity of that disorder and the phonological patterns necessary for remediation. In addition, factors related to general level of functioning, including psychosocial, neuromotor, and cognitive/linguistic abilities need to be evaluated, as well as the individual's auditory and perceptual abilities and the structure and function of the speech mechanism. If significant perpetuating etiological factors exist (e.g., otitis media), referrals will need to be made (e.g., to an otolaryngologist) in order to alleviate such factors.

5. *Remediation of Highly Unintelligible Phonologies*

5.1 *Clinical Research*

Experimental phonology clinics that accepted only highly unintelligible children were begun at the University of Illinois in 1975, at San Diego State University in 1981, and at The Wichita State University in 1989. Over 200 children between the ages of 2 and 14 years participated in these clinics. Children whose hearing and cognitive abilities were within normal limits were dismissed from these clinics as being essentially intelligible in less than 18 months.

5.2 *Cycles Approach*

The remediation approach that evolved from this research is referred to as "the phonological cycles approach" (Hodson and Paden 1991). Many of the auditory, kinesthetic, and visual stimulation techniques and production–practice procedures used in the cycles approach are similar to those used in traditional articulation therapy. The major difference between the approaches pertains to targets. Although target phonemes are still presented in production–practice words, they serve as a means to facilitate development of phonological patterns rather than as an end in themselves.

5.3 *Targets*

The speech–language practitioner selects from the child's phonological deficiencies the patterns and phonemes that are most stimulable. Each phoneme target (e.g., /st/) within the deficient phonological pattern (e.g., /s/ clusters) is presented for approximately 60 minutes before progressing to the next most stimulable phoneme target. Each major pattern is presented for a period of time ranging from two to six hours per pattern. Deficient phonological patterns are recycled until they emerge in conversational speech. The order of presentation varies for each child.

6. Underlying Concepts for Phonological Remediation

6.1 Phonological Acquisition is a Gradual Process

One of the most basic underlying concepts of the cycles approach is that phonological acquisition is a gradual process (Ingram 1976). Results of developmental phonology research (e.g., Dyson and Paden 1983) indicate that young children evidence a great deal of variability and vacillation as they learn the speech patterns of adults in their respective linguistic communities. Normally developing children do not learn one sound to perfection, and then the next, and so on. In the cycles approach, children are provided with limited, but successful, experiences in producing a target for a short period of time. While the child is internalizing the first pattern, the next pattern is presented, and so on. After all of the major deficient patterns have been targeted in succession, they are recycled until each phonological pattern emerges in conversational speech.

6.2 Children Need to Develop Appropriate Kinesthetic Images

Another important consideration is that children rely on kinesthetic images for monitoring their own productions. Most clients can identify speech errors made by someone other than themselves, but they do not seem to hear their own mistakes. They need to experience enough successful productions of the target to develop an awareness of contrasting kinesthetic images for self-monitoring purposes.

6.3 Children Learn Speech by Listening

A third underlying concept of the cycles phonological approach is that children with normal hearing typically learn the adult speech–sound system by listening. A couple of minutes of auditory stimulation, incorporating mild-gain amplification, is provided during each phonological remediation session to increase the child's auditory awareness of the target pattern. The client listens to, but does not repeat, a list of words containing the target pattern. Immediately following the listening activity while still wearing the headphones connected to the amplifier, the child repeats several carefully selected potential production–practice words. As children develop auditory awareness of the targets along with new kinesthetic images for their target patterns, they learn to monitor and correct their own speech errors.

6.4 Optimal Matches Facilitate Learning

Another basic concept is that an optimal "match" facilitates learning. Hunt (1961) theorized that optimal learning occurs if stimulation/teaching is provided exactly one step above the individual's current level of functioning. Phonological analysis allows speech–language practitioners to ascertain more precisely where and how a client's performance at the moment fits into the overall system of developing phonology. By starting at the very next step, practitioners can provide an optimal challenge for children, and at the same time allow their clients to experience success. Complexity is then gradually increased so that individuals are always optimally challenged.

6.5 Children Should be Active Participants

A concept that is now widely accepted in linguistically oriented therapy approaches is that children need to be active participants in the language-learning process. Articulation therapy procedures that were based on behaviorism principles allowed children to be passive recipients, typically imitating the practitioner's productions in order to receive extrinsic reinforcers. Children learn best if they are participating and experiencing cognitively as well as physically. Opportunities are provided in the phonological cycles remediation approach for children to understand semantic differences, to explore possible alternative productions, to test their own hypotheses about language, and to become optimally involved as they develop intelligible speech patterns.

7. Conclusion

Children who are in the process of learning to read and spell have a critical need to be intelligible. The phonological cycles remediation approach, which is still evolving, has helped expedite intelligibility gains for children with severe/profound speech disorders. A great deal more research is needed, however, to develop even more effective and more efficient services for children who are highly unintelligible in order to decrease the handicapping effects of their disordered phonologies on the development of their literacy skills.

See also: Speech and Language Handicapped: Overview; Speech and Language Disorders and the Hard of Hearing

References

Chomsky N, Halle M 1968 *The Sound Pattern of English*. Harper and Row, New York

Clarke-Klein S 1991 A phonological analysis of children's spelling errors. Doctoral dissertation, Wichita State University, Kansas

Dyson A, Paden E 1983 Some phonological acquisition strategies used by two-year-olds. *J. Childhood Communication Disord*. 7: 6–18

Fey M 1985 Articulation and phonology: Inextricable constructs in speech pathology. *Human Communication in Canada* 9: 7–16

Grunwell P 1985 *Phonological Assessment of Child Speech*. NFER–Nelson, Windsor

Hodson B 1980 *The Assessment of Phonological Processes*. Interstate, Danville, Illinois

Hodson B 1986 *The Assessment of Phonological Processes—Revised*. ProEd, Austin, Texas

Hodson B, Paden E 1991 *Targeting Intelligible Speech: A Phonological Approach to Remediation*, 2nd edn. ProEd, Austin, Texas
Hunt J 1961 *Intelligence and Experience*, Ronald Press, New York
Ingram D 1976 *Phonological Disability in Children*, Edward Arnold, London
Ingram D 1981 *Procedures for the Phonological Analysis of Children's Language*. University Park Press, Baltimore, Maryland
Jakobson R 1941 *Kindersprache, Aphasie und allgemeine Lautgesetze*, Mouton, The Hague
McReynolds L, Engmann D 1975 *Distinctive Feature Analysis of Misarticulations*. University Park Press, Baltimore, Maryland
Shriberg L, Kwiatkowski J 1980 *Natural Process Analysis*. Macmillan, New York
Stampe D 1969 The acquisition of phonetic representation. In: Binnick R L (ed.) 1969 *Papers From the Fifth Regional Meeting of the Chicago Linguistic Society*. Department of Linguistics, University of Chicago, Chicago, Illinois
Stoel-Gammon C, Dunn C 1985 *Normal and Disordered Phonology in Children*. ProEd, Austin, Texas
Templin M 1957 *Certain Language Skills in Children*. University of Minnesota Press, Minneapolis, Minnesota
Van Riper C 1939 *Speech Correction: Principles and Methods*. Prentice-Hall, New York
Weiner F 1979 *Phonological Process Analysis*. University Park Press, Baltimore, Maryland

Further Reading

Edwards H 1992 *Applied Phonetics: The Sounds of American English*. Singular, San Diego, California
Edwards M, Shriberg L 1993 *Phonology: Applications in Communicative Disorders*. College-Hill, San Diego, California
Dean E, Howell J 1986 Developing linguistic awareness: A theoretically based approach to phonological disorders. *Br. J. Disord. Commun.* 21(2): 223–38
Hodson B, Nonomuva C, Zappin M 1989 Phonological disorders: Impact on academic performance. *Semin. Speech Lang.* 10: 252–59
Ingram D 1986 Explanation and phonological remediation. *Child Lang. Teach. Ther.* 2(1): 1–19
Grunwell, P 1987 *Clinical Phonology*, 2nd edn. Williams and Wilkins, Baltimore, Maryland
Yavas M (ed.) 1989 *Desrios fonologicas nas criansas: Teoria, Pesqusa e tratamento*. Mercado Aberto, Portro Alegre

B. W. Hodson

Spelling and Grammar Instruction

It has been hypothesized by psycholinguists and language theorists that a set of common psychological, linguistic, and discourse competencies underlie all language use (listening, speaking, reading, and writing). Although different authors have developed different taxonomies and used different terminology, taken together they have accounted for the following: (a) phonological and graphophonic knowledge (a combination of the knowledge of both the phonological and graphic systems of the language and their correspondences); (b) syntactic knowledge (knowledge of the grammatical rules of the language); (c) lexical or word knowledge (knowledge of the vocabulary of the language); (d) semantic knowledge (knowledge of the concepts in language and their interrelationships); (e) background or world knowledge; (f) pragmatic knowledge (knowledge about the social uses of language); and finally (g) rhetorical or discourse knowledge (knowledge about effective uses and discourse structures of language). None of these systems works independently; in fact, they operate simultaneously and interdependently in such a way that language users draw on all of them in order to produce and understand language (see Flood et al. 1991). The teaching of the conventions and structures of language—in particular, the teaching of spelling and the teaching of grammatical structures—has been directed primarily toward the improvement of the first two of the areas in the list above; that is, phonological or graphophonic knowledge and syntactic knowledge.

In this entry the nature and validity of the assumptions surrounding the teaching of grammar and spelling will be examined, and the conclusions derived from the instructional research carried out over the past century in these two areas will be briefly reviewed. The entry will begin by examining definitions of grammar and grammar instruction, will move to an examination of the relationship between the teaching of grammar and growth in language use, and will then explore some possible interpretations of the research in the teaching of formal grammar. The entry will then move to a discussion of spelling development, followed by a review of the conclusions from the classical research in spelling instruction.

1. Grammar

Grammar study has been one of the pillars of language and literacy instruction since ancient times. Connell (1987) reported that the approach to grammar study articulated in the first century BC established the general approach that has "dominated the teaching of languages . . . until modern times" (p. 201). He identified the two main elements of learning grammar as memorization and analogical reasoning; that is, the memorization of definitions and rules paired with practice in identifying constituent elements, in identifying instances of the incorrect applications of rules in parsing sentences, and in analyzing how rules have been applied in well-formed sentences and discourse. For centuries the study of grammar provided the basis for the "advanced" study of oratory, rhetoric, stylistics, and poetics. Basic grammatical knowledge was seen as a prerequisite for the development of mature reading and writing, and correct speaking. Across the centuries, well into the twentieth century, the study of formal grammar has been one of the most pervasive and resilient areas of literary and literacy education. Hillocks and Smith (1991) claimed that "[f]or two millennia, grammar has been central to school curricula" (p. 591).

One of the reasons for the endurance of grammar as a school subject is an intuitive sense, on the part of both teachers and the public at large, that knowing the description of a language will help language users gain greater control over their own language performance; that is, that explicitly knowing the "rules of the game" will help a person "play the game" better. This assumption is particularly true in the avoidance of error in speaking and writing and in written composition. The assumption of a direct relationship between explicit knowledge about language and the ability to control and use language has helped to maintain grammar study as an important element in language and literacy programs. Hillocks and Smith (1991) suggested that proponents of grammar instruction have cited three reasons for teaching it: (a) for the insight it offers into how language works; (b) for its usefulness in mastering standard forms of English; and (c) for its usefulness in improving composition skill (p. 594). Because syntactic knowledge has been demonstrated to be an underlying component of language, it would follow that instruction in the grammatical rules of the language (i.e., instruction aimed at enhancing growth in syntactic competence) ought to enhance growth in language performance.

1.1 What is Grammar

The *Dictionary of Reading and Related Terms* defines grammar as "a linguistic description of some language—a set of statements saying how a language works. . . . In this usage, the grammar includes the phonological, morphological, syntactic, and semantic description of both the language's structure at a given time and its evolution over time" (Harris and Hodges 1981 p. 132). "Grammar" used in this way refers to a wide variety of rules that govern language use, rules about sounds, words, as well as the syntax of the language. These linguistic-descriptive notions are embodied in the first two definitions of grammar reviewed by Hillocks and Smith (1991), drawn from Hartwell (1985). The first definition ("Grammar 1") is the "set of formal patterns in which the words of a language are arranged in order to convey larger meanings"; the second ("Grammar 2") is the "scientific study (description, analysis, and articulation) of the formal patterns of the language" (Hillocks and Smith 1991 p. 591). These two definitions are similar to the definition in the above mentioned *Dictionary*.

This is not, however, the way in which the term has typically been used by teachers or by those who have researched the efficacy of grammar instruction. Nor is this the way the general public thinks about grammar. The general public generally thinks of grammar as Hartwell's "Grammar 3"—"a set of rules governing how one ought to speak or write. In this sense, grammar is prescriptive rather than simply descriptive" (Hillocks and Smith 1991 p. 591). Hartwell (1985) stated that "Grammar 3 is, of course, not grammar at all, but usage" (p. 110). Although usage is an element in the grammar taught in schools, it is only part of what Hartwell calls "Grammar 4"—"the grammar taught in schools" (Hillocks and Smith 1991 p. 591). Hartwell also discussed a fifth type of grammar, "Grammar 5"—"grammatical terms and concepts used to help teach prose style" (Hillocks and Smith 1991 p. 591).

In their discussion of grammar and usage, Hillocks and Smith defined what they called "Traditional School Grammar"—the grammatical rules typically taught in schools. They traced the development of this "grammar" in English from late eighteenth-century attempts to describe English employing the syntactic descriptions of Latin—what have become known as Latinate grammars. Hillocks and Smith stated that "[f]or the most part, current grammar texts are direct descendants of these late eighteenth-century Latinate grammars and present what we call traditional school grammar (TSG). . . . Except for less emphasis on the case and gender of nouns and mode of verbs, the declarations about the grammar of English found in most contemporary texts are essentially the same as those in their counterparts of nearly 200 years ago" (p. 592).

The formal grammar taught in schools includes study of the definitions and appropriate uses of form classes (parts of speech), study of the make-up of constituent structures (words, phrases, clauses, sentences), identification and analysis of sentence patterns, sentence types, and phrase structure rules, identification of the structures of embedded clauses and sentences, and practice in parsing sentences (breaking sentences down into their constituent structures, with particular attention paid to the syntactic functions of words, phrases, and clauses—the epitome of which was sentence analysis using diagrams). Grammar has also included the study of common standard usage errors and the mechanics of language. Traditional school grammar is typically taught analytically using deductive and prescriptive methods with practice on teacher- or text-provided examples in correction and sentence parsing—essentially the same methods (memorization and analogic reasoning) that have been employed for the past 2,000 years.

"Grammar 5: Stylistic Grammar," as laid out by Hartwell (1985 p. 124), has made an impact, however, on some teaching in schools. Teachers who have become disenchanted with traditional school grammar have sometimes taken a more "functional" approach to the teaching of language structures. As Hartwell (1985) pointed out, this more functional approach may take on either a "romantic" or a "classic" mode (p. 124). The "romantic position is that stylistic grammars, though perhaps useful for teachers, have little place in the teaching of composition. . . . The classic position, on the other hand, is that we can find ways to offer developing writers helpful suggestions about prose style . . ." (p. 124). Although neither Hillocks and Smith (1991) nor Hartwell (1985) specifically identified sentence combining as a kind of stylistic grammar, it seems that sentence-combining instruction and practice fit into Hartwell's description of stylistic grammars: "that one learns to control the language of print by manipulating language in meaningful contexts, not by learning about language, as by the study of formal grammar" (p. 125).

The instruction associated with stylistic grammars has been much more functional in that its purpose has, for the most part, been a direct transfer to student writing. For example, the Daiker et al. (1989) sentence-combining book is entitled *The Writer's Options: Combining to Composing* and includes topics such as "paragraph emphasis," "using subordination to strengthen paragraphs," "creating coherence," "changing emphasis," "revising for consistency of tone," "adding details," and "choosing paragraph patterns" (pp. v–xi). Instruction in sentence manipulation, while addressing many of the same syntactic issues as formal grammar, typically avoids the deductive–prescriptive pattern associated with traditional school grammar instruction and teaches for transfer to students' own writing. The purpose is to develop in students more mature syntactic structures and a set of syntactic options "by manipulating language for stylistic effect" (Hartwell 1985 p. 125).

1.2 Instructional Research on the Teaching of Grammar

The efficacy of teaching traditional school grammar has been challenged repeatedly. Braddock et al. (1963), in their comprehensive review of research on written composition, stated that "study after study based on objective testing . . . confirms that instruction in formal grammar has little or no effect on the quality of study compositions" (p. 37). They further reported studies that measured the effect of formal grammar instruction on both composition performance and the avoidance of error in the writing of students. They stated: "The conclusion can be stated in strong and unqualified terms: the teaching of grammar has a negligible or, because it usually displaces some instruction and practice in actual composition, even a harmful effect on the improvement of writing" (pp. 37–38).

At about the same time, Meckel (1963) published his review of the research on teaching composition and literature. His first conclusion was that "[t]here is no research evidence that grammar as traditionally taught in the schools has any appreciable effect on the improvement of writing skill" (p. 981). He also concluded that "[t]here are more efficient methods of securing *immediate* improvement in the writing of pupils, both in sentence structure and usage, than systematic grammatical instruction" (p. 981). Meckel commented, however, that there was also no conclusive research "that grammar has *no* transfer value in developing composition skill" (p. 981) and called for more research on the effects of grammar on language use. Much of the research he called for was carried out in the 30 years after his report was published.

The studies reported by Braddock et al. (1963) and Meckel (1963) were studies in which structural or traditional grammar was taught. When transformational-generative grammar appeared in the late 1950s, some researchers hypothesized that the results of previous studies showing the inefficacy of teaching grammar could be attributed to the fact that inappropriate grammars were being taught. A number of studies appeared investigating the efficacy of teaching transformational-generative grammar to students.

In general, this research has indicated that neither variety of grammar instruction has had a significant effect on language use. The most ambitious study of the effect of transformational grammar instruction on writing performance was reported by Elley et al. (1979). They conducted a three-year investigation of the effects of three different programs: one in transformational grammar, one in traditional grammar, and one in which no grammar was taught at all but in which students practiced reading and writing. They measured language performance on essay writing (style, structure, mechanics, content), usage, sentence-combining, reading comprehension, vocabulary, literature, spelling, listening, a variety of transformational sentence structures, study skills, and attitudes toward various aspects of English. They concluded that the direct effects of transformational grammar on the language growth of secondary school pupils were negligible. Similarly, those pupils who studied a course containing elements of traditional grammar showed no measurable benefits. The RW (reading/writing) group, who studied no formal grammar for three years, demonstrated competence in writing and related language skills fully equal to that shown by the two grammar groups.

Perhaps the most compelling later evidence about the effect of teaching grammar on language use came from the meta-analysis of the research on written composition carried out by Hillocks (1986). One of the focuses of instruction included in his meta-analysis was grammar and mechanics. Here, in part, is Hillocks's discussion of those data:

> Students in the grammar and mechanics treatments scored 0.29 standard deviation *less* than their peers in no grammar or mechanics treatments. The mean effect size of −0.29 is homogeneous ($H = 8.85$, $df = 4$). These

> results are supported by the pre-to-post mean effect for all treatments using grammar in experimental or control conditions. . . . Braddock and his colleagues (1963) argued that grammar study may have a possibly negative effect on composition ability. These data certainly support their contention, in the sense that nearly anything else is more effective in increasing the quality of writing. (Hillocks 1986 p. 214)

Hillocks and Smith (1991) suggested, however, that improvement in written composition may not be the only reason for teaching traditional school grammar. Along with Meckel (1963), they suggested that grammar is also taught to help students to employ standard written English. Their review of the research on the effect of grammar teaching on error reduction is that "the study of formal grammar has little effect on learning these conventions [of mechanics and usage]" (p. 597). In the Elley et al. (1979) study, for example, there were no significant differences between the mechanics ratings of students who studied grammar for three years and those who did not.

In conclusion, the research evidence does not support the teaching of traditional school grammar as a means of enhancing language performance. In fact, Hillocks and Smith's data suggested that the teaching of traditional school grammar and mechanics may negatively affect students' composition and writing performance (Hillocks and Smith 1986). It is difficult, in the face of the research evidence, not to agree with Hillocks and Smith (1986 p. 138) when they state: "If schools insist upon teaching the identification of parts of speech, the parsing or diagramming of sentences, or other concepts of traditional school grammar (as many still do), they cannot defend it as a means of improving the quality of writing."

1.3 Reasons why Grammar is Not an Effective Teaching Tool

In light of this conclusion, a valid question is: if syntactic knowledge is a basic underlying construct for language performance, why does instruction teaching the rules of the language not affect performance in language? The answer is at least threefold.

First, although researchers have found that syntactic knowledge is a significant contributor to language use, that contribution, as measured in a large number of studies, has been relatively small with students older than seven or eight. During the 1960s and 1970s a variety of studies investigated the contribution of syntactic knowledge to language use. Positive contributions were found for language development in general as well as for the four language-processing areas of listening, speaking, reading, and writing. However, although syntactic knowledge appears to be an essential component in language use, research studies have consistently suggested that syntactic knowledge, measured in a variety of ways, *alone* accounts for a relatively small amount of variance in language performance of school-age children and adults ($I^2 = 0.05 - 0.16$).

Second, it would seem that teaching syntactic rules deductively does not, in fact, increase students' syntactic knowledge, because they have already mastered the rules (though not the terminology) of traditional school grammar before they ever encounter formal grammar instruction. Carroll (1960), in an exhaustive review of the literature in language development, concluded that "by the age of six, the average child has mastered nearly all of its [language's] common grammatical forms and constructions" (p. 745).

Further studies indicated that even though the syntax of students becomes increasingly more complex after grade three, few, if any, new structures are learned. It was concluded that children learn the basic structures of their language fairly thoroughly at an early age. A variety of studies have verified that school-age children have nearly all the basic syntactic structures of the language within their language repertoire. O'Donnell et al. (1967), for example, found virtually no differences between the basic syntactic rules used in the oral language of kindergarten children and seventh-grade students. Hunt (1964), on the other hand, in studying the writing of students at three grade levels, stated: "The structures studied here are at least as complex as those studied in most school grammars. Yet they are virtually all used by fourth graders, and are used often enough to indicate that fourth graders command them" (p. 146).

That does not mean, however, that researchers have not found syntactic differences between younger and older students. Hunt (1964), for example, stated (a) that structures that were tabulated were used, almost without exception, by the youngest writers; (b) that many of those structures were used with significantly greater frequency by older students. In the great majority of instances the ones that increased were the very ones produced by sentence-combining transformations. It would appear, then, that students do not learn new rules but become more comfortable and adept at manipulating the language rules they already know. In that way, complexity in syntax is increased but new structures are not added. Learning the names of the terms and memorizing the rules do not appear to increase students' already sophisticated ability to manipulate structures either in receptive or productive language.

The final reason why students may not increase their language processing ability as a result of traditional school grammar instruction may be that the study of language as embodied in grammar is a deductive/prescriptive/analytic activity; that is, its major activities involve the taking apart of sentences. Language use in both receptive language and productive language is a synthetic and constructive process. Learning how to parse language may be so different a process from the effective use of language that students may be unable to transfer instruction in analyzing and parsing to language use (Straw and Schreiner 1982). Furthermore, intense analytic study may, in fact, interfere with the constructive nature of language use.

1.4 Stylistic Grammar: Sentence Manipulation and Writing

In response to the seeming ineffectiveness of traditional school grammar in enhancing language growth, researchers in the mid-1960s began to investigate alternatives that would build on students' tacit and intuitive knowledge of language and that would more closely resemble the synthetic nature of language processing. The instructional procedures developed were a variety of sentence manipulation activities, the main one being sentence combining. Stated simply, sentence combining is instruction in taking two or more sentences, often simple sentences, and combining them into a single, more complex sentence.

The first major study of sentence manipulation and sentence combining was carried out by Mellon (1969). He studied seventh-grade students who had been assigned to one of three groups: (a) sentence-combining instruction; (b) traditional grammar instruction; and (c) no instruction in written composition. Mellon found statistically significant growth in the group that took sentence combining, as measured by 12 indexes of written syntactic complexity. No growth was evident in either of the other two treatment groups—in fact, they were mutually indistinguishable. Not only did this study provide evidence that sentence combining can be effective in fostering language use, it also added evidence about the ineffectiveness of instruction in traditional grammar. The assertion made by Mellon was that sentence-combining practice affected the students' underlying linguistic knowledge about how to manipulate sentences which, in turn, affected their performance in written composition.

O'Hare (1973) based his research on Mellon's, but omitted the use of grammatical terminology. He found significant differences in the syntactic growth of the sentence-combining group compared with a control group that studied reading/writing units during a nine-month period. He also found that the post-test compositions of the sentence combining group were judged to be qualitatively superior to the control group's.

In more than 30 studies, the conclusion has been reached that sentence combining has significant effects on productive language. Gains in syntactic control and maturity have been found in instruction with different ethnic groups, with low- and high-ability students, with college students, with secondary students, and with elementary students. Gains have been reported against measures resulting from structural analysis and on the basis of judgments of quality and measures of syntactic maturity.

Hillocks (1986), in his meta-analysis, studied the effect of sentence combining on the quality of written composition. In the highly homogeneous studies included in the analysis, he found a mean effect size of +0.35. This mean effect size suggests that the average student working with sentence combining performs, in terms of composition quality, at approximately the 64th percentile of students in the control groups in these studies.

1.5 Sentence Manipulation and Receptive Language

The positive effect of sentence combining on the productive language performance of students led researchers to hypothesize that sentence combining might also affect receptive language performance. The hypothesis underlying this research is that if sentence combining can affect the underlying syntactic knowledge of students, which, in turn, affects their language production performance, and if the same syntactic knowledge underlies the abilities of both productive and receptive language, then it is reasonable to assume that sentence-combining activities would also affect performance in the areas of reading and listening comprehension. Stotsky (1975), in her review of the sentence-combining research, stated that "significant results [of the teaching of sentence combining on written composition] from these programs have led some researchers to suggest that enhancing children's syntactic skills in writing may also improve reading comprehension" (p. 32).

Straw and Sadowy (1990), in an analysis of the studies on the effect of sentence-combining instruction on reading, made a number of observations about the relationship between sentence-combining instruction and receptive language performance. Their first conclusion was that sentence combining appears to have a positive effect in studies in which readers were less competent, either by virtue of age or of language ability. Elementary school readers appeared to profit, in terms of comprehension, from a sentence-combining program. In addition, sentence combining appeared to be effective with students at the secondary/college level who were less competent with language, though this conclusion is more tentative than the conclusion about elementary level students.

Their second conclusion was related to the type of instruction used in sentence combining. They stated:

> One of the pervasive qualities of the studies we have reviewed is that those studies that indicate that sentence combining was actively instructed appear to be effective in increasing comprehension whereas those studies that indicate that sentence combining was merely practiced do not show positive results. It would appear, then, that sentence combining is most effective when teachers

actively instruct the method, rather than simply have students practice the exercises. (Straw and Sadowy 1990 p. 21)

Straw and Sadowy's third conclusion was that studies that found positive effects of sentence combining on measures of syntactic maturity in writing (e.g., The Syntactic Maturity Test) were more likely to show effects on comprehension than those that did not. Their final conclusion was that when sentence-combining treatments were based on or related to students' reading materials, the treatment was more likely to have a positive effect than when sentence combining was taught in isolation of students' reading.

All studies investigating the effect of sentence combining have not shown positive effects. It was pointed out, however, that in order for effects to be apparent, reading measures must be sensitive to growth in the syntactic knowledge of students.

Finally, a study of particular interest is one carried out by Straw and Schreiner (1982) which measured the effect of sentence-combining instruction on listening comprehension at fourth-grade level. They found that sentence combining significantly improved the listening comprehension of students compared with that of students who studied sentence analysis techniques. The study indicated that sentence-combining instruction in fact affects the syntactic knowledge of students as realized in a different language mode.

Although sentence combining is not the only set of procedures covered by Hartwell's (1985) "Grammar 5" category, it is probably the most well-researched. Studies of generative rhetoric fall within this category of grammar to help teach prose style and have shown some positive effects, but no single approach has been as well-researched as sentence combining. The totality of the research in sentence combining indicates that instruction in one type of grammar, a grammar that is highly functional, that involves students in the manipulation of sentence structure for a variety of purposes, that addresses the kind of syntactic growth taking place at their own level (i.e., growth in the expansion of already known structures rather than the addition of new structures), and that transfers to both the reading and writing of students, can be a positive addition to the literacy instruction carried out by teachers. Unfortunately, the same cannot be said about traditional school grammar.

2. Spelling

The issue of instruction in spelling is, in many ways, similar to grammar in that instruction appears to be most profitable when it is functional for students, when the transfer of learning from spelling lessons to real writing is made explicit, and when students can see how the study of the structures of the language (in this case the orthographic or graphophonic structures) can be applied to writing (Hodges 1991). This section will briefly discuss the development of spelling ability in students, review the classical research in teaching spelling, and attempt to conclude with guidance on how teachers might most profitably aid students in developing spelling ability.

2.1 The Development of Spelling Ability

Early models of learning to spell viewed spelling as a "mechanistic" activity. In the 1970s and 1980s, however, spelling came to be seen as a much more complex cognitive activity than merely the memorizing of the serial elements of words. Research in spelling suggests that orthographic knowledge is acquired systematically (Read 1971) and that the errors that young students make in spelling reflect a complex knowledge of lexical and graphophonic conventions.

The observation that spelling is systematic led researchers to hypothesize a number of "stages" of spelling ability, suggesting that children employed different strategies for spelling words, dependent, in part, on their literacy experiences and their knowledge of the language system. Beers (1980 p. 42) suggested that "[c]hildren between the ages of six and seven years do follow sequential spelling strategies that progress as the youngster develops." Zutell (1980 p. 59), after studying the spelling strategies of students at four grade levels, observed that "as grade level increased the children seemed to use more sophisticated spelling strategies." The stages of spelling, furthermore, are roughly correlative to children's stages of cognitive development and to the stages of children's metalinguistic awareness.

Gentry (1982) has suggested that there are five stages of spelling. The earliest stage was originally labelled the "deviant" stage, because of the apparent random use of letters to represent words or thoughts. Later, the terms "precommunicative" or "preliterate" were suggested for this stage of development. At this stage, the child appears to have little understanding of the letter–sound correspondences in language and lacks a clear notion about what a *word* is. In this stage of spelling, the child is attempting to represent oral language in written form but has little concept of how written language is structured, except that oral language may be written down. Gentry (1982) has listed a set of spelling "errors" specifically related to this stage of development.

In the second stage, referred to as "prephonetic" by Gentry in 1981 and changed to "semiphonetic," in 1982 the child has become more familiar with the alphabet and is able to produce two or three letters of a word. Typically, the speller understands that letters have sounds, and that often letters written will be consonant sounds that the child hears when pronouncing a word. At this stage, the child has developed both a basic (but often inconsistent) understanding of the word as a unit of language and has developed a concept that individual letters may stand for sounds in a word. At this stage, children rely heavily on a letter–name strategy in spelling.

The third stage, the "phonetic" stage, stabilizes for the child the letter–sound correspondences. In this stage, children demonstrate their ability to match what they hear when a word is pronounced with the letters they write. This stage is prevalent in Grade 1 children. Because of the lack of a one-to-one correspondence in English between the sounds in words and the letters that represent those sounds, this stage does not constitute correct adult spelling. The child's phonetic writing does not look like standard spelling, though it is generally readable. Children may remain in the phonetic stage for as long as 18 months or 2 years, depending on the kinds of literacy activities they are involved in. It is apparent, however, that before children move on to the next stage, this stage needs to be sufficiently well-developed that they are comfortable with their knowledge of the letter–sound correspondences.

Children then move into the "transitional" stage. In this stage, words, though still often misspelled, take on the appearance of standard English spelling. Vowels appear in every syllable, and common letter patterns (e.g., *oo*, *ou*, *ck*) appear in the child's writing. Transitional spellers are able to use common vowel patterns and inflectional endings, and many of the errors in spelling are due to a lack of knowledge of structure.

The final stage is the "standard" or "correct" stage of spelling. That is, students can spell correctly nearly all of the words they want to use in their own writing. Gentry (1982 p. 197) suggested that the correct stage of spelling "may exist at different levels. Instructionally a second grader is a 'correct speller' after mastering a certain corpus of words that has been designated 'second grade level.'"

Hodges (1991) outlined several strategies that students employ as they are learning to spell. For young children, these strategies include a "letter–name" strategy in which they confuse the name of a letter with the sound that letter makes (e.g., "are" may be spelled "R"). Later, students develop a "phonemic" spelling strategy that more closely resembles standard orthography (e.g., "cake" might be spelled "kak"). Hodges goes on to discuss two other important and later developing spelling strategies:

> A significant strategy emerges in the elementary school years for most developing spellers, as early as second grade for some . . . an *analogical* spelling strategy in which orthographic knowledge of known words is used to spell other words whose spellings have not been secured in memory. . . . Another important orthographic principle involves the spellings of words with shared roots and bases . . . in which the root spellings remain essentially the same even when the words are differently pronounced. (Hodges 1991 p. 778)

These are higher-order spelling strategies that students begin to use once they have reached the transitional or standard stage of spelling development.

2.2 Instruction in Spelling

The fact that children go through predictable stages of spelling does not address the issue of when spelling should be taught. Although there is a large body of research evidence suggesting that when spelling is taught there are some time-proven methods for doing so, it does not indicate under what circumstances spelling instruction should take place.

Research in early writing (e.g., Clarke 1988, Gentry 1982) suggests that until children reach the transitional stage of spelling, it is probably unwise to engage them in a systematic spelling program. Gentry (1982) suggested that once a child is well into the transitional stage of spelling, formal instruction appears to facilitate spelling growth. He stated that "[b]eyond the transitional stage, frequent writing experiences with some formal instruction enables children to attain spelling competency over a period of time" (p. 197).

This assertion has been supported by two Canadian studies in spelling development, one carried out by Clarke (1988) with first-grade children, the other by Williamson (1988) with second-grade children. Clarke (1988) was interested in comparing the progress of children who were encouraged to use invented spellings with those who were encouraged to use traditional "correct" spelling in their own writing. Her conclusions were that "using invented spelling, more children were able to write on their own in the early months [of grade one]. Their productions were significantly longer overall and contained significantly more spelling errors than those by children using traditional spelling" (Clarke 1988 p. 281). Clarke's data suggested that children who were encouraged to use invented spelling scored higher on the spelling posttests than children who were encouraged to use traditional spelling. However, Clarke's analysis also suggested that the differences between the two groups could be accounted for primarily by the low initial achievers. She concluded that the results suggested that the main benefits of encouraging invented spellings are for initially low-achieving children.

Williamson (1988) carried out a similar study with Grade 2 children comparing three classroom spelling environments: (a) deductive spelling instruction with occasional writing; (b) deductive spelling instruction with daily writing and conferencing; and (c) inductive spelling instruction with daily writing and conferencing. He analyzed the relative contribution of deductive spelling (an emphasis on phonic generalizations with the words for study selected by the teacher) versus inductive spelling (an "as needed" spelling approach that encouraged students to rely on invented spellings), and also considered the amount of writing that students did in class. His data indicated that students at the transitional stage profited from a deductive approach to spelling, as measured by both a standardized spelling test and an analysis of their story writing. His research indicated, as well, that there was no difference between the inductive and deductive programs in the amount of writing produced by students; that is, it appears that, with transitional spellers, being exposed to an instructional program in spelling does not interfere with writing fluency.

A number of researchers and commentators have reviewed the classical research on the teaching of spelling. Several conclusions from those studies apply when teachers decide to give direct instruction in spelling. They include focusing students' attention on the spelling of words rather than the meaning of words (e.g., presenting words in lists rather than in sentences). In addition, students should not be asked to learn to spell words whose meanings they do not know or words they are unlikely to use in their writing. Research suggests that breaking words into syllables and writing multiple copies of the correct spelling of misspelled words probably have little value in helping students to learn to spell those words. Research also supports the teaching of phonic generalizations, but only when the generalizations have wide applicability (i.e., those rules that apply 80 percent or more of the time). Students probably do not profit from more than about 15 minutes of spelling instruction and practice daily; time beyond about 60 minutes a week appears to have little effect on spelling. Finally, it is apparent that teachers who teach and test spelling should employ test-corrected test-study-retest procedures in teaching and testing. Loomer suggested that "[t]he child's correcting his own spelling test, under the direction of the teacher, is the single most important factor in learning to spell. . . . The corrected test alone contributes 90–95 percent of the achievement that comes from pronunciation, corrected test, and study" (1978 p. 6).

Although this research was carried out before the introduction of the process writing curriculum, it seems clear that when teachers choose to focus on spelling with their students, they should do so as directed by the "classical" research evidence on how to teach spelling. However, it should also be emphasized that a structured spelling program is probably unsuitable for children who have not reached at least the transitional stage of spelling and that spelling instruction should be relevant to children's own writing. Otherwise there will be little transfer value.

See also: Linguistics and Language Learning; Computer and Information Sciences: Educational Programs; Language Development

References

Beers J W 1980 Developmental strategies of spelling competence in primary school children. In: Henderson E H, Beers J W (eds.) 1980 *Developmental and Cognitive Aspects of Learning to Spell: A Reflection of Word Knowledge.* International Reading Association, Newark, Delaware

Braddock R, Lloyd-Jones R, Schoer L 1963 *Research in Written Composition.* National Council of Teachers of English, Champaign, Illinois

Carroll J B 1960 Language development. In: Harris C W (ed.) 1960 *Encyclopedia of Educational Research.* Macmillan, Inc., New York

Clarke L K 1988 Invented versus traditional spelling in first graders' writings: Effects on learning to spell and read. *Research in the Teaching of English* 22(3): 281–309

Connell W F 1987 History of teaching methods. In: Dunkin M J (ed.) 1987 *The International Encyclopedia of Teaching and Teacher Education.* Pergamon Press, Oxford

Daiker D A, Kerek A, Morenberg M 1989 *The Writer's Options: Combining to Composing*, 4th edn. Harper and Row, New York

Elley W B, Barham I H, Lamb H, Wyllie M 1979 *The Role of Grammar in a Secondary School Curriculum.* New Zealand Council for Educational Research, Wellington

Flood J, Jensen J M, Lapp D, Squire J R (eds.) 1991 *Handbook of Research on Teaching the English Language Arts.* Macmillan Inc., New York

Gentry J R 1982 An analysis of developmental spelling in GYNS at WRK. *Read. Teach.* 36: 192–99

Harris T L, Hodges R E (eds.) 1981 *A Dictionary of Reading and Related Terms.* International Reading Association, Newark, Delaware

Hartwell P 1985 Grammar, grammars, and the teaching of grammar. *College English* 47(2): 105–27

Hillocks G Jr 1986 *Research on Written Composition: New Directions for Teaching.* National Conference on Research in English, Urbana, Illinois

Hillocks G Jr, Smith M 1986 Grammar. In: Hillocks G Jr 1986

Hillocks G Jr, Smith M 1991 Grammar and usage. In: Flood J, Jensen J M, Lapp D, Squire J R (eds.) 1991

Hodges R E 1991 The conventions of writing. In: Flood J, Jensen J M, Lapp D, Squire J R (eds.) 1991

Hunt K W 1964 *Differences in Grammatical Structures Written at Three Grade Levels, the Structures to be Analyzed by Transformational Methods.* Florida State University, Tallahassee, Florida

Loomer B M 1978 *Educator's Guide to Spelling Research and Practice.* University of lowa, Iowa City, Iowa

Meckel H C 1963 Research on teaching composition and literature. In: Gage N L (ed.) 1963 *Handbook of Research on Teaching.* Rand-McNally, Chicago, Illinois

Mellon J 1969 *Transformational Sentence-combining: A Method for Enhancing the Development of Syntactic Fluency in English Composition.* National Council of Teachers of English, Urbana, Illinois

O'Donnell R C, Griffin W J, Norris R C 1967 *Syntax of Kindergarten and Elementary School Children: A Transformational Analysis.* National Council of Teachers of English, Champaign, Illinois

O'Hare F 1973 *Sentence-Combining: Improving Student Writing Without Formal Grammar Instruction.* National Council of Teachers of English, Urbana, Illinois

Read C 1971 Pre-school children's knowledge of English phonology. *Harv. Educ. Rev.* 41(1): 1–34

Stotsky S L 1975 Sentence-combining as a curricular activity: Its effects on written language development and reading comprehension. *Research in the Teaching of English* 9(1): 30–71

Straw S B, Sadowy P G 1990 Can teaching sentence-combining help our students comprehend? An historical review. Unpublished research report, Faculty of Education, University of Manitoba, Winnipeg

Straw S B, Schreiner R 1982 The effect of sentence manipulation on subsequent measures of reading and listening comprehension. *Read. Res. Q.* 17(3): 339–52

Williamson G M 1988 An investigation of different writing programs and spelling programs on the writing fluency and spelling performance of grade two students. Unpublished research paper, Faculty of Education, University of Manitoba, Winnipeg

Zutell J 1980 Children's spelling strategies and their cognitive development. In: Henderson E H, Beers J W (eds.) 1980 *Developmental and Cognitive Aspects of Learning to Spell: A Reflection of Word Knowledge.* International Reading Association, Newark, Delaware

S. B. Straw

Spencer and Education

Herbert Spencer (1820–1903) was born in Derby in the English Midlands. He was the only surviving child of William George Spencer, a respected local teacher who was also secretary of the local scientific society. When Herbert died he had, arguably, amassed one of the largest readerships of any author of nonfiction in the nineteenth century, and, at one time or another, he could include among his admirers John Stuart Mill, Thomas Henry Huxley, William James, Ivan Pavlov, George Eliot, Henry Holt, and multimillionaire philanthropist, Andrew Carnegie. Spencer's theories had both a direct, and an indirect but nontheless marked, impact on education in many countries around the world, and he can be credited with doing much to establish the claims of science to a place on the school curriculum.

1. Spencer's Impact

Spencer's books and essays were translated into many languages: his *Essays on Education* (1861) appeared in 15 languages during his lifetime. In 1902 he was nominated for the Nobel Prize in literature, which was more an acknowledgement of the volume of his publications and his influence than a testament to his prose style which was, in his contemporary, US Supreme Court Justice Oliver Wardell Holmes put it, "dull." In an interesting assessment of Spencer's contributions, Holmes said that he "writes an ugly uncharming style, his ideals are those of a lower middle-class British Philistine. And yet after all abatements I doubt if any writer of English except Darwin has done so much to affect our whole way of thinking about the universe" (Holmes, quoted in Low-Beer 1969 p.13). In a more recent assessment the historian of education, Lawrence Cremin, in *The Transformation of the School* wrote that the 1890s produced a revolution in educational thought that included the work of William James, John Dewey, Stanley Hall, and others; and "if the revolution had a beginning it was surely with the work of Herbert Spencer" (Cremin 1964 p.91). Yet, a century after that important time, Spencer's work is largely forgotten, and those few authors who have recently studied it are likely to pass over his writings on education with little or no comment (see Kennedy 1978, Turner 1985).

2. Overview of Spencer's work

Spencer was not, in the conventional sense, an original thinker. His strength lay rather in his ability to synthesize ideas from a large number of disparate realms. However, at the core of his work were ideas that reflected his nonconformist political and religious background and his interest (but lack of expertise) in the sciences of his day. He was an evolutionist long before the publication of Darwin's *Origin of Species by Means of Natural Selection* in 1859 (having been converted to this view upon reading the work of the embryologist, Karl Ernst von Baer), and it was Spencer who coined the expression "survival of the fittest." He regarded publication of Darwin's work as confirmation of his own already developed views. Partly on "evolutionary" grounds, and partly because of his nonconformist suspicion of government interference into realms where individuals need to be free to follow their own conscience, he was an advocate of *laissez-faire* economic and social policies and of "small government" (even in the realms of social welfare and public education)—positions that were to be revived more than a century later in the United States during the period of the Reagan administration. (It is arguable that late-nineteenth and twentieth-century American thought has a strong "social Darwinist" element that emanates from Spencer.)

For a synthesizer Spencer was surprisingly poorly read. He found it psychologically impossible to do more than quickly browse through authors he found difficult or with whom he suspected he might have serious disagreements, and this characteristic was heightened by a mysterious ailment that, for more than half his life, prevented him from working in more than short bursts. This intellectual defect was magnified, too, by the fact that he lacked formal education. Spencer's father had not wanted to patronize organized schooling and so his son was educated at home and, later, by his uncle: he never attended university. In adult life, much of his knowledge seems to have been gathered from conversations with friends, among whom were numbered many of the leading intellectuals of the day, including several Fellows of the Royal Society.

Despite his handicaps, during the 1850's Spencer developed his key ideas and attitudes, and mapped out an exhaustive program for applying them to a wide range of disciplines including psychology, sociology, biology, and ethics. He published his prospectus for a series of works on "synthetic philosophy" in 1860 and, partly funded by subscriptions, was able to bring this mammoth multivolume undertaking to a conclusion before his death. In a brilliant review of Spencer's lifelong work published only months after his death, John Dewey referred to his subject's patience and courage in bringing his plans to fruition, but also pointed to the severe limitation inherent in this undertaking: "The point that seems to me so significant . . . when we balance accounts with the intellectual work of Mr. Spencer, is this sitting down to achieve a preconceived idea . . . Spencer and his readers are committed in advance to a definitely wrought out, a rounded and closed interpretation of the universe. Further discovery and intercourse are not to count . . ." (Dewey 1929 p.46). In short, Spencer's last 40 years were devoted to applying (but not developing or revising) a concept that was fully crystallized by 1860.

3. *Social and Political Thought*

At the age of 22 Spencer wrote a series of letters to the journal *The Nonconformist* on "the proper sphere of government," and these were followed almost a decade later in 1851 by his book *Social Statics* (see Spencer 1893). In 1896 some of the same ideas were reiterated in his *Principles of Ethics*. He argued that government legislation should be kept to a minimum—the only valid function it had was to ensure that competition was carried out fairly and that brute force was not brought to bear by the strong on the weak. But he denied government a role in alleviating the effects of competition; that is, he opposed social welfare and even health programs and legislation. Spencer advocated the "law of equal freedom," whereby the free man was able to enjoy the rewards, but also able to suffer the consequences, of his own actions. He defined "interference" as "any arrangements which in considerable degree prevent superiority from profiting by the rewards of superiority, or shield inferiority from the evils it entails" (Spencer, quoted in Wiltshire 1978 p.138). He was, consistent with this general outlook, a supporter of free trade and an opponent of organizations (such as trade unions) or legislation that endangered the free labor market. Not surprisingly, then, he was opposed to compulsory, state-provided education, and he even attacked private philanthropy (although he was the beneficiary of philanthropic support from his friends):

> Blind to the fact that under the natural order of things society is constantly excreting its unhealthy, imbecile, slow, vacillating faithless members . . . in their eagerness to prevent the salutary sufferings that surround us, these sigh-wise and groan-foolish people [philanthropists] bequeath to posterity a continually-increasing curse. (Spencer 1893 p.151)

Underlying these closely related positions is a general view of society as a type of organism, which will only progress if the natural law of progress is allowed to operate unfettered. It was in this context, but in pre-Darwinian times, that he coined the expression "survival of the fittest" which indeed stands as a pithy summary of his position.

4. *Progress*

Spencer's theory concerning the nature and cause of progress was fundamental to much (if not all) of his thought. He published an essay "Progress: Its Law and Cause" in 1857, which is usually reprinted alongside the four essays on education which he also wrote during the 1850s. In 1862 his theory played a central role in *First Principles*, in which he outlined the future volumes he intended to write to expound his "synthetic philosophy"—a project, as mentioned above, which he indeed brought to fruition. In the opening paragraphs of his 1857 essay he cited the work of the embryologist von Baer as showing that, in the process of their development, embryos "advance from homogeneity of structure to heterogeneity of structure" (Spencer 1949 p.154). He then argued that this "law of organic progress is the law of all progress." He saw this, in turn, as a product of the physical law that all forces (i.e., all causes) produce more than one effect.

Being central to his thought, it is no surprise that the law of progress played a role in his writings on education. As one commentator has written, although there are other elements present, "belief in science, a social view of man, a materialist conception of society, and a belief in universal and inevitable laws, are all clear in Spencer's educational works" (Low-Beer 1969 p.14).

5. *Essays on Education*

The four essays on education appeared between the years 1854 and 1859 as self-contained contributions to several different journals. In 1861 Spencer collected them into one volume, and the last-written piece (which is perhaps the most famous of the four)—"What Knowledge is of Most Worth?"—became the book's opening chapter.

In this first essay he argued that, historically speaking, for the human race the ornamental had taken precedence over the useful in a variety of areas ranging from clothing to the realm of ideas. Thus, in education, unfortunately the focus is not what knowledge is of most "real worth," but "what will bring most applause, honour, respect—what will most conduce to social position and influence. . ." (Spencer 1949 p.4). Spencer concluded that in order to adjudicate between the rival claims of various subjects contending for places in the curriculum—and to go beyond mere ornament—he had to determine their relative worth, and for this endeavor a measure of value was required. Clearly, he felt, the requisite criterion was the relevance of the subject for human welfare, and especially what the subject contributed to "complete living." He wrote that the key issue was: "How to live?—that is the essential question for us. Not how to live in the mere material sense only, but in the widest sense" (Spencer 1949 p.6).

From this point he produced a classification of human activities that reflected the various tasks that face humans in the course of "living completely": first, those activities which directly minister to self-preservation; second, activities which, by securing "the necessaries of life," indirectly contribute to self-preservation; third, activities which relate to the rearing and discipline of offspring; fourth, activities contributing to the maintenance of social and political relations; and finally, "those miscellaneous activities which fill up the leisure part of life, devoted to the gratification of the tastes and feelings" (Spencer 1949 p. 7). Within the course of a couple of pages, however, Spencer had slipped from claiming this was simply a classification of activities involved in "complete living" to also claiming that this order reflected the "successively decreasing importance" of the activities (Spencer 1949 p. 10). Of course, Spencer could claim that, in a sense, his ordering reflected the biological importance of the activities; after all, in order to rear offspring, a person first had to survive, and so forth.

In the next steps of his "argument" he attempted to show several important things: first, that in each of these categories of activity, scientific knowledge was the most valuable simply as knowledge; second, that science was also the most valuable as a discipline (as "mental exercise"); and third, that although he personally valued the activities of the fifth category—those that contribute to leisure and the cultivation of taste (such as the arts and literature)—nevertheless, the logic of his classification demanded that "As they occupy the leisure part of life, so should they occupy the leisure part of education" (Spencer 1949 p. 32).

Although it may well have been this last point that led numerous commentators (see e.g., Holmes, quoted in Low-Beer 1969 p. 13) to brand Spencer as a philistine, the other portions of the essay seem to have been of great importance and influence. Spencer had produced a strange but, at the time, powerful argument for the inclusion of science in the school curriculum, and in fact, since the 1860s classics has become of less importance in the school curriculum. Certainly the dual claims that science is directly relevant to life and is a fine mental training are still part of the rhetoric of debates over the curriculum.

In the second essay, "Intellectual Education," the law of movement from homogeneity to heterogeneity made an appearance. Spencer attacked rote learning and applauded the movement to make learning pleasurable to students. He saw the "fundamental principle of tuition" as being that "the arrangement of matter and method [of education] must correspond with the order of evolution and mode of activity of the faculties" (Spencer 1949 p. 53). The term "evolution" is used here somewhat ambiguously in both its pre-Darwinian sense of "unfolding" or growth, and its Darwinian sense of "order of origin in the pre-history of the species". In the late nineteeth century, Spencer, and many others, were concerned with both aspects of evolution—a practice that became codified later in Evenst Haeckel's notorious law which stated that the "ontogeny recapitulates phylogeny."

From this basis Spencer derived several influential principles, including "education should always proceed from the simple to the complex"; "lessons should move from the concrete to the abstract, rather than vice-versa"; and "the genesis of knowledge in the individual must follow the same course as the genesis of knowledge in the race" (Spencer 1949 pp. 58–60).

Of the remaining two essays—on "Moral Education" and "Physical Education"—the former has dated rapidly. Its chief defect is that it does not treat anything that looks like morality at all, and it is, in essence, a piece of advocacy for the Rousseauian doctrine of the suffering of the natural consequences of one's actions. The final piece is a discussion—now also dated—on issues concerning the physical well-being of children.

6. Conclusion

By way of summary it is appropriate to quote from Charles W Eliot's widely read "Introduction" to the 1910 edition of Spencer's essays:

> On the whole, Herbert Spencer has been fortunate among educational philosophers. He has not had to wait so long for the acceptance of his teachings as Comenius, Montaigne, or Rousseau waited. His ideas have been floated on a prodigious tide of industrial and social change, which necessarily involved widespread and profound educational reform. (Eliot, in Spencer 1949 pp. xvi–xvii)

See also: Philosophy of Education: Historical Overview; Philosophy of Education: Western European Perspectives

References

Cremin L A 1964 *The Transformation of the School*. Vintage Books, New York

Dewey J 1929 *Characters and Events: Popular Essays in Social and Political Philosophy*. Henry Holt, New York

Kennedy J G 1978 *Herbert Spencer*. Twayne Publishers, Boston, Massachusetts

Low-Beer A (ed.) 1969 *Herbert Spencer*. Collier-Macmillan, London

Turner J H 1985 *Herbert Spencer: A Renewed Appreciation*. Sage, Beverly Hills, California

Wiltshire D 1978 *The Social and Political Thought of Herbert Spencer*. Oxford University Press, Oxford
Spencer H 1893 *Social Statics, Abridged and Revised, Together With The Man Versus The State*. Appleton, New York
Spencer H 1949 *Essays on Education and Kindred Subjects*. Everyman, London

Further Reading

Hofstadter R 1955 *Social Darwinism in American Thought*. Beacon Press, Boston, Massachusetts
Phillips D C 1966 The idea of evolution in educational thought. In: French E L (ed.) 1966 *Melbourne Studies in Education 1965*. Melbourne University Press, Carlton, Victoria
Spencer H 1937 *First Principles*, 6th edn. Watts, London
Trompf G W 1971 Essays on education and the young Herbert Spencer. In: Selleck R J W (ed.) 1971 *Melbourne Studies in Education 1971*. Melbourne University Press, Melbourne

D. C. Phillips

Sport Pedagogy, Research in

The term "sport pedagogy" is extensively used by researchers in physical education, although one encounters differences in the definition of the term. Some researchers refer to this term as "The art and science of teaching sport, exercise and expressive movement," while others have thought this definition to be too restrictive. Disagreement regarding the term is based on philosophic differences or views and is often further exacerbated by cultural differences that influence the relative meaning of language and terms. One need only review the following operational definitions of sport pedagogy from experts around the world to appreciate the complexity and diversity of opinion (Piéron et al. 1990).

Sport pedagogy is the process of translating theory into practice (Almond 1988). Supporting this popular description is the need for pedagogy to conduct: (a) first-order research, such as empirical, analytic, and interpretative research and use of critical theory; (b) development work: distilling research findings and making them accessible to practitioners; (c) second-order research: investigation into the effectiveness of translating theory into practice and understanding the problems faced by teachers/coaches in incorporating research into practice.

Sport pedagogy is considered by Piéron et al. (1990) to comprise two vital processes: (a) the academic professional preparation of future physical education teachers and coaches and (b) the professional activity of physical education teachers and coaches. This definition is used throughout the entry. Sport pedagogy is concerned with teaching and coaching, including teaching methods and other important elements tied to the concerns of professional practice in physical education and sport. Thus, in addition to teaching, sport pedagogy includes curriculum, supervision, and administration.

The largest part of research on sport pedagogy deals with research on teaching and on teacher education. Results from research on teaching should provide a sound basis to improve teacher education. In addition, research on teacher education is expected to influence strongly what is happening in a physical education class. Research on teaching concerns "what teachers do and how this affects and is related to learning and the social dynamics of the class" (Silverman 1991). Research on teacher education refers to "research which deals with any aspect of the process designed to influence what teachers will do in the execution of professional tasks" (Locke and Dodds 1984).

In this entry, two major areas of sport pedagogy will be examined: the study of the teaching/coaching process and the study of teacher/coach preparation. In each area, the knowledge derived from the research will be subdivided into categories representing the descriptive–correlative–experimental loop suggested by Rosenshine and Furst (1973). They deal with: (a) the development of procedures and techniques describing accurately the teaching/coaching act under its quantitative and qualitative aspects; (b) *Correlational studies* wherein the descriptive variables are correlated with student learning gains and various changes in their attitudes and motivation; and (c) *Experimental studies* where meaningful variables are tested in rigorously controlled settings.

1. Teaching Process in Physical Education: Descriptive Approach

The descriptive approach, the first step to understand any phenomenon, was largely used in the early 1970s to analyze physical education teaching and later the world of teacher/coach preparation and of induction of students to teaching or coaching. The first research endeavor was based mainly on observation schemes generated by deductive systems. With the emergence of the qualitative research, ethnographic methods became popular in sport pedagogy research. Cognitive techniques are emerging in the 1990s that concern teacher thinking and decision-making.

1.1 Observation by Deductive Systems

Several choices were available to observers: using existing observation systems validated for classroom observation, or devising new systems better adapted to physical education. Systems from classroom research were used in the perspective that physical education was a component of the curriculum and that physical education contributed to the overall achievement goals. The development of new observation systems was aimed at accounting for the specific nature of physical education and the characteristics of student engagement in various physical education settings.

1.1.1 Physical education teacher and sports coach behavior. A clear description of teacher behavior profile was provided. It dealt with teaching functions such as instruction or presentation of content, feedback, class organization and management, and silent observation. Significant differences in some of these functions have been observed in comparing classes according to teacher's expertise, subject matter taught, or lesson objectives. The variability of behavior profiles seems to be greater when considering program variables (objectives, subject matter, sharing decision-making between teacher and student, accountability systems) than in context variables such as grade level or gender. Compared to novices or to student teachers, expert teachers emphasized content of the subject matter reflected by the quantitative level of instructional or feedback categories. Experienced teachers (defined by number of years employed in the profession) cannot be equated with expert teachers (defined in terms of teacher skills or student achievement).

Teacher feedback is of importance when dealing with learning objectives. From the research in motor learning, it is believed that feedback plays a key role in teaching. However, teaching conditions are far more complex than those existing in motor learning experiments. It was necessary to describe feedback more accurately. In addition to the quantitative aspect, feedback was described under various structural viewpoints such as intent, form, direction, specificity, or generality of its referent and cue-relevancy. In physical education teaching as well as in coaching, the feedback was predominantly evaluative or prescriptive, given verbally to a single student or athlete.

In teaching, the following questions should be asked: Do students and athletes hear and understand the feedback message? Are they able to process the information contained in the feedback message and to restructure their motor plan? Are they able to change their motor behavior after receiving feedback from the teacher or the coach?

Important facets of feedback are still missing. Clearly, its apparent effect on student performance and its appropriateness to the characteristics of the learner will be a focus for future research. Other teacher interventions remain to be examined; to date, the presentation of content, its clarity, and ways to gain and maintain student attention have produced few studies.

Teaching and coaching settings have been compared. Coaches as well as teachers perform in communication situations and exert their actions through verbal and nonverbal interventions. Usually, their aims are more accurately defined and more explicit than those of teachers. Moreover they are more consonant to their players' aims than to the student aims. To study coach behaviors, observers frequently used the same instruments as in teaching. However, adaptations were made to better suit the specific interventions as in the Piéron and Gonçalves study (1987) or as described by Darst et al. (1989).

Descriptive studies of exceptional coaches, as well as ordinary coaches, showed that they devote a large part of their instructional behaviors to content and struggle to increase athletes' efforts and involvement. These differences were confirmed in comparisons between behaviors exhibited by the same persons performing in the two settings of coaching and teaching (Piéron and Gonçalves, 1987).

In classroom research it appeared that not all students are affected the same way by the teacher's interaction with them. Teacher expectancy studies indicated that some teachers treated high- and low-achieving students differently. In teaching physical education, the expectancy phenomenon is strongly influenced by cultural values, less apparent in Western Europe than in the United States. The phenomenon is more visible and more universal in coaching than in teaching. The high-achieving athletes received more frequent feedback, usually with positive or approving connotations, than low-achieving athletes. They received more frequent praise and positive reinforcement and less frequent scolding. In teaching as well as in coaching, if the interaction and the student/athlete engagement stay the same, the gap between high and low achievers will continue to widen.

1.1.2 Student behavior. In the 1980s, researchers studying teaching shifted part of their interest from teacher behavior to student behavior observation and more precisely to analyzing their participation in activities and motor engagement time. These variables have received strong theoretical support from the research on teaching effectiveness completed in the classroom. Its meaning for practical application is clear and based on results from the process–product studies. Authors have proposed one variable directly related to student engagement time as a substitution variable to appraise teaching effectiveness. Without denying the value of time, there is evidence that success in teaching cannot be limited to such a restrictive view. Quality of teaching will eventually be predicted only by a multidimensional approach (Telama et al. 1982). The level of success in student engagement, and the appropriateness and specificity of tasks will provide more predictive power than simple time variables. In addition to providing quantitative data, the use of a qualitative paradigm in observing students provides teachers with other more pertinent information about students.

In general, figures describing the quantitative aspects of student motor engagement are relatively bleak. Data show that students spend less than 20 percent of their time in physical activity and more than 40 percent of this time in waiting their turn to exercise. Significant differences were observed in comparing student engagement according to subject matter or objectives. Lower engagement was observed in gymnastics, organized within the context of recreational and learning objectives. High engagement was registered in dance or team sports and with fitness objectives. In coaching settings, top-level athletes were engaged in motor activities at a higher level than less advanced athletes and much higher than students in any teaching setting.

Researchers in sport pedagogy have been strongly influenced by research models and theories from classroom research, sometimes forgetting the specificity of their discipline. One typical example is that of the intensity of physical education sessions. Motor engagement, success of participation, and emotional involvement have been investigated. The specificity of the tasks or the intensity level of participation have rarely been approached in observation studies.

Some people have expressed a deep concern about the health effects of school physical activities. In many industrialized countries, children and youth are characterized by inactivity in their everyday lives. School physical education appears to induce only a low level of intensity and is unable to produce noticeable effects on cardiovascular or muscular endurance (Armstrong et al. 1990, Piéron and Vrijens 1991, Ross and Gilbert 1985). Observation systems carefully validated are able to report on student engagement and the intensity of physical education. They discriminate among levels of energy expenditure. It is expected that in the future more research will gather data on the intensity of physical education lessons.

It is easy to understand that observation cannot be limited to isolated behaviors but must concentrate on more elaborate constructs like enthusiasm, discipline, clarity of presentation, and task structure. Large research efforts are needed to understand better their meaning in relation to teaching. Researchers were committed to simultaneously gathering data from several points of origin. Interaction of teacher behavior was observed (Telama et al. 1982) at the same time as student involvement along with physiological data.

1.2 Observation by Inductive Systems: Ethnographical Approach

The teaching situation is complex and none of the research approaches deals satisfactorily with all its aspects. Data gathered through observation systems have been unable to provide the investigators with complete interpretation and understanding of the teaching process. For example, knowing the feedback rate or its structure does not indicate its appropriateness or how it was perceived and retained by the student.

Several researchers have adopted the ecological paradigm to clarify the relationship between the environmental demands (the classroom situations) and the ways used by individuals to respond to it. In following the ecological model, observers wished to enter more profoundly into the participants' world and to understand the meanings and philosophies they have developed. Qualitative research methods or naturalistic observation techniques have been used to gain a thorough understanding of life in a physical education classroom, and to explore the participants' interpretations of events. Teacher behaviors and perceptions indicated that order, compliance, and control were the main characteristics of many physical education teachers.

As an example, the application of ethnographic techniques in observation has dealt with the characterization of student behavior, the qualitative analysis of task structures, the socializing process, or the decision-making process in teacher planning. To give a further example, task structures and student participation patterns were described through participant observation. Categories of behavior were identified through the nature of task accomplishment by students engaged: a) with the task as stated by the teacher, b) in a modified task, c) in deviant off-task behavior, and d) as competent bystanders (avoiding the participation without misbehaving). Major types of accountability were apparent, formal and informal. Minimal participation, effort, or production of motor responses were the focuses of accountability systems. There were subtle interactions between student behaviors and accountability systems and the consistency of the application (Tousignant and Siedentop 1983).

The student participation as a function of gender was also approached by ethnographic observation in physical education classes. Boys and girls participated seriously only in activities traditionally considered appropriate to their sex. In other cases, the participant was reluctant or "frivolous". In coeducational classes, the interaction between boys and girls is frequently described as ignoring and separating, or hassling and responding to hassles (Griffin 1983).

Like the quantitative approach, ethnographical observation does not escape criticism. Siedentop (1987) lists some of these as follows: (a) the absence of any mechanism for public verifiability of primary data; (b) the possibility, due to the amount of time and effort needed to reduce primary data, of the intervention of persons other than the observer; (c) the temptation to make implicit attribution of causality; (d) the central role attributed to intentions; and (e) the philosophical or educational bias of the investigator.

2. Study of Teaching Effectiveness: Correlational Approach

Studies using the correlational approach have been

influenced by the research program "Beginning Teacher Evaluation Study" completed in classroom settings (Denham and Lieberman, 1980). The purpose was to answer the questions: What does make a difference between more and less effective teachers? and what are the relationships between the teaching process and student outcomes?

In physical education, when the pioneers started the research on teaching effectiveness, they adopted the same general design as in the classroom research. Studies of the magnitude of the teacher effectiveness research, however, require resources not usually available to research in teaching physical education. One alternative to the full scale process–product paradigm has been the Experimental Teaching Unit (ETU) or ETU-like studies. Their results permitted reasonable hypotheses on variables important in the success of teaching. Later, more extensive studies, very close to the reality of the physical education class, have been completed. They confirmed a large part of the results gathered in smaller ETUs.

Experimental Teaching Units are characterized by:

(a) a learning objective set forth for all the teachers involved in the study;

(b) measures of student learning developed specifically to appraise the instructional content taught in the ETU, which is administered before and after the actual ETU lessons are taught;

(c) teaching period of specified length;

(d) systematic observation of selected teacher and student behaviors conducted during the ETU lessons.

Although some differences exist in the design of the studies completed, they can be summarized and discussed according to several topics specified below.

2.1 The Improvement of Learner Performance

The teaching conditions of all the studies have resulted in some student learning gains except when tasks were too complex and inappropriate to the student ability levels. The relationship between the entry and final levels is generally high. However, it decreases when the duration of the teaching period is increased.

2.2 The Motor Engagement Time

A large number of studies have shown that time on task is important in student learning. There is strong evidence that practice is related to achievement in physical education. The number of practice trials and the difficulty levels are more important than the engagement time. Appropriate practice is positively related to achievement and inappropriate practice or unsuccessful trials are negatively related to learning gains (Silverman 1991). However, it was found that this unique variable was not satisfactorily predictive. The adequacy of any treatment must be considered under two aspects. First, the specificity of activities to facilitate a significant transfer from the activities performed in the ETU toward the final learning objective; and second, the aptitude–treatment interaction theory suggests that not every student can benefit from the same kind of activities or from the same teacher interventions. Student individual differences should be accounted for. The adequacy of the tasks to student skill level is a key to their success in learning.

2.3 Feedback Provided by the Teacher to the Student

Several studies found a significant relationship between feedback and student learning gains when the quality of performance, rather than its quantitative aspect, was considered.

It is possible to generalize results in teaching effectiveness research. They depend on the teaching conditions in terms of a) tasks practised by the students during the teaching period. A large variety of tasks have been used, from simple (hitting a ball) to complex (high jump); chosen in open (volleyball and tennis) and in closed skills (cartwheel, in gymnastics); and in individual and in team sports; b) length of the ETUs. They have ranged from a few minutes to a full unit of teaching lasting for several weeks or even three years (Graham et al. 1991); c) the students and teachers involved in the ETU: students from kindergarten to university levels and student teachers to master teachers.

Most of the criteria identified in research on teaching effectiveness have received confirmation through comparisons between expert teachers and novices. In general, studies have been characterized by a trend to become closer to the real teaching conditions. This is the problem facing the researchers and to date the implications of these studies for preservice and inservice teachers suggest that this area of investigation is far from being thorough. This research question will be improved through a higher adequacy of research instruments, an enrichment of the learning situations, and by considering more carefully the methods used by the teacher.

3. Teacher/Coach Preparation: Descriptive Studies

The teaching/coaching preparation has been a field of application of qualitative research methods. Qualities of teachers, their perception of their own success, the beliefs and values of physical education teachers, their perception of sex equity problems, the impact of principals on teachers during inservice education, and teacher socialization, have been current research questions investigated by multidimensional qualitative methods. Typical questions asked were: Why does one become a teacher of physical education? How does one acquire the skills, knowledge, values, and attitudes essential in performing the role of the physical educator? What socialization processes are involved in the development of one's teaching perspective? (Templin and Schempp 1989).

The impact of being a student on learning teaching tasks, the identification with teachers and the development of teachers' professional perspective were explored. The influence of the school setting, of teachers' colleagues, students, administrators, and school policies were analyzed. Doyle's concept of task was also used as an explicative concept within student teaching. Tinning and Siedentop (1985) concluded that for the intern, "acceptable responses" must be considered as both acceptable to the supervisors (including both university supervisor and cooperating teacher) and the class pupils. Thus, the intern may be faced with difficulties if the supervisor's expectations are at variance with what produces cooperation from the pupils. The hidden curriculum in physical education as an agent of teacher socialization was examined (Templin and Schempp 1989).

4. *Acquiring Teaching Skills: Experimental Studies*

After identifying teaching skills by descriptive methods or by the correlational approach, it was natural to seek applications in preservice preparation or inservice training. Two research methodologies have been used in studying the learning of pedagogical skills: (a) comparing experimental and control groups. The treatment group follows a specific preparation based on the learning of some observation system, on clear definition and demonstration of typical teaching behaviors. In addition, subjects receive objective feedback from the observation. (b) Behavior modification using the multiple baseline design and specific intervention to modify target behaviors. This research methodology has been systematically used (Siedentop 1981). It was based on specific interventions aimed at the acquisition of well-defined behaviors. Without entering into a detailed view of teaching skills, it emphasized variables related to teaching effectiveness, namely feedback, climate of the class, or student time-on-task. Moreover, it allowed one to individualize the preparation in matching trainee characteristics with intervention or treatment. The behavior modification related dynamically to the intervention and modification. Three options were described by Hersen and Barlow (1976): through behaviors, through subjects, and through situations. They were used in studies involving physical education student teachers or inservice teachers.

Experimental studies can be distributed in four main categories aiming at: a) changing the whole picture of the teaching relationship; b) modifying specific teacher behaviors such as increasing the feedback rate, increasing the positive and approving statements rate, decreasing the negative reactions to performance and off-task behaviors, using students' first names more frequently and decreasing the length of silent observation and organization periods; c) increasing student motor engagement time in physical education classes; and d) acquiring high inference teacher behavior such as enthusiasm. From all the studies, it must be remembered that teaching behavior or teacher student interaction can be changed by specific programs or by behavior modification techniques.

Some findings are as follows (Piéron 1988): An informative or objective feedback is efficient in changing many teaching behaviors. However, when a change has occurred it is not necessarily maintained at the level attained during the intervention phase or after the training program. Results are not automatically transferable to another educational or sport setting. Therefore it must be kept in mind that every teacher is committed to continuous inservice training or to self-improvement effort.

The more powerful factors influencing teacher preparation and field experiences include the cooperating teacher, the teaching style, the knowledge of the subject matter by the trainee, and the entry level. The motivation and the will to change teacher behavior is a key determinant in the success of any program aimed at acquiring teaching skills. The more involved the subject, the greater the chances of success.

It is easier to increase the rate of approving interventions than to decrease the rate of negative and disapproving interventions.

Second-order variables in teaching such as student motor engagement time, depending on various strategies besides teacher behavior, are more difficult to change. The modification is subject to other variables such as class organization.

Various preparation means such as peer teaching, role play, or micro-teaching were used to learn new or to change old teaching behaviors. Other styles of intervention included:

(a) Competency modules, in written form. They comprise general objectives, specific behavioral objectives, definition of teaching skills, and suggestion of practice and evaluation procedures.

(b) Target behavior adapted to the individual, presented in percentages or intervention rates.

(c) "Cueing": recalling the objective in written or verbal forms. It is stated by another student, the investigator, or by preregistered messages.

(d) Verbal and graphic feedback stated immediately after the lesson. It is provided by the investigator, the cooperating teacher, or by other student teachers.

(e) Systematic reinforcement through praise to increase the rate of desirable behaviors and to decrease undesirable behaviors.

(f) Modeling of specific behaviors, demonstrated or through videotapes.

It was observed that one specific intervention was usually less effective than a package.

5. Conclusions and Perspectives

Quantitative and qualitative descriptive analyses of teaching have confirmed the large gap between pedagogical theories and the daily reality of physical education classes. However, systematic observations have contributed to gathering data that provides a sound basis to teaching methodology. Teaching physical education can be based on reality rather than on unrealistic expectations. To date, some of the research findings have been disseminated and applied in teacher preparation and in inservice training.

It is expected that multiple data collection processes and improved strategies will add insight to the process of teaching and teacher preparation. Many problems are still ahead. They must be dealt with by in-depth analyses and longitudinal or long-term studies. Some of these problems are: the impact of some high inference teaching qualities (enthusiasm, clarity, class management), discipline and burn-out problems, teachers' induction into the career, teacher decision-making in preactive and interactive phases of teaching, and the appropriateness and quality of teacher intervention and student participation.

See also: Physical Education Teacher Education

References

Almond L 1988 What is sport pedagogy? *International Committee of Sport Pedagogy Newsletter* 4: 2–3

Armstrong N, Balding J, Bray S, Gentle P, Kirby B 1990 The physical activity patterns of 10 to 13 year old children. In: Beunen G, Ghesquière T, Reybrouck A, Claessens A (eds.) 1990 *Children and Exercise*. Enke Verlag, Stuttgart

Denham C, Lieberman A 1980 *Time to Learn*. US Department of Education, Washington, DC

Graham G, Metzler M, Webster G 1991 Specialist and classroom teacher effectiveness in children's physical education: A 3-year study. *Journal of Teaching in Physical Education* 10: 321–426

Griffin P 1983 Gymnastics is a girl's thing: Student participation and interaction patterns in a middle school gymnastics unit. In: Templin T, Olson J (eds.) 1983 *Teaching in Physical Education*. Human Kinetics, Champaign, Illinois

Hersen M, Barlow D 1976 *Single Case Experimental Design: Strategies for Studying Behavior Change*. Pergamon, New York

Locke L, Dodds P 1984 Research on teaching teachers: Where are we now? *Journal of Teaching in Physical Education*. Monograph 2: 1–85

Piéron M 1986 *Enseignement des Activités Physiques et Sportives: Observations et Recherches*. Presses Universitaires, Liège

Piéron M, Cheffers J, Barrette G 1990 *An Introduction to the Terminology of Sport Pedagogy*. ICSP, Liège

Piéron M, Gonçalves C 1987 Participant engagement and teacher's feedback in physical education teaching and coaching. In: Barrette G T, Feingold R S, Rees C R, Piéron M (eds.) 1987 *Myths, Models and Methods in Sport Pedagogy*. Human Kinetics, Champaign, Illinois

Piéron M, Vrijens J 1991 *Livre Blanc sur la Condition Physique des Jeunes en Belgique*. Fondation Roi Baudouin et Comité Interfédéral Belge, Brussels

Rife F, Dodds P 1978 Developing evidential bases for educational practice through the single subject research paradigm: Motor skills. *Theory Prac.* 3(1): 40–48

Rosenshine B, Furst N 1973 The use of direct observation to study teaching. In: Travers R (ed.) 1973 *Second Handbook of Research on Teaching*. Rand McNally, Chicago, Illinois

Ross J, Gilbert G 1985 The national children and youth fitness study: A summary of findings. *J. Phys. Educ., Recreat. Dance* 56(1): 45–50

Siedentop D1981 The Ohio State University supervision research program summary report. *Journal of Teaching in Physical Education*, Introductory Issue: 30–38

Siedentop D1987 Sport pedagogy research: Methods and assumptions. In: Rieder H, Hanke U (eds.) 1987 *The Physical Education Teacher and Coach Today*. Bundesinstitut für Sport, Cologne

Silverman S1991 Research on teaching in physical education. *Research Quarterly for Exercise and Sport* 62(4): 352–64

Telama R, Paukku P, Varstala V, Paananen M 1982 Pupil's physical activity and learning behaviour in physical education classes. In: Piéron M, Cheffers J (eds.) 1982 *Studying the Teaching in Physical Education*. AIESEP, Liège

Templin T, Schempp P1989 An introduction to socialization into physical education. In: Templin T, Schempp P (eds.) 1989 *Socialization into Physical Education. Learning to teach*. Benchmark Press, Indianapolis

Tinning R, Siedentop D 1985 The characteristics of tasks and accountability in student teaching. *Journal of Teaching in Physical Education* 4(4): 286–99

Tousignant M, Siedentop D 1983 A qualitative analysis of task structures in required secondary physical education classes. *Journal of Teaching in Physical Education* 3(1): 47–57

M. Piéron

Sri Lanka: System of Education

1. General Background

The Republic of Sri Lanka, a pear-shaped island measuring 435 kilometers from north to south and 225 kilometers from east to west with an area of 65,600 square kilometers, is located off the southeastern tip of the Indian subcontinent. The country has a typical tropical climate with heavy monsoon rains and average temperatures around 27°C in the lowlands and 10–20°C in the central highlands.

In 1990, the population was estimated to be nearly 17 million. The population growth rate declined from 1.9 in the 1960s to 1.5 in the 1990s, but the population is expected to be well beyond 20 million by the year 2000 and about 27 million by the 2040s. More than 75 percent of the population is rural. The fact that 35 percent of the population is below the age of 14 has significant implications for educational planning. Furthermore, the older age groups are becoming relatively larger than the younger ones due to the declining fertility level. This foretells a change in the demands made on the social infrastructure and consequently on education. The density of population varies widely from 2,909 per square kilometer (in the Colombo district—1989) to 36 (in the Mullaitivu district); the national average is 260 per square kilometer.

The Sinhalese comprise 74 percent of the population, Sri Lankan Tamils 12.6 percent, Indian Tamils 5.5 percent, Moors 7.1 percent, and others (Eurasians, Malays, etc.) 0.8 percent. About 69 percent of the people are Buddhists, 15.5 percent Hindus, 7.6 percent Muslims, and 7.5 percent Christians according to the 1981 census. Sinhala and Tamil are the two national languages and they are also the media of instruction, although English is a widely used second language. The multiracial, multilingual, multireligious character of the population has given rise to various types of socioeconomic problems (particularly in education) and has also been the cause of ethnic conflicts, mainly between the Sinhalese and the Tamils, which surfaced after Independence and escalated into armed confrontation in the 1980s. With the adoption of a free market economic policy in 1977 and the expansion of the modern sector of employment, there has been an increasing demand for English which is considered to be the key with which to gain access to that sector.

Sri Lanka is predominantly an agricultural country whose export income is mainly from tea, rubber, and coconut, which account for nearly 60 percent of export earnings and 26 percent of the Gross Domestic Product (GDP). The most important food crop is rice, which is also the staple food of the people. The industrial base of the economy is still weak, the main industries being cement, textiles, leather and rubber goods, paper, ceramics, and petroleum products. Nontraditional exports such as precious stones and garments are gaining in importance as foreign-exchange earners. The composition of the GDP in 1989 was: agriculture 26.0 percent; industry 25.6 percent; and services 48.4 percent. The Gross National Product (GNP) (at 1990 prices) was 284,553 million rupees, equivalent to US$7,103 million and a per capita GNP of US$418. Imports exceeded exports by about US$705 million in 1990.

Of those employed in 1991, most were in elementary occupations (39.5%) followed by skilled agricultural workers (25.2%) and crafts and related workers, machine operators, and so on (14.3%). Only about 12 percent were in senior or management level and professional occupations, or technical or similar occupations. Just over 50 percent of all working-age persons were reported to be economically active, but about 14 percent of this group were unemployed. Over 70 percent of the people between 20 and 34 years and 30 percent between 15 and 19 years of age were unemployed. Thus, there is a problem of unemployed youth, since the unemployed have a much higher educational profile than the employed.

The problem of abject poverty has driven children to work at various trades such as pavement hawkers, domestic labor, private bus conductors and criers, and in repair shops and small industries. These children are either early dropouts from school or those who were never enrolled.

Sri Lanka has been able to achieve considerable social progress despite low economic development, due to welfare measures taken by successive governments since Independence for meeting the basic needs of the people through such means as food subsidies, free education and healthcare, and nationalization of essential services. This is reflected in Sri Lanka being placed 75th in the Human Development Index (HDI) of 160 countries while its GNP rank is as low as 120 (UNDP 1991). Ironically, it is the disproportionate success of these services relative to economic development which has put inexorable pressures on the socioeconomic system of the country. Since 1989, the government has placed high priority on alleviation of poverty and launched a major trans-sectorial strategy known as the *Janasaviya* Program (JSP) aimed at combating income disparities, unemployment, landlessness, malnutrition, and the like.

With the expansion of economic activities the demand for trained personnel—especially in the fields of construction, industry, finance, tourism and other service sectors—has increased considerably. Also, increasing external demand, particularly from the Middle-East countries for skilled personnel in technical fields, further augments the necessity for trained personnel.

Sri Lanka can claim to have a satisfactory level of infrastructure for a developing country. The country has developed its electric power capacity mainly through hydro power and has a good public transport system providing access even to remote rural areas.

Sri Lanka has a well-developed health system in which both the Western and the traditional (*Ayurveda*) system function side by side focusing on primary healthcare resulting in a substantial lowering of death rates, infant and maternal mortality rates, and raised life expectancy levels.

Sri Lanka gained independence from British colonial rule in 1948 and adopted a parliamentary system of government. The country was declared a republic within the Commonwealth in 1972. Since

1987 there has been some devolution of powers from the national government to the provincial councils. The provincial council system was designed to decentralize the administration and, within the framework of a unitary state, to have a system of devolution of power. Education and education services are subjects that come within the purview of the provincial councils, which have limited and specified powers assigned to them in certain areas. The devolution of power has brought in a new dimension to educational planning and development in Sri Lanka, with implications in particular for curriculum development, teacher education, and evaluation and accreditation at the school level and for entry into tertiary-level education.

2. Politics and the Goals of the Education System

The traditional education base, which has evolved since the introduction of Buddhism in the third century BC, gradually eroded with the advent of the Western powers—the Portuguese, Dutch, and British—from the sixteenth to the twentieth centuries. Certain radical policy changes introduced in the 1940s constitute a landmark in the democratization of education. The most significant changes were the introduction, in 1945, of free education from kindergarten through to university and the adoption of the mother tongue of the child as the medium of instruction. These measures were expected to provide for greater equality of opportunity and social mobility. After Independence (1948), successive governments have declared their intention to continue with the policies of democratization of education, removal of elitism and privilege, and of providing equality of opportunity to all.

As the political pendulum swung with changes of government, each government attempted to introduce educational reforms to suit its political and socioeconomic ideologies, which contributed to a high degree of disorder in the system. A government that came into power with the support of the Sinhala–Buddhist majority introduced drastic changes to eradicate inequalities that stemmed from the existence of a Western-oriented English-educated elite and a privileged Christian denominational sector in the education system. In spite of these policy changes, most middle-class parents consider education to be the key to social mobility and demand a system which would enable their children to enter the prestigious professions in society such as medicine, engineering, accountancy, and law, or to qualify for lucrative jobs in a foreign land.

As a result, attempts to restructure the education system and make it more relevant to the socioeconomic needs and realities of the country have met with strong resistance from certain classes of parents. Such situations are invariably exploited by rival political parties to woo voters at general elections and offer professionally unsound counterproposals in their election manifestos.

The main political goals of the government in the 1990s are to eradicate poverty, to adopt a free market economic policy to encourage rapid economic growth, and to take appropriate measures to solve the ethnic conflict between the Sinhalese and Tamils and ensure national unity. The achievement of these goals would entail the modernization of the school curriculum giving special emphasis to science and technology, English and other foreign languages, multicultural understanding, and proficiency in the two national languages; strengthening nonformal basic education for the general population, and making structural changes in terms of the devolution of power to the provincial level and more effective management at the micro level.

3. The Formal System of Education

3.1 Primary, Secondary, and Tertiary Education

There are two categories of schools in Sri Lanka—government schools and nongovernment schools. The nongovernment schools consist of private schools, estate schools, *Pirivena* institutions, approved/certified schools, preschools, international schools, and special schools. *Pirivenas* are educational institutions attached to Buddhist temples catering primarily to the education of Buddhist monks and also conducting general education classes for lay students. In 1989 there were 9,805 government schools, 427 *Pirivenas*, 12 estate schools, and 37 private schools. Of these 4,430 are primary (or junior) schools having classes up to year 5 (or year 8), 3,511 up to year 11, and 1,864 up to year 13. More than 2,000 of the primary schools are considered to be "small schools" having fewer than 100 pupils and one or two teachers. There is a special category of about 30 very large prestigious schools called "national schools" having 3,000 to 6,000 pupils each.

Figure 1 outlines the structure of the formal school system. Key statistics on enrollments and resources in the major education sectors are given in Table 1. The flow through the system of a cohort of pupils entering Grade 1 is shown in Fig. 2. General education is divisible into four stages: primary (years 1–5), junior-secondary (years 6–8), senior-secondary (years 9–11), and collegiate (years 12–13).

Age of admission to school in year 1 is 5+ years and all children are expected to remain in school up to year 11 (age 15+), although there is no legal provision to enforce compulsory schooling.

There is a fairly high rate of dropout and grade repetition at different levels, as shown in Table 2. The enrollment ratios for 1986–88 as a percentage are: primary 100, secondary 71, and tertiary 4 (UNDP 1991). The school system has about 4.23 million pupils and about 180,000 teachers with a pupil–teacher ratio of 23:1 for the system and 32:1 for the

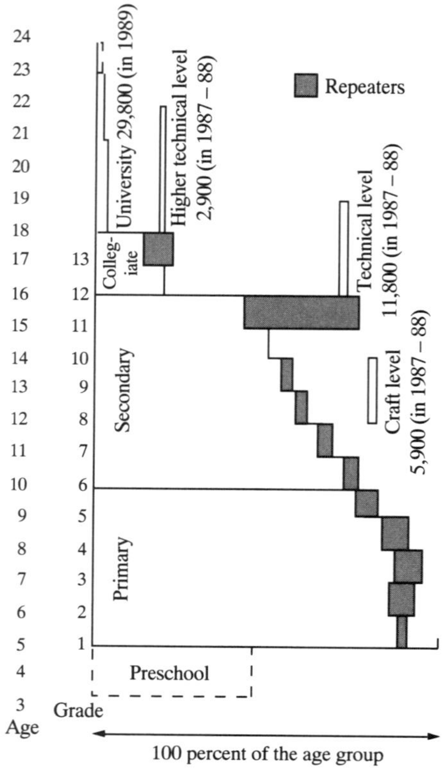

Figure 1
Sri Lanka: Structure of the formal education system 1991

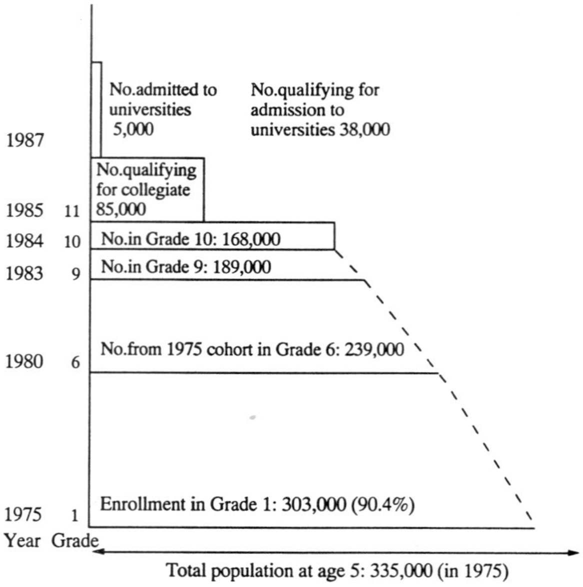

Figure 2
The flow through the formal system: Progress of an annual cohort by educational level 1975–87
Source: Based on data from the Ministry of Education School Census 1975–87

Table 1
Enrollments and government expenditure on education 1989

Number of schools (government and private)	10,253
Number of schools (government)	9,805
Number of pupils:	
primary (years 1–5)	2,085,700
secondary (years 6–11)	1,783,200
collegiate (years 12–13)	188,800
Total	4,057,700
Number of teachers	151,434
Expenditure on general and higher education (in millions of rupees)	7,477
Education budget as a percentage of:	
total government expenditure	7.9
the GNP	3.36

Sources: *School Census*, Ministry of Education 1989; *Annual Reports*, Central Bank of Sri Lanka

primary level. There is no male–female gap either in terms of access or success in school education. In regard to enrollment, "female as a percentage to male" was 100 for the primary level and 109 for the secondary level in 1987–88.

Formal school education is free at all levels in all state and state-aided institutes (except in a few fee-levying private institutions) and the medium of instruction is the mother tongue of the pupil. The essential textbooks are provided free to all students up to the senior-secondary level (year 11). A scheme to provide a free mid-day meal to all has been in operation since 1989.

The school year lasts from January to December, with three terms separated by three holiday periods, and consists of a minimum of 190 school days per year. The lower-primary level (years 1–3) has 4 hours of work per day while the upper-primary, secondary, and collegiate levels have 5.5 hours of work per day.

Since the 1940s, university education has grown so rapidly that by 1989 there were 8 universities with a total enrollment of 29,800, 12,600 of whom were females. Sri Lanka also has an open university offering a variety of academic and professional courses through distance education.

In addition, there are 10 other institutes of higher education. Action was taken in 1992 to establish nine affiliated university colleges, one in each province, to provide higher education to a large number of students who are denied educational opportunities because of the lack of places in the national universities.

3.2 Preschool Education

Preschool education is not a component of state-

Table 2
Repetition and dropout rates 1987

School year	1	2	3	4	5	6	7	8	9
Repetition rate	8.0	9.6	9.4	9.7	8.5	6.4	6.6	4.6	3.6
Dropout rate	—	0.8	2.1	3.1	5.2	6.0	6.3	6.2	7.1

Source: Ministry of Education

managed general education. However, some preschool facilities are provided by local government authorities, nongovernmental organizations, and by the private sector on a fee-levying basis. It is estimated that about 50 percent of Sri Lankan children attend preschool for periods ranging from a few months to a year. Many pupils do not receive any systematic preschool education, especially in rural areas.

3.3 Special Education

Special education is provided through two types of programs: the integrated special education program under which handicapped children attend regular schools and learn with normal children; and the non integrated special schools program where handicapped children learn in special schools which are mostly residential. As a matter of policy, handicapped children are sent to regular schools under the integrated system wherever possible. Special education programs are available for the following categories: the visually handicapped; the hearing handicapped; the mentally handicapped; and crippled children and slow learners. The Ministry of Education has a special unit to implement the special education program and coordinate other related activities, such as those concerned with health and employment, with the different ministries and departments.

3.4 Vocational, Technical, and Business Education

Vocational, technical, and business education covers a wide spectrum of vocational and technical levels and is administered by a variety of institutional arrangements under about 20 ministries and state agencies. The following are the main ministries: Education and Higher Education; Youth Affairs and Sports; Labor; Rural Industrial Development; Local Government, Housing, and Construction; Transport; and Fisheries and Health. Some private-sector institutions also offer industrial training courses catering to a small clientele.

In 1981, the government issued a white paper on educational proposals for reform which suggested several proposals for expanding and consolidating technical/vocational education both for school dropouts and those having completed general education. The main proposals consisted of: a technical stream parallel to the academic GCE (O-level) stream in years 9–11; artisan courses for school leavers at the junior-secondary level; an "Open School" providing a nonformal type of enrichment courses; technical, commerce, fine arts, and apprenticeship courses under a "Technical Education Authority"; open university courses; and professional colleges (at university level) providing courses for a wide range of established professions. Some of these proposals have yet to be implemented.

The existing technical/vocational education programs broadly fall into four categories: professional engineering education at university level; technical education at technician level; technical/vocational education at craft level; and vocational training courses, mostly short ones, for a wide range of skill levels. In addition, inservice training given by the employer and informal training provided in traditional guild form by trained craftsmen are also in existence.

Degree-level professional education is provided by the engineering faculties of two universities and the Open University. A total of 24 technical colleges and 5 affiliated units under the Ministry of Education and Higher Education offer diplomas and certificate-level courses in a wide range of fields including commerce, accountancy, stenography, and so on. In addition, full-time and part-time craft (trade) level courses are also offered by the colleges. The National Apprenticeship and Industrial Training Authority (NAITA) provides training in over 200 industrial establishments to more than 11,000 apprentices in about 150 categories of trades. These programs have a built-in linkage with industry and the employment market. The National Youth Services Council and the Ministry of Labor offer vocational training programs at different levels based on current market demands. The state and state-sponsored agencies bear the major burden of technical/vocational education and the participation of private enterprise is relatively small, generally being coordinated via NAITA. The state-sponsored programs are usually free. Apprentices of NAITA are financially supported by the state during training and absorbed into industrial ventures on completion of training. Voluntary organizations like *Sarvodaya* and some private agencies also offer vocational training programs.

Since a large number of governmental and nongovernmental agencies are involved in technical/vocational training, there is a lack of proper coordination between these programs as regards standardization and horizontal and vertical mobility, as well as higher marketability and productivity through quality improvement. In order to remedy this situation a Tertiary Vocational Education Commission (TVEC) was established.

With the expansion and modernization of the economy, new courses have been introduced and appropriate curriculum changes have been made, particularly in areas relevant to computers and informatics, tourism and the hotel industry, and the development of new nontraditional industries.

3.5 Adult and Nonformal Education

The educational needs of adults and out-of-school children did not receive high priority until the early 1980s when the Nonformal Education Division of the Ministry of Education was established and several projects launched. Nonformal education is now a part of accepted governmental policy. In 1992, there were four programs conducted by the Nonformal Education Division for children, youth, and adults: skills development programs for school leavers, literacy programs for nonschool-goers and primary-school dropouts, adult education/community education programs, and English-language classes for adults. Several new programs are being planned.

The nonformal education programs are supported by donor agencies such as UNICEF and SIDA. Existing infrastructure facilities of the formal sector are being used. A proposal to introduce an islandwide network of "open schools" to provide a variety of short-term courses for those who have left the formal school system or a more comprehensive "open learning system" is being considered in new educational reform projects. A Department of Nonformal Education has been set up at the National Institute of Education which is mainly concerned with research and development work in this field.

In the nongovernment sector, many social service and voluntary organizations conduct various types of nonformal education programs for adults and children, mainly in income generating activities such as handicrafts and farming.

4. Administrative and Supervisory Structure and Operation

The Ministry of Education and Higher Education (MOE&HE) (formerly two separate ministries, but amalgamated since 1990) is responsible for the design, implementation, control, and maintenance of general education, teacher education, higher education, and technical/vocational education in Sri Lanka. The Minister of Education and Higher Education who is the executive head of the Ministry is assisted by a State Minister of Education, a Project Minister of Education Services, and a Project Minister of Higher Education. The Secretary to the Ministry, who is also the Director General of Education, is the most senior public servant in the Ministry and is responsible for the supervision and management of the entire education system within the Ministry. An independent body named the "Education Service Committee" under the Public Service Commission is responsible for such functions as recruitment, promotions, and disciplinary matters of teachers and officers of the education service. The University Grants Commission deals with matters related to universities and other institutes of higher education. Certain functions which were formerly under the Ministry (e.g., curriculum development, research, distance education, management of the Staff College for Education Administration, etc.) have been transferred to the newly created National Institute of Education (NIE).

Educational structure and management in Sri Lanka was hitherto highly centralized. The situation has changed with the devolution of power to the provincial councils. The provincial councils have provincial ministries of education to deal with the powers and functions assigned to them by central government. Suitable organizational arrangements and appropriate structural changes in the central ministry are being worked out to ensure smooth coordination between the center, NIE, and the provincial councils.

The "school circuit" which formed the unit for administration and supervision under the Circuit Education Officer has been gradually giving way to a "school cluster system" since the early 1980s. The school clusters are managed by divisional education offices which are the subunits of the provincial education departments.

5. Educational Finance

The total government expenditure on education in 1989 was 7,477 million rupees, which was 7.9 percent of all government expenditure and 3.36 percent of the GNP. Expenditure on education has fluctuated since Independence, depending on the priorities of successive governments and their educational policies. Expenditure as a proportion of the GNP increased through the 1950s from 3 percent in 1952 to 4.8 percent in 1960. It rose to 4.9 percent in 1965 and remained between 4.0 to 4.9 up to 1972, showing a steady decline from 1973 (3.4%) to 2.8 percent in 1977 and 2.48 percent in 1984, with a gradual increase in the late 1980s to around 3 percent. Since 1983, about 37 million rupees per year were received as foreign aid. This was less than 1 percent of the recurrent expenditure on general education. About 80 percent of the education budget is spent on teachers' salaries. The distribution of current expenditure in 1990 among various levels was about 93 percent on first- and second-level education and 7 percent on tertiary education. The total recurrent expenditure per pupil per year was 906 rupees (in 1985) while the nonsalary recurrent expenditure was 136 rupees.

Since the formal system is almost entirely a state system, capital and recurrent costs are borne by the state except in the case of a few fee-levying private institutions. Schools may levy a facilities fee from pupils to cover the cost of extracurricular activities such as sports. School development societies and alumni associations sometimes assist in providing facilities for schools.

Even though education is free from year 1 up to the first-degree level in the universities, pupils from low income families need financial assistance to sustain them in school. There are several support schemes to help pupils in need of such financial assistance. The year 5 scholarship test, conducted by the Ministry of Education, and a few other schemes offer bursaries to needy pupils. Bank loans and scholarships are also available for students in higher education institutions.

6. Supplying Personnel for the Education System

The total number of teachers in state schools in 1990 was estimated to be about 184,000, of whom only 106,000 were professionally trained. The number of teaching staff at universities was about 1,785 in 1988–89.

Teachers are recruited at two levels: university graduates and those possessing a minimum of passes in three subjects at the General Certificate of Education (Advanced level) which is the examination at the end of the collegiate level (year 13). The rapid expansion of education necessitated a large number of untrained teachers to be appointed to schools. In 1990, 42 percent of all teachers still had not received a professional training. In 1992 there were four systems of initial training: a three-year program in 16 teachers colleges for nongraduate inservice teachers; a three-year pre-service program in 7 colleges of education; a distance education program administered by the National Institute of Education (NIE), and a postgraduate Diploma in Education for graduate teachers conducted by the education faculties of three universities and also by the NIE. The teachers colleges and colleges of education are administered by the Ministry of Education.

As well as initial training, the NIE and the provincial departments of education conduct inservice education programs to re-orient the teachers to changes in the curriculum and methodology. A "Master Teacher Scheme" has been in operation for this purpose. There are several special projects to train teachers of English. The NIE conducts Bachelor of Education courses in selected areas of specialization. The Department of Education Management Development of the NIE has various programs to train principals and deputy principals of schools and administrators.

7. Curriculum Development and Teaching Methodology

For purposes of curriculum development, school education may be considered to consist of the four stages outlined in Sect. 3.1 above. There is a commonly prescribed national curriculum for years 1 to 11. The lower-primary stage is characterized by a highly integrated curriculum involving first language, mathematics, environmental studies, creative and aesthetic activities, and religion. In the upper-primary stage, the curriculum is semi-integrated with more emphasis on subject-bound competencies. A "Beginning Science" course and English-as-a-second-language are also introduced. At the secondary stage the curriculum consists of the following subjects, some of which are interdisciplinary in nature: religion, first language, English, mathematics, integrated science, social studies and history, aesthetic education, health, physical education, and life skills/technical subjects. Life skills is a subject in years 7 and 8, and in year 9 pupils select one out of 53 prevocational-type courses designed to cover a wide field of vocations. Pupils may choose a technical subject out of several options in years 10–11.

At the end of year 11, which is also the end of the span of general education for all, the General Certificate of Education Ordinary-level (GCE O-level) examination—a centrally planned national school leaving examination—is held. Only those who achieve certain prescribed standards at GCE O level are permitted to enter the collegiate stage (years 12–13). Generally about 25–30 percent qualify to enter the collegiate level. The curriculum of this stage is discipline oriented and consists of a wide choice of subjects classified under three streams—arts, science, and commerce. Pupils select four subjects within any one of the streams for which they are qualified to enter. At the end of this stage the General Certificate of Education Advanced-level (GCE A-level) is held. Schools with GCE A-level science streams have a course designed to provide computer literacy.

The National Institute of Education is responsible for the preparation of syllabuses of instructions, teachers' guides, and textbooks for the school curriculum. The curriculum teams consist of specialist officers from the NIE, teacher educators, and teachers seconded for service to the respective teams. The Education Publications Department is responsible for printing and distributing the textbooks.

The last major curriculum revision at the primary and secondary levels was effected in 1986 and that of the collegiate level in 1979. However, there is an on-going process of qualitative improvement of an informal nature to infuse important changes in both content and methodology and emerging current issues. But the actual curriculum, as transacted in the classroom, does not measure up to the expectations of the prescribed specifications. The teaching methodology still remains rather traditional and didactic in spite of efforts made to introduce activity-based learning rather than a teaching-oriented approach.

Educational radio and television programs have

been developed to support the learning of science, mathematics, and English.

The lack of continuity in education policy has resulted in sudden changes in the curriculum causing hardships to teachers and pupils. The relevance and balance of the curriculum and its academic bias and lack of sufficient flexibility are often questioned by critics.

The problem of making the school curriculum relevant to the needs of both the minority, who wish to proceed to higher levels of specialization, as well as to the large majority, who fail or do not wish to do so, has hitherto remained unsolved. The examination-oriented rote-learning approach adopted by most teachers and pupils is also a major concern.

8. *The System of Examinations, Promotions, and Certifications*

A system of automatic promotion from one year to the next is practiced in principle, but there are exceptions as can be seen from the number of grade repeaters. The rule imposed in 1991 makes it compulsory for pupils to obtain the Junior Technical Certificate at year 9 to proceed further. The GCE O-level examination at the end of year 11 is the main national school leaving examination which also serves as the selection examination for the different streams of the collegiate stage. While the grades obtained at the GCE A level serve for certification, the aggregate marks are used to select students to the universities on an all-island merit basis as well as on a district quota basis.

Sri Lankan society places more faith in centrally controlled national examinations with identical criteria and standards for the entire country than on decentralized or school-based assessment procedures. School-based continuous assessment systems introduced at various times have met with strong opposition from parents and teachers and had to be abandoned. This has resulted in the classroom teaching–learning process becoming heavily examination-oriented to the neglect of more desirable objectives envisaged in the curriculum. National school examinations are conducted by the Department of Examinations.

9. *Educational Assessment, Evaluation, and Research*

The Research Division of NIE is mainly responsible for conducting and promoting research. Prior to the setting up of NIE, research and assessments were conducted in an ad hoc manner by various sections and individual officers of the Ministry. Research in universities was mainly confined to theses and dissertations submitted for graduate degrees. The Planning Division of the Ministry conducts a school census every year, processes the data and makes summary statistics available to policymakers. The Department of Examinations analyzes the results of national examinations GCE O and A levels, which provide some feedback to the system.

The Research Division of NIE has carried out or sponsored several studies on issues such as indicators of school effectiveness, management reforms, teacher requirements, school profiles, policy changes, pupil achievement, regional disparities, and so forth.

The main emphasis of research in the 1990s, as foreseen by NIE, is on problems and issues such as low achievement in certain subjects like mathematics, science, and English; establishing a minimum learning continuum for the primary level; nonformal approaches to basic education; the validity of the year 5 scholarship examination; experimental work in science; rehabilitation problems arising out of the ethnic conflict; devolution of power to the provincial councils; and quality improvement of teacher education.

There is no special allocation in the primary and secondary school budget for evaluation and research.

10. *Major Reforms in the 1980s and 1990s*

Reforms in education were initiated by the Education Reforms Committee (ERC) appointed in 1977. The ERC Report (1982) recommended certain reforms in the structure and content of the education system. The 1981 white paper on education (Ministry of Education 1981) provided a basic framework for reforms in the 1980s and was considered a major step in transforming school and technical/vocational education in Sri Lanka. The proposals were concerned with all aspects of the system and generated much public debate. Certain proposals, such as school clusters and continuous assessment, came in for public criticism. Some of these proposals were implemented, some tried out and abandoned, and some others remain to be implemented.

The government appointed a National Education Commission in 1991 to be an advisory body to the government in matters of reform and innovation, coordination, and the rationalization of educational policies. The attention of the Commission has been drawn to the need for diversifying the products of the system in close collaboration with employers and making it a multilayered and more efficient human resource development system.

11. *Major Problems for the Year 2000*

Sri Lanka has already advanced considerably insofar as quantitative progress in terms of participation and literacy rates is concerned. The challenge for the future is therefore to improve the quality and the internal efficiency of the system to meet the demands of a rapidly changing society, and to obtain a better return for the vast investment of resources made on education. The major problems in the above context are those concerned with the low internal efficiency of the system; inter-regional disparities; inter-racial harmony; lack of curriculum relevance; the backlog of untrained teachers; lack of accountability, effective supervision, monitoring, and evaluation; and failure to have national consensus and continuity in policies, which creates disorder in the system and lack of proper linkages and coordination both within and with other sectors outside the system.

Successive governments have been confronted with the problem of ensuring that the output from the educational system is capable of providing the knowledge, skills, attitudes, and values needed to improve the quality of life of the individual and to execute tasks required to achieve national goals. The "mass–elite gap" between the English-educated Western-oriented elites and the vernacular educated mostly rural masses poses major problems for policymakers and planners. The reluctance to break away from traditional models inherited from colonial times and those imposed more recently by the developed countries, and the resistance to change shown by the dominant elitist culture influenced by Eurocentric norms and biases makes the task of reform even more difficult. The overall challenge for the future is to break away from overdependence on the traditional formal system and evolve an innovative system integrating the formal, nonformal, and informal sectors and harnessing all settings for learning in society to achieve the goals of individual and national development.

References

ERC 1982 *Towards Relevance in Education: Report of the Education Reforms Committee 1979*. Ministry of Education, Colombo

Ministry of Education 1981 *White Paper on Education Proposals for Reform*. Ministry of Education, Colombo

Ministry of Education 1989 *School Census 1989*. Ministry of Education, Colombo

Sri Lanka 1990 *Annual Report for the Year 1990*. Central Bank of Sri Lanka, Colombo

UNDP 1991 *Human Development Report 1991*. Oxford University Press, New York

Further Reading

De Silva W A, Gunawardena C 1989 *Educational Policies and Change 1977–1986*. National Institute of Education, Maharagama

Gunawardena G B n.d. *A National Study on Secondary Education in Sri Lanka*. National Institute of Education, Maharagama

Herath J P 1991 *Sri Lanka Country Paper for* SAARC *Expert Group Meeting on Modernization of Curriculum*. National Institute of Education, Maharagama

Jayasuriya J E n.d. *Educational Policies and Progress during British Rule in Sri Lanka 1796–1948*. Associated Educational Publishers, Colombo

Jayaweera S 1988 *Educational Policies and Change from the Mid-twentieth Century to 1977*. National Institute of Education, Maharagama

Nyström K 1985 *Schooling and Disparities. A Study of Regional Differences in Sri Lanka*. Institute of International Education, University of Stockholm, Stockholm

Singhal R P et al. 1989 *Education and Training in Sri Lanka*, Vols 1–4. Educational Consultants India Ltd., New Delhi

Sri Lanka 1969 *Education in Ceylon (from the 6th Century to the Present Day): A Centenary Volume*, vols 1–3. Ministry of Education and Cultural Affairs, Colombo

Sri Lanka 1990a *Report of the Presidential Commission on Youth*. Department of Government Printing, Colombo

Sri Lanka 1990b *Statistical Pocket Book of Sri Lanka 1990*. Department of Census and Statistics, Colombo

Sumathipala K H M 1968 *History of Education in Ceylon*. Tisara Prakasakayo, Dehiwala

A. M. Ranaweera

Standard Setting in Criterion-referenced Testing

One of the primary purposes of criterion-referenced tests is to make mastery decisions about examinees in relation to well-defined domains of content. This requires a standard or cutoff score on the test score scale to separate examinees into two performance categories, often labeled mastery and nonmastery. Sometimes multiple standards are set to separate examinees into more than two performance categories. For example, three standards may be set to separate examinees into four mastery categories: novice, apprentice, proficient, and advanced. For the purposes of this entry, discussion will center on setting one standard, though the extension to multiple standards on the same test score scale is straightforward.

All standard-setting methods in use in the early 1990s involve judgment and are arbitrary. Some researchers have argued that arbitrary standards are not defensible in education (Glass 1978). Popham (1978) countered with this response:

> Unable to avoid reliance on human judgment as the chief ingredient in standard-setting, some individuals have thrown up their hands in dismay and cast aside all efforts to set performance standards as arbitrary, hence unacceptable.
>
> But *Webster's Dictionary* offers us two definitions of arbitrary. The first of these is positive, describing arbitrary as an adjective reflecting choice or discretion, that is, "Determinable by a judge or tribunal." The second definition, pejorative in nature, describes arbitrary as an adjective denoting capriciousness, that is, "selected at random and without reason." In my estimate, when people start knocking the standard-setting game as arbitrary, they are clearly employing Webster's second, negatively loaded definition.
>
> But the first definition is more accurately reflective of serious standard-setting efforts. They represent genuine attempts to do a good job in deciding what kinds of

> standards ought to be employed. That they are judgmental is inescapable. But to malign all judgmental operations as capricious is absurd. (Popham 1978 p. 168)

Many of the standards that are set by society to regulate behavior are set arbitrarily, but in the positive sense of the word. For example, fire, health, environmental, and highway safety standards are common and they are set arbitrarily. Professional judgment provides the basis for setting these standards. Criterion-referenced test standards are set arbitrarily too, but the process used in arriving at the standards is carefully planned and carried out by persons identified as suitable for setting the standards. Presumably sometimes standards are set too high or too low. Through experience and carefully designed validity studies of the test scores and decisions that are made, standards that are not "in line" can be identified and revised. The consequences of assigning (a) a nonmaster to a mastery state (known as a false–positive error) or (b) a master to a nonmastery state (known as a false–negative error) on a credentialing examination, however, are considerably more serious than errors made on (say) a classroom test; therefore, more attention should be given to the setting of standards on the more important testing programs.

Many of the available standard-setting methods have been described, compared, and critiqued in the measurement literature (Berk 1986, Glass 1978, Hambleton and Powell 1983, Shepard 1984). The methods can be organized into three categories: "judgmental," "empirical," and "combination." The judgmental methods require data from judges for setting standards, or require judgments to be made about the presence of variables (e.g., guessing) that influence the setting of a standard. Empirical methods are based on the analysis of actual criterion-referenced test results from two groups formed on the basis of a criterion variable. For example, the criterion variable would be a measure of success on a variable related to the contents of the criterion-referenced test. Also, empirical methods involve decision-theoretic concepts and procedures. Combination methods use both judgmental data and empirical data in the standard-setting process. Livingston and Zieky (1982) and Hambleton and Powell (1983) have developed guidelines for applying several of the methods.

Several of the popular judgmental, empirical, and combination methods are described next. Then some practical guidelines for setting standards are offered, along with a brief discussion of emerging trends and current research.

1. Judgmental Methods

With the judgmental methods, individual items are studied in order to judge how well a minimally competent examinee will perform on the test items. The minimally competent examinee is someone who has a proficiency score located right at the standard. Judges are asked to assess how or to what degree an examinee who could be described as minimally competent would perform on each item.

1.1 Nedelsky Method

With the Nedelsky (1954) method, judges are asked to identify distractors in multiple-choice test items that they feel the minimally competent student will be able to identify as incorrect. The assumption is then made that the minimally competent examinee would be indifferent to the remaining answer choices, and therefore he or she would choose one of the remaining choices at random. The minimum passing level for that item then becomes the reciprocal of the number of remaining answer choices. For example, suppose a judge reviews a test item and feels that a minimally competent examinee would recognize that two of the available five choices are incorrect. The expected score for the minimally competent examinee then is 0.33, since the assumption is made that all remaining choices (three remain) are equally plausible to the minimally competent examinee.

The judges proceed with each test item in a similar fashion, and, on completion of the judging process, each judge sums the minimum passing levels across the test items to obtain a standard. A judge's standard is the expected score on the test for the minimally competent examinee. Individual judges' standards are averaged to obtain a standard that is considered to be the best estimate of the standard.

Often a discussion of the judges' ratings will then take place, and judges have the opportunity to revise their ratings if they feel revisions are appropriate. And often judges do make revisions, since misreading of test items, overlooking of important features of test items, and even some carelessness in making the ratings are common in the item rating process. After judges provide a second set of ratings, again, each judge's item ratings are summed to obtain a standard on the test, and then the judges' standards are averaged to obtain a standard based upon the ratings of all of the judges.

The standard deviation of the judges' standards is often used as an indicator of the consensus among the judges (the lower the standard deviation, the more consensus there is among the judges on the placement of the standard). When the variability is large, confidence in the standard produced by the judges is lessened. Very often the goal in standard-setting is to achieve a consensus among the judges.

1.2 Ebel's Method

With the Ebel (1972) method, judges rate test items along two dimensions: relevance and difficulty. There are four levels of relevance in Ebel's method: essential, important, acceptable, and questionable. These levels of relevance are often edited or collapsed into two or three levels when the method is used in practice. Ebel used three levels of item difficulty: easy, medium, and hard. These levels of relevance and difficulty can be used to form a 4×3 grid for sorting the test items. The judges are asked to do two things:

(a) Locate each of the test items in the proper cell, based on their perceived relevance and difficulty.

(b) Assign a percentage to each cell representing the percentage of items in the cell that the minimally competent examinees should be able to answer.

The number of test items in each cell is multiplied by the percentage assigned by the judge, and the sum of these products, when divided by the total number of test items, yields the standard. As with all of the judgmental methods, the standards set by the individual judges are averaged to obtain a final standard.

1.3 Angoff's Method

When using Angoff's method (Angoff 1971), judges are asked to assign a probability to each test item directly, thus circumventing the analysis of a grid or the analysis of answer choices. Each probability is to be an estimate of the minimally competent examinee answering the test item correctly. Individual judges' assigned probabilities for items in the test can be summed to obtain a standard, and then the judges' standards can be averaged to obtain a final standard.

As with the other judgmental methods, it is common practice to repeat the probability assignment process following discussions among the judges about their assigned probabilities. Sometimes, too, judges are provided with item statistics, or information which addresses the consequences (i.e., passing and failing rates) of various standards to aid them in the standard-setting process.

The method has been applied successfully to multiple-choice test items, and in a modified form to performance data. For example, suppose a standard for separating masters and nonmasters on a performance task is the goal. Judges, using a variation on the Angoff method, might be asked to specify the expected number of score points on the performance task (i.e., the standard) for the minimally competent examinee. Various standards from the judges can be averaged to obtain a final standard that would be used for classifying examinees as masters and nonmasters on the performance task.

2. Empirical Methods

Two of the typical methods in this category depend upon the availability of an outside criterion, performance measure, or true ability distribution. The test itself, and the possible standards, are observed in relation to these criterion scores. An "optimal" standard is then selected. For instance, Livingston's (1975) utility-based approach leads to the selection of a standard that optimizes a particular utility function. Livingston suggested the use of a set of linear or semilinear utility functions in viewing the effects of decision-making accuracy based upon a particular standard. A standard is selected to maximize the utility function.

A second method, by van der Linden and Mellenbergh (1977), leads to the selection of a standard that minimizes "expected losses." Scores from the criterion-referenced test of interest are used with an arbitrary standard to classify examinees into two categories: masters and nonmasters. Also, an external criterion, specified in advance, is used to dichotomize the examinee population into "successes" and "failures." Then an expected loss function (the quantity to be minimized) is specified. One simple possibility is the sum of false–positive and false–negative errors. A more interesting option is to weight the two types of errors by their importance. The standard on the test is then varied to find the one that minimizes expected losses over the sample of examinees. The standard that minimizes the chosen loss function is the one that is used with the test. Essentially, expected losses occur when examinees who score high on the external criterion (successes) fail the test, or when low-scoring examinees (failures) on the external criterion pass the test. The goal is to choose a standard to minimize the expected losses, which is accomplished by locating the standard on the test so that essentially the maximum number of successful persons on the criterion pass the test and unsuccessful persons on the criterion fail the test.

Decision-oriented approaches, such as those developed by Livingston (1975), van der Linden and Mellenbergh (1977), and Hambleton and Novick (1973), are conceptually and technically appealing, but unfortunately the difficulty of obtaining criterion data, let alone suitable criterion data in most standard-setting studies, limits the applicability of the approaches. As a result, they are rarely used in practice.

3. Combination Methods

With these methods, judgments are made about the mastery status of a sample group of examinees from the population of interest. In a school context, these judgments would come from the teachers. The choice of combination method determines the nature of the required judgments. Next, one or more groups for whom mastery determinations have been made are administered the test. Details are offered next for analyzing the judgmental data and the test scores.

3.1 Borderline-group Method

This method requires that a definition be prepared

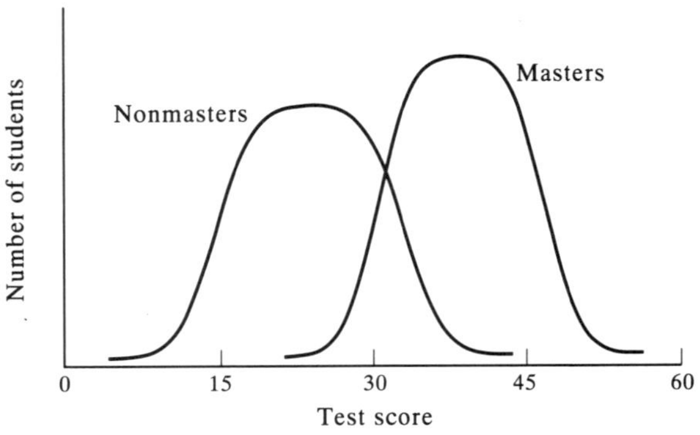

Figure 1
Constrasting groups method for standard setting

of minimally acceptable performance in the content area being assessed. For example, here is the definition of the minimally proficient Grade 4 student in mathematics on the 1992 National Assessment of Educational Progress (NAEP) in the United States: fourth-grade students performing at the proficient level should consistently apply integrated procedural knowledge and conceptual understanding to problem-solving in the five NAEP content areas.

The judges (in practice, teachers who are familiar with the academic accomplishments of the examinees) are asked to submit a list of examinees whose performances would be so close to the standard or borderline that they could not be reliably classified as masters or nonmasters. The test is administered to this "borderline" group, and the median test score for the group may be taken as the standard. Alternatively, it may be decided to pass more or less than 50 percent of those examinees judged to be minimally competent examinees.

3.2 Contrasting Groups Method

Once judges have defined minimally acceptable performance in the domain of content of interest (or perhaps, they may be provided with a definition), the judges are asked to identify those examinees they are certain are either masters or nonmasters in relation to the domain of content of interest (Berk 1976). The test is administered to the two groups, and the score distributions for the two groups are compared. The point of intersection is often taken as the initial standard. An example is given in Fig. 1. The standard can be moved up to reduce the number of false–positive errors (examinees identified as masters by the test, but who were not in the masters group formed by the judges) or down to reduce the number of false–negative errors (examinees identified as nonmasters by the test, but who were in the masters group formed by the judges). The direction in which to move the standard will depend on the relative seriousness of the false–positive and false–negative errors. If the score distributions overlap completely, no mastery–nonmastery decisions can be made reliably. The ideal situation would be one in which the two distributions did not overlap at all. Then, the standard can be positioned between the two distributions, and the assignment of examinees to mastery states would be in complete agreement with the judges.

The validity of this approach to standard setting depends, in part, on the appropriateness of the judges' classifications of examinees. If the judges tend to err in their classifications by assigning examinees to the mastery group who do not belong, the result is that standards from the contrasting groups method are lower than they should be. On the other hand, the standards tend to be higher if judges err by assigning some masters to the nonmastery group who do not belong. Like the Angoff method, or modified Angoff method, the contrasting groups method can also be applied to performance assessment data.

4. Some Practical Guidelines for Setting Standards

A number of researchers have suggested guidelines to follow in setting standards (Hambleton and Powell 1983, Livingston and Zieky 1982). An updated list of guidelines for setting standards via judgmental methods is as follows:

(a) The importance of the resulting mastery–nonmastery decisions should impact substantially on the effort that is committed to the standard-setting process. With important tests, such as those used in awarding high school diplomas, and professional licenses and certificates, substantial effort should be committed to producing defensible standards and this effort would include compiling evidence to support the validity of the standards.

(b) The design of the standard-setting process should be influenced by the judges (and their backgrounds), test length, and test-item formats. For example, inexperienced judges may require substantial amounts of training, long tests may require that subgroups of judges be formed with each group assigned a different portion of the test, and some formats such as performance measures will require modifications to the common methods for setting standards.

(c) With important standard-setting initiatives, the full process should be field-tested prior to using it operationally. Serious errors can often be avoided with carefully conducted and evaluated field tests of the standard-setting process.

(d) The selection and number of judges should be given considerable attention. Can the judges represent the main constituencies, and are there enough judges to produce stable standards? The defensibility of the resulting standards depends very much on how this question is answered.

(e) The judges should take the test (or a part) under test-like conditions. This familiarity with the test and its administration will enhance the validity of the resulting standards. This reduces the common problem of judges underestimating the difficulty of the test and setting unreasonably high expectations for examinee performance.

(f) The judges should be thoroughly trained in the standard-setting process and be given practice exercises. The judges' understanding of the process is critical to their confidence in the process and the acceptability of the standards that are produced.

(g) It is desirable to provide an opportunity for judges to discuss their first set of ratings with each other prior to providing a final set of ratings. The second set of ratings will often be more informed and lead to more defensible standards because many sources of error due to misunderstandings, carelessness, inconsistencies, and mistakes can be removed. It has also become common to provide judges with item statistics and passing rates associated with different standards so that they have a meaningful frame of reference for providing their ratings.

(h) The full process of standard-setting should be documented so that it is available if challenges to the standards arise. Every detail, from who selected the judges to the choice of method, and the resolution of differences among the judges should be documented for possible use later.

5. Emerging Trends and Research

Many researchers are still not comfortable with standard-setting methods in the early 1990s. Criticisms center on both the logic of the methods and the ways in which the methods are being implemented. Clearly, there is a need for new ideas and more research. Both new methods and improved implementation of existing methods are needed. With respect to new methods, "policy-capturing" methods are now being developed for use with performance-based assessments (Hobson and Gibson 1983, Jaeger et al. 1993). The methods require judgments about the acceptability or nonacceptability of profiles of examinee scores across a number of performance tasks. These methods seemed to have potential with performance assessments, which are becoming popular, but the relative advantages and disadvantages of these new methods compared to modified Angoff methods are unknown. With respect to improved implementation, considerable attention is being focused on the implementation of the modified-Angoff method. Every aspect of it, from the initial definition of minimally competent examinees to the selection and training of judges, and the resolving of interjudge and intrajudge differences is being researched (Jaeger 1991, Mills et al. 1991)

6. Summary

The most controversial problem in criterion-referenced testing concerns setting standards on the test score scale to separate examinees into masters and nonmasters, or certifiable and noncertifiable. It is recognized by workers in the educational testing field that there are no true standards waiting to be discovered by well-designed psychometric research studies. Rather, setting standards is ultimately a judgmental process that is best done by appropriate individuals who (a) are familiar with the test content and knowledgeable about the standard-setting method they will be expected to use, (b) have access to item performance and test score distribution data in the standard-setting process, and (c) understand the social and political context in which the tests will be used.

See also: Criterion-referenced Measurement; Tests: Different Types

References

Angoff W H 1971 Scales, norms, and equivalent scores. In: Thorndike R L (ed.) 1971 *Educational Measurement*, 2nd edn. American Council on Education, Washington, DC

Berk R A 1976 Determination of optimal cutting scores in criterion-referenced measurement. *J. Exp. Educ.* 45: 4–9

Berk R A 1986 A consumer's guide to setting performance standards on criterion-referenced tests. *Rev. Educ. Res.* 56: 137–72

Ebel R L 1972 *Essentials of Educational Measurement*. Prentice-Hall, Englewood Cliffs, New Jersey

Glass G V 1978 Standards and criteria. *J. Educ. Meas.* 15: 277–90

Hambleton R K, Novick M R 1973 Toward an integration of theory and method for criterion-referenced tests. *J. Educ. Meas.* 10: 159–71

Hambleton R K, Powell S 1983 A framework for viewing the process of standard-setting. *Evaluation and the Health Professions* 6: 3–24

Hobson C J, Gibson F W 1983 Policy capturing as an approach to understanding and improving performance appraisal: A review of the literature. *Academy of Management Review* 8: 640–49

Jaeger R M 1991 Selection of judges for standard setting. *Educational Measurement: Issues and Practice* 10: 3–6, 10

Jaeger R M, Plake B S, Hambleton R K 1993 Integrating multidimensional performances and setting performance standards. Paper presented at the meeting of the American Educational Research Association, Atlanta, Georgia

Livingston S A 1975 *A Utility-based Approach to the Eval-*

uation of Pass/Fail Testing Decision Procedures. Report No. COPA-75-01, Center for Occupational and Professional Assessment, Educational Testing Service, Princeton, New Jersey
Livingston S A, Zieky M J 1982 *Passing Scores: A Manual for Setting Standards of Performance on Educational and Occupational Tests*. Educational Testing Service, Princeton, New Jersey
Mills C N, Melican G, Ahluwalia N T 1991 Defining minimal competence. *Educational Measurement: Issues and Practice* 10: 15–16, 22, 25–26
Nedelsky L 1954 Absolute grading standards for objective tests. *Educ. Psychol. Meas.* 14: 3–19
Popham W J 1978 *Criterion-referenced Measurement*. Prentice-Hall, Englewood Cliffs, New Jersey
Shepard L A 1984 Setting performance standards. In: Berk R A (ed.) 1984 *A Guide to Criterion-referenced Test Construction*. Johns Hopkins University Press, Baltimore, Maryland
van der Linden W J, Mellenbergh G J 1977 Optimal cutting scores using a linear loss function. *Appl. Psychol. Meas.* 2: 593–99

R. K. Hambleton

Still Media, Production of

While many of the still media used for presentations have not changed in format, some of the methods used to produce them have changed significantly. Sometimes, changes in production methods have led to major changes in the results; for example, overhead projection, which now uses computer-based images shown on a liquid crystal display (LCD) panel. In other cases, the method of production has changed but the result is essentially the same as before; for example, overhead transparencies produced from computer-driven laser printers vs. those produced from electrostatic or thermal copiers.

The distinction between production changes that bring about a new result and production changes yielding the same result is critical. New results may directly change the actual process of instruction and learning because they introduce a new media format. New methods of production with the same result do not change the instruction directly. Their impact comes from changing the infrastructure supporting the instructional process; for example, making media more cost-effective or easy to produce.

Perhaps more important, the new media formats begin to blur distinctions between traditional media classes (such as "still media"). This moots some of the conventional wisdom about the effect of specific media on learning. For example, is a computer-driven presentation using limited animation and projected through an LCD panel on an overhead projector to be considered an overhead medium, even though its screen effects appear similar to those of slides or an animated motion picture loop? What if that same presentation is shown on video monitors? What medium is it? What are the generalizations about its effectiveness as a medium? Similarly, videodisks may carry still images or full motion, with or without audio. Should the production medium or the output be considered?

This entry does *not* establish strict media classifications. Rather, it looks at the three common still presentation media used in most instructional situations and briefly comments on the production of each media format. The media covered are: (a) charts, flipcharts, and presentation boards; (b) overhead projection (including computer-generated materials); and (c) slides. The accompanying charts offer a concise summary of key factors to consider when producing and using these media.

A note of caution: modern production technologies make virtually anything possible. A slide is digitally scanned and reproduced as a 3×4 foot color poster. Video frames are captured digitally, manipulated on the computer with text and graphics, and are then produced as slides. The information in the following charts represents the more common and affordable methods of media production.

1. Charts, Flipcharts, and Presentation Boards

This category covers nonprojected media—both permanent and transitory. Media in this category are generally used with smaller audiences and are almost always prepared by the instructor or trainer. Because of their simplicity and flexibility, these media remain the mainstay of instructor-centered presentations. The instructor can make changes and create (with the exception of commercially prepared maps and charts) new information during the class. Moreover, the relatively low cost of these media makes them popular when the information or the audience might change (see Tables 1 and 2).

Charts, flipcharts and presentation boards are primarily one-of-a-kind, instructor-driven media. In all uses of these media, the instructor or presenter interacts significantly with the medium. Except for commercial charts and maps, each use of the medium is a singular event—in effect, a one-time use. This is in sharp contrast to overhead transparencies and slides where materials are reused or where simple reproduction methods encourage additional copies.

2. Overhead Projection

In the space of a few decades, overhead projection has gone from occasional use to being a ubiquitous medium. Training rooms and classrooms are now routinely equipped with overhead projectors. One overlooked advantage of the overhead projector is that little has changed with the mechanics of the projector itself. In the meantime, there have been significant changes in the materials used. The overhead accommodates the oldest and simplest materials to the newest and most complex. In addition to

Table 1
Characteristics of charts, flipcharts, and presentation boards (a)

	When is information usually prepared or added?	How permanent is the information?	Who usually prepares the medium?	Maximum audience size
Charts, posters, maps (printed, usually commercial)	Prior to presentation	Permanent	Commercially prepared	Small to medium
Presentation boards (e.g., chalkboard, whiteboard)	During presentation	Transitory	Always instructor	Small to medium
Flipcharts	Prior to/during presentation	Transitory and/or permanent	Instructor (sometimes the audience)	Small to medium

Table 2
Characteristics of charts, flipcharts, and presentation boards (b)

	Flexibility (to change content)	Relative cost of first copy	Cost for additional copies	Portability	(a) Ease of production (b) Ease of use
Charts, maps (printed, usually commercially prepared)	Very low	High	May drop with large purchase	Somewhat; depends on size	(a) Hard (if commercially prepared) (b)Easy to use
Presentation boards (e.g., chalkboard, whiteboard)	Very high	Low	Remains same	Usually fixed: some may be movable	(a) Easy (to change information) (b) Easy to use
Flipcharts	Very high	Low	Remains same	Somewhat: depends on size	(a) Easy to produce (b) Easy to use

showing opaque objects and serving as a projected chalkboard, the overhead accommodates transparencies produced in a number of ways.

There are two important new developments in overhead projection. The first is the vastly increased quality of the electrostatic (xerographic) color copier—especially those with digital color. During the 1980s, the quality of transparencies increased significantly and began to rival photographic transparencies—at least, as they are displayed on most overhead projectors. In addition, the production time with xerographic copiers is significantly less than with photographic processes.

The second new development is the LCD panel. LCD panels lie on the stage of the overhead projector like any transparency. However, they use computer output (either from a direct link to the computer or from information stored in the panel's own memory) to form images. The panels themselves have evolved rapidly from relatively dim black-and-white images to brighter multicolor images which can be changed rapidly enough (through the computer) to create a rough form of animation.

Producing material for the overhead requires skill in design and production. Producing for the LCD panel, however, requires computer expertise as well. There are probably more ways to make overhead transparencies than there are production methods for any other medium. The more common ones appear in Table 3.

Because of its flexibility—the capacity to use any number of differential materials in a variety of environments—and its ubiquity, the overhead projector is the most common presentation device for meetings, presentations, and training. The overhead projector is the undisputed workhorse of the media field.

3. Slides

If the overhead is the workhorse of the presentation world, the 2×2 slide is the racehorse. The term "slide" most commonly refers to a photographic color reversal transparency in a slide mount whose *outside* dimensions are two inches by two inches (called 2×2) and are projected using a "slide projector." The

Table 3
Characteristics of production for overhead projection

Method of Production	Process and materials	Master/original required	Comments
Hand-made	Clear base (acetate) dry transfer letters; some markers; grease pencils	None; the original is the only copy made	Most flexible and quickest, but limited by the graphics skills of the producer
Thermal	Special materials which use infrared and heat process; dry, one-step process; variety of materials (black-on-clear or color; reverse or negative image; color on clear) no true color[a] reproduction	Information to be copied *must* be carbon-based on original; line reproduction only (although half-tones will copy poorly); copies are same size as original; electrostatic copiers often used to make originals when size change is needed	Also called Thermofax™; materials stay heat-sensitive and can turn dark if subjected to high heat levels
Electrostatic (xerographic black/white and color)	Xerographic process used in dry process copiers; may need special acetate (heavy enough to withstand heat and/or treated so toner will adhere); true color[a] reproduction on color machines	Any original that could be used in normal electrostatic copying; some machines allow change in size of copy. Black/white reproduction better with line than with continuous tone originals; large areas of black may not reach full density. Color may use hard copy or 2×2 slides as originals	Also called Xerox™; quick and reasonably cheap for black/white; not all copiers will make transparencies; color originals may not reproduce well as black/white
Photography black and white	Photographic process requiring large format camera (or enlarger); uses photographic materials; line or continuous tone; regular or proprietary processing methods	Any original; film type should be matched to subject (line vs. continuous tone); any size original; if appropriate reproduction equipment available	Can combine with other means; line has crisp edges and total blacks; strong lighting or long exposure often needed for some graphic arts films with low exposure index (EI)
Photography—color	Photographic process requiring large format camera or enlarger; usually color reversal film; excellent true color[a] reproduction	Any	8×10-inch color transparencies are relatively expensive but have the highest resolution of any production method
Diazo	Special materials (process similar to blueprint production); uses ammonia, requiring good ventilation; one color per foil; color on clear (or reverse); no true color[a] reproduction	Originals must be translucent; no reduction/enlargement; no continuous tone	Also called Ozalid™ and copies often called "foils"; has been largely replaced by newer methods
Multicolor processes (nonphotographic)	Mostly variants of proprietary systems used for checking color separations in printing industry; usually requires special equipment and materials	Originals can be already separated or camera will make separations through separate exposures with filters; reduction/enlargement depends on machine and system used	More commonly found in printing systems than in audiovisual production
Computer display panels	Computer drives a display panel which sits on the stage of the overhead; bluish-black on clear; multicolor panels available, but may require some room darkening for best effect	No master specifically required; displays are created stored in computer; sophistication differs with quality of panel and with software program	Display panels vary widely in quality and sophistication; advanced models can store images in the panel's memory and show can be programmed without computer; often requires dimmer room light than other overhead projection

a True color, as used here, means that the colors (including a variety of hues and tints) are reproduced as they are on the original and on a single transparency. Some methods achieve true color by separating the colors onto different transparencies and combining them to obtain a range of hues and tints most common image area for the 2×2 mount is approximately 24×36 millimeters (about 1×1.5 inches). While the slide mount may hold any sort of projectable material, the most common material is 35 millimeters color reversal film. However, the term slide is also used for other sizes of photographic transparencies, for example:

(a) $1\frac{5}{8} \times 1\frac{5}{8}$ inches image area in a 2×2 inch mount (called a superslide);

(b) $2\frac{1}{4} \times 2\frac{1}{4}$ inches (from 120 and 220 film), requiring a special projector;

(c) 3×4 inches (often called a lantern slide), also requiring a special projector.

In some circles, *any* transparency for the overhead projector is called a "slide" (perhaps from the use of 8×10 inch color transparencies). In this entry, slide refers to the color reversal transparency (usually from 35mm film in a 2×2 mount) shown through the optics of a slide projector.

Generally speaking, the slide (technically, a color reversal transparency) has more visual impact than an overhead transparency—even when both are made of the same high-resolution color transparency film. The slide's advantage derives from two factors. First, the optics of the slide projector are generally superior to those of the overhead projector. Second, slides are generally used in a much darker environment than are overhead transparencies. The better optics and viewing conditions make, in general, for a superior image on the screen. Although most slides are made through a photographic process, the input to that process may be a traditional camera, a special effects camera (capable of multiple exposures for photo and graphic effects), or computer-generated output. Slides now range in complexity from simple text on a solid background to elaborate pictorial and graphic effects.

4. *From any Input to any Output*

The introduction of the computer and, especially, sophisticated computer picture–graphics programs have blurred the traditional methods of producing still media. For example, pictorial or photographic images (from video, from electronic photography, from CD-ROM, or from high-resolution scanners) can be entered into the computer and manipulated to produce almost any imaginable visual result. That result can be: (a) shown through a video projector (conventional or LCD); (b) shown on an overhead projector using an LCD panel (black and white or color); (c) converted to a color reversal transparency (from 35mm to 8×10 inches); (d) printed on a xerographic copier or on a plotter (again, black and white or color) in sizes of 2×3 feet or larger. Thus, while the production techniques for the more traditional materials remain the same, the production techniques for high-technology still media overlap. Although computer skills (primarily the use of graphics applications) are important, good design is still paramount. Computer skills, no matter how good, are no substitute for the ability to create messages that communicate and teach.

5. *Choosing a Still Medium*

Apart from their physical limitations (e.g., the number of people who can see the medium clearly), the still media are almost interchangeable; that is, the presenter can achieve approximately the *same results* with the audience. The following are factors to consider in selecting and producing a still medium: (a) communications or training objectives; (b) presentation environment (a physical limitation); (c) audience characteristics; (d) structure and mood of the meeting; (e) production resources (other than cost); (f) cost (and cost effectiveness).

While matching the medium to the objective is generally held to be the most important consideration, the reality is that the presentation environment is the factor most presenters consider first. For example, slides may be the best choice to show subtle colors, but slides require a darkened room. If the room cannot be darkened sufficiently, slides—no matter how appropriate to the objectives—may be a poor choice of medium. The following are some common attributes of the three still media.

5.1 *Charts, Flipcharts, and Presentation Boards*

These media usually involve a high presenter interaction with medium (especially true of flipcharts). Because the size of the image is limited, the size of the audience is also limited. Because of the way they are traditionally used (with small groups, presenter adding information), flipcharts lend an air of informality and intimacy, thus encouraging audience involvement. Charts (whether already prepared or done during the presentation) can be posted around the room for reference during the presentation. These presentation media require no electricity or special room preparation, making them ideal for spontaneous, small group meetings.

5.2 *Overhead Projection*

Because the size of the image is enlarged by projection, the size of the audience can be much larger, even if the overhead is used only like a flipchart or chalkboard. The overhead can be used in a moderately lighted room as long as the light does not fall on the projection screen. Most overhead projectors have fixed focal length lenses, limiting the location of projector and screen as well as the arrangement of the room. The projector accepts a wide variety of materials—thus, presentations can be quite informal (with handwritten materials) or very structured (as with computer-generated material shown through an LCD panel) to meet the needs of the presenter. The range of materials means a wide range of costs and preparation time, depending on the technical complexity of the materials to be used. Because most overhead projectors have a brighter area in the center of the image (the so called "hot spot"), materials, especially photographic materials, must be designed and produced accordingly. Some presenters are not at ease changing and handling transparencies—in such cases, an assistant should be used.

5.3 Slides

Slides usually require a well-darkened room (special high intensity projectors are available, but are relatively expensive). Because the room is dark, some informality and audience involvement may be lost. Moreover, the presenter is less able to monitor audience reactions. The equipment set-up and the room darkening require more presentation coordination and preparation than with overheads and flipcharts. Slides generally require more production time than the other still media. The projector's size (in comparison to the overhead) and zoom lens allow more flexibility in location in the room than with the overhead projector. Dissolve units may be used with slide projectors to give the presentation a very smooth and polished look.

Keep in mind that the foregoing are generalizations and exceptions can be found to each statement. There is no single, correct medium for all presentations. The growing sophistication of production methods (especially computer-generated design and production) make it relatively easy to produce a number of media formats from the same input. The key to success is making the best of available resources in order to communicate effectively.

See also: Media in Education: Role of Still, Audio, and Audiovisual; Media Selection

Bibliography

Anderson R H 1976 *Selecting and Developing Media for Instruction*. Van Nostrand, Reinhold, New York

Reiser R A, Gagné R M 1983 *Selecting Media for Instruction*. Educational Technology Publications, Englewood Cliffs, New Jersey

Wallington C J 1987 Audiovisual methods. In: Craig R L (ed.) 1987 *Training and Development Handbook*, 3rd edn. McGraw-Hill, New York

How to Make a Better Technical Presentation. 3M Company, St Paul, Minnesota

C. J. Wallington

Stratification in Educational Systems

This entry will first address the issue of what is meant by stratification. Conceptual issues and corresponding empirical indicators at the individual level are introduced. This is followed by a discussion of the relationship between an individuals' position in the stratification and the educational system. Different connotations of "education" are distinguished. The third section considers whether these relationships are stable or differ between schools. On a more general level the structures of educational systems are also relevant. Do systems induce stratified patterns and lead to specific strategies of social groups, and are these changed after reforms in educational systems? There has been much empirical progress in this area which merits that some attention be given to methodological issues.

1. Stratification

In discussions about stratification, five issues arise. First, there is the question of whether social privileges are connected to certain discrete social classes which can be clearly distinguished, or whether social privileges are linked with a dimension of status which ranks individuals in a more or less continuous way. The former view is associated with the classical theory of Karl Marx and mostly applied to preindustrial societies with clear-cut social dividing lines. The latter view is based on the work of Max Weber, who introduced the concept of life-styles to indicate class and status.

After agreement is reached on the meaning of class and status, the second issue is the question of how many classes must be distinguished, or whether more or less homogeneous strata of persons with similar life-styles can be identified. Do persons belonging to these classes share (or lack) the same privileges? Or can individuals be ordered in a hierarchical way, where people at the top enjoy more privileges? Usually social position is defined in terms of the occupation held, even though this implies that information is available on the active employed population of men and women between 20 and 65 years of age.

The third issue is descriptive: how many persons belong to which category and what are the correlates of this class or status position with respect to other socially scarce goods, such as education, income, wealth, or consumption? Here, there are many studies which document social distributions, ranging from the classical Yankee City and Middletown studies to the contemporary social indicator reports of many countries.

A fourth issue is the degree of stability of the above-described patterns. Due to changing social conditions and economic growth, the distributions of privileged positions and occupations are changing, which creates opportunities for individuals to move upward or downward in social hierarchies. These mobility patterns may be observed during an individual's life course (intragenerational), but also between the generations of parents and children (intergenerational). The degree to which mobility within and between generations is realized is often considered an indicator for the openness or rigidity of a society. The more mobility, the less an individual is determined by his or her origins. It will be clear that much openness does not challenge the legitimacy of the social hierarchy or class system; it only means that many persons travel across socially defined borderlines.

The fifth issue is therefore whether these borderlines, the classifications or dimensions of class or status themselves, are subject to change over time. In the development of industrial societies the division of labor has led to an increased specialization and differentiation of work. Especially in the twentieth century, many occupations have disappeared due to the mechanization and automation of work. Also, new occupations have been created that did not formerly exist. This has resulted in a complete rearranging of the social hierarchies and thus of the paths according to which social mobility could develop. One of the difficult tasks in sociology is to set apart the various components of mobility: absolute versus relative rates of mobility; changes resulting from different classifications versus "real" changing patterns of mobility.

These issues are not limited to theoretical importance. Empirical research in this area is determined by the distinction between classes, status, prestige, and socioeconomic position. Socioeconomic position (and also social standing) is frequently indicated by some kind of composite measure that includes the weighted sums of occupational prestige, educational level and income. It will be clear that these kinds of indicators are unsuitable for studies of stratification and education because these variables are interrelated.

In the 1990s principally two different instruments are accepted as a standard in international and comparative research. For national research local versions of socioeconomic position are available. The *Standard International Occupational Prestige Scale* was developed by Treiman (1977) to normalize the many national status scales into one that could be used in comparative research. The scale is based on the aggregated national prestige scales that were available and in use in the 1950s and 1960s.

A further observation about status and prestige scales is that persons with the same prestige score hold a wide variety of jobs and vice versa. Thus a prestige score does not refer to a social group with more or less cohesion. Erikson and his colleagues (1979) therefore developed a ten-category (EGP) class scheme on the basis of four different job attributes: sector, employment status, skill level, and supervisor status (see Table 1).

Table 1
The Erikson–Goldthorpe–Portocarero Class Scheme (EGP)

I	Large proprietors; higher professionals and managers
II	Lower professionals and managers
III	Routine nonmanual workers
IVa	Small proprietors with employees
IVb	Small proprietors without employees
IVc	Self-employed farmers
V	Lower grade technicians and manual supervisors
VI	Skilled manual workers
VIIa	Unskilled and semiskilled manual workers
VIIb	(Unskilled) agricultural workers

Source: Erikson et al. 1979

Similarly Ganzeboom et al. (1989) applied a compressed version of this scheme to 149 mobility tables from 35 countries to discover a modest general trend toward societal openness since the Second World War. For both the Treiman and EGP scales, detailed recoding schemes are easily available from knowledge about levels of occupations (see Sect. 5).

Some authors consider gender and race as special dimensions for social stratification. These can also be considered as specifications of a general pattern of stratification. The criteria discussed, however, refer to the occupational domain and it has been argued that other criteria might be equally relevant as indicators to distinguish stratified societies. Marriage patterns (homogamy and heterogamy) have been suggested and applied, as well as educational criteria (educational mobility).

2. *Stratification and Educational Outcomes*

An important question is whether persons with higher educational performance or achievements have better mobility chances? To answer this, it is first necessary to elaborate on the meaning of "education." For the individual, the notion of educational qualification is the most relevant concept. While several distinctions regarding education can be made (cognitive, technical instrumental, noncognitive, social normative), stratification studies by and large concentrate on the cognitive outcomes of education (achievement, performance). As this information is not always available, educational certification (diploma), or simply the time spent in school (number of years), are chosen as proxies. These proxies, however, are not always comparable, as they reflect local or national characteristics, and are not stable over time. In cross-national research it is very difficult to use educational criteria and indicators which are equivalent enough to allow reliable comparisons. The practice of using number of years of education as an indicator has been frequently

Table 2
Educational scheme according to Müller et al. (1989)

1a	Inadequately completed general elementary education
1b	General elementary education
1c	General elementary education and basic vocational qualification
2a	Intermediate vocational qualification
2b	Intermediate general qualification
3a	Higher education—maturity level
3b	Higher education—lower-level tertiary certificate
3c	Higher education—upper-level tertiary certificate

discussed and rejected (see, e.g., Allmendinger 1989).

When educational certification is chosen, other problems arise: the cross-national comparison of diplomas includes both an individual component (performance) and system characteristics. Müller et al. (1989) developed a special version for their study of class (EGP) and education in nine industrial nations (See Table 2). From this scheme it is clear that the ranking of diplomas of different school types can only partially be achieved in educational systems where both a general and a vocational track exist. In addition, a separate translation table must be constructed to match national certificates to the scheme. This can be done only by experts.

What is the relation between stratification and educational outcomes? Blau and Duncan (1967) developed a model of status attainment, where educational attainment is determined by social background (occupation and education of the father), but in turn the achieved job and income of a person is determined by the level of education attained. There have been numerous replications and extensions of this basic model (for a discussion, see Treiman and Ganzeboom 1990 or Breiger 1991). This causal model approach has led to many new questions which need to be addressed. The relationship between education and mobility has been clarified, but studies on the effects of the composition of the paternal family, siblings, and peer group or educational attainment have also been carried out. In later research, studies included the role of school factors (such as organization, teachers, management style, curriculum) in the attainment process, which has led into what is known as research into effective schools.

Though considered a very productive approach, the main criticism of this research has been that progress, especially in methodology (see Sect. 5), has been at the expense of theory and explanatory power. The reason why and through which mechanisms the position of parents in a social hierarchy can affect a student's performance and achievement has thus not been solved: the research has documented mainly the degree to which this pattern exists. Various theoretical approaches have attempted to open this black box and have more or less been subject to empirical research. The influence of parents' attitudes, aspirations, and expectations was initially seen as the main determinant of educational success. Later, theories on conformity values, language codes, cultural reproduction, social capital, and networks were proposed (see *Contemporary Sociological Theories of Education; Family and Schooling*). The limitation of space restricts the elaboration of these explanations of differential educational success. It must be noted, however, that empirical support for these explanations is not always impressive. Little research has been done to test the combined effects of different or alternative explanations.

A main characteristic of these attainment studies in stages of the life-cycle is the application of models using individual longitudinal data. One of the objections to Jencks's famous *Inequality* study (Jencks et al. 1972) was to the lack of such data. A replication of this study revealed that the influence of family and schooling on earnings becomes much stronger over time, when based on longitudinal data (Jencks and Bartlett 1979).

The above approach to the study of stratification and education is typically an individualized one. The personal characteristics of the family and the student are assumed to determine to what extent he or she may be successful in school and career. Contextual information is introduced into the models at the level of interaction with peers or teachers, but a job will only be attained in competition with others, and an employer will only pay the wage that is reasonable in certain labor markets. Thus the strength of these models, that is, the rigorous testing of hypotheses by conducting appropriate analyses, is at the same time its weakness: structural and institutional effects are left out.

Others have emphasized precisely these institutional aspects. Boudon (1974) developed a dynamic model of educational and social opportunity that accounts for the increase of numbers of students with higher educational credentials. He demonstrated that an increase in educational opportunities is not necessarily matched with an increase in occupational opportunities, because at the structural level only a fixed number of vacancies (opportunities) are available. A similar point was made by Thurow (1975), who argued that employers do not select according to the absolute educational level attained, but on the relative position of an individual within a queue of applicants. Although these views have been challenged, they do direct attention to the possible importance of the institutional aspects of stratification.

3. Schools and Stratification

Schools may contribute to different educational outcomes in various ways. A stronger selection of students according to previous performance at entrance to schools (input) will raise the level of educational outcomes. As this level of performance is highly correlated with social backgrounds, the selective schools will become less heterogeneous. Within these schools, therefore, the effect of social background on educational outcomes will decrease, if not disappear. Thus the reduction of social variation within schools can be seen as a result of restricted admission, which might explain the absence of strong correlations between social background and performance at the highest educational levels (restriction of range).

However, this raises the question of whether the school is a neutral institution that only transmits inequality from the parents' generation to that of the child. Does the school act independently to weaken or reinforce the effects of stratification? Do educational outcomes still vary, having controlled for the social composition of the student body? The influence of school factors, such as organization, curriculum, or general well-being has been the focus of much school effectiveness research. In general these factors contribute up to 10 to 15 percent of the variance in addition to that already accounted for by other influences.

Research has shown that sometimes interesting contextual effects show up after controlling for student body composition. For example, Coleman and Hoffer (1987) confirmed earlier studies which focused on the higher relative performance of students in Catholic schools in the United States. Similar results were reported in Scotland by McPherson and Willms (1986), and again the question arises as to how these findings can be explained. Coleman and Hoffer (1987) have argued that stronger Catholic social capital and networks explain the difference; the Scottish authors suggest that the minority status of Catholics may be the cause. Other research, however, has resulted in inconsistent contextual effects of school, religious background, or neighborhood.

Multilevel techniques that separate the effects of individual and school variation are becoming the appropriate tools to study the issue of whether schools reinforce or weaken the ties between stratification and education. It is still too early to determine whether school effects are substantive, and to what extent they relate to properties of the school (tracking, denominational, selectivity) or of the school system (comprehensiveness).

4. Educational Systems and Stratification

Educational systems throughout the world show a large variety of structures. Systems vary with regard to the length of compulsory schooling, but also on the age that different curriculum tracks have to be chosen by the student. Some systems are decentralized, while others are highly centralized; some have little or no selection for entry, while others are very selective at early ages. It might well be that for any given society the variation in system characteristics coincides with the strength of stratification effects on education. Such inference, however, cannot be found by simply studying the blueprints of educational structures in detail, as has often been done in the past. Whether the correlation between social background and educational achievement or performance varies between educational systems can only be established by empirical research. This, however, assumes the availability of large-scale cross-national data sets with equivalent measures and samples. Unfortunately these types of data are rare and very expensive to collect.

The various IEA (International Association for the Evaluation of Educational Achievement) studies, some in more than 25 countries, are one exception, but little attention has been given to the stratification issue. The study of Passow and his colleagues (1976) attempted to establish the relationship between average academic performance and educational system characteristics using country as the unit of analysis. They found no clear relationships, possibly because the variation between countries is much smaller than that within countries. Keeves et al. (1991) conducted a study on individual student IEA data for the 10 countries which participated in the two science studies in 1970–71 and 1983–84. They reported that educational expansion has resulted in a general increase of educational opportunity, particularly in Sweden with a marked equality policy.

An alternative approach is the application of large-scale national surveys that contain data on the social background and education of respondents and their parents. These data usually are collected from individuals between 15 and 65 years old, so one can compare the relationship between social background and education for persons born in the same year in several countries. Though the number of variables in past surveys of this kind is restricted (and usually only contains achievement and no measures of performance), this cohort approach leads to interesting findings over a long time-span. In standardized analyses the change in educational opportunity seems to be comparable and constant over time for many Western countries. Exceptions to this rule are Sweden and the Netherlands where opportunities appear to have increased (Shavit and Blossfeld 1992).

Such studies on the level of educational opportunity over time become more interesting when used to evaluate the effects of specific educational transformations. Sato (1991) studied the educational system in Japan, which was transformed after 1945 from a highly selective system to a nonselective secondary school system. She concluded that while social selection in secondary education had diminished, it returned again at the university level. In this respect the system preserved its social selection mechanism, only at a later age.

In Eastern and Central Europe, great social changes took place after the Second World War. The transformation to state socialist societies with much emphasis on equal opportunity implied that the old educational systems had to be abolished and replaced by systems where selection on social grounds would not occur. Education was seen as the engine of social change and greater social justice. Unfortunately no evaluations are available on the effectiveness of these massive educational reforms. When comparing the educational achievement of generations from before and after the great transformations, the average absolute educational level has increased for every younger generation. The transformation itself provided an expansion of opportunity, but the anticipated relative improvement for lower-class children has not been observed at all. Patterns of inequality proved to be the same and almost constant over time in Hungary, Czechoslovakia, and Poland, but also in the Netherlands, where no educational change was introduced during the period under study (Peschar 1991). In fact the old patterns of school choice and achievement hardly changed, in spite of explicit policies (e.g., quota systems) to promote better individual chances for children from working-class families.

A few studies have focused on cross-national differences in the qualification structure of countries and the consequences of these structures for educational careers. Müller et al. (1989) concluded in their nine-country study that nations which have a relatively low degree of credentialism (as in the United Kingdom or Poland) show a low degree of class inequality and educational opportunity. In other nations (as Germany, France, or Hungary) the association between qualification and class position seemed to be stronger. This suggests that there are structural and institutional effects present. Also Allmendinger (1989) shows that the effects of educational attainment on occupational rewards are clearly dependent on characteristics of the educational system. For example, the relation is stronger in more stratified educational systems.

These latter studies underline the relevance of context and social structure when comparing educational systems and their outcomes. Studies on many countries from a macro perspective, with aggregated data, are unlikely to find much variation between systems. In addition to the ecological fallacy, one should be careful not to generalize from cross-national comparisons from one point in time, to developments over time in a comparative perspective. The best strategy would seem to be one which is restricted to an intensive study of a few countries over a longer period of time.

5. *Methodological issues*

The area of stratification and education is a crossroad between subject matter and methodology and statistics. Path analysis and structural equation modeling were applied first in the study of this research problem (Blau and Duncan 1967, Featherman and Hauser 1978). These developments resulted in numerous studies on the effects of social background on education, which later served as bases for large-scale evaluation programs in compensatory education.

The analysis of mobility tables, or more generally panel data, was taken up again in the beginning of the 1980s when log-linear modeling was developed (Hagenaars 1990). This procedure has led to particular progress in the area of comparative studies. To study, for instance, the effects of educational reform on social equality one needs data on educational attainment and social background for different birth cohorts. When comparing before- and after-reform cohorts, the effects of the reform can be tested rigorously with log-linear analysis, and the absolute and relative educational improvement can be identified and measured (for an application on Eastern Europe see Peschar 1991).

By 1990 more attention was being devoted to the analysis of complete life histories over time. Event history analysis has proven to be a powerful tool to investigate the role of education in career attainments for different generations (Blossfeld et al. 1988).

The development of multilevel models has been referred to previously. It may be expected that the further advancement of these models will make possible the separation of effects on the individual by factors at different contextual levels more precise (Goldstein 1987).

The growth of knowledge about stratification and education has been facilitated by the development of information technology. Apart from newly designed statistical techniques, the manipulation and processing of large data sets with numerous variables from one or more countries is now possible. This is most important as research in this area heavily depends on the (re-)analysis of existing (census) data. In addition, large (inter)national surveys about the labor market can now be made accessible for this type of research problem.

Finally, new standards and coding systems for occupations and key attainments in educational careers have been developed. Occupations can now be coded using the *International Standard Classification of Occupations* (ISCO) of the International Labour Organisation, and coding is being implemented by most national central bureaus of statistics. Sophisticated systems allow the transformation of the ISCO code into most other major coding systems, such as Treimans' international prestige scale or the EGP (Popping 1991). It is only a matter of time before the same will hold for information from the *International Standard Classification of Education* (ISCED).

See also: Family and School Environmental Measures; Family and Schooling; Measurement of Social Background; Multilevel Analysis; Social Mobility, Social Stratification, and Education

References

Allmendinger J 1989 Educational systems and labor market outcomes. *European Sociological Review* 5: 231–50

Blau P, Duncan O D 1967 *The American Occupational Structure*. Wiley, New York

Blossfeld H-P, Hamerle A, Mayer K-M 1988 *Event History Analysis. Statistical Theory and Application*. Erlbaum, Hillsdale, New Jersey

Boudon R 1974 *Education, Opportunity, and Social Inequality*. Wiley, New York

Breiger R L (ed.) 1991 *Social Mobility and Social Structure*. Cambridge University Press, Cambridge

Coleman J S, Hoffer T 1987 *Public and Private High Schools. The Impact of Communities*. Basic Books, New York

Erikson R, Goldthorpe J H, Portocarero L 1979 Intergenerational class mobility in three Western European societies: England, France, and Sweden. *Br. J. Sociol.* 30(4): 415–41

Featherman D L, Hauser R M 1978 *Opportunity and Change*. Academic Press, New York

Ganzeboom H B G, Luijkx R, Treiman D J 1989 Intergenerational class mobility in comparative perspective. *Research in Social Stratification and Mobility* 9: 3–85

Goldstein H 1987 *Multilevel Models in Educational and Social Research*. Oxford University Press, New York

Hagenaars J A 1990 *Categorial Longitudinal Data: Loglinear Panel, Trend and Cohort Analysis*. Sage, Newbury Park, California

Jencks C S, Bartlett S 1979 *Who Gets Ahead? The Determinants of Economic Success in America*. Basic Books, New York

Jencks C S et al. 1972 *Inequality: A Reassessment of the Effect of Family and Schooling In America*. Basic Books, New York

Keeves J P, Morgenstern C, Saha L J 1991 Educational expansion and equality of opportunity: Evidence from studies conducted by IEA in ten countries in 1970–71 and 1983–84. *Int. J. Educ. Res.* 15(1): 61–80

McPherson A, Willms J D 1986 Certification, class conflict, religion, and community: A socio-historical explanation of the effectiveness of contemporary schools. *Research in Sociology of Education and Socialisation* 6: 227–302

Müller W, Lüttinger P, Koenig W, Karle W 1989 Class and education in industrial nations. *International Journal of Sociology* 19: 3–39

Passow A H, Noah H J, Eckstein M A, Mallea J R 1976 *The National Case Study: An Empirical Comparative Study of Twenty-One Educational Systems*. Almqvist and Wiksell, Stockholm

Peschar J L 1991 Educational opportunities in East–West perspective: A comparative analysis of the Netherlands, Hungary, Poland and Czechoslovakia. *Int. J. Educ. Res.* 15(1): 107–121

Popping R 1991 *A Knowledge-Based System for Occupational Classifications*. iec*Pro*GAMMA, Groningen

Sato J 1991 Family background and school continuation decisions in Japan *Int. J. Educ. Res.* 15: 81–105

Shavit Y, Blossfeld H-P 1992 *Educational Opportunity in Comparative Perspective*. Westview Press, Boulder, Colorado

Thurow L 1975 *Generating Inequality. Mechanisms of Distribution in the US Economy*. Basic Books, New York

Treiman D J (ed.) 1977 *Occupational Prestige in Comparative Perspective*. Academic Press, New York

Treiman D J Ganzeboom H B G 1990 Cross-national comparative status attainment research. *Research in Social Stratification and Mobility*. 9: 105–27

Further Reading

Müller D K, Ringer F, Simon B (eds.) 1987 *The Rise of the Modern Educational System: Structural Change and Social Reproduction 1870–1921*. Cambridge University Press, Cambridge

J. L. Peschar

Stress, Coping, and Learning

Two examples of school situations that cause stress are: (a) waiting to take an important exam and discovering that one has studied the wrong material; (b) having a conflict with a teacher and being sent to the school principal. Students know these experiences and can describe how they feel and think, and what they do in such situations. It is a fact, however, that not all students will feel stress in the situations described above, and that those who do will not all react in the same way. When under stress, students report experiencing psychological symptoms such as negative emotions (anger, frustration, anxiety, or sadness), the presence of intrusive and repetitive thoughts about the cause of the stress, and behavioral and bodily changes (e.g., aggressive or passive behavior, increased heart rate, perspiration). Such stress-bound emotions, cognitions, and behavioral changes should be reduced swiftly in order to initiate or maintain adequate functioning.

In the 1980s psychologists studied how individuals of various ages reacted to stressful events (stressors). Numerous studies have examined the relationship between coping techniques and: (a) the way people experience stress (psychological symptoms), and (b) long-term adverse effects of the stress experience (e.g., psychosomatic complaints, absenteeism). The first part of this entry will describe stressful situations. Then the transactional stress model will be presented and a global review provided of the research into coping with stress.

1. Stressful Situations for Children and Adolescents

Before the 1980s stress research in children and adolescents focused on major life events. Difficult existential situations, relating to disease, death, severe loss, or separation, were identified; students' adaptive and nonadaptive reactions were recorded. A vast amount of evidence suggests that psychological and behavioral problems in students of all ages can be related to recent stressful life events. However, considerable differences in students' vulnerability to these life traumas are reported. It seems that it is not so much the stressful impact itself that causes long-term adverse effects on adaptation, development, and health, but the way in which individuals cope with the life stressor.

Research has yielded evidence that stress at school is a multidimensional construct and that daily frustrations may produce intense and chronic stress in students of all ages. Questionnaires have been constructed to measure the impact of daily frustrations. The data collected indicate that they break down factor-analytically into social conflicts related to criticism, social exposure, and social pressure on the one hand and stressful academic situations on the other. The latter group of stressors includes impediments, overloads, and failures. Any of these daily frustrations may be experienced by a student as a "difficult situation," associated with unpleasant experiences, symptoms of malaise, fatigue, or uncertainty about one's ability to keep the situation under control.

Compas et al. (1989) reported that the relationship between stressful events and psychological symptoms changes with development. In children and young adolescents (up to age 14) family stressors (e.g., pressures and expectations by parents) were most predictive of psychological symptoms. In middle adolescence (age 15–17) only peer stressors were predictive of psychological symptoms. In late adolescence (age 18–20) academic stressors (e.g., doing poorly in an exam or a paper) were the best predictors. A consistent pattern of differences emerged between males and females: females of all ages report more stress than males and are more affected by it; females are also significantly more affected by observing the stress experienced by people in their social network.

2. *Two Types of Appraisals*

It is important to note, that stress does not lie in a situation but in the way an individual perceives a potential stressor. For this reason stress is defined in terms of an individual's appraisal of a situation. The founder of transactional stress theory, Lazarus, views a person who is experiencing stress as an active organizer of the stress experience and an active responder to the taxing environment. That is, a transaction occurs when the stressor and the person mutually influence each other. Lazarus and Folkman defined stress as "a particular relationship between the person and the environment that is appraised by the person as taxing or exceeding his or her resources and endangering his or her well-being" (1984 p.19). They further explained that any new or unexpected situation calls for two types of appraisals: a primary appraisal which determines the significance of the event and a secondary appraisal which determines whether one's coping options will be sufficient to overcome the perceived or anticipated threat of the situation.

Primary appraisals assess whether a situation is beneficial, negative, or neutral for well-being. When a person does not perceive a discrepancy between the perceived task demands and his or her resources to meet these demands, he or she may feel little stress. By contrast, when an individual assesses situational demands as exceeding his or her resources, the person may experience stress and this will be further differentiated into: (a) actual harm, damage, or loss; (b) anticipated damage or loss (threat); or (c) potential gains, mastery, or benefits that will result from dealing with the event (challenge).

Secondary appraisals assess whether coping resources will be sufficient to overcome the harm, loss, damage, threat, or challenge represented by a stressful situation. The upshot of this is that whether or not stress is experienced depends on the achieved balance between primary appraisals (perception of harm, loss, or threat) and secondary appraisals (perceived coping ability).

3. *Coping with Stress*

Coping refers to efforts on the part of a student to deal with taxing situations. Lazarus and Folkman defined coping as "constantly changing cognitive and behavioral efforts to manage specific external and/or internal demands that are appraised as taxing or exceeding the resources of the individual" (1984 p.141). Coping is further delineated into two basic, universal ways of dealing with stressors, namely, problem-focused coping and emotion-focused coping. The former coping mode refers to efforts on the part of the learner to act on the source of stress (approach), whereas the latter coping mode alludes to efforts to reduce the emotional distress by moving away from the source of stress either actually or mentally (avoidance). Roth and Cohen (1986) predicted and found that approach and avoidance are highly consistent coping responses within a particular context but that they are not mutually exclusive. On the basis of a meta-analysis on coping with stressful life events, Suls and Fletcher (1986) concluded that approach and avoidance can be seen as habitual or preferential ways of dealing with stressful events, but that neither coping mode is more effective in all situations. Avoidance seems to be more effective to deal with short-term threats, whereas approach is more effective when the threat persists over time, mainly because it allows the individual to engage in cognitive and emotional efforts to deal with long-term stress.

It is important to note that coping in a school context should not be seen as an action executed at a particular moment in time. The relationship between coping and a stressful event is a dynamic process that entails a series of transactions between the student and his or her environment. For example, an open conflict with a teacher in class may produce a variety of coping responses in the same student, ranging from being angry and ignoring the teacher to attempting to make it up or engaging in distracting activities. When perceiving discouragements from fellow-learners, the student may attempt to pacify the teacher, whereas encouragements may increase aggressive behavior. Because of the dynamic nature of the coping construct, it is difficult to typify a student's characteristic coping mode. Observations of students' coping attempts reveal the existence of many different coping techniques.

3.1 Coping and Learning

Students need multiple attempts before they succeed in performing a new skill swiftly. Constraints are put on their performance by their present ability to perform the skill. When students' initial attempts at mastery fail, or when they fall back several times on older, less adequate skills, they may take this to mean that they are incapable of mastering the new skill. When such a situation arises, students may feel that their personal resources are inadequate to meet the demands of the task. Evidence from mainstream psychology indicates that social exposure, and especially anticipated social comparisons, create a concern with limited personal resources and may cause prolonged physiological arousal, reflected in increased heart rate and variability in blood pressure. Such physiological arousal, and the negative emotions it elicits, signals to the learner that something is wrong and that actions should be undertaken to restore well-being and to prevent stressful experiences from occurring now and in the future.

In the literature on stress and coping, different coping techniques have been described. Unfortunately, most authors have used their own labels to refer to these techniques, which makes it difficult to compare and contrast them. For example, Rost and Schermer (1987) identified four techniques that adolescents use to reduce, accept, or come to terms with threatening academic situations: (a) danger control, (b)anxiety control, (c) anxiety repression, and (d) situation control. Danger control and anxiety control are regarded as preventive ways of coping with anxiety, either cognitively or emotionally. The first way of control refers to adequate preparation in the form of productive study skills. The second way of control refers to strategies that reduce psychic and somatic anxiety symptoms.

Anxiety repression and situation control refer to avoidance; both of these techniques may lead to effective relief of anxiety, but neither of them modifies the underlying causes. Anxiety repression may temporarily calm down the student, whereas situation control may help the student to evade taxing demands in the confrontation phase (e.g., by cheating, or reporting sick).

Seiffge-Krenke (1989) also described the coping techniques adolescents use. She grouped them under three main headings: (a) internal coping, (b) active coping, and (c) withdrawal. The first two labels refer to the problem-focused coping mode. The term "internal coping" is reserved for techniques that are characterized by internal reflection of possible solutions, whereas the term "active coping" is used for responses that reflect active and constructive attempts to solve a problem, by gathering information about the nature of the problem or by eliciting social support. Finally, withdrawal includes defenses such as denial and repression: the student inhibits actions that might produce more stress, are embarrassing, or might get him or her into trouble. Seiffge-Krenke reported that the coping techniques used in adolescence are relatively stable over time, and that the use of internal forms of coping and the willingness to compromise increase with age. She also noted considerable culture and sex differences in the use of coping techniques.

In conclusion, it seems that most students use both the problem- and the emotion-focused coping modes in response to stressful events and that the effectiveness of the selected coping mode depends on the interaction between personal variables and situational demands. A study by Compas Forbythe and Wagner (1988) supports this view. They found that when there was a match between the student's perception of control and the selected coping mode (e.g., low perceived control and emotion-focused coping, or high perceived control and problem-focused coping) low stress was reported (and vice versa for a mismatch). A further study by Compas, Malcame and Fondacaro (1988) documented that students who demonstrated more flexibility in their coping mode over a four-week period reported lower levels of stress than students who rigidly responded to the changing demands of stressful situations. On the basis of these results it was concluded that intervention programs should teach students how and when to use different coping techniques. A vast number of intervention programs have been designed. Some of these programs concentrate on the use of relaxation techniques, whereas others focus more on problem-solving skills (for an overview, see Compas et al. 1989). Beneficial effects have been reported, including increased self-esteem, enhanced academic performance, ability to handle academic stress, ability to deal with social conflict, and decreased absenteeism.

3.2 Coping, Health, and Development

Educators and teachers often forget that students'

participation in classroom activities may also have important implications for their personality development and their health. It has already been pointed out that stressful situations, rooted in perceived academic inadequacy, in social conflict, or in both may hinder students in acquiring new knowledge and skill. When these students' ability to cope with a wide range of stressful daily situations is not enhanced, they are at risk of lagging behind or dropping out. But what is more, stressful experiences may also constitute a health risk. Boekaerts (1991) reported that some coping techniques may be beneficial from the point of view of increasing grade point average but coincide with psychosomatic complaints. Given the significance of stress and coping in the development of educational and health risks, it is crucial that preventive efforts are made to help students understand why certain coping techniques are better than others in different stressful situations. It is important to note, however, that stress and coping with it should be seen as aspects of normal development. Indeed, in major periods of transition, such as for example in the transition from elementary school to junior high school, students are confronted with new challenges, for which their habitual adaptive potential may prove to be inadequate, or unaceptable. Some students may have no trouble in meeting these new challenges, whereas others may find it difficult to bridge the gap between the new stressors and their coping repertoire. Preventive intervention programs aimed at the major transition periods should help students to use new coping techniques. Some promising results have been reported (Elias et al. 1986).

See also: Affect, Emotions, and Learning; Achievement Motivation, Development of; Motivation and Learning

References

Boekaerts M 1991 Competitive drive, coping and math achievement: What's so detrimental about avoidance behaviour? In: Hagtvet K (ed.) 1991 *Advances in Test Anxiety Research*, Vol. 7. Swets and Zeitlinger, Lisse

Compas B E, Forsythe C J, Wagner B M 1988 Consistency and variability in causal attributions and coping with stress. *Cogni. Therapy and Res.* 12: 305–20

Compas B E, Malcarne V L, Fondacaro K 1988 Coping with stressful events in older children and young adolescents. *J. Consult. Clin. Psychol.* 56(3): 405–11

Compas B E, Phares V, Ledoux N 1989 Stress and coping preventive interventions for children and adolescents. In: Bond L A, Compas B E (eds.) 1989 *Primary Prevention and Promotion in the Schools*. Sage, Newbury Park, California

Elias M J et al. (1986) Impact of a preventive social problem solving intervention on children's coping with middle-school stressors. *Am. J. Community Psychol.* 14: 259–75

Lazarus R S, Folkman S 1984 *Stress, Appraisal and Coping*. Springer-Verlag, New York

Rost D H, Schermer F J 1987 Emotion and cognition in coping with test anxiety. *Commun. and Cognition* 20(2/3): 225–44

Roth S, Cohen J 1986 Approach, avoidance and coping with stress. *Am. Psychol.* 41(7): 813–19

Seiffge-Krenke I 1989 Health related behavior and coping with illness in adolescence: A cross-cultural perspective. In: Schmidt L R, Schwenkmezger P, Weinman J, Maes, S (eds.) 1989 *Theoretical and Applied Aspects of Health Psychology*. Harwood Academic Publishers, Chur

Suls J, Fletcher B 1986 The relative efficacy of avoidant and nonavoidant coping strategies: A meta-analysis. *Health Psychology* 4: 249–88

Further Reading

Boekaerts M 1993 Being concerned with well-being and with learning. *Educ. Psychol.* 2

Bond A L, Compas B E (eds.) 1989 *Primary Prevention and Promotion in the Schools*. Sage, Newbury Park, California

Bosma H, Jackson S (eds.) 1990 *Coping and Self-concept in Adolescence*. Springer-Verlag, Berlin

M. Boekaerts

Student Cognitive Processing and Learning

In the mid-twentieth century conceptions about learning and about how instructional events help students learn underwent a transition. A new view of learning—that the learner adapts to events as they unfold in an instructional environment—replaced one that saw the learner's behavior as controlled by instructional stimuluses (Anderson and Gates 1950). Research into this adaptive process aimed to discover principles for designing instructional environments that could specify "the experiences which most effectively implant in the individual a disposition to learn . . . the ways in which a body of knowledge should be structured so that it can be most readily grasped by the learner . . . the most effective sequences in which to present the materials to be learned . . . [and] the nature and pacing of rewards and punishments in the process of learning and teaching" (Bruner 1964 pp. 307–08). A rapprochement between psychology and instructional research was underway that would sweep up the field of educational psychology within the larger cognitive revolution (Glaser 1982). As research accumulated over the next 40 years, perspectives on learning, instruction, and the learner would evolve significantly.

The view of learning that came to guide theory and research characterizes the learner as an active inquiring agent. Classifying the learner as "active" implies that he or she is continuously involved in cognition about self and environment. Elements interacting in cognition are the learner's mental structures of knowledge and the learner's current perceptions of events, people, and objects in the environment, which are developed in terms of the student's existing knowledge. Thus this conception emphasizes the intrinsic and central role of the learner's prior knowledge as a background for interpreting instruction and as a resource with which to construct new achievements in school subjects.

Characterizing the learner as "inquiring" emphasizes the central role played by hypothesis-framing and testing as the student takes part in the instructional environment. Theoretically, the student creates provisional models and theories about matters at hand; for example, how to participate in a discovery lesson, how to explain why some heavy objects float, how to gain acceptance by peers, and how to achieve personal satisfaction. Means for inquiring into phenomena, models of systems, and theories are themselves learned and can become objects of inquiry.

Finally, acknowledging the learner as an "agent" recognizes that the student does not merely observe surroundings and receive information available therein. Beyond observational and receptive qualities, the student also steps forward to define goals and to seek specific information from peers, a text, or the teacher. Thus, the learner shapes and takes actions in the instructional environment. These acts, mental and physical, elicit information which the student seeks for the purpose of guiding subsequent thinking and acting. In this way, students co-create events that comprise instructional tasks and generate their own learning-from-instruction.

1. A Framework Describing Cognition and Instruction

Many models have been proposed to characterize forms of cognition and the kinds of information that are cognitively manipulated as learners participate in instruction. Literature that predates this entry is summarized in Winne (1985, 1991a, 1991b) and Wittrock (1986). Figure 1 presents a model which describes a learner's cognitive participation in instruction. It involves three broad classes of variables: characteristics of the learner, characteristics of the instructional tasks, and events that transpire as the learner interacts with instructional tasks. Other contemporary models of instructional cognition differ primarily in the variables they assign to these different classes. Variables in Fig. 1 are representative of those in other models and, obviously, are not exhaustive.

Figure 1 should not be interpreted as suggesting that values for variables or relationships among variables are static. Over time, variables are reciprocally determined and interact. That is, changes in a variable in one class can affect other variables within that same class, and may influence variables in other classes as well. In turn, the affected variable(s) may induce changes in other variables, including the one focused on initially. In this reciprocally determined system, identifying a single "cause" is difficult because choosing the slice in time within which to observe change is arbitrary. For instance, consider the case of a section heading within a textbook chapter. At the time the student is reading the chapter, it seems that the heading (a characteristic of the task environment) induces the student to retrieve (an event transpiring when the learner interacts with the text) some particular prior knowledge (a characteristic of the student). Earlier, however, when the textbook author was writing the chapter, the decision to insert the heading (a characteristic of the task environment) was probably based on a prediction about the prior knowledge that an average reader would possess (a characteristic of the student), and on the author's understanding about how inducing students to retrieve that prior knowledge might help them to construct an understanding of information in the chapter (an event transpiring when the learner interacts with the text). At this earlier time, then, the character of learners' prior knowledge affected

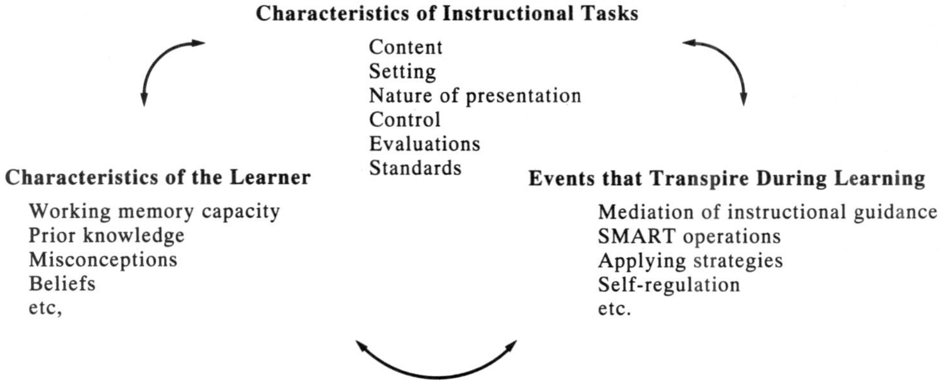

Figure 1
Contextual model of instructional information processing

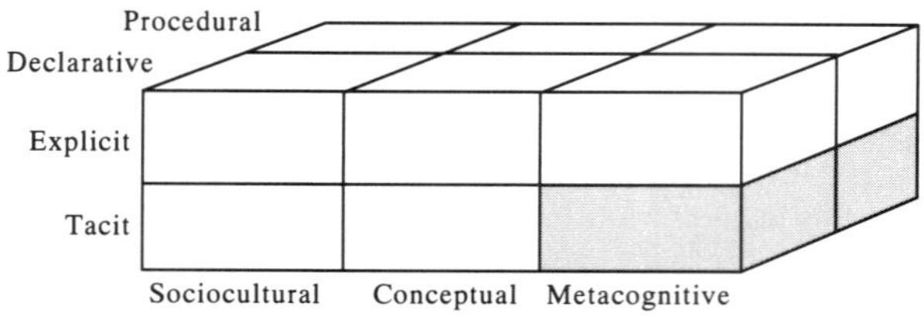

Figure 2
Facets of knowledge

the task environment by causing the author to include the heading in the text.

2. Characteristics of the Learner

Characteristics of the learner provide resources for and set limits on how a student reciprocally interprets and shapes instructional tasks. In information-processing models there are two main divisions of these characteristics: (a) features of the cognitive system that processes information; (b) kinds of knowledge (information) represented in the student's mind, both as products of information processing and as vehicles for processing information.

2.1 The Information-processing System

The mind is a biological and physical system and, hence, its functioning is influenced in part by its physical architecture (Newell 1990). While learning is partly a function of characteristics of human biological systems, those characteristics rarely have a direct, observable impact on learning in a classroom or in self-study situations. Two exceptions are notable, however.

Working memory, the metaphorical mental location where information is processed, has a limited channel capacity or span. This capacity is a joint function of the brain's neurophysiological properties and characteristics of the information being processed. Approximately 5 ± 2 information-processing events, such as maintaining conceptual knowledge in memory or performing a routine based on procedural knowledge, can be carried out simultaneously. The more structured knowledge is—chunked or schematized, in the case of conceptual knowledge; composed and automated, in the case of procedural knowledge—the greater the apparent capacity of working memory. This explains how experts can appear to have huge capacity relative to novices when the fact is that experts use highly structured or automated forms of information in approximately the same "mental volume" in which a novice processes considerably less "dense" information. In general, the interaction of properties of working memory and of information's structure jointly influence information processing during learning from instruction.

The second area where physical properties of the mind clearly influence information processing in instruction arises in cases of learners with a typical neurological conditions (e.g., specific learning disabilities [see *Specific Learning Disability*]).

2.2 Knowledge

Terms for and theories about knowledge are legion (Alexander et al. 1991). Figure 2 revises Alexander et al.'s model by distinguishing two forms for representing knowledge—declarative and procedural; two levels of awareness about knowledge—tacit and explicit; and three kinds of information in knowledge—conceptual, metacognitive, and sociocultural.

Declarative knowledge is descriptive information, or "knowledge that." It remains static until changed by learning. Hosts of terms describe organizations in which declarative knowledge is organized or stored in memory. Some of the more common are analogy, chunk, concept, frame, image, metaphor, proposition, and schema.

Procedural knowledge is rules, often called condition–action rules or if–then rules, because only if particular conditions are satisfied is this knowledge invoked. One type of procedural knowledge classifies situations based on their properties. It is typically referred to as conditional knowledge because it defines when, where, and why declarative knowledge or a rule is relevant. Conditional knowledge plays a central role in students' use of cognitive strategies. A second type of procedural knowledge, referred to simply as a rule, acts on information to transform knowledge, such as translating information into a visual image. Procedural knowledge underlies the processes that students perform, such as organizing materials and the surrounding environment in preparation for studying. The certainty of the output obtained by applying procedural knowledge can vary. Thus algorithms, which yield reliable outcomes, are distinguished from heuristics, which are predictive but do not assure a determinate result. Sets of rules, in which the conditions of some are satisfied by the output of other rules' actions, are called production systems.

Tacit knowledge (Polanyi 1966) is knowledge the learner possesses which influences cognitive processing but of which the learner is not really aware.

It is proposed to exist because, so far, it has not been possible to account fully for information processing and achievements in terms of explicit, reportable forms of knowledge. Iran-Nejad (1990) hypothesized the existence of cognitively local and relatively independent units of procedure-like knowledge that students accumulate through experience. These units are "dynamic," that is, they process information automatically and in parallel with processing that occurs in working memory, but lie "outside" working memory itself. Such dynamic components of knowledge may constitute tacit knowledge and, because of their independence from working memory, explain the apparent impenetrability of tacit knowledge.

Explicit knowledge is knowledge a learner can consciously inspect, including tacit knowledge that converts to explicit form by becoming an "object of thought" (Prawat 1989). Alexander et al. (1991) distinguish two kinds of explicit knowledge, conceptual and metacognitive knowledge, each of which is further divided.

Conceptual knowledge, according to Alexander et al. has two major divisions. The first, content knowledge, is information a student has about his or her physical, social, and mental world. It can be used informally or, especially in the context of schooling, it can be formalized into domains of study such as spelling, science, music, gymnastics, and art. Discourse knowledge, the second main kind of conceptual knowledge, represents information about common forms and functions of language, as well as other symbol systems used to represent and convey conceptual knowledge. In formalized domains of study, discourse knowledge may be unique to the domain and undergird procedures for developing new knowledge in that domain. In science, for instance, a mixture of text structures, mathematical formalisms, and graphic symbol systems are found in academic textbooks. These same discourse structures are used generatively by scientists as tools to extend knowledge of their domain.

As described above, students' extant or prior content knowledge has a powerful influence on information processing and resulting achievements (Perkins and Simmons 1988). Misconceptions may block accurate perceptions of information presented in instruction. Also, students can have difficulty translating and integrating information presented in different discourse systems, such as words and mathematical expressions (Dee Lucas and Larkin 1991), because they lack knowledge about how the two systems correspond. With instruction about what such structures are and how they can be used as schemata for building and monitoring comprehension benefits are observed in recall, problem solving, and transfer (Cook and Mayer 1988, Fuson and Willis 1989).

Metacognitive knowledge is the knowledge that provides the means by which learners actively inquire about knowledge. It is a second-order construct that represents reflections on or knowledge about knowledge, and the procedures by which a student regulates cognition and action. Since metacognition is effortful, conscious cognition, the cells in Fig. 2 where metacognitive and tacit knowledge intersect are shaded to indicate that the model's factors are not fully independent. Alexander et al. (1991) differentiate four interrelated facets of metacognitive knowledge: task knowledge, self-knowledge, strategy knowledge, and goals and plans.

Task knowledge is information a student perceives about the circumstances in which a task is situated and about features of the task itself. It is a composite of the student's prior knowledge about tasks similar to the one now being addressed, plus information provided by the teacher, peers, or directions on assignments. Typical aspects of task knowledge include the number and clarity of criteria by which progress and final products of the task will be evaluated, time allocated for the task, resources that can be acquired to assist with work on the task, whether the student or someone else controls the processes by which the task can develop, and the timing and nature of feedback about performance. These kinds of information create elements of a stable backdrop for performance and, in the case of accessible resources and feedback, new and updated information about how to work on the task and how that work is progressing relative to criteria.

Students may have misconceptions about tasks that interfere with achieving the goals of instruction. For example, Anderson et al. (1991) observed that low-achieving first-grade students often approached seatwork tasks in reading with the understanding that they were to "get the work done" rather than understand information in the task, and develop strategies for accomplishing tasks such as those assigned. In this instance, the students' views of criteria by which the tasks' processes and products would be evaluated were antithetical to developing conceptual knowledge from reading and enhancing procedural knowledge for reading with comprehension.

Self-knowledge consists of a student's idiosyncratic motivational orientations to topics and instructional tasks, plus the student's characteristic beliefs about learning. This knowledge has a fundamental impact on the goals and plans a learner adopts. Winne (1991b) described four constituents of motivational orientation. Incentives are the values—positive, neutral, and negative—that a student perceives to be associated with goals to be accomplished in a specific task. Efficacy judgments are the student's beliefs about skills, abilities, and power to achieve those goals in relation to resources and constraints in the task environment. Outcomes are the results the student predicts will follow from engaging with the task by applying knowledge and skills considered in making the efficacy judgment. Attributions identify reasons, such as a person's ability or the difficulty of a task, that explain why work on the task yields the predicted (or realized) outcomes. All four kinds of motivational knowledge combine in a descriptive profile of the task's utility relative to other approaches to this task or to other tasks.

Strategy knowledge is knowledge about how to process information in tasks to promote comprehension, learning, remembering, and transfer. More specifically, strategy knowledge consists of cognitive procedures that students can use to construct and refine conceptual knowledge, and to develop and elaborate strategy knowledge itself. Four main categories of cognitive strategies, each subclassified at two levels of tasks, basic and complex, can be identified (Weinstein and Mayer 1986). Rehearsal strategies, such as mentally repeating information or copying text, enhance remembering. Elaboration strategies, such as developing mnemonics or assembling new material with prior knowledge using analogies, construct links for encoding knowledge. Organizing strategies—for instance, developing categories or translating and extending newly presented information as spatial maps—promote the assembly of new information into chunks and schemata. Monitoring strategies identify shortcomings in performance and point toward repairs that improve it.

To use strategy knowledge productively, students need to blend several kinds of knowledge. First, they require conceptual knowledge about the subject that is the focus of the task, plus conceptual knowledge about the strategy. The latter includes knowledge of the parts or steps that comprise the strategy (declarative component), knowledge about how to perform those steps (procedural component), and knowledge about which strategies are appropriate given present circumstances surrounding particular tasks (conditional component). Finally, they need metacognitive knowledge about the task, themselves as learners, the implementation of strategies in the context of tasks, and the probable impact of each strategy on performance.

Goals and plans are mental constructions that students, as active inquiring agents, create. Goals are multifaceted representations of states to be achieved that inherently fuse affects (information that represents feelings and emotions) with the various kinds of knowledge previously discussed. Plans are mental structures that range from small, focused, one-step rules to grand and encompassing orchestrations of events. Plans give shape to a student's information processing, constituting how the student addresses instructional tasks. Metaphorically, goals are the "reason qua motive" for engaging in a task, and plans provide instrumental knowledge on which the student calls to realize goals.

Sociocultural knowledge is the accumulated collection of attitudes and beliefs that a student has acquired as a result of experiences in a social and cultural milieu. In relation to instruction, it is about the forms, content, and functions of instruction that have developed from students' previous participation in a variety of instructional tasks. Sociocultural knowledge typically resides at the tacit level; it can, however, be addressed directly, thus becoming explicit. As tacit knowledge, however, sociocultural knowledge can influence information processing without students being aware of it.

A study by Ortony et al. (1985), for example, indicated that Afro-American children who engaged often in a turn-taking verbal riposte called "playing the dozens" are in a stronger position to understand figurative language in literary tasks. More generally, students' differential experiences involving social and cultural conventions influence their abilities to recognize narrators' or speakers' use of literary devices and characters' departures from social conventions that emphasize unusual events (Beach and Hynds 1991). These differences in tacit sociocultural knowledge thus affect what students can glean from tasks and how they judge accomplishments in tasks.

3. Instructional Tasks and Student Cognition

Instructing students is an intentional act in which an instructor strives to improve the cognitive resources that students need to perform tasks. If instruction is effective, students develop more knowledge than they would develop if they were left entirely on their own. That is, the instructor presumes that, by managing students' encounters with curricular information and by guiding them in cognitively processing the subject matter, educational objectives can be achieved more effectively than if they were left to their own devices. Thus, from the point of view of an instructor, instruction consists of (a) deliberately arranging (b) features of the instructional environment (c) to guide (d) the student's modification of aptitudes (e) for performing (f) specified tasks that reflect instructional objectives. From the student's point of view, participating in instruction has three main facets: mediating instruction, learning, and demonstrating achievements.

Corresponding to elements (b) and (c) of instruction, the student perceives features of the instructional environment and decides whether and how to make use of them. The match between students' perceptions and the instructor's guidance is a first step toward instructional effectiveness. For example, an author may mark sections of a text by headings, or a teacher may use transition statements to close segments of a lesson and introduce upcoming content or activity structures. These kinds of information or mediating instruction are features of the environment by which the instructor is attempting to improve what the student might learn from a text.

For the instructor's intentions to be realized, the student must perceive these communications as a particular kind of information, namely, information about what is to be learned and the means for learning it. Moreover, the student must elect to apply particular cognitive processes to that information so that prior knowledge becomes integrated with new subject matter that will be presented in the next moments. In addressing this task, the student determines whether and how to participate in instructional events as the instructor created them.

Corresponding to part (d) of instruction is the student's processing of information—or learning—available in the instructional environment in concert with prior knowledge. To learn from the text or the lesson, the student must construct temporary structures of knowledge in working memory, such as a hypothesis about schemata useful for understanding information that will be presented next in the text or in an upcoming segment of the lesson. Then, as new information comes available, the student must integrate it with prior knowledge to modify and extend it. The dynamic events comprising students' engagements in information processing form the topics of Sect. 5.

Corresponding to parts (e) and (f) of instruction is the student's job of demonstrating learning by attempting to perform tasks that reflect instructional objectives. For example, having read a text or engaged in a lesson's activities, the student might be invited to discuss issues raised, solve problems posed by the teacher, or design an activity that requires applying information recently presented.

4. *Task Characteristics*

Because features of tasks are relatively much easier to manipulate and control than are characteristics of students, thousands of research articles have described thousands of experiments in which task characteristics have been investigated as independent variables. To organize this immense variety, five facets of tasks can be identified: conditions under which the task is performed; operations that carry out the task; products that result from operations; evaluations that feed back information about products; standards by which achievement is gauged (Winne 1991b).

Winne and Marx (1989) suggest that there are three conditions under which classroom tasks are performed. These include the content to be learned (declarative and procedural knowledge), the setting (resources available, social features, time allocation), and the nature of the presentation (the medium, goals, and performance cues). Students confronted with academic tasks develop a tentative model representing their interpretation of these conditions, and these perceptions mediate the students' development of goals, plans, and cognitive processing in response to those conditions.

Task conditions interact with the student's information processing to determine the "cognitive load" of a task. Cognitive load can be thought of as a ratio of the demands placed on the student's information-processing system relative to its capacity. Optimum load is a value less, but not greatly less, than 1. A combination of variables, such as rate of presentation, permanence of information display, and the meaningfulness, amount, and complexity of information, operationally define the cognitive load of a task. As noted in Sect. 2.1, there is a relation between information-processing capacity and the degree of organization or automaticity of a student's prior knowledge.

Another important facet of a task is the location of control of the operations needed to carry out the task. Models of instruction vary from discovery environments, in which the student controls most of the task operations, to strongly didactic environments, in which the instructor controls instructional events. When control is vested with the student, cognitive load increases, because the student must regulate most of the information processing. Under most conditions, when learners are granted control, they often exit tasks before they fully achieve knowledge of the subject.

5. *Dynamics of Learning from Instruction*

This section examines the dynamic interplay among variables and classes of variables in Fig. 1. It is divided into two parts: learning operations and the promotion of self-regulation.

5.1 Learning Operations

Winne (1991a) has described five primitive cognitive operations in which students engage while completing tasks: *s*timulating, *m*onitoring, *a*ssembling, *r*ehearsing, and *t*ranslating. In combination, they form the SMART operations. Stimulating transfers information from long-term memory into working memory, making it "the object of thought". Monitoring matches or compares features of items which are active in working memory. Assembling forms new relations between items of information. Rehearsing maintains information in working memory and can transfer it into long-term memory. Finally, translating recodes information.

Typically, these SMART operations are combined in a learning task to create three main kinds of strategies (Zimmerman 1989). Behavioral strategies lead to choices about overt behavior for pursuing a task. For example, a student might seek feedback by looking up answers after working problems in a text. Environmental strategies are those where the learner modifies conditions of a task to make them more favorable. For instance, a learner might move closer to the teacher to receive more attention. Finally, covert strategies are sequences of cognitions by which a learner guides learning. For example, a learner might mentally summarize a section in a text to improve comprehension.

Although highly automated strategies are tacit, as when an expert engages in tasks that do not challenge expertise, deliberate use of strategies is associated with greater gains in achievement when learners address new material or engage in transfer tasks. Thus, while education aims to help students acquire a large repertoire of automatic–tacit strategies, effective learners also must consciously regulate learning in response to challenging instructional tasks. Such learners are called self-regulated (Paris and Byrnes 1989, Zimmerman 1989) or self-instructive (Wang and Palincsar 1989).

In models of self-regulated learning, students first interpret a task's conditions. Next, perceptions about the values of a task's goals (incentives), judgments of competence and control over learning (efficacy judgments), and beliefs about the roles of effort and ability in learning (attributions) mediate between the student's understanding of task demands and the goals he or she adopts for learning. For example, in the face of low expectation for success, a student may choose task avoidance. In contrast, if a task's goals have high incentive and the student is moderately confident that success can be achieved with effort, setting a goal to understand is probable.

Based on the goals they adopt, self-regulated learners then develop a plan for action, grounded in prior knowledge. A central feature of this plan is obtaining feedback by monitoring intermediate products against goals. Incrementally, the learner modifies knowledge, motivational beliefs, goals, and strategies in response to that feedback. Thus, interaction with the task evolves "strategically" based on dynamic engagements involving the learner, the task and the events that transpire during learning.

Rumelhart and Norman (1978) describe three mechanisms by which new learning is acquired and integrated with prior knowledge in this process. Accretion involves monitoring new information in terms of an existing general schema and encoding the new material as a particular instantiation of that general structure. Tuning is undertaken when new information does not correspond to an existing schema and the student reorganizes elements of prior knowledge to accommodate the new information. For example, a child who has overgeneralized the concept "dog" to include all furry, four-legged animals tunes a schema to differentiate cats from dogs. Finally, restructuring is necessary when no schema adequately encompasses new information or when existing schemata are inadequate for making sense of new knowledge. Here, students construct entirely new knowledge structures by assembling existing knowledge or by inducing a new schema.

Perkins and Simmons (1988) described three classes of misconceptions that parallel Rumelhart and Norman's learning mechanisms. Naive misconceptions are characteristic of insufficient background knowledge. These misconceptions can be remedied by accretion. Ritual misconceptions arise when students have formalized knowledge but can not apply it easily or transfer it. Tuning schemata, for example, by developing analogies, can remedy this problem. Finally, Gordian misconceptions are those where complex formalized knowledge is faulty. Repairing these misconceptions requires the entire conceptual frame to be restructured, producing a personal paradigm shift.

5.2 Promoting Self-regulated Learning

To assist students in developing self-regulated learning, explicit instruction about cognitive strategies should be integrated with subject matter. In this format, subject matter knowledge grows in parallel with declarative and procedural knowledge about strategies, and with conditional knowledge that can guide choices about when to apply particular strategies under specific conditions. To promote transfer and students' independent use of strategies following instruction, metacognitive strategies can be taught that can guide students in planning how to approach tasks and in monitoring progress (Wang and Palincsar 1989). Teaching students positive motivational beliefs, such as refocusing attributions toward effortful use of strategies (Borkowski et al. 1988), is another critical element in promoting self-regulation (Paris and Byrnes 1989).

An assumption underlying students' independent use of strategies is that they consciously and reflectively choose strategies. Salomon and Perkins (1989) highlighted the importance of consciously chosen strategies in their distinction between two kinds transfer. "Low-road transfer" can be promoted by repeated experiences that involve using knowledge in a variety of contexts. It results in automatic transfer across the range of task conditions the student has experienced. "High-road transfer," in contrast, requires the student deliberately to abstract principles about applying strategies. Promoting such reflection in instruction invites the student to decontextualize principles, extending their range of application beyond past experiences. In this analysis, the process of approaching high-road transfer equates to independent use of cognitive strategies.

6. Conclusion

By viewing the student as an active, inquiring agent who constructs knowledge, rather than a mere receiver of information, theories of information processing have come to emphasize the role of a student's prior knowledge and of processes that create achievements through the student's participation in instruction. To realize these theories, researchers have devised and tested systems that characterize prior knowledge and that describe information-handling processes. Modern theories also view instruction as an interaction between features in a teaching environment and each student's prior knowledge, rather than as a unidirectional effect of instruction on students. The student's mediation of instructional events and self-regulation of approaches to learning are recognized as potent factors that influence the development of achievements. An important advance has been a gain in knowledge about ways of guiding students in mediating instruction and in regulating information processes that build knowledge. Continued research in these areas promises gains in theoretical and practical understandings about how instruction can be optimized for effectiveness relative to each student's individual differences.

See also: Teaching: Informational Processing Theories; Cognitive Styles and Learning; Learning Theories: Historical Overview and Trends

References

Alexander P A, Schallert D L, Hare V C 1991 Coming to terms: How researchers in learning and literacy talk about knowledge. *Rev. Educ. Res.* 61(3): 315–43

Anderson G L, Gates A I 1950 The general nature of learning. In: Henry N B (ed.) 1990 *Learning and Instruction*, 49th Yearbook of the National Society for the Study of Education, Pt 1. University of Chicago Press, Chicago, Illinois

Beach R, Hynds S 1991 Research on response to literature. In: Barr R, Kamil M L et al. (eds.) 1991 *Handbook of Reading Research*, Vol. 2. Longman, New York

Borkowski J G, Wehing R S, Carr M 1988 Effects of attributional retraining on strategy-based reading comprehension in learning-disabled students. *J. Educ. Psychol.* 80: 46–53

Bruner J S 1964 Some theorems on instruction illustrated with reference to mathematics. In: Hilgard E R (ed.) 1964 *Theories of Learning and Instruction*, 63rd Yearbook of the National Society for the Study of Education, Pt 1. University of Chicago Press, Chicago, Illinois

Cook L K, Mayer R E 1988 Teaching readers about the structure of scientific text. *J. Educ. Psychol.* 80(4): 448–56

Dee Lucas D, Larkin J H 1991 Equations in scientific proofs: Effects on comprehension. *Am. Educ. Res. J.* 28(3): 661–82

Fuson K C, Willis G B 1989 Second graders' use of schematic drawings in solving addition and subtraction word problems. *J. Educ. Psychol.* 81(4): 514–20

Glaser R 1982 Instructional psychology: Past, present, and future. *Am. Psychol.* 37: 292–305

Iran-Nejad A 1990 Active and dynamic self-regulation of learning processes. *Rev. Educ. Res.* 60(4): 573–602

Newell A 1990 *Unified Theories of Cognition*. Harvard University Press, Cambridge, Massachusetts

Ortony A, Turner T, Larson-Shapiro N 1985 Cultural and instructional influences on figurative language comprehension by inner-city children. *Research in the Teaching of English*. 19(1): 25–36

Paris S G, Byrnes J P 1989 The constructivist approach to self-regulation in classrooms. In: Zimmerman B J, Schunk D H (eds.) 1989 *Self-regulated Learning and Academic Achievement*. Springer-Verlag, Berlin

Perkins D N, Simmons, R 1988 Patterns of misunderstanding: An integrative model for science, math, and programming. *Rev. Educ. Res.* 58: 303–26

Polanyi M 1966 *The Tacit Dimension*. Anchor Press, Garden City, New York

Prawat R S 1989 Promoting access to knowledge, strategy, and disposition in students: A research synthesis. *Rev. Educ. Res.* 59: 1–41

Rumelhart D E, Norman D A 1978 Accretion, tuning, and restructuring: Three modes of learning. In: Cotton J W, Klatzky R (eds.) 1978 *Semantic Factors in Cognition*. Erlbaum, Hillsdale, New Jersey

Salomon G, Perkins D N 1989 Rocky roads to transfer: Rethinking mechanisms of a neglected phenomenon. *Educ. Psychol.* 24: 11–142

Wang M C, Palincsar A S 1989 Teaching students to assume an active role in their learning. In: Reynolds M C (ed.) 1989 *Knowledge Base for the Beginning Teacher*. Pergamon Press, Oxford

Weinstein C E, Mayer R E 1986 The teaching of learning strategies. In: Wittrock M C (ed.) 1986 *Handbook of Research on Teaching*, 3rd edn. Macmillan Inc., New York

Winne P H 1985 Cognitive processing in the classroom. In: Husén T, Postlethwaite T N (eds.) 1985 *The International Encyclopedia of Education*, 1st edn. Pergamon Press, Oxford

Winne P H 1991a Instructional psychology and a model of teaching. In: Short R H, Stewin L L, McCann S J (eds.) 1991 *Educational Psychology: Canadian Perspectives*. Copp Clark Pittman, Toronto

Winne P H 1991b Motivation and teaching. In: Waxman H, Walberg H A (eds.) 1991 *Effective Teaching: Current Research*. McCutchan, Berkeley, California

Winne P H, Marx R W 1989 A cognitive–processing analysis of motivation within classroom tasks. In: Ames C, Ames R (eds.) 1989 *Research on Motivation in Education: Goals and Cognitions*. Academic Press, San Diego, California

Wittrock, M C 1986 Students' thought processes. In: Wittrock M C (ed.) 1986 *Handbook of Research on Teaching*, 3rd edn. Macmillan Inc., New York

Zimmerman B J 1989 A social cognitive view of self-regulated academic learning. *J. Educ. Psychol.* 81: 329–39

P. H. Winne; D. L. Butler

Student Diversity and Classroom Teaching

Advances in theory and research, particularly since the 1970s, have generated substantial conceptual changes in the understanding of the process of learning and increased recognition that certain student characteristics can be altered through schooling. Among the most important of these characteristics are family characteristics, such as parental expectation and family involvement (Comer 1986); cognition (or the processes of learning; de Bono 1976, Feuerstein 1980); intelligence (or the ability to learn; Husén and Tuijnman 1991); and student motivation (or the willingness to learn; Zimmerman 1986). The recognition of the alterability of these characteristics has led researchers to study ways of modifying the psychological processes and cognitive operations used by the individual learner, as well as modifying learning environments and instructional strategies to accommodate learner differences (Wang 1992). Findings from research, along with the practical wisdom culled from implementing innovative school programs, have significantly contributed to the current understanding of what constitutes effective practice and how the learning of diverse students can be enhanced in the same classroom.

Although research has identified numerous variables that are related to differences in student learning and achievement, the sheer number of these variables has posed a perplexing challenge to researchers, policymakers, and practitioners. To begin to address this challenge, these variables can be divided into two groups; those internal to students (e.g., ability and motivation) and those external to students (e.g., quality of instruction and task demands).

1. Models of School Learning

Carroll (1963) introduced educational researchers to the concept of a model of school learning. In his model, he put forth six constructs. Three of these constructs pertained to student differences (aptitude, ability to understand instruction, and perseverance), while the remaining three constructs applied to the classroom environment (clarity of instruction, task appropriateness, and opportunity to learn). These constructs became a point of departure for other models of school learning that were developed during the late 1960s and 1970s (Bennett 1978, Bloom 1976, Bruner 1966, Glaser 1976). Bloom's model specifically differentiated between two types of student characteristics: cognitive entry behaviors and affective entry characteristics.

In retrospect, all of these models recognized both types of entry characteristics. With respect to cognitive entry characteristics, for example, they included constructs such as aptitude, prior knowledge, and home background. With respect to affective entry characteristics, they included perseverance, self-concept, and attitudes toward school and specific subject matters. This acknowledgement of differences among students stood in contrast to more narrow psychological studies of influences on learning, which generally treated individual differences as a source of error, and focused instead on instructional treatment variables.

In addition to student variables, each of these models of school learning gave salience to constructs related to the classroom environment. These constructs varied in generality, some being as broad as "instructional events" or "clarity of instruction," and others as narrow as "use of cues" or "feedback and correctives." Although later models brought some refinement in the ways in which individual difference variables and instructional treatment variables were defined and the ways in which they were related to one another, the primary contributions of more recent models have been in extending the range of influences considered.

The evolution of models of school learning was further advanced with the introduction of models of adaptive instruction (Corno and Snow 1986, Glaser 1976, Wang 1992). School-based implementation of models of adaptive instruction was designed to help schools create classroom environments that maximized each student's opportunities for success in school. Particular attention was paid to new variables associated with instructional delivery systems, program design, and implementation. In particular, attention was given to those features that Glaser (1982) referred to as the "large practical variables," which included efficient allocation and use of teacher and student time, a practical classroom management system, systematic teacher feedback and reinforcement of student learning behavior and progress, instructional interactions based on the diagnosed learning needs of individual students, and flexible administrative and organizational patterns responsive to program implementation and staffing needs.

Another contribution to models of school learning came from researchers concerned with the identification and characterization of effective schools. Edmonds (1979) is most strongly associated with this identification of variables for exceptionally effective schools, especially for the urban poor. Significant contributions to effective school models were also made by Brookover (1979), Brookover and Lezotte (1979), and Rutter et al. (1979). Illustrations of the types of variables characterizing effective schools include degree of curriculum articulation and organization, school-wide staff development, parental involvement and support, school-wide recognition of academic success, maximized learning time, district support, clear goals and high expectations, orderly and disciplined school environment, and principal leadership characterized by attention to quality of instruction (Purkey and Smith 1983).

These various models of school learning have contributed greatly to the understanding of the relative contributions of different influences on student achievement and practical strategies for maximizing educational outcomes across a range of educational conditions and settings. The following section provides a synthesis of the research bases that undergird the design of these models of school learning. Although individual researchers and practitioners may focus their work on particular variables or constructs, the discussion in this section is intended to provide a synoptic view of the entire canopy of influences of learning.

2. The Knowledge Base of School Learning

Focusing on identifying variables related to processes of learning and student achievement, Wang et al. (1990) completed a knowledge base review. The data sources for this review were the consensus ratings from 61 educational research experts, results from 91 quantitative research syntheses, and findings in 179 handbook chapters and narrative reviews published since 1975. Thus, findings from this "meta-review" constitute a distillation of understandings and results from large numbers of primary research studies, quantitative research syntheses, and narrative reviews. They indicate a substantial agreement on the categories of variables that exert influence on student learning, as well as those that had little influence. Table 1 provides a summary list of factors that influence student learning and selected examples of each factor. The factors are placed into one of six major categories and 30 subcategories.

Of the six major categories (see Table 1), the highest ratings overall were assigned to "Program design variables," followed by "Out-of-school contextual variables." The category reflecting the quality of instruction, "Implementation, classroom instruction, and climate variables," ranked third in importance, closely followed by "Student variables." The last two categories, "School-level variables" and "State and district variables," received markedly lower ratings overall.

In the following section, the categories that received exceptionally high ratings are highlighted. The categories representing instruction as designed and instruction as delivered are discussed first. These are followed by out-of-school context and student characteristics.

2.1 Program Design Variables

This category includes instruction as designed and the physical arrangements for its delivery. Variables included in the program design category (Category 5 in Table 1) are organized into three subcategories. The first subcategory, "Demographic and marker variables," was rated the highest of the three. Furthermore, within this subcategory, the most highly rated variables are "size of instructional group (whole class, small group, or one-on-one instruction)," "number of classroom aides," and "resources needed." Thus, the most important aspect of program design appears to be the intensity of educational services provided to each learner. More aides, smaller groups, or increased material resources are associated with significantly higher learning outcomes.

Ratings on the "Curriculum and instruction variables" suggest that the key to effective instructional design is the flexible and appropriate use of a variety of instructional strategies while maintaining an orderly classroom environment. The highest overall rating in this subcategory was for "use of classroom management techniques to control classroom disruptiveness." This variable was followed by "use of prescriptive instruction combined with aspects of informal or open education" and "presence of information in the curriculum on individual differences and commonalities," both of which explicitly relate to student diversity and individualization. Other highly rated variables referred to specific instructional strategies, including "use of mastery-learning techniques," "instructional cues, engagement, and corrective feedback," "use of cooperative learning strategies," and "use of diagnostic–prescriptive methods."

High ratings in the "Curriculum design variables" were given to the variables of "materials employ alternative modes of representation" and "degree of structure in curriculum accommodates needs of different learners," both of which reinforce the importance of offering a variety of instructional materials and approaches to accommodate individual differences. The importance of the organization of curriculum content is revealed by the two highest rated items in this subcategory: "materials employ learning hierarchies" and "material is presented in a cognitively efficient manner."

2.2 Implementation, Classroom Instruction, and Climate Variables

This category includes support of the curriculum and the instructional program; classroom routines; specific instructional, assessment, and classroom-management practices; quantity of instruction; academic and nonacademic student–teacher interaction; and classroom climate. It is by far the largest of the six major categories.

High ratings in the areas of implementation, classroom instruction, and climate point to the importance of maintaining an orderly classroom environment and providing clear, well-organized instruction appropriate to the needs of individual learners. In the overall ranking of all 30 subcategories, classroom management ranked second. Its most critical items were "group alerting (teacher uses questioning/recitation strategies that maintain active participation by all students)" and "learner accountability (teacher maintains student awareness of learning goals and expectations)." Smooth transitions from one instructional activity to another, minimal disruptions, and teacher awareness of what is going on in the classroom at all times also received relatively high ratings.

Quantity of instruction was also highly rated. This subcategory includes time spent in direct instruction, especially direct instruction on basic skills; time spent on homework; and length of the school day and school year. The importance accorded to quantity of instruction is not surprising since it has appeared in

Table 1
Variable categories of influences on learning with illustrative examples

Category/subcategory[a]	Illustrative variable
Category 1: State and district variables are associated with state- and district-level school governance and administration, including state curriculum and textbook policies, testing and graduation requirements, teacher licensure, specific provisions in teacher contracts, and some district-level administrative and fiscal variables.	
District-Level demographics and marker variables	School district size
State-level policy variables	Teacher licensure requirements
Category 2: Out-of-school contextual variables are associated with the home and community contexts within which schools function. They include community demographics, peer culture, parental support and involvement, and the amount of time students spend out of school on activities such as television viewing, leisure reading, and homework.	
Community variables	Socioeconomic level of community
Peer group variables	Level of peers' academic aspirations
Home environment and parental support variables	Parental involvement in ensuring completion of homework
Student use of out-of-school time variables	Student participation in clubs and extracurricular school activities
Category 3: School-level variables are associated with school-level demographics, culture, climate, policies, and practices. They include demographics of the student body, whether the school is public or private, and levels of funding for specific categorical programs; school-level decision-making variables; and specific school-level policies and practices, including policies on parental involvement in the school.	
Demographic and marker variables	Size of school
Teacher-administrator decision-making variables	Principal actively concerned with instructional program
School culture variables (ethos conducive to teaching and learning)	School-wide emphasis on and recognition of academic achievement
School-wide policy and organization variables	Explicit school-wide discipline policy
Accessibility variables	Accessibility of educational program (overcoming architectural, communication, and environmental barriers)
Parental involvement variables	Parental involvement in improvement and operation of instructional programs
Category 4: Student variables are those associated with students, including demographics; academic history; and a variety of social, behavioral, motivational, cognitive, and affective characteristics.	
Demographic and marker variables	Gender
Placement history variables	Prior grade retentions
Social and behavioral variables	Positive, nondisruptive behavior
Motivational and affective variables	Attitude toward subject matter instructed
Cognition variables	Level of specific academic knowledge in subject area instructed
Metacognition variables	Comprehension monitoring (plan, monitor effectiveness of attempted actions, monitor outcomes of actions)
Psychomotor variables	Psychomotor skills specific to area instructed
Category 5: Program design variables are associated with instruction as designed, and with the physical arrangements for its delivery. They include the instructional strategies specified by the curriculum and characteristics of instructional materials.	
Demographic and marker variables	Size of instructional group (whole class, small group, one-on-one instruction)
Curriculum and instruction variables	Alignment among goals, contents, instruction, assignments, and evaluation
Curriculum design variables	Materials employ advance organizers
Category 6: Implementation, classroom instruction, and climate variables are associated with the implementation of the curriculum and the instructional program, including classroom routines and practices, characteristics of instruction as delivered, classroom management, monitoring of student progress, quality and quantity of instruction provided, student–teacher interactions, and classroom climate.	
Classroom support variables	Establishing efficient classroom routines and communicating rules and procedures
Classroom instruction variables	Use of clear and organized direct instruction
Quantity of instruction variables	Time on task (amount of time students are actively engaged in learning)
Classroom assessment variables	Use of assessment as a frequent, integral component of instruction
Classroom management variables	Group alerting (teacher uses questioning/recitation strategies that maintain active participation by all students)
Student and teacher interactions: social variables	Student responds positively to questions from other students and from teacher
Student and teacher interactions: academic variables	Frequent calls for extended, substantive oral and written responses (not one-word answers)
Classroom climate variables	Cohesiveness (members of class are friends who share common interests and values and emphasize cooperative goals)

a Subcategories are listed below the description of each major category and are each illustrated with representative variables. For example, the first major category includes two subcategories, "District-level demographics and marker variables" and "State-level policy variables" many of the most widely cited models of school learning.

Student and teacher interactions were ranked highly, as were classroom climate variables. Taken together, the highly rated items in these two subcategories characterize a classroom in which teachers interact with students frequently for instructional purposes, and where students work with classmates, share common interests and values, and pursue cooperative goals. Students are actively engaged in learning and are involved in some classroom decisions. At the same time, the class is well-organized and well-planned, with a clear academic focus. Objectives of learning activities are specific and explicit, with the pacing of instruction appropriate for the majority.

High ratings were also given to the quality of the instruction provided to students, namely, the use of advanced organizers, the direction of students' attention to the content to be learned, the provision of clear and organized direct instruction, the systematic sequencing of lesson events, and the use of clear lesson transitions. Other highly rated variables included corrective feedback in case of student error, frequent academic questions, and accurate measurement of skills. Finally, the literature strongly supports the teaching of skills in the context of meaningful application, use of good examples and analogies, and teaching for meaningful understanding, together with explicit promotion of student self-monitoring of comprehension and gradual transfer of responsibility for learning from the teacher to the student.

2.3 Out-of-school Contextual Variables

This category includes variables associated with the home and community contexts within which schools function. Variables receiving high ratings under this category include peers' educational and occupational aspirations, parental involvement in ensuring completion of homework, parental participation in school conferences and related activities, and parental interest in students' schoolwork. The educational environment of the home (e.g., number of books and magazines) was also cited in numerous reference sources and received consistently high ratings. Student participation in clubs and extracurricular school activities and time spent on leisure reading were also moderately related to learning outcomes.

2.4 Student Variables

"Metacognition variables" was among the subcategories that received highest mean ratings. Highly rated variables in this subcategory include "comprehension monitoring (planning; monitoring effectiveness of attempted actions; testing, revising, and evaluating learning strategies)," "self-regulatory, self-control strategies (e.g., control of attention)," and "positive strategies to facilitate generalization of concepts." Other highly rated student variables include positive behavior and ability to make friends with peers, motivation for continual learning, and perseverance on learning tasks. These variables fall under the rubric of affective entry characteristics. Highly rated variables related to cognitive entry characteristics included general mental abilities, levels of basic skills sufficient to profit from instruction, and prior knowledge in the subject area instructed.

3. Implications for Improving Practice

Classroom teachers must respond to a multitude of influences interacting in kaleidoscopic patterns (Lockheed and Hanushek 1988, Purves 1989, Stevenson and Stigler 1992). While a large number of variables are moderately related to learning outcomes, few, if any, single variables are very strongly related to learning. Authors of original research studies and of reviews and syntheses are appropriately cautious in stating the importance of particular variables. Nonetheless, taken together, the extant research base suggests some powerful interactive effects on school learning.

Two sets of implications are particularly noteworthy. First, in contrast to the prevailing conception of the important influence of distal variables (notably, policy, demographic, and organizational), the extant research base suggests that these distal variables are relatively unimportant. One explanation of the limited impact of policy and organizational variables is that they are at least one step removed from the daily learning experiences of teachers and students. Simply implementing any one policy, such as the "extended school day," does not guarantee that students in a given classroom will receive instruction from a teacher who plans lessons with special attention to eliminating poor management practices and inefficient use of class time. Effective school policies require effective implementation by teachers at the classroom and student levels.

A second significant finding of the accumulated knowledge base on school learning is the consistent evidence of the impact of the home environment, classroom management, and metacognitive processes on student learning. There is an increasing research base that prescribes metacognitive processes and functions, such as comprehension monitoring, strategies to facilitate generalization of concepts, and self-regulatory and self-control strategies, and effective interventions, to teach metacognitive skills. Similarly, teachers must use a variety of instructional techniques, activities, and behaviors in their efforts to control classrooms and enhance learning. Examples include group alerting, learner accountability, smooth transitions, and teacher "with-it-ness." Finally, studies supporting the importance of the home environment have identified characteristics and behaviors of parents and extended family members that support student achievement. Parent behaviors such as attendance at school functions, interest in children's schoolwork, monitoring television viewing, engaging in conversations with children, and ensuring completion of homework and regular school attendance have positive effects on student achievement.

See also: Individualized Instruction; Individual Differences and Instruction; Models of Learning

References

Bennett S N 1978 Recent research on teaching: A dream, a belief and a model. *Br. J. Educ. Psychol.* 48: 127–47

Bloom B S 1976 *Human Characteristics and School Learning*. McGraw-Hill, New York

Brookover W B (ed.) 1979 *School Social Systems and Student Achievement: Schools Can Make a Difference*. Praeger, New York

Brookover W B, Lezotte L W 1979 *Changes in School Characteristics Coincident with Changes in Student Achievement*. Michigan State University, Institute for Research on Teaching, East Lansing, Michigan

Bruner J S 1966 *Toward a Theory of Instruction*. Norton, New York

Carroll J B 1963 A model of school learning. *Teach. Coll. Rec.* 64: 723–33

Comer J P 1986 Parent participation in the schools. *Phi Del. Kap.* 67: 442–44

Corno L, Snow R E 1986 Adapting teaching to individual differences among learners. In: Wittrock M C (ed.) 1986 *Handbook of Research on Teaching*, 3rd edn. Macmillan Inc., New York

de Bono E 1976 *Teaching Thinking*. Temple Smith, London

Edmonds R 1979 Effective schools for the urban poor. *Educ. Leadership* 37(1): 15–27

Feuerstein R 1980 *Instrumental Enrichment: An Intervention Program for Cognitive Modifiability*. College Park Press, Baltimore, Maryland

Glaser R 1976 Components of a psychological theory of instruction: Toward a science of design. *Rev. Educ. Res.* 46: 1–24

Glaser R 1982 Instructional psychology: Past, present, and future. *Am. Psychol.* 37: 292–305

Husén T, Tuijnman A 1991 The contribution of formal schooling to the increase in intellectual capital. *Educ. Researcher* 20(7): 10–25

Lockheed M E, Hanushek E 1988 Improving educational efficiency in developing countries: What do we know? *Compare* 18(1): 21–38

Purkey S C, Smith M S 1983 Effective schools: A review. *Elementary Sch. J.* 83: 427–52

Purves A C (ed.) 1989 *International Comparisons and Educational Reform*. Association for Supervision and Curriculum Development, Cucamonga, California

Rutter M, Maughan B, Mortimore P, Ouston J, Smith A 1979 *Fifteen Thousand Hours: Secondary Schools and their Effects on Children*. Harvard University Press, Cambridge, Massachusetts

Stevenson H W, Stigler J W 1992 *The Learning Gap*. Summit Books, New York

Wang M C 1992 *Adaptive Education Strategies: Building on Diversity*. Brookes Publishing, Baltimore, Maryland

Wang M C, Haertel G D, Walberg H J 1990 What influences learning? A content analysis of review literature. *J. Educ. Res.* 84(1): 30–43

Zimmerman B J (ed.) 1986 Discussions of role subprocesses in student self-regulated learning [Special issue]. *Contemp. Educ. Psychol.* 11(4)

M. C. Wang

Student Fees

Student fees are payments of money which are made to cover all or part of the costs of tuition in schools, colleges, universities, or other educational institutions. Fees may be paid by students themselves, or by their parents, families, or some other agency such as an employer or a central, state, or local government. In all cases the payment is made in return for tuition received by the student. However, not all educational establishments charge fees and the question of whether institutions should charge fees and what their level should be has been the subject of considerable debate in many countries.

One of the points at issue is the role of public and private institutions. In many countries public and private schools or colleges exist side by side, but the question of ownership does not necessarily determine the way in which the institutions are financed. In some countries publicly owned colleges or universities do charge fees, whereas in other cases a school or college is privately owned and administered—by a religious or charitable body, for instance—but nevertheless receives funds from central or local government and therefore does not charge fees. Elsewhere however, the debate about the level of fees is primarily concerned with the question of whether educational institutions should be under public or private ownership.

In other cases, where both public and private institutions exist, there is debate about whether publicly owned schools or colleges should charge fees. In many European countries, universities, colleges of higher education, and technical and vocational schools are owned and controlled by the government, and financed entirely out of public funds by means of institutional grants. In other countries, such as the United Kingdom, higher education institutions do charge fees, even when they are publicly owned and administered, but central or local government provide financial assistance to students to enable them to pay the fees, and in some cases the fees are paid entirely out of public funds. In the United States there has been some controversy about whether government funds should be given to public institutions to enable them to abolish or reduce fees, or whether governments should simply provide financial assistance for students to enable them to pay fees. In fact, the majority of public institutions in the United States do charge fees, but are subsidized by state governments.

The third area of disagreement concerns the question of fee differentials. Differential fees can be charged which reflect cost differences. For example, fees may be higher for graduate than for undergraduate courses, or different fees may be charged for different subjects: thus, fees for engineering may be higher than for economics on the grounds of cost differences. In some countries differential fees do not reflect cost differences but differences between students' place of residence. As a result, in many parts of the United States a student attending a public university will pay higher fees if he or she lives outside the state where the university is situated. The reason for this is that the university is partly financed by the state government, and it is argued that state government subsidies should be used primarily to benefit the residents of that state, since the funds are derived from taxing local residents. In the United Kingdom, students whose normal place of residence is outside the United Kingdom or the European Community pay higher fees than "home students," and in Australia and Canada foreign students pay higher fees than home students. All these differential fee policies have aroused controversy.

The question of whether students pay fees, and how those fees should be determined, therefore raises a number of issues concerning the finance of education and its control. Also relevant is the question of how governments provide financial assistance for students. There has been considerable debate in some countries about whether student aid should be given in the form of grants or subsidized loans, and whether governments should provide students or their parents with vouchers which can be used to pay tuition fees.

1. *Student Fees in Private Institutions*

Although in some countries the majority of educational institutions are publicly owned and administered, there are many private institutions where student fees represent the predominant or, in some cases, the only source of finance. In many countries private schools and colleges play a significant role in the provision of higher education and postsecondary vocational education and training. Some of these institutions are run by charitable organizations, but others are profit-making establishments, charging fees which are intended to cover all costs and provide a profit for the owners.

There exist a number of studies of private higher education in Asia, particularly in Japan (James and Benjamin 1988) and the Philippines (James 1991), also in Latin America (Levy 1986) and several international comparisons of the role of private institutions (Geiger 1986; James 1987, 1989; James et al. 1988). Many of these studies provide information and data on fees in private institutions. Attempts to assess the significance of private vocational schools and colleges in the United States and the United Kingdom have reavealed a great variety in the size and quality of institutions, and a similar diversity in the level of fees charged.

Economists have suggested that private institutions are likely to be more efficient than publicly owned schools or colleges, because they are wholly dependent on student fees for their income, and will therefore be more responsive to the needs of students, or employers, as well as attempting to maximize efficiency. Comparisons between public and private schools in the United States (e.g., Coleman et al. 1982, Coleman and Hoffer 1987) have generated considerable controversy. Since the late 1980s, there have been several comparative studies of public and private schools in developing countries (Psacharopoulos 1987, Jimenez et al. 1988, 1991) which concluded that private schools "are relatively more cost-effective (that is, efficient) than public schools" (Jimenez et al. 1988 p. 162), although critics argue that differences in pupil achievement are the result of selection bias and other social factors rather than greater efficiency. This issue remains controversial and it is impossible to demonstrate any general relationship between the charging of fees in private schools and efficiency. More extended treatment of this topic will be found in the section on the public–private division of education.

2. *Student Fees in Public Institutions*

In many countries all education in publicly owned institutions is provided free, including both compulsory and higher education. In some cases both current and capital expenditure is financed by means of direct grants from central or local government and no fees are charged.

Throughout Scandanavia, for example, and in many European countries, schools, colleges, and universities which are publicly owned do not charge any tuition fees. However, there are a number of countries where colleges and universities do charge fees, despite the fact that they are public institutions.

In Canada, Spain, and Japan, for example, tuition fees provide between 15 and 20 percent of the income of public universities (Williams and Fulth 1990), and Australia introduced a new Higher Education Contribution Scheme (HECS) in 1989, under which students must pay a charge of about 20 percent of average university costs, either as an "up-front fee" or by means of a deffered payment, collected through the tax system. There has been extensive debate in Australia, as in other countries, about the effects of the introduction of tuition fees on equality of opportunity and access. Tuition fees were abolished in Australia in 1974, but the Wran Committee, which recommended the introduction of HECS, quoted research which showed that "the abolition of fees had a marginal effect at best, on the accessibility of higher education for socially and economically disadvantaged groups. At worst, it provided a further benefit to the economically advantaged" (Wran Committee 1988 p. 5). The imposition of charges for tuition therefore represented, in the view of the Wran Committee, an improvement rather than a reduction in equity: "The advantaged who use and benefit directly from higher education ought to contribute more directly to the cost of the system" (p. xi).

In the United States there are wide differences between the states in the proportion of income derived from tuition fees in public universities and colleges, but on average tuition fees represent about 25 percent of average instructional costs and in many states this proportion increased in the 1970s and 1980s. The question of the role of student fees in public institutions of higher education is still very controversial in the United States. One commentator sums it up as follows:

> Two opposing doctrines have vied for acceptance: one holds that higher education is like elementary and secondary schooling, a public good whose benefits accrue to the entire nation and whose costs should therefore be written into the Social Contract and financed by the public sector through taxation; the other asserts that because higher education enhances the lives of those receiving it, they should pay for it themselves. The crazy-quilt pattern of financing higher education today reflects the inability to agree on either doctrine and the resultant compromises that have been made. Postsecondary schooling, it appears, is regarded as both a public good and a private investment and is paid for accordingly. (Finn 1978 p. 46)

In many countries the same two principles are debated among economists. On the one hand, it is argued that higher education provides benefits for the whole of society and so should be financed out of general taxation. On the other hand, since individuals gain both financial and noneconomic benefits from their education, it is argued that they should contribute to its cost by paying fees. Governments can still provide subsidies in the form of grants or loans to help students who could not afford to pay the fees without financial assistance. The argument is not about whether government subsidies should be provided for education, but whether it is better to subsidize institutions or individuals.

In the United Kingdom, for example, the Robbins Committee (1963) argued for an increase in tuition fees on the grounds that it was a source of strength that public finance should come from more than one channel, and that it was better to subsidize students than institutions. The arguments put forward for individual rather than institutional subsidies include the fact that institutions will be more efficient if they have to compete directly for students, and it is suggested that they will be more responsive to the needs of students, or their future employers, if they are dependent on student fees for their income. It is also suggested that if institutions charge fees, and governments provide financial aid to students, this will encourage institutional autonomy and diversity.

The British government introduced a new policy in 1990, which involved substantial increases in tuition fees in higher education, even though the majority of British students still have their fees paid in full from public funds. The rationale for this change is that it will give universities and other higher education institutions a greater incentive to recruit additional students and thus reduce unit costs, that it will increase the responsiveness of institutions to student demand, and will diversify sources of institutional income and reduce dependence on a single central government grant (Department of Education and Science 1989).

Tuition fee policy in Canada has been reviewed by Stager (1989), who not only provides a historical summary of the development of tuition fees, particularly in the province of Ontario, but also a detailed analysis of alternative approaches to setting tuition fees, together with a summary of research on fees and student financial aid policy in Canada and other countries.

In some developing countries tuition fees are charged at primary, secondary, and higher levels, but many governments have tried to maintain a policy of free education, despite serious financial constraints. The provision of free education is usually justified on grounds of equity, but several economists have argued that tuition fees, combined with student aid, are in fact more equitable and more efficient than universal subsidies that often favor the children of rich parents at the expense of poor taxpayers. This view has been strongly emphasized by Psacharopoulos et al. (1986), and Bray (1988) provides a useful summary of economic, philosophical, and operational issues concerning tuition fees in developing countries.

3. Differences between Public and Private Institutions

In countries such as Japan and the United States, where both public and private institutions exist side by side, there are often very considerable differences between fees in public and private colleges or universities.

Many private institutions have expressed concern about the growing differential between public and private fees which is known as the "tuition gap" in the United States. A number of proposals have been made in the United States for increased federal or state government subsidies to private institutions to overcome this problem.

There has been some research on the likely effects of different proposals (Breneman and Finn 1978) but there is still major political disagreement about the desirability of providing public subsidies to reduce differentials between public and private institutions.

4. Fee Differentials between Students

Not only are there considerable differentials between public and private institutions in several countries, but there is an increasing trend in some countries to differentiate between students in the level of fees charged in the same institution. There are two possible ways of introducing such differentials. If tuition fees represent the main source of income for colleges or universities, then it can be argued that fees should reflect differences in the costs of courses. For example, where the costs of graduate courses of study exceed the costs of undergraduate courses, then institutions may charge fees which reflect these cost differences. The problem is that it is difficult to obtain accurate cost data for different levels of education or for different subjects, even though it is well-established that some courses—for example, science, engineering, and medicine—have higher costs than others such as arts or social studies. Another problem is that the average costs of higher education may be higher or lower than the marginal costs of educating one additional student or an incremental group of students. If tuition fees are supposed to reflect cost differences, then strictly speaking they should be based on marginal, rather than average costs. Yet very little information is available on the marginal costs of different courses of study.

In the United Kingdom the government introduced a policy of "full-cost fees" for overseas students in 1980. Tuition fees for home students and those from the European Community are still subsidized, but all other overseas students pay fees which are intended to cover the full costs of their courses. In 1990 these ranged from £4,560 (US$6,980) for arts and social studies, £6,050 (US$9,260) for science and engineering, to £11,150 (US$17,060) for medicine.

This policy of full-cost fees for overseas students has attracted great controversy in the United Kingdom and in other countries. There has been extensive research on the effects of the introduction of full-cost fees for overseas students in the United Kingdom (Williams 1981; Williams 1982; Overseas Students Trust 1987; Williams et al. 1986). Fee differentials for overseas students have also been introduced in Australia and Canada, and Throsby (1986) has analyzed the economic implications of fee differentials in Australia.

The question of whether there should or should not be a fee differential for overseas students is not one which can be answered by research. It is a political question which raises a number of difficult issues concerning equity and the proper role of educational subsidies. Many people would prefer to see the same fees charged to all students, regardless of origin. Others argue that it is right that public subsidies should be provided mainly for the country's taxpayers, or children of taxpayers, but that selective aid can be provided for particular groups of students on the basis of agreed criteria. In the United States the policy in many states of charging higher fees for students whose normal residence is not in the state where they are studying raises many similar issues.

The question of fee differentials therefore brings to light a number of issues concerning who benefits from education and who should bear the cost. Countries differ in the policies which determine how these costs are shared between individuals and the public purse, and between taxpayers and citizens from other states or countries.

5. Student Aid

Countries also differ in their policies on financial aid for students, to enable them to pay tuition fees and other charges. Since the mid-1980s there have been significant changes in the type and level of financial aid for students in many countries and several comparative studies have analyzed student aid policy in detail (Johnstone 1986, Woodhall 1989).

Even where no tuition fees are charged, as in many European countries, there is still a need for student aid in order to help students pay their living expenses. Where students must pay tuition fees, however, the question of what is the most efficient and equitable method of providing financial aid for students takes on an even greater importance (see *Student Loans*).

See also: Benefits of Education; Cost–Benefit Analysis; Cost Analysis in Education; Public versus Private Schools: Research Controversies

References

Bray M 1988 School fees: Philosophical and operational issues. In Bray M, Lillis K (eds.) 1988 *Community Financing of Education: Issues and Policy Implications in Less Developed Countries*. Pergamon Press, Oxford

Breneman D W, Finn C E Jr (eds.) 1978 *Public Policy and Private Higher Education*. Brookings Institution, Washington, DC

Coleman J, Hoffer T, Kilgore S 1982 *High School Achievement: Public, Catholic and Private Schools Compared*. Basic Books, New York

Coleman J, Hoffer T 1987 *Public and Private High Schools: The Impact of Communities*. Basic Books, New York

Department of Education and Science (DES) 1989 *Shifting the Balance of Public Funding of Higher Education to Fees: A Consultation Paper*. DES, London

Finn C E Jr 1978 *Scholars, Dollars and Bureaucrats*. Brookings Institution, Washington, DC

Geiger R 1986 *Private Sectors in Higher Education: Structure, Function and Change in Eight Countries*. University of Michigan Press, Ann Albor, Michigan

James E 1987 The public/private division of responsibility for education: An international comparison. *Econ. Educ. Rev.* 6(1):1–14

James E 1989 *The Non-profit Sector in International Per-*

spective: Studies in Comparative Culture and Policy. Yale Studies on Non-profit Organizations, Oxford University Press, New York
James E 1991 Private higher education: The Philippines as a Prototype. *Higher Educ.* 21 (2): 189–206
James E, Benjamin G 1988 *Public Policy and Private Education in Japan*. Macmillan, Basingstoke
James T, Levin H, Haenel E (eds.) 1988 *Comparing Public and Private Schools*. Falmer Press, London
Jimenez E, Lockheed M, Wattanawaha N 1988 The relative efficiency of private and public schools: The case of Thailand. *World Bank Econ. Rev.* 2 (2): 139–64
Jimenez E, Lockheed M, Paqueo V 1991 The relative efficiency of private and public schools in developing countries. *World Bank Res. Obs.* 6 (2):205–18
Johnstone D B 1986 *Sharing the Costs of Higher Education: Student Financial Assistance in the United Kingdom, the Federal Republic of Germany, France, Sweden, and the United States*. College Entrance Examination Board, New York
Levy D 1986 *Higher Education and the State in Latin America: Private Challenges to Public Dominance*. University of Chicago Press, Chicago, Illinois
Overseas Students Trust (OST) 1987 *The Next Steps: Overseas Student Policy into the 1990s*. OST, London
Psacharopoulos G 1987 Public versus private schools in developing countries: Evidence from Colombia and Tanzania. *Int. J. Educ. Dev.* 7 (1): 59–67
Psacharopoulos G, Tan J-P, Jimenez E 1986 *Financing Education in Developing Countries: An Exploration of Policy Options*. World Bank, Washington, DC
Robbins Committee 1963 *Higher Education. Report of the Committee under the Chairmanship of Lord Robbins 1961–63*. HMSO, London
Stager D 1989 *Focus on Fees: Alternative Policies for University Tuition Fees*. Council of Ontario Universities, Toronto
Throsby C D 1986 Economic aspects of the foreign student question. *Econ. Rec.* 62 (179): 400–14
Williams G, Woodhall M, O'Brien U 1986 *Overseas Students and Their Place of Study*. Overseas Students Trust, London
Williams G, Fulth D 1990 *Financing Higher Education: Current Patterns*. OECD, Paris
Williams P (ed.) 1981 *The Overseas Student Question: Studies for a Policy*. Heinemann, London
Williams P 1982 *A Policy for Overseas Students: Analysis Options, Proposals*. Overseas Student Trust, London
Woodhall M (ed.) 1989 *Financial Support for Students: Grants, Loans or Graduate Tax?* Kogan Page, London
Wran Committee 1988 *Report of the Committee on Higher Education Funding*. Australian Government Publishing Service, Canberra

M. Woodhall

Student Friendships and Conflict in School

Although theories and research focused on the friendships of children and adolescents have a long history, studies of such friendships that take account of school settings are more recent, and few studies have yet appeared that are centrally concerned with conflicts among students in schools. The older tradition of research and theorizing concerned with students' friendships has produced a well-established set of findings about the relationships between student characteristics and friendship formation. The smaller body of literature focused on friendships in schools has added information about the ways in which school characteristics affect friendship formation. Investigators in both traditions have participated in a lively debate concerned with the positive versus negative influences of friends on students' behaviors in school, and they have also begun to raise questions about the nature of student conflicts.

1. Relationships Between Student Characteristics and Friendship Formation

Of all the student characteristics that might affect friendship formation, the two that have produced the most reliable findings are age and gender. Studies conducted over several decades have found that friendship formation among younger children tends to be based on shared activities, and friends tend to be described by young children as playmates and helpers. In preschools, schools, and other settings, children are expected to get along with one another and to engage in coordinated activities. To these ends, adults have often been found to intervene in the interactions of young children and in the processes of their friendship formation.

As children get older, they are more likely to choose their own friends and to construct their friendships in interaction with one another. By middle childhood, reliable gender differences in friendship patterns also begin to appear. Whereas the friendships of girls are intensively focused on one or a few friends, boys both report and are observed to have more extensive friendship networks. In middle childhood, friendships also become characterized by more expressive intimacy, especially the friendships of females, which have consistently been found to be more expressive than those of males from middle childhood through adolescence and on into adulthood and old age. Even for males, however, friendships based on shared thoughts and feelings become more common as boys move toward adolescence, and teenagers of both sexes are more likely than younger children to describe their friends as confidantes.

Only since the late 1980s has research concerned with effects of social class on friendships in schools appeared, and most of these studies have been limited to secondary schools. A review of this research by Corsaro and Eder (1990) suggests that students from middle-class backgrounds, and especially those who are members of elite groups within the high school, are more likely to base their friendships on interests and activities, often switching friends as their interests change. In contrast, students from working-class backgrounds exhibit more loyalty to their friends, often to the point of avoiding those activities in which their friends are uninvolved. As a result, their friendship networks tend to be more stable and less extensive. Members of secondary school cliques and crowds in which working-class adolescents predominate are likely to view their personal networks as the continuous element in their lives, and their resistance to the formal school culture is well documented in a variety of national contexts.

Few studies have appeared examining the effects on friendships of nationality and national context, but Shlapentokh (1984) has used research into the role of friendship in the former Soviet Union as the basis for a theory about these effects. He begins by asserting that friendships often serve as a refuge for the individual against external threats, including threats from the state. He goes on to hypothesize that, all other things being equal, the lower the sense of security among people and the weaker their confidence in the future, the more intense and vital are their interpersonal relationships. It is for these reasons, Shlapentokh (1984) argues, that people from the former Soviet Union attribute to friendship a more prominent place in their system of values than do people from the United States, and oppressed minorities have closer personal relations than those of the dominant majority.

Despite this latter suggestion, the literature concerned with race and ethnicity contains surprisingly little research that compares the characteristics of friendships across groups. Instead, the major research question about race and friendship concerns the extent to which students select as friends other students whose race or ethnicity is the same as their own. This research has yielded a large body of evidence documenting the existence of racial homophily in several national contexts. In the United States, this preference for same-race friends seems to increase during primary school, reaching its highest level in junior high school, and then remaining at about the same level throughout high school.

The principle of homophily in friendship formation has also been documented for age, gender, social class, and a wide variety of opinions and behaviors. Unlike racial homophily, both gender and age homophily seem to decrease throughout adolescence, after reaching their peak in middle childhood. Some of this decrease during the teenage years may be due to the formation of romantic or sexual liaisons, however, rather than to an increase in cross-sex or cross-age friendships per se. Although young children pay relatively little attention to such characteristics of potential friends as goals, values, or personal predispositions, students in the middle grades have been found to assign such characteristics great importance and to exhibit a strong preference for friends whose characteristics are similar to their own. This preference seems to decline slightly during the adolescent years, but there is no age group for whom similarities of any kind have been found to be negatively correlated with friendship formation.

Three major reasons have been offered to explain this strong tendency toward homophily. One of these is social pressure, which has been found by several investigators to inhibit the development of friendships that cross racial, gender, or social class lines. Adults often intervene to make certain that children select "appropriate" friends, and peers frequently do likewise. Especially among preadolescents, there seems to be a strong aversion to those who are different from themselves. In his description of a United States junior high school, Everhart (1983) gives vivid, and sometimes chilling, examples of the ways in which friendship groups demand conformity and reject anyone who deviates from the group norms for actions, interests, talk, dress, attitudes toward school, or treatment of peers.

A more benign and psychological reason for homophily in friendship selection is the set of assumptions that people tend to make about those who are similar to them. In particular, social psychologists have found that most people make the assumption that similar others will like them more than dissimilar others. This assumption, coupled with the well-documented tendency of people to like those who like them, produces more reciprocal liking among those who are similar than among those who are not. Both assumed and actual reciprocity of liking, in turn, have been found to be strong predictors of friendship selection and stability.

The third and most structural reason for homophily in friendship selection is proximity. Although it is not uncommon for researchers to find a few students who mention fantasy figures or famous personalities when asked to nominate their friends, most friends are selected from among people with whom the students have actually been in contact. Contact seems to be particularly necessary for what are called close friendships or strong ties in which students choose for their friends the same persons who choose them. Such choices, and the contacts that make them possible, depend on the available opportunities for interaction. Social structures can either facilitate or impede interactions among certain kinds of people, and considerable evidence exists to suggest that many social organizations sort and separate people who are dissimilar from one another while promoting interaction among those who are alike. This tendency is particularly noticeable in schools.

2. *Effects of School Characteristics on Friendship Formation*

Both across schools and within them, there is considerable segregation of students by age, gender, race, ethnicity, and social class. Some of this segregation is deliberately designed to promote connections among students from the same social background and to prevent contacts and friendships with students who are different. Some of this segregation is unintentional, however, and it often occurs even in those school systems that are sincerely dedicated to social integration and egalitarianism. Some of this unintended segregation is undoubtedly student initiated, but much of it seems to be perpetuated, and possibly created, by the many ways in which schools differentiate and group their students.

Epstein (1989) has identified a broad range of school characteristics that affect proximities among students and, therefore, possibilities for friendship formation. These school characteristics include architectural features of the school building and grounds, equipment and supplies, demographic features, the organization of extracurricular activities, and such characteristics of instructional methods as authority structures, evaluation and reward systems, ways of grouping students, task structures, and the amount of time teachers spend fostering exchanges of ideas among students.

Sometimes these characteristics vary across schools, with the result that some schools are friendlier than others. High participatory schools, for example, are defined by Epstein (1983b) as those in which both the school's architecture and its educational program combine to create a relatively high level of student participation in classroom decision-making. Compared to students in low participatory schools, those in high participatory schools were found to select more students as friends, to participate in more reciprocated friendships, and to select more friends from outside their own classroom.

Sometimes characteristics of classrooms within the same school have significant effects on friendship selection. One of these characteristics is curricular tracking. Such tracking includes specialized programs for academic and vocational students, student placements in core subjects on the basis of ability, and elective courses for students with particular talents or interests. Although tracking is usually designed for educational purposes, it also alters opportunities for peer interactions within the school. This opportunity structure directly affects friendship formation, and several studies have appeared showing that students are more likely to select friends from their own curricular track than from other tracks. Because the educationally relevant criteria used for tracking students are so highly correlated with their social background characteristics, tracking usually serves as a means for perpetuating segregation by age, gender, social class, race, and ethnicity.

Even though reducing proximity among students of diverse backgrounds seems to be an effective way of preventing friendships among them, encouraging contacts among diverse students does not guarantee friendly relations. In the case of race relations, for example, some studies (e.g., Bank et al. 1977) suggest that increased contact across racial lines is more likely to increase than decrease both perceptions of racial dissimilarity and interracial antipathy. Thus, the challenge for educators who would like to promote friendly behaviors among students of diverse backgrounds is to restructure school activities in ways that will help such students to see their similarities, rather than their differences, and to form positive opinions of one another. According to a growing body of research, these outcomes can be achieved if students participate in instructional groupings that are deliberately and carefully structured to meet these goals. Two interrelated group characteristics that have been found particularly likely to promote friendship formation among group members, even across racial lines, are task and reward interdependence.

In groups characterized by task interdependence, cooperation between students is emphasized by the teacher. All students in a group are expected to work together toward some common goal. Equal participation by all group members is encouraged, and tasks are structured in ways designed to equalize status differences. In some cooperative group methods, individuals are tested after their group experience and are given grades for their individual performance as well as a team score, based on the group average. In other cooperative group methods, students are praised and rewarded as a group, but not as individuals. In both cases, however, the rewards that students receive are dependent upon the help and cooperation they have given to and received from other group members.

Studies of cooperative learning generally support the conclusion that task and reward interdependence stimulate positive relations among students of different races or ethnicities, but many of these studies are experiments of relatively brief duration. Thus, it is not certain whether the positive relations among cooperative group members will continue after the group is dissolved. Nor is it clear whether task and reward interdependence among students of diverse backgrounds increases the heterogeneity of previously existing friendship groups. Nevertheless, it seems likely that schools and classrooms stressing greater proximity and cooperation among students will foster more friendships and more diversity in friendship networks than will schools and classrooms that limit contact and stress competition among their students.

3. *Influences of Friends on Students' Behaviors*

Although researchers and educators have often been willing, and sometimes eager, to seek ways to promote interracial and interethnic friendships among students, these propensities probably reflect a desire for racial harmony more than a positive view of student friendships per se. As Farrell (1990 p. 50) notes, "Many (American) teachers, in fact, fear that friendships in classrooms might work against learning and classroom management. Friends can reinforce each other to avoid work or to engage in disruptive and attention-getting behavior." This hostility toward friendships is similar to that which Vogel (1965) attributed to the Chinese Communist Party in the years after the People's Republic was established and which Shlapentokh (1984) described as the "hidden animosity toward friendship" in the state ideology of the former Soviet Union.

In support of teachers' suspicions that students' friendships undermine official educational goals, Everhart (1983) reports that the students in his ethnographic study prized their friendships above grades and rarely discussed the academic side of school with their friends. Similar findings have been reported by other researchers, especially in the United States. Csikszentmihalyi and Larson (1984), for example, asked a group of United States teenagers to carry electronic pagers for one week and to fill out reports of their activities and feelings whenever they were paged. This sampling of students' time revealed that the majority of the time these adolescents spent with friends was spent in leisure activities or maintenance tasks (such as eating or doing errands). Only 3.5 percent of the sampled time with friends was spent studying or doing other school-related productive work. Reports of students' feelings indicated that they enjoyed studying with friends more than studying alone or in the presence of family members, but they admitted to having more difficulty concentrating on studies when friends were present than when they were not.

In contrast to studies suggesting that friends have negative effects on student learning, there is considerable literature extoling the positive benefits of students' friendships. Several writers draw on the interpersonal development theory of Sullivan (1953) to argue that friendships help youngsters develop mutual respect and support, reciprocal commitment, and genuine, altruistic concern for each other. Buhrmester and Furman (1986), for example, have developed a neo-Sullivanian model of child development based on the assumption that children are actively motivated to establish new types of social relations as they get older, including the kinds of intimate, same-sex, preadolescent friendships with which Sullivan (1953) was primarily concerned. Buhrmester and Furman (1986) suggest that these new relationships benefit their participants by helping to fulfill their social needs, contributing to the growth of their social competencies, and remediating their adjustment problems.

Other positive consequences of friendship that have been argued in the literature include high or improved self-esteem, mastery of symbolic expression, realistic assessments of one's own abilities and achievements, acquisition of role-taking and communication skills, development of self-identity and autonomy, self-validation, development of creative and critical thinking, and the learning of moral principles and social rules. Regarding the latter, Youniss and Smollar (1985) have characterized close friendships as principled relationships in which adolescents learn the tenets of mutual caring, mutual respect, mutual trust, and symmetrical reciprocity. The latter principle seems to be a variant of the rule of fairness which young children are said to learn from their friendships.

Some of the claims about the influences of friendship seem contradictory. Some writers claim, for example, that close friends provide one another with the kinds of unconditional support they cannot gain in other relationships. It is hard to reconcile either this claim or the common assertion that friendships enhance self-esteem with the contention that friendships promote realistic self-assessments. Such inconsistencies may result from a lack of consensus among researchers about the best ways to measure friendships which may, in turn, account for the fact that evidence to support some of these claims is weak or inconsistent.

Another problem that characterizes some of the research concerned with the influence of friends is the failure to separate influence from selection. If, for example, friends have similar preferences, should this finding be interpreted to mean that friends influence each other's likes and dislikes, or should it be concluded that "birds of a feather flock together"? Although most research on the influence of friends continues to be cross-sectional, and thus is incapable of answering this question, some good, longitudinal studies have also appeared. In one of these, Kandel (1978) assessed the extent to which members of friendship dyads were alike in their frequency of current marijuana use, level of educational aspirations, political orientation, and participation in minor delinquency. She was able to show that about half of the similarity exhibited by the friendship pairs on these four measures was due to the process of selection in which similarity led to friendship, and the other half of the similarity resulted from the process of influence in which association led to similarity.

Whereas Kandel (1978) used behavioral self-reports, Epstein (1983a) obtained standardized achievement test scores in mathematics and English for the United States students she studied. She also asked them to nominate their three best friends from among their classmates. One year later, the achievements of these students were retested, and changes in their scores were calculated. Epstein (1983a) found that students with both high and low initial scores on achievement and high-scoring friends had significantly higher scores one year later than did students with low-scoring friends. Similar findings were obtained for report card grades in mathematics and English and for self-reports of college plans.

These findings suggest that the influence of friends is not necessarily a force antagonistic to the school's goals of achievement and academic success. Nevertheless, suspicious teachers and state authorities are correct in assuming that the influence of friends is not always supportive of official policies. Those who wish to make it so might follow the optimistic advice of Damon and Phelps (1989) concerning the ways in which educators can translate what is known about positive peer influences into an effective pedagogy that utilizes peer learning. More skeptical practitioners might heed the cautions of Cohen (1983) who argues that the friends students select for themselves have much more influence on them than nonselected peers, even if these peers are among the school elites.

4. Student Conflicts in Schools

Studies of friendships have become increasingly sensitive to the ways in which conflict is embedded in personal relationships. Preschool children tend to quarrel over possession of play materials and entry into peer groups (Corsaro and Eder 1990), and their conflicts often take the form of hitting and name-calling (Shantz 1987). Among older children, conflicts often occur when friends violate important rules, such as not helping a friend in need or breaking a promise (Shantz 1987). Among adolescents, conflicts often result from the paradoxical requirements of close friendships such as the tensions between autonomy and connection or between expressivity and instrumentality. These various kinds of conflicts rarely destroy close friendships. Instead, they are means for testing friendships and for developing social identity (Corsaro and Eder 1990).

Conflicts within friendships have also been found to be less frequent and severe than conflicts in other relationships, such as those with parents (Csikszentmihalyi and Larson 1984) or those in which a friendship group conflicts with individuals or collectivities external to the group (Everhart 1983). Regarding the latter, Fine (1981 p. 46) notes that the cruelty of the preadolescent boys he observed in the United States was "almost always expressed in the presence of friends. Insults seem(ed) to be expressed as much for reasons of self-presentation to one's peers as to attack the target." Similar observations were made by Connell et al. (1982) of boys in Australian secondary schools who often had to fight with other boys to prove their masculinity to themselves and their mates. Such findings suggest that conflicts in school can best be understood by using theories and research designs that also take account of the processes of friendship formation and influence among students.

See also: Peer Relations and Development; Peer Relations and Learning; School and Classroom Dynamics

References

Bank B J, Biddle B J, Keats D M, Keats J A 1977 Normative, preferential and belief modes in adolescent prejudice. *Sociol. Q.* 18(4):574–88

Buhrmester D, Furman W 1986 The changing functions of friends in childhood: A neo-Sullivanian perspective. In: Derlega V J, Winstead B A (eds.) 1986 *Friendship and Social Interaction*. Springer-Verlag, New York

Cohen J 1983 Commentary: The relationship between friendship selection and peer influence. In: Epstein J L, Karweit N (eds.) 1983 *Friends in School: Patterns of Selection and Influence in Secondary Schools*. Academic Press, New York

Connell R W, Ashenden D J, Kessler S, Dowsett G W 1982 *Making the Difference: Schools, Families and Social Division*. Allen and Unwin, Sydney

Corsaro W A, Eder D 1990 Children's peer cultures. *An. Rev. Sociol.* 16:197–220

Csikszentmihalyi M, Larson R 1984 *Being Adolescent: Conflict and Growth in the Teenage Years*. Basic Books, New York

Damon W, Phelps E 1989 Strategic uses of peer learning in children's education. In: Berndt T J, Ladd G W (eds.) 1989 *Peer Relationships in Child Development*. Wiley, New York

Epstein J L 1983a The influence of friends on achievement and affective outcomes. In: Epstein J L, Karweit N (eds.) 1983 *Friends in School: Patterns of Selection and Influence in Secondary Schools*. Academic Press, New York

Epstein J L 1983b Selection of friends in differently organized schools and classrooms. In: Epstein J L, Karweit N (eds.) 1983 *Friends in School: Patterns of Selection and Influence in Secondary Schools*. Academic Press, New York

Epstein J L 1989 The selection of friends: Changes across the grades and in different school environments. In: Berndt T J, Ladd G W (eds.) 1989 *Peer Relationships in Child Development*. Wiley, New York

Everhart R B 1983 *Reading, Writing and Resistance: Adolescence and Labor in a Junior High School*. Routledge and Kegan Paul, Boston, Massachusetts

Farrell E 1990 *Hanging In and Dropping Out: Voices of At-Risk High School Students*. Teacher's College Press, New York

Fine G A 1981 Friends, impression management, and preadolescent behavior. In: Asher S R, Gottman J M (eds.) 1981 *The Development of Children's Friendships*. Cambridge University Press, Cambridge

Kandel D 1978 Homophily, selection, and socialization in adolescent friendships. *Am. J. Sociol.* 84(2): 427–36

Shantz C U 1987 Conflicts between children. *Child Devl.* 58(2): 283–305

Shlapentokh V 1984 *Love, Marriage, and Friendship in the Soviet Union: Ideals and Practices*. Greenwood, New York

Sullivan H S 1953 *The Interpersonal Theory of Psychiatry*. Norton, New York

Vogel E F 1965 From friendship to comradeship: The changes in personal relations in communist China. *China Quarterly* 21: 46–60

Youniss J, Smollar J 1985 *Adolescent Relations with Mothers, Fathers, and Friends*. University of Chicago Press, Chicago, Illinois

Further Reading

Epstein J L, Karweit N (eds.) 1983 *Friends in School: Patterns of Selection and Influence in Secondary Schools*. Academic Press, London

Gottman J M, Parker J G (eds.) 1987 *Conversations of Friends: Speculations on Affective Development*. Cambridge University Press, Cambridge

Hallinan M T 1986 School organization and interracial friendships. In: Derlega V J, Winstead B A (eds.) 1986 *Friendship and Social Interaction*. Springer-Verlag, New York

Rawlins W K 1992 *Friendship Matters: Communication, Dialectics, and the Life Course*. Aldine De Gruyter, Hawthorne, New York

Rubin K H, Ross H S (eds.) 1982 *Peer Relationships and Social Skills in Childhood*. Springer-Verlag, New York

Rubin Z 1980 *Children's Friendships*. Harvard University Press, Cambridge, Massachusetts

Salzinger S, Antrobus J, Hammer M (eds.) 1988 *Social Networks of Children, Adolescents, and College Students*. Erlbaum, Hillsdale, New Jersey

B. J. Bank

Student Influences on Teaching

Teaching and learning in classrooms are complex, multiply determined phenomena. It is generally assumed that teachers, through their teaching, influence the learning of students. It is equally true, however, that students influence the ways in which they are taught. When in their classrooms, teachers may act or react on the basis of means–ends reasoning or "bounded rationality." That is, teachers adapt their methods of teaching (the means) to achieve certain goals (the ends) to differences among students. Similarly, teachers may teach students according to the expectations they have of them (see *Teachers' Expectations*).

The ways in which students influence teachers have been studied by many researchers using a variety of research methodologies. The results of these studies are presented and examined in this entry in terms of two guiding questions. First, what characteristics and behaviors of students influence teachers' classroom behavior and instructional practices? Second, what theoretical mechanisms account for teachers' differential behavior and practices?

1. Assumptions

There are two basic assumptions that guide this review. First, much of teaching is assumed to be a mindful enterprise. That is, teachers modify their actions toward different students based on some sort of means–ends reasoning. Second, teachers are assumed to be subject to influences other than those that are rational. Much theoretical and empirical work has examined the expectations of teachers, the ways in which these expectations are communicated to students, and the ways in which these expectations, once communicated, influence students. While the second assumption has been discussed widely (e.g., Rosenthal and Jacobson 1968), the first needs some elaboration.

Schools are institutions with particular social purposes (e.g., developing basic literacy and numeracy skills, cultivation of mind, socialization to cultural norms and practices, preparation for participation in the local and national economy). As the primary agents of this institution, teachers act in ways that are consistent with the attainment of some or all of these goals. This is not to say that all interactions between teachers and students are influenced by such a "bounded-rationality" conception, nor that such interactions actually optimize outcomes. Rather, it means that many of the interactions are influenced by such a conception.

Several instructional theories have been developed to examine how a bounded rationality of teaching might work in classrooms. One of the more elegant has been developed since the late 1960s by Snow (1988). The elegance in Snow's work lies in both its psychological sophistication and in its explicit reliance on how instruction can be adapted to individual differences in learners. Snow refers to these individual differences as "aptitudes," which are characteristics of the learner prior to instruction that influence the extent to which the instruction will be effective. Individual differences in characteristics such as sex, ethnicity, and prior achievement can serve as devices that teachers use to connect goals with instruction, learning, and, assessment.

2. Research on Students' Influence on Teaching

Studies of students' effects on teachers tend to focus on three characteristics of students: their sex, ethnicity, and prior level of educational achievement. Some studies have examined two, or in a small number of cases, all three of these characteristics. In a few studies, researchers have investigated interactions among these characteristics of students and the same characteristics of teachers (e.g., how the sex or ethnicity of the teacher interacts with sex or ethnicity of the students). Two lines of inquiry have been used in these studies: process–product and teacher expectancies. Much of the process–product research on classroom teaching has been based on a behavioral conception of classroom interaction. The goal of this research tradition is to identify those teacher behaviors and their antecedents that are associated with higher levels of student attainment. The research methodology is quantitative, relying on correlational and descriptive studies as well as subsequent field-based experiments to demonstrate the impact of particular teacher behaviors or clusters of behaviors on student learning. The second line of inquiry directly relevant to the ways in which students affect teaching is the research on teacher expectancies. Work along this line addresses more global or inferential dimensions of classroom action and relies on qualitative research methods such as ethnographies, case studies, and teacher narratives.

2.1 Process–Product Studies

An example of a process–product study based on a behavioral approach to studying students and teachers is that conducted by Nafpaktitis et al. (1985). These researchers were interested in teacher approval and disapproval of student behavior as a function of the students' on-task and off-task behavior. Their research methods included an interval time sampling observation procedure whereby 84 intermediate school teachers (Grades 6–9) and their students were observed for two or three 30-minute periods. Teacher approval and disapproval rates were calculated and correlated with rates of student off-task and on-task behavior. Nafpaktitis et al. found that teachers who tended to approve of off-task student behavior more often also had lower rates of on-task behavior. Similarly, teachers who tended to disapprove of off-task behavior had higher rates of student on-task behavior. Working in a similar tradition, Simpson and Erickson (1983) found that White teachers in the United States directed more verbal praise, nonverbal praises and verbal criticism toward first-grade males than toward first-grade females. However, they directed more nonverbal criticism to Black males than to any other sex–race grouping.

One of the problems with work in the genre of the Nafpaktitis et al. and the Simpson and Erickson studies is that the potential role of subject matter in conditioning the types of interactions between teachers and students and among students is ignored (Stodolsky 1988). Weber and Shake (1988), for example, examined teacher rejoinders (i.e., teachers' responses to students' answers) in the comprehension phase of reading instruction in second-grade classrooms. In the overwhelming majority of these rejoinders, teachers accepted students' answers as correct. Only about 6 percent of the rejoinders indicated that the students' answers were incorrect.

By and large, the finding that teachers tend to accept or approve of students' response has been replicated over a large number of studies, at least in United States classrooms. However, because students' understanding of these teacher responses interacts in many different ways with personal (e.g., beliefs about self as learner or what one considers valuable or worthwhile), social (e.g., norms for peer support), and situational (e.g., goal structures associated with grading practices) factors, it is difficult to make generalizable, theoretically robust predictions about student behavior based on such findings.

In a study of 36 fourth-grade mathematics classes in the United States, Fennema and Peterson (1986) found very complex interactions involving teachers' differential behavior toward boys and girls. The teachers' differential behavior also interacted with achievement differently for boys and girls, depending on whether the achievement was assessed by tasks that required higher or lower level thinking. As an example of the complexity of these findings, Fennema and Peterson stated that for lower level tasks, teachers' praise for girls' correct responses was positively related to test scores on these tasks. For boys, on the other hand, teacher praise following a correct answer to higher level tasks was associated with higher scores on high-level test items. This finding was one of several dozen complex interactions.

Undaunted by this complexity, Fennema and Peterson made a number of specific recommendations for specific teacher reaction to student responses depending on whether the goal is to increase higher or lower level achievement and if the student is a boy or a girl and if the task is higher or lower level. Over a dozen specific teacher responses were suggested.

2.2 Expectation Studies

Purely behavioral accounts of student and teacher interaction beg the question of the mechanisms that might mediate the effects of student characteristics and behaviors on the way teachers respond to students. Teaching decisions are not always based on rational decisions. They may stem from inappropriate or extraneous information such as stereotypical expectations for student behavior and performance. Such expectations may, in turn, lead to expectancy effects or self-fulfilling prophecies; that is, unwarranted differential treatment of students that reinforces or alters student outcomes. Since Rosenthal and Jacobson's (1968) study, a plethora of studies have examined the determinants and outcomes of teachers' differential expectations of students.

Studies indicate that teacher expectancies for student performance can be affected by a range of student characteristics including students' race, attractiveness, socioeconomic status, classroom conduct, and previous academic record (Dusek and Joseph 1983). Equivocal evidence has been found for expectancy effects based on several categories of student characteristics such as student gender, name stereotypes, and siblings' previous performance.

Differences in results may be attributed to several causes. First, teacher characteristics such as race and gender may influence expectancy effects (Irvine 1985). Teachers also differ on the importance they place on various student characteristics. In a study of 21 first-grade teachers, for example, Fedoruk and Norman (1991) found wide variance in the rankings teachers gave to 86 student descriptors as contributors to student success or failure. Furthermore, some teachers may be more susceptible to biasing information and expectancy effects than others

(Babad and Inabr 1982). In addition, most studies of teacher expectancies have been experimental, not naturalistic. Because experimental studies neglect contextual elements, their validity has been questioned. They usually use nonteachers as participants, are not conducted with intact classrooms, and do not consider multiple, interactive determinants of teacher expectancies.

Students' behavior or performance may confirm teachers' original expectations because of expectancy effects, perceptual biases on the part of teachers, or because teachers tend to predict achievement accurately without influencing it (Jussim 1989). Some researchers have argued that teachers tend to be accurate predictors of student achievement and that differential treatment may reflect appropriate responses to needs of individual students. It may also reflect students' frequency of participation and quality of contributions to classroom discourse (e.g., it is more difficult to call on students who do not raise their hand). Research in Canada by Clifton and Bulcock (1987) has shown that expectations of students held by ninth-grade teachers are based more on judgments of intellectual ability and prior performance than ethnicity (in this case, Yiddish- and French-speaking adolescents). In addition, there is evidence that teachers tend to modify their expectations as their experience with individual students increases (Brophy 1983, Raudenbush 1984).

2.3 Qualitative Studies

Since the early 1980s, research on teachers and classrooms has expanded to include more detailed, qualitative studies, usually with smaller sample sizes than those used in process–product or expectation studies. These studies provide a rich understanding of teachers' beliefs and conceptions and how they influence the ways in which teachers modify their teaching in reaction to students. These studies also provide information about how social, institutional, and personal contexts influence the work of teachers.

In a simulation study of expert, novice, and postulant (subject matter experts who wish to teach, but who have not yet been prepared formally) teachers, Carter et al. (1987) have shown that the expert teachers differ with respect to their understanding of students and classrooms. They further explicate the role that this understanding plays in classroom decisions and subsequent classroom interaction. For example, while all three groups use categories to describe students (e.g., discipline problems), expert teachers have a far richer understanding of the meaning that these categories have for their actions in the classroom. It is this more detailed understanding of teacher's beliefs, conceptions, and understandings that qualitative research methods uncover.

One of the findings from process–product and expectation studies is that teachers' judgments about students and their expectations for future performance are as likely to be based on realistic information from prior performance and classroom participation as they are to be based on bias and unfounded stereotype. This finding is supported by Barakett (1986) in her ethnography of English-speaking elementary school teachers in an inner-city school in Montreal, Canada. Barakett found that teachers' theories of students and instruction are to a large part based on teachers' experiences with students in their classrooms with respect to the type of activities and tasks that the teachers develop and use with these students. For example, the teachers in this school grouped children for learning using what, on the surface, might seem like conventional criteria (e.g., ability, motivation, family background). However, closer analysis suggested that classroom performance plays an even more powerful role than these conventional labels.

In a very different context, Abagi and Cleghorn (1990) found that rural and urban teachers in Kenya interpret and implement government policy about language of instruction in ways that are heavily influenced by their students' classroom performance. The policy for urban areas required that English be used as the language of instruction. The urban school teachers conformed to this policy. One of the rural schools in this study was situated geographically in the urban language policy jurisdiction. However, the students in this school largely spoke Kikuyu, not English, and the primary-grade teachers in this school used Kikuyu as the language of instruction, in violation of official policy. Clearly, in this as in many other instances in the literature, teachers modify their practices in conformance with their understanding of the students with whom they work more so than in reaction to official policy.

3. Conclusion

Early research on student effects on teaching and teachers was predicated on the search for behavioral regularities, that is, replicable statistical relationships between student and teacher behaviors. Since the early 1980s, researchers and theorists have recognized that an understanding of teachers and teaching requires an understanding of the minds of teachers and students. It is the beliefs, theories, and understandings of teachers that underlie whatever predictability that will be found between student and teacher behavior. Teachers' perceptions of students are filtered through their belief systems and mediate their behavior. Teachers continually change their teaching practice in response to students' needs and in reaction to the development of their own professional knowledge and expertise (Richardson 1991).

See also: Teachers' Beliefs and Belief Systems; Teachers' Expectations; Student Roles in Classrooms

References

Abagi J O, Cleghorn A 1990 Teacher attitudes towards the use of English, Kiswahili, and mother tongue in Kenyan primary classrooms. *Canadian and International Education* 19(1): 61–71
Babad E Y, Inabr J 1982 Pygmalion, Galatea, and the Golem: Investigations of biased and unbiased teachers. *J. Educ. Psychol.* 74(4): 459–74
Barakett J M 1986 Teachers' theories and methods in structuring routine activities in an inner city school. *Canadian J. Educ.* 11(2): 91–108
Brophy J E 1983 Research on the self-fulfilling prophesy and teacher expectations. *J. Educ. Psychol.* 75(5): 631–61
Carter K, Sabers D, Cushing K, Pinnegar S, Berliner D C 1987 Processing and using information about students: A study of expert, novice, and postulant teachers. *Teaching and Teacher Educ.* 3(2): 147–57
Clifton R A, Bulcock, J W 1987 Ethnicity, teachers' expectations, and student performances in Ontario schools. *Canadian J. Educ.* 12(2): 294–315
Dusek J B, Joseph G 1983 The bases of teacher expectancies: A meta-analysis. *J. Educ. Psychol.* 75(3): 327–46
Fedoruk G M, Norman C A 1991 Kindergarten screening predictive inaccuracy: First-grade teacher variability *Excep. Child.* 57(3): 258–63
Fennema E, Peterson P L 1986 Teacher–student interactions and sex-related differences in learning mathematics. *Teaching and Teacher Educ.* 2(1): 19–42
Irvine J J 1985 Teacher communication patterns as related to the race and sex of the student. *J. Educ. Res.* 78(6): 338–45
Jussim L 1989 Teacher expectations: Self-fulfilling prophecies, perceptual biases, and accuracy. *J. Pers. Soc. Psychol.* 57(3): 469–80
Nafpaktitis M, Mayer G R, Butterworth T 1985 Natural rates of teacher approval and disapproval and their relation to student behavior in intermediate school classrooms. *J. Educ. Psych.* 77(3): 362–67
Raudenbush S W 1984 Magnitude of teacher expectancy effects on pupil IQ as a function of the credibility of expectancy induction: A synthesis of findings from eighteen experiments. *J. Educ. Psychol.* 76(1): 85–97
Richardson V 1991 Significant and worthwhile change in teaching practice. *Educ. Researcher* 19(7): 10–18
Rosenthal R, Jacobson L 1968 *Pygmalion in the Classroom: Teacher Expectation and Pupils' Intellectual Development*. Holt, Rinehart, and Winston, New York
Simpson A W, Erickson, M T 1983 Teachers' verbal and nonverbal communication patterns as a function of teacher race, student gender, and student race. *Am. Educ. Res. J.* 20(2): 183–98
Snow R E 1988 Aptitude-treatment intervention as a framework for research on individual differences in learning. In: Ackerman P L, Sterberg R J, Glaser R (eds.) 1989 *Learning and Individual Differences*. Freeman, New York
Stodolsky S 1988 *The Subject Matters: Classroom Activity in Math and Social Studies*. University of Chicago Press, Chicago, Illinois
Weber R, Shake M C 1988 Teachers' rejoiners to students' responses in reading lessons. *J. Read. Behav.* 20(4): 285–99

R. W. Marx; R. M. B. Collopy

Student Loans

Students in higher education in many developed and less developed countries receive financial aid in the form of loans, which must be repaid after the students graduate or complete their education. Student loans, together with scholarships, grants, bursaries, or fellowships represent one of the main ways in which governments or private institutions provide financial support for students, to enable them to pay tuition fees or living expenses. However loans, unlike other forms of student support, must ultimately be repaid. There are a wide variety of student loan schemes operating in different countries, and the conditions under which the loan schemes are administered differ substantially.

Student loans are the subject of great controversy in several countries, because there is disagreement about whether students should be subsidized by means of loans or grants and scholarships. There is disagreement about the effects of loans and disagreement about the best way of providing financial aid for students. Advocates and opponents of loans argue fiercely, often ignoring the actual experience of various countries with student loan schemes. However, there is a considerable body of experience, since student loans have been widely used as a means of supporting students in higher education since at least the early 1960s. This entry will therefore summarize the type of student loan schemes operating in various countries, consider the arguments for and against loans, and review the evidence on the effects of student loans as a means of financing higher education.

The arguments about student loans concern the effect of loans compared with other forms of financial aid on access to higher education, particularly for poor students from low-income families, the equity of different methods of financing students, the effects of loans on student motivation and performance, the feasibility and costs of administering loan programs, and administrative issues such as which institutions should provide the loan, how to organize repayment, what rate of interest should be charged, how to deal with students who default on repayment, and so on.

1. Different Types of Financial Aid for Students

Governments throughout the world provide financial support for students in higher education. The extent of subsidization of education and the way in which subsidies are provided differ substantially in different countries, but in every country, both developed and less developed, governments provide a large part of the financial resources for higher education, as well as for primary and secondary education. Subsidies for higher education may be given to institutions, that is schools, colleges, or universities, or to students, to cover part or all of their living costs.

The majority of countries provide both kinds of subsidy, but there are considerable differences between countries in the balance between aid to institutions and aid to students. The following types of financial aid are provided, in various countries:

(a) Payments to institutions to cover direct costs of tuition, and therefore reduce or eliminate fees to students.

(b) Unconditional payment to all students in the form of a grant.

(c) Payments to selected students, in the form of a scholarship, grant, or bursary awarded on the basis of academic ability.

(d) Payments to selected students, in the form of means-tested grants or scholarships, awarded on grounds of financial need.

(e) Repayable loans provided to students from public funds at interest rates below the market rate, or at zero interest.

(f) Government guarantees for loans provided by banks or other private institutions, and interest subsidies to enable loans to be offered at less than market rates of interest.

(g) Payments to students for part-time work provided under special employment schemes for students.

(h) Provision of meals, accommodation, or travel at prices below market rates.

(i) Tax concessions to students or graduates.

(j) Tax concessions to students' parents.

Governments subsidize higher education for a number of different reasons. Since investment in education is judged to bring economic and social benefits, one objective of government aid to education is to ensure that there is sufficient investment in education, and another is to promote equality of opportunity by ensuring that financial barriers do not prevent students from enrolling in higher education.

Student loan programs also have a number of different objectives. In some countries the primary aim is to secure sufficient educated personnel to serve the needs of the economy, whereas in other countries the question of equality of opportunity is of crucial importance. Many countries provide a number of different types of financial aid for students. In particular, many countries provide a mixture of grants and loans, in some cases accompanied by tax concessions for students or their parents, or subsidized employment opportunities for students.

Student loans are an important form of financial aid for students in various European countries, throughout Scandinavia, in Canada, the United States, and in Japan, and they are widely used in Latin America. Some developing countries in Africa and Asia have student loan programs, but many developing countries make little use of loans, providing instead the bulk of financial aid for higher education by means of grants to institutions and grants, scholarships, or bursaries to students. Very few countries rely exclusively on student loans. Japan is one of the few countries which provides nearly all financial aid to students in the form of loans, although there has been a trend toward greater reliance on loans in several countries in the 1980s, and some countries, including the United Kingdom, have recently introduced loan programs in the early 1990s. However, there is still controversy in many countries about the desirability of introducing student loans. A few countries, for example, Japan and Sweden, provide loans for students in upper-secondary schools. However, in most cases, loans are mainly provided for students in higher education (post-secondary, technical, or vocational) rather than for those in primary or secondary education.

There have been several comparative studies of student support in Europe and the United States (Woodhall 1970, 1978, 1982, 1989, 1990; Johnstone 1986) and extensive analysis of student aid policy in individual countries, particularly the United States and the United Kingdom. From the late 1980s, the feasibility of student loans in developing countries has also attracted attention, and the International Institute for Educational Planning (IIEP) has organized a series of educational forums on student loans in the United States and Europe (Woodhall 1990), Asia (Woodhall 1991a), Africa (Woodhall 1991b), and Latin America (Woodhall 1993). The World Bank has also conducted research on student loans in developing countries, and a special issue of *Higher Education* is entirely devoted to student loans in developing countries. These studies are summarized below.

2. *Student Loan Programs*

In some countries, private institutions operate student loan programs, for example, some individual colleges or universities offer loans to their students, and some charitable funds have been established to provide loans for poor students. In the majority of cases, however, student loan schemes are operated by or for central or state governments. Many countries, including Canada, Denmark, Norway, Sweden, and Japan established government loan programs in the 1960s, while others, including Germany and the United Kingdom, have introduced loans more recently.

In the United States there are various student loan programs, operated by commercial banks, individual colleges, universities, or private agencies, but with government guarantees and interest subsidies. The first scheme was set up in 1958 and called the National Direct Student Loan Program (NDSLP), now known as "Perkins loans." This was followed by the Guaranteed Student Loan Program (GSLP) in 1965, now known as "Stafford loans", and the most recently established schemes, set up in 1981, are Parent Loans for Undergraduate Students (PLUS), and Supplementary Loans for Students (SLS). In the United Kingdom, student loans known as "top-up loans" were introduced in 1990, to supplement grants covering students' maintenance or living expenses.

In South America, the first student loans were offered in 1950 when the Colombian Institute for Advanced Training Abroad (*Instituto Colombiano de Crédito Educativo y Estudios Técnicos en el Exterior*, or ICETEX) was established. The term "educational credit" (*crédito educativo*) is used in Latin America to refer to student loans and any type of financial aid for students involving a repayment obligation. The scheme in Colombia was originally intended to help students finance higher education abroad, but in 1968 ICETEX began to provide loans to students for study in Colombia. The student loan scheme in Colombia was followed, during the 1960s and 1970s, by the establishment of student loan institutions in many Latin American countries, for example EDUCREDITO in Venezuela, and the *Instituto Nacional de Crédito Educativo* (INCE) in Argentina. The various student loan institutions in Latin America have formed the Pan American Association of Educational Credit Institutions (*Asociación Panamericana de Instituciones de Crédito Educativo*, or APICE).

3. The Main Features of Student Loan Programs

The majority of student loan programs provide long-term low-interest loans for students to enable them to finance tuition fees and/or living expenses. In Scandinavia and in other European countries loans are provided for maintenance costs only, since tuition is generally free, but in Japan and the United States loans are given to help students pay tuition fees. Most student loans have to be repaid within 10 or 20 years, but there are considerable differences in the terms of repayment, and in the rate of interest charged on student loans. Many governments subsidize student loans so that students do not usually have to pay interest while they are studying, and after graduating or completing their course the interest charged on the money borrowed is usually below market rates of interest. In the United States the different loan schemes charge different rates of interest. The most highly subsidized loans are Perkins loans, intended for students from low-income families; borrowers must pay 5 percent on Perkins loans, but 8–10 percent on Stafford loans, and between 12 and 14 percent on SLS and PLUS loans. In Canada the rate of interest varies with market rates and in Sweden and Japan interest is below commercial rates. In most cases, students undertake to repay their loans over a fixed period of time, at a fixed rate per year. Thus student loans resemble mortgages in most cases. However, in a few instances graduates may vary the rate at which they repay their loans and in several countries graduates can postpone repayment in the eventuality of illness or unemployment. The government provides guarantees in many countries, so that if a borrower dies or becomes seriously ill or handicapped, and so cannot repay the loan, the debt is written off, although in some cases borrowers must have personal guarantors.

In several countries there have been proposals to introduce income-contingent loans. This would mean that students would undertake to pay a fixed proportion of their income each year until their debt was repaid. Very few countries have so far introduced income-contingent loans, but Sweden introduced income-related repayment in 1989, which means that graduates are expected to pay 4 percent of their income until their loan is repaid. Australia has introduced a Higher Education Contribution Scheme (HECS) under which students must pay a charge which represents about 20 percent of average tuition costs; this may be deferred until after graduation and then paid, through the tax system, by means of 2 to 4 percent of gross taxable income. This scheme has been wrongly described by some commentators as a graduate tax, but in fact it resembles an income-contingent loan, collected through the tax system. The essential difference between student loans and a graduate tax is that the former involves repayment of a debt, and payment comes to an end when the debt is fully discharged, whereas a graduate tax involves a permanent obligation. In Australia a graduate's payments come to an end when the total liability is repaid.

Income-contingent loans have been advocated in the United Kingdom by Barr (1988, 1991) on the grounds that they are both more efficient and more equitable than mortgage-type loans. There have been several such proposals in the United States, but a short-lived experiment with income-contingent loans in the United States—the so-called "Yale Plan" in the 1970s—was not a success. Nevertheless, some United States economists, notably Reischauer (1989) have advocated income-related repayments, and the idea is again being examined in the United States.

In most countries, eligibility for student loans depends on the level of a student's family income, that is, they are means-tested. In many cases loans are specifically intended for needy students who would otherwise be unable to afford to pay fees or living expenses. However, in Sweden all students are entitled to receive loans, regardless of parental income, and in the United Kingdom the new "top-up loans" are also available to all students regardless of family income. In the United States the Middle

Income Student Assistance Act (MISAA) of 1978 removed any income ceiling, so that all students became eligible for GSLP loans. The result was such an increase in demand for subsidized loans, and such a heavy burden on federal government funds, that in 1981 GSLP loans were again confined to students from lower income families.

This brief summary of existing student loan programs shows that there are wide variations in the type of loan available to students in different countries. The effects of student loans will, therefore, depend on the type of loan scheme adopted, and there is still considerable controversy among economists about the relative merits of different types of loan.

4. *The Question of Loans versus Grants*

One of the fiercest controversies in the field of educational finance is whether financial aid for students should be given in the form of loans or grants. Economists in the United States and the United Kingdom have disagreed, over many years, on the subject of the desirability of student loans, as well as the advantages or disadvantages of particular types of loan. Arguments center around the following factors: (a) the supply of finance for higher education, (b) the financial benefits of higher education, (c) the equity of alternative methods of financing education, (d) the effect of loans or grants on equality of opportunity, (e) the efficiency of higher education, and (f) practical and administrative questions about the operation of student loan programs.

Advocates of student loans argue that governments should subsidize higher education on grounds of national welfare, since education brings both economic and noneconomic benefits to the community, but that a system of loans will impose less of a burden on public funds than a system of grants or scholarships, and it will also be more equitable than grants, since those who will themselves benefit from higher education, in the form of higher lifetime earnings, will contribute to the costs of their education through repaying their loans. Opponents of loans, on the other hand, argue that student loans will be less effective than grants in encouraging low-income students to continue their education, since the fear of debt may discourage poor students or women. They also argue that student loans will increase the risk of wastage or dropout, since students will be concerned about the size of their debts, and furthermore that the costs of administering a loan scheme and the problem of students who default on repayments will reduce the potential savings from introducing a loan scheme.

Much of the argument depends on what type or level of student aid is available in a country. So, for example, in the United Kingdom where the majority of university students receive a grant to cover maintenance expenses and have free tuition, the opponents of loans argue that loans will discourage working-class students, and that the threat of a "negative dowry" will discourage women from enrolling in higher education. In the United States on the other hand, where very little student aid was available until the mid-1970s, advocates of student loans argued that they would help to equalize educational opportunities by making it possible for even the poorest students to finance higher education by borrowing.

The question of equity is raised in many of the debates about loans versus grants. Advocates of loans argue that it is students from upper income families who are most likely to benefit from subsidies for higher education, and this involves a transfer of income from taxpayers with average or below average income to those who will enjoy above average income in the future as a result of their education. Thus, it is argued that loans are more equitable than grants because they ensure that those who directly benefit from higher education will ultimately pay when they repay their loans. A system of loans, it is argued, provides financial aid when it is needed, but does not involve a transfer of income from taxpayers to graduates. In the United Kingdom, for example, Prest (1966), Blaug (1970), Maynard (1975), and Woodhall (1982) all argued that a system of student loans is more equitable than a system of outright grants, as well as being more flexible and imposing less of a burden on public funds. In addition, Barr (1988, 1991) argues that income-contingent loans, collected through the national insurance or social security systems, are supported by both the "benefit principle" of taxation and ability to pay.

5. *Student Loans in Developing Countries*

The arguments about loans versus grants as a means of student support have recently been extended to developing countries. Severe financial constraints which limit public expenditure mean that governments in many developing countries have been forced to reduce public funding for higher education. Many economists have argued for increased cost-recovery in higher education, on the grounds that it is a profitable private investment, with private returns exceeding social returns, so that high levels of subsidy, including grants, involve a transfer of income from poor taxpayers to those who will in the future enjoy high earnings as a result of their higher education. Moreover, in many developing countries students in higher education are likely to come from privileged backgrounds, so that increased cost-recovery together with a substitution of loans for grants have been advocated, both for their efficiency and their equity. (Psacharopoulos and Woodhall 1985, Psacharopoulos et al. 1986).

Experience of student loans in developing countries is more limited than in industrialized countries, but loan schemes now operate throughout Latin America and increasingly in Africa and Asia. However, many of these have encountered serious administrative problems, in particular high rates of default, so that critics contend that loans are not feasible in developing countries that lack an efficient banking system or other financial infrastructure. There is a growing body of literature dealing specifically with the problems of designing student loan programs for developing countries (Woodhall 1987, Albrecht and Ziderman 1991). This depends crucially on evaluations of existing loan programs, including experience in industrialized and developing countries. This research is summarized in the following section.

6. *Evaluations of Student Loans*

There have been a number of recent evaluations of student loans as a means of financing higher education. Some of these have been carried out in the context of debates about how to reform student aid policy in particular countries. For example, in Canada a Federal-Provincial Task Force on Student Assistance presented a report in 1980 which included an evaluation of the Canada Student Loan Program (CSLP). In the United States there have been many evaluations and assessments of loans as a means of student support (Hartman 1971, Rice 1977, Hansen 1989, Gladieux 1989). An early study concluded: "The student loan program is not an unmixed blessing, nor an entirely unmitigated evil . . . In today's fiscal and educational policy circumstances loans are needed" (Rice 1977 p. 9).

More recently, Hansen concluded that "The existence of loans gives students wider access to financial assistance than would be possible if the aid were in the form of outright, non-repayable grants . . . Fiscal realities demand that we continue to rely on loans as a major source of funding for students in post-secondary education" (Hansen 1989 p. 67).

The two main concerns identified by Hansen are the fear of excessive debt burdens and high default rates, particularly in proprietary schools. These problems are partly due to the very rapid growth in student loans in the United States. Between 1978 and 1981, as a result of the increase in eligibility of GSLP loans, the total volume of lending to students rose from US$2 billion to US$8 billion, and the cost of interest subsidies rose from US$600 million in 1978 to US$2.5 billion in 1981. By 1989, total lending under federal government programs had risen to over US$12 billion, and defaults cost the federal government over US$1 billion per annum. However, Hansen concludes that this is mainly due to the rapid increase in borrowing, rather than a growing unwillingness to repay student loans. If debtors with very low incomes could be protected by means of income insurance, the default problem would be greatly reduced.

In addition to evaluations of individual countries, there has been a considerable growth throughout the 1980s and early 1990s of comparative studies which draw conclusions about the effects of different types of student loans on the basis of international experience (Rogers 1972, Johnstone 1986, Woodhall 1970, 1982, 1983, 1989, 1992, 1993, Barr 1991, Albrecht and Ziderman 1991).

Research shows that student loans are feasible in developed countries, but that certain problems remain, and many countries are still actively changing their systems of student support, and the terms of conditions of loans.

An early study of student loans in Scandinavia concluded:

> A perfect system of student aid has not yet been developed in any country. What is clear from this examination of Scandinavian experience is that to regard a system of student loans as either a panacea for educational and financial ills, or as an evil to be avoided at all costs, is equally mistaken. Some of the more exaggerated statements of both the opponents and advocates of student loans fall into perspective when viewed in the light of the working experience of other countries. (Woodhall 1970 pp. 1983–84)

This conclusion was based on the relatively early experience of several countries which had introduced student loans in the mid-1960s. At that time the rate of inflation was low in Europe and there was full employment, so that graduates experienced little difficulty in finding and keeping jobs, and the problem of default on loan repayments was not severe. A more recent evaluation of experience in Canada, Sweden, and the United States concluded:

(a) Student loan schemes can be devised to satisfy any objective of government policy, but trade-offs exist between the costs of a program and the number of students who can be assisted.

(b) The degree of subsidy involved in student loans is variable, and depends upon political decisions, but it is advisable to make both students and the public aware of the size of the subsidy, rather than have a system of "hidden grants."

(c) Default rates need not be high, provided that there are special provisions for those who are unable to pay their loans because of illness, unemployment, or low incomes.

(d) Student loans do not automatically deter working-class students or women from participating in higher education.

(e) There are no significant savings in the short run from introducing student loans, but in the long run a system of loans can produce significant saving of public funds, which can then be used to provide other forms of financial assistance—

for example, for 16–19-year olds or for adults taking part-time courses.

(f) Evaluations of student loans have shown that they are popular among students and the general public, that problems have arisen in the last 10 years as a result of inflation and high interest rates, but that these can be controlled. High rates of default, particularly in the United States, have demonstrated the importance of providing some element of insurance, such as exists in Sweden, for those who are unable to repay their loans as a result of low incomes. (Woodhall 1982 p. 7)

Johnstone (1986) showed that because most loan programs involve a substantial interest subsidy, the present value of loan repayments is actually considerably below the real value of the funds borrowed, so that there is a substantial "hidden grant" in the Swedish and German loan programs, and to a lesser extent in the United States. Albrecht and Ziderman (1991) have extended this analysis and calculated the implicit subsidy involved in 20 countries where student loans are offered at less than market interest rates. They conclude that in half the programs examined, the implicit subsidy or "hidden grant" is more than half the value of the loan, and in a few cases, such as Kenya and Venezuela, the combined effects of interest subsidies, high rates of default, and administrative costs mean that it would actually be cheaper for the government to give grants to students. Thus, the study concludes that loan programs have so far had only marginal impacts on educational finance, and that "loans have been operating only at the margins of cost recovery." Nevertheless, the authors emphasize:

> It should not be concluded from disappointing results of past experience that loan programs should be abandoned. On the contrary, we argue that reform and improvement in several key elements of program design are necessary conditions for well-functioning loan programs. (Albrecht and Ziderman 1991 p. 23)

In particular three major issues are identified: effective targeting (for example to concentrate resources on needy students); reducing subsidies while limiting debt burdens (by increasing interest rates, but linking repayments to income, as in Sweden since 1989); and finally minimizing evasion (by designing efficient recovery mechanisms, for example using the tax system as in Australia, or the social security system). Albrecht and Ziderman conclude:

> Student loans and alternative forms of deferred payments present an important policy option to assist in cost recovery, without deterring access to qualified students. In order to achieve these twin goals, however, programs require careful planning, particularly to ensure recovery. (1991 p. 49)

Another important issue is the effect of student loans on equality of opportunity and equity. Advocates of loans believe that they will be more equitable than grants because they involve less transfer of income from poor taxpayers to potentially rich students. Critics, on the other hand, believe that loans will deter working-class students. Once again, the evidence from evaluations of student loan programs shows that loans are neither as effective nor as damaging as these views suggest. On the one hand, studies in the United States and Sweden show that low-income students are not discouraged from entering higher education by the fear of incurring debts. On the other hand, the fact that loan programs are so heavily subsidized in most countries means that there is still a substantial transfer of income. So, for example, Jallade's evaluation (1974) of student loans in Colombia concluded that the loan scheme "can hardly be considered as a tool to shift the burden of higher education away from taxpayers to students, but rather as a cheaper way to channel additional funds to private universities" (Jallade 1974 p. 35).

Thus, the general conclusion of these evaluations of student loans in both developed and developing countries is that student loans can be an effective way of providing financial assistance for students but the extent to which they contribute toward cost recovery, equality of opportunity, or toward redistributing the costs of higher education depends critically on the terms and conditions of the loans and the general educational and economic situation within which a student loan scheme operates.

See also: Cost–Benefit Analysis

References

Albrecht D, Ziderman A 1991 *Deferred Cost Recovery for Higher Education: Student Loan Programs in Developing Countries*. Discussion Paper No. 137, World Bank, Washington DC

Barr N 1988 *Student Loans: The Next Steps*. Aberdeen University Press, Aberdeen

Barr N 1991 Income-contingent student loans: An idea whose time has come. In: Shaw G K (ed.) 1991 *Economics, Culture and Education: Essays in Honour of Mark Blaug*. Edward Elgar, Aldershot

Blaug M 1970 *An Introduction to the Economics of Education*. Penguin, Harmondsworth

Gladieux L (ed.) 1989 *Radical Reform or Incremental Change? Student Loan Policies for the Federal Government*. College Entrance Examination Board, New York

Hansen J 1989 Cost-sharing in higher education: The United States experience. In: Woodhall M (ed.) 1989

Hartman R W 1971 *Credit for College: Public Policy for Student Loans*. McGraw-Hill, New York

Jallade J-P 1974 *Student Loans in Developing Countries: An Evaluation of the Colombian Performance*. Staff Working Paper No. 182, World Bank, Washington, DC

Johnstone D B 1986 *Sharing the Costs of Higher Education: Student Financial Assistance in the United Kingdom, the Federal Republic of Germany, France, Sweden and the United States*. College Entrance Examination Board, New York

Maynard A K 1975 *Experiment with Choice in Education: An Analysis of New Methods of Consumer Financing to*

Bring More Resources into Education by Vouchers and Loans. Institute of Economic Affairs, London
Prest A R 1966 *Financing University Education: A Study of University Fees and Loans to Students in Great Britain*. Institute of Economic Affairs, London
Psacharopoulos G, Woodhall M, 1985 *Education for Development: An Analysis of Investment Choices*. Oxford University Press, New York
Psacharopoulos G, Tan J-P, Jimenez E 1986 *Financing Education in Developing Countries: An Exploration of Policy Options*. World Bank, Washington, DC
Reischauer R 1989 HELP: A student loan program for the twenty-first century. In: Gladieux L (ed.) 1989
Rice L (ed.) 1977 *Student Loans: Problems and Policy Alternatives*. College Entrance Examination Board, New York
Rogers D C 1972 *An Evaluation of Student Loan Programs*. US Agency for International Development, Washington, DC
Woodhall M 1970 *Student Loans: A Review of Experience in Scandinavia and Elsewhere*. Harrap, London
Woodhall M 1978 *Review of Student Support Schemes in Selected OECD Countries*. Organisation for Economic Co-operation and Development, Paris
Woodhall M 1982 *Student Loans: Lessons from Recent International Experience*. Policy Studies Institute, London
Woodhall M 1983 *Student Loans as a Means of Financing Higher Education: Lessons from International Experience*. World Bank Staff Working Paper No. 599, World Bank, Washington DC
Woodhall M 1987 *Lending for Learning: Designing a Student Loan Programme for Developing Countries*. Commonwealth Secretariat, London
Woodhall M 1989 (ed.) *Financial Support for Students: Grants, Loans or Graduate Tax?* Kogan Page, London
Woodhall M 1990 *Student Loans in Higher Education 1: Western Europe and USA*. International Institute for Educational Planning, Paris
Woodhall M 1991a *Student Loans in Higher Education 2: Asia*. International Institute for Educational Planning, Paris
Woodhall M 1991b *Student Loans in Higher Education 3: English-speaking Africa*. International Institute for Educational Planning, Paris
Woodhall M 1992 Student loans in developing countries: Feasibility, experience and prospects for reform. *Higher Education* 23 (4): 347–56 (special issue devoted to student loans)
Woodhall M 1993 *Student Loans in Higher Education 4: Latin America*. International Institute for Educational Planning, Paris.

M. Woodhall

Student Needs: Diagnosing

Optimizing student learning requires an assessment of those student aptitudes which are relevant for learning. There are several ways for the teacher to collect such diagnostic information, ranging from standardized tests to informal observations; each serves a different purpose. This entry focuses on the strengths and weaknesses of various diagnostic tools, with special emphasis on teacher diagnoses of students' learning needs.

1. *The Relevance of Diagnosing Students' Needs*

Students' needs occur are related to the attainment of basic educational goals, especially the goal of cognitive growth. Differences among students in the attainment of such goals are caused in part by differences in their cognitive characteristics (such as intelligence and prior knowledge) and their motivational characteristics (such as need to achieve, self-concept of ability, and test anxiety). To optimally foster students' cognitive and affective growth, the teacher must be able to diagnose interindividual differences in those learning characteristics. Furthermore, teachers should be sensitive to intra-individual changes over time. From this perspective, diagnosis of students' needs is not restricted to pupils with problems, deficits, or handicaps; rather, it includes the diagnosis of specific strengths and favorable prerequisites as well.

The proper diagnosis of learning-related student characteristics before, during, and after instruction is important for a variety of decisions. The scope of these decisions ranges from the planning and preparation of a single lesson to the design, presentation, and evaluation of the course of instruction. In the preactive phase of teaching, teacher decisions about the planning of instruction, the selection of appropriate materials, or the formation of instructional groups require judgments about each student's strengths and weaknesses as well as the distribution of these strengths and weaknesses in the classroom. During the interactive phase of instruction, several teacher activities are influenced by judgments about student aptitudes (e.g., posing questions or assigning tasks to students). The concept of the "steering group" is illustrative of interactive decision-making (see, for example, Clark and Peterson 1986). Many teachers determine the pacing of instruction by their perceptions of the reactions of a steering group (i.e., a reference group consisting of, for example, the students in the bottom one-fifth of the ability distribution). A major requirement for optimizing student learning is a satisfactory match between those teacher decisions and the actual needs of students.

Some teaching strategies (see *Teaching: Diagnostic-Prescriptive; Individualized Instruction*) are explicitly based on the systematic relation between the results of differential diagnoses and teachers' instructional and didactical activities. Also, in research on teacher expertise, diagnostic competence of the teacher is regarded as a core component of teacher expertise (Weinert et al. 1990). Finally, teachers' judgments about the students are central to models of teaching as decision-making. According to the influential model of Shavelson and Stern (1981), teaching is regarded as consisting of a multistep process, which includes a variety of pedagogical decisions. These decisions depend on three sets of variables: (a) individual characteristics of the teachers themselves, (b) their use of judgment heuristics, and (c) the nature of the task. These constructs, however, do not affect pedagogical decisions directly, but are mediated by teachers' judgments about the students and the content being taught.

2. Methods of Diagnosing Students' Needs

There is a large variety of methods for assessing students' needs which can be classified with respect to at least the following five dimensions.

2.1 Data Source

There are three main kinds of data sources underlying teacher diagnoses: tests (or questionnaires), direct observation of student behavior, and student work. Data from these sources must be integrated by the teacher to make judgments about the student.

2.2 Goal

Summative evaluation focuses on the final product; examples would include minimum competency tests and final course examinations. The goal is grading or classifying students. In contrast, formative evaluation focuses on the process, not the final product. The goal is the continuous assessment of students' present knowledge, and the monitoring of their learning progress.

2.3 Degree of Formality

Examples of formal diagnoses are standardized tests, as they are frequently administered in the evaluation of schools or in educational research. In contrast, informal diagnoses comprise teacher-made tests or other procedures that elicit student work, as well as implicit teacher judgments that occur many times during classroom instruction.

2.4 Standard of evaluation

Three types of evaluative standards are typically used in teacher decision-making. Social standards involve the comparison of student achievement with the distribution of a given reference group, typically the classroom. Criterial standards involve the comparison of student achievement with a previously defined "mastery standard," which, as a rule, is derived from the respective curriculum. Finally, individual standards focus not on the absolute level, but on the intra-individual change over time (i.e., the extent to which the achievement of the student has improved or deteriorated).

2.5 Consideration of Dynamics

Traditional diagnosis of student aptitude (in particular, of intelligence) has focused on the students' competencies at a given point in time. Since it is based on the actual status of achievement, this diagnosis is static in nature. In contrast, the prototype of a dynamic procedure is the "learning potential" or "dynamic assessment" approach (Feuerstein 1980, Guthke 1992). This procedure, derived from Vygotsky's concept of the "zone of proximal development", assesses how much the competency profile of a given student can be improved by means of training and systematic support, utilizing a test–train–retest design. Competence is conceptualized as the capability to benefit from training. Although this procedure has been applied primarily to the diagnosis and remedying of deficiencies of poor learners, the principles could also be applied to domain-specific aptitudes of students in general.

3. The Use of Tests for Diagnosing Students' Achievement

Traditionally, standardized tests have been used to diagnose students. Since the 1980s, however, several alternative testing procedures have been used.

3.1 Standardized Achievement Tests

A widespread method for diagnosing student achievement is the standardized test. The major advantages of standardized tests are obvious: high objectivity and reliability. Furthermore, their use is very economic. There are, however, several problems associated with the use of standardized tests.

The first problem concerns the curricular validity of the test. It is well-known that there are considerable differences in the official curriculum both between and within different states or regions. Even within the same school, teachers can often select learning materials and determine the sequence of content covered. These differences among states, regions, or teachers themselves all contribute to the problem of the curricular validity of tests. Specifically, the smaller the overlap of instructional content which was actually taught with the content of the test, the lower the curricular validity of that test.

A second problem with standardized tests concerns the effects of achievement tests on teaching and learning. The increasing use of such tests (especially, but not only, in US schools) may contribute to a strong bias in education (Frederiksen 1984) because such standardized multiple-choice tests assess predominantly basic skills and factual knowledge. This emphasis may discourage teachers' efforts to teach to other equally important cognitive goals (e.g., understanding, problem-solving, application, evaluation, and creativity).

3.2 Alternative Approaches

Most standardized tests have been developed and are administered for summative evaluation purposes and are often less appropriate for formative evaluation and remediation. Therefore, and to overcome some of the critiques mentioned earlier, there is an increasing trend toward replacing or at least complementing traditional standardized tests with informal and diagnostic tests.

Teacher-developed informal tests are a widespread tool for determining students' actual achievement profiles. Their main advantages are sensitivity to the actual content of instruction and the possibility of diagnosing errors. Informal tests usually use open-ended questions rather than the multiple-choice format. As a consequence, they are often problematic with respect to objectivity and reliability.

A second alternative is diagnostic tests, which have been developed specifically for diagnostic purposes, in particular in mathematics and reading (Nitko 1989). One major category of these tests focuses on the detection of students' errors. Ideally, such a test would provide a one-to-one relationship between a specific wrong solution (an error) and a corresponding misconception. Obviously, this kind of diagnostic test is very useful for instruction because it facilitates a detailed analysis of erroneously learned rules, missing skills, and misconceptions. In other words, the teacher can learn why certain tasks or routines are not solved, and draw implications for his or her instruction (e.g., the selection of learning materials).

4. Teacher Judgments of Student Characteristics

Teachers' diagnoses of students' learning needs are based on a variety of sources: tests, school records, past grades, casual observation of students' behavior, information provided by the parents, and the anecdotical reports of other teachers. It is obvious that successful teaching requires that these assessments be valid. As Corno and Snow (1986) point out: "If differential treatment of learners is based on invalid assessments, the teaching system may become maladaptive, even discriminatory in the extreme" (p. 607). Also, teachers' perceptions of their students' ability form the basis for their expectations, which in turn influence students' self-concepts of their ability (Stipek and Tannatt 1984). Hence, the validity of teacher judgments has become an important issue in recent research.

The starting point of this research tradition, usually labeled the "judgment accuracy approach", is that accuracy requires an objective standard against which the teacher diagnosis can be measured. Thus, accuracy of judgments is determined by comparing respective teachers' judgments with some external criterion, mostly tests or other objective instruments. This approach, however, is characterized by several methodological problems, especially when accuracy is determined by computing difference scores between judgments and objective measures. This computation leads to a confusion of widely disparate judgmental biases and errors. Although suggestions have been made as to how to overcome these methodological problems, these problems are a major reason for research in this field being nearly abandoned. Only recently has there been a renaissance of the judgment-accuracy approach in education (Funder 1987).

Teachers are typically faced with the task of diagnosing several characteristics (e.g., various learning prerequisites) of several target persons (e.g., all students in the classroom). Under these circumstances, teacher judgment can be analyzed with respect to several statistically and logically independent components (Cook 1979): level (general underestimation or overestimation of mean competence), differentiation (underestimation or overestimation of within-class variance), and rank (correlations between teacher judgments and actual competencies). Most of the research on teacher judgment accuracy has dealt with the last component. (For psychometric properties of teacher judgments in general, see Hoge 1983.)

4.1 Teachers as Diagnosticians of Their Students' Achievement and Understanding

Hoge and Coladarci (1989) reviewed 16 studies dealing with the question of how accurately teachers judge their students' achievement. In these studies correlations of teachers' ratings of their students' academic achievement with achievement test scores were explored. The data support the validity of teachers' judgments of their students' achievement. The median judgment criterion correlation was 0.62 for teacher ratings of student achievement and 0.69 for teachers' prediction of students' test scores. Interestingly, large differences among teachers in their judgment accuracy were found (see also Helmke and Schrader 1987). Future research should investigate the contextual factors and teacher characteristics that account for this variability.

Research based on a cognitively oriented paradigm has begun to investigate what teachers know about their students' intuitive knowledge, their ways of thinking, and their understanding. A series of studies conducted in the area of mathematics instruction in the elementary school (e.g., Peterson et al. 1989) has shown that teachers were, on average, rather successful in judging the relative difficulties of various types of mathematical tasks. Furthermore, most of the teachers, when faced with videotapes of first-grade children solving various word problems, were also able to judge which strategies children of that age would generally use. However, when the task was to predict which of six selected students of their own classroom would apply certain strategies and whether they would solve those problems, teachers were only moderately knowledgeable. In other words, teachers were successful in judging the general developmental level of their students, but were less successful in differential diagnosis of individual students.

4.2. *Teachers' Perceptions of their Students' Affective and Emotional Characteristics*

Although researchers and teachers agree that fostering learning must take into account factors other than cognitive student characteristics, the salience of affective, motivational, volitional, and emotional determinants of learning is still underestimated. A major reason for this state of affairs may be the predominant cognitive orientation in today's mainstream psychology. Empirical studies on determinants of achievement often include the whole range of cognitive determinants (such as intelligence and prior knowledge) but typically only a very small (and often unreliably measured) subsample of noncognitive variables. However, as Helmke (1992) has demonstrated, if one uses a broad range of noncognitive variables, their predictive power for later achievement test performance is as high as the combined impact of intelligence plus prior knowledge, and is even higher for the prediction of grades.

4.2.1 Data sources for teacher judgments of noncognitive variables. Information about noncognitive student characteristics is typically gathered by formal instruments, such as questionnaires given to students, and teachers' judgments. The use of personality questionnaires in a nonanonymous setting with possibly crucial consequences for the tested person is questionable, and will probably not yield valid results. Therefore, teachers and school psychologists should be cautious in using the results of such questionnaires for individual diagnoses.

Teacher judgments are a more promising way of getting information about noncognitive student characteristics. However, it might be very helpful for the teacher to administer questionnaires on achievement-related attitudes and subjective ratings of the difficulty of instruction on an anonymous basis to get information about salient learning issues that exist within a classroom of students.

For implicit teacher judgments about their students' noncognitive characteristics the concept of accuracy is not applicable, since the standards against which teacher diagnoses are compared may be "soft" or ambiguous. The empirical evidence about teachers as diagnosticians of noncognitive student characteristics should be interpreted within these restrictions.

4.2.2 Judgment of motivational variables: Empirical research. Most of the research concerning teacher judgments of noncognitive student variables has been conducted for achievement-related attitudes, attributions, self-concepts, emotions, and motives (Helmke and Fend 1982, Carr and Kurtz 1991). These, and most of the other studies, have shown that correlations between students' self-reports and the correspondent teacher ratings of these same variables are generally very low, ranging from about −0.10 to 0.35.

One reason for the low covariations is certainly the low psychometric quality of instruments tapping motivational variables, as compared with those measuring achievement and intelligence. There may in fact be no valid empirical indicators for the noncognitive constructs under consideration. For example, some test-anxious students may be able to hide their subjective emotional experience and to control their motor behavior. Similarly, the construct may be difficult to judge because its indicators are ambiguous. For example (as in the case of test anxiety again), there may be considerable interindividual differences with regard to its manifestation. Some students express anxiety in the form of heightened motoric, gestic, postural, and mimic activity, whereas others appear to be paralyzed. Finally, teachers may be more or less able and/or motivated to actually use existing behavioral cues for their judgments.

5. *Conclusion*

Although there is a considerable body of research on various methods and tools of teachers' diagnoses of students' needs, at least three areas are underrepresented in research on this topic.

First, attempts to analyze students' understanding and their content-specific knowledge structures, including the analysis of errors and misconceptions, are a necessary counterweight against the widespread use of standardized multiple-choice achievement tests. The growing use of computerized testing in diagnosis (Bunderson et al. 1989, Jäger 1991) appears to be very promising and is likely to facilitate and accelerate the appropriate and efficient use of diagnostic methods. Second, although there is now agreement about the importance of noncognitive student characteristics for learning, the focus of research on teacher diagnosis is strongly biased toward cognitive characteristics. Future teacher training should focus more on affective growth as an important educational outcome, and teachers should become more sensitive to observable manifestations of motivational aspects of learning. Third, this entry has concentrated on teachers' diagnoses of their students' needs. Although there is as yet little empirical research, it should not be overlooked that diagnosis by parents of their children may be important as well (Helmke and Schrader 1990).

See also: Teaching: Diagnostic-Prescriptive; Teaching: Aptitude–Treatment Interaction Model; Individualized Instruction; Individual Differences and Instruction; Classroom Assessment

References

Bunderson C V, Inouye D K, Olsen J B 1989 The four generations of computerized educational measurement.

In: Linn R L (ed.) 1989 *Educational Measurement*, 3rd edn. Macmillan, New York
Carr M, Kurtz B E 1991 Teachers' perceptions of their students' metacognition, attributions, and self-concept. *Br. J. Educ. Psychol.* 61(2): 197–206
Clark C M, Peterson P L 1986 Teachers' thought processes. In: Wittrock M C (ed.) 1986 *Handbook of Research on Teaching*, 3rd edn. Macmillan, New York
Cook M 1979 *Perceiving Others: The Psychology of Interpersonal Perception*. Methuen, London
Corno L, Snow R E 1986 Adapting teaching to individual differences among learners. In: Wittrock M C (ed.) 1986 *Handbook of Research on Teaching*, 3rd edn. Macmillan, New York
Feuerstein R 1980 *Instrumental Enrichment: An Intervention Program for Cognitive Modifiability*. University Park Press, Baltimore, Maryland
Frederiksen N 1984 The real test bias: Influences of testing on teaching and learning. *Am. Psychol.* 39: 193–202
Funder D C 1987 Errors and mistakes: Evaluating the accuracy of social judgment. *Psych. Bull.* 101: 75–90
Guthke J 1992 Learning tests—the concept, main research findings, problems and trends. *Learning and Individual Differences* 4(2): 137–51
Helmke A 1992 *Selbstvertrauen und schulische Leistungen*. Hogrefe, Göttingen
Helmke A, Fend H 1982 Diagnostic sensitivity of teachers and parents with respect to the test anxiety of students. In: Schwarzer R, van der Ploeg H M, Spielberger C D (eds.) 1982 *Advances in Test Anxiety Research*, Vol. 1. Erlbaum, Hillsdale, New Jersey
Helmke A, Schrader F W 1987 Interactional effects of instructional quality and teacher judgement accuracy on achievement. *Teaching and Teacher Education* 3(2): 91–98
Helmke A, Schrader F W 1990 Are mothers good diagnosticians of their children? Analyses of components and determinants of judgment accuracy. *The German Journal of Psychology* 14: 221–22
Hoge R D 1983 Psychometric properties of teacher-judgment measures of pupil aptitudes, classroom behaviors, and achievement levels. *J. Spec. Educ.* 17(4): 401–29
Hoge R D, Coladarci T 1989 Teacher-based judgments of academic achievement: A review of literature. *Rev. Educ. Res.* 59(3): 297–313
Jäger R S 1991 Computer diagnostics—survey of practical applications of computerized assessment—theoretical principles and perspectives. *Rev. Psy. App.* 41: 247–68
Nitko A J 1989 Designing tests that are integrated with instruction. In: Linn R L (ed.) 1989 *Educational Measurement*, 3rd edn. Macmillan, New York
Peterson P L, Carpenter T C, Fennema E 1989 Teachers' knowledge of students' knowledge in mathematics problem solving: Correlational and case analyses. *J. Educ. Psychol.* 81(4): 558–69
Shavelson R J, Stern P 1981 Research on teachers' pedagogical thoughts, judgments, decisions, and behavior. *Rev. Educ. Res.* 51(4): 455–98
Stipek D J, Tannatt L M 1984 Childrens' judgements of their own and their peer academic competence. *J. Educ. Psychol.* 76(1): 75–84
Weinert F E, Schrader F W, Helmke A 1990 Educational expertise: Closing the gap between educational research and classroom practice. *School Psychology International* 11(3): 163–80

A. Helmke

Student Perceptions of Classrooms

In contrast to earlier behaviorist views of students as passive recipients of information, late twentieth century theories of teaching and learning view students as being actively involved in their own learning and recognize the importance and relevance of student perceptions. Although this interest in students' perceptions is evident in the third edition of the *Handbook of Research on Teaching* (Wittrock 1986), it was largely absent from the first and second editions. Considerable research has provided insights into factors related to student perceptions as well as the associations between student perceptions and student outcomes.

The importance of students' perceptions is well supported by two lines of research. First, because research in numerous countries has revealed consistent differences between students' and teachers' perceptions (Fraser in press), a focus on students' rather than teachers' perceptions is likely to be more productive in attempts to improve and understand classroom learning. Second, student perceptions help to explain student outcomes beyond the effects of student abilities, instructional methods, and curricular materials (Fraser 1986, Schunk and Meece 1992). Because teacher behaviors can be considered relevant only when they are perceived as cues by students, student perceptions can be thought of as mediators between instruction and student outcomes.

Schunk and Meece (1992) edited a collection of studies of both students' self-perceptions (of their abilities, competence, interests, and goals) and their social perceptions (of teachers, peers, events, and situations). In addition to providing evidence supporting the validity of student perceptions, this collection of research studies shows that the student's perceptions not only affect his or her own behavior, but that perceptions themselves are influenced by student attributes and situational cues. For example, gender differences in student perceptions have been documented (Meece and Courtney 1992) and student perceptions of classroom climate have been related consistently to student outcomes when student aptitude differences were controlled (Fraser 1986, Haertel et al. 1981).

1. Measuring Student Perceptions of Classrooms

In the late 1960s, the Learning Environment Inventory was used as part of the research and evaluation activities of Harvard Project Physics (Welch and Walberg 1972). Around the same time, Moos began developing social climate scales for a wide variety of human environments, including the Classroom Environment Scale for use in school settings (Moos and Trickett 1987). Other instruments for assessing students' perceptions of classroom environment include the Individualized Classroom Environment Questionnaire, My Class Inventory, College and University Classroom Environment Inventory, Science Laboratory Environment Inventory, and Questionnaire on Teacher Interaction. Research involving the use of these instruments has been reviewed by Fraser (1986, in press) and Fraser and Walberg (1991) (see also *Classroom Environments*).

2. *Factors Related to Student Perceptions*

Fraser (1986) tabulated 39 studies in which students' perceptions of their classrooms were employed as dependent variables in (a) curriculum evaluation studies, (b) investigations of differences between student and teacher perceptions of actual and preferred environment, and (c) studies involving other independent variables. One promising but largely neglected use of students' perceptions is as process criteria in evaluating innovations and new curricula. A study involving an evaluation of the Australian Science Education Project (ASEP) revealed that, in comparison with a control group, students in ASEP classes perceived their classrooms as being more satisfying and individualized and having a better material environment (Fraser 1986). The significance of this evaluation, as well as Welch and Walberg's (1972) evaluation of Harvard Project Physics in the United States, is that student perceptions differentiated revealingly between curricula, even when various outcome measures showed negligible differences.

The fact that most instruments which assess perceptions have different forms for assessing actual and preferred conditions and forms for teachers and students permits investigation of differences between students' and teachers' perceptions, and differences between the actual situation and that preferred by students or teachers. Fisher and Fraser's (1983) research revealed that, first, students preferred a more positive classroom environment than they perceived as being actually present and, second, teachers perceived a more positive classroom environment than did their students in the same classrooms. These results replicate studies in school classrooms in the United States, Israel, and Australia (Fraser in press), as well as in other settings such as hospital wards and work milieus (e.g., Moos 1974).

In a study by Wubbels et al. (1992) in the Netherlands, the majority of teachers (70%) perceived the classroom environment more favorably than their students. However, the perceptions of another group of teachers (30%) were more negative than those of their students. Overall, this study suggested that teacher perceptions are shaped partly by their ideals about the learning environment (i.e., teachers' ideals can distort their perceptions of the actual learning environment). The discrepancy between teachers' and students' perceptions on average was larger for teachers who exhibited fewer behaviors that promoted student cognitive and affective outcomes than for teachers who exhibited more of those behaviors.

The third group of studies reviewed by Fraser (1986) shows that researchers in various countries have used students' perceptions as criterion variables in studies aimed at identifying how perceptions vary with such factors as teacher personality, class size, grade level, student gender, subject matter, the nature of the school-level environment, and the type of school. Studies into the transition from elementary to high school in the United States have revealed a deterioration in the perceived classroom environment when students move from generally smaller elementary schools to larger, departmentally organized lower secondary schools (Midgley et al. 1991). This decline could be attributable to less positive student relations with teachers and reduced student opportunities for decision-making in the classroom.

3. *Associations Between Student Perceptions and Student Outcomes*

A strong tradition in past research (Haertel et al. 1981) has shown that student perceptions of classroom environment account for appreciable amounts of variance in cognitive and affective learning outcomes, often beyond that attributable to background student characteristics. The practical implication from this research is that student outcomes might be improved by creating classroom environments found empirically to be conducive to learning.

Fraser (in press) has tabulated a set of 40 studies in which the effects of student perceptions of their classrooms on student outcomes were investigated in numerous countries. These studies involved a variety of cognitive and affective outcome measures, student perception instruments, and samples of students from a variety of grade levels.

The findings from prior research are highlighted in the results of a meta-analysis involving 734 correlations from 12 studies including 823 classes in eight subject areas containing 17,805 students in four nations (Haertel et al. 1981). Learning posttest scores and gains were found consistently and strongly to be associated with student perceptions of their classrooms, although correlations generally were higher in samples of older students and in studies employing collectivities such as classes and schools (in contrast to individual students) as the units of statistical analysis. In particular, higher achievement on a variety of measures was found in classes perceived by students as having greater cohesiveness, satisfaction, and goal direction, and less disorganization and friction. In a study of science laboratory classes in Nigeria, Israel, the United Kingdom, Canada, the United States, and Australia, students' perceptions were more positive in settings in which integration between theory and laboratory classes was perceived to be greater (Fraser et al. 1992).

Fraser and Fisher (1983) used a person–environment interaction framework in exploring whether or not student outcomes depend, not only on student perceptions of the actual classroom environment, but also on the match between students' preferences and the actual environment. Overall, the findings suggest that similarity between actual and preferred environment could be as important as the actual environment in predicting student achievement of important affective and cognitive aims.

4. Current Trends and Desirable Future Directions

While speculations on numerous trends and directions can be offered, three topics are treated briefly in this section. They are school psychology, constructivist learning environments, and personal forms of scales.

4.1 School Psychology

Given the school psychologist's changing role, the work on student perceptions of classrooms provides a good example of an area that furnishes a number of ideas, techniques, and research findings that could be valuable in school psychology. Traditionally, school psychologists have tended to concentrate heavily and sometimes exclusively on their roles in assessing and enhancing academic achievement and other valued learning outcomes. Understanding student perceptions of classrooms enables school psychologists to become sensitized to subtle but important aspects of classroom life. Burden and Fraser (in press) report some ways in which students' perceptions were used in the United Kingdom in helping teachers change their classroom interactive styles, and in using discrepancies between students' perceptions of actual and preferred environment as an effective basis to guide improvements in their classrooms.

4.2 Constructivist Learning Environments

Traditionally, teachers have conceived their roles to be concerned with revealing or transmitting the logical structures of their knowledge, and directing students through rational inquiry toward discovering the predetermined universal truths expressed in the form of laws, principles, rules, and algorithms. Developments in history, philosophy, and sociology have provided educators with a better understanding of the nature of knowledge development. At the level of the individual learner, there has been a realization that meaningful learning is a cognitive process of making sense, or purposeful problem-solving, of the experiential world of the individual in relation to the totality of the individual's already constructed knowledge. This sense-making process involves active negotiation and consensus building. Because a new learning environment instrument is needed to assist researchers to assess the degree to which a particular classroom's environment is perceived by students to be consistent with a constructivist epistemology, and in order to assist teachers to reflect on their epistemological assumptions and reshape their teaching practice, the Constructivist Learning Environment Survey (CLES) was developed. The CLES includes four scales: autonomy, prior knowledge, collaboration, and reflection (Taylor and Fraser 1991).

4.3 Personal Forms of Student Perception Scales

There is potentially a major problem with nearly all existing classroom environment instruments when used to identify differences between subgroups within a classroom (e.g., boys and girls) or in the construction of case studies of individual students. The problem is that items are worded in such a way that they elicit an individual student's perceptions of the class as a whole, as distinct from that student's perceptions of his or her own role within the classroom. For example, items in the traditional class form of classroom environment instruments might seek students' opinions about whether "the work of the class is difficult" or whether "the teacher is friendly toward the class." In contrast, a personal form of the same items would seek opinions about whether "I find the work of the class difficult" or whether "the teacher is friendly toward me."

A vivid example of the way in which certain subgroups of students within a class perceived different subenvironments because of the teacher's differential treatment of them is provided by a study of "target" students (i.e., pupils who monopolized the verbal interaction during whole-class activities) (see Fraser in press). It was found that target students perceived significantly greater levels of involvement and rule clarity than did nontarget students. Furthermore, these perceptions were consistent with classroom observations that the teachers directed more questions at target students and allowed them (and not other students) to call out answers without being asked. Similarly, Tobin et al.'s (1990) case studies of individual students revealed that meaningful differences in perceptions existed between certain students, and that those differences were consistent with the teacher's expectations of and attitudes toward individuals. The findings of these two studies highlight the need for a new generation of student perception instruments which are more capable of detecting the differences in perceptions between individuals or subgroups within the class.

Fraser et al. (1992) developed and validated parallel class and personal forms of both an actual and preferred version of the Science Laboratory Environment Inventory (SLEI), and reported three uses of the new personal form. First, students' perceptions on the class form were found to be systematically more favorable than their scores on the personal form, perhaps suggesting that students have a more detached view of the classroom as it applies to the class as a whole. Second, as hypothesized, gender differences in perceptions were somewhat larger on the personal form than on the class form. Third, although a study of associations between students' outcomes and their perceptions of the science laboratory revealed that the magnitudes of associations were comparable for class and personal forms, commonality analyses showed that each form accounted for appreciable amounts of outcome variance which was independent of that explained by the other form. This finding serves to justify the decision to evolve separate class and personal forms.

5. Conclusion

Outcome measures alone cannot provide a complete picture of the educational process, so student perceptions of classrooms also should be used to provide information about subtle but important aspects of classroom life. However, because teachers and students have systematically different perceptions of the learning environments of the same classrooms (the "rose-colored glasses" phenomenon), student feedback about classrooms is important in teacher education, staff development, and school improvement efforts.

See also: Classroom Environments; Classroom Culture and Social Organization, Anthropological Study of; Classroom Assessment

References

Burden R, Fraser B J in press Use of classroom environment assessments in school psychology: A British perspective. *Psychol. Sch.*

Fisher D L, Fraser B J 1983 A comparison of actual and preferred classroom environment as perceived by science teachers and students. *J. Res. Sci. Teach.* 20(1): 55–61

Fraser B J 1986 *Classroom Environment.* Croom Helm, London

Fraser B J in press Classroom and school climate. In: Gabel D (ed.) in press *Handbook of Research on Science Teaching and Learning.* National Association for Research in Science Teaching, Washington, DC

Fraser B J, Fisher D L 1983 Student achievement as a function of person–environment fit: A regression surface analysis. *Br. J. Educ. Psychol.* 53(1): 89–99

Fraser B J, Walberg H J (eds.) 1991 *Educational Environments: Evaluation, Antecedents and Consequences.* Pergamon Press, Oxford

Fraser B J, Giddings G J, McRobbie C J 1992 Assessment of the psychological environment of university science laboratory classrooms: A cross-national study. *Higher Ed.* 24: 431–51

Haertel G D, Walberg H J, Haertel E H 1981 Socio-psychological environments and learning: A quantitative synthesis. *Br. Educ. Res. J.* 7(1): 27–36

Meece J L, Courtney D P 1992 Gender differences in students' perceptions: Consequences for achievement-related choices. In: Schunk D H, Meece J L (eds.) 1992

Midgley C, Eccles J S, Feldlaufer H 1991 Classroom environment and the transition to junior high school. In: Fraser B J, Walberg H J (eds.) 1991

Moos R H 1974 *The Social Climate Scales: An Overview.* Consulting Psychologists Press, Palo Alto, California

Moos R H, Trickett E J 1987 *Classroom Environment Scale Manual*, 2nd. edn. Consulting Psychologists Press, Palo Alto, California

Schunk D H, Meece J L (eds.) 1992 *Student Perceptions in the Classroom.* Erlbaum, Hillsdale, New Jersey

Taylor P C, Fraser B J 1991 Development of an instrument for assessing constructivist learning environments. Paper presented at the annual meeting of the American Educational Research Association, Chicago, Illinois

Tobin K, Kahle J B, Fraser B J (eds.) 1990 *Windows into Science Classrooms: Problems Associated with Higher-level Cognitive Learning.* Falmer Press, London

Welch W W, Walberg H J 1972 A national experiment in curriculum evaluation. *Am. Educ. Res. J.* 9(3): 373–83

Wittrock M C 1986 Students' thought processes. In: Wittrock M C (ed.) 1986 *Handbook of Research on Teaching*, 3rd. edn. Macmillan, New York

Wubbels T, Brekelmans M, Hooymayers H P 1992 Do teacher ideals distort the self-reports of their interpersonal behavior? *Teaching and Teacher Education* 8(1): 47–58

Further Reading

Raudenbush S, Bryk A S 1986 A hierarchical model of studying school effects. *Sociol. Educ.* 59(1): 1–17

B. J. Fraser

Student Political Activism and Student Movements

Students have been important political actors in many countries and in many circumstances. Most student activism has taken place at the postsecondary level, and this entry will deal mainly with student political activism in colleges and universities. However, students have occasionally been politically involved in secondary schools as well. Student activism and student political organizations have had an immense and often ignored impact, not only on students and student cultures but also on academic institutions and sometimes on society. The most visible student organizations are activist political movements, which have received considerable attention, particularly in the aftermath of the volatile 1960s. Activist movements have not only had a significant impact on universities, but have occasionally created social unrest and sometimes revolution. However, there are many kinds of less dramatic student organizations, ranging from cultural and social organizations (including fraternities and sororities) to student publications and newspapers and athletic groups. This entry is mainly concerned with those organizations that have an impact on politics, culture, and society. It does not deal with the purely social element of extracurricular life, although for many students this is the most important aspect, or with the changing attitudes and values of students, which may influence the scope and nature of organizational life. It focuses on the organizational aspects of extracurricular life in higher education and stresses those parts that have a wider impact on both the university and society (Horowitz 1987).

The university is a particularly favorable environment for the development of organizations and movements among students. There is an active environment that stresses independent thought and analysis and intellectual values, theories, and ideals, that may call into question established social and political norms. University faculty, through their teaching and research, may also provide an atmosphere that legitimates dissent. It is the case, for example, that professors are often to the left of the broader society in their attitudes about politics and culture (Basu 1981).

In many countries, university authorities encourage extracurricular activities and organizations, often providing funds and space for them. There is a recognition that such activities are an important part of the experience of higher education and that the academic culture goes beyond the classroom. Universities are in most instances "age-graded" cultures where the majority of students are of a similar age and at a stage in life when they seek a sense of community. The academic culture also allows a considerable amount of free time to engage in extracurricular activities (Ben-David and Zloczower 1962). It is easy to communicate when students are centered on a campus. It should be kept in mind that the total combined membership of student groups is in almost all instances a minority, albeit significant, of the student population. Even in times of considerable politicization and activism, student involvement generally remains a minority phenomenon.

Academic communities also have some special characteristics that affect the nature of organizations and movements. Student generations are short, generally lasting 3 or 4 years, and thus it is sometimes a challenge to keep movements, and to a lesser extent organizations, alive through student generations. Students tend to be impatient, wanting change quickly, due in part to the brevity of student generations and in part to a certain impatience normal in young people. Students, especially in political organizations, tend to seek total solutions and be impatient with compromise. As Shils and others have pointed out, students are often antinomian—opposed to established authority—regardless of the perspectives of those in power (Shils 1969 pp. 1–34).

It is difficult to estimate the scope of student organizational involvement in different academic environments. Participation varies according to institutional tradition, period of time, facilities, and other factors. Even within a country, organizational participation may vary considerably. In the United States, elite colleges and universities with largely full-time and residential student populations generally have a higher level of involvement than "commuter schools" that attract many part-time and employed students who have little time for extracurricular activities. In many countries, there are few facilities available for organizational activities and this limits participation. There are also variations according to historical circumstances. During periods of considerable political consciousness, students tend to be involved in activist campus movements, swelling the numbers participating in organizations.

The impact of students on both university and society is often overlooked. This impact goes far beyond student political activist movements that have threatened governments. Student organizations are a major influence on the campus culture and ethos. They help to determine the self-image of the student body and strongly influence the ideas that permeate the institution. Student groups shape the political and cultural ideas of the institution as much as the faculty and curriculum. Student organizations influence and sometimes control the rules and regulations that govern campus life. For example, student opposition to *in loco parentis* in the United States at the end of the 1950s and in the 1960s forced academic institutions to give up many of the rules and regulations that governed student conduct (Horowitz 1987). In Western Europe, student reaction against deteriorating conditions during the rapid expansion of the 1960s led to significant reforms of higher education at this time (Altbach 1974). In West Germany and a few other countries, student ideas about the nature of reform had an impact on the dramatic changes that took place in many German universities at the time (Nitsch et al. 1965). Student unrest in India has led to the canceling of examinations and other major changes in academic routines. The existence of active political and social organizations, as well as organizations such as fraternities and sororities, on campus can affect the opinions of the entire student body.

1. Multifaceted Student Organizational Culture

While national and institutional student cultures vary significantly, it is worth pointing out the scope of student organizations that exist on many campuses throughout the world.

1.1 Student Newspapers and Publications

Student newspapers and other publications are highly significant organizations on most campuses. Student newspapers are sometimes completely independent of administrative control, in some cases even being published off-campus or by independent companies. They are generally the most important means of communication among students and an outlet for student opinion on a variety of topics. Newspapers may be daily or published less frequently. Some are highly professional, while others are not. In many countries, experience in campus journalism often leads to a career in journalism. There are wide variations in the nature and scope of student newspapers. Some are highly political, seeking to convince the student body of a specific political position or ideology. Some seek to provide information about campus issues while others focus on national and international matters as well as university-based issues. Student newspapers generally constitute an organizational culture for those serving on the staff. Student newspapers also exist in secondary schools, although they are naturally less professional and in most instances more directly controlled by school authorities. However, secondary school newspapers often constitute a distinct subculture, frequently with political or cultural overtones. Students involved in the campus press often work long hours and find that the newspaper is an all-consuming activity.

Other student publications are also an important part of campus life. In the United States, most colleges and universities and many secondary schools publish yearbooks, featuring stories and pictures concerning campus life. Such books are designed, written, and frequently published by student groups. Many journals and other ephemeral publications appear from time to time on campuses, usually established and edited by students. Such publications may be political, cultural, or devoted to other pursuits. Student literary journals have a long-standing tradition in many countries and sometimes serve as the source of original intellectual work. As with newspapers, the student groups involved in editing such journals are generally close-knit and active.

The student press cannot be overestimated as an important part of the organizational culture of a campus. Not only do such publications constitute a key means of communicating but they are also among the largest and most active student organizations. Newspapers can influence the campus, and other publications provide an outlet for creative writing. Student publications are among the most visible element of student organizational culture. They tend to be active even when other organizations may be dormant and can, if inclined, maintain a sense of political or social awareness in a university without overt activism. While student newspapers and other publications in secondary schools are less visible than those in higher education, they are often important, especially as a means of creating a sense of community among highly motivated students.

1.2 Fraternities and Sororities

Although limited to a relatively small number of countries, fraternities and sororities are important elements of student life. These organizations have been especially important in the United States and Germany, although their tradition goes back to medieval times. The tradition of students banding together for both social and living purposes dates back to the medieval "nations," or student communities based on country of origin in the medieval universities (Cobban 1975). In Germany, the *burschenshaften* (fraternities) have traditionally been an important part of German academic life, providing a social core to a highly fragmented academic culture. The traditional *burschenshaften* were conservative in culture and politics and often played a role in campus political affairs. They were also highly nationalistic and were a significant influence in the rise of German nationalism in the nineteenth century.

The United States fraternities and sororities provide a place to live on campus as well as a social focus for their student members. They tend to be relatively homogenous in membership, often in an effort to provide a congenial and unthreatening home for students challenged by a complex academic environment. Fraternities and sororities have seldom been overtly political in orientation, although they reflect conservative values and orientations. The "Greek movement," as the fraternities and sororities call themselves (because they have given themselves names based on letters in the Greek alphabet), has a long history in United States higher education, dating from the early nineteenth century (Allmendinger 1975). They have tended to play a more central part in campus life during relatively conservative periods. For example, their popularity declined significantly during the radical 1960s. Nonetheless, "Greeks" have been an important element in the student culture of most residential colleges and unversities and they remain active, although less important in the 1990s than in the 1950s and earlier. Relatively few other countries have significant fraternity–sorority movements. In most countries, students either live privately away from the campus or in dormitories. Fraternities and sororities are extremely rare in secondary schools.

1.3 Religious Organizations

In many countries, religious organizations constitue an important part of student life in higher education but seldom in secondary schools. In the United States, for example, religious organizations representing virtually every major and many minor denominations and religions can be found at most large universities and colleges. These groups not only provide a spiritual focus for students but often provide a social center as well. Some religious organizations also have a political orientation. In the United States, fundamentalist Christian groups have been politically active against the legalization of abortion. At earlier periods, liberal Protestant organizations were at the forefront of civil rights and other progressive causes. Religious groups are also active in other countries.

In India, nationalist-oriented Hindu organizations have been active in the universities and have involved large numbers of students in both religious and political activities as well as programs to assist the poor. In the Islamic world, fundamentalist Muslim groups have been among the strongest political influences in the universities and in some instances in society as well. The Islamic student movement is especially influential at the end of the twentieth century, dominating student political life in many Islamic countries. Islamic student organizations are powerful not only in higher education but also in secondary schools in many countries. The Islamic student movement constitutes a religious, cultural, and political force.

1.4 Student Unions and Governments

In most countries, students are organized into governmental structures to represent their interests and provide services at both the higher and the secondary levels. In some countries, there are national student unions that have both political and service functions as well as local student unions in individual universities. Generally, national student unions are federations of university-based student governments, which are in turn generally elected by the students. At times, national student unions have played an important national political role in influencing higher education policy and defending student interests (Fields 1970). National student unions, especially in Europe, have traditionally provided services to students such as low-cost travel arrangements.

Student governments or unions at individual universities and in many secondary schools often control a significant budget and provide services such as food, entertainment, reduced price tickets, and transportation. Student governments also represent student interests to the university and often appoint student representatives to academic committees and governing boards. At times, student governments have played significant political roles as well (Levine 1980). In the United States, institution-based student governments sometimes reflect broader political concerns and often are thrust into a political role by campus events. In some cases, candidates for office have specifically political platforms, although in general overt politics are not part of the culture of student governments in the United States.

In other countries, student governments are often more politically involved and elections often have a political aura. In India and other countries, established political parties run candidates in student government elections and sometimes spend considerable amounts of money on campus to ensure that their candidates are elected. While less frequent, student governments in secondary schools sometimes play an important political role, especially in countries with very small higher education sectors. In a number of African countries, for example, secondary school student governments have sometimes been active in politics.

1.5 Cultural Organizations

Culture and politics are sometimes mixed on campus. For example, nationalist student organizations have often had a cultural component and sometimes emerged from cultural groups. Groups focusing on "countercultural" activities—certain kinds of music or art and, for example in Eastern European countries, underground literature—often have a significant political as well as cultural function. Even when not overtly political, cultural organizations are an important force in most universities. Groups dealing with literature, drama, dance, and other forms of cultural expression involve many students, often providing both training and socialization for later careers.

2. Student Political Activism

Student politics is an important element of student organizations and movements. Political activism on campus is central because it has the greatest potential for affecting both the university and society. Activist movements have caused governments to topple and on a few occasions have implemented significant university reform (Walter 1968). These organizations involve highly motivated students, some of who become important in national politics. Activist movements tend to be among the best organized groups that are able to obtain very strong commitments from the students who are involved in them (Lipset 1976). It must be kept in mind, however, that student activist organizations are minority phenomena, involving a very small number of students in sustained organizational activity. Even when there are mass demonstrations on campus, those involved in them are generally a minority of the student body. This fact does not make student activist movements unimportant, but their scope and nature must be kept in careful perspective (Altbach 1989 pp. 97–110).

Activist movements are almost all oppositional in nature, opposing established governmental authority, university administrators, or others in authority. While most contemporary student movements are on the left in terms of their ideologies and politics, events in Eastern Europe, where students played a central role against Communist authorities, and in the Islamic world, where religious fundamentalism is currently the most potent political force on campus, indicate that there is no one universal student political orientation. Student political movements are both complex and highly significant to both the university and society.

2.1 Historical Perspectives

Student movements have a long history, and in many

countries this historical tradition is part of the living memory of contemporary organizations. The involvement of students in the nationalist upsurge in Europe in the nineteenth century was very significant. German nationalist ideas percolated in the universities before becoming a key political force in society. Both students and professors played a central role in the nationalist uprisings of 1848 (Altbach 1969 pp. 451–74). Students were similarly active in the Italian nationalist movement, and in both cases were important in social movements that resulted in significant change in Europe.

Nationalist ideas spread to student movements emerging in the colonial areas of Africa and Asia and students emerged as key forces for independence in much of what is now the Third World (Emmerson 1968). For example, students from the Dutch East Indies studying at universities in the Netherlands in the first several decades of the twentieth century were exposed to nationalist ideas and created the concept of an Indonesian nation. Former student leaders such as Sukarno and Hatta became the most important leaders of the nationalist movement that eventually drove the Dutch from Indonesia and created a new nation (Bachtiar 1968 pp. 180–214). The role of Indonesian students was crucial not only in developing the ideas of the nationalist movement but later in the struggle against the Dutch. Students were a central force in the Indian nationalist movement as well. Ideas of nationalism, Marxism, and secularism were part of the Indian student experience while in the United Kingdom. Western-oriented universities in India also imparted nationalist orientations. Student movements emerged during the 1920s and were active in the struggle for independence that culminated in the departure of the British in 1947. Significantly, Indian student organizations were always situated on the left of the nationalist movement, often in opposition to the tactics of Gandhi (Altbach 1968). The traditions of student activism, established during the independence struggle in both Indonesia and India, continued after Independence and remain active in the early 1990s.

Historically, secondary schools have played a significant political role, although their importance has been overshadowed by university-based activism. In many colonial countries, the higher education sector was extremely small or even absent, and in these cases high schools often were hotbeds of nationalist political ferment. During the colonial period in Africa, where there were few post-secondary institutions, high-school students were often involved in nationalist agitation. There are similar examples in many Asian countries.

Late twentieth-century student movements are, for the most part, leftist. This has not always been the case. In fact, the nationalist influences of European student movements turned some of them to the right during the period after the First World War. In Germany, the major student organizations supported the Nazis both before and after Hitler came to power (Steinberg 1977). There were, of course, many student groups that opposed the Nazis as well. Similarly, in Italy the largest student groups supported Mussolini's Fascist movement. In France there was strong support in the universities for rightist nationalist movements during this period.

Another important historical example of student political activism is the significant student movement that emerged in Latin America in the first decades of the twentieth century, and which succeeded in virtually transforming Latin American higher education by forcing the adoption of far-reaching reforms (Walter 1968). The movement started in Argentina at the University of Cordoba and spread quickly throughout the continent, affecting the major institutions from Mexico in the north, to Chile in the south. The *reforma* established student participation in virtually all elements of academic decision-making, from the election of the rector to important curricular decisions. It also enshrined the notion of the university as an autonomous institution that could claim not only the freedom to control academic decisions but whose campus could not be entered by civil authority without the formal permission of university officials. The *reforma* fundamentally changed Latin American higher education and its impact has continued to the early 1990s, although since the early 1970s severe political and economic pressures, military regimes, and the growth of private universities have weakened the power of the *reforma* ideals (Levy 1986).

Student movements are usually sporadic, seldom lasting very long. Even countries with high levels of activism exhibit considerable variation in levels of involvement and in the strength of student movements. It is to some extent possible to chart international trends in student political activism. The volatile 1960s were clearly a time of worldwide activism, and there were some international influences involved, although it seems clear that national student movements are largely motivated by national concerns.

The historical development of the United States student movement indicates the sporadic nature of student politics (Altbach 1974). While there was some campus unrest before the 1930s (including antislavery and then antidraft agitation in the period of the Civil War), the first major student movement emerged during the Depression of the 1930s, stimulated as much by foreign policy concerns (such as the civil war in Spain and a desire to keep the United States out of the Second World War) as by the economic crisis of the period. There was very little activism between 1941 and 1960. During the 1960s, student activism was stimulated by both the civil rights movement (started by Black college students in the south) and growing opinion on campus against the arms race. Escalation of the war in Vietnam brought student activism to its highest level of activity, culminating in nationwide campus disruptions and mass demonstrations in Washington, DC at the end of the decade. Once the war in Vietnam ended, campus activism declined to a very low level during the 1970s, with a minor resurgence of political interest in the late 1980s (Altbach and Cohen 1990 pp. 32–49). Similar fluctuations can be seen in student movements in other industrialized nations, although the reasons and the timing of course vary according to national, or even local, political and academic circumstances.

Historical consciousness is also important because countries that have a strong tradition of activism tend to see campus movements as more legitimate political actors than countries that have relatively weak activist traditions. It is particularly clear that where students played an important role in the shaping of national history, as in the Third World, activist movements are accepted as legitimate participants in the national political scene. In most Western countries, students have not been involved in key political events and, partly for this reason, are not generally accepted as actors on a societal political stage.

2.2 Ideological Variations

While most of the student activist movements of the post-Second World War period have been to one degree or another on the left, student movements in the 1990s show a significant, and perhaps widening, ideological range. It has been pointed out that there is considerable historical variety in student ideologies. The nationalist impulse, important historically, is difficult to characterize ideologically. Without question, nationalism continues to be an important force. The same is true of religion, particularly when it is combined with nationalism. The growth of Islamic fundamentalism as a powerful political force in the universities of the Islamic world is one of the major developments in student politics worldwide since the start of the 1980s.

It is difficult to characterize ideologically the extraordinarily important political role played by student activists in the political upheaval in Eastern Europe and to some extent in China in the late 1980s. Students were the primary motivating force in the political movement that led up to the Tiananmen Square massacre in June 1989 (Liu 1989 pp. 31–46). Chinese students seem to have been motivated by a desire for better jobs, complaints against corruption, and a demand for more democracy and freedom of expression. The students did not seem to have a clear perspective concerning their place in the ideological spectrum.

The role of students in the successful upheavals in Eastern Europe at the end of 1989 is clear. In every country (except perhaps Rumania), university students and professors were the first important groups to protest against the government, and students often articulated and to an extent shaped the discontent felt by large numbers of people in those countries. Students were in part motivated by nationalism—a desire to see their countries free of external (Soviet) influence. A desire for freedom of expression and representative government also played an important role. The students were protesting against regimes that were unsuccessful in meeting the economic needs of the people. These demands are certainly anti-regime, and as been noted above, student movements tend in virtually all cases to be against established authority, but it is not clear whether the movements are on the left or on the right. The movements seem to be "anti-statist" in terms of the control of the economy, but it is not at all clear that they are "pro-capitalist." The ideological pedigree of several of the most important student activist movements of the postwar period is unclear. It is perhaps significant that these student movements became much less prominent and active in the aftermath of the collapse of the Communist regimes in Central and Eastern Europe.

Islamic fundamentalism is without question the most powerful force among students in Islamic countries. In countries such as Iran, Egypt, Algeria, and Malaysia, student movements that were at one time highly secularist and often leftist in orientation have been transformed into Islamic movements. The underlying reasons for this dramatic change have yet to be analyzed, but the phenomenon is clear. The failure of secular-minded governments throughout the Islamic world to achieve their goals of modernization, the continuing challenge of the Arab–Israeli conflict, and the breakdown of traditional values and the absence of widely accepted new norms may have all contributed to the rise of Islamic fundamentalism. So far, only Iran has become a fundamentalist state, although governments in many other countries from Malaysia to Algeria have become more religious in their orientation. These governments are also worried about political stability and about the future of the educated elite in the context of the new trend in the universities. There is no doubt that the power of the Islamic idea will remain a key force in the Islamic world.

Students have often tended to adhere to an all-encompassing ideology and to seek massive social change in an effort to create a utopian society. The rise of the Islamic movement may reflect such goals. More commonly in the twentieth century, students have looked to ideologies of the left to provide the path to a more perfect social order. The impact of Marxism and other socialist ideas has been perhaps the most important influence on student movements around the world (Levitt 1984). During the 1960s, virtually all the powerful student movements of the period identified with the left and very often with Marxism, but without adherence to the Soviet Union or any other communist movement. There has been significant change since the 1960s, and the appeal of leftist alternatives has diminished.

The ideological orientation of student movements is less clear at the end of the twentieth century than it has been since the 1940s. The "failure" of countries identified with socialism to build just and successful societies, the rebirth of nationalism in many countries, the continuing problems of modernization and development in the Third World, and new issues such as the environment have all contributed to a lack of clarity concerning the ideological underpinnings of student activist movements.

2.3 Sociological Generalizations

While the research literature on student political movements is limited, relatively little is known about the backgrounds and motivations of student activists in most countries, and it is only possible to speculate about the causes of student unrest, some sociological generalizations are possible (Klineberg et al. 1979). While there are some counterexamples, the following generalizations reflect the realities of many countries in the 1990s. Although very little is known about secondary school activism, there is some evidence that the generalizations noted here, based on research on university students, are applicable to high-school students as well.

Student activists come largely from the social sciences and to some extent from the humanities. Fields such as sociology and political science produce a significant proportion of student leaders. The content of the curriculum in these fields may contribute to an interest in activism; the social sciences are concerned with the problems of society. There is probably a degree of self-selection involved as well, with students who have an interest in social issues gravitating to disciplines that focus on these questions. Further, professors in these fields tend to be among the most liberal or radical in the university, no doubt contributing to such attitudes and values among students (Ladd and Lipset 1975). The intellectual atmosphere in the social sciences is more congenial to activism in both thought and action. At the other end of the activist spectrum, highly vocational fields such as management and agriculture tend to be much more conservative in terms of the attitudes of both faculty and students; the curriculum is vocationally focused as well. The culture of such fields does not seem to promote either radical ideologies or a tendency to become involved in activist movements.

Activist students have some common characteristics. Not surprisingly, they are more politically conscious and concerned about ideological issues than the majority of students. They tend to come from families with a higher level of income and education than the average student population. Students in most countries come from significantly more affluent families than the general population. The educational background of the parents tends to be much higher than average, and very often the political attitudes of the families of activists are to the left of the general population. Thus, activist students are very often from highly elite groups in their societies—groups that have benefited from existing societal arrangements. Activists tend to come from urban and cosmopolitan families. This is a key variable in developing countries where the majority of the population is rural and relatively uneducated. During the 1960s, much was made of a perceived "generational conflict" between student activists and their families (Feuer 1969). However, the data show that there is relatively little conflict among activists and their families (Keniston 1971).

3. Conclusion

It is said that students learn as much outside the classroom as in it during their university years. Without question student organizational culture plays an extraordinarily important role in the collegiate experience of students. Student groups provide socialization, give students a sense of belonging in what can be a difficult and sometimes alienating environment, and set up networks of support that often last throughout life and provide valuable skills.

The organizational network in most colleges and universities is highly complex and dense. Few realize how many student groups exist on campus or how they affect students. In the 1990s, as university authorities have yielded control over extracurricular activities to students, there is probably less concern about the nature of extracurricular organizational life than in the past, at least in the United States. Student organizations range from overtly political groups to purely social associations. Religion, culture, athletics, self-improvement, and aspects of the academic curriculum are all represented by such groups. The growing numbers of foreign students have their own nationality-based associations. In some cases, these groups are not very active and have only small numbers of participants. Other student groups are large and have significant budgets.

Student organizational culture varies from country to country and among academic institutions within a country. Traditionally, European universities have not had as strong a network of extracurricular organizations as United States universities. European students are older than their United States compeers and, except in the United Kingdom, there are few traditions of organized extracurricular life. In developing countries, there is often a large number of student groups, ranging from radical political movements to many social and religious organizations. There are also frequently more controls by campus administrators. There are significant variations within countries. In the United States, for example, student organizational life varies significantly from being very active in residential institutions to being much less dense in commuter schools and community colleges. Some institutions place emphasis on political organizations while others have a more active religious life.

The nature of both student culture and student political activism in secondary schools is much less clear everywhere. Except in periods of significant social unrest, secondary school students are generally not involved directly in politics. There are some exceptions to this generalization. For example, high school students were involved in the cultural revolution in China (Lin 1991, Chan 1985) and students have been sporadically involved in politics in some African countries where there are few university students. The relationship between political education and socialization in secondary schools and political activism is unclear (Massialas 1972).

This entry has focused significantly on political organizations and movements because they tend to be the most visible and vocal and they have had the greatest direct impact on both the educational system and society. Yet in terms of numbers of students involved or perhaps even in long-term effect on those involved in student organizations, activist movements are not necessarily the most important. The entire nexus of organizations and their different constituencies and functions are among the most important elements of contemporary academic life.

See also: Youth Cultures and Subcultures

References

Allmendinger D F 1975 *Paupers and Scholars: The Transformation of Student Life in Nineteenth Century New England*. St. Martins, New York

Altbach E 1969 Vanguard of revolt: Students and politics in Central Europe, 1815–1948. In: Lipset S M, Altbach P (eds.) 1969 *Students in Revolt*. Beacon, Boston, Massachusetts

Altbach P (ed.) 1968 *Turmoil and Transition: Higher Education and Student Politics in India*. Basic Books, New York

Altbach P 1974a *Student Politics in America: A Historical Analysis*. McGraw-Hill, New York

Altbach P 1989a Perspectives on student political activism. *Comp. Educ.* 25: 97–110

Altbach P, Cohen R 1990 American student activism: The post-sixties transformation. *J. Higher Educ.* 61: 32–49

Bachtiar H 1968 Indonesia. In: Emmerson D (ed.) 1968 *Students and Politics in Developing Nations*. Praeger, New York

Basu A 1981 *Culture, Politics and Critical Academics*. Archana, Meerut

Ben-David J, Zloczower A 1962 Universities and academic systems in modern societies. *European Journal of Sociology* 3(1): 45–84

Chan A 1985 *Children of Mao: Personality Development and Political Activism in the Red Guard Generation*. Macmillan, London

Cobban A B 1975 *The Medieval Universities: Their Development and Organization*. Methuen, London

Emmerson D (ed.) 1968 *Students and Politics in Developing Nations*. Praeger, New York

Feuer L 1969 *The Conflict of Generations: The Character and Significance of Student Movements*. Basic Books, New York

Fields A B 1970 *Student Politics in France: A study of the Union Nationale des Etudiants de France*. Heinemann Educational, London

Horowitz H L 1987 *Campus Life: Undergraduate Cultures from the End of the Eighteenth Century to the Present*. University of Chicago Press, Chicago, Illinois

Keniston K 1971 *Youth and Dissent: The Rise of a New Opposition*. Harcourt Brace Jovanovich, New York

Klineberg O, Zavaloni M, Louis-Guerin L, Benbrika J 1979 *Students, Values and Politics: A Cross-cultural Comparison*. Free Press, New York

Ladd E C, Lipset S M 1975 *The Divided Academy: Professor and Politics*. McGraw-Hill, New York

Levitt C 1984 *Children of Privilege: Student Revolt in the Sixties*. University of Toronto Press, Toronto

Levine A 1980 *When Dreams and Heroes Died: A Portrait of Today's College Student*. Jossey-Bass, San Francisco, California

Levy D 1986 *Higher Education and the State in Latin America: Private Challenges to Public Dominance*. University of Chicago Press, Chicago, Illinois

Lin J 1991 *The Red Guards' Path to Violence: Political, Educational and Psychological Factors*. Praeger, New York

Liu S C 1989 The 1989 Peking student pro-democracy movement in retrospect. *Issues and Studies* 25:31–46

Massialas B (ed.) 1972 *Political Youth, Traditional Schools: National and International Perspectives*. Prentice Hall, Englewood Cliffs, New Jersey

Nitsch W et al. 1965 *Hochschule in der Demokratie*. Luchterhand, Berlin

Shils E 1969 Dreams of plentitude, nightmares of scarcity. In: Lipset S M, Altbach P G (eds.) 1969 *Students in Revolt*. Beacon, Boston, Massachusetts

Steinberg M S 1977 *Sabers and Brown Shirts: The German Students' Path to National Socialism, 1918–1935*. University of Chicago Press, Chicago, Illinois

Walter R J 1968 *Student Politics in Argentina: The University Reform and Its Effects, 1918–1964*. Basic Books, New York

Further Reading

Altbach P (ed.) 1974b *University Reform: Comparative Perspectives for the Seventies*. Schenkman, Cambridge, Masschusetts

Altbach P (ed.) 1989b *Student Political Activism: An International Reference Handbook*. Greenwood, Westport, Connecticut

Astin A, Astin H, Bayer A, Bisconti A 1975 *The Power of Protest*. Jossey-Bass, San Francisco, California

Barkan J 1975 *An African Dilemma: University Students, Development and Politics in Ghana, Tanzania and Uganda*. Oxford University Press, Nairobi

Caute D 1988 *The Year of the Barricades: A Journey Through 1968*. Harper and Row, New York

Cerych L, Sabatier P 1986 *Great Expectations and Mixed Performance: The Implementation of Higher Education Reforms in Europe*. Trentham Books, Stoke-on-Trent

Chu D 1989 *The Character of American Higher Education and Intercollegiate Sport*. SUNY Press, Albany, New York
Fass P 1977 *The Damned and the Beautiful: American Youth in the 1920s*. Oxford University Press, Oxford
Fields A B 1989 France. In: Altbach P (ed.) 1989b
Gitlin T 1987 *The Sixties: Years of Hope. Days of Rage*. Bantam, Toronto
Hazary S C 1987 *Student Politics in India*. Ashish, New Delhi
Hendrick I G, Jones R L 1972 *Student Dissent in the Schools*. Houghton Mifflin, Boston
Jayaram N 1989 India. In: Altbach P (ed.) 1989b
Krauss E S 1974 *Japanese Radical Revisited: Student Protest in Postwar Japan*. University of California, Berkeley, California
Laqueur W 1962 *Young Germany: A History of the German Youth Movement*. Routledge and Kegan Paul, London
Liebman A, Walker K, Glazer M 1972 *Latin American University Students: A Six Nation Study*. Harvard University Press, Cambridge, Massachusetts
Lipset S M 1976 *Rebellion in the University*. University of Chicago Press, Chicago, Illinois
Touraine A 1971 (trans. Mayhew LFX) *The May Movement: Revolt and Reform*. Irvington, New York

P. G. Altbach

Student Progress, Charting of

A common approach to measuring a student's achievement is to administer a test and to record the questions he or she answers correctly. In modern test theory (see *Rasch Measurement, Theory of; Item Response Theory*), the resulting record of right and wrong answers leads to an estimate of that student's standing on an achievement continuum. This continuum is marked out and defined operationally by the test questions that students attempt and so provides a framework for charting progress over time.

This methodology is particularly appropriate if the aim of an instructional program is to provide students with a body of facts, skills, and procedures. Test questions can be written to assess the presence or absence of specific items of learning on any given occasion and students' performances on those items can be scored either right or wrong. But not all learning is a matter of absorbing and reproducing provided information. An important form of learning occurs when students change the way they conceptualize aspects of a subject. Progress occurs when a student discards a naive model or representation of a phenomenon in favor of a more expert conception. Traditional achievement tests are not well suited to the identification of the conceptions that students bring to problems. To chart progress in conceptual understanding, an alternative testing methodology is required. This entry describes recent advances in developing such a methodology.

1. Learning as an Active Process

Implicit in much of our current measurement theory and practice is a view of learners as passive absorbers of provided wisdom. Most items on standard achievement tests assess students' abilities to recall and apply facts and routines presented during instruction. Some require only the memorization of detail; they seek evidence that students have absorbed factual details presented in class and are able to reproduce these on command. Other achievement items, although supposed to assess higher-level learning outcomes like "comprehension" and "application," often require little more than the ability to recall a formula and to make appropriate substitutions to arrive at a correct answer.

Test items of this type are consistent with a view of learning as a passive, receptive process through which new facts and skills are added to a learner's repertoire in much the same way as bricks might progressively be added to a wall. The process is additive and incremental: students with the highest levels of achievement in an area are those who have absorbed and can reproduce the greatest numbers of facts and formulae. The practice of scoring answers to items of this type either "right" or "wrong" is consistent with the view that individual units of knowledge or skill are either present or absent in a learner at the time of testing. Under this approach, diagnosis is a simple matter of identifying unexpected holes or gaps in a student's store of knowledge. These are subareas of learning in which knowledge is "missing" and in which there is a need for remedial teaching to fill a deficit.

This approach to the measurement of achievement may be appropriate for some forms of learning. However, in recent decades, significant advances have occurred in our understanding of the ways in which students learn. In particular, there has been an increased awareness of the active, constructive nature of most forms of human learning and of the important role that students' personal conceptions and representations of subject matter play in the learning process. Rather than being a passive process of absorbing new material as it is encountered, meaningful learning is increasingly being recognized as an active process through which students construct their own interpretations, approaches, and ways of viewing phenomena, and through which learners relate new information to their existing knowledge and understandings. Under this view of learning, the difference between beginning and advanced learners is seen not so much as a difference in amount of factual knowledge (although this is usually an important aspect of competent performance), but as a difference in the types of conceptions and understandings that students bring to a problem, and in the strategies and approaches that they use.

Support for this view of learning can be found in recent studies in a number of areas of investigation. In cognitive science, comparisions of novices and experts in various fields of learning (Chi et al. 1981, Larkin 1983, McCloskey et al. 1980) show that expertise typically involves much more than mastery of a body of facts: experts and novices usually have very different ways of viewing phenomena and of representing and approaching problems in a field. Expert-novice studies suggest that the performances of beginning learners often can be understood in terms of the inappropriate or inefficient models that these learners have constructed for themselves.

Similar observations have been made in the field of science education (see Driver and Easley 1978, Osborne and Wittrock 1983, Posner et al. 1982). Research into students' science learning has drawn attention to the frequent mismatch between intuitive understandings that students bring to the classroom and the conceptual frameworks assumed by teachers. Caramazza et al. (1981) observe that the scientific "principles" that students abstract from everyday experience are often strikingly at variance with the most fundamental physical laws. These misunderstandings can go undetected by teachers if correct answers to test questions depend only on superficial knowledge of formulae and formula manipulation techniques (Clement 1982). There is evidence that students can succeed in high school and even college science courses while still maintaining many of their misconceptions and without acquiring an understanding of underlying principles (White and Horwitz 1987).

Related work in Sweden (Marton 1981, Dahlgren 1984, Säljö 1984) has used clinical interviews to explore the different understandings that students have of key principles and phenomena in a number of fields of learning. These interviews have revealed a range of student conceptions of each of the phenomena that these studies have explored and have illustrated the importance of forms of learning which produce "a qualitative change in a person's conception of a phenomenon" from a lower-level, more naive conception to a more expert understanding of that phenomenon (Johansson et al. 1985 p. 235).

Under this view of learning, a student is rarely considered to have no understanding or no strategy when addressing a problem. Even beginning learners are considered to be engaged in an active search for meaning, constructing and using naive representations or models of subject matter. Rather than being "wrong," these representations frequently display partial understanding and are applied rationally and consistently by the individuals who use them. In arithmetic, for example, "it has been demonstrated repeatedly that novices who make mistakes do not make them at random, but rather operate in terms of meaning systems that they hold at a given time" (Nesher 1986).

An implication of this view of learning for the assessment and monitoring of student learning is that much greater cognizance must be taken of the understandings and models that individual students construct for themselves during the learning process. In many areas of learning, levels of achievement might be better defined and measured not in terms of the number of facts and procedures that a student can reproduce, but in terms of his or her levels of understanding of key concepts and principles underlying a learning area.

2. *Conventional Achievement Testing*

Techniques for constructing achievement tests have been developed and refined over many decades. Most achievement tests begin with a statement of the instructional objectives to be assessed. According to Bloom et al. (1971 p. 28), these objectives should be stated as directly observable student behaviors which can be reliably recorded as either present or absent. They should be "stated in terms which are operational, involving reliable observation and allowing no leeway in interpretation." To achieve this degree of reliability, test constructors are encouraged to write items to assess students' abilities to perform unambiguous, observable tasks like "stating," "listing," "naming," "selecting," "recognizing," "matching," and "calculating" (Bloom et al. 1971 p. 34).

This emphasis on specifying and testing precise student behaviors has led to the construction of achievement tests composed of discrete items, each relating to a particular behavioral objective, and each scorable as either right or wrong. Multiple choice items have become especially popular in achievement tests because they can be scored quickly, unambiguously, and even by machine. In some areas of education, machine-scored multiple choice tests are now the principal mode of evaluating student learning.

The advantages of traditional achievement testing include the fact that it provides a close link between curriculum objectives which can be expressed in behavioral terms and the resulting measures of student achievement. By constructing standard conditions and establishing unambiguous right/wrong scoring rules, standardized achievement tests reduce subjectivity in assessment and provide results which are comparable over time and across students.

A potential disadvantage of conventional achievement tests is that, because of the emphasis these tests place on precisely-defined student behaviors, they can encourage students to focus their efforts on relatively superficial forms of learning. An alternative approach is to base achievement testing not on the detailed specification of many observable student behaviors each of which can be recorded as either present or absent, but on a consideration of the key concepts, principles, and phenomena that underlie a course of instruction and around which factual learning can be organized. Rather than recording students' understandings of these concepts as either "right" or "wrong," this alternative approach recognizes that learners have a variety of understandings of phenomena, and that some of these understandings are less complete than others.

3. Testing for Conceptual Understanding

An achievement testing methodology based on an active, constructive view of learning differs from more traditional approaches in that its prime focus is on revealing how individual students view and think about key concepts in a subject. Rather than comparing students' responses with a "correct" answer to a question so that each response can be scored right or wrong, the emphasis is on understanding the variety of responses that students make to a question and inferring from those responses students' levels of conceptual understanding.

One area of learning in which a great deal of work has been done to understand how students think about and approach phenomena is the area of physics education. Studies in a number of countries have explored students' understandings of such concepts as acceleration (Trowbridge and McDermott 1981); mole concept (Lybeck et al. 1988); electric charge, enthalpy and entropy, force and motion (Viennot 1979); gravitation (Champagne et al. 1980, Gunstone and White 1981); light and the transmission of heat, momentum, potential difference, proportionality, torque, and such principles and models as Newton's laws, conservation laws, the atomic model, and electron flow models for circuits.

A common technique in these studies is to use drawings of simple physical systems and to ask students to describe what is happening in each drawing (e.g., to predict what will happen to an object, to describe the forces acting on a body, or to draw the trajectory that an object will follow). During these interviews, students are asked to explain their responses and their explanations are tape recorded (Johansson et al. 1985, McCloskey 1983).

In other studies, students are asked to manipulate apparatus in a laboratory to achieve particular effects (e.g., to apply a force to make a body move in a particular direction) and students' explanations and comments have been tape recorded and transcribed (McDermott 1984). Still other researchers (e.g., diSessa 1982, White, 1983) have developed interactive software for this purpose. In these studies, students are asked to apply "forces" to simulated objects on a screen to make them move to specified positions, to speed up, to slow down, and so on.

The observations made in these studies suggest that students do not simply make random "errors" but operate in terms of naive theories about physical phenomena. In the area of force and motion, these theories can be "remarkably well articulated, . . . quite consistent across individuals, . . . and strikingly inconsistent with the fundamental principles of classical mechanics" (McCloskey 1983 p. 299). In his studies of students' attempts to control a simulated object on a screen, diSessa (1982 p. 38) found "a surprising structure of discrete and definite theories" about how forces influence motion. And, through their interviews with Swedish students about aspects of science learning, Johansson et al. (1985) arrive at a similar conclusion

> In our case, a discovery of decisive importance was that for each phenomenon, principle, or aspect of reality, the understanding of which we studied, there seemed to exist a limited number of qualitatively different conceptions of that phenomenon, principle, or aspect of reality. (Johansson et al. pp. 235–36)

A number of researchers have observed that the same naive conceptions can be found among students of different ages and with different educational backgrounds. McCloskey (1983), for example, found the same types of naive physical theories among students who had never taken physics, among high school physics students, and among college physics students. The only difference was in the frequencies of occurrence of these different understandings. McDermott (1984) reports an identical observation in a Norwegian study of high school physics students, future high school science teachers, and physics graduates.

A significant finding of these studies is that some students can succeed on traditional achievement tests and graduate from high school and even college physics courses with their naive conceptions of physical principles largely unchanged. Through their physics courses students are able to "master certain methods of calculation without having adopted the conceptualization underlying them" (Johansson et al. 1985 p. 235). Indeed, a misconception "may go undetected because a student's superficial knowledge of formulas and formula manipulation techniques can mask his or her misunderstanding of an underlying concept" (Clement 1982 p. 66). The result is that "many students emerge from their study of physics and physical science without a functional understanding of some elementary but fundamental concepts" (McDermott 1984 p. 31).

These findings invite a reconsideration of the way in which we think about and attempt to measure student learning. Clearly, many students are succeeding on precise, operationally-defined objectives without developing an understanding of the material that they are learning. For many science educators, the answer is to place greater emphasis not on the learning of scientific facts and formulae, but on changing students' ways of thinking about scientific phenomena:

> The formal learning of science can be viewed as involving, at least in part, a shift from one set of beliefs about the physical world to another, one set of conceptions to another. (Osborne and Wittrock 1983 p. 81)

and

> In our view, learning (or the kind of learning we are primarily interested in) is a qualitative change in a

3 Students who take this approach solve the problem by focusing on relative speed and relative distance. They focus on the "gap" as the distance that Martha must run. She closes this gap at the "catching speed." The ground appears to be automatically conditioned out of consideration, indicating a sophisticated understanding of speed as a relative quantity. Most students in this category solve the problem using:

$$\text{time to close gap} = \frac{\text{size of gap}}{\text{catching speed}}$$

2 Students who take this approach consider the motion of each runner separately with respect to the ground. Typically, they set up two separate equations of motion and attempt to solve those two equations simultaneously. Alternatively, they may solve the problem graphically by finding the intersection of two separate straight lines on a distance–time graph. Almost all students taking this approach understand that Martha and Arthur run for the same time t and use this fact in the solution. Some students are able to arrive at a solution: e.g.,

distance Martha runs = *distance Arthur runs* + *gap*

i.e., $V_m \times t = V_a \times t + gap$

Others fail to solve the problem because they do not incorporate the initial distance between Martha and Arthur: e.g., time Martha runs = time Arthur runs

i.e., $t = d_m / V_m = d_a / V_a$.

1 Students who take this approach focus on the motions of Martha and Arthur separately and, rather than attempting to derive a general algebraic or graphical solution, adopt a "trial-and-error" approach. Typically, they divide the continuous motion into discrete pieces and consider the relative locations of the two runners after fixed intervals of time or after one of them has run a particular distance. This may or may not lead to a solution of the problem.

0 A small number of students when presented with this problem in written form fail to display an understanding of the problem or of an appropriate approach. These students may produce one or more equations of motion and attempt to substitute into these equations, but they show little evidence of understanding and invariably become lost. This category includes all students who fail to demonstrate the levels of understanding reflected in categories 1, 2, and 3.

Figure 1
Response categories for physics question

person's conception of a certain phenomenon or of a certain aspect of reality. (Johansson et al. 1985 p. 235)

4. *Constructing Ordered Outcome Categories*

A methodology for charting progress in conceptual understanding first identifies a range of key concepts in an area of learning and then develops questions or tasks that can be used to explore the different understandings that students have of those concepts. For each of these questions, a set of ordered categories is defined corresponding to different levels of conceptual understanding. This notion of order is basic to a view of learning as a "shift" or "change" in a student's understanding. Such a change constitutes "learning" only if it involves a change from a lower level, more naive understanding to a higher level, more expert conception.

In practice, the set of ordered categories for a question is constructed by first exploring the variety of responses that students give when confronted with that question and asked to explain their thinking about it. In other words, the data from which ordered categories are constructed for a question are usually collected through student interviews. The resulting categories provide a framework for recording future responses to that question and introduce the possibility of basing measures of achievement on inferences about students' levels of understanding.

The construction of categories of response from interview data is part of the method used by Marton (1981) and his colleagues at the University of Gothenburg. These researchers interview students to explore their understandings of particular concepts and principles, transcribe tape-recordings of these interviews, and then carry out detailed analyses of transcripts. "The aim of the analysis is to yield descriptive categories representing qualitatively distinct conceptions of a phenomenon." These categories form an "outcome space" which provides "a kind of analytic map" of students' understandings of each phenomenon. Learning is thought of as "a shift from one conception to another" on this map (Dahlgren 1984 p. 2431).

"The difference in velocities (in m/sec) is how much Martha would gain on Arthur if the following equation is used:

V = Martha's velocity − Arthur's velocity.

3 Once we know how much Martha would gain on Arthur per second, we can then divide the original distance between them by V to find out how long it would take Martha to catch Arthur, in seconds:

$$\text{time taken to catch Arthur} = \frac{\text{original distance between runners}}{V}$$

2 "In the time t, Martha will travel $V_m.t$ and Arthur will travel $V_a.t$ . . . But given that Martha has to travel an extra d, we'll take that away from the distance and then they'll be in the same place:

$V_m.t - d = V_a.t$".

1 "Work out the time taken for Martha to travel the initial distance (S_i) between them. i.e., time = S_i/V_m. Use this time to find out how far Arthur ran. Then find our how long it takes Martha to run this extra distance. Then find out how far Arthur ran in this time.

Keep doing this until they have run the same distance (i.e., Martha has caught up to Arthur)."

0 "v = speed Martha, u = speed of Arthur,
s = distance between the two, t = time.

$$s = ((v+u)/2).t"$$

Figure 2
Student responses illustrating the categories

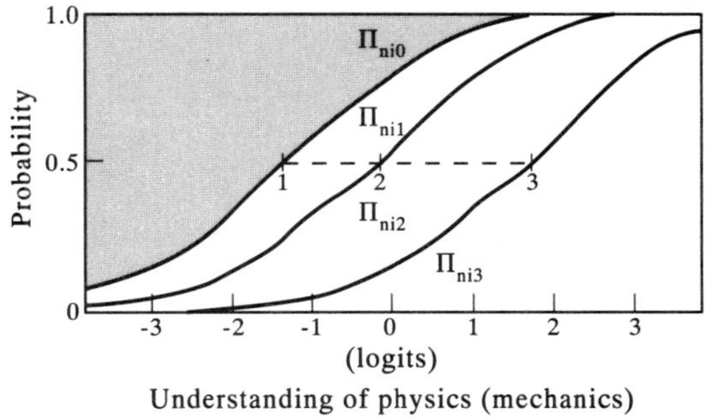

Figure 3
Modeled probabilities for "Martha and Arthur" question

5. Collecting Observations

While interviews with students are essential for identifying the variety of understandings that learners have of phenomena and for constructing ordered categories for individual questions, interviews are not practicable as a basis for achievement testing. For the purposes of assigning students to the categories that have been defined for test questions, alternative observation formats must be used. In general, this requires imaginative new kinds of tests capable of providing information about the conceptions that students bring to questions.

One approach to exploring students' levels of understanding is through computer-administered tasks. When students enter their responses to questions into a computer, these can be matched to libraries of common responses. In this way, particular kinds of errors and misunderstandings can be identified and inferences made about students' levels of understanding.

Alternatively, a student's initial response might trigger additional hints and subquestions designed to provide further information about the nature of that student's understanding. Through additional questioning of this kind it may be possible to emulate in a crude way the type of exploration that can be done through an interview to reveal a student's conception of a phenomenon.

Achievement tests constructed to reveal students' models and representations of phenomena may bear little resemblance to traditional achievement tests. As diSessa (1982) and White (1983) show, a great deal of information can be collected about individuals' naive theories of force and motion by asking them to move simulated objects on a screen. A computer can be used to keep detailed records of when students apply forces, in which directions they apply those forces, and how they respond to the motion that they produce. Automatic analyses of student records can then be used to infer students' understandings of the relations between force and motion.

6. Constructing Measures of Achievement

The construction of achievement measures from observations recorded in sets of ordered outcome categories requires a psychometric method analogous to the methods that have been developed for the analysis of right and wrong answers to test questions, but designed for ordered response categories. Such a method is described by Masters (1982) and Wright and Masters (1982). This psychometric method (see *Partial Credit Model*) proposes that the probability of a person scoring x rather than $x-1$ on a particular item i will increase steadily with ability in an area of learning such that

$$\frac{\pi nix}{\pi nix - 1 + \pi nix} = \frac{\exp(\beta n - \delta ix)}{1 + \exp(\beta n - \delta ix)} \tag{1}$$

where π_{nix} is the probability of person n responding in category x ($x = 1, 2, \ldots, m_i$) of item i, β_n is person n's level of ability in this area of learning (to be measured by this set of items), and δ_{ix} is a parameter that governs the probability of a response being made in category x rather than in category $x-1$ of item i.

The consequence of applying the simple logistic expression (1) to the transition between each pair of adjacent outcome categories for each item, is that a connection is formed between the ordered categories for that item and the underlying variable that the set of items is used to measure. It is this connection that enables performances on each item to be used to estimate students' locations on the underlying variable. This model permits measures of achievement to be constructed from inferences of students' levels of understanding of each of a number of concepts or phenomena in an area of learning.

6.1 Example 1

The methodology outlined in this entry has been used in a number of studies to measure levels of conceptual understanding in science. In one study (Bowden et al. 1992, Ramsden et al. 1992) 14 physics problems were developed, each designed to explore students' conceptual understandings of an aspect of mechanics. Students attempted each problem during an interview and their explanations were tape recorded and transcribed. Interview transcripts were then analyzed and students' responses were grouped to form a hierarchy of qualitatively different levels of understanding of the phenomenon addressed by each question.

One of these 14 questions addressed students' understanding of speed as a relative quantity:

> Martha and Arthur are running along a straight road at constant speed. Arthur is ahead of Martha. Arthur's speed is less than Martha's speed. How far must Martha run before she catches up to Arthur, and how long will this take her?

A detailed analysis of several dozen student transcripts led to the identification of six different strategies these students used to answer this question. These have been combined in Fig. 1 to define four

Figure 4
Response categories and levels for a "living things" question

	Level
Responses that include a list containing a number of the usually identified characteristics of living things. The answer need not be complete in biological terms	3
Responses that focus on movement	2
Responses that focus on growth	2
Responses that focus on the appearance of the object	1
Responses that suggest *poking at* or touching the object with a stick. A reason for poking or touching the objects is not provided	1
Uninterpretable responses	0

ordered outcome categories for this question. The most sophisticated understanding is reflected in the approach described in category 3. Students assigned to category 0 show very little understanding and may refer to the "acceleration" of Martha or rely on equations that relate the relevant variables but that are inappropriate. Excerpts from students' verbal and written explanations illustrating these four categories are shown in Fig. 2.

An important difference between the four categories in Fig. 1 and illustrated in Fig. 2 and more usual approaches to defining ordered levels of response to an item is that, rather than being defined in terms of stages in the solution of a problem, these categories reflect qualitatively different strategies and understandings. In this study, ordered categories were defined for each of the 14 physics questions and used to construct measures of student understanding in this area of physics.

The application of the partial credit model (1) to this physics question is illustrated in Fig. 3. This figure shows the modeled relationship between the variable being measured by the set of 14 questions and the response probabilities for the "Martha and Arthur" question. It can be seen that, under the model, the greater a student's general understanding in this area of physics, the more likely the student is to display a sophisticated understanding of speed as a relative quantity.

The points labeled 1, 2, and 3 in Fig. 3 mark boundaries between the four categories defined for this question. Measures of conceptual understanding on the horizontal variable in Fig. 3 can be referred to the category boundaries for all 14 items to provide an interpretation of the kinds of understandings that typify each measure. A student with an estimate of 1.0 logits on this scale will probably respond in category 1 but below category 3 (i.e., in category 2) to the "Arthur and Martha" question, for example.

6.2 Example 2

A second application of the methodology described in this entry is found in the Victorian Science Achievement Study by Adams et al. (1990) of students' understandings of a number of different science phenomena (see also Doig and Adams 1991). The Victorian Science study began with a detailed review of the science education research literature to establish the kinds of student misconceptions reported in earlier studies. This review of previous research provided a guide to the construction of ordered response categories for each of the questions used in the study.

The questions used in the Victorian Science study were based on short comic-strip sequences around particular themes (e.g., living things, earth and space, force and motion). Each question invited students to respond to the discussion in the comic strip and to explain some aspect of science in their own words. An example of one of the open-ended questions used with fifth-grade students is shown at the top of Fig. 4.

The range of responses that students might give to

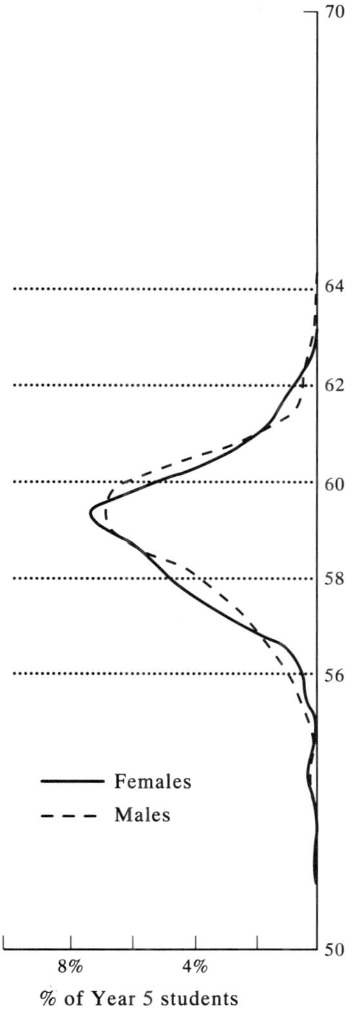

Figure 5
The "living things" variable
Students are able to use scientific terminology in supporting evidence; for example, to make distinctions between living and non-living things.
Some evidence that students are able to relate observations, provide multiple reasons to justify their responses, and draw inferences from evidence provided.
Students have some basic scientific knowledge such as humans are animals. Students can provide justifications for their responses but that justification is often unscientific and direct.
Student understandings are unscientific. They provide responses based upon folklore. Little or no justification or supporting evidence is provided for responses.
Students provide responses that are uninterpretable.

this question can be anticipated to some extent from previous research evidence (e.g., Bell 1981, Trowbridge and Mintzes 1988). The six different categories of response in Fig. 4 were identified in the written responses of fifth-grade students in the Victorian study. On the right of Fig. 4, these six responses have been clustered to form four "levels" of performance on the question. The lowest level of response is labeled 0, the highest is labeled 3. In this way, all responses to the question were assigned to one of four ordered response levels.

Students' responses to all eight Living Things questions were then analysed using the partial credit model (1) and the results of the analysis were used to construct the variable shown in Fig. 5. The text on the right of Fig. 5 describes increasing levels of understanding of the characteristics of living things.

On the left of Fig. 5 are the distributions of male and female fifth-grade students' levels of performance. It can be seen that very few fifth-grade students demonstrated an ability on this set of questions to "relate their observations," to "provide multiple reasons to justify their responses," or to "draw inferences from evidence."

The methodology described in this entry and illustrated in these two examples can be used to mark out a measurement variable in terms of qualitatively different levels of understanding. Measures derived and interpreted in this way are capable of providing a more instructionally-useful basis for charting student learning than some more traditional testing methods.

See also: Learning Activity; Bilingualism; Cognitive Development: Information-processing Approach; Cognitive Styles and Learning

References

Adams R J, Doig B A, Rosier M 1990 *Science Learning in Victorian Schools.* Australian Council for Educational Research, Hawthorn, Victoria

Bell B F 1981 When is an animal not an animal? *J. Biol. Ed.* 15(3): 213–18

Bloom B S, Hastings J T, Madaus G F 1971 *Handbook on Formative and Summative Evaluation of Student Learning.* McGraw Hill, New York

Bowden J et al. 1992 Displacement, velocity, and frames of reference: Phenomenographic studies of students' understanding and some implications for teaching and assessment. *Am. J. Physics* 60:3

Caramazza A, McCloskey M, Green B 1981 Naive beliefs in "sophisticated" subjects: Misconceptions about trajectories of objects. *Cog.* 9(2): 117–23

Champagne A B, Klopfer L E, Anderson J H 1980 Factors influencing the learning of classical mechanics. *Am. J. Physics* 48(12): 1074–79

Chi M T H, Feltovich P J, Glaser R 1981 Categorization and representation of physics problems by experts and novices. *Cognit. Sci.* 5: 121–52

Clement J 1982 Students' preconceptions of introductory mechanics. *Am. J. Physics* 50(1): 66–71

Dahlgren L-O 1984 Outcomes of learning. In: Marton F, Hounsell D, Entwistle N (eds.) 1984 *The Experience of Learning.* Scottish Academic Press, Edinburgh

diSessa A 1982 Unlearning Aristotelian physics: A study of knowledge-based learning. *Cognit. Sci.* 6: 37–75

Doig B A, Adams R J 1991 The Victorian Science Achievement Study: Implications for practice. *Aust. Sci. Teach. J.* 37(4): 25–31

Driver R, Easley J 1978 Pupils and paradigms: A review of literature related to concept development in adolescent science students. *Stud. Sci. Educ.* 5: 61–84

Gunstone R, White R 1981 Understanding of gravity. *Sci. Educ.* 65(3): 291–99

Johansson B, Marton F, Svensson L 1985 An approach to describing learning as change between qualitatively different conceptions. In: West L H, Pines L A (eds.) 1985 *Cognitive Structure and Conceptual Change.* Academic Press, Orlando, Florida

Larkin J H 1983 The role of problem representation in physics. In: Gentner D, Stevens A (eds.) 1983 *Mental Models.* Erlbaum, Hillsdale, New Jersey

Lybeck L et al. 1988 The phenomenography of "the mole concept in chemistry." In: Ramsden P (ed.) 1988 *Improving Learning—New Perspectives.* Kegan Paul, London

Marton F 1981 Phenomenography—describing conceptions of the world around us. *Instr. Sci.* 10(2): 177–200

Masters G N 1982 A Rasch model for partial credit scoring. *Psychometri* 47(2): 149–74

McCloskey M 1983 Naive theories of motion. In Gentner D, Stevens A (eds.) 1983 *Mental Models.* Erlbaum, Hillsdale, New Jersey

McCloskey M, Caramazza A, Green B 1980 Curvilinear motion in the absence of external forces: Naive beliefs about motions of objects. *Science* 210(4474): 1139–41

McDermott L C 1984 Research on conceptual understanding in mechanics. *Physics Today*: 1–10

Nesher P 1986 Learning mathematics: A cognitive perspective. *Am. Psychol.*, 41(10): 1114–22

Osborne R J, Wittrock M C 1983 Learning science: A generative process. *Sci. Educ.* 67(4): 489–508

Posner G J, Strike K A, Hewson P W, Gertzog W A 1982 Accommodation of a scientific conception: Toward a theory of conceptual change. *Sci. Educ.* 66(2): 211–27

Ramsden P et al. 1992 Phenomenographic research and the measurement of understanding: An investigation of students' conceptions of speed, distance and time. *Int. J. Educ. Res.* 19(3): 301–16

Säljö R 1984 Learning from reading. In: Marton F Hounsell D, Entwistle N (eds.) 1984 *The Experience of Learning.* Scottish Academic Press, Edinburgh

Trowbridge D E, McDermott L C 1981 Investigation of student understanding of the concept of acceleration in one dimension. *Am. J. Physics* 49(3): 242–53

Trowbridge D E, Mintzes J J 1988 Alternative conceptions in animal classification: A cross age study. *J. Res. Sci. Teach.* 25(7): 547–71

Viennot L 1979 Spontaneous reasoning in elementary dynamics. *Eur. J. Sci. Educ.* 1(2): 205–21

White B Y 1983 Sources of difficulty in understanding Newtonian dynamics. *Cognit. Sci.* 7(1): 41–65

White B Y, Horwitz P 1987 Thinker Tools: Enabling children to understand physical laws. Proc. 9th Annual Conf. of the Cognitive Science Society, Erlbaum, Hillsdale, New Jersey

Wright B D, Masters G N 1982 *Rating Scale Analysis*. MESA Press, Chicago, Illinois

G. N. Masters; R. J. Adams; M. Wilson

Student Roles in Classrooms

In the first edition of the *International Encyclopedia of Education*, student roles were conceptualized as behaviors characteristic of persons in a context (Tisher 1985). Researchers in the 1970s and early 1980s found that students in the typical classroom assumed a passive role, spending most of their time listening to the teacher (Goodlad 1984). Students talked no more than 30 percent of the time and this followed the teacher initiation–student response–teacher evaluation pattern (IRE) identified by Mehan (1979). Tisher (1985) suggested that classroom context influenced teachers' and students' observed behavior. For example, teachers in open classrooms asked more higher level cognitive questions than teachers in traditional classrooms. Thus, students in open classrooms received more opportunities to engage in higher level responding than those in traditional classrooms.

Since 1985, researchers have shifted away from a view of classroom roles and practices that focus only on teachers' and students' observed behavior, toward a view that also considers the understandings and perspectives of students and teachers within the social context of classrooms and schools. According to this view, roles are created by participants within a social situation such as a classroom. An understanding of student roles, then, involves understanding not only the observed roles of students in classrooms, but also teachers' and students' assumptions and beliefs about these roles.

1. A New Role for Students in Classrooms

During the late 1980s and continuing into the 1990s, curriculum development efforts in literacy and mathematics have focused on creating a more active role for students (Anderson et al. 1984, National Council of Teachers of Mathematics 1989). In order for students to assume such a role, however, changes in the traditional conceptions of knowledge, tasks, and discourse are needed.

Underlying the student's traditionally passive classroom role is a conception of knowledge that places the authority for knowing with the teacher. The teacher's role is to transmit knowledge to students who simply receive the knowledge transmitted. Underlying the new role for students is a conception of knowledge as an active construction of meaning by the learner, often in collaboration with peers.

Classroom tasks in traditional classrooms involve the use of basal texts in reading and mathematics and an endless array of worksheets that teach skills. Reformers recommend that teachers engage students in new kinds of tasks such as reading authentic children's literature, working on real problems, interpreting texts from a variety of perspectives, solving mathematics problems using a variety of strategies and tools, keeping journals that document learners' thinking, writing for real audiences about topics of students' own choice, and having students pose and solve mathematics problems for themselves.

Finally in traditional classrooms, teachers typically control the discourse. They ask convergent, factual questions for which they know the answers. Students respond by providing specific answers and generating few questions of their own (Mehan 1979). New discourse patterns in literacy instruction include teacher–student and peer conferences that provide students with their peers' perspectives and interpretations of their reading and writing (DiPardo and Freedman 1988). New discourse patterns in mathematics classrooms involve students in negotiating mathematical meaning, discussing and explaining their thinking and strategies for solving problems, justifying their answers, and creating and posing new mathematical problems for themselves (Lampert 1990).

1.1 Student Responses and Teacher Diagnosis

The active role of students has been conceived as involving more extended student responses than has been typical in traditional classrooms. Students have the opportunity to engage in authentic tasks involving reading, writing, solving mathematical problems, and using mathematical tools. While the teacher controls classroom discourse, students have opportunities to provide ideas. The role of the teacher is to construct knowledge, diagnose students' needs, and develop instruction accordingly, while attempting to make learning meaningful for students. The student's role is to acquire this knowledge in a meaningful way.

An example of such a program in literacy is Reading Recovery. Developed in New Zealand to help children having trouble learning to read, Reading Recovery is designed to serve the lowest achieving readers in first-grade classrooms (Clay 1982). Teachers provide daily 30-minute lessons to individual children during which they involve students in reading small books and in writing their own messages. The teachers respond to the students on a minute-to-minute basis according to the student's strengths, needs, and interests. The teacher introduces students to predictable books that they often reread to develop fluency. Additionally, the student has the opportunity to read a new book each day to become familiar with important ideas in stories. While the student is reading, the teacher watches and records substitutions, self-corrections, and omissions to aid in selecting materials for the next day. Students also compose a message each day with the aid of the teacher (Pinnell et al. 1990). Research conducted in New Zealand indicated that students at risk of failure made accelerated progress while enrolled in the Reading Recovery program (Clay 1985). Studies in Ohio showed that students who had participated in Reading Recovery scored significantly higher than comparison children and retained their gains at least two years after the intervention (Pinnell 1989).

Stevenson and Stigler (1992) have portrayed a similar approach to mathematics teaching in their vignettes of selected Japanese classrooms. They have argued that the success of mathematics teaching in Japanese classrooms is related to several important features of active student roles. Students work on real world problems and manipulate concrete objects to model problem solutions. Students discuss their solution strategies in a small or large group. Finally, the teacher diagnoses and remediates students' misconceptions during group discussion. The student's role is to manipulate objects and construct representations; the teacher's role is to assure that correct representations are produced. Class discussion emphasizes meaning, yet is teacher-controlled.

1.2 Learning Expert Strategies from Experts

Some educators have attempted to make students more autonomous, active learners using programs designed to teach strategies that researchers have identified as being employed successfully by experts. These programs are characterized by direct modeling of strategies by the teacher or a student with students gradually assuming more responsibility. Conceptions of knowledge often derive from social constructivist notions, suggesting the importance of teacher scaffolding instruction for the learner (Vygotsky 1978) or from cognitive scientists' ideas of identifying strategies of experts or those more knowledgeable than the student and then teaching these strategies to novices (Romberg 1982). Again, these tasks are structured to promote a gradual internalization of problem-solving processes, emphasizing the learner's assuming metacognitive control (Baker and Brown 1984). Classroom discourse is often initiated by the teacher, but students gradually take over aspects of the dialogue and teach peers. Students assume an active role while receiving continued assistance from a person with greater expertise such as the teacher.

Palincsar and Brown (1989) developed what they term "reciprocal teaching" to increase both reading comprehension and the use of metacognitive strategies. Their premise is that students will come to internalize dialogue about text that is modeled by the teacher. The dialogue is structured around four strategies used by expert readers: summarizing, self-questioning, predicting, and clarifying. The teacher models these strategies and provides support as students gradually acquire the strategies to use independently in their reading, and students gradually take on more active roles in controlling the discourse. Reciprocal teaching has increased the reading comprehension of elementary- and junior-high students significantly; students were able to use the strategies independent of the teacher and to provide help to other students.

The Kamehameha Early Education Program (KEEP) has focused on altering discourse patterns during the reading of text to become more culturally congruent with the participation structures of native Hawaiians outside the classroom. Teachers use the experience–text–relationship (ETR) method that involves activating children's background experiences relevant to the text, close literal reading of the text, and the integration of information read with prior knowledge and experience. Teacher–student interactions are characterized by the talk story pattern in which students answer the teacher's questions without being called upon, building upon one another's answers. Studies suggest that a careful match between patterns of interaction and instructional goals can facilitate learning. The social organization of lessons permits students to show initiative and supports the transfer of control over text comprehension from teacher to student (Au and Kawakami 1986).

Cognitively Guided Instruction (CGI) is based on research on the development of young children's strategies for solving mathematics word problems (Carpenter and Moser 1982). The developers of CGI begin by sharing two research-based knowledge frameworks with teachers: (a) the framework of strategies that young children use in developing increasingly sophisticated approaches for solving mathematics word problems, and (b) the framework of problem types that children are able to solve. The assumption is that children construct knowledge by proceeding through a sequence of strategy development, and that the teacher's role is to facililate the children's development of increasingly sophisticated problem-solving strategies. In CGI classrooms, elementary mathematics teaching is characterized by a focus on solving word problems and other nonroutine problems; use of multiple strategies by students to solve problems, including counters and other mathematics tools; and listening to students explain and show their strategies and solutions for solving problems. Students in CGI classrooms tended to achieve higher on tests of mathematical problem-solving than students in traditional classrooms, and to recall their number facts with equal or greater facility (Peterson et al. 1989).

1.3 Collaborative Roles in Learning

In this conception of the active learner, students are seen as being actively involved in the negotiation of shared meaning with others in a learning community. Like Dewey (1916), these educators see communication as both the means of learning and the substance of what is learned. Communication is intertwined with the notion of community, developing what Dewey referred to as "participation in a common understanding." Teachers and students, then, are jointly responsible for learning.

In collaboration with others in their learning community, students choose the tasks and materials they use and communicate and collaborate with one another in order to develop new knowledge. Students' roles are dynamic and changing, depending on the text or problem in which they are engaged. As advocated by Freire (1986) in teaching Brazilian students, "the teacher is no longer merely the-one-who-teaches, but one who is himself taught in dialogue with the students" (p. 67).

Within this conception of the active learner, educators have developed student-led "book clubs" and "literature circles." Students use the book clubs for several purposes including sharing their written responses to a text, clarifying points of confusion, discussing main themes in a book, relating the text to other texts, identifying an author's purpose, critiquing an author's success, and relating the text to their personal experiences (Raphael et al. 1992). In literature circles, students have choices about which books to read before joining the circle. The types of discussion questions depend on readers' interests. These discussions take the form of reacting to the book, reading aloud favorite parts, and raising questions about parts they do not understand. Members of the circle often present the book to the rest of the class (Harste et al. 1984). Smagorinsky and Fly (1992) suggested that such student-led discussions can be very successful, especially when the teacher has made the interpretive process explicit at an earlier point in time.

Peer writing conferences or response groups consist of small groups of students who respond to each other's written texts. DiPardo and Freedman (1988) suggested a variety of purposes for these conferences depending on teachers' and students' goals, including responding to writing, thinking collaboratively, writing collaboratively, and editing written text. Groups provide a forum for discussing the writing process, generating ideas, understanding the functions of an audience, and providing support for engaging in writing. The assumption is that students benefit from talking together because the writer's knowledge becomes available in the discourse; the beginner's work is supported through questions, comments, and suggestions of others; beginning writers have opportunities to practice orally ways of using written language; and talking about text makes clear to writers the value of their work (Florio-Ruane 1988). Studies suggest that peer groups for writing collaboratively or responding to writing can positively influence students' writing (Dahl 1988). The nature of the discourse is an important element in determining the kinds of revisions that students make in their texts (Gere and Abbott 1985). Finally, the quality of the discourse influences the learning of individual students (Daiute 1985, Fitzgerald and Stamm 1990).

Lampert (1990) discussed approaches to mathematics teaching where learning mathematics involves the negotiation of shared meaning among students and the teacher within the mathematical community which exists in each classroom. Students assume authority for knowing mathematics and for explaining and justifying their mathematical thinking to others in their community. Students' ideas and knowledge become available for debate and discussion as part of the classroom discourse. New ways of thinking and mathematical ideas are developed and learned by all members of the community, and learning occurs on the part of the teacher as well as the students.

2. *Making Sense of Classrooms*

Three ways that educators have conceived of students as playing more active roles in the classroom have been described. These conceptions should result in rather different classroom scenarios; different from traditional classrooms and different from each other. But how will developers' conceptions impact on what actually happens in classrooms and how will the actors—teachers and students—actually construe their roles?

Although new curricula, tasks, and discourse structures that embody more active roles for learners have been designed, these new curricula, tasks, discourse structures, and roles will be transformed by the participants in their particular contexts (Bruce and Rubin 1993). The roles students actually play in each classroom will depend on how curricula, tasks, discourse, and role structures are created and recreated within classrooms. Influential factors include the beliefs of the participants and the culture of the classroom.

2.1 Teachers' and Students' Beliefs About Subject Matter

Nickerson (1992) reviewed studies that show how the pupil's role in United Kingdom classrooms can vary dramatically according to the view of mathematics projected by the teacher. She contrasted pupil's roles as "accepting" versus "questioning" and suggested that pupils' participation in these different roles is related to the ideas they develop about mathematical knowledge. Similarly, Schoenfeld (1992) has shown how students' roles are intertwined with teachers' and students' existing beliefs about mathematical knowledge. Schoenfeld's analysis produced the following set of students' beliefs about the nature of mathematical knowledge.

(a) Mathematics problems have one and only one right answer.

(b) There is only one correct way to solve any mathematics problem, usually the rule the teacher has most recently demonstrated in class.

(c) Ordinary students cannot be expected to understand mathematics, they expect simply to memorize it and apply what they have learned mechanically and without understanding.

(d) Formal proof is irrelevant to processes of discovery or invention.

(e) Mathematics is a solitary activity, done by individuals in isolation.

(f) Students who have understood the mathematics they have studied will be able to solve any assigned problem in five minutes or less.

(g) The mathematics learned in school has little or nothing to do with the real world.

These beliefs have definite implications for students' roles. Students are expected to find the correct answer; to work alone; to memorize and apply procedures that are demonstrated by the teacher; to work quickly and efficiently; and to view their role as a "student" in school rather than as a lifelong "learner" in school and out.

Similarly, in the area of literacy, children and adults have a set of beliefs about text: what is, who created it, and how to evaluate it (Garner and Alexander in press). Once again these beliefs imply certain roles for students in the classroom.

2.2 Teachers' and Students' Beliefs About Teaching and Learning

The role of the student and what it means to be an active learner in the classroom also depend on the beliefs teachers and students have about learning and teaching. For example, among 20 teachers who were implementing Cognitively Guided Instruction (CGI) in their classrooms, Peterson et al. (1989) observed substantial differences among teachers related to their beliefs about the role of the student and the teacher. Teachers who continued to see their roles as presenting knowledge rather than listening to students or facilitating children's construction of knowledge, implemented CGI by engaging in direct instruction and presenting the correct answer and correct mathematical strategy to be learned. Teachers who saw their roles as actively facilitating children's construction of knowledge created CGI classrooms where everyone listened to students' strategies for solving problems, tried to understand children's thinking, and encouraged the development of mathematical understanding.

In implementing new approaches to literacy learning, such as process writing and reciprocal teaching, teachers have "proceduralized" the substantive intervention and recreated the innovation within their existing conceptions of the learner, the teacher, and knowledge (Bruce and Rubin 1993). Florio-Ruane and Lensmire (1990), for example, found that teachers adopted and taught the steps of process writing, but did not alter their understandings of what it meant to be a good writer or the knowledge of authority relationships among teacher, student, and text.

2.3 The Culture of the Classroom and the School

The role of the student is one that is created solely within the context of the school. The role of the learner as conceived in school, however, is very different from the role of the learner in the contexts of work, family, and play where children and youth also learn (Resnick 1987). Outside of schools, children and youth often learn in authentic situations, such as apprenticeships (Collins et al. 1989) in which participants' work has real economic value and significance. What would happen if the role of learner were conceptualized within a community that is unbounded by school walls, but that encompasses the experiences of home and other learning contexts?

3. Transforming the Roles of Children and Youth as Learners in Schools and Out

Heath (in press) describes how effective organizations for inner-city youth in the United States differ from formal learning contexts in the ways in which learning and knowledge are conceived and the roles that youths play. She argues that formal learning contexts, such as schools, should change to encompass the following features.

(a) Effective youth organizations have open frank discussions and make learning possible primarily through demonstration, apprenticeship, extensive practice, and peer evaluation.

(b) Youth organizations place the control of knowledge within the group as team members committed to a central goal. Knowledge and skills blend together. The facts of a myth for a Ballet Folklorico dance go along with the skill inherent in specific dance routines.

(c) Learning is cumulative, multidirectional, and displayed through a variety of different kinds of symbols: verbal, kinesthetic, musical, and visual.

(d) Learning and thinking of the self as a learner for a set of purposes and goals of joint identification become synomous with one's life, just as knowing oneself as a member of a family unconsciously merges with an individual sense of identity (Heath in press).

Heath argues for changing schools to become more like effective youth organizations in order to create a "seamless life of thinking, development and learning." If such changes do come about, then in the next edition of the *International Encyclopedia of Education* this entry will be transformed and retitled to reflect the role of the student as merged within the multifaceted roles of young learners growing up in a global community.

See also: School and Classroom Dynamics; Teachers' Roles

References

Anderson R C, Hiebert E H, Scott J A, Wilkinson I A G 1984 *Becoming a Nation of Readers: The Report of the Commission on Reading*. The National Institute of Education, Washington, DC

Au K H, Kawakami A J 1986 The influence of the social organization of instruction on children's text comprehension ability: A Vygotskian perspective. In: Raphael T E (ed.) 1986 *The Contexts of School-based Literacy*. Random House, New York

Baker L, Brown A L 1984 Metacognitive skills and reading. In: Pearson (ed.) 1984 *Handbook of Reading Research*, Vol 1. Longman, New York

Bruce B B, Rubin A 1993 *Electronic Quills: A Situated Evaluation of Using Computers for Writing in Classrooms*. Erlbaum, Hillsdale, New Jersey

Carpenter T P, Moser J M 1982 The development of addition and subtraction problem-solving skills. In: Carpenter T P, Moser J M, Romberg T A (eds.) 1982 *Addition and Subtraction: A Cognitive Perspective*. Erlbaum, Hillsdale, New Jersey

Clay M M 1982 *Observing Young Readers*. Heinemann, Portsmouth, New Hampshire

Clay M M 1985 *The Early Detection of Reading Difficulties*. Heinemann, Portsmouth, New Hampshire

Collins A, Brown J S, Newman S E 1989 Cognitive apprenticeship: Teaching the crafts of reading, writing, and mathematics. In: Resnick L (ed.) 1989 *Knowing, Learning and Instruction: Essays in Honor of Robert Glaser*. Erlbaum, Hillsdale, New Jersey

Dahl K 1988 Peer conferences as social contexts for learning about revision. In: Readance J (ed.) 1988 *Dialogues in Literacy Research*. National Reading Conference, Chicago, Illinois

Daiute C 1985 Do writers talk to themselves? In: Freedman S W (ed.) 1985 *The Acquisition of Written Language: Response and Revision*. Ablex, Norwood, New Jersey

Dewey J 1916 *Democracy and Education*. Macmillan, New York

DiPardo A, Freedman S W 1988 Peer response groups in the writing classroom: Theoretic foundations and new directions. *Rev. Educ. Res.* 58: 119–49

Fitzgerald J, Stamm C 1990 Effects of group conferences on first-grader's revisions of writing. *Written Communication* 7: 96–135

Florio-Ruane S 1988 How ethnographers of communication study writing in school. In: Readance J (ed.) 1988 *Dialogues in Literacy Research*. National Reading Conference, Chicago, Illinois

Florio-Ruane S, Lensmire T J 1990 Transforming future teachers' ideas about writing instruction *J. Curric. St.* 22: 277–89

Freire P 1986 *Pedagogy of the Oppressed*. Continuum Publishing, New York

Garner R, Alexander P (eds.) in press *Beliefs about Text and about Instruction with Text*. Erlbaum, Hillsdale, New Jersey

Gere A R, Abbott R D 1985 Talking about writing: The language of writing groups. *Research in the Teaching of English* 19: 362–85

Goodlad J I 1984 *A Place Called School*. McGraw-Hill, New York

Harste J C, Woodward V A, Burke C L 1984 *Language Stories and Literacy Lessons*. Heinemann, Portsmouth, New Hampshire

Heath S B in press Play for identity: Where the mind is everyday for inner-city youth. In: Mangieri J, Block C C (ed.) in press *Mindfulness: Increasing Thinking Abilities*. Harcourt, Brace, Jovanovich, New York

Lampert M 1990 When the problem is not the question and the solution is not the answer: Mathematical knowing and teaching. *Am. Educ. Res. J.* 27: 29–64

Mehan H 1979 *Learning Lessons*. Harvard University Press, Cambridge, Massachusetts

National Council of Teachers of Mathematics 1989 *Curriculum and Evaluation Standards for School Mathematics*. National Council of Teachers of Mathematics, Reston, Virginia

Nickerson M 1992 The culture of the mathematics classroom: An unknown quantity? In: Grouws D A (ed.) 1992 *Handbook of Research on Mathematics Teaching and Learning*. Macmillan, New York

Palincsar A S, Brown A L 1989 Classroom dialogues to promote self-regulated comprehension. In: Brophy J (ed.) 1989 *Advances in Research on Teaching*, Vol 1. JAI Press, Greenwich, Connecticut

Peterson P L, Carpenter T, Fennema E 1989 Teachers' knowledge of students' knowledge in mathematics problem solving: Correlational and case analyses. *J. Educ. Psychol.* 81: 558–69

Pinnell G S 1989 Reading Recovery: Helping at-risk children learn to read. *Elem. Sch. J.* 90 (2): 161–82

Pinnell G S, Fried M D, Estice R M 1990 Reading Recovery: Learning how to make a difference. *Read. Teach.* 43: 282–95

Raphael T E et al. 1992 Research directions: Literature and discussion in the reading program. *Lang. Arts* 69 (1): 54–61

Resnick L B 1987 Learning in school and out. *Educ. Researcher* 16 (9): 13–20

Romberg T 1982 An emerging paradigm for research on addition and subtraction skills. In: Carpenter T P, Moser J P, Romberg T A (eds.) 1982 *Addition and Subtraction: A Cognitive Perspective* Erlbaum, Hillsdale, New Jersey

Schoenfeld A 1992 Learning to think mathematically: Problem solving, metacognition, and sense making in mathematics. In: Grouws D A (ed.) 1993 *Handbook of Research on Mathematics Teaching and Learning*. Macmillan, New York

Smagorinsky P, Fly P K 1992 Patterns of discourse in small group discussions of literature. Paper presented at the Annual Meeting of the American Educational Research Association, San Francisco, California

Stevenson H, Stigler J 1992 *The Learning Gap*. Summit Books, New York

Tisher R P 1985 Student roles in the classroom. In: Husén T, Postlethwaite T N (eds.) 1985 *The International Encyclopedia of Education*, 1st edn. Pergamon Press, Oxford

Vygotsky L S 1978 *Mind in Society: The Development of Higher Psychological Processes*. Harvard University Press, Cambridge, Massachusetts

S. J. McCarthey; P. L. Peterson

Student Support Systems: Administration

The purpose of this entry is to describe the nature and range of student affairs programs and services in institutions of higher and continuing education. Student affairs is the administrative unit typically designated to respond to students' welfare needs and, to a lesser extent, social interests. Student affairs personnel also buffer faculty members and academic administrators from demands considered peripheral to the institution's academic mission. In the United States in particular, the range of student affairs programs has expanded to encourage students to take advantage of learning and personal development opportunities outside of the classroom, laboratory, and library.

This presentation relies extensively on information about higher and continuing education in the United States for two reasons: (a) little systematic research on student affairs programs and services around the world is available; and (b) student affairs administration in the United States is more fully developed than in other countries, due in part to American traditions of egalitarian social values and mass higher education. As a result, United States colleges and universities have developed programs and services for students with a wide range of intellectual ability and social and emotional needs and interests (Fenske 1989). When appropriate, illustrations from other countries are used for purposes of comparison and contrast, although comparisons across cultures and hemispheres must be made with extreme caution. Systems of higher and continuing education evolve at different rates, influenced by circumstances such as economic productivity and issues of social justice. As with curriculum and other administrative functions, student services are a product of available resources and personnel, student characteristics, institutional philosophy and educational priorities, educational and cultural traditions of the host country and region, and innovative responses to local conditions.

1. History of Student Affairs Work

In the middle ages, student life in European countries was characterized by concerns that remain quite familiar today: food and housing, town-gown relationships, concern about excessive noise and aberrant student behavior, financing of university study, legal rights of students, and the role of students in university governance (Prins 1983). In general, the president and faculty members in United States colleges accepted responsibility for all aspects of a student's education. Harvard College in the United States adopted the residential model in use at Cambridge and Oxford in England. Residence halls contained classrooms, the chapel, the sleeping rooms both for students, who were often as young as 13 or 14 years of age, and the clergy who were their professors and tutors (Cowley 1934). Intellectual and moral discourse were fostered by faculty members and students living together, although this arrangement also contributed to a paternalistic system of discipline and the close supervision of student life (Brubacher and Rudy 1976).

As institutions of higher education became more complex organizations, administrative roles were created to bring an all-campus or all-university frame of reference to questions of policy and practice (Clark 1983). "The proliferation of administrators . . . [included] first a secretary of the faculty, then a registrar, and then in succession a Vice-President, a Dean [of students], a Dean of Women, a Chief Business Officer, an Assistant Dean, a Dean of Men, a Director of Admissions" (Rudolph 1962 pp. 434–35). These administrators were expected to free faculty members from activities that were not directly related to the academic program, such as student housing, social life, and discipline (Fenske 1989).

In 1890, Harvard College appointed the first college dean whose responsibilities, in addition to teaching, included discipline and the enrollment and registration of students. By 1920 nearly every sizable American college or university had a dean of men and a dean of women. Unlike most other administrative areas, women exerted considerable influence on the philosophy and methods used to work with students. The first separate services to appear—discipline, admissions, record keeping, living group supervision, food service, and advice for foreign students—were manifestations of a desire for organizational efficiency and effectiveness and a custodian of culture and parental substitute (Bursch 1962).

1.1 The Personnel Movement

The First World War spawned the development of intelligence and vocational aptitude tests and created a demand for personnel trained to administer and interpret these instruments which were subsequently adapted for use in higher education. Due to increasing specialization of academic disciplines and concomitant changes in the professional role, the focus of the faculty member shifted from a holistic approach to student learning and development to an emphasis on classroom teaching and scholarly interests, particularly in large universities. Through the first five decades of the twentieth century, student affairs personnel emphasized control and student welfare programs such as discipline, vocational guidance, health, financial aid, and housing to enable students to perform as efficiently as possible without being distracted by potentially debilitating conditions. Taken together, the testing movement, an expanding curriculum that attracted a more diverse student population with different expectations for college, and changes in the faculty role created a demand for college student affairs personnel in the United States and many other countries.

1.2 Student Development Movement

Williamson (1961) presciently predicted the student development movement in American higher education which gained momentum in the 1970s: "The fundamental purpose of personnel workers is not to perform a service per se but to use a service to help students develop into full maturity" (p. 52). With roots in psychology and counselling (Rogers 1961, Williamson 1961), the student development philosophy advocates managing and restructuring environmental conditions and applying principles from human development theories to encourage students' cognitive and affective development (Miller and Prince 1976). This position is consistent with the espoused value of most United States institutions that the integration of students' social and emotional (affective) behaviors with intellectual (cognitive) skills is important in order to foster the development of the whole person (Brown 1972). The student development movement was also fueled by student demands for more autonomy and the demise of *in loco parentis* as a guiding philosophical framework which historically made legitimate the control and welfare functions of student affairs work. By the late 1960s, the *in loco parentis* philosophy was no longer legally, morally, or socially tenable in most institutions.

2. Purposes and Philosophy of Student Affairs

As an applied field of professional practice, student affairs is primarily concerned with the immediate needs and concerns of the institution and students (Knock 1988). The emphasis given to behavior control, student welfare, and student development varies by country and institution. For example, student affairs staff in some East European countries select students with political attitudes and vocational aspirations compatible with the state's social and economic plans. Student life policies are designed to discourage student challenges to state interests. This approach stands in contrast to United States goals of student affairs: to help students realize their potential and become responsible, self-directed citizens. However, some purposes are common to many countries and result in services to meet financial, health, cultural, recreational, and social needs, blending moral education with the academic, concern with the practical application of knowledge, and a trend toward centralization of student affairs programs and activities (Forrest 1968).

Institutional philosophies also shape institutional policy and program development. Four schools of philosophy shape student affairs practice: pragmatism, neohumanism, existentialism, and rationalism (Knock 1988). Pragmatism and neohumanism have influenced the field to a greater degree than existentialism and rationalism. By emphasizing "what works," pragmatism values specific and particular student experiences over universal truths. Through concrete learning experiences from student government or organizational leadership roles, students discover values and solutions to problems through learning by doing. While acknowledging the duality of thought and action and reason and emotion, neohumanism emphasizes concern for development of the whole person. Thus, through providing extracurricular outlets for recreation and social interaction, student affairs manifests higher education's interest in encouraging development of talents and skills in addition to the cultivation of reason and knowledge.

Existentialism suggests that students are free and responsible for their own decisions; each choice moves an individual closer to the person he or she is becoming. For example, an existential view assumes the individual student determines his or her own learning and development. Rationalism argues that the cultivation of the intellect is the primary goal of higher education. The control and discipline functions of student affairs, such as maintaining environmental conditions that permit students to learn free from disturbance, are manifestations of rationalism (Knock 1988).

Two core assumptions that reflect themes emphasized in these philosophical bases guide student affairs practice: (a) the institution's educational missions are pre-eminent; and (b) student life policies and practices should enhance and be consistent with the institution's educational philosophy and purposes and promote attainment of students' learning and personal development objectives. Statements have periodically been issued to translate the guiding philosophical tenets of the field into goals and priorities. The first codification, *The Student Personnel Point of View* (American Council on Education 1937), established the development of the whole person as the primary goal of student affairs and identified student services and programs considered necessary for student success. Following the Second World War, this statement was revised to emphasize the importance of education for democracy, international understanding, and amelioration of societal problems (American Council on Education 1949). In the mid-1970s, several guiding statements conceptualized the primary role of a student affairs worker as a student development educator (American College Personnel Association 1975, Council of Student Personnel Associations 1975).

In 1987, the National Association of Student Personnel Administrators produced *A Perspective on*

Student Affairs which set forth guiding assumptions and beliefs for student affairs in American higher education. The statement includes a list of functions and responsibilities that can be expected of student affairs by students and institutions. The 1987 statement also reaffirmed that student affairs exist to enhance and support the academic mission of the institution, to advocate for the common good, and champion the rights of the individual through encouraging intelligent risk taking and setting limits on behavior, and to encourage independent thought and interdependent behavior by students.

3. Theoretical Perspectives for Practice

Student affairs staff work with individuals, groups, and organizations. Theories from four applied fields are considered useful in understanding and performing student affairs work: counseling and personality theory, human development theory, human ecology or theory of environments, and organizational and management theory. These theories reflect the dominant philosophical bases for the fields mentioned above—pragmatism and neohumanism.

Counseling and personality theories are helpful for understanding students' personal adjustment, personality functioning, individual motives and aspirations, and behavior in small groups. Many of these theories acknowledge the individual's inherent need to grow "in a basically positive direction" (Rogers 1961 p. 26) and are consistent with a holistic, neohumanist view of student development in which the intellect and affect are viewed as inextricably intertwined (Forrest 1989).

Human development theories address the issues of intellectual and ethical or moral development (Gilligan 1982, Kohlberg 1971, Perry 1970), psychological development (Erikson 1968, Katz 1968, Sanford 1962), development on various affective and cognitive dimensions (Chickering 1969), and specific behavior such as vocational choice (Holland 1985). For the most part, these theories are based on research on White, traditional age (18–23) male students. Rodgers (in Delworth and Hanson 1989) provides an excellent summary of these theories (see also the paper by Stage and Kuh in the same volume).

To understand individual and group behavior, environmental influences on behavior must be understood. Walsh (1973) reviewed different perspectives on environments that inform student affairs practice including behavior setting, subcultures, personality types, and social climate. Environmental assessment techniques such as ecosystem approaches (Huebner 1979) are also becoming popular in the United States.

Organizational and management theories are used to interpret processes such as allocating resources, policy-making, managing personnel, leading, revitalizing institutions, and terminating programs. Some organizational theories, such as the political model, explicitly acknowledge the relationships among external groups and behavior in institutions of higher education; thus, organizational theory offers insights about the context in which student development and student affairs work takes place (Kuh 1989).

4. Organization of Student Affairs Functions

No single organizational structure is appropriate for all institutions, given the differences in historical and cultural traditions and institutional missions, purposes, and size. In general, the larger the institution, the greater the diversity of students and the larger the number of services needed by the student body. Not all student services and programs are assigned to an administrative unit labeled student affairs or the equivalent. For example, admissions, registration, and academic advising functions often report either to the president or chief academic officer. In other institutions, these functions may report to the chief student affairs officer.

In institutions in the former Federal Republic of Germany, no single university office directs student activities and services (Stibbs 1966). An assistant to the rector handles university visitors, foreign students, the student club, and academic ceremonies. As with United States institutions, many areas of student services in Australia, Belgium, and the Netherlands tend to report to an administrator whose title indicates responsibility for student services, such as a director for student services or dean of students. In Germany, the *Studentenwerk*—which is directly responsible to the state ministry of education—provides student services on behalf of institutions in a specified geographical area (Prins 1983). The coordination and management of services in the United Kingdom is often the responsibility of the secretary of the university rather than a director of student services (Gurowitz 1988). In France, increasingly autonomous student services centers report to the director of the National Center for Student Services in Paris which represents student services for the government (Prins 1983). In general, United States institutions have the autonomy to determine which services will be provided; however, the range of services may be influenced by policies established by state systems of higher education or coordinating boards. Student services in many countries in Africa tend to be decentralized with many responsibilities remaining at the level of the academic department or individual faculty member; that is, faculty members are responsible for dealing with students' tutoring needs and academic as well as career advice.

In Belgium student services are supported by the government; support received by the institution is determined by law on an amount per student basis (Prins 1983). In United States universities, student services are typically funded through a combination of student fees, charges for the use of services such as health care, income generated by auxiliary services such as dining facilities, and general fund revenues.

4.1 Student Unions

Not all student welfare services are provided by the institution. In Scandinavia and Western Europe, many student services are provided through student unions; cooperative enterprises are established and operated by students. A variant of the student union, albeit on a limited scale, is becoming popular in some areas of the United States such as California. Services available through membership in the union or co-op may include housing, health services, psychological counseling, restaurants, snack shops, grocery stores, travel bureaus, photo services, cleaning services, and so on (Mullen 1987). The membership fee is sometimes refundable at graduation or after resigning from the co-op. While the co-op is usually independent of the institution, the institution may provide space for union services. Student unions are successful often because salaried student managers, on leave from their studies, employ professionals to oversee the variety of operations (Kuh 1979).

Another variant of the student union is the political action organization. For example, any Chinese student may join the All-China Students' Federation (ACSF) which has over 100,000 member unions with a combined enrollment of over 60 million students across secondary schools, colleges, and universities. Through collective action, the ACSF advocates on behalf of students to the university and government. ACSF-sponsored activities include interdisciplinary symposia, cultural performances, weekend parties, photography exhibitions, film and opera reviews, student games, work study programs, and contests of encyclopedic knowledge (Klepper 1988).

5. Student Affairs Programs and Services

Student affairs units may administer a variety of programs and services: admissions, registration, orientation, financial aids, housing and food services, student activities, academic advice, discipline, career planning and placement; health services, including psychological counseling; special services for groups such as fraternities, veterans, sight- and mobility-impaired students, and students with learning disabilities; recreational sports, social and educational programming for the campus community and for particular groups such as racial and ethnic groups, older students, and women; and other services deemed necessary by the institution. For example, some institutions provide free or low-cost legal services and childcare for students. Student characteristics, such as age, ability, maturity, and commitment to intellectual activity, vary considerably and dictate in part the need for certain programs and services. The range and nature of student affairs programs and services are also influenced by the perceived role and responsibility of the student in the learning enterprise. Students in many West European countries and Scandinavia are expected to be self-sufficient. In addition, in some countries, such as Japan and Nigeria, the family plays a more active role in a student's life, thus reducing the need for institutionally provided services.

Only selected programs and services can be described here. More complete descriptions of these and other services and programs can be found in Delworth and Hanson (1989), Packwood (1977), and Rentz and Saddlemire (1988).

5.1 Admissions

The emergence of an office to coordinate new student admissions was the direct result of expanding duties of college registrars, although similar activities were performed by the "major beadle" in the medieval university (Kuh 1977). Admissions officers implement faculty or government policies designed to facilitate an appropriate transition from a student's previous educational experience to university study. National universities in many countries, such as the United Kingdom, Japan, Kenya, Nigeria, and the Republic of China, use established "cut-off" scores on one or more entrance examinations to determine who can matriculate. In the United Kingdom, applications for undergraduate study are made through the Universities and Colleges Admissions Service (UCAS), a process similar to that in the United States at the City University of New York. Because of the popularity of Oxford and Cambridge, these universities offer places before other universities, which permits the UCAS to allocate the remaining students to departments at other British universities (Frisz 1979).

In the former German Democratic Republic, France, and Switzerland, the government determines admissions standards. In some East European countries, admissions policies originate from the Communist Party. Candidates take a common national entrance examination and submit references from the Party, Student Communist League, or trade union for their fields, and others. Stricter screening procedures may be applied to applicants for politically and socially sensitive fields (Forrest 1968). However, private colleges and universities in most countries use factors in addition to examination scores to determine admission.

The proportion of a college-age cohort participating in higher education in the former Soviet Union (about one third) is closer to that of the United States and Japan, where participation exceeds 40–50 percent, than other areas such as Australia and Eastern or Western Europe. In the United Kingdom, about 10–20 percent of the eligible population participate. In Kenya, only about half of 1 percent of students entering primary school have been permitted to participate in higher education.

Because of declining birthrates in the United States, the numbers of traditional-age college students (17–22) has declined. As a result, admissions personnel have developed institutional marketing strategies to attract students in order to maintain stable enrollments (Hossler 1984). Some institutions in Australia, the United Kingdom, and South Africa have begun aggressive marketing techniques to recruit foreign students. Also, concern for social equity coupled with demands for economic productivity have influenced admission policies so that persons from more varied educational and social backgrounds can participate in higher education, particularly in the United States. In general, however, members of many minority groups remain concentrated in lower division institutions, such as community colleges in the United States, and some are significantly underrepresented throughout all levels of higher education.

5.2 Orientation

Common to United States and some Australian institutions, but rare elsewhere, are programs designed to introduce new students (and often their parents and/or spouse and children) to college life. Programs range in length from several hours during the summer designed primarily to disseminate academic information, to week-long initiatives offered immediately preceding the start of the first semester, to semester- or year-long courses that carry academic credit (Dannells and Kuh 1977). Illustrative orientation activities include tours of facilities such as the library, programs that address study skills, academic advice and career planning, and activities designed to establish social affinity groups.

5.3 Registrars

In the United States registrars often have a faculty appointment and are responsible for monitoring students' academic progress, maintaining student records, verifying institutional requirements for completion of programs of study, and implementing related academic policies. In some countries, such as the United Kingdom, the registrar role carries additional status and responsibility for university governance. In other countries, such as Japan and Kenya, registrars are intimately involved in the entrance examination process. Institutions in Western Europe do not typically maintain comprehensive student files. Academic records, when they exist, are kept by faculty members. In East European countries, the Student Communist League sometimes maintains records of student achievements (Forrest 1968).

5.4 Financial Aid

Student financial aid includes any funds, other than those provided by the student and his or her family, that either reduce college costs or minimize the pressure of such expenses while enrolled in college (Dannells 1977). Student aid may be either direct or indirect. Direct aid goes from a government agency to the individual student; indirect aid is channeled through the institution to the student (Coomes 1988).

Three forms of aid are available: grants, loans, and employment. Grants represent resources that do not require repayment and include scholarships based on academic performance or some other talent such as music or athletics. Loans are funds that are to be repaid in whole or part, with or without interest, and may be available through commercial lending institutions, the college or university, or directly from a government agency to the student. Student employment includes part-time jobs or jobs secured through the college to assist students in meeting their expenses.

The administration of financial aid, including part-time work on or off the campus, is a primary function of student affairs personnel in the United States, where the two largest sources of aid are the federal government and institutional resources. In general, selection of recipients and determination of award amounts are made by administrators using the criteria established by faculty committees, government agencies, and other groups. In the United Kingdom, France, Germany, and Switzerland, the major criteria for receiving aid are academic performance and financial need; in the United States the latter has become more important in an effort to make higher education accessible to all citizens. Switzerland uses local commissions of faculty and lay persons to determine recipients and aid amounts. Although students do not pay tuition to French universities, as with Kenya and Scandinavia, scholarships for living expenses may be awarded by the national government and from institutional funds. Japan has an intricate system of grants provided by the national government, local governments (municipality or prefecture), and private organizations (Kuh and Nuss 1986). In many institutions in Africa and Eastern Europe, governments award scholarships to persons whose fields of study are integral to the country's economic plan (Forrest 1968, Hughes 1990). In Australia financial support to cover living expenses is available to all full-time students who meet the strict criteria of a means test on family income.

5.5 Housing

The range of student housing options, including single-sex, coeducational, and family, and allied services, such as dining facilities, varies greatly around the world. Depending upon the size, location, and educational mission of the institution, virtually all or only a few students may live in college-owned housing. Many institutions in the United States emphasize the importance of learning about individual differences through educational and social programs presented in the residence hall (Schuh

1988). Although most United States universities have resident advisors in residence halls, their functions are not as well integrated with the curriculum as those of their counterparts (tutors) at, for example, Cambridge University in England. In the United States faculty members rarely live in residence halls.

At some institutions in African countries and in England, faculty members called wardens are responsible for residence halls and the personal and social welfare of students, and are often assisted by subwardens—junior members of the academic or administrative staff (Gurowitz 1988). Wardens live in or near the hall and are expected to monitor the living/learning environment, resolve conflicts, and advocate for students with problems (Hughes 1990). The warden works closely with the hall council, an elected body of student residents responsible for social, cultural, and sports activities of the hall. In some universities in the United Kingdom and Germany, dormitories serve as centers for academic teaching, recreation, and social interaction.

In general, institutions in countries other than the United Kingdom, Australia, and the United States provide relatively little university-owned and operated student housing. For example, students in Scandinavia obtain their own housing; in some instances, student unions have built dormitories using student membership fees (Kuh 1979). Student dormitories built by the government but supervised by institutions are provided for about half the students in colleges and universities of Eastern Europe (Forrest 1968). Swiss universities provide dining facilities but typically do not provide dormitories. The French government builds, owns, and supervises student cafeterias in residence halls. Other countries, such as Japan and Nigeria, provide student housing on a limited basis but offer little or no educational programming in student housing. At Japan's Tsukuba University about 4,000 students (29% of the student body) live in university-owned housing. Kyoto University is more representative of student housing in Japan as only 2 percent of the student body are provided with accommodation, in five small dormitories (Kuh and Nuss 1986).

In some developing countries, many students have their first experience of cafetaria service, hot and cold running water, and flush toilets when living in a residence hall. In 1966, the largest building in Afghanistan was a residence hall at Kabul (Hawley 1966). However, dormitory living is less feasible at institutions where the majority of students are older, attend college part-time, and extend their studies over a period of four to eight years or more.

5.6 Discipline

The degree to which student discipline is an institutional priority depends upon the age of students and cultural expectations for the relationship between the institution and the student. In Scandinavia and many West European countries, institutions do not monitor student out-of-class behavior; students are expected to be self-sufficient and few live in college-owned housing. In some institutions, the discipline function may also include adjudicating violations of the academic code, such as plagiarism. When discipline is a major concern, the chief student affairs officer is typically the responsible institutional agent. Often review boards with representation by students, faculty, and administrators are employed to adjudicate violations of academic and social conduct codes. The Student Communist League in the former German Democratic Republic and some student unions in other countries conduct discipline hearings and determine sanctions (Forrest 1968).

5.7 Health Services

Most institutions in the United States, particularly those that attract large numbers of residential students, provide campus-based medical assistance funded in part by student fees. The use of community-based health services and user fees, that is, pay for services when rendered, has increased because of escalating costs of medical services. West European universities, excluding those in the United Kingdom, do not generally provide health services on the campus, although most have compulsory health insurance plans (Prins 1983). In countries where student unions are prevalent, the union may contract with health service providers in the community to offer members reasonably priced services, including psychological counseling.

Universities in developing countries have been slow in recognizing the importance of counseling because of the need to emphasize economic over social development and dominant cultural mores that dictate preferred responses to psychological problems. For example, in Nigeria psychological disorders are often addressed by "wise men," conferences of elders, or family gatherings rather than through assistance from professional counselors (Mack 1979).

5.8 Extracurricular Activities

In most colleges and universities, students form clubs or organizations to pursue special interests, either with or without the sanction of the institution. Faculty or student affairs staff often advise institutionally sanctioned student organizations, such as student government or discipline-based groups such as a history or biology club. In France, governmental agencies organize clubs (Prins 1983). In the United Kingdom and Germany, students assume more responsibility for these activities than in the United States. Students in the United Kingdom are admitted to the university by a department or faculty which usually sponsors its own social and sports activities. At Cambridge University the senior tutor at each college acts in a capacity similar to a dean of students and supervises clubs (Gurowitz 1988).

In Japan, clubs—particularly for sports and music—are very popular, perhaps because of the limited social interaction in the few dormitories and absence of opportunities to participate in institutional governance (Kuh and Nuss 1986). In East European countries, the Student Communist League sponsors out-of-class activities including sports, social events, academic discussion and study groups, and fine arts (Forrest 1968). In general, Swiss university students generally perceive a lack of utility in such activities (Prins 1983).

5.9 College and University Unions

The college union is common to most institutions in the United States and the number of unions is expanding in countries such as Australia, Canada, and Japan. The college union is a facility or designated part of a campus building that serves as the gathering place for student government, clubs, and organizations—the campus counterpart of a community center with an educational and recreation mission. The college union should not be confused with a labor union or student political action union. Indeed, the first college union—literally a "union" of three debating societies—was established in 1815 in the United Kingdom, 50 years before the first labor union was organized and 130 years before student political action unions were formed in Europe, Asia, and Africa following the Second World War.

The college union is often the only facility provided to meet the dining needs of students and faculty who do not dine where they live, particularly on smaller residential campuses. Other services include an information desk, computers, lockers, telephones, bookstores, financial services, newspapers and periodicals, recreation facilities, meeting space, and so forth. College unions are usually self-supporting, particularly in the United States. Funds are derived from revenues generated by food service, bookstore sales, recreational areas, and space rentals. Fees are sometimes charged to students as a means of funding debt services and daily operations (Association of College Unions-International 1982).

5.10 Career Development and Placement

As higher education becomes more expensive, students increasingly expect to obtain employment commensurate with their training after college. Thus, assistance by the institution in helping students identify suitable positions has become increasingly important. Placement services may be centralized in one office or decentralized to various academic units such as the School of Technology, School of Business, or School of Pedagogy or Education. In some countries, such as France, Germany, and Switzerland, the placement function is performed by faculty who use personal relationships with prospective employers and employment agencies to help students locate jobs (Prins 1983). In the United Kingdom the appointment (admissions and placement) officer does some vocational counseling (Gurowitz 1988). Placement functions in United States universities typically include a career development focus in which students examine the congruence between personal interests, abilities, and aspirations, and the demands of a vocation (Kroll and Rentz 1988).

Little vocational guidance or academic counseling is available in many European universities. In general, students must choose a major and vocation before applying to college where they will have a rigidly prescribed course of study; they will also find difficulty in changing their major or transferring to another institution, and must enter a vocation assigned by the state upon graduation. In the countries of Eastern Europe, vocational guidance often takes the form of recruiting students in their last year of secondary school into the scientific and technological fields prioritized in the economic plan. Thus, a student's vocational field is influenced by the number of openings in various areas of study as well as the financial inducements offered as part of the admission procedure (Forrest 1968).

5.11 Foreign Student Counseling

As the world becomes more of a global village, international understanding is essential. Foreign student advisors provide information to foreign nationals about the institution and governmental regulations affecting their student eligibility status. They also assist foreign students in locating suitable housing, obtaining necessary medical treatment, and with other matters required for a successful university experience. Most colleges and universities designate someone, often the registrar, to serve as the foreign student liaison. At Japan's University of Kyoto, for example, four professional staff work with the more than 400 non-Japanese students (Kuh and Nuss 1986). Colleges and universities in the United States—particularly large universities—have developed numerous programs and services to assist international students.

6. Credentials of Student Affairs Staff

A chief student affairs officer (CSAO), the dean of students, or vice-president for student affairs, in United States institutions may be a faculty member or a professional student affairs administrator with an advanced professional degree in student affairs administration, higher education, or counseling. In other higher education systems, such as Japan and The People's Republic of China, the chief student affairs officer is likely to be a faculty member. In some countries, such as Japan, student affairs staff other than the CSAO sometimes report to government officials, such as the Ministry of Education (Kuh and Nuss 1986). In the former German Democratic Republic, institutions usually had an assistant president for student affairs whose responsibilities were similar to those of the United States dean of students. However, a comparable officer does not exist in the former Soviet Union, Hungary, Bulgaria, France, the former Federal Republic of Germany, Switzerland, or the United Kingdom (Forrest 1968, Gurowitz 1988, Prins 1983). The dean in some of these systems tends to spend more time with individual students, does not have the extensive formal training of the American counterpart, and has minimal staff and bureaucracy to manage (Forrest 1968).

7. Main Issues

Many pressing concerns facing student affairs are perennial: helping students make a successful transition to college life; reviewing programs and services to make certain they are responsive to changing student characteristics, needs, and interests; student involvement in national politics; and encouraging students to be responsible and to conform to legal requirements and community standards with regard to the use of alcohol and other substances. Relatively little attention has been given by institutions in countries other than the United States to developing policy statements addressing students' academic and social rights and responsibilities. In many countries in Western Europe, student housing policies, health insurance arrangement, and access by the general public to university-sponsored programs and events lack clarity and consistency (Prins 1983).

In some parts of the world, the link between students' out-of-class life and the quality of the college experience is being recognized for the first time. For example, the Burmese Central Regional College Supervisory Committee recently developed a master plan for cultural affairs, vocational guidance, sports, and other activities. In Australia and West European countries, as with the United States, students are becoming increasingly involved in university governance, and a more professional approach to developing programs and services has been noted (Prins 1983).

Two specific issues warrant some elaboration—enrollment management and the implications of an increasingly diverse student body, particularly with regard to racial and ethnic background.

7.1 Enrollment Management

Enrollment management is unique to the United States (Hossler 1984). It is an institution-wide initiative designed to enhance student satisfaction with college life and to increase the proportion of students who will remain at the institution to complete their educational program. High attrition rates are a natural consequence of efforts to make higher education accessible to all. The guiding proposition is that because institutional programs and services are interrelated, through purposeful coordination of services, an institution can be more responsive to students' needs. Thus, the enrollment management model satisfies both the institution's instrumental need for stable tuition and fee revenues, which insures institutional survival, and the student's desire to obtain a college education.

7.2 The Multiculturalism Imperative

As students become increasingly diverse in terms of age, ability, and cultural and ethnic heritage, institutions will have to develop strategies that acknowledge and celebrate these differences. Such differences cannot only, or perhaps best be addressed in classrooms. Students affairs personnel, in cooperation with others, will be expected to encourage students to establish meaningful patterns of interaction that result in understanding, respect, and appreciation of cultural differences. Responding affirmatively to ethnic and cultural differences is one of the most significant challenges facing higher education, and student affairs staff will be expected to play a major role in shaping institutional policy and student attitudes and behavior.

8. Conclusion

Student affairs emerged because of increasing institutional size and complexity resulting in the diversification of general administrative functions. Initially student affairs assumed the necessary and sometimes unpopular tasks abandoned by trustees, administrators, and faculty. Student affairs staff have subsequently reaffirmed the development of the whole person as a *raison d'être* of the field.

Student affairs work is difficult. Deans must meet the expectations of the university and their superiors who typically desire decorous, orderly campuses. Students usually resist regulation and wish to participate in university self-governance and exercise free speech. Students expect student affairs staff to understand and respond to their needs and demands; presidents, other administrators, and faculty members often perceive student affairs staff as too lenient or supportive of student requests. Student affairs personnel often work with issues marked by tension, therefore, because of the need to mediate the needs and expectations of students with those of the institution.

Student affairs personnel will continue to be challenged by the tensions and dilemmas that characterize college and university life. Each student is unique; yet students are expected to be treated equitably. Certain policies and practices and campus traditions contribute to a sense of community, but may also cause some members to suffer indignities, particularly those of ethnic and racial minorities.

Responsible citizenship demands that unjust institutional norms, policies, and practices be questioned, yet public criticism of institutional policies is often unsettling (National Association of Student Personnel Administrators 1987) and is sometimes the proximate cause of civil unrest in a nation. Encouraging students to take advantage of learning and personal development opportunities while in college remains the primary goal of student affairs. Working in concert with faculty, other administrators, and students, student affairs programs and services enhance the quality of the college experience for all students.

See also: Administration of Education as a Field of Study; Student Political Activism and Student Movements

References

American College Personnel Association 1975 A student development model for student affairs in tomorrow's higher education. *J. Col. Stud. Personnel* 16: 334–41

American Council on Education 1937 *The Student Personnel Point of View*. American Council on Education, Washington, DC

American Council on Education 1949 *The Student Personnel Point of View*. American Council on Education, Washington, DC

Association of College Unions-International 1982 *College Unions: Fifty Facts*. Association of College Unions-International, Bloomington, Indiana

Brown R D 1972 *Student Development in Tomorrow's Higher Education: A Return to the Academy*. American Personnel and Guidance Association, Washington, DC

Brubacher J S, Rudy W 1976 *Higher Education in Transition*, 3rd edn. Harper and Row, New York

Bursch C W 1962 The vice president or dean of students. In: Burns G P (ed.) 1962 *Administrators in Higher Education*. Harper, New York

Chickering A W 1969 *Education and Identity*. Jossey-Bass, San Francisco, California

Clark B R 1983 *The Higher Education System: Academic Organization in Cross-national Perspective*. University of California Press, Berkeley, California

Coomes M D 1988 Student financial aid. In: Rentz A L, Saddlemire G L (eds.) 1988

Council of Student Personnel Associations 1975 Student development services in postsecondary education. *J. Col. Stud. Personnel* 16: 524–28

Cowley W H 1934 The history of student residential housing. *Sch. Soc.* 40: 705–12

Dannells M 1977 Financial aid. In: Packwood W T (ed.) 1977

Dannells M, Kuh G D 1977 Orientation. In: Packwood W T (ed.) 1977

Delworth U, Hanson G R (eds.) 1989 *Student Services: A Handbook for the Profession*, 2nd edn. Jossey-Bass, San Francisco, California

Erikson E 1968 *Identity, Youth, and Crisis*. Norton, New York

Fenske R H 1989 Historical foundations of student services. In: Delworth U, Hanson G R (eds.) 1989

Frisz R H 1979 A comparison of student services in England and the United States. *J. NAWDAC* 42: 10–15

Forrest A 1968 Student personnel services in higher education in Communist East Europe. *NASPA J.* 5: (1)17–23

Forrest L 1989 Guilding, supporting, and advising students: The counselor role. In: Delworth U, Hanson G R (eds.) 1989

Gilligan C 1982 *In a Different Voice*. Harvard University Press, Cambridge, Massachusetts

Gurowitz W D 1988 *A Fulbright to England*. Cornell University, Ithaca, New York

Hawley K 1966 Developing Afghanistan. *NASPA J.* 3(3): 8–10

Holland J L 1985 *Making Vocational Choices: A Theory of Vocational Personalities and Work Environments*, 2nd edn. Prentice-Hall, Englewood Cliffs, New Jersey

Hossler D 1984 *Enrollment Management: An Integrated Approach*. College Entrance Examination Board, New York

Huebner L A (ed.) 1979 *Redesigning Campus Environments*. Jossey-Bass, San Francisco, California

Hughes R 1990 Development of student services abroad—An African case study. *NASPA J.* 27: 336–43

Katz J (ed.) 1968 *No Time For Youth*. Jossey-Bass, San Francisco, California

Klepper W M 1988 Student governance in China. *NASPA J.* 25: 169–73

Knock G H 1988 The philosophical heritage of student affairs. In: Rentz A L, Saddlemire G L (eds.) 1988

Kohlberg L 1971 Stages of moral development. In: Beck C M, Crittenden B S, Sullivan E V (eds.) 1971 *Moral Education: Interdisciplinary approaches*. University of Toronto Press, Toronto

Kroll J, Rentz A L 1988 Career planning and placement. In: Rentz A L, Saddlemire G L (eds.) 1988

Kuh G D 1977 Admissions. In: Packwood W T (ed.) 1977

Kuh G D 1979 Student unions: The Scandinavian counterpart to American university student services. *J. NAWDAC* 42: 3–9

Kuh G D 1989 Organizational concepts and influences. In: Delworth U, Hanson G R (eds.) 1989

Kuh G D, Nuss E M 1986 Student affairs work in Japanese colleges and universities. *NASPA J.* 23(3): 39–49

Mack D E 1979 Counseling in a Nigerian university. *Pers. Guid. J.* 57(9): 457–61

Miller T K, Prince J S 1976 *The Future of Student Affairs*. Jossey-Bass, San Francisco, California

Mullen M A 1987 College unions, student activities, and student services in Japanese colleges and universities: Does the college union idea lose something in the translation? Proc. 67th Annual Conf. of College Unions-International, Boston, Massachusetts

National Association of Student Personnel Administrators 1987 *A Perspective on Student Affairs*. American College Testing Program, Iowa City, Iowa

Packwood W T (ed.) 1977 *College Student Personnel Services*. C Thomas, Springfield, Illinois

Perry W Jr. 1970 *Forms of Intellectual and Ethical Development in the College Years*. Holt, Rinehart and Winston, New York

Prins D J 1983 Student services and policies: An outdated privilege or a necessary part of higher education? *Int. J. Inst. Mangt. in Higher Educ.* 7: 149–56

Rentz A L, Saddlemire G L (eds.) 1988 *Student Affairs Functions in Higher Education*. C Thomas, Springfield, Illinois

Rodgers R 1989 Student development. In: Delworth U, Hanson G R (eds.) 1989
Rogers C R 1961 On Becoming a Person. Houghton Mifflin, Boston, Massachusetts
Rudolph F 1962 *The American College and University: A History*. Knopf, New York
Sanford N 1962 Developmental status of the entering freshman. In: Sanford N (ed.) 1962 *The American College*. Wiley, New York
Schuh J H 1988 Residence halls. In: Rentz A L, Saddlemire G L (eds.) 1988
Stibbs J H 1966 The free university. *NAPSA J.* 3(3): 6–8
Walsh W B 1973 *Theories of Person-Environment Interaction: Implications for the College Student*, American College Testing Program, Iowa City, Iowa
Williamson E G 1961 *Student Personnel Services in Colleges and Universities: Some Foundations, Techniques and Processes of Program Administration*. McGraw-Hill, New York

Further Reading

Barr M J (ed.) 1988 *Student Services and The Law: A Handbook for Practitioners*. Jossey-Bass, San Francisco, California
Knefelkamp L, Widick C, Parker C A (eds.) 1978 *applying New Developmental Findings*. Jossey-Bass, San Francisco, California
Kuh G D (ed.) 1983 *Understanding Student Affairs Organizations*. Jossey-Bass, San Francisco, California
Kuh G D 1984 A framework for understanding student affairs work. *J. Col. Stud. Personnel* 25: 25–31
Kuh G D, Whitt E J, Shedd J D 1987 *Student Affairs Work 2001: A Paradigmatic Odyssey*. American College Personnel Association, Alexandria, Virginia
Sandeen A 1988 Issues influencing the organization of student affairs. In: Delworth U, Hanson G R (eds.) 1989

G. D. Kuh

Student Support Systems: Adult Education

The demand for, and expansion of, adult education is greater than ever. Due to their special needs, adults often require as much or more support than younger learners. Arrangements to promote and reinforce adult efforts to intiate and continue education are taking increasingly varied forms and are incorporating many functions of traditional services such as advising, counseling, tutoring, orientation, financial assistance, and peer support networks. However, the forms for rendering these functions may differ because they evolve from the matrix of challenges and resources in the adult learners' contexts. These support systems are increasingly dependent on personnel who are not trained in traditional support or personnel services. By recognizing that counseling helps adult learners on two levels, first to assimilate or engage in the new experiences, and second to accommodate or develop changed perspectives and behaviors from processing new experiences, one can realize that untrained personnel can assist in the first function, while the second, more complex function can be addressed by trained personnel. Examples of governmental and collaborative support systems are given now. They are intended to illustrate the range of systems which are coming into existence to support adult learning. The development of such support systems depends on alliances between educational, economic, and political entities.

1. Background and Philosophy of Support Systems for Adult Learners

In spite of philosophical and pragmatic arguments in favor of adult education, one cannot deny that institutions of adult education have generally attracted only a minor portion of their potential audience, even when there were few economic constraints. Perhaps more disheartening is the problem of retaining adult learners. Many adult education programs suffer from high attrition due to an array of problems which confront the students. Although support systems have been shown to promote enrollment and retention, there has been a general failure to offer support systems, much less integrate them with recruitment and provision.

Adult learners usually face multiple barriers to resuming their education. The need to attend to family obligations and the lure of other activities competes for both time and energy. Success is far more likely when learners have the active support of employers and others significant to them. Long absences from school may also have created anxieties about the capacity to continue learning across the whole lifespan, and impatience with pedagogy that fails to take into account the differences between the young and older learners. In addition, the competence of adult learners must be acknowledged and they must be allowed to play a more active role in the development of course syllabi and goals. Moreover, they may need active intervention with instructors, employers, and others, and support from counselors and tutors (Chuma 1991). Services may also need to enlighten employers about absorbing more women and retrained older workers into the workforce and about underwriting their employees who are engaged in adult education (Gooderham 1991).

Unfortunately, heightened appreciation of the importance of adult education coincides with financial crises befalling most of the world's educational systems. The specter of reduced educational budgets and resources underscores the need to promote andragogical innovations as well as systems to support them. Approaches which are the most systemic and involve the largest network should go the furthest in securing the educational goals of all concerned. And the more integrated the support systems, both horizontally and vertically, the higher the likelihood of success.

2. Student Support Systems at the Government Level

Some types of support by central or local governments enjoy almost universal appeal. Examples of these are: paid educational leave, state-sponsored childcare, scholarships, guarantees of employment following formal studies, vocational training on apprenticeships, and linking employment and education through cooperative education. Also important in supporting adult education is the provision of multiple options, alone or in concert with industry. One may even view increasing accessibility as a major support system in itself. The People's Republic of China, for instance, offers one of the most comprehensive systems for facilitating access. Prospective learners may choose to study independently, via correspondence or televised courses, part-time or full-time at an established residential college, or through workshops in the factory or farm. About half of the workers in industrial and commercial enterprises attend short-term training courses (see *China, People's Republic of: Adult Education*).

Outside of Europe, national sponsorship of free education has led to increased access, but there has been diminishing attention or resources expended in support of efforts beyond the narrow context of institutional, classroom-based supervision. Some exceptions can be found in nations as diverse as the United States (where substantial aid is given to categories of adults on the basis of factors such as financial need), France (liberal work-study programs), and Singapore (scholarships and loans are available for poor students if they pursue need-driven academic majors) (Salmi 1992).

2.1 Efforts in Rural Areas

Governmental systems have long been a feature of agricultural education. These efforts often illustrate one of the few instances of true long-range thinking in the provision of education for adult learners. In the United States, agricultural extension guidance, publications, and experimental farms have been an integral part of many public universities since their initial establishment.

It is crucial that the instruction does not occur in a vacuum. Appreciation for the more conservative audiences found in rural areas needs to take the form of teaching within the context of local traditions and with the support of individuals who command respect within the smaller community (Roberts 1989). Indonesia's *Dikmas* program exemplifies a large-scale approach that integrates literacy, vocational education, and exposure to developments occurring in the more sophisticated parts of the nation (see *Literacy Education: Southeast Asia*). Elsewhere in Asia, Thailand's *Khit-Pen* and Japan's *Kominkan* programs are similarly attuned to enhancing the general educational level of rural communities (Duke 1989). Amongst African countries, rural adult education is offered full-time development workers who provide instruction and support the establishment of women's clubs at the village level. These clubs meet twice weekly to upgrade the quality of life in a variety of spheres, e.g., home economics, child rearing, and agricultural production, and are often dependent on self-help principles (Kamfwa 1992).

2.2 Regional Centers

Governments have established centers in support of adult learners who are beyond the reach of conventional institutions. Some centers are rather modest in scope. One in Papua New Guinea, for example, simply offers weekly tutorial services for extension students enrolled in correspondence courses. A better funded example is Malaysia's Center for Off-Campus Studies. The "Center" has an umbrella of 12 regional centers which support a Distance Education program by providing tutors, technical receivers and transmitters, meeting venues for student discussions, and laboratory equipment. Each center's operation is integrated with, and supported by, the local secondary school and regional library, as well as the Universiti Sains Malaysia, and presents a model which other tertiary learning programs may wish to emulate (Indrus and Zin 1992).

Spain's Popular Universities, which have counterparts in Latin America, illustrate a more eclectic system in support of adult education. In 1990 some 500,000 adults either enrolled in one of the 87 sites' 2,000 courses, or participated in one of the 4,000 cultural events offered. Depending on local needs, the Popular Universities also include as part of their offerings social intervention and back-up educational programs, creation of cooperatives and small businesses in rural areas, and training for entry into the job market. The ability to respond to a variety of adult learner needs is due, in part, to each site's varied infrastructure and variable teams of instructors, which facilitates adaptability (Lopez 1992).

2.3 United States Community Colleges

Integrated support systems are found in many of the North American Community Colleges (also known as Two-Year or Junior Colleges). Although these institutions traditionally fall under the public school system, the range of support services goes well beyond the expectations of adolescents. The Community College usually makes available a comprehensive range of services provided by trained professionals housed within a division known as Student Services or Student Affairs. These are usually available to students and include not only personal, financial, and academic counseling, but also services which address health and disability problems, childcare for dependents, social interests, employment referral, and career guidance.

3. Cooperative Support Systems

One of the most cost-effective models for adult education is the Study Circle. These consist of populist learning activities which link clusters of individuals in the community, educational associations, firms, and public institutions. Although common primarily in the Nordic countries, Germany, and Japan, variants can also be found in Tanzania and other developing nations.

In Sweden, where it has reached its fullest development, the study circle brings together 5–20 friends or associates. Under the direction of one of the group's members, they assemble a planned study of a subject or problem area. One of 10 national associations then sanctions the plan and the leader, and makes the study circle eligible for state funding. There have been more than 300,000 study circles in Sweden alone, which have run the gamut from studying the theater, union education, aesthetics, immigrant language skills, and international studies. There have even been 4,000 study circles at the university level (see *Study Circles*).

Similar to the Study Circle are "self-help" groups organized at the work site. These generally meet on a regular basis following initial assessment and identification of needs by outside educators or consultants in collaboration with the management. Employer support can take the form of paying start-up costs, allowing the use of premises, and paid release time. However, it is unusual for employers to pay for formal support services such as counseling.

In the United Kingdom a major component of continuing vocational education is known as PICKUP (Professional, Industrial, and Commercial Updating). It was stimulated by the Thatcher government's desire to see education take a more "free market" stance by making itself self-financing or at least cost covering. The basic premise is that by increased private sector involvement the full expertise of the universities can be made available to the various professions, industry, and commerce (Hester 1991). Implicit in such models with strong employer involvement is the expectation that the learners' studies are linked directly to their current employment.

Throughout the world employees find themselves engaged in on-the-job training. In the United States it has been estimated that business and industry spends between US $40–200 billion on employee training and development—more than equal to the annual budget of all United States postsecondary institutions combined. North American businesses now teach over a thousand college credit courses and some even offer degree programs (Smith 1984). For the most part, what is known as market financed or Industry-Based Training (IBT) is provided by professional trainers within the organization, or by educators brought in from outside. The curriculum is driven by the needs which the employer perceives. The high level of employer support and commitment for the programs is attested to by the fact that employers nearly always pay the full cost (Dahlgren and Stone 1990). However, these expenses seldom include student support beyond formal teaching (see *Measurement of Industry Training; Training Costs: Measurement*).

An interesting example of market financed education exists in Finland. The employers' "cash-for-services" approach consists of an initial analysis of educational needs, and then a demand for as local a level as possible of educator customization of curriculum, and procurement of materials and teachers (Marjomaki 1990).

Such training is naturally more reflective of worker needs and more state-of-the-art since traditional academic criteria—for example, prerequisites, credentialing, academic periods, and degree objectives—do not delimit the trainer. Lessons can be "sandwiched" between periods of employment, or conducted on-the-job. Greater success can be achieved when these efforts are backed by systems which support the learners in getting the most out of the instruction. This trend may also help stem the current imbalance in many parts of the world between overeducation in low-demand fields and undereducation in high-demand ones, for example, in Indonesia, Morocco, and Thailand (Salmi 1992) (see *Overeducation*).

4. Conclusion

Considering diminishing budgets for education together with demands for the retraining or upgrading of adult learners, it seems inevitable that alliances between educators and employers will have to be made. These alliances, however, will also need to integrate input from professional associations and/or trade unions affiliated with the skills at issue. Each entity has a vested interest that goes beyond the narrower focus of any single private or public employer (Knox and McLeish 1989). In the United States, union-sponsored efforts for its members illustrate benefits which include not just the individual worker, but the family and local educational institutions, as well as the employer.

In many parts of the world the endorsement or active participation of religious leaders or agencies may also help to encourage reluctant or apprehensive workers to change old ways to suit new market conditions and to accommodate modernism. In short, efforts to support the adult learner need to include diverse groups and be integrated with one another at all levels. This is demanded not only because it represents the most efficient delivery of services, but because societies can ill afford to squander their human resources.

See also: Counseling Adult Students; Dropout in Adult

Education; Outreach in Adult Education; Participation Motivation in Adult Education; Participation in Adult Education: Antecedent Factors

References

Chuma P 1991 People's participation in continuing education: A case study of extension studies of the University of Zambia. *Int. J. Univ. Adult Educ.* 30(2): 35–40

Dahlgren J, Stone J R 1990 Industry perceptions of industry-based training provided by technical colleges. *J. Voc. Tech. Educ.* 7(1): 46–56

Duke C 1989 Provision in Southeast Asia. In: Titmus C J (ed.) 1989 *Lifelong Education for Adults: An International Handbook*, Pergamon Press, New York

Gooderham P 1991 Socioeconomic outcomes from adult education. *Adult Educ. Q.* 41(4): 203–16

Hester M 1991 The changing face of British university adult education—with specific reference to Exeter University. *Int. J. Univ. Adult Educ.* 30(3): 55–70

Idrus R, Zin A–R 1992 Supporting adult learners in distance education at the centre for off-campus studies, Universiti Sains Malaysia, Malaysia. *Int. J. Univ. Adult Educ.* 30(1): 51–62

Kamfwa F 1992 Contributions of women's clubs to rural development in ndola rural east. *J. Adult Educ.* 1(1): 42–54

Knox A B, McLeish J A B 1989 Continuing education of the professional. In Titmus C J (ed.) 1989 *Lifelong Education for Adults: An International Handbook* Pergamon Press, New York

Lopez V 1992 Popular universities in Spain. *Int. J. Univ. Adult Educ.* 31(2): 1–7

Marjomaki V 1990 Towards market financed education. *Adult Educ. in Finland* 27(2): 35–38

Roberts H W 1989 Integrated rural developments: Specialized training programs. In Titmus C J (ed.) 1989 *Lifelong Education for Adults: An International Handbook*. Pergamon Press, New York

Salmi J 1992 The higher education crisis in developing countries: Issues, problems, constraints and reforms. *Int. Rev. Educ.* 38(1): 19–33

Smith W 1984 The future impact of lifelong learning. *Standard Education Almanac*. Professional Publications, Chicago, Illinois

Further Reading

Bojuwoye O 1992 The role of counselling in developing countries: A reply to Soliman. *Int. J. for the Advancement of Counseling* 15(1): 3–16

Dominice P 1992 Continuing education and the burden of schooling. *European Educ.* 24(1): 55–67

Garry A, Cowan J 1992 Opinion: Self-help continuing professional development groups in the workplace—A case study to determine their potential and viability. *Educational and Technology Int.* 29(1): 6–27

Gibson C 1992 Current trends and social issues: Alphabet soup is coming your way. *Adult Learning* 4(2): 18–9

Hill N 1991 AISES: A college intervention program that works. *Change* 23(2): 24–6

Kaeley G 1991 Break in studies and post secondary mathematics performance. *Int. J. Univ. Adult Educ.* 30 (2): 49–64

Kamvnema A 1982 A study of the low attendance and performance of adults in high schools. *J. Adult Educ.* 1 (1): 60–72

Kuh G, Schuh J, Whitt, E 1991 Some good news about campus life: How "Involving Colleges" promote learning outside the classroom. *Change* 23(5): 48–55

Mohle H 1992 The development of adult distance education: The 15th world conference on distance education, Cavacus 1990 *Int. Rev. Educ.* 38(2): 189–93

Soliman, A M 1991 The role of counseling in developing countries. *Int. J. for the Advancement of Counseling* 14 (1): 3–14

C. Healy; H. Martin

Student Teaching and Field Experiences

Classroom experience is critical to the development of skill as a teacher, but there are disagreements about the appropriate weight to be given to practical experience relative to theoretical principles of teaching and learning. This entry provides a general introduction to the problem, reports on variations in teacher education programs in the provision of classroom experience, reviews research-based criticisms of the effects of such experience and the roles played by those who supervise the experience, identifies recommendations for change, and indicates some directions for future research.

1. Introduction

The general purpose of early field experiences and student teaching is to provide prospective teachers with classroom practice in a supportive environment, enabling them gradually to assume the range of responsibilities associated with full-time professional practice. Early field experiences typically begin with structured observations in classrooms, and may proceed to tutoring individual pupils and eventually include teaching isolated lessons to small groups of pupils. Placement within a classroom is usually of short duration (a few hours distributed over a few weeks). Student teaching typically involves more extended practice (e.g., full days for 1–6 weeks) in one setting and often culminates with the prospective teacher planning and teaching all lessons for several days.

Student teaching and field experiences are the major vehicles for providing practical experience in any teacher education program. This is the program area, therefore, where the traditional conflict between theory and practice is felt most strongly. Leavitt (1991) notes that program content is one of eight worldwide issues in teacher education, and says that the problem derives from the fact that teacher education must answer to both the university and the school. University pressures are for more subject-matter content and more research-based pedagogical content. School system pressures are for more practice-oriented courses and more practical experience in classrooms. The amount of time devoted to student teaching and field experiences in any teacher education program is determined by which of these two pressures is stronger in the given setting. There is clear variation among programs, both between and within countries.

2. Types of Variation

Student teaching and field experiences vary in the point in the program where initial placement occurs, the number and variety of placements for a given student, the duration of individual placements, the total hours in all placements, the frequency of supervision by college/university personnel, and the degree of responsibility for evaluation accorded the cooperating teacher in whose classroom a student teacher is placed.

2.1 Variation Between Countries

An examination of three universities in three different countries reveals some of the variations that exist.

University of Western Ontario, Canada. The one-year post-baccalaureate teacher preparation program in operation at the University of Western Ontario involves most students in a total of ten weeks of practice teaching in three periods (October, February, and April) at three different sites. The placements are split to provide practice in a student's two areas of certification. Supervision and evaluation are shared between university supervisors and teachers (called "associate teachers" here, and "clinical instructors" or "cooperating teachers" in other programs) in classrooms where students are placed. However, the university supervisor may see a student teacher only once in the entire year, as each supervises many students who are dispersed over a wide geographical area. Associate teachers therefore shoulder the bulk of the supervisory responsibility.

Yokohama National University, Japan. The undergraduate teacher preparation program at Yokohama National University in Japan engages students in education courses during the last two years of college. An early field experience in the junior year is one week long, involving two days of observation and two days of lectures and discussions led by university professors, school administrators, and school teachers. Student teaching in the senior year lasts four weeks. Students observe their own class and other classes at the same level. They gradually increase the number of lessons taught and must teach from one to three full days of classes. In the final week they prepare one particularly detailed lesson plan, and a college professor observes that lesson. All other evaluation is done by the "mentor" teacher (called "cooperating teacher" elsewhere in this entry). All mentor teachers are selected by their school principals.

University of New Hampshire, United States. The five-year preparation program at the University of New Hampshire, in the United States, culminates in a year-long teaching apprenticeship. Cooperating teachers noted for their excellence are carefully chosen by the university and provided with additional training. Some participate as instructors in weekly student seminars. Student teachers are placed in schools in clusters, contributing to a close working relationship between the university and the schools. University supervisors often offer informal consultation and assistance to the cluster schools.

2.2 Variation Within Countries

Ben-Peretz and Rumney (1991) describe sharp variations between universities and teacher education colleges in Israel. Universities prepare teachers for junior and senior high schools, stress theoretical subjects, and require only 14–40 total practicum hours during a two-year preparation program. Teacher education colleges, in contrast, require 80–150 hours of observation and teaching for prospective elementary and secondary teachers in each of three to four years of study.

The Research About Teacher Education (RATE) study in the United States reports on data from 90 teacher education institutions organized by level of degree offered (bachelor's, master's, or doctorate) (AACTE 1990). Time spent in student teaching and field experiences across these institutions varies from 0 to 400 hours, with secondary education candidates spending less time than elementary or special education candidates. The average times for all students are 75–100 hours in early field experiences and 12 weeks at 40 hours per week in student teaching. Half the institutions surveyed have no stated requirements to become an associate/cooperating teacher and rewards for this contribution are minimal, averaging US$113 per teacher. College supervisors are primarily graduate students and assistant professors. Cooperating teachers surveyed consider student teachers well-prepared, but college supervisors are less enthusiastic. Similar differences are noted in perceptions of teacher education faculty at institutions offering only bachelor's degrees (i.e., they think student teachers are well-prepared) compared to those offering doctorates (i.e., they think student teachers are less well-prepared).

3. Criticisms of Approaches

Criticisms of typical approaches to student teaching and field experiences abound, with most reflecting the tension between theory and practice.

3.1 Criticism of what is Learned

Joyce (1988) cites studies indicating that the general effects of field experience are poorer attitudes toward pupils, suspicion of innovative teaching methods, and negative views of educational research and theory. Furthermore, teacher candidates tend to imitate the attitudes and behavior of their cooperating teachers, resulting in a limitation of the variety of teaching strategies practiced, rather than development of an expanded repertoire.

Feiman-Nemser and Buchmann (1987) concur that experience is not necessarily the best proving ground for prospective teachers. They argue that effective student teaching must differentiate between appropriate and inappropriate lessons of experience, and they present case studies which demonstrate that experiential learning can be misdirected despite the best intentions. They note that cooperating teachers may not take their responsibilities as teacher educators seriously and should have special preparation for this new role.

Kagan (1992) reports on a review of 40 qualitative learning-to-teach studies, and identifies five components of professional growth associated with classroom experiences of prospective and beginning teachers. These are: increased awareness of their knowledge and beliefs about pupils and classrooms; reconstruction of idealized and inaccurate images of pupils and of self-as-teacher; shifts in attention from self, to instructional issues, and then to pupil learning; development of standardized routines for management and instruction; and development of problem-solving skills that are multidimensional and context-specific. Kagan concludes that student teaching would be more beneficial if teacher education programs presented more information about classroom routines, encouraged students to explore images of self-as-teacher, provided for extended interaction with pupils in early field experiences, and placed students with cooperating teachers holding beliefs different from their own, to promote cognitive dissonance.

Grossman and Richert (1988) have observed and interviewed student teachers to identify their perceptions of the comparative contributions of coursework and fieldwork to their knowledge of teaching. They report that fieldwork is cited as a source of knowledge slightly more frequently than coursework. Coursework is seen as providing conceptions of subject matter, theoretical principles of learning/instruction/management, and "images of the possible." Fieldwork is seen as providing practical survival skills, knowledge of pupil interests and difficulties with subject matter, and additional learning about specific topics within the subject content.

Other studies have used questionnaires to examine prospective teachers' feelings of readiness to teach successfully, termed "self-efficacy." Canadian students responding just prior to each of three student teaching experiences, distributed over time, exhibited high ratings of self-efficacy in October, before any actual classroom experience, and these positive feelings grew progressively stronger with each classroom placement (Housego 1990). The greatest changes over time were in perceptions of skills in classroom management and instructional planning. Areas of least change included questioning skills, motivating individual learners, and assessment of pupil learning.

A study conducted in the United States (Weinstein 1990) has examined feelings of self-efficacy associated with early field experiences. Weinstein asked students to predict their own effectiveness as student teachers and first-year teachers compared to other students in their teacher education program. Prior to their field experience the large majority of students saw themselves as well above average in ability to teach. After the field experience their optimism declined somewhat, but an "unrealistic optimism" (p. 280) still remained. A matter of particular concern to Weinstein was that interpersonal relations were regarded as a more important reason for personal success than the academic dimensions of teaching.

Weinstein recommended use of alternative materials in college classes (videotaped teaching sessions and written cases depicting critical classroom events) to promote more astute observation and thoughtful reflection on teaching and learning. She also supported the use of field placements that prompt students to re-examine their beliefs by confronting them with the differing beliefs of a successful cooperating teacher.

Another United States study (Ellwein et al. 1990) used semistructured interviews during which student teachers were asked to describe one successful and one unsuccessful lesson and explain why the lessons were successful or unsuccessful. Successful lessons were defined on the bases of pupil interest and participation, effective implementation (challenge to pupils, relevance to pupil experience), and use of unique materials or activities. Unsuccessful lessons were defined on the bases of pupil reactions (lack of interest or engagement) and problems with behavior management, lesson organization, or clarity of goals. A large majority of the student teachers showed a willingness to be self-critical, acknowledging their own contribution to lack of success in the unsuccessful lessons; yet they were not sophisticated in their use of self-criticism, probably because their teaching situations only nominally encouraged such activity.

3.2 *Criticism of Supervisory Roles*

Questions about what is learned during student teaching and field experiences lead inevitably to questions about the roles of college supervisors and cooperating teachers in providing feedback to prospective teachers. Christensen (1988) analyzed feedback of university supervisors in the United States and compared patterns to results of a similar study of cooperating teachers' feedback. Discussions between student teachers and college supervisors involved predominantly evaluative comments about the lesson from both participants. This contrasts with patterns observed in discussions between student teachers and cooperating teachers, which predominantly involved simple reviews of events and student teaching activities. Cooperating teachers were described as dominant and directive in the interviews, telling student teachers what to do and how to do it, apparently assuming that what works in their own situation will be appropriate for other situations, regardless of classroom context. College supervisors, on the other hand, encouraged student teachers to think, and modeled problem-solving and decision-making approaches to classroom problems.

Ben-Peretz and Rumney (1991) report other differences between cooperating teachers and university supervisors in Israel. In discussions between student teachers and cooperating teachers, evaluative comments by cooperating teachers dominated the conversation. Suggestions about alternative procedures were rare or nonexistent, as were any references to educational theory by cooperating teachers. University supervisors' meetings with the same student teachers dealt with alternative instructional methods and educational theory. Student teachers were less passive in meetings with university supervisors.

Koerner (1992) provides some possible explanations for the conferencing behavior of cooperating teachers, based on journals they kept on their experiences in these discussions. These teachers reported that student teachers interrupted classroom instruction, displaced the teacher from the central role in the classroom, disrupted and replaced carefully established classroom routines, and shifted the cooperating teachers' time and energy from instruction of their pupils to instruction of the student teacher. A more positive effect is the breaking of teachers' isolation by providing the opportunity to discuss classroom experiences with another adult. However, teachers felt that the "university ideas" student teachers brought with them were not relevant to their classrooms.

4. *Some Trends and Recommendations for Change*

Several types of change are proposed to address the problems associated with student teaching and field experiences revealed by research.

4.1 Changes in Duration of Experience

Despite the clear controversy about the value of what is typically learned in student teaching and field experiences, trends in many nations involve some increase in the time that prospective teachers spend in field settings. In some cases this increase is mandated by governmental policy changes. For example, a 1991 regulation by the Ministry of Education in Japan increased the minimum student teaching time required for secondary education candidates from two weeks to four. In 1986, the National Council for the Accreditation of Teacher Education (NCATE), a nongovernmental agency in the United States, issued new guidelines which mandated an increase in student teaching time from eight to ten weeks.

4.2 Changes in Field Settings

Teacher educators, who are aware that quality is at least as important as quantity, have initiated more collaborative arrangements between schools and universities for the provision of field experiences. The Holmes Group, an association of 100 research universities in the United States with teacher preparation programs, has issued a call for the establishment of "professional development schools" (PDSs) (Holmes Group 1990). A PDS is envisioned as an institution formed by a partnership between schools and universities that can provide clinical experiences for the development of prospective teachers, as well as opportunities for the continued professional development of experienced teachers. A PDS is also a site for research and development activities conducted collaboratively by teachers and university professors. A number of universities have collaborated with schools to establish such sites, but the movement is still young and it is too early to tell how successful this innovation will be.

This movement is not limited to the United States. The University of Western Ontario in Canada is working to establish Teacher Education Centres (TECs). Each TEC would involve a small number of schools with several student teachers in each school. All supervision of student teachers would be handled by the associate (cooperating) teachers; university faculty would provide liaison between the school and university. The TECs are expected to provide sites for observation, demonstration, practice, research, and evaluation.

In Spain, a 1986 order published in the *Generalitat* Official Bulletin discussed the possibility of setting up Classified Practice Centres (CPCS), and noted the conditions that would make such schools qualified to take on prospective teachers as trainees. These CPCs are experimental and limited in number. Professors at the University of Barcelona have developed a model to guide the provision of practical experience for students in their program (Fernández et al. 1988). This model specifies essential qualifications for the teacher-tutor (cooperating teacher), including both theoretical and practical knowledge of teaching and training in group dynamics. The student teaching experience is envisioned as a period of cooperative problem-solving, involving the student teacher, the teacher-tutor, and the college tutor (supervisor) working together. The planners acknowledge two major difficulties in implementing this model. First, there are problems inherent in negotiating permission for the college tutor to enter the school classroom to observe teaching practice. Second, the attitudes of some college lecturers interfere with the establishment of cooperative relationships with schools.

4.3 Changes in Preparation for Classroom Experience

Most criticisms of traditional approaches to student teaching and field experiences, as well as many recommendations for improvement in the effectiveness of these experiences, focus directly on the field setting. In the continuing debate about theory versus practice, advocates of learning from practice propose increases in the length of time spent in the field setting and the enhancement of the role and status of the cooperating teacher. Advocates of learning from theory propose changes in the nature of overall professional development in the field setting by involving experienced teachers in classroom-based research and development.

Some alternative recommendations for improvement focus on changes in preparatory experiences provided in college courses. These recommendations stem from assumptions that locate the problem not in the field setting, but in the preconceptions that prospective teachers bring to their teacher education programs. Advocates of these alternative approaches discuss the need for conceptual change, requiring prospective teachers to confront their limited conceptions of teaching and learning and replace them with more inclusive concepts.

Describing these preconceptions as "world images," Wubbels (1992) suggests that the logical or technical language of teacher education courses is not suited to change. A more appropriate language is that of imagery or metaphor. Exploration of alternative metaphors for the teacher (e.g., entertainer, ship's captain, lion tamer) may encourage prospective teachers to consider new perspectives and raise questions about the types of classroom they want to create. The use of aphorisms, like "when the teacher stops teaching, the students start learning" might help teachers realize that effective teaching involves more than clear explanations. Wubbels also recommends the use of visual images through photographs and video, and encouraging students to choose between illusory alternatives, for example authoritarian and *laissez-faire* classroom settings.

5. Future Research

Most research in the area has tended to focus on perceptions and beliefs of prospective teachers, cooperating teachers, and college supervisors, with limited attention to observations of interaction among them. Furthermore, minimal reference has been made to academic or social outcomes for the pupils instructed by student teachers. These types of data should be included in future studies, particularly in those that evaluate new approaches such as professional development schools.

References

American Association of Colleges for Teacher Education 1990 *RATE 4, Teaching Teachers: Facts and Figures*. (Research About Teacher Education Project). AACTE, Washington, DC

Ben-Peretz M, Rumney S 1991 Professional thinking in guided practice. *Teaching and Teacher Education* 7 (5/6): 517–30

Christensen P A 1988 The nature of feedback student teachers receive in post-observation conferences with the university supervisor: A comparison with O'Neal's study of cooperating teacher feedback. *Teaching and Teacher Education* 4(3): 275–86

Ellwein M C, Graue M E, Comfort R E 1990 Talking about instruction: Student teachers' reflections on success and failure in the classroom. *J. Teach. Educ.* 41(5): 3–14

Feiman-Nemser S, Buchmann M 1987 When is student teaching teacher education? *Teaching and Teacher Education* 3(4): 255–73

Fernández M, González R, Subirats A 1988 The tutor's role in teaching practice in initial teacher training. *European Journal of Teacher Education* 11(2/3): 123–30

Grossman P L, Richert A E 1988 Unacknowledged growth: A re-examination of the effects of teacher education. *Teaching and Teacher Education* 4(1): 53–62

Holmes Group 1990 *Tomorrow's Schools: Principles for the Design of Professional Development Schools*. The Holmes Group, East Lansing, Michigan

Housego B E J 1990 Student teachers' feelings of preparedness to teach. *Can. J. Educ.* 15(1): 37–56

Joyce B R 1988 Training research and preservice teacher education: A reconsideration. *J. Teach. Educ.* 39(5): 32–36

Kagan D M 1992 Professional growth among preservice and beginning teachers. *Rev. Educ. Res.* 62: 129–79

Koerner M E 1992 The cooperating teacher: An ambivalent participant in student teaching. *J. Teach. Educ.* 43: 46–56

Leavitt H B 1991 Worldwide issues and problems in teacher education. *J. Teach. Educ.* 42(5): 323–31

Weinstein C S 1990 Prospective elementary teachers' beliefs about teaching: Implications for teacher education. *Teaching and Teacher Education* 6(3): 279–90

Wubbels T 1992 Taking account of student teachers' preconceptions. *Teaching and Teacher Education* 8(2): 137–49

Further Reading

Calderhead J 1991 The nature and growth of knowledge in student teaching. *Teaching and Teacher Education* 7(5/6): 531–35

Griffin G 1986 Issues in student teaching: A review. In: Raths J, Katz L (eds.) 1986 *Advances in Teacher Education*, Vol. 2. Ablex Publishing, Norwood, New Jersey

Guyton E, McIntyre D J 1990 Student teaching and school experiences. In: Houston W R (ed.) 1990 *Handbook of Research on Teacher Education*. Macmillan, New York

G. Morine-Dershimer; K. Leighfield

Students' Curriculum Experiences

Students in curriculum is a relative newcomer as a topic in the literature. However, it is acknowledged sufficiently throughout various literatures on education that it merits inclusion. Such literatures may be categorized as follows: (a) historical inclusion of students in curriculum development and deliberation, especially in progressive education literature; (b) biographical and autobiographical studies of students' sense of meaning and direction, derived from curriculum; (c) ethnographic studies of students' responses to curriculum; (d) empirical and interpretive studies of student interpretations of school and nonschool curricula; (e) critical and phenomenological interpretations of students' curriculum experiences; and (f) stories. Some of the literature exemplifies more than one of these categories; consequently, there is some overlap among them. Nevertheless, they represent a meaningful scheme to subdivide this emergent area of inquiry.

Erickson and Shultz (1992) have made another attempt to draw together research that illuminates student perspectives on curriculum. They discuss conceptions of student experience, noting origins in writings of John Dewey, the absence of treatments of student experience in current discourse, the need for perspective, and the classroom as a scene for student experience of curriculum. In considering relevant research, they draw perspectives from anthropology and educational history, review the "manifest curriculum" or subject matter, and indicate useful findings of studies of the implicit or hidden curriculum. They conclude by setting forth substantive questions for research agendas and methods of inquiry for investigating them.

1. Historical Inclusion of Students in the Curriculum

The literature on curriculum contains very few books prior to the 1980s that directly relate to the student or children in either historical accounts (e.g., Kliebard 1986, Schubert and Lopez-Schubert 1980) or synoptic texts over several decades (see, e.g., Caswell and Campbell 1935, Smith et al. 1950, Taba 1962, Schubert 1986). Most curriculum books that tried to portray comprehensively the emergent field of study contained reference to approaches derived from Dewey's theory of education.

Dewey's theory of education is highly complex and is most fully developed in *Democracy and Education* (Dewey 1916) and *Experience and Education* (Dewey 1938). To fully understand Dewey's work on education, however, one must recognize, as does historian and biographer Westbrook (1991), that Dewey was a philosopher who contributed to all major categories of philosophical discourse: metaphysics, epistemology, axiology, ethics, aesthetics, politics, and logic. Dewey's philosophy posits a world of flux in which human intelligence establishes values through inquiry that is saturated with aesthetic perception of patterns and relationships, and with ethical attention to the consequences of action. Logic is the kind of reason that best decides what to do in the course of everyday experience. Education is experience that more finely tunes the capacity to meet dilemmas; to transform them into meaningful and well-clarified problems; to search for precedent for action in previous lived experience; to imagine possibilities and their consequences; to choose a course of action; to act; to monitor the overt and covert consequences of action; to continuously revise action until the dilemma is satisfactorily overcome; and then to move to a similar action–inquiry process with dilemmas that continue to emerge.

Dewey (1902) referred to the curriculum organization that best serves this "education embedded in life experience" as moving from the psychological to the logical. The "psychological" for Dewey was the interest, concern, and sense of meaning and purpose of the individual or group. The "logical" was extant knowledge, the disciplines, whatever (formally or informally) constituted the funded knowledge of the human race. He argued that education moved back and forth on a continuum between the psychological and the logical, and that the most sound pedagogical starting point for curriculum usually resides in the psychological. Thus, the curriculum should be designed not primarily from pre-ordained adult conceptualizations of what students need, but should begin with students' own experiences, perceived needs, interests, concerns, and wonderings. In short, it should acknowledge as worthy of inquiry and study that which genuinely grows out of student experience.

Many labels may be found in the history of curriculum writing that represent attempts to put the students' interests and concerns at center stage in the curriculum. Most of these acknowledged Dewey as a principal influence. For example, Kilpatrick (1918) described an approach known as "the project method" which led students to engage, often in small groups, on cooperative projects to learn more about problems that they encountered in school or life outside of school. Rugg and Shumaker (1928) set forth an environment and methods for engaging children in salient decisions about their own learning. The progressive educator (taking his or her cue from Dewey) learns about what both curricular content and method ought to be from authentic efforts to understand the learning experience of students.

Hopkins called this "integration" (1937) and its social vehicle "interaction" (1941). For Hopkins, integration was more than a mere joining of subjects, it should be a joining of the most central understandings from school experiences with perspectives fashioned from life experience as a whole. In short, integration was a blending of Dewey's "psychological" and "logical". Interaction enhances integration, by enabling democratic communication of many experiential repertoires about what happens, both in and out of school. It builds one's perspective on life and in turn enhances subsequent problem-solving efforts.

Sometimes authors noted the gradations of student participation in curriculum-making with different levels. For instance, Alberty (1947), used the term "core" to refer to the bases upon which curriculum is designed. He distinguished a hierarchy of six types of core, as follows: (a) separate subjects; (b) informal correlation of subjects; (c) formalized correlation of required subjects; (d) fusion of two or more subjects; (e) common needs, problems, and interests of students; and (f) curriculum based on teacher–pupil planning of activities without reference to any formal structure (pp. 167–91). Similarly, Smith et al. (1950) laid out four types of curricular organization leading increasingly to greater student participation, naming them as follows: (a) the subject curriculum, (b) the activity curriculum, (c) the core curriculum, and (d) the community school (pp. 376–617). A lesser-known text, *The Third Curriculum* by Robert Frederick (1959), deals at length with a variety of student activities and contrasts them with the required and the elective curriculum. Nevertheless, his discussion is limited mainly to activities that occur in school. Only by implication, therefore, does Frederick treat the nonschool curricula.

Perhaps the most elaborate treatment of student roles in curricular practice during the first half of the twentieth century is in the Eight-year Study. The Progressive Education Association, which met regularly in the United States from 1919 to the mid-twentieth century to further progressive positions first advanced by Dewey, decided in the late 1920s to pioneer a comparative study of secondary students who attended progressive schools and those who attended conventional schools. Over a period of eight years (1933–41), ranging through high school and college, students from 30 school systems in the "experimental group" (progressively educated) were compared with those from traditional schools. An overview of the study was prepared by its director, Wilford Aikin (1942), in *The Story of the Eight-Year Study*, and elaborated in four subsequent volumes that deal respectively with the curriculum, success in college, evaluation, and stories of the 30 schools. The Eight-year Study revealed that students educated through progressive approaches that recognized their input into curriculum, exceeded, on almost every comparative measure, students who experienced traditional curriculum which allowed little, if any, student input into what was taught and learned. Comparisons included an array of indicators that stretched across a wide range of social, psychological, academic, attitudinal, and other dimensions of growth and development.

The main point of interest in the Eight-year Study for this entry is that of student involvement and commentaries, found in the final volume. Several of these schools, the ones that deviated most from the traditional schools, used curricula that emerged from projects of learning created by teacher/student collaboration. These were projects in which most of the learning experiences came from student concerns and interests. When shared, the pursuit of the projects became democratic experience. As problems were addressed, new skills and knowledge had to be learned. As students became more immersed in an area of mutual concern, they began to see their own problems as reflective of basic human problems, such as freedom, equality, love, goodness, beauty, and justice. In project-oriented curricula, these concepts were discussed not as abstract entities, but in the context of actual situations. In some cases, curricular patterns were developed in conjunction with communities for mutual benefit. Hanna (1938) provides concrete examples of this, as does Collings (1923). In contrast to the work of Hanna and Collings, who predated the publication of the Eight-year Study, the reflections of Rice and Rice (1988) were drawn directly from their experience as teachers in the Denver, Colorado School, one of the experimental schools in the Eight-year Study. They told of students who designed projects that grew from previous projects throughout the high school years, supplemented only by electives of a mini-course variety, and culminating in a senior year self-designed study of the good life which they deemed valuable since they were about to embark on the project of creating their adult life. Such students far exceeded those of the control group in the variety of measures indicating success in college.

2. *Biographical and Autobiographical Studies*

Students' sense of meaning and purpose are often best revealed through their autobiographies or biographies. While autobiography and biography have emerged to a level of considerable prominence in curriculum literature since the early 1980s, stories of student experience have dotted literary and historical writings for centuries. The writings cover an enormous range, from Dickens, Rabelais, and Goethe, to lesser known authors such as Edward Eggleston's *The Hoosier Schoolboy* (1883), *Andre Laurie's Schoolboy Days in Russia* (1892), and C.E. Pascoe's *Everyday Life in Our Public Schools* (1883). Both fiction and nonfiction are included, indicating that both, when well-done, can make valuable contributions to the understanding of students in relationship with curriculum and teachers.

A range of writings have emerged that portray student experiences with curriculum. Some of these are of the biographic and autobiographic varieties, while others are brief and anecdotal about students written by teachers. The popular writings of Holt (1982), Kohl (1984), Paley (1990), Rose (1990), Rodriguez (1982), and the Schoolboys of Barbiana (1970) are at once autobiographical, biographical, and anecdotal.

Biographical, autobiographical, and anecdotal work on students' curricular experience provides the advantage of a broad context of forces (social, cultural, political, economic, geographical, and historical) that the learner brings to the teaching–learning encounter. It has the shortcoming of being idiosyncratic, lacking generalizability. Nonetheless, a powerful and insightful treatment, even if anecdotal, may give insights for one's own situation. The powerful insight from one situation, like that in fiction, may yield perspective for other situations that at first glance do not seem similar in context or character.

3. *Ethnographic Studies*

Using field study methods derived from anthropology and sociology, researchers are beginning to reveal more about the lives of students. Usually couched as studies of schooling, ethnographic writers spend considerable time immersed in schools, other educative settings, and their communities. Peshkin, for instance, has produced several book-length treatments, one of the first (Peshkin 1978) being a study of the impact of schooling in a rural community, and more recently, another (Peshkin 1991) which examines the influence of ethnicity and race in an urban school and community. Similarly, Sedlak et al. (1986) investigate bargains in which teachers and students engage to actually reveal how they too frequently exchange academic studies for social tranquility.

Ethnographic studies need not focus exclusively on students in school. The tradition of work established by Opie and Opie (1959, 1969) reveals the need to study the lore of children, including their language, stories, and games, if one is to understand them as whole persons and in their various group contexts. In curriculum studies, this implies the need to learn about the out-of-school learnings and implicit curricula of homes and families, peer groups, mass media, nonschool organizations from sports to street gangs, avocations, and vocations (Schubert 1986).

4. *Empirical and Interpretive Studies of School and Nonschool Curricula*

"Empirical," interpreted as based in experience, and interpretive studies of the impact of nonschool life on school are wide ranging and offer considerable perspective for understanding school curriculum. Schubert (1981), for instance, argues that educators are only in a defensible position to offer curriculum that has meaning for students in schools when they have an understanding of the nonschool educative forces in student lives. These forces constitute implicit curricula that emanate from parents, extended families, television, friendships, hobbies, books and magazines, movies and videos, and a range of other sources. Fantini and Sinclair (1985) identify each of the following categories as "educators": families, workplaces, museums, religious institutions, youth serving agencies, media, and technology. They draw upon experts in each of these dimensions of life to explain how they are educational. Schubert (1981, 1986) further contends that these dimensions embody elements of curriculum. For instance, they could be studied for their implicit purposes, selection of learning experiences, organizational patterns, and evaluation, to draw upon Tyler's model of curriculum. Politically, the design could be analyzed relative to Walker's (1971) naturalistic conceptualization that emphasizes beginning with a "platform" of basic perspectives and proceeds through a process of "deliberation" in which human interaction and dialogue create the "design" or what is actually practiced with learners. Another possibility is to interpret these educative settings in light of the influence of Tyler's four commonplaces on each other: teachers, learners, subject matter, and milieu (Schwab 1973). Using the latter, one might first identify who the teachers and learners are in any of the nonschool learning settings, what the nature of subject matter is, and the ways in which the interpersonal atmosphere and physical environment (milieu) contribute to the character and influence of that setting on the outlook of participants in it.

Each sphere of nonschool curriculum contributes to the emerging perspective of each person. When such persons enter schools and are designated students they are better served if those who develop and design curriculum know something of their perspectives (i.e., the outlook that nonschool curricula have forged for them). Such knowledge puts educators in a better position to promote what students ought to have. If, as is widely contended, curriculum is that which is deemed worthwhile to know or experience, it seems reasonable to ask, "Reasonable for whom?" If curriculum developers have little knowledge of the impact of the larger context of student lives on the way they perceive, interpret, and negotiate with the world, they are distinctly disadvantaged. Conversely, they are advantaged if they do know about such sources of influence. They can better address and discover skills, knowledge, and values that enhance students as they seek to become more fully human and as they contribute to society and the world. Moreover, study of nonschool curricula may also reveal overlooked and valuable approaches to teaching and learning that schools could profit from incorporating.

Studies, divergent though they are, reveal the complexity of conceptualizing school curriculum due to its embeddedness in nonschool realms. Cognitive psychologists point to the multifaceted origins of cognitive development and the subtle nuances that contribute meanings to learning any subject (Haertel 1991). The complexity of natural thinking processes are illuminated by Gardner (1991) and reconstructed in terms of implications for ways in which schools should teach, drawing upon a rich variety of interdisciplinary knowledge as well as from the history of apprenticeship and the modern interactive museum.

Other empirical attempts to understand student curricular experience focus on portrayals of students who do not seem to fit the mold of schooling. In this regard, Weis et al. (1989) focus on dropouts and Page (1991) explores the experience of lower-track classrooms. Both of these studies point to the need to see origins of problems in the larger fabric of society, culture, and historical forces. Treatments of the lives of children and youth outside of school (again the nonschool "curriculum") illuminate life situations that enhance awareness of reasons that students do not fit the mold of curricula designed by and for persons from quite different backgrounds. The central point here is that such treatments symbolize the nonschool context that is essential for understanding the multifarious ways students experience curriculum.

5. *Critical and Phenomenological Interpretations*

Closely connected with the type of literature mentioned above, one often finds an enhanced concern for social justice. Critical accounts of students, mostly of the ethnographic variety, deal with justice or equity of educational opportunity to engage high quality curricular experience. In these studies, questions of whose knowledge is represented in school and who benefits from its being there come to the forefront of attention. Asking such questions reveals that matters of race, class, gender, health, ableness, place, appearance, ethnicity, and nationality are prominent factors. Anyon (1980) produced ethnographies of schools in four different social class areas, concentrating on student images of routes to success in each. In lower-class and lower-working class schools she found that students are taught that one succeeds by following the rules. Middle-class students, however, learn that success emanates from discovering how to give "the right" answers (i.e., what teachers want to hear). Students of professional classes learn to be creative, and those of executive class background learn to succeed by manipulating the system.

While these teachings are rarely a direct feature of the overt or intended curriculum, they constitute a powerful message in the covert or hidden curriculum. The hidden curriculum reflects dominant values, hierarchies, and structures of the larger society that surrounds schooling. Similarly, Willis's (1977) modern educational classic *Learning to Labor* reveals how school and nonschool lives of working class lads in England are structured to reproduce working class jobs. In an ethnography on politics of an urban high school Fine (1991) integrates Black and feminist literatures to show how societal structures and ideologies actually frame student dropouts. In a more story-like manner, Best (1983) portrays the scars wrought by gender inequality in elementary schools, while McNeil (1986) shows that the controlling structure of secondary schools and reform policies designed to ensure improvement teach an outlook that values credentials more than genuine education. McLaren (1989) explains a critical pedagogy derived from his dual standpoint of teacher and theorist in an inner city school.

Brazilian educator and theorist Freire, broke new ground with his classic *Pedagogy of the Oppressed* (1970) by emphasizing both a critical consciousness of oppressive societal structures and the potential of human beings to learn through the phenomenological sources of meaning in their own lives. He did this by describing his work with Brazilian peasants, particularly how he engaged them in "problem posing" about their own experience, teaching them literacy by enabling them to name their world rather than by the "banking system" of education usually employed. His theory and approaches have circulated widely around the globe since the early 1970s.

Phenomenological perspectives on pedagogy involve what van Manen (1991) calls "pedagogical thoughtfulness and tactfulness," an attempt to be pedagogic by approaching the deeper sources of meaning in the lives of students. This invokes a relationship of being with students that embodies at once a moral intuitiveness, an openness to learning from students, a improvisational involvement with them, and an ongoing interpretive reflection. It involves what Berman et al. (1991) call a "curriculum for being." Without this orientation, one finds a condition that Suransky (1982) calls "the Erosion of Childhood." Work from phenomenological perspectives has been portrayed regularly since the early 1980s in *Phenomenology and Pedagogy*, a Canadian journal (with an international editorial board) founded by Max van Manen.

6. *Stories*

Educational researchers have shown growing recognition of stories as valuable sources of insight about students. Witherell and Noddings (1991) show the richness of story in the lives of teachers and learners, Willis and Schubert (1991) provide stories of educators who in turn were influenced by stories in art and literature, and Schubert and Ayers (1992) provide stories of teachers who share what they have learned from experience with their students, calling the latter "teacher lore." Stories may be true life renditions, such as those provided by Granger and Granger (1986) based on their own child's encounter with special education, they may be an author's investigation of schooling, or they may be fictional (Hesse 1968). Whether it occurred in part or not, the fictional account can be as illuminative as the ethnography. It need not even be about school to provide insight. Coles (1989) discusses the "call of stories" throughout history, stories being essential sources of moral imagination that can shape new forms of teaching and curriculum, while Egan (1986, 1992) argues that story and imagination should be the heart of the curriculum that good teaching makes available to student experience.

7. Conclusion: On the Curricular Value of Student Experiences

At least three main themes run throughout this entry. First, curriculum is more defensible if a wide range of student experience is known and used as a basis for designing it. Second, serious attempts to understand student experience of curriculum in schools reveals the need to probe more deeply into the social and cultural conditions that make schools and their curricula what they have come to be. Third, since at least the time of Dewey, there has been a succession of calls for involvement of students in curriculum design and development.

In order to better understand these themes, a range of writing that could be labeled "student lore" has begun to emerge. Looking carefully at the lives of students in and out of school could, among other things, highlight the profound differences among the manifest or intended curriculum of policy statements, the taught curriculum of teacher practices, and the curriculum as students experience it when it becomes part of their own perspectives.

See also: Dewy, Pragmatism, and Education

References

Alberty H 1947 *Reorganizing the High School Curriculum*. Macmillan, New York

Anyon J 1980 Social class and the hidden curriculum of work. *J. Educ*. 162(1): 67–92

Berman L M et al. 1991 *Toward a Curriculum for Being. Voices of Educators*. State University of New York Press, Albany, New York

Best R 1983 *We've All Got Scars: What Boys and Girls Learn in Elementary School*. Indiana University Press, Bloomington, Indiana

Caswell H L, Campbell D S 1935 *Curriculum Development*. American Book Company, New York

Coles R 1990 *The Call of Stories. Stories and the Moral Imagination*. Houghton Mifflin, Boston, Massachusetts

Collings E 1923 *An Experiment with a Project Curriculum*. Macmillan, New York

Dewey J 1902 *The Child and the Curriculum*. University of Chicago Press, Chicago, Illinois

Dewey J 1916 *Democracy and Education: An Introduction to the Philosophy of Education* Macmillan, New York

Dewey J 1938 *Experience and Education*. Macmillan, New York

Egan K 1986 *Teaching as Story Telling*. Routledge, London

Egan K 1992 *Imagination in Teaching and Learning. Ages 8 to 15*. Routledge, London

Erickson F, Shultz J 1992 Students' experience of the curriculum. In: Jackson P W (ed.) 1992 *Handbook of Research on Curriculum*. Macmillan, New York

Fantini M, Sinclair R (eds.) 1985 *Education in School and Non-School Settings*. Eighty-fourth yearbook of the National Society for the Study of Education, Part I. University of Chicago Press, Chicago, Illinois

Fine M 1991 *Framing Dropouts*. State University of New York Press, Albany, New York

Freire P 1970 *Pedagogy of the Oppressed*. Continuum, New York

Gardner H 1991 *The Unschooled Mind. How Children Think and How Schools Should Teach*. Basic Books, New York

Granger L, Granger B 1986 *The Magic Feather*. Dutton, New York

Haertel G D 1991 Cognitive psychology and curriculum In: Lewy A (ed.) 1991 *The International Encyclopedia of Curriculum*. Pergamon Press, Oxford

Hanna P R 1936 *Youth Serves the Community*. D Appleton-Century, New York

Hesse H 1968 *Beneath the Wheel*. Bantam, New York

Hopkins L T (ed.) 1937 *Integration: Its Meaning and Application*. D Appleton-Century, New York

Hopkins L T 1941 *Interaction: The Democratic Process*. D C Heath, Boston, Massachusetts

Kilpatrick W H 1918 The project method. *Teach. Coll. Rec*. 19: 319–35

Kliebard H M 1986 *The Struggle for the American Curriculum 1893–1958*. Routledge and Kegan Paul, Boston and London

McLaren P 1989 *Life in Schools*. Longman, New York

McNeil L 1986 *Contradictions of Control. School Structure and School Knowledge*. Routledge, New York

Opie I, Opie P 1959 *The Lore and Language of School Children*. Oxford University Press, Oxford

Opie I, Opie P 1969 *Childrens Games in Street and Playground*. Clarendon Press, Oxford

Page R N 1991 *Lower-Track Classrooms*. Teachers College Press, New York

Peshkin A 1978 *Growing Up American*. University of Chicago Press, Chicago, Illinois

Peshkin A 1991 *The Color of Strangers, The Color of Friends*. University of Chicago Press, Chicago, Illinois

Rice T, Rice C 1988 The Eight-year Study at East High School, Denver, Colorado. In: Kridel C (ed.) 1988 *Curriculum History*. University Press of America, Lanham, Maryland

Rugg H O, Shumaker A 1928 *The Child-centered School*. World Book, New York

Schoolboys of Barbiana 1970 *Letter to a Teacher*. Random House, New York

Schubert W H 1981 Knowledge about out-of school curricula. *Educ. Forum* 45(2): 185–99

Schubert W H 1986 *Curriculum: Perspective, Paradigm, and Possibility*. Macmillan, New York

Schubert W H, Lopez-Schubert A L 1980 *Curriculum*

Books: The First Eighty Years. University Press of America, Lanham, Maryland
Schubert W H, Ayers W (eds.) 1992 *Teacher Lore: Learning from Our Own Experience*. Longman, New York
Schwab J J 1973 The practical 3: Translation into curriculum. *School Rev*. 81: 501–22
Sedlak M W, Wheeler C W, Pullin D C, Cusick P A 1986 *Selling Students Short*. Teachers College Press, New York
Smith B O, Stanley W O, Shores J H 1950 *Fundamentals of Curriculum Development*. World Book, New York
Suransky V P 1982 *The Erosion of Childhood*. University of Chicago Press, Chicago, Illinois
Taba H 1962 *Curriculum Development: Theory and Practice*. Harcourt, Brace and World, New York
van Manen M 1986 *The Tact of Teaching*. Heinemann, New York
Walker D F 1971 A naturalistic model for curriculum development. *School Rev*. 80: 51–65
Weis L, Farrar E, Petrie H G (eds.) 1989 *Dropouts from Schools. Issue, Dilemmas and Solutions*. State University of New York Press, Albany, New York
Westbrook R B 1991 *John Dewey and American Democracy*. Cornell University Press, Ithaca, New York
Willis G, Schubert W H (eds.) 1991 *Reflections from the Heart of Educational Inquiry: Understanding Curriculum and Teaching Through the Arts*. State University of New York Press, Albany, New York
Willis P 1977 *Learning to Labor*. Saxon House, New York
Witherell C, Noddings N (eds.) 1991 *Stories Lives Tell: Narrative and Dialogue in Education*. Teachers College Press, New York

W. H. Schubert; A. L. Lopez

Students, Grading and Evaluation of

In the United States the type of system teachers use to assign grades (or marks) to students is often determined at the district or school level. Most teachers have little choice of whether an "A through F," "Excellent–Good–Satisfactory–Unsatisfactory," or numerical (e.g., 0–100 points) system is used. However, teachers do have considerable flexibility in deciding how the grades are assigned to students within the system.

1. Types of Comparison used in Grading Students

Assigning a grade to a student typically involves some type of comparison. A student's classroom performance can be compared with the performance of other students (norm-referenced grading), established standards of excellence, mastery, or minimal competency (criterion-referenced grading), the student's aptitudes, the student's effort, or the student's improvement in his or her performance. Each of these types of comparison has advantages and disadvantages.

1.1 Comparisons with Other Students

This approach to grading is often referred to as "grading on the curve." Grading on the curve means that the grade assigned to a student is based on the performance of other students in the class. Certain percentages of the class are assigned A's, B's, C's, D's, and F's, depending upon how they performed relative to others, regardless of their absolute level of performance. A student who answers 50 percent of the items on a test correctly might get an A, F, or any grade in between, depending on how his or her score of 50 percent compares with the scores of other students in the class. A school may encourage grading on the curve by suggesting the approximate percentages of students who should be assigned various marks. For example, 10 percent may be assigned A's and F's, 20 percent may be assigned B's and D's, with the remaining 40 percent assigned C's.

Table 1
Distribution of Students based on standard deviations

Standard deviations from the mean	Letter grade	Approximate percentage of students
+1.50	A	7
+.75 to +1.49	B	16
mean ±.74	C	54
−.75 to −1.49	D	16
−1.50	F	7

The main advantage of such a system is that it simplifies grading decisions. There is no apparent need for deliberation over what scores constitute cut-offs for the various grades since these cut-offs can be provided by reference to the distribution of scores (e.g., the top 10 percent of the students receive A's). Assuming the distribution of scores follows the normal or bell-shaped distribution, standard deviation units from the mean can be used to determine divisions between the marks. For example, Table 1 shows the percentages of students that may be assigned to each of five grade categories for a normally distributed set of scores.

Statistical techniques (see Kubiszyn and Borich 1993) may be used in selecting and revising test items to assure the required normal or bell-shaped distribution. In practice, however, grading on the curve is often used with non-normal distributions by selecting asymmetrical cut-off scores around the mean with which desired percentages can be obtained.

There are several disadvantages with grading on the curve. First, this approach fails to consider differences due to the overall ability level of the class. Imagine the disappointment that would result if such a system were imposed on a class of intellectually gifted students, none of whom had ever earned less than a B. Suddenly, 77 percent would be transformed into C through F students. Regardless of their achievement, in such a system some students will always get A's, some will always get F's.

Another disadvantage involves specifying percentages: why have 5 percent A's, not 15 percent A's? These percentages, or the standard deviations from the mean from which they are derived, are often arbitrarily set. Furthermore, the meaning of an A may not be clear: Has the "A" student mastered all course content? Or, was the student graded with a class of less able learners? Such a system fails to indicate *absolute* achievement, which makes comparisons across grades and schools difficult.

1.2 Comparison with Established Standards

In this approach it is possible for all students or no students to get A's or F's or any grade in between. The performance of the rest of the students in the class is irrelevant to a student's grade. All that is relevant is whether a student attains a defined standard of achievement or performance. This approach is sometimes labeled "criterion referenced." In a criterion-referenced system, letter grades may be assigned based on the percentage of test items answered correctly. Answering correctly 85 percent of the items or more may earn an A, while answering between 75 and 84 percent correctly might earn a B. Decreasing percentages can be used to differentiate grades of C, D, and F. Thus, a student who answers 79 percent of the test items correctly earns a B, regardless of whether the rest of the class did better, worse, or about the same. The successful use of this approach requires some prior knowledge of what level of achievement or performance it is reasonable to expect from students given the difficulty of the test.

There are several advantages to such a system. First, it is possible, in theory, for all students to obtain high grades if they show sufficient effort (assuming the percentage cut-offs are not unreasonably high). Second, the assignment of grades is simplified. A student either has answered 75 percent of the items correctly or has not. As with comparison with other students, there is no apparent need to deliberate over assigning grades, once the desired percentages are selected. Finally, assuming that ability levels of incoming students remain fairly constant and that tests remain comparable in validity and difficulty, teachers who work to improve their teaching effectiveness should see improvement in grades with the passage of time.

Such a system also has some disadvantages. Establishing standards may be difficult. What it is reasonable to expect for an "A" may vary from school to school, across time, across students, across communities, and across curricula. For example, should the same standards be maintained for a gifted or a less able class as for a class of average learners? Another limitation is that some parents and administrators may have difficulty accepting a grading system that potentially allows everyone to make an "A."

Table 2
Relationships between aptitude, achievement, and marks in marking systems based on comparisons of achievement with aptitude

Aptitude level	Achievement level	Marks
High	High	High
	Average	Average
	Low	Low
Average	High	High
	Average	High
	Low	Average
Low	High	High
	Average	High
	Low	High

1.3 Comparisons with Aptitude

Aptitude is another name for potential or ability. In an approach based on aptitude, students are compared neither to other students nor to established standards. Instead, they are compared to themselves. That is, grades are assigned according to how close their achievement is to their potential. Thus students with high aptitudes who are achieving at high levels would get high grades, since they would be achieving at their potential. Those with high aptitude and average achievement would get lower grades, since they would be achieving below their potential. Students with average aptitude and average achievement would also get high grades, since they would be considered to be achieving at their potential. Although such a system appears attractive, several problems exist, as illustrated in Table 2.

Table 2 illustrates that the concept of assigning grades based on the congruence of a student's achievement with the student's aptitude may be reasonable for high-aptitude students but not for low-aptitude students. If a student's aptitude is very low, it would be unlikely the student would achieve below his or her potential. Thus, the student would always be achieving at or above the expected level. Thus, this approach might not be fair to students of moderate and high ability. Perhaps more importantly, this approach greatly complicates interpreting grades. For example, a C for a high-aptitude student might indicate 70 percent mastery, while for an average-aptitude student it might indicate 60 percent, and perhaps 50 percent mastery for the low-aptitude student. The same grade may mean very different things in terms of absolute achievement.

Another drawback is the tendency for the achievement scores of lower aptitude students to increase and the achievement scores of higher aptitude students to decrease on repeated testing. This phenomenon is called the "regression toward the mean" effect; the more extreme an achievement score, the further it can be expected to "regress" or fall back toward the average or mean of all students at another testing. Finally, this approach requires more complex record-keeping than the first two approaches discussed.

1.4 Comparison of Achievement with Effort

Approaches that compare achievement with effort are similar to those that compare achievement with aptitude. Students who obtain average test scores but have to work hard to get them are given high marks. Students who get average scores but do not have to work hard are given lower marks.

Several problems exist with approaches to grading based on effort. First, there may be no known acceptable measures of effort. Unlike aptitude, for which reliable and valid measures exist, effort is at best estimated by informal procedures. Second, some students may be punished for excelling quickly, while others are rewarded for taking a longer time to master concepts. Third, there is once again the problem that the grades themselves may not represent academic achievement. Effort may not coincide with academic attainment, making grades all the more difficult to interpret. Finally, record-keeping is once again complicated.

The advantage cited for grading based on effort is that it serves to motivate the slower or poorly motivated students. However, it may also serve to discourage the brighter students who would quickly see such a system as unfair. Whatever the case, the primary function of grading—to provide feedback about academic achievement—is less likely to be achieved by teachers who use this approach.

1.5 Equating Achievement with Improvement

In this approach, the amount of improvement between the beginning and end of instruction is used to assign grades. Through a system of pretesting and posttesting, students who show the most progress are awarded the highest grades. However, a problem occurs for students who do well on the pretest. Improvement for such students is likely to be less overall than for students who do poorly on the pretest. More proficient learners sometimes have been known to "underperform" on pretests on purpose when this approach is used. Other shortcomings include the statistical problems mentioned with regard to regression toward the mean and the added burden of constructing and administering pretests.

1.6 Selecting the Best Approach

Since each approach has advantages as well as limitations, many schools and districts have adopted multiple marking systems, such as assigning separate grades for achievement and effort or for achievement, effort, and improvement. As long as the achievement portion of the grade reflects *only* achievement, such systems are defensible. Two disadvantages of such systems are worth noting, however. First, they increase the number of grades to be assigned and interpreted, leading to an increase in record-keeping and in the time needed to report the grades to others. Second, unless the purpose of each grade is explained clearly on the report card, multiple marking systems are often difficult for parents to decipher. When feedback about academic achievement is the primary goal, comparison with established standards is the method of choice.

2 Types of Symbols

Within grading systems, a variety of symbols has been used. The more common types are letter grades, numerical grades, pass–fail grades, and checklists.

2.1 Letter Grades

The use of letter grades is the most common kind of grading. Over 75 percent of the high schools in America use the letters A–F to report marks (Kubiszyn and Borich 1993). Sometimes, plus and minus signs are used to indicate finer distinctions between the letter grades, providing as many as 15 separate symbols. This system along with its variation (Excellent, Good, Satisfactory, Unsatisfactory) has several advantages that have led to its widespread adoption and popularity.

First, the letter system is widely understood. Students, teachers, parents, administrators, and employers understand, at least in a general sense, that grades of A represent excellent or exceptional performance and grades of D to F represent marginal or poor performance. Second, such a system is compact, requiring only one or two spaces to report a summary mark of the work for a grading period. Third, such a system has about the optimal number of levels that can be easily distinguished without the use of interpretative aids.

Limitations of this system can also be noted. First, the specific meaning of letter grades varies from class to class and from school to school. Different schools and districts tend to use different grading systems and also tend to combine and weight the components of a grade differently. Consequently, a grade of A in one school or school district may represent performance similar to a grade of B or even C in another. Second, letter grades fail to indicate clearly the student's actual level of mastery. There is often a considerable difference between the achievement of a "low B" student and that of a "high B" student. Finally, averaging letter grades often results in a loss of information or misinterpretation of the student's actual achievement. When averaging letter grades, it is necessary to go back to the actual numerical grades to obtain the "correct" average.

2.2 Numerical Grades

Such a system usually employs 100 as the highest mark, and report cards often carry letter grade equivalents for the range of numerical grades. For example: A (90–100), B (80–89), C (70–79), D (60–69), and F (below 60).

Numerical grades have three main advantages. First, like letter grades, they provide a convenient summary mark for a term's or year's work. Second, unlike letter grades, numerical grades are easily averaged to obtain the "correct" final marks. Third, they are widely understood—most pupils and parents understand that there are substantial differences between a mark of 95 and one of 75.

There are also disadvantages to such a system. First, the number of possible discriminations may be greater than an untrained user can make reliably. For example, few individuals could make the 40 distinctions required between the grades of 61 and 100 reliably. In other words, it may not be possible to determine the real difference between a grade of 67 and a grade of 68 or between a grade of 95 and a grade of 96. Second, as with letter grades, it may not be possible to know what a grade means, since standards may vary considerably from school to school.

2.3 Pass–Fail Grades

Pass–Fail (P–F) is another grading symbol system. Few schools, however, employ this approach today because of its many shortcomings. The major weakness is that such symbols do not provide sufficient information. "P" could mean the student exhibited anywhere from exceptional to marginal performance in the class. This makes it difficult for employers and admissions officers to evaluate applicants. Students themselves often complain about the same lack of information; that is, they do not know how well they actually did or how much they must improve. Finally, students tend to do the minimum necessary to earn a "P" under such systems.

2.4 Checklists

A common adjunct to a letter or numerical symbol system is a checklist. Since both letter and numerical symbol systems fail to define just what a student can or cannot do, many report cards include skill checklists (specifying, e.g., independence, thoroughness, effort) to accompany their grade symbols for each subject. Checklists are also used to provide information about nonacademic aspects of the learner. For example, checklists are often used to identify problems in the areas of conduct, social skills, responsibility, and organization. Properly utilized checklists represent useful supplements to letter or numerical grades and can convey more detailed information about the student without contaminating or confusing the interpretation of a student's overall achievement level. More detail on this and the other systems and symbols for grading may be found in Kubiszyn and Borich (1993).

3. New Trends in Grading

A recent trend in grading and testing has been the "performance assessment of learning." Following the work of Resnick and Resnick (1989), performance assessment of learning calls for the evaluation of student work in the form of oral reports, extended projects, portfolios of work, scientific investigations, creative scores and scripts, and physical models. These and other similar overt signs are attempts to determine whether acquired "bits" of knowledge have been successfully converted into an "integrated performance" in a context different from that in which they were learned. Performance assessments typically take place over a period of hours or days in which students work at their own pace. Based on guidelines provided by the teacher, students select the tasks and projects with which to demonstrate their competence against a set of published criteria.

The goal of performance assessment is to reduce the importance of artificial knowledge that may be unintentionally promoted by the exclusive or heavy reliance on true–false, multiple choice, and some types of essay tests, and to increase the importance of verbal explanations and justifications, critical thinking, and problem-solving related to authentic professional and social responsibilities pertaining to adult life. A secondary goal is to diminish the implicit weight generally accorded to traditional test-taking skills in grading students, especially for those for whom such skills are determined to be weak.

The performance assessment of learning involves the use of checklists, scales, or numerically equivalent codes in the form of ratings and awards which indicate the success of a learner in meeting established standards for the specific production to be evaluated. For example, a typical "production" might require the learner to complete a scientific investigation, scale model, or literary script on his or her own that would include essential features of adequacy (for example, theoretical understanding, planning, design, use of procedures and equipment, and possible alternative solutions). The product would be compared with established guidelines or an existing model, rated, and given a particular code of achievement.

The performance assessment of learning is not so much a new method of grading as it is an increase in emphasis upon higher order cognitive processes which include decision-making, problem-solving, independent judgment, and creativity. For this reason it shares much in common with the comparison with established standards approach of grading and the checklist method of reporting. A distinctive feature of the performance assessment of learning lies with the fact that the codes of achievement obtained are reported separately on the grade report rather than as part of a letter grade.

See also: Evaluation, Nature of; Evaluation: Formative, Summative and Goal-free

References

Kubiszyn T, Borich G 1993 *Educational Testing and Measurement: Classroom Application and Practice*, 4th edn. Harper Collins, New York

Resnick L, Resnick D 1989 *Assessing the Thinking Curriculum: New Tools for Educational Reform*. University of Pittsburgh, Learning Research and Development Center, Pittsburgh, Pennsylvania

Further Reading

Lyman H B 1986 *Test Scores and What They Mean*. Prentice-Hall, Englewood Cliffs, New Jersey

Popham W J 1988 *Educational Evaluation*, 2nd edn. Prentice-Hall, Englewood Cliffs, New Jersey

G. Borich; T. Kubiszyn

Students in Classrooms, Gender and Racial Differences Among

The concept of "differences" in education is problematic. The term can be used, among other things, to celebrate diversity, to denote injustice, or to ascribe inferiority and powerlessness. It is also a concept used more by educational psychologists than sociologists or teachers. The latter two groups are more likely to conceptualize the problem of educational difference in terms of the manifestation of unequal power relations in schools or in addressing educational equality and inequality. In contrast, psychologists have tended to focus on gender and race at psychological and interpersonal levels rather than infusing their studies with an understanding of how a social order maintains dominance or how school relations perpetuate existing unequal social relations. Moreover, exploration of educational differences has a higher profile in studies of gender compared with those of race, possibly because racial differences are far more complex than the relatively clear male/female dualism.

1. Historical Perspective

It is important to see theories of difference as they have emerged historically. Biological attributions of gender and racial inferiority held in the nineteenth and early twentieth centuries have lost ground in the second half of the twentieth century as societal and educational factors emerged as more important, reliable, and acceptable. There has also been some debate about the nature and extent of gender and racial differences. For example, in their extensive survey of sex differences, Maccoby and Jacklin (1974) found relatively little overall difference between the performance of females and males. Further, the educational effects of sociological factors such as low income and the relative heterogeneity of different cultural groups have rendered the identification of racial differences very problematic.

Moreover, the possibility that identifying difference will lead to an increase in educational equality within a fundamentally unequal society has been challenged.

Sarup (1986) poses the following question: "If society is differentiated on the basis of power, wealth, and education, how can children coming into the educational system from various parts of that differentiated society ever, as it were, line up equally?" (p. 3). Nevertheless, researchers have explored and identified patterns of educational inequality, mostly focusing on gender but with some consideration of race. These are now provided in some detail.

2. Language

Language has been identified as one means by which male, White dominance of power relationships is sustained and recreated. Spender (1980) criticized the ways in which language, both in the classroom and more generally, is used both to subordinate girls and women and to define them sexually. The dominant male experience is both reflected and constructed through language so that women are defined principally in sexual or domestic servicing roles.

Language has also proved problematic for Black and ethnic minority students. For example, the dialects used by Black American and British African-Caribbean students were originally thought of as simply mispronounced and poorly spoken Standard English: hence, the emergence of linguistic deficit hypotheses which accord little respect to dialects. However, in the 1960s, this position was reconsidered by social scientists who began to see Black English as a valid dialect of Standard English. However, problems arising from linguistic differences still continue, as emphasis on Standard English is increasingly being promoted, for example, in the British National Curriculum. A strategy to overcome these differences suggested by Cooper and Stewart (1987), is to point out differences without critizing student speech, thus highlighting linguistic difference rather than linguistic deficit.

Further, gender differences in writing style and reading choice are also evident. Female students are likely to read more widely and gain greater enjoyment from reading fiction than their male counterparts who tend to focus their reading on informational, nonfictional texts (Gorman et al. 1988). It is argued that these reading patterns have an effect on writing styles, resulting in female students' preference for essay-type narratives in contrast to male students' preference for factual, briefer forms of communication (Stobart et al. 1992).

3. Student Self-concept

How students feel about themselves has been perceived as crucial to their school performance: thus, studies of differences in student self-concept have been of much interest. However, research evidence is inconclusive: findings range from little evidence of difference in self-perception between male and female students (Chapman and Boersma 1983) to males having far higher self-images (Connell et al. 1975).

The similar claim that Black children come to see themselves as failures and are nonachievers because of their negative self-concept and low esteem has also been challenged. Milner (1983), for example, suggests that Black people who are ashamed of their color feel this way because White society has forced them to accept its own appraisal of them. In contrast, Stone (1981) found the British research on Black self-concept and self-esteem to be inconclusive and contradictory. In her view, there is no basis for the belief that Black children have poor self-esteem and negative self-concept; rather the negative self-concept hypothesis serves to obscure the real issues which are of power, class, and racial oppression.

4. Socialization

Socialization into masculinity and femininity, and/or being Black or White, it is argued, begins within the family from the moment a child is born. Milner (1983) maintains that the socialization process is the most important determinant of prejudice. Similarly, Nash (1979) argues that children learn to apply stereotypes, whether in relation to gender or to racial differences before they start school. Cultural factors such as language, literature, and art also contribute to stereotypical and prejudicial thinking by conventionally using whiteness as a metaphor for all things good and pure, and blackness to denote badness and evil. Schools condone rather than challenge these stereotypes. Thus, just as parents give more attention to their sons and are more likely to reprimand them, the same patterns of differential treatment of the sexes is apparent at school.

5. Teachers' Perceptions of Students

Teachers are more likely to chastise male students and pay them more attention, while at the same timecreating greater dependency in their treatment of female students (Fagot 1977). Hence, both male and female teachers encourage in their female students stereotyped traits of obedience and passivity yet prefer their male students to adopt the more male-identified characteristics of aggression and independence (Etaugh and Hughes 1975).

Research has also shown that teachers have lower expectations of female students (as do parents and students themselves), are more intellectually encouraging and demanding of male students, and are more likely to reward female students for good behavior and tidy presentation. Teachers also direct male and female students into conventional subjects and careers and believe female careers to be less important than male ones (Arnot and Weiner 1987). Further, they are likely to be sexist in their allocation of tasks within school; for example, at elementary level, choosing girls to help keep the classroom clean and tidy and the often physically smaller boys to move furniture or equipment (Clift 1978).

Similarly, Black and ethnic minority children are perceived as problems rather than potentially enriching to school life. Teachers also have lower expectations of these children's abilities and potential achievements. For example, Proctor (1984) found that low expectations of students are associated with minority group membership, nonconforming personality, and nonstandard speech. There is a tendency to encourage Black students' sporting and musical abilities to the detriment of their academic studies. Further, teachers are apparently more severe in disciplining Black students, blaming "bad" behavior on what teachers see as the inadequacies of Black family life (Brah and Minhas 1985; Phoenix 1987).

Whether teachers are male or female has been found to be important in terms of their interactions with students in the classroom. In a study of 6th and 11th grade classes, Griffin (1972) found that male teachers were generally more direct and authoritarian, and female teachers warmer and less direct. However, there is little evidence to indicate that male and female teachers differ in their generally traditional and stereotypical treatment of male and female students.

6. Curriculum

Attention has focused on both the formal and hidden (implicit) school curriculum. In terms of the formal curriculum, syllabuses and content tend to exclude the experiences of girls and women whether Black or White; textbooks and reading schemes generally portray a traditional view of middle-class family life (Deliyanni-Kouimtzi 1992). Where choice is available, female students opt for the humanities, languages, and social sciences while male students select mathematical, scientific, and technological subjects despite various initiatives to counter this trend (Elkjaer 1992). Furthermore, the hidden curriculum exerts enormous pressure on students (and teachers) to conform in sex-specific ways.

At the institutional level there are gender-specific

regulations on clothing (especially in the United Kingdom with its increasing adoption of school uniform) and discipline. Similarly, sexual harassment and verbal abuse have been found to be common features of school life (Lees 1987).

Black and ethnic minority experience is also under-represented in the content of school syllabuses and texts; racist institutional practices inhibit the progress of Black students in climbing the educational ladder. For example, there is evidence to show that irrespective of their actual ability, Black students are assigned to lower ability groups than their White counterparts. These students are consequently restricted in the level of school qualifications open to them (Wright 1987), and future channels into higher education, and the labor market (Brennan and McGeevor 1990).

7. *Student Performance and Achievement*

Attempts to establish differences in intelligence between various social groups have proved less than successful. In fact, Pidgeon (quoted in Goldstein 1987) argues that any differences emerging from tests are manufactured rather than "natural." Similarly, contemporary cultural assumptions and expectations influence test construction resulting in relatively poor performances from lower status groups (Gould 1981). According to Pidgeon, differences, say, between male and female students' test performances are likely to be due to differences in the balance of items favoring one sex or the other. Thus, it is possible for "fair" tests to be constructed where appropriate selection of items will yield tests without gender or cultural bias.

It has also been found that forms of testing are likely to affect the relative performance of male and female students, with male students achieving better on multiple choice examinations and female students on essay-type questions (Stobart et al. 1992). There is little research on the different test responses of different ethnic groups. Ethical decisions now confront test constructors as to whether it is legitimate, as is currently the case, to formulate a theoretical description of achievement which is sexually and culturally biased (Goldstein 1987), or should test constructors be working toward a more gender and culturally fair mode of assessment, as Stobart et al. (1992) suggest?

The appearance of differences between social groups in subject areas has been less controversial. Female students tend to perform better in reading, spelling, and verbal skills while male students, in the later school years, tend to excel in mathematics and problem solving (Maccoby and Jacklin 1974). Further, girls tend to be academically ahead in the elementary school phase. One perceived reason for this is that the elementary atmosphere is more "feminine" and thus more comfortable for girls. Another is that girls are relatively more mature than boys, though the concept of maturity in relation to academic achievement has been heavily critized by Goldstein (1987).

As female students progress through the school, however, their achievement levels slip, particularly in mathematics and science (Becker 1981). A variety of reasons have been given for this finding. For example, female students favor serialistic learning (proceeding from certainty to certainty, learning, remembering, recapitulating) whereas male students are likely to take a holistic approach (more exploratory, working towards an explanatory framework). Scott-Hodgetts (1986) suggests that male students are likely to be more successful learners, say in mathematics, because they are more versatile and capable of switching learning strategies where necessary.

Other studies have found that female students are more likely than their male counterparts to display "learned helplessness" (Licht and Dweck 1983). Whereas male students are more likely to attribute success to their ability and failure to a lack of effort, female students tend to relate success to effort and failure to lack of ability. Female students show a stronger tendency to view their successes as due to factors such as "luck," which implies some uncertainty about their ability to succeed in the future (Nicholls 1979).

8. *Classroom Context*

Mixed-classroom studies have repeatedly found that male students receive more teacher attention than do female students (e.g. Galton et al. 1980). Teachers tend to place more importance on male learning and give male students more teacher time. Yet, it is often male students themselves who demand attention by asking questions or by making heavier demands on the teacher in other ways. Teacher attention need not necessarily be thought of as positive. In her ethnographic study of a comprehensive school in Birmingham, England, Wright (1987) found that African-Caribbean students, both male and female, received more attention than their White counterparts, but that this attention was demoralizing and prejudicial in achievement terms.

A study by Sikes (1971) of seventh and eighth grade classrooms found that the many more contacts that male students had with teachers related not only to misbehavior (negative attention) but to academic contexts, both teacher and student initiated (positive attention). This study also found that male students were asked a higher percentage of abstract (rather than factual) questions and showed a greater willingness to guess when unsure of the answer. Female students had a higher percentage of positive contacts with their teachers, but they were more likely to remain silent in classroom discussion. While these patterns of classroom interaction have been found at all levels of education, there are some specific age-related factors.

8.1 Elementary or Primary Classrooms

A review of British primary schools by Brophy and Good (1974) found that, although boys are criticized more often than girls, they are praised as often and sometimes more often. Teachers not only check on boys' work more but also tend to question them more during the lesson. Further, boys are more likely to call out answers and thus, proactively, make greater demands on the teacher. A study by French and French (1984) similarly revealed that boys are far more able to make their comments heard and to be addressed by the teacher. In addition, certain boys in the class develop strategies which increase their chances of being asked a question by their teachers and which ensure, during the lesson, that they become the focus of attention for the whole class.

On average, elementary boys appear to misbehave much more often and more intensively than girls, thus eliciting more frequent criticism and punishment for misbehavior. However, this praise and criticism is not distributed equally among all boys in the classroom. Brophy and Good (1974) found that a large proportion, sometimes even the majority of the criticism, may be directed to a small group of boys who are perceived as likely to misbehave and who are often low achievers. In Britain, this group typically includes an overrepresentation of Black and ethnic minority students. Meanwhile, a high proportion of praise (for academic accomplishment) goes to another small group of generally White boys who are high achievers.

Overall, then, the data suggest that differences between elementary boys and girls in patterns of interactions with their teachers are as likely to be due to differences in the behavior of the students themselves as due to the tendency of teachers to treat the two sexes differently.

8.2 High-school or Secondary Classrooms

As has been discussed, the advantage in achievement held by girls at the elementary school level is not sustained as they move to the secondary school. Moreover, it is claimed that this slippage is due to the prevention of older, female students from achieving their academic potential because of inappropriate teacher expectations and other aspects of institutionalized sexism in the school system (Becker 1981).

Significantly, early high school studies found striking differences in the teachers' treatment of males and females, invariably favoring the male students. Jones (1971), for example, found that all kinds of interactions favored male students. Particularly significant were the number of direct questions, open questions, student-initiated contacts, teacher-initiated work contacts, and positive teacher–student contacts. In addition, male students received more behavioral warnings and criticisms than did their female counterparts.

As male students get older and move toward college and university, the conflict that once seemed to have existed between the student role and the male sex role disappears. The converse happens to female students as their perceived future domestic role as wife and mother narrows their career aspirations. Since achievement in school is perceived as a stepping stone toward later performance as either the family "breadwinner" or the family "carer" occupation becomes a basic part of student expectations. At the same time, familiar patterns of interaction between teachers and students continue. Stanworth (1983) found that British female secondary students found it more difficult to engage successfully in conversation with the teachers and that they were more "invisible." Hence, many of the teachers in Stanworth's study found difficulty in recalling girls' names and admitted to the fact that they could not, in some cases, distinguish one female student from another.

9. Social Relationships within the School

Many student experiences in the school context are shaped by the way they are perceived by their peer group. Evidence is now emerging that students are profoundly affected by these experiences. Two British studies illustrate this concern; the first regarding the subjective world of adolescent girls (Lees 1987), and the second the impact of racism on children's lives (Troyna and Hatcher 1992).

Lees' study aimed to explore the system of social relations in the school, Specifically how boys treat girls and how girls respond in the classroom. What emerged was that, regardless of social class or ethnic group, adolescent girls are concerned and anxious about their sexual reputation; that is, whether they are "slags" (girls who sleep around) or "drags" ("nice" girls who do not and who are considered by boys as marriageable rather than "easy lays"). Lees commented on the sheer volume of denigratory terms for women and the tight control exercised over female students' autonomy with the intent of protecting their sexual reputations.

Offensive labeling also plays a part in Black children's lives. In their study of predominantly White primary schools, Troyna and Hatcher (1992) found, first, that race and racism are significant features of school life, and that racist name-calling is by far the most common expression of racism.

> There is a wide variation in black children's experiences of racist name-calling. For some it may almost be an everyday happening. For others it is less frequent, with occurences remembered as significant events whose reoccurrence remains a possibility in every new social situation. For all, it is in general the most hurtful form of verbal aggression from other children. (p. 195)

Significantly, differences between the experiences of children in different schools were accounted for in terms of the effectiveness of the stance of staff and particularly the head (principal) in dealing with racist incidents. Again, as in the Lees (1987) study, verbal harassment was found to induce fear and construct systems of control over Black students.

10. Conclusion

Males and females, and students of different races, experience schooling quite differently. They are perceived and treated differently by their teachers and their classmates (particulary those of the opposite sex or from different races). They are assigned or select different curriculums. They achieve at different levels, partly because of the type and form of tests administered. They develop different interests and preferences, and they may come to perceive themselves and their abilities quite differently.

The importance of research on gender and racial differences is that findings derived from such research can raise consciousness about current inequalities in the schooling system and thus enable changes to be made. At the same time, however, raising consciousness does not guarantee that the necessary improvements will be made. Substantial improvement will probably require fundamental changes in the economic and social structures within which schools currently operate.

See also: Individual Differences and Instruction; Learning Potential and Learning Potential Tests; Sex Differences in Behavior and Behavioral Development; Cognitive Development: Individual Differences; Gender and Education

References

Arnot M, Weiner G (eds.) 1987 *Gender and the Politics of Schooling*. Hutchinson, London

Becker J 1981 Differential teacher treatment of males and females in mathematics classes. *J. Res. Math. Educ.* 12(1): 40–53

Brah A, Minhas R 1985 Structural racism or cultural difference. In: Weiner G (ed.) 1985 *Just a Bunch of Girls*. Open University Press, Milton Keynes

Brennan J, McGeevor P 1990 *Ethnic Minority and the Graduate Labour Market*, Commission for Racial Equality, London

Brophy J, Good T 1974 *Teacher–Student Relationships: Causes and Consequences*. Holt, Rinehart and Winston, New York

Chapman J W, Boersma F J 1983 A cross-national study of academic self-concept using the Student's Perception of Ability Scale. *N. Z. J. Educ. Stud.* 18(1): 69–75

Clift P 1978 And all things nice. . . . Unpublished paper, Open University, Milton Keynes

Connell W F, Stroobant R E, Sinclair K E, Connell R W, Rogers K W 1975 *Twenty to Twenty*. Hicks Smith, Sydney

Cooper P, Stewart L 1987 *Language Skills in the Classroom: What Research Say to the Teacher* National Educational Association, Washington, DC

Deliyanni-Kouimtzi K 1992 "Father is out shopping because mother is at work": Greek primary school reading texts as an example of educational policy for gender equality. *Gender and Education* 4(1–2): 67–79

Elkjaer B 1992 Girls and information technology in Denmark—An account of a socially constructed problem. *Gender and Education* 4(1–2): 25–40

Etaugh C, Hughes V 1975 Teachers' evaluations of sex-typed behavior in children: The role of teacher sex and school setting. *Dev. Psychol.* 11: 394–95

Fagot B I 1977 Consequences of moderate cross-gender behavior in pre-school children. *Child Dev.* 48(3): 902–07

French J, French P 1984 Sociolinguists and gender divisions: In: Acker S (ed.) 1984 *World Yearbook of Education 1983–84: Women and Education*. Kogan Page, London

Galton M, Simon B, Croll P J 1980 *Inside the Primary Classroom*. Routledge and Kegan Paul, London

Goldstein H 1987 Gender bias and test norms in educational selection. In: Arnot M, Weiner G(eds.) 1987

Gorman T, White J, Brooks G, Maclure M, Kispala A 1988 *Language Performance in Schools*. Review of APU Language Monitoring 1979–83 HMSO, London

Gould S J 1981 *The Mismeasure of Man*. W W Norton, New York

Griffin J 1972 Influence strategies: Theory and research a study of teacher behavior. Doctoral dissertation, University of Missouri, Columbia, Missouri

Jones V 1971 The Influence of teacher–student introversion, achievement and similarity on teacher–student dyadic classroom interactions. Doctoral dissertation University of Texas, Austin, Texas

Lees S 1987 The structure of sexual relations in school. In: Arnot M, Weiner G (eds.) 1987

Licht B G, Dweck C S 1983 Sex differences in achievement orientations: Consequences for academic clones and attainments. In: Marland M (ed.) 1983 *Sex Differentiation and Schooling*. Heinemann, London

Maccoby E M, Jacklin C N 1975 *The Psychology of Sex Differences*. Oxford University Press, London

Milner D 1983 *Children and Race: Ten Years On*. Ward Lock Educational, London

Nash S C 1979 Sex role as mediator of intellectual functioning. In: Wittig M A, Petersen A C (eds.) 1979 *Sex Related Differences in Cognitive Functioning: Developmental Issues*. Academic Press, Orlando, Florida

Nicholls J 1979 Development of perception of any attainment and causal attributions for success and failure in reading. *J. Educ. Psychol.* 71(1): 94–99

Phoenix A 1987 Theories of gender and black families. In: Weiner G, Arnot M (eds.) 1987 *Gender Under Scrutiny*. Hutchinson, London

Proctor C P 1984 Teacher expectations: A model for school improvement. *Elem. Sch. J.* 84(4): 469–81

Sarup M 1986 *The Politics of Multiracial Education*. Routledge, London

Scott-Hodgetts R 1986 Girls and mathematics: The negative implications of success. In: Burton L (ed.) 1986 *Girls into Maths Can Go*. Holt, Rinehart and Winston, London

Sikes J 1971 Differential behavior of male and female teachers with male and female students. Doctoral dissertation, University of Texas, Austin, Texas

Spender D 1980 *Man Made Language*. Routledge and Kegan Paul, London
Stanworth M 1983 *Gender and Schooling: A Study of Sexual Divisions in the Classroom*. Unwin and Hyman, London.
Stobart G, Elwood J, Quinlan M 1992 Gender bias in examinations: How equal are the opportunities. *Br. J. Educ. Res.* 18(3): 261–76
Stone M 1981 *The Education the of Black Child in Britain: The Myth of Multiracial Education*. Fontana, London
Troyna B, Hatcher R 1992 *Racism in Children's Lives: A Study of Mainly-White Primary Schools* Routledge, London
Wright C 1987 The relations between teachers and Afro-Caribbean pupils: Observing multicultural classrooms. In: Weiner G, Arnot M (eds.) 1987 *Gender Under Scrutiny*. Hutchinson, London

G. Weiner

Study Circles

A study circle is a circle of friends or associates assembled for common and planned study of a predetermined subject or problem area. The study circle is a form of education capable of attracting people with a short previous education who are often unaccustomed to taking part in adult education programs.

The study circle is now generally recognized as a modern method of adult education and has even drawn attention from areas outside of popular education, for example, in the case of industry training circles in large firms in Germany and Japan. Study circles have their roots in the inadequacies prevalent in nineteenth-century society in Sweden. They developed alongside the popular movements that emerged at that time.

This entry describes the historical background and the development of the study circle, and discusses its ideology and pedagogical ideas. The study circle is a part of popular education in all Nordic countries, but there are differences in historical development and in how the study circles are organized. This entry deals primarily with Sweden, a country where roughly one-fourth of the adult population takes part in study circles each year.

1. Definition

The study circle is a small group of people (normally between 5 and 12), who over an extended period of time, and on a regular basis, meet to study or to take part in a cultural project under the guidance of a leader. Most study circles last two or three months, during which time the participants normally meet once a week for two to three hours (see *Group Learning*).

2. Historical Background

2.1 The Growth of the Popular Movements

During the second half of the nineteenth century so-called "popular movements" emerged in the Nordic countries. First came the free Church movement followed by the temperance movement and the labor movement. Lack of knowledge was seen as an impediment to organizational development and to the desired transformation of society. The knowledge needed for bringing about radical social change was not offered as part of the traditional school curriculum. Despite inauspicious circumstances, many workers studied on their own. The study circles offered not only an opportunity for learning, but they also played an important role in establishing social and cultural networks (see *Nordic Countries: Adult Education; Worker Education and Labor Education*).

2.2 Orientation of Study Circles

The study circles served mainly two goals, although in practice these were often combined. First, the education offered by the circles was seen as "ammunition" for the trade unions and the political movement—a means of engaging in, and preparing for, class struggle and social transformation. Second, the circles were intended as a means of raising the level of general education of the working class.

Both goals are reflected in the arrangement and methods of the studies, which can be summarized as follows:

(a) People studied in small groups, often in their homes.

(b) They had little to draw on in the way of study materials.

(c) They had no teachers, nor did they feel the need for any. The leader of the group was primarily an organizer and administrator with no special theoretical qualifications.

(d) To supplement their studies, people would attend lectures or meetings.

(e) The people who studied in this way had no academic background, but they had acquired an abundance of practical experience.

(f) People learned to discuss, to argue, to show consideration for others, to accept defeat, and share responsibility.

(g) They experienced a sense of solidarity and community.

(h) The knowledge they acquired was immediately relevant and applicable to everyday life.

(i) They began studying at their own level, and the studies were directed by their own needs.

The form of education which thus evolved within the popular movements later provided the foundation of what came to be known as the "study circle". The first real study circle is customarily said to have been founded in 1902 by Oscar Olsson, a keyperson in the temperance movement. He was inspired by a visit to the United States and observation of the successful Chautauqua movement (see *Community Education and Community Development; North America: Adult Education*).

2.3 State Grants

At a very early stage, each of the popular movements developed special organizational arrangements for educational activities—usually in the form of an adult education association. In Sweden, the activities of these associations are mainly financed by grants from the state and the municipal authorities. As early as 1912, the Swedish Parliament voted to give grants for the purchase of books.

State funding of study circle activities, which was introduced in 1947, has played a vital role in enabling Swedish popular education to develop. For example, during the 1970s, the number of study hours qualifying for public aid rose from 5.5 million to 12 million. At the same time as these grants were introduced, rules and conditions were drawn up which gave a definition of the study circle with the aim of preserving its distinctive character.

From the 1960s onwards, public institutions have often chosen to distribute information on vital social issues through the organized adult education associations.

3. The Pedagogy of the Study Circle

3.1 Philosophy

Study circles make use of a great variety of methods and subjects. It is therefore relevant to ask whether the study circle demands special teaching and learning methods.

There is a basic study circle philosophy which is close to Paulo Freire's ideas concerning the pedagogy of the oppressed (see *Conscientization and Mobilization*). The views of the popular movements concerning society, people, and knowledge govern the choice of methods in the study circles. This pedagogy is based on the ideals of community development and principles of emancipatory democracy involving the struggle for freedom, justice, and equality. Study circles therefore seek to establish an environment which is conducive to personal development and the enhancement of inner creative abilities.

3.2 Context

A fundamental idea in the pedagogy of the study circle is that people have an innate desire to learn. Educational efforts do not necessarily demand a monetary or nonmonetary reward. The new knowledge the participants acquire will be important insofar as it enriches their everyday lives. This is why the precise cognitive targets of the study circle cannot be defined in advance.

Instead, the common efforts of the members, as well as the use of the acquired knowledge, indicate new needs and problems to be dealt with. The study circle must have sufficient flexibility to adjust its activities in accordance with the resulting redefinition of learning goals to be attained. Through their studies, the members must be enabled to view their own lives in a wider social context. This means that the members of the study circle must learn how to deal with problems through their studies and how to work out solutions to problems that cannot be foreseen in advance by the producers of study materials, the study circle leader, or the circle members themselves.

3.3 The Common Goal

Characteristic of the study circle is the collective nature of learning. In dialogue with others, the participants constantly appraise their knowledge, comparing notes and helping each other to discover new insights and to find new knowledge. In order for a study circle to function adequately, certain principles have to be observed by all its members, including the leader. Above all, everyone must be actively engaged in pursuing the common learning goals. It is only then that dialogue and equal participation, as well as sharing of responsibility, can exist.

The knowledge and experience is used as an input into the learning activity, but it is not enough. New information is also required in order to progress. All members of the study circle share a responsibility for ensuring that studies are meaningful. Even if the leader's knowledge of the subject is an asset, the leader should not assume the traditional role of a teacher. It is his or her job to assist the participants by providing information, indicating means of problem solving, and ensuring the active participation of all members.

The learning process within the study circle builds on the participants' knowledge, experiences, and perceived learning needs. Members are not only reponsible for themselves, but also for the learning progress achieved by the other members of the study circle. However, the knowledge communicated in the study circle is not universal and common to all. All participants receive and process the material in accordance with their own needs. Hence no two study circles are alike, nor should they be.

4. Trends and Developments

4.1 Freedom from Rules

In Sweden, during the 1980s, demands grew stronger for abolishing the formal rules that had been associated with the system of state grants since 1947. In order to meet future challenges, the educational associations required continued freedom to develop the study circle approach. Since the early 1990s, the state no longer sets formal regulations for the study circles: only some basic goals are defined.

4.2 International Scope

Interest in the study circle has increased even outside the Nordic countries. The study circle approach is gaining recognition in Canada and the United States. The Nordic educational associations are engaged in development projects in Central and Eastern Europe. There is also an interest in the Scandinavian experience of popular education in Latin America. FoNoLa (The Society for Exchange of Popular Education Scandinavia–Latin America) is one of the organizations that supports developments involving study circles.

See also: Nordic Countries: Adult Education; Folk High Schools; Community Education and Community Development; Experiential and Open Learning for Adults; Cooperative Learning

Bibliography

Arvidson L 1985 *Folkbildning i rörelse*. Liber Förlag AB, Malmö

Arvidson L 1989 Popular education and educational ideology. In: Ball S, Larsson S (eds.) 1989 *The Struggle for Democratic Education: Equality and Participation in Sweden*. Falmer Press, London

Arvidson L 1991 *Folkbildning och självuppfostran*. Tidens Förlag, Stockholm

Byström J 1983 *Studiecirkelns pedagogik*. Brevskolan, Stockholm

Freire P 1970 *Pedagogy of the Oppressed*. Continuum, New York

Ginner T 1988 *Den bildade arbetaren*. Linköping University, Linköping

Oliver L P 1987 *Study Circles: Coming Together for Personal Growth and Social Change*. Seven Locks Press, Washington, DC

J. Byström

Study Habits and Strategies

Study habits and strategies refer to activities carried out by a learner during the learning process for the purpose of improving learning. This definition has three components, concerning the what, when, and why of study habits and strategies, respectively. First, study habits and strategies are behaviors that the learner produces. Second, they occur at the time of learning. Third, they are intended as aids to learning. This definition also corresponds to a definition of learning strategies (Mayer 1987, Weinstein and Mayer 1986) (see *Learning Strategies, Teaching and Testing for*). Examples of study strategies for reading a textbook lesson include underlining key terms, creating an outline, and taking elaborative notes.

For students—including children in elementary schools, youngsters in secondary schools, and adults in colleges or training programs—learning from teachers and books becomes a dominant activity in their lives. They are expected to become professional learners, but they are rarely given any training in how to learn (Mayer 1992, Norman 1980, Weinstein and Mayer 1986). In spite of their importance, study habits and strategies often remain part of the hidden curriculum (i.e., material that is not heavily taught but that students are expected to learn). Successful students somehow acquire study strategies even though "strategy instruction has not been incorporated into the curriculum on a large scale" (Presley 1990 p. 7). In contrast, some learning disabilities can be described as cognitive processing deficits (Swanson and Keogh 1990).

1. Cognitive Processes and Outcomes During Learning

The basis for a theory of study strategies comes from the information-processing approach to human learning (Mayer 1984, 1987, Sternberg 1985). Figure 1 summarizes aspects of an information-processing model that are most relevant to a discussion of study strategies. The model highlights three memory stores represented as boxes—namely sensory memory, short-term memory, and long-term memory—and three cognitive learning processes represented by arrows—namely, selecting, organizing, and integrating.

The arrow from sensory memory (SM) to short-term memory (STM) refers to the process of selecting relevant information, such as paying attention to the important principles stated in textbook lesson. Mayer (1984, 1987) describes this process as focusing attention whereas Sternberg (1985) describes it as selective encoding. The arrow from STM back to itself refers to the process of organizing the incoming information, such as noting that one event is the cause of another

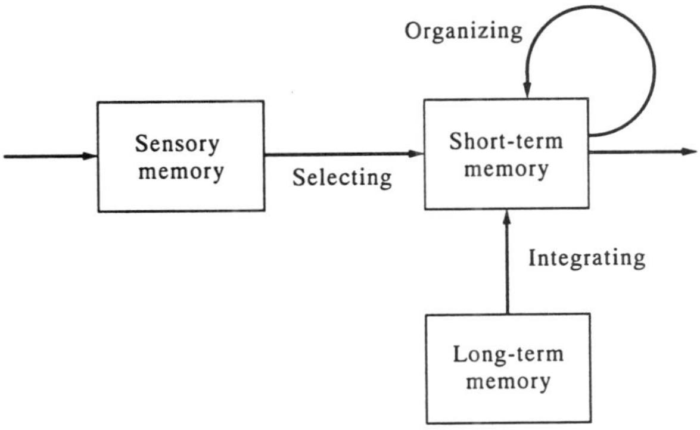

Figure 1
An information-processing model of cognitive processes in learning

event. Mayer (1984, 1987) calls this cognitive activity building internal connections while Sternberg (1985) calls it selective combination. Finally the arrow from long-term memory (LTM) to STM refers to the process of integrating incoming information with existing relevant knowledge from LTM, such as relating a lesson on radar to one's existing knowledge about a ball bouncing off a wall. Mayer (1984, 1987) refers to this cognitive activity as building external connections and Sternberg (1985) calls it selective comparison.

The information-processing model in Fig. 1 suggests four possible learning outcomes. First, if the learner fails to select relevant information, no learning will occur. Consequently, the student will perform poorly both on retention tests, which cover the presented material, and transfer tests, which require applying the material in new situations. Second, if the learner pays attention to the material but does not work on organizing it, then nonmeaningful learning will occur. In this case, the student would be expected to perform well on retention tests, but poorly on transfer tests. Third, partially meaningful learning occurs when the learner selects and organizes relevant incoming information but fails to integrate it with existing knowledge. This learner would perform well on retention and on certain types of transfer tests. Fourth, when all three learning processes are engaged, the learner builds a meaningful learning outcome that supports good retention and transfer performance.

2. *Guiding Cognitive Processes During Learning*

Study habits and strategies are intended to elicit and guide one's cognitive processes during learning. A self-directed learner possesses appropriate study strategies and uses them at the appropriate times and places during learning. Knowing when to use or modify use of a study strategy is a kind of metacognitive skill (see *Learning Strategies, Teaching and Testing for*).

When the learner's goal is solely good retention performance, then study strategies that promote the selecting process are important. When the learner's goal is good transfer performance (as well as good retention performance), then study strategies should be used that engage selecting, organizing, and integrating processes.

Study strategies can be categorized in terms of the cognitive processes they affect; strategies to promote selecting, organizing, and/or integrating. Underlining and verbatim copying of selected words in a textbook lesson are examples of a study strategy aimed primarily at the selection of relevant information. These kinds of activities are most likely to guide the learner's attention toward the material that is copied or underlined. Outlining the material in a textbook is an example of a study strategy which affects both selecting relevant information and organizing it into a coherent structure. Writing a description in one's own words of how the material relates to something else, may elicit all three of the major learning processes. By encouraging the learner to go beyond the information presented, elaboration strategies cause learners to use their existing knowledge in long-term memory to make sense out of the incoming material.

Pressley and his colleagues (Pressley 1990) have suggested several study strategies that could become part of the curriculum. They include summarization strategies, text-structuring strategies, and question-asking strategies. Summarization strategies involve writing or stating the content of a passage or lecture in condensed form. Since summarization strategies can be expected to activate the cognitive processes of selecting relevant information, they should improve students' retention performance. Research supports this expectation. For example, students who were asked to write a single sentence to summarize a paragraph retained more of the information than students who simply read the paragraph (Doctorow et al. 1978). Similarly, elementary-school students who were taught how to write a single-sentence summary of a paragraph were subsequently better able to retain the main ideas from paragraphs they read than were untrained students (Rinehart et al. 1986).

In some cases, summarization strategies that emphasize outlining of the material can encourage learners both to select and organize relevant information, resulting in good performance on retention and on some types of transfer tests. For example, Barnett et al. (1981) asked some students to listen to an 1800-word lecture on the history of roads whereas other students were asked to identify and outline the main ideas as they listened. The students who outlined recalled more than twice as much of the information as those students who listened only. Similarly, seventh-grade students who were taught how to write hierarchical outlines for social studies lessons outperformed untrained peers on recalling key information and answering questions about social studies passages they had read (Taylor and Beach 1984). Other forms of outlining instruction that have improved student learning include network training (Dansereau et al. 1979) and concept mapping (Novak and Gowin 1984).

Text-structuring strategies involve selecting pieces of information from a passage that fit within a general structure. For example, the structure of a story may include a main character, a place, a time, one or more major events, and a final outcome. When elementary school children who were poor readers were taught to find these kinds of elements in stories that they read, their retention test performance improved toward the level of good readers (Idol and Croll 1987, Short and Ryan 1987). In contrast to narrative prose, expository prose can be organized in several ways: generalization (i.e., a main idea followed by supporting pieces of information); enumeration (i.e., a list of facts all related to the same topic); sequence (i.e., a series of steps in a process); classification (i.e., a set of categories and subcategories); or comparison (i.e., a description of similarities and differences between two or more things along several different dimensions). Cook and Mayer (1988) taught junior college students how to recognize and outline paragraphs from their textbooks based on these kinds of text structures. On a post-test involving new expository passages, trained students remembered more of the relevant information and solved more transfer problems than untrained students.

Question-generation strategies occur when a reader creates questions based on text material. When the learner generates transfer questions that require integration and extension of the material in the passage, he or she is encouraged to engage in selecting, organizing, and integrating processes which result in superior retention and transfer performance. For example, Davey and McBride (1986) taught elementary-school students how to generate transfer questions for expository texts. On subsequent tests trained students performed better than untrained students on remembering and comprehending text passages. In another study, King (1990) taught college students how to generate transfer questions based on a lecture that they had just heard. Again, trained students who were asked to generate questions performed better on a post-test involving retention and transfer questions than untrained students who were simply asked to discuss the lecture.

3. Future Research on Study Habits and Strategies

Research on study habits and strategies has made clear that successful learners do more than read (or listen to) every word in a lesson; when necessary, they also engage in what Wittrock and his colleagues (Doctorow et al. 1978) have called "generative processes" (i.e., active strategies aimed at improving learning). Research on cognitive strategy instruction also suggests that many study strategies are domain-specific; that is, they can be used mainly for studying a single kind of material such as mathematics, science, or literature (Pressley 1990). For example, strategies for how to represent algebra story problems as diagrams (Lewis 1989) are useful for learning to solve story problems, but not for learning to solve problems in history or computer programming. Future research is needed to determine the specific study strategies used by skilled learners in each subject-matter field and to devise methods for teaching these strategies to unskilled learners who have failed to learn them otherwise. These strategies are likely to include more effective methods for note-taking as well as for studying with peers.

See also: Learning Strategies and Learning to Learn; Learning Strategies, Teaching and Testing for; Learning to Learn: Adult Education

References

Barnett J E, DiVesta F J, Rogozinski J T 1981 What is learned in note taking? *J Educ. Psychol.* 73: 181–92

Cook L K, Mayer R E 1988 Teaching readers about the structure of scientific text. *J. Educ. Psychol.* 80: 448–56

Dansereau D F et al. 1979 Development and evaluation of an effective learning strategy program. *J. Educ. Psychol.* 71: 64–73

Davey B, McBride S 1986 The effects of question generation training on reading comprehension. *J. Educ. Psychol.* 78: 256–62

Doctorow M, Wittrock M C, Marks C 1978 Generative processes in reading comprehension. *J. Educ. Psychol.* 70: 109–18

King A 1990 Enhancing peer interaction and learning in the classroom through reciprocal questioning. *Am. Educ. Res. J.* 27: 664–87

Idol L, Croll V J 1987 Story-mapping training as a means of improving reading comprehension. *Learning Disability Quarterly* 10: 214–29

Lewis A B 1989 Training students to represent arithmetic word problems. *J. Educ. Psychol.* 81: 521–31

Mayer R E 1984 Aids to text comprehension. *Educ. Psychol.* 19: 30–42

Mayer R E 1987 *Educational Psychology: A Cognitive Approach*. Harper Collins, New York

Mayer R E 1992 Guiding students' cognitive processing of scientific information. In: Pressley M, Harris K, Guthrie J (eds.) 1992 *Promoting Academic Competence and Literary in Schools* Academic Press, Orlando, Florida

Norman D A 1980 Cognitive engineering and education. In: Tuma D T, Reif F (eds.) 1980 *Problem Solving and Education*. Erlbaum, Hillsdale, New Jersey

Novak J D, Gowin D B 1984 *Learning to Learn*. Cambridge University Press, Cambridge

Pressley M 1990 *Cognitive Strategy Instruction That Really Improves Children's Academic Performance*, Brookline Books, Cambridge, Massachusetts

Rinehart S C, Stahl S A, Erickson L G 1986 Some effects of summarization training on reading and studying. *Read. Res. Q.* 21: 422–28

Short E J, Ryan E B 1987 Metacognitive differences between skilled and less skilled readers: Remediating deficits through story grammar and attribution training. *J. Educ. Psychol.* 76: 225–35

Sternberg R J 1985 *Beyond IQ: A Triarchic Theory of Human Intelligence*. Cambridge University Press, Cambridge

Swanson H L, Keogh B (eds.) 1990 *Learning Disabilities: Theoretical and Research Issues*. Erlbaum, Hillsdale, New Jersey

Taylor B M, Beach R W 1984 The effects of text structure instruction on middle-grade students' comprehension and production of expository text. *Read. Res. Q.* 19: 134–46

Weinstein C E, Mayer R E 1986 The teaching of learning strategies. In: Wittrock W C (ed.) 1986 *Handbook of Research on Teaching*, 3rd edn. Macmillan, New York

R. E. Mayer

Substitute Teachers

The use of substitute teachers when regular classroom teachers are absent varies widely from country to country. Only in those countries where more pressing educational needs such as adequate school facilities, reasonable class size, relevant instructional materials, and well-trained teachers have been addressed, does the provision of substitute teachers become a factor in classroom instruction. The purposes of this entry are to: (a) discuss the relationship between teacher absenteeism and substitute teachers, (b) describe the characteristics of substitute teachers, (c) explore the problems confronted by substitute teachers, and (d) examine the costs associated with the practice of employing substitute teachers.

1. Teacher Absenteeism and Substitute Teaching

Teachers are absent from work between seven and ten percent of the days schools are in session (Brace 1990, Trotter and Wragg 1990). The causes of teacher absenteeism are as varied as the schools in which they occur. In the United States, as teachers take advantage of contract provisions for personal and professional leave, substitute teachers are used more frequently (Deay and Bontempo 1986). In the United Kingdom substitute teachers are used to provide teaching services during inservice training for regular classroom teachers (Trotter and Wragg 1990). Latin American rural teachers are often absent to take reports or attend meetings at a distant central office, while Kenyan rural teachers may take a period of time off from teaching to work at a second job. In many developing countries, teacher absence is often determined by location of teacher residence, availability of reliable transportation, existence of roads, and status of local health conditions (Montero-Sieburth 1989, Roy 1980).

Like the causes of absenteeism, ways of covering teacher absences vary widely. In more developed countries where an approved list of substitutes is available, different administrative procedures for contacting substitutes when they are needed may be used. Teachers may be responsible for securing their own substitute, principals or their designées may make the contact, or a specified district or regional office employee may call substitute teachers for several schools. The size of the district or region is often a factor in determining the routine to be followed, with larger districts or regions likely to have a more formalized, centralized procedure (Koelling 1983).

In less developed countries, substitutes are not always available. The demand for teachers in these countries has exceeded the supply as universal primary education has been adopted (Hajjar 1983). Seventy students or more is a normal class size, and schools often operate two or more shifts (British Council 1985); therefore, staffing is a major problem and qualified substitute teachers are an unaffordable and unavailable luxury. When teachers are absent, students are supervised either by a close-by teacher with a large class of his or her own or an older student (Montero-Sieburth 1989).

2. Characteristics of Substitute Teachers

Many substitutes are certified teachers who for a variety of reasons are not currently full-time employees. They may have recently moved, are taking time out to raise families, are retired, or are just taking a career break. Most substitutes who are not certified teachers have some college training or a college degree. In some cases college students preparing for a career in teaching are called upon to substitute (Morris 1981). Also called on at times are librarians, counselors, or other classroom teachers who give up planning time or cancel classes (Meara 1983). Most substitute teachers are female with a wide range of teaching experience (from 1 to 30 years) (Trotter and Wragg 1990, Rose et al. 1987).

People substitute teach for a number of reasons. Trotter and Wragg (1990) found that flexibility in scheduling and remuneration were the two most frequently cited advantages of substitute teaching. There are demands on a person's time that preclude full-time employment (such as caring for children or elderly parents). Flexibility in scheduling allows these people to be employed on a part-time basis, choosing the days they work. Also, while substitute pay is not equivalent to what full-time teachers make, it usually averages from $25.00 to $50.00 daily; this daily rate is sufficient to attract a pool of part-time workers (Koelling 1983).

A reason that prospective teachers substitute teach is that preferential consideration is often given to substitute teachers when administrators are looking for full-time teachers (Rose et al. 1987). Retired teachers and other retired people substitute because it keeps them in touch with children and schools, while allowing them time to pursue their own interests.

3. Problems Associated with Substitute Teaching

Substitute teachers are often called at inconvenient hours to go to unknown locations, to work with people they do not know, to do a job for which they may or may not be prepared (Simmons 1991). Thus, despite the advantages discussed in the section above, it is not surprising that substitutes, when surveyed, mention disadvantages as well. Certain factors make the job of substitute teacher more stressful. Having no lesson plans or poor lesson plans left for them, teaching outside their area of certification or expertise, and being given little or no information about the students regarding seating charts, classroom rules, and schedules are the major causes of apprehension in substitute teachers (Johnson 1988).

Trotter and Wragg (1990) found that substitutes listed lack of knowledge of the school, their colleagues, and particular children with difficulties as the greatest disadvantages in substitute teaching. These studies echo the findings of Deay and Bontempo (1986) who found that substitute teachers felt they most needed information about the following items in order of preference: (a) classroom plans and procedures, (b) school rules and regulations, (c) their professional role, (d) organizing and managing learning experiences, (e) discipline procedures, (f) knowledge of learner differences, and (g) knowledge of school programs. These issues reflect concern primarily with the immediate class situation and how to maintain order and the continuity of learning. Lack of advance information about these areas contributes to less than effective use of substitute teachers' time and makes their jobs more difficult.

Substitute teaching is often a marginally rewarding activity. Clifton and Rambaran (1987) found that substitutes often experience anxiety and do not feel satisfied, competent, or recognized as part of the education community. They see themselves as holding low status and prestige in the school and feel their efforts in classrooms often are unappreciated. Also, the substitute teachers in this study mentioned that they rarely received positive feedback in their work. They felt principals and other staff members saw them as one-day employees not worth much time and effort. Because they had no real authority over student progress, they occasionally felt that students did not see them as legitimate figures in the educational setting. All of these factors combined to create problems.

4. *Costs Associated with Substitute Teaching*

There are two types of costs associated with substitute teaching: financial and instructional. Of the two, financial costs are easier to estimate because specific amounts of money can be traced to the cost of teacher absenteeism and hiring substitute teachers. For example, a study conducted in Chicago, Illinois, by Meara (1983) examined costs over three years and found that approximately $54,000,000 a year was spent on all costs associated with teacher absence and substitute coverage (e.g., substitute pay, sick leave, and extra compensation for staff diverted from regular duties). This figure represented about 8.4 percent of the total annual amount budget for teacher salary expenditures.

The results of a study conducted in New York City supported the Chicago findings (Willerman and McGuire 1986). In this study approximately $71,500,000 was found to be spent on substitute teacher costs, a figure which represented approximately 9 percent of total teacher salary expenditures. Thus, the costs of substitute teachers are a major administrative concern in days of upwardly spiralling school budgets.

Large as the financial costs are, the instructional costs may be even larger and are certainly more difficult to calculate. Classroom time is defined partly in terms of the activities that occur within it; thus student achievement is directly related to the way in which time is allocated and used in classrooms (Fisher and Berliner 1985). Schools are time-oriented; time should not be wasted through idleness, boredom, or passivity (Pronovost 1986).

One of the basic problems associated with substitute teaching, whether in a more developed country where trained substitutes are available or in a less developed country where older students are called on to monitor when a teacher is absent, is that it often leads to marginally functional activity on the part of students (Koelling 1983). Gaps in the continuity of learning occur when the regular classroom teacher is absent; often busywork assignments rather than meaningful learning activities are given to keep students occupied and quiet. Given that students on average may spend as much as 10 percent of their school time with someone other than the regular classroom teacher, sizable loss of meaningful student learning experiences can be inferred as instructional costs associated with substitute teaching.

5. *The Future of Substitute Teaching*

Three generalizations can be offered regarding the future of substitute teaching. First, as developing countries become better able to provide quality education services, the availability of a cadre of qualified substitute teachers to maintain meaningful student learning when teachers must be absent will become a more important instructional issue. Second, ways of integrating substitute teachers into the school community are likely to result in greater commitment on the part of substitute teachers and, ultimately, improved instructional opportunities for the students they encounter. Third, as costs of providing quality education services escalate, and as the demand for higher student achievement increases, better ways for substitute teachers to maintain continuity in learning when teachers are absent must be found. These may involve having specific staff development sessions for substitute teachers, developing a separate certification system for substitute teachers, developing a district or regional pool of trained substitutes for a specific school or content area, and/or implementing policies and practices which provide more thorough advance information for substitute teachers when they are called into service.

See also: Teachers as Professionals

References

Brace D L 1990 Establishing a support system for substitute teachers. NASSP *Bull.* 74(526): 73–77

British Council—English Language and Literature Division 1985 *English Teaching Profile: Malawi*. British Council, London

Clifton R A, Rambaran R 1987 Substitute teaching: Survival in a marginal situation. *Urban Educ.* 22(3): 310–27

Deay A M, Bontempo B T 1986 Helping substitute teachers contribute to school effectiveness. *Clearing House* 59(8): 359–62

Fisher C W, Berliner D C 1985 *Perspectives on Instructional Time*. Longman, New York

Hajjar H 1983 *Intensive Training Courses on Microplanning and School Mapping Report*. (Omdurman: Democratic Republic of Sudan). International Institute for Educational Planning, Paris

Johnson J M 1988 Apprehensions of substitute teachers. *Clearing House* 62(2): 89–91

Koelling C H 1983 Substitute teachers—School policies and procedures in the north central region. *Education* 104(2): 155–71

Meara H 1983 *Class Coverage in the Chicago Public Schools: A Study of Teacher Absences and Substitute Coverage*. Chicago Panel on Public School Policy and Finance, Chicago, Illinois

Montero-Sieburth M 1989 *Classroom Management: Instructional Strategies and the Allocation of Learning Resources*, BRIDGES Research Report Series No. 4. Cambridge Institute for International Development, Harvard University, Cambridge, Massachusetts

Morris J E 1981 The use of student teachers as substitutes: A survey of practices and opinions. *Teacher Educ.* 17(2): 22–32

Pronovost G 1986 Introduction: Time in a sociological and historical perspective. *Int. Soc. Sci. J.* 107: 5–18

Rose T L, Beattie J R, White R 1987 *Current Practices and Procedures in the Use of Substitute Teachers*. Office of Special Education and Rehabilitative Services, Washington, DC

Roy A 1980 School and communities: An experience in rural India. *Int. Rev. Educ.* 26(3): 369–78

Simmons B J 1991 Planning to improve the quality of the substitute teacher program. NASSP *Bull* 75(531): 91–98

Trotter A, Wragg T 1990 A study of supply teachers. *Res. Papers Educ.* 5(3): 251–76

Willerman M, McGuire J 1986 Substitute effectiveness in a school for behaviour disordered students. *Planning Changing* 17(4): 233–38

L. W. Anderson; C. Gardner

Sudan: System of Education

1. General Background

The Republic of Sudan is the largest country in Africa, with a surface area of 2.5 million square kilometers. It is situated in the north-east of the continent between latitudes 4 and 22 degrees north and longitudes 22 and 38 degrees east. The land ranges from desert in the north through rich grasslands in the center to thick jungle in the south. Only 12 percent of the land is currently cultivated, while 22 percent is forest. The climate is hot, reaching temperatures of 45 centigrade at times, being dry in the north with little seasonal rain, and tropical in the south. Sudan shares borders with nine countries: Egypt, Libya, Chad, Zaire, the Central African Republic, Uganda, Kenya, Ethiopia, and Eritrea. Conflict and famine in the region have resulted in Sudan in the early 1990s playing host to well over one million refugees, predominantly from Eritrea, Ethiopia, and Chad, which puts great strain on its limited social welfare system.

The country is entirely landlocked, except for some 630 kilometers of coastline on the Red Sea, where the only port is situated. The capital, Khartoum (which is actually made up of the three towns of Khartoum, Omdurman, and North Khartoum), is situated some 1260 kilometers along the country's main highway from the coast, at the confluence of the Blue and the White Nile rivers. The size of the country, its widely scattered population, and the lack of an extensive transport network make communications difficult and impose obvious restrictions and costs on the provision of even the most basic goods and services.

In 1990 Sudan's population was estimated at just over 25 million, with 45 percent being under the age of 14. The annual population growth rate is estimated at 2.7 percent, having declined slightly from a high of 3 percent. The population has more than doubled in 30 years and is expected to reach over 33 million by the year 2000. Such a large increase puts an enormous strain on public services, in particular the provision of education and health care.

Sudan is one of the world's poorest and least developed countries. Life expectancy in 1990 stood at 50.4 years, having improved from an estimated 39 years in 1960. The infant mortality rate in the same year was 102.4 per 1000 inhabitants. While being a great improvement from a figure of 170 in 1960, this is still very high. Health care, like education, is unevenly distributed, with isolated and sparsely populated rural communities being particularly underresourced. Illiteracy is still very high, with the latest estimate being 72.9 percent of the population (in 1956 it was 86%); 88.3 percent of females are illiterate, whereas the figure for males is 57.3 percent.

In 1988 GNP per capita was US$380 per annum, having declined by 1.8% since 1980. The Sudan's external debt stands at US$15.3 billion, an enormous burden for such a poor country. However, it has experienced some economic growth since 1990.

Sudan's population is overwhelmingly rural, with two-thirds engaging in agricultural activity, most of it subsistence farming. Over 2 million people are estimated to be still entirely nomadic. Ninety-five percent of the country's exports are agricultural products. It has great scope for agricultural development as only 2 percent of its potential arable land is under irrigation.

The latest official estimate is that only 22 percent of the population is urbanized. However, unofficial squatter camps on the edge of major towns are likely to make the figure higher. Refugees from neighboring countries and large movements of Sudanese people during the 1984–5 drought brought an estimated 3 million people into the capital, Khartoum, swelling its population to 5 million (26% of the total population). This figure has decreased somewhat with the voluntary or enforced repatriation of some refugees.

Sudan's people are ethnically very diverse. The 1956 census identified 597 tribes, with 19 major tribal groupings. Arabs in the north form the largest group (40% of the total); the second largest group are the Dinka in the south (at 12%). Over 115 languages are spoken, 26 by more than 100,000 people. Approximately 60 percent of the population are Muslim, 4 percent are Christian (the majority in the south), and the remainder, mainly in the south and west, are animist. There has been a policy of progressive Islamicization of the population over the years. Arabic is the official language of the country, although in the south English is widely used as a lingua franca.

For 56 years, Sudan was the Anglo-Egyptian Condominium, in effect a British colony. Its borders were artificially drawn by the British to include Africans in the south and west, Arabs in the north, and Hamites in the east, the result being a nation of very diverse ethnic groupings sharing no common culture, language, or religious faith. However, the traditional division in the country has always been perceived as being between the dominant Muslim Arab north and the African, largely animist, south. Lack of contact between the two parts of the country and the development of separate political and social systems, which the British encouraged (until as late as 1944 education in the south was provided totally by Christian missions), was to contribute much to the later mistrust and lack of mutual interest between the two sides.

Even before independence in 1956, the longstanding animosity between northerners and southerners, fuelled by the growing economic and political dominance of the north during the last years of British rule, was to erupt into a civil war which has engulfed the country for all but 11 years of its post-independence history. Although the 1972 Addis Ababa peace agreement gave a high degree of autonomy to the south, absorbed the region into formal political life, and allowed for some development to take place, Sudan returned to full-scale civil war in 1984 when President Numeiri introduced Islamic law (*Sharia*) throughout the country. The conflict has continued since then and has completely devastated the south, where 25 percent of the country's population used to live. Many have died from the fighting or from famine, while others have fled to northern Sudan or to neighboring countries. Public services including education have almost totally ceased to function outside the main towns. The war is estimated by the International Monetary Fund (IMF) to cost the government US$2 million a day, with 22 percent of the total government budget being allocated to defense. This has had an obvious negative impact on budgetary allocations to other sectors, including education.

In addition to the civil war, Sudan has experienced much political instability. There have been only three short-lived periods of democratically elected government. The remainder of the time the country has been under military rule. The longest, and with hindsight relatively peaceful, period of continuous government was the military dictatorship of Jaafar Numeiri (1969–84). The latest military regime took power in June 1989. It has pursued a radical Islamic social and economic policy, combined with liberalization of the economy. The nature of the regime and its support for Iraq during the Gulf War have led to the country's political and financial isolation from the majority of its former Arab and Western allies, who have cut off much of their aid. In addition, Sudan's inability at the present time to pay interest on its debts to the IMF means that it is unable to borrow further on the international finance markets.

Administratively, Sudan is divided into nine regions, one of which is the capital, Khartoum, and three of the regions are situated in the south. These nine regions are in turn divided into a total of 19 provinces. In 1991 the government introduced a federal system of government, with the regions becoming states, each with its appointed governor and regional ministers. In the south this has little meaning at the present time (1993).

In terms of skilled labor, the Sudan economy has suffered from a massive brain drain of skilled workers and professionals to the oil-rich Arab states starting in the mid-1970s, although many were obliged to return in the aftermath of the Gulf War. In 1983 the Food and Agriculture Organization (FAO) estimated that there were 350,000 Sudanese working abroad, with up to 50 percent of those trained in some professions having left the country. In education, very large numbers of teachers have gone abroad, in particular university lecturers and graduate teachers. While the brain drain has brought in badly needed hard currency remittances, the cost in terms of the loss of skilled personnel for the country's development effort has been incalculable.

Despite the generally pessimistic economic picture, the early 1990s government has launched an ambitious educational reform program aimed at achieving universal basic education by the year 2001, diversifying secondary education, and doubling the intake to higher education. The cost of the program is not known. Although economic performance has improved since 1990, it has grown from a very low base which was the result of declining performance during the 1980s. It is too early to judge how effective the recent economic liberalization program will be in increasing revenue. However, without very large and sustained economic growth, and a reversal of the sharp decline in public expenditure for education experienced during the late 1980s, the educational reforms cannot become a meaningful reality and can only result in existing resources being spread ever more thinly through an already chronically underfunded service. In the south, there will need to be a massive reconstruction and retraining program if education is to become a normal activity again.

2. *Politics and the Goals of the Education System*

The various governments of Sudan have all viewed education as playing an important role in the economic and social development of the country through meeting the requirements for educated and skilled workers. Until the mid-1980s they regularly apportioned 10–15 percent of the national budget to education. However, in response to public pressure, they have allowed secondary and higher education to expand at the expense of primary. Also, despite efforts to promote technical secondary education and nonarts-based higher studies according to declared policy, the trend has been overwhelmingly in favor of academic education. This has meant that there is an excess of arts graduates from both secondary and higher institutions, while there is still a serious shortage of middle-level technicians. At the same time, the whole educational system has expanded much more rapidly than the economy, with the result that there are large numbers of educated unemployed (one source estimates 20,000 unemployed university graduates).

With these imbalances in mind, the present government is seeking through its recent reforms to expand basic education and at the same time make it more terminal and more relevant to the economic needs of the country. It is also attempting to inject a greater degree of technical and vocational education into the secondary and tertiary levels, while allowing expansion to take place in the appropriate subject areas. Throughout, the curriculum is to be revised in order to better reflect national values and Islamic principles in line with the government's political and social ideology.

Limited political decentralization was introduced during the early 1980s, which included some devolution of educational responsibility to the regions. This has been taken much further by the recent introduction of a federal system of states. In education, all but major policy decisions will be taken at the state level.

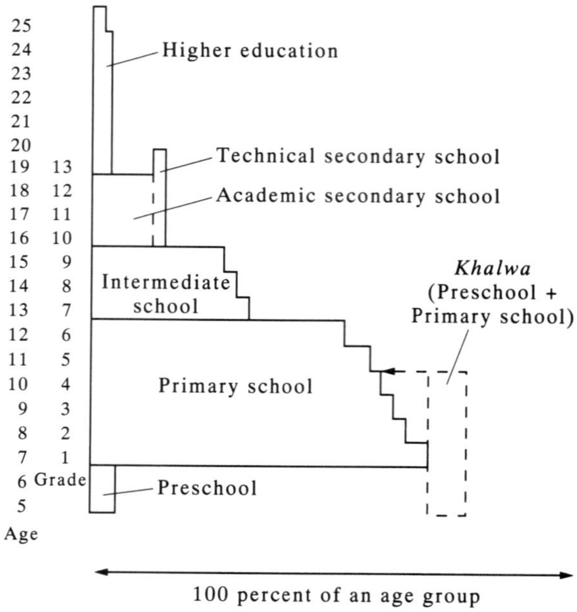

Figure 1
Sudan: Structure of the formal education system 1989 (Northern regions only)

3. *The Formal System of Education*

Figure 1 outlines the structure of the formal edu-

Table 1
The Sudan educational system 1990

Level	Numbers Enrolled	Male	Female	Number of Institutions	Teachers
Primary	2,026,519	1,146,263	880,256	7,939	60,048
Intermediate	413,321	224,944	188,377	2,421	23,654
Academic secondary	247,896	141,880	106,016	485	7,884
Technical secondary	23,003	16,430	6,573	72	1,103
Primary teacher training	5,328	2,452	2,876	16	683
Higher education	60,134	35,970	24,164	18	2,522
(1989) of which University	54,558	32,065	22,493	8	1,933

cational system as it existed in 1990. Key statistics are provided in Table 1.

3.1 Primary, Secondary, and Tertiary Education

Reforms to education at the primary to secondary levels were announced in 1991 as part of a ten-year plan for general education and took effect from the 1992–93 school year. At the tertiary level, reforms were announced in 1989 and took effect in 1991–92.

Under the previous system, which was introduced in 1970, primary education lasted for six years, intermediate for three years and secondary for a further three years (or four years in the case of technical schools), with entry at age 7 years. In southern Sudan, village schools, offering only the first four years of primary schooling, were also common. Entry to intermediate and secondary education was by competitive examination at the end of the preceding cycle. Pupils who achieved the highest grades in the intermediate school certificate were offered places in general (academic) secondary schools, while some of those with lower grades would find places in technical and commercial schools, or in primary teacher training institutes.

In 1990, 47 percent of primary schools were coeducational, but at the intermediate level fewer than 3 percent were. At the secondary level under 6 percent were coeducational, and these were either Catholic mission schools or southern schools. Government secondary schools in the north are all single sex.

An alternative, but less widely available, route through the educational system is offered by religious schools, with children attending primary level education in Islamic *khalwa* schools, then moving on to religious schools at the intermediate and secondary levels. However, there are only 37 schools at the intermediate level and 20 at the secondary level. Students in religious schools sit the same intermediate and secondary school-leaving examinations as those studying in the secular schools. Those with the highest grades can gain places at Islamic universities.

The 1991 reforms set out a radical restructuring and expansion program for schooling. The 6–3–3 system was replaced by eight years of basic education, followed by three years of secondary education, resulting in 11 instead of 12 or 13 years of formal schooling as the maximum available. The school entry age has also been lowered to 6 years. At the secondary level, academic and technical schools will be integrated, offering a mixture of academic and technical subjects alongside a core curriculum. For males who are eligible to proceed to higher education, a period of national service is now compulsory before they may continue their studies.

At the tertiary level, prior to the 1991 reforms, there were eight universities (the oldest being the University of Khartoum) and about ten specialist higher institutes in Sudan. All but two of these universities are situated in the capital, Khartoum. The University of Cairo runs a Khartoum branch, which is funded by the Egyptian Government and administered and staffed by the University of Cairo. There is also an Islamic University of Omdurman. The two regional universities specialize in rural-based studies, one in Gezira province and the other in Juba (the capital of the south). There are also two privately funded universities, Ahfad University for Women and Ahlia University. The Sudan's only polytechnic became the Sudan University of Science and Technology in 1989. In 1989, 91 percent of higher education students were in universities.

The specialist higher education institutions include institutes of music and drama, physical education, hygiene, nursing, radiography, and mechanical engineering (in Atbara). There are also two graduate institutions within the University of Khartoum, the Institute of African and Asian Studies and the Development Studies Research Center.

Competition for places in higher education is fierce. Prior to the reforms, only about 7.5 percent of those sitting the secondary school leaving certificate could expect to find places in higher education. As a result, many young Sudanese were studying abroad and the government was obliged to provide them with hard currency at a subsidized rate. In 1992, an estimated 11,000 were studying abroad, representing some 22 percent of Sudanese undergraduates. In 1984, as many as 21,700 were studying abroad.

The 1991 Higher Education Act was aimed at increasing the annual intake, distributing it more evenly around the country, and increasing the numbers enrolled in nonarts-based courses. It was also hoped that this expansion would encourage those studying abroad to continue their studies at home. The initial aim was to increase the intake to higher education from 11,336 in 1989 to 22,716 in 1991. Of the eight universities created since 1991, six are situated in the regions. Two are intended for the south. However, the lack of security in the region will make it extremely difficult for these to become a functional reality in the foreseeable future. Indeed, the University of Juba has had to move to temporary premises in Khartoum because it became impossible to operate in a war zone.

In addition, eight new private institutions of higher education have been established. These will offer degree and diploma courses in subjects such as civil engineering, aviation, business administration, computer studies, and Islamic religion. There is also a distance education institution (Open University). These private institutions will receive some financial support from the government and will be supervised by a special committee of the National Council for Higher Education.

Schooling is not compulsory in Sudan and is by no means available to all those who wish to attend. At independence, educational provision was very limited, and during the 1960s and early 1970s, the country witnessed an enormous expansion in educational provision, in particular at the secondary and higher levels. During the 1960s school enrollments at all levels grew at a rate of around 10–11 percent annually. Between 1970 and 1981 primary enrollments doubled, intermediate and academic secondary grew sixfold while technical secondary grew ninefold. During the 1980s growth rates at all levels slowed down, but secondary enrollments doubled again between 1981 and 1991. As a result, at the primary level the gross enrollment ratio increased from 30.5 percent of the 7–12 age group in 1970 to 38.8 percent in 1980 to 49.8 percent in 1985 to 58 percent in 1989 (the latter figure for the six northern regions only). At the intermediate level, the enrollment ratio increased from 26 percent of the 13–15 age group in 1981 to 28.2 percent in 1985, but this had dropped to 24 percent by 1989 (still an increase in total enrollments because of the growth in the size of the age group). At the secondary level, the enrollment ratio increased from 12.8 percent of the 16–18 age group in 1981 to 16.6 percent in 1985, but this had dropped to 15.8 percent by 1989. At the tertiary level, despite enormous growth, still only 2.9 percent of the 19–23 age group were able to find places in higher education in 1989.

These figures do not reflect the wide discrepancies in provison of education between regions, between urban and rural areas, and between males and females. Traditionally the greatest opportunity for education is found in the Khartoum area and in the northern and central regions (now states), while the least opportunity has always been in the south. For example, in northern Sudan primary enrollment ratios in 1989 were highest in the northern region, at 75 percent of the relevant age-group, and lowest in the eastern region, at 42.5 percent. At the intermediate level, they were highest in Khartoum at 32 percent, and lowest in Darfur region (in the west) at 12.6 percent. At secondary level the highest enrollment ratio was again in Khartoum, with 32 percent, and lowest in Darfur, at 3.8 percent. In the south the ratios are consistently lower than those in the north. For example, in 1986 (the last available such figures for the south) primary enrollments were highest in Equatoria region, at 40.2 percent, and lowest in Bahr-el-Ghazal region, at 9.5 percent. Given that, in the early 1990s, there is very little educational provision in the south outside the major towns, the current ratios would be even lower. However, some schools have relocated temporarily to Khartoum, where many of the southern refugees are to be found.

Likewise, urban areas have always been favored over rural areas and males over females. Girls have been traditionally underrepresented in education, largely for socioeconomic and cultural reasons, but the gap has been slowly narrowing. In 1989, 42.2 percent of primary school pupils were female (representing 52.6 percent of the relevant female age group, as compared to 62.8 percent of the male age group). At the intermediate level 44.7 percent of pupils were female, and at the secondary level, 42.7 percent. At the tertiary level, the figure is 40 percent. Although females are still underrepresented at all levels of education, the gap is much smaller than in many other African countries, especially in higher education.

The school day lasts six hours, six days per week, officially for 200 days in the year (but the real figure is likely to be much lower due to shortages of teachers, books, electricity, water, and other basic amenities). The average teacher–pupil ratio in 1990 was 34:1 at the primary level, 18:1 at intermediate, 31:1 at academic secondary, and 21:1 at technical secondary. However, actual class size frequently exceeds 60 at all levels and can reach 100. Dropout rates are relatively high: in 1989 only 80 percent of those who had entered Grade 1 reached Grade 6.

In the northern Sudan, the language of instruction throughout primary and secondary education is Arabic. At the tertiary level it was English until 1990. However a continuing decline in the standard of English among both students and lecturers, combined with a desire for greater national and cultural relevance, led the government to decree that Arabic was to become the language of instruction, albeit progressively. This has presented considerable difficulties due to the shortage of appropriate textbooks and materials in Arabic.

In the south, it has been customary for local languages to be used as the medium of instruction for the first three to four years of primary education, with English used at all subsequent levels. The future status of English in southern education is not clear, as Arabic is not widely spoken and its introduction would be culturally unacceptable.

Under the reforms, the 1991 first year intake to primary education of 61.2 percent of the age group is to be increased to 81 percent by 1994 and to 99 percent by the year 2000, making basic education available for all school-age children. This is a very ambitious target. With a projected primary school population of 5.4 million in the year 2000, this would require an absorption of at least 3 million children into basic education. The government itself has estimated that reducing the school entry age from 7 to 6 years alone will require places for an additional 960,000 children, constructing nearly 20,000 classrooms and engaging an additional 26,000 teachers.

A considerable number of schools in Sudan are nongovernmental. The highest proportion are academic secondary schools. Approximately 20 percent of intermediate schools and 50 percent of secondary schools are nongovernmental. However, few of these are elite private schools. These are only located in the major towns and charge high fees. Several of the elite schools are run by Catholic missions.

The majority of nongovernmental schools are schools which have been built through private donation or through community contributions on a self-help basis (*ahlia* schools). They charge low fees. These schools have been established largely in response to the enormous public demand for education which the government has been unable to satisfy. They are usually of poor quality with a high number of untrained teachers. There are also around 30 Egyptian schools staffed by Egyptian teachers and 30 Catholic mission schools (both types having a number of schools at each level).

In 1990 pupils in private schools accounted for less than 1 percent of all primary level enrollments, 11 percent of intermediate, 43 percent of academic secondary and 18 percent of technical secondary school enrollments. At the preschool level, almost all provision comes from outside the government system, either through private nursery schools or religious *khalwa* schools.

In higher education, as already mentioned, the government is encouraging the creation of private institutions, and government institutions are urged to seek ways of raising additional revenue from private sources.

3.2 Preschool Education

Approximately 6 percent of the 5–7 age group were in kindergarten in 1990. In addition an unknown number of preschool age children were among the 162,000 children attending some 3700 Islamic *khalwa* schools, where they learn to recite the Koran. Of children studying in *khalwas* 77 percent are boys. Many of the preprimary age children will transfer to state basic (exprimary) schools at the age of 6 (formerly 7), while a small minority will continue up the educational ladder through the parallel religious route.

Under the reforms, the aim is to provide preschool education for all 4–6-year olds by the year 2000. This is to be done, first by providing places automatically to children of preschool age as new *khalwas* are set up as part of the expansion program, second by opening nursery classes in existing primary schools, and third by encouraging the creation of private or community-run nursery schools.

3.3 Special Education

There is very limited provision of special education in the Sudan. There are seven institutions for the disabled, which cater for around 700 individuals (both children and adults); five of the institutions are based in the capital. Teachers are provided by the Ministry of Education and the Ministry of Social Welfare. In the late 1980s a vocational training center for the disabled was set up in Khartoum with ILO/World Bank support.

3.4 Vocational, Technical, and Business Education

Numerous public statements have been made over the years regarding Sudan's need for more technical education at secondary and higher levels, but a lack of planning and coordination, inadequate resources, and pressure from the public to expand academic education has meant that schooling in Sudan is still overwhelmingly of an academic nature. In particular the fact that half the academic secondary schools are in private hands has meant that much of the expansion has been carried out outside the government's control in a direction contrary to declared policy. Likewise at the tertiary level, over half the students prior to the expansion were at the University of Cairo, Khartoum branch, which offers predominantly courses in the arts, social sciences, and commerce, and which is also outside the control of the Sudan government.

In 1990 only 13 percent of Sudan's 557 secondary schools were technical (72 schools). Industrial and commercial courses dominated, with home economics also being available for girls. Usually places in technical schools were less sought after than those in the academic secondary schools, as technical jobs are much less well paid and considered to be of lower status than those open to academic school graduates.

Under the reforms, academic and technical secondary schools will be integrated to become diversified schools offering three streams of study (academic, technical, and religious). At the same time, the government aims eventually to increase the proportion of students studying technical subjects to 60 percent of the total (from 10% at the present time). Students taking technical subjects will be able to compete on equal terms with those taking academic subjects for entry to higher education. (Under the previous system graduates from technical secondary schools were usually limited to places in technical institutes and at Khartoum Polytechnic.)

In the new diversified schools, all streams will study religion, Arabic language, English language, elementary mathematics and a number of other subjects in their first year. In their second and third years they will specialize. The courses available for specialization include science, religion, industry, commerce, agriculture, animal welfare, and arts and letters. Schools are able to choose courses to suit their environment and to make a selection of the subjects offered within each course. However the shortage of teachers at the secondary level, especially in mathematics and science-related subjects, and the shortage of suitable textbooks and materials will constrain the options available to all but the most generously supported schools.

At the higher education level, there are opportunities at the Sudan University of Science and Technology to undertake vocational, technical, and business studies. Cairo University also has a large Faculty of Commerce and Ahfad University for Women offers a degree course in secretarial studies. Commercial and business studies are popular because of the higher salaries found in private enterprises. There are also a number of private institutes offering advanced secretarial studies.

Under the 1991 reforms many of the existing universities are to have new faculties or colleges added to them, in specialist areas such as environmental studies, business administration, computer studies, information technology, accountancy, and textile technology. Some of these have already opened but the lack of suitable buildings, specialist staff, and course materials and textbooks in Arabic, as well as financial constraints are likely to make it difficult to run a wide range of courses.

Opportunities also exist for technical and vocational training in the nonformal sector (see Sect. 3.5).

3.5 Adult and Nonformal Education

Several ministries, including the Ministries of Education, Labor, Youth, and Social Affairs are responsible for running programs in adult and nonformal education. During the 1980s the World Bank and a number of donors gave considerable support to nonformal programs.

In 1990 there were 59,000 registered students in adult education. The Ministry of Education was running 17 vocational training centers, with just over 2,000 students. These are open to those who have completed intermediate schooling and offer two to three year courses.

The Sudan Ministry of Youth also runs a number of Youth Training Centers which provide training in income-generating activities for uneducated or poorly educated youth from low-income families. Courses usually last for 2 years.

During the 1980s around 24 integrated rural education centers (IRECs) were set up around the Sudan with ILO/World Bank support. These were intended to serve as multipurpose educational establishments, combining formal primary schooling with rural-oriented adult education. However they no longer function as originally planned.

The National Council of Literacy, under the auspices of the Ministry of Education, has been running literacy campaigns since the early 1960s. This has been the major area of activity in nonformal adult education in the Sudan. In 1991 a new council was set up to run a national campaign providing classes in schools, clubs, workplaces, and mosques, with trade unions, political organizations and national service and popular defense personnel being involved in running classes.

The problems experienced by all nonformal programs in the Sudan are inadequate funding, lack of nationwide coherent organization, and lack of equipment, resources, and suitably trained personnel.

4. Administrative and Supervisory Structure and Operation

Under the new federal system of government set up in 1991 each of the nine former regions became states (only nominally so in the case of the three southern regions). Each state has its own minister of education and director-general of education. The administration of basic and secondary education are the responsibility of the states, the latter having been previously a central government responsibility. However, higher education remains the responsibility of the central government, which has also taken over teacher education, since this is now part of higher education (see below). Basic and secondary level teachers will continue to be recruited and administered by the individual states.

Inspectors will continue to be appointed by the central government. Major policy decisions relating to education will also continue to be made by the central government, but the administration of schools will, as before, be carried out at the district and provincial level under the authority of the individual state.

5. Educational Finance

Public education is nominally free at primary and secondary level. However, given inadequate government financing, parents are being increasingly obliged to make contributions towards building and recurrent costs and to provide textbooks and other materials for their children. Because of the huge demand for education which the government cannot meet, many schools have been built and furnished by local communities, but frequently the government has been unable to provide teachers for them.

All community-financed and private schools must follow Ministry of Education regulations concerning teachers' terms of service (including salaries), the curriculum and examinations.

In higher education institutions, student fees are levied for all but those from the poorest families. The level of fees is determined by the level of parental income. Students used to receive free board and accommodation (where appropriate) but this is being phased out.

During the 1960s and 1970s, between 12 and 19 percent of annual government expenditure was allocated to education. In 1974 education accounted for 14.8 percent of total government expenditure (and 5.5% of GNP) but by 1980 this figure had fallen to 9.1 percent (4.8% of GNP). It rose again to 15 percent (4% of GNP) in 1985 but has since declined rapidly to stand at only 1.7 percent in 1991. However, whereas in the past the bulk of the financing of education came from central government, a much greater share is now expected to be provided by the states. Only higher education will continue to be funded centrally (together with teacher education).

In 1990, expenditure per student was: SD 670 (US$51.6) per primary pupil, SD 1206 (US$92.9) per intermediate pupil and SD 1636 (US$126) per academic secondary pupil; 84.3 percent of the education budget went on salaries and wages.

6. Supplying Personnel for the Education System

In 1989 50 percent of primary teachers were female, as were 39 percent of intermediate teachers and 21 percent of secondary teachers. Only 16 percent of higher education teachers were female. At the preschool level, 100 percent of kindergarten teachers were female, but 95 percent of *khalwa* teachers were male.

At all levels there are shortages of trained and experienced teachers. In 1989, 23 percent of primary teachers, 32 percent of intermediate teachers and 53 percent of academic secondary teachers in government schools in the Northern regions were untrained. In community-financed schools, the figures would be even higher.

The rapid expansion of schooling at all levels has put great strain on teacher training facilities. In addition, the rapid decline in status and remuneration of teachers has also meant that large numbers of trained teachers have deserted the profession, or have sought more lucrative teaching posts abroad. The result is that many secondary school graduates have been recruited as primary and intermediate teachers without any initial training. The shortage of trained teachers has always been particularly acute in the south, where there were limited training facilities, general educational levels were considerably lower than in the north, and teachers were often not paid regularly.

Under the old system, primary teachers were trained in primary teacher training institutes (PTTIs). There were 16 such institutes in 1992 (although the three in the south were not functioning). The average annual intake of the PTTIs was 150, with 80 percent completing their training successfully. Students entered after completing intermediate schooling and underwent four years of training. Primary teachers taught all subjects at primary level.

Intermediate teachers were trained in intermediate teacher training institutes (ITTIs), of which there were eight in 1992. Two more are currently under construction. Only one is situated in the South (at Maridi). The intake for intermediate training was taken from secondary school graduates, who underwent two years of training. This two-year training period was reduced to one year during the 1980s to speed up the availability of trained teachers to meet the requirement of the rapidly expanding intermediate sector. This returned to two years at the end of the 1980s. The average intake is 100–150 per annum.

At the secondary level, teachers are university graduates. Usually they have received no special training. Although the three Faculties of Education (at Khartoum, Juba, and Wadi Nil Universities) produce graduates in education, almost all seek employment abroad or outside the education sector. Among secondary school teachers, there are particular shortages of teachers of science, mathematics, and English. In 1990 39 percent of mathematics teachers were neither subject specialists nor trained, as were 17 percent of science teachers and 13 percent of English teachers. This has led the Ministry of Education in the past to seek teachers of these subjects abroad. Science and mathematics teachers were usually recruited from Egypt and English teachers from the United Kingdom. Specialist training institutes exist for the teaching of English Language, Arabic, and Islamic religion.

To meet the growing need for trained teachers, an alternative training route was established in 1972, first for primary and then for intermediate teachers through the Inservice Educational Institute (ISETI), which trained practicing teachers in regional centers. The untrained teachers were released one and a half days per week over a two-year period to attend their nearest center. Since 1991 this function of ISETI has been dropped and the institute now concentrates on inservice courses for head teachers, inspectors, and for practicing teachers, in particular with regard to the new basic education system.

Under the new system, efforts are to be made to increase the number of graduate teachers. In 1991 six new faculties of education were established in the new universities for the training of secondary school graduates. The current output of the existing faculties is about 350 graduates per annum.

To meet the training requirements for the new basic education teachers, seven new colleges of education, to be affiliated to the faculties of education, will open during 1993. These will be created from the existing primary and intermediate training institutes. They will be the joint responsibility of the central Ministry of Education (for finance and administration) and the faculties of education (for academic and technical matters). They will take their recruits from the ranks of existing primary and intermediate teachers and from new secondary school graduates. Basic level teachers holding a teacher's certificate will have the opportunity to obtain graduate status by returning for BEd studies after a period of teaching in schools. The ultimate aim is to have an all-graduate teaching profession.

7. Curriculum Development and Teaching Methodology

A national compulsory curriculum exists at all levels

of schooling. Curriculum development remains a central government responsibility and has traditionally been undertaken at Sudan's oldest teacher training institute at Bakht-er-Ruda, which recently became the National Center for Curriculum Development and Educational Research. Teaching materials are prepared there and tried out in local schools. Dissemination is undertaken by the central Ministry of Education. The syllabuses and course books for all subjects at the basic level are currently being rewritten, with the aim of increasing relevance of content and providing a better integration of course material. Extensive curriculum development is also taking place at the secondary level, where academic and technical education are being integrated.

In the north, under the old system, English was introduced as a compulsory subject in the first year of intermediate schooling and French was introduced as a compulsory subject in the first year of secondary school. The language competence of teachers of these two subjects is usually low.

The south has always followed its own development in syllabuses and course books, to reflect its different cultural background. English is both a taught subject and the medium of instruction from the fourth year of primary schooling.

Classroom methods are on the whole very traditional, with blackboard and chalk being the only teaching aids in many cases (and sometimes even these are absent). Severe shortages of trained teachers in the different subjects on the curriculum, and of textbooks, teacher's manuals and basic classroom equipment continue to undermine the quality of education in most schools.

8. The System of Examinations, Promotions, and Certifications

There is no official policy of automatic promotion from one grade to another in Sudanese schools. Pupils are expected to pass the end-of-term examinations, which are set and marked independently within each school (usually by the class teacher). At the end of each cycle (now only basic and secondary), the school-leaving examinations are the responsibility of the state education authorities. Under the old system, the secondary leaving certificate (the Sudan School Certificate) was the responsibility of the central authority, but this has now passed to the individual states. In 1990, 59.4 percent of those who sat the Sudan School Certificate examinations passed (a progressive decline from 67.1% in 1985).

9. Educational Assessment, Evaluation, and Research

These activities are very limited in scope. The traditional role of the inspector is to assess the teachers, largely on classroom performance. It is not usually seen as including an advisory or supportive role. However, the Inservice Educational Training Institute runs courses for inspectors to help them expand their role within the educational system.

Most educational research is carried out at Bakht-er-Ruda, although some education-related research is also done at the University of Khartoum (e.g., at the Development Studies Research Center and at the Faculty of Education) and also by the National Council for Research.

10. Major Reforms in the 1980s and 1990s

There were no major reforms to the educational system during the 1980s. The current reforms, initiated in 1989–91, which have already been discussed, are the most sweeping reforms for decades.

11. Major Problems for the Year 2000

The ambitious reforms set out above will require strenuous efforts at both the central and the state level if they are not to remain mere rhetoric. They are aimed at both very high rates of expansion at all levels and an improvement in quality and relevance. This will involve major construction work, training and retraining of large numbers of teachers, and competent curriculum development. Sudan in the early 1990s does not possess either a highly committed and motivated teaching force or an efficient bureaucracy, so that implementation of the reforms will be difficult. In particular, there will be a chronic shortage of competent teaching staff in the new specializations offered in higher education. Moreover, the reforms will require substantial increases of funding, which will only be forthcoming if there is considerable economic growth, which in turn is necessary if jobs are to be found for those who graduate from an expanded educational system.

References

Government of Sudan 1991 *Comprehensive National Strategy, Social Development Sector. The Ten-Year Plan for General Education.* General Education Committee, Khartoum

Government of Sudan 1991 *Comprehensive National Strategy Conference Report of the Higher Education Committee.* Higher Education Committee, Khartoum

Further Reading

Beshir M O 1969 *Educational Development in the Sudan 1898–1956.* Clarendon Press, Oxford

Brown G N, Hiskett M (eds.) *Conflict and Harmony in Education in Tropical Africa.* George Allen and Unwin, London

Daly M 1992 *Sudan.* Clio Press, Oxford

Economist Intelligence Unit 1993 *Sudan Country Profile 1992–3.* Economist Intelligence Unit, London

Griffiths V L 1975 *Teacher-Centred Quality in Sudan Primary Education 1930 to 1970*. Longman, London
Ministry of Education 1991 *Summary of Educational Statistics*. Educational Planning Secretariat, Section of Educational Statistics, Khartoum
Ministry of Education 1992 *Educational Statistics Academic Year 1989/90*. Educational Planning Secretariat, Section of Educational Statistics, Khartoum
Sanyal B C, Yacoub S A 1975 *Higher Education and Employment in the Sudan*. UNESCO IIEP, Paris
Sanyal B C, Yaici L, Mallasi I 1987 *From College to Work: the Case of the Sudan*. UNESCO IIEP, Paris
Twose N, Pogrund B 1988 *War Wounds: Development Costs of Conflict in Southern Sudan*. Panos, London
UNESCO 1991 *Development of Education in Africa: A Statistical Review*. Sixth Conference of Ministers of Education and Those Responsible for Economic Planning in African Member States, Dakar, July 1991. UNESCO, Section of Statistics on Education, Division of Statistics, Paris
UNESCO 1991 *Statistical Yearbook*. UNESCO, Paris
UNESCO 1991 *World Education Report*. UNESCO, Paris

F. Leach

Supply of Teachers

A recurring policy concern in many countries is whether there will be enough skilled teachers to educate all children. This entry describes economic factors that affect the supply of teachers, and summarizes evidence on how these factors impact on the career decisions of potential teachers, current teachers, and former teachers. It is these decisions that determine the supply of teachers.

1. *Factors Affecting Teacher Supply*

Key determinants of the supply of teachers in a particular country are salaries and working conditions for teachers relative to those in other occupations, and the cost of preparing to become a teacher relative to the cost of preparing for other occupations.

1.1 Salaries and Working Conditions for Teachers

At the center of the economics perspective on the determinants of teacher supply are salaries in teaching relative to salaries in other occupations. Barro and Suter (1988) have documented that the ratios of teachers' salaries to those in other occupations vary widely across countries, suggesting that the attractiveness of teaching as an occupation of choice also varies across countries. Table 1 presents Barro's estimates for ten industrialized countries of the average elementary school teacher salary and the average secondary school teacher salary expressed as a percentage of per capita gross domestic product.

Two patterns are evident from the Table. First, the attractiveness of teaching salaries relative to a measure of per capita income level varies enormously across countries, ranging from relatively low levels in Sweden and the United States to quite high levels in South Korea. Second, while in some countries, such as the United States and Sweden, elementary and secondary school teachers are paid approximately the same salaries, in other countries, such as the Netherlands and Denmark, secondary school teachers earn considerably more than elementary school teachers. As the next section documents, there is evidence that the supply of teachers is sensitive to relative salary levels.

The limited evidence from developing countries suggests the importance of living and working conditions in determining teacher supply. Ankhara-Dove (1982) and Klitgaard et al. (1985) point out that difficult living and working conditions in rural areas make it difficult to attract teachers to these areas, even when there is a surplus of teachers in cities.

In principle, working conditions should also influence the supply of teachers in industrialized countries. It has proven difficult, however, to collect meaningful data on working conditions because, as Johnson (1990) has explained, teachers care about difficult-to-measure variables such as the availability of materials, and the quality of administrative support. As a result, there is almost no solid evidence on the impact of working conditions on teacher supply in industrialized countries.

1.2 Opportunities in Other Occupations

In evaluating whether salaries and working conditions in teaching are sufficient to attract an adequate supply of skilled teachers, the critical concept is how well they stack up against the best alternatives available to potential teachers. In most countries, teachers are paid according to a uniform scale in which salaries depend on amount of formal education and years of teaching experience, and *not* on the

Table 1
Average salaries of elementary and secondary school teachers relative to per capita gross domestic product, selected countries and years

Country	Year	Ratio (elementary)	Ratio (secondary)
Sweden	1984	1.15	1.37
United States	1984	1.37	1.44
Netherlands	1982	1.54	2.33
United Kingdom	1984	1.62	1.69
Denmark	1982	1.67	2.40
West Germany	1982	1.72	1.96
Japan	1984	1.84	2.03
Canada	1984	1.90	2.14
New Zealand	1986	2.02	2.54
South Korea	1984	3.32	3.32

Source: Barro and Suter 1988 Table 3

field of subject specialization. Since college graduates trained in certain fields, such as chemistry and physics, can earn more in business and industry than graduates trained in the liberal arts, any single salary scale for teachers will appear more competitive for liberal arts graduates than for chemistry and physics graduates. For this reason, some countries, including the United States, have greater difficulty in staffing the schools with an adequate supply of chemistry and physics teachers than they do in finding a sufficient number of history teachers (Murnane et al. 1991). This illustrates the importance of identifying subject fields in analyzing teacher supply. Because of differences in opportunities in other occupations, the teaching profession is much more attractive to college graduates with certain subject specialties than to graduates with other specialties.

In some countries, the teaching profession has been able to attract relatively large numbers of women and minority group members because they have been denied access to occupations with better pay. Social changes resulting in improved access to other professions for women and minorities reduces the ability of the education sector to attract women and minority groups at relatively low salaries. One illustration of this phenomenon is the change in the occupational choices of Black female college graduates. Among those graduating in the late 1960s and entering the full-time work force, seven in ten became teachers. By 1980, the comparable figure was one in four (Murnane et al. 1991). While the attraction of teaching also declined for other groups of college graduates during the 1970s, for no other group is the change so great. This illustrates the general point that the supply of teachers is influenced not only by salaries and working conditions in the teaching profession, but also by the quality of alternative career opportunities available to potential teachers. As a result, changes in opportunities in other fields are likely to have a significant impact on teacher supply.

1.3 Cost of Preparation

Many countries specify that potential teachers must satisfy certain conditions before obtaining a license permitting them to teach. Typically, these conditions include completion of a minimum number of years of formal education, and also frequently include completion of particular training programs, or achieving above a prespecified score on a test of subject matter knowledge or knowledge of pedagogy. The goal of these regulations is to assure that students are taught by competent teachers. However, they also restrict the number of people who choose to teach, by increasing the cost of entering the profession. The costs include not only tuition and fees for the formal education required for entry, but also forgone income during the training period. In addition, test score requirements reduce the supply of teachers by eliminating potential teachers who score below the cutoff score, and by deterring from teacher training potential teachers who fear that they may not pass the licensing test.

1.4 The Quality Dilemma

A major limitation in research on teacher supply is the difficulty in measuring quality. This is important because, in many countries, the primary adjustment mechanism when there is a shortage of "skilled" teachers is not that schools are closed; instead, the schools are staffed with teachers who lack the skills to teach effectively. A consequence of this adjustment mechanism is that research should focus on the supply of skilled teachers, recognizing that the need to staff schools with unskilled teachers may be almost as great a cost as denying schooling to children altogether. The difficulty in implementing this idea is that it has proven very difficult to identify variables that reliably distinguish skilled teachers from unskilled teachers. As Harbison and Hanushek (1992) explain, the number of years of formal education is not a strong predictor of teaching effectiveness, especially in industrialized countries where all teachers have completed at least 14 years of schooling. Teachers' scores on tests of cognitive skills are positively related to teaching effectiveness, as measured by students' test score gains. But even these variables explain only a small part of the variance in teachers effectiveness, as measured by the test score gains of students. Consequently, available research evidence suggests that the criteria many nations use to license teachers do not reliably distinguish competent teachers from incompetent ones.

This inability to study the supply of skilled teachers is a major limitation of existing research. In particular, in interpreting research on teacher supply, one should be aware that almost no studies shed light on the impact of salaries and working conditions on the quality of the teaching force.

2. The Career Pipeline

The supply of teachers is determined by the career decisions of potential, current, and former teachers. This section summarizes the evidence on the roles which salaries, working conditions, and training costs play in influencing these career decisions.

2.1 Whether to Become a Teacher

Dolton (1990) has shown that the occupational decisions of college graduates in the United Kingdom are extremely sensitive to salaries. The more favorably teacher salaries compare to salaries in other occupations, the more likely graduates are to choose teaching.

Manski (1987) used information on college students in the United States in the 1970s to explore the role of salaries and test scores in the decision to become a teacher. He found that teaching salaries have marked effects on the size of the pool of college graduates who enter teaching: the higher the salaries, the larger the pool. He also found that salary levels did not have a marked impact on the ability distribution of the set of college graduates who enter teaching. The inference Manski drew from his analysis is that a strategy for upgrading the quality of new entrants to teaching must include salary increases and entry requirements that screen out weaker applicants. The difficulty in implementing Manski's strategy is identifying a variable that reliably distinguishes weaker candidates from stronger ones.

Murnane et al. (1991) have shown that the representation of Black college graduates in the pool of newly licensed teachers is extremely sensitive to test score requirements. They report that in the first four years after the state of North Carolina reinstituted a test score requirement for obtaining a teaching license, the proportion of Black graduates in the pool of new licensees fell from 20 percent to 10 percent. Smith (1987) has shown that even small changes in the minimum passing scores on written licensing tests have a large impact on the number of minority group applicants who obtain teaching licenses.

2.2 How Long to Stay in Teaching

The length of time teachers remain in teaching has a marked influence on the adequacy of the supply of teachers. For example, if two million teachers are needed to staff a nation's schools, and 20 percent of the existing stock leaves the classroom each year, then 400,000 replacements are needed each year. If the attrition rate is 5 percent, only 100,000 replacements are needed.

As Grissmer and Kirby (1991) have explained, the average attrition rate for a stock of teachers is highly sensitive to the age and experience distribution. The reason is that the attrition rate is relatively high for novice teachers, especially young ones. The attrition rate is low for middle-aged, experienced teachers, and rises only as teachers approach retirement age. As a result, changes in the age and experience distribution of a stock of teachers affects the attrition rate even when there is no change in the attrition rate for teachers of a specific age with a specific amount of teaching experience.

Recent studies by Murnane et al. (1991) and Grissmer and Kirby (1991), based on data from the United States, have shown that the attrition rate of novice teachers is very sensitive to salaries and opportunities in other fields. Novice teachers who are relatively well-paid are less likely to leave teaching after only one or two years than are less well-paid novices. Novice chemistry and physics teachers, who tend to have well-paying alternative career options, are more likely to leave teaching than novice social studies and language arts teachers, who face less well-paying career alternatives. Novice teachers who score well on standardized tests, and who consequently are most likely to do well on the examinations required for entry to training programs for highly paid fields such as the legal profession, are more likely to leave teaching than are novices with lower test scores.

While the effects of salaries in teaching and in other occupations have strong effects on the decisions of novice teachers, they do not significantly affect the career decisions of teachers with more than seven or eight years of experience. As a result, the effect of salaries on the overall attrition rate is very sensitive to the proportion of novice teachers and very young teachers in the teaching stock: the larger the proportion of novices and young teachers, the larger the impact salary changes will have on the average attrition rate.

2.3 Where to Teach

A number of studies have shown that, as a result of geographical differences in salaries and working conditions, teacher surpluses and teacher shortages within a country can exist simultaneously. For example, Klitgaard (1985) reports the coexistence in Pakistan of an aggregate unemployment rate of more than 50 per cent for licensed teachers and a shortage of teachers in rural areas. Ankhara-Dove (1982) describes the conditions in rural areas of developing countries that make it difficult to attract skilled teachers and lead to extremely high teacher turnover rates.

Ferguson (1991) examined the role of salaries in attracting academically talented teachers in 900 local school districts in Texas, each of which sets its own salary scale. He documents that districts paying high salaries attract higher percentages of teachers who score well on standardized tests than do neighboring districts paying low salaries. Moreover, Ferguson shows that teachers' scores on this test predict student test scores. As a result, this study differs from almost all other studies of teacher supply in that it indicates that salaries affect teacher quality, as well as the number of college graduates who want to teach.

2.4 Whether to Return to Teaching

One of the surprising findings of recent studies on teacher supply in the United States is that the majority of newly hired teachers are not new college graduates making an initial career choice. Instead, they are older graduates either returning to teaching after a career interruption, or entering teaching after either raising children or working in another occupation (Kirby et al. 1991). This has led to significant interest in the concept of the "reserve pool," defined as individuals licensed to teach, but not currently teaching.

While the evidence on the reserve pool is restricted to the United States the lessons for teacher supply about the importance of demographic trends are generally applicable and significant. In the United States, the reserve pool is large for two related reasons. First, as a result of the baby boom of the 1950s and 1960s, the age cohorts currently in their late thirties and early forties are very large. Second, many college graduates in these age groups obtained teaching credentials in the late 1960s and early 1970s when jobs in teaching still seemed abundant, but were not able to find or retain teaching jobs in the late 1970s when the earlier baby boom was followed by a marked declined in the birthrate.

As the United States looks ahead to growing demand for teachers in the 1990s, a critical question is whether the reserve pool will continue to be the major source of supply that it was during the 1980s. It is unlikely that this will be the case because the large baby boom cohorts will be followed by smaller cohorts, reducing the size of the reserve pool, and also because the projected slow rate of labor force growth should create strong alternative career opportunities for college graduates, giving members of the reserve pool a variety of occupational choices.

3. Conclusion

The literature on teacher supply provides three basic lessons. The first is that incentives matter. Evidence from a variety of countries shows that the supply of teachers is sensitive to salaries and working conditions in teaching relative to those in other occupations. Second, demographics play a major role. Trends in birthrates and cohort sizes have long-term effects on the supply of teachers, both by influencing the number of potential teachers, and by influencing the likelihood that individuals who do prepare to teach will find teaching positions. Third, the important policy questions do not concern the generic issue of teacher supply, but rather the more detailed issues of: the supply of teachers of particular subjects, the quality of individuals entering and staying in the teaching profession, and the willingness of teachers to work in particular geographical areas.

Important questions concerning teacher supply about which little is known, and which are in critical need of study include: the effects that changes in licensing requirements have on the supply of teachers, factors influencing the timing of teachers' retirement decisions, the impact of working conditions on teacher supply, and the extent to which geographically specific pension plans inhibit teacher mobility.

See also: Teacher Unionization, Economics of; Demand and Supply Elasticities for Educated Labor

References

Ankhara-Dove L 1982 The deployment and training of teachers for remote rural schools in less-developed countries. *Int. Rev. Educ.* 28(1): 3–27

Barro S M, Suter L 1988 *International Comparisons of Teachers' Salaries: An Exploratory Study*. National Center for Education Statistics, Washington, DC

Dolton P 1990 The economics of UK teacher supply: The graduate's decision. *Economic J.* 100(5): 91–104

Ferguson R F 1991 Paying for public education: New evidence on how and why money matters. *Harvard J. Legislation* 28(2): 465–98

Grissmer D W, Kirby S N 1991 *Patterns of Attrition Among Indiana Teachers, 1965–1987*. The Rand Corporation, Santa Monica, California

Harbison R W, Hanushek E A 1992 *Educational Performance of the Poor: Lessons from Rural Northeast Brazil*. Oxford University Press, New York

Johnson S M 1990 *Teachers at Work: Achieving Excellence in Our Schools*. Basic Books, New York

Kirby S N, Grissmer D W, Hudson L 1991 *New and Returning Teachers in Indiana: Sources of Supply*. The Rand Corporation, Santa Monica, California

Klitgaard R E 1985 The economics of teacher education in Pakistan. *Comp. Educ. Rev.* 29(1): 97–110

Manski C F 1987 Academic ability, earnings, and the decision to become a teacher: Evidence from the national longitudinal study of the high school class of 1972. In: Wise D A (ed.) 1987 *Public Sector Payrolls*. University of Chicago Press, Chicago, Illinois

Murnane R J, Singer J D, Willett J B, Kemple J J, Olsen R J 1991 *Who Will Teach: Policies That Matter*. Harvard University Press, Cambridge, Massachusetts

Smith G P 1987 *The Effects of Competency Testing on the Supply of Minority Teachers*. National Education Association and the Council of Chief State School Officers, Washington, DC

Further Reading

Bobbitt S A et al. 1991 Characteristics of stayers, movers, and leavers: Results from the teacher followup survey, 1988–89. National Center for Education Statistics, Washington, DC

Hafner A, Owings J 1991 Careers in teaching: Following members of the high school class of 1972 in and out of teaching. National Center for Education Statistics, Washington, DC

Kershaw J A, McKean R N 1962 *Teacher Shortages and Salary Schedules*. McGraw-Hill, New York

Murnane R J, Olsen R J 1989 Economics of the education industry: Will there be enough teachers? *American Economics Review Papers and Proceedings* 79(2): 242–46

R. J. Murnane

Suriname: System of Education

1. General Background

The Republic of Suriname, with an area of 164,000 square kilometers, is situated on the northeast coast of South America, bordered by Guyana, French Guiana, and Brazil. It is a former Dutch colony which became a constituent part of the Kingdom of the Netherlands in 1954 and attained political independence in 1975. The last census in 1980 recorded a population of 355,000, showing a 6.5 percent decrease from 1972 to 1980. The decrease was mainly due to emigration to the Netherlands immediately before and after Independence. Since 1980, after a military coup, there has again been a high emigration to the Netherlands, both recorded and unrecorded. Since 1986, when civil war activities started in the eastern and southern regions opposed to the military regime, a flight of refugees in significant numbers took place to French Guiana. Inward migration especially from Guyana has offset this emigration in recent years. In 1989 the population was estimated to be 403,000. The annual population growth rate was 2.1 percent between 1964 and 1972. In the 1980s the annual growth rate was estimated at 1.4 percent.

Almost 90 percent of the population resides on the coastal strip which is approximately 40 kilometers wide. Two-thirds of the population is concentrated in two of the ten districts—approximately 1 percent of the total area. The two districts, Paramaribo (the capital city with 205,000 inhabitants) and the district of Wanica (which surrounds the capital city with 70,000 residents) are forming a population conglomerate. Therefore, senior-secondary and higher level schools and most educational services are concentrated in and around the capital city. As the remaining population is scattered in the country, school mapping becomes critical since it takes much effort to bring schools and other education facilities to the sparsely populated and rural areas. Some 39 percent of the population are below the age of 15 and 53 percent below the age of 22.

Demographic conditions include ribbon developments in the rural areas and some tribe-based settlements in the interior along the rivers. The latter are populated by Bush Negroes—former slaves (40,000)—and Native Americans (6,000). Except for Native Americans, the citizens have their origins in several other parts of the world and belong to different ethnic groups, including Blacks and Creoles (Blacks mixed with others), Hindustanis, Indonesians, Chinese, and Europeans. All have lived in Suriname for generations but have still preserved much of their original cultures and languages. One-third of the population consists of Blacks and Creoles, around a third are Hindustanis, and one-fifth Indonesians. Sranang Tongo (a mixture of English, different African languages, Dutch, and Portuguese) serves as a *lingua franca*. Dutch is the official language in government and education. For the vast majority, Dutch is a second and foreign language to be mastered in the early school grades. This bilingual characteristic of the different ethnic groups and the multilingual situation of the nation set extra requirements on the curriculum and instructional methods for the early years. One of the major objectives of preschool and early primary education is a sufficient command of Dutch to proceed in the school system where Dutch is the instructional language.

Between 1975 and 1980 the Gross Domestic Product (GDP) in real terms (constant 1975 guilders) grew at an average rate of 3.4 percent. This growth was due mainly to government investments from Dutch development aid funds and an extra bauxite levy. The 1980s, however, were difficult economic times. Growth of GDP was hampered by discontinuation of the flow of Dutch funds from 1983 onwards and the recession in the bauxite industry, followed by an upturn in the late 1980s. Sectorial contributions to GDP in 1989 were as follows: primary 19 percent, secondary 27 percent, and tertiary 54 percent. The bauxite industry contributes a third of government revenue. Government expenditure increased in size from 26 percent in 1975 to 41 percent in 1985. At the beginning of the 1990s it was running at a level some 35 percent above revenues. Per capita income in real terms (constant in 1980 guilders) in 1989 was G3,540 (US$1=G1.77). Between 1980 and 1989, exports increased slightly from G888 million to 966 million, while imports decreased from G925 million to 791 million.

Some 20.5 percent of the population in 1989 was economically active. Employment distribution by sector is as follows: primary 7 percent, secondary 17 percent, and tertiary 76 percent (including government 50 percent). Labor surveys estimated unemployment to be 15.8 percent in 1986, 19.5 percent in 1987, and 18.1 percent in 1989.

The military coup of February 25, 1980 resulted in a radical change of the government structure. The parliament was abolished and a military authority (three members) together with a policy center (two military members and the civilian prime minister) became the principal authorities for legislation and policy-making. The President, the head of the state, was appointed by these bodies in consultation with functional organizations. The board of ministers consisted of civilian and military members. The judiciary remained independent while the Constitution was replaced by a decree including basic human rights. Following some unsuccessful counter coup attempts, military actions resulted in the killing of 15 prominent citizens including academics, lawyers, journalists, and union leaders in December 1982. The Dutch government, as a reaction to this traumatic event, stopped the flow of treaty funds, causing the national economy to deteriorate in the mid-1980s.

There was a growing dissatisfaction with the political situation and the military regime. Forced by external and internal opposition forces calling for the restoration of democracy, military leaders agreed to hold a general election in November 1987. This brought about a coalition government of the three major political parties. After a conflict with military leaders, the civilian government was again overthrown by a military coup in December 1990, and replaced by an interim government. The main task of the interim government was to organize general elections since the coup leaders were in favor of a new government. The election was held in May 1991. Delegations from interested democratic nations and international institutions were present for observation purposes. The same coalition with the addition of a fourth party won the election. A national assembly, consisting of 52 elected members, became responsible for legislation and elected the President who has executive power. The central government consists of 16 ministries including dependent directorates, each headed by a minister of cabinet rank.

One of the forces opposed to the military regime was the armed Jungle Commando. It started its guerrilla-like revolt against the military regime in 1986 in the eastern and southern parts of the country. The armed combat in these regions caused dramatic demographic movements: approximately 6,000 refugees moved to French Guiana. These refugees, including 2,000 children who were deprived of basic education, were still in French Guiana in 1991 awaiting arrangements for repatriation. Furthermore, around 5,000 Blacks and some Native Americans migrated to Paramaribo and are camped in extremely poor conditions on the outskirts of the city.

2. Politics and the Goals of the Education System

The main political goals of the Suriname government include: restoration of democracy and reinforcement of democratic institutions, recovery of production (agriculture and industry) and economic growth, expansion of employment (job creation), a fair share for all the people in prosperity and welfare, and improved participation of the people in socioeconomic development.

In consequence, efforts will be concentrated to improve the performance of the education system and to provide educational opportunities for all. This involves making the education system more life- and work-oriented than it is now. Vocational and, more particularly, technical education has become a sector of special interest. The goal is to achieve a better match with labor requirements. Due to the social and economic setback, school buildings and other facilities have deteriorated while teaching–learning materials have become scarce. The government is in search of external funds for the recovery of facilities and the supply of educational materials.

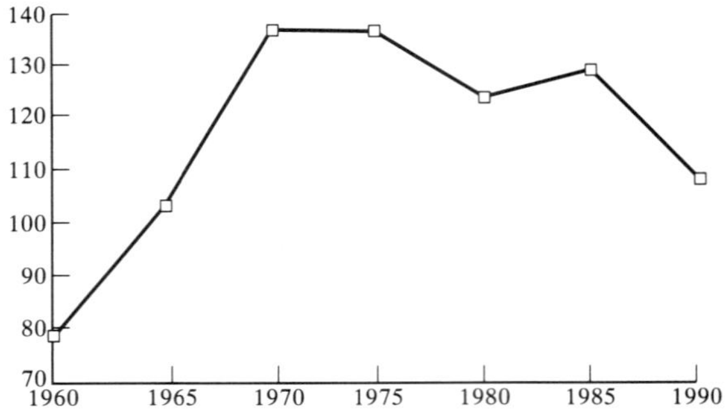

Figure 1
Total school enrollment 1960–89

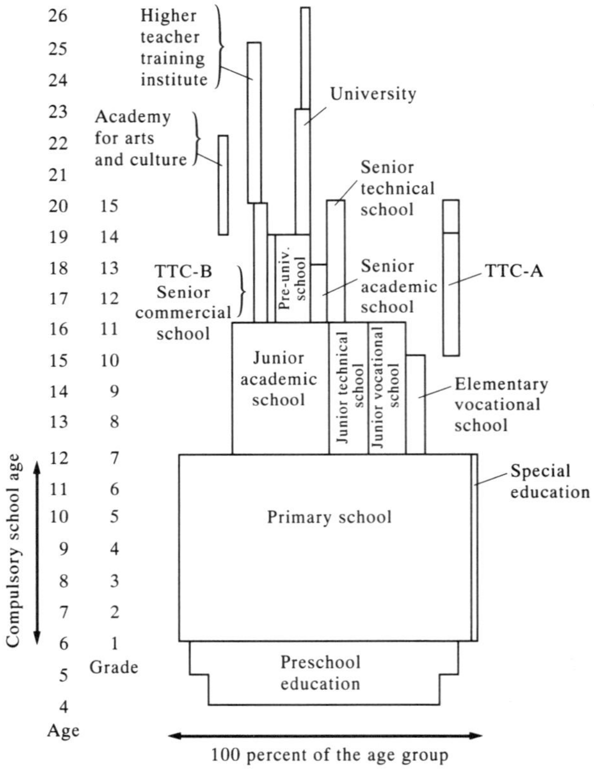

Figure 2
Suriname: Structure of the formal education system 1991

3. The Formal System of Education

3.1 Primary, Secondary, and Tertiary Education

Since 1876, primary education has been compulsory for children aged 6–12 years. Until 1950, there were three types of schools: the primary school offering elementary education (Grades 1 to 6), the extended primary school (Grades 1 to 8), and the more extended primary school (Grades 1 to 10). Children were entitled to enroll in each of these schools at age 6. Most primary schools had a kindergarten for children aged 5. For vocational and professional training, including teacher training, a few evening courses were offered.

The requirements of the economy and the growing demand for education have resulted in a tremendous

Table 1
Student enrollments and teachers by level and type of education 1989

Level and type of education	Student enrollment	Percentage male	Teachers	Pupil–teacher ratio
Preschool	16,711	51	652	25.6
Primary	61,435	51	2,733	22.5
Junior-secondary	24,810	49	1,767	14.0
Senior-secondary	8,355	38	722	11.6
Higher education[a]	4,234	46	495	8.5
Special education	1,954	65	180	10.9
Total	117,489	50	6,549	17.9

Source: Ministry of Education, Department of Planning, 1991
a Higher education teachers include 412 part-time teachers

increase in enrollment and the establishment of various types of school at the secondary level since 1950. Total school enrollment rose from 37,000 in 1950 to just over 135,000 in 1970 and 1975 and dropped thereafter. After an upturn around 1985, it dropped again to less than 118,000 in 1989 (see Fig. 1). This decrease was mainly due to migration to the Netherlands. The education system at the beginning of the 1990s (see Fig. 2) originated from, and is modeled on, that of the Netherlands. Enrollments and teacher statistics are presented in Table 1. Formal education at all levels became free upon Independence in 1975.

Primary education, lasting 6 years, is almost universal in the coastal areas where the participation rate is approximately 90 percent. A school year in preschool and primary education has around 200 days. A school day lasts for 3.5 hours of tuition in preschool and in primary Grades 1 and 2, and 4.5 hours in higher primary grades. Primary schools are distributed among almost all rural areas and settlements in the interior. A large number of these schools are very small and have a remote location. Staffing these remote schools and supplying them with the necessary material and supporting services puts a considerable strain on the administrative authorities. Nationwide, the number of government schools is almost the same as that of private schools at preschool and primary school level. The distribution of pupils and teachers among government and private schools is also equal at these levels.

Secondary education is offered in a wide variety of schools on two levels: junior and senior. Junior-secondary education is available for either 3 or 4 years. Three-year courses are offered as final schooling in a technical or service trade in elementary vocational schools. Approximately 90 percent of the pupils at this level are enrolled in four-year courses in either an academic type or a technical or vocational type of school. Graduates from these courses can enter the employment market or proceed with schooling at the senior level. At the junior level a school year consists of 200 days and a school day lasts 5 hours. The academic schools are distributed across all the districts, but the technical and vocational schools are, with a few exceptions, concentrated in the capital city. Enrollments in government schools and in private schools are equal, and participation of both sexes at this level is the same.

At the senior level there are also both types of courses: academic type (including preuniversity education) and technical and vocational schools. These courses vary in duration from 2 to 4 years. The academic and technical schools at this level have entry examinations for admission. Entry examinations are not required for admission to the teacher-training college and the senior commercial school. The senior technical school offers courses for the technician level in chemistry, mining, mechanics, electricity, and construction. A school year at senior level has 190 days and a school day consists of 5 hours of instruction. Surprisingly, participation of females at this level increased from 47 percent in 1981 to 62 percent in 1989. Except for one teacher-training college, all schools at the senior-secondary level are government schools.

There are three institutes for higher education, all located in Paramaribo: the University of Suriname, the Higher Institute for Teacher Training, and the Academy for Arts and Culture. The University, founded in 1968, has three faculties: medicine, social sciences, and technical sciences. Law and economics are included in the faculty of social sciences. With 2,164 students in 1989, enrollment had increased by almost 200 percent in ten years. The distribution of students among the faculties was as follows in 1989: 20 percent in medicine, 65 percent in social sciences, and 15 percent in technical sciences. Females constitute 44 percent of the student body. The Higher Institute for Teacher Training offers two- to five-year courses for teacher training for secondary education. Except for a few, most are part-time and evening courses. The upper-level secondary school certificate is required for admission. In 1989 approximately 90 percent of enrollment consisted of teachers already inservice but taking courses for upgrading purposes. Females constituted 65 percent of students and total enrollment was 1,850 in 1989. The Academy for Arts and Culture, established in 1985, has three faculties, each offering a wide variety of courses, and each of three years' duration. The faculties are: plastic arts, cultural education, and study of literature and communication. Total enrollment in 1989 was 210, with a female participation rate of 70 percent.

3.2 Preschool Education

Preschool education is now included in almost all primary schools, and is offered to children aged 4 and 5. In the capital city Paramaribo, there are also a few private institutes offering only preschool programs, but on payment of fees. A growing portion of 4- and 5-year olds attend preschool programs before commencing primary education at the prescribed age of 6. In general the preschool programs focus on social learning and learning of the Dutch language through structured play. The enrollment rate in preschool was 82 percent in 1989.

3.3 Special Education

Special education programs are provided for children with physical, intellectual, and emotional disabilities. It is provided in special classes in some primary schools, and in special schools or institutes. In 1989 there were 18 special classes and 18 special schools, providing programs for about 2000 children, which is about 1.7 percent of total enrollment in formal education. Almost two-thirds of the total enrollment are male. There are two levels, an elementary level focusing on the "three R's" and an advanced level preparing for the world of work through training in a handicraft. Approximately 20 percent is enrolled in an advanced-level program. In 1989 the pupil–teacher ratio was 10.9. There were 180 teachers.

There are three special institutes in Paramaribo: an institute for the hearing impaired, one for the vision impaired, and one for the physically handicapped. There are also two institutes for severely intellectually retarded children in Paramaribo. These are all charity-based private institutes, but they are almost completely financed by the government.

A department for special education named the Pedological Institute was founded in 1967 and provides the required support and counseling services in this sector. The services include testing, the placement and guidance of pupils in cooperation with other agents, curriculum development, and the inservice training of teachers.

3.4 Vocational, Technical, and Business Education

Vocational, technical, and business education is available in the formal system at the junior- and senior-secondary levels. Demand for this type of education is less than for the general or academic type of education. Total enrollment in vocational, technical, and business education amounts 40 to 45 percent of secondary school population. Allocation to the three types of courses is, in most cases, determined by the selective entry tests at both junior and senior level.

Evening schools offer a wide variety of technical and business courses with a duration of 1 to 4 years. Two evening senior technical schools provide four- to five-year courses for the training of technicians in the civil, mechanical, and electrical domains. One is administered by the Ministry of Education and the other by the Ministry of Public Works. All of these evening schools, including the evening senior business school, are government schools and free of fees. There are some private institutes that provide management training and accounting courses for a fee in the evening.

The Ministry of Labor has two training centers, each providing elementary craft training of 1 to 2 years' duration to the unemployed over 16 years of age. Each year approximately 150 students take a full-time course in a civil, mechanical, electrical, or related trade. Courses in fishery and agriculture extension services are provided by the Ministry of Agriculture. The Ministry of Home Affairs conducts inservice initial and upgrading courses for civil servants. An average of 300 to 400 civil servants are enrolled each year in these evening courses of 1 to 2 years' duration. A few private and semi-government business concerns have their own centers for inservice training of their employees. In addition, the two bauxite companies and the telephone company maintain their own apprentice training.

3.5 Adult and Nonformal Education

Nonformal education is provided by a wide variety of public and private sources. Government efforts in this field have been intensified since the late 1970s.

A nationwide literacy program was initiated in 1981 by the Ministry of Education targeting all illiterates above 12 years of age (19% of the population). As the results were not satisfactory, a more ambitious program, named Alfa '84, was launched in 1984 with technical assistance from UNESCO. Due to financial and organizational constraints Alfa '84 was not successful. With technical assistance from the Regional Center of Adult Education and Literacy for Latin America and the Caribbean (CREFAL) a new literacy program was developed in 1987 by the Department of Adult Education. This program included the creation of a nationwide nonformal education mechanism with regional offices, to be established and administered in cooperation between government and nongovernment agencies. Classes in the regions were conducted by formal teachers in schools during out-of-school hours with teaching–learning materials developed centrally by the Department of Adult Education. After 3 to 4 years, illiterates can be awarded a certificate equivalent to a primary-school certificate. Due to lack of funds the program is presently being implemented on a very small scale, and only in a few regions. In 1991, a total of approximately 500 adults were enrolled in literacy classes.

Literacy programs in the tribe-based settlements in the interior are also provided by some religious foundations including the Summer Institute of Linguistics. The objective of these programs is, however, conversion to the Christian faith.

4. *Administrative and Supervisory Structure and Operation*

There are both public and private schools at primary and secondary levels. At the primary and junior-secondary levels some 50 percent of enrollments are in private schools, most being denominational and administered by a religious body (school board), that is, Catholic, Protestant, Hindu, or Moslem. At the senior-secondary level only about 10 percent of enrollments are in private schools. All higher education institutes are government-run.

Except for a very small portion of administrative costs, private schools are subsidized completely by the government. All schools, public and private, operate under the jurisdiction of the Ministry of Education and Community Development. This ministry (hereafter to be referred to as the Ministry of Education) is in charge of formulating educational policy and is headed by a minister of cabinet rank. Science, culture, and sports are also under the jurisdiction of this ministry. Except for having to meet prescribed minimum educational standards for registration and funding purposes, private schools are free from close government direction.

While private schools are staffed and administratively controlled by their respective boards, public schools are staffed and controlled by the Ministry of Education. The state inspectorate monitors all schools (both private and public). The Ministry has two administrative sections, the larger education section and the culture section, each headed by a permanent secretary. The education section comprises four divisions: supervision, finance and administrative services, technical services, and developmental services. Each division is supervised by an assistant permanent secretary, reporting to the permanent secretary for education. Administrative control is centralized and all divisions operate from the capital city where the Ministry is located. Only the inspectorate is decentralized to the district level.

However, in addition to their monitoring role, district inspectors arrange for and coordinate all other services for schools in their areas. At primary and junior-secondary level the schools (public and private) are geographically grouped into school clusters (6 to 12 schools), allowing them to share facilities and services. Individual clusters form a network for communication, cooperative thinking, and collaborative work between teachers. School clusters are considered as target systems for the provision of supervision and consultancy services.

5. *Educational Finance*

Education, including private schools run by religious bodies, is almost entirely financed from the recurrent budget of the Ministry of Education. The technical ministries, the Ministry of Labor, and some private institutions and industries also provide training and education. It is difficult, however, to determine the educational expenditure of these agents.

Recurrent expenditure of the Ministry of Education has risen rapidly since Independence in 1975, increasing by a factor of 3.4 between 1977 and 1990. As a proportion of the total government budget there was an increase in this period from 12.4 to 22.4 percent. As a percentage of the GNP it rose from 5.9 to 9.1 percent. The budget of the Ministry was G72.4 million in 1977 and G249.5 million in 1990. In addition to inflation and higher unit costs at all levels, the increase resulted mainly from the linear expansion of the secondary system.

The breakdown of the 1990 budget of the Ministry of Education was: administration 7.5 percent, first level including preschool 47.6 percent, second level 30.8 percent, third level 8.8 percent, adult and nonformal education 0.6 percent, special education 0.2 percent, and scholarships 2.4 percent. The capital budget for education is not a part of the Ministry's budget. Instead, it is included in the budget of the Ministry of Public Works. Capital investments are financed mainly from Dutch, European, American, and international development funds.

6. *Supplying Personnel for the Education System*

At the first and second levels of schooling, the overall teacher–pupil ratio is relatively low (see Table 1). For these levels, the supply from teacher-training colleges is sufficient to keep up with the demand for new teachers and the replacement of the brain drain of qualified teachers in the late 1980s. The teaching force at the preschool and primary levels is completely qualified. Some 95 percent of teachers are qualified at the junior-secondary level, but there is an enduring shortage of qualified teachers at senior-secondary and higher levels. At the senior-secondary level only one-fourth of the teaching force is completely qualified, half is partly qualified, and the remaining fourth is unqualified. The supply of teachers at these levels continues to come partially from external sources. In addition, in higher education a large proportion of teachers work part-time.

There are three types of teacher-training colleges: the A-level teacher-training college, the B-level teacher-training college, and the Higher Institute for Teacher Training.

The A-level teacher-training college offers a four-year course after 2–3 years' junior-secondary education, qualifying graduates for preschool and primary teaching (Grades 1 and 2). An optional one-year course qualifies graduates for supervision of a kindergarten. Although there are no formal restrictions for males, only female students enroll.

The B-level teacher-training college is also a four-year course. The certificate of four-year junior-secondary school (academic course) is required for entry. B-level teachers are qualified to teach in primary schools.

The Higher Institute for Teacher Training offers two- and five-year subject-oriented evening courses, which qualify teachers for the junior- and senior-secondary levels respectively. Courses for teaching in special education are also provided. Entry requirement is the B-level qualification or another senior-secondary certificate.

7. Curriculum Development and Teaching Methodology

With the establishment of the Ministry of Education's development services division (including a Curriculum Department) in 1980, an infrastructure was created for curriculum development and related services. The first step was taken for the development of a new nationwide common school curriculum. Disparity among the regions, and in many cases among schools, had caused a long-felt need for a new nationwide standard core curriculum for primary and secondary level. Core curricula and timetables are prescribed by central authorities of the Ministry of Education.

A major project for primary education curriculum reform launched in 1980 was near completion in 1990. With the exception of geography, curricula and teaching–learning materials were developed, piloted, and implemented for all subjects in all grades. Primary-school subjects are: language, reading, writing, arithmetic, geography, history, science, creative arts, and physical education. Except for girls, who can attend needlework classes in some schools, there are no electives in primary education. Denominational schools are entitled to provide religious education in addition to the core curriculum. In primary schools teachers are assigned to a specific grade and they teach all subjects involved.

The update and reform of curricula for the different types of secondary education started in the mid-1970s and continued in the 1980s. For some school types curriculum reform resulted in the extension of the cycle time with one year (i.e., junior technical and vocational schools). Subject matter qualification is required for teaching in secondary schools. English as a foreign language is compulsory in all secondary schools, while Spanish as a second foreign language is compulsory only in the junior academic school.

The development of curricula and teaching–learning materials is performed by a variety of agents including sections of the curriculum department, special committees and teams, subject matter specialists and experienced teachers, working either on a part-time or full-time basis. Once developed and approved, the curricula and materials are produced and distributed by the Ministry of Education. Dissemination of materials is performed by the Department of Educational Guidance through its network of guidance officers and school clusters. This department is also in charge of improving teaching methods and practices by means of classroom observation, consultation, and inservice training of teachers. State inspectors or supervisors ensure the proper implementation of prescribed curricula and teaching methods. In the early 1990s it is foreseen that all curricula and other quality-related activities will be concentrated into a Learning Resource Center.

8. The System of Examinations, Promotions, and Certifications

Admission to preschool and primary school is based on age, respectively 4 and 6 years. Promotion to subsequent grades in primary and secondary schools is based on internal assessment. Primary schools award a certificate upon successful completion, normally at the age of 12 years.

For most secondary schools, the primary school certificate together with a nationwide entry examination is required for admission. The examination is selective and this, in spite of some efforts to equalize schools, leads to stratification in the secondary-school system. Social demand for the academic types of schools is the highest. Promotion within schools takes place through internal assessment.

For diagnostic purposes a nationwide test is taken at the completion of Grade 5 in primary education. This test makes it possible to compare the achievements of individual pupils, groups of pupils, schools, and geographical areas. Following the comparison of these data, remedial and other corrective measures are taken for improvement.

Transition from junior- to senior-secondary schools varies. In some cases the certificate of the junior-level school is sufficient; in other cases an entry examination is required, and in still other cases both are needed. This entry examination, taken nationwide, is again a selective one, strengthening stratification of the system.

All nationwide entry examinations and the diagnostic test are developed and taken by the central Examination Office of the Ministry of Education. This office is also involved with the core portion of the terminal examination of most of the school types in the secondary system.

9. *Educational Assessment, Evaluation, and Research*

Rapid increase of education expenditure on the one hand, and dissatisfaction with the performance of the system on the other, have resulted in the need for assessment and evaluation of the system. In the 1980s several ad hoc attempts at assessment and evaluation were made. They were all undertaken by designated committees and focused on a particular sector or part of the education system. A mechanism for a thorough assessment of the educational system has not yet been established.

The outcomes of the annual nationwide entry examinations for secondary education at both junior and senior level and final school examinations are used as performance indicators of the system. As standardization of these examinations is not guaranteed, their validity and reliability are questionable. This is, however, the only evaluative information available. A Ministry-commissioned study of education expenditure in 1987 concluded that (a) the repetition rate decreased from an average of 25 percent in the 1960s to an average of 21 percent in the mid-1980s; and (b) entry examination results were very low with a high variability in the last 10 years; at junior-secondary level it varied between 35 and 46 percent and at senior level between 23 and 35 percent.

This information reflected a very low internal efficiency of the system. With regard to the external validity of the school programs, there is a general feeling of dissatisfaction, especially related to the vocational schools.

10. *Major Reforms in the 1980s and 1990s*

As a consequence of a study performed in cooperation with UNESCO (Rensch et al. 1979), a major project for primary education curriculum reform was launched in 1980. This project consisted of three programs: (a) inservice training of teachers and education officers (change agents), (b) development of new syllabuses through nationwide discussions with teachers, and (c) development of curricula and teaching–learning materials for all subject areas. The project was almost completely implemented by 1990.

The military coup of 1980 gave rise to many revolutionary ideas and evoked considerable changes in the early 1980s. Many were poorly prepared and the results failed to materialize. One of these attempts was the very ambitious literacy program (Alfa '84), which had to be changed in scope and pace in 1987.

In continuation of the primary-education curriculum reform project a more inclusive program for the improvement of the quality of primary education started in 1986. It will include the construction and furnishing of a Learning Resource Center which will have departments for curriculum development, educational guidance, educational assessment and research, planning, a central library, and the examination office. Training facilities will also become available in the Center. Total costs are estimated at US$10 million, 80 percent of which should come from a loan from the Inter-American Development Bank (IDB). The execution of the project, originally planned for 4 years, has been severely delayed and is now estimated to take 6 to 8 years.

There is a discrepancy between the output of the educational system and labor force requirements, quantitatively and qualitatively. Although there is a shortage of technically trained people, the labor market is oversupplied with people with a service type of education. The government, recognizing the importance of proper vocational education for the development of the economy, started a major project for improvement in 1990. With Dutch technical assistance, the project included changes in the education structure, its contents, and its administration so as to achieve a better match with the labor market.

11. *Major Problems for the Year 2000*

Rising educational costs in connection with the growing demand for senior-secondary and higher education will be a problem. In this context education cost analysis together with strategies and measures for improvement of the internal efficiency of the educational system will become a challenge in the 2000s. Development of an appropriate vocational and technical education sector will put an extra burden on scarce resources.

The pressure of the brain drain will increase in the future if social and economic conditions remain poor. The training of higher-level teachers and academics in key disciplines will remain an issue of vital importance. However, it will require much more effort to retain them in the country as Suriname moves toward a global market and global economy. The capability to cope with these issues will largely determine the quality of the nation's education and economy.

References

Rensch E S, Murdoch J P, Van Kemenade J A 1979 *Preparing for Change in Education. Draft policy document.* Minov/Paramaribo and UNESCO, Paris

Suriname, Ministry of Education 1987 *National Report on Progress and Achievements in the Framework of the Major Project in the Field of Education in Suriname.* Ministry of Education, Paramaribo

Further Reading

Dwarkasing W W 1976 *Development of an In-service Education System in Suriname: A Proposal.* UNESCO IIEP/IP76/4.1, Paris

Dwarkasing W W, Belfor F, Gulpen E, Tjon H 1987 *Eindverslag werkgroep: evaluatie onderwijsuitgaven.* Ministerie van Onderwijs, Paramaribo

Marshall E K 1975 The beginning of educational planning in Suriname. *J. Int. Soc. Educ. Planners* 3(4): 81–92
Mathijsen A, Pollen P, Dundas J, Roell S, Meijer M 1990 *Beroepsonderwijs en volwasseneducatie in Suriname. Voorstellen tot herstructurering*. Factfinding Mission, Amsterdam
Mys A A 1973 Onderwijs en ontwikkeling in Suriname. Doctoral thesis, University of Amsterdam, Amsterdam
Netherlands Universities Foundation for International Cooperation (NUFFIC) 1989 *Onderwijs in Suriname, verslag van de identificatiemissie technische samenwerking onderwijs*. NUFFIC, The Hague
Suriname 1991 *National Accounts Statistics*. General Bureau for Statistics, Paramaribo

W. W. Dwarkasing

Survey Research Methods

Survey research methods in education describe procedures for the collection of information associated with education. This information is used to extend understanding of educational issues and to assist in the development of educational policy. General works on survey research methods include Fowler (1988), Karweit (1982), and Miller (1991).

Three developments have influenced the methodology of survey research. First, the technology of sampling has reached a high level. Second, many techniques have been developed for collecting valid and reliable information from survey respondents. Third, the availability of computers and survey research software have facilitated the analysis of this information.

This entry is concerned with the purposes of surveys, the distinction between a census and a sample survey (which, while alternatives, are also complementary in nature), and the steps taken in the conduct of survey research. These steps form a cycle of activities, which involve: (a) formulation of the research questions, (b) definition of a conceptual framework, (c) development of survey instruments, (d) collection of data, (e) preparation of the data for analysis, (f) conduct of analyses, and (g) reporting the findings from the survey. In the fourth step attention is given in sample surveys to the problems of sampling and the problems of ensuring the participation and cooperation of the respondents. Subsequently in the analysis stage, the data in a sample should be adjusted to compensate for different response rates and the characteristics of the sample design.

1. Purpose of Surveys

Surveys are conducted to accomplish two main purposes. First, descriptive or enumerative surveys are used to obtain descriptive information. Second, analytic, explanatory or comparative surveys are designed to examine relationships between measures and variables in the survey. The users of surveys for these two purposes are characterized by Groves (1989 p. 3) as "describers" and "modelers."

There are, in general, two types of surveys. First, there is the complete census of all members of the target population. Second, there is a sample survey in which a known proportion of the target population is under survey. The collection of data from a complete population is generally both costly and a burden on the people involved. Thus a sample survey not only reduces costs, but may ensure that the data collected are of high quality. However, the major limitation of a sample survey is the inability to provide detailed information for all members of particular subgroups when needed. A census can achieve better coverage and response rates than sample surveys, although this is not always true. With a well-designed sample, and high-quality procedures of data collection, it may be possible to allocate resources so as to obtain a very high level of response and a greater range of information.

A third source of survey data exists and may be accessed from administrative registers. The "annual census" of the population of most school systems is not so much a census but more a collection and compilation of information that is necessarily held in a standard form in administrative registers. Such information is inexpensive to collect, available when required, and generally accurate and detailed.

Sample surveys and population censuses must be seen to be complementary rather than alternatives, for sometimes within a census it is desirable to include a component that is a sample survey. In this way it is possible to obtain rich and complex data from only a known fraction of a population at the same time as obtaining a complete enumeration of the entire population with respect to a limited amount of information (see Kish 1987).

When a sample is selected for a descriptive survey, the results obtained from the sample must be generalized to the population from which the sample was drawn (the target population). One example is a survey to measure student achievement in literacy and numeracy. Such surveys can be conducted at various levels: school, school district, region, country, or cross-national. Another example is a survey to provide norms for standard tests for students at specified grades or ages, or for specified subgroups of the population defined in terms of sex or locality.

Analytic surveys typically collect information on a range of predictor or explanatory variables that are hypothesized to influence the criterion variables of interest. For example, the main criterion in the Second Science Study of the International Association for the Evaluation of Educational Achievement (IEA) was the science achievement of the students in the participating countries. However, rather than merely reporting the mean levels of science achievement, the data were analyzed to investigate how differences in the science achievement of students were explained by factors such as their home background and their school experiences (Keeves 1992, Postlethwaite and Wiley 1992, Rosier and Banks 1990). Underlying surveys of this type are conceptual models which the researchers wish to examine, in order to improve understanding of the network of factors influencing educational processes. In general, in these survey studies, a sample was drawn, but in some school systems a complete population was tested.

As in the IEA studies, the descriptive and analytic purposes of surveys are not mutually exclusive, since researchers in education commonly wish to fulfill both purposes in a single survey. Although a dual-purpose survey may be less expensive than conducting two separate studies, such a survey may be more complicated, especially in terms of sampling designs and analyses. An efficient sample used to provide descriptive characteristics of a population (population parameters) may not be as efficient for estimating the strength of the relationships in an explanatory model (Kish 1987 p. 46).

Reasons for undertaking surveys vary. Some are undertaken by researchers to investigate a scientific hypothesis, perhaps with funding from individual universities or national research funding agencies. Some are carried out under the auspices of government agencies to evaluate educational and social policy programs. Some, such as the studies carried out by the IEA or the United States National Assessment of Educational Progress (NAEP), aim to monitor levels of achievement, making comparisons across countries or national regions and across time.

The purposes of a survey influence the formulation of the research questions to be examined, the way it is conducted, and the presentation and dissemination of the findings. Many surveys are proposed or sponsored by those responsible for the administration of educational systems. In this case the aims of the study are largely determined by the sponsoring agency, often for the purpose of evaluating some aspect of educational policy. The researchers and the administrators may need to negotiate in order to reach agreement about the aims of the survey so that the intentions of the administrators may be met by the survey.

Most surveys are "cross-sectional," measuring the population at one point in time. However, the major weakness of a cross-sectional survey is that it is not possible with data from such a survey to establish causal relationships. To examine such relationships with data from a cross-sectional survey requires the assumption that variables measured at one point in time may be ordered in a causal sequence. An untestable assumption that a spurious correlation is not present must be made.

This problem of making causal statements from

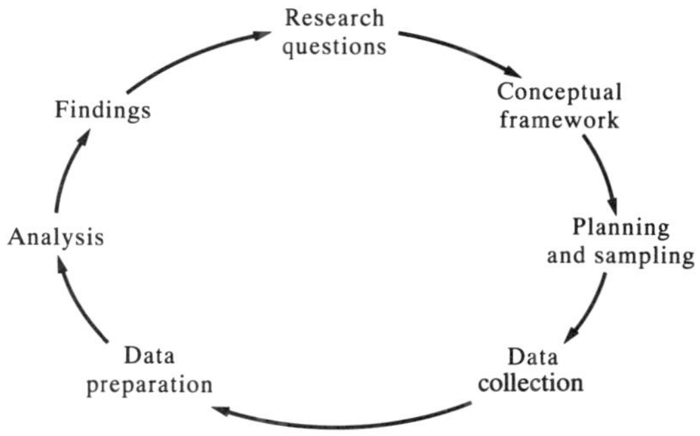

Figure 1
Survey research cycle

cross-sectional studies may be remedied by taking repeated measures from the same respondents in a "longitudinal" study (Menard 1991). For example, a longitudinal study is required to measure the effectiveness of individual teachers in enhancing the achievement of their students. The students' achievement is measured at several points in a period of time (such as several weeks or months). Any changes in achievement may then be linked directly to the contribution of their teacher over that time period.

A key task of analytic studies is to examine causal paths, where the explanatory factors that influence outcomes are identified. A significant path can provide an empirical justification for interventions to change behavior associated with that variable. For example, if it can be shown that a more structured curriculum leads to higher achievement in elementary school science classrooms, this can provide the basis for policy decisions about the development of science curricula.

A variation on the simple cross-sectional survey involves "replication," where the same basic survey is carried out in several regions or countries, as in the IEA studies. This permits stronger generalizations of relationships to be made across the range of different educational environments represented by the regions or countries. As another form of replication, the study may be repeated at a later stage, to strengthen the generalizability of the results across time. This also enables trends to be monitored.

2. *Survey Research Cycle*

One helpful way to understand the range of components of a typical survey is in terms of a "survey research cycle." A detailed description of the series of steps involved in surveys is given in Runkel and McGrath (1972). Thinking about survey research in terms of a cycle highlights the need to consider a survey project as an entity which is repeated after an interval of time. Each stage has implications for later stages, and in practice there is feedback from the later stages to modify earlier stages. Both in its planning and execution a survey may be conducted more effectively by reference to the logical demands of the cycle, as is summarized in Fig. 1.

3. Research Questions

The starting point for a survey is a clear statement of the research questions it is designed to answer. The finishing point is a set of results which addresses these research questions. In defining the questions it is customary to identify the relevant demographic, social, and administrative contents. The questions should preferably be stated in "normal" language rather than in "statistical" language. As the study proceeds through its cycle it becomes necessary to adopt the procedures and terminology of statistics, but ultimately the survey should provide responses to the original research questions in normal language. Especially for sponsored surveys, it is often necessary to convert the general aims of the survey into specific research questions that are amenable to investigation by survey research methods.

4. Conceptual Framework

At the second stage of the cycle, the ideas or components included in the research questions should be specified more precisely in conceptual terms. Where an explanatory survey is being undertaken, the hypothesized relationships between concepts should be expressed in terms of a "conceptual framework," from which models to be examined can be derived. The conceptual framework should be based on a review of previous research studies.

Educational researchers operate in an incremental way in which each survey adds its contribution to what was previously known. Where the basic conceptual framework is complex it may be desirable to proceed by forming a series of reduced frameworks. The incremental approach could operate here as well, by enabling a complex model to be examined in stages corresponding to the simpler frameworks or models.

5. Survey Instruments

The term "instruments" refers to the range of questionnaires, interviews, tests, and attitude scales used for the collection of data in a survey. The instruments should be linked to the concepts included in the conceptual framework. They should be designed for the collection of data that are suitable for conversion into variables for subsequent analysis. The numbers associated with a variable represent a quantification of the underlying concept. The subsequent statistical analyses do not involve the concepts themselves, but the quantified abstractions associated with the concepts.

The researcher has the choice of using existing instruments or of developing new instruments to measure and to collect data (De Vellis 1991). The advantage of using existing instruments is that the work of development and validation has generally been undertaken and published. On the other hand, these instruments may not adequately operationalize the concepts needed for the particular study. Although more work is involved in creating new survey instruments than in using existing instruments, the researcher may have greater confidence in the ability of the new instruments to measure the concepts.

5.1 Types of Survey Instruments

Instruments for use in analytic surveys may be classified into four broad categories, dealing with the measurement of (a) background characteristics, (b) subject matter achievement, (c) attitudes, and (d) behavior. The term "background characteristics" refers to the range of personal, social, economic, and demographic measures that are typically used as explanatory variables in research on educational outcomes; for example, the sex of a student, the educational level of a parent, the age of a teacher, the enrollment of a school, or the population of a town.

In educational settings, subject matter achievement is typically measured by tests requiring written answers, although other measures of performance are possible; for example, inquiry skills in science may be measured by means of practical laboratory exercises requiring manipulation of equipment. Attitudes and opinions are often measured by setting out a range of statements on a topic, and asking the respondents to indicate the extent to which they agree or disagree with the statements. Attitudes and knowledge may both manifest themselves in behavior. The measurement of behavior usually requires direct observation, with the respondent's acts being rated according to a defined protocol. In this area, for example, instruments have been developed for measuring the behavior of teachers and students during their lessons as in the IEA Classroom Environment Study (Anderson et al. 1989).

5.2 Development of Survey Instruments

The development of a new survey instrument starts with a statement about the scope and purpose of the instrument in terms of its operationalization of a key concept, such as science achievement or attitude to science. After the initial trial version has been prepared, there will be a cycle of pretesting using respondents similar to those who will be included in the final survey, revising the structure or wording of the instrument, and repeating the pretesting and revision until the instrument is appropriate for its designed purpose, with satisfactory levels of reliability and validity.

Pretesting also provides the opportunity to check that the respondents understand the meaning of the questions or statements (Converse and Presser 1986), to gauge whether test items are at an appropriate level of difficulty, to develop suitable code values for responses, and, generally, to ensure adequate reliability and validity of the instruments. Even where existing instruments are to be used in a survey they should be pretested to ensure that they are suitable. Where possible, the pretesting should be extended as a pilot study to follow the complete cycle, so that procedures for data collection, data preparation, and analysis can be refined prior to the commitment of resources to the main data collection program.

6. *Data Collection*

The data collection stage of the survey research cycle involves identifying the survey respondents and collecting the desired information from them. Survey information is collected from people in their natural surroundings; for example, from students in their normal classes. In this way surveys differ from experiments in which the participants are assigned to specified treatment and control groups for the purposes of the research. It is possible to link studies involving other research methods to a survey. For example, information from a survey may be used to identify members of the survey sample for use in a case study requiring detailed qualitative observation.

The data collection stage of a survey is usually the most time-consuming and expensive. If it is not done well the time and resources expended on the survey research study have been largely wasted.

6.1 Populations under Survey

Kish (1987) identified four populations involved in a survey: (a) survey population, (b) frame population, (c) target population, and (d) inferential population. The "inferential population" is that population about which inferences are drawn from the data collected and to which generalizations that are made will apply; for example, all 14-year old students in a country or school system. There may, however, be some students in the inferential population who are inaccessible in a survey, because they are unable to read and write, being in certain special schools, and are unable to respond to an achievement test or questionnaire. Such students must be deliberately excluded from a survey, and the "target population" is formed after their exclusion. The target population may, however, not be fully accessible, because of errors in listings of schools and students. The population which in practice can be investigated, because of being in an incomplete frame and missing units is called the "frame population."

Finally there is the "survey population," which is less than the frame population because of lack of responses and incomplete or missing data. It is the relationship between the survey population and the inferential population and the extent of the discrepancies between them that determines the strength of the inferences that may be drawn from the survey data. The specification of these four distinct populations serves to clarify the sources of error in the drawing of inferences and the steps that must be taken in order to collect sound data.

In the specification of the population to be surveyed, Kish (1987) identified four different characteristics that must be considered. These are: (a) content, for example, student achievement in science; (b) units of investigation, for example, students, teachers, schools; (c) extent of domains in subclasses that are compared, for example, schools, school districts, boys and girls; and (d) period, for example, 10-year old students and 14-year old students, or 1970–71 compared with 1983–84, as in the Second IEA Science Study (Keeves 1992). Only after these characteristics of the populations have been specified is it possible to proceed with the design of a study.

6.2 Sample Surveys

Irrespective of whether a census or a sample survey is carried out, the four populations need to be considered and the four characteristics of the populations to be surveyed need to be specified. The costs, in terms of money, and the labor, in terms of human resources, are typically so high for a census that a sample survey must of necessity be conducted. Sample surveys differ from investigations in so far as probability samples are drawn with a known probability of selection of the units into the sample. Investigations on the other hand are carried out—possibly with care and often with considerable control—so that groups can be meaningfully compared, but without the random allocation that is required by experiments or the random selection with a known probability as required by sample surveys.

The advantages of undertaking a sample survey over an investigation are that the population parameters that are estimated have a known error of sampling and as a consequence inferences can be drawn as to the probability that a parameter is significantly greater than zero, or that the estimates of the parameter for two subgroups are different from each other. It is the known probability of selection of the elements in the sample from the populations under survey, together with the lack of bias, that is the result of discrepancies between the populations, that permits inferences to be made from the sample data to the inferential population. In statistical writing the term "probability sampling" is generally considered to be synonymous with the term "random sampling," although in common usage random sampling tends to be used loosely to imply the taking of *any* part (Kish 1965).

Since the drawing of samples is so widely employed in educational research there are special entries in this *Encyclopedia* that consider both survey sampling and sampling errors (see *Sampling in Survey Research; Sampling Errors in Survey Research*). As a consequence the material contained in these entries is not replicated here, and the reader is referred to these entries. There are, however, several general principles of importance that need to be emphasized (Skinner et al. 1989).

(a) In educational research it is rarely possible to draw a simple random sample of students, and a two-stage sample (of schools at the first stage of sampling and students within schools at the second stage) is commonly drawn. This cluster design of schools and students within schools must be taken into consideration in the estimation of sampling errors.

(b) In any analysis of data the cluster design of sample data and indeed of census data, which the sample data seek to mirror, must be modeled in the data analysis. Thus multilevel strategies of analyses must be employed (see *Multilevel Analysis; Hierarchical Linear Models*).

(c) More efficient estimates of parameters, such as population mean values, can be achieved by stratification of the sample design, if the stratifying variables are strongly related to the parameter being estimated. However, only a limited number (<10) of stratification categories is effective for each stratifying variable employed in sample surveys.

(d) Where sample survey data are subjected to multivariate analysis, it is necessary to control for the effects of stratification by the inclusion of the stratifying variable in the analysis.

(e) Since there are always administrative and cost constraints on the size of a sample to be drawn in a sample survey study, the design of the sample is necessarily influenced by the need to minimize the errors of sampling within the constraints of cost and sample size on which costs depend. Sample design takes into consideration both the use of cluster sampling and stratification.

(f) Since some losses commonly occur in sample surveys there is a need to compensate for such losses, by either the weighting of data or by replacement of missing data by inferred values (see *Missing Data and Nonresponse in Survey Research*).

6.3 Conduct and Cooperation in a Survey

In addition to the development of the sample design, there are many practical aspects involved in the conduct of the data collection stage of a survey. At an early stage, the appropriate administrative authorities should be approached for their support for the survey, which may also require their permission to collect data. It may also be necessary to approach regional or local administrative units for their support. The authorities should also be asked for relevant census data, since these data are generally necessary for the preparation of the sampling frame, for the choice of a sample design, and for subsequent testing of the adequacy of the achieved sample.

The funding for the study should entail adequate resources for obtaining the cooperation of the authorities who provide the support and of the respondents who provide the data. Both the authorities and the respondents should be persuaded that the survey is relevant and important. Their cooperation is crucial since the value and credibility of surveys depend on high response rates: that is, the percentage of units from whom data are actually obtained. Surveys also depend on the quality of the data, in the sense that the respondents must cooperate in responding to the instruments.

One of the problems with longitudinal survey studies is the need to maintain contact with the members of the original group over the duration of the study. This problem increases as the time gap between data collection stages increases. It is necessary to check that the characteristics of the reduced groups at the later stages are similar to the characteristics of the original group. In planning longitudinal survey studies, it is advisable to collect a variety of contact information from the members of the original group surveyed. For example, it is desirable to collect the names and addresses of the members of the original group to assist in locating them at a later stage.

For surveys where data are collected from students in schools, the data collection procedures should be designed to be interesting for the students and to minimize disruption to the normal school program. Considerable effort and resources should be expended to provide useful feedback to the students and schools about the results of the survey; for example, details about the performance of the students on achievement tests included in the survey.

6.4 Ethical Considerations

An important aspect of the contact with respondents is the assurance that the information provided would be used only for the stated purposes of the survey, with any published reports presenting findings in a manner that would prevent the identification of individual respondents. This is not the same as advocating that all information should be collected anonymously. Where the names of respondents are known, it is much easier to apply follow-up procedures to urge nonrespondents to reply.

Increasingly, countries and institutions are controlling the kinds of research data that may be collected, and the procedures to be followed for maintaining the privacy of the records and for enabling research workers to receive access to the data. In addition, many institutions and funding agencies require that the proposal for a study should be reviewed by an "Ethics Committee" or similar body to ensure that the confidentiality and privacy provisions are adequate. In any case, it is advisable to keep all identifying data, such as the names and addresses of respondents, separate from files containing the other data collected from the respondents.

The students included in a survey, and their parents, should be fully informed about the nature of the study. They should be told who is sponsoring the study, who is conducting it, the amount of time to be taken in participating, and the likely benefits arising from the study. This is often achieved by means of a letter sent to the parents of the students. Many educational systems require that the parents should have the option of withholding permission for the participation of their children. Indeed, especially for studies seeking information of a more sensitive nature, the active written consent of the students and their parents may be required.

6.5 Quality of Data Collection

The final task in the process of collecting data is to assess the adequacy of the procedures employed. In practice there are usually differences between the plans for the survey as originally developed and the actual administration. Reports of a survey should contain a comparison of the designed and achieved numbers of respondents, from which response rates can be calculated. If the response rates differ across strata, the balance may be restored by weighting procedures, although weighting procedures cannot fully compensate for data lost due to different and reduced response rate. Reports of the study should always include details of the different populations, the designed sample, the achieved sample, the response rates, and the weights employed in the analysis of the data.

The adequacy of an achieved sample may also be examined by comparing known characteristics of the population with corresponding characteristics of the sample. Such marker variables may include the percentage of male students, the mean enrollment of schools, or the level of teacher qualifications.

No item of information should be collected in a survey without a clear idea of where it fits into the logic of the research questions or conceptual framework guiding the study. Each item of information collected should have a specified place in the analyses that are linked to the original research questions posed by the survey. It is easy to distort a survey by attempting to collect too much information, which may alienate the respondents and hence reduce the validity and reliability of their responses.

7. Data Preparation and Management

The data preparation stage of the cycle starts with the raw information as collected from the respondents, and concludes with the data carefully organized as computer files ready for analysis. This stage is concerned with checking and coding data, and building the data files. The intended answers of the respondents must be transferred as accurately as possible into a form in which they may be analyzed.

7.1 Coding

Most of the data collected in educational survey research are derived from the respondent's written responses to the survey instruments. Often the items in the questionnaires are precoded, so that the respondent selects one of the options presented, as in multiple-choice items for achievement tests. Otherwise, respondents may write their own responses which are subsequently coded by the researchers. For most survey studies, numerical code values are used so that quantitative analyses can be conducted. A codebook is prepared which specifies the location of each item of the data on the computer file, together with a description of characteristics of each variable: the name of the variable, the valid code values, and the code values for missing data.

In association with the coding of responses, it is necessary to include an editing stage, when anomalies and omissions may be detected. It may be possible to return to the respondents for the resolution of anomalies, or for the completion of omitted items. More commonly, the researcher develops a set of rules to resolve these problems at the coding stage.

7.2 Data Entry

After coding, the responses are normally transferred to a computer file. This is commonly accomplished by typing the coded responses from the survey instrument into a computer file using a program designed for data entry.

Procedures are available to circumvent this labor intensive data entry. For example, the respondent may mark sheets or cards that can be read by optical scanning methods with the coded values being transferred directly to the computer files, although this method will involve some additional human editing where the equipment has not been able to read the marks properly. Alternatively, the respondent's answers may be entered directly into the computer, as in computer-aided telephone interviews.

7.3 Checking and Verification

Once the initial data file has been established, further checking and verification procedures should always be carried out. At one extreme this may involve an independent punching of all responses with a comparison of the two versions in order to resolve any discrepancies. More commonly, a sample of the completed instruments is selected for independent verification. An important check is to ensure that all data have been entered into the correct column locations on the computer file. The actual responses from some of the questionnaires should be compared to the data in the variables on the computer file.

For each variable there will be a range of valid values. An initial stage of checking involves detecting and correcting any values outside the valid range. It is then necessary to return to the original questionnaire completed by the respondent to find the valid value. It is also desirable to include checks of logical consistency; for example, to ensure that educational qualifications are consistent with stated occupations.

Further consideration, in terms of the technology now available, of the tasks of code book preparation, data entry, data clearing, and database design and management are considered in the entry on data management in educational survey research (see *Database Management Systems in Education*). There are relatively few published accounts of the practical aspects of data preparation and management, and notable treatments of this field are provided in Rossi et al. (1983) and Sonquist and Dunkelberg (1977).

8. *Analysis*

Analysis can commence once the data file has been adequately prepared. In terms of the logic of the survey research cycle, the earlier stages of the cycle should anticipate the analysis stage. The construction of instruments and the coding of responses should anticipate the manipulation of numerical data. The sample design should also ensure that there are sufficient cases or respondents for the planned analyses.

8.1 *Variable Construction*

An initial stage in analysis is to construct new variables from the basic data. For achievement test data this may involve the development of test scores according to defined rules. For attitude scales this may result in scale scores, often based on factor analysis. For questionnaires, a typical constructed variable would be an index of socioeconomic status of the student's home.

8.2 *Univariate Analysis*

The plans for a survey will include a description of the analyses to be undertaken. The analyses may be classified in terms of the number of variables involved. "Univariate" analysis deals with the variables individually. "Bivariate" analysis involves pairs of variables. "Multivariate" analysis is concerned with the simultaneous effects of more than two variables.

For all surveys, the initial analyses involve examining the basic univariates for all variables. For data recorded at the categorical level, the univariates would display the frequency of the number of cases for each code value for each variable. For continuous data, such as test scores, the corresponding basic univariates would be the mean, number of cases, standard deviation, skewness, and kurtosis for each variable. The univariates enable the researcher to gain an initial view of the data for each variable. This should be done before submitting data to further analysis. Weaknesses such as highly skewed variables, and variables with large amounts of missing data, may distort the results of more complex analyses.

Where univariates derived from a sample are published, they should incorporate estimates of the sampling errors (standard errors of sampling). Where the data from a sample are used to estimate parameters in a population, the sampling errors indicate the degree of uncertainty associated with the estimates of the corresponding parameters in the population. Data derived from complex samples or stratified sample designs that depart from simple random sampling procedures should be adjusted to compensate for the "design effect" which measures the extent to which the complex sample is less efficient than a simple random sample, with the same number of cases (see *Sampling Errors in Survey Research*).

8.3 *Bivariate Analysis*

The main bivariate statistics are "cross-tabulations" and "correlation coefficients." With modern computers it is tempting to generate large numbers of cross-tabulations, often involving several nested levels. Classification of data by using cross-tabulations may assist the researcher to gain a good overview of the data, but the method is very inefficient for examining relationships. Most situations in education are complex, involving many interrelated variables.

Matrices of correlation coefficients are useful for summarizing bivariate relationships. In particular they provide an initial opportunity to assess which explanatory variables are strongly associated with each other and with dependent variables. From the correlation matrix it is easy to identify variables that are only weakly linked to a criterion. There is little value in including these variables in explanatory analyses. The correlation matrices may also provide the starting point for multivariate analyses.

8.4 *Multivariate Analysis*

The multivariate stage of the analysis is designed to unravel the complex interrelationships between the variables. The analysis is guided by the conceptual framework which has identified the likely patterns of relationship.

Many multivariate analysis techniques are available, of which Stevens (1986) provide an overview.

One of the most common techniques used in the analysis of survey data is multiple regression analysis, which is used to estimate the relative strengths of several explanatory variables acting simultaneously on a criterion. Underlying the regression analysis should be a statistical model of the relationships between the explanatory variables and the criterion, derived from the conceptual framework on which the study is based.

An extension of multiple regression is the development and estimation of structural equation models (Bollen 1989) in which the explanatory variables may be arranged in a causal sequence. For example, the significant paths associated with achievement indicate where policy changes may most fruitfully be introduced to enhance the levels of achievement.

The use of multistage sampling reflects the hierarchical nature of most educational settings, with students in classes in schools in school districts, and so on. Multilevel analysis is a form of multivariate analysis that takes account of the differences between students within classes and between classes (Raudenbush and Willms 1991). For example, it shows the extent to which differences in achievement depend on the students' membership of a given class or school, and isolates the relative contribution of the individual and the group to the criterion under consideration. This procedure may also be used to estimate the sampling errors and design effects associated with multistage sampling (see *Multilevel Analysis; Hierarchical Linear Models*).

In some larger surveys, the researcher may carry out analyses separately for each stratum or group of strata, particularly where these strata or groups represent independent administrative units. In effect, each separate analysis is itself a replication. Stronger generalizations may be made where patterns of relationships occur across the replicated analyses.

The ultimate purpose of the analysis stage is to produce sets of statistics that summarize the data: frequencies, proportions, percentages, means, standard deviations, correlation coefficients, regression coefficients, and so on. These should relate to the original conceptual framework or models. The statistics serve to confirm or negate the models and the associated propositions that were to be examined. Reports of the survey should contain sufficient information to enable interested readers to make their independent judgments about the reliability of the data that were collected, the appropriateness of the analysis that was undertaken, and the statistical conclusions that were drawn.

9. Findings

The last stage of the survey research cycle involves the presentation of the findings, which should link to the original questions. This final stage should also include a discussion of the strength of the findings, and of the extent to which they may be generalized. Distinctions should be made between findings that are strong and those that are tentative, and between findings of high generalizability and those that are limited in scope.

The ways in which the findings are disseminated may depend on the sponsorship of the study. Findings couched in statistical language may be appropriate for a scientific audience. For surveys dealing with public policy, every effort should be made to present the findings in language suitable for policymakers who may not have a strong statistical background. It is difficult to present complex findings in a form that can be reported in the print and electronic media without being distorted, but strenuous efforts should be made to do so.

10. Documentation and Secondary Analysis

There is increasing recognition that carefully documented data files, especially from larger surveys, should be lodged in data archive systems. Some funding agencies require the archiving of data as a condition of the grant. National centers for data archives exist in most countries, and there are also international networks for social science data, such as the Inter-University Consortium for Political and Social Research based at the University of Michigan. The lodging of data files with a data archives system facilitates the use of the data by other researchers for secondary analysis. The usefulness of the data for any particular secondary analysis depends on the quality of the associated documentation, so that the secondary analyst can gain a full understanding of the original data collection process, and the relevance of the variables in the survey to the aims of the secondary analysis.

11. Conclusion

The underlying theme of this entry is that the conduct of survey research should follow a logical process, interpreted here as a cycle. The success of a study is not guaranteed by following the cycle, but it may enhance confidence in the management of the survey. No single study can ever identify all the important research questions or find all the answers, so that one cycle may lead to another as findings from one survey lead to new questions for future surveys.

See also: Cross-sectional Research Methods; Data Banks and Data Archives; Longitudinal Research Methods; Secondary Data Analysis; Educational Achievement: Comparative Studies; Sampling in Survey Research

References

Anderson L W, Ryan D W, Shapiro B J (eds.) 1989 *The IEA Classroom Environment Study*. Pergamon Press, Oxford

Bollen K A 1989 *Structural Equations with Latent Variables*. Wiley, New York
Converse J M, Presser S 1986 *Survey Questions: Handcrafting the Standardized Questionnaire*. Sage, Beverly Hills, California
De Vellis R F 1991 *Scale Development: Theories and Applications*. Sage, Beverly Hills, California
Fowler F J Jr 1988 *Survey Research Methods*, 2nd edn. Sage, Beverly Hills, California
Groves R M 1989 *Survey Errors and Survey Costs*. Wiley, New York
Karweit N L 1982 Survey research methods. In: Mitzel H E 1982 *Encyclopedia of Educational Research*, 5th edn. Free Press, New York
Keeves J P (ed.) 1992 *The IEA Study of Science III: Changes in Science Education and Achievement: 1970 to 1984*. Pergamon Press, Oxford
Kish L 1965 *Survey Sampling*. Wiley, New York
Kish L 1987 *Statistical Design for Research*. Wiley, New York
Menard 1991 *Longitudinal Research*. Sage, Newbury Park, California
Miller D C 1991 *Handbook of Research Design and Social Measurement*. Sage, Beverly Hills, California
Postlethwaite T N, Wiley D E (eds.) 1992 *The IEA Study of Science II: Science Achievement in Twenty-three Countries*. Pergamon Press, Oxford
Raudenbush S W, Willms J D (eds.) 1991 *Schools, Classrooms, and Pupils: International Studies of Schooling from a Multilevel Perspective*. Academic Press, San Diego, California
Rosier M J, Banks D K 1990 *The Scientific Literacy of Australian Students*. Australian Council for Educational Research, Hawthorn
Rossi P H, Wright J D, Anderson A B 1983 *Handbook of Survey Research*. Academic Press, New York
Runkel P J, McGrath J E 1972 *Research on Human Behavior: A Systematic Guide to Method*. Holt, Rinehart and Winston, New York
Skinner C J, Holt D, Smith T M F (eds.) 1989 *Analysis of Complex Surveys*. Wiley, New York
Sonquist J A, Dunkelberg W C 1977 *Survey and Opinion Research: Procedures for Processing and Analysis*. Prentice Hall, Englewood Cliffs, New Jersey
Stevens J 1986 *Applied Multivariate Statistics for the Social Sciences*. Erlbaum, Hillsdale, New Jersey

M. J. Rosier

Swaziland: System of Education

1. General Background

The Kingdom of Swaziland is the smallest country in Southern Africa, covering an area of 17,364 square kilometers with a length of 193 kilometers north to south and a width of 145 kilometers east to west. The country is surrounded by the Transvaal and the Natal provinces of South Africa, except in the northeast, where the country borders on the Republic of Mozambique for a distance of 97 kilometers. Swaziland's four geographical regions are the Highveld, the Middleveld, the Lowveld, and the Lubombo. These cover 29, 26, 37, and 8 percent respectively. The capital city of Mbabane is situated in the mountainous Highveld. The Middleveld and Lubombo are at somewhat lower altitudes (610 to 762 meters), and the Lowveld is a region of bush vegetation at altitudes from 152 to 305 meters. The climate is temperate in the highlands and subtropical in the lowlands. The population of the country was estimated at 681,000 persons in the period 1976–86 and the annual average population growth rate was estimated at 3.2 percent. Nearly half of the population lives in the Middleveld which has some of the best soils in Swaziland.

Swaziland became a British High Commission territory in 1907 and remained such until gaining independence in 1968. Executive authority is vested in the king and exercised through a cabinet presided over by a prime minister. The country is divided into chieftaincies, each of which elects two members to the electoral college. In each of the nation's four regions, a council made up of members of the college is responsible for implementing government policies.

The nation's main economic base is agriculture, in which a high percentage of the labor force is engaged. The major crops for both export and consumption are sugar, maize, cotton, and pineapples. Cattle farming dominates the country's livestock sector, but there is rapid development in goats, sheep, poultry, and pigs. Other activities include forestry, mining construction, and manufacturing.

In religion and official language, the country reflects its colonial background. Around 60 percent of the population is Christian (Protestant and Roman Catholic), while the remainder adheres to traditional African beliefs. The official languages are English and Siswati, a Bantu language related to Zulu.

The King is Head of State and is advised by a cabinet of Ministers responsible to a two-chamber parliament. On the other hand, he is advised by the Supreme Council of State, which is traditionally responsible to the Swazi Nation Council made up of all Swazi adults. The political dualism created by the role of the monarchy has distinctly shaped the nation's administration and the way of life of the Swazi people and is thought to ensure a balance in the political power structure and also to prevent any rift between the modern (westernized) elite and the traditional (conservative) majority.

Western education was introduced in Swaziland around the beginning of the twentieth century by missionaries, with the colonial government later becoming involved. Schools were developed along ethnic lines, with separate schools for Africans, for Europeans, and for Euro-Africans. By mid-century a large number of the schools for Africans were limited to a four-year primary course, which later was extended to six years. Although enrollments grew over the decades, by the 1950s more than half of school-age African children still did not attend

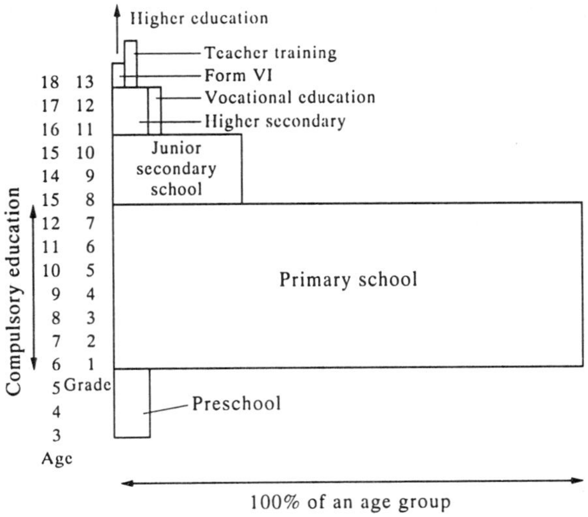

Figure 1
Swaziland: Structure of the formal education system

school, and more than half of the teachers were untrained (Pott 1955). The period between the close of the Second World War and the attainment of independence witnessed a more rapid increase in educational opportunities. Whereas only 11,600 pupils attended 207 primary schools in 1945, there were 172,908 pupils in 1991 and this enrollment is projected to increase to nearly 200,000 by 1995. Over the same period, secondary school enrollment increased from 318 students to 44,085 students in 1991 and the projection for 1995 is 58,220.

2. Politics and the Goals of the Education System

Since independence, the government has had a goal of universal primary education. For primary education the aims are the development of children's moral, intellectual, cultural, spiritual, and aesthetic values in order to prepare them for life. For secondary education the aims are to develop the individual by building upon and strengthening the foundation that was laid in primary school, and to provide the type of education which will support the development of those qualities and skills that will be of benefit to the individual and society, through both academic and vocational streams. Higher education focuses on the production of high-level and middle-level personnel and on academic learning.

3. The Formal System of Education

Figure 1 presents the structure of the Swaziland system of education. The system consists of seven years of primary school, three years of junior secondary school and two years of senior secondary school.

3.1 Primary, Secondary, and Tertiary Education

The age of entry into primary school is 6 years and the cycle or duration is seven years, which means children theoretically finish when they are 12 years old after they have written an examination awarding the Swaziland Primary Certificate (SPC).

Secondary education is divided into two sublevels; the first is known as junior secondary. However, there are two schools in the country which go beyond these sublevels. The junior level has a duration of three years while the senior is two years and the two exceptional schools have one extra year.

The students who pass the junior level obtain a Junior Certificate and proceed to take the Cambridge O-level examination which offers a General Certificate of Education (GCE) for entry to tertiary institutions and to university, whereas the two schools beyond O level offer an A level. This latter certificate allows students to enter directly into the second year of a four-year course at the local university.

In 1993 there were not sufficient places at the secondary schools to permit all students to progress from primary to secondary schools, if they were all to pass the SPC examination. However, the ministry has taken steps to provide, as much as possible, the necessary facilities in the form of classrooms, teachers' houses and furniture at both the primary and the secondary levels. With the limited budget allocation, government together with community effort provide the facilities, but due to the high demand for education, this is not always sufficient to meet the annual requirements.

The University of Swaziland is the only institution in the country offering degree programs and to which other tertiary institutions are affiliated. It offers degree and diploma programs in agriculture, education, natural sciences, humanities, and social sciences, and it also has an extramural services division that offers courses in adult education, management, and business studies. Table 1 presents enrollment data for selected years.

3.2 Preschool Education

Preschool education provides care for children between the ages of 3 and 5 years with emphasis on their socialization, development of their audio-sensorial skills, communication skills in Siswati and English, potential aptitudes, enhancement of their personality and character building, and preparation for entry into the school system.

While the country waits for preschool education to be universally available, primary schools are not allowed to consider preschool education as a prerequisite for entry into their first year. In 1993, some of these preschools were owned and run by communities, religious organizations, private individuals, and companies. In 1990, there were 260 preschools with an enrollment of 6,113 children.

Table 1
Enrollment data at primary, secondary, and tertiary education for 1991, 1993[a], and 1995[a]

	1991	1993	1995
Primary			
Students	172,281	181,359	197,599
Teachers	5,584	6,133	7,059
Pupil–teacher ratio	32.3	29.6	28.0
Secondary[b]			
Students	44,085	50,662	58,220
Teachers	2,430	2,927	3,523
Pupil–teacher ratio	18.1	17.3	16.5
University			
Agriculture	258	242	—
Education	138	165	—
Humanities	261	252	—
Science	300	298	—
Social science	778	773	—

a Projected Values b Source: Ministry of Education c Source: University of Swaziland

3.3 Special Education

The purpose of special education is to provide educational opportunities to children with disabilities. These include the physically and mentally handicapped, and those with visual and hearing disabilities. In 1993 special education was offered at four centers or schools that offer formal courses of instruction, and suitable facilities for disabled students.

3.4 Vocational, Technical, and Business Education

In 1993 there were three colleges offering vocational education: (a) the Swaziland College of Technology which offers both vocational and technical programs with Junior Certificate and O-level admission requirements; (b) the Vocational and Commercial Training Institute (VOCTIM), with a minimum entry qualification of Junior Certificate, but also taking O-level graduates due to the competition for entry; and (c) the Manzini Industrial Training Center (MITC) which provides trades training for students who have not graduated from the regular school system and who do not have the prerequisites for admission to other vocational training institutions. MITC is run as a business with training occurring in tandem with repairs and production activities carried out by the students for outside clients. The goal of the administration of MITC is to become self-sufficient as a result of the proceeds of these businesses.

3.5 Adult and Nonformal Education

Adult education is intended to provide an opportunity to adults and youths who either had no formal education or who benefited little from their education. The aim is to educate and inculcate literacy and numeracy skills so that each individual can participate and contribute effectively both to his or her overall well-being and to society.

Adult education is offered on a nonformal basis through various institutes, rural education centers, agricultural and industrial training centers, and the Division of Extramural Services administered by the Faculty of Education at the University of Swaziland.

There is also a system of distance education, the purpose of which is to provide correspondence and continuing education and inservice correspondence education training. The students include those who have bypassed the formal school system as well as working youths and adults. The students who pass their examinations rejoin the formal school system or continue to further their education through correspondence. Inservice teacher education is also conducted through distance education.

4. Administrative and Supervisory Structure and Operation

All schools, colleges, and the university operate under the jurisdiction of the Ministry of Education, which is headed by a minister and deputy minister. Subordinate to these political appointees is a principal secretary, who is supported by a director of education, an undersecretary, and a research and planning unit; a chief inspector, subject inspectors, and regional education officers. The chief inspectors for primary schools and secondary schools direct the activities of the inspectors in individual subjects who visit the schools to monitor the quality of teaching.

5. Educational Finance

Of the state budget, 28.5 percent is spent on education. Of this, 37.2 percent is spent on primary education, 29.3 on secondary education, and 17.9 on higher education. The student unit costs are E 492 (US$180) at primary, E 1,577 (US$576) at secondary, and E 12,236 (US$4468) at tertiary.

Although universal primary education has been achieved, there are problems in having sufficient schools and classrooms to meet the demand in secondary education, and parents and communities are expected to help finance or build the classrooms needed.

6. Supplying Personnel for the Education System

There are three teacher training colleges: Nazarene Teachers' College and Ngwane Teachers' College, both of which produce primary school teachers, and William Pitcher Teachers' Training College, which produces both primary and secondary school teachers. The training of primary school teachers is being phased out at this last college. All of these teacher training colleges have a three-year resident course. The minimum entrance requirement is O level.

Commercial and technical teachers are trained at the Swaziland College of Technology. The University of Swaziland also trains primary school teachers and secondary teachers, including specialization in agricultural education, prevocational agricultural education, and home economics. The Swaziland College of Technology offers a three-year program and the University of Swaziland offers a four-year degree program for secondary school teachers. The number of expatriates teaching in secondary schools has been reduced.

Inservice teacher training both at the university and through distance education is an important feature. Following independence, the nation was faced with a critical shortage of qualified teachers so that a large number of unqualified people had to be employed to staff primary school classrooms. However, by 1993, only 7 percent of primary school teachers were unqualified.

7. Curriculum Development and Teaching Methodology

The National Curriculum Center is responsible for curriculum development and coordination at the primary and secondary levels. The development of the primary school curriculum is well advanced; the center is planning to focus on strengthening its role in secondary curriculum development in the coming years. One of the center's main concerns is that the curriculum at one level should be linked to ensure a smooth transition to the next level because now it is being diversified to offer even more subjects. For example, practical arts subjects have been introduced in a number of schools in Grade 7. Hence, in Form I or Grade 8, the woodwork curriculum should begin at the point where the Grade 7 curriculum left off.

8. The System of Examinations, Promotions, and Certifications

Promotion from one grade to the next within the cycle of education is determined by the students' performance during the year. In order to ensure a continuous progression in the system, donor assistance has been obtained through the Education Policy Management and Technology Project (EPMT) for the development of methodologies and teacher training. Assessment will be criterion-referenced, that is, pupils will attain skills to a specified standard at each stage of their education. All primary teachers will be trained in methodology and remedial approaches required to assist pupils in reaching the criteria. In the light of the introduction of continuous assessment and of examination system improvements, the examinations at the end of Grades 7 and 10 will be phased out and replaced by a system of diagnostic testing. The Education Testing, Guidance, and Psychological Services Section of the Ministry of Education is being strengthened in order to fulfill its task of assisting in continuous assessment and diagnostic testing. Its major tasks will include conducting diagnostic tests to detect learning strengths and weaknesses, administering a centralized continuous assessment system for the maintenance of uniform standards in the country, and identifying students' abilities, talents, and inclinations. Specific activities will include internships for local personnel in institutions abroad to provide training in testing and continuous assessment, in-country training for teachers and headmasters, long-term training to Master's degree level in guidance, and the production of test materials and the development of guidance strategies.

9. Educational Assessment, Evaluation, and Research

The Research and Planning Section of the Ministry of Education is responsible for the production of statistics about areas of concern in the education system. It is also responsible for evaluating and assessing the impact of educational projects that have been implemented. Research work conducted in the 1980s included tracer studies from school to work, school mapping exercises, wastage studies, and a preschool sector study as well as work for sector reviews.

Small scale research projects were also undertaken by the University and other institutions in the period 1990–93. These included: distribution of textbooks, skills for the future, a tracer study of prevocation students output, and auditing of school revenue and expenditure.

10. Major Reforms in the 1980s and 1990s

At the preschool level the reforms in the 1980s were the establishment of:

(a) qualified teacher leaders;

(b) health checks (i.e., immunization and other medical care);

(c) feeding schemes in some rural and urban schools;

(d) assistance in the form of grants from government and donor funds to preschools;

(e) parent/community involvement in the development of self-help schemes for preschools;

(f) administrative services of the ministry of education to strengthen preschool education at headquarters and at the regional level.

At the primary school level, universal primary education was achieved in 1985 and the curriculum has been diversified to some extent to include practical subjects. Proposals for a nine-year basic education were made and plans for developing the curriculum for both academic and prevocational education in secondary schools were begun. Finally, the introduction of master's programs at the university was initiated.

11. Major Problems for the Year 2000

The reforms of the education system will have serious cost implications in procuring and maintaining equipment for the prevocational stream. The inservice training of teachers to adapt to the above reforms will involve carefully planned training, both at home and abroad.

Many schools need to be upgraded and new ones need to be built.

The nationalizing and changing of the examination will bring about changes in the present system to which Swazis have been accustomed for quite some time. The introduction of new technologies will necessitate year-to-year inservice teacher programs.

References

Pott D 1955 *Swaziland: A General Survey*. South African Institute for Race Relations, Johannesburg

Further Reading

Government of Swaziland 1973 *Second National Development Plan 1973–77*. Government Printing Office, Mbabane

Government of Swaziland 1985 *National Review Commission Report*. Government Printing Office, Mbabane

Government of Swaziland 1991–92, 1992–93, 1993–94, 1994–95 *Rolling Development Plan*. Government Printing Office, Mbabane

Swaziland Ministry of Education 1986 *Wastage in the Education System*. Ministry of Education, Mbabane

Swaziland Ministry of Education 1990, 1991 *Education Statistics Reports*. Ministry of Education, Mbabane

Swaziland Ministry of Education 1992 *Education Preparatory Study*. Ministry of Education, Mbabane

E. Dlamini

Sweden: System of Education

1. General Background

Sweden is located in northern Europe and has an area of 450,000 square kilometers. Its length from north to south is 1,650 kilometers. The present borders were fixed in 1815. Sweden's population has increased from nearly 2.5 million inhabitants in 1800 to 5.1 million in 1900 and 8.4 million in 1992. The birthrate has been low since the 1920s. However, this has been counteracted by an increased average life expectancy and increased immigration. The population density is low, with only 20 inhabitants per square kilometer.

Table 1
Percentages of workers in types of industry 1990

	Percentage
Agriculture, forestry, fishing, and hunting	3.9
Mining, manufacturing, construction, electricity, gas, and water service	29.5
Wholesale and retail trade, restaurants, and hotels	14.5
Transport, storage, and communication	7.0
Finance and insurance	8.3
Services	36.9

Ethnically, the population was homogeneous until the 1950s. Small national minorities include the Lapps in the north and a Finnish-speaking population along the northeastern borders. The remainder, excluding some small groups, from the Swedish majority population with Swedish as their national language. The dominant religion is that of the Lutheran State Church. Since 1950 immigration has exceeded emigration. Immigrants and their children now number 1 million and they live almost exclusively in the cities. This has considerably affected the school system. Swedish-as-a-foreign-language was introduced as a school subject in 1974. Nearly all immigrant students are also taught their mother tongue at school.

The economically active population numbered 4.7 million in 1990. The percentage breakdown by type of sectoral employment is shown in Table 1. Since the early 1970s the number of employees in manufacturing and mining has slightly decreased and the number in health, social services, and education has increased. Government policies on labor, salaries, and general welfare have resulted in considerable equalization and overlapping of socioeconomic classes. The differences in disposable income and working conditions seem to be smaller than in any other country.

Sweden is a constitutional monarchy with a parliamentary representative democracy written into its Constitution. Universal suffrage was introduced in 1908 for men and in 1919 for women. In local political elections, immigrants have the right to vote in the district in which they live. Elections are held every three years. A significant factor for reform activities in general has been Sweden's political stability. The dominant political party has been the Social Democrats. Between 1932 and 1976, they were in power practically without interruption. However, during 1976–82 Sweden had, and since 1991 has again had a right-wing liberal government. The same political situation has prevailed, by and large, in local government. Political stability has been paralleled by a comparatively conflict-free labor market.

An additional factor of importance has been the growth of material prosperity. Using the Gross Domestic Product (GDP) per capita as a yardstick, Sweden is usually ranked as one of the richest countries in the world. Through social welfare legislation, there are high standards for all in such matters as unemployment insurance, basic old-age and supplementary income-related pensions, public health and medical care, as well as child and housing allowances. The reforms in the educational system from preschool to higher education are part of this welfare program. It includes benefits for everyone, such as free schooling and higher education.

2. Politics and the Goals of the Education System

In 1950, Parliament decided upon a general strategy for the future development of the whole school system. The main objective was to raise the general level of education. The period of compulsory schooling had to be lengthened. At the same time, there was a desire to "democratize" the school system, by improving educational opportunities for previously underprivileged groups and by replacing the tripartite system of schools at secondary level with a comprehensive system, thereby creating greater equality of educational opportunity. Practical training was to receive equal status with theoretical ("academic") training. These objectives comprised both a social and an educational program.

After 12 years of experimental activities throughout the country, a new school structure was decided upon in 1962. In the school laws, statutes, and central curricular guidelines, the development of the individual student according to his or her inherent aptitudes was pronounced as the first and major goal of education. The second general goal put society at the center: school was to educate the individual for participation in the affairs of society for productivity and for social usefulness. The third goal concerned the handing down from the older to the younger generation of traditions and values—the cultural heritage. In interpreting these goals, equality and justice are the right of everyone, regardless of social, economic, ethnic, or geographical conditions.

3. The Formal System of Education

From 1962 to 1972, a nine-year compulsory comprehensive school (*grundskola*) was introduced all over the country. In 1971, an integrated upper-secondary school (*gymnasieskola*) was likewise introduced throughout the country, comprising academic, general and technical—vocational education within the same organization. The preschool structure was reorganized in 1967 and 1971, and higher education (universities and corresponding tertiary institutes) in 1975, 1977, and 1992.

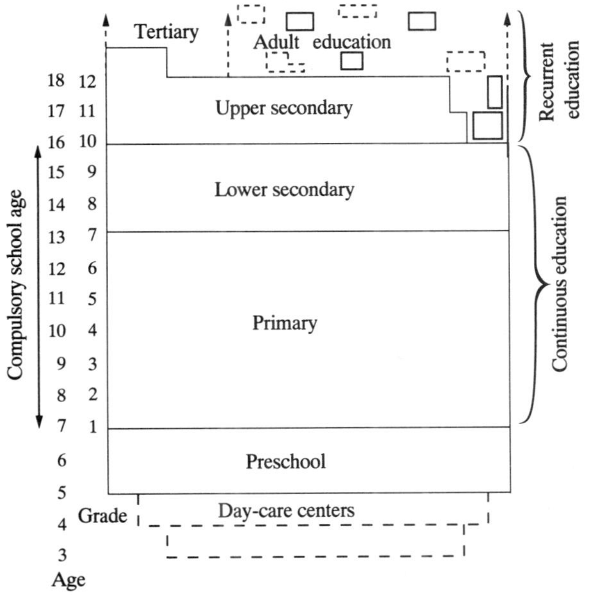

Figure 1
Sweden: Structure of the formal education system

Thus the traditional stages of preschool, primary school, and secondary and vocational school were restructured as precompulsory, compulsory, and postcompulsory (see Fig. 1). The inconspicuous part played by private schools is typical. The Education Act (1962) does not place any obstacles in the way of private persons or groups wishing to provide their own education for their children. They can also receive the same state and municipal grants as the regular municipal schools, provided they follow the basic governmental school statutes.

Most children aged 7–16 years attend the *grundskola*. The private school population is only 2 per cent. The school year starts in late August and ends in mid-June. It encompasses 40 weeks. The school year is basically the same for primary, secondary, and higher education. Until 1978 the maximum class size was 30. The average size was 22.6 in the compulsory schools and 24.0 in upper-secondary schools. In 1992 it was similar. However, as a result of increased possibilities for working with small groups or single individuals, the student–teacher ratio is much lower. Owing to this and other changes during the 1980s (mainly reduction of the teachers' annual tuition load) the compulsory school had 9 full-time teachers per 100 students in 1992. The corresponding figure for the upper-secondary school was 7.5.

The most important dividing line in Swedish public education is at age 16 when compulsory, full-time, and continuous schooling ends. Students then move to a postcompulsory school, not necessarily full-time and continuous, but often part-time and recurrent.

The traditional upper-secondary school can be used in a more flexible way, as can higher education and various kinds of adult education to an even greater degree. Recurrent education can vary in timing, length, and content depending on how a single individual wishes to plan his or her studies and work.

3.1 Primary, Secondary, and Tertiary Education

Since 1972, there have been no separate official secondary schools before the postcompulsory stage. English is compulsory in grades 3 to 9. Grades 1 to 6 usually have class teachers. Grades 7 to 9 have specialized teachers, most of them in two school subjects. In Grades 7 to 9, the students have a common course except for 10 to 15 percent of the time when they have elective subjects—either a second foreign language or extra courses in their general subjects. Regardless of electives, a complete nine-year school course qualifies students to study in the upper-secondary school.

As a consequence of the introduction of the 9-year comprehensive school a new type of postcompulsory upper-secondary school has developed. In 1971, all types of postcompulsory schools were brought together into an integrated upper-secondary school (*gymnasieskola*). As an official national school this seems to be unique in the world. An important aim was to give equal status to academic, general, and technical–vocational education at this level: general academic education should be "vocationalized" and technical–vocational education should be "generalized." The integrated upper-secondary school has three main sectors of study: arts and social subjects, economics and commercial subjects, and scientific and technical subjects. In each one of these three sectors there are academic, general, and vocational courses. The majority of students have so far taken one of 25 tracks. These tracks have had a length of two to four years. This integration in the *gymnasieskola* explains why there is no special description of vocational, technical, and business education later in this entry.

In principle, students enjoy a free choice of study routes in the upper-secondary school. The school has places for all who finish the compulsory school, and more than 90 percent of them continue with upper-secondary training. Because of limited availability of places in certain programs, the students cannot always get their first choice. Whenever the number of applicants exceeds the supply of student places, admission preference is accorded on the basis of marks earned in comprehensive school and occasionally on other qualifications such as work experience. The students' preferences are strongly influenced by the labor-market situation.

Dropout used to be a problem in the traditional Swedish secondary school. In the nine-year compulsory school this has now been eradicated, although it happens that a few students end with an "incomplete" final grade. In the integrated upper-secondary school, nearly a fifth "dropout" of their courses, but most of them return later to upper-secondary or adult education to complete these courses or take others. In the context of recurrent and lifelong learning the concept of "dropout" is now being redefined.

In 1975, Parliament approved general principles for a new higher education system. Undergraduate studies were organized into study programs grouped into five sectors (technical, administrative–economic–social welfare, medical–paramedical, teaching, and cultural–informational) as well as into single courses. Efforts to create greater diversity in available undergraduate programs were an important part of a policy which aimed at reaching new categories of students. Development of the content and structure of study programs was seen as a necessary complement to the new admission rules for reaching new categories of students.

For centuries Sweden had only two universities: Uppsala, founded in 1477, and Lund, founded in 1668. Institutes of higher studies in Stockholm and Göteborg were reorganized into universities during the 1950s and 1960s. An annex to Stockholm University was created at Linköping, one to Göteborg University at Karlstad, one to Uppsala at Örebro, and one to the University of Lund at Växjö. The most popular subjects within the faculties of humanities (social sciences and mathematics–natural sciences) were offered at the branch campuses. The university annex at Linköping was organized as an independent university in 1970.

Regional development policies were taken into account in planning higher education. North of Uppsala—within an area covering more than two-thirds of Sweden's total area—there were no resources for higher education and research. A university was established at Umeå in 1963, and an institute of higher education was also founded at Luleå to provide higher technical education and research.

Since 1977, higher education has included state-run institutes of higher education in 14 towns in addition to those 7 which had already been allotted resources. Most of these towns already had post-secondary schools or professional colleges of various kinds. In 1990, the Swedish universities and other tertiary training institutes had 165,000 students, of whom 92,000 were women.

Vocational, technical, and business education has in this way been integrated with upper-secondary and higher education as parts of the municipal secondary and the governmental postsecondary education systems. Only a few schools and institutes for these purposes are now run on a nonpublic basis.

3.2 Preschool Education

The establishment of day homes, nursery schools,

Table 2
Number of children in day homes and nursery schools

	Day homes[a]		Nursery schools[b]	
Age	1981	1990	1981	1990
0–4	87,800	162,000	2,300	1,600
5	27,500	49,400	14,300	11,000
6+	26,600	54,800	79,000	50,500
Total	141,900	266,200	95,600	63,100

a Full-time b Some part-time

kindergartens, and corresponding preschool-care institutions has predominantly been seen as a social welfare enterprise. Centrally, and usually also locally, preschool institutions are managed by the boards of health and social welfare and not by the boards of education. Compulsory school does not start until the age of 7. An earlier start has long been discussed. In 1973, parliament decided to retain the starting age of 7, but also decided that preschool should be available for all 6-year old children ("common preschool year"). However, an earlier school start is being reinvestigated by a governmental committee.

The treatment of preschool care and education as primarily a social question has given Swedish preschool institutions some unique features. They have a low child–adult ratio (seldom more than 5:1 or 6:1). They also have a special responsibility for children with difficulties and special needs, for instance, immigrant children. The statistics in Table 2 are from 1981 and 1990. These figures should be seen in relation to the birthrate in Sweden, which in the 1980s, was about 100,000 per year.

3.3 Special Education

Mentally retarded children are educated at special schools and training centers. Similarly, children who are blind, deaf, suffering from severe eyesight or hearing difficulties, or who have severe physical disabilities receive their schooling at special institutions. However, these students account for only 1 percent of the school-age population. Regular schools also provide special education. Such a provision has been developing since the late 1800s. Slow-learning students were taught in "help-classes." In 1942 these classes acquired their own structure when special training for their teachers started. In the nine-year compulsory *grundskola*, special classes were also organized for children judged as insufficiently mature to start schooling, as well as for children with reading disabilities and for students with social and emotional problems.

From the 1960s onward these special classes were gradually replaced by a system of special lessons for students taught individually or in small groups in so-

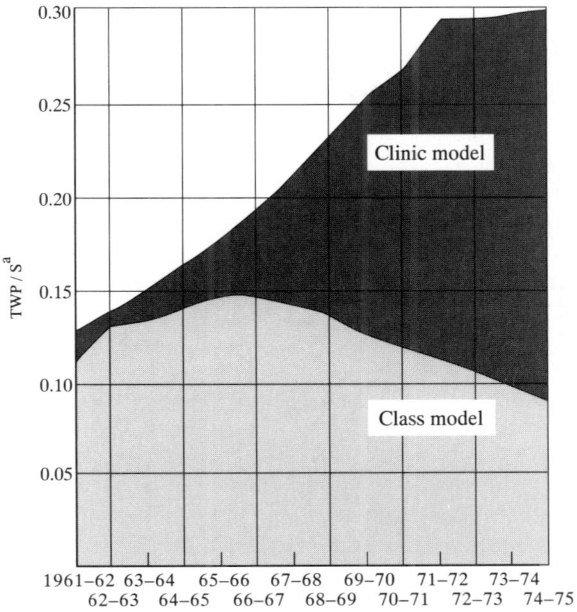

Figure 2
Development of special education in Swedish compulsory schools 1961/62–1974/75
a Proportions of Teacher Weekly Periods per Student (TWP/S) in Class teaching (lower part) and Clinic teaching (upper part)

called "clinics" parallel to teaching in special classes. Figure 2 indicates how the proportion of these two kinds of special education developed during the implementation of the new comprehensive school system. The total amount of special education doubled from 1961–62 to 1974–75, measured as the amount of "Teacher Weekly Periods per Student" (TWP/S) spent on special education. The lower part of the figure represents the amount of teaching in special classes, whereas the upper part represents special education in clinics, individually or in small groups. The clinic model increased from the mid-1960s at the same time as the class model decreased.

The proportions of the two models have generally remained unchanged since 1974–75. In 1972, an upper limit for special education was set at 0.30 TWP/S. This meant that approximately every fifth teacher in *grundskola* was a special teacher. In 1978 this limit was abolished when special education became subject to decisions by local authorities, although still within the overall framework for state grants. There are no official statistics about special education since 1978.

3.4 Adult and Nonformal Education

Adult and nonformal education in Sweden is of three kinds: popular-movement education, municipal adult education, and labor market training.

Popular-movement education is of two types: folk

high schools and evening study circles. The first folk high schools were founded in 1868. In 1992, they numbered more than 100. They are run by county councils, and special organizations and associations. They provide a general civic education, mostly as two or three-year full-time courses in boarding schools, with the aim of giving students an insight into their responsibilities as human beings and as members of society. Each school designs its own program. Folk high schools try to meet educational needs not fulfilled by the regular schools. The minimum age of eligibility is 18 years.

An evening study circle is a nonformal group of adults, usually 5 to 20, meeting for a minimum of 12 evenings over a period of at least 4 weeks. One of the members leads the circle. There are 11 nationwide adult education associations that operate folk high schools and study circles; all are entitled to state grants. These associations have links with various organizations, such as blue-collar and white-collar trade unions, political parties, and churches. The adult education associations collaborate with libraries and other cultural institutions. They cover a broad range of subjects varying from one association to another. In 1990, nearly two million people participated in study circles.

In 1967, Parliament decided that the local school authorities should also be responsible for providing opportunities for adult education. The number of adult students then grew quickly. During the 1970s and 1980s more than 200,000 people participated in such programs every year. This is as many as are trained in the regular upper-secondary schools. Municipal adult education aims at providing preparation for continued studies or for an occupation. About one-fourth took comprehensive-school courses. Nearly half were in upper-secondary courses, and almost one-third were in special vocationally oriented courses. Municipal adult education is provided within all of Sweden's 280 municipal districts.

Labor-market training provides vocational education for those are unemployed or in danger of losing their jobs. It is paid for by the government and is conducted at special training centers and within the regular educational system. The main emphasis is on manufacturing operations. Participation in labor-market training varies from year to year. In 1981 it had 40,000 trainees. In 1991 it had increased to 125,000.

4. *Administrative and Supervisory Structure and Operation*

Primary and secondary education (the latter including vocational and technical education) are subordinate to local school boards, one in each district. At the central level they are subordinate to the government, including the Ministry of Education.

Table 3
Primary- and secondary-school costs in selected years, with 1950–51 as a base year

	1950–51	1960–61	1970–71	1980–81	1989–90
Costs					
Total	100	214	395	640	636
Per student	100	192	262	411	405
GDP	100	138	206	242	241
Costs as percentage of GDP					
State	1.3	2.1	2.8	3.5	2.9
Municipality	1.0	1.6	2.5	3.6	3.1
Total	2.3	3.7	5.3	7.1	6.0

Until 1991, Sweden had a special administrative body—the National Board of Education (NBE)—corresponding to what in most other countries constitutes the administrative nonpolitical branch of the Ministry of Education. The NBE had a fairly free and independent position but was subordinate to the government as a whole and not just the Ministry of Education. Thus, for instance, the far-reaching school reform activities in the period 1950 to 1980 in compulsory and postcompulsory schools was led and executed by the NBE, within relatively general guidelines given by the government.

In 1991, the NBE was replaced by a smaller central authority called the Central Agency for Education (CAE). This change was a consequence of a far-reaching decentralization of responsibility for further development of the schools from the central government to local authorities. The local districts were made bigger and fewer (from approximately 2,500 in 1950 to 1,000 in 1953, 800 in 1962, and 280 in 1974).

A school inspectorate for upper-secondary education, attached to the NBE, was abolished in 1980. For compulsory education, a corresponding system of regionally attached inspectors was abolished in 1991. Their responsibilities were taken over by the local district boards and the heads of schools.

Universities and colleges have their own boards. At the central level, they are under the government and have long since been administered by a National Board of Universities and Colleges. In 1992 this board was replaced with four smaller administrative units.

5. *Educational Finance*

The extent to which school costs have increased can be seen in Table 3. For comparison purposes, figures for 1950–51 have been put at 100. In 1989–90 (39 years later), costs in a fixed currency increased nearly 6 times (from 100 to 636). Per student costs increased from 100 to 405.

Since the 1950s, Sweden's material wealth also increased considerably (the GDP rose from 100 to

245). In 1950, some 2.3 percent of the GDP went to schools; 40 years later it was 6.0 percent. However, this increase seems to have stopped. According to World Bank statistics, Sweden, Denmark, and Norway seem to have the most expensive school systems in the world. The annual cost for a student in 1989–90 was US$7,600 in the compulsory comprehensive school and US$8,300 in the integrated upper-secondary school. These costs are shared roughly evenly by the state and the municipality.

6. *Supplying Personnel for the Education System*

Before 1968, the major part of teacher training was clearly divided into two levels. Primary-teacher training was mostly conducted at the preuniversity level and was of an apprenticeship type, with training in academic subjects and teaching practice. Secondary academic teachers were trained at the postsecondary level, usually at universities and with a final preparatory pedagogical year (or half-year) to provide a formal qualification for teaching. Teachers in arts, music, home economics, physical education, or manual instruction had special kinds of training somewhere between these two types.

From 1968 onward different types of training (for primary, secondary academic, and secondary nonacademic teachers) were gradually placed in the tertiary education system. There have also been steps taken to equalize salaries and teaching conditions. Training has usually been two years for preprimary teachers, two and a half or three years for primary teachers, and four years (minimum) for secondary teachers. In 1988 the training of teachers for compulsory schools was extended to three and a half to four and a half years, depending on the type of specialization.

From 1952 to 1972, Sweden had a severe teacher shortage, due primarily to the introduction of extended compulsory education and a broadening of postcompulsory education. Since 1972, there has been a fair balance between supply and demand of teachers.

7. *Curriculum Development*

The major aim of the first six school years is to give the pupils basic skills in reading, writing, and arithmetic and a general social and science orientation. As early as Grade 3 a foreign language (English) is introduced as a compulsory subject. Since 1970, all primary teachers have been formally qualified to teach English.

A national curriculum for the compulsory school was introduced in 1962 with many electives in Grades 7–8 and 9 streams in Grade 9. In 1969 streaming was banned all through the compulsory school. Some 15 percent of instructional time in Grades 7 to 9 (lower-secondary) was allocated to electives where the student could choose between a second foreign language (German, French, or mother tongue for immigrants), technical subjects, economics, and art. In 1980, Parliament decided that the choice of postcompulsory training could be made independently of the choice of electives in the preceding compulsory education.

The upper-secondary curriculum is clearly tracked but all tracks include Swedish, civics, and physical education. A total of six tracks are predominantly academic with more than 10 subjects in each. However, as from 1993, the system of tracks with fixed combinations of subjects will be replaced by a system of 16 so-called "study programs," within which students will have some possibility for composing their own curricula. The central curricular guidelines for compulsory, as well as postcompulsory, schools were were being revised, again in 1992. The implementation of this revision was expected to take place sometime in the period 1993 to 1995.

8. *The System of Examinations, Promotions, and Certifications*

There are no final examinations in the compulsory comprehensive school (*grundskola*) and the integrated upper-secondary school (*gymnasieskola*). In the compulsory school the pass–fail concept was abolished. With few exceptions all students move to the next grade at the end of the school year.

In the compulsory school, students are awarded subject marks at the end of the Autumn and Spring terms in Grades 8 and 9. The latter make up the basis for further studies in postcompulsory schools. There the students receive marks in all subjects at the end of the Autumn and Spring terms. Marks are given on a five-point scale, where 1 is lowest and 5 highest. The basis for selection of students to higher education is the average mark in Grade 12 (and, for some kinds of higher education, in Grade 11).

Since 1977, admission to tertiary education can also be granted on the basis of a voluntary central entrance test of "suitability for higher studies." Around 40 percent of available training places are filled by persons having taken the entrance test, and around 60 percent on the basis of marks from preceding schools. In each case, the applicants must fulfill both general requirements and special requirements for admission. The former is usually the completion of secondary school, but can also be experience of other kinds. The latter are mostly secondary-school marks in subjects relevant to the specific training for which application was made.

At the tertiary level most faculties and corresponding bodies set a basic exam (*högskoleexamen*), usually after three or four years of full-time studies. Some faculties also have a master's degree or a licentiate degree between this basic exam and the final doctoral degree. Exams are judged as "well approved," "approved," or "not approved."

In Sweden, certification for a number of professions following tertiary studies has disappeared for many occupational areas. The medical and legal professions usually demand special certificates after fulfilled studies, but for most other professions tertiary examination in relevant subjects is usually enough.

9. Educational Assessment, Evaluation, and Research

In the "new" school as of 1962 it was said that assessment should be continuous, regardless of how often students received formal marks. Standardized central achievement tests had existed since 1944 in primary schools for reading, writing, and mathematics, and from 1959 for English. Tests in these subjects, plus physics, chemistry, German, and French (and for some time also in business economics and accountancy), were introduced in upper-secondary education.

The standardized tests for primary education were at first voluntary for teachers, but 90 to 95 percent used them. As from the 1980s the tests became compulsory but were restricted to Grades 8 and 9. In upper-secondary school the central tests became mandatory upon their introduction in 1971. The tests were constructed by a special department at the NBE, but from 1982 this task was decentralized to a number of educational research institutes. The main objective of these tests was to help teachers make students' marks comparable all over the country. The results were not registered in the students' final certificates.

Another kind of assessment is the National Evaluation of Compulsory Education, an on-going project started in 1989. It is based on a national sampling of classes in Grades 2, 5, and 9 every three years. Student achievements in all major school subjects are measured. Methods of how students work, learn, and communicate are also studied.

Since the 1960s, Sweden has also participated in international studies of student achievement. The largest project so far has been organized by the International Association for the Evaluation of Educational Achievement (IEA) for samples of 10-year old, 14-year old, and preuniversity-age students. In general, Sweden achieved average or above-average results.

In addition to achievement studies of this nature, the Swedish government has, since 1962, set aside special resources for educational research. These funds have been administered by the NBE, and from 1991 by its replacement, the CAE. During the first decade of activities, funds were predominantly used for so-called "development projects"; these included studies of methods and materials, and development of learning aids according to the "educational technology" of the time. Since then the scope of studies has broadened to include many other kinds of studies. The amount of funding increased until 1977–78, when the NBE provided resources equivalent to US$7.5 million for educational research and development. This was 0.4 percent of the government school budget. Since 1978 the annual sum has decreased to sums less than half of that amount.

10. Major Reforms in the 1980s and 1990s

Compared with the period 1950 to 1980, when the Swedish education system was almost totally reshaped, the 1980s became a period mostly characterized by quiet and stabilization. New national curricular guidelines for the compulsory school were established in 1980. The 1980s was also the decade of decentralization to local authorities of responsibility for the development of the school. State grants could, within a wide national framework, be used locally for varying organizational arrangements. Elective subjects in Grades 7 to 9 (lower secondary) could, from 1980, be extended courses in any of the school subjects in the curriculum, even in cross-disciplinary local subjects. Practical vocational orientation with local employers, previously restricted to 2 weeks in Grade 8, was extended to 6 to 10 weeks spread over Grades 1 to 9. It was broadened to "working life orientation" and was decided upon locally.

In the period 1985 to 1988 the upper-secondary school (Grades 10–12) was the focus of varying local experiments concerning internal study forms and external organizational structures. These experiences became the starting point for later changes from the "track system" to the "study program system," to be introduced in the period 1993 to 1995.

In higher education the most far-reaching change will be the replacement of the five general "study lines" by more freely composed programs for professional training. This will begin in 1993.

11. Major Problems for the Year 2000

Prospective major questions will probably concern how to find a new and constructive balance of the two main forces in social and educational policy-making which have been operating since the 1950s. Left-wing forces, promoting a "democratized" education with extended schooling and delayed differentiation in comprehensive systems will, more than before, be counteracted by right-wing liberal forces demanding more freedom for "profiling" school and education independent of central policy-making.

Such a dialogue between forces and opinions will include general as well as specific issues such as the balance between educational policy-making and social welfare policy-making. One of the long-discussed but still unresolved questions is the transition of children from preschool to compulsory school. In

1993 the age of transition was 7 years. It might change to 6 in the year 2000 or even before that time.

Bibliography

Gurgsdies E 1975 *Schulreform und Chancengleichheit. Ergebnisse der schwedischen Gesamtschulreformen.* Dietz, Berlin

Hörner H 1970 *Demokratisierung der Schule in Schweden, Erziehungswissenschaftliche Forschungen*, Vol. 4. Beltz, Weinheim

Jüttner E 1970 *Der Kampf um die schwedische Schulreform.* Mannheim

Marklund S 1980 *The Democratization of Education in Sweden: A UNESCO Case Study*, Studies in Comparative and International Education, No. 2. Institute of International Education, Stockholm University, Stockholm

Marklund S 1980 The role of central government in educational development in Sweden. In: Hoyle E, Megarry J (eds.) 1980 *Professional Development of Teachers. World Yearbook of Education 1980.* Kogan Page, London

Marklund S 1981 Sweden: Setting up the comprehensive school. *Prospect* 11(2): 161–79

Marklund S 1984 Sweden. In: Hough J R (ed.) 1984 *Educational Policy. An International Survey.* Croom Helm, London

Marklund S 1984 Effects of educational research on educational policy-making: The case of Sweden. In: Husén T, Kogan M (eds.) 1984 *Educational Research and Policy. How Do They Relate?* Pergamon Press, Oxford

Marklund S, Bergendal G 1979 *Trends in Swedish Educational Policy.* The Swedish Institute, Stockholm

OECD 1981 *Educational Reforms in Sweden*, Reviews of National Policies for Education. OECD, Paris

Sweden, Ministry of Education and Cultural Affairs 1991 *"Growing with Knowledge." A Reform of Upper-Secondary and Municipal Education in Sweden. Government Bill and the Decisions of Parliament in June 1991.* Ministry of Education and Cultural Affairs, Stockholm

Sweden, Skolöverstyrelsen (various years) *Läroplan för grundskolan 1962, 1969 och 1980.* Skolöverstyrelsen, Stockholm

Sweden, Skolöverstyrelsen 1970 *Läroplan för gymnasieskolan 1970.* Skolöverstyrelsen, Stockholm

Sweden, Skolöverstyrelsen 1990 *Anslagsbetänkanden för åren 1950/51–1990/91.* Skolöverstyrelsen, Stockholm

Sweden, Statistiska Centralbyrån 1991 *Statistisk Årsbok, åren 1950–1991.* Statistiska Centralbyrån, Stockholm

Wieser K 1974 *Bildungspolitik und Gesellschaft in Schweden. Dargestellt unter besonderer Berücksichtigung der Einführung der Gymnasieschule als Berufsgrundschule.* Jobst Schultze, Hamburg

S. Marklund

Switzerland: System of Education

1. General Background

Switzerland is a small country in the heart of Europe, covering an area of roughly 41,300 square kilometers or 15,945 square miles (about one-fourth of it being unproductive). Geographically, the country is made up of three main parts: the Jura, the Central Plain, and the Alps. Its rivers, which have their sources in the Alps, flow into the North Sea, the Mediterranean Sea, and the Black Sea. Founded in the year 1291 (with three cantons), Switzerland grew at different stages and found its present shape at the beginning of the nineteenth century, after the Napoleonic wars (25 cantons; a 26th canton was established in 1978).

In 1990, the population reached 6,751,000 inhabitants, 1,127,000 (16.7 percent) of whom were foreigners. With an average annual growth rate of 0.6 percent between 1980 and 1990, the total population is growing slowly. There are, however, significant changes in the age structure of the population: between 1950 and 1990, the age group 0–19 years has decreased from 30.6 to 23.4 percent, whereas the age group above 65 increased from 9.6 to 14.6 percent. This trend toward a society of more and more elderly people has important repercussions on the level and structure of qualifications and causes specific educational needs: since fewer new qualifications are brought to the active population by the young generation, updating and refreshing of the economically active people's qualifications by further training is gaining in importance. The average life expectancy still on the rise, is 80.8 years for women and 74.1 years for men. Due to its geographical situation (its neighbors being Germany, Austria, France, Italy, and Liechtenstein) and also to political will, Switzerland is a multicultural and multilingual country. Some 65 percent of the population speak German, 18.4 percent French, 9.8 percent Italian, and 0.8 percent Rhaeto-Romanic, the remainder being foreigners with other mother tongues. As to religious denomination, 47.9 percent are Roman Catholics, 44.3 percent Protestants, 3.2 percent belong to other religions, and 4.9 percent are without professed religion.

Economically, Switzerland has followed the general evolution of European countries from an agrarian to an industrial and, finally, to a service-dominated economy. Whereas in 1800, roughly 65 percent of the active population worked in the primary sector, this figure diminished to 5.6 percent by 1990; the corresponding figures for the secondary sector are roughly 25 and 34.9 percent (with a peak of almost 50 percent around 1965), and for the still growing tertiary sector which was less than 10 percent in 1800 but was 59.5 percent in 1990. This change in the economic structure was accompanied by a process of urbanization: in 1990, 14.2 percent of the population was living in towns with more than 100,000 inhabitants, 28.5 percent in communities with 10,000–99,999 inhabitants, and 57.3 percent in small localities (sometimes suburban) with less than 10,000 inhabitants; on the whole, 59.8 percent of the population live in urban and 40.2 percent in rural settings. The Swiss economy depends heavily on exports, mainly of high-quality products (imports, however, normally exceed exports—in 1990, by 9.5%) and on a high proportion of foreign labor (26.8% in 1990). Women account for 37.5 percent of the total labor force. National income per inhabitant (nominal US$ 30,600 in 1990) is one of the highest in the world.

Politically and administratively, the country is structured into three main levels: the Confederation, the 26 cantons, and the 3,029 communes, each of which has its own legislative and executive political power. The modern state in its present form was founded on the basis of the Federal Constitution of 1848. The central government (Federal Council), formed by seven ministers, is a coalition representing the four most important political parties; it is characterized by great stability.

Legislative power at the federal level consists of two houses, the National Council (200 deputies representing 10 political parties) and the Council of States (46 deputies). Adopting a very simple right-center-left model, it can be said that, in 1990, 138 deputies of the National Council belonged to the center and the right, and the other 62 represented the left. Neutrality in foreign affairs (increasingly being questioned with the possibility of Switzerland joining the European Community), a free market economy, and increasing social security are some salient points of long-term government policy. Decreasing interest and participation in voting at elections is one of the contemporary problems of the Swiss democratic system.

2. Politics and Goals of the Education System

Formal schooling started in the monastery schools of the Middle Ages with the purpose of ensuring the supply of priests. From the twelfth century onwards, so-called "small schools" catered for the needs of the rising bourgeoisie, teaching languages, elementary mathematics, and geography. Schooling was intensified with the Reformation and Counter-Reformation, but the middle schools and Latin schools were limited to the cities, whereas schools in rural areas continued to be dominated by religious instruction. The Age of Enlightenment brought some liberation from this domination, and the teaching of mathematics and science was reinforced. In that period, Rousseau (1712–78), born in Geneva, developed his concept of education, and Pestalozzi (1746–1827), working as a practitioner and a theoretician of education, founded and directed his schools and wrote his books.

The nineteenth century—with the emergence of the modern state, the economic revolution, and the spread of new ideas—brought general compulsory schooling. It was recognized that the education of the young generation was one of the most important public goals to be achieved. The cantons created school laws, established primary schools, and founded cantonal secondary schools (*Kantonsschulen*). Both existing universities (Basle and Geneva) were reorganized, and new universities were founded. The public educational system as it still essentially exists today was created.

One of the preeminent features of Switzerland's political system is the permanent search for an equilibrium between federal and cantonal power. Education essentially lies within the competence of the cantons, the federal state having very little to say in this field; consequently there is no federal ministry of education. Attempts to give more power to the central state in educational matters failed in 1874, when the constitution was totally revised, and again in 1973, when a constitutional amendment was accepted by a small majority of the voters, but rejected by the smallest possible majority of cantons. These failures show that the cantons are very anxious to safeguard their almost exclusive authority in educational matters. Therefore, there is no Swiss system of education: there are 26 cantonal systems. The following description of the "Swiss system" tries to underline both the differences between and the features common to the cantonal systems.

As there is no central authority in education and therefore no real educational planning at national level, the goals of the educational system are not easy to define. Goals for compulsory schooling are defined in each of the 26 cantonal school laws; for upper secondary education, they are formulated in the federal law on vocational training and the federal maturity regulation. Generally, these goals cover three dimensions: (a) personal development; (b) socialization in the sense of integrating the young generations into the local, national, and to an increasing extent into the European and the global society by means of introducing them into the essential cultural and other values; (c) economic qualification.

3. The Formal System of Education

Figure 1 presents an overall picture of the Swiss system of education. There are, however, marked differences between the 26 cantonal systems both in structure and in the richness and variety of educational provision. Thus, the educational provision in some small rural cantons with low per capita income is sometimes limited to preschool education, compulsory including special education, and just one gymnasium and one vocational school at the upper-secondary level, there being no provision at all (apart from private adult education) at the tertiary level. At the other extreme, there are urban cantons with high per capita income, offering an extremely rich variety of educational institutions at the upper-secondary and the university and nonuniversity tertiary level. Given the short distances in a small country, attending higher education institutions in another canton constitutes no major problem for students of small rural cantons. A system of cantonal

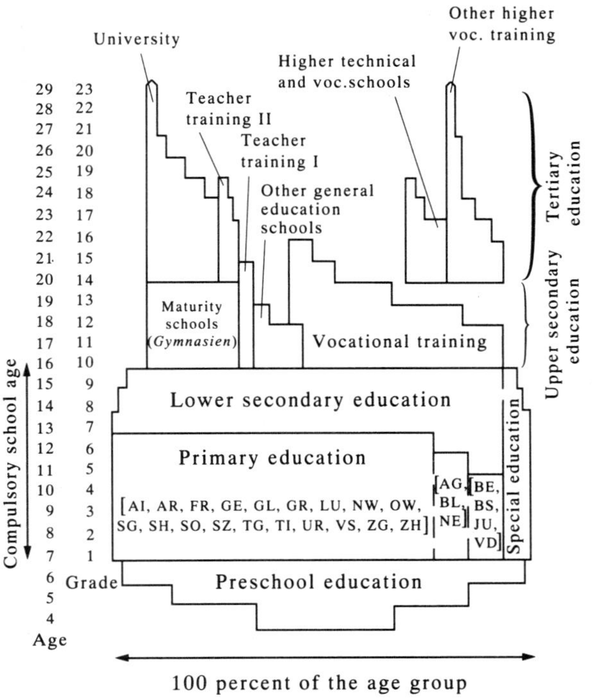

Swiss cantons:

AG	Aargau	NW	Nidwalden
AI	Appenzell(Inner-Rhoden)	OW	Obwalden
AR	Appenzell(Außer-Rhoden)	SG	St Gall
BE	Berne	SH	Schaffhausen
BL	Basel–Country	SO	Solothurn
BS	Basel–Town	SZ	Schwyz
FR	Fribourg	TG	Thurgau
GE	Geneva	TI	Ticino
GL	Glarus	UR	Uri
GR	Graubünden	VD	Vaud
JU	Jura	VS	Valais
LU	Lucerne	ZG	Zug
NE	Neuchâtel	ZH	Zurich

Figure 1
Switzerland: Structure of the formal education system 1990–91

scholarships, subsidized by the national government, widely provides for educational opportunities for economically underprivileged students.

3.1 Primary, Secondary, and Higher Education

The duration of compulsory schooling, divided into primary and lower-secondary education, has gradually been extended; in 1992, it was 9 years in almost all cantons. The enrollment rate at this level is virtually 100 percent (see Fig. 1).

Primary education, with all pupils in the same type of school, lasts 4 years in 4 cantons, 5 years in 3, and 6 years in the other 19 cantons (see Fig. 1). Since the end of primary education is the first point of selection in the system, there is a tendency in the first-mentioned cantons to prolong it by 1 or 2 years. From a curricular point of view, the period 1975 to 1990 was characterized by a reform of mathematics and the introduction of a foreign language as early as the fourth or fifth grade.

A feature of growing importance in the Swiss educational system is the high number of foreign pupils and students. As shown in Fig. 2, the proportion of foreign-origin and foreign-language schoolchildren in compulsory education varies between more than 40 percent in the canton of Geneva and less than 5 percent in the cantons of Nidwalden and Obwalden. The Swiss average is 17.5 percent. The Swiss Conference of Cantonal Ministers of Public Education has issued several recommendations concerning the schooling of foreign-language children. Roughly speaking the policy in this field can be characterized by three different stages: assimilation (in the 1960s), integration (in the 1970s and early 1980s), and intercultural education (from the mid-1980s onwards).

The average class size in 1990–91 was 19 pupils in primary education (with a minimum of 15.3 in the canton of Jura and a maximum of 21.4 in the canton of Thurgau) and 17.8 students in secondary education (with a minimum of 14.2 in Graubünden and a maximum of 19.9 in Ticino).

Lower-secondary education takes place in different types of school. Some cantons have organized their lower-secondary level in a comprehensive form; in others, the different types of schools may be classified into two groups: schools with basic requirements and schools with extended requirements. In 1991, 31.3 percent of the total number of pupils attended the first type and 68.7 percent the second type.

Upper-secondary education can be divided into four major types: *Maturitätsschulen*, designed for university entrance; other general education schools; teacher-training institutions; and vocational training institutions (see Sect. 3.4).

Unlike other schools, *Maturitätsschulen* are governed by a federal regulation. Originally, there were only two types of *Matura* (the final examination providing access to university): Type A (with emphasis on Greek and Latin) and Type B (Latin and modern languages). Type C (mathematics and science) was added in 1925 and Types D (modern languages) and E (economics) in 1972. In 1992, a proposed revision of this federal regulation was made in order to reduce the different types to just one, offering a great number of individual options. A decision will be taken after consultation with all interested parties.

Until the Second World War, *Maturitätsschulen* were reserved for a small elite; after the war, and particularly after 1960, enrollment increased spectacularly. It almost doubled between 1960 and 1970 and again between 1970 and 1980. In 1991 the total

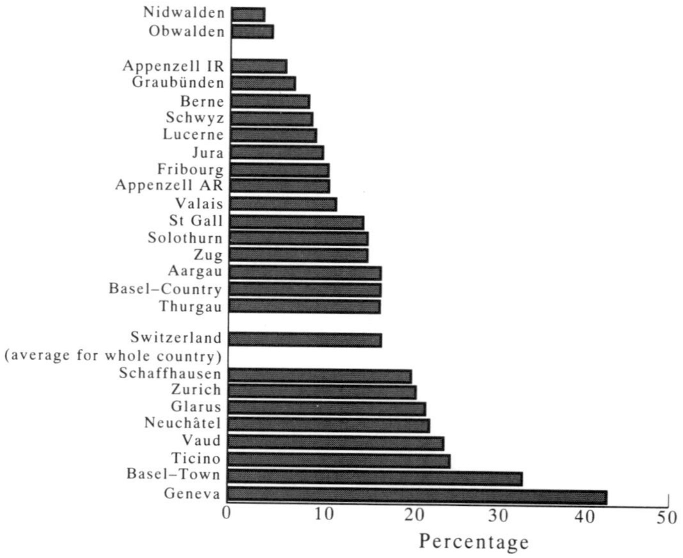

Figure 2
Compulsory schooling: foreign-origin and foreign-language school children by canton 1988–89

enrollment was 54,300. This increase was a response to two objectives of educational policy: to provide highly qualified personnel for the economy and to reduce inequality of educational opportunity by geographical region, social stratum, and sex. The means by which this increase took place were mainly decentralization of *Maturitätsschulen* and the development of the system of educational grants.

The other general education schools at this level (total enrollment in 1991: 12,000) prepare students primarily for certain nonuniversity professions (such as in the paramedical and social fields).

The main and traditional part of tertiary education is university education, but there is also a growing and increasingly diversified extrauniversity tertiary sector.

Academic education is provided for in the two federal institutes of technology (Zurich and Lausanne), in the seven cantonal universities: Basle (founded in 1460), Berne (1834), Freiburg (1889), Geneva (1559), Lausanne (1890), Neuchâtel (1909), and Zurich (1833), as well as in the School of Economics, Law, and Social Sciences of St Gallen. The increase in enrollment since 1960 has been spectacular and is expected to continue for some time to come. Thus, the total number of students in the above-mentioned university level institutions has grown as follows: 1960: 21,300; 1970: 42,200; 1980: 60,500; and 1991: 86,000.

The extrauniversity tertiary sector is characterized by diversity. This is not so much the result of a deliberate central policy as of a desire to provide pragmatic and specific answers to emerging needs. Admission normally depends on diplomas or certificates acquired in upper-secondary education. Six professional fields can be distinguished: (a) teaching; (b) higher technical and agricultural professions; (c) social work; (d) health professions; (e) commerce, traffic, administration, and communication; and (f) liberal arts. In addition to this, there are higher vocational courses and examinations in most of the trades which are accessed by apprenticeship. In 1990–91, a total of 52,000 students were enrolled in extrauniversity tertiary education, about two-thirds being part-time and the rest full-time students. In Switzerland, the extrauniversity tertiary enrollment as a proportion of total tertiary enrollment is higher than in most other countries. Of particular note are the higher technical institutes (*Höhere Technische Lehranstalt* or HTL) and the higher business and administration institutes (*Höhere Wirtschafts- und Verwaltungsschule* or HWV). There is general agreement that the engineers and middle-level staff trained in these institutes play an important role in the development of Swiss business and industry. In order to guarantee full international recognition of the diplomas conferred in the extrauniversity sector, tertiary teaching and training institutions providing a high quality education of at least three years' duration will obtain the status of specialized university institutes (*Fachhochschulen*).

3.2 Preschool Education

Normally, Swiss children spend one or two years in kindergarten before going to primary school. Preschool attendance in 1990–91 was 24.9 percent for 4-

year olds, 75 percent for 5-year olds, and 98.4 percent for 6-year olds (this last figure representing, however, a mixture of preschool and school attendance). There are notable differences between urban and rural regions. Total enrollment in 1990–91 was 139,800; the enrollment rate has steadily increased and will probably continue to do so.

As these figures show, preschool attendance is not compulsory. It is considered to be complementary to family education. About two-thirds of the cantons have preschool regulations at the cantonal level; the most important public body in preschool education, however, is the commune. The trend is to leave preschool education as noncompulsory, but to offer parents, by cantonal legislation, the opportunity of a one- or two-year enrollment for every child. Special measures such as the setting up of peripatetic kindergartens are sometimes taken in rural regions. The trend is also away from private to public preschool institutions. However, the former still play an important part. Besides the traditional (in some areas often church-run) private institutions, new forms of mostly parent-run playgroups are growing in importance. Special attention is given to the transition from preschool institutions to primary schooling.

As far as the philosophy and ideology of preschool education are concerned, there is a difference between German-speaking Switzerland, whose system is based on Fröbel (1782–1852), and the French- and Italian-speaking parts of the country, whose system is mainly based on Claparède (1873–1940), Ferrière (1879–1960), and Montessori (1870–1952). This difference, however, seems to be on the decrease in practice.

3.3 Special Education

For the duration of compulsory schooling, special education is offered to handicapped children (total enrollment in 1990–91: 36,000, which was 5% of pupils in compulsory schooling). As in many other countries, the development in this field was characterized by the separation versus integration debate in the early 1990s. In order to keep the growing proportions of children with learning difficulties within normal classes, and also in order to reduce the class repetition rates (14% of the children repeat a class in the course of compulsory schooling), different forms of special learning assistance (*Stütz- und Förderunterricht*) have been developed and play an important role in a growing number of cantons.

3.4 Vocational, Technical, and Business Education

By far the largest proportion of the young (more than 70% of an age group; total enrollment in 1991: 221,000) enter vocational training after compulsory schooling (normally from about age 16 to about age 19). This is mostly in the form of apprenticeship, consisting of two basic elements: practical training on the job in an enterprise (3.5 to 4 days per week), and theoretical and general instruction in a vocational school (1 to 1.5 days per week). A third element, basic courses in training centers, bringing together apprentices of the same craft or trade for some weeks, is becoming more popular. Following a very old tradition going back to preindustrial times, apprenticeship is regulated by a contract between master (employer) and apprentice. Craft and trade associations play an important part in establishing job descriptions, training programs, and examination rules. Vocational training is regulated by federal law; responsibility in the central administration is with the Federal Office of Industry, Trades, and Labor in the Federal Department of Public Economy. Leaving aside agriculture and public health, there are recognized apprenticeships (of two to four years' duration) in about 280 vocations in the fields of industry, handicrafts, and different service sectors. At the beginning of the 1970s, the vocational school with an augmented curriculum (*Berufsmittelschule*) was introduced for particularly gifted or ambitious apprentices.

In relation to the transformation of the extrauniversity tertiary institutes (*Fachhochschulen*, see Sect. 3.1) and also influenced by the educational policy of the European Community (EC), an important reform will be introduced in the field of basic vocational training: apprentices will be offered the opportunity of additional general education (about 1,200 lessons) resulting in an examination (Berufsunatuvität) offering access to the specialized university institutes in the corresponding vocational field. On the other hand, graduates from the upper-secondary general education schools with an additional year of vocational practice will also be admitted to these specialized university institutes.

Two main types of higher vocational training can be distinguished: higher technical and vocational schools (mostly full-time, sometimes also part-time) and other higher vocational training (mostly part-time, see Fig. 1). As explained above, most of the higher technical and vocational schools (total enrollment in 1990–91: 15,000) will be transformed into specialized university institutes (*Fachhochschulen*). However, this is not the case for the so-called technicians' schools (total enrollment in 1990–91: 5,000). Other higher vocational training (total enrollment in 1990–91: 32,000) consists mainly of part-time courses preparing for higher vocational examinations known as the master examinations in the trades. Access is by successful completion of an apprenticeship. The conferment of a Master (*Meister*) title allows the holder to train apprentices.

3.5 Adult and Nonformal Education

Adult education is almost completely a private matter. On the vocational side, industry and other economic sectors organize a wide range of further training courses on an intra- or interfirm level, whereas general adult education is offered by a great number of organizations and associations, sometimes on ideological grounds and sometimes on a commercial basis. About 90 of the most important associations and institutions form the Swiss Federation for Adult Education, founded in 1951. Courses organized by the federation are attended by about 900,000 participants each year, totalling about 17 million participant hours. In vocational further training alone, the number of participants per year is about 500,000, corresponding to about 17 percent of the population in the 25–64 age group.

Participation in continuing education is very clearly a function of the level of basic education: the higher it is, the higher the participation rate in continuing education. One third of the population with a university degree is active in continuing education, whereas the participation rate is only about one-tenth for persons without postcompulsory basic education.

4. Administrative and Supervisory Structure and Operation

As already mentioned, responsibility for education lies essentially with the cantons. Each canton has its own school law and its own system of education. Cantonal governments all have a department of education. In a number of cantons, the government is assisted by an elected consultative body in educational matters (*Erziehungsrat*). The next level of the supervisory structure in many cantons, but not in all, is the district (*Bezirksschulrat*). Local decisions are taken by the local educational authority (*Schulpflege* or *commission scolaire*), a body elected and formed by members of the communal population, in which the local teacher representatives have a consultative voice. Each teacher is supervised by an inspector. In some cantons, these are part-time fellow teachers or lay persons and in other cantons full-time staff of the department of education. As a result of this decentralized multilevel structure, the link between the population and its educational system is very close. On the other hand, since all important decisions are voted on by the population, changes in the system of education are normally very slow.

An educational system characterized by decentralization and by cantonal authority calls for harmonization and coordination. This is the main task of the Swiss Conference of Cantonal Directors of Education (SCCDE), which was founded in 1897, but which has significantly extended its activities since about 1970. Its main constituent bodies are the Concordat on School Coordination (dating from 1970), a number of commissions, and a few institutions. The Concordat stipulates the compulsory school-entrance age (6 years), the duration of compulsory schooling (at least 9 years), and the beginning of the school year. This last point has been widely discussed and put to the vote in a number of cantons (in some of them several times) over a period of more than 10 years. Since the cantons were unable to solve this organizational problem on their own, a popular initiative had finally to be voted on at federal level: by decision of the Swiss population, the school year in all cantons now starts between August and October.

More importantly the provisions of the Concordat aim at common principles for the programs, common textbooks and manuals, and so on. Among the different coordinating bodies of the Conference, the Pedagogical Commission, founded in 1972 and responsible for compulsory school affairs, is probably the most important. Its activity is characterized by a close link between coordination and pedagogical reform.

The SCCDE has a permanent secretariat, and also four regional conferences with regional secretaries: French- and Italian-speaking Switzerland, northwestern, central, and eastern Switzerland (all three of them German speaking). These regions are culturally more homogeneous than the country as a whole and play an important role as an intermediate structure between the national level and the cantons. However, final decisions in most matters are taken by the cantons.

The SCCDE runs several national institutions: the Swiss Educational Documentation Center in Geneva, the Swiss Coordination Center for Research in Education in Aarau, and the Swiss Center for In-service Education of Secondary School Teachers in Lucerne. The first two are institutions common to the conference and the federal government; in this they are an expression of what is called cooperative federalism in education. The same is true for the Swiss University Council (*Schweizerische Hochschulkonferenz*), an intercantonal and federal planning and coordination body for university education. On the other hand, the federal government is assisted in scientific and educational affairs (as far as federal competence goes) by the Swiss Science Council, a consultative body.

5. Educational Finance

Of the total public expenditure for education and research for the year 1989, 53.2 percent of the funds went to compulsory education, 14.5 percent to vocational schools, 12.5 percent to upper-secondary education (other than vocational), 17.7 percent to universities and federal institutes of technology and research, and 2.1 percent to other educational matters. The classification by sources of funding, on the other hand, shows that 12 percent of total public expenditures for education and research were from the confederation, 53.8 percent from the cantons, and 34.2 percent from the communes.

Overall spending on education and research in 1989 was 14,560 million Swiss francs, corresponding

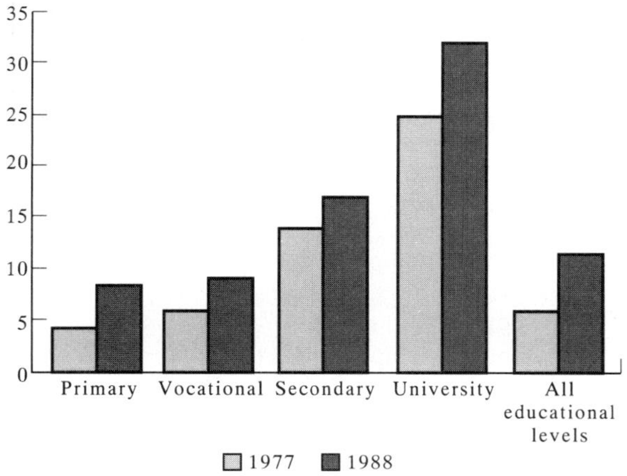

Figure 3
Approximate public expenditure per pupil by educational level (in thousands SF) 1977 and 1988

to 18.6 percent of total public expenditure, making education the recipient of the highest percentage of public spending. Public expenditure on education as a percentage of gross domestic product was about 5 percent.

The financing of universities was originally completely a cantonal matter. The cantons were unable, however, to meet the increase in expenditure resulting from the fast-growing number of students after 1960. In 1968, the federal law of subsidy to the cantonal universities (*Hochschulförderungsgesetz*) was implemented. When the Confederation's financial budget began to meet difficulties in the 1970s, the number of financial resources for the universities had to be enlarged again. Since students from all cantons are enrolled in the eight cantonal universities, the university cantons asked the nonuniversity cantons to contribute to the financing of the universities. In 1981 for the first time, the nonuniversity cantons paid a per capita contribution for each of their students to the university cantons.

Figure 3 shows the approximate public expenditure per pupil/student by educational levels. In 1988, public expenditure per pupil in compulsory schooling varied in the different cantons between 6,739 and 14,421 Swiss francs; 11 cantons spent less than 8,000, 10 cantons between 8,000 and 10,000, and 5 cantons more than 10,000 Swiss francs per pupil.

6. *Supplying Personnel for the Education System*

Despite the diversity of teacher-training institutions, two main types can be identified. The traditional one is the *Seminar*, starting after compulsory schooling and training teacher candidates in a program of typically four years' duration. There is no strict separation in the curriculum between general education and professional preparation. When, in the late 1960s and early 1970s, the *Seminar* became the object of growing criticism, its training being judged insufficient, two alternative solutions were put forward: (a) maintaining the structure of the *Seminar*, but extending the duration to five or six years, and (b) changing the training to a type which already existed in Basle and Geneva. In this second type, candidates first finish upper-secondary education with a *Matura* certificate, thus consolidating their general education, and then undergo professional training of two years' duration at university or in an extrauniversity tertiary education institution such as a *Höhere Pädagogische Lehranstalt* (HPL). In the 1970s, there were reforms in a number of cantons, with a clear trend toward the second type, but the extended *Seminar* type nevertheless retained much of its traditional importance. For at least some time to come, the two types will probably coexist. The teachers trained in the above-mentioned institutions are certified for teaching in primary and, in some cases, lower-secondary education.

Teachers for upper-secondary education obtain their qualification on completion of full academic studies in the field in which they are going to teach. There is an almost general agreement that the professional aspect of their training (courses in pedagogy) should be strengthened. In the part-time vocational schools for apprentices there are different teachers for general education and for vocational specialization. Whereas the latter are normally master artisans with little teacher training, the former are now trained in the Swiss Institute for Vocational Education (*Schweizerisches Institut für Berufspädagogik*), created by the Confederation at the beginning of the 1970s. For all categories of teachers, further training is considered very important; it is partly voluntary and partly compulsory, partly organized by the educational authorities and partly by teacher associations on a cantonal, regional, or sometimes national, level. A few cantons have also created full-time further-training institutes to which teachers can return after a certain number of years of practical work. Such courses normally last six months, during which teachers receive their full salary.

Most teacher-training reforms are heavily influenced by the report "Teacher Training of Tomorrow" (*Lehrerbildung von morgen*), commissioned by the Swiss Conference of Cantonal Directors of Education and published in 1975. Its recommendations include detailed proposals for structure, curriculum, didactic principles, supervision at the beginning of professional activity, and further training. This basic study in teacher training has been completed by official national reports on teacher training for lower-secondary education (1983), upper-secondary education (1989), and further teacher training (1991).

In 1990–91, 8,100 teacher students were trained in over 50 institutions at the upper-secondary level, and

Table 1
Estimate of teaching staff 1987–88

	Primary	Lower secondary
Total	27,000	19,000
Women	16,000	6,000
Men	11,000	13,000

3,900 were trained in around 120 institutions at the extrauniversity tertiary education level; the first figure has decreased (from 9,900), the second figure has increased (from 3,100) over the last ten years, thus confirming the trend toward tertiary level teacher training.

Teacher statistics at the national level still do not exist. Table 1 shows an estimate of total teaching staff for compulsory schooling; in primary education there are more women than men, whereas the opposite is true for lower-secondary education.

Compared with other countries, teacher salaries in Switzerland are among the highest: for the early 1990s, the average salary of a primary teacher having reached the top of his or her salary scale has been estimated at US$57,900. However, there is considerable variation between the different cantons.

Teacher assessment other than by the traditional inspectorate has become an issue in the early 1990s. Some cantons are likely to introduce salary effective assessment systems, one model being based on external evaluation, and the other more on self-evaluation.

7. *Curriculum Development and Teaching Methodology*

As with most functions of the educational system, curriculum development is a cantonal matter. Basically, each canton has its own curricula for compulsory schooling. In the 1970s and 1980s, almost all cantons revised their curricula. The development process normally involves a considerable number of cantonal commissions and working parties (overall, by level, and by subject matter) including relevant teacher participation. Two of the four educational regions have founded regional research and development institutions, the *Institut romand de recherches et de documentation pédagogiques (IRDP)* for French- and Italian-speaking Switzerland and the *Zentralschweizerischer Beratungsdienst für Schulfragen (ZBS)* for central Switzerland. Among other tasks, these institutes are in charge of developing common curricula for all of the cantons in their region. At the national level—but this only holds for mathematics and foreign language teaching—there is some curriculum coordination by general recommendations and so-called "meeting points" (setting subject standards which should be met at given levels of compulsory schooling).

At the level of upper-secondary education, there are centrally developed curricula for vocational training and, for the first time in the history of Swiss education, national curricula recommendations for *Maturitätsschulen*, published in 1992 (*Rahmenlehrpläne für Maturitätsschulen*).

In teaching methodology and instruction materials, the individual teacher usually has considerable freedom. In addition to a few compulsory textbooks (regulation varies from canton to canton), he or she can normally choose among a wide range of optional learning materials. There are many reform and development projects in the field of teaching methodology, with a general trend toward more group work and individualized learning (e.g., the important regional project "Enlarged learning forms" or *Erweiterte Lernformen* of the early 1990s in north-western Switzerland).

8. *The System of Examinations, Promotions, and Certifications*

One of the characteristics of the Swiss educational system underlined by the OECD (1991) in its review of the Swiss national policy for education is its selectivity. The first important and often decisive point of selection is the transition from primary to lower-secondary education. The decision whether a pupil will attend either the basic or extended lower-secondary education is normally taken (in varying ways in the different cantons) on the basis of school performance during the last year of primary education and/or a special examination and/or teachers' advice and/or parents' opinion, the latter two factors becoming more and more important. As far as promotion from one grade to the other is concerned, one out of six pupils misses promotion to the next grade at least once in the course of compulsory schooling; this means that he or she has to repeat that grade.

Normally there is no special examination and therefore no special certificate at the end of compulsory education, but at the end of upper secondary education there is one. Apprenticeship ends with a final examination (the same all over the country) and a certificate. *Maturitätsschulen* also end with a final examination according to national regulations; the *Matura* certificate gives free access (without additional admission examination) to all Swiss universities.

9. *Educational Assessment, Evaluation, and Research*

Research in education has a relatively long tradition in French-speaking Switzerland, where Edouard Claparède (1873–1940) and Pierre Bovet (1878–1965)

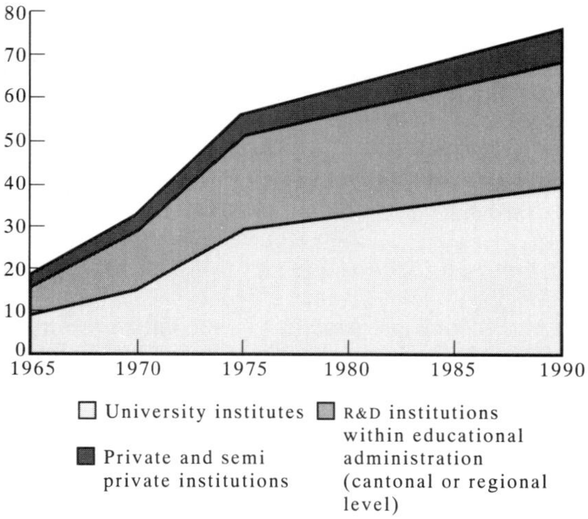

Figure 4
Quantitative evolution of R&D institutions in education 1965–90

founded the Jean-Jacques Rousseau Institute in 1912. Jean Piaget (1896–1980) also worked in this institute, which has now become the Faculty of Psychology and Education Sciences of the University of Geneva. In German-speaking Switzerland, educational research was almost exclusively philosophically based until the Second World War. Experimental and empirical research in education started with research institutes being founded in the late 1960s and the early 1970s (see Fig. 4). Three main types of institutions can be distinguished: (a) university institutes, mostly in the fields of education, psychology, or sociology; (b) institutions within the framework of educational administration at the cantonal or regional level (most of them with an emphasis on development activities); and (c) private and semipublic institutions. The importance of research in education was officially underlined by the Swiss Science Council on several occasions. In its 1973 report on urgent research needs, research in education was among the few disciplines to be given top priority.

The establishment, in 1971, of the Swiss Coordination Centre for Research in Education was a result of an initiative of the Science Council. This center, whose main task consists of promoting research and coordination between research, teaching practice, administration, and politics, publishes information on research and development projects. These continuing surveys show that research, on the whole, is still fairly scattered and dispersed, that small projects dominate, and that only a few institutions are able to work with effect and continuity.

There were and are three large nationwide projects. *Education et vie active* (Education and Active Life 1979–85) was a national research program, financed by the Swiss National Science Foundation. The program had three parts: (a) personality development and vocational training in the work situation, (b) organizational problems in vocational training institutions and the organization of teaching and learning processes, and (c) transition problems in careers and the life cycle. *Überprüfung der Situation der Primarschule* (General Review of the Situation of Primary Education, 1978–86) had four parts: (a) goals of primary education—claims and reality, (b) functions and forms of pupil evaluation, (c) transition from preschool to primary education, and (d) cooperation between schools and parents. The National Research Program "The Efficiency of our Education and Training Systems," 1991–97, again financed by the Swiss National Science Foundation, aims at increasing the self-evaluation and innovation capacity of educational subsystems and institutions.

The increasing vitality of research in education in Switzerland and a growing consciousness of its importance are also demonstrated by the foundation, in 1975, of the Swiss Society for Research in Education (SSRE). The society publishes a scientific review called *Bildungsforschung und Bildungspraxis/ Education et Recherche* (Research and Practice in Education), and in 1988, it presented a "Development Plan for Educational Research in Switzerland."

Since the end of the 1980s, Switzerland has also been participating in the international projects of the International Association for the Evaluation of Educational Achievement (IEA). In 1992, a National Coordination Conference for Educational Research Policy, involving the most important federal and cantonal authorities in this field, was founded.

10. Major Reforms in the 1980s and 1990s

The major reforms in the 1980s and 1990s were:

(a) earlier start of second language learning (fourth or fifth grade of primary education);

(b) curricula revision in mathematics as well as most other subjects of compulsory education;

(c) introduction of the computer into lower- and upper-secondary (and sometimes primary) education;

(d) measures aiming at closing the gap between general and vocational education at the upper-secondary level (introduction of a vocational *Matura* certificate);

(e) revision of the *Matura* examination regulations;

(f) restructuring of the extrauniversity tertiary level of education (*Fachhochschulen*);

(g) ongoing reform of basic and further teacher training.

11. Major Problems for the Year 2000

Any prognosis of future problems is partially subjective, the appraisal of the future depending, among other things, on value judgments which differ from political party to political party. Nonetheless, some of the major problems which may have to be faced by the Swiss educational system around the year 2000 are given below.

As in many other countries, Switzerland, in the first half of the 1990s, is suffering from financial restrictions in public expenditure, not excluding education. This might have an impact on the quality of education (i.e., teacher–student ratio, failure to create necessary new chairs at university level, postponement of planned reforms, etc.). Depending upon the economic development in the second half of the 1990s, relative lack of public financial resources for education might still be a major problem around the year 2000.

Given the fact that the Swiss system of education has a federal structure, one of its permanent problems—and this will be the same around the year 2000—is the search for the degree of coordination and harmonization at national level judged necessary even in a decentralized structure. With a more strongly integrated Europe—irrespective of whether Switzerland will be a member of the EC or not—and other factors, the trend seems to be toward strengthening coordination and harmonization and thereby also strengthening the national aspects of educational policy. To state it simply, the question is: will Switzerland—in spite of its federal structure—have a national policy of education or not?

Some limited progress has been made toward the equalization of educational opportunity. Nevertheless, socioeconomic origin, gender, and regional origin still play an important role in a school career. Thus, measures which favor equal educational opportunity will still be a major problem in the year 2000.

If one accepts the hypothesis that, on the one hand, the growing complexity of life calls for even more education in the future, and that, on the other hand, duration of initial formal education should not be further prolonged (the discrepancy between the biological and socioeconomic status of many young people being most probably one of the roots of youth unrest), then the challenge arises to provide more education without prolonging initial education. The solution to this problem may be sought among the principles of lifelong and recurrent education. This would require structural changes in tertiary and upper-secondary education and have an impact on the whole system of education. It could at the same time provide for an extension of adult education and its gradual integration into the system. Given the participation structure in further education, it will be difficult not to widen the gap between the relatively well-educated and the relatively poorly educated parts of the population.

Other structural reforms will probably focus on lower-secondary education in an attempt to reduce the qualitative differences between schools with basic and schools with extended requirements. Reforms of teacher training for this level of education will have to be introduced, along with structural reforms.

It may be assumed that education has the following fundamental functions: (a) development of the personality (in a broad sense); (b) qualification (in a restricted economic sense); (c) socialization (transmission of values, integration into society); and (d) distribution and legitimation of social status. For the coming years, and even decades, increasing conflicts between some of these functions can be predicted (personality development versus qualifications asked for by the economy, or social-status aspirations versus qualifications needed by the economy). Therefore, the search for an equilibrium between these functions is likely to be a problem in the near future.

References

Organisation for Economic Co-operation and Development (OECD) 1991 *Reviews of National Policies for Education: Switzerland*. OECD, Paris

Schweizerische Konferenz der kantonalen Erziehungsdirektoren (EDK) 1975 *Lehrerbildung von morgen*. EDK, Bern

Schweizerische Konferenz der kantonalen Erziehungsdirektoren (EDK) 1992 *Rahmenlehrpläne für die Maturitätsschulen*. EDK, Bern

Schweizerischer Nationalfonds zur Förderung der wissenschaftlichen Forschung (SNF) 1991 *Die Wirksamkeit unserer Bildungssysteme angesichts der demographischen und technologischen Entwicklung und angesichts der Probleme in der mehrsprachigen Schweiz*. Ausführungsplan zum Nationalen Forschungsprogramm 33, SNF, Bern

Swiss Co-ordination Centre for Research in Education *Permanent Inquiry into Educational Research*. Swiss Coordination Centre for Research in Education, Aarau

Further Reading

Bundesamt für Statistik (BFS) 1990 *Der Weiterbildungsbereich—Entwicklung, Strukturen, Forschungsstand*. BFS, Bern

Bundesamt für Statistik (BFS), Schweizerische Konferenz der kantonalen Erziehungsdirektoren (EDK) 1993 *Bildungsindikatoren Schweiz*. BFS, EDK, Bern

Federal Statistical Office, Federal Administration of Finances, CESDOC 1991 *The Swiss Educational Mosaic—A Study in Diversity*. Swiss Federal Statistical Office, Bern

Schweizerische Gesellschaft für Bildungsforschung (SGBF/SSRE) 1988 *Entwicklungsplan der schweizerischen Bildungsforschung. Sondernummer von Bildungsforschung und Bildungspraxis*. Schweizerische Koordinationsstelle für Bildungsforschung, Aarau

Schweizerische Konferenz der kantonalen Erziehungsdirektoren (EDK) 1983 *Die Ausbildung der Lehrer für die Sekundarstufe I*. EDK, Bern

Schweizerische Konferenz der kantonalen Erziehungsdirektoren (EDK) 1986 *Primarschule Schweiz. 22 Thesen zur Entwicklung der Primarschule*. EDK, Bern
Schweizerische Konferenz der kantonalen Erziehungsdirektoren (EDK) *Bildung in der Schweiz von morgen*. Literaturanalyse 1988, Expertenbefragung 1989, Schlussbericht 1990. EDK, Bern
Schweizerische Konferenz der kantonalen Erziehungsdirektoren (EDK) 1992 *Reform des Fremdsprachenunterrichts in der obligatorischen Schule*. EDK, Bern

A. Gretler

Syllabus

Syllabi are organizers of course content and are undoubtedly one of the oldest teaching tools in formal education. They are vehicles by which organization and structure of intended learnings are communicated from teacher to learner and teacher to teacher, and by authorities in systems of education to teachers and learners.

1. Need for Syllabi

As frameworks, syllabi by definition are the organizing documents in areas of instruction. Under some systems of instruction they become highly formalized, authority-oriented instruments which control the amount of decision-making that teacher and learner can take. In other systems they are more informal documents, operating as general guides to the teacher.

Despite a paucity of literature and studies of the organization and influence of syllabi on curriculum, teachers, and learners, syllabi are a focal point in curriculum and are given considerable attention in all systems of education. In developing countries where national systems of education are under formulation, it is customary to induce organization and achieve coordination through the writing of syllabi for curriculum areas that traverse grade levels. Thus syllabi are viewed as fundamental instruments for the shaping of curriculum and the guiding of curriculum processes. They are both implicitly and explicitly needed by those who give direction to curriculum, whether they are classroom teachers or administrative authorities who exercise educational and political control over curriculum (Tyler 1977).

2. Variety of Syllabi

Syllabi take many forms and shapes and are of varying lengths. They may be simple one-page course descriptions; they may describe a course that is presented for a fixed period of time, such as one semester or one year; they may be lengthy documents covering the full range and organization of subject matter and suggested ways of implementing it in classrooms over several years, such as syllabi on a science or mathematics program spanning kindergarten through grade eight. Notwithstanding the apparent difference in documents, which could range from one page to 300 pages, they share a common concern of transmission of knowledge on how to formulate and organize a curriculum area. In some countries the organization and issuing of syllabi are solely invested in a central authority. In other decentralized systems of education the formulation and use of syllabi is left almost exclusively to the teachers who are directly concerned with the transmitting of subject matter in the classroom. Between these two extremes there are a number of positions on the development and use of syllabi, and they are frequently the chief products of curriculum development activities in instructional departments of a school, school system, or state educational agency.

3. Legal Status

Syllabi have a mixed status in the legal codes of political systems inasmuch as their enforcement in classroom use is compounded by other variables involved in determining teacher competency and efficiency. In the United States, where syllabi are frequently adopted (upon presentation of a written product) by formal action of the governing political authority, the School Board, they achieve a legal status. Similarly the determination and legal enforcement of course content through syllabi in institutions of higher education has been upheld by the courts: "Governing bodies of colleges, universities and other schools acting through their deans, department heads and duly constituted faculty committees, have a right to develop curriculum, determine course content, and impose methods of institution, and teachers are obligated to comply with their directions in this regard" (Riggin 1986 p. 630). However, a search of the United States case law on teacher court trials for incompetency and inefficiency failed to turn up cases where a teacher's dismissal hinged specifically on failure to abide by the syllabus for their courses. In court cases where a teacher was charged with incompetency and inefficiency and the charge of failure to follow a prescribed syllabus was made, the charge was buried within a series of others, (e.g., failure to observe proper classroom discipline, lack of knowledge of prescribed content, failure to organize and prepare for class, failure to maintain a climate conducive to pupils' learning, failure to carry out responsibilities to cooperate with other faculty members on curriculum and scheduling, failure to accept advice from supervisors on instructional improvement, or lack of self-control in the classroom) (Root 1977). Failure to follow a syllabus, when included, was not a singular charge; and while giving credence to the belief that a syllabus is a document commanding legal status in the educational world it did not assume in the court records a commanding position on which a teacher's continued employment was solely contingent. Informal conversation with teachers and administrators in the northeast United States found that they viewed the syllabus not as a legal contract, but as a guide assisting them with direction and organization of content to enable learners to move smoothly from one level or grade to the next with a mastery of essential subject matter concepts. This is not to imply that teachers feel no pressure to abide by the syllabus, for this pressure stems from other sources—most commonly, required and centrally administered examinations which are curriculum validated. Teachers whose students perform poorly on these examinations are seen to be accountable for the student's poor performances and their teaching competency is called into question. A syllabus and its implementation in the classroom is more likely to be enforced through an examination system than through a more cumbersome legal system.

When syllabi are formulated by centralized national systems to direct the subject matter to be taught, they take on the dominant political ideology of the government. Under these conditions, what are viewed by professional educators as technical tools to assist the teacher in selecting and organizing large bodies of subject matter can become documents over which political battles ensue as contending factions attempt to entrench their brand of prescribed wisdom in the chief educational documents that determine the subject matter to be selected and taught to students. Certain subject areas, such as the social sciences (history, government, and economics), and to a lesser extent the sciences, are focuses for these ideological battles. In the social sciences they are sparked by differing interpretations of the "facts," or disagreement over which facts should receive priority. In some instances the strength of feeling of advocates is so high that not only are selected facts presented, but opposing facts are suppressed (Auster 1991). In the sciences they revolve around theories, particularly evolution, and factual interpretations that confront religious beliefs.

The social sciences are prone to influence from politicians and interest groups who see syllabi as mechanisms for promoting special interests. These conflicts have erupted in strained relations between countries since the start of the 1980s, as in the case of the Republic of China and Japan over the interpretation given in course materials to the Japanese incursion into China in the 1930s which led into the Second World War and the devastation of both countries. The Chinese government at the start of the 1990s desires more explicit coverage of these events in Japanese course materials as acts of Japanese aggression upon a peaceful, nonthreatening, neighboring country. It also wants the content of the courses to convey a sense of the immorality and injustice of nationalistic aggression. Japanese educational authorities have not been receptive to these suggested emphases (New York Times 1989).

Within any country, tensions between cultural and special interest groups in controlling and directing syllabus content are similar to international disputes, except the parties to the dispute have convenient forums in the schools and communities. In one well-known dispute over a revision in a social studies syllabus for use in California schools, special interest groups who wanted their point of view added to the curriculum fought their cause at the state level and continued the battle in the adoption of course materials at the local school level.

Where teachings in science confront religious beliefs, syllabi become focuses for political action and targets for suppression. The theory of evolution and its consequences for organizing and interpreting scientific data has been a source of contention in syllabus writing and adoption. Of interest to the professional educator in these conflicts is the preoccupation with the inclusion or exclusion of subject matter, neglect of teacher and peer influence on student attitudes, and how these attitudes are shaped in the transmission of subject matter. In most of these cases it appears that passion overrides knowledge of cognitive psychology (Shulman 1986).

As organizers of instruction, syllabi have a long tradition in formal education. In a sense, textbooks were a result of an attempt to organize the instructional area conceptually so that it could be transmitted in a more efficient, consistent manner by many teachers. Syllabi gave educational authorities some confidence that there was a body of knowledge being consistently transmitted to a number of learners by different teachers. Control of syllabi has been seen as a way of controlling curricula, and attempts to shape curricula rely heavily upon syllabi as the vehicles. Most syllabi come in written form: course outlines, units of work, guides, lists of materials to be taught, and suggested or prescribed methodology for the teacher. A new development is the electronic storage and production of subject matter whereby control of subject matter and the way students can interact with it are largely within a computer. The building of syllabi constitutes, in most educational systems, the major curriculum development effort. There are different philosophical positions on how best to develop a syllabus in order to guarantee its implementation in the educational system, and this is the subject of curriculum development literature. The common framework of a syllabus includes the provisioning of curriculum constructs (Mosback 1990).

4. *Content of Syllabi*

Not all curriculum components are provisioned in every syllabus but there are implicit assumptions as decisions are made on the way subject matter and learning activities are organized in a unit of instruction (Niedermeyer 1990). The first step in syllabus organization is to establish a rationale for the unit of instruction being planned. Within this rationale, curriculum developers will ordinarily assume a position on why subject matter should be taught, usually involving the society in which the learner will live or the learner's need for the subject matter. Decisions in the area of rationale are crucial because they predicate many other decisions on provisioning of constructs within the syllabus. There are positions that reconcile the needs of the society and the needs of the learner, as well as positions that advocate the preeminence of one or the other in the decision-making process (Dewey 1948). Once the rationale is explicated, the other constructs of aims and objectives, organization of specific subject matter (scope and sequence), modes of transaction (methodology of instruction), and evaluation are usually provisioned for the user of the syllabus. Syllabi can be developed for learners as well as for teachers.

4.1 Aims and Objectives

Aims and objectives define the conceptual map on which a syllabus will be based. There is a wide range of formats for statements of aims and objectives. They may be quite vague and considered implicit in the provisions made for the other curriculum constructs. If a syllabus is developed by a central authority, careful attention will usually be given to aims and objectives, for they are seen as guides to classroom activity and to shaping and directing a curriculum from a central authority. Whether aims and objectives will be fixed or evolve from activities of students or subject matter is another continuum for curriculum writers of a syllabus. Whether aims and objectives are prescribed or discretionary for the teacher/learner will also shape the framework and the use of the syllabus. Moreover, it is not uncommon for there to be a priority listing of aims and objectives to order them within the unit of instruction, across several units of instruction, or within the total scope of subject matter across school grades or systems of education. Most syllabus writers assume some hierarchy of instruction as they write aims and objectives. For example, a student who is not going to become a mathematician or pursue activities that require in-depth knowledge of advanced mathematics has different goals in the study of mathematics than one who is going to pursue it as a major life activity or be involved in a profession where it is required for success.

Objectives in a syllabus may be macro, that is, tying together large elements of subject matter; or they may be micro, where they specify intended learning outcomes for a student and categorize them according to the type of learning involved. An example of this difference would be the macro objective,"the student will understand the importance of being a contributing citizen to his or her country through work, participation in the support of government, and willingness to defend his or her country." An example of a micro objective, which would be contributory towards this macro objective, would be: "the student will be able to do basic addition in day-to-day activities in which he or she encounters the use of numbers in buying products, or necessities of life."

The organization of subject matter, particularly the scope (what is taught) and sequence (the order in which it is taught), has occupied a major place in syllabi. The organization of subject matter may provide a list of intended learning outcomes as stated within the subject matter framework (Romenets et al. 1985). Syllabi usually limit the scope, since subject matter in most instructional areas has increased to a level whereby a major curriculum development activity involves choosing what should be taught or ignored. Setting the scope of subject matter is often undertaken by a central authority, especially where political goals are pursued through the educational system. Examination of curricula for bias is often done through review of the scope for inclusion or exclusion of subject matters.

The sequence of a curriculum may be organized through several approaches making assumptions about whether the logical organization of subject matter, or the psychological approach of the learner, ought to be of primary consideration. The organization of the conceptual map of a syllabus is the reconciliation of logical relationships in subject matter with a sequence, consistent with the individual's learning process (Lynch 1987). The quality of scope and sequence is critical to the ease with which students absorb the learnings of the instructional area and to the development of longer-term learner interest in material. Another form used in syllabi along with conceptual maps is flow charts, depicting the relationships between the complex skills to be taught. Much of the controversy over syllabi revolves around scope and sequence activities and reflects different assumptions about the way subject matter is organized and the way learning proceeds (Schwab 1983).

4.2 Modes of Transaction (Methodology)

Syllabi directed at teachers are often exclusively oriented to specification of the modes of transaction that are to be used in the curriculum. These teacher prescriptions are featured where the methodological approach is viewed as a major learning outcome for students and as critical to their advancement in the subject matter (Geographic Education National Implementation Project 1989). Where there is an abundance of pedagogical resources, syllabi assist teachers in selecting among them for greater efficiency in student learning. The learner verification of materials, a new development in the creation of instructional materials, helps teachers to know what types of learner outcome to expect. Frequently, the syllabus will contain a list of essential materials that must be purchased and incorporated into the curriculum if the syllabus is to be implemented as written. In some newer approaches where syllabi are becoming part of an electronics instructional system, formed around computers and word processors, the modes of transaction are specified by the way the subject matter is controlled and presented to students (Smith and Sherwood 1976). If there is a highly structured approach to the modes of transaction, authorities are moving to the position that the prescribed mode should be learner verified in advance of their commitment to a syllabus which then becomes the authorized course of study. Some syllabi provide the modes of transaction as an instructional plan which presents in sequence: (a) what each unit is about; (b) what the desired aim or learning outcomes of each unit are; and (c) prescribed general teaching strategies to accomplish intended learning outcomes.

4.3 Evaluation in Syllabi

Evaluation tools for use by teachers and learners are frequently part of the syllabus framework. They may be written tests or other types of measurement instruments placed within the instructional process either to give the student immediate feedback, or to inform the teacher or other educational authority whether the student is achieving those aims and objectives. Syllabi will at times give attention to the main effects of learning outcomes as products that are idiosyncratic to the interaction of teacher, learner, and subject matter. Consequently, syllabi may provide suggestions on ways of gathering data on side effects, as well as main effects, of instruction. Where evaluation is directed toward controlling effects of curriculum and teaching, procedures of evaluation may become separated from the syllabus; the teacher and learner will know only that there will be an evaluation from an outside source the syllabus, its use, and learning outcomes. This form of outside examination is used where the curriculum is determined by a central authority and uniformity across the diversity of contexts is important.

5. Utilization and Future of Syllabi

There has been relatively little systematic evaluation of syllabi although the way the constructs are provisioned, the attention given to the paradoxes, and contradictions are a rich source of information for the evaluation of a curriculum framework in syllabus form (Eash 1970, 1972, 1974; Newfield 1982). The syllabuses examined for this entry overwhelmingly reflect an engineering rather than a scientific approach to learning. Where they are influenced by the curriculum recommendations of major societies, they reveal a greater awareness of research on instruction and learning (Fleming 1991). Publishers' uses of syllabi to guide the development of textbooks ranged from close attention to no attention. The future of curriculum syllabi is guaranteed by the need for more formal education in increasingly larger sectors of populations. The form of future curriculum syllabi is not as clear. With increased knowledge about the individual's ability to process information, and the further knowledge of the way subject matter can be conceptually organized so that the network of concepts becomes more readily available in less time to a greater number of learners, it might be expected that frameworks and forms of syllabi will rapidly change from the traditional written statements that have been characteristic of the syllabi of the past.

See also: Curriculum as a Field of Study; Curriculum, History of; Curriculum: Sociological Perspectives; Evaluation: A Tylerian Perspective; Evaluation, Nature of

References

Auster L 1991 The Mondo baffo of the New York regents: A report from Albany. *Measure* 100: 1–3

Dewey J 1949 *Reconstruction in Philosophy*, enlarged edn. Beacon, Boston, Massachusetts

Eash M 1969 *Evaluation of instructional materials for exceptional children and youth.* A preliminary instrument. Resources in Education. Educational Resources Information Center (ERIC). Document No. ED 040-540. National Institute of Education, Educational Resources Information Center, Washington, DC.

Eash M 1972 Developing an instrument for evaluating instructional materials. *Curric. Theo.* 8–9: 193–220

Eash M 1974 *Evaluating instructional materials.* In: Hitchens H (ed.) 1974 *Selecting Media for Learning. Readings from Audio Visual Instruction.* Association for Education Communications and Technology, Washington, DC

Fleming D B 1991 Social studies reform and global education: California and New York and the report of the National Commission on the Social Studies. *Social Studies* 82(1): 11–15

Geographic Education National Implementation Project 1989 American Geographical Society, Association of American Geographers, National Council for Geographic Education, National Geographic Society

John Root versus Board of Education of the Fulton Consolidated School District, Fulton, New York and Glenn W. Clark, as Superintendent, respondents. Supreme Court Appellate Division, Fourth Department, November 14, 1977. *New York Supplement 2d series* 399 p. 785

Lynch D J 1987 How to write a curriculum guide to specify content and sequence objectives. *Southern Social Studies Quarterly* 13(2): 65–71

Mosback 1990 National syllabus and textbook design on communicative principles: English every day *ELT Journal* 44(1): 18–24

Newfield J 1982 Teacher influence: A key concept for writing useful curriculum guides. *Education* 102(4): 389–98

New York Times 8 October 1989 Japan and the War: Debate on censors is renewed. 1: 8,1
Niedermeyer F C 1990 Educational technology looks at industry-sponsored Economics programs *Soc. Educ.* 54(2): 96–99
Richard E Riggin versus Board of Trustees of Ball State University and Robert P Bell as President of Ball State University. Indiana Court of Appeals. 1986. *North-eastern Reporter 489 2nd Series* pp 629–30.
Romenets V A et al. 1985 An interdisciplinary approach to the development of curricula and syllabi at the Moscow Institute of Steel and Alloys. *Higher Educ. Eur.* 10(4): 60–66
Schwab J 1983 The Practical 4: Something for curriculum professors to do. *Curric. Inq.* 13(3): 239–65
Shulman L A 1986 Paradigms and research programs in the study of teaching. In: Whittrock M C (ed.) 1986 *Handbook of Research on Teaching* (3rd edn.) Macmillan, New York
Smith S G, Sherwood B A 1976 Educational uses of the Plato computer system. *Science* 192: 344–52
Tyler R W 1977 Desirable content for a curriculum syllabus today. In: Molnar A, Zahorik J A (eds.) 1977 *Curriculum Theory*. Association for Supervision and Curriculum Development, Washington, DC

Further Reading

Godwin D 1970 The Structure of Knowledge. *Educ. Theory* 20(4): 319–28
Greeno J 1976 Cognitive objectives of instruction: Theory of Knowledge for solving problems and answering questions. In: Klahr D (ed.) 1976 *Cognition and Instruction*. Erlbaum, Hillsdale, New Jersey
Popham W J, Baker E L 1970 *Systematic Instruction*. Prentice-Hall, Englewood Cliffs, New Jersey
Posner G, Strike K 1976 A categorization scheme for principles of sequencing content. *Rev. Educ. Res.* 46(4): 665–90
Posner G J, Rudnitsky A N 1982 *Course Design: A Guide to Curriculum Development for Teachers,* 2nd edn. Longman, New York
Tyler R W 1950 *Basic Principles of Curriculum and Instruction: Syllabus for Education*. University of Chicago Press, Chicago, Illinois

M. Eash

Syria: System of Education

1. General Background

Historically, "Syria" was the name of the fertile strip between the eastern Mediterranean coast and the desert of northern Arabia, covering almost all the present northern Arabic countries of the Middle East except for Iraq. In 1992, Syria is a relatively small country on the eastern side of the Mediterranean sea.

The geographical shape of the state was determined at the beginning of the French mandate in 1920. Syria is bordered by Turkey on the north, Iraq on the east, Jordan and Israel on the south, and Lebanon and the Mediterranean Sea on the west. Its total area is 185,180 square kilometers, of which eight million hectares are arable.

The principal result of the First World War for the Middle East was the termination of the Ottoman occupation of Syria which had lasted for four centuries (1516–1918), and the setting up of a Hashemite kingdom under King Faisal I. This lasted until July 1920, when Syria and Lebanon were occupied and controlled by France under a League of Nations mandate. The French forces left Syria in April 1946 and Independence was declared.

Between 1945 and 1958, a representative regime was installed; but it was frequently interrupted by military coup d'états. A political union with Egypt, under the name of the "United Arab Republic," was declared in 1958; but this was terminated in September 1961. Since then, the country has been known as the "Syrian Arab Republic." The regime installed by the military forces in 1961 was abolished by a second military coup in March 1963. Since 1963, the Baath Socialist Party has been in power.

The present constitution of Syria was approved and promulgated in 1973. It defines the Syrian Arab Republic as a democratic sovereign, and socialist state. The political regime can be viewed as a mixture of a presidential and a representative regime. It gives the president, the chief executive, the predominant share of power. The president, who is elected for a seven-year term, chooses the vice president, the prime minister, and the cabinet ministers. The legislative function is vested in the People's Assembly, which has grown to 250 members. The number of parties allowed to operate in Syria is limited. They recognize the leadership of the Baath Party and run under its umbrella. These parties are represented through the ruling "National Progressive Front" and the government.

The Front obtained two-thirds of the seats in the parliamentary election held in May 1990. Independents, of whom 21 are women, received the other third of the seats.

Arabic is the mother tongue of more than 80 percent of the Syrian population: estimated to be 12,116,000 in the middle of 1990. Arabic is also the official language and is spoken by all of the population. The other spoken languages are: Kurdish, Armenian, Turkish, Circassian, Syriac, and Hebrew. English and French are the main foreign languages taught in the schools.

The population is concentrated mainly along the coast and in the plain region parallel to the coast, with probably equal settlement in 1990 in rural and urban areas. The highest density of population is in western and southern regions. The overall density is relatively low: 66 inhabitants per square kilometer. The low density is due to two main factors: (a) an important part of the territory is desert; and (b) the country's historical background of being susceptible to invasion—an unfavorable condition for the settlement of people. The demographic growth, which is one of the highest rates in the world, increased from 3.28 percent per annum between 1960 and 1970 to 3.35 percent per annum between 1970 and 1981. It has remained at this high level. Thus, the age structure of the Syrian population is very young with more than 49 percent of the people below the age of 15.

The main demographic factors influencing education and development are:

(a) a high population growth rate;

(b) an increasing proportion of children below the age of 15 among the total population;

(c) an unequal distribution of population growth throughout the country: the rural—urban migration is declining but is still significant. (Urban areas are still growing at a higher rate than rural ones (3.9 vs. 2.9) due essentially to the migration from rural to urban areas.)

Historically, Syria's economy has been agriculturally based. However, industrialization campaigns since the early 1960s have built a good-sized industrial base. The Syrian economy showed slight changes in terms of the structure and distribution of employment in the 1980s.

Employment in agriculture accounted for about one-third of the labor force (16% of GDP in 1980). At the end of 1980s, it dropped to about one-fourth of the GDP, and remained approximately the same in 1990. Similarly, the industrial sector, which accounted for 28 percent of the labor force and 37 percent of the GDP in the early 1980s, showed little variation (one-third for employment) at the beginning of the 1990s due to stagnation in the economic situation during this period. In fact, the main changes in the structure and the distribution of employment were achieved in the 1970s.

Some 44 percent of the Syrian population is of working age; 15- to 59-years old. Only one-fourth of the total population comprised the labor force in 1990, of which 6 percent were unemployed. Female participation in the labor force was 16 percent. The dependence ratio is high as a result of the youthful concentration of the age structure and low female participation in the labor force. For the country as a whole, there are four dependents for each active person. Consequently, the rapid economic development is difficult to achieve, particularly when a significant level of investment is oriented to satisfy the basic social needs of the population (i.e., education, health).

On the other hand, the labor market shows sectoral imbalance between supply and demand (shortage, excess) in several jobs and specialties in the labor force.

Syria was the site of many great cultural centers in ancient times, with famous names like Ugarit, Mari, Elba, Palmira, Damascus, and Aleppo. The earliest known alphabet, dating back to the fourteenth century BC, was discovered in Ugarit.

During the Ottoman occupation (1516–1918), the schools' objective was to teach the Koran; the principles of religion; and the rudiments of reading, writing, and arithmetic. *Sharia* and language were taught to adults. Through contact with the West, the introduction of some educational reforms led gradually to the foundation of Ottoman state schools in the 1850s which prepared students to serve the ruling authorities. Education was extended outside the control of the Ottoman authorities by foreign mission schools and Christian communities with the protection of foreign powers. Only some of them taught Arabic. Thus, the model of the modern schools in terms of their content, methods, and materials appeared as both a revolutionary innovation and a rupture.

Syria had more state schools than other Arab provinces, but Ottoman expenditure on Syrian education was very limited. Most people remained illiterate. Education was restricted to the sons of famous people and civil servants, and Turkish was the medium of instruction.

The Arab State under King Faisal (1918–20) had a beneficial impact on education by initiating some important and symbolic educational projects. It made Arabic the instructional language; founded new schools based on the Occidental models; and established the Academy of Arabic, the Arab Scientific Society, the School of Law, and the Institute of Medicine.

The constitution of 1928, initiated under the French Mandate (1920–46), provided that:

(a) Education should be free and the primary level should be compulsory.

(b) Arabic should be the official language in the public sector.

(c) Technical education should be imposed as compulsory in order to meet the country's needs for technical personnel.

Only some of the above reforms were implemented before the mandate ended. The French authorities managed education according to their objectives. In 1945, only 5 percent of the state budget was allocated to education and the schools were located mainly in towns.

Soon after Independence, many decisions were taken, such as the opening of the Higher Teachers' College in 1946, the establishment of the National Cultural Committee for the Organization of Education, the Law on Vocational Training, the regulation for primary education in 1948, the standardization of textbooks in 1949, and so on. In 1947, the budget of the Ministry of Education rose to 16 percent of the state budget and the number of students increased by about 40 percent from the 1946 level. During the Period of Unity with Egypt (1958–61) the conversion from a five- to six-year primary school, with automatic promotion from grade to grade, was introduced. An attempt to unify primary and secondary schools curricula between the two countries was also undertaken.

2. *Politics and the Goals of the Education System*

Education was strongly supported by the government in the 1960s, particularly when the Baath Party came to power. However, the policy and the content of education were, to some extent, influenced by its principles and ideology.

The established educational and curriculum goals are stated in several articles in the 1973 Constitution:

> The educational and cultural system shall aim to bring up a national Arab generation who are socialist and scientific in their manner of thinking, attached to their land and history, proud of their heritage . . .. The national socialist culture shall be the basis of building up the unified Arab society. It shall aim at enhancing moral values, realizing the ideals of the Arab Nation . . .. Science, scientific research and all scientific achievements constitute a mean for the progress of Arab socialist society. The state shall give it full support. Education shall be a right guaranteed by the state. It shall be free at all stages and compulsory in the primary steps. The state shall endeavor to make other stages compulsory, shall supervize education, and direct it in a manner ensuring its adaptation to the needs of society and production.

These objectives can be best interpeted by taking them out of their general framework and making them the basis for the curriculum strategies.

3. *The Formal System of Education*

Figure 1 presents the formal system of education.

3.1 Primary, Secondary, and Tertiary Education

The education system of Syria consists of 1–3 years of preprimary education, 6 years of primary education, 3 years of lower-secondary and intermediate education, and 3 years of secondary education. Post-secondary education may be undertaken at a university, higher institute of technology, or an intermediate institute.

In 1990, school enrollment was close to 100 percent for boys and 95 percent for girls at the primary level. Before 1981, primary education was free but not compulsory. To achieve compulsory education, a large campaign was mounted to encourage parents to enroll all children of primary school age. Special measures were taken to enroll children between 10 and 12 years of age. A new Department for Compulsory Education was created in the Ministry for

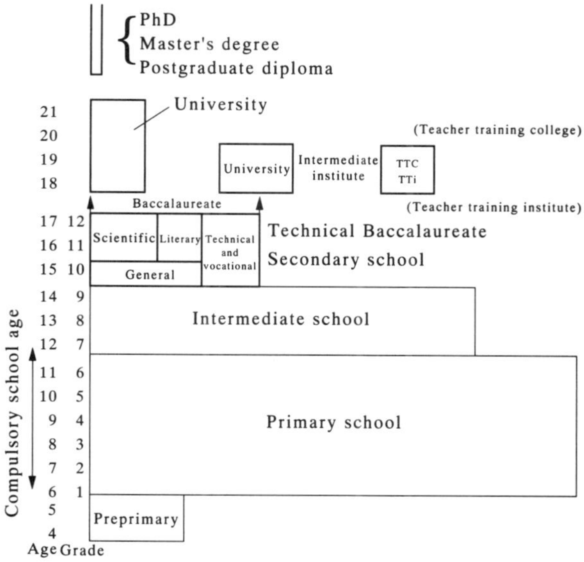

Figure 1
Syria: Structure of the formal education system.

monitoring and evaluating school attendance. Despite this, some differences still exist among geographic regions and between the sexes. However, three Governorates (Deir Elzhor, Hama, and Rakkha) have an enrollment rate between 95 and 98 percent. The factors impeding complete enrollment are: nomadism, poverty, lack of facilities in some remote areas with small populations, and lack of coordination between official parties involved in the compulsory law.

The primary course lasts six years and children begin at the age of six. The primary school day normally lasts for about 5 hours and the school year for around 200 days. Most schools are run by the government, but a small proportion (less than 3%) are private. UNRWA provides 2 percent. Both the private sector and UNRWA use the curriculum of the Ministry of Education (MOE). All pupils who have successfully completed the primary level can enter intermediate schools. Before 1970, there was an entrance examination for Grade 7 but this has been abolished.

The lower-secondary (or intermediate) level lasts 3 years and is free but not compulsory. The curriculum includes all the subjects taught at primary level, with the addition of English, French, and "female education." At the end of Grade 9, there is a examination for the Intermediate Level Diploma. In 1990, the enrollment rate in Grade 7 was close to 80 percent. The total enrollment in intermediate level was 631,000 pupils. Most schools are run by the government, but a small proportion (less than 4%) are private and 2% are provided by UNRWA. Both the private sector and UNRWA use the curriculum of the MOE. Since 1970, successive educational plans have included objectives to merge primary and intermediate levels (grades 1 to 9) into a basic cycle and to extend compulsory education to cover it. This aim had not been achieved by 1992, but it can be achieved if the financial situation of the state improves. The upper-secondary level also lasts 3 years and is free of charge. It includes grades 10 to 12. There are two types of upper-secondary schooling: general and technical. Entry is selective and based on the Intermediate Diploma examination at the end of Grade 9. Pupils who are 15-years old are free to choose either general or technical schools, but those beyond this age must enter technical schools. The total enrollment in secondary education in 1989–90 was 273,000.

The general school continues to be the most popular, accounting for 78 percent of the total secondary enrollment in 1990. The first year of the general program is an introductory one, after which pupils enter one of two streams: scientific or literary. About three-fourths of pupils opt for the scientific stream. Upon completion of the course, pupils sit for the Secondary Diploma (or baccalaureate). This diploma is the sole qualification to grant automatic entrance to higher education institutions. About 90 percent of general secondary schools are provided by the government and 10 percent are private.

Technical and vocational schools cover industrial, commercial, and agricultural specializations, as well as the "female" specializations of home economics and nursing. Their respective percentages within technical education in 1989–90 were 51, 22, 7, and 20. Technical secondary schools are run by the MOE, except for agriculture schools which are run by the Ministry of Agriculture. The 76 industrial schools give instruction in 10 engineering trades.

On the other hand, intermediate industrial and banking institutes also provide instruction in 17 engineering specializations. Timetables consist of 18 hours of instruction per week and 20 hours of practical training. Pupils who fail their practical examinations must repeat the grade. At the end of the course, students take the technical baccalaureate, but holders have only limited opportunities for further education. The top students proceed to university. The remainder can enroll in intermediate institutes belonging to the Ministry of Higher Education. The other specialization streams (agricultural and female education) do not lead to the baccalaureate examination.

Religious education is run by the *Awkaf* Ministry and provides a six-year course parallel to the intermediate and secondary cycles in the secular system. The number of pupils in religious schools is less than 1 percent of those in the secular schools. Curricula are substantially different from those drawn up by the MOE.

Higher education is comprised of universities, higher, and intermediate institutes. There are four universities (Damascus, Aleppo, Lattaquieh, and Homs), one Higher Institute for Political Science, one Higher Institute of Administrative Science, and 47 intermediate institutes with total enrollments of 138,700 and 44,200 for universities and institutes respectively in 1986. The growth of attendance has been very rapid since the early 1960s. The expansion has stabilized in the early 1990s. The University of Damascus is the oldest and largest university, having 15 faculties. Aleppo, Lattaquieh, and Homs universities now have 9, 7, and 6 faculties respectively. A significant proportion of university students study abroad. Some of them have scholarships, but the majority are studying at their own expense. The other type of higher education is the two-year post-secondary intermediate institute which provides training at technician level. These institutes are administered by technical ministries: Agriculture, Industry, Natural Resources, Public Works, and so forth. The Secondary Diploma is required for entry, and most courses last two years. Entry to those institutes controlled by the Ministry of Higher Education is limited to graduates of the general secondary schools. Those controlled by the Ministry of Education and other technical ministries are open to graduates of the technical and vocational secondary schools. The government hopes to accommodate an increasing percentage (almost 50) of technical–vocational secondary school graduates in this type of higher education.

The Law of Absorption, promulgated in 1973, gives the right to any student who passes the general secondary diploma to enter the university. However, in practice there is a *numerus clausus*. Only the previous year's secondary school graduates are admitted, and applicants are accepted according to their grades within the quotas specified for each subject by the Council of Higher Education. In general, holders of the technical secondary schools cannot apply for admission to university. The faculties of Medicine and Engineering require very high marks from their prospective students.

University education is free as long as the student passes his or her final examinations. Degree courses last between four and six years. At the graduate level, a diploma takes one year, a master's degree a further year after the diploma, and the PhD a further two years after the master's. However, few opportunities exist to study for a doctorate in Syria.

The medium of instruction in Syrian universities is Arabic. However, English is used as a medium of instruction in some subjects at both undergraduate and graduate level.

3.2 Preschool Education

Preprimary education is optional and is run on a fee-paying basis. It lasts 3 years (from age 3 to 5 years).

However, it is provided on a limited scale and proposals for increased provision are being considered. Some classes are attached to public primary schools; others are run by private groups (for more than 60% of children) or by the General Union of Syrian Arab Women or by the Teacher's Union. In 1989–90, there were 84,800 children (about 5% of an age group) enrolled in pre-primary, and 793 kindergardens and 2,711 teachers. Preprimary education was relatively neglected in the 1960s and 1970s. The state now supports the extension of this education due to the increasing percentage of working women. The 1928 Constitution included compulsory education as an aim for the primary level—it took more than half a century to achieve it.

3.3 Special Education

Reliable information concerning disabled persons is not available. Syria has started to include disability statistics in its population census. Pupils with mild difficulties attend ordinary schools. Their needs are generally unidentified and they tend to drop out at the primary level.

The notion of special education as a part of the educational system is unknown in Syria. Opinion is divided in the educational community between regular and special education. The Ministry of Social Affairs and Labor administers 20 centers for the social care of the deaf, dumb, and blind providing "special programs and services" for almost 2,500 disabled students. This represents less than 0.7 per 1,000 of the pre-university student population.

3.4 Vocational, Technical, and Business Education

The technical and vocational secondary school system, as well as the intermediate industrial schools, were dealt with in section 3.1 above. A great deal of trade training is undertaken under the umbrella of adult and nonformal education (see section 3.5 below).

3.5 Adult and Nonformal Education

There are two types of nonformal education. The first is literacy education, while the second covers a wide range of vocational and cultural activities.

In 1990, the literacy rate was estimated to be 70 percent. In 1972 and 1978, two literacy campaigns were undertaken under the supervision of the Higher Council for Literacy. The Ministry of Culture is in charge of coordinating all programs and administering literacy classes. Each Governorate also has its own regional literacy committee. The literacy curriculum comprises two parts: basic training lasting six months (360 hours) and a second three months devoted to integrated training. Other technical ministries and agencies involved in literacy training and functional projects are: the ministries of Social Affairs and Labor, Agriculture, and Industry; the General Federation of Women's Trade Unions; farmers; and students. The last campaign, which began in 1978, succeeded in eradicating the illiteracy of 434,511 persons by 1989.

The Ministry of Culture runs adult education centers and institutes of popular culture. These centers offer a number of part-time vocational courses (knitting, sewing, housekeeping, arts, music) throughout the day, for people who have completed primary schooling and are over 15 years of age. At the same time, the Ministry of Social Affairs provides craft centers which provide classes in the traditional skills of carpet weaving and rug making.

The Ministry of Social Affairs provides, through its community development centers, courses and activities such as home economics, nursing education, veterinary medicine, and film shows. The Ministry of Agriculture provides long- and short-term training courses for literate farmers above 16 years of age. Since 1975, farmer training has been the responsibility of the General Union of Peasants. This para-governmental organization has training centers in each Governorate. These centers run courses in cooperative management every year.

The Ministry of Industry is in charge of several vocational training courses for literate adults. These include accelerated training for basic-entry-level job skills, long-term industrial apprenticeship courses preparing skilled workers of 15 to 18 years of age for public industries, a specialized training program for new skills, and on-the-job training to meet the needs of the public sector. There are two types of programs offered in factory schools or training centers respectively. These courses are open only to the employees of public enterprises who are preparatory school graduates. Training centers offer more general training in subjects like electronics, electricity, textiles, drafting, and so on. The Ministry of Public Works also operates several centers for accelerated training in the building and construction trades. Some other international nongovernmental agencies or organizations undertake nonformal education activities but they operate generally through national authorities. Almost all these activities and centers are financed by the central budget, but detailed statistics about them are not available.

4. Administrative and Supervisory Structure and Operation

Educational administration (and the overall administrative system) in Syria is very centralized. There are two levels in the administration of education: the central level and the local level. Education in Syria is primarily the responsibility of the central government. However, organizational changes instituting local administration took place in the 1970s and 1980s. The main philosophy of the reform is the centralization of conception and planning and the decentralization of implementation. The directorates of education in the Governorates create primary and secondary schools and decide on their location, as well as deciding pedagogical orientation within the region. They appoint teachers, distribute teaching materials, organize training programs, and manage primary schooling.

There are two ministries which are exclusively concerned with education: the Ministry of Education and the Ministry of Higher Education. However, other ministries are in charge of some vocational or technical education. UNRWA and the private sector have a limited role in this field. (More than 95% of enrollments are in the public sector.)

The Ministry of Education controls all pre-university education (except for agricultural secondary schools which are under the Ministry of Agriculture) as well as some of the intermediate institutes training teachers for primary, intermediate, or technical schools, and for all levels in some specializations (music, handicrafts, physical education). The ministries define policy guidelines, carry out the major programs, and allocate resources to main subsectors and Governorates. The MOE designs teaching programs and textbooks. Implementation of programs, which are the same for the whole country, is maintained through inspectorates. The Ministry, through its Establishment for Schools Books, prints and distributes textbooks for all schools (these are free at the primary level only).

The Ministry of Higher Education controls and coordinates the four universities, the Higher Institute of Political Science, the Higher Institute of Administrative Sciences, and the other intermediate institutes. Coordination among these institutions is maintained through the Council of Higher Education which is the major executive body in higher education and is presided over by the Minister. This Council is also responsible for planning, policy guidelines, academic programs, funding, and entrance quotas.

In addition, there are several other ministries involved in different types of education and training (formal or nonformal): these include the ministries of Health, Planning, Information, Industry, and Agriculture—all of which control institutes designed to meet certain specific needs.

Communal and foreign schools were nationalized in 1967. Since then, private schools have been strictly controlled by the MOE, which appoints their principals. However, due to the financial crisis and the international political evolution at the beginning of the 1990s, the educational authorities are beginning to realize the limits of the expansion of public education. It is therefore possible that a new orientation may appear gradually, granting greater recognition and autonomy to the private sector in the various educational levels. Thus, the private sector will probably be called upon to play a greater role in this field.

5. *Educational Finance*

It is difficult to compare, in absolute terms, the present budget with the budgets in the 1940s and 1950s since data in constant prices are not available. However, it can be said that the budgets of the 1970s and 1980s had nothing in common with the budget of 1946. In relative terms, the total budget (current and capital expenditure) of education (excluding the third level) between 1975 and 1987, as a percentage of the consolidated government expenditure, increased from 7.8 percent in 1975, to 11.8 percent in 1985, and to 14 percent in 1987. As a percentage of GDP, the evolution was 3.9 percent in 1975, 6.1 percent in 1985, and 4.7 percent in 1987. The percentage of the current education expenditure, in the consolidated government expenditure, was 12.6 percent in 1987, 11.4 percent in 1988, 12.1 percent, in 1989, and 12.7 percent in 1990. The corresponding percentages for higher education were: 2.95 in 1987, 3.2 in 1988, and 3.05 in 1989.

UNESCO figures concerning the evolution of public current and capital expenditure on education at constant prices (base year 1980) gave 96 for 1986 (57 in 1975). After substantial increases in current and capital expenditure on education between 1975 and 1985, the 1990 level is lower than it was in 1980. After 1986, the rate of inflation was generally higher than the annual rate of increase of public expenditure. On the other hand, the per pupil expenditure, expressed in units of GNP per capita, for all levels of education did not vary between 1980 and 1987, and at 0.14, is amongst the lowest in the region. This overall figure masks a decrease in higher education expenditure and a slight increase at the secondary and primary levels.

The 1990 education budget allocation was 81 percent for prehigher education and 19 percent for higher education. For the same year, the prehigher education funds were distributed as follows: 49 percent for primary and preprimary, 27 percent for intermediate and general secondary, 8 percent for technical secondary, 11 percent for school building projects, and 5 percent for others. It should be noted that local administration pays for part of primary school expenditures. The percentage of teaching materials and scholarships dropped from 5.9 and 2.5 percent respectively in 1975 to 2.6 and 0.6 percent in 1987. On the other hand, teachers salaries and emoluments account for more than 90 percent of total current expenditure.

Since other ministries are also involved in education, their expenditures must be added to the figures of the two ministries of education. Consequently, the percentages mentioned above must be considered as a minimum.

6. *Supplying Personnel for the Education System*

Nearly 145,000 teachers were employed in schools

in 1990. About 92,000 teachers were employed in primary and preprimary schools and 51,000 in all types of secondary schools. Some 75 percent of primary school teachers are female.

Until the late 1980s, there were teacher shortages at all levels. Auxiliary teachers and contractual teachers (on temporary or part-time basis) were employed at that time. The implementation of compulsory education (and the extension of preprimary education) has created a continuous demand for teachers in the public sector. The main requirements for this level in the 1980s were met by employing female teachers. Their number increased by a factor of two between 1980 and 1990. The expected expansion of the preprimary level will create a demand for even more teachers. On the other hand, the number of teachers in the intermediate and secondary schools has decreased since 1986–87. In the intermediate schools, the enrollment has been almost static since 1986–87, whereas enrollment has been decreasing since 1988–89 for general education and since 1984–85 for technical education. However, enrollment in the vocational secondary schools has slightly increased since 1989. The pupil–teacher ratio has declined somewhat, but is still high: 31:1 in primary schools, 36:1 in intermediate schools, and 35:1 in secondary schools.

Primary teachers and intermediate school auxiliary teachers are trained in the 20 two-year postsecondary teacher-training colleges and 22 two-year postsecondary auxiliary teacher-training institutes (in those subjects for which there is a shortage of teachers) under the Ministry of Education. Intermediate and secondary school teachers may attend a one-year course at the Faculty of Education of Damascus following their university degree. However, this training is not obligatory. The universities and the intermediate institutes run by the MOE are the main sources of trained instructors and trainers for the technical and vocational secondary schools.

Regular inservice training is not common in Syria. In 1988, 24,097 persons (including administrative and pedagogical staff) were involved in different training courses managed by the training department of the MOE at all levels. Their number dropped to 6,000 in 1989.

7. *Curriculum Development and Teaching Methodology*

The curriculum is uniform and nationwide. A detailed syllabus is developed by the central authorities. The Department of Curriculum and Research at the MOE is in charge of the development of courses, learning materials, and teaching methods. Additionally, it is responsible for trying out the learning materials at all preuniversity levels. In primary education, the curriculum includes Arabic, mathematics, religious instruction, elements of science and health education, social and national education, art, music, and physical education. Fewer than 300 primary schools provided four hours a week of rural education in Grades 4, 5, and 6 in 1989. In the intermediate and general secondary schools, the curriculum includes all of the subjects taught at the primary level with the addition of English or French and practical work and female education (rural education for boys). In the technical secondary schools, two-thirds of the curriculum is oriented towards scientific and practical training.

For many years, curriculum was characteristically traditional and theoretical, putting emphasis on the humanities and factual data rather than on scientific concepts, attitudes, skills, and values. The MOE intends to develop curricula by defining successively pedagogical objectives, content, teaching methods, and, finally the practical exercises for the evaluation of pupil achievement. At the end of the 1980s, various attempts at curriculum reform for primary and secondary schools and for teacher-training college were made. These aimed at introducing some practical aspects related to productive work, and nutritional, environmental, and population subjects. These reforms are on-going and no appraisal of how far they have been successful has yet been undertaken.

One experiment introduced foreign language teaching into Grades 5 and 6 in some primary schools. Again, the results of the experiment are not yet known.

The private sector is authorized to add a few hours of foreign language teaching to the official curriculum. In some areas, the directorate of education in the Governorates can decide to make additions to the intermediate school courses in agricultural subjects.

Teaching methods are rather didactic and verbal. Inservice and self-training have not yet developed to any degree in Syria. Some attempts are being made to introduce educational radio and television, especially in general and languages teaching, and cultural programs. An Educational Materials Production Center has been created by the Department of Materials and Equipment in the MOE. The authorities consider it to be a base for Arabic cooperation in the development of teaching materials and intend to promote it as such.

8. *The System of Examinations, Promotions, and Certifications*

There is automatic promotion based on age in primary education. However, in order to sit for the final grade, the pupils must score a 50 percent in Arabic and an overall average of 50 percent. Grading is left to the discretion of the teacher; there is no standardized national examination. At the end of the intermediate (Grade 9) and the secondary levels, there is a public nationwide examination for the intermediate and secondary diploma. At the end of the technical secondary school, students take the technical secondary diploma. Only the top students have access to the universities. The percentage of grade repeaters in the first and second levels declined from 10 and 16 percent respectively in 1975 to 7 and 13 percent in 1987.

Any student who passes the secondary diploma has the right to enter university, but there is a *numerus clausus* determined by the authorities. The diplomas awarded by universities are: the bachelor's degree, the master of arts or science, and the PhD in some fields such as law and Arabic literature.

University degrees, especially the highest (i.e. the PhD), have traditionally been held in great esteem. The social and economic value of these diplomas has decreased due to the increasing number of graduates coming from Eastern and Western countries and from Egypt.

Examinations in Syria are based on memorization and affirmative modes rather than ways of thinking, attitudes, and skills. The Syrian educational system relies on written or oral formative evaluation, on the one hand, and summative evaluation in the form of final examinations, formal teacher evaluation by inspectors, and comparisons of pupil performance on general examinations for school evaluation on the other. General examinations are still "considered as aims in themselves" and contribute to the rigidity of the curriculum. In fact valuable feedback is rarely provided to those developing curriculum.

9. Educational Assessment, Evaluation, and Research

In general, the main focus of the MOE—as a management structure—is on monitoring resource inputs rather than pupils outcomes. Evaluation and assessment are rarely applied. In practice, evaluation is perceived as a monitoring process and no clear criteria are identified for its implementation. At the preuniversity level, the Department of Planning and Statistics and the Department of Curriculum and Research are in charge of educational research and studies. The first conducts sectoral and diagnostic studies, whereas the second focuses on educational processes. The main studies which have been undertaken (the results of which are supposed to be used by the planning process and decision-making) are: (a) the introduction of environmental, population, and health education into school curriculum; (b) the introduction of basic education into the educational system; (c) the development and implementation of school mapping as a regional planning tool at secondary and university levels; (d) the development of computer data in managing the educational system and in research; (e) creating the conditions for teaching foreign languages at the primary level; (f) monitoring the impact of educational television programs; and,(g) monitoring some aspects of dropout in the educational system. Research at the university level is undertaken by faculties as a part of graduate programs.

10. Major Reforms in the 1980s and 1990s

Population education is being introduced into Syrian secondary schools. As an on-going reform, it consists of revising the curriculum at the secondary level and determining the concepts to be integrated. On the other hand, teaching materials are expected to be produced (teacher guide, reference book in population education). The project was initiated in 1986 and the second phase is expected to be achieved in 1994. Other reforms that have also been proposed include: the establishment of a Research Center for Pedagogical Development; the establishment of vocational courses lasting 1 to 3 years after basic education; the opening of channels or pathways between the technical secondary schools, intermediate institutes, and the related departments in the universities having the same specialization; the establishment of a special department for scientific research in each university with ad hoc financial resources; and, the establishment of basic compulsory education (from Grades 1 to 9).

11. Major Problems for the Year 2000

There are two problems that seem to be outstanding: the extension of compulsory school education to Grade 9 and improvement in the quality of education. The government is conscious of the limits of existing strategy, but the major constraint for the designing and implementation of the two reforms is financial. In fact, the two problems are interdependent. The first problem implies that, with the introduction of basic compulsory education, an in-depth revision of the present curriculum, the reform of teacher preservice and inservice training, and a redistribution of the main resources such as teachers and schools will be necessary. The second implies, among other things, revising the curriculum and pedagogical methods, introducing foreign languages, eliminating the multigrade teacher in the primary schools, and improving inservice teacher training.

In 1987 objectives were formulated to bring about: the orientation of 60 percent of the pupils, after basic education, towards the labor market and 40 percent towards the secondary schools at the beginning of the 1990s; and the orientation of 70 percent of the enrollment in secondary schools towards the technical and vocational secondary schools (60% vocational and 10% technical) and the remainder (30%) towards general secondary in 1995. The two reforms mentioned above should be considered as a means to implement these objectives.

Bibliography

Akrawi M 1967 *Arab Education During Fifty Years*. Amman

Alrabaa S 1985 Sex division of labor in Syrian school textbooks. *IRE* 31: 335–48

Azzam M 1985 Syria: system of education. In: Husén T, Postlethwaite TN (eds.) 1985 *International Encyclopedia of Education*, 1st edn. Pergamon Press, Oxford

British Council 1979 *Syria, Education Profile*. British Council, London

Central Bureau of Statistics 1991 *Syrian Arab Republic: Statistical Abstract 1991*. Central Bureau of Statistics, Damascus

Gennaoui A 1990 Etude régionale: Bilan et Perspective de la Planification et de la Gestion de l'Education dans les pays arabes. Congrès International de Mexico 1990. UNESCO Paris

Ministère de l'éducation 1990 *Le Développement de l'Education en RAS* 1989–1990, *ICE 42ème session* Genève. Ministère de l'éducation, Damascus

Ministry of Education 1990 *Education in SAR for the school year 1989–1990*. Ministry of Education, Damascus (in arabic)

UNDP 1990 *Development Co-operation, Syrian Arab Republic. 1989 Report*. UNDP, Damascus

UNESCO 1991 *Statistical Yearbook 1991*. UNESCO, Paris

A. Gennaoui

Systems Approach to Design and Development

The *International Dictionary of Education* defines the systems approach in education as follows:

> Conscious use of systems analysis and systems design techniques in an endeavor to identify and solve complex problems in learning or instructional systems. The components of the approach include the establishment of a systems boundary, the identification of all actual or possible inputs and outputs to the system and examination of their interaction. (Page and Thomas 1978)

This definition, however, probably raises more questions than it answers. What are systems analysis and systems design techniques and how are they relevant to the solving of complex problems in education? What are the meanings of such terms as input, output, and boundary in the context of educational planning? What is the relevance of such an approach, seemingly borrowed from engineering, to the social context of educational planning? In addition to such questions springing directly from the formal definition of systems approach, there are questions or misunderstandings that have arisen from several decades of the practical use of this term to describe procedures in the area of educational planning and instructional design and development. To many outside observers of educational technology or the instructional design and development process, the systems approach appears to be a systematic procedure of stages through which a project should go in order for it to be easily managed.

However, the term "systems approach" grew out of general systems theory and cybernetics as a creative and heuristic approach to the understanding and improvement of complex, probabilistic systems (Romiszowski 1981). Cybernetics grew up as an interdisciplinary science seeking the commonalities between diverse areas where complex and probabilistic systems have to be in some way controlled, or designed, or put to work effectively (Ackoff 1960, Pask 1961). The systems approach was originally a way of looking at a complex reality in the awareness that it was not completely controllable in a deterministic manner as many simpler mechanical systems might be (Romiszowski 1970, Beer 1959). From this realization came the basic principles of the systems approach, which involve the careful analysis of interrelationships existing between interacting subsystems and the interpretation of these interactions in terms of predicting what may happen in other parts of the system if certain changes are made in a particular part (Neil 1969). Another important principle, the cybernetic principle of control by feedback, grew out of the realization that complexity cannot be planned and implemented successfully the first time around, but only by an iterative process where a first-attempt solution is followed by evaluation of what worked and what did not, and by revision and reevaluation (Neil 1970). The whole process is in fact heuristic rather than algorithmic, creative rather than mechanistic, and systemic rather than merely systematic.

It has been convenient to describe the process as a set of phases or stages but it is unfortunate that this description has often been presented by some form of flowchart that has then been interpreted by later generations as a directive algorithm to be slavishly followed and not modified in the light of the actual situation. The systems approach is principally a way of thinking (Emery 1969) which enables a person to have the vision necessary for effective needs analysis, innovative design, and critical evaluation.

However, in addition to the systems thinking connotation, the systems approach does also involve a systematic process by which complex problems may be analyzed and appropriate solutions designed and implemented (Singleton 1974). The following sections will examine the systems thinking connotation and then the systematic process connotation of the systems approach.

1. Systemic Thinking

The term "system" describes a rather abstract concept. Traditional definitions, such as "a set of components or elements, interacting together towards a common goal" do not provide much help toward understanding the concept. It may be said that a system exists because someone has defined it as such.

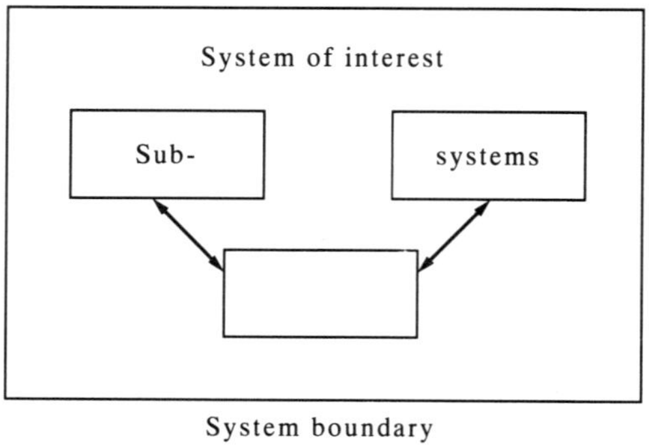

Figure 1
Some basic systems terminology

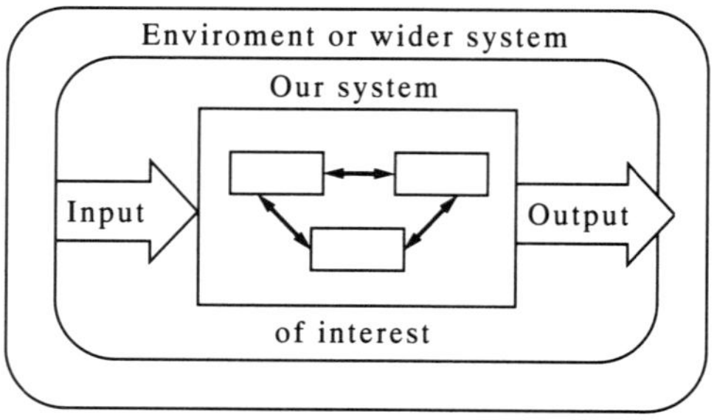

Figure 2
The wider system

A bicycle may be viewed as a system with clearly defined components—wheels, pedals, chain, handlebars, etc. Most people would agree as to the purpose or goal of a bicycle (to provide a means of propelled transport) and on the bicycle's essential components. However the bicycle might be considered as but one component of a wider system (of a rider–machine system, for example, whose objective is to maximize the efficiency of transformation of the rider's energy into the bicycle's motion) or an even wider system (the bicycle as one component in a city's transport system, which involves cars, trucks, trains, buses, roads, etc.). Alternatively, the three-speed gear in the hub of the back wheel can be considered quite a complex system on its own.

Thus, for practical purposes, a system exists because people have chosen to consider it as that. A boundary has been drawn that limits the extent of the system, thus defining the components, or subsystems that compose the "system of interest" (see Fig. 1).

Once defined in this way, the principal connections between this system and its environment can be identified, as can the inputs from the environment to the system and the outputs from the system to its environment (see Fig. 2).

The first step in systems analysis is to define the system of interest, its boundaries, and the chief inputs and outputs across these boundaries. Quantifying these inputs and outputs defines the system's purpose and to some extent its efficiency. For the time being, the complexity inside the boundary may be ignored. The system is treated as a "black box."

There is usually some means of controlling the output from outside the black box. A ministry of education may (to a point) control the output of a school system by manipulating output criteria, input resources, and capacity without detailed knowledge of the instructional processes going on in the schools. A teacher may (also to a point) control the learning of a student by observing the outputs (new capabilities or behaviors) and manipulating the inputs (type of information, type of task, frequency and repetition, duration of practice, etc.) without any detailed knowledge of the internal learning processes that are going on inside the student.

When this mode of control fails, there is a situation that might possibly justify the time and effort of more detailed system analysis. When external controls fail, the ministry of education begins to be interested in the inner workings of curriculum design, teacher training, teaching methods, and other aspects of the process. When teachers have exhausted their resourcefulness in adapting instruction to individual needs by the "input–output–feedback" approval of behaviorism, they begin to study the cognitive processes occurring in the students' minds.

At this point, the real complexity of the internal structure and the nondeterministic nature of the ongoing processes have to be faced. It is here that systemic thinking is of particular value to the analyst or designer. Basic concepts and principles from general systems theory, such as the laws governing a system's entropy, or the law of requisite variety, help to explain and predict the system's behavior. The ability to visualize the system's structure and the internal relationships between the component subsystems makes it possible to maintain a "systems view" or "big picture" while engaged on detailed analysis or design of one of the components. The extensive use of block diagrams by systems engineers is an attempt to promote and document this "systems view."

2. *Systematic Problem-solving*

The procedural or systematic aspect of the systems approach is related to its focus on the analysis and solution of problems in complex and probabilistic systems. Two points need to be made for clarification. First, the emphasis on complexity and indeterminism emphasizes that a problem-solving approach should be iterative in nature, developing tentative solutions and putting them to the test in order to refine them as required. Second, the very nature of what is meant by a problem should be further defined. In the most general terms, a problem is a discrepancy between a current state or situation and a desired state or situation. This may result from dissatisfaction with the status quo, but it may equally result from the perception of an opportunity to "go somewhere where we have never gone before." The definition of this "problem" is tantamount to defining the purpose of a given system analysis and design project.

In order to "define the problem," the following steps can be taken. First, it is necessary to identify the system that best defines the problem in input–output terms. Second, the problem should be defined as a discrepancy between the current state of the system and the desired state (in input–output terms). Third, attempts should be made to quantify the change that would be acceptable as a measure of a successful solution.

No mention has been made of any specific solution—nor should there be at this stage. Indeed, this should be avoided to evade the trap of mixing up problems with solutions, or confusing aims and means. All too often premature decisions are made about the form of the solution before the person making them has really come to terms with the problem. But effective problem-solving is concerned with the selection of the best solution from amongst alternatives. The criteria for such a selection must spring from the specific problem; hence the emphasis on first defining the problem. Thinking in systems terms helps to define the problem as clearly and as completely as possible. It also helps in the analysis of the problem in order to identify possible alternative solutions. It helps in selecting from among the alternatives and in developing the most viable solution. Finally, it helps to implement the solution, to evaluate its effectiveness and real worth, and to improve it if necessary.

Hence the systems approach, though essentially a way of thinking about problems in systems terms, is also a methodology—scientific method applied to the design and development of complex systems. It follows the general stages of: (a) problem definition in systems terms; (b) analysis to generate alternatives; (c) selection and synthesis of an optimal solution; (d) controlled implementation; and (e) evaluation and possible revision.

3. Systems Approach: Systemic or Systematic?

The five steps or stages in the problem-solving process described above have been adopted as the basis for development of a plethora of instructional design and development models, quite often represented in the literature by more or less complicated flowcharts. Over time these have led to an emphasis, maybe an overemphasis, on the systematic procedural aspects of the systems approach. Perhaps for this reason, the systems approach has for many become analogous to anticreative, mechanistic approaches to the design and development of instruction.

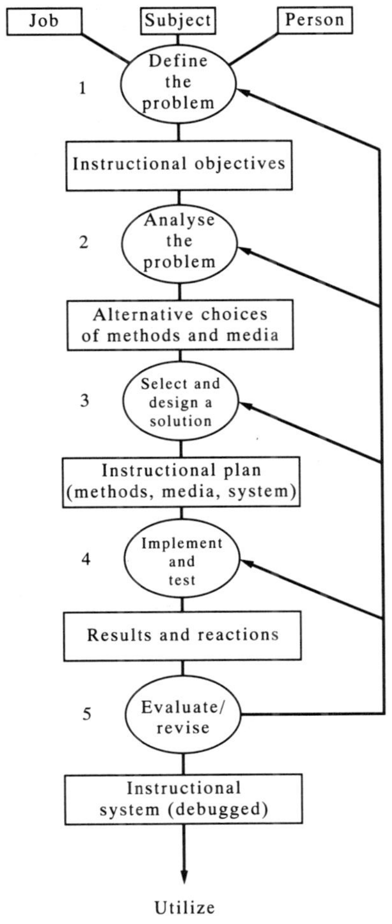

Figure 3
Systems approach at the micro level applied to instructional design

In order to rectify this viewpoint somewhat, Fig. 3 is presented in flowchart form, but utilizes a unique graphic convention of rectangles to indicate key products and circles or ovals to indicate stages at which heuristic decision-making and creative thinking must occur in order to produce the products. Figure 3 illustrates the process of designing instruction. The outcome of defining the problem, or the gap between "what is" and "what should be," results in a specification of instructional objectives. However, the process of selecting and defining these objectives is by no means algorithmic, step-by-step, and mechanistic.

The instructional objectives or goals are next used to generate a list of alternative choices of instructional methods and media with the related costs and priorities that could be used for making a final selection. Once more, the process of identifying these

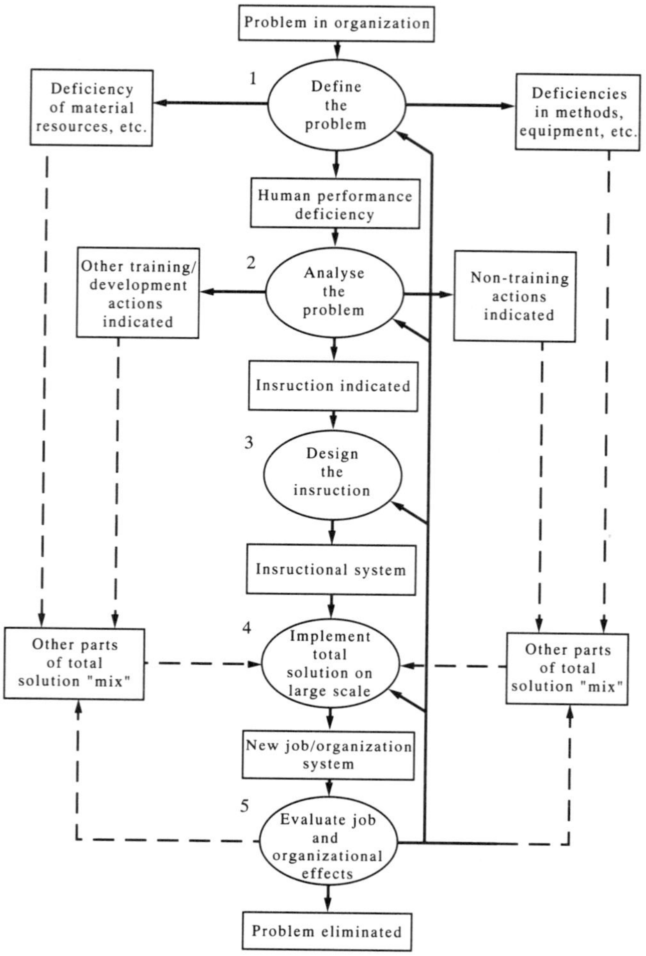

Figure 4
Systems approach at the macro level applied to the solution of any problem in the organization

alternatives is a complex heuristic, often creative, decision-making process. The further stages of selecting and designing a solution, implementing and testing, and then evaluating and revising are similarly considered to be heuristic decision-making processes rather than step-by-step mechanistic procedures. Thus, although Fig. 3 is a form of flowchart, it is by no means an algorithm.

The general applicability and versatility of the systems approach as a problem-solving process can be further illustrated by Fig. 4, which illustrates the same five stages of problem-solving applied in the more general or macro context of organizational analysis as may be carried out as part of an organizational development program.

Step 1 will now involve establishing clear and measurable organizational or job performance objectives and identifying the environmental conditions required to make these objectives relevant and viable.

Step 2 will now be the analysis of the causes of actual performance problems or discrepancies, to identify all possible solutions and solution components, to evaluate the alternatives, and to select the optimal mix of interventions (instruction, other types of training/development activity, plus other actions such as organizational change, job design, modified selection procedures, etc.).

Step 3: all the components of the mix will now have to be developed in coordination (often difficult, since they may be the responsibilities of different departments in the organization). It is worth concentrating on the instruction component however. If there is an instruction component to develop, its contribution to the total solution is by now defined. The following sequence would be followed: (a) develop instructional objectives; (b) generate alternatives for instructional methods or media; (c) develop the chosen solution; (d) implement experimentally; and (e) evaluate. All of the micro-level application of the systems approach (illustrated in Fig. 3) is compressed into Step 3 of the macro-level application illustrated in Fig. 4.

Step 4: parallel with this activity, the other components will undergo a similar process of systems development. Large-scale implementation brings together the various (already independently evaluated) components of the solution, and implements them jointly in the real organizational setting.

Step 5: evaluation now occurs at the organizational and long-term effects level, to check that all aspects of the original diagnosis and of the developed solutions are correct.

Fig. 4 illustrates the potential multidisciplinarity of the systems approach. Although the figure only elaborates on a possible instructional component of a solution, it implies that there may be several other components in a total solution to the multiplicity of problems and multiple causes of these problems that may exist in the organization. It illustrates, therefore, that although the procedure to be followed for problem-solving is in some respect systematic, the view that the problem solver has to take of the problem and its context has to be systemic.

4. Application of the Systems Approach in Education

In this last section, several examples of systems approach applications in the educational context will be given. These have been selected to illustrate important applications and also to illustrate the different levels within educational systems at which the systems approach may have value. The presentation will start at the lower or micro levels and work up to higher or macro levels.

At the level of instructional materials design and development, the systematic, procedural aspects of the systems approach have been embodied in many of the practical methodologies for the design and development of text, audiovisual materials, and computer-based instructional materials. One such model that has been widely used is the one proposed by Dick and Carey 1985). The systemic aspects of the systems approach have in the past been ignored in the context of materials design and development. However, instructional product developers have now turned away from the design and development of materials, destined for clearly defined target populations, that seek to achieve precise, preagreed performance objectives and toward the creation of knowledge bases that may be used under learner control for a multiplicity of purposes by learners who have a multiplicity of entry level skills. The focus has turned toward the systemic analysis of the structure of knowledge. The creation of a Hypertext knowledge base, for example, is a project that depends on a high level of systemic thinking applied to the analysis of the structure of a particular domain of knowledge, the design of an appropriate way of representing this structure within a database, and the evaluation of the way that a variety of potential users may best benefit from the resultant materials.

A good example of a methodology for materials development that embodies quite clearly both the systematic and systemic aspects of the systems approach is the Information Mapping methodology developed by Robert Horn and his associates (Horn 1976, 1989). ("Information Mapping" is a trademark of Information Mapping Inc., Waltham, Massachusetts, United States.) This methodology, initially developed in the 1960s and 1970s for the production of paper-based materials for both learning and reference, is now finding increased application as a design methodology for Hypertext and Hypermedia systems.

At a somewhat higher level of system resolution, the integration of materials and other activities into lessons and course modules may also be planned according to the systems approach methodology. Procedural models, such as the Dick and Carey model mentioned before, may serve to organize the process systematically. However, understanding the complex forces that exist within a teaching or learning situation will be enhanced by the adoption of a systemic view of the participants and how they interrelate with each other and their environment. An excellent example of this latter aspect is given by Tubbs in his book *A Systems Approach to Small Group Interaction* (Tubbs 1978). This book studies the work of small groups and the work of facilitators, or teachers, with such groups, looking at small groups as examples of open systems of simultaneously interacting forces. These forces include relevant background factors of the group members, the internal influences or group processes, and the consequences of the interaction of these factors. Systems concepts and terminology are used throughout the book for the following purposes: (a) to describe the group process phenomenon and to explain the working of groups with a generic model; (b) to analyze the background or environmental factors of group members that are relevant to their behavior in the group; (c) to describe and analyze the environmental impact and the internal structure of the group itself; (d) to analyze aspects of the status, power, leadership, and social influence processes as they impinge on the group process; (e) to analyze and evaluate aspects of communication as it occurs between group members and its influence on overall group behavior; and (f) to analyze the methods of decision-making and conflict resolution within groups.

At a yet more "macro" level, the overall planning of educational curricula and courses from a systems viewpoint may be considered. Here again, the systematic procedural aspects of commencing by defining the problem and proceeding through the five stages of problem-solving continue to demonstrate their effectiveness. In a consulting mission, the author was involved with approximately 40 European experts in a curriculum planning exercise for the development of new university courses on European Studies that might help to develop professionals with appropriate skills for accelerating the East–West integration of Europe. At the beginning of the exercise, most of the 40 experts were quite convinced that the purpose for their coming together was clearly and precisely understood by all. After being taken through a two-hour exercise in "defining the problem," the experts found a vast divergence of views about the real nature of the problem to be solved. The first step was to resolve these differences. The subsequent work of curriculum-planning was much accelerated and the quality of decision-making much improved as a result of the time devoted initially to clarifying the problem that the team was attempting to solve.

The systemic aspect of the systems approach can also be implemented in curriculum planning by the adoption of structural visualization techniques such as those suggested by the DACUM process (Adams 1975). This process for designing a curriculum is characterized by noting down all decisions and contributions of all team members on separate cards, and then organizing them in different ways in order to visualize alternative structures for the emerging curriculum.

Moving finally to the level of the organization as a whole reveals the most active and promising area for the application of systems approaches. The concept of systemic analysis and planning is long-established in the context of educational or training systems design (Romiszowski 1970, Banathy 1973). Perhaps one of the first attempts to design a whole educational institution by consciously basing the process on the systems approach was the case of the British Open University (Neil 1970). In the corporate context, the methodologies of organizational development that took root in many companies through the 1970s and 1980s were firmly based on the concepts of systems and the application of systems approaches (French and Bell 1973). The power of systemic thinking in the analysis of complex, real-life educational systems was well-illustrated by many authors who used these concepts to make sense of apparently intractable problems associated with the lack of effectiveness and efficiency of American education (Green 1980, Sarason 1990).

Whereas the systems approach seemed to lose much in popularity and gain much in terms of misunderstanding through the 1980s, it would appear that in the 1990s this trend is reversing and a strong return to systemic thinking and systems approaches in educational reform is being evidenced. Educational reformers and academics are tending to present their views ever more in terms of systems concepts and methodologies (Banathy 1991, Reigeluth 1988, 1992). By the early 1990s practical reformers, policymakers, and even politicians were beginning to use the terminology and sometimes the methodologies of the systems approach. A headline in *Education Weekly* read: "Fed up with tinkering, reformers now tout systemic approaches to school redesign." Later in the article, this "modern" concept of systemic reform was defined as "really what you're trying to do is develop the system so it can support really serious local creativity in the context of a common vision."

In conclusion, the 1990s show the completion of a cycle and a return to the theoretical principles developed by the cyberneticians of the 1950s. They emphasized that the major contribution of systems theory to practical problem-solving was the systemic view, which allows a clear vision of the complexity of the real problems involved in any attempt at reform or innovation. Far from being an antiquated and redundant set of concepts and methodologies, it would appear that the systems approach in its true meaning is only now coming to be realized for what it is and for what it can contribute to the process of educational innovation and improvement.

See also: Educational Technology: Scope of the Field; Planning Education: Overview; Educational Planning: Models and Methods

References

Ackoff R L 1960 Systems, organizations and interdisciplinary research. *General Systems Yearbook*, Vol. 5. Society for General Systems Research

Adams R E 1975 *DACUM Approach to Curriculum Learning and Education in Occupational Training*. Department of Regional Economic Expansion, Yarmouth

Banathy B H 1980 *Developing a Systems View of Education*. Intersystems Publications, Salinas, California

Banathy B H 1991 *Systems Design of Education: A Journey to Create the Future*. Educational Technology Publications, Englewood Cliffs, New Jersey

Beer S 1959 *Cybernetics and Management*. English Universities Press, London

Dick W, Carey L 1985 *The Systematic Design of Instruction*, 2nd edn. Scott, Foresman, Glenview, Illinois

Emery F E (ed.) 1969 *Systems Thinking*. Penguin, Harmondsworth

French W L, Bell C H Jr 1973 *Organization Development: Behavioral Science Interventions for Organization Improvement*. Prentice-Hall, Englewood Cliffs, New Jersey

Green T F 1980 *Predicting the Behavior of the Educational System*. Syracuse University Press, Syracuse, New York

Horn R E 1976 *How to Write Information Mapping*. Information Mapping, Waltham, Massachusetts

Horn R E 1989 *Mapping Hypertext*. Lexington Institute, Lexington, Massachusetts

Neil M W 1969 An operational and systems approach to research strategy in educational technology. In: Mann A P, Brunstrom C K (eds.) 1969 *Aspects of Educational Technology*, Vol. 3. Pitman, London
Neil M W 1970 A systems approach to course planning at the Open University. In: Romiszowski A J (ed.) 1970 *A Systems Approach to Education and Training*. Kogan Page, London
Page G T, Thomas J B 1977 *International Dictionary of Education*. Kogan Page, London
Pask G 1961 *An Approach to Cybernetics*. Hutchinson, London
Reigeluth C M 1988 The search for meaningful reform: A third-wave educational system. *J. Instr. Dev*. 10(4): 3–14
Reigeluth C M 1992 The imperative for systemic change. *Educ. Technol*. 32(11): 9–13
Romiszowski A J 1970 Systems approaches to education and training: An introduction. In: Romiszowski A J (ed.) 1970 *A Systems Approach to Education and Training*. Kogan Page, London
Romiszowski A J 1981 *Designing Instructional Systems*. Kogan Page, London
Sarason S B 1990 *The Predictable Failure of Educational Reform: Can We Change Course Before it's too Late?* Jossey-Bass, San Francisco, California
Singleton W T 1974 *Man–Machine Systems*. Penguin, Harmondsworth
Tubbs S L 1978 *A Systems Approach to Small Group Interaction*. Addison-Wesley, Reading, Massachusetts

A. J. Romiszowski

T

Tanzania: System of Education

1. General Background

Tanzania is a republic on the East Coast of Africa. It lies between latitudes 1 and 11 South and longitudes 30–40 East. It attained its independence as Tanganyika in 1961 within the British Commonwealth of Nations and it declared complete independence with republic status in 1962. In 1964, Tanganyika united with the then newly formed People's Republic of Zanzibar, an island off the coast of Tanganyika in the Indian Ocean, to form the United Republic of Tanzania. There is one union constitution although two governments operate, one in Zanzibar with autonomy over the internal affairs of Zanzibar. The Union government has overall responsibility for defence, home affairs, foreign affairs, and a number of other subsectors such as higher education, civil aviation, post, and telecommunications. Some other sectors, for example primary, secondary, and vocational education, agriculture, and industry are not Union concerns.

Tanzania covers an area of 945,087 square kilometers and is divided into 25 administrative regions. It has a population of about 25 million with an average growth rate of 2.8 percent. The economy is predominantly agricultural, although steady progress is being made toward industrialization.

2. Politics and the Goals of the Education System

Since the Arusha Declaration in 1967, Tanzania has followed an ideology of socialism and self-reliance, an ideology well-articulated in various documents including *Socialism and Rural Development* (1967) and *Freedom and Socialism* (1968). The goals and objectives aspire to achieve the building of a society in which all members have equal rights and equal opportunities, in which justice is observed and where exploitation is not tolerated. Up to 1992, the country had a one-party political system but in that year, the country opened the way for a multiparty system.

The country's education system is based on the *Education for Self-reliance* (1967) philosophy which is derived from the major policy of socialism and self-reliance. The philosophy propounds the merging of individuals and communities, a reflection of the idea of education and society being inseparable. It proposes a functional education combining skills and academic learning geared toward opening up the future for the individual learner.

Education in Tanzania is called upon to play an important role in producing the needed knowledge and skills for national development. The importance Tanzania places on education for every citizen cannot be overemphasized. The National Constitution (1977, amended in 1984) safeguards the right of the individual to learning opportunities. Education Act no. 25 of 1978 also stipulates that "every citizen of the United Republic of Tanzania shall be entitled to receive such category, nature and level of education as his ability may permit". Hence, equal opportunity exists for everyone to pursue one or other type of education.

The general aims and objectives of education can be summarized as follows:

(a) to provide all the population with the basic tools of education, namely reading, writing, and numeracy;

(b) to provide Tanzanians with such knowledge, skills, and attitudes as are appropriate and essential for development;

(c) to develop in each citizen an inquiring mind, self-confidence, creativity, and a scientific outlook necessary for an informed and rational choice of strategies needed to improve the quality of life;

(d) to enable learners to appreciate, emulate, and promote national, social, and cultural values.

3. The Formal System of Education

3.1 Primary, Secondary, and Tertiary Education

Primary education in Tanzania is a right for every child. The age of entry is 7 years and primary education lasts for seven years. In Zanzibar, the first cycle of school includes the seven years of primary education and three of secondary education. In mainland Tanzania the gross enrollment rate was 81.3 percent (1991); in Zanzibar it was 65.0. Pupils in mainland Tanzania are promoted to secondary education only after sitting for and passing a national examination set and administered under the supervision of the National Examinations Council of Tanzania (NECTA). Promotion to secondary school depends on the number of vacancies available and the level at which the pupil passed the examination. The transition rate from primary to secondary education was 15.4 percent in 1991.

The primary school curriculum consists of eight subjects, namely Kiswahili (the national language), English, mathematics, home economics, health, science, practical arts, and religious studies.

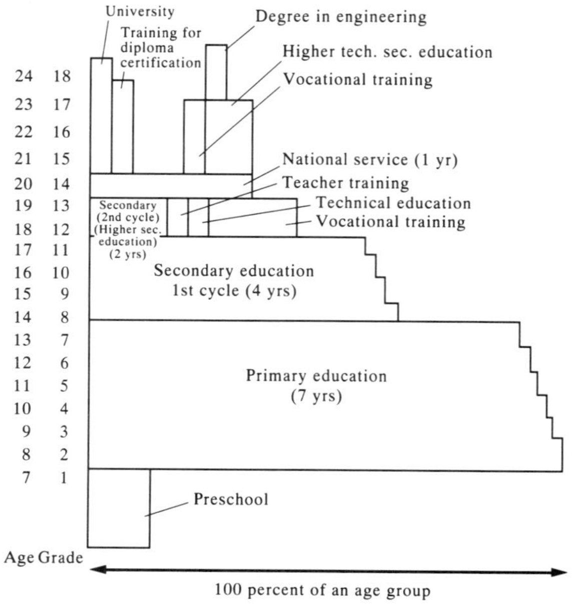

Figure 1
Tanzania: Structure of the formal education system

Most primary schools are owned by the local government. Some are owned and managed by nongovernment organizations and a few by the central government. Consequently, the teaching/learning materials and facilities are provided by the owners and managers of the schools. Staff for the schools are trained and allocated centrally by the central government.

Secondary education has two cycles. The first cycle consists of four years, at the end of which a national examination is taken. Promotion to the next two-year cycle depends on the number of available places and a student's performance in the national examination. After another final examination at the end of the second cycle, a student may secure entry into a university, other tertiary education colleges or vocational training colleges, or secure employment.

Secondary schools are owned by both the government (central and local), and nongovernmental organizations, and secondary education is not free of charge. There is a nominal fee determined by the government. In 1993 the fee was 5,000 Tanzania Sh (US$11.30) per year for a day student and 8,000 Sh (US$18.13) for a boarding student in a government-owned school. This fee, however, covers only a small part of the cost of providing education, which is about 186,000 Sh (US$426) for a day student and 242,000 Sh (US$554) for a boarder. The major part of the cost is funded by the government. The fee payable by students in nongovernment secondary schools is 35,000 Sh (US$80) for a day student and 45,000 Sh (US$103) for a boarder. The curriculum, as in primary education, is centrally controlled. Within the curriculum, students have to study seven core subjects, comprising Kiswahili, English, mathematics, unified science, social studies, computer literacy, and religious instruction. In addition, students are encouraged to study three more subjects from either the sciences or the arts or they can drop the combined course and opt for separate pure science or arts subjects (e.g., physics, chemistry, biology, geography, and history).

Tertiary education is provided in technical colleges and universities. In 1993 there were three advanced technical colleges situated in Dar es Salaam, Arusha, and Mbeya and three universities, namely the Sokoine University of Agriculture at Morogoro, the University of Dar es Salaam with its affiliate college, the Muhimbili College of Medical Sciences, and the Open University based in Dar es Salaam. All institutions offering higher education are government owned and are under the umbrella of the Ministry of Science, Technology, and Higher Education. The universities are semiautonomous and manage their own affairs under the vice-chancellor, who is appointed by the President of Tanzania. However, their running costs are subsidized by the government.

3.2 Preschool Education

Prior to the 1980s, preschool institutions were managed by private institutions. There was no proper coordination and no clear curriculum. There are now clear policies on the care of children below age three (day care centers), and for the provision of education to children between ages 4 and 7 (preschool education). The Ministry of Education and Culture registers the schools, trains the teachers, supervises them, and develops the curriculum. The curriculum comprises activities in language, arithmetic, nature study, art, music, physical education, health education, good behavior, and character training. There were 134 preprimary schools in mainland Tanzania in 1991 while in Zanzibar there were 18 such government preschools (Ministry of Education and Culture 1992).

3.3 Special Education

In 1992 there were 118 educational institutions (government and nongovernment) catering for the education of disabled students. Of these, 100 provided primary education. The rest were at secondary and college level. Some of these schools were special in that they received pupils with special learning needs only. The children in these schools were isolated in terms of the nature of their handicap. In 1992 there were 14 such schools. The rest of the schools catering for the handicapped were ordinary integrated boarding and/or day schools. Most physically handicapped students and Albinos had access to education in the ordinary schools. This is to enhance interaction with other students and bring up the handicapped children in a natural environment.

Emphasis tends to be on itinerant teaching programs rather than special schools.

All schools for handicapped students use the same syllabuses and textbooks as ordinary schools. However, the former employ additional specialized equipment and materials and have to teach extra learning skills depending on the nature of the handicap. Blind children are taught sense perception, braille reading and writing, typewriting, and mobility. In addition to the normal school subjects, deaf and partially hearing students are taught speech, lip-reading, auditory training, and vocational skills in agriculture, tailoring, and carpentry.

In contrast to the control and management of normal primary education which is concentrated at the regional level, special education is monitored and controlled at both the ministerial and regional levels. There is a unit at the Ministry of Education and Culture headquarters which directly coordinates efforts, both national and international, directed toward the improvement and expansion of special education.

3.4 *Vocational, Technical, and Business Education*

In Tanzania the learning of skills useful for life starts formally at the primary level. The curriculum requires that pupils learn skills such as agriculture, technical skills, home craft, and commerce so that after leaving school, they can be usefully employed. The secondary school curriculum also requires the student to study at least one vocational subject which will be accompanied by practical applications in the school setting. These subjects include agriculture, technical subjects, home economics, commerce, and accounts. These are taught at a level which will be of immediate use after school. Vocational training is offered after completion of any one level or cycle of formal education. There are vocational colleges/centers and institutes which train primary school leavers in various trades. Some of these centers are under the department of primary education of the Ministry of Education and Culture but the majority are under the Ministry of Labor and Community Development. A few others are managed by non-government organizations. Vocational training is not free. For government-owned centers a government-stipulated fee is paid, while for the other institutions a fee is charged for every subject or skill learnt, with rates being dependent on the market demand for the skills. Vocational training is also offered to young women and men who have completed the first and second cycles of secondary education; most institutions offering training at this level are run by the government under respective ministries.

Entry into these institutions is based on examination results, performance at work after secondary education, and individual preference for the course. Certification at the end of the course is either ministerial or national, that is, awarded by the National Examination Council of Tanzania (NECTA). Curriculum at these institutions is not centralized but its quality is controlled by the respective ministries.

Technical education starts at the first cycle of secondary education in some designated schools. Those performing well in this field at the end of the cycle are selected for further technical education and training in the technical colleges or at the Faculty of Engineering at the University of Dar es Salaam. A relatively small number of students sometimes pursue such studies at universities outside the country.

The curriculum in the technical colleges is centrally prescribed and examinations and certification are national. The technical colleges are multifaculty. Subjects and trades include electronics, electrical, mechanical, and structural engineering, plumbing, welding, woodwork, and foundry.

3.5 *Adult and Nonformal Education*

The objective of adult literacy is to help adults (especially in rural areas) to find solutions to problems like hunger, ignorance, and disease including malnutrition. Programs include the provision of, among other things, functional literacy skills to adults in their respective communities; other skills include simple techniques in agriculture, rural construction, health education, home economics, and civics.

Adult literacy programs were initiated in 1968 on an experimental basis in four regions: Mara, Mwanza, Shinyanga, and Kagera. In 1970, a nationwide campaign against illiteracy was launched. The operational objectives of adult education were to create ideological awareness as well as imparting skills which would be functional and instrumental in improving the rural or agricultural settings in which the majority of the population live.

Several subprograms and projects have been initiated. In 1970, "The Choice is Yours" campaign was launched. This emphasized participative democracy in decision-making and development. The national literacy campaign, inspired by the functional literacy approach, was launched in 1972–75. In 1973 there was a campaign known as "Man is Health," which emphasized the need to observe good health habits for a prolonged lifespan, while in 1974 the "Agriculture for Life" campaign was launched. In these campaigns, important technical information about the respective themes was transmitted to the people.

There are three main categories of adult literacy classes. These are: (a) literacy classes which deal with reading, writing, and numeracy; (b) those for the retention of acquired literacy skills; and (c) those aimed at the application and extension of knowledge and skills.

Adult literacy programs are organized in eight stages. Stages 1–4 involve different categories of adults based on their ability to read and write and the utilization and/or comprehension of the literacy skills; stages 5–8 are for those adults who wish to continue after stage 4. Students in both literacy and postliteracy programs are provided with the necessary books and materials free of charge.

Apart from this formal program, there are supporting programs which offer services in the following domains:

(a) Education through radio; this keeps contact with learners every week.

(b) Folk development colleges (FDCs) which offer short courses of one to three weeks and long courses of up to two years in handicrafts, home economics, mechanics, and so on.

(c) Rural libraries, functioning in about a third of the villages in the country.

(d) Rural newspapers; these are published in each of the seven zones in the country and sold at low prices to postliteracy adult education students.

The management and coordination of adult education is the responsibility of the Department of Adult Education at the Ministry of Education and Culture. Apart from the Department, there is an Institute of Adult Education, a semiautonomous public institution which is charged with the duty of providing continuing education to adults through short and long courses, workshops, seminars, and distance learning mainly by correspondence. An open university has been established through which adults can acquire university education through correspondence. Nonformal education has existed in Tanzania for years although without the guidance of any clearly defined policy. However, programs have been implicitly recognized through guidelines, statements, resolutions, and educational policies issued at different times since Independence in 1961.

Out-of-school education programs can be categorized according to the needs of the out-of-school population. These include semiscientific-oriented activities resulting in vocational training institutions, backyard garages, traditional tin-smithing, watch repair works and the like. Examples are:

(a) activities which deal with distributive business and community services, such as fishmongers, street vendors, and so on;

(b) small-scale farming including vegetable growing, poultry keeping, and pig keeping;

(c) dress making, cobbling, and handicrafts;

(d) professional-oriented activities, such as secretarial services and commercial consultancy services;

(e) cultural and recreational activities.

A common feature of these programs is that they are specific and need oriented. Categories of program include:

(a) those under industries, such as small-scale industry programs;

(b) programs under nongovernmental organizations including church organizations such as YMCA, YWCA, CARITAS, Tanzania Family Planning Association, and the Tanzania Red Cross Society;

(c) programs which are offered by private companies and individuals (e.g., computer distribution companies, secretarial services companies, and private garages).

The out-of-school programs are normally small in size, having about 10 to 60 students at a time. The clientele for the programs consists essentially of primary school leavers, school dropouts, and various target groups in search of continuing education or certain skills. Admission involves individuals' efforts to apply for a course and for most programs basic literacy is essential. In some programs, students are admitted on the basis of competitive examinations. The length of a course varies according to its objectives. Most of the prevocational programs range from six months to two years. Courses to upgrade the skills of those already employed vary from a few days to two years.

The financing of most programs, particularly those run by nongovernmental organizations, is through voluntary contributions. Privately owned institutions charge fees. Staffing is through the institution's own initiatives except for government-run programs where staffing is organized by government.

4. *Administrative and Supervisory Structure and Operation*

The Minister for Education and Culture is responsible for the development and implementation of all education plans in the country. The Minister is assisted by an Advisory Council. The Principal Secretary is the chief executive of the Ministry. Under the Principal Secretary, there are two Commissioners; the Commissioner for Education who is the chief advisor to the Minister on education policies and practices and the Commissioner for Culture who advises the Minister on cultural affairs and coordinates the departments and units involved in culture and sports.

The headquarters of the Ministry is organized into various departments: the departments of primary, secondary, teacher and adult education, educational planning, administration, and personnel. Others include the school inspectorate, arts, games and sports, and national museums. There are also units responsible for national antiquities and archives. The departments are headed by directors, who manage and coordinate the activities of the institutions in their respective levels of education. The day-to-day functions of the primary and adult education departments are decentralized and are administratively under the Ministry of Regional Administration and Local Government. The regional and district education officers are representatives of the Ministry of Education and Culture at the regional and district levels respectively.

In its efforts to ensure effective deployment of its specialist staff in the design and proper implementation and evaluation of educational programs, the Ministry established independent and semigovernmental institutes which perform specialist functions. The Institute of Curriculum Development (ICD) is responsible for the development of education content and instructional materials, while the Institute of Adult Education (IAE) ensures the development of programs for adult literacy and postliteracy education. The National Examination Council of Tanzania (NECTA) specializes in the design and administration of national examinations and the certification of candidates. These organizations work closely with the office of the Commissioner for Education. Other semigovernmental organizations include the Tanzania Library Services (TLS), which ensures the national readership and promotion of school libraries, and The Tanzania Elimu Supplies (TES) which deals with the distribution of educational materials countrywide.

The universities and higher technical colleges which were formerly under the Ministry of Education and Culture are now under the umbrella of the Ministry of Science, Technology, and Higher Education.

5. *Educational Finance*

Since Independence the financing of education has been largely the responsibility of the central government. Since the mid-1980s parents and owners of schools have been required to contribute more toward meeting the ever-increasing costs of education. During the 1970s, the government spent 15–20 percent of its total annual recurrent budget on education for most of the years. In 1980 to 1984 about 12 percent of the central government's budget was allocated to education. Since 1984/85 it has ranged between 4.8 percent and 7.9 percent. In 1990/91, it was 6.3 percent.

Part of this decline has been offset by cost-sharing initiatives. At the preschool level, privately owned kindergartens determine their own fees. Government-owned preschools do not charge fees but parents contribute toward the cost of school meals and play materials. The contributions range from 400 Sh (US$0.9) per child per year in rural schools to 12,000 Sh (US$27) per child per year in urban areas. At primary school level, the government requires parents to contribute 200 Sh (US$0.5) per child per year toward the cost of learning materials. In overall terms, the financing of primary education is low. In 1991, per capita expenditure was 3,200 Sh (US$7) per child while actual requirement stood at 17,000 Sh (US$39) per student per year.

Pupils in government-managed day secondary schools pay 5,000 Sh (US$11.3) per pupil per year while boarding pupils pay 8,000 Sh (US$18.13) each. A nongovernment secondary school pupil pays between 30,000 (US$69) and 46,000 Sh (US$105) depending on whether he or she is a day or boarding student in the first or second cycle of secondary education.

The cost of training teachers and that for providing adult education is the responsibility of the central government.

Up until 1991 costs of preparing examinations administration, supervision, and correction of scripts were covered by the government. Since then, every pupil sitting for the national examinations, except for primary school students, has to pay a small fee to subsidize the cost of materials and examination administration. Development projects in education are heavily dependent on external financing. Up to 75 percent of development projects funding is external.

6. *Supplying Personnel for the Education System*

The training of teachers is a central government responsibility. Student teachers for primary schools are recruited mainly from successful applicants from the first cycle of secondary education. These receive residential training in teachers colleges for two years and if they successfully complete the course they become Grade A teachers.

Similarly, applicants from the second cycle of secondary education receive training for two years to be awarded a Diploma in Education; they may teach in secondary forms 1–4 (the first cycle of secondary education).

Teachers trained at the university level teach in both cycles of secondary education and in teacher training colleges. Selection to teacher training is based on the prospective candidate's level of pass in the requisite examination, and vacancies for training available in the institutes or colleges. Each educational institution is headed by an education officer appointed by the Ministry. The appointment criteria are mainly academic merit, management, and leadership competence. Seniority may also contribute toward these appointments. Staffing and transfers of personnel are implemented by the ministries concerned. Discipline of staff is handled by the head of the school or college in collaboration with a school/college board. Staff discipline is also handled by the Ministry headquarters and the Teacher Service Commission (TSC). The commission is also charged with the responsibility of hiring teachers, and proposing teacher promotion, on behalf of the government. Heads of schools and colleges have no power to dismiss staff. Certification and registration of teachers is done by the Commissioner for Education.

7. Curriculum Development and Teaching Methodology

Curriculum development for kindergartens, schools, teacher training colleges, postprimary technical centers, and special education programs in mainland Tanzania is the responsibility of the Institute of Curriculum Development (ICD). It operates through a system of subject panels and curriculum boards.

A subject panel examines the selection and organization of the subject matter of a specific subject at the different levels of education and recommends the outcomes for approval and use in schools by the Commissioner for Education.

In the early 1990s, the ICD, in consultation with the Ministry of Education and Culture, proposed significant changes in the design of the curriculum offered at primary, secondary, and teacher training levels. The focus is mainly on the reduction of the number of subjects for easy management by students and teachers and on methods for improving instruction. As part of the curriculum reform, consideration was given to a number of key issues including:

(a) problems in the old curriculum package;

(b) educational demands by parents, students, teachers and employers;

(c) research findings;

(d) the philosophy, goals, and objectives of education in Tanzania as reflected in government policy and statements;

(e) trends of curriculum reforms which had been taking place globally in the 1980s;

(f) contemporary theories and practices in education;

(g) the need to balance theoretical content and practical skills and to diversify the provision of vocational and life skills in every school to give students a wider choice of subjects to pursue through a definition of core, obligatory choices, work-oriented and optional subjects.

Redefinition and streamlining of the curriculum package for teacher training programs has been made with more emphases on studies in the principles of education and teaching, educational psychology and counselling, and teaching methods in order to improve the quality of teachers.

In 1993, the ICD was revising syllabuses, instructional materials, equipment, charts, and other audiovisual aids. Induction and orientation into the new content and materials were planned for all teachers.

8. The System of Examinations, Promotions, and Certifications

At the end of every level of formal education there is a final examination which also determines whether a student is promoted to the next level or not. The examinations include national examinations at the end of primary Grades 4 and 7. Failure in the primary grade 4 examination does not terminate a pupil's primary education but gives the educators information about the progress of the pupil. The Grade 7 examination is terminal. Those who do not gain access to secondary education enter the economy.

The examinations administered at secondary school level are: the National Form 2 (Grade 9) Examination, the Certificate of Secondary Education Examination (CSEE) and the Advanced Certificate of Secondary Education Examination (ACSEE). While the last two are terminal, the Form 2 examination provides information about the learners' progress.

Teacher certification examinations are administered for trainees of various courses, namely Grade B, Grade A, and Diploma student courses.

9. Educational Assessment, Evaluation, and Research

Teachers assess their pupils both in their classroom work and also in practical skills as demonstrated by self-reliance activities, attitudes toward manual work, and commitment to community endeavors. In practice, however, teachers are able to assess factual knowledge only.

Educational administrators at ward, district, and regional level, heads of schools, subject teachers, the National Examinations Council of Tanzania (NECTA) and the Inspectorate are all involved in one way or another in the evaluation of education.

School inspectors evaluate the teaching of various subjects, the general administration of the educational institutions, financial management, and other matters relating to the organization of these institutions.

A coordinating unit for Educational Research and Evaluation has been established at the Ministry of Education and Culture headquarters. It conducts and supports the conduct of different types of small- or large-scale studies. Further, it renders advisory services to various researchers, facilitates research clearances, and organizes or takes part in collaborative research endeavors with other institutions. It plays a significant role in feeding planners with information about development trends in education so as to influence policy direction.

10. Major Reforms in the 1980s and 1990s

Major educational reforms in the 1980s and 1990s resulting from policy reviews included:

(a) The Special Education School Inspection Services, introduced in 1980.

(b) The first attempt in setting a direction for education toward the year 2000 by the Presidential Commission on Education.

(c) The National Conference on Education held in 1984 to discuss and adopt the recommendations of the 1982 Presidential Commission on Education report.

(d) The introduction of an Early Childhood Education Project following the resolutions and recommendations of the National Committee for the International Year of the Child. The project, which was launched on a pilot basis 1983 to 1985, continues to operate on a small scale but is expected to be integrated into the mainstream of the education system by July 1993.

(e) Increasing intersectoral collaboration in education. Health and environmental projects since 1985 included the following projects:

- (i) Child Survival Development Program;
- (ii) School Feeding Program;
- (iii) AIDS Education and Prevention;
- (iv) Health Education and Environmental Sanitation;
- (v) Family Life Education.

(f) Establishment of an open university to cater for the needs of the out-of-school population necessitated the appointment of a special committee in 1988 to undertake a needs assessment survey and make recommendations for action.

(g) The establishment of the Ministry of Science, Technology, and Higher Education in 1990 was prompted by the need for Tanzania to deal with the development of science and technology more effectively while the establishment of the Ministry of Community Development, Women's Affairs, and Children was promoted by the need for the country to deal with issues of gender and the rights of women and children more realistically.

(h) Review of the education system for the twenty-first century in the light of technological change was undertaken in 1992 with the ultimate goal of producing an education policy for mainland Tanzania.

(i) Revision of the curriculum and the introduction of the new curriculum package which includes science and technology, environmental education, cultural values, civics, and social studies.

(j) National inservice teacher workshops for primary teachers have continued under the "Mpango wa Tanzania/UNESCO/UNICEF" (MTUU) programs.

(k) A national Education Conference was held in 1991 as a follow-up to Jomtien Conference on Education for All.

(l) A survey on the needs of special education in Tanzania to cater for the disabled was begun in 1991.

(m) A national conference on special education was held with the purpose of expanding and promoting education so as to integrate disabled students into ordinary schools, and looking into possibilities of establishing a teacher training college.

(n) An early childhood education (ECE) workshop was held in 1991. It was organized by the Ministry of Education and Culture in collaboration with the Aga Khan Education Services Tanzania to revitalize ECE provision and to establish an ECE association.

(o) National, subregional, and regional workshops for inservice teachers were supported by the Australian government under the Education Program for Southern Africa (EPSA).

(p) Through the financial assistance of SIDA, short-term upgrading teachers courses and seminars were conducted to develop teachers' aptitudes, skills, and competence.

(q) There has been a re-structuring of the Ministry of Education, integrating it with culture with a purpose of promoting education for cultural development.

11. Major Problems for the Year 2000

As the year 2000 approaches the following major issues will have to be addressed:

(a) eradication of remaining illiteracy;

(b) ensuring full primary education for all school-age children;

(c) improving the quality of basic education;

(d) emphasizing science and technology.

References

Ministry of Education and Culture 1992 *National Report of the United Republic of Tanzania*. International Conference on Education, 43rd session, Geneva 1992. Ministry of Education and Culture, Dar es Salaam.

Further Reading

Ministry of Education 1986 *National Report of the United Republic of Tanzania*. International Conference on Education, 40th Session Geneva 1986, Ministry of Education, Dar es Salaam

Ministry of Education 1989 *Education for All: Meeting Basic Learning Needs, to the Year 2000, Tanzania National Document*. Ministry of Education, Dar es Salaam

Ministry of Education 1990 *National Report of the United Republic of Tanzania*. International Conference on Education, 42nd session, Geneva 1990. Ministry of Education, Dar es Salaam

Ministry of Education and Culture 1992/93 Budget speech. Ministry of Education and Culture, Dar es Salaam

B. N. V. Buretta

Task Analysis

Task analysis is a process used to develop understanding of what is involved in performing and/or learning to perform a task: either a skill, a procedure, or an area of content. In most cases its purpose is to help determine appropriate methods for improving performance of that task, primarily by helping an instructional designer to decide what to teach (content) and how best to teach it (methods). The present entry defines task analysis and describes various purposes it can serve. Major techniques, key questions, and important research issues are discussed.

1. What is Task Analysis?

In a general sense, task analysis determines what is involved in meeting a given goal or need. It follows the process of needs assessment, through which the designer determines where learning or some other form of performance enhancement is required. Thus, task analysis is a process used to develop understanding of what is involved in performing and/or learning to perform a task. This includes the skills and knowledge that are relied upon, the thought processes engaged in, and/or the actions taken in performing the task. Task analysis can also provide information on such factors as the environment where performance takes place, the criticality of the task, typical errors, and the consequences of good or poor performance. In a general sense, the task analyst asks what has to be done by whom, how, when, where, and with what level of skill. Task analysis results in a representation of the task—for example, a list of visual map of task elements and their relationships—that is useful in facilitating performance and/or designing instruction.

The term "task analysis" is often used rather broadly to include analysis of subject matter or content. Related processes that are sometimes considered types of task analysis include job analysis, skills analysis, goal analysis, and instructional analysis.

2. Purposes of Task Analysis

Jonassen et al. (1989) have identified five functions for task analysis, the last three of which are instructional purposes: inventorying tasks, describing tasks, selecting tasks for instruction, sequencing tasks (and subtasks) in instruction, and analyzing task and content level (for selecting instructional strategies). Task analysis information can be useful in such areas as worker selection, training selection, performance appraisal, job design, instructional design, and others. For worker selection, workers can be selected for a job based on their preparation in terms of the skills and knowledge identified by the task analysis. For training selection, a worker might be required to complete only those aspects of a training program that match task elements where his or her skills are lacking. For performance appraisal, results of the task analysis can be used as criteria for evaluating performance, making it easier to identify areas of deficiency. For job design, it is frequently possible to find ways to improve the person–job system (e.g., the task environment or the way the task is performed). For example, the task representation can serve as a job aid, placing knowledge in the world rather than in performers' heads. As this implies, task analysis often eliminates the need for further work; learning simply to use the aid rather than to remember task steps may be all that is required. For instructional design, designers of courses and curricula use information from a task analysis primarily to identify what individuals need to learn, how instruction should be sequenced, and what instructional strategies and tactics should be used.

Task analysis offers the potential benefit of helping a designer to avoid (or eliminate) content that is irrelevant to achieving the goal. This can decrease costs by reducing training time and reducing the need for learning on the job. On the other hand, it is possible that omitted content could have had unanticipated benefits, say in helping the learner understand other aspects of a job. Therefore, while benefits can be great, task analysis has potential to limit the designer's thinking to those aspects of performance which can be observed and explicitly stated. It is prudent to view task analysis as an aid rather than a prescription in designing, and to analyze problems logically and pose solutions creatively. Further areas where task analysis information is useful include troubleshooting, resource allocation, manual development, and test construction. Task analysis is also a powerful tool used by engineers to increase reliability and reduce error. This entry will focus on task analysis for purposes of instructional design.

3. How Is Task Analysis Carried Out?

Techniques for carrying out task analysis can be grouped into at least five major categories: those which identify subordinate learning skills; those which identify procedural steps; those which identify causal models underlying complex cognitive tasks; those which identify content elements; and those which help the designer to select appropriate instructional strategies. Each of the first four techniques seeks to determine the elements of the task or content area, the relationships among those elements, and the organizing principle that ties all elements together. The fifth technique seeks to determine the kind of learning involved so that appropriate instructional strategies and tactics can be selected. Selection of a particular technique depends primarily on the type of goal involved or the purpose of the analysis, and such classification is typically the first step in conducting the analysis.

Task analysis of subordinate skills assumes that learning a complex skill involves mastery of a number of more simple subskills. If those subskills can be identified and sequenced according to learning prerequisite relations, then learning should be more effective and efficient. The most widely used technique is the learning hierarchy (Gagné 1968), a representation of the task as a visual map of prerequisite skills. Learning entry-level skills at the base of the hierarchy is expected to lead, or "positively transfer," to learning intermediate skills (enabling objectives) in the middle, and to learning the goal (terminal objective) at the top. This technique is especially useful in criterion testing, selection, and placement, and in sequencing instruction. It is often selected when the goal involves performance of an intellectual skill. A disadvantage is that the hierarchy does not show procedural relationships.

Procedural task analysis assumes that tasks are performed as sequences of specific cognitive processes and actions. Hence, task acquisition and performance can be facilitated by identifying steps and representing them in algorithmic form, for example, in a flowchart or decision table. There are two major kinds of procedural task analysis: that which merely identifies the order of steps in a procedure (see e.g., Merrill 1976), and that which also arranges different versions of the task in order of complexity, such as Merrill's (1976) path analysis technique or the Elaboration Theory's simplifying conditions method for procedural content (Reigeluth 1992). Procedural task analysis is often selected when the goal is a physical action or psychomotor task, or an intellectual skill with a fairly limited number of ways it can be performed by experts. It is not appropriate for complex cognitive tasks that vary greatly from one performance to another.

Task analysis of complex cognitive tasks assumes that such tasks are not performed by experts as a sequence of steps; rather experts have an underlying body of knowledge—a set of principles or causal models—that they use to generate an appropriate performance for each particular situation. Therefore, such tasks require a type of task analysis that identifies the underlying principles or causal models that experts use to perform them. There are also two major kinds of complex-cognitive-task analysis: that which merely identifies the underlying principles, and that which also arranges different versions of the task in order of complexity (see e.g., the Elaboration Theory's simplifying conditions method for causal models—Reigeluth 1992). This technique is selected only when the goal is a complex cognitive task.

Task analysis of content elements assumes that some important knowledge is not tied to any one specific task (or goal), such as an understanding of some basic principles of economics or biology. This technique results in some sort of visual map of content, such as an outline, a content taxonomy, or a chart. A content map can provide a powerful tool for a designer to sequence instruction and for a learner to grasp relationships, but it does not identify what the learner should be able to do as a result of learning. That is, the skills or learning outcomes are not made explicit by the map. In carrying out an analysis of content (and in using most other techniques), analysts often employ a card sort method, writing elements on cards, sorting, selecting, and organizing the cards, and then linking them together.

Task analysis of kinds of learning differs from the above kinds of task analysis in that it does not break down a task into parts; rather it classifies the parts in order to select appropriate instructional tactics. It is based on the assumption that different kinds of learning are best taught with different kinds of instructional tactics. This intact classification of task elements is based on a taxonomy, such as Bloom's or Gagné's (1986) or Merrill's (1983). After a task element has been classified as to the type of learning involved or desired, a set of tactics is assigned for teaching that kind of learning for that element. The most common categories include cognitive, affective, and psychomotor learning, and, within the cognitive domain, memorizing information, understanding relationships, applying skills, and using generic (domain independent) skills (Leshin et al. 1992). The strategy or tactics are then adapted and supplemented based on the learning situation (content, learners, and learning environment).

Often, the learning goal leads to selection of a certain task analysis technique. For example, a psychomotor task such as operating a machine can be expressed as an algorithm fairly easily. Just as often, however, the nature of the goal is not so easily classified, and several different techniques are candidates. Also, the analyst can select one technique, but one technique provides a single perspective. It is often wise to use more than one technique or to combine several. For example, algorithmic elements could be identified for a subordinate skill, or subordinate skills could be identified for a procedural step. Content elements might be attached to either. Reigeluth and Merrill's (1984) extended task analysis procedure represents such a combination.

The techniques described above are representative. Other techniques include path, critical incident, fault tree, pattern noting, and matrix analysis. See Jonassen et al. (1989), Zemke and Kramlinger (1982), and Carlisle (1986) for descriptions of these and many other techniques, and for sample task representations.

The selection of a task analysis technique or techniques will be influenced greatly by the purpose of the analysis. A variety of purposes was listed in the previous section of this entry, but even within the instructional design focus selected here, purpose can include selecting and sequencing the course content (which is the purpose of most of the above-described techniques) or selecting instructional strategies and tactics.

Regardless of the purpose within the instructional design focus, the role of task analysis is to provide information needed for good instructional design decisions. Thus, selection of methods of task analysis should be driven by the information needs at each point in the design process. Task analysis should not be viewed as an activity totally independent from design. In many cases, the instructional theories that a designer selects will specify what those information needs are, because the theories prescribe methods for different situations, particularly for different types of tasks. In effect, theories of instruction require the analyst to seek certain types of information about the tasks in order to select appropriate content, sequences, strategies, and tactics. Therefore, theories of instruction can be seen as having corresponding task analysis methods (although those methods can also be used independently of a given instructional theory). In cases where instructional theory is driving the design, the goal of task analysis becomes not just identification of elements and relationships, but doing so in a manner which supports designing instruction according to the theory.

After a task analysis technique (or combination of techniques) has been chosen, information about the task must be collected. Sources of information for task analysis include various levels of job performers (e.g., novices and experts), supervisors, instructors, content experts, and learners. Also useful are reference guides, training materials, manuals, logs, and other documents, and potentially anything that exists in the physical environment. Data are gathered using unobtrusive participant observation of the job, individual interviews, structured or unstructured group interviews, surveys, and study of documents (Jonassen et al. 1989).

Task analysis tools have been developed that reveal some information on processes that previously remained implicit in performance. For example, cognitive task analysis (Roth and Woods 1989) requires performers to think aloud as they perform tasks. Analysis of the resulting think-aloud protocols gives at least partial evidence of the thought processes performers engage in during performance of the task. These data are believed superior to retrospective reports. That is, the performer describing task performance after the fact often constructs a hypothetical argument of what he or she may have done, as opposed to what really occurred. Of course, skill components that cannot be verbalized, for example, procedures that are performed "automatically" and are no longer consciously controlled, will not appear in a protocol.

4. *Key Questions*

Perhaps the most difficult questions to answer in conducting a task analysis are where to start and where to stop. When task analysis is employed for creating instruction, the first question, where to start, is difficult but manageable. The analysis should begin with the goal, the broadest statement of what learning is sought, and move to progressively greater levels of detail. This goal is never completely clear, and is much less clear at the outset, but it can at least tentatively be stated and agreed upon.

The second question, where to stop, is more challenging. What to include and what to exclude and how much detail to add or cut are rarely easy decisions. Generally, the learners' abilities and prior knowledge are the major basis for making these decisions. That is, the instruction should start at the learners' current level of skill and knowledge. Ultimately, it is a question of risk management, which must assess the tolerance for error and the consequences of including too much or too little content.

5. *Issues and Directions*

It is important to recognize that the types of task elements that are identified—for example, subskills, steps in a procedure, underlying principles or causal models, or content elements—and the processes used in breaking the task down, are based on theories of human performance, knowledge, or learning. As those theories advance, new methods of task analysis are developed. Furthermore, different methods of task analysis are compatible with, and useful for, different kinds of learning and different approaches to learning. Thus, analysts break a task down in a particular way because they believe it will be most useful for their situation and philosophy of learning and instruction.

For example, techniques based on a behavioral tradition identify types of behaviors or kinds of learning outcomes (Gagné 1986). In contrast, techniques based on cognitive psychology attempt to describe mental processes that underlie those outcomes. In the case of procedural tasks, the two traditions may often identify the same elements, but in the case of complex cognitive tasks, the differences are great.

Techniques such as cognitive task analysis appear to have much potential. Task analysts or "knowledge engineers" seek to describe the knowledge of experts and to express that knowledge in computer software programs known as expert systems. Significant progress has been made in this area, and expert systems have been developed which do a fair job of solving some problems as experts do. However, a number of constraints on development of expert systems remain, including a primitive understanding of cognitive processes underlying performance, the domain-specificity of expertise, and—as a major consequence of these two factors—the great amount of time needed to develop a single system.

Efforts to understand performance in terms of the mental processes involved include Sternberg's (1983) componential analysis and Rasmussen's SRK or skills, rules, and knowledge (see Goodstein et al. 1988). However, intellectual performance may also be influenced by such things as beliefs and social processes. Furthermore, although general characteristics of experts have been described, there is the clear notion that much of the knowledge and skill of an expert in one domain does not transfer to another. As a result, task analysis or "knowledge acquisition" processes must be repeated for each and every domain. It is also important to note that these techniques, while appropriate to building systems that imitate the behavior of an expert, are not necessarily appropriate as pedagogical tools. The gap between an expert and a novice may be made clear, but how best to help a novice become an expert remains a matter of instructional design.

Since the mid-1980s, increasing credence has been given to a "constructivist" epistemology which views learning as the active development of meaning on the basis of experience. Learning is seen as a constructive act, and the designer should provide for rich experiences by situating activities in authentic contexts and provide for exploration and sharing of multiple perspectives. The implication of this view for task analysis is that, for some learning situations, the learning environment should not be limited to specific task elements and relationships. The analyst may still seek a core of information to make available to all learners, but should avoid setting boundaries on what information is deemed relevant and included for such learning situations. The goals and methods of task analysis from this perspective, and how results can be implemented in instructional systems, are not entirely clear, but efforts are under way in this area.

A second issue concerns when task analysis should be conducted. Task analysis can be seen as a process engaged in after needs assessment and before design. But the costs of performing a task analysis are often high and, therefore, resources are infrequently committed before a clear goal or performance gap is identified. Nevertheless, an iterative process may yield better results. That is, task analysis can inform needs assessment, and design can inform both needs assessment and task analysis. A cyclical approach with feedback and feedforward is implied. A rapid prototyping methodology such as that offered by the Elaboration Theory's simplifying conditions method (Reigeluth 1992) may offer a key to managing such a cyclical process, particularly with a large project and a large design team.

A final issue relates to the potential for computers to assist the analyst, for example, in reducing the amount of time and effort needed to develop an expert system. An example of a computer program designed to help the task analyst is SNOWMAN, or System for Knowledge Management. The potential for computers to assist designers in these and other processes have been explored. Gayeski (1991) raises some questions regarding the nature of such programs, that is, where and for what types of problems such systems, at least as conceived at that time, are appropriate and useful.

See also: Problem-solving and Learning: Computer Modeling; Constructivism and Learning; Instructional Design Theories; Instructional Psychology (as a Contributing Field to Instructional Design); Job Analysis in Corporate Education; Learning Processes and Learning Outcomes; Models of Learning

References

Carlisle K E 1986 *Analyzing Jobs and Tasks*. Educational Technology Publications, Englewood Cliffs, New Jersey

Gagné R M 1968 Learning hierarchies. *Educ. Psychol.* 6(1): 3–6

Gagné R M 1986 *The Conditions of Learning*, 4th edn. Holt, Rinehart, and Winston, New York

Gayeski D M 1991 Software tools for empowering instructional developers. *Performance Improvement Quarterly* 4(4): 21–36

Goodstein L P, Andersen H B, Olsen S E (eds.) 1988 *Tasks, Errors, and Mental Models*. Taylor and Francis, London

Jonassen D H, Hannum W H, Tessmer M 1989 *Handbook of Task Analysis Procedures*. Praeger, New York

Leshin C, Pollock J, Reigeluth C M 1992 *Instructional Design Strategies and Tactics*. Educational Technology Publications, Englewood Cliffs, New Jersey

Merrill M D 1983 Component display theory. In: Reigeluth C M (ed.) 1983 *Instructional Design Theories and Models: An Overview of their Current Status*. Erlbaum, Hillsdale, New Jersey

Merrill P F 1976 Task analysis: An information-processing approach. *NSPI Journal* 15(2): 7–11

Reigeluth C M 1992 Elaborating the elaboration theory. *Educ. Tech. Res. Dev.* 40(3): 80–86

Reigeluth C M, Merrill M D 1984 *The Extended Task*

Analysis Procedure: User's Manual. University Press of America, Lanham, Maryland

Roth E M, Woods D D 1989 Cognitive task analysis: An approach to knowledge acquisition for intelligent system design. In: Guida G, Tasso C (eds.) 1989 *Topics in Expert System Design: Methodologies and Tools*. North Holland, Amsterdam

Sternberg R J 1983 Components of human intelligence. *Cog*. 15 (1–3): 1–48

Zemke R, Kramlinger T 1982 *Figuring Things Out: A Trainer's Guide to Needs and Task Analysis*. Addison-Wesley, Reading, Massachusetts

Further Reading

Duffy T M, Lowyck J, Jonassen D H (eds.) 1993 *Designing Environments for Constructive Learning*. Springer-Verlag, Berlin

G. Rowland; C. M. Reigeluth

Taxonomies of Skill Development

Skill development programs are operated by many different public agencies in many different settings. Training is also provided in the workplace as an ancillary activity to production (on-the-job training) in both public and private sectors. Lastly, training is offered by proprietary firms that specialize in skill development. In some countries, a piece-by-piece approach to building a system of skill development has created serious problems with respect to coordination and coverage. This entry proposes a taxonomy of skill development programs to guide appropriate placement and sponsorship of particular training programs in an integrated system of skill development. The taxonomy should also be useful in clarifying the appropriate distribution of financial responsibilities to assure adequate and stable funding for training programs. The overall objective is to assist in designing systems of skill development that are productive, efficient, and equitable.

1. Some Characteristics of Preferred Training Systems

A preferred training system will be accountable for maintaining standards of skill development in industrial fields that allow sustained economic growth to take place. Neither qualitative deficiencies nor quantitative shortages of skills should be bottlenecks in the process of economic development. A related objective is to avoid surpluses of trained workers in given occupations. A preferred training system will also ensure a rising standard of competence among workers in the social sectors (health, education, community development). In both the industrial and the social sectors, desired worker characteristics include problem-identifying and problem-solving abilities, the capacity to communicate in oral and written forms, and the flexibility to master new tasks as work processes change. Not all actual or potential training agencies have equal capacity for high quality skill development. For example, if the objective is to produce top-flight electronics technicians, a large firm with a strong commitment to research and development will likely offer a better kind of training than a village workshop. Not all agencies have the same degree of flexibility to meet the shifting demands of the labor market. Public agencies with more or less fixed budgets and tenured trainers may have difficulty in responding quickly to sharp increases or decreases in demand for particular types of workers.

A preferred training system will be efficient. The trainers will be proficient in the skills they are teaching and they will be well-motivated. The mix of theoretical and practical learning will be appropriate to the tasks the graduates will perform. The equipment available in training sites will be technologically up-to-date, in good repair, and heavily utilized. The trainees will have their motivation to learn enhanced by seeing a clear connection between their acquiring a high standard of proficiency and career advancement. The opportunity costs of trainees will be at an appropriate minimum. Rates of student wastage will be low and long interruptions in training will be avoided. A creditable system of student assessment and program evaluation will be in place. In a preferred training system, all agencies will have a stable and adequate level of funding. Stable and adequate funding appears to be best achieved when the costs of training are distributed to the direct beneficiaries of skill development. Direct beneficiaries are ordinarily of two main classes: trainees and employers. In particular cases, either class of beneficiary, or both together, may contribute to cost recovery.

Lastly, a preferred training system will be equitable, in the sense that access to give training opportunities is truly meritocratic, not determined by family status or caste. Taking account of the fact that potential trainees are likely to be dispersed geographically, to have different needs for support systems, and to display different tastes for ways in which training is presented, a certain amount of redundancy in the training system is probably helpful in attaining the equity objective. No single agency should necessarily be solely responsible for developing a particular set of skills. Redundancy, however, can be nonfunctional and interfere with attainment of the efficiency objective.

2. Forms of Skill Development

The usefulness of a taxonomy of skill development is underscored by the great variety of multiple location, multiple delivery programs for training that are in place in the early 1990s. A prime example of such diversity is the United States. In the public sector, Wirt et al. (1989) have reported that skills training is provided in comprehensive secondary schools, specialized secondary schools, part-day regional training facilities for secondary students and adults, community colleges, technical institutes, and subsidized programs of "community based organizations." Also in the public sector are residential programs for low-income youth (Job Corps), short-term training for entry-level workers and displaced workers (Jobs Training Partnership Act), a vast amount of military training (of which a high proportion is in skills transferable to the civilian sectors), and programs in correctional institutions. In the private sector, apprenticeship programs, other forms of formal on-the-job training, informal on-the-job training, privately subsidized off-the-job training, and a flourishing set of proprietary training institutions can all be found.

The plethora of training sites notwithstanding, Carnevale (1991) offers comparative evidence that the United States workforce is on the whole, underskilled. For example, most of the 19 studies of economic returns to vocational education in secondary schools conducted since the early 1970s failed to establish positive significant effects on wage rates, as reported in Benson et al. (1991). Information on on-the-job training in the United States has been sparse, but a study by Lynch (1992) indicates that (a) the characteristics influencing participation in formal on-the-job training are primarily race and gender, with women and non-Whites being much less likely to receive training; (b) on-the-job training is associated with higher wages in the given firm but is not readily portable; and (c) the stronger influence on wage rates, being of an even stronger influence on wages than seniority.

In other countries, there is generally less internal diversity in locuses of skill development, but there remain strong differences between countries in patterns of training. In Japan, as Hashimoto (1991) notes, there is major reliance on on-the-job training (OJT). On-the-job training in Japan is characterized by a great deal of flexibility. The long tenure of most employees in Japan reduces the need for portability of skills and, hence, for strict regulation of skill development processes (as in, e.g., Germany). The job rotation system helps insure that workers acquire "intrafirm general skills," reducing layoffs when product demand shifts. "Training in Japanese firms is a long-term process for which the major input is time spent exchanging information and transferring knowledge among employees as well as between management and employees" (Hashimoto 1991 p. 165). In the United Kingdom, as Vickers (1991) notes, the 1980s witnessed the development of a mixed mode of training, implying intensified competition for youth aged 16 to 18 as between training programs in formal institutions of education (mainly in colleges of further education), paid for largely by government, and the "internal" programs of employers assisted by the state (Youth Training). The internal programs have come to be more firm-specific, offering less portability of skills; at the same time, the proportion of costs borne by employers has increased. Germany has its renowned "dual system." The firm-based apprenticeship provides credentials that are respected and portable, but it is problematical employers in many other countries could accept the strict standards and regulatory machinery on which the German apprenticeship is based.

As Schweitzer (1985) has observed, it is the practice of the Egyptian Ministry of Education to attach specialized secondary schools to major firms, with the intent that students receive their theoretical instruction in school and their practical training in the workshops of the plant. There is a close nexus between the teachers of theoretical instruction and the skilled artisans, the latter being seconded by the firm into full- or part-time teaching duties. When skill demands shift, the artisan teaching force can be readily adapted to the change. The same practice of enclosing secondary schools within the compound of major firms is followed to some extent in Bulgaria. However, the chief means to heighten relevance of instruction to work in Bulgarian secondary technical schools is to include production-for-sale in the school day and week. Profits from the production units are shared by faculty and students.

In a study of returns to on-the job training in Kenya and Tanzania, De Beyer (1990) found much greater differences in average predicted earnings for trained workers with formal education relative to those without formal education. In other words, the combination of formal education and training had a big financial payoff. The relationship between creation of human capital, measured in terms of earnings differentials, and human capital inputs, may be defined as "human capital elasticity," namely, the ratio of the proportionate change in the amount of human capital to the proportionate change in the amount of any one of the inputs. De Beyer suggests there may be interdependencies between three components of a human capital production function: formal education, training, and experience, in which the human capital elasticity of any one of these three inputs depends on the levels of the other two.

Latin American countries rely heavily on SENA-type (Servicio National de Aprendizaje) programs of skill development. (SENA is based in Colombia.) The programs function outside the formal educational system, and employers have the largest voice in their operation. The systems are financed mainly by a payroll tax on large firms, and offer both short-term training (upgrading) and longer term apprenticeships. The closeness of connection to employers and the willingness of employers to second their own skilled workers to train other workers appears to ensure relevance of training to job markets. As Bowman (1990) notes, SENA-type programs generally have had positive evaluations.

3. An Illustrative Taxonomy of Skill Development

To gain greater coherence in design of systems of skill development, taxonomies of training programs may be helpful. What is illustrated here is a heuristic taxonomy for a hypothetical developing country, using an industrial classification as the key variable. The two questions the taxonomy is intended to deal with are (a) what type of agency should be providing training? and (b) how shall training be paid for?

With regard to the first question, the main matter to be decided is whether training should be given in an institution that specializes in training, whether publicly or privately controlled, or in an organization whose main function is production. This is not, however, an all-or-nothing matter. On-the-job training could be supplemented by theoretical instruction provided in a school or college; alternatively, schools or colleges could be sited at the workplace.

There is a similar complexity with respect to the second question. Financing can take a number of forms. These include the use of general tax revenue; assumption of costs by individual firms; payroll tax levies, possibly with differential rates by industrial sector, to subsidize costs in firms that conduct on-the-job training; fees paid by trainees; foregone income (as in apprenticeships); and levies on workers as a group (in the United States union dues are sometimes used to finance apprenticeships). These various means of financing can be used in combination.

Selection of an appropriate site for training is related to the inherent characteristics of those sites. Ordinarily, public institutions operate under tight budgets; they are also likely to offer security of employment to trainers, and these are generally employed on a full-time basis. These conditions make it difficult for public institutions to respond quickly to changes in the technology of production; they cannot, for example, replace trainers who know the old technology with trainers who know the new. Likewise, public institutions may lack the means to keep instructional equipment up-to-date and in functioning order. In lines of work where technological change is rapid, or where production processes are regarded as proprietary, on-the-job training would appear to be the preferred mode. Likewise, if trainees need to be exposed—for motivational or other reasons—to the processes in which they are to become engaged, on-the-job training has an advantage. Nevertheless, training in public institutions offers standards of depth and comprehensiveness of instruction that many work-based training schemes fail to meet.

Choice of financing is similarly complex. Where jobs meet important social needs where at the same time earned income is low—teachers and nurses, for example—a high level of public subsidy is called for. The way financing is arranged can affect incentives. If workers pay for training, they have an incentive to make careful choices in selecting the training program that is right for them and then to study hard. When employers pay for training, they have an incentive to see that training is conducted in an efficient manner and that the skills produced are of a sufficient standard to meet their needs.

The taxonomy below deals with the broad middle swathe of occupations. Jobs requiring university training are excluded, as are unskilled jobs. The hypothetical developing country of the illustration has six main industrial sectors, with corresponding workforce skill requirements, as follows:

(a) A small but growing modern industrial sector, chiefly manufacturing but including extractive and construction activities. The technology level is middle to high (IND-M).

(b) An informal industrial sector consisting of village-based firms but including precision workshops in support of the agricultural sector, that is, production and repair of farm machinery (IND–I).

(c) A commercial sector, including standard office skills, basic accounting, marketing, banking, and insurance (COM).

(d) Health services, at the level of health assistant and junior nurse (HEA).

(e) Agriculture, at the level of lead worker on larger estates and agricultural extension worker, junior grade (AGR).

(f) Primary school teaching (PST).

Here, then, are some illustrative elements of a taxonomy of skill development:

Item 1. Predictability of Demand for Skills

Low	*Middle*	*High*
IND-M	IND-I	HEA
	COM	PST
	AGR	

The low predictability of skills in the modern industrial sector is related to technological change and shifts in the product mix (in response to demands in international markets). Requirements for trained workers in the health and primary education sectors are related strongly to population growth and migration, which are predictable to a relatively high degree of accuracy. Low predictability of demand suggests on-the-job training or a SENA approach. High predictability fits with training in formal, publicly administered institutions of education.

Item 2. Rate of Change in Technical Content of Skills

Low	*Middle*	*High*
COM	IND-I	IND-M
PST	HEA	
	AGR	

A high rate of change in technical content of skills

indicates placement of training in on-the-job or in a SENA-type system. A low rate is consistent with use of state-owned institutions (formal education).

Item 3. Rate of Change in Technical Processes of Production

Low	*Middle*	*High*
PST	IND-I	IND-M
	AGR	COM
		HEA

Item 3 is a "lead indicator" for Item 2. It may be that important changes loom on the horizon in automation of modern sector industrial processes, in the introduction of computerized workstations in banking and insurance firms, and in putting specialties of nuclear medicine in hospitals. Hence, the government might wish to start to develop more advanced training curricula for these three fields.

Item 4. Range in Skill Complexity

Low	*Middle*	*High*
PST	COM	IND-M
	HEA	IND-I
	AGR	

In modern sector factories, there is a need for a limited number of people to repair complicated equipment, and some of the jobs in automation and control require a great deal of technical knowledge. On the other hand, factories employ large numbers of people with middle levels of skill. In the informal industrial sectors, skills range from making lamps from tin and food processing (low) to machining and tool design. Where the range in skill complexity is high, on-the-job training may need to be supplemented by a certain amount of formal, theoretical instruction.

Item 5. Opportunity for Trained Workers to Take Initiative and Be Innovative

Low	*Middle*	*High*
	IND-M	IND-I
	COM	HEA
	PST	AGR

Certain work settings are bureaucratic and others allow for a lot of individual action. Rural craftspeople, agricultural extension agents, and health workers fall into the latter category. One may surmise that theoretical understandings of a line of work helps people to be constructively innovative. Hence, trainees in IND-I, HEA, and AGR should receive theoretical instruction, either in a training institution or as a supplement to on-the-job training.

Item 6. Market Demand for Alternative Uses of Trainers' (Instructors') Time

Low	*Middle*	*High*
HEA	COM	IND-M
PST	AGR	IND-I

Where the market demand for trainers' time is high, it would seem especially important to locate training in, or adjacent to, the workplace, or to use the SENA model.

Item 7. Size of Trainer (Instructor) Labor Pool

Small	*Middle*	*Large*
IND-M	COM	PST
IND-I	AGR	
HEA		

Here, small means both few in number and not readily expandable. Item 7 reinforces the conclusions of Item 6, but adds HEA to workers who should be trained in a setting in, or adjacent to, the workplace (hospitals, clinics).

Item 8. Requirements for Equipment in Training Programs

Small	*Middle*	*Large*
PST	IND-I	IND-M
	COM	HEA
	AGR	

Where requirements for equipment are large, it would seem best to place the training in or near the workplace. Governments often are unwilling to spend the necessary money to purchase and maintain equipment, nor do they always choose the right kinds. Also, public institutions often have difficulty in protecting valuable equipment from theft. Proprietary institutions tend to concentrate on skills training in fields, such as COM, that do not require massive expenditures on equipment.

Item 9. Rate of Change in Types of Equipment Used in Work Processes

Slow	*Middle*	*Fast*
PST	IND-I	IND-M
	COM	HEA
	AGR	

Even though a training process may not need a lot of items that are individually expensive, a high rate of technical obsolescence makes it difficult for a free-standing training institution to keep up-to-date. Where a rapid rate of change is expected, training should be at or near the workplace.

Item 10. Basic Familiarity of Trainees with the Nature of the Workplace

Low	*Middle*	*High*
IND-M	IND-I	AGR
COM		PST
HEA		

All teacher trainees know something about primary schools and many rural youth are familiar with the farm as a workplace. However, most youth know little about what activities are carried out in modern sector factories, offices, and hospitals/clinics. Where basic familiarity is lacking, placing training in or near the workplace may heighten the motivation of students to work hard in their instructional programs.

As a practical matter, this would seem to be more important in IND-M than in COM or HEA.

Item 11. Fungibility of Skills between Modern and Informal Sectors

Low	*Middle*	*High*
AGR	IND-I	IND-M
	PST	COM
		HEA

This is a question of whether people who have received training with the intent that they upgrade small-scale rural enterprise have the opportunity to transfer to modern sector employment and to become urbanized. It is also a question of whether those who have been trained for modern sector roles have the opportunity to move back into their villages and start their own small firms. Where fungibility is high, government might seek a training strategy that recruited people who seemed already to have made the choice to stay in the right job in the right place. Fungibility appears to increase with length of schooling. Without clear commitment toward rural development, postsecondary training may be unsuitable for skills that are deemed strategic in the countryside, at least in the early stages of economic development.

Item 12. General versus Specific Skills

General	*Specific*
IND-I*	IND-M
COM	HEA
	AGR
	PST

This and the following two items bear upon the question of who should pay for training. The employer or government should pay for training for specific skills and the employee should meet the expenses of getting general skills (possibly through foregone income). This statement is made under the conventional argument, which applies in full to perfectly competitive labor markets: that general skills, being widely marketable at a going wage rate, hold value for the employee but not for the employer in whose workplace those skills may have been created, while specific skills, being confined in use to that given workplace, hold value only for the employer.

Item 13. Creation of External or Intergenerational Benefits

Low	*High*
IND-M	HEA
IND-I	AGR
COM	PST

External benefits are received by households and employers in equal amounts, regardless of whether any particular household or employer contributed resources toward their production. An example: among the presumed external benefits of literacy is protection of life and property afforded by living in a stable democracy. Intergenerational benefits are future benefits: such things as higher standards of health and education in the rising generations. In general, individual households and employers resist making voluntary purchases of external and intergenerational benefits. The distribution in Item 13 suggests that HEA, AGR, and PST could appropriately be financed from general tax revenue. IND-I and COM might better be paid for by trainees (Item 12), and the costs of IND-M would fall to the employer.

Item 14. Expected Earnings of Graduates of Training Programs

Low	*Middle*	*High*
HEA	IND-I	IND-M
AGR	COM	
PST		

Most developing countries supply HEA, AGR (for example, agricultural extension services), and PST to their populations at low prices per unit of service. In turn, this implies that workers in these fields receive salaries that are relatively low. To maintain private benefits of training for these lines of work at tolerably high levels, it appears important to subsidize training heavily in HEA, AGR, and PST.

The 14 items in this simple, common-sense-derived taxonomy appear to encourage certain recommendations. For example, training for modern sector industry, especially the job-specific components, should (a) be conducted in or near the workplace, (b) be supplemented by off-the-job theoretical instruction for higher categories of workers, and (c) be paid for by employers, either through individual contributions, payroll tax levies (ignoring here questions of incidence), or a combination of the two. Primary school teachers should be trained in institutions of formal education owned and run by government, with costs of training heavily subsidized by government. The placement of training for workers in other industrial sectors is a more complicated matter to decide. The interested reader may experiment with the taxonomy to draw further illustrative results, for example, by consulting case studies of Vocational Training in Europe, the United States, or Japan, as well as in Africa and Latin America.

4. Conclusion

The form of skill development taxonomies is open to refinement, depending on insight, availability of data, and research results. (Indeed, efforts to create training taxonomies might suggest new avenues of research.) It should be questioned whether skill development taxonomies would really be useful guides to planning. A few positive observations follow.

(a) Any actual use of a skill development taxonomy

would likely deal with less aggregated sets of training activities than were used in the above discussion. Even in the obvious case of modern sector industry, it might turn out that some training exercises did not fit the on-the-job, employer-financed mode very well.

(b) The signals for training in fields other than modern sector industry and primary school teaching do not all point in the same direction. In these cases, the taxonomy can be used to sort out and clarify the arguments for and against a proposed training strategy.

(c) Where the signals do not all point in the same direction, the taxonomy could be helpful in devising combinations of training and financing. It would probably be useful to view training in a less monolithic fashion than is commonly done. A particular training exercise need not be all on-the-job or all formal. Nor need the financing of a given project be drawn from a single source. Appropriate combinations of on-the-job training and formal instruction might be more efficient, and cost sharing, if wisely done, could have positive motivational effects on those who supply or receive training.

See also: Vocational Training Modes: Sweden, Germany, and Japan; Vocational Education and Training: Western Europe; Training, Government Role in; Planning for Vocational Education and Training; Vocational Education and Training: Improving Cost-effectiveness in Developing Nations; Educational Financing; Latin America: Articulation of Education, Training, and Work; Informal Sector: Vocational Education and Training; Sex Equity: Assumptions and Strategies; Gender and Education; Gender and Occupational Segregation

References

Benson C S, Ibser M H, Klein S G 1990 *Economic Returns to Vocational Education and Other Types of Occupational Training*. Graduate School of Education, Berkeley, California

Bowman M J 1990 Overview essay: Views from the past and the future. *Econ. Educ. Rev.* 9(4): 283–308

Carnevale A P 1991 *America and the New Economy. How New Competitive Standards Are Radically Changing American Workplaces*. Jossey-Bass, San Francisco, California

De Beyer J 1990 The incidence and impact on earnings of formal training provided by enterprises in Kenya and Tanzania. *Econ. Educ. Rev.* 9(4): 321–30

Hashimoto M 1991 Training and employment relations in Japanese firms. In: Stern D, Ritzen J M (eds.) 1991 *Market Failure in Training? New Economic Analysis and Evidence on Training of Adult Employees*. Springer-Verlag, New York

Lynch L M 1992 Private-sector training and earnings of young workers. *Am. Econ. Rev.* 82(1): 299–312

Schweitzer J 1985 *Egypt: Special Study of Formal and Non-Formal Education and Training and Linkages to Employment*. World Bank, Washington, DC

Vickers M 1991 *Building a National System for School-to-Work Transition: Lessons from Britain and Australia*. Jobs for the Future, Somerville, Massachusetts

Wirt J G, Muraskin L D, Goodwin, D A, Mayer R H 1989 *Summary of Findings and Recommendations: Final Report: National Assessment of Vocational Education*. US Department of Education, Washington, DC

Further Reading

Middleton J, Ziderman A, Adams A V Skills for Productivity: *Vocational and Technical Education and Training in Developing Countries*. Oxford University Press, Oxford

United Nations Development Programme 1990 *Human Development Report*. Oxford University Press, Oxford

C. S. Benson

Teacher Burnout

A sense of alienation and loss of enthusiasm about teaching characterize a significantly large number of teachers in urban schools in many developed nations. Excessive job stress and the absence of support by school administrators lead many teachers to feel exhausted, unproductive, and prone to denigrate their students. Organizational and individual factors determine which teachers are most likely to burn out. Burnout has been implicated in teacher absenteeism, entrapment, and the desire to quit teaching; it also makes difficult any school district's efforts to implement new programs to raise student achievement.

1. Two Perspectives on Burnout

Both psychologists and sociologists hypothesize that excessive stress associated with the teaching role precipitates burnout. However, the psychological view sees burnout as a clinical problem with the proactive development of coping skills as the suggested treatment. The sociological view emphasizes the nature of organizational and social support mechanisms which affect burnout and proposes organizational, rather than individual, solutions to the problem of burnout.

1.1 Psychological View of Burnout

The concept of burnout was first coined by Freudenberger (1974), who described it as a condition in which human service professionals wear out. Maslach and Jackson (1981) developed the most widely used scale for assessing burnout, the Maslach Burnout Inventory (MBI), an instrument that taps three central psychological dimensions of the construct: exhaustion, the loss of a sense of personal achievement, and depersonalization. The first reflects Freudenberger's view that burnout represents a sense of wearing out.

Individuals report being too tired and too drained to maintain enthusiasm for their work. Maslach and Jackson's second dimension of burnout is expressed as a sense that one is not achieving one's goals; that one's work efforts produce no satisfying results; in essence, that one sees one's work as meaningless. Finally, burnout involves an emotional separation of the worker (in this case the teacher) from the client (or student). The student is viewed as an object to be processed and a nuisance, rather than as a person of worth. Further, a blaming mechanism evolves in which burned-out teachers fault their students for the teachers' own sense of failure. Thus, students are also seen as enemies who deflect one from achieving desired ends. Research by Friesen et al. (1988), using a sample of teachers from Australia and Canada, suggests that the dimensions of burnout assessed by the MBI may not function in unison, nor may they be caused by the same factors. Their study reveals that job-related stress is more associated with exhaustion than with either depersonalization or the lack of personal accomplishment.

Investigators have identified five progressive stages in burnout: physical, intellectual, social, psycho-emotional, and spiritual (Cedoline 1982 pp. 23–37). Numerous symptoms characterize each of the stages, with fatigue and exhaustion being most common in the first stage; impaired decision making and obsessive thoughts about work during the second stage; social withdrawal, cynicism, irritability, and rudeness at the third stage; denial, blame, anger, and depression in the fourth stage; and poor work quality, absenteeism, the desire to escape, and the tendency to see the needs of students as a threat during the last stage.

Central to many of the views of burnout is the role of stress (or distress) as noted by Cedoline (1982), or strain as portrayed by Cherniss (1980). While some level of stress characterizes most human endeavors, excessive stress that is perceived by the individual as threatening and dysfunctional (hence, distress) is likely to tax the individual's coping capacity. The linkage between stress and burnout has led some investigators to use the terms interchangeably (see, e.g., the work on stress burnout by Riggar 1985, or the work of Kyriacou and Sutcliffe 1978). Farber (1984) and Pines and Aronson (1988) note, however, that stress per se does not produce burnout. Individuals can thrive and achieve substantially in stress-laden environments, provided that they have a sense of doing meaningful work. However, Pines and Aronson (1988) point out that when the activities appear to be devoid of meaning, they become tedious. Pines et al. (1981) have conceptualized burnout as the end-product of tedium.

The psychological view is generally clinical in nature and offers clinical solutions to problems of burnout. With burnout often seen as the end-product of distress, stress-reduction strategies are offered to individuals to mitigate such strains and reduce burnout (see e.g., Maslach 1976, Spaniol and Caputo 1979, Cherniss 1980, and Cedoline 1982).

While still offering clinical solutions to burnout, several researchers have viewed burnout as the product of elevated stress caused by the conjoined effects of work overload, role conflict, and role ambiguity. Kahn et al. (1964), Schwab and Iwanicki (1982), and Haney and Long (1989) view excessive work demands, demands that are mutually exclusive and/or contradictory, and demands in instances where resources are lacking or where one is not given the necessary authority to secure the cooperation of others, as causes of distress, which then results in burnout. By focusing upon roles and organizational variables, these investigators provide the beginnings of a sociological perspective on burnout.

1.2 Sociological View of Burnout

The sociological view does not deny the significant role of stress or distress in the creation of burnout. However, its emphasis is upon societal and demographic factors, and elements in the school setting and the nature of the training of teachers which heighten the likelihood of burnout. The importance of feelings of meaninglessness and powerlessness, which are found in some psychological views of burnout, is even more salient to sociologists. Burnout is thought of as a form of role-specific alienation, generally driven by stressors, which themselves have origins in the social structure of the society and the organizational structure of the school. As such, sociologists look to structural and organization changes as mechanisms which can reduce burnout.

As a form of alienation, teacher burnout is the product of a perceived gap between expectations, often developed during the preservice training of teachers, and the teacher's experiences in the classroom (Dworkin 1985, 1987; LeCompte and Dworkin 1991). Many enter teaching because of a desire to make a significant difference in the lives of children. Preservice teachers often expect that they will be able to educate and influence children, plan and develop new curricula, evaluate student learning, manage classrooms, maintain discipline, and perhaps, serve as role models and surrogate parents for children. Most important is the assumption that teachers are granted professional status and autonomy. Cherniss et al. (1976) and Sarason (1977) see colleges of education as failing to prepare teachers for educational bureaucracies in which autonomy is severely restricted. Teachers are also unprepared for an environment in which there is an excess of paperwork, where the children, their parents, other teachers, and administrators appear to be unconcerned about learning, where there are significant class and cultural differences between the teachers and their students, and where the larger community does not respect teachers. Hence, teacher burnout is often greatest in large, urban school districts, and especially among inexperienced teachers (Cedoline 1982, Russell et al. 1987, Dworkin 1987).

Agreements across the psychological and sociological paradigms support a view of burnout as composed of each of Seeman's (1975) dimensions of alienation: meaninglessness, powerlessness, isolation, normlessness, and estrangement. However, on the basis of a large sample of urban teachers, Dworkin (1987) concluded that feelings of meaninglessness and powerlessness were central to the responses of burned-out urban teachers. Dworkin defined teacher burnout as "... an extreme form of role-specific alienation characterized by a sense that one's work is meaningless and that one is powerless to effect changes which could make the work more meaningful" (1987 p. 28). Dworkin and Townsend (1991) utilized both the MBI and Dworkin's own scale, finding that the exhaustion and depersonalization components of psychological burnout diminish as the meaninglessness and powerlessness components of sociological burnout increase among experienced teachers. The result is that burnout, as alienation, can insulate teachers from the psychological element of exhaustion, and thus can be a coping mechanism for more experienced teachers.

2. *Magnitude of the Burnout Problem*

It is difficult to arrive at an accurate figure to assess the burnout rate among public school teachers, although most researchers agree that the rates are high. Furthermore, much of the research estimates stress rather than burnout levels. Litt and Turk (1985) report that 79 percent of public school teachers feel that their job is a major source of stress in their lives, compared with 38 percent for other college-educated workers. There is some variation in stress levels across school districts and societies (Menlo and Poppleton 1990). In the Consortium for Cross-cultural Research in Education's five-nation study of job attitudes, conducted between 1986 and 1988, only 10 or 11 percent of the teachers in England, the United States, Japan, and Singapore reported low levels or no stress, while 21 percent of the West German teachers reported the relative absence of stress (Poppleton 1990). Furthermore, one-third or less of the teachers (and only 15% in England) reported that staff morale in their schools was generally good (Poppleton 1990). The five-nation survey did not address burnout per se.

Many burnout studies are based upon small ethnographic and case studies, thereby mitigating generalizability. Cedoline (1982) estimated that the burnout rate among teachers in the United States is somewhere between 10 percent and 80 percent, a range too great to be of value. Dworkin (1987) and LeCompte and Dworkin (1991) rely upon data on urban and suburban teachers to arrive at a burnout rate of 37.3 percent prior to the implementation of educational reforms, which mandated more accountability of teachers, and 64.1 percent after the reforms. Rates for urban teachers were slightly higher than for suburban teachers. Kalekin-Fishman's (1986) study of metropolitan secondary school teachers suggests that burnout is widespread in Israel; however, percentages are not available.

Some researchers have compared the components of the MBI across several nations, not so much to ascertain burnout rates, as to determine differences among the components of burnout. Sarros and Sarros (1990) found that Australian teachers experienced less of the emotional exhaustion aspect of burnout than teachers in the United States, but more emotional exhaustion than Canadian teachers. In contrast, the depersonalization form of burnout was highest in some samples of teachers in the United States, and lower both among Australian and Canadian teachers. Finally, Australian teachers suffered the highest levels of diminished personal accomplishment, followed by the Canadian teachers, and finally teachers in the United States.

3. *Teachers Most Likely to Burn Out*

While burnout is a widespread phenomenon in urban schools in many societies, not all groups of teachers are equally susceptible to burning out. Psychologists have isolated personality and individualistic factors associated with the likelihood of burnout, while sociologists have concentrated on group, organizational, and social structural factors.

3.1 *Individualistic Factors*

Many psychologists have looked for personality types who are more likely to burn out because they cannot cope as easily with stress as other individuals. Kahn et al. (1964) suggested that neurotics and introverts experience more stress in teaching, and may be more likely to experience the loss of job idealism. They also held that flexible and democratic thinkers (who often cannot say "no" to excessive organizational demands and who have difficulty working under rigid and autocratic administrators) tend to experience increased stress and a heightened chance of burnout when they are assigned to teach in rigid school systems. Finally, Mazur and Lynch (1989) noted that Type A personalities (individuals who have trouble relaxing), as well as individuals with an external locus of control (who believe that their life chances are controlled by fate or by powerful others) are more likely to burn out than are individuals with Type B personalities and individuals with an internal locus of control. Kyriacou's (1980) teachers in the United Kingdom and Dworkin's (1987) teachers in the United States were more likely to burn out if they had an external locus of control.

3.2 Demographic and Organizational Factors

Demographic factors refer to membership categories to which groups of teachers belong that affect their social status in the larger society, or in the work setting (school) to which they are assigned. Included among such demographic factors are age and teaching experience, race, ethnicity, social class, and gender. Among the organizational factors are school size (as well as the extent of bureaucratization of the school), grade level taught, and the management style of the campus administrator.

Generally, burnout is more a malady of inexperienced teachers than of those with five or more years in the classroom (Cedoline 1982, Dworkin 1987, Mazur and Lynch 1989). Cherniss et al. (1976) reported that the absence of adequate preservice training, a problem of many new teachers, increased the chance of burnout. Russell et al. (1987) found that the number of reported stressors (sources of burnout) diminished with age and experience.

Racial isolation contributes to teacher burnout (Dworkin 1987). In urban schools in the United States, White movement to the suburbs and/or to private schools has resulted in urban districts in which most students are members of racial and ethnic minorities. Many White teachers find themselves racially isolated from their students and even feel threatened by them. Likewise, minority teachers in suburban school districts, where the majority of the students are White, report feelings of racial isolation. Frequently, parents voice preferences that their children be taught by teachers of their own race, with the result that racially isolated teachers feel intimidated, unwanted, and alienated. However, minority teachers are less likely to experience burnout than are majority teachers; this is due, in part, to the greater degree of racial isolation of White teachers in the inner city than of minority teachers in the suburbs (Dworkin 1987).

Social class differences between teachers and students often observed in American urban schools contribute to a sense of culture shock for teachers, regardless of their race (LeCompte 1985). While most public school teachers come from middle-class backgrounds (Dworkin 1980), the majority of students in urban schools are from working-class or lower-class families. These differences reflect distinctive lifestyles, expectations, aspirations, values, and even communication patterns (see LeCompte and Dworkin 1991). Many parents feel that the teachers are inaccessible and unresponsive (Richardson-Koehler 1989). Ogbu (1974) noted that when middle-class teachers made extra efforts to help low income, minority children, they were shown no appreciation. In fact, the parents, with incomes substantially lower than that of the teachers, felt that the teachers were sufficiently well-paid and needed no additional thanks. Kyriacou (1980) and Kyriacou and Sutcliffe (1978) found similar frustrations among teachers in inner-city schools in the United Kingdom.

There is mixed evidence regarding the relationship between burnout and gender. Male teachers in Canada (Burke and Greenglass 1989) and the United States (Russell et al. 1987) report more stress associated with the teaching role and were more likely to experience the depersonalization form of burnout than were female teachers. Women in the study reported experiencing greater amounts of social support than did men, and this support reduced the risk of burnout. By contrast, gender differences evaporated in a multivariate model (Dworkin 1987).

The size of a school affects its likely level of bureaucracy. In turn, bureaucratization increases the sense of isolation of teachers; it also increases the likelihood of role conflicts, role ambiguities, and ultimately burnout, as teachers are forced to comply with mandates from many organizational layers. Jackson (1968) and Maslach and Pines (1979) find lower stress levels and less burnout in small schools, while Russell et al. (1987) find that larger class sizes contribute to burnout.

If burnout is associated with class and organizational size, then it might be expected that burnout levels should be highest in secondary schools, which are generally large, and lowest in elementary schools, which are generally small. However, the data are not conclusive, suggesting that the relationship between grade level and burnout is complex. Some investigators noted that male secondary school teachers reported greater levels of depersonalization burnout than did elementary school teachers (Russell et al. 1987). In contrast, Anderson and Iwanicki (1984) noted a curvilinear relationship between grade level and burnout, with early secondary (middle or junior high) school teachers displaying more burnout than did elementary and secondary school teachers. Other investigations found that, while middle school is characterized by high levels of job stress, burnout levels are highest in elementary schools (Dworkin 1987). This is because elementary school teaching tends to be quite intense, with the children placing greater interpersonal demands upon the teacher. In the absence of departmentalization, teachers have day-long contact (without even a free period) with the same students. Such prolonged interactions are stressful (Jackson 1968).

Some researchers have noted that the management style of the principal significantly affects teachers morale and burnout levels in schools (Kyriacou 1980, Murphy and Paddock 1986, Dworkin 1987, Firestone and Rosenblum 1988, Dworkin et al. 1990). Authoritarian principals and those whose styles are too *laissez-faire* are associated with higher levels of burnout among their teachers than are those whose styles are more democratic (Murphy and Paddock 1986). In addition, any substantial discrepancy between the administrative style of the principal as desired by the teachers and the actual style of that principal contributes to teacher burnout (Dworkin 1987). Further, management styles that are perceived by teachers to be unsupportive and that treat teachers as dispensable and diminish the teacher's role in campus decision-making contribute to burnout.

4. *Social Support and Burnout*

Much of the medical sociology literature on stress has suggested that an effective buffer against stressful events is a network of social support (see Kaplan 1983 for a survey of this research). Investigators have also spoken of the significant role of social support in mitigating burnout (see, e.g., Maslach 1976, Freudenberger 1974, Cherniss 1980, and Cedoline 1982). However, there is a disagreement about the persons who can be most supportive. The above-mentioned investigators have argued that co-worker support provides an effective buffer for teachers. By contrast, Russell et al. (1987), Dworkin (1987), and Dworkin et al. (1990) found that supportive principals, who offered positive feedback to teachers and treated them as valued colleagues, involving them in campus decision-making, retarded burnout. Supportive co-workers, however, did not reduce burnout. In fact, in the absence of principal support, co-worker support can elevate stress and burnout among younger teachers (Dworkin et al. 1990). This is due to the tendency for co-workers to feed on one another's stress and anxiety, creating rumors and emotional contagion. In a survey of burnout in 21 Dutch companies (rather than schools), Marcelissen et al. (1988) reported that strain tends to heighten negative interactions and burnout among co-workers, rather than co-worker interactions reducing strain and burnout.

In one study of principal support (Dworkin 1987), teachers who were assigned to a school where the principal was seen as supportive experienced lower levels of burnout than teachers who were assigned to schools where the principal was seen as unsupportive. When burnout did occur among teachers with supportive principals, individual teacher characteristics, rather than job stress, were implicated in the burnout; however, burnout among teachers assigned to unsupportive principals was driven by job stress. It is important to note that the reported job stress levels were statistically equal in schools with supportive and unsupportive principals. It appears that a supportive principal, who treats teachers as valued colleagues, informs them that their work is meaningful, thereby breaking the functional connection between stress and burnout. Support by co-workers alone did not affect the relationship between stress and burnout. In light of the role of principal support in mitigating burnout, it seems reasonable to rethink the clinical strategy to reducing burnout levels among teachers. The clinical solutions involve the teaching of coping skills (Maslach 1976, Cherniss 1980), the use of holistic health practices (Tubesing and Tubesing 1982), and relaxation and self-suggestion therapy (Swick and Hanley 1983). However, if the improvement of managerial skills among principals can retard burnout, then in large school districts with thousands of teachers and hundreds of principals, it is more cost-efficient to change the management styles of the principals than to provide therapy for the multitude of teachers. Changed administrator behaviors will also reduce the need to offer additional classes in coping skills for each new cohort of teachers.

Collegial support varies somewhat across the five-nation survey (Poppleton 1990). While over 80 percent of the teachers reported their colleagues to be supportive at least some of the time, only in England and the United States did more than half of the teachers report that their colleagues were supportive most of the time. By contrast, only in England were immediate superiors seen as helpful most of the time by at least half of the sample of teachers. In West Germany, a mere 17 percent of the teachers felt that their immediate superiors were helpful most of the time (Poppleton 1990).

5. *Teacher Burnout, Turnover, and Entrapment*

Public school teachers tend to have an above-average job turnover rate, but one that is similar to that in other female-dominated semi-professions (Price 1977). In the United States, the turnover rate grew during the 1980s as a result of educational reform efforts that demanded greater teacher accountability and paperwork (LeCompte and Dworkin 1991), and the expansion of job opportunities in other, better-paying, fields (Mark and Anderson 1985). However, one-third of all teachers who quit eventually return to the classroom, with many recycling back and forth throughout their careers (Heyns 1990).

Burnout is strongly implicated in the desire to quit a job (Calamidas 1979, Cherniss 1980, Cedoline 1982, Dworkin 1987). It is also linked to high rates of absenteeism (Calamidas 1979). However, actual turnover does not seem to be caused by burnout (Cherniss 1980, Jackson et al. 1986, Dworkin 1987). In fact, the most burned-out teachers are quite unlikely to quit (Jackson et al. 1986). Job turnover appears to depend upon the availability of other job opportunities outside of teaching. With the exception of teachers whose specialties can translate into valued skills in the corporate sector (e.g., mathematics, science, industrial arts, business, etc.), most teachers must either retrain or accept lower-status, poorer-paying employment if they leave the field of education (Dworkin 1987, LeCompte and Dworkin 1991).

The five-nation study by the Consortium for Cross-cultural Research in Education found that slightly less than half of the teachers from West Germany and the United States, around one-fifth of the teachers from England, and fewer than one-fifth of the teachers from Japan and Singapore would, if given the chance, again choose to become teachers (Poppleton 1990). Nevertheless, Poppleton (1990) reports that two-thirds of the teachers from the United States and three-fourths of the teachers from Japan and Singapore expect still to be teaching five years from when they were surveyed (the results for England and West Germany were not reported).

Burned out, wanting to quit, but unable to find work elsewhere, many teachers remain in disliked jobs much of their working lives. In fact, in a five-year follow-up study of urban public school teachers, Dworkin (1987) found that nearly three-fourths of the burned-out teachers who wanted to quit had not left teaching. In another study, 37 percent of the burnouts attempted to leave but could not find satisfactory work (LeCompte and Dworkin 1991). They were clearly entrapped.

Teacher entrapment represents a problem for both teachers and school districts. It is a human problem for the teacher, as there are many personal, emotional, and psychophysical costs associated with the continuation of a career that is disliked or even hated. It is an organizational problem for schools. Teacher entrapment exacerbates staffing problems. School districts, which depend upon turnover to balance budgets through the replacement of higher-paid teachers with lower-paid new teachers, discover that some of the teachers they might like to see quit do not. Furthermore, it becomes all the more difficult for school systems to introduce new programs aimed at raising student achievement when, to implement the programs, districts must rely upon unenthusiastic burned-out teachers who depersonalize their students.

References

Anderson M B, Iwanicki E F 1984 Teacher motivation and its relationship to burnout. *Educational Administration Quarterly* 20(2): 109–32

Burke R J, Greenglass E 1989 The client's role in psychological burnout in teachers and administrators. *Psychol. Reports* 64(3): 1299–1306

Calamidas A 1979 Distress and burnout will kill productivity. In: Cedoline A J (ed.) 1982

Cedoline A J (ed.) 1982 *Job Burnout in Public Education: Symptoms, Causes, and Survival Skills*. Teachers College Press, Columbia University, New York

Cherniss C 1980 *Professional Burnout in Human Service Organizations*. Praeger, New York

Cherniss C, Egnatios E S, Wacker S 1976 Job stress and career development in new public professionals. *Prof. Psychol.* 7(4): 428–36

Dworkin A G 1980 The changing demography of public school teachers: Some implications for faculty turnover in urban areas. *Sociol. Educ.* 53: 65–73

Dworkin A G 1985 *When Teachers Give Up: Teacher Burnout, Teacher Turnover, and Their Impact on Children*. Hogg Foundation for Mental Health, Austin, Texas

Dworkin A G 1987 *Teacher Burnout in the Public Schools: Structural Causes and Consequences for Children*. State University of New York Press, Albany, New York

Dworkin A G, Haney C A, Dworkin R J, Telschow R L 1990 Stress and illness behavior among urban public school teachers. *Educ. Admin. Q.* 26(1): 60–72

Dworkin A G, Townsend M L 1991 Burnout as a coping mechanism: Or how to survive in an urban public school. Paper presented at the Southwestern Sociological Association meetings, San Antonio, Texas

Farber B A 1984 Teacher burnout: Assumptions, myths, and issues. *Teachers College Record* 86(2): 321–38

Firestone W A, Rosenblum S 1988 Building commitment in urban high schools. *Educ. Eval. Policy Anal.* 10(4): 285–99

Freudenberger H J 1974 Staff burn-out. *J. Social Issues* 30(1): 159–65

Friesen D, Prokop C M, Sarros J C 1988 Why teachers burn out. *Educ. Res. Q.* 12(3): 9–19

Haney C J, Long B C 1989 Role stress, coping effectiveness, and health concerns of physical education teachers. *Educ. Res. Q.* 13(4): 34–42

Heyns B 1990 The changing contours of the teaching profession. In: Hallinan M T, Klein D M, Glass J (eds.) 1990 *Change in Societal Institutions*. Plenum, New York

Jackson P 1968 *Life in Classrooms*. Holt, Rinehart, Winston, New York

Jackson S E, Schwab R L, Schuler R S 1986 Toward an understanding of the burnout phenomenon. *J. Applied Psychol.* 71(4): 630–40

Kahn R L, Wolfe D M, Quinn R P, Snoek J D, Rosenthal R A 1964 *Organizational Stress: Studies in Role Conflict and Ambiguity*. Wiley, New York

Kalekin-Fishman D 1986 Burnout or alienation? A context specific study of occupational fatigue among secondary school teachers. *J. of Res. Develop. in Educ.* 19(3): 24–34

Kaplan H B 1983 Psychological distress in sociological context: Toward a general theory of psychosocial distress. In: Kaplan H B (ed.) 1983 *Psychosocial Stress: Trends in Theory and Research*. Academic Press, New York

Kyriacou C 1980 Sources of stress among British teachers: The contribution of job factors and personality factors. In: Cooper C L, Marshall J (eds.) 1980 *White Collar and Professional Stress*. John Wiley, New York

Kyriacou C, Sutcliffe J 1978 Teacher stress: Prevalence, sources, and symptoms *Br. J. Educ. Psychol.* 48(2): 159–67

LeCompte M D 1985 Defining the differences: Cultural subgroups within the educational mainstream. *The Urban Rev.* 17(2): 111–28

LeCompte M D, Dworkin A G 1991 *Giving Up On School: Student Dropouts and Teacher Burnouts*. Corwin Press, Newbury Park, California

Litt M D, Turk D C 1985 Sources of stress and dissatisfaction in experienced high school teachers. *J. Educ. Res.* 78(3): 178–85

Marcelissen F H G, Winnubst J A M, Buunk B B, de Wolfe C J 1988 Social support and occupational stress. *Soc. Sci. Med.* 26(3): 365–73

Mark J H, Anderson B D 1985 Teacher survival rates in St. Louis, 1969–1982. *Amer. Educ. Res. J.* 22(3): 413–21

Maslach C 1976 Burned-out. *Human Behavior* 5(9): 16–22

Maslach C 1978 Job burnout: How people cope. *Public Welfare* 36(4): 56–58
Maslach C, Jackson S 1981 The measurement of experienced burnout. *J. Occupational Behavior* 2: 99–113
Maslach C, Pines A 1979 Burnout: The loss of human caring. In: Pines A, Maslach C (eds.) 1979 *Experiencing Social Psychology*. Knopf, New York
Mazur P J, Lynch M D 1989 Differential impact of administrative, organizational, and personality factors on teacher burnout. *Teaching and Teacher Ed.* 5(4): 337–53
Menlo A, Poppleton P 1990 A five-country study of the work perceptions of secondary school teachers in England, the United States, Japan, Singapore, and West Germany (1986–88). *Comp. Educ.* 26(2–3): 173–82
Murphy J W, Paddock J T 1986 The "burnout syndrome" and management style. *The Clinical Supervisor* 4(4): 35–44
Ogbu J U 1974 *The Next Generation*. Academic Press, New York
Pines A, Aronson E, Kafry D 1981 *Burnout: From Tedium to Personal Growth*. The Free Press, New York
Pines A, Aronson E 1988 *Career Burnout: Causes and Cures*. The Free Press, New York
Poppleton P 1990 The survey data. *Comp. Educ.* 26(2–3): 183–210
Price J L 1977 *The Study of Turnover*. Iowa State University Press, Ames, Iowa
Richardson-Koehler V (ed.) 1989 *School Children At-Risk*. Taylor and Francis, Philadelphia, Pennsylvania
Riggar T F 1985 *Stress Burnout*. Southern Illinois University Press, Carbondale, Illinois
Russell D W, Altmaier E, Van Velzen D 1987 Job-related stress, social support, and burnout among classroom teachers. *J. Applied Psychol.* 72(2): 269–74
Sarason S B 1977 *Work, Aging, and Social Change*. The Free Press, New York
Sarros A M, Sarros J C 1990 How burned out are our teachers? A cross-cultural study. *Austral. J. Ed.* 34(2): 145–52
Schwab R L, Iwanicki E F 1982 Received role conflict, role ambiguity, and teacher burnout. *Ed. Admin. Q.* 18(1): 60–74
Seeman M 1975 Alienation studies. *Ann. Rev. Sociol.* 1: 91–123
Spaniol L, Caputo J 1979 *Professional Burn-out: A Personal Survival Kit*. Human Services Associates, Lexington, Massachusetts
Swick K J, Hanely P E 1983 *Teacher Renewal: Revitalization of Classroom Teachers*. National Education Association, Washington, DC
Tubesing N L, Tubesing D A 1982 The treatment of choice: Selecting stress skills to suit the individual and the situation. In: Paine W S (ed.) 1982 *Job Stress and Burnout: Research, Theory, and Intervention Perspectives*. Sage, Beverly Hills, California

Further Reading

Maslach C 1982 Understanding burnout: Definitional issues in analyzing a complex phenomenon. In: Paine W S (ed.) 1982 *Job Stress and Burnout: Research, Theory, and Intervention Perspectives*. Sage, Beverly Hills, California
Poppleton P (Issue ed.) 1990 Work perceptions of secondary teachers: International comparisons. *Comp. Educ.* 26(2–3)

A. G. Dworkin

Teacher Certification and Standards

What qualifications does a person need to become a teacher? The answer to this question lies at the heart of teacher licensure and certification decisions. In fact, there are multiple answers, depending on the country and the time period in which it is asked.

Some countries require different levels of education (e.g., 2 or 3 years vs. 4 years) or types of education (e.g., teacher training institutes vs. universities) for primary school and secondary school teachers; other countries require essentially the same level and type for all teachers. Similarly, some countries require prospective teachers to pass licensure or certification examinations before being licensed or certified, while others do not (Holmes 1983, Kurian 1988, Farrell 1989).

Licensure and certification standards also depend on the relationship of teacher supply and demand. Tarvin and Faraj (1990) have stated this relationship quite succinctly: "In periods of rapid expansion of student population, low standards of qualifications have been accepted in hiring teachers" (p. 92). They illustrate this generalization with examples from China, Nepal, Sri Lanka, and Pakistan. Lockheed and Verspoor (1990) provided specific data to highlight the magnitude of this problem. In separate studies, 54 percent of primary school teachers in Zimbabwe and fewer than 10 percent of primary school teachers in Haiti were classified as qualified. In Kano State in Nigeria only 9 percent of the primary teachers held formal teacher certification.

When licensure and certification standards are lowered, status is decreased. As Lockheed and Verspoor (1990) have asserted, "in countries experiencing rapid expansion of their educational systems, underqualified applicants are recruited to meet the growing demand for teachers; this further lowers the public perception of the occupation's prestige" (p. 64).

Issues concerning teacher licensure and certification, then, are quite different in developing and industrialized countries. In many developing countries, the problem is how to attract prospective teachers and educate them to meet minimal standards. In the words of Altbach (1987), "In the Third World, there is concern that a sufficient number of teachers be provided and that these teachers have appropriate training" (p. 326). In many industrialized countries, on the other hand, the problem is inherent in the standards themselves. The major questions in these countries are as follows. What licensure and certification standards should be established? Who should establish them? What evidence is needed to determine whether the standards have been achieved?

In light of the previous discussion, this entry focuses primarily on industrialized countries, with most of the examples taken from the United States. At the same time, however, the concepts and ideas presented and discussed are applicable to virtually all countries. For, as Altbach has written:

> Concern about the teaching profession is worldwide. Many countries have realized that teachers are at the center of the educational process and that without good teachers, all other innovations are doomed to failure. . . . There is also widespread dissatisfaction with the current situation of schooling in many nations—and teachers have come in for their share of criticism. (Altbach 1987 p. 326)

1. Certification, Credentialing, and Licensure

In the first edition of this *Encyclopedia* Zimpher (1985) noted that the terms "certification," "credentialing," and "licensure" are frequently used interchangeably in the field of education. In this entry, "licensure" will refer to quality control excercised by states, while "certification" will refer to quality control exercised by peer review.

There are two primary reasons for these definitions. First, they are consistent with the use of the terms in most professions and occupations requiring state authorization to practice. In these fields, the term "licensure" is used to indicate that the state has authorized an individual to practice. In contrast, the term "certification" indicates peer approbation, usually provided at the conclusion of some specified minimal period of practice, after completion of a course of study to achieve some specialty, and/or after success on an examination covering the speciality. If teaching were to use terms consistent with the practice of other fields, communication with those in the recognized professions and the general public would be enhanced.

Second, in 1987 the National Board for Professional Teaching Standards (NBPTS) was created in the United States. "The mission of the NBPTS is to establish high and rigorous standards for what accomplished teachers should know and be able to do, to develop and operate a national voluntary system to assess and certify teachers who meet these standards, and to advance related education reforms for the purpose of improving student learning in American schools" (NBPTS 1991 p. 1). With the advent of this form of professional certification, clarity of communication will be improved if the term "license" is used to signify a state authorization to practice in the public schools, and the term "certification" restricted to denoting professional recognition of accomplished practice.

2. The Policy Context for Certification and Licensure

In a 1990 review of literature on "Roles and Authority of States in Policies for Teachers and Teaching," Scannell noted that since the 1960s there have been three major shifts in the locus of educational decision-making in the United States. These shifts have had an impact on the standards and processes for licensure of teachers.

Timar and Kirp (1988) credited the 1954 Supreme Court decision in Brown v. Board of Education for causing the movement of much decision-making in education from the local level to national and state levels. In contrast to many other developed countries, the United States has a tradition of local decision-making with final authority vested at the state level. Thus, the Brown v. Board of Education decision resulted in states moving some delegated authority from local districts to the state level; it also caused the federal government to become involved because of the need to monitor desegregation efforts and by virtue of increased federal spending for education. The publication in 1983 of *A Nation at Risk* (National Commission on Excellence in Education 1984) caused a second shift in the locus of decision-making by advocating a reduced federal role, insisting that schooling is essentially a state and local matter. The third shift, according to Darling-Hammond (1988), occurred in 1986 when a second wave of reform reports in the United States advocated a change from centralized, highly regulated decisions by state policymakers to control at the local level by professionals. It might also be contended that the third shift has evolved into a fourth—one in which decision-making is done by local schools and teachers within a renewed emphasis on nationalization. This context includes national education goals, national curriculum standards, national assessment programs for teachers, and teacher education programs.

3. Processes Associated with Certification and Licensure

The purpose of licensing is to protect the public. Licensing is a method of quality control at the level of the individual applicant for admission to the field of teaching. As was noted by Zimpher (1985), legal authority for licensure in the United States is at the state level, but in many other countries authority for certification is vested in national ministries or national councils. In the United States the process for awarding licenses has been administered by State Departments of Education (SDEs). Standards, and to some extent processes, have been established by State Boards of Education, sometimes with the assistance of advisory boards of teachers, administrators, and teacher educators. These standards are usually enacted by state legislatures and, therefore, can be changed only through legislative action. (Some states have autonomous standards boards that recommend standards and processes for certification and teacher education program approval directly to the state board of education or the state legislature. Autonomous boards are discussed at greater length later in this entry, but these boards are an exception to the prevailing policies.) The processes used for awarding a license to teach can be ordered into five categories: (a) the approved program approach, (b) transcript analysis or credit count, (c) testing, (d) alternative certification, and (e) regional certificates.

3.1 The Approved Program Approach

Since the 1980s the system most widely used by SDEs to award licenses has been based on the graduation of candidates from "approved programs." This process is quite similar to accreditation (see *Accreditation and Standards: Teacher Education*). Institutions undertake a self-study and, using a specified format, prepare reports. Visiting teams of educators are appointed by the SDE, which visit the institutions to verify the institution's reports and prepare their own report. Final decisions are made by the State Board of Education, a lay-body either elected directly or appointed by the state governor. After this process has been completed, graduates of the approved programs have usually been automatically granted a license.

3.2 Transcript Analysis

A second approach is called "transcript analysis" or "credit count." This procedure is used to provide an avenue to licensure for people graduating from institutions that do not have approved programs and for individuals who have earned course credits from a number of institutions. The process involves an assessment of a candidate's transcript(s) to ascertain whether the aspiring teacher has taken courses that are likely to have included the knowledge and skills implied by the state's standards and to ascertain whether the credits earned in the teaching field meet the state's requirements, in terms of both number of credits and the content of courses taken.

3.3 Testing

The use of testing as part of the licensure process has increased dramatically in the United States since the publication of *A Nation at Risk* in 1984. Some states have contracted for the development of tests for this purpose, but typically states have used commercially available tests. Among these, the National Teacher's Examination (NTE) published by the Educational Testing Service (ETS) has been most widely used.

The areas covered in teacher testing include basic skills, general education, pedagogy, and teaching field content. In many states basic skill testing is done near the midpoint of the baccalaureate program and adequate scores are required for admission to teacher education programs. The other components of the test are normally administered after graduation. In many states the standards for the award of a license are stated as "graduation from an approved program and successful completion of the licensure tests."

3.4 Alternative Certification

As states have increased the formal standards for access to a teaching credential, they also have created permissive policies for emergency licenses and alternative certification (Scannell 1988). Darling-Hammond and Berry (1988) observed, "Ironically, even as states have increased their influence over teacher preparation programs, they have created or expanded loopholes allowing more candidates to avoid these same requirements" (p. 9). In 1991, 30 states had some form of alternative certification program not driven by teacher shortages.

Although alternative certification programs vary across states, a common pattern is to use test scores to establish a baseline for acceptance of college graduates into the program, provide candidates with some exposure to pedagogy in an intensive, short summer workshop, and provide a temporary permit for the candidate to teach for one year. During this time an experienced teacher is to serve in a mentoring capacity, the candidates meet periodically for seminars, and often additional coursework in pedagogy is required within a specified period of time.

3.5 Regional Certification

A relatively novel approach to credentialing is a regional "certificate" developed by states in the northeastern part of the United States. Teachers credentialed in one of the participating states can apply for a regional credential which authorizes the person to teach in any of the states (Newton et al. 1989). The regional certificate can be thought of as a form of reciprocity among the participating states, one that facilitates movement of teachers within the region. More traditional forms of reciprocity are based on agreements among states that have similar accreditation standards and a large number of states will credential out-of-state applicants who have graduated from accredited institutions.

4. Issues and Trends

Several initiatives have been undertaken to raise the status of the teaching occupation, which by some definitions has not achieved the characteristics of a true profession. One of these, noted earlier, is the NBPTS which expects to award its first certificates recognizing accomplished teaching in 1994. During subsequent years additional fields will be brought online until all fields are operational. Although the NBPTS has engendered significant financial and moral support, it also has its critics.

Eligibility requirements for NBPTS applicants include graduation from a regionally accredited institution and three years of teaching experience. Critics who support the Board's goal of professionalizing teaching cite the eligibility requirements as inadequate, noting that other professions require graduation from an institution that holds specialized accreditation. In addition, applicants to the NBPTS process do not have to hold the state license to teach;

in some parts of the United States, a license is not required to teach in private schools. The counter arguments to the criticisms are that the significant proportion of private school teachers should not be excluded and that if the standards are rigorous, candidates will have to develop high skill levels through either formal education or effective self-directed study.

It is important to note again that the NBPTS does not grant licenses: this authority is vested in state governments. Even so, it is having an impact on state licensing requirements and processes. An organization has been established by the Council of Chief State School Officers to create recommendations for state licensure requirements that are appropriate for beginning teachers and that reflect the standards the NBPTS will use for recognizing accomplished teaching. The Interstate New Teacher Assessment and Support Consortium (INTASC) has the direct involvement of 17 states, both major teacher unions and several major educational organizations. An additional 22 states have expressed interest in participation and will facilitate public review of the draft standards.

Two major advantages will be achieved if INTASC is successful. First, there will be widespread agreement on what a beginning teacher needs to know and should be able to do, and thus there will be common standards in most of the states. Second, an articulation between standards for novices and accomplished teachers will contribute to a better integration of initial, or basic, teacher education programs with continuing professional development programs.

Zimpher (1985) cited as a recent trend the issue of who would control the licensure and certification process—the traditional state board comprised of lay people or professional standards and practices boards (PSPBs) comprised of educators? At that time three states had delegated responsibility for the process to autonomous PSPBs—California, Oregon, and Minnesota. The question needs to be cited again as a trend and issue.

In 1989 Scannell et al. noted that the original group of three states had been increased to four but that 44 additional states had advisory PSPBs. Since 1989 several additional states have converted advisory boards into autonomous boards to bring the number to nine (AACTE 1990), and teacher unions continue to work for the creation of additional autonomous boards. Within the major efforts to professionalize teaching, it seems likely that additional autonomous boards will be created.

4.1 Testing Teachers

As was noted earlier, one of the first and most widespread reactions following the publication of *A Nation at Risk* was an increase in teacher testing. Testing was introduced as a requirement for entry into teacher education programs and as a final hurdle to qualify for the initial license. Support for these policies came more from outside than inside the educational establishment. Those who support the practice asserted that testing would weed out the incompetents and at the same time restore public confidence in teachers. The opposition formed ranks around two major issues, questions of validity and the differential effect of testing on ethnic and racial groups.

Most teacher tests have been paper-and-pencil multiple-choice tests. Publishers and users of these tests have conducted studies to establish curricular and occupational validity. Even so, major questions remain about whether the tests can adequately assess the personal qualities needed for effective teaching and the ability to use the knowledge of pedagogy effectively.

The concern about differential failure rates centers on the assertion that minorities and people for whom English is a second language do not perform well on written, multiple-choice tests. To this concern is added the observation that the minority presence in the teaching work force, once over 12 percent, is falling rapidly toward 5 percent, at the same time as the percentage of minority students in public schools is increasing rapidly. These concerns have led to the development of a variety of assessment practices to determine the competence of both beginning and experienced teachers. A key component in both the NBPTS and INTASC efforts is the use of multiple assessment strategies. Included are portfolios that encompass: peer assessments; examples of teacher artifacts and student work; videotapes of classroom performance; and assessment center activities including structured interviews, inbasket exercises, simulations, and written tests.

4.2 Required Coursework

An increasingly important issue in the credentialing of teachers is the distribution of coursework to be required for the initial license. The trend in the early 1990s in the teacher education curriculum in the United States is toward undergraduate majors in an arts or science field followed by a year of pedagogy and clinical experiences. In addition, the content of the teaching field is being modified in response to new standards being created by professional groups. The field furthest advanced is mathematics, although science, English, social studies, and other fields are engaged in the creation of national "frameworks." It seems likely that majors based on new standards in academic fields will continue to expand as the norm for preservice teacher preparation.

Related to the issue noted above is a question of whether a separate license is needed for the middle grades. Sparked by the publication of *Turning Points* (Carnegie Council on Adolescent Development 1989), considerable energy has been invested in developing a unique middle school curriculum and teacher preparation consistent with the program. The past practice of allowing elementary and secondary teachers also to qualify for the middle grades seems virtually certain to be discontinued. As a result, new standards for middle-level teacher education will be developed and implemented.

5. The Future of Teacher Licensure and Certification

There are five major questions that will guide the setting of standards and processes for licensure and certification in the immediate future. The questions are likely to be applicable throughout the world.

First, who will control licensure? The issue here is whether professionally dominated, autonomous boards will be given the opportunity to serve roles commonly assigned to other professional fields.

Second, what will be the balance among content, theory, and clinical practice required for the initial license? Subject-matter baccalaureate majors followed by a period of pedagogy and clinical practice seem to be the trend. This includes increased time spent in clinical experiences and the addition of an internship year.

Third, how will established standards be assessed? Performance assessment seems likely to become more prevalent, at least in the short run. However, there will remain an issue of whether other forms of competency assessment will continue to supplement graduation from an approved program or perhaps replace program approval entirely.

Fourth, how will requirements for continuing professional development relate to standards for initial licensure and how will accomplished practice be assessed? It seems likely that the future will see a rational continuum of expectations from those for novice teachers to those for peer approbation of accomplished practice. If NBPTS and INTASC are successful, major advancement toward professional status for teaching will be achieved.

Fifth, will policymakers continue to support "backdoor entry" into teaching or will policies support the movement toward the professionalization of teaching? Teacher shortages provided the motivation for creating emergency and alternative routes to licensure. Teacher education critics expanded the alternative routes to attract career changers on the assumption that knowledge of an academic field was adequate for successful teaching.

Several of these questions (especially the second, fourth, and fifth ones) create a tension between policymakers and educators. How these questions are resolved will have a major impact on the future of teaching as a profession and as a career.

See also: Teacher Education Programs: Curriculum; Teacher Evaluation

References

American Association of Colleges for Teacher Education 1991 *Teacher Education Policy in the States: A 50-State Survey of Legislative and Administrative Actions.* AACTE, Washington, DC

Altbach P G 1987 Teaching: International concerns. *Teach. Coll. Rec.* 88(3): 326–29

Carnegie Council on Adolescent Development 1989 *Turning Points.* Carnegie Council on Adolescent Development, Washington, DC

Council of Chief State School Officers 1992 *Model Standards for Beginning Teacher Licensing and Development: A Resource for State Dialogue.* Interstate New Teacher Assessment and Support Consortium, Washington, DC

Darling-Hammond L 1988 Policy and professionalism In: Lieberman A (ed.) 1988 *Building a Professional Culture in Schools.* Teachers College Press, New York

Darling-Hammond L, Berry B 1988 *The Evolution of Teacher Policy.* Rand Corporation, Washington, DC

Education Testing Service 1992 *The Praxis Series: Professional Assessments for Beginning Teachers.* Education Testing Service Princeton, New Jersey

Farrell J P 1989 International lessons for school effectiveness: The view from the developing world. In: Holmes M, Leithwood K A, Mussella D F (eds.) 1989 *Educational Policy for Effective Schools.* OISE Press, Toronto

Holmes B (ed.) 1983 *International Handbook of Education Systems. Vol. 1: Europe and Canada.* Wiley, Chichester

Kurian G T (ed.) 1988 *World Education Encyclopedia.* Facts on File, New York

Lockheed M E, Verspoor A M 1990 *Improving Primary Education in Developing Countries: A Review of Policy Options.* World Bank, Washington, DC

National Board for Professional Teaching Standards 1991 *Toward High and Rigorous Standards for the Teaching Profession*, 3rd edn. National Board for Professional Teaching Standards, Detroit, Michigan

National Commission on Excellence in Education 1984 *A Nation at Risk: The Imperative for Educational Reform.* United States Department of Education, Washington, DC

Newton A et al. 1989 *Implementation of a Northeast Regional Credential for Educators in New England and New York.* Regional Laboratories, Andover, Massachusetts

Scannell D P, Andersen D G, Gideonse H D 1989 *Who Sets the Standards?* Association of Colleges and Schools of Education in State Universities and Land-Grant Colleges and Affiliated Private Universities, Las Vegas, Nevada

Scannell M M 1988 Factors influencing state policies restricting entry to teaching. (Doctoral dissertation, George Washington University)

Tarvin W L, Faraj A H 1990 The quest for qualified teachers in developing countries of south and southeast Asia. *Int. Rev. Educ.* 36(1): 89–101

Timar T B, Kirp D L 1988 *Managing Educational Excellence.* Falmer Press, New York

Zimpher N L 1985 Certification and licensing of teachers. In: Husén T, Postlethwaite T N (eds.) 1985 *The International Encyclopedia of Education*, 1st edn. Pergamon Press, Oxford

Further Reading

McDonnell L M, Elmore R F 1987 Getting the job done: Alternative policy instruments. *Educ. Eval. Policy Anal.* 9(2): 133–52
Scannell M M 1990 *Roles and Authority of States in Policies for Teachers and Teaching*. American Association of Colleges for Teacher Education, Washington, DC

M. M. Scannell; D. P. Scannell

Teacher Development

Teacher development is the professional growth a teacher achieves as a result of gaining increased experience and examining his or her teaching systematically. This entry presents a conceptual model of teacher development, then the significant factors influencing teacher development are identified. The entry concludes by examining the effects of the processes intended to foster teacher growth.

1. The Concept and Related Terms

As Little (1992) notes, teacher development is marked by four types of growth—growth in knowledge, growth in skill, growth in judgment (all of which are classroom-related), and growth in the contributions teachers make to a professional community. Leithwood (1992) posits six increasingly complex levels of such development: (a) developing survival skills, (b) becoming competent in the basic skills of teaching, (c) expanding one's instructional flexibility, (d) acquiring instructional expertise, (e) contributing to the professional growth of colleagues, and (f) exercising leadership and participating in decision-making. Obviously there is a value judgment implicit in Leithwood's analysis, namely, that professional development finds its highest expression in the exercise of leadership. Not all teachers share that value, since many expert teachers seem satisfied to devote all their energies to teaching.

Teacher development can be differentiated from two closely related concepts, "career development" and "staff development." Career development is the growth that occurs as the teacher moves through the professional career cycle; this experiential growth is typically conceptualized as occurring in several clearly demarcated and sequential stages. Staff development is the provision of organized inservice programs designed to foster the growth of groups of teachers; it is only one of the systematic interventions that can be used for teacher development.

2. Factors Influencing Teacher Development

There are three groups of factors that seem to influence teacher development: those involving the teacher as a person, those relating to the context in which the teacher lives and works, and those involving specific interventions to foster teacher development. As shown in Fig. 1, these three factors interact in a complex manner, affecting each other and in turn influencing teacher development. The personal and contextual factors will be examined in this section; and the intervention processes designed to foster growth will be analyzed in the final section of this entry.

2.1 Personal Factors

Most researchers who have examined the personal factors factors influencing teacher development have taken a developmental perspective. Specifically, they have examined chronological age, ego development, moral development, interpersonal development, cognitive development, career development, and motivational development (see Burden 1990). Of these factors, the ones that seem to play the most significant role are the teacher's cognitive development, career development, and motivational development.

2.1.1 Cognitive development. The teacher's cognitive development is usually equated with the extent to which the teacher can reason conceptually. Building upon Hunt's work in conceptual development, Glickman (1981) posited three levels of abstract thinking—low, moderate, and high. Teachers at a low level think more concretely, differentiate fewer concepts, and tend to see problems simplistically; those at a high level can reason abstractly, see connections between disparate elements, and enjoy complexity.

Studies using conceptual level as the variable have concluded that teachers at the high level (as contrasted with those at the low level) are more adaptable and flexible in teaching style, are more empathetic, provide more varied learning environments, are more tolerant of stress, are more effective with students of diverse ethnic backgrounds, and prefer

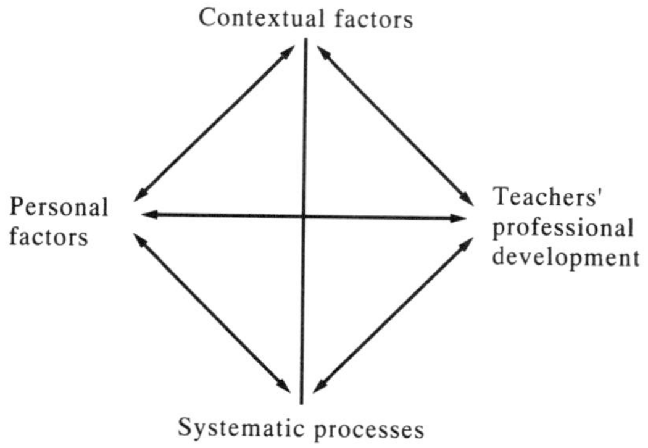

Figure 1
The nature of teacher development

to learn through a discovery model. Although it would seem that cognitive level would be difficult to change, Sprinthall and Thies-Sprinthall (1983) provide evidence that cognitive development can be facilitated by placing persons in significant role-taking situations (such as mentoring), along with continuous guided reflection and ongoing support.

2.1.2 Career development. As noted above, "career development" denotes the growth experienced as teachers move through the stages of their professional careers. Several researchers have investigated the patterns of growth and stagnation that emerge as teachers remain in the profession, each using different terms to identify the stages. The conceptualization that seems to be the most rigorous in its formulation is that advanced by Huberman et al. (1989) (see also Huberman 1989 for a summary of the research).

Huberman's synthesis of the theory and research on career development posits five stages of the professional career, demarcated in terms of years of teaching experience. "Career entry," from the first to the third year, is a time of both survival and discovery. The survival theme is the one most often sounded in studies of beginning teachers; however, many beginning teachers report a sense of discovery as they work with their own pupils and become part of a collegial group. Teachers having from four to six years of teaching experience seem to move into a "stabilization" period when tenure is granted, a definitive commitment to the career of teaching is made, and a sense of instructional mastery is achieved.

Teachers having from 7 to 18 years of experience enter a divergent period. Some report this period as one of experimentation and activism, when they try out new approaches, develop their own courses, and confront institutional barriers. Others report this period as one of self-doubt and reassessment, when disenchantment with the system leads many to consider changing professions.

Divergence also occurs for teachers with 19 to 30 years of experience. For many, it is a time of relaxed self-acceptance and serenity, accompanied by a developing awareness of greater relational distance from their pupils. For others, this period is one of conservatism, with these teachers tending to complain a great deal, criticizing the administrators, their colleagues, and their students.

The final period, from 31 to 40 years of teaching experience, is a stage of disengagement, a gradual withdrawal as the end of the career looms. For some, it is a time of serenity; for others, a time of bitterness.

2.1.3 Motivational development. "Motivation" refers to the strength of the inner drive to achieve professional goals. Glatthorn (1990) has identified several factors that influence a teacher's motivational level. The first is a supportive environment consisting of five features: positive relationships with students and parents, the presence of effective leadership, adequate physical conditions, positive school climate, and a manageable teaching assignment. The second factor is meaningful work. The teacher has an appropriate degree of autonomy and believes in the significance of his or her work.

The third factor is the teacher's belief system. The following beliefs are essential for a high level of motivation. "I can perform successfully." "The actions I take will achieve the results I want." "The results I achieve will be recognized by rewards that I value." Rewards are particularly important. In the United States, teachers are more motivated by such intrinsic rewards as the satisfaction of improving student learning than they are by extrinsic ones such as merit pay (Dilworth 1991). However, a comparison of teachers in France and the United Kingdom concluded that inner-city French teachers are much less likely to perceive teaching as a means of giving meaning to life and are more likely to see it simply as a means of earning a living (Broadfoot and Osborn 1987).

The fourth factor is the teacher's goals. The teacher's level of motivation is more likely to be high when the teacher's goals are shared by peers, when the goal-setting process is a collaborative one, when the goals are specific, and when the goals are challenging but attainable.

The final factor in teacher motivation is the type and frequency of feedback. Several studies suggest that the teacher's level of motivation is more likely to increase when the teacher makes continuing assessments of student learning and uses positive results as reinforcement. Frequent and positive feedback from administrators and supervisors can also increase the level of teacher motivation.

2.2 Contextual Factors

Contextual factors include all those elements of the environment that impact upon teacher development. McLaughlin and Talbert (1990) have identified five embedded contextual layers. The most remote (but not necessarily the least influential) layer is the community and society. Increasing proximal layers are the school system or school district, the school, the teaching team or department, and the classroom.

2.2.1 Society and the community. Although the societal and community contexts have not been given a great deal of attention in the literature on teacher development, there is evidence that they do play an influential role. The way in which society at large perceives teachers and teaching would likely affect the way teachers view their development. Louis (1990) discusses national differences in this regard.

In Denmark, the general perception is that teachers are collectively responsible for carrying out their job; their craft knowledge is highly valued. As a consequence, teachers are expected to be responsible for the design of improvement efforts. In France, on the other hand, teaching is seen as comprising highly analyzable skills, and teacher autonomy is protected by civil service and union regulations. Although the system is highly centralized, bureaucratic policies sharply limit what teachers can be expected to do relative to their professional development. Japan presents a third model. As Louis notes, cultural traditions there support a view of teachers as good technical experts, motivated by strong norms of collective professional behavior. It is not unusual for Japanese teachers to respond to a perceived problem by forming a voluntary Saturday morning study group.

2.2.2 The school system. The school system, the next layer of influence, affects teacher development in several ways. Its policies on teacher supervision and evaluation might either constrain or facilitate the professional development of teachers. Its practices and procedures relative to staff development would similarly affect how teachers grow. During the 1980s, school systems in the United States, for example, based most of their staff development programs on a rather narrow conceptualization of the skills of direct instruction, an emphasis that in retrospect probably inhibited significant growth for many experienced teachers who had already internalized those basic skills.

2.2.3 The school. The school level, the third layer of influence, has been studied more often than any other. The research suggests that, in general, two elements are most influential at the school level: the culture of the school (as manifested in its values and norms of behavior), and the nature of school leadership.

An analysis of the literature on school culture indicates that five beliefs play an instrumental role in teachers' professional development (Fullan 1990, Corcoran 1990, Rosenholtz 1989, Little 1990, Rutter 1987). First, the school is a cooperative community where people act with trust and collegiality. They value the cohesiveness that characterizes such a community. Hargreaves (1992), however, notes the dangers of what he terms "contrived collegiality"—superficial cooperation imposed by administrators in the guise of peer coaching.

Second, there is a belief in common goals. As Rosenholtz (1989) observes in her study of eight elementary schools, a strong consensus about goals leads the principal and the teachers toward a dynamic sense of community, in which professional growth is viewed as an essential part of professionalism. Third, school improvement can be achieved through a problem-solving orientation. Furthermore, professionals will spend the time necessary to solve important school-based problems. Fourth, all those in the school can achieve success; relatedly, people must hold high expectations for themselves and others. Finally, administrators and teachers believe that instruction is their highest priority. Thus, while professional development is essential, it is pursued as a means of improving instruction, not as an end unto itself.

The importance of school leadership in fostering teacher development has been noted in several publications; Leithwood (1992) presents perhaps the most fully developed conceptualization. Focusing upon teacher development as the most central function of instructional leadership, he offers four guidelines for discharging that function more effectively: (a) treat the teacher as a whole person, emphasizing psychological development along with the development of expertise; (b) establish a school culture based on norms of collaboration and professional inquiry; (c) diagnose the starting points for teacher development; and (d) recast routine administrative activities into powerful teacher development strategies.

2.2.4 The teaching team or department. Teaching peers or colleagues can also influence teacher development. Peers influence each other in three crucial ways: they affect the decision-making of colleagues through informal exchanges in departmental offices, they influence each other in determining the predominant teaching style, and they establish and reinforce informal norms about peer interactions and professional development (Glatthorn 1990). Johnson (1990) underscores the strong influence exerted by department heads as they provide both internal leadership and external advocacy.

2.2.5 The classroom. The final and most immediate layer is the classroom. A teacher who serves time with unmotivated students, lecturing and drilling, will see little need for professional growth. On the other hand, as Lieberman and Miller (1992) argue, teachers who engage students in problem-solving, who provide opportunities for students' primary research, who use students as teachers, and who connect school life with community life, are in reality growing by teaching. Such a learning-rich environment, they contend, will compel the teacher to grow in significantly new ways.

3. *Fostering Teacher Development*

Given the strength of those influential factors, what can school administrators, supervisors, and teachers do to foster teacher development? The answers to this question will be presented below from three perspectives: standard approaches to teacher development, alternative processes for teacher growth, and the likely future for teacher development.

3.1 Standard Approaches to Teacher Development

For several decades prior to the 1990s, school administrators and supervisors in most developed nations have relied upon clinical supervision and teacher evaluation as the primary means of fostering teacher development. While these approaches have achieved some success, the evidence tends to suggest that they might have outlived their usefulness for competent experienced teachers.

3.1.1 Clinical supervision. While clinical supervision takes many forms, almost all models include several common elements: a pre-observation conference, an observation of classroom performance, the analysis of observational data, and a post-observation debriefing conference. In a review of 25 studies from 1973 to 1983, Pavan (1983) concluded that the evidence on the effectiveness of clinical supervision was, at best, inconclusive. She also pointed out the pervasive methodological flaws in much of the research she reviewed. In contrast, in a review of studies conducted from 1978 to 1981, Adams and Glickman (1984) concluded that the clinical model has a positive effect on teacher attitude and teacher performance.

In addition to these somewhat mixed findings, clinical supervision has been questioned on other grounds. Glatthorn (1990) pointed out that clinical supervision suffers from several drawbacks: (a) an undue focus on the basic skills of teaching; (b) a failure to differentiate the needs of experienced teachers from those of novices; and, (c) a frequent superficiality in its application, since it is labor intensive. Similarly, Smyth (1989) observed that it has lost its original collaborative emphasis and has degenerated into a sophisticated mechanism of inspection and surveillance.

3.1.2 Teacher evaluation. By the early 1990s, the evaluation of teachers had received a great deal of attention, especially in the United States, where it has developed as a somewhat predictable consequence of the concern for teacher accountability. In its standard form, a supervisor or an administrator takes to the classroom an observational "scorecard," which lists criteria loosely derived from the research on teacher effectiveness. The evaluator observes the class, completes the scorecard, and confers with the teacher in a conference that has been characterized as a "good news/bad news" session. Typically, the evaluator makes two or three such evaluative observations in the course of the school year and then arrives at a summative assessment that determines whether the teacher will be granted or denied tenure, dismissed or retained, promoted or not promoted.

The effect of these evaluations or inspections on teacher development has been almost totally negative, despite the claims by school systems that the evaluation process was designed to improve instruction (Glickman 1991). Stodolsky (1990) has identified several significant limitations of such observations. First, they do not yield insight into teachers' thinking. Second, they do not provide information on how teachers plan. Third, they give no data on how teachers work with colleagues, students, and parents.

In the light of such criticisms, experts in the field have proposed several alternatives. They are: (a) the use of self-assessment; (b) the development of a cumulative professional portfolio; (c) the administration of performance tests, in which teachers are expected to demonstrate skills and knowledge; and (d) the use of goal-based systems that focus on growth, not evaluation (Millman and Darling-Hammond 1990).

3.2 Alternative Approaches to Teacher Development

There are four alternative approaches to teacher development that seem to be gaining wide currency: self-directed development, cooperative or collegial development, change-oriented staff development, and new roles for teachers.

3.2.1 Self-directed development. In self-directed models of teacher development, the teacher typically identifies a significant goal related to his or her professional development. That goal may be derived from one or more of several sources: the school improvement plan, the advanced skills of teaching, or new knowledge about the subject or students for which the teacher is responsible. The teacher then identifies the means by which he or she will achieve that goal, the resources needed, and the way in which accomplishment will be assessed. In such a self-directed model, the principal or supervisor acts as a facilitator, clarifying goals and methods, providing resources, and sharing in the assessment process.

Clark (1992) has designed a set of seven guidelines for implementing self-directed development: "Write your own credo of teaching." "Start with your strengths." "Make a five-year plan." "Look in your own backyard (use your own classroom as the locus of growth." "Ask for support." "Go first class (pursue quality ventures)." "Finally, blow your own trumpet (let others know about your accomplishments)."

Self-directed models are reported to be effective by those advocating their use. One potential weakness is that growth requires objective feedback; some self-directed models do not provide for this.

3.2.2 Cooperative or collegial development. "Cooperative professional development" is a term used by Glatthorn (1987) to describe his model of collegial development. In this model, small teams of teachers develop and implement their own approach to professional growth. They choose from several options: professional dialogues—structured discussions focusing on current educational issues that affect them directly; curriculum development—collaborative development of curriculum units and teaching materials; peer supervision—peer observations and debriefing sessions; peer coaching—the development of specific teaching skills through staff development and peer assistance; and action research—collaborative inquiry about a real problem.

The results of several pilot tests suggest that the cooperative model seems to be effective only when the following conditions are in place. First, it grows out of a collaborative organizational environment and is not the result of "contrived collegiality." Second, it has the strong support of administrators. Third, teachers are provided with sufficient time. Finally, teachers are given the training they need to implement the model successfully.

3.2.3 Change-oriented staff development. Change-oriented staff development programs are recommended by several experts in the field. Rather than offering staff development programs that respond to some new fad, these experts argue that all staff development should be directly related to the school improvement process. Fullan (1990) is among those who have instituted such programs and reports initial success. In the Fullan model, the teacher-as-learner is seen as the central cog linking classroom improvement to school improvement. Throughout the three phases of the change process (initiation, implementation, and institutionalization), teachers work collaboratively to develop the skills and knowledge they need to effect significant and long-term school improvement.

3.2.4 New roles for teachers. Expanding teachers' roles is seen as a means of both improving the school and facilitating teachers' growth. Typically, such "job-enhancement" strategies provide the teacher with expanded opportunities to make decisions which, in turn, lead to significant professional growth. Conley (1991) identifies four components of school management as possible focuses for increased teacher participation: direction (e.g., determining teaching assignments); organization (e.g., setting schedules for teachers and students); support (e.g., mentoring); and monitoring (e.g., evaluating performance). In all these components, she notes, the critical issue is not involvement, but influence. That is, do teachers have increased influence in the decision-making process?

3.3 Future Directions for Teacher Development

Extrapolating from trends in the larger society and the profession, several trends in teacher development are likely in the 1990s. First, there will be increased coordination between the preservice and inservice education of teachers. The wide acceptance and early success of "Professional Development Schools" (schools that function as the site of much of the preservice training) should encourage teacher-training institutions to see professional development as an uninterrupted and well-coordinated sequence of experiences.

Second, the use of technology as the central means for delivering staff development programs will increase. The hardware is already available to enable teachers to interact with a distant expert, to participate in professional networks with teachers all across the country, to observe and critique their own teaching, to learn from electronic simulations, and to retrieve and synthesize information. Whether school systems have the resources, the will, or the know-how is uncertain.

Finally, there should be increased contact and collaboration with professionals from other human service organizations. Educators realize that the problems of poverty and ignorance do not stop at the classroom door. As a result, several school systems in the United States have taken a leadership role in using the local school as a one-stop center for families who need help. If services are to be coordinated, the next logical step is to engage teachers, social workers, therapists, and physicians in collaborative professional development.

See also: Teacher Education: Inservice; Teachers, Professional Socialization of; Teachers' Roles; Teaching, Realities of

References

Adams A, Glickman C 1984 Does clinical supervision work? A review of research. *Tennessee Educational Leadership* 11: 28–40

Broadfoot P, Osborn M 1987 Teachers' conceptions of their professional responsibility: Some international comparisons. *Comp. Educ.* 23(3): 287–301

Burden P 1990 Teacher development. In: Houston W R (ed.) 1990 *Handbook of Research on Teacher Education*. Macmillan, New York

Clark C M 1992 Teachers as designers in self-directed professional development. In: Hargreaves A, Fullan M G (eds.) 1992 *Understanding Teacher Development*. Cassell, London

Conley S 1991 Review of research on teacher participation in school decision-making. In: Grant G (ed.) 1991 *Review of Research in Education*, Vol. 17. American Educational Research Association, Washington, DC

Corcoran T B 1990 Schoolwork: Perspectives on workplace reform. In: McLaughlin M W, Talbert J E, Bascia N (eds.) 1990 *The Contexts of Teaching in Secondary Schools*. Teachers College Press, New York

Dilworth M E 1991 *Motivation, Rewards, and Incentives*. American Association of Colleges for Teacher Education, Washington, DC

Fullan M G 1990 Staff development, innovation, and institutional development. In: Fullan M G, Joyce B, Bruce B B 1990 *Changing School Culture through Staff Development. Yearbook of the ASCD*. Association for Supervision and Curriculum Development, Alexandria, Virginia

Glatthorn A A 1987 Cooperative professional development: Peer-centered options for teacher growth. *Educ. Leadership* 45(3): 31–35

Glatthorn A A 1990 *Supervisory Leadership*. Scott Foresman, Glenview, Illinois

Glickman C D 1981 *Developmental Supervision*. Association for Supervision and Curriculum Development, Alexandria, Virginia

Glickman C D 1991 Pretending not to know what we know. *Educ. Leadership* 48(8): 4–10

Hargreaves A 1992 Cultures of teaching: A focus for change. In: Hargreaves A, Fullan M G (eds.) 1992 *Understanding Teacher Development*. Cassell, London

Huberman M 1989 The professional life cycle of teachers. *Teach. Coll. Rec.* 91(1): 31–57

Huberman M et al. 1989 *La Vie des Enseignants*. Delachaux et Niestle, Lausanne

Johnson S M 1990 The primacy and potential of high school departments. In: McLaughlin M W, Talbert J E, Bascia N 1990 *The Contexts of Teaching in Secondary Schools*. Teachers College Press, New York

Leithwood K A 1992 The principal's role in teacher development. In: Fullan M, Hargreaves A (eds.) 1992 *Teacher Development and Educational Change*. Taylor and Francis, London

Lieberman A, Miller L 1992 Teacher development in professional practice schools. In: Levine M (ed.) 1992 *Professional Practice Schools*. Teachers College Press, New York

Little J W 1990 Conditions of professional development in secondary schools. In: McLaughlin M W, Talbert J E, Bascia N (eds.) 1990 *The Contexts of Teaching in Secondary Schools*. Teachers College Press, New York

Little J W 1992 Teacher development and educational policy. In: Fullan M, Hargreaves A (eds.) 1992 *Teacher Development and Educational Change*. Falmer Press, London

Louis K S 1990 School and community values and the quality of teachers' work life. In: McLaughlin M W, Talbert J E, Bascia N (eds.) 1990 *The Contexts of Teaching in Secondary Schools*. Teachers College Press, New York

McLaughlin M W, Talbert J E 1990 The contexts in question: The secondary school workplace. In: McLaughlin M W, Talbert J E, Bascia N (eds.) 1990 *The Contexts of Teaching in Secondary Schools*. Teachers College Press, New York

Millman J, Darling-Hammond L (eds.) 1990 *The New Handbook of Teacher Evaluation*. Sage, Newbury Park, California

Pavan B N 1983 Clinical supervision: Does it make a difference? Paper presented at annual meeting of the Council of Professors of Instructional Supervision, DeKalb, Illinois

Rosenholtz S J 1989 *Teachers' Workplace: The Social Organization of Schools*. Longman, New York

Rutter R A 1987 *Facilitating Teacher Engagement*. National Center on Effective Secondary Schools, Madison, Wisconsin

Smyth J 1989 Problematizing teaching through a "critical" perspective on clinical supervision. Paper presented at meeting of American Educational Research Association, San Francisco, California

Sprinthall N A, Thies-Sprinthall L 1983 The teacher as adult learner: A cognitive–developmental view. In: Griffin G (ed.) 1983 *Staff Development* (82nd yearbook of the National Society for the Study of Education). University of Chicago Press, Chicago, Illinois

Stodolsky S S 1990 Classroom observation. In: Millman J, Darling-Hammond L (eds.) 1990

Further Reading

Feiman S, Floden R E 1981 *A Consumer's Guide to Teacher Development*. Institute for Research on Teaching, East Lansing, Michigan

Hughes P (ed.) 1991 *Teachers' Professional Development*. Australian Council for Educational Research, Hawthorn, Victoria

A. Glatthorn

Teacher Education and Adult Development

Age theories suggest a pattern of tasks that confront adults throughout their life cycles. Beginning teachers in their 20s may be concerned with initial commitments to teaching, living arrangements, and relationships. In subsequent life-cycle periods such as their 40s, teachers may question their priorities and values as they realize that time is finite and success and achievement have limitations. At each age-related transition, a person's developmental task is to create a better fit between the life structure he or she has defined and the reality of life's challenges.

The concept of structure building and structure changing (Levinson 1986) is particularly important to a conception of life periods in adulthood. A number of extensive reviews of life-age and life-cycle theories were completed in the 1980s by researchers such as Chickering, Havighurst, Neugarten, and Hagestad. These researchers discussed sociological changes (political, technological, economic, and demographic), age norms, the social clock, and on- and off-time crises that can result in life-cycle changes which may have a significant impact upon the functioning of the individual.

1. Teachers' Professional Life Cycles and their Careers

A variety of researchers have used age-related life-cycle literature to understand better the phases of a teacher's career. Since space in this entry does not permit a detailed review of these studies, readers are referred to the literature review by Burden (1990); A few studies are mentioned in this section to give the reader a general picture of the research in this area.

Huberman's (1989) life-cycle research with Swiss teachers used collaborative autobiography to analyze teacher career paths and attitudes toward teaching. His work raised issues about the disjointed nature of teachers' development which can result in either rigid or flexible endpoints.

Fessler and Christensen (1992) provided descriptions of the complex environmental factors which may influence a teacher's career and the major characteristics of each career cycle: induction, competency building, enthusiasm and growth, career frustration, stability, wind-down, and exit. Their work discussed growth needs as well as the incentives and support systems for each phase in a teacher's career cycle.

Vonk and Schras (1987) focused on professional development during the first 4 years of teaching in the Netherlands, and Burden (1990) presented an extensive review of research on preservice teachers and inservice teacher development, mostly in the United States. This research produced suggestions for effective ways to educate new teachers and to train experienced teachers as mentors.

2. *Stages of Teacher Development*

Cognitive–developmental stages are not defined by age; teachers at the same age are frequently at different stages of development. Stage theorists have focused on underlying patterns of thought and problem-solving which play a central role in determining an individual's approach to the world. The stages are structural in nature, qualitatively different from one another, hierarchically integrated, and emerge—according to these theories—in an unvaried sequence or progression. The sequence of development progresses from simpler to more complex and differentiated modes of thought and functioning. Levine (1988) has reviewed stage theories in teacher development.

3. *Moral/Ethical Development*

A number of researchers have used a Kohlbergian perspective, referred to as a "morality of justice," to determine teacher stage and level of moral judgment. There are two ways of collecting data—a moral judgment interview based on dilemma situations, or an objective questionnaire called the Defining Issues Test (DIT). Six stages of development have been identified, ranging from preconventional through conventional to postconventional thinking.

Johnson (1989) found a positive relation between moral reasoning levels and teachers' understanding of individualized instruction. She also summarized a number of previous studies that led to the conclusion that moral developmental levels are related to teachers' understanding of curriculum, student–teacher roles, management issues, rules, and teaching practices. Thomas and Rest (1987) investigated moral sensitivity in 30 student teachers and found that moral judgment was related to teaching performance, though the magnitude was not large.

Yeazell and Johnson (1988) investigated levels of moral judgment of faculty and students in a teacher education program. They found that the faculty were able to recognize principled postconventional moral judgments while none of the three student groups (undergraduate beginning teacher education students, student teachers, or graduate students) exhibited similar abilities. They were surprised that the three different student groups did not differ from each other in their moral judgment scores, even though they represented different educational levels and many of the graduate students were full-time teachers. As a result of their findings, Yeazell and Johnson called for increasing attention to the important teaching competency called "moral sensitivity."

Finally, in a study of 27 teachers in Perth, Australia, MacCallum (1991) found that teachers' moral judgments were related to various aspects of discipline. Thus, the importance of challenging teachers to address the moral issues inherent in the teaching/learning environment was confirmed.

3.1 *Moral Reasoning and the School Environment*

The influence of the school as a workplace on the moral development of teachers is an important topic of research. For example, Oser and Zutavern (1987) described an inservice program in which teachers analyzed the extent to which they created a "just community" for their students. In the process, they deepened their understanding of moral and social theories, the school atmosphere, democratic decision-making, and transformation procedures with respect to the authority of teachers and principals. Similarly, Miserandino (1989) discussed a successful case study of a teacher workshop which was designed as part of a staff development program and focused on the moral development of teachers in one school. Teachers were provided with a work environment that demanded choice, autonomy, dialogue, reflection, and teachers' close collaboration with the principal and the students.

3.2 *Women's Moral/Ethical Development*

Researchers investigating women's development have identified a pattern referred to as a "morality of response and care" (Gilligan 1988). This pattern consists of three developmental levels and two transitional phases in a spiraling evolution of care and responsibility to oneself and others. Gilligan et al.'s research challenged the dominant developmental models that equated maturity with separation, independence, and self-sufficiency. Through the lens of Gilligan's theory, a primary focus on attachments and relationships can be understood, validated, and added as another important perspective of the moral/ethical domain.

3.3 *Moral Perspectives on Justice and Care*

The research on the two moral perspectives of care and justice suggested that women and men do raise both justice and care concerns in describing moral conflicts, but they tend to focus their attention on either justice or care, elaborating one set of concerns and minimally representing the other. This tendency to focus on one perspective means that loss of the other perspective is a liability that both men and women share.

Gilligan (1988) suggested that adult moral maturity can be defined by the ability to see in at least two ways and to speak in at least two languages, the voice of justice and the voice of care. Lyons (1990) used the care and response perspective to explore the nature and meaning of the moral dilemmas teachers encounter in their work as they respond to and interpret the tasks of learning and teaching. Through analyses of teacher narratives, she revealed how the teachers' perspectives toward knowledge and their views of themselves and their students as knowers enter into their work and can at times be part of their continuing adult development. The work of Gilligan and Lyons has been followed by teachers and researchers who continue to focus on the themes of connection and separation in the paradoxical struggle to become autonomous within the context of relationships (see, e.g., Witherell and Noddings 1991).

4. *Ego Development*

Ego development theory may have strong potential for explaining observed differences between teachers and administrators. A growing number of researchers have used Loevinger's (1976) model of ego development in investigating teacher development. Ego development includes moral and personality development, cognitive complexity, and interpersonal style. Ego development, especially at the preconventional and conventional ego stages, can be measured by a well-researched test, the Washington University Sentence Completion Test (SCT), using Loevinger's self-training manuals. The post-conventional stages of adult development and an additional transitional stage are defined more clearly and scored more adequately using methods reported by Cook-Greuter (1990).

Teachers at different stages respond to and need different environments. In a study of 58 Canadian teachers, Cummings and Murray (1989) found that views on issues such as teacher role and sources of knowledge differed significantly by ego level.

Richardson and Thompson (1982) surveyed 70 principals and 308 teachers using the SCT to measure each principal's ego development level and the teachers' perceptions of each principal's reliance on different power bases. The SCT scores of these principals clustered at conventional levels: the conformist, self-aware, and conscientious ego stages. With this restricted sample, the results showed no statistically significant differences in the patterns of power base used by the principals according to levels of ego development. Studies of this type will be important for the future; however, an extended sample which includes principals scoring at post-conventional stages will be necessary.

Kegan and Lahey (1984) illustrated how teachers and principals operating at different stages of ego development have conflicting perceptions regarding leadership and authority in a school. At a time when administrators and teachers are being urged to work much more collaboratively in strategic planning and restructuring for the twenty-first century, educators need to consider the impact of ego development on their work.

5. *Cognitive, Intellectual, and Epistemological Development.*

Piaget (1972) postulated continuing cognitive development through adulthood in two ways. Initially, there is a transition from concrete operations into the stage of formal abstract thought, evidenced by the ability to reason, to view a situation from a variety of perspectives, and to use alternative problem-solving solutions. Later, a stabilization of formal abstract thought occurs, evidenced by increasing application of abstract thinking processes to progressively more complex issues in religion, politics, management, and interpersonal relationships. Subsequent investigations supported the finding that cognitive development was not completed in adolescence; research among adults suggested that even when abstract thinking levels have been attained, they may not be retained across the life span.

Significant cognitive development can take place during adulthood. Thus, any inservice program which assumes that adults have attained abstract operations in all aspects of their thinking is likely to encounter problems. Efforts need to be made to aid teachers in the transition from concrete to abstract modes of thought in new areas of teaching and learning. In some contexts an appropriate educational goal would be to foster development beyond abstract operations to a stage of problem-posing and to foster cognitive development of a different sort, such as dialectical thought.

5.1 Teachers' Conceptual Levels

Research in conceptual development (for a review, see Miller 1981) is particularly applicable to teacher education. Stages of conceptual level are defined by degree of abstractness as well as by degree of interpersonal maturity. Hunt's (1971) work provided a key empirical and theoretical bridge connecting developmental concepts to classroom teaching. Key concepts from Hunt's work were developmental match and constructive mismatch as ways for educators to plan for growth of teachers in ways that would be appropriately challenging and continuously supportive.

This research suggested that teachers at higher stages are more flexible, more tolerant of stress, and more adaptive to changing circumstances than teachers at lower stages. These higher stage teachers are more able to function in highly student-centered environments where their role is to utilize the learner's frame of reference and to encourage students to question and hypothesize. Furthermore, teachers at higher stages are able to assume multiple perspectives, utilize a wide variety of coping behaviors, employ a broader repertoire of teaching models, and consequently be more effective with a wide range of learning styles and needs of students.

Subsequent researchers found that teachers at higher levels of development were also more effective in supervisory interactions with preservice teachers (see review by Burden 1990).

Perry's (1981) longitudinal research provided vivid descriptions of the emotional turmoil connected with intellectual growth. Perry identified four main positions and five transitions of intellectual growth from dualism through multiplicity, from relativism to commitment. As a person progresses through these intellectual positions in response to new experiences and learning, personal identity is affirmed. Perry's account of intellectual development is helpful in understanding the growth of reflective judgment, reasoning in action, and the teacher's ability to be a reflective practitioner. Significant new work in teacher reflective thinking was evident in Simmons et al. (1989).

5.2 *Women's Intellectual/Epistemological Development*

Another approach to the study of intellectual development is that of Belenky et al. (1986). Analyzing interview data from 135 women, these researchers identified five different epistemological positions that represent women's experience of themselves as knowers. The positions are silence, received knowledge, subjective knowledge, procedural knowledge, and constructed knowledge. In the fifth position of constructed knowledge, speaking and listening are used equally in active dialogue with others, in situations in which knowledge is constructed by persons who experience themselves as equals. This work highlights the gender-related aspects of women's educational experience.

One of the most important findings is the evidence of two subcategories at the procedural level: separate and connected knowing. The separate way of knowing functioned under standard rules and conventions of rational thought, much like that described in Perry's model, and focused on principles and critical thinking procedures. In the connected way of knowing, knowledge and reason were gained through personal experience and relationships. Women at all levels preferred connected rather than separate modes of learning, a finding which has significant applications to teaching. Connected knowing describes an educational environment in which individuals value personal individual experience; nurture each other's thoughts to maturity; construct truth through consensus rather than conflict; bridge private and shared experience; accord respect to each others' unique perspectives; and base authority on cooperation, not subordination.

6. *Staff Development and Collaborative Problem-solving*

Oja's research with her colleagues (for a summary, see Oja 1991) consisted of four staff development programs whose goals were increased ego maturity, moral reasoning, conceptual complexity, and interpersonal functioning as a means to improve teacher effectiveness. This work suggested that collaborative action research could create a school-based problem-solving environment which stimulated postconventional stages of adult development. These researchers noted that teachers who were developing toward postconventional stages preferred the conditions of the action research team in contrast to the more permanent context of the school environment. The action research team context was nonhierarchial and self-managed; it had norms of collegiality and experimentation; power was diffused among the team; teachers developed their own tasks and flexibly undertook a variety of roles and responsibilities; the setting allowed reflective thinking and cognitive expansion; decision-making was participatory and collaboratively shared. A subsequent study found that teachers and administrators who self-selected to be involved in collaborative supervision and who sustained their involvement in the program over a period of years were at the postconventional stages. The collaborative supervisory teams in the action research program had both challenged and supported postconventional stage educators.

7. *Conclusion*

The research summarized in this entry, drawn from a larger body of research on adult development and teacher education, suggests that adults at different developmental stages exhibit different attitudes toward teaching and learning, attitudes toward decision-making and change, perceptions of group organization and process, and perceptions of leadership, supervision, and evaluation. This knowledge base can be used to understand how teachers change throughout their careers. It also can be used to promote teacher development with the proper use of supervision and a series of appropriate staff development programs.

See also: Lifespan Development; Human Development, Stages in; Teacher Development

References

Belenky M F, Clinchy B M, Goldberger N, Tarule J 1986 *Women's Ways of Knowing: The Development of Self, Voice, and Mind*. Basic Books, New York

Burden P R 1990 Teacher Development. In: Houston W R (ed.) 1990 *Handbook of Research on Teacher Education*. Macmillan, New York

Cook-Greuter S 1990 Maps for living: Ego-development theory from symbiosis to conscious universal embeddedness. In: Commons M M et al. (eds.) 1990 *Adult Development*, Vol. 2. Praeger, New York

Cummings A L, Murray H G 1989 Ego development and its relation to teacher education. *Teaching and Teacher Education* 5(1): 21–32

Fessler R, Christensen J C (eds.) 1992 *The Teacher Career Cycle: Understanding and Guiding the Professional Development of Teachers*. Allyn and Bacon, Boston, Massachusetts

Gilligan C 1988 *A Contribution of Women's Thinking to Psychological Theory and Education Mapping the Moral Domain*. Harvard University Press, Boston, Massachusetts

Huberman M 1989 *Vie Des Enseignants: Evolution et Bilan d'une Profession*. Delachaux et Niestle, Paris/Neuchâtel

Hunt D E 1971 *Matching Models in Education: The Coordination of Teaching Methods with Student Characteristics*. Ontario Institute for Studies in Education, Toronto

Johnston M 1989 Moral reasoning and teachers' understanding of individualized instruction *Journal of Moral Education* 18(1): 45–59

Kegan R, Lahey L L 1984 Adult leadership and adult development: A constructivist view. In: Kellerman B (ed.) 1984 *Leadership: Multidisciplinary Perspectives*. Prentice-Hall, Englewood Cliffs, New Jersey

Levine S 1988 *Promoting Adult Growth in Schools: The Promise of Professional Development*. Allyn and Bacon, Boston, Massachusetts

Levinson D J 1986 A Conception of adult development. *Am. Psychol*. 41(1): 3–13

Loevinger J 1976 *Ego Development: Conceptions and Theories*. Jossey-Bass, San Francisco, California

Lyons N 1990 Dilemmas of knowing: Ethical and epistemological dimensions of teachers' work and development. *Harv. Educ. Rev*. 60(2): 159–80

MacCallum J A 1991 Teacher reasoning and moral judgment in the context of student discipline situations. Paper presented at the Annual Meeting of the American Educational Research Association, Chicago

Miller A 1981 Conceptual matching models and interactional research in education. *Rev. Educ. Res*. 51(1): 33–84

Miserandino A 1989 *Supervision for Growth: A Practitioner's Perspective*. Paper presented at the Annual Meeting of the American Educational Research Association, San Francisco

Oja S N 1991 Teacher and supervisor development: A report of four studies from 1978 to 1988 In: Campos B P (ed.) 1991 *Psychological Intervention and Human Development*. Instituto de Consulta Psicologica, Formacao e Desenvolvimento, Porto

Oser F, Zutavern M 1987 *Berufsethos von Lehrer/innen*. Pädagogisches Institut, Universität Fribourg, Fribourg

Perry W G 1981 Cognitive and ethical growth: The making of meaning. In: Chickering A W (ed.) 1981 *The Modern American College*. Jossey-Bass, San Francisco, California

Piaget J 1972 Intellectual evolution from adolescence to adulthood. *Hum. Dev*. 15(1): 1–12

Richardson R, Thompson B 1982 Ego development and power base reliance of school principals. Paper presented at the Annual Meeting of the American Educational Research Association, New York

Simmons J M et al. 1989 Exploring the structure of reflective pedagogical thinking in novice and expert teachers: The birth of a developmental taxonomy. Paper presented at the annual meeting of the American Educational Research Association, San Francisco

Thomas S J, Rest J 1987 Moral sensitivity and judgment in the development and performance of student teachers. *Moral Education Forum* 12(3): 15–20

Vonk J H C, Schras G A 1987 From beginning to experienced teacher: A study of the professional development of teachers during their first four years of service. *European Journal of Teacher Education* 10(1): 95–110

Witherell C, Noddings N (eds.) 1991 *Stories Lives Tell: Narrative and Dialogue in Education*. Teachers College Press, New York

Yeazell M I, Johnson S F 1988 Levels of moral judgment of faculty and students in a teacher education program: A micro study of an institution. *Teach. Educ. Q*. 15(1): 61–70

Further Reading

Holly M L, McLoughlin C S (eds.) 1989 *Perspectives on Teacher Professional Development*. Falmer Press, London

Huberman M (ed.) 1989 Research on teachers' professional lives. *Int. J. Educ. Res*. 13(4): 341–466

Loucks-Horsely S et al. 1987 *Continuing to Learn: A Guidebook for Teacher Development*. The Regional Laboratory for Educational Improvement of the Northeast and Islands, and the National Staff Development Council, Andover, Maryland

Oja S N, Smulyan L 1989 *Collaborative Action Research: A Developmental Approach*. Falmer Press, Basingstoke

S. N. Oja

Teacher Education and Special Education Needs

It is widely accepted that special training is central to the efficacy of special educational provision. Indeed, some countries have formal policies which emphasize the need for specialist training. In the United States, for example, certification requirements are used to establish minimum criteria for individuals to be regarded as qualified special education teachers. However, the lack of specially trained staff frequently makes the implementation of such policies impractical and specialist training is far from the norm, even in developed countries. For example, in the United States, in spite of the certification system, Huebner and Strumwasser (1987) report major variations between states in the extent to which they allow uncertificated teachers to teach students who are blind and visually impaired and make other exceptions to the general certification regulations. Similarly in the United Kingdom, the Advisory Committee on the Supply and Education of Teachers (1984) reported that less than 30 percent of the qualified teachers in special schools have a recognized additional qualification specifically related to special educational needs. In Japan, while it is necessary, in principle, to have a specialist teacher's certificate in addition to an ordinary teacher's certificate to teach in a special school, in practice it is common for those holding only ordinary certificates to do so (Ministry of Education, Science and Culture 1991). In developing countries, the availability of specially trained staff is even more limited (Aminah 1991).

1. The Relationship Between Educational Provision and Training

In considering the nature of, and the need for, special educational training it is important to recognize the relationship between the nature of the special educational provision which exists in a country and the training which is needed by the staff who work within that system. In many countries (e.g., Japan and Germany) the concepts of "disability" and "handicap" still play a fundamental role in the definition of special education, while in others (e.g., the US, Canada, and the UK) they have increasingly limited relevance. Categorical definitions are seen negatively and have been replaced by more positive constructions of educational need. In the United Kingdom, for example, the concept of special education has been broadened to cater to a much larger group of children and young people, and to focus on educational needs irrespective of the handicap or disability (Blackhurst et al. 1987). At the same time, much effort has been concentrated on making provision for these children, where possible, in mainstream schools. Integration has become the catchword.

The implications which these changes have for training are far-reaching and in some ways render international dialogue about training difficult. In countries where the concept of special needs has been broadened in the way described above, attention has to be given to training a much larger group of people to be able to recognize and cater for children with special educational needs and, in consequence, training has tended to shift from specialist to more generic forms of training. This has not meant the end of specialist courses; within the context of an emphasis on generic training it is still important to understand the needs of children with visual impairments and to have specialists who can provide support for other teachers and for individual children. The same is true for most of the handicapping conditions to which attention has been given traditionally. However, in the international context it is not possible to translate ideas about training generated in one educational system to another without carefully considering the objectives which that training is intended to meet within the context of that educational system.

It is important to realize that no one approach to teacher education is necessarily better than any other. This is particularly relevant in relation to developing countries, where all too often special educational training has been modeled on that of developed countries with virtually no change to make it meaningful in the local context. The need for training to reflect the local situation has been increasingly recognized by those who work in programs of international collaboration. Boucebi and Brau (1981), for example, argue that

> In countries of the Third World, the urgency and the immensity of the need for staff trained in the care of the mentally handicapped calls for the formulation of training programs which can be rapidly and realistically implemented, but which can be integrated into medium and long-term programs. These programs should not be modelled on the sophisticated and expensive techniques and structures developed in the industrialized countries, which are ill-suited to local socio-cultural conditions. (p. 105)

At the same time, it is important that training in any country reflects well-confirmed knowledge about special educational needs and is informed as fully as is realistically possible by an awareness of international trends and developments. In relation to international development projects, this suggests the need for collaborative programs which arise out of local needs but which reflect the best of Western experience. Ainscow (1991) provides a good example of such collaborative planning and development on a multinational basis.

2. Initial Teacher Education

2.1 General Teacher Education Courses

Regardless of the educational system and the way in which special education is defined, a concern for special educators must be the extent to which teachers in ordinary schools understand the nature of special education and the role which they can play in ensuring that the needs of special children are met. In countries where integration is the focus of development this is vital, for, as Young (1990) argues, the effectiveness of integration is heavily dependent on the willingness and ability of all teachers to do their part in meeting the needs of the children involved. The extent to which special educational needs are adequately met depends on the ability of ordinary teachers to "differentiate" their teaching to meet the full range of individual differences which exist in any class. In countries where there is little emphasis on integration and where special education is delivered primarily through segregated special school placement, teachers in mainstream schools have an important role to play in the identification of children with special needs.

In consequence, a primary concern in initial teacher education must be to familiarize all would-be teachers with the nature of special education and to provide them with appropriate skills to meet the needs of any such children with whom they come into contact. In the United Kingdom, an attempt has been made to ensure that this happens by introducing accreditation criteria for all initial teacher education courses which relate to special educational needs. These state that, on completion of their course, students should have developed:

(a) an understanding of the different ways in which pupils develop and learn and the ways in which pupils' work can be planned to secure clear progression;

(b) the capacity to use a range of teaching methods appropriate to the different abilities and other needs of pupils and organize their work accordingly;

(c) the capacity to identify gifted pupils and pupils with special educational needs or learning difficulties, and to understand the ways in which the potential of such pupils can be developed;

(d) skills in the evaluation of pupil performance;

(e) the capacity to guard against preconceptions based on the race, gender, or other attributes of pupils.

Such intentions are shared by special educators in many countries but whether they are successful in achieving these aims is not clear. In the United Kingdom, requirement (c) above is commonly met, but the others are less adequately addressed. There is some evidence that the situation is changing (Ramasut 1989), but subject specialists who have expertise (and interest) in the teaching of their subject to children with special educational needs are not common in any country.

2.2 Specialized Courses

In many countries, special education training is provided at the pre-service level. Such training is most commonly directed toward specific categories of handicap but can be related to more generic concepts of special need. This has proved to be an effective way of encouraging highly motivated young people to enter the teaching profession. In four or five years they can be trained to a very high level of expertise within their area of specialization. This approach, however, has been rejected in some countries (e.g., Canada) because of the limited experience such people inevitably have of normal development. In these countries, it has been argued that special education teachers should have training and experience in ordinary education before undertaking specialist training.

3. Further Professional Development

3.1 Specialist Courses

Most commonly, specialist training is provided at an advanced level for experienced regular teachers. Specialist training is frequently related to a particular handicapping condition, such as visual impairment or learning disabilities, but the growing emphasis on integration has drawn attention to the importance of generic or noncategorical training programs as the most appropriate form of training for the majority of special education teachers. Such training varies in length, but the norm in many countries has been a one-year full-time course. There has been an increasing emphasis, however, on part-time training of inservice teachers as a cost-effective way of maximizing the potential for staff development within fixed training budgets. For a discussion of the curriculum for specialized teacher preparation, see Reynolds (1990).

3.2 Other Courses

Changing concepts of special education have also brought with them the need for the inservice education of a larger group of teachers and other workers who may come into contact with special needs children as a result of integration/mainstreaming. In particular, there has been a recognition of the need for administrators and those who hold management posts within schools to be trained in order to ensure that the provision for which they are responsible is catering adequately to children with special educational needs. Equally, the need to train support staff paraprofessionals, such as classroom assistants, has been increasingly recognized.

4. New Demands

4.1 The Extension of Special Education

In many countries, it has been recognized that special education should extend above and below the conventional ages of school attendance and this has focused attention on the need for extended training emphases. Since the mid-1960s, a lot of attention has focused on training for the early years, but the needs of handicapped young people and adults beyond school age and in higher education have only begun to be addressed comparatively recently. However, while much progress has been made at this level (e.g., in the UK), much remains to be done to ensure the availability of a cadre of teachers who understand the needs of people in the postschool age group (Department of Education and Science 1987).

4.2 Cooperation with Parents/Other Professionals

The benefits which may accrue from cooperation between teachers and parents and other professionals is widely recognized as having particular relevance to the education of children with special educational needs. While the efficacy of multidisciplinary teamwork has not been evaluated with any rigor, personal experience suggests that interdisciplinary communication is rarely good. Similarly, while many special educators stress the importance of parent–school liaison, practice rarely equates with the rhetoric. A possible explanation for this is that these issues are inadequately addressed in pre-service and inservice teacher-training programs. A review of the literature reveals little relevant material, although an example of interest is provided by Heron and Harris (1982) who outline a training manual for working with other professional groups and parents. There is a clear need for thought to be given to ways in which special education teachers can be trained more effectively for collaborative work (Kroth 1975).

4.3 School-focused Training

Traditional patterns of training have assumed that training should be carried out in institutions of higher education such as universities and colleges. However, this assumption has been increasingly challenged and there has been growing pressure in many countries for courses to be more school-based and to involve a higher level of cooperation between schools and teacher-training institutes. Responses to this have been many and varied but have generally resulted in courses which have (a) a greater focus on teaching skills than knowledge of theory or research, (b) a greater involvement of serving teachers in the planning and delivery of courses, and (c) a greater proportion of course components actually being delivered in schools (e.g., methods of subject delivery are often taught in schools jointly by teachers and the staff of the training institution).

There has been a similar trend toward school-focused inservice training. The introduction of teacher appraisal in the United Kingdom, for example, has led to an increased emphasis on the identification of individual training needs, while the introduction of local school management and the devolution of funds for inservice training from central government has focused attention on meeting the needs of schools and local education authorities. Once again the responses of institutions of higher education have varied, but the trend has been toward more collaboration with schools and education authorities on the planning and delivery of courses, the accreditation of training provided by schools and local authorities, and a growing emphasis on "on-the-job" training. The increased awareness of the need for cost-effective training has also led in many countries to more part-time course provision at the expense of full-time training and a greater focus on skills-based training at the expense of the study of theory and the findings of research. The study of traditional disciplines such as educational psychology, the philosophy of education, and the sociology of education as pure academic pursuits has become increasingly unpopular.

4.4 Modes of Delivery

The development of new technology has highlighted the potential value of new and innovative approaches for the delivery of both preservice and inservice education. Developments in micro-technology, desk-top publishing, and satellite communication, together with continuing improvement in transport and postal and telephone communications have opened the way for the development of distance learning on a grand scale. This has particular relevance for special education. For example, Mason and Miller (1991) discuss the potential of distance learning in the provision of highly specialized training courses. McConkey and Bradley (1991) give an illustration of the value of video courses in developing countries, an area in which much future development could be profitably focused.

5. Challenges for the Future

The primary issue which has to be addressed in most countries is the preparation of adequate numbers of specially trained staff to make the delivery of special education maximally effective. In order to achieve this, there is a need to look critically at provisions for special educational training in the 1990s. Equally, there is a need to consider what current training needs are and to think through how training programs could be devised to meet those needs more effectively. In undertaking these tasks it is important to bear in mind: (a) the need for training to be embedded in its educational context; (b) the need for a coherent training program which takes into account the needs of specialists and generalists, classroom teachers and school administrators, and which allows continued professional development; and (c) the need for a flexible program which is responsive to changing patterns of provision and priorities in special education.

See also: Teacher Education: Onservice; Teacher Education: Inservice; Special Education, History of; Special Education, Sociology of

References

Advisory Committee on the Supply and Education of Teachers 1984 *Teacher Training and Special Educational Needs*. Department of Education and Science, London.

Ainscow M 1991 Towards effective schools for all. In: Upton G (ed.) 1991

Aminah S 1991 Special education in ASEAN countries. Paper presented at the 11th APEID Regional Seminar on Special Education at the National Institute of Special Education, Japan, October 14–19, 1991
Blackhurst A, Bott D, Cross D 1987 Noncategorical special education personnel preparation. In: Wang, M C, Reynolds M C, Walberg H J (eds.) 1987 *Handbook of Special Education: Research and Practice. Vol. 1 Learner Characteristics and Adaptive Education*. Pergamon Press, Oxford
Boucebi M, Brau M T 1981 Training specialized staff for the mentally handicapped. *Assignment Children* 53–54: 105–14
Department of Education and Science 1987 *A 'Special' Professionalism*. HMSO, London
Heron T E, Harris K C 1982 *The Educational Consultant*. Allyn and Bacon, Boston, Massachusetts
Huebner K M, Strumwasser K P 1987 State certification of teachers of blind and visually impaired students: Report of a national study. *Journal of Visual Impairment and Blindness* 81(6): 244–50
Kroth R 1975 *Communicating with Parents of Exceptional Children*. Love, Denver, Colorado
Mason H, Miller C 1991 Training teachers of children with special needs at a distance. In: Upton G (ed.) 1991
Ministry of Education, Science and Culture, 1991 *Special Education in Japan*. Monbusho, Tokyo
McConkey R, Bradley A 1991 Videocourses: A modern solution to an age-old problem. In: Upton G (ed.) 1991
Ramasut A (ed.) 1989 *Special Educational Needs: The Whole School Approach*. Falmer Press, London
Reynolds M C 1990 Educating teachers of special education students. In: Houston W (ed.) 1990 *Handbook of Research on Teacher Education*. Macmillan, New York
Young M J 1990 Australia: A country report. In: *Final Report of the Tenth APEID. Regional Seminar on Special Education*. Japan National Institute of Special Education

Further Reading

Hegarty S, Moses D 1988 *Developing Expertise: INSET for Special Educational Needs*. NFER–Nelson, Windsor
Holmes Group 1986 *Tomorrow's Teachers: A Report of the Holmes Group*. Holmes Group, East Lansing, Michigan
Robson C, Sebba J, Mittler P, Davies G 1988 *In-service Training and Special Educational Needs*. Manchester University Press, Manchester
Sayer J, Jones N (eds.) 1985 *Teacher Training and Special Educational Needs*. Croom Helm, Beckenham
Teacher Education and Special Education Council for Exceptional Children, Reston, Virginia
Upton G (ed.) 1991 *Staff Training and Special Educational Needs*. David Fulton, London

G. Upton

Teacher Education, Case Methods in

Case methods can be defined as "the methods of pedagogy employed in conjunction with teaching cases" (Shulman 1992 p. 19). It is useful to distinguish between case methods, a form of pedagogy, and case study methods, a form of qualitative research. A good case study may at times be useful for pedagogical purposes, whereas case studies are generally not written with that aim in mind. This entry includes discussions of the following topics: the context for research on case methods; case methods in law and business; a heuristic of case methods in teacher education; and finally, some issues for future research.

1. The Context for Research on Case Methods

The first edition of this *Encyclopedia* (Husén and Postlethwaite 1985) did not include an entry on case methods in teacher education. Since its publication, however, research on how cases can contribute to the teacher education curriculum has burgeoned. In the United States, the growing interest in case methods can be partly attributed to Shulman's (1986) seminal conceptualization of the knowledge base of teaching. Shulman asserted that cases have an important role to play in the education of teachers, and that case knowledge is a key component of the knowledge base of teaching. Interest in case methods since the mid-1980s can also be traced to the pressure exerted by politicians to professionalize teaching. For example, the Carnegie Forum on Education and the Economy (1986) recommended that the case method be introduced into teacher education programs. Thus, some teacher educators have studied the preparation of professionals in more prestigious fields, such as law, medicine, and business, and concluded that the apparently efficacious methods of preparing these practitioners also has a role to play in teacher education. As Sykes and Bird (1992) noted, "proponents of case teaching for teacher education frequently argue by analogy to case teaching in other fields of professional education" (p. 458).

Finally, since the mid-1980s, some teacher educators have turned away from science and the university as a source of knowledge for teaching and have looked instead to the practical setting. In rejecting the "applied science" conception of teaching, for example, proponents of craft knowledge argue that teaching is so highly contextual that knowledge for teaching is found in the situated knowledge of teachers. As Carter (1990) wrote:

> New ways of talking about the knowledge of teaching have emerged, many of which have signaled a need to rethink the conduct of teacher education and to explore richer ways of representing what experienced teachers know about classrooms and what new teachers need to know to function successfully in such inherently complex environments. (p. 109)

The study of cases is held to accord with this new view of teacher knowledge, which gives emphasis to the complexity of the practice setting, to reflection on experience, and to teacher wisdom. For these and other reasons, "the case idea" (Sykes and Bird 1992) has caught the imagination of many teacher educators.

This is not to say that using case methods in teacher preparation programs is a new idea. Case collection and study formed a part of teacher education programs at New Jersey State Teacher's College at Montclair during the 1920s (Sperle 1933). Merseth (1991) reported that the faculty of the Harvard Graduate School of Education briefly considered—but ultimately rejected—such a method for its programs in the 1920s. Furthermore, casebooks for use in both preservice and inservice programs have been published throughout the twentieth century (McAninch 1991). Indeed, it is interesting to speculate as to why case methods became a mainstay in the preparation of a whole range of professionals from lawyers to social workers, but not teachers. Before proceeding to a discussion of case methods in teacher education, it is useful to survey briefly the case methods in law and business, the two fields which have received the most attention from teacher educators interested in developing a case method for their own field (Kleinfeld 1992, Merseth 1992).

2. *Case Methods in Law and Business*

It is useful to study case methods in fields other than teacher education in order to underscore the idea that case methods, and what constitutes a case, vary. There is an array of case methods across professional disciplines, and even within disciplines. In addition, the literature that has emerged in other professions indicates some of the theoretical issues associated with case teaching.

2.1 *The Case Method in Law*

The case method in legal education is associated with Harvard Law School and its first dean, Christopher Columbus Langdell, who was appointed in 1870 (Stevens 1983, Thorne 1973). Langdell argued that decided opinions of the courts formed the basic data for rendering the study of the law scientific and therefore worthy of university status. The earliest casebooks were collections of appellate court cases, offered without commentary or materials. Further, he maintained that the curriculum should consist entirely of the study of cases, which reinforced the Common Law view that judges pronounce the law. Finally, Langdell asserted that students should be taught by the Socratic method, so that they could induce the skein of legal precedent themselves, rather than merely be told what the law said through didactic methods.

Early in the twentieth century, when adherence to Common Law fell from favor, Langdell's successors rhetorically shifted the rationale of the case method to teaching students the process of legal reasoning. Yet, as Stevens noted, Langdell's case method remains virtually intact to this day:

> Throughout the hierarchy of law schools, from the most famous national ones to the most locally-oriented, it is the analysis of the appellate decisions through case classes which takes pride of place. The skills developed in today's students tend to be substantially the same as those inculcated in the students of the 1870s largely because the structure of legal education has remained unchanged. Law teaching, no matter how differently the case method is used, is still predominantly a matter of a single professor dissecting innumerable cases before a class consisting of large numbers of students. (Stevens cited in Thorne 1973 p. 107)

This model of the case method and legal education in general have been attacked on various grounds. Some critics, for example, argue that the legal case method develops technical skills at the expense of fostering a concern for the moral consequences of any given outcome (Stevens 1983).

2.2 *The Case Method in Business*

The use of cases in business education originated at Harvard Business School in the early part of the twentieth century. Unlike the field of law, however, where cases are generated by the practice itself, business cases had to be formulated for the curriculum. A business case is generally a written account of a business problem that demands action on the part of an executive or group of executives. In 1920, the Harvard Business School allocated funds specifically for the purpose of case development and a group of graduates was employed to go out into the field to collect and write-up "real" business problems. Later, case writing became an activity of business school faculty.

The literature on the case method in business education suggests a much more eclectic approach than is in law. Dooley and Skinner (1977) found nearly endless variations of case use in business classes. Van Woerden (1988) listed a variety of case formats, including in-baskets and simulations.

Unlike the case method in law, the emphasis in business is on group process and discussion for the purpose of developing problem-solving and decision-making skills (Christensen and Hansen 1987). Because the aim of this method is the development of executive judgment, business cases are generally open-ended and allow for more than one credible solution. The role of the professor is that of discussion leader, rather than Socratic questioner. In comparing these two models of case methods, Shulman (1992) characterized one of the key distinctions:

> Where legal case methods typically ask students to discern underlying principles, business cases are more likely to press students to examine the likely consequences of each action they propose. Legal cases focus student attention on judgments and reasons; business cases focus on actions and consequences. (p. 29)

One final point must be made before moving to an examination of case methods in teacher education. For all the rhetoric attesting to the efficacy of case methods in law, business, and other fields, there is a dearth of research which supports the conclusion that they are more effective in meeting instructional goals than other discussion methods or didactics (Shulman 1992).

3. A Heuristic of Case Methods in Teacher Education

Extending the work of Merseth (1991), research on case methods can be usefully organized into categories representing various conceptual orientations of teacher education programs. The classification scheme used here is advanced by Feiman-Nemser (1990), who divided programs into five categories or orientations: (a) academic, (b) practical, (c) technological, (d) personal, and (e) critical/social. She asserted that each orientation "has a focus or thesis that highlights certain aspects of teaching, learning, and learning to teach; directs attention to a central goal of teacher preparation; and manifests itself in particular practices" (p. 221).

3.1 The Academic Orientation

The academic orientation "is primarily concerned with the transmission of knowledge and the development of understanding . . . the academic orientation emphasizes the teacher's role as intellectual leader, scholar, and subject-matter specialist" (Feiman-Nemser 1990 p. 221). This conception is exemplified by the work of Shulman (1986, 1992) and Broudy (1990).

Shulman's (1986) essay on the knowledge base of teaching is an excellent starting point for a review of literature on case methods in teacher education. His paper remains one of the most important theoretical contributions in this area. According to Shulman, not only are there different types of content knowledge, but also different forms of knowledge, one of which is case knowledge. Case knowledge stands in contrast to knowledge represented in propositional form. Shulman defined case knowledge as "knowledge of specific, well-documented, and richly described events. Whereas cases themselves are reports of events or sequences of events, the knowledge they represent is what makes them cases" (p. 11). Cases represent theoretical knowledge: thus, cases and theory are inextricably linked.

> To call something a case is to make a theoretical claim—to argue that it is a "case of something," or to argue that it is an instance of a larger class. A red rash on the face is not a case of something until the observer has invoked theoretical knowledge of disease. (Shulman 1986 p. 11)

Thus, Shulman argued, there can be no case knowledge without theoretical knowledge. Furthermore, he pointed out that "generalizability does not inhere in the case, but in the conceptual apparatus of the explicator. An event can be described; a case must be explicated, interpreted, argued, dissected, and reassembled" (p. 12). Shulman thus called for the development of cases in teacher education which would illuminate this relationship between the concrete and the theoretical.

There are three types of cases: prototypes, precedents, and parables. Prototype cases exemplify and illustrate the theoretical propositions. Precedents provide guidelines or models to follow. Parables serve to communicate a moral or value, which Shulman regarded as particularly useful in teacher socialization.

A single case may serve more than one function, as in the following example.

> A teacher was confronted with repeated incidents of students coming to class without pencils. Rather than either supplying them with replacements (thus making it possible for them to keep up with their work, although running the risk of reinforcing their poor habits), or forcing them to sit through the lesson without benefit of participation, the following strategy was reported. The teacher kept a box of very short pencil stubs in his desk. Whenever a student approached who had forgotten to bring a pencil, the teacher produced the shortest stub available and lent it to the student, who was then expected to use it in completing all of that day's work. (Shulman 1986 p. 12)

Shulman noted that this case serves as both a precedent for managing classroom problems and a prototype for the principle of avoiding accidentally reinforcing inappropriate behavior.

Also in the academic tradition, Broudy (1990) argued that the development of a case literature can help teacher educators develop a "consensus of the learned" regarding the key concepts and "canonical literatures" of the field, a consensus he considered woefully lacking in teacher education. A consensus, Broudy contended, is more likely to emerge around a set of problems than a set of taxonomies or theories. For that reason, he maintained that the identification of "paradigmatic problems"—problems that are so generic and important that virtually all teachers will be familiar with them—was a vital element in the professionalization of teaching.

At the University of Illinois, a case method project developed by Broudy and his colleagues has sought to identify standard problems from teacher surveys and their portrayal on videotape. A final component of the project has been the collection of a body of scholarly literature to accompany each case (Broudy 1990).

3.2 The Practical Orientation

The practical orientation, according to Feiman-Nemser (1990),

> focuses attention on the elements of craft, technique, and artistry that skillful practitioners reveal in their work. It also recognizes that teachers deal with unique situations and that their work is ambiguous and uncertain . . . the practical orientation endorses the primacy of experience as a source of knowledge about teaching. (p. 222)

Teacher educators working within this tradition have generally proposed two different types of case methods. Kleinfeld (1992) and Merseth (1991, 1992) have argued that teaching is in some important ways analogous to the field of business, and maintained that the business case method is the appropriate model for the field. Teaching, like the business world, is an "ill-structured domain" (Merseth 1991), a view also reflected in the casebook developed by Silverman et al. (1992). In contrast, Carter (1990, 1992) argued for the importance of learning how experienced teachers understand the complexity of classrooms and helping others acquire those understandings through cases (see also Silberstein and Tamir 1991).

Kleinfeld (1992) reported her work at the University of Alaska at Fairbanks in developing cases for a problem-based fifth-year teacher education program entitled "Teachers for Alaska." She listed five objectives of case teaching: (a) to provide students with vicarious experience, (b) to show students how an expert teacher constructs educational problems, (c) to model an expert teacher's process of inquiry, (d) to rehearse and broaden the students' repertoire of teaching strategies, and (e) to develop the habit of reflection.

Merseth (1991, 1992), working within the context of the business model, has developed cases written especially for pedagogical purposes. In one case, entitled "It ain't fair!," a novice teacher attempted to use a cooperative learning methodology in a multiracial, urban school setting. In the case discussion, participants analyzed the situation and suggest plans of action. The instructor focused the discussion on answers to two major questions: "Why would you do that? What are the implications of your proposed actions?" Thus, Merseth aimed at helping teacher candidates think through alternative courses of action and their consequences.

The casebook by Silverman et al. (1992) also embraced the business case method model and emphasized student problem-solving and analysis in preparation for the "real world of teaching" (p. xv). Each case describes a dilemma facing a classroom teacher. The authors wrote that the aim of the text is "to encourage student generated analysis rather than teacher-manufactured solutions" (p. xv). Thus, the cases, which dealt with topics such as classroom management and effective teaching, were open-ended and intended to promote the development of possible action plans.

Finally, Carter (1990, 1992) focused on the value cases may have in communicating expert teachers' knowledge and comprehension of classrooms to novices. The cases she developed, all dealing with classroom management, were comprised of three parts: (a) general description of the management structure of a teacher's classroom based on observations, (b) an account of the teacher's reaction to unforeseen managerial problems, and (c) a metaphor suggested by Carter to capture the way in which the teacher seemed to think about management. In the cases describing more successful classroom managers, for example, she found the metaphors "pathfinder" and "pacesetter" useful, while she described less successful managers' actions using metaphors such as "arbiter of adult conscience" or "defender of a territory" (Carter 1990 p. 110). A portion of her case discussions is devoted to analyzing how apt the metaphor is as an attribution to the teacher described in the case.

3.3 The Technological Orientation

The technological orientation in teacher education aims to prepare teachers who can carry out teaching tasks proficiently. Teachers are expected to acquire principles and practices derived from the scientific study of teaching (Feiman-Nemser 1990). Advocates of the case method who work within this tradition focus on the opportunities cases provide to practice a model of rational decision-making or the application of theoretical or scientific principles to instances. Like the teacher educators working within the practical tradition, those working within this tradition, frequently emphasize decision-making and analysis. Unlike the practical orientation, however, the technological conception stresses a specific decision-making procedure which yields effective decision-making. In short, university-generated knowledge takes pride of place. A casebook which reflects this perspective is that produced by Greenwood and Parkay (1989). Also within this tradition, Gliessman (1984) and others (see Sykes and Bird 1992 for a review) used videotape cases to facilitate teachers' acquisition of skills and behaviors derived from research on teaching.

Greenwood and Parkay posed the question "Why do so many teachers not learn to use research-based theory and research in their decision-making activities?" (1989 p. 7.). They asserted that teachers lack a procedure for doing so and suggested a six-step process for incorporating research into decision-making. The first four steps involve examining the situation, collecting and interpreting data, searching for alternatives, and making a decision on the basis of the inquiry. The last two steps consist of reviewing the earlier steps and evaluating the course of action chosen. Research enters into the decision-making process, as each of these steps is to be carried out in light of a single theoretical perspective. In other words, the analysis is to proceed consistently from a Skinnerian perspective or a Piagetian view throughout the inquiry. In this way, the teacher candidate rehearses the rational decision-making procedure for addressing future teaching problems.

Gliessman (1984) used videotape and film protocols to portray teacher skills and behavior derived from empirical research on teaching, and coupled the protocols with instruction aimed at acquisition of the skills portrayed in the film. The skills are treated as concepts to be attained by the teachers. The use of the videotapes facilitated the acquisition of these concepts, a key factor in changing teacher performance.

3.4 The Personal Orientation

According to Feiman-Nemser (1990), the personal orientation stresses the personal growth and development of teacher candidates: "Learning to teach is construed as a process of learning to understand, develop, and use oneself effectively" (p. 225). The personal orientation "places the teacher-learner at the center of the educational process" (Merseth 1991). As in the practical orientation, teacher experience is highly valued here, but a person's own experience and their reflection on it is seen as central.

Approximately 50 cases are contained in *The Mentor Teacher Casebook* (Shulman and Colbert 1987), which was written by mentor teachers working in the Los Angeles Unified School District (LAUSD). The cases are intended to be first a guide to understanding that will help other mentor teachers learn about some important issues related to mentoring. Second, the cases might serve as a guide to action. The idea that the cases can serve as precedents suggests that this orientation is based on the legal case method model, rather than the business case method which underlies much of the work done in the practical orientation. Shulman and Colbert (1987) were quick to point out that the cases are not meant to be prescriptive or open-ended, nor do they beg a response from the reader. Rather, they are cases that enable mentors to see how other mentors confront situations similar to their own.

The cases included in *The Mentor Teacher Casebook* are generally relatively brief descriptions of a conflict or problem. Some of the narratives are followed by a brief reaction of another mentor teacher. Shulman et al. (1990) reported that, in debriefing over their finished work, many of the mentor teachers commented that their casebook had a tremendous ego-building effect and that the experience was valuable for its positive affective outcomes for the mentors.

Richert (1991) argued that two program structures found in professional education programs in other fields help foster reflection. One is the provision of opportunities for students to interact and collaborate among themselves and with faculty. The second is the use of artifacts, such as records, charts, or blueprints. Richert claimed that a case methodology "combines the artifactual and social elements . . . . The artifactual component is the case itself, which is typically a description of an actual teaching situation" (pp. 135–36). The social element occurs during the case discussion. Richert wrote that case discussions are particularly empowering: "Working together, contemplating the dilemmas of practice and building on each other's ideas, are at the core of the method" (p. 144).

3.5 The Critical/Social Orientation

The critical/social orientation, which has its roots in social reconstructionism, "combines a progressive social vision with a radical critique of schooling" (Feiman-Nemser 1990 p. 226). To date, teacher educators working within this tradition have generally expressed little interest in case methods. While not espousing either a particular rationale or proposal for the use of cases, or a particular theory of teacher education, the texts developed by Soltis and his colleagues (see, e.g., Feinberg and Soltis (1992), can be usefully included under this heading. These texts, designed for social foundations courses, contain teaching cases that address broad social issues and topics that critical theorists see as fundamental to the study of education: ideology, hidden curriculum, power, gender, race, class, and so on.

Feinberg and Soltis's (1992) text consists of seven chapters which review theories of the relationship between school and society. The final chapter of the book contains approximately 20 cases which describe incidents related to the theoretical content in the previous six chapters. For example, in one case entitled "College or Workforce?" a Hispanic parent complained to a high school principal about the over representation of Hispanic students in the school's vocational track. The principal confronted the guidance counselor, who defended her advising practices. This case raises issues related to class, race, and equal educational opportunity in schooling, among others. Thus, these texts contain useful case materials for teacher educators working within the critical tradition.

4. Issues for Research

While teaching with cases is a promising pedagogy for teacher education, it is not without its disadvantages. Much of the literature on case methods in teacher education and in other fields cites the inefficiency of this type of teaching. Case methods are slow, and cases are "episodic, discontinuous, hard to structure and organize into larger wholes in the minds of students" (Shulman 1992 p. 27). In addition, teaching by the case method is a difficult form of discussion and places an extra demand on teacher educators who may already be overburdened. Finally, the enthusiasm for case methods in teacher education is more a matter of conjecture and faith than of evidence. One important direction for future research is to assess empirically the contribution teaching with cases can make compared to other instructional methodologies.

This brief review of the research on case methods gives some indication of the various directions of inquiry and harks back to Broudy's point about diversity in teacher education. Can case methods, or any form of pedagogy, make a lasting contribution to the field before prior questions are answered regarding the aims and purposes of teacher education? As Broudy wrote, "Delightful and interesting as this diversity may be, it makes a shambles of the claim of teacher education to a consensus of the learned" (1990 pp. 450–51). Questions fundamental to the development of case methods that can have a transformative impact on teacher education, such as what constitutes a case, what are the aims and purposes of case teaching, and what is a successful case, all seem to hinge on greater agreement than teacher education enjoys regarding its aims and purposes in the early 1990s. Whether, as Broudy hopes, the identification of standard problems leads to greater consensus remains to be seen.

See also: Teacher Education Programs: Curriculum

References

Broudy H 1990 Case studies—why and how. *Teach. Coll. Rec.* 91(3): 449–59

Carnegie Forum on Education and the Economy/Branscomb L 1986 *A Nation Prepared: Teachers for the 21st Century*. Carnegie Forum, New York

Carter K 1990 Meaning and metaphor: Case knowledge in teaching. *Theory Pract.* 29(2): 109–15

Carter K 1992 Toward a cognitive conception of classroom management: A case of teacher comprehension. In: Shulman J H (ed.) 1992 *Case Methods in Teacher Education*. Teachers College Press, New York

Christensen C R, Hansen A J 1987 *Teaching and the Case Method: Text, Cases, and Readings*. Harvard Business School, Boston, Massachusetts

Dooley A R, Skinner W 1977 Casing case method methods *Academy of Management Review* 2(2): 277–89

Feiman-Nemser S 1990 Teacher preparation: Structural and conceptual alternatives. In: Houston W R, Haberman M, Sikula J (eds.) 1990, *Handbook of Research on Teacher Education*. Macmillan, New York

Feinberg W, Soltis J F 1992 *School and Society*, 2nd edn. Teachers College Press, New York

Gliessman D 1984 Changing teaching performance. In: Katz L G, Raths J D (eds.) 1984 *Advances in Teacher Education*, Vol 1. Ablex, Norwood, New Jersey

Greenwood G E, Parkay F W 1989 *Case Studies for Teacher Decision Making*. Random House, New York

Husén T, Postlethwaite T N (eds.) 1985 *The International Encyclopedia of Education* 1st edn. Pergamon Press, Oxford

Kleinfeld J 1992 Learning to think like a teacher: The study of cases. In: Shulman J H (ed.) 1992 *Case Methods in Teacher Education*. Teachers College Press, New York

McAninch A R 1991 Casebooks for teacher education: The latest fad or lasting contribution? *J. Curric. St.* 23(4): 345–55

Merseth K 1991 The early history of case-based instruction: Insights for teacher education today. *J. Teach. Educ.* 42(4): 243–49

Merseth K 1992 Cases for decision-making in teacher education. In: Shulman J H (ed.) 1992 *Case Methods in Teacher Education*. Teachers College Press, New York

Richert A E 1991 Case methods and teacher education: Using cases to teach teacher reflection. In: Tabachnick B R, Zeichner K M (eds.) 1991 *Issues and Practices in Inquiry-Oriented Teacher Education*. Falmer, London

Shulman J H, Colbert J A(eds.) 1987 *The Mentor Teacher Casebook*. ERIC Clearinghouse on Educational Management, University of Oregon, Eugene, Oregon

Shulman J H, Colbert J A, Kemper D, Dmytriw L 1990 Case writing as a site for collaboration. *Teach. Educ. Q.* 17(1): 63–78

Shulman L S 1986 Those who understand: Knowledge growth in teaching. *Educ. Researcher* 15(2): 4–14

Shulman L S 1992 Toward a pedagogy of cases. In: Shulman J H (ed.) 1992 *Case Methods in Teacher Education*. Teachers College Press, New York

Silberstein M, Tamir P 1991 The expert case study model: An alternative approach to the development of teacher education modules. *J. Educ. Teach.* 17(2): 165–79

Silverman R, Welty W M, Lyon S 1992 *Case Studies for Teacher Problem Solving*. McGraw-Hill, New York

Sperle D H 1933 *The Case Method Technique in Professional Training*. Teachers College, Columbia University, New York

Stevens R 1983 *Law School: Legal Education in America fro the 1850s to the 1980s*. University of North Carolina Press, Chapel Hill, North Carolina

Sykes G, Bird T 1992 Teacher education and the case idea. In: Grant G (ed.) 1992 *Review of Research in Education, 18*. American Educational Research Association, Washington, DC

Thorne B 1973 Professional education in law. In: Hughes E C, Thorne B, DeBaggis A M, Gurin A, Williams D, 1973 *Education for the Professions of Medicine, Law, Theology, and Social Welfare*. McGraw-Hill, New York

Van Woerden W M 1988 Interaction as a key factor in the teaching-learning process of the case-method. In: Klein H E 1988 *Case Method Research and Case Method Application: An International Forum*. World Association for Case Method Research and Case Method Application, Needham, Massachusetts

A. R. McAninch

Teacher Education, Economics of

Policies aimed at improving compulsory education in Organisation for Economic Co-operation and Development (OECD) member countries include proposals for reform in teacher education. The reforms have important economic dimensions, although the economic aspects have not always figured prominently in the research or policy debates (see, e.g., Neave 1987, Blackburn and Moisan 1987, OECD/CERI 1993). Nonetheless, costs and financing, and their relationship to effectiveness, are essential elements for informed choices among alternative options for teacher education. This entry presents an elaboration of these elements, drawing on the situation and experiences in OECD member countries with regard to the education of primary and secondary school teachers.

1. Demand for and Supply of Teacher Education

As with all forms of education, the demand for teacher education can be regarded principally as a derived demand. It is derived from the demand for teachers or, more appropriately, for teaching services. From this perspective, the stocks of knowledge and skills to be embodied in teachers are seen to depend both on the expectations placed on schools (what children are expected to learn) and on the ways in which teaching and learning are organized within schools. It is important to note that differences exist among and within countries on these matters (see, e.g., Hanushek 1981). Furthermore, school "inputs" (teacher effort, student effort, materials, equipment, and facilities) can be combined in different ways to achieve comparable schooling results. It follows that, for any given school level and subject specialization of teacher, there is no single profile for the specific mix of the stocks of knowledge and skills. The profiles demanded may differ from one school to another, and these demands may change over time.

One key aspect which influences the demand for teacher education is the cyclical pattern of growth in the size of the teaching force in most OECD countries. Particularly during the postwar period (and dating back to the nineteenth century in Germany), large increases in the number of teachers have been followed by years in which the increases were relatively low. The cycles result from particular demographic trends (in pupil numbers and in the age distribution of the teaching force), a volatile pattern of policy-driven changes in curricula and educational standards, and trends in opportunities and conditions in teaching as compared to other occupations (OECD 1990). Annual new entrant teacher requirements in the United Kingdom (England and Wales only), for example, were estimated at 14,800 for 1980–81 to 1984–85, 11,400 for 1985–86 to 1989–90 and 16,400 for 1990–91 to 1994–95 (with most of the differences expected at the secondary level). In the states which formerly constituted the Federal Republic of Germany, owing in part to declines in new teacher demand, the absolute volume of students enrolled in teacher-training programs fell by more than 50 percent from 1977 to 1988 (OECD 1992).

The supply of teacher education differs both among and within countries, with respect to structure (e.g., by level and timing over the teaching career), content, and methods. In the area of the OECD, the most common pattern has been to elaborate different initial teacher education requirements by level and type of teacher. While there are exceptions, aspiring primary school teachers receive their training in non university higher education and the study program devotes particular attention to pedagogy and child development. Candidates seeking posts as secondary teachers commonly follow a regular first degree course at university, with specialized study in education and practical training taken either as part of their coursework (Japan and the United States, for example) or mostly on completion of the first degree (as in Germany, France, and the Postgraduate Certificate of Education (PGCE) course in the United Kingdom). Within the area of the OECD, the trend has been to move toward an "all graduate" profession, by requiring all aspiring primary school teachers to complete university or university-level education. Greece, Spain, and France have implemented reforms which take just this step.

Differences also exist among and within countries in the nature and scale of organized inservice education and training (INSET) activities. Such activities extend from long, credit-bearing courses to short, formal off-site training for individual teachers, to on-site school development activities for the entire school staff. Relatively greater weight appears to be given in Belgium (Flemish community) to formal courses than to school-based activities, although there is a general trend in the area of the OECD toward INSET which is provided in short sessions, at the school site, and in relation to overall school development.

2. Costs of Teacher Education

A full economic accounting of the costs of teacher education includes direct program expenses (wages of training staff, use of equipment and facilities, and certain "overhead" costs), direct expenses incurred by the participants (books and materials, relevant transportation costs), the costs of the participants' time, and the implicit costs of the time devoted by the staff to the activity. The calculation of these costs is not easy for methodological and practical reasons (see, e.g., Drake 1973, Bolam 1982, Levin 1983, Ryan 1991). As a result, comprehensive, detailed comparative information in the area of the OECD on program-level and system-wide costs of teacher education are not readily available.

2.1 Costs of Participants' and Staff Time

In estimating the costs of teacher education, the costs of participants' and trainers' time are the most difficult to gauge and the most frequently miscalculated.

In Germany, for example, teacher candidates in the second phase of initial teacher training receive stipends. As these candidates will teach during part of this phase of their training, some portion of the stipend should be considered as payment for service rather than as a cost of training. In contrast, for beginning teachers who take part in induction activities (as in Australia, Japan, and the United States among other countries), a portion of their salaries should be considered as a cost of training. With regard to INSET, provision is often made for full or partial replacement of teachers who participate in training during regular school hours. However, to the extent that the replacements are not full and complete substitutes (in the economic sense) for those in training, the budgeted costs may understate the actual costs as other teachers are required to make up the difference (if levels of student learning are to be maintained).

Available estimates suggest that the costs of participants' time are considerable, ranging in the United Kingdom (England and Wales) from 33 percent of annual costs of university-based initial teacher education to 56 percent of the annual costs of initial teacher education provided in colleges (Drake 1973). One implication of these estimates is that changes in resources used directly by teacher education programs (reflected, for example, in student–staff ratios or program "unit" costs as conventionally measured) will have a limited effect on the full economic costs of initial teacher education. The length of initial teacher education is perhaps the most important determinant of its costs.

In Germany and other OECD countries, the costs of staff time set aside in schools for supervision and mentoring of teacher candidates are not always calculated. These costs may be explicit, such as when the difference between the regular class load and the reduced class load is assigned to supervising teachers, as well as implicit, for instance, when other teachers assume heavier class loads to cover for the reduced loads of both the supervising teacher and the teacher candidate. Proposals in the United Kingdom (England and Wales) to increase the "school-based" component in initial teacher education to 80 percent have brought this question to the surface. While it is envisaged that schools which accept teacher candidates for such training will be compensated, the level of compensation has not been worked out. Apart from increased costs during an implementation period, there are indications that the recurrent costs of locating a larger share of initial teacher training in the schools are as considerable as, and may be greater than, the costs of traditional, formal initial teacher education courses (OECD/CERI 1993).

2.2 Forms of Teacher Education

Estimates from England and Wales also reveal large differences in costs according to the type of the initial teacher-training program: annual student costs in colleges were half of student costs at universities and 77 percent of student costs in advanced full-time further education (Drake 1973). The sources of differences are to be found in the running and capital costs of the different programs. It should be pointed out that such annual cost differences may be justified by differences in the results or effectiveness of the programs (i.e., differences in amounts and mixes of the stocks of knowledge and skills acquired by graduates, dropout rates and "jointly produced" results such as improved knowledge about teaching and learning which accompanies, and is accompanied by, the production of qualified teachers).

Cost considerations, as well as considerations of effectiveness, are raised by the introduction of "alternative routes" to teaching. Initial teacher education provided under alternative route schemes found in the United States and the United Kingdom (England and Wales) are relatively short in duration and combine actual teaching with part-time training. In the mid-1980s, the mean cost per participant for United States "alternative route" programs was about US$5,000; the median cost was about US$2,200 (Adelman 1986). Most participants had completed first degrees. The costs of participants' time are not included in these figures; the average salary in 1985–86 for beginning teachers was about US$17,500 (part of which, as noted above, should be considered as payment for service).

2.3 Scale and Variation in Participant Flows

The teacher education effort in most OECD member countries is large. One indication of the magnitude of the effort is simply the relative size of the teaching force. Other things being equal, even modest rates of replacement and new teacher demand imply significant recruitment from initial teacher training. Graduates with teaching credentials account for 12 percent of new graduates in the United States and 8 percent of new graduates in Germany, although not all of these graduates will become teachers (OECD 1992).

The scale of requirements for the inservice education and training of teachers is similarly large. Quite apart from the development and delivery costs of such training, the direct and indirect costs of teacher participation can be considerable. In Japan, the equivalent of an estimated 8 percent of the total work year is given over to various inservice activities. In the Nordic countries, it is estimated that 1.5 to 2.5 percent of the working year is given over to INSET. In Sweden, about 12 percent of the teaching force annually follow inservice education courses each year, and all teachers must take part in five days of school-based inservice training each year. In the Netherlands, the cost of inservice training in education amounts to an estimated 1 percent of the education wage bill, a share that is nonetheless smaller than the 4 to 6 percent share found in some Dutch industry training budgets. The volume of training to be delivered implies that alternative approaches need to be judged in terms of cost-feasibility as well as cost-effectiveness.

Given the magnitude of the overall teacher education effort, less costly alternatives are being sought. Such options include distance learning and the use of new information technologies. While these strategies can reduce the overall unit cost of training, it is not clear that this is always the case (Nielsen and Tatto

1991). Moreover, such approaches also may lead to an increase in the economic costs borne by some participants (see, e.g., Kemmerer and Wagner 1985, 1986; Kurland 1984).

Attention should be given to changes in the Netherlands, Finland, and Sweden, where steps have been taken to widen both the age-span and subject coverage of teacher education and teacher qualifications. The development reverses a trend toward greater specialization in teaching. The impact on the effectiveness of teaching and learning aside, such changes enable education authorities to minimize the extent of underutilization and overutilization of the available capacity of teacher education, with consequent moderation of effects on unit costs (per student, per graduate, or per new teacher placement). Indirectly, these changes respond to the limits of basing teacher education provision on detailed forecasts of teacher demand and supply, and to the rigidities present in most countries which prevent rapid adaptation of teacher employment and teacher education to conditions found at different levels and segments of the education system.

3. *Sources and Methods of Financing*

In most OECD member countries, the course of studies of a student pursuing initial education for entry into teaching is financed in ways similar to studies in other postsecondary education fields. Direct study costs are subsidized, to a greater or lesser extent, through grants made directly to the institutions providing the education or through grants to students who then must pay fees. There are different approaches to financing participants' time. Similar to other postsecondary students, those following courses in initial teacher education have at least part of the costs of their time subsidized by below-cost provision of housing and meals (e.g., in France), stipends (e.g., second phase of teacher education in Germany, and also France) and/or subsidies implicit in student loans. Earnings forgone in excess of these subsidies are borne by students or their families.

The trend in most OECD member countries is to reduce subsidies, and so increase the share of costs—instruction and forgone earnings—borne by students and their families. However, authorities in some countries offer additional support or subsidies for students in initial teacher education. In the United States, such students may qualify for special grants, scholarships, or loans which offer forgiveness of principal and interest if the student, upon graduation, enters and remains in teaching for a minimum number of years. In France, special grants are offered in regions and subject areas experiencing shortages.

With respect to the inservice education and training of teachers, the variation in provision among and within OECD member countries is accompanied by wide differences in the ways in which the costs are financed. Dedicated budgets for inservice education cover principally the salaries of the trainers (whether they are employed full-time for this purpose or they are employed in other jobs and take on specific, short-term assignments for nominal fees). The salary costs of teachers participating in training during working hours are sometimes absorbed within the teacher salary budget at the appropriate level (but, as noted above, replacements may only partly substitute for teachers undergoing training during regular working hours and thus require other teachers to share the training costs through their own additional effort). Teachers participating in INSET outside of regular class hours bear the implicit costs of the time spent in training and, as in the United Kingdom (England and Wales) among other countries, sometimes the fees as well.

Since INSET is usually provided as an expectation or requirement for the continued employment or career progression of the teacher, the share of costs borne by the employers (education authorities) is usually not treated as personal income of the participating teacher for the purposes of income taxation. This tax treatment implies another "partner" in the costs of INSET, namely the finance authorities which forgo tax payments on the value of inservice training provided by education authorities to teachers.

Notwithstanding how the costs of teacher education are shared among the various stakeholders, the methods of financing are being changed in a number of OECD countries in the early 1990s. The most recent trend is to provide clearer signals and incentives to providers of inservice education via criteria included in categorical funding mechanisms, as in Norway and the United Kingdom (England and Wales), and to introduce competition by allowing authorities at the appropriate levels in the countries concerned (schools, municipalities, regions) to purchase inservice training from a provider offering the best training at the lowest cost (as in Sweden, Denmark, and the United Kingdom). These financing methods are believed to promote efficiency in the sense that provision has been "steered" toward priority areas, new knowledge or techniques have been diffused widely in the schools, and budgeted costs per participant appear to have been reduced in various ways.

4. *Internal Efficiency*

Much of the extant research in teacher education in OECD member countries focuses on the effectiveness of different approaches, although the results of this work are seldom presented in ways which permit comparisons among approaches or the assessment of internal and external efficiency (the latter requires cost data). In these studies, the outputs —the knowledge and skills to be learned by prospective or practicing teachers—are defined by teacher education faculty or teacher trainers and shaped to a greater or lesser extent by criteria set down by relevant education authorities.

One key issue in this area is the balance to be struck between on-site, "practical" training and education provided in formal courses in professional education subjects such as sociology of education or child psychology. The debates have centered on questions of changes in observed teaching practice (e.g., to what extent does broad knowledge of educational theory enable and encourage teachers to employ specific teaching techniques? To what extent does greater attention to practical training at the expense of the study of educational theory foreclose the development in the teacher of an ability to "work through" solutions to the unique educational situations confronted by individual students?). On these matters, the research base is limited and diverse, but suggestive (see, e.g., Smith and O'Day 1988, Gran 1989). The main conclusions with regard to teacher education are that there needs to be a balance between theoretical subjects and practical training (neither extreme appears to be appropriate), and that teachers acquire skills best when the training is grounded in the reality of schools and classrooms.

The implications of the present and likely future profile of the teaching force for the internal efficiency of teacher education, including the balance between its theoretical and practical elements, has been studied less. Under quite reasonable assumptions, it may well be that new entrants into teaching will be more diverse in abilities, interests, background, and motivation. In these circumstances, the balance to be struck between formal courses in education subjects as opposed to practical training might differ according to the characteristics of prospective teachers and the ways teachers with different characteristics will be employed within individual schools.

A second key issue concerning internal efficiency is the balance between initial teacher preparation and inservice education and training. The question here is whether the knowledge and skills required by teachers might be best acquired over a longer period of time, rather than through the "front-loaded" approach characteristic of teacher education in most OECD member countries in the early 1990s. Differences exist among countries, with Japan placing relatively less weight on preservice and more weight on inservice than is the case in Sweden. One view is that appropriate, substantial, and in-depth initial teacher education may equip teachers with the stocks of knowledge and skills which enable more efficient inservice education and training, that is, fewer instances of formal inservice training, of shorter duration, which are more effectively assimilated by the participating teacher (see, e.g., Eraut 1989). However, a shift in the timing of teacher education toward inservice could provide a more effective and less costly response to evolving career paths and profiles in the teaching force, including a growth in part-time teaching, intermittent periods inside and outside of the profession, mid-career recruitment in some countries, and cyclical patterns of new teacher demand.

One important consequence of a shift toward inservice teacher education and training is that it may be possible to use the system's present capacity for initial teacher training more effectively. This capacity could be applied to inservice education and so reduce the costs arising from the tendency of programs aimed at initial teacher preparation to operate above or below capacity.

5. *External Efficiency*

Teacher education can also be evaluated with respect to outcomes, particularly the effects on pupils attributable to the stocks of knowledge and skills acquired by teachers via teacher education. In the United States, experiments have shown that training teachers to behave in effective ways did lead to changes in classroom practice which were associated with relatively greater increases in student achievement than alternative approaches (in which teachers continued to use their conventional ways of teaching). However, the effects apparently vary by school level, student characteristics, subject matter, and the type of achievement being measured. Moreover, such a specific approach to training seems to lead to diminishing returns; that is, the gains decrease as certain teacher behaviors are more intensively and comprehensively used. More generally, teacher education in the United States (and other OECD member countries) is criticized because it has failed to develop in prospective or practicing teachers the knowledge and skills required for effective teaching in actual classrooms (Smith and O'Day 1988). In other words, programs may be internally efficient, in that teachers acquire the skills and knowledge imparted by the programs, but these programs nevertheless fail to meet external efficiency criteria, inasmuch as knowledge and skills are either inappropriate for the settings or pupils, or are inappropriately used (Cohen 1990).

Evidence exists with regard to another dimension of the outcomes of teacher education, namely the employment experiences of those who are qualified to teach. Compared to other fields of study, initial teacher education develops skills and abilities which are more directly linked to a specific employment sector and job (e.g., in France, the number of openings in teacher training courses are set according to estimates of new teacher demand). As a result, teacher education graduates are more likely to be found in teaching, either initially or at mid-career, than graduates of other fields are to be found in occupations closely related to their training (OECD

1992). Evidence on the effect of inservice training on the subsequent careers of teachers is limited. Apart from systems in which additional formal training is a prerequisite for advancement (and so provides clear benefits to the individual teacher), wider effects commonly have neither been gauged nor weighed against costs. A study in the United Kingdom suggested that successful participation in long, award-bearing courses provides a signal to authorities about the enhanced skills and abilities of the participant (Howard and Bradley 1992).

However, owing both to the particular structure of the labor markets for graduates with qualifications and to the requirements for entry into teaching, differences in the employment experiences of newly qualified graduates can be seen among countries. In Japan, for example, about 2 out of 10 recipients of teaching certificates in the mid-1980s were placed into teaching posts; the ratio for Finland is estimated to be about 8 out of 10. Those who do not enter teaching appear to be able to find employment in other sectors, and in posts which draw upon the knowledge and skills acquired in teacher education. In Germany, for example, a mid-1980s study revealed that unemployed teacher education graduates who subsequently were employed outside of teaching often found jobs related to their training. About two-thirds (64 percent) of these graduates considered their jobs to be satisfactory; 34 percent regarded their jobs as a provisional expedient (OECD 1992).

Moreover, teacher education may enable students to acquire field-specific knowledge which is of value outside of formal paid work. In this case, such training might prepare parents to contribute more effectively to the intellectual and social development of their own children as a complement to the teaching and learning which takes place in schools and classrooms. Indeed, the profiles of teachers and their careers (female, married, part-time, intermittent employment) imply that the perceived value of the use of the acquired skills and abilities in the home or family may be one of the motivations for following a course in teacher education.

Finally, initial teacher education programs are seen by some to serve purposes other than enabling prospective teachers to acquire the skills and abilities necessary for teaching per se. One of these purposes is to convey a status commensurate with the perceived requirements of the job of teaching. In this view, completion of teacher education at the university level will lead to a more appropriate level of remuneration (as provided in public sector pay schedules which are differentiated by educational qualifications) as well as to confer on teaching a status that makes teaching more attractive. The effects on recruitment of differences in the educational level required for entry into teaching have not been fully explored. Raising entry qualifications is a costly way to improve recruitment and retention, although strengthening the content and rigor of teacher education by raising it to university level has been advocated on the grounds of improved effectiveness of teaching. An interesting issue is the extent to which individuals differ in their valuations of the status conferred by different levels of qualifications. Different forms and requirements of teacher education might discriminate better among pools of prospective teachers than salaries or other monetary incentives.

Another purpose set out for initial teacher education programs is to provide for the orderly development of the knowledge base on teaching and learning. While the effects and costs of this aspect of existing teacher education programs are difficult to gauge, some general issues regarding the efficiency of different structures can be developed.

6. Conclusion

While teacher education assumes a vital role in the development and improvement of schooling in OECD member countries, careful analyses of the costs, financing and efficiency of provision are limited in number and breadth. This entry has drawn on developments in the area of the OECD in teacher education and training in an attempt to set out more clearly their economic dimensions. Four conclusions have emerged as crucial to an evaluation of teacher education from such a perspective. First, a full accounting of economic costs includes the costs of participants', trainers', and other staff time. These costs are the most difficult to gauge and most frequently miscalculated. Second, the scale of provision introduces an important issue of cost feasibility. Some effective and efficient approaches may be impossible to implement system-wide. Third, the efficiency of provision must be gauged against the organization of schooling and labor market structures in individual countries. Finally, the effectiveness and efficiency of alternative forms of teacher education are related to the characteristics and abilities of participants; the particular way in which the teaching force evolves will determine the choice of approach to teacher education.

See also: Cost-effectiveness Analysis

References

Adelman N E 1986 *An Exploratory Study of Teacher Alternate Certification and Retraining Programs.* Policy Studies Associates, Washington, DC

Blackburn V, Moisan C 1987 *The In-Service Training of Teachers in the Twelve Member States of the European Community.* Presses InterUniversitaires Européennes, Maastricht

Bolam R 1982 *In-Service Education and Training of Teachers: A Condition of Educational Change.* OECD/CERI, Paris

Cohen D K 1990 A revolution in one classroom: The case of Mrs. Oublier. *Educ. Eval. Policy Anal.* 12(3): 327–45

Drake K 1973 The economics of teacher education. In: Lomax D E (ed.) 1973 *The Education of Teachers in Britain*. Wiley, London
Eraut M 1989 Review of research on in-service education: A UK perspective. In: Wilson J (ed.) 1989 *The Effectiveness of In-Service Education and Training of Teachers and School Leaders*. Swets and Zeitlinger, Amsterdam
Gran B 1989 *Research on Swedish Teacher Training*. School of Education, University of Lund, Malmö
Hanushek E 1981 Throwing money at schools. *Journal of Policy Analysis and Management* 1: 19–41
Howard J, Bradley H 1992 *Patterns of Employment and Development of Teachers after INSET Courses*. Cambridge Institute of Education, Cambridge
Kemmerer F, Wagner A 1985 The economics of educational reform. *Econ. Educ. Rev*. 4(2): 111–21
Kemmerer F, Wagner A 1986 *Limits on the Use of Educational Technology in Developing Countries: A Reappraisal of the Costs*. IREDU, University of Dijon, Dijon
Kurland N D 1984 *The Role of Technology in the Education, Training and Retraining of Adult Workers*. Kurland & Associates, Delmar, New York
Levin H M 1983 *Cost-Effectiveness: A Primer*. Sage, Newbury Park, California
Neave G 1987 Challenges met: Trends in teacher education 1975–85. In: Council of Europe Standing Conference of European Ministers of Education 1987 *New Challenges for Teachers and their Education*. Council of Europe, Strasbourg
Nielsen H D, Tatto M T 1991 *The Cost-Effectiveness of Distance Education for Teacher Training, Bridges Research Report Series*, No. 9. USAID, Washington, DC
OECD 1990 *Teacher Demand and Supply: The Labour Market for Teachers*. (Restricted), OECD, Paris
OECD 1992 *From Higher Education to Employment*, Vol. I–III (country reports). OECD, Paris
OECD/CERI in press *The Training of Teachers*. OECD/CERI, Paris
Ryan P 1991 How much do employers spend on training? An assessment of the 'Training in Britain' estimates. *Human Resource Manag. J*. 1: 55–76
Smith M S, O'Day J 1988 *Teaching Policy and Research on Teaching*. Stanford University Press, Stanford, California

A. Wagner

Teacher Education, Evaluation in

The effect that a teacher education program has on the knowledge, skills, and dispositions of its graduates is a constant source of inquiry at teacher preparation institutions. The practice in the field, however, is not advanced. This entry describes the application of educational evaluation methods to the preparation of teachers.

1. Background Literature

Almost 90 percent of teacher education institutions in the United States collect program evaluation data (Adams and Craig 1983), and for the majority the reason is one of external accountability. Such evaluations are based on quite diverse philosophical underpinnings. Medley (1977), using the behaviorist process–product paradigm, defined program evaluation as "the extent that the training experiences produce the competencies defined as objectives of the training program" (p. 69). In contrast, Stufflebeam (1982) stated that evaluation is "the process of delineating, obtaining, and applying descriptive and judgmental information about the worth or merit of some program's goals, design, implementation, and impact in order to promote improvements, serve needs for accountability, and foster understandings" (p. 138). What is common to the philosophies of these two definitions is that for program evaluation to be meaningful it must address the needs of the local audiences, and must be focused on obtaining data for making judgments about the degree to which the program meets its stated goals.

2. Evaluation Models

The initial impetus for the growth of program evaluation can be traced to the increasing number of social programs. To begin with there were few guidelines as to what constituted acceptable evaluation. Thus, evaluators typically applied research methods to social settings. As the need for reliable information that could be used to demonstrate the worth and merit of a program increased, project planners needed methods which were both flexible (to be applied in natural setting) and systematic. As a result, models of evaluation were developed, which incorporated research methods from various disciplines.

Popham (1975), for example, described an objectives-based model in which the judgment about a program is determined by the extent to which the program meets its stated objectives. Stake (1967), on the other hand, designed the more comprehensive "countenance" model which borrowed from qualitative research methods. This model was composed of antecedents (that is, those conditions which existed when the program was begun); transactions (that is, those events which transpired during the program); and outcomes (that is, those intended and unintended results of the program). Stufflebeam et al. (1971) developed an evaluation model with four dimensions: contexts, (the conditions under which the program began); inputs (the resources and commitments necessary to operate the program); processes (the events which occurred during the operation of the program); and products (the results or outcomes of the program).

3. Applications to Teacher Education

Galluzzo and Craig (1990) labeled program evaluation teacher education's "orphan," as it is one of the more poorly practiced aspects of the field. The application of educational evaluation models to teacher education lacks the rich history one would expect to find in an area where the literature is almost 50 years old. In a seminal analysis of teacher education program evaluation Troyer and Pace (1944) documented the evaluation efforts at a variety of institutions. They examined the methods used to evaluate the contributions of various program components (including general education, professional education, and student teaching), and conducted a more general analysis using follow-up studies. While their contribution may be considered dated, remarkably the impression is that practice at the end of the twentieth century is only slightly more sophisticated.

The most visible model for program evaluation in teacher education was developed by Sandefur (1970) who outlined in his monograph the necessary features of an evaluation model for teacher education. Like Popham (1975) Sandefur viewed the evaluation of a program as measuring the degree to which students can demonstrate the competencies which serve as the outcomes of the program. Included in his model are assessments of teaching skill, classroom personality, and students' perceptions of teacher preparation.

More recent models have challenged Sandefur's competency-based, quantitative approach to evaluation. Borrowing from the research methods of anthropology, de Voss and Hawk (1983) developed a model based more on documentation than on assessment. In their model, students and faculty are not data points; rather, they are informants who characterize the processes and the outcomes of the program.

Some approaches use both documentation and assessment. Zimpher and Loadman (1986), for example, described a large-scale documentation and assessment system that included data on students when they began the program, throughout the program, upon completion, and in follow-up.

Nelli and Nutter (1984) applied Stake's "countenance model" to teacher education. Throughout their application, they suggested building evaluation around the questions that a program faculty would want to ask in each of the antecedents, transactions, and outcomes phases of the evaluation.

More recently, Rickards and Diez (1992) described an essentially outcomes-based program evaluation effort for teacher education, but the nature of the outcomes, many of which are nonbehavioral, challenged conventional notions of such programs. Their model included a mix of quantitative and qualitative data on each student.

There has been one debate that challenges the utility of evaluation in teacher education. In 1981 Katz et al. raised the question of whether what is learned from program evaluation studies justifies the resources expended. Following a review of 26 follow-up studies, Katz et al. identified major threats to the validity of the investigations, including sampling, the validity of the conclusions, and the evaluation method. They concluded that the methodological shortcomings were sufficiently great to call into question the worth of the findings. In response, Adams et al. (1981) claimed that the review methods used had been more appropriate for research studies than for evaluation studies, and thus Katz et al. had drawn erroneous conclusions.

4. *Impediments to Quality Evaluation*

Many weaknesses beset program evaluators beside those singled out by Katz et al. They include the identification of criterion variables and independent variables, as well as issues concerning the design of the evaluation.

4.1 Criterion Variables

Criterion variables fall into four broad categories: (a) knowledge, (b) teaching skill, (c) affective dimensions, and (d) perceptions of preparation. Teacher knowledge can be divided into three areas: general knowledge, subject-matter knowledge, and professional knowledge. Galluzzo (1983) followed 19 preservice teachers from their point of entry into professional education as freshmen through to their graduation in order to assess the growth in their knowledge over the four years of professional preparation. At the beginning of the freshman year, the students were administered the National Teachers Examination; each spring thereafter, they were measured with alternative forms of the same test. The results indicated no significant differences in their general knowledge but, in contrast, there were significant and positive differences in scores on the test of professional knowledge.

Later interpretations of teacher knowledge have regarded it as beyond simple measurement on a paper-and-pencil test. Shulman (1986) contended that teacher knowledge is the application of knowledge to simulated teaching settings, and thus focused on the way teachers use knowledge, not only the knowledge they possess.

Teaching skills typically evaluated using performance assessments include, among many others, the teacher's use of higher order questioning, the use of praise, and the ability to stop misbehavior in a timely and accurate manner. Many instruments to measure teaching skills have been developed based on the teacher effectiveness research (Borich 1977, Cooper 1983).

There is a great deal of debate surrounding the direct observation of teaching. Compelling arguments exist concerning the timing of the observation, the teacher's expectation for the lesson, and the teacher's expectation for the students. Context greatly influences classroom processes, and yet it is rare for direct observations to consider the role that context plays in what is being observed.

There is a persistent belief that attitudes toward teaching or children influence how teachers teach. It follows, then, that programs in teacher education should have certain expectations for the attitudes held by beginning teachers and that the program should help foster appropriate attitudes. The measurement of teachers' attitudes occupies a great deal of the literature, but has not been highly conclusive. Either the instruments lack validity or it is difficult to trace the resultant scores to the effects of the program. Perhaps the most promising work in this area is that contributed by Katz and Raths (1986). According to Katz and Raths, a disposition is a cognitive orientation which is operationalized as the tendency on the part of the teacher to act in a consistent manner. The concept of dispositions introduces a more powerful interpretation to the important and confusing area of affective criterion variables.

Perceptions of programs typically refer to how satisfied teachers are with their preparation. Perceptions are usually gained through mailed questionnaires, and the resultant data usually define program effectiveness. Lindsay (1985) has outlined a set of procedures for conducting useful surveys of graduates, but unfortunately, many researchers do not follow them. Thus, while satisfaction is the most frequently measured criterion, it is also the least validly and reliably measured.

4.2 Independent Variables

This next area of weakness is somewhat more obscure in the literature, but is nonetheless potent. The critical question is whether the teacher education program should really be expected to affect students in substantial ways. Galluzzo and Pankratz (1990) argued that a teacher education program must be grounded in a knowledge base that includes a set of beliefs, a body of supportive literature, and a set of clearly articulated expectations for students. All too often teacher education is a collection of courses which offer no consistent image of what it means to teach, nor what it means to learn to teach. This allows students to proceed through their programs confirming what they already believed teaching to be and rejecting or ignoring those concepts and practices which are inconsistent with their preconceived notions of teaching.

4.3 Design Problems

Teacher educators must organize a systematic strategy for collecting data that can be used to conduct meaningful evaluation of the program. Program evaluation efforts in teacher education are typically institution-specific studies designed to inform the local setting and the findings are rarely generalizable to other institutions. Given these limitations, it is incumbent on the faculty members who teach in the program to be clear as to their purposes, processes, and outcomes.

5. Model Efforts to Evaluate Teacher Education Programs

Over time, researchers have attempted to conduct evaluations that are useful for meeting accountability concerns, for improving programs, and for contributing to the body of literature. This section summarizes some of the more promising of these efforts.

Hummel and Strom (1987) used a survey to study the relationship between the graduates' perceptions of their preparation and the number of years the graduates had been teaching. Graduates with less teaching experience viewed their preparation more positively than did graduates with more teaching experience. Specifically, graduates with two or more years of experience were significantly less positive in their perceptions than were those who had taught for only one year.

Pigge (1978) also surveyed recent graduates. He reported a high correlation between teachers' perceived need for a particular competency and their proficiency at it. He also found the teachers reporting that "high need" competencies were developed in the workplace and not during the teacher education program. Unfortunately, teachers also reported that "low need" competencies in teaching were developed in the teacher education program.

Gideonse (1988) asked his colleagues to list the names of students who had great potential as teachers and then interviewed the resulting 43 nominees. The interview method allowed the researcher to gather the rich and anecdotal data that is so often lost in a mailed survey. Gideonse was able to quote students to make his points, and the categories of strengths and weaknesses were created jointly by the interviewees and the researcher.

A highly useful volume is the summary of an international conference on the preparation of science teachers held in Jerusalem (Tamir 1985) which contains several papers from researchers in many countries, outlining problems in the preparation of science teachers. These papers focused both on the content of science and science curriculum materials. Generalizations emerged on the role of science in society, the role of science education, and the role of the science teacher.

Perhaps the most comprehensive study is that conducted by Furlong et al. (1988) in the United Kingdom. Included in the design were direct observations; interviews with students, professors, and mentors; survey questionnaires; and anecdotal record-keeping. The subjects were 75 students enrolled in four programs. Although the focus of the study was on learning to teach, there was an emphasis on becoming a thoughtful, analytic, and reflective teacher. The work of Furlong et al. is an excellent example of what can be accomplished with available resources.

Because of the institution-specific nature of program evaluation efforts it is difficult to make generalizations, nonetheless, a few notable themes emerge. Internationally, there is difficulty in linking theory to practice. Students report that programs are effective in teaching the preactive skills of teaching (e.g., planning, materials development, materials selection) and less effective in teaching the interactive skills of teaching (e.g., alternate instructional strategies, classroom management and discipline, and lesson development). Research appears to be most necessary on the effects of teacher education programs on these interactive skills. Little is known about why students rate their preparation programs as less effective in these areas.

6. Conclusion

In this entry, the application of educational evaluation processes to teacher education has been outlined briefly. Concerns for program evaluation increase when concerns for accountability increase. At the same time, however, it is important to recognize that program evaluation can serve multiple purposes besides accountability, namely, in improving programs, fostering an understanding of the programs, and contributing to the body of literature on teacher education and program evaluation. The future of practice in this area is dependent on the degree of importance accorded to researchers' conceptions of teacher education as a field of inquiry. Internationally, there is still a great deal to learn about the extent to which teacher education affects teachers' knowledge, behavior, dispositions, and perceptions, and how to measure these effects.

See also: Evaluation Models and Approaches; Evaluation of Educational Personnel

References

Adams R, Craig J 1983 A status report of teacher education program evaluation. *J. Teach. Educ.* 34(2): 33–37

Adams R, Craig J, Hord S, Hall G 1981 Program evaluation and program development in teacher education: A response to Katz et al. 1981 *J. Teach. Educ.* 32(5): 21–24

Borich G 1977 *The Appraisal of Teaching: Concepts and Processes.* Addison-Wesley, Reading, Massachusetts

Cooper J 1983 Basic elements in teacher education program evaluation: Implications for future research and development. In: Howey K R, Gardner W E (eds.) 1983 *The Education of Teachers: A Look Ahead.* Longman, New York

de Voss G, Hawk D 1983 Follow-up models in teacher education. *Educ. Eval. Policy Anal.* 5(2): 163–71

Furlong V, Hirst P, Pocklington K, Miles S 1988 *Initial Teacher Training and the Role of the School.* Open University Press, Milton Keynes

Galluzzo G 1983 An evaluation of a teacher education program. Paper presented at the annual meeting of the American Educational Research Association, New Orleans. ERIC Document No. ED 229 373

Galluzzo G, Craig J 1990 Evaluation of preservice teacher education programs. In: Houston W (ed.) *Handbook of Research on Teacher Education: A Project of the Association of Teacher Educators.* Macmillan, New York

Galluzzo G, Pankratz R 1990 The five essential attributes of a teacher education program knowledge base. *J. Teach. Educ.* 41(4): 7–14

Gideonse H 1988 Follow-up study of a selected sample of elementary and secondary education graduates. Unpublished manuscript. University of Cincinnati, Cincinnati, Ohio

Hummell T, Strom S 1987 The relationship between teaching experience and satisfaction with teacher preparation: A summary of three surveys. *J. Teach. Educ.* 38(5): 28–36

Katz L G, Raths J D 1986 Dispositions as goals for teacher education. *Teaching and Teacher Education*, 1(4): 301–307

Katz L, Raths J D, Mohanty C, Kurachi A, and Irving J 1981 Follow-up studies: Are they worth the trouble? *J. Teach. Educ.* 32(2): 18–24

Lindsay M 1985 Procedures for follow-up studies of teacher education graduates. *J. Teach. Educ.* 35(2): 29–33

Medley D M 1977 *Teacher Competence and Teacher Effectiveness: A Review of Process–Product Research.* American Association of Colleges for Teacher Education, Washington, DC (ERIC Document Reproduction Service No. ED 143 629)

Nelli E, Nutter N 1984 *A Model for Evaluating Teacher Education Programs.* National Institute of Education, Washington, DC

Pigge F 1978 Teacher competencies: Need, proficiency, and where proficiency was developed. *J. Teach. Educ.* 29(4): 70–6

Popham W J 1975 *Educational Evaluation.* Prentice-Hall, Englewood Cliffs, New Jersey

Rickards W, Diez M 1992 Integrating multiple internal and external data sources in the institutional evaluation of teacher education. Paper presented at the American Educational Research Association, San Francisco, California

Sandefur J T 1970 *An Illustrated Model for the Evaluation of Teacher Education Graduates.* American Association of Colleges for Teacher Education, Washington, DC

Shulman L 1986 Those who understand: Knowledge growth in teaching. *Educ. Researcher*, 15(2), 4–14

Stake R 1967 The countenance of educational evaluation *Teach. Coll. Rec.* 68(7): 523–40

Stufflebeam D 1982 Explorations in the evaluation of teacher education. In: Hord S, Savage T, Bethel L (eds.) 1982 *Toward Usable Strategies for Teacher Education Program Evaluation.* University of Texas R & D Center for Teacher Education, Austin, Texas

Stufflebeam D, Foley W, Gephart W, Guba E, Hammond R, Merriman H, Provus M 1971 *Educational Evaluation and Decision-making.* Peacock, Itasca, Illinois

Tamir P 1985 *Preservice and Inservice Education of Science Teachers.* ERIC Document Reproduction Service No. ED 258 839

Troyer M, Pace C R 1944 *Evaluation in Teacher Education.* American Council on Education, Washington, DC

Zimpher N, Loadman W 1986 *A Documentation and Assessment System for Student and Program Development*. American Association of Colleges for Teacher Education, Washington, DC

G. R. Galluzzo

Teacher Education for Language Arts and Literature

Language arts and literature teacher education encompasses all of the processes by which individuals are educated to become elementary or secondary teachers of the language arts and literature. The term "language arts" originated during the Second World War amid growing concern about illiteracy in the American armed services, and was revived in the mid-1960s by a group of British educators interested in the linguistic and personal growth of the child. Today, the term is most often used to describe instruction at the primary or elementary school level—specifically, instruction in which students are engaged in purposeful learning acts involving the interrelation of reading, writing, speaking, and listening.

Literature study, as it originated just prior to the start of the twentieth century, involved historical and philological treatments of English and American literary works. More recently, the term "literature education" has come to include the personal, social, and cultural dimensions of readers' understanding of and responses to literary texts. Although literature education has traditionally been associated with the secondary school curriculum, proponents of "whole language" and "integrated language arts" perspectives have argued for the vital role of literature in both the preschool and in the primary or elementary school curriculum.

Finally, the term "teacher education" (as opposed to "teacher training") implies the lifelong development of pedagogical and disciplinary knowledge in relation to an understanding of theories of learning and development, the historical and philosophical contexts of education, and the ability to adapt instruction to a variety of learning situations.

1. Changing Views of Language Arts and Literature Education

Since the early 1960s, theories of language arts and literature education have undergone a substantive transformation, while pedagogical practices have often remained intractable. This gap between theory and practice has powerful implications for the preparation of language arts and literature teachers.

Prior to this transformation, language arts and literature instruction emanated largely from a set of academic, text-based assumptions. Because texts could easily be broken down into constituent parts (i.e., letters, words, sentences, paragraphs), it was assumed that the teaching of language and literature should proceed according to the same part-to-whole logic. Furthermore, it was thought that learners should be instructed in basic skills such as vocabulary, phonics, spelling, and handwriting, before they could read and write whole pieces of discourse.

In the early elementary school grades, for instance, students were taught basic printing and handwriting skills, and read basal texts that had been systematically designed to promote reading skills at increasing levels of difficulty. In the later elementary school grades, students were taught rules of grammar and punctuation, and occasionally wrote short texts in various genres on teacher-assigned topics.

At the secondary school level, literature instruction was organized around an accepted canon of literary texts, and involved the study of literary genre, history, and terminology. Grammar instruction often involved practice in sentence diagramming and a knowledge of grammatical terms. Writing instruction, when it was offered at all at the secondary level, usually followed a classical rhetorical model, which focused on stock principles of invention, organization, style, and a knowledge of textual forms. Oral language was virtually ignored as a deliberate part of the curriculum.

From the early 1960s onward, researchers and scholars began to challenge commonly held beliefs about the nature of language and learning. The results of these scholarly research endeavors, as well as the influence of international symposia such as The Anglo-American Conference (also known as the "Dartmouth Conference"), eventually led to a shift from a focus on texts or products to a focus on learners and their cognitive, social, and linguistic growth.

1.1 From Text-Centered Models to Learner-Centered Models

Largely through the influence of British educators in the 1960s (Britton 1970, Dixon 1967), the language arts were no longer envisioned as discrete and distinctly developing processes. The "language across the curriculum" movement established the idea that language was a way of learning, not just an outcome of learning, and should be a fundamental aspect of every curricular area.

The "writing process" movement, which arose from a large body of research on the cognitive processes of writers and the enthusiasm generated from the National Writing Project in the United States, popularized the notion of writing as a recursive process, requiring multiple drafts, responses from peers and teachers, and attention to substance rather than form, until the publication stage.

On the preschool and elementary level, movements such as "whole language" (Goodman 1986) and "emergent literacy" (Clay 1975, Sulzby and

Teale 1991) have stressed the purposeful reading and writing of whole texts of language; the interrelationship of reading, writing, speaking, and listening; and the value of collaborative learning experiences with teachers and peers.

Largely inspired by the work of Louise Rosenblatt (1978), the "reader response" movement has placed the reader, and not the literary text, at the center of critical and scholarly attention. Since the early 1970s, theorists from a poststructuralist orientation have argued that texts, responses, and readers' identities themselves are socially and culturally constructed.

1.2 Changing Roles of Teachers

The shift from an academic, text-centered perspective to a more learner-centered perspective has implications for the entire enterprise of language arts and literature teacher education. The role of the classroom teacher has changed from one of knowledge-giver to one of facilitator or nurturer. Students are expected to grow toward greater independence and engage in authentic transactions, not just with the teacher, but with other students as well. Theories of teaching are no longer based on a "transmission model" (Barnes et al. 1984), where teachers are at the top of the classroom hierarchy, but on a more egalitarian, transactive model, where students learn with help of peers and teachers.

While there are vehement arguments for teaching an accepted canon of literary texts and a recognized body of cultural knowledge (Hirsch 1987), there is a corresponding movement toward a "cultural transformation" model (Barnes et al. 1984). This model stresses inclusivity, multiculturalism, and an expansion of the traditional canon to include more socially and culturally representative works.

Changes such as these have challenged commonly held notions of teacher education. Transformations in the traditional roles of teachers, as well as the power structure of classrooms, demand new definitions of the knowledge base, attitudes, and professional experiences required for teachers of language arts and literature in the 1990s and beyond.

1.3 Gap between Theory and Practice

Studies in the 1980s and early 1990s have shown that, despite changes in pedagogical theories, the teaching of language arts and literature remain entrenched in rather traditional techniques and perspectives. Several years after the publication of Britton et al.'s (1975) landmark study of students' writing in the United Kingdom, researchers have documented that writing in classrooms consists mostly of artificial, short-answer summaries of the teacher's knowledge, as opposed to more extended writing involving personal speculation or exploration (Applebee 1981).

Although many teachers are now familiar with process-oriented models of instruction, these models are still not being implemented to any great extent in classrooms (Applebee 1989). Similarly, although elementary school teachers are familiar with the principles of emergent literacy, whole language, or integrated language arts, they often engage in practices which contradict these philosophies. Opportunities for oral language are usually absent from the curriculum altogether (Barnes et al. 1984).

At the secondary level in the United States, literature instruction is still the mainstay of the English curriculum, and is organized by genre from middle school to tenth grade (age 15), and by historical period in eleventh and twelfth grades. Teachers still select literary works largely from the traditional literary canon, and focus on textual analysis, rather than more personal responses or interpretations (Applebee 1989, 1992).

This gap between theory and practice makes the preparatory and continuing education of teachers in language arts and literature increasingly problematic. Over the years, there has been a great deal of controversy over the roles of universities, school systems, and accreditation agencies in the education of teachers.

2. Models and Programs for Teacher Education in Language Arts and Literature

There has been little empirical inquiry in the area of teacher education specific to language arts and literature education. Much current wisdom about language arts and literature teacher education is in the form of prescriptions for what should be included in teacher education programs, or descriptions of innovative programs, rather than systematic studies of the efficacy or results of particular teacher education models.

2.1 Defining the Knowledge Base for Teaching

Through the years, there have been calls for the professionalization of teachers and the establishment of a recognized knowledge base for teaching. Criteria for teaching certification and teacher assessment often include some combination of specific "content knowledge" and an understanding of pedagogical skills. Shulman (1987 p. 6) criticizes many research and policy perspectives for "bifurcating content and teaching processes." He argues that, rather than a generic set of principles of effective teaching, or the knowledge of subject area content, expert teachers rely upon a variety of knowledge bases.

One important knowledge source, Shulman states, is "pedagogical content knowledge," or "that special amalgam of content and pedagogy that is uniquely the province of teachers, their own special form of professional understanding" (1987 p. 8). Competent teachers, in Shulman's view, not only have a knowledge of a particular subject matter, but they are also able to call upon a variety of strategies to make that knowledge accessible to students.

The unique dimensions of "pedagogical content knowledge" appropriate for teachers of language arts and literature are just beginning to be explored. Grossman (1990) compared first year English teachers who had graduated from teacher education programs with first-year English teachers who had entered teaching from college literature programs, without professional preparation in a teacher education program. She discovered differences between the two groups in the following sources of pedagogical content knowledge: beliefs about purposes for teaching literature, beliefs about what it means to write, understanding of the primary concerns of English as a discipline, beliefs about the selection and organization of content, and an understanding of students' knowledge, needs, and motivations.

Grossman concluded that graduates without a teacher education background paid little attention to the teaching of writing, based most of their curricular decisions on the literary worth of texts rather than the needs of students, and most often chose texts from the traditional literary canon. Graduates of teacher education programs, on the other hand, based curricular decisions on the needs of students, often planned a thematic approach to teaching, and tended to choose texts that were not from the traditional literary canon. She further concluded that teachers tend to reproduce the curriculum within which they have been taught, and that content area methods courses allow prospective teachers to extend beyond their own experiences as students in the university, and to think about curricular choices that are more appropriate for the particular students they will teach.

2.2 Role of Reflection in Teacher Education

As theories of learning have changed, so theories of teaching effectiveness and teacher education have also changed. Effective teaching is no longer defined by a set of discrete teacher behaviors, a recognized body of knowledge, or student success on performance measures. Teaching effectiveness cannot be determined in isolation from the contexts within which teachers function or the subject matter of their teaching.

In addition to pedagogical content knowledge, teachers need to develop a reflective stance, within which they can make conscious and careful decisions about practice (Schön 1983). It has been argued that the development of critical inquiry and reflective practice among teachers is the main avenue to the professionalization of teaching.

The recent "teacher-as-researcher" movement has succeeded in bringing the richness of teachers' reflections into the research base from which teachers of language arts and literature make decisions about pedagogy. This movement has also brought the university researcher out of the role of expert or distanced observer, and into more collaborative relationships with classroom teachers. Finally, the movement has succeeded in involving teachers in the kind of systematic reflection-in-action (Schön 1983), essential to their lifetime development.

3. Developments in Language Arts and Literature Teacher Education

As students are being empowered to take control of their own learning, teachers of language arts and literature are being encouraged to generate their own theories on which to base their teaching.

3.1 Changing Relationships between Schools and Universities

Over the years, there has been a consistent debate over the roles of universities and schools in teacher education. Teachers often report that methods courses are irrelevant and should focus more on teaching strategies and techniques for classroom management than on philosophical or theoretical perspectives. On the other hand, university professionals argue that experiences in methods courses will allow preservice teachers to become change agents in a rather traditionally entrenched field.

There is often a deep disparity between what preservice teachers learn in the university and what they actually encounter in schools (Zeichner and Tabachnick 1981). Given the time demands on university supervisors and cooperating teachers, there are often weak relationships between teacher education programs and schools. Furthermore, preservice teachers in the most tenuous and demanding phases of their career are not likely to suggest methods that might run counter to a cooperating teacher's expectations or preferences. General dissatisfaction with the disparity between field placements and university experiences has resulted in a call for closer partnerships between universities and schools, as well as for the support, mentoring, and involvement of competent practicing teachers with a commitment to becoming teacher educators.

3.2 Role of Collaboration in Teacher Education

Peer-mentoring models and the vast array of grassroots teacher support networks in language arts and literature are evidence of a movement to place inservice teacher education more firmly in the hands of classroom teachers. The result has been a move toward more collaborative relationships among classroom teachers, researchers, and teacher educators.

The image of the classroom teacher as isolated from colleagues and from those outside the school setting is gradually changing. The National Writing Project has provided a network for teachers as they learn to implement a "writing process" model in their own classrooms. The Bread Loaf School of English in the United States has provided development opportunities and small grants to support teachers as they engage in classroom inquiry projects. Such organizations have helped teachers to develop pedagogical theories from the accounts of other teachers, as well as their own careful and systematic reflection. Cross-visitation programs are being collaboratively developed by universities and schools in order to help teachers observe and learn from each other.

School and university partnerships are also being developed for the purpose of involving preservice teachers and their mentors in study groups, seminars, and research projects. Such collaborative efforts are beginning to blur the once distinct lines between universities and schools in the preparation and continued development of teachers.

4. Future of Teacher Education in Language Arts and Literature Education

Arguments for the professionalization of teaching stem from the need to grant teachers more legitimacy, status, and economic benefits. There have been calls for the establishment of national tests and licensing boards for teachers, higher standards of admissions in teacher education programs, increased years of preparation for teachers, and the recruitment of students from liberal arts programs into teaching. At the same time, however, alternative certification programs have begun to appear in response to teacher shortages, and some certification agencies have begun to accept teachers with liberal arts backgrounds and little or no experience in educational methods, foundations, or supervised field experiences typically provided by faculties of education.

While there are no agreed-upon solutions, there is general consensus that teaching will only acquire professional status when its constituents begin to identify the intellectual attributes, attitudes, and practical experiences that distinguish the professional educator from the nonprofessional. The ongoing challenge of teacher educators will be to identify and develop the unique blend of pedagogical content knowledge, intellectual abilities, and professional experience required for teachers of language arts and literature in the 1990s and beyond.

See also: Literacy; Reading, Learning and Instruction of

References

Applebee A N 1981 *Writing in the Secondary School: English and the Content Areas*. National Council for the Accreditation of Teacher Education (NCATE), Urbana, Illinois

Applebee A N 1989 *The teaching of literature in Programs with Reputations for Excellence in English*. Report Series 1.1, Center for the Learning and Teaching of Literature, State University of New York, Albany, New York

Applebee A N 1992 The background for reform. In: Langer J A (ed.) 1992 *Literature Instruction: A Focus for Student Response*. NCATE, Urbana, Illinois

Barnes D, Barnes D, Clarke S 1984 *Versions of English*. Heinemann Educational, London

Britton J 1970 *Language and Learning*. Penguin, London

Britton J, Burgess T, Martin N, McLeod A, Rosen H 1975 *The Development of Writing Abilities (11–18)*. Macmillan Education for the Schools Council, London

Clay M M 1975 *What Did I Write?* Heinemann Educational, London

Dixon J 1967 *Growth through English: A Report Based on the Dartmouth Seminar, 1966*. NCATE, Urbana, Illinois

Goodman K 1986 *What's Whole in Whole Language?* Heinemann, Portsmouth, New Hampshire

Grossman P L 1990 *The Making of a Teacher: Teacher Knowledge and Teacher Education*. Teachers College Press, New York

Hirsch E C 1987 *Cultural Literacy: What Every American Needs to Know*. Houghton Mifflin, Boston, Massachusetts

Rosenblatt L 1978 *The Reader, the Text, the Poem: The Transactional Theory of the Literary Work*. Southern Illinois University Press, Carbondale, Illinois

Schon D 1983 *The Reflective Practitioner: How Professionals Think in Action*. Basic Books, New York

Shulman L S 1987 Knowledge and teaching: Foundations of the new reform. *Harv. Educ. Rev.* 57(1): 1–22

Sulzby E, Teale W 1991 Emergent literacy. In: Barr R, Kamil M L, Mosenthal P B, Pearson P D (eds.) 1991 *Second Handbook of Reading Research*, Vol. II. Longman, New York

Zeichner K M, Tabachnick R 1981 Are the effects of university teacher education "washed out" by school experience? *J. Teach. Educ.* 32(3): 7–11

Further Reading

Jordell K O 1991 Learning to teach through teaching and being taught. *Scand. J. Educ. Res.* 35(2): 131–44

Langer J A 1992 Rethinking literature instruction. In: Langer J A (ed.) 1992 *Literature Instruction: A Focus on Student Response*. NCATE, Urbana, Illinois

Lester N B, Mayher J S 1987 Critical professional inquiry. *English Education* 19(4): 198–210

Lytle S L, Fecho R 1991 Meeting strangers in familiar places: teacher collaboration by cross-visitation. *English Education* 23(1): 5–28

Perl S, Wilson N 1986 *Through Teachers' Eyes: Portraits of Writing Teachers at Work*. Heinemann, Portsmouth, New Hampshire

S. Hynds

Teacher Education, Governance of

Nations establish policies to recruit and prepare teachers and maintain and enhance their skills because the heart of any nation's educational system is to be found in the quality of its teachers. The governance of teacher education embraces the *structures* of government agencies and teacher preparation institutions responsible for addressing such policy matters. It embraces also the *processes* employed by those structures in arriving at policy (e.g., sources of initiative, advisory input, opportunities for review, accountability schemes). Finally, governance includes the *functions* of teacher education policy (e.g., establishing entrance qualifications, levels of preparation, nature of the preparation program, exit standards).

Given the centrality of teachers to national education systems, it is surprising that so little scholarly literature exists on the governance of teacher education. Most of what exists either focuses on Western or developed countries or is found in the literature coming from the same sources. Educational systems are always deeply rooted in their cultures. Given the increasing complexity, diversity, and vigor of cultural expression in the world, as the astounding developments in the early 1990s in Central and Eastern Europe and Asia attest, conceptualizing across cultural and national boundaries can be extremely risky. In considering the governance of teacher education, therefore, the potential for bias exists not only as to the meaning of specifics addressed in the literature but also as regards the very frames established for understanding the issues of governance in the first place.

While expertise on these matters does exist, it has not been generated by members of the scholarly community. Rather, expertise resides in the experiences of the practitioners of policy; that is, those who have lived through or have been affected by its processes and products. Practitioners of policy do not frequently write of their experiences, but they are often deeply knowledgeable. Mindful of the particular perspectives their roles and positions may have afforded them, individuals who have served in or who currently occupy positions in teacher education policy can be important sources of valuable information and insight into the structure, processes, and functions of the governance of teacher education. The absence of a substantial literature, however, means each new generation must discover these matters anew.

A final caveat, taking something of the form of a conundrum, deserves mention. The very concept of governance implies a degree of purposiveness and rationality that is often belied by reality. Scholars of governance warn of the rationalistic fallacy—the belief that orderly argument, well-marshalled data, and careful logic will determine policy (see Clark and McNergney 1990; Hawley 1990). The reality is much less neat and much more political.

1. Governance Structures: Policy

Any conceptual framework for analyzing the governance of teacher education should begin with those structures that develop policies affecting teacher education. The term "policy" embraces decisions about rules, criteria, incentives, priorities, and resources. The term "Structure" refers to the institutional forms, including their interrelationships, with formal responsibility for making such decisions.

Throughout the world, national ministries of education are the most common structural arrangement for determining policy and for governing teacher education. These ministries are sometimes devoted exclusively to education (e.g., in China, Cuba, Finland, Italy, Jamaica, Spain, Turkey, and Uganda). Sometimes, however, the education portfolio is combined with others, as in Bolivia (Ministry of Education and Culture), Japan (Ministry of Education, Science, and Culture), Norway (Ministry of Education, Research and Church Affairs), or the Philippines (Ministry of Education, Culture, and Sports). In yet other instances, the governance responsibility is bifurcated. An example is Bolivia where urban teacher education is governed by the Ministry of Education and Culture and rural teacher education by the Ministry of Rural Affairs.

Nations that are federal in structure (e.g., Australia, Brazil, Canada, Germany, Switzerland, or the United States) have vested responsibility for education in the ministries of education (or their equivalent) at the province or state level. However, for economic as well as for policy reasons, the role of the federal counterpart to the provincial or state authorities is becoming increasingly more vigorous worldwide.

A second source of governance authority over teacher education is legislative or parliamentary. Instances of legislative action directly impacting teacher education are found in the 1988 Education Act for England and Wales, Norway's 1973 Act concerning teacher education, and Italy's 1973 Act on the legal status of teachers. Policies handled in some nations by executive decision within a ministry may instead be proposed to a parliament and determined legislatively, or initiated within the legislative body; on adoption, these policies establish the ministry's administrative responsibilities.

A third structural form is where the teaching profession itself is granted authority to make important governance decisions. Typically, these structures are known as "professional standards boards," or "professional standards and practices boards." In the United States, for example, such boards exist in the states of Oregon, California, Nevada, and Minnesota; and in Canada, in British Columbia. In Scotland, the board is called the General Teaching Council.

The mechanisms that exist rarely exercise comprehensive governance responsibilities affecting teacher education. For example, they typically cannot make major resource commitments to teacher education. Rather, their policy actions impact on entrance qualifications to teacher education, specifications for preparation programs, and exit standards for candidates including, possibly, the definition and implementation of professional licensure examinations. Where the board also has responsibility for standards of practice, it will have important obligations for defining and enforcing expectations about how teachers and other licensed education personnel perform their duties. One of the most vigorous of such bodies is the California Commission on Teacher Credentialing (Mastain and Brott 1992).

Many countries approach the governance of teacher education by formally specifying advisory bodies to their ministry of education. Although authority for making decisions is retained by the administrative entity to whom the body is advisory, such structures provide formal means for injecting ideas into policy processes and for subjecting policy proposals to review prior to implementation. The Teacher Training Council (Denmark), the Federal Council of Education (Germany), the National Council for Teacher Education (Finland), the National Education Committee (Nepal), the National Council for Teacher Education (Norway, and also India), and the National Council for Education (Zambia) are examples of advisory bodies.

A fifth form of governance structure can be labeled "voluntary." One form of such an organization is the private foundation; from time to time these support systematic innovation in teacher education. Examples of this, both in the United States and especially in developing nations, may be seen in the work of the Ford, Carnegie, and Exxon Foundations. In the United States, the accreditation function for teacher education units has been undertaken at national level by a voluntary association, the National Council for Accreditation of Teacher Education (NCATE). The governing board of NCATE is weighted in four equal parts representative of teachers, teacher educators, policy bodies responsible for education, and so-called "specialty groups", such as learned societies and organizations representing various teaching specializations. A voluntary organization of a somewhat different, supranational sort, is the Organization for Economic Cooperation and Development (OECD). Through the mechanism of country reviews as well as through its subsidiary Centre for Educational Research and Innovation, OECD has had an impact on policy development in member countries.

A final structural device is the temporary commission or task force. Sometimes established by government, sometimes not, commissions and task forces can give high-level attention for a specified period of time to an issue or issues. This work culminates in a set of recommendations for established structures to consider. The Plowden Commission in the United Kingdom, the 1983 Commission on Educational Excellence in the United States, or the Congress of Education and Instruction organized every five years in Romania are examples.

2. Governance Structures: Teacher Education Programs

Within the policy literature, distinctions are made between policy formation (governance) and policy implementation (administration). Despite the locus of governance responsibility for teacher education policy in government agencies or professional associations, in most countries throughout the world real autonomy exists for the colleges and universities responsible for the initial preparation of teachers. While important policy guidelines may be established by ministerial, parliamentary, or professional bodies, teacher preparation programs often have a fair amount of latitude within which to operate. Thus, understanding the governance of teacher education programs is of considerable importance.

The governance of higher education institutions is a domain of interest in its own right, not without its own complexities and contradictions. While traditions of collegial faculty governance are strong, the collegial governance of the teacher education unit can be deeply affected by the collegial governance of the larger or superior governance unit at the college or university level. Administrative officers within the college or university can wield great power. In addition, formal and informal advisory bodies may exist, affording avenues for students, practitioners, alumni, and others to affect programs. Finally, collaboration between teacher education programs having clinical and/or field components, and schools and school authorities, places special constraints on the governance of programs.

3. Functions of Governance for Teacher Education

A handful of core functions engage the bulk of governance attention in teacher education. Entrance qualifications, levels of preparation, length of training, nature of the preparation program, and exit requirements are principal among these.

Entrance qualifications are governed in a variety of ways. Completion of specified levels of schooling is one approach. In Austria, for example, the secondary school certificate (*Matura*) is required in order to enter the teacher-training colleges. Achieving a pass score on one or more examinations may be required for entry into or continuation in a program. In some jurisdictions in the United States, for example, pass scores on specified basic skills tests may be a requirement.

The level of preparation is often differentiated as to the type of licensure sought. It is not uncommon to have nursery school, kindergarten, and elementary school licensure accomplished through a secondary school (e.g., in Bulgaria, China, Cuba, Ecuador, Egypt, and Libya). In contrast, secondary licensure almost universally requires preparation at the university level. Where resources permit, there has been a slow but steady trend throughout the world toward moving all licensure programs to the college or university level.

One of the most visible governance functions in teacher education is the specification of the elements of the training program itself. This governance function is undertaken in several ways. Where ministries of education operate the training colleges (as in Algeria, Cuba, Malawi, the Netherlands, Norway, and Saudi Arabia, for example), they exercise direct control over the teacher preparation curriculum. In other countries, licensure standards are defined by the appropriate authority, and preparing institutions develop curricula to meet those standards. A program-approval process is then employed where the institutions proposing to certify teachers in terms of the licensure standards are examined by the agency to determine whether the programs are consistent with the standards as defined (most jurisdictions in the United States follow this procedure, for example). In the United Kingdom, a subsidiary agency, the Council for Accreditation of Teacher Education, has been established to undertake the program examination.

Governance authorities also establish exit requirements, which are sometimes defined in terms of preparation-program completion. Requirements may also be defined in terms of completion of an internship or other successful teaching experience following, or instead of, a preparation program (e.g., as in New Zealand, and in alternative certification programs in the United States). These requirements may also take the form of a pass mark on a specified examination, which may be designed and administered by the ministry (e.g., in, Algeria, Austria, Egypt, France, Germany, the Philippines, and Turkey), or may be devised by another agency to which the ministry has given sanction (e.g., the privately developed National Teacher Examination used by a number of states in the United States).

The governance of teacher education can include the specification and provision of incentives for individuals to undertake preservice teacher preparation. These may take the form of subsidized enrollment at teacher preparation institutions, or scholarships, or fellowships (e.g., as in Australia, Germany, Norway, New Zealand, or Saudi Arabia), or forgivable loans to attend preparation programs in instructional areas of special needs (e.g., science, languages, or specified handicapping conditions).

Governance has also included indirect or partial provision of teacher education programs. As noted above, direct provision is where a ministry operates teacher preparation programs as part of its overall responsibility. Indirect provision occurs when resources are made available to preparing institutions, either preservice or inservice, to help subsidize the type of program the ministry has defined as being desirable.

Finally, governance includes the specification of continuing education requirements. Such requirements may be directed to induction programs or to continuing education needs which may, in turn, be defined either locally or centrally. They may also take the form of additional educational qualifications necessary for securing a permanent license. At least one system, that of Japan, seems to place even greater emphasis on continuing professional education than on preservice preparation.

4. *Governance Processes*

Education is an intensely political function for any society, but it is also, at least in the eyes of its principal actors, a professional endeavor. This dual character, awareness of which is increasing worldwide, has made advisory input into political governance processes critically important. Claims for advisory access may come from a wide range of stakeholders: teachers' and parents' organizations, preparation faculty (both professional and academic), preparation program administrators, employers of teachers, and many others.

Opportunities for policy review prior to promulgation is another process consideration. Authorities may not always wish or be able to provide such opportunities. Reviews of this kind may create delays, not only for the review process itself but also as a consequence of having to address questions that may be raised. Prepromulgation review increases the likelihood that all relevant considerations will be examined before decisions are taken.

Two kinds of accountability processes can be identified. The first is policy accountability, a subsidiary question of structure. Administrative authority is responsible to the legislature in a parliamentary system, to the elected executive in presidential systems, and essentially to itself in nondemocratic systems. For legislatively derived policy, accountability is ultimately to those who elect the legislative body. For professional standards and practices boards, accountability is to the appointing bodies and, ultimately, to the authority responsible for authorizing the board structure.

The second kind of accountability is performance accountability. For teacher education, especially, the dictum that the operations *are* the policy is well-remembered. Economic considerations, intentions that exceed a nation's current capacity, or mutually incompatible policy provisions may affect performance (for instance, in Malta teachers have received formal designation as professionals equal to other professionals but remain severely constrained by administrative control—see Farrugia 1992). Incapacity, disagreements over policy, or recalcitrance respecting policy may also figure in the discrepancy between policy intentions and actual performance. Sanctions in such instances may range from denial of individual licenses to loss of appropriations, program approval, or employment.

5. Issues in Governing Teacher Education

This final section briefly illustrates three categories of issues and topics that need to be considered in the course of governing teacher education. They are: substantive topics, governance topics, and meta-questions of governance.

5.1 Substantive Topics

The substantive topics are numerous. Questions concerning entry and exit qualifications of candidates, length and level of preparation, character of program, incentives to encourage candidacy, types and requirements of full licensure, and continuing education expectations remain to be answered.

Special circumstances frame the governance of teacher preparation in particular national contexts. Belgium's complex cultural mix has generated a policy structure with five education ministers. Bolivia's mountainous geography and isolated rural populations create special problems for teacher education. Rapid democratization of schooling in, say, Algeria and the People's Republic of China (plus the sheer size of China's 8.7 million teaching force) challenges aspirations to maintain or enhance standards.

Teacher education in Botswana confronts rural migrations to urban areas and a school curriculum ill-suited to the immediate needs of the population. Compensation arrangements compromise the ability of many Latin American countries to convene university faculty for purposes of program conceptualization. Indonesia, the world's fifth most populous country, is culturally extremely diverse and spans an archipelago embracing 13,000 islands.

Nations associated with former colonial empires must address the superimposition of European forms on indigenous cultures (e.g., Bolivia, Nicaragua, Nigeria, and Ghana). South Africa's system of four separate school systems for Blacks, Whites, Coloureds, and Asians will almost certainly undergo new challenges as a result of the dismantling of apartheid.

5.2 Governance Issues

A second set of issues focuses on governance itself. Examples include the balance between political and professional authorities in governance; the method of representating various professional specialties in teaching; the necessity for governance; and the relative weight to be given to national, regional, and local interests.

5.3 Meta-questions of Governance

Fundamental considerations of the nature of teaching, the role of the teacher in the facilitating the learning of others, and the part that expertise plays in carrying out a teacher's responsibilities also impact on the governance of teacher education. So too does the critically important "chicken-and-egg" question—how the desired new kinds of teachers can be prepared and placed if schools themselves are not transformed first.

Teaching, for example, may be conceived as the transmission of knowledge and skills or as the process of helping children reconstruct that knowledge for themselves. The teacher may be thought of as an authority, or as speaking on behalf of authority, or as a facilitator for developing the independent authority of the learner. High-quality teaching may be viewed as more a commitment to values and effective adult models and less a question of technical facility in the arts and crafts of curriculum, instruction, evaluation, and managing student behavior. Finally, when current schools and the conditions of practice in them are perceived to be antithetical to better models of teaching that might be advanced, the governance of teacher education may well become inseparable from the governance of new kinds of schools embracing state-of-the-art practice.

See also: Governance: Relations among Levels of Government

References

Clark D L, McNergney R F 1990 Governance in teacher education. In: Houston W R, Haberman M, Sikula J (eds.) 1990 *Handbook of Research on Teacher Education*. Macmillan, New York

Farrugia C J 1992 Authority and control in the Maltese educational system. *Int. Rev. Educ.* 38(2): 155–72

Hawley W D 1990 Systematic analysis, public policy-making, and teacher education. In: Houston W R, Haberman M, Sikula J (eds.) 1990 *Handbook of Research on Teacher Education*. Macmillan, New York

Mastain R, Brott R 1992 The California Commission on Teacher Credentialing: Seeking the ingredients for change. In: Gideonse H D (ed.) 1992

Further Reading

Ashton P T (ed.) 1991 Theme: Comparative teacher education. *J. Teach. Educ.* 42(5): 322–78

Churukian G A, Kissock C (eds.) 1991 Teacher education: Perspectives from abroad. *Action Tchr. Educ.* 13(3): 1–64

Gideonse H D (ed.) 1992 *Teacher Education Policy: Narratives, Stories, and Cases*. State University of New York Press, Albany, New York

Gumbert E B (ed.) 1990 *Fit to Teach: Teacher Education in International Perspective*. Georgia State University, Atlanta, Georgia

Leavitt H B 1992 *Issues and Problems in Teacher Education: An International Handbook*. Greenwood Press, Westport, Connecticut

Rust V D, Dalin P (eds.) 1990 *Teachers and Teaching in the Developing World*. Garland, New York

Tisher R P, Wideen M F (eds.) 1990 *Research in Teacher Education: International Perspectives*. Falmer Press, London

Vos A J, Brits V M 1990 *Comparative Education and National Education Systems*. Butterworths, Durban

H. D. Gideonse

Teacher Education: Inservice

The abbreviation INSET is widely used to refer to the inservice education and training of teachers. Two types of definition are in common use: official and functional. The official definition comprises all activities supported by INSET budgets. In practice, this can mislead even the officials who use it, because the budget rarely accounts for the total cost. The teaching may be conducted by teacher educators, inspectors, or teachers whose salaries are paid by other budgets. Thus, financial arrangements often reflect the somewhat marginal role allocated to INSET by educational planners and policymakers. Greenland (1983) divides INSET into the following four categories:

(a) INSET for unqualified teachers (mainly certification courses);

(b) INSET to upgrade teachers;

(c) INSET to prepare for new roles, such as principal or teacher educator;

(d) Curriculum-related INSET (mainly courses linked to planned curriculum change or ad hoc refresher courses).

Where there are large numbers of unqualified teachers, both full-time and part-time provision can be found. In China, for example, there is a network of dedicated inservice colleges and a national television channel transmitting programs for part-time students. Several African countries combine full-time provision with part-time correspondence courses supplemented by visits and residential summer schools. Other countries, however, employ very few unqualified teachers; thus, their definition of INSET often excludes them.

The most widely used functional definition of INSET is that developed by an Organisation for Economic Co-operation and Development (OECD) project which characterized INSET as:

> those education and training activities engaged in by primary and secondary school teachers and principals, following their initial professional certification, and intended mainly or exclusively to improve their professional knowledge, skills, and attitudes in order that they can educate children more effectively. (Bolam 1982 p. 3)

This definition includes activities which are not courses and which are not officially funded, but still requires that INSET is the main intention. However, teachers also learn a great deal from participation in activities such as curriculum development which would not be classified under INSET. Participation in these activities will be accommodated under the heading "staff development," which is defined in this entry as that dimension of school life which concerns the professional learning of staff.

1. *Orientations toward INSET*

Underpinning much of the debate about INSET are three distinct yet complementary rationales. Human resources development (HRD) is concerned with (a) ensuring an adequate supply of appropriately trained and prepared people for all positions in the system; and (b) maximizing the potential of all current personnel. HRD is a form of investment in human capital, which seeks to enhance people's experience and develop their expertise to meet future demands. Since such demands are not wholly predictable, HRD focuses on enhancing people's general capability, resourcefulness, flexibility, and capacity to change.

The management of planned change (MPC) has been given by far the greatest attention in the education literature. MPC is generally associated with top-down or center–periphery strategies, although the "top" may be either central or local government, or even the principal of a school. Chin (1967) made an important distinction between three centralist approaches: empirical–rational, normative–reeducative, and power–coercive—although the term "political–administrative" (CERI/OECD 1973) is perhaps more appropriate for the third. These distinctions are important because they affect both the power relationships and the perceived purpose of any accompanying INSET.

The third rationale is based on self-development by schools and teachers supported by various kinds of external funding, advice, and learning opportunities. The arguments in favor of it are threefold. First, schools and teachers will be more committed to changes they have initiated and planned themselves. Second, that change will be institutionalized, "real" change, rather than token change. Third, needs and priorities are best decided at local level, because it is only there that people have sufficiently detailed knowledge of situations and circumstances.

In practice, strategies tend to be mixed. Effective self-development at the school or district level requires expertise in needs assessment and the management of change that is still very scarce. Hence, an appropriate HRD program is often required to make it work. Once a school or district has identified a need for change, it may be able to develop its own response unaided. More often, however, a search for relevant ideas, practices, and materials is required. Support systems for schools can play an important role in aiding such a search, by fostering social interaction among schools, districts, and higher education.

Introducing schools to new ideas and approaches is an important purpose of INSET. However, this introduction is often conducted within the rationale of a district or university which adopts a somewhat patronizing, normative–reeducative approach to change rather than having the school gather intelligence about ideas, materials, and practices which it may want to use. Moreover, INSET of this kind is rarely well-designed for the purpose. School representatives are not well-briefed for their intelligence-gathering role, and are given very little scope to pursue it systematically. Independent assessment of products by school representatives is rare, and those few occasions are dominated by the uncritical accounts of the products' proponents. It is usually only in the higher education context that more critical approaches are encouraged.

The political–administrative approach to change involves either mandated change or sponsored change. Mandated change arises when new policies are introduced, and INSET is needed to guide and support the implementation. Sponsored change occurs when government provides special funding or advice to facilitate particular changes. In some contexts this is simply a mechanism for enabling schools to adopt unusually expensive or complex innovations or to support a local trial of a new idea. In others, sponsorship is perceived as coming very close to a mandate, and schools believe that refusal will jeopardize their relationship with their district.

A further dimension is added when one considers the role of individual decision makers. Attendance at voluntary INSET and the adoption of approved innovations are means by which teachers can attract the attention of district officials and possible support for their further education or promotion. Career progress can also be an important explanatory factor for a district official's own behavior. Thus, in practice, there is a continuum of central influence between mandated change at one extreme and support for independent school-based change at the other.

Both centralized and decentralized approaches to change are dependent on effective INSET; furthermore, many combinations of centralized and decentralized strategies are possible. However, competition between the two approaches will always be uneven. Griffin (1987) points out that mandated change is rarely accompanied by sufficient additional resources, so the system has to redirect resources to meet the new requirements. "The implementation (of mandated change) pulls away energy, time and other resources, often well beyond the expected level of effort that might be allocated to a competing staff development program" (p. 22). Hence there are clear limits to the amount of mandated change a school system can handle without rendering impotent attempts to develop school-based staff development programs. Since research on the implementation of mandated change suggests that schools need internal staff development programs in order to develop the capability to implement and institutionalize change properly, the issue of the right balance between external and internal initiatives is crucial (Steadman et al. 1992).

2. The Identification and Prioritization of INSET Needs

The prevailing view that INSET planning should be based on assessment of need poses more questions than it provides answers. Whose needs are to be assessed? Those of a particular group of pupils, an individual teacher, a department within a school, the school itself, the district, or even the nation? Moreover, who will be making the assessment? One clear finding of research is that, if INSET participants do not recognize a need as having sufficient priority for them, activities aimed at meeting that need will be judged irrelevant. Yet it would be undemocratic if teachers were to be regarded as the sole definers of INSET needs without considering the views of other members of society. This suggests two possible strategies for INSET managers: (a) considerable effort is devoted before or during INSET to convincing participants of the importance of certain needs, or (b) the needs assessment process is decentralized so that schools and teachers define their own needs, with some safeguard to ensure that views of other groups are taken into account.

Devolution of the needs assessment process, however, is no guarantee that it will be properly conducted. Logically, to define a need implies: (a) some view of the current situation, and (b) aspirations for, or expectations of, a future situation that is different. The quality of the needs assessment will depend on both these factors. For example, a person's view of the current situation will comprise:

(a) Information about context, conditions, processes, activities, intentions and outcomes;

(b) Standards, values and criteria by which these are judged; and

(c) Frameworks and perspectives which determine how it is interpreted and understood (Eraut 1989a).

Such a view may be constructed from existing perceptions with little further inquiry or reflection. On the other hand, there may be considerable effort to go beyond first thoughts by collecting new information, becoming more aware of other perspectives and interpretations, and reflecting more on this evidence and underpinning educational values. This process would itself be a process of staff development.

Similarly, thinking about the future must necessarily involve the following:

(a) Some awareness of alternatives to current policy and practice,

(b) Some assessment of the feasibility of these options, and

(c) Some evaluation of the desirability of options and their anticipated outcomes (Eraut 1989a).

Once again, such thinking is enhanced by INSET, particularly by the kind of intelligence gathering mentioned above. The dangers are that awareness of alternatives will remain rather superficial and that significant changes will be prematurely dismissed as impractical without serious study.

2.1 School Self-review

Bollen and Hopkins (1987) argue that school self-review is a necessary but not sufficient condition for school improvement, and that developing schools' capability for self-review should be a priority for HRD programs. However, this argument does not prevent schools without such capability from formulating school INSET plans in a more pragmatic, though probably less effective, way. Ongoing monitoring by teachers and awareness of innovations and practice elsewhere are capable of generating more needs than many schools are able to fulfill. Schools in the United Kingdom are becoming accustomed to producing development plans for their governors and for internal planning of change. They also are required to produce INSET plans in order to get government funds to support their INSET programs. These plans play an important role in determining and coordinating INSET activities at a time when there is an exceptionally high level of externally mandated change.

2.2 Individual Teacher Needs

School INSET plans also have to take into account individual needs, which in the United Kingdom are identified through school-based systems of teacher appraisal. The central purpose of such appraisal is professional development, and targets are jointly agreed and/or reviewed on each occasion (Bradley 1991). These targets may relate to classroom strategies, wider school roles, or career development. Part of the "bargain" is the provision of support, including if necessary the use of some of the school's own INSET funds.

It is important that this support is not just short-term and instrumental in nature. Teachers also need encouragement to participate in external professional meetings in order to widen their horizons, stimulate their thinking, and prevent the school from becoming too insular. On the whole, the privacy of an appraisal interview appears to offer a better context for the expression of need than a more public school self-review; however, more evidence is needed to confirm this hypothesis. Whatever the system, the crucial research question still remains to be answered: under what conditions and circumstances will teachers diagnose their own learning needs, engage in the collection of evidence to deepen that diagnosis, or agree with a diagnosis made by another person?

3. The Development of Professional Knowledge and Learning

One of the more critical developments in educational research during the 1980s and early 1990s has been an attempt to characterize the nature of teachers' professional knowledge and to study how it gets used (Eraut 1994). As a result, the problems facing the INSET designer can now be better understood. For any practical situation there is a large amount of potentially relevant theoretical knowledge which can contribute to its understanding; however, its relevance may not become apparent until it has become part of each teacher's conceptual framework. In other words, theory acquires relevance through use, and use involves thought and discussion in periods of time set aside for that purpose.

On the other hand, practical knowledge is partly tacit in nature, and is not easily articulated or explained. Some INSET goals cannot be achieved by words alone, as teachers have to experience and do things for themselves. The concomitant problem is that what teachers do is unlikely to be fully understood and only partly under their critical control. Thus, if INSET is to develop new and valid practice, it will have to combine the use of theoretical and practical knowledge in some kind of dialogical relationship, involving close linkage between off-the-job reflection and ongoing classroom experience. The models of professional learning discussed below have all been developed as responses to these problems.

3.1 Joyce and Showers' Approach to Skill Development

Joyce and Showers' (1988) approach was designed to expand teachers' repertoires by teaching them new teaching techniques such as inquiry teaching, higher order questioning, or groupwork. Although they identify five essential components of their model, the model's most distinctive feature is a substantial period of off-the-job practical training (not dissimilar to that used in microteaching) followed by transfer into the normal classroom supported by coaching. The contribution to learning of each component is clearly explained.

(a) An exploration of theory through discussions, readings, and lectures is necessary for understanding the rationale. "Study of theory facilitates skill acquisition by increasing one's discrimination of the demonstrations, by providing a mental image to guide practice and clarify feedback, and by promoting the attainment of executive control" (p. 68).

(b) The demonstration or modeling of skills through

video, or live in the training setting. There are advantages in interweaving the theory and demonstration components, as each facilitates the understanding of the other.

(c) Practice under simulated conditions, teaching either a group of peers or small groups of children. For a technique of medium complexity, this practice requires 20 to 25 trials over a period of 8 to 10 weeks in a setting which approximates the normal workplace.

(d) Feedback can be provided by peers under guidance, once the model has been understood. Audio or video recording is desirable, and feedback should be as soon as possible after practice.

(e) Coaching provides continuing support during the difficult process of transferring acquired skills into the normal classroom setting.

Joyce and Showers refer to their final goal as not just the use of new skills in the classroom, but the acquisition of "executive control," which is defined as "the consistent and appropriate use of new skills and strategies for classroom instruction" (1988 p. 68). They expect flexibility in multiple situations, not the delivery of a blueprint. Coaching must be attached to a proper training program and should remain under its overall guidance even when most of it is provided by peers. Thus the transfer of training, supported by coaching, is seen as the experimental component of a period of continuous study. Interaction between theory and practice takes place throughout the program.

3.2 Reflective Models

While Joyce and Showers' model can be seen as a method of introducing into schools techniques and approaches whose credibility derives from research, reflective models aim to build on teachers' own experience by increasing their capacity to learn from it. They are a deliberate attempt to counteract the "dailiness" of teaching by encouraging teachers to attend to different features and seek new information about the flow of classroom events, then put aside time to reflect upon it and discuss it with others. As Schutz (1967) has noted, an "act of attention" is required to distinguish an "experience" from the flow of life in order that it can be reflected upon. Furthermore, a reflective glance may penetrate more or less deeply depending on its purpose and how much is taken for granted. Reflective models, therefore, are highly dependent on teachers' willingness to attend, to reflect, and to take greater control over their practice.

Reflective models have received considerable impetus from research into teachers' thinking which has presented an increasingly sophisticated account of teachers' professional knowledge, much of which has been found to be tacit and intuitive. Classroom behavior is characterized by routines interspersed with rapid intuitive decisions which require instant interpretations of the developing situation and almost immediate responses. The appropriateness of such decisions can only be considered during reflection after the event, if there is the time and the will to do it. The argument as to why teachers should engage in reflection is essentially moral, and is derived from teachers' responsibility for the progress and well-being of the students in their classes. This argument is underpinned by a particular view of teachers' professionalism and accountability. Thus, Eraut (1994) argues that being a professional teacher implies:

(a) A moral commitment to serve the interests of students by reflecting on their well-being and their progress and deciding how best it can be fostered or promoted.

(b) A professional obligation to review periodically the nature and effectiveness of one's practice in order to improve the quality of one's management, pedagogy, and decision-making.

(c) A professional obligation to continue to develop one's practical knowledge both by personal reflection and through interaction with others.

Although there is considerable debate about how these goals can best be promoted, it is possible to describe the range of practices which have been tried in terms of their experiential and reflective components. The experiences to be reflected upon may be based, on either (1) normal occurrences in a teacher's own classroom, possibly enhanced by the collection of more information than usual (e.g., recordings, children's views, observations by a colleague, analysis of children's work); or (2) changes or experiments and their effects. The reflection which follows may include (3) a discussion of the above, possibly aided by questions or issues previously agreed; and/or, (4) action-planning for some modified practice or experiment. Finally, the whole process may be supported by, (5) readings to illuminate (or divert?) the discussion; and/or, (6) an internal or external consultant as a facilitator and/or resource person.

According to the context, the combination of (1) and (3) has been described as mutual observation, peer-assisted review, self-evaluation, or even needs assessment. The sequence (1),(2),(4),(2),(3) is often described as "action research," although Elliott (1991) raises the question of whether the starting point should not be (2) rather than (1). In this, he refers to two rather different accounts of how teachers might reflectively develop their practices:

(a) The teacher undertakes research into a practical problem and on this basis changes some aspect of his or

her teaching. The development of understanding precedes the decision to change teaching strategies. In other words, reflection initiates action.
(b) The teacher changes some aspect of his or her teaching in response to a practical problem and then self-monitors its effectiveness in resolving it. Through the evaluation the teacher's initial understanding of the problem is modified and changed. The decision to adopt a change strategy therefore precedes the development of understanding. Action initiates reflection, (Elliott 1991 p. 23)

Elliott adds that the first account may constitute "a projection of academic bias into the study of teachers' thinking," while the second "may reflect the natural logic of practical thinking more accurately" (1991 p. 23). Another interpretation might be that the first account is more typical of a deliberately created action research group or project (Stuart 1991), the second of ongoing reflective practice by individual teachers who have developed a strong self-monitoring capability.

Research on reflective models gives little guidance on the relative effectiveness of these different approaches, but consistently draws attention to the enabling or disabling effect of school management and ethos. The main personal barriers to participation appear to be the commitment of time and the loss of self-esteem which accompanies initial confrontation with new evidence from one's own classroom. Appropriate support can help overcome these problems, where the teacher accepts the underpinning view of teacher professionalism.

Eraut (1989b) has argued that while reflection at the level of self-monitoring is an ongoing professional obligation, reflection at the level of self-review ought to be treated more as a periodic activity. It is unrealistic to expect major changes in classroom practice to arise from waves of innovation, inadequately resourced for INSET support, or an accumulation of small adjustments triggered by school-based staff development and an appraisal system. Continual disturbance may actually lower the quality of teaching by reducing teachers' sense of efficacy and allowing too little time for any specific change to take root. The question arises as to whether it would not be better to build periods of self-renewal into the professional life cycle of teachers, so that every 5–10 years they engage with a few colleagues in a period of reflection and action research with proper support. Such a strategy would make sense to teachers, establish such interludes as a normal part of professional life, and focus support structures more effectively on teacher development.

3.3 Project-based Models

Project-based models originated within advanced courses provided by higher education. These are best placed within the HRD approach to inservice education, since most participants are preparing to take up more senior positions at school or district level, or posts in teacher education. The types of projects used in such courses range from research into classroom events or institutional problems, through evaluations of courses, materials or policies, to design or development work. Relevant theory and research is required, and the quality of analysis is what a university would expect.

The primary goal is to develop the students' capacity to work independently and collaboratively as reflective professionals, a goal which is supported not only by their own project experience but by accompanying discussion, comparison, and contrast with accounts in the literature and the work of their fellow-students. A secondary goal is to make a positive contribution to students' own institutions, which helps to sustain their support for the course. Some far-seeing schools see it as a cheap form of consultancy! While some universities place projects at the end of courses, others construct courses around a series of projects, which are informed by and fed into ongoing seminar discussions.

Project-work of this kind is chosen by teachers and combines a high degree of authenticity with a more rigorous analysis than is commonly found in schools. Not only does it prepare people for leadership roles but it improves the general quality of professional work (Vulliamy and Webb 1991). Experience of supporting such projects also improves the knowledge-base of the university, leading to better consultancy services and improved teaching and research.

3.4 Professional Development Opportunities

At the beginning of this entry, it was noted that professional learning can occur during many activities not primarily intended for that purpose. Much more use can be made of these professional development opportunities (PDOs) if they are recognized in advance and consciously used for learning purposes. In order to do so, there is a need for:

(a) prior recognition of a professional development need, perhaps as a result of appraisal;

(b) agreement that engaging in a particular activity will provide a learning opportunity relevant to that need; and

(c) planning for an experiential learning cycle of setting targets, providing support, self-evaluation, and feedback from others.

Thus personal PDOs are jointly created by a teacher and a support person, either by selecting some of the teacher's normal professional tasks for special attention or by choosing some special learning activity to assist in the achievement of agreed learning goals. Examples of the former might be conducting an unusually thorough review of the progress of a particular student causing concern, or giving special attention to preparing for the teaching of a new topic. Targets would include both professional quality reports on the task (important for confidence and sustaining a sense of professionalism) and learning goals (with potential for transfer to other cases and situations). Examples of the latter might include studying practice in another classroom (or even another school), shadowing another member of staff prior to taking on some new responsibility, or chairing a school committee. In all such cases, there is a clear learning focus agreed at the beginning; advice and support are provided as appropriate (not only by the designated support person, who may negotiate for additional help); and self-evaluation of what has been achieved and what has been learned is followed by constructive feedback from others.

While PDOs may be weak on the theoretical side, they are highly motivating and relevant for the teacher. Moreover, they are less difficult to initiate than the other models discussed earlier. Although they have been discussed in terms of purely school-based activity, they are equally applicable to the professional development of educational personnel outside schools. Such activities can also be incorporated into INSET courses, to which they bring a wealth of fresh experience to stimulate discussion. Eraut (1988), for example, discusses their use on management courses to change the attitudes and perceptions of those who apparently know all. Similarly, Day (1990) describes how reflective models can be built into INSET courses of 10 to 30 days duration.

4. *Conditions for Effective* INSET *and Staff Development*

Fullan (1987) identifies four factors as crucial for successful staff development:

(a) redefining staff development as a process of learning,

(b) the role of leadership at the school level,

(c) organizational culture at the school level, and

(d) the role of external agencies especially at the local or regional level.

To understand the significance of these factors it is useful to distinguish between three facets of INSET/staff development:

(a) its management (that is, decisions about what to do, for what purpose and with what support; the provision of support; and the evaluation of INSET programmes and policies);

(b) its design and conduct; and

(c) its ongoing interaction with the life of schools and the behavior and intentions of individual teachers.

All those involved need to have some understanding of each of these factors if the process of professional learning is to be understood, the purposes of programs are to be agreed, and the culture of the school is going to have a positive rather than negative influence on development.

Other entries in this encyclopedia focus on issues such as the role of the principal, school improvement, and the effective school. All emphasize the importance of leadership and organizational culture in school development. INSET/staff development is an integral part of that development. However, rather than regarding effective leadership and a positive organizational culture as preconditions for successful INSET/staff development, it is perhaps more constructive to ask how INSET/staff development can help to create the necessary leadership and culture. There is a strong argument that, while the role of principal will always be the most important, the function of leadership should be quite widely distributed for a school to be effectively run. Thus management development programs should be an important component of INSET planning. In addition, the staff development role is important at every level of management. The person best placed to support a teacher's development is usually the senior teacher in his or her subject or grade-level group. Many schools have also evolved roles such as mentor, professional tutor, appraiser, or INSET coordinator whose *raison d'être* is staff development. All these people need training to strengthen their roles.

At a practical level, schools have to create time for INSET and staff development, while still preserving continuity of teaching (Hewton and Jolley 1991). In many countries staff development days are set aside for this purpose, though schools do not always have the expertise to make good use of them (Ekholm 1988). However, time is still needed for functional groups to meet in school and teachers to attend courses and meetings outside school. The former can be timetabled and teachers can be replaced when away; both require careful advance planning by a capable and committed principal.

5. *Role of External Agencies*

Very strong evidence exists to show that substantial external support is needed for all three INSET orientations (Fullan 1991, Louis et al. 1985, Tangyong et al. 1989). Three strategies can be distinguished:

(a) Support for the change process in general, as opposed to specific innovations. This includes (i) INSET directed at building up schools' capacity for managing change (both internally and externally initiated); and (ii) ongoing management consultancy on school-based review and development, including staff development.

(b) Training school-based trainers and supporting them through a specific program of change. This includes (i) INSET for teachers designated as school-based trainers and (ii) follow-up support with their own internal programs.

(c) Direct training of teachers for a specific program of change. This includes (i) externally provided INSET for all teachers concerned in the change, and (ii) follow-up support in their classrooms.

Each strategy has been described in terms of both an INSET component and a follow-up component. Evidence is now overwhelming that follow-up is essential for effective implementation (Huberman and Miles 1984, Bradley 1991). Since proper follow-up is highly dependent on the schools themselves, as well as external agencies, strategies (b) and (c) above will be wasted if schools lack the capacity to manage the process of change. Hence strategy (a) has to be given first priority. Strategy (c) is extremely expensive, but can provide a useful means of developing practical experience and expertise prior to switching to strategy (b).

Although strategy (b), involving the training of trainers, tends to be favored, it is rarely employed effectively. The main mistakes are:

(a) limited school capacity for change, resulting from insufficient attention to strategy (a) above;

(b) failure to train the trainers as change-agents and INSET providers, as well as classroom implementers;

(c) failure to provide continuing support for trainers throughout the implementation phase; and

(d) the provision of training of insufficient length and breadth.

Significant benefits have also been noted from training pairs of trainers from each school rather than individuals. Not only can they assist and encourage each other, but there is also a safeguard against staff mobility and illness.

6. Conclusion

The capacity of school districts to implement any of the above strategies must be called into question. Often innovations fail because district staff lack expertise in INSET/staff development and the management of change. INSET leaders may lack sufficient practical experience of the innovations they are promoting (Noor Azmi 1991). The level of investment per teacher in most INSET programs is too low to make significant changes in classroom practice a likely outcome for the majority of participants.

Some countries control INSET at national level, which can make communication with schools very difficult. However, it does offer the opportunity to mount a coherent INSET program. The proliferation of uncoordinated initiatives has been a major weakness of INSET planning in multilevel governments and has often undercut schools' attempts to manage the process of change properly. Hence, Blackburn and Moisan (1987) suggest that INSET is best organized through a system of local, regional, and national networks, which can foster social interaction, build INSET teams, and coordinate INSET efforts. Many countries are beginning to address a wide range of problems as increasing recognition is paid to the role of INSET in improving the quality of education. It remains to be seen whether, during a period of economic stringency, the funding will match the rhetoric.

See also: Teacher Education: Onservice; Teacher Education Programs: Curriculum; Teacher Education Programs: Structure

References

Blackburn V, Moisan C 1987 *The In-service Training of Teachers in the Twelve Member States of the European Community*. Presses Interuniversitaires Européenes, Maastricht

Bolam R 1982 *In-service Education and Training of Teachers: A Condition of Educational Change*. Final Report of CERI Project on INSET. OECD, Paris

Bollen R, Hopkins D (eds.) 1987 *School Based Review: Towards a Praxis*. International School Improvement Project, OECD, Paris

Bradley H 1991 *Staff Development*. Falmer Press, London

Chin R 1967 General strategies for affecting change in human systems. In: Morphet E, Ryan C (eds.) 1967 *Designing Education for the Future*. Citation Press, New York

CERI/OECD 1973 *Case Studies of Educational Innovation IV: Strategies for Innovation in Education*. CERI/OECD, Paris

Day C 1990 In-service as consultancy: *The Evaluation of a Management Programme for Primary School Curriculum Leaders*. In: Aubrey C (ed.) 1990 *Consultancy in the United Kingdom*. Falmer Press, London

Ekholm M 1988 *In-service Teacher Education and School Development: Overview and Soliloquy* Swedish National Board of Education, Stockholm

Elliott J 1991 *Action Research for Educational Change*. Open University Press, Milton Keynes

Eraut M 1988 Learning about management—The role of the management course. In: Day C, Poster C (eds.) 1988 *Partnership in Educational Management*. Routledge, London

Eraut M 1989a Review of research on in-service education: In: Wilson J (ed.) 1989 *The Effectiveness of In-Service Education and Training of Teachers and School Leaders*. Swets and Zeitlinger, Amsterdam

Eraut M 1989b Teacher appraisal and/or teacher development: Friends or foes? In: Simons H, Elliot J (eds.) 1989 *Rethinking Appraisal and Assessment*. Open University Press, Milton Keynes

Eraut M 1994 Developing professional knowledge within

a client-centred orientation. In: Guskey T, Huberman M (eds.) 1994 *New Paradigms and Practices in Professional Development*. Teachers College Press, New York
Fullan M 1987 Implementing the implementation plan. In: Wideen M F, Andrews I (eds.) 1987 *Staff Development for School Improvement*. Falmer Press, New York
Fullan M G 1991 *The New Meaning of Educational Change*, 2nd edn. Cassells, London
Greenland J (ed.) 1983 *The In-Service Training of Primary School Teachers in English-Speaking Africa: A Report*. Macmillan, London
Griffin G A 1987 The School in society and social organization of the school: implications for staff development. In: Wideen M F, Andrew I (eds.) 1987 *Staff Development for School Improvement*. Falmer Press, New York
Hewton E, Jolley M 1991 *Making Time for Staff Development*. Occasional Paper 14, University of Sussex Education Area, Brighton
Huberman M, Miles M 1984 *Innovation Up Close: How School Improvement Works*. Plenum Press, New York
Joyce B, Showers B 1988 *Student Achievement through Staff Development*. Longman, New York
Louis K S, Van Velzen W G, Loucks S, Crandall D 1985 External support systems for school improvement. In: Van Velzen W G et al. (eds.) 1985 *Making School Improvement Work*. International School Improvement Project, OECD, Paris
Noor Azmi I 1991 Inservice training in Malaysia for the new primary curriculum (KBSR). In: Lewin K M, Stuart J S (eds.) 1991 *Educational Innovation in Developing Countries: Case-Studies of Changemakers*. Macmillan, Basingstoke
Schutz A 1967 *The Phenomenology of the Social World*. Northwestern University Press, Evanston, Illinois
Steadman S, Eraut M, Fielding M, Horton A 1992 INSET effectiveness. Report to the Department of Education and Science, London
Stuart J S 1991 Classroom action research in Africa: A Lesotho case study of curriculum and professional development. In: Lewin K M, Stuart J S (eds.) 1991 *Educational Innovation in Developing Countries: Case-Studies of Changemakers*. Macmillan, Basingstoke
Tangyong A F, Wahgudi R, Hawes H 1989 *Quality through Support for Teachers: A Case-Study from Indonesia*. University of London Institute of Education, London
Vulliamy G, Webb R 1991 Teacher research and educational change: An empirical study. *Br. Educ. Res. J.* 17(3): 219–36

M. Eraut

Teacher Education, Microteaching in

The term "microteaching" is used to describe a cluster of teacher education techniques which allow teachers, especially beginning teachers, to acquire, practice, or refine teaching skills in a setting of reduced complexity. The term itself and the approaches underlying it were formulated at Stanford University in the United States in the early 1960s. The aim was to provide for more effective teacher education than the process of "theoretical discussion followed by trial by fire" (Bush 1968.)

In one of the early descriptions, microteaching was depicted as a "scaled-down encounter in class size and class time" (Allen et al. 1965 p. 1). Later, Allen and Ryan (1969) suggested that the basis of microteaching was to be found in five essential propositions, namely: (a) microteaching is real teaching, in which (b) the complexities of normal classroom teaching are reduced, in which (c) there is a focus on training for the accomplishment of specific tasks, which (d) allows for the increased control of practice, and which (e) greatly expands the normal knowledge-of-results or feedback dimension.

Although later writers have offered a variety of different descriptions and definitions of microteaching, it is clear that the early Stanford models and descriptions provided the basis for the development of microteaching around the world. As Batten (1979) put it, differences in program descriptions "merely reflected different purposes and resources of the user, and overall the format developed at Stanford for the microteaching experience was followed elsewhere" (p. 8).

1. *The Essence of Microteaching*

A typical microteaching encounter begins with a preparation phase in which the teaching skill to be practiced is introduced, perhaps through videotaped models. This introduction is followed by a practice or "teach" phase in which students are given an opportunity to undertake their own practice of the modeled skill. Next, a feedback or "critique" phase takes place in which a videotape replay of the "teach" session is viewed and discussed by student and supervisor. This phase might be followed by a "reteach" phase in which the student repractices the skill in light of initial feedback and then reviews the second performance.

While many variations of this approach have occurred, what remains constant is the opportunity to practice teaching in an environment reduced in complexity through a decrease in class size and lesson length and through focus on only one aspect or skill of teaching at any one time. Although these scaling-down factors are the defining characteristics of microteaching, microteaching also offers the opportunity to scale-up or increase the intensity both of the precision of the preparation for the teaching encounter and of the opportunity for trainees to gain detailed feedback on the effects of their teaching. Microteaching not only gives teacher educators an excellent chance of gaining greater control of their students' learning-to-teach experiences, but also, by its very controllability, it provides opportunities for researchers into teaching and teacher education to explore systematically the effects and effectiveness of different educative techniques. The very nature of microteaching, with its distinct phases and components, means that controlled experimentation can readily occur.

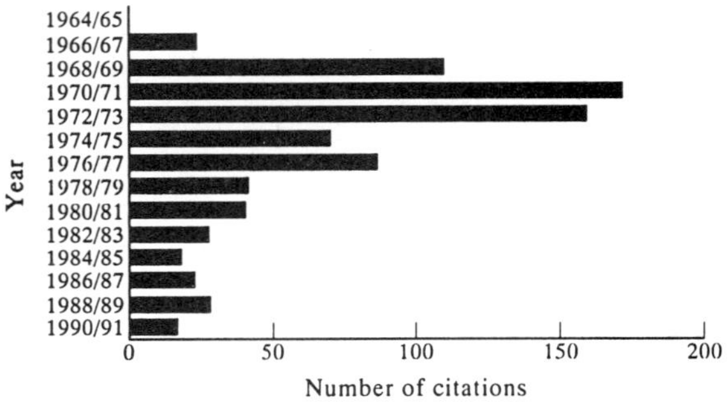

Figure 1
Citations of the keyword "microteaching" in the ERIC database 1964–91

As a result, microteaching enjoyed immense popularity both as a teacher education technique and as a focus of research interest in the 1970s. Use of the approach became rapidly widespread in teacher education institutions throughout the United States (Jones 1979) and major research or development programs were identifiable within the United States (Allen and Ryan 1969), in Australia (Turney et al. 1973), and in the United Kingdom (Brown 1975).

2. *Research on Microteaching*

Shortly after its development, microteaching became the focus of intense research interest. Figure 1, which charts the citation incidence of the keyword "microteaching" in the ERIC database, gives an indication not only of the sudden explosion of research interest in microteaching but also of the almost equally dramatic decline in research and publication on the topic.

Much of the early work on microteaching was concerned with experimental studies on the components of microteaching while later efforts concentrated more on the overall effects of microteaching, on the transfer of skills performance from a microteaching setting to the classroom, and on developing or exploring some of the concepts or models underlying microteaching. This entry follows a similar pattern in that it first provides summaries of research on the preparation, practice, and feedback components of microteaching. This discussion is followed by an outline of conceptual models underlying microteaching and a brief discussion of the overall outcomes of microteaching.

2.1 Research on the Preparation Phase

Reviews of research on the preparation phase have been provided by MacLeod (1985) and Pegg (1985). In general, much of this work has focused on modeling and has been guided by Bandura's work on social learning theory (Bandura 1977), especially the work demonstrating that film-mediated models could be as effective as live models (Bandura et al. 1963).

One of the early interests was the relative efficacy of positive and negative models. Studies by Koran et al. (1972) and Gilmore (1977) showed that the use of positive models was more effective than the use of negative models, although it was demonstrated that negative models were also useful aids to skill acquisition. MacLeod (1985) pointed to difficulties of interpretation of these outcomes in the light of possible differences in the information value of the positive and negative models provided to the subjects.

Researchers who have compared the effects of symbolic (written materials) and perceptual media (film or videotape) have demonstrated a slight favoring of perceptual over symbolic modeling (Phillips 1973). This difference has been attributed to the greater motivational or attention-drawing value of perceptual models. As Bandura (1977) put it, people "rarely have to be compelled to watch television, whereas oral or written reports of the same activities would not hold their attention for long" (p. 40). Perhaps more significant than the intended experimental comparisons of these studies was the clear demonstration that modeling, no matter what the medium, was a powerful facilitator of skill acquisition.

Research on focus in modeling indicated that where cueing, coding, or labeling of the modeled activities was provided, the effectiveness of the modeling treatment was greater (Allen and McDonald 1967). This effect was particularly strong when focus was provided through some form of discrimination training whereby trainees learned to code and label appropriate and inappropriate behaviors (Wagner 1973). Studies by MacLeod et al. (1977) and Pegg (1985) suggested that modeling with discrimination training may be sufficient for at least some skill acquisition. Pegg's study further revealed that a modeling/discrimination treatment may be at least as favorably received by trainees as the practice/feedback component of microteaching.

2.2 Research on the Practice Phase

Practice of skills in microteaching has been so readily assumed to be necessary that there are very few direct studies of its efficacy. In the initial Stanford programs, practice of skills was seen as a central part of the process. In an intriguing follow-up of work on discrimination training and modeling, Pegg (1985) compared the effects of discrimination training including modeling with the effects of skill practice on the acquisition of two teaching skills, variation and higher order questioning. These two skills were selected by Pegg to reflect differences on a posited dimension of "behavioral–cognitive" so that this dimension might be used in an explanatory way if the obtained results of the experimental comparison required it. On higher order questioning there were no performance differences between the groups; on variation, students who had undertaken the discrimination training significantly outperformed those who had undertaken skill practice. Pegg concluded that "practice was not an essential requirement for skill acquisition, at least for the two skills used in his study" (p. 227).

More commonly, questions about practice in microteaching have been concerned with the role of the reteach component in microteaching. Several studies (e.g., Wragg 1971) indicated that the benefits of the reteach were perhaps less than had been supposed. The surveys of microteaching usage cited above indicated that most institutions did not see the value of the reteach session in microteaching and only a minority of microteaching programs were making use of it at the time of the surveys.

2.3 Research on the Feedback Phase

Research on feedback in microteaching has tended to focus on experimental comparisons of different modes of mechanical feedback, such as videotape or audiotape, or different modes of supervisory feedback, but with little recent development of the field being apparent. Griffiths (1974) reviewed a series of studies that compared audiotape with videotape feedback. On the basis of the mixed and sometimes complex results of these studies, Griffiths concluded that "videotape feedback is not necessarily more effective than audiotape feedback [and] the contribution of mechanical feedback within microteaching is . . . more complex than some writers admit" (p. 6). Some 10 years later, in his review of feedback in microteaching, Levis (1985) drew a similar conclusion and suggested that it "has more often been assumed than tested" (p. 3356) that videotape feedback is more effective than other forms of feedback. Levis further suggested that the work he reviewed on feedback in microteaching demonstrated the importance of powerful modeling procedures as a determinant of student skill performance.

Studies of supervisory feedback in microteaching have also been disappointing in that they reveal very little about the effectiveness of different approaches, except that the outcomes are complex and probably represent an interaction of a variety of factors (Claus 1969). Typical of the inconclusive research of this kind was an experimental study of the effects of four supervisory treatments on the acquisition of the skill (Griffiths et al. 1977). With one minor exception, no skill-related differences were found among the groups assigned to the four treatments. Instead, subjects in each of the groups asserted that what they wanted was that which had *not* been provided to them in the carefully controlled experimental treatments. "If the supervision was direct, they wanted more opportunity to discuss their own perceptions, but if the supervision was directed, they wanted to know more about how the *supervisor* had perceived the lesson; if the supervision had concentrated upon their strengths, they wanted to have advice on how they could *improve* their use of the skill, but if the supervision had concentrated on suggesting alternatives, they wanted to be told what they were *doing well* already" (MacLeod and McIntyre 1977 p. 256).

3. Models Underlying Microteaching

Questions about the overall effectiveness and contribution of microteaching depend upon the aims of particular microteaching programs. Those aims are themselves dependent upon the models of participant learning underlying the program. From the literature on microteaching, four distinct but sometimes overlapping models may be discerned: pragmatism, behavior modification, social skills, and the cognitive model.

First, there was the apparent "easy pragmatism" of the early programs. Microteaching was seen within a general training paradigm; concepts from psychology, such as modeling and reinforcement, were freely borrowed, and the emphasis was upon "what worked." In the words of Allen and Ryan, "the decisions as to what skills should be developed . . . were not made in light of any set of rules about what good teaching consists of or what teachers need to know, but resulted from the discussions and debates of the microteaching staff" (Allen and Ryan 1969 p. 14). Thus, the criteria for success were skill acquisition and measures of general teaching effectiveness. The task for research on microteaching was to discover the optimal combinations of the components of microteaching for effective skill acquisition.

Behavior modification as a model for microteaching has been espoused strongly by McDonald, one of the original researchers at Stanford. Teaching skills are simply sets of behaviors which may be acquired through the application of classical, well-established behavior modification procedures. Other than research of a very simple practical kind, "there is very little else about microteaching as a methodological device that is worth studying" (McDonald 1973 p. 73). However, few microteaching programs have operated according to behavior-modification principles, leading McDonald to write that "many users of microteaching did not see the relevance of behavior modification procedures" (p. 72). Furthermore, McDonald contended that the "most undesirable consequence of the promotion of microteaching was that the role of behavior modification . . . was obscured" (p. 73).

The social skills training model of Argyle (1969) has been applied in a microteaching context by Brown (1975). Teaching skills, like other social skills, are seen as analogous to perceptual and motor skills, so that the focuses of Brown's training program related to the selection of aims, the selective perception of relevant cures, motor response (or practice), and feedback and correction. McIntyre (1983) suggested that Argyle's model has not been fully utilized by researchers on microteaching and that, in particular, the cognitive processes involved in the coordination and organization of skilled performance have been neglected. Thus, although the model has been used as a means of conceptualizing the skills involved in microteaching, it has had little applicability to the design of programs planned to facilitate acquisition of these skills.

A cognitive model for microteaching, emphasizing participants' thinking about their teaching, was proposed by MacLeod and McIntyre (1977). This model was based on inferences drawn from the results of research on microteaching and suggested that microteaching should be viewed as a procedure facilitating long-term changes in student teachers' thinking about teaching rather than short-term changes in their teaching behavior. Attention was drawn to the importance of students' conceptual structures when they entered a microteaching program, to the apparent stability of these structures, and to the effects upon these structures of academic discipline or teaching-subject background. This cognitive model was set within a framework of an analysis of classroom life which drew attention to the heavy information-processing demands imposed by the complexity of classroom environments and the cognitive strategies that teachers use to cope with that complexity. The cognitive model assumes that teaching skills should be reconceptualized as "ways of thinking" rather than as "ways of behaving," and that the effectiveness of microteaching should be assessed in terms of whether it provides "for the development and induction of functional and adaptive cognitive structures" (MacLeod and McIntyre 1977 p. 26). Pegg's (1985) study of the effects of practice on skill acquisition was carried out within the framework of this cognitive model and in general produced results supportive of the model.

4. *Outcomes of Microteaching*

Like many educational programs, the effectiveness of microteaching is judged in terms of both behavioral and affective outcomes. In this section, attitudinal outcomes are discussed, followed by a discussion of performance outcomes.

4.1 Attitudinal Outcomes of Microteaching

Perhaps the most consistently reported outcome of research on microteaching is that participants find it a valuable and enjoyable activity (Gregory 1986), with favorable assessments being reported from both preservice and inservice participants. Among teacher educators, attitudes toward microteaching have been mixed. Although many immediately accepted and implemented the innovation, others questioned the assumptions implicit in the practice of microteaching. In particular, doubt was cast upon whether the complex and dynamic art of teaching could readily be dissected into component parts or skills.

4.2 Performance Outcomes of Microteaching

A meta-analysis by Butcher (1981) provided a clear demonstration that microteaching produces short-term change in teaching behavior. What is much less clear is whether microteaching produces long-term behavioral change or the transfer of teaching skills to classroom settings. MacLeod (1981) carried out a detailed review of five experimental studies that attempted to assess the effectiveness of microteaching through use of skill acquisition as a criterion and two experimental studies that attempted to assess the effectiveness of microteaching through use of a pupil performance criterion. He concluded that the results of these studies did little to alleviate ignorance of the effects of microteaching and that it was difficult to conceive of any satisfactory test of the effectiveness of microteaching that made use of student performance criteria. In general, the results of these studies lent support to McIntyre's (1980) "commonsense generalization [that] patterns of teaching are commonly successful in attaining the goals towards which they are most commonly directed" (p. 6).

5. *Conclusion*

Despite some 30 years of research effort, there are few definitive conclusions that can be drawn about the effectiveness of microteaching other than that the participants tend to have favorable attitudes to the experience. It is clear that microteaching enjoyed almost faddish popularity after its introduction and that this produced a plethora of studies on it; however, only a few useful generalizations could be drawn from the results of the studies. Similarly, it is also very clear that there has been no recent sustained research program that has attempted to draw both on these generalizations and the lessons learned in the execution of the early research.

Simple verdicts on the effects of microteaching are unlikely to be reached. Microteaching, like any other teaching method, is complex: complex in terms of the variety of components it uses, the aims it attempts to achieve, and the conceptual models that underlie these aims. It is evident that much of the early experimental research was sterile, providing only a situation-specific evaluation of particular and local sets of training components rather than a testing of coherent and generalizable theory about learning to teach, its form and function. Nonetheless, microteaching did represent a major breakthrough in thinking about teacher education and its advent clearly sparked a major research enterprise which contributed substantially to teacher education thinking and practice.

See also: Teacher Education: Onservice; Teacher Education, Supervision in

References

Allen D W et al. 1965 *Microteaching: A Description*. School of Education, Stanford University, Stanford, California

Allen D W, McDonald F J 1967 *Training Effects of Feedback and Modeling Procedures on Teaching Performance*. Stanford Center for Research and Development in Teaching, Stanford University, Stanford, California

Allen D W, Ryan K 1969 *Microteaching*. Addison-Wesley, Reading, Massachusetts

Argyle M 1969 *Social Interaction*. Methuen, London

Bandura A 1977 *Social Learning Theory*. Prentice-Hall, Englewood Cliffs, New Jersey

Bandura A, Ross D, Ross S 1963 Imitation of film-mediated aggressive models. *J. Abnorm. Soc. Psychol.* 66(1): 3–11

Batten H D 1979 Factors influencing the effectiveness of microteaching in a teacher education programme Doctoral dissertation, University of Stirling, Stirling

Brown G A 1975 *Microteaching: A Programme of Teaching Skills*. Methuen, London

Bush R N (ed.) 1968 *Microteaching: A description*. Stanford University, Stanford, California (mimeo)

Butcher P M 1981 An experimental investigation of the effectiveness of a value claim strategy unit for use in teacher education. Master's dissertation, Macquarie University, Sydney

Claus K E 1969 Effects of modeling and feedback treatments on the development of teachers' questioning skills. Technical report No 6, Stanford Center for Research and Development in Teaching, Stanford University, Stanford, California. ERIC Document Reproduction Service No. ED 033 081, Washington, DC

Gilmore S 1977 The effects of positive and negative models on student teachers' questioning behaviours. In: McIntyre D I, MacLeod G R, Griffiths R (eds.) 1977 *Investigations of Microteaching*. Croom Helm, London

Gregory I 1986 Third World–First World: Time for another look at microteaching. *Journal of Education for Teaching* 12(3): 173–88

Griffiths R 1974 The contribution of feedback to microteaching technique. Paper presented at the APLET/NPLC Conference, Reading

Griffiths R, MacLeod G R, McIntyre D I 1977 Effects of supervisory strategies in microteaching on students' attitudes and skill acquisition. In: McIntyre D I, MacLeod G R, Griffiths R (eds.) 1977 *Investigations of Microteaching*. Croom Helm, London

Jones P E 1979 A survey of microteaching in secondary teacher education programs of NCATE accredited colleges and universities. Paper presented at the AERA Conference, San Francisco, California. ERIC Document Reproduction Service No. ED 173 336, Washington, DC

Koran J J, Koran M L, McDonald F J 1972 Effects of different sources of positive and negative information on observational learning of a teaching skill. *J. Educ. Psychol.* 63(5): 405–10

Levis D S 1985 Feedback in microteaching. In: Husén T, Postlethwaite T N (eds.) 1985 *The International Encyclopedia of Education*, 1st edn. Pergamon Press, Oxford

MacLeod G R 1981 Experimental studies of the outcomes of microteaching. *South Pac. J. Teach. Educ.* 9(1): 31–42

MacLeod G R 1985 Microteaching: Modelling. In: Husén T, Postlethwaite T N (eds.) 1985 *The International Encyclopedia of Education*, 1st edn. Pergamon Press, Oxford

MacLeod G R, Griffiths R, McIntyre D I 1977 The effects of differential training and of teaching subject on microteaching skills performance. In: McIntyre D I, MacLeod G R, Griffiths R (eds.) 1977 *Investigations of Microteaching*. Croom Helm, London

MacLeod G R, McIntyre D I 1977 Towards a model for microteaching. In: McIntyre D I, MacLeod G R, Griffiths R (eds.) 1977 *Investigations of Microteaching*. Croom Helm, London

McDonald F J 1973 Behavior modification in teacher education. In: Thoresen C E (ed.) 1973 *Behavior Modification in Education*. University of Chicago Press, Chicago, Illinois

McIntyre D I 1980 The contribution of research to quality in teacher education. *South Pacif. J. Teach. Educ.* 4(1/2): 4–19

McIntyre D I 1983 Social skills training for teaching: A cognitive perspective. In: Ellis R, Whittington D (eds.) 1983 *New Directions in Social Skills Training*. Croom Helm, London

Pegg J E 1985 The effect of practice on the acquisition of teaching skills. Doctoral dissertation, University of New England, Armidale, New England

Phillips W E 1973 Effects of a videotaped modeling procedure on verbal questioning practices of secondary social studies student teachers. Final report, Fairmont State College, Fairmont, West Virginia. ERIC Document Reproduction Service No. ED 079 967, Washington, DC

Turney C, Clift J C, Dunkin M, Traill R 1973 *Microteaching: Research, Theory and Practice*. Sydney University Press, Sydney

Wagner A C 1973 Changing teaching behavior: A comparison of microteaching and cognitive discrimination training. *J. Educ. Psychol.* 64(3): 299–305

Wragg E C 1971 The influence of feedback on teachers' performance. *Educ. Res.* 13(3): 217–21

G. MacLeod

Teacher Education: Onservice

The training, retraining, and updating of practicing teachers are widely recognized as essential factors in the development of teacher quality. Teacher quality is a major, perhaps the major, factor contributing to improved learning outcomes of students. It is both vital and appropriate that the education and training of practicing teachers should receive increasing attention.

1. Definitions of Teacher Training

The most common distinction adopted in discussions of the education and training of teachers is that between the provision made before teachers begin teaching (preservice) and that which takes place after

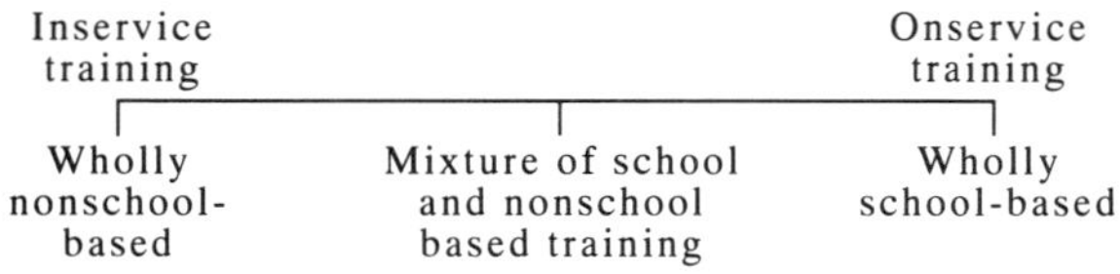

Figure 1
Continuum from in-service to on-service training

they are employed as teachers (inservice). However, this distinction is too simple. While preservice training is often equated with initial training, the term does not apply when teachers are employed without training and must obtain qualifications on the job. Similarly, while in general all postappointment training has been called inservice and the use of the acronym INSET (for Inservice Education and Training) has become commonplace, this term also covers a range of provision.

A different distinction is necessary because of the wide variety of practice that exists throughout the world. In this regard, inservice and onservice are suggested as two broad categories of practice.

1.1 Inservice and Onservice Training

The spectrum of postappointment training can be represented by a continuum. At one end is a form of training that takes place wholly away from the school, possibly in some specifically designed training environment. At the other end of the continuum are practices where all the training takes place in the schools in which the teachers normally work. We might call the one end "inservice" (INSET) and the other, "onservice" (ONSET). (See Fig. 1). Between the two poles of the continuum might be a series of practices that provide training to greater or lesser degrees in or out of school.

Edelfelt (1985) has adopted a different approach and has associated "onservice training" with unqualified teachers and "inservice training" with qualified teachers. This distinction has not been adopted in this entry, although it recognized that the difference in teachers' backgrounds will have important effects on how training is arranged and received.

1.2 A Philosophy for Postappointment Training and Retraining

The basic tenet of inservice and onservice training is that teachers need continual renewal of their knowledge and their capabilities to provide appropriate learning strategies for their students. Commitment to the ongoing training of teachers is evident from the universal practice of providing opportunities for teachers to meet and receive such training. This commitment may be small in many education systems—indeed, it may be one of the first areas of an educational budget to be cut during periods of austerity. Nonetheless, nearly all education systems do attempt to provide for the continuing professional stimulation of teachers during their careers. The frequency, duration, and value of the training may be open for discussion, but the availability and organization of training continue to receive attention from educational planners, managers, and teachers.

The mechanism for the provision of postappointment training is as important as the training itself. The practice of providing short courses (perhaps 1–2 hours) at long intervals has given way to the recognition that the frequency of professional contact is of the greatest importance. The emergence of local places for teachers to meet has been a signal development since the late 1970s. The teachers center, which may be part of an overall network linking teachers across a state, has been widely recognized as having great potential for influencing professional practice. The need for teachers to meet to exchange ideas and work together to define and solve common problems has been accepted, and the value of peer interaction among teachers has been stressed as a means to instill confidence to bring about change in classroom practices. Countries such as Kenya, with its teachers center and subcenters, and Tanzania, with its community education centers, provide just two examples where locally based resource facilities intended to support teacher development have received support not only from the central authorities but also from teachers at large.

2. Three Case Studies

Three case studies, from Indonesia, India, and Pakistan, are useful in examining the value of onservice training. While the first two have many similarities, the third provides an important contrast.

2.1 The Active Learning through Professional Support Project (ALPS)

As a result of the 1973 increase in oil prices, Indonesia was able to undertake a massive program of expansion of primary education. It swiftly provided near-universal access to primary education. While Indonesia was highly successful in quantitative terms, considerable concern was expressed about the qualitative aspects of primary education. An in-depth study conducted in 1976 showed that there was significant underachievement in primary schools. The study examined factors that might explain this problem and identified the teacher as being the most consistent factor affecting school quality. It was decided to establish a program to improve quality. The resulting project became known as the Cianjur Project after the district in which it was located.

The Cianjur Project took as its starting point the proposition that it is possible to identify specific aspects of teacher behavior that might be modified in order to bring about improvements in classroom practice. Preparing realistic teaching plans, encouraging children's investigations, encouraging children's talk and interaction, marking books and providing feedback, and keeping appropriate records were some of the aspects of teacher behavior targeted for change. It was also realized that in order to bring about these changes, which represented a step forward in the learning process from Indonesia's traditional didactic mode, teachers would need support. Such support had to be directed at the teacher and be provided where it was needed most, namely in the classroom and school, and not in a college environment some distance from the school.

Some direct training was provided for teachers at an induction course organized in local schools, but this component was kept to a minimum, largely because of cost. One main part of the support for teachers was provided through the reexamination of the roles of head teachers and the local inspectors, both of which had been seen as almost solely administrative. Head teachers and inspectors were encouraged to adopt more professionally oriented stances, which in turn raised important questions about the ability of these categories of staff to support innovations in practice. Neither the headteachers nor the inspectors resisted the innovations, but for each category problems arose. For the headteachers, the new approach required a reorientation of thinking for them and their staffs to the interventions that they could or should make in the classroom. For the inspectors, it demanded a restructuring of their schedules to permit them to spend more time in schools with teachers to help them bring about the required changes.

It was recognized by all involved that opportunities to meet were needed to discuss problems as well as ways of moving forward. A series of "clubs" were established, one for each category of staff. The schools were divided into groups and the teachers from the schools within each group met on a regular basis. Similarly, the head teachers and inspectors met separately, normally on a monthly basis.

After the start of the Cianjur Project in 1980, the introduction of activity-based learning spread to other provinces in Indonesia. By 1990, 7 out of 27 provinces had become involved. While the model for the provision of support remained basically the same (i.e., induction courses in a school, school groups, teacher clubs, heads and inspector clubs and teachers centers, and provision of a meeting place with some resources), there have been wide variations in the ways in which the detailed arrangements are organized. In particular, attendance at the teachers clubs varies considerably. Tangyong et al. (1990) recorded that in Cianjur teachers attended clubs four to six times a year. However, in other areas the teachers attended monthly (as in South Sulawesi), or even weekly (Lampung). These variations in the application of the model arose from the process of decision-making about implementation, where the

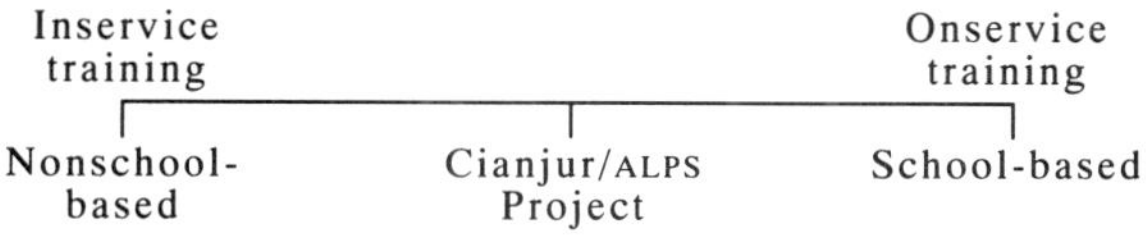

Figure 2
Cianjur/ALPS project on the training continuum

emphasis was upon the selection of priorities for support by local officials at the provincial level.

In the Cianjur Project, which in 1987 became known as the Active Learning through Professional Support (ALPS) project, the emphasis has been upon small groups of teachers meeting frequently to help each other. These meetings have taken place in school, during school time, and dealt with issues identified by the group members as important. In some areas these are essentially staff meetings at an individual school, the staff of which are, by regulation, expected to meet on Saturday mornings. These staff meetings were intended for minor school administrative issues, but their purpose has been revised to provide opportunities for discussion of professional concerns and the agreement of action to be taken in the ensuing period.

ALPS as a project was reviewed by Tangyong et al. (1990). The spread of the model led to the adoption of active learning as a national policy for education. Experiential learning was then included in the new national curriculum (1994), with textbooks prepared to complement this approach to learning in the primary school. With the implementation of Indonesia's nine-year Basic Education cycle, active learning will spread to higher classes and eventually will be common practice for classes 1–9 (6–15 years of age) throughout Indonesia.

The position of the Cianjur/ALPS Project on the inservice–onservice continuum is shown in Fig. 2. The conduct of courses in a school did require teachers to be absent from classes and for some of them to leave their school to attend meetings elsewhere. The same applied to attendance at the teachers clubs. However, the brevity of these absences from the classroom might suggest that the meetings were more directly based on school problems and realities than on conventional inservice courses, which may offer a set program for professional orientation that is not directed fully at immediate and local interests. As a consequence, the ALPS Project might be positioned slightly to the right of the center on the continuum to reflect the school-based nature of the professional development that takes place.

2.2 The Andhra Pradesh Primary Education Project (APPEP)

The second project is the Andhra Pradesh Primary Education Project (APPEP) in India. This project, funded by the United Kingdom Overseas Development Administration, has many features similar to those of ALPS (also funded by the Administration). APPEP started in 1985 with a large pilot project involving 328 schools and 794 teachers in 11 (out of 23) districts of Andhra Pradesh, one of the poorest states of India. Originally the districts were selected to represent different climate zones in Andhra Pradesh and the locations for training activities were chosen to provide for the poorest areas. The pilot project (now called Phase I) was essentially a building program with a training element. Again, the intention of the training program was to bring about changes in teaching styles toward a more activity-oriented and investigative approach to learning in the primary school. An evaluative study in 1987 showed a satisfactory implementation of the basic ideas of APPEP. Full-scale state-wide dissemination of APPEP to 175,000 teachers in 50,000 schools commenced in 1989 with a five-year program in each district.

There are some important differences between ALPS and APPEP. Although the basic educational philosophy, with its emphasis on "hands-on" experience, was common to both, differences in the structure of the training were obvious. In the case of ALPS, the provision of courses for induction was dependent upon the local supply of funds to support the program. In the case of APPEP, however, funds were provided through bilateral aid for an agreed-upon program of training. This program provided for not only the induction of teachers but also the preparation of tutors able to conduct the training of the teachers.

In order to reach all teachers in the period allotted and to include all new appointees, a highly coordinated program was needed, directed by a project headquarters. There was no room for local initiative and action in the training program. Teachers (and local inspectors) were sent to the District Institute of Education and Training (DIET) (previously the government teacher training institutes, which had been upgraded in 1986 under the National Policy on Education) or to local centers. These courses all took place during the school year. In some areas the schools were closed for a period while all teachers attended courses.

Another common feature of ALPS and APPEP was teachers' meetings. Under APPEP the teachers clubs of ALPS were called "teacher centers." All teachers in a group of schools were expected to attend a compulsory meeting at the center on the third Saturday of the month. On that day the schools were closed and children were free. In some cases groups of children were taken to the centers to participate in demonstration lessons, a regular feature of programs at the centers.

One feature that was different in APPEP was the role of the head teachers and the local inspectors. With an average teacher–school ratio of 3.5:1, and

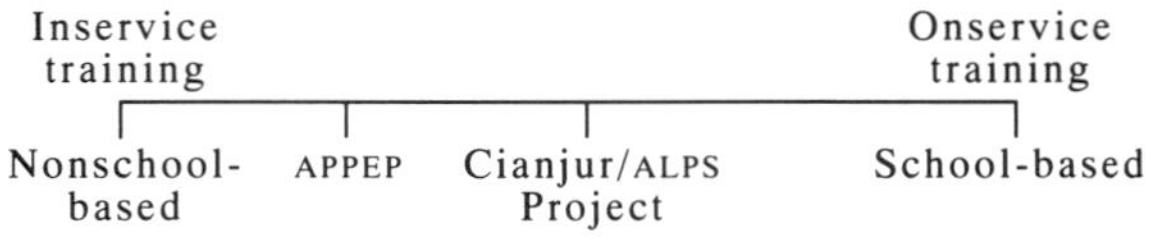

Figure 3
APPEP project on the training curriculum

with many schools having only two teachers, the system was severely understaffed. There were many schools without a formally appointed head teacher. In these schools one of the staff acted in a senior coordinating capacity. Elsewhere heads were usually also full-time class teachers and hence had little opportunity or will to attempt to bring about the large-scale changes demanded by APPEP. Most of the local inspectors were too absorbed in administration to be able to undertake professional development. Nonetheless, they all agreed that such engagement should be part of their contribution to the overall improvement of the quality of primary education in Andhra Pradesh. With the absence of support from head teachers and inspectors, progress in the adoption of the project's principles was dependent upon: (a) the quality of the induction course provided, and (b) the extent to which the teacher center meetings were attended.

In combining elements of inservice and onservice training, APPEP was a large and ambitious project. However, in placing APPEP on the continuum, it might be appropriate to locate it more toward the inservice end and to the left of ALPS. In APPEP the whole of the training and, for most teachers, the attendance at teacher center meetings required teachers to leave their schools for shorter or longer periods of time. Like the ALPS teachers, teachers in the APPEP project who showed particular interest and ability were encouraged to assume leadership roles in the centers. These teachers emerged spontaneously. Their activities were confined to leading meetings of teachers, and as such they made a valuable contribution to the success of a vital part of the project. It would have been better if these teachers had been given sufficient assistance to enable them to provide more direct help to their fellow teachers on a more regular basis. Administrative structures did not permit the creation of posts equivalent to the Advisory Teacher in the United Kingdom's system, where teachers have the opportunity to interact on a one-to-one basis with a colleague who could assist with the development of improved strategies. The World Bank in creating a project (Primary Education Quality Improvement Project—PEQIP) parallel to ALPS in Indonesia attempted to create posts of field tutors, but difficulties arose over the status, role, and functions of such posts as well as over the qualifications of those who might have filled them.

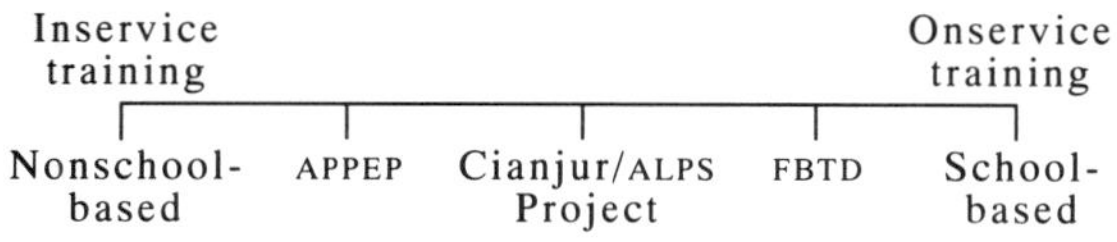

Figure 4
FBTD Project on the training continuum

2.3 Field-based Teacher Development Program (FBTD)

The third project is of a different character and conforms more easily to all the criteria established for onservice provision (see Fig. 4). The Field-based Teacher Development (FBTD) program in the northern areas of Pakistan was initiated in 1984 to provide training for unqualified teachers (Bude 1991). Large numbers of unqualified teachers were working in primary schools in this part of Pakistan. The small capacity of the only government elementary teacher-training college, at Gilgit, did not permit a rapid increase in the supply of qualified teachers. At a time of increasing enrollments in primary schools, there was a need for a new approach to initial training. Through the joint initiative of the government of Pakistan and the Aga Khan Foundation, FBTD was introduced.

FBTD tried to improve the quality of primary education by (a) providing on-the-job training in specially designated courses for untrained primary teachers; (b) providing general inservice courses of two weeks' duration, open to every primary school teacher in the area.

The on-the-job training took place in middle or high schools under the supervision of qualified and experienced "master trainers." The primary section of a middle or high school was turned into a center, the qualified teachers were transferred to the centers, and the centers took in unqualified teachers for training. The maximum number of trainees was limited to ten. Two untrained teachers were put in charge of each class, one teaching and the other observing in turn.

The trainees were supervised by a master trainer and an assistant master trainer, who were selected for their outstanding teaching capabilities. They received a short period of training before joining a center and then guided the trainees in the conduct of the classes. They observed the trainees, made careful notes on their performance, and from time to time demonstrated better teaching techniques. At the end of the school day the master trainers and the trainees met to review the day's work and plan for the next day. In addition, time was spent on those subjects the trainees had to pass to obtain the primary teacher's certificate (e.g., school administration, child development, arts and crafts). Some additional help was also provided for the trainees with the content of primary-school subjects.

The government teacher-training college at Gilgit also prepared manuals in the five main primary school subjects for use by the trainees in preparing their lessons. Inservice courses of two weeks were conducted twice yearly for 120 primary school teachers. Trainees took part along with other teachers.

In reviewing the progress of the FBTD program Bude (1991) noted that over 4 years 320 teachers had been trained, 88 percent receiving the primary teacher's certificate on their first or second attempt. The FBTD used different schools throughout the period, with 27 schools participating in the training of the trainees. Only two Aga Khan Foundation and three government schools were used twice. By using different schools every year, FBTD was spread throughout the northern area.

3. Conclusion

These three examples of postappointment training for primary teachers represent different patterns of organization. FBTD is similar to arrangements for teachers in the Sudan, where in the mid-1970s the Omdurman Teachers' College provided coordinated in-college and in-school programs for professional development. The emphasis in the FBTD on the provision of direct support in schools took advantage of the possibilities of drawing upon the services of qualified staff near at hand. The use of a master trainer was a feature that depended on their ready availability, a situation that could be exploited in the northern areas of Pakistan.

In both the Indonesian and Andhra Pradesh studies there was little opportunity to draw upon other more senior staff. Schemes had to be developed that relied entirely on available expertise and facilities within the primary school system. Hence, in these cases there was less reliance on outside support. Rather, there was a tendency to look for what could be provided through mutual support, with teachers, head teachers, and local inspectors having a role to play. Essentially in ALPS and APPEP the mainspring of development was at ground level, with teachers taking the leading role. Through their frequent meetings and the exchange of ideas, a climate for professional growth was created which stimulated innovative approaches to teaching. For the most part, this stimulus was provided in the schools and formed the basis of the onservice training provided.

Onservice training seeks to encourage professional development and change without removing teachers from the everyday realities of the classroom. The conduct of training in schools, with teachers and their problems forming the main focus of programs, means that the daily demands of the school are not forgotten as ideas for classroom practices are investigated. This constant reminder of the possibilities and limitations of classroom change may have a retarding impact on the introduction of new practices as teachers carefully examine the implications of what is being requested of them. On the other hand, the detailed revision of possible ideas against a framework of school and classroom does ensure that ideas, once examined and accepted, have a better-than-average chance of being accepted and introduced into practice. Perhaps future developments will include a lessening of the reliance on courses—short or long—at a college or center where teachers are taken from the classroom, and a greater acceptance of school-based training. If so, then perhaps onservice training may be seen to be more cost-effective and more likely to lead to professional development and growth.

See also: Teacher Education: Inservice; Teacher Education, Supervision in

References

Bude U 1991 *Improving Primary School Teaching*. Deutsche stiftung für Internationale Entwicklung (DSE), Bonn

Edelfelt R 1985 *An Analysis of Policy Needs for In-service Education in Indonesia*. The International Learning Co-op (IMTEC), Oslo

Tangyong A F et al. 1990 *Quality through Support for Teachers: A Case Study from Indonesia*. Office of the Educational and Cultural Research and Development, Ministry of Education and Culture, Jakarta/DICE, Institute of Education, London

Further Reading

Bell L, Day C 1991 *Managing the Professional Development of Teachers*. Open University Press, Buckingham

Hopkins D, Wideen M 1984 *Alternative Perspectives on School Improvement*. Falmer, Philadelphia, Pennsylvania

Joyce B, Showers B 1980 Improving inservice training: The messages of research. *Educ. Leadership* 37: 379–85

McMahon A, Bolam R 1984 *A Handbook for LEAS*. Chapman, London

R. Gardner

Teacher Education: Philosophical Issues

Material on teacher education occupies many handbooks, encyclopedias, and large areas of library shelving. Much of this material is, however, predictably and rightly empirical. In this entry, the focus is on the philosophical issues raised by the preparation of teachers to work in schools. They include the relationship between the aims of education and teacher education, the theory and practice debate, the nature and role of reflection in teacher education, and the place of philosophy of education within it.

1. Teacher Education, School Education, and the Nature of Society

The theoretical knowledge, skills, and dispositions that teachers are thought to need will be related to the view taken of the aims of education and how these are best realized (see, e.g., Martin 1987). Several influential views can be used to illustrate how different views of the aims of education and their realization have given different emphases to the content and extent of teacher education. For those who hold that schooling should consist almost entirely of the transmission of traditional academic knowledge, teacher education will emphasize the need for an appropriate grounding in the academic disciplines with some understanding of the conditions in which young people might learn these. Some who hold this view may regard any formal teacher education as unnecessary, holding that people need first and foremost to be good historians, good scientists, and so on to be good teachers. Anything else can be picked up on the job. In what might be loosely referred to as the child-centered tradition, however, where the main aim of education is thought to be the realization of children's potential, the task of the teacher will be to tend the children's intellectual and moral growth and to provide the conditions in which they can best flourish. To equip teachers for this task, teacher education will need to give student teachers a particularly thorough grounding in psychology of education. The teacher will need to be able to recognize the stages of intellectual and moral growth and particularly when children are "ready" for certain kinds of learning. In the United States an amalgam of these two views has been developed, in which the inducting of students into knowledge is taken to be the central aim but where the bringing about of this understanding is held to be something in which the teacher must play an active and demanding role. Indeed teachers' professionalism consists precisely in adapting the knowledge in which they are competent for teaching to particular learners in particular contexts. This will involve a wide-ranging professional preparation, including, for instance, detailed work on subject matter, understanding of learning styles, and the influence of social context on learning.

There are also views of purpose that consider a major aim of schooling to be the creation of democratic citizens. Teachers will need to know how to pass on knowledge (including knowledge that extends beyond the academic disciplines) and also how to foster in their school students the skills and dispositions appropriate to democratic citizens. If, in addition, it is thought that some of this learning is best achieved through the ethos and organization of the school, this will demand teacher preparation that prepares student teachers to contribute to such a professional educational community.

Clearly there are overlaps in the nature of teacher education on these different views of the aims of education, but there are also major differences, not only in content but also in the degree of preparation thought appropriate.

The nature of teacher education will also be affected by the role it is thought appropriate for professional teachers to play in the formulation and critical commentary on educational policy. To take two extremes: if teachers are expected to be similar to civil servants, executing the educational policies of the state, their preparation will be rather different from a situation in which they are expected to contribute as autonomous professionals to the formulation, execution, and monitoring of educational policies. These extremes may be variously combined with different views taken of the aims of education. If an academic knowledge-centered view of the aims of school education is taken, for instance, the formulation, monitoring, and so on of educational policy may be left wholly within the control of teachers or these tasks may be given to another body (e.g., a government agency). A view that sets democratic citizenship as a major aim of school education, depending on the position taken on how education is appropriately controlled in a democracy, may similarly give its teachers more or less power over the determination of policy.

2. The Relationship between Theory and Practice

All views about teacher education, including those discussed above, will involve assumptions about the nature of the relationship between theory and practice. This relationship is embodied in three major models of teacher education.

2.1 The Apprenticeship Model

This view focuses on teaching as a practical activity and claims that the best way to learn it is on the job, taught by successful practitioners. The model itself covers a range of possibilities. At one extreme is the idea that the new entrant, unencumbered by theory, more or less copies the practice of the professionals (O'Hear 1988). More sophisticated versions recognize, however, that practice is inescapably theory-laden: theory is present in any teaching situation even if the teacher does not attend to it. On this view, those practitioners (sometimes called "mentors" in the United Kingdom and United States) charged with the job of inducting entrants into the profession will have some grasp of explicit elements of the theory. Drawing in part on this, they will introduce student teachers to the best contemporary practice. They will also encourage them to develop a professional awareness, to be on the lookout for new and more successful methods and to experiment. What this approach will exclude is any academic study of education involving a wide-ranging exploration of the empirical (e.g., psychological, sociological) and value assumptions underpinning educational practice.

In its sophisticated versions this seems a most plausible model for teacher education. It rightly puts the practice of teaching in the center of the picture. It aims to produce teachers who are professionally alert and not simply content to carry out their responsibilities in a routine way. It also correctly sees the new entrant not operating as an isolated individual but as joining a professional community. Problems arise, however, with the criteria for successful practice. In one sense the process of intelligent trial and error, on which this model relies for the improvement of practice, is capable of making massive improvements to current practice. This happens, however, only within a given framework of empirical and value assumptions. It is not hard to imagine that progressively careful refinement of practices over decades would, within a different framework, be condemned because they were based on faulty psychological or philosophical assumptions or on values, perhaps sexist or racist ones, later regarded as, at the least, controversial.

2.2 The Rationalist Model

The problem with the apprenticeship model, even in its most sophisticated versions, seems to be that it leaves teachers embedded in a particular set of practices, without the intellectual tools to subject those practices to sufficiently far-reaching critical scrutiny. A response to this shortcoming—one that was fashionable in the United Kingdom in the 1960s and 1970s (Tibble 1966)—is to provide teachers with the tools necessary for scrutiny. Teacher education practiced on this view, therefore, has included a grounding in the so-called foundation disciplines of philosophy of education, sociology of education, psychology of education, and history of education. Such a grounding, with teacher educators judiciously selecting appropriately from the disciplines, can have a prominent place, even in preservice teacher education (perhaps especially at that level, indeed, so that new entrants to the profession are not "contaminated" by the fads and fashions of current practice). This grounding will supply new entrants with a whole set of theoretical frameworks from which general principles and empirical considerations relevant to successful practice can be derived. Provided with such a set of principles and considerations, which have been subjected to appropriately rigorous testing procedures within the disciplines, new entrants must apply them to the practical teaching situations in which they find themselves.

The rationalist view is strong where the apprenticeship model is weak. It is strong on the need for teachers to be equipped critically to assess in the most far-reaching way the practices and institutions in which they find themselves. However, in seeking to make practice subject to fundamental criticism, it vastly underplays the importance of the practice of teaching and the knowledge and expertise found within the professional community. It skews the relationship between educational theory and practice by making it a matter of rationalistically applying principles generated by disciplines to the complex matter of education.

Is it possible for a conception of teacher education to do justice to the emphasis on induction into a community of practitioners in the apprenticeship model, while not losing sight of the importance of the need for fundamental examination of the educational community's work?

2.3 The Reflective Model

A fruitful starting point from which to look for such a conception as that described above might be Schön's (1987) influential idea of teachers as reflective practitioners. Schön argued that, traditionally, professional knowledge and action have been understood (as in the rationalist model above) in terms of technical rationality, with professionals applying their knowledge to problems in a rule-governed fashion. This, he argued, is a totally inadequate way of understanding how teachers (and other professionals) operate. Teachers, for instance, do not try to fit the behavior of a particular group of school students into some preexisting mental grid on the basis of which they automatically devise what action to take. They draw on past experiences to interpret the situation and their interpretation to some degree shapes that situation. The action they then take on the basis of that interpretation in turn has certain consequences which demand further reflection. Professional activity is therefore a constant process of interpretation, action, reflection, and adjustment.

Schön's account seems to capture the nature of professional activity rather more sensitively and accurately than it appears in the rationalist or even the apprenticeship model. It has affinities with Shulman's (1987) work on the special body of knowledge or expertise teachers must possess and with the work of Carr and Kemmis (1986), who have followed the "action research" tradition and have been influenced by the critical theory of Habermas. They stress particularly the collaborative nature of teachers' professional work as teacher-researchers and their political responsibilities to the wider community. If, however, the notion of the teacher as a reflective practitioner is to have any effect on teacher education, it is necessary to look more closely at the precise character of the successful teacher's reflection.

Hirst (1990) suggested three levels at which reflection occurs. The first involves teachers in reflection on their practice in relation to the given principles and criteria that are taught as current professional knowledge. If their practice is to be defensible, however, teachers will also need to reflect critically on the adequacy of those principles and criteria themselves. In addition further questions can be raised about the more general beliefs and values—about human nature, human society, and so on—that inform the principles and criteria of current professional knowledge.

Educating reflective practitioners at the preservice stage will clearly involve making them reflective about their practice at the first level, just as the sophisticated versions of the apprenticeship model do. It will also involve, however, encouraging them to reflect at the second level on the adequacy of the principles with which they are working and acquainting them with the significance of the more far-reaching reflection at the third level. In-service education will involve work at the second level and, for those with the inclination and aptitude for more wide-ranging reflection, the rigorous critical examination of empirical and value frameworks at the third level.

How do these three conceptions of the relationship between theory and practice fit the different conceptions of the aims of education that inevitably shape teacher education? One frequent conjunction and one rather tighter link can be proposed. The apprenticeship system, in both its crude and its sophisticated versions, is often thought to be appropriate to train teachers who are mainly required to pass on traditional academic knowledge (O'Hear 1988). There is no necessity about this, however. Teachers could equally well be trained to become reflective practitioners in the passing on of academic knowledge. Indeed the research of Shulman and others (see Wilson et al. 1987) into teachers' knowledge of subject matter and the role it plays in teaching suggests that there is much more to be discovered about how teachers should conceptualize their teaching subject in relation to wider considerations, such as educational aims. It is, nonetheless, hard to see how the aim of the creation of democratic citizens might be successfully accomplished other than via the reflective model. For the achievement of this aim requires not only that the curriculum provides suitable knowledge and skills but that the ethos and organization of a school instantiates democratic values and also contributes, not least by providing a context for fostering appropriate personal qualities, to the education of future democratic citizens. Setting up and maintaining an educational institution in which curriculum, organization, and ethos all harmoniously contribute to democratic education demands that school staff are sensitive to, and knowledgeable about, for instance, the intended and unintended consequences of different organizational arrangements. Since whole school policies are involved, this will demand that in the staff as a whole there are the intellectual resources to reflect at the second and third levels on the school's rules and customs.

3. Philosophy of Education in Teacher Education and Educational Policy

The view taken of the aims of education and of the theory–practice relationship will affect the role assigned to philosophy of education in teacher education. A view that envisages a crude apprenticeship system, adequately preparing people to pass on traditional academic knowledge, will have little place for philosophy of education. In the education of reflective practitioners aiming to educate future citizens of a democracy, philosophy will play another, larger role.

How might that work? In preservice work, philosophy of education should ideally engage with student teachers' critical reflections on the practical principles they are mastering. For instance, student teachers will be in a professional milieu where people will be talking about children as intelligent or not; or saying that it is the teacher's job to foster their moral development; or that music or science education is of prime importance; or talking about problems of assessment. All of these topics, and others, could benefit from the insights philosophical discussion, offered at the appropriate time, could bring. The insights, important in their own right, would also indicate to prospective teachers the contribution that philosophy of education can make to reflection on the educational thinking on which their practice is ultimately based. It would be inappropriate to suggest in this entry what this might mean in terms of courses and teaching arrangements, since such maters depend also on the availability of resources. It is worth emphasizing however, that whatever the context it is important that philosophical work engages with the new teacher's current concerns (see Barrow 1984).

At in-service level, philosophy of education can be expected to make a large contribution. This might include, for instance, discussion of the aims of education, as well as the elucidation of the nature of particular aims of education; the qualities of mind that education seeks to foster (e.g., imaginativeness, creativity, independence of mind); aspects of moral education and educational issues raised by the social context (e.g., issues to do with the rights of parents, children and the state, the nature of multicultural education). This list is illustrative rather than exhaustive. At this level, philosophy of education can be expected to contribute not only to the work of individual teachers and schools, but also more broadly to the formulation, monitoring, and critical debate about educational policies within a democratic society. Indeed, in the United States a number of philosophers of education have offered philosophical perspectives on the important Holmes Group's report *Tomorrow's Teachers* (Soltis 1987).

4. Conclusion

Philosophical discussion impinges on teacher education in relation to the aims envisaged for education—a topic that has been too little discussed in relation to teacher education. It also does so in attempting to characterize the appropriate relationship between theory and practice in education, a matter that has considerable implications for the structure of teacher education courses. There are also questions to be answered about the contribution of philosophy of education to preservice and inservice teacher education which can only be tackled in relation to the first two issues.

See also: Philosophy of Education: Historical Overview; Teachers as Professionals

References

Barrow R 1984 *Giving Teaching Back to Teachers.* Wheatsheaf Books, Brighton
Carr W, Kemmis S 1986 *Becoming Critical: Education, Knowledge and Action Research.* Falmer Press, London
Hirst P H 1990 The theory–practice relationship in teacher training. In: Booth M, Furlong J, Wilkins M (eds.) 1990 *Partnership in Initial Teacher Training.* Cassell, London
Martin J R 1987 Reforming teacher education, rethinking liberal education. In: Soltis J (ed.) 1987 *Reforming Teacher Education: the Impact of the Holmes Group Report.* Teachers College Press, New York
O'Hear A 1988 *Who Teaches the Teachers?* A contribution to public debate of the DES Green Paper. Social Affairs Unit, London.
Schön D 1987 *Educating the Reflective Practitioner: Toward a New Design for Teaching and Learning in the Professions.* Jossey-Bass, San Francisco, California
Shulman L 1987 Knowledge and teaching: Foundations of the new reform. *Harv. Educ. Rev.* 57(1): 1–22
Soltis J (ed.) 1987 *Reforming Teacher Education: the Impact of the Holmes Group Report.* Teachers College Press, New York
Tibble J (ed.) 1966 *The Study of Education.* Routledge and Kegan Paul, London
Wilson S M, Shulman L S, Richert A E 1987 150 different ways of knowing: Representations of knowledge in teaching. In: Calderhead J (ed.) 1987 *Exploring Teachers' Thinking.* Cassell, London

Further Reading

Grimmett P P, Erickson G L (eds.) 1988 *Reflection in Teacher Education.* Pacific Educational Press, Vancouver
Hirst P H 1983 Educational theory. In: Hirst P H (ed.) 1983 *Educational Theory and Its Foundation Disciplines.* Routledge, London
Pearson A 1989 *The Teacher: Theory and Practice in Teacher Education.* Routledge, New York

P. White

Teacher Education: Professional Ethics

Traditionally, professional ethics has been associated with ethical codes of conduct and standards as formulated by and within different professional communities, as, for example, medicine, law, or education. The value and role of such codes will be discussed below. All these codes and standards have been developed in the context of a way of thinking, or paradigm, that originated in the Enlightenment in the eighteenth century. As the paradigm guiding the evolution of the modern Western world, this way of thinking has provided, ever since, a framework for professional ethics and the institutional behavior of a variety of professional associations.

A new paradigm has emerged since the 1980s requiring a fundamental reassessment not only of professional ethics, but of schooling and teacher preparation as well. This paradigm envisions a more intrinsically intimate relationship between knowledge and moral values than has been generally acknowledged in theory or practice. Its basic dimensions are being articulated across academic disciplines at the same time as they are beginning to affect the practice of many other traditional professions, especially law and medicine (Jennings 1987). Common aspects of this new paradigm can be identified in such seemingly unrelated factors as international political developments and the enduring strength of the feminist movement in the United States and Europe. The growing environmental crisis and the collapse of hegemonic communism have both contributed to new ways of perceiving connection and interdependence across gender lines and national boundaries, as well as between species and the natural environment. The new paradigm can best be characterized as ecological in nature, insofar as it focuses attention on ecosystems, both natural and human, and their interdependent relationships. In contrast, much modernist thinking has been based in sharp categorical distinctions, not only between natural and human social environments, but in dualistic divisions, for example, between mind and matter, or ethics and knowledge.

In the 1990s and beyond, both the institution of schooling and the ethical responsibilities of teachers will require an ecological perspective. Such a perspective is not ecological in the limited sense of simply relating human behavior to the natural environment. In fact, the ecological orientation envisioned here requires that schools and classrooms be acknowledged as types of ecosystems in their own right, not unlike those existing in nature. Such systems, natural or social, are interactive, holistic, and embody diversity, interdependence, and self-modification. To appreciate the systemic condition of human environments is thus to conceive of them in terms of intrinsic relationships between culture, and language and thought; this implies in turn the need to locate educational responsibility in relation to social and cultural dimensions of human nature and development. Given the central moral character that defines education as an enterprise, teachers will increasingly need to see their work in terms of an ethical worldview encompassing international multicultural diversity and ecological literacy. Since the early 1980s, a number of labels have been attached to different aspects of the nature and structure of the new paradigm, but the most common of these include "postmodern" (Griffin 1988), "postliberal" (Bowers 1987), "poststructural" (Cherryholmes 1988), or "postpositivist" (Giarelli and Chambliss 1989).

These "post-" labels notwithstanding, many of the basic categories of criticism comprising new paradigm thinking were formulated by John Dewey, among others, early in the twentieth century. Dewey's writings on education conceived schooling as essentially a sociocultural enterprise (see, e.g., Dewey 1916). In his rejection of the dualistic categories of the Enlightenment, as in the Cartesian mind/body separation, Dewey foreshadowed postmodernism. Moreover, in his contextualism, as well as in the intimate relationship he envisioned between ends and means, or between educational aims and the means used to achieve them, Dewey laid the groundwork for much recent literature reflecting the thought characterized as "new paradigm." In this sense, then, Dewey might appropriately be seen as postmodern; however, it must be noted that postmodernism has come to signify diffuse contradictions and complex meanings not consistent with, or embodied in, Dewey's major works, or his legacy.

1. Essential Features of New Paradigm Thinking

In areas ranging from physics (Gleick 1988) to the legal profession (Tribe 1989)—including teacher education and schooling—three major assumptions can be singled out to demarcate essential characteristics of the older "modernist" paradigm which are being called into question. They are the following: (a) the primacy of rationality (and its modern expression in science and technology) as a solution to all important human problems; (b) the unqualified faith in human progress as linear and inevitable; and (c) the presumption that individualism as an expression of total human emancipation from tradition and enculturation is the ultimate achievement of civilization (Bowers 1987).

These three deeply rooted assumptions can be traced back to Isaac Newton and the birth of modern science, and to the philosopher René Descartes, the quintessential representative of the Enlightenment and its exaltation of reason as the distinctive trait separating humanity from all other species. Descartes also saw in Newtonian science (as indeed did Newton himself) physical evidence that the universe obeyed divinely ordained laws, as absolute and immutable as they were rational and comprehensive. The development of modern technology has similarly been perceived as a natural extension of Cartesian thought. In their dramatic twentieth-century manifestations, technological advances have been extolled for their capacity to extend and refine the principle of scientific prediction and control, as applied to nature, and even to human nature (Skinner 1971).

Such unlimited faith in reason, science, and technology is supported by an equally deep-seated belief in the Western world in the inevitability of human progress, another idea to emerge from the Enlightenment. Apparent setbacks to this progress have been held to originate in irrational or nonrational aspects of human nature, and such human weaknesses were thought to be correctable through education. Accordingly, as schooling became more widely available, it was assumed that democratic institutions would naturally emerge to replace authoritarian structures and would effect a general emancipation of humanity. Widespread emancipation of individuals would in turn facilitate the emergence of social contracts, political and economic, in the service of infinitely expandable human betterment.

If the paradigm out of which such views originated and developed is morally and ethically appealing, it serves as a reminder that human knowledge and belief are intimately linked to a vision of what ought to be. Indeed, the three assumptions outlined above, reflecting the Enlightenment's faith in reason, progress, and individual emancipation, constituted the dominant mind-set in the West for more than three centuries. Both as ideas and ideals, these premises fostered considerable material and economic progress during this period, along with the development of democratic institutions and processes. Nonetheless, it has become painfully evident in the latter half of the twentieth century that science and technology cannot resolve the most profound moral and ethical problems, nor can they guarantee the continuance of linear progress in economic or social terms.

Moreover, failure to acknowledge in theory and practice the inherently social–cultural nature of the individual has severely limited and distorted the effectiveness of educational reform. Inappropriate promotion of excellence over equity and competitiveness over cooperation are only two of many educational mandates which derive their institutional legitimacy from the Newtonian/Cartesian legacy as it has evolved in modern Western thought. Policies based on these mandates continue to enjoy widespread acceptance and even some degree of success in the homogeneous cultures of nations such as Japan (Leestma and Walberg 1992). However, in countries like the United States, profound cultural diversity, together with the equally disparate economic and social circumstances in which children are born and reared, consigns these same educational policies to failure, and not merely in the schools. These policies generate miseducative outcomes in the form of misdirected anger and alienation, drug addiction and crime, and a costly waste of human potential imprisoned in expensive penal institutions.

In summary, if it is assumed that most developed nations are either already multiculturally diverse, are becoming so, or that they perceive the need to interact in morally responsible ways with other cultures, then the emergence of a new paradigm sanctioning radically different educational policies and behaviors should be welcomed. Similarly, there may come a time when the demise of a historically potent paradigm that has legitimated an often hostile competitive quest for dominance over, and exploitation of, the earth's finite resources is appreciated.

It is in the context of considerations such as these that the nature and role of professional ethics as it relates to the enterprise of schooling and, ultimately, to the education of teachers must be examined. Educational responsibilities entail moral development as well as cultural transmission, and the ethical obligations of teachers clearly require that attention be focused on social and environmental concerns. Specifically, such a mission must be informed by an ecological orientation exhibiting the interdependence of, and connections between, human beings around the globe, and their collective mutual dependence upon a viable environment that recognizes no national boundaries. In addition, professional ethics will need to be recast to take full cognizance of the profoundly conservative ways in which humans are molded culturally. The fact is that much of human nature is impervious to, or misshaped by, educational efforts based on organizational structures derived from Enlightenment beliefs. In this vein, traditional ways of analyzing and categorizing professional ethics are not unimportant, but they do not typically reflect priorities like those outlined here.

2. *Codes of Professional Ethics: Assets and Limitations*

Nearly every profession that has emerged in the twentieth century takes pride in defining itself, at least in part, in reference to a code of ethics. The ethical code of the National Educational Association (NEA) is therefore an appropriate document to consider in any attempt to characterize the role and nature of professional ethics.

Initially, it is interesting to note that, not unlike the Ten Commandments in the Old Testament of the Bible, the list of ethical obligations in the NEA Code of Ethics is framed almost wholly in negative terms: while 8 of the biblical Ten Commandments are phrased as "Thou shalt not" admonitions, 15 of the 16 responsibilities in the NEA Code are listed as "shall nots." Unfortunately such negative exhortations as the religious commandment, "Thou shall not kill" are unambiguous only if understood literally. Many Christians who have taken this commandment seriously have made systematic and numerous exceptions to its literal meaning throughout history. Furthermore, restraint from killing does not preclude a variety of possibilities involving infliction of injuries short of causing someone's death. In similar fashion, the NEA Code can affirm, for example, that a teacher "shall not unreasonably deny the student access to varying points of view" (Strike and Soltis 1992 p.x). Although again the literal meaning may not be ambiguous, the variety of situations affecting or precluding its possible or appropriate application are almost limitless. Quite apart from legitimate professional disagreements over what constitutes a relevant point of view to which students might be exposed, the extent to which teachers may be constrained, explicitly or tacitly, from acting according to conscience, integrally depends upon the school and community in which they work. Controversial issues involving, for instance, AIDS, religion, or sexual orientation, routinely proscribe teachers from discussing such issues even in what is deemed an intellectually defensible way. Thus the ethical injunction not to restrict "unreasonably" students' access to different sides of various issues is often rendered impotent, rightly or wrongly, in the context of cultural diversity and value conflicts in the wider community. What is more significant is that a similar line of reasoning could be applied to almost all negative ethical injunctions.

It is certainly true that guidelines couched in such terms can be helpful to teachers and the public alike in clarifying the ethics of the profession; but especially if framed negatively, they are much less helpful in the equally important function of setting forth in unambiguous terms the positive proactive ethical obligations of teachers, let alone their possible interpretations in the classroom. Moreover, simply to "react" to educational policies and proposals, whether set forth at the national, state, or local level, is not to assume responsibility commensurate with professional status.

What is becoming increasingly clear as the twenty-first century approaches is that the teaching profession needs to emulate to a far greater extent the professions of law and medicine by playing a greater proactive role in formulating and clarifying in practice both policies and professional standards. As in medicine and law, the range of policy issues to which teachers need to give attention is broad. In relation to the educational enterprise the economic and social questions which define an equitable society must be addressed as ethical, and not merely political, responsibilities. The survival of meaningful forms of democracy in the United States and other countries is directly relevant to the development of viable democratic governments and institutions throughout the world.

It is axiomatic that such patterns and directions cannot be achieved except through the education of a globally conscious, responsible citizenry. While it is possible for education to occur outside of schools, it is primarily through institutionalized education that the pluralistic social and cultural needs of students can be addressed in a purposive way. No code of ethics for teachers could adequately identify or direct the complex tasks involved in interpreting and accomplishing a moral mission with a broad agenda such as this.

3. Management-based versus Ecologically-based Educational Models

In addition to the enterprise of schooling as a whole, professional ethics and teacher education are beginning to undergo a profound shift in the way they have been conceptualized since the middle of the twentieth century. This reconceptualization appears to have become well-established in the United States and Canada in particular (Boyd 1990), but will probably gain acceptance in other countries with strong or developing democratic traditions and relatively stable economic systems.

In the social and multicultural context of advanced democracies, serious questions have arisen about the adequacy of what has been termed the "management paradigm" (Bowers and Flinders 1990) as a model for addressing a vast range of educational problems and challenges. From preschool initiatives to university preparation programs for teachers, the management model has characteristically approached education in piecemeal fashion. In other words, educational problems have been typically defined reductionistically in line with the positivistic philosophical orientation which has dominated thought about educational reform. This orientation has rested upon the assumption that all important educational questions or issues could only effectively be addressed in isolated and separate categories rendering them susceptible to rational or scientific analysis. Such analysis was alleged to open the way for possible subsequent technological treatment, or at least for solutions achieved through further concise logical or statistical manipulation.

In essence this mode of thinking harks back to the Cartesian Enlightenment quest for clear and distinct ideas. As a model for thought, moreover, this paradigm has long underpinned much scientific and technological advancement. Cartesian rationalism and Newtonian science together paved the way for the emergence in the twentieth century of the basic features of the management paradigm. As in positivistic science, the management model has utilized the power of rational analysis and scientific reductionism to explain, predict, and ultimately control many of the important dimensions of education and schooling. Indeed, on a larger scale, until recently the material and scientific advances that have often dramatically marked Western civilization seemed a logical corollary to the direction set by the Enlightenment paradigm.

It has thus come as a profound shock for Western culture and thought to have to acknowledge that the rationalistic worldview has no way of addressing the question of the very survival of the planet. Accordingly an ecologically based paradigm for education has emerged as a new mode of perceiving and thinking, calling into question the basic assumptions and conceptual foundations of the management-based paradigm. In short, this postmodern, or post-structural, orientation, as previously characterized, requires a release from patterns of thinking and feeling based on ideas that have taken maturing centuries to evolve; the notions must be relinquished that change is progressive or even predetermined, that reason or science can avert catastrophe, and that unencumbered individualism is the capstone of Western civilization. The emergence of this ecological paradigm has profound implications for the education of teachers.

4. Reconceptualizing the Teacher Preparation Program

It has become commonplace to note that there is a necessary and essential connection between the education of teachers and the reform of schooling. Equally clear is Goodlad's contention that "The moral responsibilities we want for both children and teachers are best cultivated in moral school cultures." (1992 p. 92). Goodlad's focus on the education of teachers highlights the intrinsic connection between the moral mission underlying the education of teachers and the primary ethical responsibility of teachers themselves; put simply, "enculturing the young into our social and political democracy and introducing them broadly to the human conversation" (p. 90).

What is critical in the emphasis upon the ethical component of professionalization becomes dramatically apparent in the face of major educational reform proposals that have attracted attention in the United States in the 1990s. Labaree (1992), for example, sees in particular grave shortcomings in both the Holmes study (Holmes Group 1986) and the Carnegie report (Carnegie Task Force 1986). Despite the many merits in each of these investigations Labaree suggests that they "may well do more for teacher educators than for teachers or students" (pp. 151–52). As the editors of the journal in which Labaree's article appeared pointed out, the Carnegie and Holmes studies both illustrate the tendency to minimize the moral components of teachers' work even as they primarily "promote the rationalization of classroom instruction by generating momentum toward an authoritative, research-driven, and standardized vision of teaching practice" (Labaree 1992 p. 123). If it is agreed that classrooms and schools are themselves moral cultures, it follows that teacher preparation needs to be based in a vision balancing the acquisition of pedagogical skills and technical expertise with the attainment of ethical perspectives rooted in moral sensitivities (see Purpel 1989).

5. The Liberal Arts Dimension of Teacher Education

Another major issue concerning teacher education programs is the extent to which prospective teachers are exposed to a sound liberal arts educational experience. It is commonly agreed that teachers need to develop an appreciation of traditional academic disciplines. This is usually provided in the form of course requirements in the humanities, the social sciences, and the natural sciences. However, in line with the growing need for ecological enlightenment embracing the social and natural world, serious issues in higher education have arisen as to the most effective ways to provide teachers with an adequate intellectual framework to perform their duties. In this connection, many colleges and universities have begun to experiment with new and different combinations of academic studies emphasizing the interdisciplinary and global nature of many of the world's most serious problems.

Such a vision of a liberal arts education inherently questions traditional programs based largely on the isolation of academic disciplines and their orientation toward graduate study. An interdisciplinary course of studies in various formats would seem more compatible with developing a vision of the need for institutional reform and with imparting an intellectual framework for connecting theory with practice, and knowledge with values. Such a conception of liberal education reflects new paradigm thinking as previously outlined, and serves to direct attention away from excessive concern for individual morality in isolation and toward the idea that educational institutions, among others, need to be seen and characterized as exhibiting moral attributes (Goodlad 1992). In turn, perhaps, a more balanced perspective may be created in which whole institutions, and not simply individuals judging and acting alone, can be deemed responsible for achieving what is right and good. On a larger scale, this point is precisely what Bellah et al. (1991) attempt to stress in their study of United States society and culture.

6. Ethics for Teachers in a Pedagogical Framework

As the twenty-first century approaches, the ethical dimension of teacher education will certainly reflect not merely elements of new paradigm thinking, but will also incorporate greater attention to experiential aspects of moral decision-making. Ethical theorizing will still remain a part of teacher education programs, if only because theory itself is useful for creating order from chaos and for reminding teachers that rationality and conscience can and often do complement one another. Familiarization with ethical concepts and terminology can also serve to make teachers aware of the relevance of ethics to their daily activities in ways they may never have suspected. As a case in point, deontological and consequentialist reasoning can focus appropriate attention not only on the ethical aspects of educational policy questions, but also upon concrete school or student-related issues as they are experienced (Strike and Soltis 1992).

It must nonetheless be acknowledged that cultivation of a code of professional ethics, however abstract or refined, begins in emotional responsiveness to human conflicts and concerns. Thus, the nonrational and intuitive aspects of ethical decision-making deserve, and doubtless will receive, more attention than they have been given in the past in the education of teachers. These emphases have been underlined by Gilligan (1982) who successfully introduced the perspectives of women into ethical theorizing and, in so doing, invited correspondingly greater attention to contextual concerns arising out of concrete experiences (see also Kittay and Meyers 1987). Strike and Soltis (1992) also pay homage from a more analytic perspective to noncognitive factors in ethical decision-making processes in education, as does Scheffler (1991) on a broader philosophical level. Accordingly, teacher education programs will need to utilize in greater measure role-playing ethical conflicts involving a wide range of educational issues. These programs also need to make better use of similar pedagogical strategies, as a means of rendering ethics more meaningful to teachers on an experiential level.

7. *Community and Culture in Institutional Change*

Finally, Dewey's recognition early in the twentieth century that "moral principles . . . are inherent in community life . . . [as well as] in the working structure of the individual" (1909 p. 58) needs to be accorded renewed emphasis. Teacher education for the twenty-first century will need to demonstrate the relation between professional ethics on the one hand, and community and culture on the other. Teachers will need to see themselves and their students as deeply embedded in cultural contexts and as members of ever-widening circles of communities. And just as cultural bridges are required to open paths between diverse communities, so communicative competencies are needed to transform fears of cultural difference into occasions for learning and growth.

In facilitating students' development in such directions, teachers will have to draw upon and refine authority patterns as they emerge within the indigeneous subcultures of children and youth. Appeals to reason and rationality will increasingly fail to motivate or sustain interest in children lacking roots in stable family life and religion. In the absence of traditional voices of authority stemming from family and church, the teacher's burden necessarily expands, especially insofar as it entails preserving and transmitting social values which cement the survival of a democratic way of life. Nothing less than the systematic cultivation of classroom communities, together with the conscious attempt to make schools into moral cultures, would appear to begin to address such societal needs.

It deserves mention here that the Association for Moral Education, an international scholarly organization of university and school faculties, convened an international conference in Canada in November, 1992, in which the entire focus of its program was concentrated upon multicultural and multiracial issues as they impinge upon the moral and ethical life of teachers (Ontario Institute for Studies in Education 1992). Clearly, this type of conference foreshadows the future direction of teacher education by acknowledging in its very content the intimate relation between professional ethical responsibility and human cultural identity. Moreover, as democratic patterns take root and grow, whether in the new sovereign states of the former Soviet Union (Long 1990) or in more monolithic cultures such as Japan (Shimahara 1992), it is equally certain that the educational constraints and liberating tendencies which form an integral part of culture, community, and social institutions as ecosystems, will attract increasing attention. Such a focus is warranted particularly as ecological and other global problems arise to highlight human interdependence and finite planetary limits (Orr 1991). No vision of educational reform or professional ethical responsibility, which does not take such factors into consideration, can be regarded as realistic or morally sound.

At the same time, new positively framed codes of ethics will need to be devised that are less focused on individualistic aspects of educational endeavor and more on the cooperative nature of the work of facilitating human growth and development. Professional standards will also require reformulation if they are to help educators welcome ethical responsibility, not shun it; such revised standards will encourage teachers to regard themselves as less alienated from their collective and shared commitment to one another, their students, their local communities, and a common global environment.

See also: Ethics, Moral Philosophy, and Education; Moral Education: Philosophical Issues; Teacher Education: Philosophical Issues

References

Bellah R N, Madsen R, Sullivan W, Swider A, Tipton S 1991 *The Good Society*. Alfred A Knopf, New York

Bowers C A 1987 *Elements of a Post-Liberal Theory of Education*. Teachers College Press, New York

Bowers C A, Flinders D J 1990 *Responsive Teaching: An Ecological Approach to Classroom Patterns of Language, Culture, and Thought*. Teachers College Press, New York

Boyd D 1990 Professionalization and the moral jeopardy of teaching, *Philosophy of Education 1989:* (Proc. 45th Ann. Meeting Philosophy of Education Society, Illinois State University, Normal, Illinois) 45: 102–18
Carnegie Task force on Teaching as a Profession 1986 *A Nation Prepared: Teachers for the 21st Century*. Carnegie Forum on Education and the Economy, Washington, DC
Cherryholmes C H 1988 *Power and Criticism: Post-Structural Investigations in Education*. Teachers College Press, New York
Dewey J 1909 *Moral Principles in Education*. Houghton Mifflin, Boston, Massachusetts
Dewey J 1916 *Democracy and Education*. Macmillan, New York
Giarelli J M, Chambliss J J 1989 John Dewey on moral development and education: Context, conception, and legacy. *Discourse* 9(2): 82–103
Gilligan C 1982 *In a Different Voice: Psychological Theory and Women's Development*. Harvard University Press, Cambridge, Massachusetts
Gleick J 1988 *Chaos: Making a New Science*. Viking Penguin, New York
Goodlad J I 1992 The moral dimensions of schooling and teacher education. *Journal of Moral Education* 21(2): 87–97
Griffin D R (ed.) 1988 *Spirituality and Society: Postmodern Visions*. State University of New York, Albany, New York
Holmes Group 1986 *Tomorrow's Teachers*. The Holmes Group, East Lansing; Michigan
Jennings B (ed.) 1987 *The Public Duties of the Professions*. Hastings Center, Hastings-on-Hudson, New York
Kittay E F, Meyers D T (eds.) 1987 *Women and Moral Theory*. Rowman and Littlefield, Lanham, Maryland
Labaree D F 1992 Power, knowledge, and the rationalization of teaching: A geneology of the movement to professionalize teaching *Harv. Educ. Rev.* 62(2): 123–54
Leestma R, Walberg H J (eds.) 1992 *Japanese Educational Productivity*. University of Michigan Press, Ann Arbor, Michigan
Long D H 1990 Continuity and change in Soviet Education under Gorbachev *Am. Educ. Res. J.* 27(3): 403–23
Ontario Institute for Studies in Education (OISE) 1992 Conference on "Power Within Diversity: Confronting Moral Issues in Multiracial/Multicultural Community and World." Toronto, November 12–14
Orr D W 1991 *Ecological Literacy: Education and the Transition to a Postmodern World*. SUNY Press, Albany, New York
Purpel D E 1989 *The Moral and Spiritual Crisis in Education: A Curriculum for Justice and Compassion in Education* Bergin and Garvey, Granby, Massachusetts
Scheffler L 1991 *In Praise of the Cognitive Emotions and Other Essays in the Philosophy of Education*. Routledge, Chapman and Hall, New York
Shimahara N K 1992 Overview of Japanese education: Policy, structure, current issues. In: Leestma R, Walberg M J (eds.) 1992
Skinner B F 1971 *Beyond Freedom and Dignity*. Bantam Books, New York
Strike K A, Soltis J F 1992 *The Ethics of Teaching*, 2nd edn. Teachers College Press, New York
Tribe L H 1989 The curvature of constitutional space: What lawyers can learn from modern physics. *Harvard Law Review* 103(1): 1–39

Further Reading

Goodlad J, Soder R, Sirotnik K A (eds.) 1990 *The Moral Dimensions of Teaching*. Jossey-Bass, San Francisco, California
Green T F 1984 *The Formation of Conscience in an Age of Technology*. Syracuse University Press, Syracuse, New York
Rich J M 1984 *Professional Ethics in Education*. Charles C. Thomas, Springfield, Illinois
Sergiovanni T J 1992 *Moral Leadership: Getting to the Heart of School Improvement*. Jossey-Bass, San Francisco, California
Sizer T R 1992 *Horace's Compromise: The Dilemma of the American High School*. Houghton Mifflin, Boston, Massachusetts

T. H. Smith

Teacher Education Programs: Curriculum

The curriculum of preservice teacher education programs across different countries and cultures may vary in important aspects, such as institutional context, content areas, time allocations, and the forms of practical experiences for students. In spite of this variability, however, most programs share some common curricular features.

The curriculum of teacher education programs is generally based on four components: subject-matter studies (whether taught concurrently or consecutively with other studies), foundation of education studies, professional studies (such as method courses), and the practicum (supervised practice). In this entry each of these components is treated separately. Curricular concepts, such as the hidden curriculum (Martin 1976) and the "null curriculum" (Flinders et al. 1986), are presented and curricular issues and some future directions are discussed.

1. Institutional Context

Programs may be housed in special institutions for teacher education, which may or may not be connected to a university system. Examples are the special institutions for training primary teachers in the United Kingdom, India, or Israel (McNamara 1990, Govinda and Buch 1990, Ben-Peretz 1990, Tisher and Wideen 1990). Programs in such institutions are mostly characterized by a "concurrent" curricular mode; namely, the simultaneous study of subject areas and professional subjects.

In many cases, programs for the education of secondary teachers are university-based and are likely to reflect a "consecutive" curricular mode; namely, candidates study professional courses and participate in the practicum after they have completed their subject courses and received a university degree. Examples are programs in the United Kingdom (McNamara 1990), the Netherlands (Kieviet 1990), Germany (Klinzig 1990), and Japan (Sato and Ushiwata 1990). In Japan in 1986, 28 percent of university graduates earned teacher certificates (Sato and Ushiwata 1990).

Teacher education programs may also be situated in schools. Several such programs have been established in the United Kingdom (MacLennan and Seadon 1988). Indeed, from the 1980s onward there has been a movement toward the increased provision of such courses. The reasoning behind this movement is that teacher education must start from classroom practice so that educational theory is then considered in its proper professional context.

2. *Subject-matter Studies*

The teaching of subjects during the training of secondary teachers is often in the hands of the various disciplinary departments of a university (Loewenberg-Ball and McDiarmid 1990, Houston et al. 1990). On the other hand, elementary teachers tend to take a range of courses in a variety of disciplines in liberal arts departments. In most programs, the professional training in colleges does not concern itself to a large degree with the subject-matter knowledge that prospective teachers need in order to teach. Edmundson (1990), discussing a Study of the Education of Educators (SEE) in 29 institutions, states that "not one institution in our study has substantial coordination and integration across general and professional studies" (p. 718).

In rare cases the curriculum integrates subject-matter studies with professional studies such as courses on teaching methods. An example of such integration is provided by the teacher education programs of the Kibbutz movement in Israel. In these programs, subject domains are taught in a college of education with concurrent emphasis on educational and instructional issues. These programs may be more appropriate for the preparation of teachers because they tend to focus on pedagogical content knowledge, and not solely on the substantive knowledge of a discipline (Shulman 1987). Such programs reflect an orientation toward specific, rather than generic, aspects of learning to teach.

Loewenberg-Ball and McDiarmid (1990) claim that until the mid-1980s it was taken for granted that the teaching of subjects to trainee teachers was adequate and appropriate. Since the mid-1980s, however, questions have been raised concerning the adequacy of such preparation. Kennedy (1991), for example, argued that "majoring in an academic subject in college does not guarantee that teachers will have the kind of subject matter knowledge they need for teaching" (p. 14). Treatment of subject matter in a way that relates it to pedagogic issues may yield more valid and useful knowledge for prospective teachers. An emphasis on knowledge about an academic discipline and the development of positive dispositions toward the subject studied have been considered by some writers to be essential components of teacher education curricula (Loewenberg-Ball and McDiarmid 1990, Kennedy 1991).

3. *Foundation of Education Studies*

The nature of educational foundation studies in the curriculum of teacher education is a matter of some dispute among teacher educators. Sirotnik (1990) included history, philosophy, and sociology of education, as well as the study of contemporary issues and educational policy. Borman (1990) cited a study in which 20 different "foundation of education" courses offered in public and private institutions across the United States were examined. Multicultural education, philosophy of education, and history of education were the most frequently listed courses. Borman concluded that during the 1980s educational foundations as a field became more involved with educational equity issues. This emphasis contrasts with the earlier apolitical, more strictly disciplinary, and academically focused foundation studies.

Sirotnik (1990) claimed that students have perceived foundation courses as irrelevant and marginal and warned of the possibility of a serious erosion of foundational studies in teacher education programs. Similarly, Edmundson (1990) reported that foundation courses are usually an early element of programs and consist of haphazard collections of themes and topics. In reviewing studies undertaken in Japan, Sato and Ushiwata (1990) found that foundation studies, even though viewed as promoting professional development, were characteristically vague in their approach.

A proposed remedy to this situation is the integration of foundation studies with practical experience throughout the curriculum of teacher education (Sirotnik 1990). Borman (1990) argued for the need to strengthen the role of educational foundations in teacher education and claimed that "by developing normative, interpretive, and critical perspectives on the teaching and learning process and on institutional patterns and societal practices more generally, foundations scholars and teachers can and do play an important role in teacher education" (p. 401). It is apparent that educators in the 1990s have suggested curricular approaches that emphasize the construction of a dialectical relationship between theory and practice, placing theory in its concrete, real-life context.

4. *Professional Studies*

Professional studies may include methods courses, curriculum courses, and courses based on knowledge generated through research on teaching. The common prevailing view concerning the professional content of teacher education perceives it to be a component of preparation for which institutions of teacher education are specifically responsible. The skills and knowledge taught in these courses are supposed to have a direct bearing on professional practice.

Tom and Valli (1990) examined the professional knowledge base of teacher education from the point of view of contrasting epistemologies—positivistic, interpretive, and critical—and clarified the knowledge–practice relationship implied by each. For instance, in the positivistic epistemology, generalizations and rules specify a direct link between knowledge and practice using a "logistic" approach. The movement of competency-based teacher education (CBTE) exemplifies such an approach. Interpretive scholarship, on the other hand, may reveal and clarify unknown aspects of teaching. "Revealing the underlying complexities of teaching is generative in the sense that these revealed complexities can suggest novel means for teachers to achieve practical ends" (Tom and Valli 1990 p. 386). Finally, critically oriented teacher educators strive to examine inequalities in education and society and to encourage a commitment to social values and to emancipatory actions.

Methods courses that focus on rules of conduct for teachers may often lack an interpretive and critically oriented knowledge base, which draws on case studies and on learning from cases. A case literature in teacher education is developing, providing resources for more interpretive frames of relating theory to practice in professional studies (see *Teacher Education, Case Methods in*).

Two of the major categories suggested by Shulman (1987) as constituting the professional knowledge base of teaching, are pedagogical content knowledge and curriculum knowledge. Curriculum studies in teacher education programs serve to develop this knowledge base. The aim of such studies is to provide teachers with the knowledge and skills needed in order to implement and use available curricular materials and to participate in school-based curriculum development. There has been a growing demand for inclusion of curriculum studies as specific courses in teacher education (Ben-Peretz 1984, Goodman 1986). In this regard, Silberstein (1991) distinguished between generic curriculum courses, applicable to any subject taught in school, and curriculum courses oriented toward subject matter.

5. *The Practicum*

In many countries, the practicum is the most favorably viewed component of teacher education. Tisher (1990), focusing on teacher education in Australia, claimed "school experience to be an extremely important, practical, satisfying component of preservice education! The trainees say they gain a lot from it; that it is the most realistic aspect of their courses, helps reduce their anxiety about teaching, fosters their practical teaching skills . . . they feel it should be increased" (p. 75). The literature from Germany has viewed the practicum as a necessary and valuable, though also doubtful, component of teacher education programs (Klinzig 1990). Supervised practice is a central part of the German *Studienseminar*, a mandatory, postgraduate component of the teacher education process, focusing on induction into school life.

The time devoted to practice teaching varies greatly between institutions although there is a growing tendency to increase field-based experiences. An interesting view of the practicum was expressed by White (1989) who saw it as a "rite of passage" which allows neophytes to acquire cultural knowledge about teaching. One of the major strengths of the practicum is its focus on specialized teaching activities, thus counteracting one of the criticisms of teacher education programs; namely, their concentration on general aspects of schooling and lower regard for specialized activities (Lortie 1975).

Distinctions have been made between four different levels of the practicum (Furlong et al. 1988). Level (a) is direct practice; i.e., teaching experiences in schools. Level (b) is indirect practice; i.e., training conducted in classes or workshops in teacher education institutions. Level (c) is practical principles; i.e., the study of principles of practice. Finally, level (d) is disciplinary theory, the study of practice and its principles in the light of research and theory. The authors claimed that traditional teacher education programs engage students in levels (b), (c), and (d), before introducing them into direct practice. However, more school-based teacher education programs have been evolving (MacLennan and Seadon 1988).

Though the practicum tends to be highly valued by student teachers and practitioners, questions concerning the value of learning from these experiences have been raised (Feiman-Nemser and Buchman 1983). Edmundson (1990) claimed that student teaching experiences do not provide students with opportunities for reflective inquiry. Tom (1987) argued that teacher education curricula should replace pedagogical knowledge with pedagogical questions, using the reality of teaching as their starting point and addressing both moral and craft elements of teaching. Tom states that "as compared to topically organized knowledge, practice-based study tends to be a more potent form of learning for novice teachers" (p. 16). In a similar vein, Pearce and Pickard (1987) warned that "the practicality of practical studies cannot be rooted in a particular predetermined content. No checklist of skills or body of theory can correlate with the complexity of what it is to be a teacher, because what teachers do is necessarily bound up with what teachers are" (p. 42).

An example of an innovative teacher education program that reflects an approach to teacher education rooted in a personal practical knowledge perspective was described by Clandinin et al. (1992). In this program a collaborative group of 28 student teachers, 6 university teachers, and 28 school teachers worked together. Through sharing and responding to each other's stories, a new opportunity for teacher education was created. Dialogue journals, response groups, and renegotiated assignments were planned collaboratively and became central components of the curriculum of this alternative teacher-education program.

6. The Hidden Curriculum and the Null Curriculum

A discussion of the curriculum of teacher education programs is incomplete without reference to the hidden curriculum. Ginsburg and Clift (1990) conceptualized the hidden curriculum of teacher education as the messages transmitted to students through the institutional context, as well as the structure and processes of the programs themselves. They claimed that these messages relate to several themes. First, teaching is a low-status profession and teachers as a professional group lack power. Their field experiences expose student teachers to the low professional status of teaching. Their coursework communicates the message that college teachers hold power only over students and are "subordinated to administration, university professors and politicians" (Parsons and Beauchamp 1985 p. 55). The perception of teachers' lack of power is further reinforced by the notion that curriculum decision-making is not a central component of teachers' professional role (Ginsburg and Clift 1990).

Second, the hidden curriculum of teacher education tends to communicate a fragmented view of knowledge, both in coursework and in field experiences. Moreover, knowledge is "given" and unproblematic. These views of knowledge are likely to become quite problematic as teachers gain experience.

Teacher education programs can also be characterized by their "null curriculum"; that is, what is not included in the curriculum (Flinders et al. 1986). Examples include the ethics of teaching and the biological roots of human behavior. The development of professional dispositions (e.g. the disposition to suspend judgment about children, the consideration of alternative interpretations of situations) is not commonly included as a goal of teacher education programs (Katz and Raths 1985). Uncovering the null curriculum of teacher education programs may have far-reaching implications for the development of programs.

7. Issues and Possible Directions

Several questions can be posed to highlight some of the basic curriculum issues confronting teacher educators. First, should the curriculum focus on generic or on specific aspects of the knowledge of teaching? The curriculum may aim at introducing students to generic aspects of teaching, such the use of varied instructional strategies. Conversely, the curriculum may attempt to provide students with methods that can be used to teach specific subject matters in a variety of educational settings.

Second, what is the proper relationship between theory and practice? Theory may be seen as guiding practice through a process of translation and application. In contrast, theory may be seen as being derived from practice. That is, practice is itself a fluid and changeable theory in action (McKeon 1952).

Third, what is the role of the innovative curriculum in teacher education? Innovation can impact on the choice of content to be included in the curriculum, on the institutional context of teacher education programs, and on the structure of courses included in a program. For example, rather than have separate courses in educational foundations, it may be possible to have "reflective seminars in which students could discuss critically their daily experiences in schools and relate them to their foundational studies" (Sirotnik 1990 p. 716).

It is important to note that reform movements such as the Holmes Group (1986) and the Carnegie Forum on Education and the Economy (1987) have proposed that preservice teacher education should be extended and made more academically demanding. At the same time, however, students are being called on to play a more active role in planning and directing their programs and the educational experiences they encounter within them.

See also: Teacher Education, Case Methods in

References

Ben-Peretz M 1984 Curriculum theory and practice in teacher education programs. In: Katz L G, Raths J D (eds.) 1984 *Advances in Teacher Education*, Vol. 1. Ablesc, Norwood, New Jersey

Ben-Peretz M 1990 Research on teacher education in Israel: Topics, methods and findings. In: Tisher R P, Wideen M F (eds.) 1990

Borman K M 1990 Foundations of Education in Teacher Education. In: Houston W R, Haberman M, Sikula G (eds.). 1990

Carnegie Forum on Education and the Economy (Task Force on Teaching as a Profession) 1987 *A Nation Prepared: Teachers for the Twenty-first Century*. Carnegie Commission on the Improvement of Teaching, New York

Clandinin D G, Davis A, Hogan P, Kennan B 1992 *Learning to Teach, Teaching to Learn: Stories of Collaboration in Teacher Education*. Teachers College Press, New York

Edmundson P G 1990 A normative look at the curriculum in teacher education. *Phi Del. Kap*. 71(9): 717–22

Feiman-Nemser S, Buchman M 1983 Pitfalls of experience in teacher education. In: Tamir P, Hofstein A, Ben-Peretz M (eds.) 1983 *Preservice and Inservice Education of Science Teachers*. Balaban International Science Services, Philadelphia, Pennsylvania

Flinders D G, Noddings N, Thornton S J 1986 The null curriculum: Its theoretical basis and practical implications. *Curric. Inq.* 16(1): 33–42
Furlong V T, Hirst P H, Pocklington K, Miles S 1988 *Initial Teacher Training and the Role of Schools*. Open University Press, Milton Keynes
Ginsburg M B, Clift R T 1990 The hidden curriculum of pre-service teacher education. In: Houston W R, Habberman M, Sikula G (eds.) 1990
Goodman J 1986 Teaching preservice teachers a critical approach to curriculum design: A descriptive account. *Curric. Inq.* 16(2): 179–201
Govinda R, Buch M B 1990 Indian research in teacher education: A review. In: Tisher R P, Wideen M F (eds.) 1990
Holmes Group 1986 *Tomorrow's Teachers*. Holmes Group, East Lansing, Michigan
Houston W R, Haberman M, Sikula G (eds.) 1990 *Handbook of Research on Teacher Education*. Macmillan Inc., New York
Katz L G, Raths J D 1985 Dispositions as goals for teacher education. *Teaching and Teacher Educ.* 1(4): 301–07
Kennedy M M 1991 Some surprising findings in how teachers learn to teach. *Educ. Leadership* 49(3): 14–17
Kieviet F K 1990 A decade of research on teacher education in the Netherlands. In: Tisher R P, Wideen M F (eds.) 1990
Klinzig H G 1990 Research on teacher education in West Germany. In: Tisher R P, Wideen M F (eds.) 1990
Loewenberg-Ball D L, McDiarmid G W 1990 The subject matter preparation of teachers. In: Houston W R, Haberman M, Sikula G (eds.) 1990 *Handbook of Research on Teacher Education*. Macmillan Inc., New York
Lortie D 1975 *Schoolteacher: A Sociological Study*. Chicago University Press, Chicago, Illinois
MacLennan S, Seadon T 1988 What price school based work? Reflections on a school sited PGCE method course. *Camb. J. Educ.* 18(3): 387–403
Martin J R 1976 What should we do with a hidden curriculum when we find one? *Curric. Inq.*,6(2): 135–51
McKeon R 1952 Philosophy and action. *Ethics* 62(2): 79–100
McNamara D 1990 Research on teacher training in a changing society: The case of Britain in the late 1980s. In: Tisher R P, Wideen M F (eds.) 1990
Parsons G, Beauchamp L 1985 The hidden curriculum of student teacher evaluation. ERIC Document Reproduction Service ED 261983, Washington, DC
Pearce G, Pickard A 1987 Being a teacher: towards an epistemology of practical studies. In: Smyth G (ed.) 1987 *Educating Teachers: Changing the Nature of Pedagogical Knowledge*. Falmer Press, London
Sato A, Ushiwata G 1990 Research on teacher education in Japan. In: Tisher R P, Wideen M F (eds.) 1990
Shulman L S 1987 Knowledge and teaching: Foundations of the new reform. *Harv. Educ. Rev.* 57(1): 1–22
Silberstein M 1991 Curriculum studies in teacher education. In: Lewy A (ed.) 1991 *International Encyclopedia of Curriculum*. McGraw-Hill, London
Sirotnik K E 1990 On the eroding foundations of teacher education. *Phi Del. Kap.* 71(9): 710–16
Tisher R P 1990 One and a half decades of research on teacher education in Australia. In: Tisher R P, Wideen M F (eds.) 1990
Tisher R P, Wideen M F (eds.) 1990 *Research in Teacher Education: International Perspectives*. Falmer Press, London
Tom A R 1987 Replacing pedagogical knowledge with pedagogical questions. In: Smyth M (ed.) 1987 *Educating Teachers: Changing the Nature of Pedagogical Knowledge*. Falmer Press, London
Tom A R, Valli L 1990 Professional knowledge for teachers. In: Houston W R, Haberman M, Sikula G (eds.) 1990
White J W 1989 Student teaching as a rite of passage. *Anthropol. Educ. Q.* 20(3): 177–95

M. Ben-Peretz

Teacher Education Programs: Structure

The structure of programs for the initial preparation of teachers is examined in this entry from several perspectives: (a) the nature of the institutional setting in which the program is offered, (b) the length and sequence of the program, and (c) the structure of the knowledge and skills included in the program. A brief examination of each perspective follows, along with a discussion of the relationship of initial teacher education to induction into the profession and ongoing inservice education.

1. Structure of Settings for Initial Teacher Preparation

Although there is variation in the design and structure of preparation programs nearly all are found within institutions of postsecondary education. Types of institutions of higher education offering programs range from those that exist for the sole purpose of preparing teachers to large universities in which teacher education may be just a small part of the overall instruction, research, and service mission.

1.1 Teachers' Colleges

Professional schools are a relatively new phenomenon in the history of higher education. Until the nineteenth century most professions consisted of individuals who were considered generally well-educated, either by virtue of having had a university education (baccalaureate) or as a result of private tutoring, and who had served a period of apprenticeship under an established practitioner of the profession. However, as a profession, teaching fell short even of this standard; it was regarded simply as the transmission of information and values. Consequently, there was an expectation that if one "possessed" the knowledge, then one could transmit it to others with little or no formal preparation in teaching. Teachers for primary grades could have as little as 8 years of schooling. During the twentieth century the number of years of formal education required for teachers has steadily increased. In the 1990s, in nearly all countries, 3 to 4 years of college/university preparation is the standard.

The history of teacher education in the United Kingdom provides a common example. Until the late nineteenth century, teachers in the primary schools were basically required to be of good character and to have mastered the content they were to teach only at the level of mastery of the grade level they were to teach. Preparation of teachers for the secondary schools was nonexistent. Universal education of the citizenry at the secondary level did not exist. Only the small portion of the populace destined to become well-educated had the privilege of a secondary education, and secondary teachers were selected from among those who had studied an academic discipline at the university level (Thomas 1990).

In the late 1800s, specialized institutions for the preparation of teachers began in the United Kingdom and the United States with the founding of "seminaries" or "normal schools." These were single-purpose institutions only serving students preparing to become teachers, and usually offering programs which extended 2 years beyond the completion of a secondary school program. In the United States the movement to require secondary teachers to undergo pedagogical training was accompanied by extension of the two-year programs for elementary teachers in normal schools to full four-year programs leading to the baccalaureate degree. Normal schools also offered degrees for secondary teachers, usually with an academic major in "secondary education," which included concentrated study in an academic discipline.

The expansion to four-year degrees required extensive growth in the curricular offerings in the liberal arts and sciences in order to provide sufficient breadth and depth. With the move to four-year status, the "normal schools" became "teachers' colleges," both in name and in purpose. Similar institutions, called Colleges of Advanced Education, were established in Australia in the mid-1900s.

Few institutions of higher education at the close of the twentieth century include the term "teachers' college" in the institutional title. Most institutions which began as "normal schools" subsequently became "teachers' colleges," then "state colleges" (offering liberal arts degrees and a limited range of professional programs) and many today include the term "university" in their title. The distinguishing characteristics of these institutions, regardless of title, are that they have maintained a clear primary purpose of preparing teachers, the range of other baccalaureate programs is limited, and they offer few, if any, graduate programs (usually only master's degrees in education.) With few exceptions, these population. The commitment to teacher education exemplified by these institutions is reflected in the principles of the Renaissance Group (1990), including a commitment to campus-wide involvement in teacher education.

1.2 Liberal Arts Colleges

The liberal arts colleges are smaller institutions that provide education at the baccalaureate level with a primary focus on in-depth studies within an academic discipline and a well-rounded "general education" in the liberal arts and sciences. Offering teacher education programs is a relatively new objective for many liberal arts colleges. The majority of liberal arts colleges are private, rather than publicly supported, and the majority of these private colleges are supported by, or affiliated with, one or more religious organizations.

The liberal arts colleges have limited historical links to the professions—primarily restricted to providing baccalaureate study, which is seen as preparatory to entry to the ministry and to the medical professions. As professional programs have been added these have been cast in the context of the general goals of the liberal arts institution. Students undertaking a teacher education or a nursing curriculum have often been expected to complete coursework in these areas as electives within an overall program with the same graduation requirements as those for students not in professional programs.

Liberal arts colleges tend to share the following characteristics. Professional programs have a lower priority within them than liberal arts programs, as the allocation of institutional resources reflects. Graduate program offerings have been limited, if they have existed at all, but the situation is changing in this respect as financial conditions have led many liberal arts colleges to develop focused master's degree programs to serve a local area adult student population. The colleges are relatively small (20–50 teacher graduates per year) and attract primarily a state and regional student population (exceptions would be the few best known liberal arts colleges, which serve a national and international student population). Finally, teacher education programs in these institutions are usually administered by a Department of Education, whose faculty members teach the courses in pedagogy and supervise field experiences.

1.3 Comprehensive Colleges and Universities

There exists a large number of colleges and universities which either were created as multipurpose institutions or evolved as such from single-purpose institutions. For those institutions within this group which offer only the baccalaureate degree, the primary factor which distinguishes them from teachers' colleges and liberal arts colleges is the fact that they award a significant portion of their degrees in two or more professional or occupational disciplines such as engineering, business administration, nursing, and education. Within these institutions, however, teacher education typically does not hold any special priority.

Included within this group are institutions which

offer graduate programs through the master's degree. In the United States approximately 60 percent of these institutions are public institutions and 40 percent are private. Characteristics of these institutions include a heavy commitment to instruction and service and less emphasis on research, some degree of role confusion and ambivalence as to future aspirations of the institution (particularly in relationship to growth in breadth of program offerings and addition of graduate programs), and a separate college or school of education as an administrative unit on par with schools or colleges of arts and sciences, business, and engineering.

1.4 Research and Doctorate-granting Universities

The final type of higher education institution in which teacher education programs are found is the university which offers doctoral programs. In the United States these institutions are further categorized by the Carnegie Foundation for the Advancement of Teaching into two subtypes. "Research Universities" offer a full range of programs up to and including the doctorate, award at least 50 doctorates annually, give a high priority to research, and receive significant federal grant funds to support research. "Doctorate-Granting Universities" also offer a full range of programs through to the doctorate, usually award fewer doctorates annually in fewer program areas, place less emphasis on research as an institutional priority, and have limited federal grant funding in support of research.

In both types of doctorate-granting institutions the teacher education program is typically located in a separate school or college of education. Programmatic relationships between the school or college of education and other schools or colleges in the university tend to focus more on relationships based on doctoral programs and faculty research than on the basic teacher preparation program. In the United States approximately 100 of these institutions are members of and have endorsed the principles of the Holmes Group (1986) or the Renaissance Group (1990).

2. Structure of Programs: Time and Organization

The number of countries in which teacher preparation begins in upper secondary school is diminishing rapidly. The worldwide trend is toward requiring a minimum of a bachelor's degree for programs to prepare teachers. Ghani (1990) summarized data gathered in the mid-1980s on teacher preparation in developing countries in four regions of the world. He found the total number of years of education (primary/elementary, secondary, postsecondary) for primary/elementary teachers in 24 countries to range from 8 in Nigeria, to 16 in Sri Lanka. For secondary teachers in these 24 countries the total years of education ranged from 14 in Nepal and Afghanistan, to 18 in Malaysia (for "upper-level secondary"). Ghani reported a trend toward requiring more general education as well as more extensive professional/pedagogical training.

Distinctions between the amount and nature of educational preparation for primary teachers and secondary teachers are also disappearing. An example of this is the increase from 2 years to 4 years in professional preparation required for elementary teachers in Taiwan, a change that was implemented in 1988. In several states in the United States an additional year of postbaccalaureate study is required. In fact, some institutions of higher education have chosen to offer their teacher education programs only at the postbaccalaureate level. Consequently, worldwide there are a number of arrangements whereby the teacher candidate engages in preparation for the profession.

2.1 Four-year Programs

The majority of teacher preparation programs are conducted within the context of a four-year program leading to a baccalaureate degree. The exceptions are of two types: those programs designed intentionally to take 5 years, and those programs to which requirements have been added, either within the pedagogical component of the program or in academic major disciplines, with the result that it has become impossible for students to complete the program in 4 years.

Four-year programs may be further described in three types of program organization.

(a) *Continuous four-year programs*. In these programs the student is admitted to the professional education program at the beginning of college studies, with the professional or pedagogical component of the baccalaureate studies beginning in the first year and continuing through to the completion of the degree program.

(b) *"One-plus-three" programs*. These programs require students to complete 1 year of college work in general studies and/or the academic major prior to formal admission to the professional teacher education program. In these programs professional or pedagogical studies typically begin in the second year of college and continue through to the completion of the baccalaureate program.

(c) *"Two-plus-two" programs*. The third design for four-year programs is the "two-plus-two" design, in which students are admitted after the completion of 2 years of college study. During the first 2 years they are generally expected to have completed general education or "core" studies as well as significant work on a major in an academic discipline. This third type of program design is found most frequently in institutions with strong links to junior (or community) colleges that offer the first 2 years of college study.

2.2 Five-year Programs

A small number of institutions of higher education offer programs of study for prospective teachers which are intentionally designed to take five full academic years to complete. These programs also vary as to point of entry, in the same manner as the four-year programs. Some institutions grant a baccalaureate degree at the completion of the five-year program; some grant a baccalaureate degree at the completion of the first 4 years (when requirements for a liberal arts degree have been met) and grant a master's degree upon completion of the fifth year.

2.3 Fifth-year Programs

An increasing number of institutions have developed teacher preparation programs which are conducted entirely at the postbaccalaureate degree level. These programs require that students hold a baccalaureate degree with a major in the liberal arts or sciences for admission. All professional coursework and field experiences are offered within the context of a master's degree program. During the 1960s and early 1970s a number of Master of Arts in Teaching programs were developed in order to qualify persons who had already completed a liberal arts degree.

The Carnegie Forum on Education and the Economy recommended, in the report of its Task Force on Teaching as a Profession (1986), that all teacher education become a graduate-level enterprise, built upon substantive study in the arts and sciences at the undergraduate level. The graduate degree, to be offered by graduate schools of education, would emphasize systematic study of teaching and clinical experiences. The Holmes Group (1986), a consortium of schools of education in American research universities, has also adopted this position. A number of American universities offer master's degree programs of this kind.

3. Structure of Learning in Teacher Education Programs

Teacher education programs are organized and structured according to a sequence of courses and the balancing of on-campus and in-school experiences. Another basis for structuring teacher education programs uses learning as the framework. The different components of knowledge and skills that teachers need become the basis for organizing the program. This approach establishes program structure on an established knowledge base.

In the United States, the National Council for Accreditation of Teacher Education (1992) has outlined parameters for a knowledge base. The first of its standards for accreditation of programs states that "professional education programs are based on essential knowledge, established and current research findings, and sound professional practice" (p. 47). Judgments about accrediting a teacher education program are based on the degree to which faculty have developed, and students have an understanding of, this knowledge base.

Galluzzo and Pankratz (1990) have described five attributes of a knowledge base: (a) a collectively held and systematically reinforced set of beliefs that guides program development and instruction; (b) a focus on organizing those beliefs in a manner that reflects the ultimate purpose of the program; (c) explicit descriptions of the knowledge, skills, and dispositions that a program graduate should possess; (d) a set of source documents that describe the essential knowledge that a program graduate needs; and (e) a model or a series of models that show how the various elements form an integrated program.

In the past, major distinctions existed between the knowledge that future teachers needed to acquire in regard to subject matter and pedagogy. In fact, these two domains of knowledge were formerly presented by higher education faculty housed in separate schools or departments. The future teacher had the implicit responsibility of synthesizing and integrating knowledge learned about subject matter from one group of faculty members with knowledge learned about pedagogy from a different faculty. This dichotomy is dissolving in the 1990s and there is a new appreciation of the importance of integration of learnings from different fields. Four general domains of knowledge are now being addressed in the preparation of teachers.

3.1 General Education

There is a body of knowledge and skills that all college graduates should possess as educated citizens. These expectations are true for all students across the campus, regardless of academic major or professional aspirations. This domain includes the ability to communicate in written and oral language, basic computational and mathematical skill, the uses of technology, and general knowledge of history, literature, the arts, and the sciences.

3.2 Content Knowledge

Teachers need to have an in-depth knowledge of the subject matter they will be teaching. The depth of knowledge expected will vary by the level of teaching that is anticipated. For example, preschool through fifth grade (elementary school) teachers should have basic subject-matter knowledge across a number of fields, since they will be expected to teach a wide array of topics. In contrast, grades 6–8 (middle-school) teachers are expected to have in-depth knowledge in two subject fields, since they will most likely be part of an interdisciplinary team and be teaching in two subject areas. Grades 9–12 (high school) teachers are expected to have extensive knowledge of a subject matter in one area, which will be their primary teaching assignment. However, knowledge of subject matter alone is not sufficient preparation to become an effective teacher.

3.3 Pedagogical Knowledge

Knowing how to teach is another critical domain for successful teaching. Future teachers need to develop an array of knowledge and skills related to the act of teaching. Many of these tend to be independent from the subject matter and level being taught. Pedagogical knowledge includes such areas as learning theories, strategies for assessing student learning, classroom management, use of technology in teaching, and multicultural issues in education.

3.4 Pedagogical Content Knowledge

Perhaps the most important of these four domains and certainly the most complex is that of pedagogical content knowledge (PCK). Shulman (1986) proposed the concept of PCK as a result of studies of novice and expert teachers. PCK represents more than a simple combination of general knowledge, content knowledge, and pedagogical knowledge. While it is an amalgam of these, it is also a representation of additional knowledge and skills that expert teachers possess.

Included in PCK is knowledge of typical misconceptions that students will have when learning a particular concept. PCK entails having knowledge of and the ability to draw upon powerful analogies, illustrations, examples, explanations, and demonstrations that will make sense to specific students. It also includes knowledge of the background of experiences and culture that learners bring to the classroom and the frames of reference they bring to the learning of specific subject-matter concepts and principles. The concept of pedagogical content knowledge has become an organizing force in the redesign of teacher education programs (Cochran 1991).

4. Relationships Among Preservice, Induction, and Inservice

Since the mid-1980s there has been a rapid growth in induction programs designed to provide special training, support, and evaluation for beginning teachers. All of these aspects of professional development of a teacher may be described in a continuum of shared involvement between higher education and the schools. Both are involved throughout the career of a teacher, with the institution of higher education having the greatest involvement in the earliest stages of formal teacher preparation, less involvement as the teacher moves through induction, and still less as the teacher undergoes inservice education throughout his or her career. Conversely, although they are involved throughout all stages, the level of involvement and responsibility of the schools in the professional education and development of teachers follows an inverted path to that of institutions of higher education. Formal partnerships between colleges or universities and schools have resulted in this shared responsibility becoming more systematic, effective, and efficient.

See also: Teacher Education Programs: Curriculum; Teacher Education, Governance of; Teacher Educators, Characteristics of

References

Carnegie Forum on Education and Economy Task Force on Teaching as a Profession 1986 *A Nation Prepared: Teachers for the 21st Century*. Carnegie Forum on Education and the Economy, New York

Cochran K F, King R A, DeRuiter J A 1991 Pedagogical content knowledge: A tentative model for teacher preparation. Paper presented at the annual meeting of the American Educational Research Association, Chicago. ERIC Document Reproduction Service No. ED 340 683, Washington, DC

Galluzzo G R, Pankratz R S 1990 Five attributes of a teacher education program knowledge base. *J. Teach. Educ.* 41(4): 7–14

Ghani Z 1990 Pre-service teacher education in developing countries. In: Rust V D, Dalin P (eds.) 1990 *Teachers and Teaching in the Developing World*. Garland, New York

National Council for the Accreditation of Teacher Education 1992 *Standards, Procedures, and Policies for the Accreditation of Professional Education Units*. NCATE, Washington, DC

Shulman L S 1986 Those who understand: Knowledge growth in teaching. *Educ. Researcher* 15(2): 4–14

The Holmes Group 1986 *Tomorrow's Teachers: A Report of the Holmes Group*, The Holmes Group Michigan State University, East Lansing, Michigan

The Renaissance Group 1990 *Teachers for a New World: A Statement of Principles of the Renaissance Group*. The Renaissance Group, College of Education, University of Northern Iowa, Cedar Falls, Iowa

Thomas J B (ed.) 1990 *British Universities and Teacher Education: A Century of Change*. Falmer Press, London

Further Reading

Collins K A 1989 The development of teacher education in Japan 1868–1980s. *Teaching and Teacher Education* 5: 217–28

Goodlad J L, Soder R, Sirotnik K A (eds.) 1990 *Teachers for Our Nation's Schools*. Jossey-Bass, San Francisco, California

Houston W R (ed.) 1990 *Handbook of Research on Teacher Education*. Macmillan, New York

Howsam R B, Corrigan D C, Denemark G W 1985 *Educating a Profession*. American Association of Colleges for Teacher Education, Washington, DC

National Institute for Educational Research (NIER) 1989 *Teacher Training in Japan*. NIER Occasional Paper 03/89. NIER, Tokyo (ERIC Document Reproduction Service No. ED 313 360)

Reynolds M (ed.) 1989 *Knowledge Base for the Beginning Teacher*. American Association of Colleges for Teacher Education, Washington, DC

Smith B O 1980 *Design for a School of Pedagogy*. US Office of Education (ERIC Document Reproduction Service No. ED 193 215)

Voorbach J T, Prick L G M 1989 *Teacher Education 5: Research and Developments on Teacher Education in the Netherlands*. SVO, The Hague

M. J. Gimmestad; G. E. Hall

Teacher Education, Supervision in

Supervision in teacher education programs occurs mainly during field experiences and, particularly, during student teaching. Supervision of teacher education students is conducted primarily by a college or university supervisor and a cooperating teacher, the teacher in whose classroom the teacher education student is working. This entry examines the purposes of supervision and the roles of these two major actors in the supervision process. It also identifies problems and issues related to the supervision of teacher education students, reviews major research findings and conceptual models for conducting supervision, and presents emergent trends and issues.

1. Purposes of Supervision

The major purpose of supervision is to help the teacher education student become a competent teacher. Through a variety of field experiences in elementary or secondary classrooms, including student teaching, teacher education students attempt to implement what they have learned in their teacher education courses as well as gaining practical experience in teaching and managing a classroom. Although teacher education students consistently describe their student teaching as the most valuable element in their preparation for teaching, many researchers criticize student teaching as being atheoretical, lacking a standard structure, and being overly dependent on an outmoded apprenticeship model. During student teaching both the cooperating teacher and the university supervisor supervise and guide the student teacher's development.

Unfortunately, the goals of supervision are too often not agreed upon, unarticulated, or lack congruence with the rest of the teacher education program. The student teaching experience, where most supervision occurs, seems to have two contrasting major conceptualizations, perhaps best articulated by Dewey (1904). One conception is that of apprenticeship, where university supervisors and cooperating teachers assist students in gaining techniques and feelings of self-confidence that will help them survive more comfortably within existing school situations, without questioning the status quo. A number of researchers conclude that this apprenticeship model predominates in teacher education. The other conception is more akin to a laboratory experience where the student teacher receives supervisory assistance in developing habits of personal inquiry and reflection about teaching and the contexts in which it occurs. In this conception, student teachers are taught and encouraged to consider a range of possibilities beyond the existing school situation.

Depending on which of these two conceptualizations is held by the university supervisor and cooperating teacher, their expectations for themselves and the student teacher will differ remarkably. One study that examined 122 cooperating teachers and 25 university supervisors (Cleary 1988) found that cooperating teachers exhibited significantly more conventional thinking than university supervisors and stifled student teachers' inclinations to function as agents of change. In other words, they were more inclined toward the apprenticeship model than the laboratory model.

2. The Role of Cooperating Teachers and University Supervisors

Both cooperating teachers and university supervisors are important to the success of the student teaching experience. However, as might be expected, they play somewhat different roles.

2.1 Cooperating Teachers

Cooperating teachers are expected to be exemplary practitioners of teaching so that student teachers can observe and emulate good practice. In addition, cooperating teachers' perceptions of their roles as supervisors include helping student teachers develop competence in classroom management, lesson planning, and lesson delivery (O'Neal 1983).

Grimmett and Ratzlaff (1986) compared studies from the United States and Canada regarding expectations about the role of cooperating teachers as held by student teachers, university supervisors, and cooperating teachers. In both countries, cooperating teachers were expected to hold conferences with their student teachers and to provide instruction on skills of presentation and classroom management. The same researchers found that cooperating teachers were generally unprepared for the task of student teaching supervision. Boothroyd (1979) found similar results in England.

Zimpher et al. (1980) reported that many cooperating teachers were not interested in observing student teachers. They perceived student teachers as aides who could help lessen their workload. Thus, being an effective classroom teacher does not ensure that an individual will be an effective cooperating teacher.

Evidence from a number of studies suggests that training cooperating teachers for their roles is effective and is a policy supported by the teachers themselves. For example, in a study at a Canadian university, Twa (1984) found that, as a result of training, cooperating teachers valued their clinical-supervision expertise, improved their supervisory skills, felt more comfortable as supervisors, and were more eager to accept student teachers. By common assent, the skills that are needed by cooperating teachers include the ability to observe well, to provide constructive criticism to guide student teachers in their practices, and to provide encouragement and support.

What are the incentives for teachers to become cooperating teachers? Guyton (1987) found that teachers wanted to work with student teachers because they believed student teaching to be important, felt they had something to offer and had a professional responsibility to prepare new teachers, thought they would gain new ideas, believed they would enhance their pupils' performance by having two adults working in the classroom, thought they would enjoy sharing ideas and working with another adult and thereby revitalize themselves as teachers. Others have identified money, recognition of the cooperating teacher's role, special status, and the opportunity to take tuition-free university courses as incentives. Although money may be a motivation for some, cooperating teachers are poorly compensated by universities for their services. Honoraria for supervising a student teacher in the United States in the early 1990s typically ranged from US$25 to US$500, with the average approximately US$100 or less.

Although the processes for the selection of cooperating teachers vary, colleges and universities typically have little control over the settings in which they place student teachers and in the selection and qualifications of the cooperating teachers in those settings. Schools, rather than universities, assign cooperating teachers and often make the assignments on the basis of who volunteers, whose turn it is, or for other political or administrative reasons. As a consequence, quality control is often a problem.

2.2 *University Supervisors*

In many ways the role of the university supervisor overlaps that of the cooperating teacher. Both are expected to observe, provide feedback, and encourage and support the student teacher's development as a professional. Although some studies show that university supervisors have as much or more influence with student teachers in comparison with cooperating teachers (Boschee et al. 1978), many more studies indicate that cooperating teachers have the major influence on student teachers (Koehler 1984, Yee 1969, Zimpher et al. 1980). In a survey of 500 randomly selected student teachers in England and Wales, for example, almost 75 percent reported that their cooperating teachers were of greater help than their university supervisors (Yates 1982). This finding is hardly surprising, since the cooperating teacher works in close contact with the student teacher for 300 hours or more during the student teaching practice or practicum, while the university supervisor is unlikely to spend more than 10 to 20 hours with the student teacher.

At many universities the supervision of student teachers has low status and is often assigned to junior faculty, graduate students, or tenured faculty members who are not regarded as having a useful function in other areas. Student teachers and cooperating teachers generally perceive few differences in the supervisory effectiveness of university faculty and graduate students, and between those who had had significant teaching experiences and those who had not (Lamb and Montague 1982).

Supervisors typically visit student teachers once a week or every other week, spending 30–90 minutes with each student. Full-time university supervisors may be assigned as few as 12, or as many as 36 student teachers. Heavy assignments are common and often reduce the time a supervisor can spend working intensively with the student teacher. Consequently, many university supervisors are unable to provide substantial observation, data collection, and feedback for the student teacher. Their role is often reduced to one of liaison and moral support (Koehler 1984).

3. *Problems of Supervision*

Communication among the members of the student teaching triad (student teacher, cooperating teacher, and university supervisor) is often reported to be a problem. Areas of difficulty include uncertain role expectations, university–school communications, and interpersonal interactions. Yee (1969) observed that groups consisting of three members are inherently unstable since there is a strong tendency for two members of such groups to bond together and isolate the third member. Since the cooperating teacher and the student teacher work together for long periods of time each day, whereas the university supervisor is only periodically a member of the group, the supervisor is most likely to become the isolated member of the group. Stones and Morris (1972) also reported considerable research evidence of conflicting values among student teachers, cooperating teachers, and supervisors.

Inadequate training and lack of time also create difficulties for cooperating teachers and supervisors. One study in the United States reported that most schools, colleges, and departments of education have fewer than 20 percent of their cooperating teachers trained in supervision (Johnson and Yates 1982), even though, as mentioned, considerable evidence exists that shows the training of cooperating teachers for their roles to be effective and that cooperating teachers support the idea of special training for themselves. Lack of time and funding seem to be the major impediments in supporting these training programs.

Evaluation of student teachers is another problem area. Gatekeeping, or determining entrance to the profession, is one of the major functions of the student teaching experience. In most programs, assigning the final grades for student teaching is the responsibility of the university supervisor, but the cooperating teacher often has a say. The possibility of disagreements occurring is quite real, particularly if poor communication has existed.

For the university supervisor, having the dual responsibilities of helper and evaluator often creates problems in developing a close, trusting relationship with the student teacher. The evaluation function of supervision may lead some student teachers to attempt to project a positive image of themselves to the supervisor, rather than admitting a weakness or problem area. Differences in opinions between the supervisor and the cooperating teacher regarding the performance of the student teacher is another potential area of tension.

4. Models of Supervision

Several models of supervision have been proposed. These differ in terms of the theoretical underpinnings and the extent of their application.

4.1 Contrasting Approaches

Most of the models of supervision have been developed with, and applied to, the supervision of experienced teachers. These include clinical supervision (Goldhammer 1969, Cogan 1973), counseling supervision (Mosher and Purpel 1972), and developmental supervision (Glickman 1985). Little research exists about supervisory practice in teacher education based on the application of these models. In a review of research on university supervision of student teaching, Zimpher (1987) identified three contrasting supervisory approaches that have been studied in preservice teacher education: Siedentop's use of an applied behavioral approach; Gitlin's model of horizontal supervision; and Copeland's studies of directive and nondirective supervision.

Siedentop's research program was designed to develop a model of supervision based on behavior analysis that could impact student teacher behavior. The model enables supervisors and others: (a) to agree on a set of teacher behaviors or competencies; (b) to design a reliable and valid system for observing the behaviors; (c) to observe significant student teacher behavior change as a result of the observation/feedback intervention; and (d) to ensure continuation of the behavior change through regular feedback and follow-up.

In Gitlin's horizontal supervision, supervisors and student teachers together established and defined goals. Lessons focusing on the goals were observed and comparisons were made of the student teachers' practice compared with the intent. Case studies of this model in action demonstrated that its use led to more reflective and self-evaluative prospective teachers, who viewed teaching holistically rather than as a set of technical skills.

Copeland conducted a series of studies comparing directive supervision (offering the teacher immediate and useful advice for overcoming instructional problems) and nondirective supervision (asking questions to solicit the teacher's opinions and suggestions, reflecting the teacher's ideas, and offering information only as the teacher requested it). Copeland discovered that student teachers preferred the directive approach early in the internship but progressed toward a preference for the nondirective approach by the end of the teaching experience. He concluded that the university supervisor and the cooperating teacher might well initiate conferences and feedback more directly early in student teaching, but move toward a more nondirective approach as the student teacher gained the ability to be more self-analytic toward teaching.

Copeland's findings are consistent with Glickman's (1985) theory of developmental supervision, in which the supervisor uses a directive, collaborative, or nondirective orientation to supervision depending on the teacher's ability and willingness to assume responsibility for improvement. Copeland's results may help to explain how such contrasting approaches as Siedentop's and Gitlin's can each be viewed as effective. That is, they show, depending on the student teacher's maturity and ability to be self-analytical, that both highly prescriptive and reflective approaches to supervision can work. This suggests, however, that the supervisor and cooperating teacher need to assess the student teacher's capabilities and to modify their supervisory approaches as the student teacher develops greater reflective abilities.

4.2 Theoretical Paradigms

May and Zimpher (1986) examined the theoretical underpinnings of different approaches to supervision and concluded that most seem to be rooted in three major world views or paradigms: (a) positivism; (b) phenomenology; (c) critical theory. The positivist's perspective in supervisory practice shows itself as behavioristic, technical, or rationalistic. A supervisor with a positivistic view would tend to diagnose problems during observation, prescribe effective courses of action with reinforcement, and evaluate to see if the objectives were mastered. Siedentop's model of supervision reflects a positivistic perspective.

The phenomenological view of supervisory practice reflects humanistic concerns. Supervisors who work from this perspective care about student teachers' values, their views of the classroom, and their feelings. Such supervisors see their role as helping student teachers develop their own teaching styles, based on their own values and attitudes. Knowledge and teaching are highly individualized and personal. The supervisor's role is more that of counselor than trainer and ranges in style from nondirective to collaborative.

The critical theorist supervisor wants to help to create a better world and addresses the question of "what ought to be." Values of justice, equality, and happiness guide the critical theorist supervisor's work with student teachers. Such supervisors work to help prospective teachers assume a greater role in shaping educational environments that exemplify these core values. They believe that teaching is a reflective, moral, and ethical action. Gitlin's model of horizontal supervision exemplifies a critical theory perspective.

May and Zimpher (1986) concluded that supervisory practice in teacher education programs has been eclectic, rather than rooted in any one theoretical position. Moreover, the array of labels and models of supervision has often confused and masked the underlying belief systems that guided particular supervisory approaches.

Sergiovanni (1982) urged the development of a theory of supervisory practice concerned with three major questions, each of which can be addressed in the three paradigms of thinking described above: What is going on in this classroom? What ought to be going on? And what do these events, activities, and aspirations mean? He goes on to say:

> Establishing what is requires the development of accurate descriptions and explanations of the real world of teaching. Establishing what ought to be requires that one give attention to stated values and attempt to discover those more implicit in teacher and teaching. Establishing what events mean requires a closer study of classroom life and its events in pursuit of understanding. Establishing meaning requires that supervisors cultivate the art of interpretation (p. 68).

Effective supervisors, then, need to be able to answer each of these questions regardless of which of the three paradigms the supervisor embraces.

4.3 *Alternative Approaches*

Dissatisfaction with traditional types of student teaching supervision has resulted in various proposals to remedy the problems. At one extreme are proposals to abolish the role of the university supervisor, based on empirical evidence that cooperating teachers are more influential and university supervisors add little of value. Such proposals would simply shift issues of evaluation to the cooperating teacher and enhance the apprenticeship model of learning to teach, a model that has many critics.

A more promising alternative is that proposed by Emans (1983), who reviewed the professional literature on student teaching and supervisory practices and concluded that the roles of university supervisor and cooperating teacher should be redesigned. He proposed changing the functions of university supervisors so that they would have less direct responsibility for the supervision of student teachers and would instead work with school personnel, particularly cooperating teachers, on curriculum development and the improvement of teaching. The university supervisors would become the major agent for bringing about change in schools and in teacher education. They would continue to provide the liaison teacher education between university and schools and would still be available for troubleshooting. Their main influence, however, would be on the cooperating teacher and, indirectly, on the school environment.

Emans likened this redefined supervisor's role to that of the agricultural agent in colleges of agriculture, who works to see that the latest research and best practice are accessible to the farmer (i.e., the teacher). Under this model, the cooperating teacher would receive much greater training and assume more responsibility for the supervision of the student teacher, but would receive ongoing support from the university supervisor. Barriers to the implementation of this proposal might include (a) school personnel, who might feel threatened by having university faculty members so intimately involved in their operations; (b) university faculty members, who might be reluctant to engage in school change; and (c) universities, which might be reluctant to commit resources to the improvement of schools.

5. *Emergent Trends and Issues*

Although dissatisfaction with the dominant supervisory patterns in teacher education permeates the professional literature, these patterns have proven remarkably resilient. The existence of the student teaching triad, the dominant influence of the cooperating teacher on the student teacher, the relatively infrequent visits by the university supervisor, inadequate training for cooperating teachers, the atheoretical nature of the student teaching experience, and reliance on the apprenticeship model seem to be in little danger of extinction. Many examples exist of instances where the negative effects of these patterns have been counteracted through training or new models. However, on the whole, they have not succeeded in replacing these long-standing dominant patterns.

Why is this the case? There are several plausible explanations. First, teacher education is an underfunded enterprise in higher education: training and adequately compensating cooperating teachers, and lowering student teacher to university supervisor ratios, require money that all too often is unavailable. Second, the supervision of student teachers is a low-status activity for university faculty members who consequently expend little time and effort on the endeavor. Reward structures within higher education would have to be changed for faculty members to spend more time in schools. Third, the atheoretical nature of student teaching and its dependence on the apprenticeship model is often a reflection of the teacher education program. Where teacher education programs have coherence or a thematic orientation (e.g., teacher as a reflective practitioner), the student teaching experience is more likely to exhibit that theme and provide a common understanding of the experiences and outcomes expected of student teaching.

One emerging trend in the United States that has the the potential to address some of the problems related to supervision in teacher education is the concept of "professional development schools." These schools would be the educational analogue of a teaching hospital, where best practice, induction for new professionals, and inquiry into educational problems and issues pertinent to that school would all exist. Creating such sites where university faculty, teacher trainees, and teachers and administrators in the school work together to achieve these three goals would go a long way toward providing a context in which research on learning, teaching, and supervision could flourish.

See also: Teacher Education Programs: Structure; Teacher Education, Governance of

References

Boothroyd W 1979 Teaching practice supervision: A research report. *British Journal of Teacher Education* 5(3): 243–50

Boschee F, Prescott D R, Hein D D 1978 Do cooperating teachers influence the educational philosophy of student teachers? *J. Teach. Educ.* 29(2): 57–61

Cleary M J 1988 Thinking styles of supervisors and implications for student teaching. *Teacher Educator* 24(1): 16–23

Cogan M L 1973 *Clinical Supervision*. Houghton Mifflin, Boston, Massachusetts

Dewey J 1904 The relation of theory to practice in education. In: McMurray C A (ed.) 1904 *The Third Yearbook of the National Society for the Scientific Study of Education*. Public School Publishing, Bloomington, Illinois

Emans R 1983 Implementing the knowledge base: Redesigning the function of cooperating teachers and college supervisors. *J. Teach. Educ.* 34(3): 14–18

Glickman C D 1985 *Supervision of Instruction, a Developmental Approach*. Allyn and Bacon, Newton, Massachusetts

Goldhammer R 1969 *Clinical Supervision: Special Methods for the Supervision of Teachers*. Holt, Rinehart and Winston, New York

Grimmett P P, Ratzlaff H C 1986 Expectations for the cooperating teacher role. *J. Teach. Educ.* 37(6): 41–50

Guyton E 1987 Working with student teachers: Incentives, problems, and advantages. *The Professional Educator* 10(1): 21–28

Johnson J, Yates J 1982 A national survey of student teaching programs. ERIC Document Reproduction Service No. ED 232 963, Washington, DC

Koehler V R 1984 The instructional supervision of student teachers. ERIC Document Reproduction Service No. ED 271 430, Washington, DC

Lamb C E, Montague E J 1982 Variables pertaining to the perceived effectiveness of university student teaching supervisors. ERIC Document Reproduction Service No. ED 212 613, Washington, DC

May W T, Zimpher N L 1986 An examination of three theoretical perspectives on supervision: Perceptions of preservice field supervision. *Journal of Curriculum and Supervision* 1(2): 83–99

Mosher R L, Purpel D E 1972 *Supervision: The Reluctant Profession*. Houghton Mifflin, Boston, Massachusetts

O'Neal S 1983 An analysis of student teaching cooperating teacher conferences as related to the self-concept, flexibility, and teaching concerns of each participant. ERIC Document Reproduction Service No. ED 234 030, Washington, DC

Sergiovanni T J 1982 Toward a theory of supervisory practice: Integrating scientific, clinical, and artistic views. In: Sergiovanni T J (ed.) 1982 *Supervision of Teaching*. Association for Supervision and Curriculum Development, Alexandria, Virginia

Stones E, Morris S 1972 *Teaching Practice: Problems and Perspectives: A Reappraisal of the Practical Element in Teaching Preparation*. Methuen, London

Twa J 1984 Teacher associate perceptions of the effectiveness of the clinical supervision workshop. ERIC Document Reproduction Service No. ED 269 855, Washington, DC

Yates J W 1982 Student teaching: Results of a recent survey. *Educ. Res.* 24: 212–15

Yee A 1969 Do cooperating teachers influence the attitudes of student teachers? *J. Educ. Psychol.* 60(4): 327–32

Zimpher N 1987 Current trends in research on university supervision of student teaching. In: Haberman M, Backus J M (eds.) 1987 *Advances in Teacher Education*, Vol. 3. Ablex, Norwood, New Jersey

Zimpher N L, deVoss G, Nott D 1980 A closer look at university student teacher supervision. *J. Teach. Educ.* 31(4): 11–15

Further Reading

Boydell D 1986 Issues in teaching practice supervision research: A review of the literature. *Teaching and Teacher Education* 2(2): 115–25

Goodman J 1988 University culture and the problem of reforming field experiences in teacher education. *J. Teach. Educ.* 39(5): 45–51

Stones E 1987 Teaching practice supervision: Bridge between theory and practice. *European Journal of Teacher Education* 10(1): 67–79

Turney C et al. 1982 *The Practicum in Teacher Education: Research, Practice, and Supervision*. Sydney University Press, Sydney

J. M. Cooper

Teacher Education, Technology in

Through the expansion of computer-related possibilities, technology is presenting the educators of teachers with new issues and challenges. Two of the major challenges are: (a) educating teachers to use technology in educationally effective ways, including teaching them about computer-related technology; and (b) incorporating technology within the delivery of teacher education. The first challenge relates to technology as content, and the second to technology as a tool or delivery channel.

1. Technology as Content

Teacher education has long included as part of its content domain the effective use of technologies as learning tools and resources. Different technologies have been emphasized at different times: text materials, still pictures, overhead transparencies, slides, filmstrips, films, audiotapes, language laboratories, radio, television, computers, multimedia productions, and telecommunications (Saettler 1990). However, the impact of these various technologies on teacher behavior and student learning remains unclear (Clark 1983, Collis 1991). Consequently, an abiding issue in teacher education is how to organize more effectively instructional experiences related to the understanding and use of technology in schools and classrooms for both preservice and inservice teachers.

These instructional experiences must be organized so that teachers: (a) develop an overall awareness of how technologies can be used in education and learn adequate skills in handling these technologies; and (b) gain insights into how the context for the application of these technologies in a particular educational setting affects the implementation of the technologies and their influence on student learning. Together, these two aspects define technology as a content area in teacher education.

This content focus began as early as the 1920s, with the appearance in teacher education programs of courses in visual instruction and visual aids. Over time, these were replaced by courses in audiovisual media as teaching aids, generally with a skill and production orientation.

1.1 Computer-related Technology as a Content Area

This area has received intensified interest with the arrival of computer-related technologies as educational tools. As early as 1970 "a basic computer appreciation course" was being advocated as part of the initial training of all teachers (Lewis and Tagg 1988). By the early 1980s a variety of forces, including parents, groups of teachers, and major government initiatives, began to call for all teachers to become "computer literate" and receive training in how to use computers in their teaching. Instead of computer appreciation, a much broader challenge emerged: "We face the need to train, as rapidly as possible, the entirety of the teaching profession to use the new technologies" (Organisation for Economic Cooperation and Development 1986, cited in Eraut 1990 p. 17). Throughout the world, different projects and initiatives arose which were strongly influenced by experts from outside the field of education who tended not to be conversant with specialists in other areas of educational technology or teacher education (Eraut 1989). These projects generally included broad-scale, computer-related teacher education as part of their scope (see Commission of the European Communities 1989 for a European review).

The push for computer use in schools led to challenges for teacher education with regard to organization, content, and staffing. In addition, issues concerning the delivery of instruction on technology and ways of preparing teachers to teach about technology were being raised and addressed.

1.1.1 Issues relating to organization. A major issue for teacher education relating to computers is the organizational structure in which such education is offered. Two questions in this respect are: where and how does computer-related technology fit into existing "technology courses" in teacher education? The general response is that it should not be integrated into them, but requires newly developed courses, separate from both the traditional courses in educational technology and the traditional methodology courses in teacher education programs.

This was the case, for example, in preservice education in Canada in 1984 (Collis and Muir 1986) and in most of the inservice short courses that appeared in European countries (Commission of the European Communities 1989). Surveys in the United States do not show much change in this overall pattern, with some form of "computers in education" course being taught as a separate (and generally required) course for preservice education students within most colleges or faculties of education (Brownell 1990, Lintner et al. 1991). More internationally, the International Association for the Evaluation of Educational Achievement (IEA) "Computers in Education" survey of 19 national educational systems found that the most frequent form of inservice training experienced by teachers relating to the application of computers in education was an introductory computer-specific course. It was followed by other types of computer-specific courses (Pelgrum and Plomp 1991).

1.1.2 Content considerations. The content of these courses has been a subject of debate since their inception. In the early 1980s the argument was often between those who advocated learning programming and technical skills (including those who wished to allow teachers to develop their own educational software), and those who felt that a more general approach was more appropriate (including topics such as applications of computers in society) (see Collis 1988 for a review). The next aspect of the content debate concerned the role of applications software in the content of teacher education courses (e.g., should all teachers be taught how to use word processors and database software?). Another major issue related to the application of computer-related technology within curriculum areas. All of these topics and others were expected to be covered in a limited time, which provoked much discussion as to the most appropriate balance of content.

Although consensus did not emerge, a survey of required preservice computer courses in the United States in 1991 indicated some convergence on content, as also happened in other countries. The content that was chosen for more than two-thirds of the required computer-related preservice courses in the United States included: LOGO as a programming language; applications software—word processing, database, and spreadsheet; an introduction to educational software; hardware topics; computer ethics; and future uses of computers (Lintner et al. 1991). These findings concur with the those from the IEA 1991 survey, in which the categories "Applications of Computers" and "Problem Analysis and Programming" were found to be the two major topic categories included in most inservice teacher training programs (Pelgrum and Plomp 1991).

In contrast to earlier computer-focused content lists, then, there has continued to be an evolution of opinion on the appropriate content for teacher education relating to computers. Programming is typically being dropped as a content area and the reference to computers is being changed to a broader range of "new communications and information technologies." The recommendations for the inclusion of information technology (IT) in initial teacher training made by the United Kingdom Department of Education and Science (1992) summarized emerging thinking in the field.

> The IT capability of all students completing their initial teacher training should be sufficient for them to make effective use of IT in the classroom and at the same time provide a sound basis for their subsequent development in this field. This capability should encompass at least:
> (i) The ability to make confident personal use of a range (albeit limited) of software packages and IT devices appropriate to their chosen subject and age range;
> (ii) The ability to review critically the relevance of software packages and IT devices . . .;
> (iii) The ability to make constructive use of IT in their teaching . . .;
> (iv) The ability to evaluate the way in which the use of IT changes the nature of teaching and learning. (p. 1)

1.1.3 Staffing considerations. Another issue of considerable significance for teacher education is that of appropriate qualifications for the deliverers of computer-related teacher education. Since the field is so new, few persons working as professional teacher educators have completed a sequence of professional training in the area of computer applications in education or have had personal classroom experience with computer applications in teaching. In the 1989 report of the Council of Europe's Standing Conference of European Ministers of Education it was noted that "the importance of observing proper practices in the use of NICT (new information and communication technologies) in actual teaching and learning situations, whether for initial or for in-service training, cannot be overrated. . . Teacher training is no doubt also affected by the fact that the trainers themselves do not possess sufficient knowledge or experience" (cited in Eraut 1990 p. 152). This problem will remain critical, given the importance in effective teacher education of providing models, coupled with the regular emergence of new forms of computer-related technologies such as multimedia and telecommunications (Moonen and Collis 1991).

One implication is that a great deal of teacher education in the computer-related area is undertaken by groups outside the mainstream teacher education field. It is common for teachers with classroom computer-use experience to "move up" to become inservice providers and leaders. More generally, the 1991 IEA survey showed that universities and teacher training colleges do not have a leading role in inservice teacher education relating to computers in the majority of countries (16 of the 19) responding to the survey. Most frequently a mixture (often uncoordinated) of different agencies provide inservice instruction, including ministries of education and local education authorities; associations (teachers' associations, or computer science associations); business and industry (computer manufacturers, software developers); educational support institutes (national curriculum centers, local resource centers); teachers; parent groups; and universities and teachers' colleges. This mixture varies from country to country. The questions of who can provide leadership and how quality and continuity can be monitored in this sort of conglomeration are critical issues for teacher education.

1.1.4 Delivery issues. Much debate has centered on the best style of inservice delivery, with considerable criticism of the most frequently used model—that of a short-term course away from the teacher's school (see, e.g., Rhodes and Cox 1990). The importance of ongoing support and context-specific inservice training (i.e., offered within a teacher's own school) frequently cited. However, the logistics and costs of providing these options remain prohibitive.

1.1.5 Preparation for teaching about technology. Besides teaching teachers about computer-related technology and how to apply it in instruction, another demand on teacher education relates to the fact that a new subject area has evolved in schools in many different countries, a subject area with a title such as "computer literacy," "principles of information technology," "informatics," "computer science" (Pelgrum and Plomp 1991). There has developed a "moral imperative to teach today's pupils about the role and function of the computer" (Tucker 1987 p. 37) and teacher education is expected to prepare teachers for this new subject area.

Although many of the issues and problems involved in preparing teachers for teaching a new subject area are the same as those already examined with respect to preparing teachers for the application of computer-related technology in their overall teaching, certain aspects are noteworthy. One of these is that no convergence has occurred in schools as to what should be the content or measurable goals of these often compulsory new courses. Only in 1991, for example, did the National Council for the Accreditation of Teacher Education in the United States adopt a set of standards for teacher education institutions preparing teachers for specializations in computer-related education (International Society for Technology in Education 1991). Earlier standards had been suggested for the preparation of computer science or informatics teachers (Task Force on Curriculum for Secondary School Computer Science 1985), but no sense of a methodology and curriculum for teacher preparation has emerged internationally.

A second issue relates to the role definition of the computer-specialist teacher in the school. Frequently such a teacher is not only called upon to teach computer-related courses but is also expected to assume a broad range of responsibilities in the school. These responsibilities include providing inservice training, providing ongoing dissemination of information, advising the administration about technology, providing leadership in the change process relative to integrating technology throughout the school, evaluating software, and serving as the school technical expert. How to prepare teachers adequately for this wide range of responsibilities remains a challenge for teacher education.

2. *Technology as a Tool and Delivery Channel*

A second element in a discussion of technology and teacher education concerns advances in the use of technology as a tool within teacher education, not in conjunction with learning about technology and its applications, but as a tool for purposes that may in themselves have nothing to do with technology. This component, which might be called "technology as a tool and delivery channel," can be discussed under two major headings: the impact of technology in non-technology-related teacher education, and the use of technology to expand options in teacher education at a distance.

2.1 *Use of Technology within Teacher Education Courses*

Outside courses where the goal is to have students learn about applications of technology in the teaching and learning process, to what extent are teacher educators actually using technologies for educational delivery? Comprehensive data on this matter are difficult to find, although occasional reports describe interesting examples, generally involving video or interactive video. It is evident that widespread use is made of "simple" traditional media such as books, overhead projectors, and slides.

As regards computer-related resources, the use of computer-based tools for word-processing, desktop publishing, and computer-based library searches are now commonplace personal skills expected of preservice teachers. Teachers may also learn to use statistics software or gradebook software as research or professional tools. Despite these examples of the use of personal tools, however, it seems in general that the use of computer-related technology is employed relatively infrequently as an instructional medium in teacher education itself.

2.2 *Technology for Teacher Education at a Distance*

An exception to the situation described above is one rapidly growing variation on the delivery of teacher education, namely the move toward distance delivery of some of its components. This movement is most relevant for inservice teacher education, in which there are benefits for the teacher (both practical and pedagogical) of being able to study in a flexible way from his or her home or school rather than attend a course fixed in time and place of delivery.

There are many international examples of the use of telecommunications to support teachers in distance participation in teacher education. These can be placed into one of two general categories: those relating to course delivery at a distance and those enabling teachers to participate in a variety of other aspects of professional education (e.g., special projects or activities, or to provide "just-in-time" or ongoing opportunities for teacher education). Central to these distance opportunities are several kinds of technologies: telephone, cable television, radio and television broadcasting, audio and video recordings, video, audio, and computer conferencing, other forms of computer-mediated communication, and audiographic technology (see Roberts et al. 1990).

2.2.1 Course delivery at a distance. Examples of inservice courses being delivered at a distance entirely or partly by means of a computer-steered telecommunications channel can be found in many countries, including Canada (with a sophisticated and extensive system in terms of organization, technology, and pedagogy), the United States, Malaysia, and Denmark. The LEARN Network in Denmark, for example, has developed and delivered a number of inservice courses via telecommunications to Danish and Norwegian teachers, all of whom can remain at home and work while participating in the courses (Larsen and Malmberg 1991).

2.2.2 "Just-in-time" or ongoing teacher education. Outside the framework of inservice courses, many other opportunities for teacher inservice education are occurring through the medium of telecommunications. In the category of special projects, the PLUTO International Network Project is a noteworthy example (UNESCO 1991). The Project has used a telecommunications infrastructure to connect European teacher education institutions. In this way, educators of teachers, preservice teachers, and classroom teachers in 10 European countries are able to identify and experience new forms of classroom activity. Distance education is a new model for teacher education.

There are other examples of how the concept of inservice teacher education is being expanded in terms of delivery and organization. More fundamentally, there is a move away from the situation where a teacher education institution decides on an appropriate sequence and timing of inservice education and toward a "just-in-time" model based on teacher choice. Throughout the world, information networks, accessible through telecommunications, are giving teachers access to collections of instructional materials, to dialogues with computer educators and other teachers about particular educational issues (not necessarily involving technology), and to large amounts of pedagogically relevant information. For example, in the United States, the Educational Native American Network connects teachers in schools for Native American students with each other and also with a wide range of informational and teaching resources including resources specifically aimed at teacher education. A similar service, the Campus 2000 Network, operates in the United Kingdom, with targeted services for special education teachers as well as teachers in general. The "Physics Forum" has provided, via an online system, different types of inservice support and education to more than 1,000 secondary school science teachers throughout North America. In the Netherlands the PTT (national telephone utility) cooperates with the National Curriculum Institute to provide a similar on-line information and communication service to teachers. Other examples could be cited, together showing that the distinction between teacher education and ongoing professional support and development is rapidly blurring.

3. Implications of Technology for Teacher Education

The emergence of new technologies—computer-related, multimedia, telecommunications—is presenting new challenges and opportunities for teacher education. Just as the teacher may no longer be able to be considered the primary source and organizer of learning for his or her students in the information society of the twenty-first century, so too will it be difficult for a teacher education institution be able to provide adequately for or structure teacher education as it relates to technology. Responding to these challenges will require the best efforts of everyone involved in teacher education.

See also: Technology and the Classroom Teacher

References

Brownell G 1990 The first course in computer education: A survey. *Journal of Computing in Teacher Education* 7(2): 15–19

Clark R E 1983 Reconsidering research on learning from media. *Rev. Educ. Res.* 53: 445–59

Collis B A 1988 *Computers, Curriculum, and Whole-Class Instruction*. Wadsworth Publishing, Belmont, California

Collis B A 1991 Anticipating the impact of multimedia in education: Lessons from the literature. *Computers in Adult Education and Training* 2(2): 136–49

Collis B A, Muir W 1986 A survey of computer education courses in Canadian faculties of education. *The Canadian Journal of Higher Education* 16(1): 61–71

Commission of the European Communities 1989 *The Introduction of New Information Technologies into Education: Report 1983–1987*. Task Force Human Resources, Education, Training and Youth, Brussels

Eraut M (ed.) 1989 *The International Encyclopedia of Educational Technology*. Pergamon Press, Oxford

Eraut M (ed.) 1990 *Education and the Information Society: A Challenge for European Policy*. Cassell Educational, London

International Society for Technology in Education (ISTE) 1991 *Curriculum Guidelines for Accreditation of Educational Computing and Technology Programs*. ISTE Eugene, Oregon

Larsen I B, Malmberg A C 1991 *LEARN Report: Education via Network*. The Royal Danish School of Educational Studies, Copenhagen

Lewis R, Tagg E D (eds.) 1988 *Informatics and Education: An Anthology of Papers Selected from* IFIP TC 3 Publications Since the Establishment of TC 3 in 1963. Elsevier, Amsterdam

Lintner M et al. 1991 The required computer course for education majors: A national perspective. *Journal of Computing in Teacher Education* 7(3): 17–23

Moonen J, Collis B A 1991 *Multimedia in het onderwijs: een verkenning*. Ministry of Education, Zoetemeer

Organisation for Economic Co-operation and Development 1986 *New Information Technologies: A Challenge for Education*. OECD, Paris

Pelgrum W, Plomp T 1991 *The Use of Computers in Education Worldwide: Results from the IEA "Computers in Education" Survey in 19 Educational Systems*. Pergamon Press, Oxford

Rhodes V, Cox M 1990 *Time for Learning*. Kings College Centre for Educational Research, London

Roberts N, Blakeslee G, Brown M, Link C 1990 *Integrating Telecommunications into Education*. Prentice-Hall, Englewood Cliffs, New Jersey

Saettler P 1990 *The Evolution of American Educational Technology*. Libraries Unlimited, Englewood, Colorado

Task Force on Curriculum for Secondary School Computer Science 1985 Proposed curriculum for programs leading to teacher certification in computer science. *Communications of the ACM* 28(3): 275–79

Tucker R N 1987 *Studies on the Incidence of the Training of Educational Staff for the Introduction of Information Technology into General Education*. UNESCO, Paris

UNESCO 1991 *Final Report of the Seminar A European Platform to Develop a Mechanism for Co-operation in the Field of Information Technologies in Education*. UNESCO, Paris

United Kingdom Department of Education and Science 1992 *Information Technology in Initial Teacher Training*. HMI (Ref. 49/92/NS), London

Further Reading

Cuban L 1985 *Teachers and Machines: The Classroom Use of Technology Since 1920*. Teachers College Press, New York

Journal of Computing in Teacher Education. ISTE, Eugene, Oregon

Office of Technological Assessment 1988 *Power On! New Tools for Teaching and Learning*. Congress of the United States, Washington, DC

B. A. Collis

Teacher Educators, Characteristics of

The body of research on teacher educators is meager. As Lanier and Little (1986) have written:

> research on teaching teachers stands in stark contrast to research on teaching youngsters . . . . Teachers of teachers—what they are like, what they do, what they think—are systematically overlooked in studies of teacher education. (p. 528)

That same year, Ducharme (1986) conducted a review of research literature in the field. He was able to locate only seven references to teacher educators, most of which focused on education faculty in general. Based on his review, Ducharme concluded that teacher educators knew very little about themselves and, furthermore, that the term "teacher educator" was ill-defined.

While teacher educators have been largely absent from refutable research literature, traditionally they have not been ignored by the literature of hyperbole, innuendo, and quasi-research. Kramer's (1991) polemic, *Ed School Follies*, followed the line of argument earlier expounded in Koerner's (1963) *The Miseducation of American Teachers*. Even Clark (1987) in his scholarly work *The Academic Life: Small Worlds, Different Worlds* relied on anecdotal barbs to make his points about education faculty.

In the late 1980s, however, things began to change. A series of books and reports appeared which systematically examined teacher education and teacher educators. Books by Warren (1989), Clifford and Guthrie (1988), Goodlad et al. (1990), and Wisniewski and Ducharme (1989) included lengthy sections on teacher educators. Howey and Zimpher's (1990) chapter "Professors and Deans of Education" in the *Handbook of Research on Teacher Education* reviewed studies of teacher educators; their *Profiles of Pre-service Education: Inquiries into the Nature of Programs* (1989) includes insightful sections on teacher educators and their work. *Phi Delta Kappan*, the *Journal of Teacher Education*, and other journals have either run feature issues on teacher educators or have published articles on the topic. The RATE committee of the American Association of Colleges for Teacher Education (AACTE) has annually published monographs based on annual surveys of education faculty and cooperating teachers. By the end of the first five years of surveys, over 12,000 faculty and more than 200 cooperating teachers had completed questionnaires.

1. Demographics of Teacher Educators

The AACTE studies from 1987 to 1991, the Ducharme and Agne data (1982, 1989) and the Howey et al. data (1978) are the major sources of information about teacher education faculty in the United States. Based on these data, a composite teacher educator can be described. This teacher educator is a White male in his late forties or early fifties, tenured at either the full or associate professor level. He acquired a doctorate while studying part-time and has been at his current place of employment for over 15 years, during which time he has published six or seven articles in refereed publications. He taught for a minimum of three years in the lower schools prior to his employment in higher education.

This composite teacher educator is from either a middle or lower middle class background. Scholars have contended that teacher educators, inasmuch as they generally come from the ranks of teachers, reflect the social class origins of teachers. Mattingly (1975), Powell (1980), Lanier and Little (1986), and Ducharme and Agne (1989) agree on this point: all suggest that the lower and lower middle social-class origins affect professional lives in higher education. Lanier and Little (1986), by way of summary, observed that:

> A disproportionately large number of faculty teaching teachers most directly have come from lower middle-class backgrounds. It is very likely that they obtain conformist orientations and utilitarian views of knowledge from their experiences at home, educational opportunities in school, and restrictive conditions of work as teachers before coming to higher education. (p. 535)

Lanier and Little's observation that teacher educators likely have "utilitarian views of knowledge" is provocative; if accurate, it may account for the high comfort level many teacher educators have historically had with such utilitarian, mechanistic movements as Competency Based Teacher Education.

This hypothetical faculty member fails, of course, to reflect the variation among teacher educators. For example, in-depth analyses of the data indicate that recently hired, generally younger faculty entered higher education faculty ranks earlier in their careers than did their older teacher education colleagues. Based on their early productivity, it can be predicted that they are likely to publish more in their careers than have the older faculty; they anticipate moving at least once in the future. They are somewhat more likely to be female, but less likely to be non-White.

These demographic data raise provocative issues for analysis and further study. For example, the teaching ranks in United States elementary schools remain largely female, while those who teach them are predominantly male. The hordes of female graduates of these programs take positions in elementary schools, the majority of which have male principals. Surely these conditions relay a direct message to prospective and practicing female teachers: you can teach, but those who prepare you to teach and those who administer the schools in which you will teach are likely to be male. A "plantation mentality" may prevail as a consequence of these conditions, irrespective of good intentions. Teacher education faculty—both male and female—would do well to provide prospective teachers with better models, to confront a sometimes sexist professional world and a curriculum and set of experiences that will enlighten and empower them to live and teach effectively in that world.

Female teacher educators perform more field work than do males. They are more likely to supervise students in early field experiences and in student teaching than are their male counterparts. They are also likely to have more advisees, and spend more time in advising and in committee work, even while reporting that they spend about the same number of hours per week doing their own work. Significantly, they report spending less time on scholarly and research activities (AACTE, 1989, 1990).

Female teacher educators also hold lower faculty ranks than do males. In the 1989 AACTE survey, for example, women comprised 28 percent of the teacher education professoriate. However, only 12 percent of the faculty at the rank of full professor were female (AACTE 1990).

The reasons for these conditions are unknown. Various explanations occur, and while all of them might explain part of the matter, no single explanation suffices. Among the explanations are their later entry into the ranks of higher education; interrupted careers to bear and raise children; lower scholarly output; inappropriate assignment or acceptance of duties with heavy emphasis on "nurturing" tasks; prejudice and bias, and a lack of a female counterpart to the "old-boy" network (including mentoring while in doctoral work). These explanations are likely to be interrelated. For example, lower scholarly productivity may be a function of an interrupted career pattern, inappropriate assignments, lack of mentoring, or all three.

The demographics on race contain an even more pernicious message. With the exception of faculty in historically Black colleges, there are virtually no Black or other minority faculty in teacher education. Year after year in the AACTE studies, regardless of the area of teacher education under study (elementary education, secondary education, educational foundations), the percentage of minority faculty never rises above 10 percent.

Teacher education units may take some solace from the fact that this is the condition in higher education generally, but this would be an unjustifiably complacent attitude. The increasingly strident voices of those administering accreditation of teacher education are calling for faculty and student diversity. Teacher education must face this issue and move toward some new manifestation of diversity if it is to be an effective force in the preparation of educators for the twenty-first century.

2. *Research and Scholarship of Teacher Educators*

There is a lack of clarity about the degree and kind of research and scholarship in which teacher educators engage. Judge (1982) contended that research is the major driving force in the large private and state flagship universities. The AACTE studies show clear differences in scholarly productivity among faculty at institutions catering for bachelors only and those providing master's and doctoral degrees, with faculty scholarly productivity growing as the level of institutional complexity increases. Critics such as Koerner (1963) and Kramer (1991) contended that what *is* published by teacher education scholars is of little merit in any event. While Ducharme and Agne (1982) suggested that research and scholarly productivity of education faculty is at about the level of higher education faculty generally (a view consistent with the successive AACTE reports), there is little from which sound, empirically based conclusions about education faculty scholarship can be drawn.

There is, however, a widely held belief that education faculty may be less *interested* in research and scholarship than are faculty in other disciplines—indeed, someone spending time on a higher education campus might draw a similar conclusion for many of the education faculty. What is the reason for this? Ducharme (1986) and Lanier and Little (1986), among others, have speculated that the years spent in the lower schools with their low priority for active scholarship and high priority for long hours of work may contribute to some individual teacher educators' low scholarly productivity. For some, old workplace habits may be too ingrained for them to change behaviors to meet the loosely applied but rigidly held scholarly standards of higher education. Ducharme (1993) found that the 34 teacher education faculty whom he interviewed were, in the main, highly productive, despite differing views of the value of such work among the different generations represented in his interviewees and despite their attending a variety of types of institutions.

Faculty scholarship is uneven among institutions and individuals. Ducharme and Agne (1982) concluded that faculty have an average of slightly more than five refereed publications during their lifetime. This conclusion has also been supported by the AACTE studies. In RATE V, for example, the average number of lifetime publications for faculty in refereed journals was 5.4 and in nonrefereed journals was 4.7 (AACTE 1992). Focusing only on the average may be misleading, however. Some faculty members have as many as 26 refereed publications; others have none.

The AACTE data also suggest that younger faculty are publishing at a pace that indicates that they will surpass their older colleagues. Schuttenberg et al. (1985) have argued that younger education faculty value scholarship more highly than more mature faculty and also believe their potential for scholarship to be higher. Ducharme and Agne (1989) have contended that new faculty increasingly come with a predisposition toward becoming scholars. The rise in scholarly orientation among incoming faculty raises a new question. Will the increased emphasis on and interest in research and scholarship distance teacher educators from the field of practitioners (with whom many of them have historically worked, thus forming a bridge between theory and practice)?

It is clear from every indicator of faculty productivity that not all faculty publish extensively, nor do they want to do so. Likewise, faculty do not teach or provide professional service on an equal basis. It is important that units contain faculty who produce exemplary scholarship, teach well, and provide effective service. Such a constellation of faculty might well be the rallying cry for units in the late 1990s and early twenty-first century.

3. *Working Conditions of Teacher Educators*

Demographics and working conditions are in some ways inextricably related. That is, who people are and where they come from often condition what they do. Nonetheless, there are some unique conditions of teacher education faculty life that merit discussion.

Teacher educators spend considerable time in primary and secondary schools. Nash (1993) observed that the nature of the work of teacher educators is such that they are in frequent conflict with both the field of practice and their own institutional values. Ducharme (1986) stated this point in the following way: "Professors of education are caught between the traditional scholarship and research norms of higher education and the professional and technical demands of practitioners" (p. 1). While some emphases may change, it seems likely that the split responsibilities and lack of understandings of role will endure.

Faculty who specialize in elementary school teaching methods reported that they spent an average of more than 28 hours per month in the schools (AACTE 1989). What faculty do while in the schools cannot be divined precisely, but the AACTE data suggest that they likely divide their time among the following activities: observing student teachers, meeting with supervisors, conducting pre- and postconferences with student teachers, or—more unlikely—providing inservice or workshop activities for teachers, or conducting research in the schools. The faculty reported that they spend 6.8 hours per month in student teaching supervision and 1.6 hours per month in research activities.

As teacher educators assess their roles and responsibilities, they might consider the amount of time they spend in school settings and determine how that time might be better coordinated and used more effectively. Key questions such as the following can be used to guide this examination. Is that time well spent? Can the time and the faculty be better organized? What are the research questions implied in this condition?

Teacher education faculty spend more time in schools among teachers and children than do any other group of higher education faculty. This condition makes sense in terms of their students and their responsibilities, but it may also partially explain the low esteem in which they are held. The banal axiom that the closer a professional works to children the less esteem he or she gathers may well apply. Preschool staffs, Head Start teachers, day care center employees, elementary school teachers—all are held in low regard by various elements of the greater society. Why, then, should those who prepare them expect to be accorded much esteem from the highly structured and hierarchical world of higher education?

4. *Summary and Conclusion*

Teacher education has come a long way from Allison's (1989) depiction of the itinerant early professors of education in Tennessee; these were individuals whose hard work, practical know-how and entrepreneurship were not matched by their academic integrity. There is a body of literature, as Wisniewski and Ducharme (1989) pointed out, that suggests that teacher education faculty have achieved status on university campuses. For some, their presence on campuses is vital for the income their programs generate; for others, for the service they provide; for still others, for the inquiry into teaching and learning they conduct.

But while the process of teaching is ageless, the profession of teacher educator is relatively young. Studies are beginning to show the value of teacher education in the preparation of teachers. Evertson et al. (1985), Ashton and Crocker (1987), and Ferguson and Womack (1993) have built a case for the proposition that professional teacher preparation makes a difference in the lives of teachers and, perhaps more importantly, in the lives of their students. Despite the remarkable advances made by these and other researchers, much more study is needed. The hope for teacher educators is that they can retain their reputation for being caring individuals while continuing to develop meaningful and effective ways of preparing teachers. In a world that appears increasingly to lean to the empirical while yearning for the spiritual, teacher education has the potential to satisfy both aspirations.

See also: Teacher Education: Inservice

References

Allison C 1989 Early professors of education: Three case studies. In: Wisniewski R, Ducharme E R (eds.) 1989

American Association of Colleges for Teacher Education (AACTE) 1988 *RATE I: Teaching Teachers: Facts and Figures*. AACTE, Washington, DC

AACTE 1989 *RATE II: Teaching Teachers: Facts and Figures*. AACTE, Washington, DC

AACTE 1990 *RATE III: Teaching Teachers: Facts and Figures*. AACTE, Washington, DC

AACTE 1991 *RATE IV: Teaching Teachers: Facts and Figures*. AACTE, Washington, DC

AACTE 1992 *RATE V: Teaching Teachers: Facts and Figures*. AACTE, Washington, DC

Ashton P, Crocker L 1987 Systematic study of planned variations: The essential focus of teacher education reform. *J. Teach. Educ.* 38(3): 2–8

Clark B 1987 *The Academic Life: Small Worlds, Different Worlds*. Carnegie Foundation for the Advancement of Teaching, Princeton, New Jersey

Clifford G, Guthrie J W 1988 *Ed School: A Brief for Professional Education*. University of Chicago Press, Chicago, Illinois

Ducharme E R 1986 *Teacher Educators: What Do We Know?* ERIC Digest 15. ERIC Clearing-house on Teacher Education, Washington, DC

Ducharme E R, Agne R 1982 The education professorate: A research-based perspective. *J. Teach. Educ.* 33(6): 30–36

Ducharme E R, Agne R 1989 Professors of education: Uneasy residents of academe. In: Wisniewski R, Ducharme E R (eds.) 1989

Ducharme E R 1993 *The Lives of Teacher Educators*. Teachers College Press, New York

Evertson C, Hawley W, Zlotnik M 1985 Making a difference in educational quality through teacher education. *J. Teach. Educ.* 36(3): 2–12

Ferguson P, Womack S 1993 The impact of subject matter and education coursework on teaching performance. *J. Teach. Educ.*

Goodlad J, Soder R, Sirotnik K (eds.) 1990 *Places Where Teachers are Taught*. Jossey-Bass, San Francisco, California

Howey K, Yarger S, Joyce B 1978 *Improving Teacher Education*. Association of Teacher Educators, Washington, DC

Howey K, Zimpher N 1989 *Profiles of Pre-service Education: Inquiry into the Nature of Programs*. State University of New York, Albany, New York

Howey K, Zimpher N 1990 Professors and deans of education. In: Houston W R (ed.) 1990 *Handbook of Research on Teacher Education*. Macmillan Inc., New York

Judge H 1982 *American Graduate Schools of Education: A View from Abroad*. The Ford Foundation, New York

Koerner J 1963 *The Miseducation of American Teachers*. Houghton Mifflin, Boston, Massachusetts

Kramer R 1991 *Ed School Follies: The Miseducation of America's Teachers*. Free Press, New York

Lanier J, Little J 1986 Research on teacher education. In: Wittrock M C (ed.) 1986 *Handbook of Research on Teaching*, 3rd edn. Macmillan Inc., New York

Mattingly P H 1975 *The Classless Profession: American Schoolmen in the Nineteenth Century*. New York University Press, New York

Nash R J 1993 Rita Kramer's follies: The misrepresentation of America's teacher educators. *J. Teach. Educ.*

Powell A 1980 *The Uncertain Profession: Harvard and the Search for Educational Authority*. Harvard University Press, Cambridge, Massachusetts

Schuttenberg E, Patterson L, Sutton R 1985 Self-perceptions of productivity of education faculty: Life phase and gender differences. Paper presented at the annual meeting of the American Educational Research Association (AERA), Chicago, Illinois (ERIC Document Reproduction Service No. ED 257 807)

Warren D (ed.) 1989 *American Teachers: Histories of a Profession at Work*. Macmillan Inc., New York

Wisniewski R, Ducharme E R (eds.) 1989 *The Professors of Teaching: An Inquiry*. State University of New York, Albany, New York

E. R. Ducharme

Teacher Evaluating Behavior

Teacher evaluating behavior refers to the feedback teachers provide for their students during classroom instruction regarding the progress that students are making toward identified goals. Teacher evaluating behavior in relation to two major learning tasks will be examined, followed by a discussion of emerging issues related to teacher evaluating behaviors.

1. Introduction

Examining classroom life is a complex problem. If one stands close to the classroom and focuses on micro aspects of teaching, such as types of questions or wait time, the larger activity in which these behaviors are embedded may be obscured. If one stands far from the classroom and focuses on macro aspects of teaching, such as the instructional leadership provided by the principal or the impact of achievement tests on teaching and learning, teaching itself will not be illuminated. The vantage point that has come to be seen as a productive middle distance between micro verbal and nonverbal actions of teachers and macro school level variables is the instructional task.

A task, according to Doyle (1983), is the work in which students engage in the classroom. A task consists of a product students are to develop, the procedures they are to follow in developing the product, and the resources they are to use. Doyle asserts that four types of tasks can be found in schools: (a) memory tasks, in which students are to reproduce information; (b) procedural tasks, in which students are to apply a formula; (c) comprehension tasks, in which students are to transform information, solve problems, and make predictions; and (d) opinion tasks, in which students are to reveal preferences. A similar list of tasks developed by Bennett and

Desforges (1988) consists of incremental tasks, restructuring tasks, enrichment tasks, and practice tasks.

These tasks are compressed into two by Rosenshine and Meister (1992): well-structured tasks and less structured tasks. Well-structured or knowledge acquisition tasks are those that students can achieve directly by following a fixed sequence of steps (e.g., following the subtraction algorithm). The task product is invariable; that is, there is a single product that can be evaluated with a single criterion or set of criteria. Less structured or higher-order thinking tasks are those for which there exists no fixed sequence of steps for the student to follow. For these tasks (e.g., reading comprehension, science problem-solving), the teacher can provide a temporary heuristic as a model of the process to be followed or product to be developed, but the student must interpret, transform, and modify this instructional aid to accomplish the task. In higher-order thinking tasks the teacher can influence the student's thinking, but the teacher cannot lead the student to the acceptable completion of the task because the routes to completion as well as the product that is produced by the student are personal and variable.

Although there undoubtedly are generic teaching behaviors that are appropriate for any instructional task, it seems reasonable to assume that since different tasks focus on different products, procedures, and materials, different teaching techniques are required. Thus, while many teacher evaluating behaviors fit any task structure, some are especially appropriate for knowledge-acquisition tasks, while others are required for higher-order thinking tasks.

2. Knowledge-acquisition Tasks and Teacher Evaluating Behavior

In knowledge-acquisition tasks the teacher's purpose is to enable students to learn some predetermined concept or skill. To ensure success, teachers should provide appropriate learning activities and materials and engage in appropriate verbal interactions with students. The behaviors that the teacher uses following student acts are referred to as teacher evaluating behaviors. These behaviors are critical because they inform students of the appropriateness of their actions in terms of the goal. If students have no knowledge of the results of their actions, learning progress is halted. Successes need to be confirmed; errors need to be identified and eliminated.

The process–product researchers of the 1970s and early 1980s did not explicitly set out to study teaching related to knowledge-acquisition tasks. Since, however, this research focused primarily on the teaching and learning of reading and mathematics at the elementary school level and used standardized achievement test scores as a measure of teaching effectiveness, the knowledge acquisition basis for the research was evident. Summaries of this research reveal the types of teacher evaluating behavior that are related to student achievement on knowledge acquisition tasks (Brophy and Good 1986).

Having examined scores of studies, Brophy and Good conclude that effective teacher evaluating behavior varies with the quality of students' responses. For correct responses the teacher should publicly indicate that the answer is correct with some overt oral behavior (e.g., "Right!") or nonverbal behavior (e.g., nod affirmatively). The purpose of the acknowledgement is to confirm that the answer was correct. Effusive praise is not needed, and may actually detract from learning. For partly correct responses, the teacher should indicate the correct part and rephrase the question, give students clues, or actually provide the correct response regarding the incorrect part. Finally, for incorrect responses the teacher should first indicate that the answer is incorrect by using simple negative feedback rather than personal criticism. Next, the teacher should rephrase the question and/or provide clues that allow the student to attempt a correct response. The correct answer plus an explanation of why the answer is correct can also follow the negation. Brophy and Good further suggest that teachers encourage students to answer every question asked, even if only to say that they do not know the answer. Rephrasing, clueing, or providing the correct answer should then follow.

Rosenshine's (1983) review of process–product research yields similar suggestions regarding teacher evaluating behavior. Correct, quick, and firm student responses should be followed by another question or a short acknowledgement statement that does not interrupt the flow of the lesson. If the response is correct but the student is hesitant the teacher should provide short statements of acknowledgement and feedback concerning why the answer is correct. Incorrect but careless answers should be followed by a teacher correction and then movement to the next question. For incorrect answers caused by knowledge deficiency the teacher should provide clues or ask simpler questions or, when the student error is substantial, the teacher should reteach the material. Rosenshine emphasizes that the important point, according to research, is that "errors should not go uncorrected" (p. 343) because uncorrected errors result in subsequent learning problems.

A review of nearly 8,000 process–product studies at both the elementary and secondary school level conducted by Fraser et al. (1987), a team of Australian and United States researchers, found that teacher reacting behavior in the form of cues, reinforcement, and correctives (i.e., suggestions for making corrections) is a critical element in learning. Examining teacher reacting behavior in general, rather than in relation to the quality of students' responses, Walberg (1991) found that cuing can take a variety of forms: advance organizers or brief overviews, adjunct or key questions, goal setting, sequenced learning, and pretests. Reinforcement in the form of praise, Walberg found, has a small positive effect, but may be less effective than token rewards for younger students and grades or personal standards for more mature students. Corrective feedback or reteaching to eliminate error was found to have a moderate effect on student learning.

3. Higher-order Thinking Tasks and Teacher Evaluating Behavior

In contrast to teaching associated with knowledge-acquisition tasks, which is based largely on a behavioral conception of learning, teaching associated with higher-order thinking tasks is based on a constructivist view of learning. In terms of the latter tasks, teacher evaluating behavior serves not to strengthen associations between stimuli and responses, but to help students to build and enrich their internal knowledge structures. From the constructivist perspective, learning is a matter of establishing or constructing a network of relationships by connecting new knowledge to existing knowledge. Growth in knowledge, according to Resnick (1985), is a "result of learners' self-modification of their own thought processes and knowledge structures" (p. 2579).

The types of teacher evaluating behavior that facilitate student construction of the personal knowledge that higher-order thinking tasks require consist of supporting, linking, challenging, and modeling. These types of teacher evaluating behavior increase student self-evaluation and promote critical thinking.

3.1 Supporting

Supporting, or what Nystrom and Gamoran (1991) refer to as high-level evaluation, is behavior that occurs naturally in conversation and signals to the speaker that his or her thoughts are being taken seriously by the listener. It serves to maintain engagement with substantive ideas. Comments such as "That's an intriguing point" build on what students say, encourage students' thinking, and maintain classroom discourse at a high level. Through meaningful discussion, in contrast to more typical question–answer–evaluation recitation, students can construct their own meanings.

3.2 Linking

Linking refers to tying main ideas together, to providing a structure of ideas that students can use to build their own knowledge structures. The teacher who uses linking evaluating behavior points out the relationship of new knowledge to other new knowledge or to prior knowledge. Ausubel's (1978) advance organizers, when made in reaction to a student comment, can be viewed as linking acts. They provide an organization of major concepts into which supporting facts and details can be inserted.

Likewise, Shulman's (1986) content transformation is a form of linking. When teachers use analogies, examples, and illustrations to portray content, they are relating unknown content to known content. In response to students' real or anticipated misunderstandings, teachers can relate new content to previously taught content, to students' out-of-school experiences, and to content embedded in hypothetical situations (Zahorik 1992).

3.3 Challenging

Sigel (1984) suggests that to generate thinking and to cause students to integrate ideas and refine their knowledge structures, teachers should, "draw a child's attention to a discrepancy, contradiction, or inconsistency" (p. 21). The value of creating puzzlement is also supported by Gallagher and Wansart (1991). Coming to see gaps in understanding can result from teacher evaluating behavior, but it can also be a product of individual or group work on various projects.

3.4 Modeling

Modeling refers to giving students a model, heuristic, or guide that they can use to get started on an activity and to which they can refer to judge the adequacy of their actions or the progress of their thinking. The model can be given to students as products (that is, what is to be accomplished) or processes (that is, how the student is to accomplish what is expected). Examples of modeling include the provision and demonstration of guide questions (King 1989), process sequences (Taylor 1985), plan sheets (Englert et al. 1991), and cue cards (Billingsley and Wildman 1984). Each of these types of assistance provides students with a set of suggested ideas to be used in attempting to write a paragraph, summarize a story, or perform some other higher-level thinking task.

Another type of modeling is what Palinscar and Brown (1984) refer to as reciprocal teaching. The teacher and students take turns being the teacher. The teacher models the process for students. When students "teach" the process, they use the teacher's model as a guide and their progress is revealed to the teacher.

Building on the work of Vygotsky (1978), Rosenshine and Meister (1992) and others suggest that scaffolding be used when providing models. Scaffolding is a form of temporary guidance in which the model is presented but then gradually withdrawn as students become more independent and self-reliant in their actions. The effectiveness of providing models through scaffolding has been well documented by Collins et al. (1989).

Although all of the teacher evaluating behavior associated with higher-order thinking tasks seeks to make students their own evaluators as they construct knowledge, modeling differs somewhat from the other techniques in that it provides the means to determine adequacy in advance.

4. Emerging Issues

In regard to teacher evaluating behavior and knowledge acquisition tasks, there seems to be little controversy. Praise, reinforcement, and knowledge of results from the teacher can facilitate the learning of simple skills and basic content by students. In regard to teacher evaluating behavior and higher-order thinking tasks, however, a number of issues are emerging. The main issue is the amount of help or direction that students should be given as they attempt to understand ideas and reform existing cognitive structures through problem-solving and related activities. In this regard, one could look at supporting, linking, challenging, and modeling as existing in a hierarchy, with linking and modeling being used early in a learning sequence when students are unclear about task demands, and supporting and challenging being used later after students have formed meaningful connections and have gained confidence in their structures.

In contrast, one could see these two pairs of evaluating behavior as conflicting and incompatible acts. Some might question whether the links and models provided by the teacher stimulate or stymie students' development of their own knowledge structures, because the teacher link or model could be perceived by the student as a firm structure rather than a heuristic device. It could be argued that if one is serious about helping students develop personal knowledge structures, the less directive techniques of support and challenge would encourage students to be more self-monitoring. This argument is particularly compelling if these acts are used in conjunction with learning activities and problems that are highly meaningful to students. It is to be hoped that future research will deal with the comparative nature of various types of teacher evaluating behavior used with higher-order thinking tasks.

See also: Classroom Environments; Questioning Strategies; Teaching, Synthesizing Research on

References

Ausubel D 1978 In defense of advance organizers: A reply to the critics. *Rev. Educ. Res.* 48(2): 251–57

Bennett N, Desforges C 1988 Matching classroom tasks to students' attainments. *Elem. Sch. J.* 88(3): 221–34

Billingsley B, Wildman T 1984 The effects of pre-reading activities on the comprehension monitoring of learning disabled adolescents. *Learning Disability Research* 4(1): 36–44

Brophy J, Good T 1986 Teacher behavior and student achievement. In: Wittrock M (ed.) 1986 *Handbook of Research on Teaching*, 3rd edn. Macmillan, New York

Collins A, Brown J, Newman S 1989 Cognitive apprenticeship: Teaching the crafts of reading, writing, and mathematics. In: Resnick L (ed.) 1989 *Knowing, Learning, and Instruction: Essays in Honor of Robert Glaser*. Erlbaum, Hillsdale, New Jersey

Doyle W 1983 Academic work. *Rev. Educ. Res.* 53(2): 159–99

Englert C, Raphael T, Anderson L, Anthony H, Stevens D 1991 Making strategies and self-talk visible: Writing instruction and special education classrooms. *Am. Educ. Res. J.* 28(2): 337–72

Fraser B, Walberg H, Welch W, Hattie J 1987 Syntheses of educational productivity research. *Int. J. Educ. Res.* 11(2): 73–145

Gallagher J, Wansart W 1991 An assimilative base model of strategy–knowledge interactions. *Rem. Spec. Educ.* 12(3): 31–41

King A 1989 Effects of a metacognitive strategy on high school students' comprehension of lectures. Paper presented at the annual meeting of the American Educational Research Association, San Francisco, California

Nystrom M, Gamoran A 1991 Student engagement: When recitation becomes conversation. In: Waxman H, Walberg H (eds.) 1991 *Effective Teaching: Current Research*. McCutchan, Berkeley, California

Palincsar A, Brown A 1984 Reciprocal teaching of comprehension-fostering and comprehension-monitoring activities. *Cognition and Instruction* 1(2): 117–75

Resnick L 1985 Instructional psychology. In: Husén T, Postlethwaite T N (eds.) 1985 *International Encyclopedia of Education*, 1st edn. Pergamon Press, Oxford

Rosenshine B 1983 Teaching functions in instructional programs. *Elem. Sch. J.* 83(4): 335–51

Rosenshine B, Meister C 1992 The use of scaffolds for teaching higher-order cognitive strategies. *Educ. Leadership* 49: 26–33

Shulman L 1986 Those who understand: Knowledge growth in teaching. *Educ. Researcher* 15(2): 4–14

Sigel I 1984 A constructivist perspective for teaching thinking. *Educ. Leadership* 42(3): 18–21

Taylor B 1985 Improving middle-grade students' reading and writing of expository text. *J. Educ. Res.* 79(2): 119–25

Vygotsky L 1978 *Mind in Society: The Development of Higher Psychological Processes*. Harvard University Press, Cambridge, Massachusetts

Walberg H 1991 Productive teaching and instruction: Assessing the knowledge base. In: Waxman H, Walberg H (eds.) 1991 *Effective Teaching: Current Research*. McCutchan, Berkeley, California

Zahorik J 1992 Connection making in teaching. Paper presented at the annual meeting of the American Educational Research Association, San Francisco

J. A. Zahorik

Teacher Evaluation

Teacher evaluation is a two-step process. The first step is to obtain information about each teacher who is to be evaluated. The second step is to use that information to form an evaluative judgment about the teacher. Although there is some question about how information about teachers should be used in evaluating them, there is no question that the validity of an evaluation depends on the accuracy and relevance of the information upon which it is based. This entry deals with the first step only. Procedures presently used to obtain information are described and ways of improving their accuracy and relevance are discussed.

1. Types of Information

Ideally, all evaluations of teachers should be based on information about teacher effectiveness. However, because direct information about teacher effectiveness is not always available when decisions must be made, many teacher evaluations are based on information about teacher competence or teacher performance.

Information about teacher performance is not available until the teacher can be observed on the job. Decisions about preservice teacher education students and candidates for teaching certificates or licenses must therefore be based on information about their competence obtained in artificial or "test" situations.

Most decisions about practicing teachers (i.e., decisions about hiring, firing, tenure, and promotion) must be made and implemented without information about teachers' effects on students. Evaluations of teachers meant to inform such decisions must therefore be based on information about teacher performance.

Underlying the use of information about competency and performance to evaluate teachers are two assumptions. The first is that the effectiveness of a teacher depends on how well the teacher performs on the job. The second is that how well a teacher performs on the job depends on how competent the teacher is. If these assumptions are valid, it seems reasonable also to assume that evaluations based on information about teacher competence and performance contain information about teacher effectiveness.

2. Evaluating Teacher Competence

Evaluations based on information about teacher competence may be and are used for two main purposes. One is to monitor the progress of students enrolled in preservice teacher education programs and programs designed to increase teacher competence. Most of the information is obtained with paper and pencil examinations designed to measure knowledge.

In many parts of the world, government agencies exist whose function it is to prevent incompetent teachers from practicing in their jurisdictions. They therefore require all teachers to present evidence of competence before they are given certificates or licenses to teach. While some agencies accept graduation from a preservice program as evidence of competence, an increasing number require the candidate to pass one or more examinations specially constructed for the purpose, called teacher competency tests. Most teacher competency tests are paper and pencil tests very similar to the examinations used in teacher preparation programs.

2.1 Teacher Competency Tests

A typical teacher competency test is designed to measure knowledge of two kinds: content knowledge and professional knowledge. The content knowledge tested usually includes both knowledge of the specific subject matter the teacher is expected to teach and general knowledge of the kind that any educated adult is expected to possess. The importance of knowledge of the subject matter to be taught is generally taken for granted. The importance of general knowledge reflects the fact that most teachers serve as role models as well as instructors. For some children, the teacher may be the first educated adult they get a chance to observe closely.

Professional knowledge consists of knowledge about the kinds of teacher behavior believed or known to be effective in helping students progress toward important educational goals. While most of it comes from the accumulated experience of the profession, some comes from systematic research in disciplines on which teaching is based and some from what is known as process–product research, that is, research intended to discover relationships between teacher behavior and student learning (see Brophy and Good 1986). In the early 1990s, some findings of research intended to discover relationships between students' classroom activities and student learning started to appear (see Berliner 1990). However, there is much less agreement about the importance of professional knowledge than of content knowledge.

2.2 Validity of Teacher Competency Tests

There is only one teacher competency test in the United States that has been used long enough and often enough to generate a useful amount of information about the validity of scores on such tests, the National Teacher Examinations (NTE) (Educational Testing Service 1940–1976). Because of the care taken to ensure that the content of these tests represented the best current wisdom of the profession, the content validity of these examinations was at least as high as that of any similar test.

Some 50 studies of the predictive validity of the so-called Common Examinations of the NTE have been conducted. In these studies scores on the Weighted Common Examinations (WCE) were correlated with measures of teacher performance and measures of teacher effectiveness. A review of these studies revealed no evidence that the correlation either between WCE scores and ratings of teacher performance or between WCE scores and measures of teacher effectiveness was greater than zero (see Quirk et al. 1973).

These findings provide no empirical support for the assumption that scores on this or any other teacher competency test contain information about teacher effectiveness. They also raise serious questions about the validity of current teacher competency tests for making decisions about prospective teachers.

2.3 Improving Teacher Competency Tests

One way to account for these findings is to make a distinction between academic knowledge, that is, knowledge useful in performing well on paper and pencil tests, and functional knowledge, that is, knowledge useful in performing well in the classroom. The fact that the NTE has high content validity (i.e., its content includes most of the things that educators believe to be important to teachers) can be taken as evidence that the test measures academic knowledge. The fact that it has low predictive validity (i.e., possession of this knowledge is unrelated to classroom performance) can be taken as evidence that it does not measure functional knowledge.

The implications of this distinction for the direction that future efforts to improve teacher competency tests should take are clear. Changes in test content are unlikely to increase either the content or predictive validity of the tests. However, modifications in what the tests require students to do with existing content might increase the predictive validity. Current tests include items that require prospective teachers to apply their knowledge to teaching problems. But the skills used to answer such items correctly are of no use when the prospective teacher is trying to apply the same knowledge to similar problems when they are encountered in the classroom.

It is clearly time to abandon the printed test booklet filled with multiple-choice items, and replace it with something else. A likely place to find a replacement is among the new modes, sequences, and formats made available by innovative technological tools such as personal computers, videotape and videodisc recorders, and the like.

One alternative to teacher certification based on competency test scores is performance-based teacher certification. All teaching candidates are allowed to teach from one to three years without having demonstrated competence. During this time their performance is rated one or more times; if the ratings are satisfactory, the teacher receives a certificate or a license to teach.

There are two disadvantages to this approach. One is its cost, which is very high. The other is that its adoption defeats the purpose of certification by permitting incompetent teachers to teach for up to three years before they are barred from the classroom.

2.4 Issues in Evaluating Teacher Competency

Some fundamental questions have been raised about the usefulness of the professional knowledge that teacher competency tests are designed to measure. Some question whether there is anything to know; others assume that there is, but question whether the amount of this knowledge that is known is great enough to make a difference. In other words, would a teacher who knew all that teacher educators can teach him or her be any more effective than one who possessed none of it?

The answer to this question depends on whether teaching should be regarded as one of the so-called learned professions. The nature of such a profession is that its practitioners help others deal with a category of difficult human problems by applying to them a specialized body of knowledge which is incomplete (i.e., which does not contain solutions to all problems in that category). If teaching is a profession, then its members are obligated to know and use whatever there is to know, however inadequate it may be.

A second question that has been raised concerns the nature of a teacher's professional knowledge. The question hinges on whether the competencies necessary for effective teaching of different subjects and grades, and even of different topics in the same subject or grade, may be so different that no valid common examination can be constructed. Instead, many different instruments must be developed for evaluating competence to teach different subjects and topics. A project to develop a national teacher assessment program using such multiple instruments is under way (see Haertel 1991).

These assumptions may be appropriate for the project described, since its focus is on teacher excellence, but they are inappropriate for present uses of competency tests which focus on entry-level competence. It is widely agreed that excellence can only be acquired from extensive experience, and may well be highly specific to the content taught. The survival skills beginning teachers need, however, which must be acquired before they have any experience, may have little to do with the specific content they are to teach.

3. Evaluating Teacher Performance

Teacher performance has been evaluated in one way or another as long as there have been teachers to evaluate. It has been evaluated by the teachers' employers, by the parents of their pupils, and by the pupils themselves. And rarely has the validity of any of these evaluations been questioned.

Almost anyone who watches a teacher for a few minutes forms a definite impression of how "good" the teacher is; and for most of the history of education, teachers were evaluated in just this way. In many schools supervisors still observe and evaluate teachers on the basis of global impressions formed in much the same way. Growing concern about the competence of some supervisors to make valid evaluations in this fashion has led to the adoption of the multifactor teacher rating scale.

3.1 Teacher Rating Scales

A multifactor teacher rating scale is an instrument used by evaluators while observing teachers. The instrument specifies the number and duration of the observations to be made and defines the aspects of the performance that are to be observed and judged. It also provides a numerical or graphic scale on which the evaluator's judgment, or rating, of each factor or item is recorded. Raters are instructed to rate each item on its own merits and without regard to ratings on other items.

The overall evaluation of the teacher is obtained later by combining the separate ratings into a composite description. Sometimes teachers' profiles on individual items are used to diagnose teacher difficulties and plan corrective action.

3.2 Validity of Teacher Ratings

The influence of the evaluator's expertise on the validity of evaluations made with a rating scale should be reduced or eliminated because the aspects of teacher performance to be evaluated are predetermined. Validity is further enhanced if the items to be rated reflect aspects of performance known or believed to be related to teacher effectiveness.

Just as the content validity of a test depends on the items it contains, so does the content validity of a rating scale. Thus, the items on a valid teacher competency test should correspond to the items on a valid teacher rating scale. Much wisdom and effort has gone into the construction of rating scales to ensure that the items incorporate the best available knowledge and current beliefs about effective teacher performance; the best of them can be said to have high content validity (for examples, see Kowalski 1978). As was the case with teacher competency tests, however, content validity of rating scales does not guarantee their validity as predictors of teacher effectiveness.

It is therefore important to establish the predictive validity of each rating scale empirically; that is, by testing whether the ratings correlate with direct measures of teacher effectiveness. The number of studies of this kind that have been reported is surprisingly small, and the findings of the few that have been reported have been consistently negative. There is no empirical evidence that correlations between supervisors' ratings of teacher performance and direct measures of teacher effectiveness differ from zero. Thus, they apparently do not contain the information about teacher effectiveness they are assumed to contain (see Medley and Coker 1987).

One likely reason for these findings is the strong tendency for ratings on individual items to be distorted by the rater's overall impression of the teacher, a distortion known as the halo effect (see Cooper 1981). The halo effect manifests itself in unduly high correlations between ratings of the same teacher by the same rater on different items. It is not unusual to find that different items on a teacher rating scale correlate extremely highly. The key to valid ratings lies in the reduction or elimination of the halo effect so that the ratings depend on the item content they purport to measure.

3.3 Improving Ratings

The most practical way to increase the validity of teacher ratings is to take steps to decrease the influence of halo on the ratings. Halo is most likely to distort ratings when no behavior relevant to an item to be rated is observed. In such cases the rating must be based either on behavior irrelevant to the item or on the rater's overall impression of the teacher, neither of which yields a valid rating.

The risk of this occurring depends first of all on the item itself. The rating scale used should include behaviors that may be expected to occur frequently enough to make it likely that the rater will see them in the classroom of each teacher who is to be rated. The duration and frequency of periods of observation should be sufficient to provide ample opportunity for behaviors relevant to every item on the scale to occur, and raters should undergo enough training, practice, and retraining so that they will see and recognize relevant behaviors when they occur.

3.4 Issues in Performance Evaluation

A more drastic step that has been proposed is to abandon teacher rating scales entirely, and replace them with "low-inference observation schedules." A low-inference observation schedule consists of a list of observable items of behavior. When an item of behavior occurs, it is recorded by the observer. There is no explicit indication of the factors on which the evaluation is based or which item is relevant to which factor. Scores on the factors are obtained by applying objective scoring keys to the record (see Medley et al. 1984).

Instruments of this type have less face validity and are more costly to develop than rating scales, and are considered less sensitive to the complexities of classroom behavior. However, scores on them have been shown to be much less susceptible to the effects of halo than ratings. Also, unlike teacher ratings, they have been shown to predict teacher effectiveness in research studies (see Brophy and Good 1986).

4. Evaluating Teacher Effectiveness

Evaluations of teachers based on measures of students' gains on achievement tests of educational goals have great appeal to the lay public as a basis for decisions about teachers regarding hiring, firing, tenure, and promotion. Methods for deriving information about teacher effectiveness from their students' scores on achievement tests are available, but educators are reluctant to use these methods for reasons which will be examined later in this section.

4.1 Measuring Teacher Effectiveness

Before teacher effectiveness can be evaluated it must be clearly defined. The definition must specify in measurable terms both the outcomes to be achieved and the kind of student with whom they are to be achieved. The outcomes may be specified in measurable terms by selecting a valid test of achievement of those outcomes. The test chosen should be administered to the students in a class taught by each teacher who is to be evaluated at the end of a school term. Scores on this test will be referred to as posttest scores.

The type of student to be affected by the teacher may be defined by specifying one or more measurable student characteristics. The most important of these is student ability, defined for this purpose by students' scores on an achievement test administered at the beginning of the term (pretest scores). This test should be equivalent to the posttest, or as nearly so as possible. Other student characteristics such as sex, ethnic origin, and attitude toward school may also be used.

Pretest and posttest scores of students in each class are used to set up a within-class regression equation for predicting future posttest scores from pretest scores in each class. When the specified pretest score (or set of scores) is entered into this equation, an estimate of the posttest score the student(s) would be expected to get in that class is obtained. Since the equations are different in different classes, the expected outcomes will also be different in different classes.

The expected posttest scores in each class estimate how much students should learn in that class in light of their pretest scores. Differences in these expectations in different classes are partly due to differences in teacher effectiveness and partly due to differences in the classes.

Among the class characteristics most likely to affect the amount a student learns are the mean ability and the range of abilities of the students in the class. The mean and standard deviation of pretest scores in the class serve as convenient measures of these factors. The effect of these two factors is dealt with by setting up a between-class regression equation in the group of teachers for predicting expected posttest scores from class characteristics. When the characteristics of a class are entered into this equation, a second estimate of the defined student's expected posttest score in that class is obtained.

When the estimated posttest score obtained from the between-class equation in a class is subtracted from the one obtained from its within-class equation, the difference may be interpreted as a measure of the effectiveness of the teacher of that class. How accurate the estimate is depends on how many of the class characteristics that affect student learning have been identified and eliminated.

4.2 Validity Problems

The fact that the achievement test used to measure student achievement by the process just described is valid is no guarantee that measures of teacher effectiveness based on that test will also be valid. On the contrary, using students' scores for such a purpose will almost certainly destroy the validity of the test.

Suppose, for example, that a school administrator notices that scores on the reading test administered annually as part of the school's testing program have been going down, and announces a campaign to improve the teaching of reading in the school. Henceforth all reading teachers will be evaluated on the basis of their students' performance on the test, and extra supervisory assistance will be given to teachers whose students' scores are below par. The intention, of course, is to improve the teaching of reading.

If past experience is any guide, at that point the primary goal of most if not all of the reading teachers in the school will change from teaching students to be better readers to teaching them to get better scores on the reading test. Instead of improving, the quality of the teaching of reading in the school will begin to decline. The administrator will not know this, because the action he or she has taken has destroyed the validity of the reading test. Instead of declining (as they would if they measured reading achievement), scores will begin to rise. Under these conditions the test measures how effective teachers are in raising students' test scores, not how effective they are in teaching them to read.

4.3 Using Measures of Teacher Effectiveness

Valid measures of teacher effectiveness can be derived from students' achievement test scores if and only if they are used for other purposes than the evaluation of individual teachers. Perhaps the most important use that can be made of such measures is to monitor and, if necessary, help increase the validity of the rating scales that are actually used to evaluate teachers.

If a school routinely administers a battery of achievement tests to its students for other purposes, as many do, the data needed to do this are available at little or no extra cost. Simple correlation coefficients between ratings of teachers and measures of their effectiveness derived from the test data will clearly indicate whether more effective teachers tend to get higher ratings than less effective ones, as they should. If they do not, correlations between ratings on individual items and the same measures of teacher effectiveness can be used to identify items that are not working so that they can be revised or replaced. It should not be necessary to point out the importance of protecting the anonymity of the teachers when this is done.

5. Conclusion

There is no consensus either about how teachers should be evaluated or about the uses to which the evaluations should be put. The main objectives of this entry have been to describe the procedures most educators use to obtain information about teachers on which to base their evaluations and to offer suggestions for strengthening these procedures.

All but the most primitive procedures for evaluating teachers assume the existence of a body of professional knowledge, knowledge of ways of teaching that maximize teachers' effectiveness in helping students achieve defined educational goals. Competence to teach is defined in terms of possession of two kinds of knowledge, knowledge of subject matter and professional knowledge, and training programs are developed to help students become competent in this sense. Prospective teachers are required to demonstrate minimum competence before they are recognized as teachers. The main instruments used to collect information to be used in evaluating teacher competence are paper-and-pencil tests of knowledge called teacher competency tests.

Once teachers are deemed competent, decisions about their employment are based on evaluations of their ability to use their knowledge on the job. The principal tools used to obtain information about teacher performance are observation instruments called teacher rating scales. Finally, teacher effectiveness is estimated by collecting data about the teacher's influence on the progress a specified kind of student makes toward a defined educational goal. Procedures for collecting data on teacher effectiveness are most appropriate for verifying and adding to the content knowledge base that is used for evaluating teacher competence and teacher performance.

See also: Evaluation, Nature of; Teacher Preparation, Conceptions of Teaching, and Evaluation: Alternative Policies; Teachers, Characteristics of Prospective; Evaluation of Educational Personnel

References

Berliner D C 1990 What's all the fuss about instructional time? In: Ben-Peritz M, Bromme R (eds.) 1990 *The Nature of Time in Schools: Theoretical Concepts, Practitioner Perceptions*. Teachers College Press, New York

Brophy J E, Good T L 1986 Teacher behavior and student achievement. In: Wittrock M C (ed.) 1986 *Handbook of Research on Teaching*, 3rd edn. Macmillan, New York

Cooper W H 1981 Ubiquitous halo. *Psych. Bull.* 90(2): 218–44

Educational Testing Service 1940–1976 *The National Teacher Examinations*. Educational Testing Service, Princeton, New Jersey

Haertel E H 1991 New forms of teacher assessment. *Rev. Res. Educ.* 17: 3–29

Kowalski J P 1978 *Evaluating Teacher Performance*. Educational Research Service, Arlington, Virginia

Medley D M, Coker H 1987 How valid are principals' judgments of teacher effectiveness? *Phi Del. Kap.* 69(2): 138–40

Medley D M, Coker H, Soar R S 1984 *Measurement-based Evaluation of Teacher Performance: An Empirical Approach*. Longman, New York

Quirk T J, Witten B J, Weinberg S F 1973 Review of studies of the concurrent and predictive validity of the National Teacher Examinations. *Rev. Educ. Res.* 43: 89–113

Further Reading

Bell L (ed.) 1988 *Appraising Teachers in Schools: A Practical Guide*. Routledge, London

Gorth W P, Chernoff M L 1985 *Testing for Teacher Certification*. Lawrence Erlbaum Associates, Hillsdale, New Jersey

Millman J, Darling-Hammond L 1990 *The New Handbook of Teacher Evaluation: Assessing Elementary and Secondary School Teachers*. Sage Publications, Newbury Park, California

Mitchell J V, Wise S L, Plake B S 1990 *Assessment of Teaching: Purposes, Practices, and Implications for the Profession*. Lawrence Erlbaum Associates, Hillsdale, New Jersey

Poster C, Poster D, Benington M 1991 *Teacher Appraisal: A Guide to Training*. Routledge, London

Smith D C (ed.) 1983 *Essential Knowledge for Beginning Educators*. ERIC Clearinghouse on Teacher Education, Washington, DC

Wragg E C 1987 *Teacher Appraisal: A Practical Guide*. Macmillan Education, Basingstoke

D. M. Medley; D. M. Shannon

Teacher Expertise

The root word for experience and expertise is the same. At one time the two terms apparently signified the same thing. An experienced worker—for example, a brewer, a tanner, or a jewelry maker—had a form of knowledge that was beyond that possessed by ordinary individuals. Guilds and unions, through their apprenticeship systems, portrayed the senior members of their associations as experts. It was obvious, however, that some of those experienced individuals were superior to others and therefore not all who were experienced deserved to be called expert in their work. Thus the notion of expertise eventually became independent from the notion of experience, though the meanings of the terms are entangled and the latter is probably the most important prerequisite for the building of the former.

Experts attain their status through experience of a special kind. In the domains in which they are acquiring their abilities, developing experts learn more from experience than do other people.

Although expertise is generally admired, it was not systematically studied by psychologists and others until comparatively recently. Certain areas in psychology were related to contemporary scholarship on expertise, however, such as research on idiot savants; training studies on the acquisition of complex skills, such as diagnosis in medicine or in electronic systems repair; and research on the acquisition of psychomotor skills. The training of telegraphers at the turn of the twentieth century by William Bryan and his student, Noble Harter (1899), was a remarkable example of the latter, revealing the importance of practice, organization, and automaticity in the development of expertise.

> The learner must come to do with one stroke of attention what now requires half a dozen, and presently in one still more inclusive stroke, what now requires 36. He must systematize the work to be done and must acquire a system of habits corresponding to the system of tasks. When he has done this he is master of the situation in his [professional field]. . . . Automatization is not genius, but it is the hands and feet of genius. (Bryan and Harter p. 375)

1. *The Development of Exemplary Performance*

As experience is gained in teaching and other areas, such as computer programming, nursing, piloting an airplane, or playing chess, some individuals get better at what they do. Psychological theories of performance acquisition, corresponding to both common sense and empirical data, usually specify three levels or stages of development—a novice stage, where errors are frequent; an intermediate stage, where some consolidation of learning takes place and automaticity is developed; and, finally, for some who work hard at acquisition of their skills, there is a stage where high levels of performance occur (see Shuell 1990 for reviews of some of these models). The developmental model of Dreyfus and Dreyfus (1986) is a little more complex, but with adaptations, fits the data collected on the acquisition of pedagogical expertise. This heuristic model specifies five stages as an individual moves from novice to expert.

1.1 Stage 1: Novice Level

A teacher at this stage may be called a greenhorn, a raw recruit, or a novice. The commonplaces of the school and classroom environments must be discriminated, the elements of the tasks to be performed need to be labeled and learned, and a set of general (i.e., context-free) rules must be acquired. The novice teacher is taught the meaning of terms like "higher-order questions," "reinforcement," and "learning disabled." Novices are taught rules such as "give praise for right answer," "wait three seconds after asking a higher-order question," and "never criticize a student." This is a stage for learning the objective facts and features of situations and for gaining experience. It is the stage at which real-world experience appears to the learner to be far more important than verbal information. Student teachers and many first-year teachers may be considered novices.

1.2 Stage 2: Advanced Beginner Level

As experience is gained, the novice becomes an advanced beginner (see Bullough 1989 for a case study of a teacher in the transition from a novice to an advanced beginner). Many second- and third-year teachers are likely to be in this developmental stage. In this stage experience can become melded with verbal knowledge, where episodic and case knowledge is built up. Similarities across contexts are recognized. Without meaningful past episodes and cases to which experience of the present can be related, individuals are unsure of themselves; they do not know what to do or what not to do. In education advanced beginners might have difficulty knowing what to do when a child challenges the teacher's authority, neurotically seeks the teacher's attention, or boasts of their "A" performance. Strategic knowledge—when to ignore or break rules and when to follow them—is also developed in this stage as context begins to guide behavior. For example, teachers learn that praise does not always have the desired effect, as when a low-ability child interprets it as communicating low expectations. They also learn that criticism after a bad performance by a usually good student can be quite motivating. Experience is affecting behavior but the advanced beginner may still have no sense of what is important.

The novice and the advanced beginner, though intensely involved in the learning process, often fail to take full responsibility for their actions. This failure occurs because they are labeling and describing events, following rules, and recognizing and classifying contexts, but not yet actively determining through personal agency what is happening. The acceptance of full personal responsibility for classroom instruction occurs when one develops a sense of personal agency, willfully choosing what to do. This acceptance occurs in the next stage of development.

1.3 Stage 3: Competent Level

With further experience, and some motivation to succeed, most of the advanced beginners become competent teachers. Not all advanced beginners, however, are likely to reach this level. Evidence exists that some teachers remain "fixed" at a less than competent level of performance (Borko 1992, Eisenhart and Jones 1992). Nevertheless it is believed that many third- and fourth-year teachers, as well as most experienced teachers, reach a level of performance that is considered to be competent.

There are two distinguishing characteristics of competent performers of a skill. First, they make conscious choices about what they are going to do. They set priorities and decide on plans. They have rational goals and choose sensible means for reaching the ends they have in mind. Second, while enacting their skill, they can determine what is and what is not important. From their experience they know what to attend to and what to ignore. As a consequence, they also learn not to make timing and targeting errors. In this stage teachers learn to make curriculum and instruction decisions, such as when to stay with a topic and when to move on, based on a particular teaching context and a particular group of students.

Because they are more personally in control of the events around them, following their own plans and responding only to the information they choose, teachers at the competent stage tend to feel more responsibility for what happens. They are not detached and thus often feel emotional about success and failure in their area in a way that is different and more intense than do novices or advanced beginners. They also have more vivid memories of their successes and failures. Competent teachers are still not yet very fast, fluid, or flexible.

1.4 Stage 4: Proficient Level

Perhaps in about the fifth year, a modest number of teachers may move into the proficient stage of development, a stage at which intuition or know-how becomes prominent. To use an analogy, at some point in learning a dance step individuals no longer think about the kinds of adjustments needed; they stop counting their steps to keep time to the music, and develop a more "intuitive" sense of the situation.

Furthermore, out of the wealth of experience that the proficient individuals have accumulated comes a holistic way of viewing the situations they encounter. They recognize similarities among events that the novice fails to see. For example, the proficient teacher may notice, without conscious effort, that today's mathematics lesson is faltering for the same reason that last week's spelling lesson failed. At some higher level of pattern categorization, the similarities between disparate events are understood. This holistic recognition of patterns as similar allows the proficient individual to predict events more precisely, since they see more things as alike and as having been experienced before.

1.5 Stage 5: Expert Level

If the novice is deliberate, the advanced beginner insightful, the competent performer rational, and the proficient performer intuitive, the expert might be categorized as often arational. Experts have an intuitive grasp of the situation and seem to sense in nonanalytic and nondeliberative ways the appropriate response to be made. They show fluid performance, as most people do when they no longer have to choose their words when speaking, or think about where to place their feet when walking. People simply talk and walk in an apparently effortless manner.

Experts perform in a way that is qualitatively different from the novice or the competent performer. They are exemplified by a science teacher who reports that the lesson moved along so well today that she never really had to teach. Experts are not consciously choosing what to attend to and what to do. They are acting effortlessly and fluidly, and in a sense this is arational because it is not easily described as deductive or analytic behavior. Though beyond the usual meaning of rational, since neither calculation nor deliberative thought are involved, the behavior of the expert is certainly not irrational. Insight into the behavior of the expert can be obtained from the writings of Schon (1983), as he discusses knowledge-in-action, and from the work of Polya (1954), in his discussion of the role played by tacit knowledge in problem-solving.

Tasks carried out by experts usually work, and thus, when matters proceed without any trouble, experts are not solving problems or making decisions in the usual sense. When anomalies occur, when matters do not work out as planned or something atypical is noted, deliberate analytic processes are brought to bear upon the situation. When things are going smoothly, however, experts rarely appear to be reflective about their performance.

2. Descriptive Propositions about Teacher Expertise

The theory of the development of teacher expertise has heuristic value for thinking about educating and evaluating teachers. It is also reasonably well-supported by data collected since the late 1980s (Berliner 1987, Berliner et al. 1988). For example, Bents and Bents (1990) studied the transitions that occur between novice, advanced beginner, and expert teachers and verified the sensibility of these stages. They characterized the transition as moving from a teacher-centered or self-centered novice, to a more student-centered advanced beginner, to a stage in which the expert teacher was a much more integrated individual.

Almost all studies of pedagogical expertise have been small-scale and nonexperimental. However, there is some consistency across these studies, and there are a number of strong propositions about expertise in pedagogy. While some of these overlap with the general characteristics of experts, others are specific to the domain of teaching.

2.1 Proposition 1: Domain and Context

The first proposition is that experts excel mainly in their own domain and in particular contexts.

Chi et al. (1988) and Glaser (1987) note that experts excel primarily in a single domain because they have a great deal more experience in some domains than in others. In studies by Lesgold and his colleagues (1988) expert radiologists were estimated to be looking at their 100,000th X-ray. Chess experts have spent 10,000–20,000 hours staring at chess positions (deGroot 1965, Newell and Simon 1972, Chase and Simon 1973). With the lengthy time commitments that are necessary to become expert in complex areas of human functioning, it is not surprising that individuals generally excel in only a single domain.

Time and experience play a similar role in the development of pedagogical expertise. Anecdotal reports suggest that teachers will not hit their peak performance until at least five years of on-the-job experience have been obtained. The expert teacher, say with 10 years experience, has spent a minimum of 10,000 hours in classrooms as a teacher, preceded by a least 15,000 hours in classrooms as a student, though it is unknown if the latter experience is of any value. Experience alone certainly will not make a teacher an expert, but it is likely that almost every expert pedagogue has had extensive classroom experience.

The domain-specific knowledge that is acquired through lengthy experience is quite contextualized. For example, expert teachers have reported that their expertise depends, in part, on knowing their students. They know the cognitive abilities of the students they teach regularly, giving them insight for determining the level at which to teach. They know their students personally, so that in their classrooms they do not need to rely on bureaucratic and formal mechanisms of control while teaching. Finally, their students knew about them and had certain expectations about what their teaching would be like. Expert teachers had students who expected to be well taught and to learn a great deal, even if they were pushed to their intellectual limits (Berliner et al. 1988).

2.2 Proposition 2: Automaticity

The second proposition is that experts often develop automaticity for the repetitive operations that are needed to accomplish their goals.

Glaser (1987) notes the efficient decoding skill of the expert comprehender in reading as an example of the way automaticity frees working memory to allow other more complex characteristics of the situation to be dealt with. The automaticity or routinization of some teaching functions among expert teachers serves the same purpose. For example, Leinhardt and Greeno (1986), in studying elementary school mathematics lessons, compared an expert's opening homework review with that of a novice. The expert teacher was found to be quite brief, taking about one-third less time than the novice. This expert was able to pick up information about attendance, about who did or did not do the homework, and was also able to identify who was going to need help later in the lesson. She elicited mostly correct answers throughout the activity and managed also to get all the homework corrected. Moreover, she did so at a brisk pace and never lost any control of the lesson.

In contrast, when the novice was enacting an opening homework review as part of a mathematics lesson, she was not able to get an understanding on who did and did not do the homework, she had problems with taking attendance, and she asked ambiguous questions that led to her misunderstanding of the difficulty of the homework. Of importance is that the novice showed a lack of familiarity with well-practiced routines. She seemed not to have habitual ways to act. Students, therefore, were unsure of their roles in the class. Additional research supportive of this proposition has been conducted by Brooks and Hawke (1985), Carter et al. (1987), Krabbe and Tullgren (1989), and Hawkins and Sharpe (in press).

2.3 Proposition 3: Task Demands and Social Situations

The third proposition is that experts are more sensitive to task demands and social situations when solving problems.

Housner and Griffey (1985), in a study of experienced and novice physical education teachers, provide evidence of the sensitivity of experienced teachers to task demands and social situations. They found that the number of requests for information made by experienced and novice teachers during the time they were planning instruction was about the same. Each group made reasonable requests for information about the number of students they would be teaching, their gender, their age, and so forth, but in two areas the experienced teachers made many more requests than did the novice teachers. They needed to know about the ability, experience, and background of the students they were to teach, and they needed to know about the facility in which they would be teaching. In fact, five of the eight experienced teachers in this study of planning and instruction demanded to see the facility in which they would teach before they could develop their plan. Novices made no such requests.

Experienced teachers were sensitive to the social and physical environment under which instruction was to take place. When actually teaching they implemented changes in their instruction more often than did novices, using social cues to guide their interactive instructional decision-making. They used their judgment about student performance as a cue to change instruction 24 percent more often than did novices. They used their judgments about student involvement as a cue 41 percent more often, student enjoyment of the activities as a cue 79 percent more frequently, and their interpretation of mood and student feelings 82 percent more often.

The novices used student verbal statements about the activity as their primary cue for instituting a change in their instructional activity. They responded to these cues 131 percent more often than did the experienced teachers. Clearly, the novice teachers changed what they were doing primarily when asked to; however, they seemed unable to decode the social cues emitted by students about the ways in which instruction was proceeding. The experienced teachers, on the other hand, were far more sensitive to the social cues emitted in the situation, and they used these social cues for adjusting their instruction. Other examples of this sensitivity to the task demands and social setting abound (Nelson 1988, Cushing et al. 1989, and Hawkins and Sharpe in press).

2.4 Proposition 4: Opportunism and Flexibility

The fourth proposition is that experts are more opportunistic and flexible in their teaching than are novices.

Glaser (1987) reports that experts are opportunistic in both their planning and their actions. They take advantage of new information, quickly bringing new interpretations and representations of the problem to light. Borko and Livingston (1988) use the term "improvizational performer" to characterize the opportunistic quality of the lessons of expert teachers. They see the expert teachers as having a well-thought-out general script to follow, but being very flexible in following it in order to be responsive to what students do.

Professor Richard Snow of Stanford University once described teaching using the metaphor of "the teacher as a Bayesian sheepdog." The image is that of the teacher or sheepdog letting the students or flock wander, to a certain extent, but bringing them back into line if they stray too far. The teacher can be flexible and opportunistic, but based on remembrances of past experiences (the Bayesian calculation of prior probabilities) the teacher also keeps the students on a course that has them conclude at an appropriate place.

2.5 Proposition 5: Approach to Problems

The fifth proposition is that experts represent problems in qualitatively different ways than do novices.

Chi et al. (1988) note that experts seem to understand problems at a deeper level than do novices. Experts apply concepts and principles that are more relevant to the problem to be solved. The understanding of novices seems to be at a more superficial level, with fewer instances shown of principled reasoning.

Nelson (1988) conducted a study in which expert and novice physical education teachers were the subjects. She concluded that experts displayed a greater variety of application of sound principles of teaching than did novices. The experts were also more creative and thorough in descriptions of ways to address teaching problems, and provided more solutions to each problem that they addressed. Similarly, Peterson and Comeaux (1987) found that the comments of experienced teachers reflected an underlying knowledge structure, while those of novices did not.

Expert teachers also differ in the inferences they make about the student cognitions used in answering an item. Experts seemed to have a fund of knowledge about the way students think and how those thoughts interact with the content of the specific mathematics or science items. In addition, the experts seemed able to think through the misalgorithms that students might apply. The experts had more experience dealing with student errors and therefore knew what types of errors students might make. Novices rarely discussed the issue of misalgorithms that students might apply to solve a problem.

2.6 Proposition 6: Interpreting Patterns

The sixth proposition is that experts have fast and accurate pattern-recognition capabilities. Novices cannot always make sense of what they experience.

The accurate interpretation of cues and the recognition of patterns reduces a person's cognitive processing load. Quick pattern recognition allows an expert chess player to spot areas of the board where difficulties might occur. Novices are not as good at recognizing such patterns, and when they do note them they are less likely to make proper inferences about the situation.

The ability of novices or other relatively inexperienced teachers to interpret classroom information in some reliable way is limited precisely because of their lack of experience. The information related to pedagogical events may be so rich and complex that novices and advanced beginners simply cannot agree on what is seen. In a study in which three television screens had to be monitored simultaneously, advanced beginners seemed to experience difficulty in making sense of their classroom observations and in providing plausible explanations about what was occurring within the classroom (Sabers et al. 1991). As a group, these first-year teachers seemed unable to make sense of what they saw. They experienced difficulty monitoring all three video screens at once. Thus, they often reported contradictory observations and appeared confused about what they were observing and about the meaning of their observations.

Carter et al. (1988) also found differences in the interpretive competency of experts and novices. In this study, novice, advanced beginner, and expert teachers were asked to watch a series of slides depicting science or mathematics instruction in a high school. The teachers held a remote control and were told to go through the 50 or so slides at their own pace, stopping to comment on any slides that they found interesting. The experts, more often than the subjects in the other groups, found the same slides worth commenting about, and made the same kinds of comments.

This reduction in variance by the experts is particularly noteworthy. It means they have learned to pay attention to some of the same things and to interpret visual stimuli in the same way. This similarity in what is attended to and how it is interpreted is what people hope for when they visit an expert ophthalmologist or automobile mechanic. Novices or advanced beginners—anyone in the early stages of skill acquisition—will not have acquired enough experience for that.

2.7 *Proposition 7: Meaningfulness and Patterns*

The seventh proposition is that experts perceive meaningful patterns in the domain in which they are experienced.

The superior perceptual skills of experts are readily apparent, but there is no reason to believe they are the result of any innate superior perceptual abilities (Chi et al. 1988). Rather, their superiority can be attributed to the way in which experience affects perception. After 100,000 X-rays, or the 10,000th hour of observing students, what is attended to and how that information is interpreted is likely to have changed for anyone motivated to learn from their experience. In this regard, Carter et al. (1988) asked expert, novice, and advanced beginners to view some slides of classrooms and describe what they saw. The slides were flashed on the screen for only a very brief time. The responses of the novices and advanced beginners to the slide were clearly descriptive, and usually quite accurate. In contrast to these literal descriptions typical of novices and advanced beginners, some of the expert teachers often responded with inferences about what they saw. For experts, the information that was often deemed important was information that had instructional significance, such as the age of the students or the teaching/learning activity in which they were engaged. They perceived more meaningful patterns than did novices.

In any field, the information that experts extract from the phenomenon with which they are confronted, stems, in part, from the concepts and principles that they use to impose meaning on phenomena in their domain of expertise. That is, experts in all domains appear to be top-down processors. They impose meaning on the stimuli in their domain of expertise.

2.8 *Proposition 8: Problem-solving Characteristics*

The final proposition is that, although experts may begin to solve problems slower, they bring richer and more personal sources of information to bear on the problem that they are trying to solve.

In Hanninen's (1985) study of expert and less expert teachers of gifted children, the mean time for a novice to read through a scenario and begin writing about ways to help solve the problems of a particular child was 2.6 minutes. The experienced teachers, who had no background in gifted education, took 3.0 minutes. The mean time for teachers with experience/expertise in teaching gifted children was 9.8 minutes. That is, from the start of reading their problem up to the start of presenting their solutions, it took the experts three or four times as long as the other two groups. When one knows a good deal more about teaching, or some other domain, more time seems to be needed to represent the problem and to access the relevant knowledge needed to address the problem. If one does not have much information in storage, one need not look too long for relevant information.

Experts, unlike novices, can bring to bear rich personal stores of knowledge when they begin to address the problems they face. Peterson and Comeaux (1987) found that their experienced teachers "often gave more elaborated answers to the questions and gave more justifications for their decisions or comments." Nelson (1988) found that experts "provide longer and more detailed analyses of situational data; were more creative and thorough in descriptions of ways to handle various teaching concerns; provided more solutions to problems; were more thoughtful to needs of individual students; [and] displayed a greater variety of application of sound principles of teaching."

3. *Conclusion*

Capturing the uniqueness of expert teaching performance is difficult. All of the studies to date have been small, generally qualitative, and highly interpretive. Furthermore, they have tended to be descriptive rather than experimental. As a consequence, there are continuing problems in adequately identifying expert, proficient, and competent teachers, and these questions lead to problems with theory development.

On the other hand, the problem is not insurmountable for those in search of a heuristic rather than a scientifically adequate theory about the development of expertise. Theory, it should be remembered, is not to be judged on its truthfulness, but on its usefulness. The five-stage theory presented in this entry fits data well enough to allow educationalists and researchers to think sensibly about the development of knowledge and skill in teaching.

Generalizing from studies in this domain is not too difficult. The propositions offered by Glaser (1987) from studies of expertise across disparate fields are highly compatible with the ones derived from studies of teaching. Thus, teacher expertise provides an interesting case in which many imperfect studies, across many different fields, have yielded a coherent body of knowledge and a heuristic theory to think about the acquisition of expertise in teaching.

Individuals who excel at a task, whether it be physics, medical diagnosis, chess, or teaching are of great interest, and provide psychology with subjects that have unique perceptual, conceptual, and psychomotor skill. When people have reasons to master some domain, and the opportunity to do so, they can reach levels of competency, proficiency, and expertise not ordinarily achieved.

References

Bents M, Bents R 1990 Perceptions of good teaching among novice, advanced beginner, and expert teachers. Paper presented at the meeting of the American Educational Research Association, Boston, Massachusetts

Berliner D C 1987 In pursuit of the expert pedagogue. *Educ. Researcher* 15: 5–13

Berliner D C et al. 1988 Implications of research on pedagogical expertise and experience for mathematics teaching. In: Grouws D A, Cooney T J (eds.) 1988 *Perspectives on Research on Effective Mathematics Teaching*. National Council of Teachers of Mathematics, Reston, Virginia

Borko H 1992 Patterns across the profiles: A critical look at theories of learning to teach. Paper presented at the meeting of the American Educational Research Association, San Francisco, California

Borko H, Livingston C 1988 Expert and novice teachers' mathematics instruction: Planning, teaching, and postlesson reflections. Paper presented at the meeting of the American Educational Research Association, New Orleans, Louisiana

Brooks D M, Hawke G 1985 Effective and ineffective session opening teacher activity and task structures. Paper presented at the meeting of the American Educational Research Association, Chicago, Illinois

Bryan W L, Harter N 1899 Studies of the telegraphic language: The acquisition of a hierarchy of habits. *Psychol. Rev.* 6: 345–75

Bullough R 1989 *First Year Teacher: A Case Study*. Teachers College Press, New York

Carter K, Cushing K, Sabers D, Stein P, Berliner D C 1988 Expert–novice differences in perceiving and processing visual information. *J. Teach. Educ.* 39 (3): 25–31

Carter K, Sabers D, Cushing K, Pinnegar P, Berliner D C 1987 Processing and using information about students: A study of expert, novice, and postulant teachers. *Teaching and Teacher Education* 3: 147–57

Chase W G, Simon H A 1973 Perception in chess. *Cognit. Psychol.* 4: 55–81

Chi M T H, Glaser R, Farr M 1988 *The Nature of Expertise*. Erlbaum, Hillsdale, New Jersey

Cushing, K S, Sabers D, Berliner D C 1989 Expert–novice research studies: Implications for teacher empowerment. In: Kerrins J A (Ed.) 1989 *Empowering the Teaching Learning Process*, Proc. 6th Annual Conf. on Issues and Trends in Educational Leadership. Colorado Springs, Colorado

deGroot A D 1965 *Thought and Choice in Chess*. Mouton, The Hague

Dreyfus H L, Dreyfus S E 1986 *Mind over Machine*. Free Press, New York

Eisenhart M, Jones D 1992 Developing teacher expertise: Two theories and a study. Paper presented at the meeting of the American Educational Research Association, San Francisco, California

Glaser R 1987 Thoughts on expertise. In: Schooler C, Schaie W (Eds.), *Cognitive Functioning and Social Structure over the Life Course*. Ablex, Norwood, New Jersey

Hanninen G 1985 Do experts exist in gifted education? (Unpublished manuscript, University of Arizona, Tucson, Arizona)

Hawkins A, Sharpe T in press Field system analysis: In search of the expert pedagogue. *The Journal of Teaching in Physical Education*

Housner L D, Griffey D C 1985 Teacher cognition: Differences in planning and interactive decision-making between experienced and inexperienced teachers. *Research Quarterly for Exercise and Sport* 56: 44–53

Krabbe M A, Tullgren R 1989 A comparison of experienced and novice teachers' routines and procedures during set and discussion instructional activity segments. Paper presented at the meeting of the American Educational Research Association, San Francisco, California

Leinhardt G, Greeno J 1986 The cognitive skill of teaching. *J. Educ. Psychol.* 78: 75–95

Lesgold A et al. 1988 Expertise in a complex skill: Diagnosing X-ray pictures. In: Chi M T H, Glaser R, Farr M 1988

Nelson K R 1988 Thinking processes, management routines, and student perceptions of expert and novice physical education teachers. (Unpublished dissertation, Louisiana State University, Baton Rouge, Louisiana)

Newell A, Simon H A 1972 *Human Problem Solving*. Prentice-Hall, Englewood Cliffs, New Jersey

Peterson P L, Comeaux M A 1987 Teachers' schemata for classroom events: The mental scaffolding of teachers' thinking during classroom instruction. *Teaching and Teacher Education* 3: 319–31

Polya G 1954 *How to Solve It*. Princeton University Press, Princeton, New Jersey

Sabers D, Cushing K, Berliner D C 1991 Differences among teachers in a task characterized by simultaneity, multidimensionality, and immediacy. *Am. Educ. Res. J.* 28: 63–88

Schon D 1983 *The Reflective Practitioner*. Basic Books, New York

Shuell T 1990 Phases of meaningful learning. *Rev. Res. Educ.* 60: 531–48

D. C. Berliner

Teacher Managerial Behaviors

The classroom setting, including the myriad demands placed on the teacher's attention by large numbers of pupils, is a complex context. Order and cooperation are necessary in such a setting to conduct activities in which learning can occur. Teacher managerial behaviors organize the setting, establish appropriate behavior, prevent problems, and deal with disruptions. These actions can be viewed as a process starting with planning and preparation at the beginning of the school year or term and continuing with maintenance of the behavior setting over time.

1. The Classroom Context

Classrooms are busy places, full of children or adolescents, not all of whom are present by choice. Securing cooperation so that learning can take place is a necessary goal of the classroom teacher. Thus, providing instruction and managing behavior are complementary aspects of the teacher's classroom role.

To appreciate the complexity of the teacher's managerial task, it is instructive to consider a few cross-sectional glimpses of classroom life—a teacher providing instruction using a small group format, for example. In this activity, the teacher instructs a small group of students while the remainder of the class works independently. To prepare for the activity, the teacher needs to attend to the following issues: where to meet with the small group, how to move students to and from the small group location, what activities are suitable for the students not in the small group, what materials to use in the small group and with the students working independently, what routines to use for monitoring and providing assistance, and what procedures to establish governing student talk and movement. Even as seemingly straightforward an activity as presenting a lesson in a whole class format needs sound management. The physical setting must be arranged, appropriate materials prepared and kept at hand, and expectations for student participation made clear.

In addition to these planned, preactive aspects of management, other more reactive managerial behaviors continue throughout the conduct of the activities. The teacher monitors student behavior, captures and recaptures student attention, fends off interruptions and intrusions, and, when necessary, deals with disruptions to the activity. The on-going management of students during instruction is complicated by the rapidity with which behaviors occur, calling for split-second, seemingly reflexive decisions. Time for reflective contemplation of potential actions and for a careful balancing of long- and short-range outcomes is in very short supply during the active phases of teaching.

Other features of classroom teaching that are significant for teacher management are the "groupness" of instruction, the teacher's isolation from other teachers during much of the workday, and the social and organizational structure of schools and teaching. In most schools, teachers instruct students in groups for most of the day. Consequently, many managerial decisions must be made and carried out in full view of all students in the group, even if they involve only one student or a small number of students. Thus, the impact of a behavior or strategy on the total class must be considered, and the teacher is usually constrained by the necessity of monitoring the whole class while reacting to individual problems. The absence of other adults in the classroom, except for occasional evaluation visits, limits the amount of external feedback the teacher receives.

Standardized data on pupil progress comes only once a year, if that, so changes in the teacher's managerial behaviors are affected mainly by students' immediate reactions. Teachers generally feel some pressure to cover the grade-level curriculum, especially at the elementary level in basic skills subjects and at the secondary level in subjects that are prerequisite to further work. Instructional and managerial problems arise as individual differences in student interests, temperament, abilities, and achievement intersect the rigidity of the curriculum and available time.

2. Critical Concepts

Establishing and maintaining classroom order has long been accepted as one of the teacher's major roles. Although some assistance from school administrators is expected by most teachers, chiefly in the form of dealing with insubordinate students, most teachers accept the responsibility for managing behavior in their own classrooms.

2.1 Teacher Control of Students

By implication, accepting responsibility for establishing order becomes a duty to control students. As Denscombe (1985) notes, teachers lack technological and material resources to control students (although some special education settings may provide exceptions), so must rely on personalized authority and personal commitments. Denscombe places control strategies into one of three general categories: domination, cooptation, and classwork management.

"Domination" strategies autocratically impose the teacher's ideas of order on the students through restricted activities, consequences, and insistence on obedience. "Cooptation" seeks to win over the students' cooperation by involving the students in governance, emphasizing choices and logical consequences rather than punishments, and developing more involving curricula. "Classwork management" strategies focus on creating lessons that keep students on-task, so that cooperation with the lesson structure prevents misbehavior. In effect, the teacher controls the students indirectly, via the requirements of the activities; control is accomplished through maintaining a smooth activity flow, limiting diversions from the primary "vector of action," and preventing competing secondary vectors of action from becoming established (Doyle 1986). While the three strategies are conceptually distinct, most teachers' practices are a mixture, with the degree of utilization of each strategy a matter of values, training, and personal experiences.

2.2 Classroom Activities

Activity structures (Berliner 1983) are unique features of classrooms that influence teacher managerial behaviors. An "activity" can be defined as a predictable pattern of teacher and student behaviors occurring for a segment of time. Transitions between activities are marked by significant shifts in the teacher's and the students' behaviors. Some of the more common activities in classrooms are whole class, teacher-led, presentations, recitations, and discussions; small group instruction and small group projects; individual seatwork; and tests. Some subjects have unique activities (e.g., the science laboratory or the choir performance), but most activity types cross content boundaries. The teacher must arrange a sequence of activities so that proper instruction can take place within the constraints imposed by the available time. Activities are thus building blocks for instruction. Because different activities, by definition, require different behaviors, the teacher needs to understand the behavioral requirements of each and be prepared to teach these to the students, to monitor compliance, and to redirect behavior when necessary.

2.3 Routines and Procedures

Efficient routines and procedures, characteristic of the classrooms of expert teachers, are important aids to management because they provide recurrent, predictable patterns of behavior that simplify the students' and teacher's task of making their way through the complexities of the behavioral environment (Berliner 1988). A "procedure" is a simple behavior designed to accomplish something specific; a "routine" is usually a combination of several procedures. Once students have learned the routines and procedures that are used in a class, the teacher's management task is simplified.

If, however, routines are not available or practiced for commonly used activities, then the lack of structure can result in lost instructional time and difficulty in group management. If a secondary teacher fails to establish a routine for the beginning of the class period, students might wander about the room, talk excessively, and delay the start of instruction, while at the same time the teacher might have difficulty taking attendance, enforcing school rules for tardiness, managing previously absent students, and beginning the day's content development activity.

2.4 Preventive and Reactive Strategies

Conceptualizations of teacher managerial behaviors frequently distinguish between "prevention" and "reaction." Preventive strategies include arrangement of the physical setting, establishing general rules and routines to guide student behavior, establishing predictable consequences, developing an efficient work system, and conducting lessons in ways that maintain student involvement (Emmer et al. 1989). The goal of preventive strategies is to set up an environment that has strong cues for appropriate behavior and that encourages student engagement in class activities. Reactive strategies occur in response to a lack of cooperation; for example, to student behaviors that interfere with the flow of appropriate behavior in an activity, to noncompliance with school or classroom rules, and to aggressive or disruptive behaviors.

Reactive strategies (Kerr and Nelson 1983, Stoner et al. 1991) vary in complexity. Those requiring little time or teacher effort include eye contact or other signals and verbal desists. Somewhat more time-consuming or involving strategies are brief removal of the student from the activity, using an established consequence, or changing the task requirements for the student. Still more complex and time-consuming are strategies such as arranging a contract for appropriate behavior, holding a conference with the student or parents, or developing a contingency management program to reduce inappropriate behavior and to establish desirable behavior. When choosing to react, key considerations for the teacher are the amount of time available for intervention, the seriousness of the problem (will it spread or become more intense?), and whether the problem can be dealt with in the classroom and during the on-going activity.

2.5 Academic Tasks

The concept of the "academic task" (Doyle and Carter 1984) helps bridge the domains of managerial behaviors, the curriculum, and instructional behaviors. An academic task is defined in terms of the products or outcomes produced by the student, such as a writing sample, a completed set of problems, or an oral performance, and the resources available to help the student achieve the outcome. Classroom resources include curricular materials, the teacher, other students, and available time. Teacher managerial behaviors thus support student achievement to the extent that they facilitate or make available the resources needed by students.

Similarly, curricular planning and instruction influence management, according to the degree to which the academic task structure engages students and promotes success. Discipline problems occur most frequently in classrooms in which there are large numbers of students with a poor match between the academic task structure and their interests and prior academic achievements. Dealing with the situation as purely a managerial or disciplinary problem will address only one side of the equation; curricular and grouping/tracking practices must be altered in order to achieve a better solution (Slavin 1989, Jones 1989).

3. Integrative Analysis: A Comprehensive Perspective of Teacher Managerial Behaviors

Research on the managerial behaviors of teachers has been extensive and multidisciplinary. It has included detailed ethnographic analyses of (usually) one or a few classes and teachers; other forms of naturalistic inquiry, such as observational studies in the tradition of ecological psychology and of sociolinguistics; large-scale process–product studies; and applied behavior analysis. Other research has been a hybridization of methodologies, reflecting crossfertilization in the field of research on teaching. This research has yielded a substantial amount of knowledge.

3.1 Classroom Management and the Beginning of the School Year

Although much of the research in classrooms takes a cross-sectional view of events, some longitudinal studies have included observations of the first few days and weeks of school, as well as interviews with teachers about their management strategies at the beginning of the year (Everston and Emmer 1982). These studies indicate that teachers who have well-managed classrooms later in the year have a well-developed conception of what student behaviors are desirable and undesirable. In addition, they have a good idea of the procedures and routines that will be needed in their classrooms. In other words, classroom management begins before students arrive.

In a sense, all prior experiences of teachers contribute to their cognitive and behavioral maps of the classroom, and planning for management is comingled with thinking about the curriculum and instruction. Yet it is clear that teachers develop a distinct system of management that includes arranging the physical setting (to facilitate monitoring and accessibility; to limit distractability), identifying specific procedures and routines in many areas (e.g., talk and movement in particular activities, out-of-room policies, handling previously absent students, use of materials, communicating assignments), planning general or specific rules or guidelines (some teachers make this a cooperative effort with students), deciding what consequences (rewards and penalties) will be used, and planning initial activities to use during the first week or so of school. These areas of management are worked out before students arrive; if not, then there is a higher risk of students learning inappropriate behaviors at the beginning of the year, and greater demands being placed on the teacher's ability to monitor student behavior and react to problems as the year progresses.

3.2 Initial Meetings with Students

Teacher managerial behaviors at the start of school can be viewed broadly as directed at socializing students into the classroom setting and putting into place the procedures and routines that define the management system. In effect, students need to learn what behaviors are appropriate in the various activities. Students are made aware of norms directly when the teacher states expectations about particular behaviors, explains procedures, and directs students' activities. Often a set of rules or guidelines for behavior are presented to (or developed cooperatively with) students.

Students also learn about appropriate behavior as the result of feedback from the teacher and consequences of their behavior. In addition, students learn about expectations indirectly by observing other students' behaviors and the consequences that occur or do not occur. Classroom norms become established over time, in the context of the activity structure used by the teacher, rather than as some unique task divorced from instruction. In the early grades, the socialization process occurs over many weeks or even months; in later grades, the process takes place more rapidly, as teachers and students draw upon prior experience in familiar activities.

3.3 On-going Teacher Management: Maintaining Activity Flow

The establishment and maintenance of appropriate behavior and the prevention of inappropriate behavior depend substantially on the teacher keeping students productively engaged in academic activities. In a well-respected set of naturalistic studies, Kounin (1970) and his colleagues identified a rich set of concepts to describe group management strategies.

During whole class activities, teachers can foster student involvement and keep activities free of disruption by nipping incipient misbehavior in the bud ("withitness") before it spreads or becomes more intense. "Overlapping," that is, handling simultaneously two or more events or situations, also helps keep order in the busy classroom. Activities that are conducted smoothly (minimal teacher-induced interruptions and irrelevances) and with good momentum (briskly paced) are the goals. Teachers also can use alerting or focusing strategies (signals or statements that capture whole class attention), accountability (communicating that student work or performance will be checked or observed), and activity formats that require more than just passive sitting and listening.

Management of independent seatwork activities is aided by greater task and format variety and by teacher comments which engender interest in and motivation for the activities. Transitions between activities can be the source of behavior problems, both during transitions and spilling over into the subsequent academic activity; however, such problems can be reduced by teacher structuring and monitoring of student behavior during the transition (Arlin 1979).

3.4 Teacher Management of Problem Behaviors

In addition to preventive management and to the ongoing management of student behaviors via maintenance of activity flow during instruction, teachers must deal with disruptive and other problem student behaviors. Although much research in different countries (e.g., Wheldall and Glynn 1989, Doyle 1986) indicates that the predominant forms of misbehavior are individually not very threatening or destructive (e.g., talking out of turn, wasting time, wandering around the classroom), their presence in large amounts can be very detrimental to the maintenance of order and to the conduct of academic activities. Furthermore, some forms of misbehavior such as aggressive acting out, interference with the activities of the teacher or other students, abusive language, or frequent refusal to follow reasonable classroom rules and routines, are encountered to some degree by most teachers.

Many of the recommended strategies for teachers were developed initially for special populations, such as behavior-disordered students. Generally, the strategies draw heavily from the field of applied behavior analysis, although they may also include components from psychotherapeutic and psychoeducational perspectives (Gallagher 1988, Maurer 1988). Examples of specific strategies that have some research base in the applied behavior analysis literature include time-out, partial exclusion, self-recording of behaviors, charting behaviors, individual concrete rewards, token reward systems, group activity rewards, goal setting, withholding rewards or privileges systematically, response cost systems, providing differential feedback and attention, and reducing distracting cues.

Applied behavior analysis strategies begin with a careful assessment of the classroom environment (and possibly external settings) to determine cues for the problem behavior and its consequences. A similar analysis is often done for desirable behaviors that can substitute for the problem behaviors. Then an intervention, which typically has goals of reducing the problem behavior and substituting more desirable ones, is implemented. Intervention usually requires altering the environment (e.g., teacher's behavior, materials, other students' behaviors, seating arrangements, assignments) to eliminate cues for the inappropriate behavior and to establish signals for the desirable alternative. The intervention usually will include changes in the consequences for the behaviors. Typically, reinforcers for the undesirable behavior will be eliminated and rewards for the desirable behavior will be added or strengthened. Since generalization of the acquired behaviors is often a problem, fading of extrinsic reinforcement is needed in order to have the best chance of producing a lasting change in behavior.

Therapeutic interventions generally attempt to alter the students' cognitions as well as behaviors. Although many such interventions are designed for long-term use by professionals outside the classroom, some have been specifically developed for teachers. A widely applied approach has been Glasser's "reality therapy."

A teacher following this intervention model initially meets with the student. After the nature of the problem behavior is clarified, the teacher works with the student to evaluate whether the behavior is helpful or harmful and to obtain a commitment to change the behavior. A plan for change is agreed upon and tried out. Failure to follow the plan results in another conference or in agreed-upon consequences. The assumption in working with the student is that behavior is a matter of choice, and that acceptance of responsibility for behavior and understanding its consequences go hand in hand. Evaluations of this approach to dealing with problem behaviors indicate support for its effectiveness in reducing a variety of disruptive behaviors (Emmer and Aussiker 1990).

4. Emergent Trends and Issues

Greater attention has been given in research to the role of teacher and student cognition in the management process. Cognitive processes such as teacher and student attributions about causes for behaviors, efficacy beliefs, and evaluations influence teacher decision-making about management strategies. Furthermore, research has begun to focus more attention on students' views of teacher managerial behaviors (Allen 1986), providing a more balanced view of effects. As more of the research on teacher and student cognition moves from analog and questionnaire formats to naturalistic studies in classrooms, a clearer picture should appear of the relationships between these cognitive factors and managerial behaviors and outcomes.

Although the education of children and adolescents occurs in a variety of contexts, most research on teacher management has been done in traditional classrooms. Examination of teacher managerial behaviors in such settings as cooperative learning groups, computer-dense classrooms, and alternative schools would be very useful, as more and more communities experiment with varied forms of schooling. Some of the findings from initial looks at management in nontraditional contexts suggest that new conceptions may be needed. For example, Cohen (1991) reports on the negative effects of teacher direction in group instruction formats focused on higher order thinking objectives. Thus, some of the emphasis on structuring activities and tasks may be inappropriate for management in this setting.

Research on teacher managerial behaviors generally does not take into account the complex interplay of teacher emotion and behavior, nor has the field taken advantage of advances in knowledge from behavioral science research. Yet, the enormous range of emotions surrounding teaching and, especially, discipline would seem to make this a fertile field for inquiry. For example, Cambone (1990), in a year-long study of a teacher's struggle to manage and teach a group of seriously disturbed children, makes a strong case for love as a core category to explain the teacher's motivation and behavior. Thus, knowledge about teacher managerial behaviors is building upon a strong behavioral research base, while moving toward a broadened view of relevant settings, teacher and student characteristics, and underlying processes.

See also: Classroom Rules and Routines; Teacher Planning, Approaches to; Discipline in Schools

References

Allen J D 1986 Classroom management: Students' perspectives, goals, and strategies. *Am. Educ. Res. J.* 23(3): 437–59

Arlin M 1979 Teacher transitions can disrupt time flow in classrooms. *Am. Educ. Res. J.* 16(1): 42–56

Berliner D C 1983 Developing conceptions of classroom environments. *Educ. Psychol.* 18(1): 1–13

Berliner D C 1988 *The Development of Expertise in Pedagogy*. American Association of Colleges for Teacher Education, Washington, DC

Cambone J 1990 Teachers and teaching. Tipping the balance. *Harv. Educ. Rev.* 60(2): 217–36

Cohen E G 1991 Classroom management and complex instruction. Paper presented at the annual meeting of the American Educational Research Association, Chicago, Illinois

Denscombe M 1985 *Classroom Control: A Sociological Perspective*. Unwin-Hyman, London

Doyle W 1986 Classroom organization and management. In: Wittrock M (ed.) 1986 *Third Handbook of Research on Teaching*. Macmillan, New York

Doyle W, Carter K 1984 Academic tasks in classrooms. *Curric. Inq.* 14(2): 29–49

Emmer E T, Aussiker A 1990 School and classroom discipline programs: How well do they work? In: Moles O C (ed.) 1990 *Student Discipline Strategies: Research and Practice*. State University of New York Press, Albany, New York

Emmer E T, Evertson C M, Sanford J, Clements B, Worsham M 1989 *Classroom Management for Secondary Teachers*, 2nd edn. Prentice-Hall, Englewood Cliffs, New Jersey

Everston C M, Emmer E T 1982 Effective management at the beginning of the year in junior high classes. *J. Educ. Psychol.* 74(4): 485–98

Gallagher P A 1988 *Teaching Students with Behavior Disorders*. Love, Denver, Colorado

Jones N (ed.) 1989 *School Management and Pupil Behavior*. Falmer Press, London

Kerr M M, Nelson C M 1983 *Strategies for Managing Behavior Problems in the Classroom*. Merrill, Columbus, Ohio

Kounin J S 1970 *Discipline and Group Management in Classrooms*. Holt, Rinehart and Winston, New York

Maurer R E 1988 *Special Educators Discipline Handbook*. Center for Applied Research in Education, West Nyack, New York

Slavin R E (ed.) 1989 *School and Classroom Organization*. Lawrence Erlbaum, Hillsdale, New Jersey

Stoner G, Shinn M R, Walker H M (eds.) 1991 *Interventions for Achievement and Behavior Problems*. National Association of School Psychologists, Silver Spring, Maryland

Wheldall K, Glynn T 1989 *Effective Classroom Learning: A Behavioral Interactionist Approach to Teaching*. Basil Blackwell, Oxford

Further Reading

Bowers C A, Flinders D J 1990 *Responsive Teaching: An Ecological Approach to Classroom Patterns of Language, Culture, and Thought*. Teachers College Press, New York

Good T L, Brophy J E 1987 *Looking in Classrooms*, 4th edn. Harper and Row, New York

Jones V F, Jones L S 1989 *Comprehensive Classroom Management*, 3rd edn. Allyn and Bacon, Boston, Massachusetts

Pitcher G D, Poland S 1992 *Crisis Intervention in the Schools*. Guilford Press, New York

E. T. Emmer

Teacher Planning, Approaches to

Planning is an essential component of teaching. Teachers are responsible daily and over the course of the year for selecting and designing subject matter-based learning experiences reflecting a school curriculum and community learning goals. A teacher must also be ready to respond to student needs and interests and be ready to make the most of unanticipated learning opportunities arising in instructional interactions. Doing this successfully requires preparation.

1. Conceptions of Planning

Planning and preparation have been the object of educational theory and research since the early 1950s. Since then, there have been major shifts in philosophy, disciplinary theory, and research methods. Dominant conceptions of teaching have moved from scientific, to managerial, to professional. Likewise, research on teaching has shifted from being dominated by psychological conceptions to incorporating concepts from sociology, anthropology, linguistics, and philosophy.

Within psychology, orientations have changed from entirely behavioral to cognitive and sociocultural. Research methods have expanded during these years from almost exclusively laboratory-based and experimental to embrace naturalistic, field-based approaches. The findings of research on teacher planning and the emerging conceptions about planning's role in teaching are best understood in the context of this dynamic research environment. Research on teacher planning can be characterized as a shift from technical to psychological to ecological conceptions of planning and instruction.

1.1 Technical Conceptions

Prior to 1970 the study of teacher planning was largely confined to theoretical prescriptions focusing on the form that good plans should take. These models, similar to rational decision making models defining rational practice in other fields, recommended four basic planning steps: (a) specify objectives, (b) select learning activities, (c) organize learning activities, and (d) specify evaluation procedures (Tyler 1950, Popham and Baker 1970). Underlying this model was the dominant assumption that student learning is under the control of the teacher and that careful design and management of small units of instruction is the major determinant of student success. This assumption undergirded scientific and technical models dominating teaching in the 1950s and 1960s. It expressed itself in the almost exclusive focus on precise (usually behavioral) specification of learning objectives and instructional tasks (Mager 1962).

1.2 Psychological Conceptions

In 1970 educational researchers began to study the actual planning processes of classroom teachers. One factor leading to this interest was the observation that the linear, objective-driven planning procedures that dominated teacher education were rarely found useful by experienced and successful classroom teachers. Were teachers abandoning rationality for expediency or was there another form of reasonableness in their practice? In effect, this question framed research on teacher planning from 1970 to the mid-1980s.

Early empirical studies in the 1970s confirmed the hypothesis that teachers' instructional planning did not tend to follow the prescribed planning models. Taylor's (1970) study of course planning strategies reported by teachers in British secondary schools found that the needs, abilities, and interests of pupils rather than predetermined objectives dominated syllabus planning. Zahorik (1975) found similar results in his examination of the reported use of behavioral objectives and the "separate ends–means" model in comparison to the "integrated ends–means" model proposed by Eisner (1967) that viewed objectives as implicit in learning activities. Planning decisions most frequently listed by teachers in his study related to pupil activities, and just over half of the teachers said they began their planning by making decisions about lesson content.

Studies observing teacher decision-making during simulated or controlled classroom planning sessions in the mid-1970s yielded findings similar to those above. Peterson et al. (1978) examined teachers' plans as they prepared to teach an unfamiliar group of students in a laboratory situation. They found teachers spent the largest proportion of their planning time on the content to be taught, the next largest amount on strategies and activities (instructional processes), and the smallest portion on objectives.

Morine-Dershimer and Vallance's (1976) study of written plans collected for experimenter-prescribed lessons found teachers paid little explicit attention to behavioral objectives, diagnosis of pupils' needs, evaluation procedures, and alternate courses of action in their written plans. However, the teachers reported that writing plans for researcher-prescribed lessons was not typical of their planning, and observations of their classroom teaching revealed that much of what the teachers had planned was not reflected in their written outlines (Morine-Dershimer 1979).

The growing influence of cognitive psychology on research on teaching in the 1970s led to research questions and studies focusing on describing the mental processes involved in teacher planning. Laboratory studies of teachers' decisions and judgments during planning (Clark and Yinger 1979, Shavelson and Borko 1979) confirmed the self-reports from earlier studies that content and student concerns rather than well-specified objectives were the focus of planning deliberations for most teachers. These studies also suggested that the instructional activity was an important organizing framework for teacher thought and behavior.

An extended classroom case study of teacher planning by Yinger (1980) combined process-tracing methods from cognitive psychology with ethnographic methods from anthropology to create a broad description of planning processes over the course of a school year. The most significant finding of this study was the complex ways in which planning deliberations were embedded in a particular teaching context. Lesson planning was found to be situated in and dependent upon a complex network of yearly plans, term plans, unit plans, and weekly and daily plans. The teacher's knowledge and experience with the particular students and subject matter materials from one day to the next contributed to a highly responsive and recursive mode of planning and teaching.

These observations and a review of research on planning in other professional fields led Yinger (1980) to propose a cyclical process model describing planning as a progressive elaboration of both goals and activities over time, based on a teacher's knowledge of past successes and failures and the ability to fine-tune instruction in response to anticipated student needs and abilities. Though this model was focused on describing teachers' mental planning processes, it clearly revealed the degree to which teacher thought and action is situated in complex social, cultural, and historical contexts.

This grounding of teacher thinking was dramatically revealed in a later study by Yinger and

Clark (1982) when they asked teachers to judge the quality of plans for language arts instructional activities. A process tracing analysis of these teachers' judgments revealed that they were unwilling and unable to judge quality or usefulness without mentally projecting and visualizing the plans as they played out in their own classrooms with their current set of students. Smith and Sandelbach (1979) found similar mental projections in the unit planning of sixth grade teachers' science instruction.

1.3 Ecological Conceptions

Research since 1980 has moved from examining planning as an individual psychological process and has begun investigating the connections between planning and classroom interaction, the ways planning and teaching respond to subject matter content, and the give and take that occurs in classrooms. Carnahan (1980) studied the planning and subsequent instructional behavior of nine fifth-grade teachers teaching the same mathematics unit. He found that the main relationship between written plans and instructional interaction was organizational and structural rather than predicting and specifying particular verbal behavior. These findings are similar to those in Clark and Yinger's (1979) survey of the planning of 78 teachers who reported that written plans rarely serve the purpose of providing detailed lesson scripts to be implemented by the teacher in class. Instead, the teachers' written responses to why they plan fell into three clusters:

(a) planning to meet immediate personal needs (e.g., to reduce uncertainty and anxiety, to find a sense of direction, confidence, and security);

(b) planning as a means to the end of instruction (e.g., to learn the material, to collect and organize materials, to organize time and activity flow); and

(c) direct use of plans during instruction (e.g., to organize students, to get an activity started, to aid memory, to provide a framework for instruction and evaluation).

McLeod's (1981) study based on stimulated recall interviews with 17 kindergarten teachers found that on the average an equal amount of intended learning outcomes are formulated during classroom interaction as during planning. These, as well as other studies examining planning and interaction (Acosta 1986, Broeckmans 1985, Peterson et al. 1978, Zahorik 1970) taken together, suggest that teacher planning does influence opportunity to learn, content coverage, grouping for instruction, and the general focus of classroom processes. They also highlight that the finer details of classroom interaction are unpredictable and, therefore, are not planned. Planning frames the broad outlines of what is possible or likely to occur while teaching (Creemers and Westerhof 1982), but once interaction begins, planning moves to the background and instructional improvisation becomes more important (Yinger 1987).

The trend in research on teaching has been to study teaching and classroom practices from a more holistic perspective. Fewer studies have focused on planning as a separate teaching component. Rather, planning is being described and analyzed as it is connected to classroom practices and teacher knowledge. For example, Leinhardt and her colleagues have sought to understand how teachers use subject matter knowledge in planning lesson frameworks ("agendas") and during interactive instruction (Leinhardt et al. 1987). In her study comparing expert and novice mathematics instruction (Leinhardt 1989) she found mathematics lessons composed by expert teachers incorporating rich agendas, consistent but flexible lesson structures, and clear, understandable explanations.

Borko and Livingston (1989), in their study of beginning and experienced teachers of mathematics, also found that much of the success of experienced teachers lay with their abilities to think more broadly and long-term about intended outcomes, to draw upon a richer representational repertoire for lesson content and structure, and to be more responsive to incorporating students' questions and interests into lessons. These and other classroom studies of teaching practice (e.g., Dillard 1992, Lampert 1986) indicate that both planning and classroom interaction are responsive, compositional, and situated (i.e., contextualized).

2. Classroom Interaction and Teacher Planning

Studies of language and social interaction in classrooms describe the social and cultural nature of lessons (Cazden 1986). Though teachers enter classrooms with purposes and plans, these studies detail how both teaching and learning are jointly constructed, socially negotiated, and embedded in an interactional history (Mehan 1979). Not only are memories, understandings, and actions present on an individual basis, but studies of sustained interaction in learning communities indicate that memory and meaning are created and shared synergistically and often are known only in the actions of the group (Wertsch 1987).

A number of studies of teacher interaction suggest that improvisation rather than implementation or decision-making is a more powerful way of describing the performance skills of many teachers (Borko and Livingston 1989, Buswinka 1990, Haley-Oliphant 1990, Yinger 1987). The ability to respond to the give-and-take of learners and situations is largely based on a sophisticated repertoire of subject matter appropriate knowledge and activity frameworks. Skillful teaching, these studies suggest, is deeply

Planning	Interaction
Intention (individual)	Intention (individual and jointly constructed)
Knowledge (individual)	Knowledge (individual and shared)
Interaction (individual: mental and physical)	Interaction (social and mutual)
Place (deliberate: known and envisioned)	Place (interactive: experienced and created)
To create ↓	To create ↓
Frames for action (plans) Frames of mind (preparation)	Activity, understanding, and relationship

Figure 1
Differences between planning and interaction

situated (contextualized) both within the subject matter and the place of the classroom, school, and community.

Portraying the interactive components of teaching as responsive, compositional, and situated helps explain the findings of much of the research on teacher planning. Getting ready for interaction as dynamic as that which occurs during instructional lessons seems to be less a matter of prediction and control and more a matter of preparation and responsiveness. In this framework, planning that produces more general, flexible, and activity-based plans will be more useful than narrowly specified, objective-oriented plans. Also, plans become more useful if they are not designed to be implemented as a means of controlling interaction, but rather as a framing device that provides a starting point of instructional interaction.

Rather than seeing planning and classroom interaction as separate activities or processes, then, research findings highlight their connectedness and similarity. Goals, purpose, and intention are a part of both planning and interaction. Both processes are highly interactive and sensitive to context and place.

3. *Differences Between Planning and Interaction*

As Fig. 1 outlines, the major difference between planning and interaction is that intention, knowledge, and interaction in planning are limited by the individual's knowledge and experience and the inability to control, predict, or even comprehensively understand what is to come in the future. Planning seeks to anticipate activities, conversations, questions, responses, and relationships in classrooms. Often, the best that planning can accomplish is to prepare teachers to participate thoughtfully and effectively in classroom interaction. Planning produces frames for action; preparation produces a frame of mind.

Once instruction begins, intention, knowledge, and interaction must respond to a created context and to multiple participants. Intentions become negotiated, knowledge shared, and interactions mutual. A well prepared teacher can harness this dynamic energy to achieve the understanding and relationships important to student learning. Exactly how this gets accomplished in a particular situation becomes part of a teacher's repertoire of knowledge and experience and thus a potential contributor to future planning and preparation.

See also: Teachers' Roles; Planning for Effective Teaching in Developing Nations; Frame Factors

References

Acosta J M 1986 Pensamiento del Profesor y la Planificación de la Enseñanza. Paper presented at the 1st International Congress on Teacher Thinking and Decision Making, La Rabida

Borko H, Livingston C 1989 Cognition and improvisation: Differences in mathematics instruction by expert and novice teachers. *Am. Educ. Res. J.* 26: 473–98

Broeckmans J 1985 Developments in student-teachers' preactive teaching. Paper presented at International Study Association on Teacher Thinking conference, Tilburg University, Tilburg

Buswinka H F 1990 A Change in practice: A case study of teacher thinking-in-action. Doctoral dissertation, University of Cincinnati, Cincinnati, Ohio

Carnahan R S 1980 *The Effects of Teacher Planning on Classroom Processes*. Wisconsin R & D Center for Individualized Schooling, Madison, Wisconsin

Cazden C 1986 Classroom discourse. In: Wittrock M C (ed.) 1986 *Handbook of Research on Teaching*, 3rd edn. Macmillan, New York

Clark C M, Yinger R J 1979 Three studies of teacher planning. Paper presented at American Educational Research Association, San Francisco, California

Creemers B P M, Westerhof K 1982 *Routinization of Instructive and Management Behaviors of Teachers*. Educational Research Institute, North Haren
Dillard J A 1992 Voice in the conversation of practice: A case study of teacher thinking-in-action. Doctoral dissertation, University of Cincinnati, Cincinnati, Ohio
Eisner E W 1967 Educational objects: Help or hindrance *Sch. Rev*. 75: 250–60
Haley-Oliphant A 1990 Classroom ecology in a science class: A description of interaction patterns in the margins of lessons. Doctoral dissertation, University of Cincinnati, Cincinnati, Ohio
Lampert M 1986 Knowing, doing and teaching multiplication. *Cognition and Instruction* 3(4): 305–42
Leinhardt G 1989 Math lessons: A contrast of novice and expert competence. *J. Res. Math. Educ*. 20(1): 52–75
Leinhardt G, Wideman C, Hammond K M 1987 Introduction and integration of classroom routines by expert teachers. *Curric. Inq*. 17(2): 135–76
Mager R F 1962 *Preparing Instructional Objectives*. Fearon Publishers, Belmont, California
McLeod M A 1981 The identification of intended learning outcomes by early childhood teachers: An exploratory study. Doctoral dissertation, University of Alberta, Edmonton
Mehan H 1979 *Learning Lessons: Social Organization in the Classroom*. Harvard University Press, Cambridge, Massachusetts
Morine-Derschimer G 1979 *Teacher Plan and Classroom Reality: The South Bay Study*. Institute for Research on Teaching, East Lansing, Michigan
Morine-Derschimer G, Vallance E 1976 *Teacher Planning*. Far West Laboratory, San Francisco, California
Peterson P L, Marx R W, Clark C M 1978 Teacher planning, teacher behavior, and student achievement. *Am. Educ. Res. J*. 15: 417–32
Popham J W, Baker E L 1970 *Systematic Instruction*. Prentice-Hall, Englewood Cliffs New Jersey
Shavelson R J, Borko H 1979 Research on teachers' decisions in planning instruction. *Educational Horizons* 57(4): 183–89
Smith E L, Sandelbach N B 1979 Teacher intentions for science instruction and their antecedents in program materials. Paper presented at the American Educational Research Association, San Francisco, California
Taylor P H 1970 *How Teachers Plan Their Courses*. National Foundation for Educational Research, Windsor
Tyler R W 1950 *Basic Principles of Curriculum and Instruction*. University of Chicago Press, Chicago, Illinois
Wertsch J 1987 Collective memory: Issues from a sociohistorical perspective. *Quarterly Newsletter of the Laboratory of Comparative Human Cognition* 9(1): 19–22
Yinger R J 1980 A study of teacher planning. *Elem. Sch. J*. 80(3): 107–27
Yinger R J 1987 By the seat of your pants: An inquiry into improvisation and teaching. Paper presented at the American Educational Research Association, Washington, DC
Yinger R J, Clark C M 1982 *Understanding Teachers' Judgments about Instruction: The Task, the Method, and the Meaning*. Institute for Research on Teaching, East Lansing, Michigan
Zahorik J A 1970 Effects of planning on teaching. *Elem. Sch. J*. 71: 143–51
Zahorik J A 1975 Teachers' planning models. *Educ. Leadership* 33(2): 134–39

Further Reading

Borko H 1970 An examination of some factors contributing to teacher preinstructional classroom organization and management decisions. Paper presented at the American Educational Research Association, Toronto, Ontario
Mintz S L 1970 Teacher planning: Simulation study. Paper presented at the American Educational Research Association, San Francisco, California

R. J. Yinger; M. S. Hendricks-Lee

Teacher Preparation, Conceptions of Teaching, and Evaluation: Alternative Policies

This entry has a dual agenda, namely, to recount the links between conceptions of teaching, teacher evaluation, and teacher preparation *and* to do this for both traditional and emerging alternative conceptions. For North American writers the task is as much an imaginative one as it is one of practical description since the three areas—conceptions of teaching, teacher evaluation, teacher preparation—are mostly separate functions in North America both at the level of policy formulation and in practice. There is more need for, and a tradition of, integrated policy formulation and coordinated practices among these areas in Third World countries (Sharpes 1988, Chapman and Carrier 1990). Various government (e.g., Fullan and Connelly 1987), academic/university (e.g., Holmes Group 1990), and private (e.g., Carnegie Forum 1986) policy task forces and commissions exist. However, these tend to parallel the decentralized administrative structure of educational functions and are, therefore, fragmented reports mostly done in isolation from other functions. Nevertheless, there is a growing literature on educational reform in developing countries which emphasizes the policy and management environment as important contexts for teacher preparation and instructional improvement (Chapman and Carrier 1990). This entry approaches these matters through the published research literature and gives the appearance of more links among the three functions than actually exist in practice. Since 1988, there has been an explosion of published research on teacher preparation (e.g., Houston 1990) and teacher evaluation (Millman and Darling-Hammond 1990). There has not been a similar explosion of research on conceptions of teaching.

1. Traditional Conceptions of Teaching and Teacher Evaluation

1.1 Traditional Conceptions of Teaching

Medley (1982) identified five conceptions of the

effective teacher based on the following factors: personal traits, teaching methods, classroom atmosphere, competencies, and decision-making. Here Medley's list is adapted and three conceptions are discussed: trait, input–output, process–product. Other constructions of this literature are, of course, possible.

The trait view, in use in the early 1990s in teacher recruitment and induction practices, has a research history going back to the turn-of-the-century. In its "strong" form it is assumed that teachers are born, not made, and that anyone may be a judge of teachers since everyone has been at school. The research format is to ask students, principals, parents, and others to remember their best teacher and then to describe that person's characteristics. In an illustrative study, Charters and Waples (1929) concluded that adaptability, considerateness, enthusiasm, good judgment, honesty, and magnetism were the six most important traits.

A more scientific version of the trait view emerged in the use of observational rating forms. Rating forms contain lists of traits (personality, knowledge, skill, beliefs) which raters either mark as present or absent, or present to a degree. Instrument validity and reliability are low (Ryan 1986). Consequently, there is little valid and reliable knowledge about the traits of effective teachers and, therefore, little that is of help in the designing of teacher preparation programs, in establishing certification criteria, and for the hiring and evaluation of teachers (Stiggins and Duke 1988).

Input–output studies are black box studies of school effects. According to this conception, teaching, and teachers, are considered to be effective only in so far as there is residual output variance not accounted for by input variance on such matters as economic levels, student ability, and socioeconomic status. Coleman et al.'s (1966) study of the equality of educational opportunity, along with its subsequent analysis (e.g., Jencks et al. 1972), helped create a climate of opinion that teachers and teaching have little effect on student achievement. While the methodology of this work has been criticized, the net effect of the input–output view of teaching has been to make educators at all levels more conscious of the limitations of schooling. In developed countries, there are no direct consequences of this conception for either teacher preparation or teacher evaluation policy and practice. There are, however, political consequences for how willing legislators might be to provide resources for the reform of teacher preparation. Furthermore, in developing countries caught in a squeeze of expanding school population and tight resources, the question of what influence the school has on achievement, especially on literacy and numeracy, has received research attention. The general result is that certain teacher preparation characteristics are now considered to be important variables in school achievement (Fuller 1990).

The process–product conception assumes that it is what teachers do, rather than what they are, that makes a difference to educational outcomes. Much process–product research focuses on teacher behavior but the category also includes instructional processes and instructional context. Dunkin and Biddle's (1974) model of research on teaching was influential in defining process–product studies although it, of course, grew out of earlier work. The model consists of four sets of variables:

(a) presage variables (e.g., teacher characteristics);

(b) context variables (e.g., student characteristics);

(c) process variables (e.g., classroom interactions);

(d) product variables (e.g., achievement).

Concrete results have been inconclusive and disappointing. Medley's enthusiasm: "we now have the first clear-cut usable findings obtained in eighty years of research in teacher effectiveness" (1982 p.1898) is not shared by researchers such as Ryan (1986) who directed the IEA Classroom Environment Study. Ryan concluded that "our efforts to use a process–product research model to generate knowledge of effective teacher behaviours . . . failed to yield such knowledge . . . the product–process model of teacher effectiveness research failed far short of what we need to move from research findings to implications for improving teaching and learning" (pp.41–42). Very little research has been done on what teachers do in developing countries (Fuller 1990).

The most widely quoted teacher-preparation-based process–product study, the Beginning Teacher Evaluation Study (Powell 1980), yielded little evidence that discrete teacher behaviors can be linked to student learning (Wise et al. 1987). Accordingly, notwithstanding the explosion of teacher effectiveness research in the 1960s, 1970s, and early 1980s, the picture of research-based design for teacher evaluation and teacher preparation is not markedly more promising than it was when based on the trait conception and the discouragements of the input–output conception.

1.2 Policy Issues

There are two teacher preparation policy issues that are related to these conceptions of teaching: governance and the integration of inservice teacher preparation with pre-service teacher preparation. "Governance" refers to the control of entry and exit to the profession and includes certification, procedures for dismissal, and standards. The process is political and varies according to different systems of government. In centralized settings, governance tends to be under the jurisdiction of a national government whereas in state and provincial systems such as United States and Canada, governance is ordinarily the responsibility of the local state and province. Decentralization has led to state-by-state and institution-by-institution variation and to low public confidence within the United States.

Little is known about the quality of teacher preparation programs approved by certification. It is common for teachers to have permanent certification withheld pending successful completion of one or more years of teaching but, again, evaluations tend to be perfunctory. The political need to staff classrooms means that in times of shortage, teachers are often granted interim certification without completing formal requirements. Various accrediting associations (e.g., National Council for the Accreditation of Teacher Preparation) have developed in the United States to establish more common criteria and standards and to increase public confidence (Houston 1990). In the United States and the United Kingdom there is a trend in the late 1980s and early 1990s to increased government control of teacher certification (Adams and Tulasiewicz 1989). In continental Europe, an opposite trend toward less control is emerging (Kron 1989). The political changes in Europe will undoubtedly influence this trend.

Two alternatives to traditional patterns of certification are in evidence in North America. The first is a shift to more collaborative forms of governance. Collaboration is associated with the assignment of more certification responsibility to employing boards of education. Shanker (1987), President of the American Federation of Teachers, wants to take this a step further in the United States by making the profession central to certification. A second trend in the United States is toward the testing of teacher competencies as a prerequisite to certification. However, existing teacher tests have limited validity. In the United States, the National Board for Professional Teaching Standards has been formed. By 1993 it is anticipated that the board will begin testing teachers for certification. While this American program is an exception, generally speaking neither traditional nor emerging alternative programs are strongly based on research, nor is there a strong research/evaluative tradition associated with the introduction of new programs which might be of use for governance policies.

Traditionally, pre-service and inservice teacher preparation are separate functions (Fullan and Connelly 1987). Centralized governments often make it mandatory for inservice teachers to attend workshops to study new government curriculum policy but the conception of teaching as a lifelong career in which pre-service teacher preparation and inservice education are linked is a relatively recent notion. There is, however, an emerging research tradition on teacher development and teachers' careers which may have policy consequences for the continuum. Much of this research is oriented to showing how learning to become a teacher is a lifelong activity. The first few years of teaching are especially important in this regard. As a result, for countries where teachers may be expected to make a career of teaching, or to stay in teaching for several years, the link between pre-service and inservice education, and the provision of inservice teacher preparation, is an increasingly important policy area (Clandinin 1989, Connelly and Clandinin 1988).

1.3 Teachers' Views of Traditional Conceptions of Teaching

Most traditional teacher evaluation is carried on in a "perfunctory bureaucratic" way (Wise et al. 1987) and tends to be isolated from system planning, from teacher goals and purposes and from a conception of the continuum of a teaching career. There is only a modest literature on teachers' views of this process and most of it suggests that teachers are unsympathetic. Lawton et al.'s (1986) six conclusions represent the state of the art:

(a) Teachers do not believe that teacher evaluation improves teaching.

(b) Teachers prefer a counseling and interview approach over observation.

(c) Teachers believe their superiors should be evaluated if teachers are evaluated.

(d) Teachers believe that summative and formative evaluation should be separated.

(e) Teachers believe that peer- and self-evaluation are best.

(f) Teachers believe that several evaluation methods used together give the best picture.

There is a marked symmetry between the minimal effects of teacher effectiveness research and teachers' more intuitionally unsympathetic responses to it. For a system of teacher evaluation to be effective in the long run, it needs not only a reliable and valid research base but also the understanding and support of its users. Consistent with Lawton et al.'s fifth conclusion, Wise et al. (1987) argue for a peer-based teacher evaluation system which they believe would ultimately increase the quality of teaching by enhancing teacher professionalism. The success of peer-based methods is presumably related to the educational levels of teachers, and these vary markedly throughout the world. In countries where teaching tends not to be a career, peer-based methods would appear to have less potential for combining teacher evaluation with teacher inservice education than in countries where people choose teaching as a career.

An anomaly of traditional teacher preparation is that it is tenaciously embedded in many societies without the benefit of a strong research and knowledge base and in the context of a commonly held view that teacher preparation makes little difference to how one learns to be a teacher. Teachers' views of pre-service teacher preparation tend not to be markedly more positive than they are of teacher evaluation. Wideen and Holborn (1986) found that in Canada, university preparation is "not held in high esteem by students, teachers, or principals" (p.574) whereas the practicum was the most valued part of teacher preparation. Research in the United States on teachers' perceived value of teacher preparation and of the value of practical experience over formal university studies tells a similar story. There are few qualitative follow-up studies of teachers entering a profession or of work such as Clandinin's (1989) narrative case study work of teachers' actual thinking and practices during their first year of teaching and later which would contribute an explanatory basis for these observations. The customary response to negative teacher views of pre-service teacher preparation is to fine tune the program in hopes of generating more positive experiences. However, a more comprehensive view would begin with a conception of teaching, take into account the practical learning that occurs during teaching, integrate a professional development-oriented teacher evaluation plan, and only then consider what a pre-service program might contribute.

2. Traditional Conceptions of Teacher Preparation

Historically, teacher preparation passed through several steps: no training or on-the-job training; training by religious orders; government-based training in "normal schools"; teachers colleges; and university faculties, schools, and departments of education. This "evolutionary" outlook on the history of teacher preparation (Ginsburg 1988) is not unlike the situation in the professions generally. Schön (1984 p.8) refers to this evolution as the "success of the professionals," a success which is generally attributed to increasing professional reliance on a knowledge base. The shift of teacher preparation from the normal schools into the universities constituted a transition from reliance on practical wisdom to academic knowledge and represented practical losses, as well as theoretical gains, in the capacity to educate teachers. The evolutionary view of theory-driven teacher development as a basis for improved professional performance is being criticized from both reflective practice (Schön 1983) and critical theory (Ginsburg 1988) outlooks. Zeichner and Liston (1990) have outlined four traditions of reform which are apparent in teacher preparation programs in the early 1990s: research-based, social efficiency, developmental, and social reconstructionist.

Traditional teacher preparation curricula contain discipline components of two sorts, instrumental subject matter and liberal arts and science background areas. Policy versions of both discipline types have come and gone more or less as fads in teacher preparation. Structure of knowledge and disciplinary inquiry were, for example, key words in the late 1950s and 1960s. The preoccupation with knowledge in the 1990s (see Sect. 3.2 below) is mostly a replay of the traditional discipline focus. Private foundation-supported discipline-based teacher preparation programs sprang up in the best United States universities in the 1970s and 1980s. Two American reports, those of the Holmes Group (1990) and the Carnegie Forum (1986), found fault with traditional teacher preparation programs in terms of their limited requirements for disciplinary knowledge. They propose making academic liberal arts and science degrees prerequisites to entering teacher preparation programs.

Within universities, methods courses (see also Sect. 2.4) have been considered a bridge between the disciplines, knowledge of teaching, and the practice of teaching. The traditional bridging conception is one of "technical–rational" application (Schön 1983), that is, what is known about the disciplines and about teaching are applied in methods courses to the development of skills and techniques for effective practice. This conception is under heavy attack by people working in an alternative reflective practice tradition. One of the central dilemmas for teacher preparation in the 1990s is essentially one of thinking through alternative theories of teaching practice and how practice may be methodologically related to disciplinary knowledge and to traditional research conceptions of teaching. Revised notions of teaching practice need to be connected to a teacher preparation continuum (see Sect. 1.2) and to a more integrated notion of education, evaluation, and the role of research.

Turning to the practicum it is important to recall Dewey's (1904) distinction between apprenticeship and laboratory programs. In apprenticeship programs, teachers model their actions on others (e.g., watching films, reading case studies, working under associate and mentor teachers) and in laboratory programs teachers engage in inquiry and learn by solving practical problems. Several practicum programs have become well enough established to be given names—for instance, "micro-teaching," "peer teaching," "demonstration," "inquiry." It may safely be assumed that these traditional practicum programs, and the ones described below in Sect. 3 as alternatives, are mostly apprenticeship and laboratory variations.

3. Alternative Conceptions of Teaching and Teacher Preparation

In the 1990s, as research on teaching and teacher

preparation has become better funded, there have developed a number of "new" conceptions of teaching with attendant policy implications for teacher preparation and teacher evaluation. What follows is a summary of some of the dominant alternative conceptions.

3.1 The Expert–Novice Conception

Much research has focused on identifying the skills, strategies, cognitive structures, and models of teaching that effective "expert" teachers use. "Expert" teachers are normally named by researchers as fulfilling certain researcher-specified criteria or are identified through reports by others whose judgment the researchers accept. What constitutes "expertness," however, is a highly contentious matter which is mostly overlooked in the literature because of the working assumptions that researchers can recognize expertness and that expertness is one thing commonly agreed to by all. For the most part, this research is rooted in psychological models of human behavior and has been conducted by educational psychologists. Three lines of research, identified with three groups of researchers, are illustrative.

The "management skills of expert teachers" line of research has identified sets of management skills used by "expert" teachers (e.g., questioning and control strategies, use of praise, and use of instructional time). Hunter (1984), for instance, identified skills and strategies of experts which are different from those of "less expert" teachers and used this knowledge to develop management workshops for boards of education.

A second line of research, "cognitive skills of expert teachers," identifies the cognitive skills and decision-making patterns of "expert" teachers. The research identifies the kind of information expert teachers collect and the ways in which they process such information to arrive at decisions regarding students and instructional and evaluation strategies. Berliner's (1986) work on expert teacher decision-making and cognitive judgment skills as differing from novice teachers' skills is illustrative of this conception of teaching.

In the third line of research—"models of teaching"—different teaching approaches used by experts are identified and described. Joyce and Weil (1980), for example, identified, described, and classified into four categories a number of distinct models of teaching used by "expert" teachers.

The overall thrust of teacher preparation approaches based on the expert–novice conception is to provide a detailed description and analysis of the identifiable skills of experts as distinct from novices. The work of teacher preparation, then, is to provide these skills to novice and less expert teachers and thereafter to "coach" these teachers until they are able to adequately perform the skills. Teachers acquire these skills using strategies such as "clinical supervision," "peer teaching," and "coaching" of the less expert teachers by more expert teachers or others.

3.2 Subject Matter Knowledge Conception

In the 1980s, a conception of teaching emerged which refocused attention on subject matter knowledge. For the most part, this work identifies the structures of knowledge in each subject matter area, the main concepts and topics in the area, and the possible ways that knowledge can be transformed for pedagogical purposes (see also Sect. 2).

This conception is associated with researchers such as Shulman (1987) and colleagues (in areas such as English literature and biology), and several teams at the Michigan Institute for Research on Teaching (working on several subjects). In this conception, the processes by which teachers transform subject matter knowledge to pedagogical knowledge and action through pedagogical reasoning and reflection are identified. Shulman's conception of teaching, which is a model of pedagogical reasoning and action, involves comprehension, reasoning, transformation, and reflection. The conception of pedagogical reasoning emphasizes the intellectual basis for teaching performance rather than behavior alone.

There are several significant possibilities for teacher preparation that follow from the subject matter knowledge conception of teaching. First, prospective teachers must either have or acquire disciplinary knowledge. They can learn ways of transforming this knowledge to pedagogical knowledge. For this purpose, laboratory exercises (Dewey 1904) using exemplars, case studies of effective transformations, simulations where prospective teachers engage in pedagogical transformations, and other forms of simulations which require pedagogical reasoning and reflection may be designed.

3.3 Organizational Models Conception

A third conception of teaching follows from organizational models in which school boards, schools, and universities work together. These organizational models constitute a conception of teaching in which administrative arrangements for teacher preparation (e.g., practicum, induction) are collaboratively negotiated among various stakeholder groups.

One line of collaborative research is Lieberman's (1986) research and development in the Seattle–Puget Sound Consortium. This work "has potential for producing knowledge when teachers define the problems of their work. Their definitions are rooted in the complexities of practice" (p.32). This conception of teaching creates a "structure for cooperation." The process of team deliberation produces organizational change in building "a sense of colleagueship."

There have been efforts to re-organize the university teaching staff in education and liberal arts and sciences to create a more coherent approach to teacher preparation (Brandt 1991). More complex organizational developments are evident in the creation of professional development schools in which university faculty, teachers, and student teachers work together (Holmes Group 1990).

The research and development on teacher centers in the United Kingdom also emerged from a similar conception of teaching. These centers are seen as organizational models which bring teachers together in more collaborative ways for purposes of cooperation. A related organizational model involves teachers taking control of their own ongoing development through teacher inquiry groups (see, e.g., the Among Teachers Community—Clandinin and Connelly 1991).

Organizational models of teaching lead to more collaborative relationships among universities, teachers, school boards, and government for the planning of teacher preparation. Such matters as certification requirements, teacher selection, pre-service curricula, practica, and inservice offerings are all possibilities. Collaborative relationships become, therefore, the context in which teacher preparation is negotiated.

3.4 Reflective Practice/Teaching as Inquiry Conception

A conception of teaching as reflective practice is discussed in much research on teaching. Here, teaching is viewed as reflective dialogue among teachers, students, subject matter, text, and context. Teaching is conceptualized as a process of inquiry in which teachers' knowing in action is continually constructed and reconstructed in teaching practice. Of the several reflective practice lines of inquiry, four are illustrative.

Schön's (1983) "reflection in, and on, practice" conception emerges from a view of the context of practice as marked by "complexity, uncertainty, instability, uniqueness, and value conflicts" (1983 p.14) and yields a practice-based conception of professional knowledge. "Our knowing is in our action" (Schön 1983 p.49) and is "ordinarily tacit" he says. In Schön's view, teachers are thinkers who turn thought back on action in what he terms "reflection in, and on, action." This conception of teaching is, then, one of the practice as a process in which the teacher "reflects on the understandings which have been implicit in his action, understandings which he surfaces, criticizes, restructures, and embodies in further action" (p.50).

A second line of inquiry, "narrative/personal practical knowledge," as adapted to educational studies, refers to the making of meaning through personal experience via a process of reflection (Connelly and Clandinin 1988). In this conception, teaching is a process of living one's personal and professional stories in an ongoing experiential text and telling one's stories in words as one reflects upon life and explains oneself to others. In this conception, teachers are always in a process of living a personal and social story, telling stories to themselves and others, retelling those stories as new situations emerge, and reliving their stories in their classrooms. This conception allows a focus on gender and culture in teacher preparation (Acker 1989).

In a third line of inquiry, "teaching as inquiry," Duckworth (1986) conceives of teaching as an ongoing reflective process of inquiry. Teachers' practices are seen as processes of inquiry in which data is collected through observation and reflection. In practice, these data are examined and reflected upon in a process of sense-making. She conceives the teaching process as an ongoing process of research.

A fourth line of inquiry, "critical reflective practice," treats the "nature of teachers' work as a form of intellectual labour" which permits and encourages "teachers to question critically their understandings of society, schooling and pedagogy" (Smyth 1987 p.155). The purpose of those working with this conception tends to be radical social reform.

There are three main consequences of the reflective practice/teaching as inquiry conception of teaching. First, the focus of academic interest and, therefore, of policy interest is shifted from theory to practice. Unlike the case in the subject matter conception where teachers' prior knowledge and what is taught to them is most important, in reflective practice it is what and how teachers learn from practice that is most important. Second, it is the person (i.e., the teacher) and what that person feels, does, and learns from teaching that is the policy interest rather than things (e.g., curriculum materials) and ideas (e.g., subject discipline). Finally, reflective practice puts its trust in the teaching profession to generate reform whereas other conceptions tend to put their trust in policymakers and researchers.

4. Alternative Conceptions of Teacher Evaluation

4.1 What is New in Teacher Evaluation?

When researchers enthuse that "programs emphasizing . . . objectives do better on tests . . . designed to measure those objectives than programs of different emphases. This generalization is robust" (Shavelson et al. 1986 p.53), the thin potential of teacher evaluation research is evident. Conclusions such as this also signal a renewed interest on the place of subject matter in teacher evaluation (see also Sects. 2 and 3). The teacher testing program in the Unites States is an example. Specific research versions of this work are Stodolsky's (1988) situation-specific activity-structure approach and Ryan's (1986) task-accomplishment view. In Stodolsky's work, an array of factors (e.g., subject matter) are used to characterize activity structures which are divided into activity segments which, in turn, are characterized by key features such as instructional format, pacing, and cognitive level. Ryan's emphasis is similar although her stress is more on what teachers accomplish than on what they do. Ryan's approach is to create a prespecified set of task structures on which to assess teachers' performance. In both of these lines of work, an extremely refined picture of teaching emerges which, at the stage their work had reached in the early 1990s, is too detailed to easily imagine practical possibilities for school system administrators concerned with teacher evaluation. There are no readily evident policy consequences of this work for teacher preparation or teacher evaluation.

Qualitatively oriented nontesting approaches to teacher evaluation are also emerging (see Sects. 2 and 3). Peer- and self-evaluation are two such ideas. The main debate over these ideas in the early 1990s is the extent to which they function as an administratively contrived vehicle to enforce collegiality for the purpose of shaping teacher behavior to prespecified system purposes or the extent to which they are genuinely collegial activities geared to reflective practice. The debate intensified as system-oriented goal-shaping coaching techniques became popular with boards of education and others concerned with the practice of evaluation for system purposes.

4.2 Supervised Reflective Practice: A Curriculum Conception

This section is concluded by proposing a notion of evaluation designed to be consistent with a reflective practice conception of teaching while recognizing the curricular context within which teaching and teacher evaluation take place. Teaching and teacher evaluation exist in the context of four commonplace matters: the teacher, the student, the subject matter, and the milieu (Schwab 1962). From either the standpoint of research, or from the actual practice of evaluation at a system level, a curriculum view requires not only that subject matter and teachers, but also that students and social context, enter into the evaluative matrix. Such matters as the educational policies of government, local school boards, and specific schools all bear on standards of effectiveness. Teacher evaluation from a curriculum point of view is, therefore, a process of relating school outcomes and school processes to the intentions of schooling. It is a process that requires an analysis of policy as well as an analysis of achievement outcomes, teaching processes, skills and performances, lesson activities, and subject matter. Furthermore, in a curriculum view, site-to-site variation is part of the evaluation system since curricula are ultimately intended to be adapted to the local circumstances within which they are taught.

To help understand what is meant by a curriculum conception of evaluation one may imagine a set of three overlapping circles representing government curriculum policy, local conditions, and teacher classroom practices (see Fig. 1). The overlap creates seven possible cells, each of which needs to be analyzed and used to characterize the context for a particular evaluation.

The ideal setting according to this view is where policy is developed to represent both local conditions and existing teacher practices and, in turn, where teachers adapt government policy to meet local conditions and to reflect their own teaching practices (Cell 7). But in the ongoing business of teaching, the ideal is seldom realized. To take only one simple example, imagine the case where teacher classroom practices and local conditions overlap but fail to overlap with policy (Cell 4). According to traditional evaluation lore, teachers not following policy would be negatively evaluated. But, according to a curriculum conception, the fact that teaching occurs outside of policy is insufficient grounds for a negative evaluation. Other curriculum factors may justify the local adaptation at work and may highlight limitations in policy rather than in teacher performance. It is clear that a curriculum conception of teaching and teacher evaluation complicates the evaluation problem since no simple position may be adopted: one cannot reduce the evaluation to behavior, to subject matter, to outcomes, to policy, or to local need, but must at all times consider all of these matters as important matrix factors.

This view, as described thus far, is essentially a curriculum one. It lends itself especially well to a supervision-evaluation setting which can be termed "supervised reflective practice." This is a setting where the supervisor is neither an "inspector," ensuring that policy is adequately adhered to, nor a "consultant," acting as an on-call resource for teachers but, instead, simultaneously represents the teachers' interest, the pull of local conditions (e.g., parents, community), and policy. Every supervision-evaluation setting would require its own balanced assessment.

A supervised reflective practice conception of evaluation would, then, be one in which supervisors (consultants, coordinators, administrators, inspectors) entered into consultative dialogue with teachers over teacher practices. Curriculum commonplaces and overlapping areas of policy, local conditions, and teacher practices would define the scope of deliberations. The purpose of supervised reflective practice is not to shape teacher behavior through pointing out teachers' faults and coaching them to permissible behaviors. Rather, its purposes are twofold: to generate a complex curricular assessment as an evaluative basis for planning instruction; and, through the reflective process of discussion with involved teachers, contribute to their inservice education. Supervised reflective practice is, therefore, a curriculum-based notion designed to integrate teacher

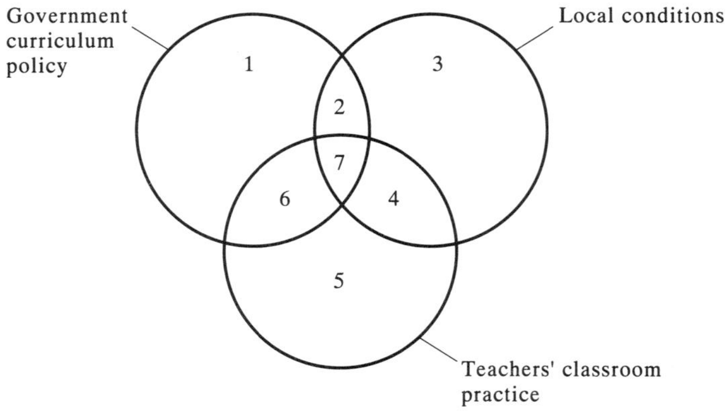

Figure 1
Supervised reflective practice: A curriculum conception

preparation and teacher evaluation into a more coherent educational process.

5. Conclusion

As this entry is being written in the early 1990s, teacher preparation is a preoccupation in many countries throughout the world concerned with educational reform. The investment in curriculum, curriculum policy, and in administrative re-organization in the 1950s and later had disappointing effects on the quality of education. The massive investments in implementation both in research and in school systems that followed these curriculum and administrative reforms have also been disappointing. In the early 1990s, there is a sense that if educational reforms are to take hold, the involved people—teachers, principals, and others—need to be central not so much as implementors but as reformers in their own right. Furthermore there is a sense that teacher preparation reform needs to be treated in a more general context of school reform. Accordingly, teacher preparation is at the core of restructuring schools in many nations (Schlechty 1991, Thiagarajan 1990).

However, the sort of research reviewed above, much of which was done in North America and England, gives little hope that the emerging teacher reforms are likely to be noticeably more effective than the earlier curricular and administrative reforms. Most of the research is pursued in isolation of other educational issues and, while it may not be desirable to create tightly linked systems of teacher preparation, teacher evaluation, and research, a more coherent, educationally sound view than tends to be evident in most of the English-speaking literature would be desirable for policy purposes. It is difficult, in fact virtually impossible, to imagine policy consequences of research conducted in isolation of policy and of other educational functions. This entry ends with a proposal for one such linked system which might have policy consequences because of its potential for a more integrated view (see Sect. 4.2).

It is important to bear in mind that policy reflects national political systems. As Sharpes says, there is a "wide range of social and political influences on teacher preparation in the world" and, for example, "significantly different concepts and practices of education will exist in Brazil compared to Camaroun or Thailand" (1988 p.1). As Sharpes notes, "colleagues in the third world have significant contributions to make to all teacher educators" (p.1). The fact that Third World countries are organized in politically different ways, often with more coherent social visions than is common in countries where most of the available research is conducted, means that it is possible to imagine different policy contexts and different roles for research in those settings. Perhaps the next wave of insight into teacher preparation, teacher evaluation, and research will come not from new North American and British programs but, instead, from rethinking the relationship of politics to policy and thence to teacher preparation, teacher evaluation, and research in a Third World context.

See also: Planning Educational Reforms: Use of Contingency Approach; Planning for Effective Teaching in Developing Nations; Politics of Educational Planning; Teacher Education, Evaluation in; Teacher Education: Inservice; Teacher Education: Philosophical Issues; Teacher Evaluation

References

Acker S 1989 Rethinking teachers' careers. In: Acker S (ed.) 1989 *Teachers, Gender and Careers*. Falmer Press, New York

Adams A, Tulasiewicz W 1989 UK education in the late 1980s: Pressure and contexts for change. In: Tulasiewicz W, Adams A (eds.) 1989 *Teachers' Expectations and Teaching Reality*. Routledge, London

Berliner D 1986 In pursuit of the expert pedagogue. *Educ. Researcher* 15(7): 5–13

Brandt R 1991 On teacher education: A conversation with John Goodlad. *Educ. Leadership* 49(3): 11–13

Carnegie Forum on Education and the Economy 1986 *A Nation Prepared: Teachers for the 21st Century*. The Report of the Task Force on Teaching as a Profession. Carnegie Corporation, New York

Chapman D W, Carrier C A 1990 Introduction: Improving educational quality in developing countries. In: Chapman D W, Carrier C A (eds.) 1990 *Improving Educational Quality: A Global Perspective*. Greenwood Press, New York

Charters W W, Waples D 1929 *The Commonwealth Teacher Training Study*. University of Chicago Press, Chicago, Illinois

Clandinin D J 1989 Developing rhythm in teaching: The narrative study of a beginning teacher's personal practical knowledge of classrooms. *Curric. Inq.* 19(2): 121–41

Clandinin D J, Connelly F M 1991 *Among Teachers Community*. Centre for Research for Teacher Education and Development, Faculty of Education, University of Alberta and Joint Centre for Teacher Development, Ontario Institute for Studies in Education and Faculty of Education, University of Toronto, Toronto

Coleman J S et al. 1966 *Equality of Educational Opportunity*. Government Printing Office, Washington, DC

Connelly F M, Clandinin D J 1988 *Teachers as Curriculum Planners: Narratives of Experience*. Teachers College Press, New York

Dewey J 1904 The relation of theory to practice in education. In: Murray C (ed.) 1904 *The Relation of Theory to Practice in the Education of Teachers*. Third Yearbook of the National Society for the Scientific Study of Education, Part I. Public School Publishing Co., Bloomington, Illinois

Duckworth E 1986 Teaching as research. *Harv. Educ. Rev.* 56(4): 481–95

Dunkin M J, Biddle B 1974 *The Study of Teaching*. Holt, Rinehart & Winston, New York

Fullan M, Connelly F M 1987 Teacher education in Ontario: Current practice and options for the future. A position paper written for the Ontario Teacher Education Review (with Heller M, Watson N, Scane J). Ontario Ministry of Education/Ministry of Colleges and Universities, Toronto

Fuller B 1990 What investments raise achievement in the Third World? In: Chapman D W, Carrier C A (eds.) 1990 *Improving Educational Quality: A Global Perspective*. Greenwood Press, New York

Ginsburg M B 1988 *Contradictions in Teacher Education and Society: A Critical Analysis*. Falmer Press, New York

Holmes Group 1990 *Tomorrow's Schools: Principles for the Design of Professional Development Schools*. The Holmes Group, Inc., East Lansing, Michigan

Houston W R (ed.) 1990 *Handbook of Research on Teacher Education: A Project of the Association of Teacher Educators*. MacMillan, New York

Hunter M 1984 Knowing, teaching and supervising. In: Hosford P (ed.) 1984 *Using What We Know about Teaching*. Association for Supervision and Curriculum Development, Alexandria, Virginia

Jencks C et al. 1972 *Inequality: A Reassessment of the Effect of Family and Schooling in America*. Basic Books, New York

Joyce B R, Weil M 1980 *Models of Teaching*. Prentice-Hall, Englewood Cliffs, New Jersey

Kron F W 1989 The nature and limitations of teachers' professional autonomy. In: Tulasiewicz W, Adams A (eds.) 1989 *Teachers' Expectations and Teaching Reality*. Routledge, London

Lawton S B, Hickcox E S, Leithwood K A, Musella D F 1986 *Development and Use of Performance Appraisal of Certificated Education Staff in Ontario School Boards*. Province of Ontario, Canada. Ontario Ministry of Education, Toronto

Lieberman A 1986 Collaborative research: Working with, not working on . . . *Educ. Leadership* 43(5): 28–32

Medley D M 1982 Teacher effectiveness. In: Mitzel H E (ed.) 1982 *Encyclopedia of Educational Research*. Free Press, New York

Millman J, Darling-Hammond L 1990 *The New Handbook of Teacher Education: Assessing Elementary and Secondary School Teachers*. Sage, Newbury Park, California

Powell M 1980 The beginning teacher evaluation study: A brief history of a major research project. In: Denham C, Lieberman A (eds.) 1980 *Time to Learn*. National Institute of Education, Washington, DC

Ryan D W 1986 *Developing a New Model of Teacher Effectiveness: Lessons Learned from the IEA Classroom Environment Study*. Province of Ontario, Canada. Ontario Ministry of Education, Toronto

Schlechty P C 1991 *School for the Twenty-First Century: Leadership Imperatives for Educational Reform*. Jossey-Bass, San Francisco, California

Schön D A 1983 *The Reflective Practitioner: How Professionals Think in Action*. Basic Books, New York

Schwab J J 1962 The teaching of science as enquiry. In: Schwab J J, Brandwein P F (eds.) 1962 *The Teaching of Science*. Harvard University Press, Cambridge, Massachusetts

Shanker A 1987 Tomorrow's teachers. In: Soltis J F (ed.) 1987 *Reforming Teacher Education: The Impact of the Holmes Group Report*. Teachers College, Columbia University, New York

Sharpes D K 1988 *International Perspectives on Teacher Education*. Routledge, New York

Shavelson R J, Webb N M, Burstein L 1986 Measurement of teaching. In: Wittrock M C (ed.) 1986 *Handbook of Research on Teaching*. MacMillan, New York

Shulman L S 1987 Knowledge and teaching: Foundations of the new reform. *Harv. Educ. Rev.* 57(1): 1–22

Smyth J 1987 Transforming teaching through intellectualizing the work of teachers. In: Smythe J (ed.) 1987 *Educating Teachers: Changing the Nature of Pedagogical Knowledge*. Falmer Press, London

Stiggins R J, Duke D L 1988 *The Case for Commitment to Teacher Growth: Research on Teacher Evaluation*. State University of New York Press, New York

Stodolsky S S 1988 *The Subject Matters*. University of Chicago Press, Chicago, Illinois

Thiagarajan S 1990 An integrated approach to primary teacher support and training. In: Chapman D W, Carrier C A (eds.) 1990 *Improving Educational Quality: A Global Perspective*. Greenwood Press, New York

Wideen M F, Holborn P 1986 Research in Canadian teacher education: Promises and problems. *Can. J. Educ.* 11(4): 557–83

Wise A E, Darling-Hammond L, Berry B 1987 *Effective Teacher Selection: From Recruitment to Retention*. The Rand Corporation, Santa Monica, California
Zeichner K M, Liston D P 1990 Traditions of reform in US teacher education. *J. Teach. Educ.* 41(2): 3–20

F. M. Connelly; D. J. Clandinin

Teacher Recruitment and Induction

There is widespread agreement that the achievement of successful schooling is crucially dependent on the quality of the teaching force. This quality, in turn, is significantly influenced by the effectiveness of the processes of recruiting and inducting beginning teachers. This entry focuses on these two processes, outlining the factors that affect their formulation, implementation, and effectiveness, including those in the broader policy context. It does not deal directly with such related matters as the supply and demand for teachers, teacher accreditation, the characteristics of beginning teachers, or the induction of experienced teachers who have changed schools.

1. Recruitment

Teacher recruitment policies of all governments are affected by basic factors such as their economic policies (specifically, the amount of money they allocate to education), increases or decreases in birthrates, and teacher supply and demand. These policies are also influenced by country-specific factors. Normally, for example, strategic decisions about the numbers to be recruited into initial teacher education and the qualifications needed to be a teacher are made nationally within the context of each government's policy for teacher supply. Thus, teachers are usually required to be college graduates, but this is not always true in developing countries. In Pakistan, for instance, only 9 percent of primary school teachers held a bachelor's degree in 1989. Similarly, although the majority of teachers are usually female, especially in the primary school sector, in Islamic countries qualifications are not the essential ingredient since a common aim is to recruit more women to teach girls. In some African countries, recruitment and selection decisions may be influenced by tribal allegiances, in India, caste is important; and in several countries, political and union affiliations may be considered.

The status of teachers in the eyes of society at large and, more concretely, their salaries and career prospects, must also be taken into account. Teachers are often civil servants with severely restricted "professional" autonomy. Indeed, the very concept of the "professional," about which so much is written in English-speaking countries, has no apparent equivalent in many other languages. Hence, teaching is much more likely to be regarded as just another occupation in non-English-speaking countries.

The nature of the career structure also varies a great deal among countries. In the United Kingdom the head teacher of a school may earn over four times the salary of a beginning teacher and the intervening career ladder offers substantial salary incentives at each stage. In Spain, by contrast, headteachers are elected by their colleagues, receive only a nominal salary increase, and there are no salary incentives, nor any significant career ladder, for teachers. Women have relatively poor career prospects in teaching and are significantly underrepresented in senior positions. Nevertheless, they continue to constitute the majority of teachers in most countries.

In those countries such as Germany, Ireland, Belgium, and Japan, where there was an overall surplus of teachers in the 1980s and 1990s, teacher unemployment, linked to a highly competitive entry process, has been the main issue in recruitment policy. In other countries there has been an overall shortage. However, the notion of a shortage is problematic. A shortage may occur for demographic or economic reasons, because of inaccurate forecasting and planning, or because of related policy decisions. The indisputable shortage that exists in developing countries is due quite simply to the fact that there is an insufficient number of qualified people.

In countries such as the United Kingdom, the numbers entering teacher training are strictly controlled on the basis of national demographic projections. In others, such as Italy, effectively no initial training for secondary teachers existed until relatively recently. In some countries, such as Greece, there is a pool of unemployed, qualified teachers. However, this is not true in those countries, particularly in the Third World, in which a teaching qualification is sought primarily as a means to a better paid job in industry or commerce. Virtually all countries have shortages in highly marketable subjects such as science, mathematics, and computing, but even here there are exceptions. Again in Greece, there has been an oversupply of physics teachers in the late 1980s and early 1990s.

Shortages in particular student age-ranges or geographic regions are also common, but the reasons are often country-specific. The nature and scope of these shortages are partly contingent on related policy decisions; for example, those on teacher–student ratios and class size, which affect the number of teachers to be recruited.

1.1 Teacher Recruitment and Teaching Quality

Most governments aim to improve the quality of their teaching force via teacher recruitment. Once again, their approaches vary. For instance, in most European countries candidates for higher education and teacher training must pass a rigorous academic examination at age 18 and, as a result, the national debate about quality is focused on subject knowledge and teaching skills rather than on basic academic competence. By contrast, many states and some school districts in the United States have introduced their own entry testing procedures to try to ensure that prospective teachers have a satisfactory level of competence in basic literacy and numeracy skills. In Europe, each member state of the European Community is now able to recruit teachers from the other states, thanks to mutual recognition of national teacher training qualifications. This in itself is a powerful new factor in promoting teacher recruitment and teaching quality throughout Europe.

1.2 Approaches to Teacher Recruitment

In centralized systems of education, including those in developing countries, teachers are usually recruited by a national unit within the framework of a national plan and then deployed by national, state, or regional administrators. The individual teacher and school have little say in the decision. Thus, new teachers are recruited to the total teaching force and may then be allocated to a school in a remote part of the country. Redeployment and promotion decisions are frequently taken in the same manner.

In systems that are relatively decentralized, such as those of the United States and the United Kingdom, on the other hand, such decisions are taken at the local or school level. Specific vacancies are advertised locally or nationally and the successful candidates are appointed after passing through a selection process conducted by the local education authority or by the governing body of the individual school. Hence, both new and experienced teachers have optimum choice over where they can apply to teach, while schools and local authorities can decide whom to select.

In general, several recruitment methods are being tried out by national and local authorities. They include the following. First, flexible entry routes and preparatory access courses are used to help candidates who are underqualified on normal criteria. Second, new forms of initial training and teacher licensing are being introduced. Third, courses for qualified candidates from other fields, for teachers wishing to switch subjects or types of school, and for married women "returners" are being converted and updated. Fourth, qualified teachers from other countries are being recruited. Fifth, specific incentives such as higher salaries, job sharing, creche facilities, and inexpensive housing are being offered to increase recruitment in shortage areas. The relative effectiveness of these various methods is unclear and, in any case, most of the available research is highly context-bound.

2. Induction

The term "induction" refers to the process of support and training that is increasingly being seen as necessary for a successful first year of teaching. Policymakers tend to be more interested in induction when there are recruitment problems, regarding it as a means of improving retention rates by encouraging a greater proportion of beginning teachers to stay on beyond the first year. Professionals tend to be interested in it as a bridging period between initial and inservice training and, hence, as the foundation of continuing professional development.

The first year of teaching has been the focus of considerable research and development since the 1960s, although principally in only a few countries (e.g., the United Kingdom, the United States, Australia, New Zealand, Canada, and Hong Kong). In other developed countries, interest in induction into teaching varies. In Germany, for example, the final two years of initial training have for many years incorporated what is, in effect, an induction period. Similarly, in the Netherlands, induction has been the subject of much research. In developing countries, induction is far less important than the improvement of initial teacher training.

The first year of teaching has several strands to it. The term "beginning teacher" is commonly used in North America, and to a lesser extent elsewhere, to refer to teachers who have completed their initial training, have received some form of professional accreditation, are employed by a school district, and are in their first year of service, with a more or less normal teaching work load. The first year is often coterminous with a period of probation during which the provisional licensure acquired by the teacher during or at the end of initial training is subject to ratification.

2.1 Principal Components of Induction Programs

By the end of the 1970s informed professional opinion and published research in the United States, United Kingdom, and Australia were, broadly speaking, in agreement regarding the principal components of a successful induction program. They are as follows: (a) additional release time, that is, time away from teaching for the beginning teacher; (b) school-based support from a colleague acting as a mentor or professional tutor, who also receives some additional release time plus training; (c) planned and systematic school-based activities, including discussion groups, classroom observation and support; (d) planned and systematic externally based activities organized by the local education authority (LEA) and university staff; and (e) the explicit and active support of school principals and other administrators. During the 1980s induction increasingly came to be considered within the broader context of staff development; since schools only recruit beginning teachers periodically, staff development is the most cost-effective way of managing the organization and staffing of the school's induction scheme.

There was, and probably still is, less operational agreement about the fundamental aims of induction.

Where it is coterminous with probation, the two tend, in practice, to become conflated and confused. This situation is related to a more basic dilemma, namely, should the aim be to induct new teachers into the knowledge, skills, and values promoted by the national system, the employing LEA, the particular school, or the wider profession? The understandable response from program organizers is that a balance must be struck between all four. However, in practice, they are usually influenced by the program's funding body (i.e., the Government, the LEA, or the school) and consequently it is the fourth aim which tends to be underplayed or even omitted. Thus, few induction programs follow the approach adopted by many initial training institutions in aiming to equip new teachers to make informed, independent, professional judgments about a range of curricular and pedagogical issues or about the worthwhileness of the current policies and practices of their national or local system or school.

This "fact of life" is hardly surprising, not only from the perspective of *realpolitik*, but also because the evidence is clear that new teachers are overwhelmingly concerned with the practical problems with which they have to deal in their classrooms, departments, and schools. This concern of new teachers can be attributed largely to the "reality shock" they encounter when they move from their relatively sheltered position in initial training to a situation where they are accountable for all aspects of their professional work. Specifically they are responsible for the learning of groups of students who are frequently uncooperative or even actively hostile, while simultaneously undergoing what may be radical change in their personal lives. Small wonder that the first year of teaching is often experienced and portrayed as traumatic. Unlike most other beginning professionals, teachers work in relative isolation, behind the classroom door.

2.2 *Induction Programs, Relevance, and Mentoring*

Beginning teachers judge the effectiveness of induction programs primarily in terms of their practical relevance to their own current problems. They tend to be skeptical about external courses which emphasize administrative and legal information or are overly theoretical. They do value the opportunity to meet with other new teachers in "neutral" settings, such as a university, where they may be relieved to discover that their problems are not peculiar to them, and where they are able to discuss them with sympathetic peers and supportive, more experienced group leaders. Above all, they value time to plan, to mark students' work, and to think. Thus, a reduced teaching load coupled with the provision of practical help given by colleagues whom they respect and who have the skills and time to help them, are needed.

It is partly for this reason that there has been much greater emphasis since the early 1980s on mentoring. The importance of support teachers was evident much earlier, for example in the British professional tutor role. During the 1980s, however, the mentor concept was developed, partly in the light of industrial models, in relation to initial training and principal training as well as induction. While definitions vary, mentors are experienced school colleagues who are responsible for helping beginning teachers. This help may be given directly or indirectly. Mentors may provide information, conduct orientations, observe classrooms and give feedback on what they saw and heard, engage in discussion groups, provide liaison with other staff, the LEA, and the university, and, sometimes, perform assessments and evaluations. Although this list would probably attract general agreement, there are many program-specific approaches to mentoring. They include, for example, the degree of emphasis on subject knowledge (and, hence, on whether or not the mentor should have expertise in the same subject or age-range specialism as the inductee) and pedagogical expertise. Many of the skills needed by mentors (for instance, those associated with classroom observation, clinical supervision, reflective practice, and coaching) are familiar in other contexts but they do require careful adaptation to mentoring.

3. *Emerging Trends, Issues, and Research*

Many trends are, of necessity, specific to particular countries. In England and Wales, for example, the abolition of the probationary year, the introduction of a national teacher appraisal scheme, the introduction of school-controlled and school-based initial training, and the possible introduction of a General Teaching Council, all have significant implications for both recruitment and induction. More generally, several countries are introducing forms of restructuring that will have direct consequences for recruitment and induction, again as illustrated by experience in England and Wales. Under the system of school-based management that is now well-established there, school governors, advised by parent and community representatives, are responsible for staff appointments and for both the overall school and staff-training budgets.

The risk of a parochial and inward-looking recruitment policy being adopted in this situation is evident. Moreover, given the limited budgets available, there are strong pressures for governors to appoint less costly beginning teachers, often on short-term contracts, in preference to experienced but more expensive teachers. Governors are also likely to be reluctant to spend money from the training budget on induction training and support unless it is earmarked for that purpose within the funding formula. The logical next step in this system of school self-management, especially since it is associated with the promotion of competition between schools within a regulated market approach, is the introduction of site-level pay bargaining together with performance-related pay linked to appraisal. The implications of such developments for recruitment and induction will be considerable.

While these policy-related issues will require careful monitoring, there are several technical matters that also should be studied. Recruitment and retention are underresearched topics, partly because they are so context-bound within particular national systems. Nevertheless, it would be instructive to see which selection methods, including the interview, were effective and under what circumstances; to do the same for innovative recruitment strategies, such as the articled and licensed teacher schemes in the United Kingdom; and to study the implications of these methods and strategies for other national systems.

Several theoretical perspectives can be used profitably to study induction, including those arising from work on teacher socialization, adult learning, teacher cognition, teacher effectiveness, and teacher biographies. There is a need for further research on the roles and training needs of mentors; the role of competence-based methods in induction; the implications of the distinctive features of curriculum subjects for induction; and the relationship of induction to staff development and human resource development.

However, the most fundamental research priority arises from an issue of policy. Although the research evidence is sometimes less than robust and must always be interpreted in relation to the national context within which it was produced, the messages about the value of induction, the main components of an effective induction scheme, and, to a lesser extent, the impact of induction on retention rates, are consistently positive. It comes as some surprise, then, that so few induction programs have become established. In the United States, for example, Conant's (1963) report advocated systematic induction and six years later the National Association of Secondary School Principals (Hunt 1969) produced a set of practical guidelines which were, in their essentials, indistinguishable from those still being advocated in the early 1990s. Similarly, in England and Wales, following the recommendations of the influential James Report on the need for systematic induction (United Kingdom, Department of Education and Science 1972), a series of government-funded research and development activities resulted, by 1978, in national agreement on the nature, scope, and practical details of successful teacher induction. At the same time, however, several subsequent studies by the national inspectorate reported that induction support is patchy and sometimes nonexistent.

In both countries, induction has moved up and down the policy agenda since the 1960s, apparently depending on the perceived scale and political significance of the teacher recruitment and retention problem. A major task for policy researchers, therefore, should be to study two issues. First, how can better use be made of existing technical knowledge about the design and implementation of effective induction schemes? Second, what kind of policy and structural changes are needed for such schemes to become firmly institutionalized in a national inservice teacher education system? Only when these issues are resolved will educators be in a position to establish whether or not induction can make a consistent and positive impact on teacher recruitment and retention.

References

Conant J B 1963 *The Education of American Teachers*. McGraw-Hill, New York

Hunt D W 1969 *Project on the Induction of Beginning Teachers*, Booklets 1–3. National Association of Secondary School Principals, Reston, Virginia

United Kingdom, Department of Education and Science 1972 *Teacher Education and Training* (James Report). HMSO, London

Further Reading

Ashton P T (ed.) 1992 Editorial—Special issue: Induction and mentoring. *J. Teach. Educ.* 43(3): 162

Bolam R 1987 Induction of beginning teachers. In: Dunkin M J (ed.) 1987 *International Encyclopedia of Teaching and Teacher Education*. Pergamon Press, Oxford

Cooke B L, Pang K C 1987 Experiences and needs of trained and untrained beginning teachers in Hong Kong: A pilot study. *Educ. Res. J.* 2: 18–27

Earley P 1992 *Beyond Initial Teacher Training: Induction and the Role of the* LEA. National Foundation for Educational Research (NFER), Slough

Education, Science and Arts Committee 1990 *Second Report: The Supply of Teachers for the 1990s*, Vol. 1. HMSO, London

Huling-Austin L, Odell S J, Ishler M, Kay R S, Edelfelt R A 1989 *Assisting the Beginning Teacher*. Association of Teacher Educators, Reston, Virginia

Instance D 1990 *The Teacher Today: Tasks, Conditions, Policies*. Organisation for Economic Co-operation and Development, Paris

Le Métais J 1990 *The Impact on the Education Service of Teacher Mobility*. National Foundation for Educational Research, Slough

Little J W, Nelson L (eds.) *Mentor Teacher: A Leader's Guide to Mentor Training*. Far West Laboratory for Educational Research and Development, San Francisco, California

Maclean R 1992 *Teachers' Careers and Promotional Patterns: A Sociological Analysis*. Falmer, London

Oldroyd D, Hall V 1991 *Managing Staff Development: A Handbook for Secondary Schools*. Chapman, London

United Kingdom Department of Education and Science 1988 *The New Teacher in School*. HMSO, London

Veenman S 1984 Perceived problems of beginning teachers. *Rev. Educ. Res.* 54(2): 143–78

Wise A E, Darling-Hammond L, Berry B 1987 *Effective*

Teacher Selection: From Recruitment to Retention. Rand Corporation, Santa Monica, California

Zeichner K, Gore T 1990 Teacher socialization. In: Houston W R, Howsam R, Sikula J (eds.), 1990 *Handbook of Research on Teacher Education*. Macmillan, New York

R. Bolam

Teacher Responsibility

Teacher responsibility deals with teachers' professional moral tasks. A procedural morality is suggested and discussed in this entry, with the aims of avoiding problems like relativism and enhancing student responsibility.

1. The Necessity of Professional Responsibility in Teaching

Control over the well-being, the interests, or the fate of someone includes, from an ethical point of view, certain obligations or a responsibility toward that person (Jonas 1987 p. 176). This responsibility can be defined legally. An authority (e.g., society, the parents) gives the teacher the responsibility to deal appropriately with the students, and the teacher's actions are judged (and possibly sanctioned) by these authorities. Responsibility can also be defined ethically as the individual obligation to act according to a set of moral or ethical principles to ensure the students' well-being and interests ("responsibleness"). According to both definitions, teachers have great responsibilities; however, the legal requirements placed upon teachers set only minimal standards (Strike 1990), they are often contradictory, and they vary from country to country. Further, they may be ethically questionable. The teachers' personal moral responsibility hence takes precedence over the legal one.

The traditional research on moral responsibility rests on the following basic premises:

(a) Research on responsibility is still dominated by "should's" (i.e. normative requirements demanded of teachers or sets of virtues that the teacher is expected to satisfy but which are, in reality, unattainable). Responsibility is often linked with the "character" or the "personality" of a teacher, with the presupposition that a given person either has the corresponding virtues or does not. This means that responsibility cannot be learned.

(b) Most research on responsibility is based on a relativistic concept of morality (an example, Nash 1991, is discussed below). The point of view that moral values are evaluations of actions generally believed by the members of a given society to be either "right" or "wrong" (social relativism) is problematic for several reasons. For example, it seems unacceptable to regard it as morally right if a group of people believes it is entitled to harm or even kill another group, and acts accordingly (as happened in the Third Reich and still happens in many places).

(c) Researchers who study teacher responsibility tend to forget that a teacher is a person with a private life and extraprofessional responsibilities. The distinction between private life and schoolwork calls for a conception of professional morality where, as in private morality, any value (including extraprofessional values) can conflict with any other value.

These basic premises can account for serious deficits in the research on responsibility with, among others, the following consequences:

(a) There is almost no empirical research in the domain of responsible action in school.

(b) In teacher education, teachers usually do not learn to deal effectively with responsibility (Bergem 1992).

(c) Teachers do not think about responsibilities and values very often (Oser et al. 1991).

(d) Teachers often believe that responsible action such as caring for specific students reduces their effectiveness with respect to the students' knowledge acquisition (see, e.g., McLaughlin 1991). Thus, responsibility and effectiveness are dealt with separately in research.

There have been some attempts to remedy these deficiencies. Nash (1991), for example, has proposed three conceptions of applied ethics. First, a language of rules and principles is necessary to help teachers think in a formal and disciplined way about their daily ethical dilemmas. However, the "test of which ethical decision is 'right' is whether the justification is sufficiently convincing to impartial observers" (p. 165). This is a relativistic position.

Second, a deeper exploration of motives, intentions, ideals, and feelings on the part of the primary moral agent as well as the larger societal influences on one's ethical actions is called for. Again, this approach is relativistic since the basis of decision-making is the individual's intuitions about what is right and the norms of important reference groups, rather than a rational argument based on universal principles.

The third conception concerns "the private world of individual consciousness where each of us chooses our moral ideals, attempts to make sense of our deepest beliefs, and tries to ground the messages" (p. 169). If these beliefs are taken as moral rules, again, a relativistic viewpoint is defended: right is the moral rule of the individual.

Nash has pointed out that all three approaches must be seen together. However, all of them are relativistic (premise (b)). Further, while the first premise is taken care of to some degree, the third is not. Consequences (a) and (d) are not accounted for at all.

In contrast to the basic premises and to Nash (1991), a nonrelativistic moral responsibility is necessary. Ethical decisions must be based on principles which are universally valid. In Kohlberg's (1981) approach, the moral frame of reference is based on two principles: (a) "People are of unconditional value" and (b) "Every person has the right to an equal consideration of his or her claims in every situation, not just those codified into law" (p. 164). In research on the teachers' professional ethos, two additional principles turned out to be equally important (Oser et al. 1991): (c) "Any person in need has the right to be helped" (caring, see also Gilligan 1982) and (d) "In social situations, people have the obligation to be truthful in the sense of being authentic."

The three claims which are essential in teacher responsibility, namely justice (according to (b)), care (c), and truthfulness (d) are discussed below. Further, within a professional ethic, extraprofessional obligations should also be considered. A procedural approach can satisfy these requirements. Instead of a set of "should's" or of virtues, the focus is on how problems can be solved without losing universal requirements (in contrast to Nash's approach).

2. *What Does "Responsibility" Mean?*

Responsibility deals with a person's choice. When a person doesn't have any choice (either because people do not influence the state of affairs, or because the particular person is denied choice or is not able to choose because of insufficient knowledge or for other reasons), he or she cannot have responsibility (Heid 1991). However, the freedom of choice is often underestimated. Many situations with apparently only one possibility contain other options as well, although most of them may have strong negative personal consequences. For instance, one has almost always the option of resistance against coercion. Whether the resistance can reasonably be expected, and if so, whether it is the most responsible solution, remains to be seen. It is clear that if the teacher is given sufficient autonomy, however, the teacher has more freedom to decide what solution is really the best; hence, autonomy is closely linked with responsibility (see Bull 1990).

The choice is always between two or more opposing values (i.e., between values that cannot be satisfied simultaneously). Dealing appropriately with such problems requires a clear distinction between descriptive statements and value judgments (including prescriptions) and the acknowledgment that each type of statement needs a different form of justification. This is not as easy as it seems. The two goals "tolerance" and "critical thinking," for instance, are so widely accepted that researchers (as well as teachers) often do not see them as values at all (Damon 1992).

3. *Responsible Teaching*

A teacher is in control of the classroom situation. The teacher, then, could decide how to operate within the classroom without consulting anyone. However, in most cases, a procedure-oriented approach with participation of all concerned people would seem to be more appropriate: the solutions are more likely to be justified (i.e., more in agreement with the universal principles), and the participants are more likely to be eager to put them into practice. Two kinds of situation can be differentiated: dilemma situations and situations where the students are supposed to acquire knowledge. In both, a procedural approach means that responsibility is delegated to the student.

3.1 Dilemma Situations

The first kind of situation is concerned with ethical dilemmas (i.e., with problems in which several values are at stake which cannot be satisfied simultaneously). In the procedural approach, instead of giving specific values or norms as to the outcomes of the decisions, some principles of the decision-making process are given which ensure that the interests and needs of all people involved in the particular situation are dealt with appropriately.

The steps of such a process are presented in Fig. 1. First, the teacher must decide for a given situation whether the problem is important enough to engage into a discourse process (1b) or whether other responsibility issues are more important (1a). If he or she decides that he or she is in charge, the central problem is how to coordinate three major moral criteria in cooperation with all concerned persons (the second level in Fig. 1). These criteria are justice (2a), care (2b), and truthfulness (2c). After balancing the three values, he or she must decide at the third level how much commitment he or she is willing to give to the solution (3b)—a commitment which might inhibit the realization of other needs, such as extraprofessional values (e.g., family life or stress reduction) (3a).

In a conflict situation, even if they feel they are treated justly (2a), students may not feel "cared for" (2b) or believe the teacher was not sufficiently truthful (2c). Perhaps the attempt to reconcile all these values is too stressful for the teacher, so that after some time he or she has a nervous breakdown (3a vs. 3b). In this regard, Oser and his colleagues

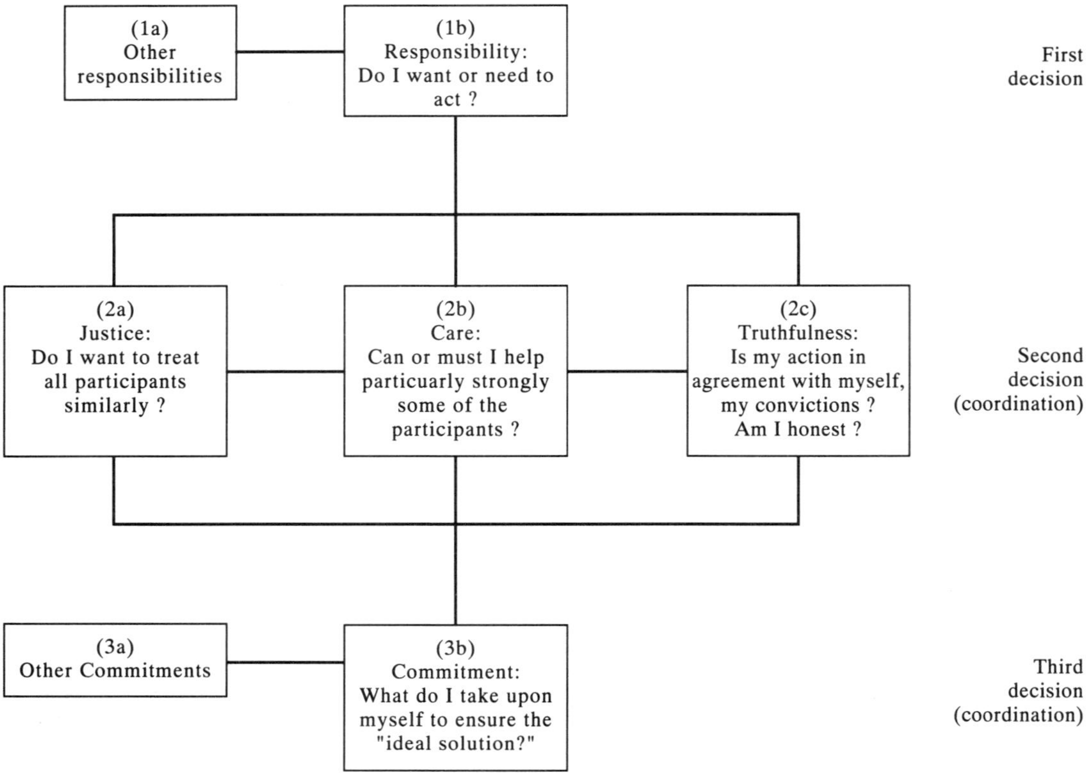

Figure 1
A model of the decision steps to solve a conflict situation

(Oser et al. 1991, Oser 1992) have found that teachers have a one-sided balancing behavior, that is, on level 2, they prefer care over the other two values (see also Dempsey's interviews reported in Rogers and Webb 1991).

When trying to coordinate the different issues five types of decision-making can be identified. First, there is avoiding behavior in which the teacher is aware that morality is at stake but doesn't deal with it: 1a is seen as more important than 1b. Second, the teacher can delegate responsibility. The teacher is aware of his or her responsibility (1b) and acts accordingly, but decides that someone else (e.g., the principal, the school psychologist, or some other agency) can deal more appropriately with the problem. The decisions on level 2 are hence shifted to other people, and the third level can then be left out. Third, there is unilateral decision-making in which the teacher decides to act, but the responsibility (decisions on levels 2 and 3) rests only on his or her intuition and reflection. There is either no information about other people's claims, needs, and feelings, or the teacher alone decides which claims, needs, and feelings are valid and which are not. Fourth, the teacher can engage in "incomplete discourse." Here the teacher explains his or her reasons and listens to the concerned students and other participants, but does not include all people involved in the situation or does not allow full responsibility to all of them, believing that he or she must in the end assume the responsibility and thus try to coordinate.

Only the fifth type of decision making, "complete discourse," allows a full coordinated balancing among justice, care, and truthfulness. Here, the leader presupposes that the child can take responsibility and can participate in the decision-making even in very difficult situations. The important point is that the responsible teacher shifts responsibility to the participants (particularly to the child) without giving up all responsibility.

Four principles are crucial in this fifth type of decision-making (Oser 1992):

(a) The teacher must create the possibility for a discourse ("round table situation").

(b) The teacher must assume two compatible roles: as participant who defends his or her own needs, and as organizer who coordinates the different needs, demands, justifications, and explanations, and who ensures that the rules of discussion are kept.

(c) The teacher must presuppose that all participants (including the students) are able and willing to take responsibility, to search for the "truth," to decide autonomously, and to balance different requirements.

(d) Finally, the teacher must be convinced that whenever the first three principles are realized, solutions will be found which are in the interest of all and which have a morally legitimate character.

The model of decision-making, the five types of decision-making, and the four underlying principles of discourse were the topic of an extended empirical research project (Oser et al. 1991). Using both questionnaires and interviews, teachers were found to solve value conflicts in professional moral situations in different ways. Some practiced more discourse than others, and some practiced discourse in situations where others did not. Thus, the results showed there was a high person–situation interaction. However, Althof's (1993) analysis indicated that the higher the moral competence of teachers, in the sense of Kohlberg's (1984) model, the more consistent the teachers were across situations (either discursive in all situations or nondiscursive in all situations).

It is obvious that responsible action is not simply an application of general moral judgment competence to professional issues. For instance, in moral judgment competence one can say "the more (i.e., the higher the stage), the better." In conflict resolutions, one can only say "the more discursive decision making, the better," particularly if the conflict is a serious one. There are situations in which discursive problem solving would be inappropriate. However, qualitative analysis seems to suggest that moral judgment competence of a certain level (i.e., a stabilized stage 3 according to Kohlberg's stage theory) is important for an adequate understanding of and responsible dealing with interpersonal conflicts; beyond this level, contextual and biographical differences prevail (Althof 1993).

In an intervention study Oser et al. (1991) found that teachers can be trained to use the complete discourse model. Through training, they can develop an increased awareness of the difficult nature of ethical problems in general and the importance of consideration of people's needs and legitimate claims, yielding the recognition that there is not only one solution to the problem, but that there are several "truths." They can also increase their acknowledgment of the specific values of justice, care, and truthfulness, some of which had been neglected or not even recognized before the intervention.

3.2 Knowledge Acquisition Situations

The second type of situation concerns teaching in the narrow sense (i.e., situations in which the main aim is that the students learn content). Research has shown that very little is learned by someone who does not take the learning in his or her own hands (see, e.g., Salomon 1992). For optimal learning to occur, then, the students must be given responsibility for their own learning. The balance between teacher control and student control is a crucial issue in the discussion of responsibility and effectiveness. The teacher and the student both assume responsibility for learning, but they assume different aspects of the responsibility. The teacher sets the conditions of learning, tries not to hinder learning, and gives the necessary information (in what way this should be done is a question of effectiveness which cannot be dealt with here). The student is the active creator and controller of the learning process.

Salomon (1992) has called this teacher's role "exploration orchestration," which means that the teacher is the conductor of an orchestra but the musicians (children) play the instruments and often improvise (many examples are discussed in Oser et al. 1992). Among the many particularities of orchestration one is particularly important: grading. Learning that follows the principles of orchestration is more strongly based on a problem-solving approach than on memory learning. Thus, the trial-and-error phase is particularly important. In this phase children are not criticized for making errors rather they have the opportunity to check them out. If every action of or every product produced by children is graded, the students do not have the freedom to make errors. Grading, then, narrows the learning possibilities. It seems more appropriate to separate the phase of self-controlled learning and the phase of self-controlled grading, and to have the children well-informed about which phase is currently in action. Of course, grading then cannot be used as a motivator; however, it is not an appropriate means for motivating children anyway.

The point here is not that teachers give up control. Rather, control assumes another function. Furthermore, the amount of control may (and in fact should) vary from lesson to lesson (or even from situation to situation within a lesson; see Patry 1993). For instance, it is quite conceivable to lecture from time to time (high control, little orchestration) and then to have the children work on the information with a much higher degree of freedom.

4. Becoming a Responsible Teacher

As mentioned above the procedural-oriented approach can be learned. Student teachers, then, should acquire some competencies, develop their own value priorities, justify these priorities in the light of universals, and learn to act both in accordance with their convictions and in a discursive manner without becoming overwhelmed by the multitude of demands. To become a responsible teacher, however, additional qualities are necessary.

4.1 Moral Competence

A first necessary but not sufficient condition for responsible action is that the subject has a high moral competence (i.e., a high stage according to Kohlberg's [1984] stage theory). The higher the stage, the better; the minimal requirement seems to be stage 3 (Althof 1993). Moral education is possible in teacher training; the main principles are described in *Attitudes and Values, Acquiring*.

A high moral competence does not guarantee analogous action. Moral competence deals with justice only, whereas responsibility involves other values (such as care and truthfulness) as well. In addition, behavior in general is not only determined by moral judgments, but also by situational conditions as well as other goals of the actor and other dispositions (Oser 1987). Further research is needed in this area, but at least a few conditions can be stated. The most important are concern for the child and awareness of values problems.

4.2 Concern for the Child

The discourse approach includes the teacher's presupposition of the child's competence and willingness to participate responsibly in the coordination process in order to balance justice, care, and truthfulness. In a more general way Fuller (1969) calls this "concern." Concern theory is part of responsibility theory. As Fuller (1969) and Janssen (1987) have shown, concern for the child has a very low priority for most teachers; on the other hand, there is some evidence that concern for the child may enhance the children's achievements (e.g., Marsh and Penn 1987–88).

Concern for the child does not mean unconditional acceptance of all that a child does. This type of acceptance would be shifting over all of the responsibility to the child, instead of establishing a balance between the teacher's and the child's responsibility. It does, however, mean unconditional acceptance of the child as a person, as an autonomous individual. Like care (Rogers and Webb 1991), concern has two aspects: making sound decisions about students and their educational needs ("concern for the future") and helping to fulfill a child's basic need for security and attachment ("concern for the present").

Concern for the child, as described above, issues from a deliberate effort to be with the child, to understand the child, and to acknowledge that children are different from adults. This requires at least empathy (see Kurt-Schai 1991) and knowledge about the psychological development and the developmental stages of children; not only about the development of intelligence (Piaget 1963) but also of self-concept (Kegan 1982), moral judgment competence (Kohlberg 1984), social behavior (Selman 1980), developmental tasks (Havinghurst 1972), and crises (Erikson 1968).

Concern for the child means decision-making on behalf of the child, based on knowledge the child may not have. Implicitly, it contains all elements of the complete discourse approach mentioned above, including particularly the (possibly contrafactual) presupposition of the child's competence to decide and the use of "advocatory discourse" (Oser et al. 1991). Such decisions, then, will necessarily be those of orchestration and not of power imposition. Concern for the child can be learned.

4.3 Ability to Deal with Values

Several studies (Oser et al. 1991, Bergem 1992, Damon 1992) show that teachers do not think about their values. This could be remedied in teacher education. The problem of access to one's own values has been addressed in moral research studies using the method of "value clarification" (e.g., Simon et al. 1972). In this approach, strategies are used to prompt participants to present their values. A typical example is to ask them to decide which three objects they would take with them to a deserted island—the chosen objects are an indicator for their values or preferences.

It is important to note that value clarification in this context is only used as a means to enhance the teachers' awareness of the values they think are important (like Nash's [1991] three approaches discussed above). By no means does this imply that those values are appropriate or justified; this would be relativistic (Oser and Althof 1992) and hence inappropriate. Rather, once one has identified one's own value system, it is necessary to justify those values based on universal principles. If the values are not in accordance with these principles, teachers are required to restructure their value systems. This corrected value system then represents the system with respect to which the moral obligations are accepted by the individual (the reference system for responsibility in the sense of responsibleness).

5. Responsibility and Effectiveness

One of the oldest scientific superstitions of humans is the notion that morality inhibits effectiveness. Considering some of the complex problems that teachers must confront on a daily basis, there is a tendency to think that the most effective teachers are the tough, single-handed decision makers who manage the classroom without concerning themselves with matters of justice, truthfulness, and caring.

However, research on management has shown that success in fact depends on the so-called "lived value system" (Peters and Waterman 1982). Similarly in schools, a teacher who cares about students and about the learning taking place in the classroom is going to be more effective in the long run than one who does not (e.g., Solomon et al. 1992). In this sense, effectiveness and responsibility are complementary.

This complementarity, or "the new synthesis" (Oser et al. 1992), is not always obvious, neither in the research nor in the practical work of teachers. Although there are many examples of successful "syntheses," we still lack comprehensive research programs which address these issues in a systematic way. The theoretical framework is available (see Oser et al. 1992); it needs now to be criticized and specified.

See also: Attitudes and Values, Acquiring; Moral Education: Philosophical Issues; Ethics, Moral Philosophy, and Education; Teacher Education: Philosophical Issues; Feminist Ethics and Moral Education

References

Althof W 1993 Teachers' moral judgment and interpersonal problem solving in the classroom. In: Olechowski R, Svik G (eds.) 1993 *Experimental Research on Teaching and Learning*. Ludwig Boltzmann Institut, Vienna

Bergem T 1992 Teaching the art of living: Lessons learned from a study of teacher education. In: Oser F, Dick A, Patry J-L (eds.) 1992

Bull B L 1990 The limits of teacher professionalization. In: Goodlad J, Soder R, Sirotnik K A (eds.) 1990 *The Moral Dimensions of Teaching*. Jossey-Bass, San Francisco, California

Damon W 1992 Teaching as a moral craft and developmental expedition. In: Oser F, Dick A, Patry J-L (eds.) 1992

Erikson E 1968 *Identity, Youth and Crisis*. Faber and Faber, London

Fuller F F 1969 Concerns of teachers: A developmental conceptualization. *Am. Educ. Res. J.* 6(2):207–26

Gilligan C 1982 *In a Different Voice: Psychological Theory and Women's Development*. Harvard University Press, Cambridge, Massachusetts

Havinghurst R J 1972 *Developmental Tasks and Education*, 3rd edn. McKay, New York

Heid H 1991 Problematik einer Erziehung zur Verantwortungsbereitschaft. *N. Sammlung* 31:459–81

Janssen S 1987 What are beginning teachers concerned about? Paper presented at the first Joint Conference of the "Arbeitsgruppe für Empirische Pädagogische Forschung" and the "Onderzoeksthemagroep Onderwijsleerprocessen", Düsseldorf

Jonas H 1987 *Das Prinzip Verantwortung. Versuch einer Ethik für die technologische Zivilisation*, 7th edn. Insel, Frankfurt

Kegan R 1982 *The Evolving Self. Problems and Process in Human Development*. Harvard University Press, Cambridge, Massachusetts

Kohlberg L 1981 From *Is* to *Ought*: How to commit the naturalistic fallacy and get away with it in the study of moral development. In: Kohlberg L (ed.) 1981 *Essays on Moral Development. Vol. 1: The Philosophy of Moral Development. Moral Stages and the Idea of Justice*. Harper and Row, San Francisco, California

Kohlberg L 1984 *Essays on Moral Development. Vol. 2: The Psychology of Moral Development. The Nature and Validity of Moral Stages*. Harper and Row, San Francisco, California

Kurt-Schai R 1991 The peril and promise of childhood: Ethical implications for tomorrow's teachers. *J. Teach. Educ.* 42(3):196–204

Marsh D D, Penn D M 1987/1988 Engaging students in innovative instruction: An application of the stages of concern framework to studying student engagement. *Journal of Classroom Interaction* 23(1): 8–14

McLaughlin H J 1991 Reconciling care and control: Authority in classroom relationships, *J. Teach. Educ.* 42(3): 182–95

Nash R J 1991 Theme: The ethical responsibilities of teaching. *J. Teach. Educ.* 42(3): 163–72.

Oser F 1987 Das Wollen, das gegen den eigenen Willen gerichtet ist: Über das Verhältnis von Urteil und Handeln im Bereich der Moral. In: Heckhausen H, Gollwitzer P M, Weinert F E (eds.) 1987 *Jenseits des Rubikon. Der Wille in den Humanwissenschaften*. Springer, Berlin

Oser F 1992 Morality in professional action: A discourse approach for teaching. In: Oser F, Dick A, Patry J-L (eds.) 1992

Oser F et al. 1991 Der Prozess der Verantwortung. Berufsethische Entscheidungen von Lehrerinnen und Lehren. Bericht zum Forschungsprojekt 1.188–0.85 und 11.25470.88/2 des Schweizerischen Nationalfonds zur Förderung der wissenschaftlichen Forschung. Freiburg Pädagogisches Institut, Freiburg

Oser F, Althof W 1992 *Moralische Selbstbestimmung. Modelle der Entwicklung und Erziehung im Wertebereich. Ein Lehrbuch*. Klett-Cotta, Stuttgart

Oser F, Dick A, Patry J-L (eds.) 1992 *Effective and Responsible Teaching: The New Synthesis*. Jossey-Bass, San Francisco, California

Patry J-L 1993 Situation specificity in teaching. In: Olechowski R, Svik G (eds.) 1993 *Experimental Research on Teaching and Learning*. Ludwig Boltzmann Institut, Vienna

Peters T, Waterman R 1982 *In Search of Excellence—Lessons from America's Best-run Companies*. Harper and Row, New York

Piaget J 1963 *The Origins of Intelligence in Children*, Norton, New York

Rogers D, Webb J 1991 The ethic of caring in teacher education. *J. Teach. Educ.* 42 (3): 173–81

Salomon G 1992 The changing role of the teacher: From information transmitter to orchestrator of learning. In: Oser F, Dick A, Patry J-L (eds.) 1992

Selman R L 1980 *The Growth of Interpersonal Understanding. Developmental and Clinical Analyses*. Academic Press, New York

Simon A B, Howe L W, Kirschenbaum H 1972 *Value Clarification. A Handbook of Practical Strategies for Teachers and Students*. Hart, New York

Solomon D, Watson M, Battistich V, Schaps E, Delucchi K 1992 Creating a caring community: Educational practices that promote children's prosocial development. In: Oser F, Dick A, Patry J-L (eds.) 1992

Strike K A 1990 The legal and moral responsibility of teachers. In: Goodlad J, Soder R, Sirotnik K A (eds.) 1990 *The Moral Dimensions of Teaching*, Jossey-Bass, San Francisco, California

F. K. Oser; J-L. Patry

Teacher Roles and Teaching Styles: Adult Education

The concepts of role and style in teaching have evolved as researchers and practitioners try to make sense of the ways in which teachers of adults habitually practice their craft, and of the learned, seemingly instinctual, responses that teachers develop to the constant dilemmas and tensions of practice they face. On closer examination, however, the concepts of role and style can be seen not as static constructs through which we can understand the essential nature of teaching, but rather as contextually bound, fluid and capable of multiple interpretation.

The experience of teaching is reported by teachers as being one of sustained ambiguity. In ethnographic studies of teachers' learning and thinking (Calderhead 1987, 1989), teaching is reported to be multifaceted, contextual, and even chaotic. Given this phenomenological reality, proposing neat delineations of adult teachers' roles and fixed concepts of teaching styles becomes problematic. The roles which teachers of adults can play in particular settings are inevitably constrained by a host of contextual variables, which can be as diverse as the political ethos of the educational institution and of the wider society, the expectations, motives and experiences of the learners involved, or individual teachers' own personalities. Similarly, what can be described as a particular teacher's style is not a static, discrete phenomenon. It is true that teachers of adults may have political orientations, habitual ways of practicing, deeply-etched personality traits, and clear philosophical rationales, all of which frame how they approach their practice. However, the extent to which these elements comprise a distinctive style, and the extent to which any such style can be imposed or allowed, depends much on the shifting contexts, constraints and distortions of practice.

1. Teacher Roles

Multiple roles have been proposed for adult teachers, including those as diverse as counselor, analyst, resource, model, and mediator. Most roles fall into one or other of two distinctive categories representing the liberal and critical traditions in the field. These approaches are those of teachers as facilitators and teachers as critical animators.

1.1 Teachers as Facilitators

The concept of adult teachers as facilitators is prominent in the literature of adult education (Brookfield 1986, 1989, Galbraith 1991). The concept has its roots in the ideas of Carl Rogers which have been interpreted for a wide audience by Knowles (1984). Teaching as facilitation is a role description which emphasizes the pre-eminence of student learning and the development of student self-insight. It regards as suspect the promulgation of teachers' agendas and the notion of the teacher as a repository of approved knowledge. The teacher's role becomes that of process analyst rather than content expert, and there is an assumption that good adult educational activities attempt to meet learners' needs as these are felt and expressed by the learners themselves. Three interpretations of the function of the teacher as facilitator are evident in the literature of adult education: the teacher as facilitator of self-directed learning, the teacher as andragogue, and the teacher as learning analyst.

The teacher as facilitator of self-directed learning is a role designation which has had an enormous impact on adult education practice (Candy 1991, Brockett and Hiemstra 1991). According to this conception, the teacher's task is to act as a nondirective resource person. Those who consider themselves as facilitators of self-directed learning seek to honor learners' wishes. The development of self-confidence, which accompanies the attempt by learner's to exert control over the planning, conduct, and evaluation of their learning activities, is the objective. The concept of self-directedness has been criticized for its practical, conceptual, and methodological ambiguities (Brookfield 1988) and for its avoidance of social commitment (Collins 1991).

The teacher as andragogue is a concept that is associated with Knowles's work (1984), and it focuses on the importance of teachers working cooperatively with learners to develop methods and curricula which are grounded in the needs and experiences of adults. Teachers and learners are seen as equals and there is an emphasis on consensus building, rather than conflict, and on the liberating aspects of learning rather than on the difficulties learning often involves. The importance of connecting education to the circumstances and problems of adult life is stressed, and there is an acknowledgement of the integrity and educational value of learners' past experiences. Proponents of these ideas have been criticized for adopting an overly technicist approach to teaching adults, for decontextualizing adult education from wider political issues, and for oversimplifying the complex nature of educational and learning processes (Hartree 1984, Tennant 1986).

The teacher as learning analyst is a role designation which focuses on teachers helping learners to understand their own learning patterns and processes so that they can overcome certain habits, inclinations, and dispositions that are harmful or constraining. In adult education this approach to facilitation has come to be associated chiefly with the work of R M Smith (1990). Smith (1990 p. 4) lists nine activities which can be considered as learning to learn, including increasing the capacity for self-reflection, broadening people's repertoires of learning styles, and helping learners make informed choices from the range of educational options available. As is the case with andragogy, the conceptual and practical components of this idea tend to proliferate and overlap with those of allied concepts such as metacognition, reflective judgement, and learning style.

1.2 Teachers as Critical Animators

The adult teacher as critical animator is a role conception which is grounded in a very different intellectual tradition to that of teachers as facilitators. The concept of facilitation is primarily psychological, whereas the concept of critical animation draws from a stream of sociological and political analysis. Politically, facilitation might be thought of as a liberal concept and critical animation as a socialist concept. It is no surprise, therefore, that political cultures in which socialist ideas are an accepted part of normal political discourse (even if a majority of people do not subscribe to these) tend to be those in which many adult educators are likely to regard their role as that of critical animator.

Those teachers of adults who see their role as being that of a critical animator share three basic assumptions about the practice of adult education. The first of these is that teachers should encourage learners to engage in critical thinking; that is, to scrutinize carefully their taken-for-granted assumptions, to consider alternative ways of interpreting and living in the world, and to become aware of how oppressive economic, political, and social structures do psychological, economic, and physical violence to human beings. A second assumption is that the critical animator should encourage learners to engage in a praxis of action and reflection, that analysis by itself is not enough. Finally, animators regard their practice as geared toward the realization of egalitarian values and structures, often of a democratic socialist nature.

Two clear strands of writing are evident in the critical animation tradition. The first of these draws upon the work of the Frankfurt school of critical social theory (Collard and Law 1991, Collins 1991) and upon the ideas of Antonio Gramsci, the Italian political economist (Armstrong 1988). This stream of thought emphasizes the crucial role of education in social transformation and interprets the adult teacher's role in an activist sense. The teacher's role is to educate in, and for, social action, so that social movements stand a better chance of breaking down oppressive structures. This emphasis on teaching as a component of social action is evident in the lives and ideas of Horton and Lindeman in the United States, Coady in Canada, Grundtvig in Denmark, Tawney and Williams in the United Kingdom, Freire in Brazil, Lovett in Northern Ireland, and in workers and trades union education movements throughout the world. Although the relative emphasis on either socialism or social democracy would vary among these figures and movements, all involved see adult education's basic justification as being that it is a force for fundamental social change.

The second strand of writing in this tradition acknowledges the importance of social transformation but, in addition, interprets critical thinking as occuring in contexts other than the purely political, such as personal relationships, the workplace, and interactions with the media (Brookfield 1987, Marsick 1988, Mezirow 1991). The teacher's role is to assist learners to recognize the epistemic, psychological, and political constraints which prevent them from living their lives according to their own, clearly realized, sense of rightness. These writers share many of the ideological biases of the social transformation stream of animation and they frequently stress the need for teachers to become involved in collective social action. But they argue that teachers of adults can also help to engender significant personal or small group transformations which do not necessarily have to be part of a major social action movement. This form of practice has been criticized for appearing to be more radical than it really is, and for being an essentially liberal, rather than socialist, perspective on transformative practice (Griffin 1988).

2. Teaching Style

As an anthology on teaching style in adult education recently acknowledged (Hayes 1989), the concept of teaching style eludes clear definition. At the core of most treatments of this concept is the idea that a style comprises a set of habitual dispositions—typical ways of approaching practice and of working through tensions and dilemmas—which can be observed over time. Sources which can be seen as framing teaching style range from personality, gender, culture, and class to the espoused theory, values, and political ethos of a field of practice, all of which are interpreted in the context of teachers' daily classroom experiences. In explorations of teacher learning and thinking (Calderhead 1987, 1989) teachers report that while they may begin their careers with firm philosophical and methodological preferences, the contextual realities and constraints of practice mean that these are usually substantially modified. Indeed, teachers' biographies often record either a detaching from a deeply-etched style, or a broadening of typical ways of practicing. Pratt (1989) has observed how the changing perspectives which teachers take on their practice, and the transitions in self-concept they experience, can be understood as recognizeable developmental stages. Teaching becomes a journey into ambiguity, in which teachers pass through an initial period of regarding teaching as the mastery of skills and procedures, followed by an increased emphasis on clinical problem-solving, until they come to incorporate as a permanent feature of their practice some critical reflection on the problematic nature of their activities. In this regard what might, in the early stages of a teacher's life, be viewed by the teacher as the reassuringly fixed components of his or her style can, over time, be reinterpreted as a constraining dependence on inappropriate, uncritical, habitual reactions. The ways in which teachers change their conceptions of practice can thus be interpreted as an adult learning process characterized by dialectical thinking, reflective judgment, and critical analysis.

2.1 Teaching Style as Practical Theory Development

One useful perspective on the development of teaching style is to interpret this as a process of what has been described as "practical theory development" (Usher and Bryant 1989).

Practical theory originates in situationally based insights regarding problems, tensions, and dilemmas of adult education practice. All practitioners develop informal, contextually grounded theories of practice to help them understand their work environment. Sometimes, however, the opportunity arises to subject such theories to critical analysis. Without this critical analysis informal theories risk remaining at the level of anecdotal, idiosyncratic reminiscence. They are little more than a collection of unconnected experiential travelers' tales from the front lines of practice. Those adult educators who do undertake a critical analysis of their informal theories can accomplish this in two ways. First, they can engage in a form of collaborative experiential scrutiny in which their hunches, instincts, and intuitions (i.e. their informal theories in use) are compared to those of other educators working in similar and allied contexts. Second, these evolving, informal theoretical tenets can be reviewed through the perspectives embedded in formal theories.

Consequently, the process of practical theory development is one in which informal theories are continuously subjected to particular and universal analysis. Particular analysis comprises the experiential comparisons mentioned earlier. Universal analysis comprises the comparison to formal theory. This constant interplay between the particular and the universal can be described as a "reflexive" or dialectical process. The evolution of a teaching style can be viewed as a form of practical theory development in which teachers' methodological preferences and philosophical inclinations are critically reinterpreted over time. Accompanying the recognition that teachers have developed a reliance on habitual ways of practicing, comes the realization that these may not always be appropriate. As teachers encounter the constraints and dilemmas of practice they learn to distrust some of their habitual, instinctive reactions and to adopt a more contextual approach. The development of this kind of insight is a gradual process distinguished by a continual praxis of experimentation, reflection, formal review, and experiential comparison. This is in marked contrast to the idea that style is a stable construct—a fixed pedagogic genetic trait or a way of practicing learned during a period of professional preparation—which is consistently applied to the world of practice.

2.2 Teaching Style and Learning Style

Many analyses of teaching style explore the connections between this concept and that of learning style. Teachers' practices can be reviewed regarding the extent to which these match the various learning styles of their students. Teachers' own teaching styles can also be analyzed for the extent to which they are grounded in their own personal learning styles.

Some interesting work has been done on the intersection of adult teaching styles and adult learning styles (Conti 1985, 1989), particularly the extent to which an andragogical or collaborative style of teaching is most suited to adult learners. Studies have been conducted on whether or not a collaborative teaching style is correlated with higher levels of student attendance (Beder and Carrea 1988), on the extent to which students with certain learning styles deliberately choose certain kinds of educational programs (Loesch and Foley 1988), and on cross-cultural differences and similarities in preferred teaching and learning styles (Pratt 1988). No clearly definitive picture emerges from this research regarding the desirability of matching one uniquely adult teaching style to the dieverse styles of adult learners. Indeed, a strong personal and social case can be made that at times it is as important to teach against students' preferred learning styles as it is to teach to them (Brookfield 1990 p. 67–70).

Teachers' own teaching styles can also be investigated regarding the extent to which these develop, sometimes unconsciously, out of teachers' own experiences. Those teachers who study their own histories as learners, and who explore the manner in which their experiences as learners have shaped their practices as teachers, may well be surprised to discover just how much of what they imagined to be their objective, rationally applied pedagogy actually reflects their own autobiographies (Tripp 1987). In fact, one fruitful but neglected approach to faculty development is to encourage teachers to place themselves regularly in the role of a learner who is trying to learn something new and difficult, to reflect on what was affirming and demeaning about this experience, and to review their own teaching practice from this unfamiliar phenomenological perspective (Brookfield 1990 pp. 40–42).

3. Adult Teaching Styles

Although no clearly definitive statement is possible concerning uniquely adult teaching styles, three observations can be made. The first concerns the contextual ambiguity of adult teaching and the essentially fruitless nature of any quest to discover all-embracing, context-free styles. What is likely to be more useful is to study how teachers' styles evolve as a process of practical theory development with emerging insights examined critically through comparison with the experiences of others in allied contexts and reviewed through the perspective of formal theory. Second, analyzing the link between teachers' evolution of certain styles and their own personal histories as learners could reveal some important but hitherto neglected connections. The ways in which teaching styles are influenced by, or an outgrowth of, teachers' own preferred learning styles is an important area for research. An important practice connection could be the development of inservice and initial preparation programs which use teachers' own experiences of learning as the means for prompting them to review their own teaching practice. Third, of overarching concern to adult learners seem to be the questions of teacher credibility and teacher authenticity. More important to learners than individual variations in teaching role or teachers' styles are the fundamental ethical and moral questions learners ask concerning their teachers: Can I trust this person? What does this person stand for? Is it worth my while being in this person's presence?

4. Teacher Credibility and Authenticity

In an integrative summary of research on the ways in which adults experience formal education (Brookfield 1990) the fundamental significance to learners of teachers being perceived as both credible and authentic was highlighted. It seems as if adults can tolerate wide variations in teaching roles and styles if, at a fundamental level, they trust their teachers to be credible and authentic. In programs of inservice, professional development, and also during periods of initial preparation, much greater attention needs to be paid to helping teachers of adults examine their own practice for the extent to which credibility and authenticity is evident. When learners perceive these qualities to be in place, the trust in teachers that is so fundamental to significant learning stands a much greater chance of being developed.

"Credibility" refers to the sense that learners report of feeling that it is in their own best interests to be in the presence of a particular teacher. Teacher credibility is, not surprisingly, reported to be of greatest significance to those adults for whom a learning activity represents an anxiety-ridden journey into unfamiliar territory. The indicators of credibility most frequently cited by adults are: (a) the teacher's demonstrable subject, content, or skill mastery; (b) the length, breadth, depth, and intensity of a teacher's experience; (c) the sense learners have that a teacher's actions are guided by a well-thought through rationale; and (d) the perception that teachers stand for something, that is, that they have a confident belief in the value of what they teach and the importance of the tasks they ask students to undertake. This emphasis on credibility contradicts much writing on the role of teacher as facilitator, which tends to downplay the significance of the teacher's actions within the learning group, preferring instead to conceptualize the teacher as one among equals. In contrast, the critical animation tradition is one which acknowledges the teacher possessing a declared moral vision, that is, an explicit commitment to certain social values and political ideals. As Freire comments, adults have a right to expect "critical competence" in their teachers (Shor and Freire 1986 p. 172).

"Authenticity" refers to the sense that students report of perceiving their teachers as being honest and open with them. Five indicators of trustworthy, authentic behaviors that are frequently mentioned are: (a) an observed congruence between teachers' words (especially their espoused philosophical beliefs about education) and their actions; (b) teachers' readiness to allow aspects of their personalities outside of their educational role to show themselves in their practice; (c) a readiness to listen to students' voices and to be open to changing practice as a result of students' suggestions; (d) teachers' attempts to make full, repeated disclosure of their agendas and expectations so that learners do not feel they are subject to arbitrary decisions or evaluative criteria which are kept secret until the last minute; and (e) teachers' readiness to admit to errors. Regarding this last indicator, it is interesting to note the crucial importance of timing for such admissions of teacher error. When teachers speak about their own mistakes, errors, and inadequacies at the outset of a class then students report that their own anxieties are raised to an almost unendurable pitch. However, once students trust the teacher's essential credibility, then perceiving a teacher's fallibility is symbolically powerful for many adults. It induces a sense of relief and release, a feeling that making mistakes is a normal part of learning and that learners do not have to exemplify perfection to gain teacher approval.

Striving to establish credibility and authenticity is both risky and riven with potential contradictions. In overemphasizing the components of their credibility teachers may be perceived as engaging in an arrogant and boastful display of their skill, knowledge, and experience. In striving to be authentic by admitting to error teachers risk leaving students with a perception that the most distinguishing characteristic of their teaching is its ineptness. So of all the complex balances teachers try to attain, maintaining credibility and authenticity in a point of congenial tension is one of the most problematic. However, striving for this balance, even with the realization that it can never be satisfactorily realized, means that adult teachers' efforts stand a much better chance of creating in learners the trust that is such an essential underpinning of significant learning in adulthood.

See also: Teachers' Roles

References

Armstrong P F 1988 L'Ordine Nuovo: The legacy of Antonio Gramsci and the education of adults. *Int. J. Lifelong Educ.* 7(4): 249–59

Beder H, Carrea N 1988 The effects of andragogical teacher training on adult students' attendance and evaluation of their teachers. *Adult Educ. Q.* 38(2): 75–87

Brockett R G, Hiemstra R 1991 *Self-Direction in Adult Learning: Perspectives on Theory, Research and Practice*. Routledge, London

Brookfield S D 1986 *Understanding and Facilitating Adult Learning: A Comprehensive Analysis of Principles and Effective Practices*. Jossey-Bass, San Francisco, California

Brookfield S D 1987 *Developing Critical Thinkers: Challenging Adults to Explore Alternative Ways of Thinking and Acting*. Jossey-Bass, San Francisco, California

Brookfield S D 1988 Conceptual, methodological and practical ambiguities in self-directed learning. In: Long H B (ed.) 1988 *Self-Directed Learning: Application and Theory*. Department of Adult Education, University of Georgia, Athens, Georgia

Brookfield S D 1989 Facilitating adult learning. In: Merriam S B, Cunningham P M (eds.) 1989 *Handbook of Adult and Continuing Education*. Jossey-Bass, San Francisco, California

Brookfield S D 1990 *The Skillful Teacher: On Technique. Trust and Responsiveness in the Classroom*. Jossey-Bass, San Francisco, California

Calderhead J (ed.) 1987 *Exploring Teachers' Thinking*. Cassell, London

Calderhead J (ed.) 1989 *Teachers' Professional Learning*. Falmer Press, London

Candy P C 1991 *Self-Direction for Lifelong Learning: A Comprehensive Guide to Theory and Practice*. Jossey-Bass, San Francisco, California

Collard S, Law M 1991 The impact of critical social theory on adult education: A preliminary evaluation. Proc. Adult Education Research Annual Conference No. 32. Center for Continuing Education, University of Oklahoma, Norman, Oklahoma

Collins M 1991 *Adult Education as Vocation: A Critical Role for the Adult Educator*. Routledge, London

Conti G J 1985 The relationship between teaching style and adult student learning. *Adult Educ. Q.* 35(4): 220–28

Conti G J 1989 Assessing teaching style in continuing education. In: Hayes E (ed.) 1989

Galbraith M W (ed.) 1991 *Facilitating Adult Learning: A Transactional Process*. Krieger, Malabar, Florida

Griffin C 1988 Critical thinking and critical theory in adult education. In: Zukas M (ed.) 1988 *Papers from the Transatlantic Dialogue*. School of Continuing Education, University of Leeds, Leeds

Hartree A 1984 Malcolm Knowles' theory of andragogy: A critique. *Int. J. Lifelong Educ.* 3(3): 203–10

Hayes E (ed.) 1989 *Effective Teaching Styles*. Jossey-Bass, San Francisco, California

Knowles M S (ed.) 1984 *Andragogy in Action*. Jossey-Bass, San Francisco, California

Loesch T, Foley R 1988 Learning preference differences among adults in traditional and nontraditional baccalaureate programs. *Adult Educ. Q.* 38(4): 224–33

Marsick V J 1988 Learning in the workplace: The case for reflectivity and critical reflectivity. *Adult Educ. Q.* 38(4): 187–98

Mezirow J M 1991 *Transformative Dimensions of Adult Learning*. Jossey-Bass, San Francisco, California

Pratt D D 1988 Cross-cultural relevance of selected psychological perspectives on learning. In: Zukas M (ed.) 1988 *Papers from the Transatlantic Dialogue*. School of Continuing Education, University of Leeds, Leeds

Pratt D D 1989 Three stages of teacher competence: A developmental perspective. In: Hayes E (ed.) 1989

Shor I, Freire P 1986 *A Pedagogy for Liberation: Dialogues on Transforming Education* Bergin and Garvey, South Hadley, Massachussetts

Smith R M (ed.) 1990 *Learning to Learn Across the Lifespan*. Jossey-Bass, San Francisco, California

Tennant M 1986 An evaluation of Knowles' theory of adult learning. *Int. J. Lifelong Educ.* 5(2): 113–22

Tripp D H 1987 *Theorizing Practice: The Teacher's Professional Journal*. Deakin University Press, Victoria, Australia

Usher R S, Bryant I 1989 *Adult Education as Theory Practice and Research: The Captive Triangle*. Routledge, London

S. Brookfield

Teacher Stress and Burnout

The study of stress has captured the interest of both researchers and practitioners since the concept was first defined and explored by Seyle in the mid-1940s. According to Gmelch (1988), over 100,000 books, journals, and articles have focused on the phenomenon of stress. This entry focuses specifically on stress in the teaching profession. Common terms are defined, major sources of stress are identified, the effects of stress are described, ways in which teachers can cope with stress are suggested, and future directions for research are offered.

1. Defining Teacher Stress and Burnout

Seyle's (1946) early work defined stress as the nonspecific response of the body to any demand made upon it to adapt, whether that demand produces pleasure or pain. Since Seyle posited his initial definition, scholars have debated its validity and have tried to establish a common definition, of stress that incorporates current knowledge about the phenomenon. While contemporary scholars have not generated a common definition, they agree that stress is an integrated, multidimensional response that occurs when people perceive that the demands of a situation exceed their ability to meet or cope with those demands. This response includes the physiological, cognitive, and behavioral systems of the individual. (For a more complete explanation see Hiebert and Farber 1984.)

As in the case of stress, defining "burnout" has been a focus of debate among researchers. Freudenberger (1974) is credited with being the first to describe and define this phenomenon. He used the term to describe people in helping professions who experienced a state of exhaustion and fatigue brought on by working too long, too much, and too intensely with needy clients. Freudenberger's work was anecdotal and conjectural in nature rather than research-based. His work was important, however, because it laid the groundwork for subsequent empirical studies that focused on helping professionals.

Maslach was one of the first people systematically to study job burnout in the helping professions. Maslach and her colleagues at the University of California at Berkeley initiated a series of large-scale studies that included such human service professionals as social workers, counselors, day care workers, police officers, and public defense lawyers. According to Maslach (1982) burnout is the behavioral response of people who experience constant stress from working in occupations that require continual, intensive interactions with people. Those who cannot effectively cope with this work-related stress develop feelings of emotional exhaustion, negative attitudes toward their clients, and a sense that they are no longer accomplishing anything worthwhile in their job. These feelings are quite different from those experienced by helpers early in their career. A common one-liner by stress researchers is "you cannot burn out if you were never on fire to begin with."

Several large-scale international studies have extended Maslach's work to the field of teaching (e.g., Schwab and Iwanicki 1982a, Dewe 1986, Kremer-Hayon and Goldstein 1990, Friesen et al. 1988). While researchers may differ in their exact definition of teacher burnout, all indicate that it is a response of teachers who have trouble coping with the stress of the job. They also agree that the three types of behavioral reactions described in the following paragraphs are typical for teachers experiencing burnout.

One of the first symptoms of burnout is the development of chronic feelings of emotional exhaustion. Teachers in this stage express feelings of being tired, irritable, and emotionally drained. Affected individuals often express dread at having to get up in the morning to go to work. Emotionally exhausted teachers often develop negative, cynical attitudes toward their students. This change in attitude from "warm and caring" to emotionally removed is the second aspect of burnout and is often referred to as depersonalization. This stage is evidenced in various ways. A common way that teachers display depersonalized attitudes is by withdrawing from contact with students. For example, teachers who never stray from behind their desk may well be physically withdrawing from their students. Teachers may also psychologically withdraw from students by ignoring or refusing to acknowledge them. Treating students as impersonal objects, calling them derogatory names, or using labels to describe individual students are further indications of depersonalization.

A third aspect of burnout occurs when teachers begin to feel they are no longer accomplishing anything worthwhile in their work. Teachers enter the profession hoping to help students gain knowledge and to make a positive impact on society. When teachers feel they are no longer making a difference in students' lives they find that their profession offers few other rewards such as money or recognition. Low feelings of accomplishment combined with the effect of the other two aspects of burnout may reduce motivation to the point where failure becomes a way of life. Social psychologists refer to this as "learned helplessness."

There are many adverse consequences for both the individual and his or her organization as a result of teacher burnout. Those experiencing burnout are more likely to have a lower quality of personal life, be absent from work more often, exert less effort in teaching, and spend a considerable amount of time looking for a new line of work. In terms of health, the afflicted individual is more inclined to develop substance abuse problems and experience stress-related phenomena such as insomnia. Regardless of whether the consequences affect the individual or the organization, the teacher's students are the ultimate losers (Dworkin 1987).

2. *Sources of Stress*

The sources of stress for any individual teacher or school staff vary greatly. While research has identified several environmental and personal/background factors that are related to aspects of burnout, it has not been able to place these in any defensible order or hierarchy of importance. Figure 1 presents a framework for describing the stress cycle as it affects teachers.

As indicated in Fig. 1, individuals react differently to environmental stress. How a person reacts to stress depends upon the nature of the stress encountered and his or her individuality. Noted stress researchers French and Caplan (1972) refer to this as "goodness of fit' between job demands and individual abilities. As illustrated in Fig 1, if the fit is one of incongruence, then the individual's psychological reaction could be burnout. Furthermore, when feelings of burnout persist, the person is more likely to develop behaviors that have negative consequences for the individual, the organization, and the students.

2.1 *Societal Sources*

Societal sources include those factors that are beyond the direct control of the individual or the organization in which he or she works. Most industrialized, as well as Third World countries, hold high expectations for

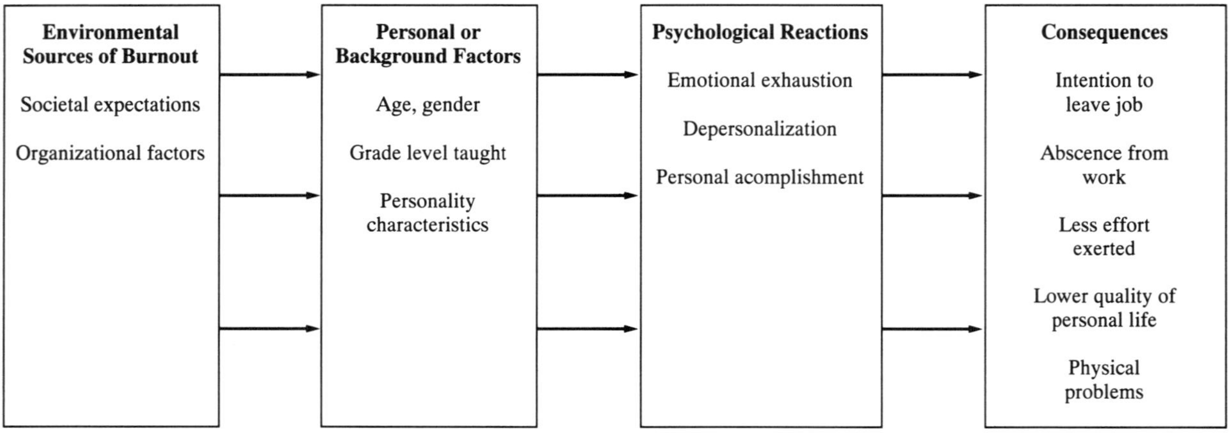

Figure 1
The stress cycle as it affects teachers

their teaching force. While the historical context, organizational structure, and societal values may differ across cultures, some expectations are consistent. Teachers are expected to instill values, teach basic and higher order thinking skills, nurture the development of students to become independent learners, and encourage students to collaborate to achieve common goals. Further, educational institutions are seen as the key to economic growth and development which places an additional stress on teachers. While most societies have high expectations for what education can do, teachers perceive that the resources to accomplish this task are limited (Kremer-Hayon and Goldstein 1990).

An issue identified as a major stressor by teachers around the globe concerns the attitudes of students they are responsible for educating (Kyriacou 1987). Teachers indicate that the poor work attitude of students and their lack of motivation are among the most stressful issus faced on a daily basis. For example, Friedman and Farber (1992) report that student misbehavior, lack of attentiveness, and low enthusiasm for learning material are significant contributors to burnout in Israeli educators. Similar findings have been reported in separate studies with teachers from New Zealand (Dewe 1986), Japan (Ninomiya and Okata 1990), the United Kingdom (Kyriacou 1987), the West Indies (Payne and Furnham 1987), Canada (Byrne 1992), and the United States (Goodlad 1984).

2.2 Organizational Sources

Organizational practices at the school and district level have been identified as major sources of stress for teachers. Two of the more frequently recognized organizational contributors to teacher burnout are role conflict and role ambiguity (Crane and Iwanicki 1986, Schwab and Iwanicki 1982a, Byrne 1992). Role conflict occurs when an individual is faced with two conflicting sets of inconsistent but expected role behaviors. Stress results from the individual's inability to reconcile the inconsistency. Role ambiguity is the lack of clear, consistent information regarding the rights, duties, and responsibilities of a person's occupation and how they can best be performed (Kahn et al. 1964). Stress results from this ambiguity.

Schwab et al. (1986) found that in addition to role conflict and role ambiguity other organizational factors contributed to higher stress levels. First, individuals with lower levels of burnout felt they had more freedom and autonomy in deciding what and how to teach. Second, teachers who believed they were able to participate in school-related decision-making processes also reported a lower incidence of stress. Third, teachers who felt their organization had a system for providing contingent rewards for good work and contingent punishments for sub-par efforts were less stressful.

The absence or presence of an effective collegial social support network in the work setting has been shown to be related to all aspects of burnout (Blase 1986, Jackson et al. 1986, Rodgers-Jenkinson and Chapman 1990). In this regard, it is important to note that social support from one's colleagues has been shown to be more important than administrator support. An effective support group includes people who provide emotional comfort, confront the individual in humane ways when the individual's behaviors are inappropriate, provide work-related support, present technical challenges that promote individual growth, serve as active listeners, and share similar values, beliefs, and perceptions of reality (Pines et al. 1981).

The majority of research studies that have examined the relationship of organizational variables to levels of teacher burnout have depended upon self-reported survey instruments. Samples of teachers have been primarily cross-sectional, while a few studies have used individual schools as the unit of analysis (Hubert et al. 1990). These studies have often used regression analysis or similar statistical procedures to identify stress factors having the highest relationship with burnout scores. Even the most complete and sophisticated studies explain only 20 to 40 percent of the variance in burnout. Thus, one might hypothesize that individual differences account for a great deal of variation in how stress is handled by teachers or that other environmental factors have not been identified.

2.3 Individual and Background Variables

Unfortunately, the science of personality inventories and tests is far from perfect, and comprehensive instruments are difficult, time-consuming and expensive to design and administer. Consequently, many studies have examined isolated personality characteristics and their relationship to teacher burnout, rather then holistically looking at personality differences and their contribution to burnout.

For example, Mclntyre (1984) and Lutz and Maddirala (1990) found that teachers with an external locus of control were more likely to experience burnout than those with an internal locus. Teachers with an external locus of control are inclined to feel that their destiny is not in their own hands and their lives are controlled by others. They believe luck, fate, or powerful others are responsible for what happens to them. Individuals with an internal locus feel that events in one's life are within one's own control.

Anderson and Iwanicki (1984) and Malanowski and Wood (1984) found that when teachers felt that their higher order needs were addressed in their work they were less likely to experience job burnout. Higher order needs include self-actualization (i.e., need for success, achievement, achieving full potential) and self-esteem (i.e., self and others' respect for what one does).

In addition, several background factors are related to levels of burnout. Studies have shown that men are more likely to experience burnout than women, teaching at elementary school is less stressful than at the middle and secondary level, single people experience higher levels of stress than married individuals, and teachers in larger and urban schools experience more stress (Burke and Greenglass 1989, Farber 1991, Schwab and Iwanicki 1982b, Malonowski and Wood 1984).

3. Coping with and Alleviating Stress

Research on the effectiveness of intervention strategies to alleviate teacher stress is limited. The few studies that exist have focused on isolated aspects of managing stress. For example, Jenkins and Calhoun (1991) found teachers who received training in personal stress-reducing activities did engage in those activities more frequently after completing the workshops. They were not able to determine whether or not participating in those activities reduced stress levels. Only one study was found that examined an intervention on the organizational level and it had limited results. Schwab (1991) studied the effectiveness of different organizational approaches to establishing support groups for teaching interns. While his studies found some benefits when placing several teaching interns in the same school and holding regular support group meetings, he found little difference in stress levels of interns who participated in the alternative approaches.

4. Research Issues

The good news regarding the status of research on teacher stress and burnout is that a great deal more is known about the topic in the early 1990s than was known 20 years before. The bad news is that much more needs to be known about the dynamic nature of how environmental factors interact with individual differences to cause burnout and what can be done about it. The following research activities should shed some light on these and other issues of importance.

First, there is a glaring need for longitudinal studies that focus on the complex interaction of personality type and environmental stressors. One-time, cross-sectional studies are fine for answering some questions but not for understanding the complexity that occurs within the dynamic interactions of personality and environment over time.

Second, valid and reliable inventories that accurately measure personality differences, levels of stress, and potential environmental factors that cause stress need to be refined and in some cases developed. Many valid and reliable instruments exist that look at pieces of the puzzle while comprehensive measures that could be useful in developing intervention strategies are limited.

Third, holistic intervention strategies that address organizational factors and individual coping strategies should be developed by interdisciplinary teams including psychologists, social psychologists, organizational behaviorists, medical researchers, educational administration researchers, and psychometricians. Studies that monitor the effectiveness of these intervention strategies must be longitudinally studied in order to determine if stress levels can be reduced and then sustained at these lower levels. Knowledge about the phenomenon is sufficient to begin such studies.

Finally, school reform and restructuring is occurring around the globe. As school restructuring efforts evolve, cross-cultural comparisons will present an exciting area of inquiry. For example, in the United States the move to site-based management, teacher involvement in decision-making, mainstreaming of all students into regular classrooms, outcome-based instruction, and numerous other advocated changes will have a direct effect on teachers. Will they reduce stress or create new pressures that lead to burnout?

5. Conclusion

The expectation that teachers can correct the ills of society, instill values, teach basic and higher order thinking skills, and prepare students for a globally competitive marketplace is unlikely to change in the future. There is little doubt that over the 1990s schools will be changing to address these multiple needs. Consequently, the subject of teacher stress will continue to be a major concern of those within and outside the profession.

See also: Teachers as Professionals; Teachers' Beliefs and Belief Systems; Teachers' Expectations; Teacher Evaluation; Motivation and Learning; Stress, Coping, and Learning

References

Anderson M B, Iwanicki E F 1984 Teacher motivation and its relationship to teacher burnout. *Educational Administration Quarterly* 20(2): 94–132

Blase J 1986 A qualitative analysis of sources of teachers stress: Consequences for performance. *Am. Educ. Res. J.* 23: 13–40

Burke R J, Greenglass E R 1989 Psychological burnout among men and women in teaching: An examination of the Cherniss model. *Hum. Relat.* 42(3): 261–73

Byrne B M 1992 Investigating causal links to burnout for elementary, intermediate, and secondary teachers. Paper presented at the American Educational Research Association Annual Meeting, San Francisco, California

Crane S, Iwanicki E F 1986 Perceived role conflict, role ambiguity, and burnout among special education teachers. *Rem. Spec. Educ.* 7(2): 24–31

Dewe P 1986 Stress: Causes, consequences & coping strategies for teachers. ERIC Document Reproduction Service No. ED 280 807, Washington, DC

Dworkin A G 1987 *Teacher Burnout in the Public Schools: Structural Causes and Consequences for Children.* SUNY Press, Albany, New York

Farber B A 1991 *Crisis in Education: Stress and Burnout in the American Teacher.* Jossey Bass, San Francisco, California

French J R Jr., Caplan R D 1972 Organizational stress and individual strain. In: Marrow A J (ed.) 1972 *The Failure of Success.* Amacom, New York

Friedman I, Farber B A 1992 Individual and socially reflected aspects of professional self-concept as predictors of teacher burnout. *Journal of Education Research* 38(2): 28–35

Freudenberger H J 1974 Staff burn-out. *J. Soc. Issues* 30: 159–65

Friesen D, Prokop C M, Sarros J C 1988 Why teachers burn out. *Educ. Res. Q.* 12(3): 9–19

Gmelch W 1988 Research perspectives on administrative stress: Causes, reactions, responses and consequences. *J. Educ. Adm.* 26(2): 134–40

Goodlad J I 1984 *A Place called School.* McGraw Hill, New York

Hiebert B, Farber I 1984 Teacher stress: A literature survey with a few surprises. *Can. J. Educ.* 9(1): 14–27

Hubert J A, Gable R K Iwanicki E F 1990 The relationship of teacher stress to school organizational health. In: Bacharach S B (ed.) 1990 *Advances in Research and Theories of School Management and Policy.* JAI Press, Greenwich, Connecticut

Jackson S E, Schwab R L, Schuler R A 1986 Toward an understanding of the burnout phenomenon. *J. Appl. Psychol.* 71(4): 630–40

Jenkins S, Calhoun J F 1991 Teacher stress: Issues and intervention. *Psychol. Sch.* 28(1): 60–70

Kahn R L, Wolfe D M, Quinn R P, Snoek J K, Rosenthal R A 1964 *Organizational Stress: Studies in Role Conflict and Ambiguity.* Wiley, New York

Kremer-Hayon L, Goldstein Z 1990 The inner world of Israeli secondary school teachers: Work centrality, job satisfaction and stress. *Comp. Educ.* 26(2–3): 285–98

Kyriacou C 1987 Teacher stress and burnout: An international review. *Educ. Res.* 29(2): 146–52

Lutz F W, Maddirala J 1990 Stress, burnout in Texas teachers and reform mandated accountability. *Educ. Res. Q.* 14(2): 10–21

Malanowski J, Wood P 1984 Burnout and self actualization in public school teachers. *Journal of Psychology* 117(1): 23–26

Maslach C 1982 Understanding burnout: Definitional issues in analyzing a complex phenomenon. In: Paine W S (Ed.) 1982 *Job Stress and Burnout: Research, Theory, and Intervention Perspectives.* Sage, Beverly Hills, California

McIntyre T 1984 The relationship between locus of control and teacher burnout. *Br. J. Educ. Psychol.* 54(2): 235–38

Ninomiya A, Okato T 1990 A critical analysis of job-satisfied teachers in Japan. *Comp. Educ.* 26(2–3): 249–57

Payne M A, Furnham A 1987 Dimensions of occupational stress in West Indian secondary school teachers. *Br. J. Educ. Psychol.* 57(2): 141–150

Pines A, Aronson E, Kafry D 1981 *Burnout from Tedium to Personal Growth.* Free Press, New York

Rodgers-Jenkinson F, Chapman D W 1990 Job satisfaction of Jamaican elementary school teachers. *Int. Rev. Educ.* 36(3): 299–313

Schwab R L 1991 Stress and the intern teacher: An exploratory study. In: Conley S C, Cooper B S (eds.) 1991 *The School as a Work Environment: Implications for Reform.* Allyn and Bacon, Boston, Massachusetts

Schwab R L, Iwanicki E F 1982a Perceived role conflict, role ambiguity, and teacher burnout. *Educational Administration Quarterly* 18(1): 60–74

Schwab R L, Iwanicki E F 1982b Who are our burned out teachers? *Educ. Res. Q.* 7(2): 5–16

Schwab R L, Jackson S E, Schuler R A 1986 Educator burnout: Sources and consequences. *Educ. Res. Q.* 10(3): 14–30

Seyle H 1946 The general adaptation syndrome and diseases of adaptation. *Journal of Clinical Endocrinology* 6(2): 117–230

R. L. Schwab

Teacher Training For Vocational Technical Subjects

Although poor teacher quality will seriously impede innovation and improvement in technical and vocational education and training (TVET), few studies have been made of the training of such teachers. This entry, focusing on teacher training for schools, seeks specifically to draw attention to problems and practices in particular low income countries which are believed to be worthy of study by policy makers elsewhere. It is based principally on Thompson et al. (1992).

1. The Teaching Force

Improving the technical/vocational content of education as a major contribution to the solution of problems of national economic development and labor supply has proved difficult. Deficiencies in provision mean that the teachers who must operate the system may be called upon to perform miracles with the minimum of tools and materials, to devise locally relevant adaptations of basic syllabuses, and to bridge the gaps between trainers, clienteles, and employers, and between the teaching of general education subjects and their application in the world of work. Staffing weaknesses have led to questioning among aid agencies of the cost-effectiveness of TVET approaches to which many national governments remain committed.

There is commonly a shortage of qualified technical/vocational teachers. A range of expedients has been adopted to staff the schools, including the use of untrained artisans as in Colombia and Nigeria, of primary trained teachers in secondary schools as in Nigeria, and of part-time teachers as in Mexico.

In several countries, decisive steps are being taken to set appropriate standards for the recruitment of technical teachers as well as to establish institutional structures for their training. However in view of the numbers needed and the cost not merely of training but of employing teachers of high quality, it seems likely that less well-qualified teachers will continue to be pressed into service for some time. This will impede the introduction of more sophisticated programs of technical and vocational education and of a design element into skill focused courses, a development of great relevance to countries where lack of resources demands improvization and the creation of locally relevant technology. In these circumstances considerable attention needs to be directed to the manner in which well-qualified teachers are both trained and deployed so as to maximize their contribution.

2. Initial Teacher Education

2.1 Organization

Staffing shortages have tended to lead to high priority being allocated to initial teacher training. A quite remarkable variety of institutional structures is being employed, including teachers' colleges where technical teachers are trained alongside other kinds of teachers, multitechnic colleges where teachers are trained alongside noneducation staff of various kinds, specialized institutions exclusively for the training of technical teachers, and nonresidential distance and inservice organizations.

The principal development has been of major specialist institutions, such as Luanshya College in Zambia, the new National Technical Teachers' Training College (TTTC) in Pakistan, Cameroun's Higher National TTTC (ENSET), Sri Lanka's TTTC Dehiwalla, Botswana's Polytechnic, TTTC Dhaka in Bangladesh, Malaysia's TTTC Kuala Lumpur, and the Kenya TTC.

The large new national institutions have a number of potential advantages:

(a) economic use of scarce experienced and qualified training staff;

(b) financial attractions: economies of scale, and appeal to international aid donors;

(c) enhancement of the status of technical and vocational subjects and institutions;

(d) stronger capacity of such institutions to engage in curriculum development and research activities and to link these to teacher training; and

(e) greater leverage in dealings with the range of government departments involved in technical and commercial undertakings, and with employers and others, than would be possessed by dispersed staff.

The disadvantages of such institutions are less obvious, but significant:

(a) distance from the field and particularly from the more disadvantaged and remote rural regions where problems of TVET are often particularly acute;

(b) remoteness from the schools and from the teachers they have trained, limiting feedback and inhibiting ongoing reinforcement of these teachers;

(c) the temptation to become institution-bound, inward-looking, more concerned with academic qualifications and with research and publication than with practical training; and

(d) the danger that separate training of technical teachers may lead to differential treatment in their professional careers and may reinforce the separation of technical from general education.

In practice, what has frequently emerged is a mixed

system, the new major national institution being added to, and operating alongside, a variety of older kinds of technical teacher training provision including the sometimes improvised use of specialist technician training institutions for this purpose. The resulting mixed system may indeed be better able to respond to local training needs and to associate in a potentially beneficial manner the training of teachers of particular technical specialisms with that of other kinds of staff in those fields. Institutions which provide teacher training in this kind of context include Jordan's Amman Community College (engineering), Egerton University College in Kenya (agriculture), the Natural Resources and Development College in Zambia (agriculture), and three Egyptian industrial schools.

Many countries, seeking to extend TVET to all pupils entering secondary education, have quite properly given priority to the development of training programs for teachers of the junior secondary stage. The task of training more senior staff has been largely left to the universities whose progress in this respect has been unconvincing, although there are grounds for optimism in the development of distance learning programs for technical teachers at the new open universities being developed in Colombia, Pakistan, and Jordan for example, and in the growth of technical teacher training in polytechnics as in Botswana, Nigeria, and Malawi. It may well be appropriate that technical teachers be trained in the technically oriented context offered by polytechnics (and, as in Jordan and Malaysia, universities of technology). However competition from universities tends to reduce the quality of polytechnic entrants. There may be interest therefore in the Malawi polytechnic which is effectively a college of the university allowing inter-institutional competition to be minimized.

The coordination of diverse provision is commonly hindered by divided management. This may arise partly from the perception of TVET as a special set of subjects which cannot be adequately provided for by regular management structures, and partly from the crude addition of new management structures to the existing organization. In consequence, in Cameroun for instance, ENSET is under one ministry but technical schools are under another. In Zambia, technical teacher education is largely provided by three institutions each under a separate ministry, with secondary schools, the secondary inspectorate, and the Curriculum Development Center under a fourth. In Nigeria, however, a National Board for Technical Education has oversight of all technical curricula, including teacher education, and rigorously accredits college courses. In Kenya it is intended to establish a single organization for the planning of all technical teacher education.

The coordination of teacher education is, however, only one aspect of the problem. The efficient management of resources requires that teacher education be linked with curriculum development on the one hand, and with supervisory and support agencies on the other. This is often seriously impeded by management disjunction. In this connection it may be of interest to note the management structure arrived at in Pakistan where teacher education, both initial and inservice, is linked to curriculum and textbook development and to examinations through a federal curriculum bureau and a network of provincial curriculum bureaux.

Problems of disjunction may, however, be increased by the new management arrangements being introduced in some countries. In Malaysia a specialist division of the Ministry of Education known as TAVED was set up in 1964 to assess the technical needs and training provision in the country, operating alongside but separately from the Teacher Education Division, the Curriculum Development Center, and the Educational Planning and Research Division. In Sri Lanka a new Technical Training Authority has been set up alongside existing structures. In Mexico, CONALEP, a body concerned with the integration of technical studies related to the needs of industry and responsible for 240 schools and 12,000 teachers in 1992, is legally independent of the Ministry of Education.

The practice of national labor force forecasting as the basis for educational planning has proved inadequate for the fine tuning of the curriculum to meet local and regional needs. There is little evidence that employers and interested agencies such as institutes of appropriate technology are effectively involved in the planning and implementation of technical education schemes and that functional relationships are being maintained between schools and local industries and employers.

In this connection there may be considerable interest in the development of the National Apprenticeship Service (SENA) in Colombia. SENA, which is semiautonomous and funded from a payroll tax on industry, has developed considerable expertise in teacher training and curriculum development. An agreement has been reached though not yet implemented for tapping this expertise to provide inservice training for technical teachers by distance techniques, using UNISUR, a pilot open university founded in 1981. The process whereby industrial revenues may be recycled into technical education and training and thereby promote the active involvement of employers is one which will be of considerable interest at least to those countries which have a sufficiently well-established industrial base.

2.2 Other Factors

Whatever the institutional and management structure, the quality of the teachers produced will be largely determined by three factors: the resources available, the staffing, and the quality of the trainees themselves.

The high cost of technical facilities and funding constraints commonly affect the efficiency of the training provided, notably in respect of the provision and maintenance of equipment and supply of consumable materials. Greater concern is often needed for making the most effective use of human and material resources and for the exploitation of all available supplementary sources of revenue. This will necessitate greater attention to proper training of all staff, including those responsible for the auxiliary functions of servicing equipment and maintaining stores, and maximum use of shared resources and facilities.

There is commonly a dearth of technically qualified trainers with substantial experience both of teaching technical subjects and of the world of work. The creation of prestigious national institutions should enable them to attract the best staff available but does not guarantee that appropriately and fully qualified staff will in fact be available or be retained for long. For some time there is likely to be a demand for technically well-qualified and able people, not merely for key posts in educational administration but in other branches of government and in the private sector, and there is a growing flow of qualified teachers from some poorer to richer countries. Free transfer of staff between education sectors may offer flexibility and promotional opportunities to staff but may well inhibit the development of the all-important critical mass of experience in technical cadres.

Provision for training the trainers appears generally inadequate, although some efforts are made in Malaysia and in Mexico's Training the Trainers program (see Sect. 3). Elsewhere little specific preparation for the task is provided, except through overseas training which is not easily geared to specific national needs. It is worthy of note that Malaysia is, in the early 1990s, using a firm of educational consultants (TECHINT) to achieve a better match between training needs and course provision in other countries.

Entry into teacher training remains highly competitive in most countries, reflecting the dearth of alternative secure employment and, in some countries, the availability of scholarships. Entry into technical teacher training is generally on a par with other teaching and demands good academic standards although, until technical education in the schools is more fully developed, specifically technical criteria will tend to be understressed.

It is not clear that high entry and retention levels will be maintained if economic development offers alternative opportunities. The impact of teacher training programs upon the quality of teaching in the schools will continue largely to depend upon the pattern of incentives offered to technical teachers by the teaching profession.

2.3 Curricula of Initial Teacher Training

There have been few significant departures from conventional teacher training practice to meet the (often) very different needs of technical teacher trainees and of new TVET approaches. Consequently technical teacher training, in addition to its own special problems, has tended to suffer from many traditional defects.

(a) Lengthy residential courses are of doubtful cost-effectiveness. In general the high costs of teacher training need to be challenged and justified.

(b) The curriculum tends to be too theoretical and examination-focused. Technical teacher training must balance not merely educational theory and classroom practice but pedagogy and technical skills.

(c) Teacher training programs too often aim to instil mere teaching competence and do not seek to develop problem-solving abilities. TVET demands more managerial expertise and initiative than conventional education (Lauglo and Narman 1988 p. 255), particularly where quite rapid changes are being introduced with relatively little experience to build on, when few senior officials are themselves experienced in technical fields, and when classroom implementation demands improvisation.

(d) Competition for time and status between subject studies and professional studies is exacerbated in technical teacher training by the relatively low standards of technical knowledge and skill in entrants and by the desirability of affording intending teachers the substantial experience in industry, commerce, or agriculture which they will need to make their teaching effective. In Zambia the structure of the Luanshya program which requires acquisition of subject skill during the first 14 months of training prior to 10 months specializing in pedagogy has much to commend it, in that competition between the subject areas for time and for the attention of trainees is avoided and the timetable for the pedagogy element can be more flexibly and imaginatively designed.

(e) The problem of providing work experience is most acute in less highly developed economies and where training institutions are situated far from commercial and industrial centers. A further problem is that teachers of the newer and broader orientational courses may need a variety of industrial, commercial, and agricultural experiences. Rarely has adequate attention been given to means of overcoming these problems. The simulation of industrial practices within the training institution, as in the Kenya TTC and in the training of agricultural teachers in Malaysia, cannot effectively provide teachers with experience of the real-life commercial or industrial situation. In Cameroun, it may be noted, all initial technical teacher training courses include work experience but in addition serving teachers may apply for a period of attachment to a business enterprise as part of their inservice training.

(f) The preparation of young people for working life may demand that the whole curriculum should carry the appropriate work orientation and not merely the "technical" section, commonly the least prestigious. However, there is little evidence of appropriate change in the training of general subject teachers. The consequence may be that TVET will remain an isolated element even where in theory part of an integrated education program.

(g) In times of rapid curriculum change, the specialist skill pattern which still predominates involves training institutions in the expensive and laborious extension of their range of technical options, limiting their ability to adapt quickly to changes in the schools. Common core multicraft approaches in training, which are being introduced in some countries, may help to create more flexible teachers.

(h) In the absence of adequate inservice provision, training programs often constitute once-and-for-all approaches, seeking to meet all the career-long needs of teachers, and are clearly inadequate for all the purposes they seek to serve.

(i) Almost all technical teacher training is addressed to the school system. In few countries is specific training provided for instructors in technician training institutions which rely on untrained but technically qualified staff. Even more rarely has effective provision been made to train instructors for the nonformal sector of TVET which largely relies upon recruitment of skilled artisans for this purpose.

Husén has described teacher education as "the most rigid and conservative part of national education systems" (Husén 1979 p. 33; see also Thompson 1990 pp. 219–20). Remedying the above weaknesses is unlikely to be easy.

3. *Inservice Teacher Training*

Even where an efficient system of initial training and support services exists, experience suggests there will be a need for a highly developed inservice training system to enable serving teachers to adapt to changing circumstances. Technical teachers will need additional opportunities to update their industrial experience.

The main need perceived by teachers generally is for upgrading of their qualifications to allow them professional advancement. Qualified technical teachers commonly have less opportunity in this respect than their colleagues, sometimes leaving them with the choice of changing career or seeking training overseas. Often, however, priority must be given to training serving but unqualified technical teachers.

In most countries a range of refresher and updating courses is offered by ministries of education in association with inspectorates and training institutions, but such provision is rarely systematic, effectively coordinated, or properly evaluated. Colleges have tended to leave inservice training and support to other agencies, notably inspectorates. Consequently initial and inservice training have evolved separately, and often the most competent teacher educators are only marginally involved in the latter. In Jordan, however, a number of purpose-built certification and inservice teacher training institutes have been set up to enable unqualified teachers to achieve qualified teacher status and to provide refresher courses for qualified teachers.

More systematic inservice provision may be made when demanded by a specific curriculum innovation. The establishment under the Life Skills Project of a specialist Teacher Training Center at Naiwala in Sri Lanka to provide short residential courses for volunteer serving teachers is an example of this.

With careful organization, certain kinds of training may be provided cheaply and with minimum disturbance to the work of the schools, and much interest is being shown in methods which take the training to the teachers instead of the reverse. This permits the training of groups of staff in a school rather than of isolated individuals and may also facilitate teacher participation in the design and conduct of inservice training. Thereby the training may serve not merely to improve the skills and knowledge of teachers but to enhance their morale and motivation, making more likely the effective application of skill and knowledge. Consequently the experience of distance techniques being employed in Colombia and Mexico will be of wider interest.

Colombia lacks adequate initial training provision and most technical teachers are recruited directly from the schools. However a potentially cheap but effective form of inservice training is being pioneered principally by technical teachers. From 1979 some 20 auxiliary centers (CASD) have been established to supplement the facilities available in local secondary schools. These have given rise to a wide range of "microcenters," each consisting of up to 15 teachers drawn from one or several schools who diagnose their own needs and design their own inservice training. This is then assessed by an inservice coordinator at district level and may be approved for professional credit.

Again in Colombia, in the absence of detailed

syllabuses for many technical options, teachers are permitted to prepare their own syllabuses according to very general guidelines and are expected to have these vetted by "experimental pilot centers" (CEP). Bogota CEP brought together a large group of technical teachers to devise common syllabuses with expert help, a process in which curriculum development was effectively combined with inservice training and professional development. Botswana also will seek to involve teachers in curriculum development in a manner which promises to develop their competence and confidence. Education centers are to be set up at district level for developing instructional methods and materials as part of the Junior Secondary Improvement Program.

Models such as these which capitalize on and thereby strengthen the motivation of the teachers, and which appear to be effective even where teacher morale is not thought to be good, may be of considerable interest, particularly in countries which have sought to decentralize educational administration and where school cluster patterns of organization are being developed, as in Sri Lanka, Thailand, and Indonesia.

An alternative and more systematic approach is being developed in Mexico for lower secondary technical teachers, who generally lack formal teaching qualifications, by the Directorate General for Technical Secondary Education. This program, known as "Training the Trainers," provides selected teachers with courses extending over 1 year, upon completion of which they will be expected to transmit the training to other teachers within their own schools and districts. The success of this "cascade" model in the north-east of the country has persuaded the authorities to extend the system to three other regions immediately.

At senior secondary level, teachers within the separate CONALEP school system receive training by distance techniques using materials developed by CONALEP itself. Over 600 qualified and experienced technical teachers have been trained since 1981 to serve as "monitors" in the schools, responsible for presenting a 60-hour introductory course to colleagues, following which they are able to follow 18 separate teacher learning packages, satisfactory completion of all of which leads to the award of a CONALEP diploma.

In addition to these two key programs the Department of Technical Secondary Education is developing one-year courses for five levels of senior staff ranging from heads of academic departments in schools to heads of departments in the state administration.

Mexico appears to have been able thus far to maintain quality and avoid the dilution factor common to cascade models of training for four reasons:

(a) The training provided is rigorous, based upon well-prepared packages of material.

(b) The trainers are carefully selected, are well-prepared initially, and then are fully supported and closely monitored. In consequence they are more effective and acceptable to their colleagues than would otherwise be the case.

(c) The training provided may lead to the teachers receiving full-time appointments or even promotion; consequently motivation is good.

(d) The provision of training at five career levels is likely to help diffuse the spirit and the content of the training throughout the system.

4. Conclusion

It is clear that important steps have been taken or are in hand in many countries to improve the quality and quantity of technical teacher training. A considerable number of the projects being undertaken possess innovative features of great interest to other countries. There is, however, grave danger that many of these will wither unnoticed particularly when, as pilot projects, they reach the immensely difficult stage of dissemination or of rationalization by bureaucratic forces. Too often they will be regarded as temporary expedients and be absorbed into conventional staff development systems, thereby losing their unique qualities. Support needs to be given to the refinement, development, and evaluation of such projects, notably those which involve a large element of self-help on the part of participant teachers and trainers and those which appear most realistically adapted to local needs and resources. This may be a fruitful area for the application of aid funding.

See also: Quality Assurance in Vocational Education and Training

References

Husén T 1979 Patterns and structures for teacher education. In: Gardner R (ed.) 1979 *Teacher Education in Developing Countries, Prospects for the Eighties*. London University Institute of Education, London

Lauglo J, Narman A 1988 Diversified secondary education in Kenya, In: Lauglo J, Lillis K (eds.) 1988 *Vocationalizing Education: An International Perspective*. Pergamon Press, Oxford

Thompson A R 1990, Alternatives in the structure, management and quality of teacher training and staff development. *Int. J. Educ. Dev.* 10(2–3): 219–26

Thompson A R et al. 1992 *Technical Teacher Education in Twelve Developing Countries*. University of Bristol School of Education, Bristol

Further Reading

Commonwealth Secretariat 1982 *Directory of Technical Teacher Training Facilities in Commonwealth Countries*. Commonwealth Secretariat, London

Commonwealth Secretariat 1982 *Technical Teacher Training, Report of a Commonwealth Regional Workshop,*

Mombasa, Kenya, April 1980. Commonwealth Secretariat, London
Commonwealth Secretariat 1985 *Technical Education Examinations, Directions for Commonwealth Cooperation*. Commonwealth Secretariat, London
National Institute for Educational Research 1982 *Vocational and Technical Teacher Preparation in Asia and the Pacific*. National Institute for Educational Research, Section for Educational Cooperation in Asia, Tokyo
UNESCO 1982 *World Directory of Selected Research and Teacher Training Institutions in the Field of Technical and Vocational Education*. UNESCO, Paris

A. R. Thompson

Teacher Unionization, Economics of

1. Introduction

Teacher unionization, defined as the formal organization of teachers for the purpose of bargaining collectively with their employer, is a relatively recent phenomenon. However, organizations representing the interests of teachers both in schools and in the political arena have been well-established in most industrialized countries for a longer period of time. Freedom of association for teachers is enunciated, for example, in the "Recommendation Concerning the Status of Teachers" adopted at an intergovernmental conference convened by UNESCO in 1966 (Pepin 1990). Again, formal collective bargaining is typically a more recent phenomenon. In the United States, for example, organizations representing public-school teachers experienced phenomenal growth in the 1970s, despite a general decline in enrollment during the same period. The two major teacher unions in the United States, the American Federation of Teachers (AFT) and the National Education Association (NEA), increased their ranks from 770,000 in 1960 to over 2 million by 1990, representing about 86 percent of the public-school teachers in the United States. Evidence provided by Saltzman (1985) suggests that the rapid growth of teacher unionization in the United States during this period was both a result and a cause of the public-sector bargaining laws enacted during that period.

Teacher unions are even more prevalent in other industrialized countries. For example, 95 percent of Australia's 180,000 teachers are formally represented and virtually all government-employed teachers in France are members of a national union. Although almost all teachers are covered by some form of collective bargaining contract in many industrialized countries, the nature and geographical scope of the bargaining process differs substantially. The United States, in particular, has very fragmented bargaining compared to other industrial countries, reflecting the autonomy of its more than 15,000 school districts. Even though many local bargaining units are members of state and national umbrella organizations, each local bargaining unit negotiates directly with the district and bargaining outcomes differ across these districts. France provides an example of the other extreme in which a national teacher association bargains with a centralized national educational system and yields a uniform contract for all teachers (Duclaud-Williams, 1985). Australia represents an intermediate case. Teacher unions have formed around the state- and territory-wide educational systems. Within each Australian territory or state (except Victoria) unions have emerged as dominant bargaining and policy-making organizations (Blackmore and Spaull, 1987).

Teacher unions affect the educational system in various ways, each one with a magnitude that depends upon its bargaining strength. For example, labor unions affect the salaries and working conditions of their members and provide a process to redress grievances. Unions also influence the availability of funds to education and the policies determined at local, state, and national levels. Results in these areas, in turn, have ramifications for the outcomes of schools—the educational achievement of students. Most of the literature on teacher unions has focused on the bargaining process and bargaining outcomes as they relate to salaries, fringe benefits, and hiring practices. However, the general public's concern lies principally with the ultimate effects of unions on the cost and quality of education.

This entry reviews the theory and empirical results of the effects of teacher unionization, with particular emphasis on student outcomes. It offers an evaluation of the effects of collective bargaining on student achievement within a framework based on educational production functions, which link the resources available to education to the various results of education. The evaluation proceeds in four stages. First, the entry surveys a list of primary determinants of student outcomes (typically measured by gains in standardized test scores) emphasized in the literature. Second, it examines the effects of collective bargaining on these various determinants. Third, it reviews studies that directly estimate the effects of collective bargaining within an educational production function framework. Finally, it summarizes evidence on the effects of teacher unionization on the cost of instruction.

2. Determinants of Educational Outcomes

The framework for looking at the possible effects of teacher unions is embedded in the literature on the determinants of educational outcomes, as described by what are referred to as "educational production functions," which are also sometimes called "input–output functions." These functions relate differences in student achievement gains to differences in school resources and other relevant factors.

Within this framework, the linkage may be traced between collective bargaining and student achievement. For instance, if collective bargaining increases class size, and students do not perform as well in larger classes, then slower student progress can be traced to teacher unions, and the same with other factors. Making the connection requires two significant relationships: the link between educational "inputs" and educational outcomes, and the link between collective bargaining and educational inputs.

The educational process is sufficiently complex that concentrating only upon class size or teachers, or aspects of the interaction between teacher and student, is not sufficient to assess the overall effect of collective bargaining. However, space does not permit a discussion of the details of educational production functions; the theory and empirical findings in this area are included in several entries in this *Encyclopedia* (see *Education Production Functions; Joint Production of Education; Political Economy of Educational Production*). In addition, the literature abounds with empirical studies of this sort. Hanushek (1986) reports that between 1966 and 1986 some 147 separate factors affecting educational outcomes were reported in the literature. Despite the widespread interest in educational production functions, only a handful of researchers have included union representation as a factor in formal educational production analysis.

It is, however, sufficient to posit a simple model of the educational process that identifies five basic groups of determinants of student outcomes and then to summarize briefly their relative importance as described in the literature. The groups are: (a) student and student-background characteristics, (b) teacher characteristics, (c) time spent by teachers and students performing various tasks, (d) modes of instruction, and (e) administrator characteristics.

At the risk of misrepresenting the richness of the results reported in the educational production function literature, it is nevertheless useful to summarize the findings and isolate the most important classes of determinants. A study by Eberts and Stone (1984) utilizes a nationwide sample of 14,000 fourth-graders in 328 elementary schools that was collected under the Department of Education's Sustaining Effects Study (SES). Student achievement is measured by the gains on standardized mathematics pre- and posttest.

Findings by Eberts and Stone are generally consistent with other studies and point to a number of teacher- and principal-related factors that are important determinants of the educational process. The factors that contribute most positively to achievement gains are the time teachers spend in instruction and preparation, the teacher–student ratio, the total experience of teachers, and the time principals spend assessing and evaluating math programs. The positive effects related to the teacher–student ratio and teacher experience are not found by all studies, as noted by Hanushek (1986). The evidence found by Eberts and Stone may be stronger because of their ability to link individual student achievement to explicit measures of the resources devoted to that student (e.g., instructional time, teacher attributes, and class size). Most studies attempt to link average student achievement to school or district averages to obtain broad determinants of student achievement.

3. Effects of Unionization on Determinants of Student Outcomes

The literature on the effects of unionization deals primarily with the effects on various immediate or intermediate determinants of student outcomes, rather than directly upon educational outcomes for students. These studies may be divided into those that address issues of resource allocation (e.g., salaries, class sizes, instructional modes, and the like), those that address attitudes among teachers and administrators important to their effectiveness, and those that address broader issues related to local and national policies.

3.1 Resource Allocation

The majority of studies of the effects of unionization on determinants of student outcomes deal directly or indirectly with issues of resource allocation. For example, several studies of teacher markets in the United States show that teacher unions increase the wages of their members (or those in the bargaining unit) relative to nonmembers. However, in the early 1970s, when teacher organizing efforts were relatively new, the effect was only marginal (see Kasper 1970, Perry 1979). Baugh and Stone (1982) show that the union-wage premium increased dramatically during the 1970s, from a 7 percent premium in 1974 to a 14 percent premium in 1977. The 14 percent union wage differential is comparable to the average union wage premium in the private sector. Baugh and Stone attribute the higher union wage premium to the growth in legislation favorable to teacher collective bargaining and the maturation of relatively new teacher unions during the 1970s.

Teacher unionization also affects staffing ratios through shifts in resources caused by higher salaries and through explicit contractual constraints, such as restrictions on class size and mandated preparation time. Using data from the Sustaining Effects Study of 6,000 elementary teachers Eberts (1984) shows that districts in which collective bargaining is practiced have more teachers and administrators per student but employ fewer clerical staff and aides per student. Estimates reveal that union districts have 10 percent more teachers per student and 5 percent more administrators per student. These increases are partly offset by a 7 percent reduction in clerical staff.

In addition, collective bargaining affects the composition and attributes of the instructional staff. Higher union salaries attract and retain teachers, and the negotiated salary structure rewards teachers for obtaining additional years of education. Eberts (1984) shows that elementary teachers covered by a collective bargaining contract have one to two years of additional teaching experience. Milkman (1989) finds similar results for a national sample of high-school teachers.

By establishing rules and procedures that govern a teacher's time, collective bargaining can affect the amount of time in which teachers engage in productive, instruction-related activities. For example, contracts commonly contain provisions that explicity specify the amount of time for class preparation, guarantee a duty-free lunch, and discourage participation in after-school meetings. Using the SES database, Eberts (1984) finds that teachers covered by collective bargaining agreements spend less time in instruction, more time in preparation and performing administrative and clerical duties. Based on a 180-day school year, collective bargaining reduces instruction by an equivalent of 5 schooldays a year and increases class preparation time by an equivalent 6.5 schooldays.

3.2 Attitudes of Teachers and Administrators

Attitudes among teachers and administrators can also be important, if intangible, factors in student achievement. The impact of collective bargaining on such attitudes is complex and subtle. Collective bargaining provides teachers with both the opportunity to voice their opinions on a wide range of district and school issues and with some degree of power to make their opinions count. Indeed, it is the union function as a voice for its members that specialists in industrial relations typically highlight as the most fundamental contribution of collective bargaining (see Hirschman 1970, Freeman and Medoff 1984).

Studies confirm that teachers derive great psychological value from pedagogical and professional activities (Lortie 1977). Relationships between teacher and student, relationships between teacher and administrator, organization of the classroom, selection of curriculum and materials, nonteaching responsibilities, and the perceptions and pressures of parents and community are all important.

According to Eberts and Stone (1984), union and nonunion teachers perceive the importance of these various issues differently. For instance, union and nonunion teachers differ in their views about the ingredients that make schools a satisfying place in which to work. Teachers covered by collective bargaining appear less concerned with the personnel policies of the district than their nonunion colleagues. It is possible that this decline in interest is due to a greater reliance on the part of union members on the union to take care of personnel matters, as well as to more structured personnel practices in union districts. Union teachers, on the other hand, appear more sensitive to class size than nonunion teachers. Unionized teachers also appear to be less satisfied in general with their workplace than their nonunionized counterparts, although the lower level of satisfaction may be an explanation rather than a consequence of collective bargaining.

3.3 Local and National Policy

Collective bargaining can also affect the educational process by influencing the formulation of state and local educational policy. For example, in the United States the two major teacher unions—the American Federation of Teachers and the National Education Association—have launched national lobbying and media campaigns that stress the importance of quality education to the national economy and individual well-being. Teacher unions in the United States have also become involved in the movement toward more choice in education, typically taking a stance opposing this initiative. In Australia, teacher unions have influenced, and often initiated, progressive educational policies on curriculum innovation, school organization, noncompetitiveness assessment, and participation of students, teachers, and parents in local and regional administrative bodies (Blackmore and Spaull 1987). Consequently, by influencing national policy and resource allocation decisions, teacher unions can affect the educational process. Indeed, in many countries the primary focus of national teacher unions is on issues of educational finance and policy at the national level.

4. Effect of Unionization on Student Outcomes

It is not possible to assess the overall effect of teacher unionization on student achievement from simply looking at the effects of components of the educational production process. Collective bargaining works in many opposing directions. For example, it appears to reduce student achievement on the one hand by reducing time spent in instruction, but increases it on the other by increasing the time teachers spend in preparation and the teacher–student ratio.

Several studies have analyzed the net effect of collective bargaining on student achievement for a variety of student groups. Most studies find that students in union districts perform better on average than students in nonunion districts. The basic approach in most studies has been to enter a measure of union representation into a standard educational production function. Eberts and Stone (1984, 1987) estimate a variant of this approach, by estimating separate equations for *individual* fourth-grade students in union and nonunion school districts. The student outcome measure records the difference in the pre- and post-test scores of each of 14,000 fourth-grade students on a standardized mathematics test. The educational production functions account for differences in student, teacher, administrator, and district characteristics, as well as the home environment. By controlling for these factors, the predominant factor explaining remaining differences in student test-score gains between students in union and nonunion districts should be teacher unionization.

Test-score gains of students in union districts are on average 8 percent higher than those of students in non-union districts. Half of the net effect is attributable to union-induced differences in resources and other educational factors between the two types of districts; half is due to union–nonunion differences in the effectiveness of these resources.

The effects of collective bargaining found by Eberts and Stone appear to vary for students of different achievement levels: union districts do better with average students. However, union districts do less well with students either well above or well below average; nonunion schools are more productive with these students, by about the same margin. These differences appear to arise from two major factors. First, union districts rely to a greater degree than nonunion districts on standard classroom instructional techniques, which work best for the majority of "average" students. However, the exposure for significantly below or above average students to specialized programs and instructional techniques is significantly greater in nonunion districts. This standardization of instructional techniques is similar to union behavior in many private sector industries. A second major source of union advantage is the greater effectiveness of instructional leadership activities by school principals in union districts. In organized districts, for example, instructional leadership by school principals may be much more effective both because specific principal actions are conditioned by teacher opinion and because the effectiveness of particular actions is enhanced by improved communication and coordination.

Milkman (1989) follows the same approach as Eberts and Stone in examining the effects of collective bargaining on the achievement gains of high school students. However, Milkman emphasizes the effect of collective bargaining on achievement of social minority group students. In schools and districts where minority group students are in the numerical minority, teacher unionization is associated with decreases in achievement by these students. However, in schools and districts where minority group students are in the numerical majority, unionization is associated with increases in their achievement. Milkman interprets this set of findings as further confirmation of the hypothesis that the standardization of curriculum and instructional techniques associated with collective bargaining explains the gains by average students in unionized districts, as well as the losses by the atypical students in the same districts.

A related study by Grimes and Register (1991) finds that Black high school students attending union districts perform better on SAT tests than Black students in nonunion districts. Their results show that a Black student in a union district scores 13.11 percent higher than a comparable Black student in a nonunion district. Register and Grimes do not distinguish whether the effects differ according to whether minority group students are in the numerical minority or majority. The use of SAT scores is also problematic because students taking SAT tests for college admission are typically above average achievers. Register and Grimes attribute their results to the fact that union work rules reduce the possibility of discriminatory practices by school staff.

Kleiner and Petree (1988), using aggregate state-level data for the period 1972–82, find that students in union districts score higher on SAT and ACT scores than students in nonunion districts. However, Kurth (1987) reports the opposite result: a negative relationship between union strength and SAT scores across states and time. This finding by Kurth has been criticized for the absence of controls for trend or regional factors, which are used in the study by Kleiner and Petree.

5. *Effect of Unionization on Costs of Instruction*

The higher average productivity of teacher unions is not without cost. The smaller classes and higher salaries enjoyed by union teachers require additional resources, or a significant shift away from other resources. The question is whether or not the additional gains in student achievement exceed the costs of obtaining these gains.

Evidence on the influence of teacher unionization on district expenditures is mixed, but most find, not surprisingly, that collective bargaining increases expenditures. Gallagher (1979) estimates that union districts have an operating budget approximately 9 percent larger than that of nonunion districts. In contrast, Hall and Carroll (1975) conclude that higher salaries negotiated in union districts are completely offset by larger class sizes, resulting in no significant difference in total operating expenditures between the two district types. Chambers (1977) also finds that collective bargaining reallocates resources within the district without significant increase in total operating expenditures.

However, none of these studies deals directly with the issue of overall union–nonunion cost differentials with the quality of education held constant. To do this, Eberts and Stone (1986) estimate an expenditure equation that specifies district operating expenditures per pupil as a function of variables that reflect the quality of education, community preferences and fiscal capacity, the size of the district, and urban and geographical characteristics. The results indicate that organized districts spend on average 12 percent more per pupil than nonorganized districts, even with achievement measures and student and community characteristics held constant.

The cost effects of teacher unions can be classified into three categories: compensation effects, factor-use effects, and productivity effects. The first two appear to increase the cost of education per unit of output, while the last effect appears to reduce the unit cost of providing education services. The factor-use effect relates to contract constraints placed on school administrators that may prevent them from allocating resources in the most efficient manner. As reported earlier, class-size restrictions, reduction-in-force limitations, and other contract provisions significantly affect the use of resources in unionized districts.

The three effects can be placed in perspective by using the estimates reported by Eberts and Stone. Of the three union effects considered, the productivity and factor-use effects appear roughly to offset one another. That is, the cost advantage associated with the higher productivity of unionized districts is of roughly the same magnitude as the cost disadvantage associated with higher teacher–student ratios in unionized districts. Because the productivity and factor-use effects tend to cancel each other out in this way, the union-induced teacher compensation premium dominates the estimated cost differential. This conclusion is further supported by the fact that multiplying the midrange estimate of the union salary premium (about 17 percent) by the typical ratio of teacher personnel costs to total costs (about 0.7) yields an estimate of the union cost differential (12 percent) consistent with the midrange of the direct estimates presented by Eberts and Stone. Thus, the union cost differential appears primarily to represent a transfer from taxpayers to teachers, with little detrimental change in average student achievement.

On a more speculative note, over a much longer period of time the higher compensation in unionized districts could enable such districts to attract and retain more productive teachers, partially offsetting the union cost differential.

6. Conclusion

Teacher unionization is a crucial force in the operation, effectiveness, and cost of public schools. Evidence to date, primarily from the United States, suggests that unionized teachers receive higher salaries, teach smaller classes, spend less time in instructing students, and have more time for classroom preparation. The net effect of teacher unions on these important factors in the educational process is to make unionized districts slightly more effective than nonunionized districts in educating the average student. This gain appears to be related to a greater standardization of instruction in unionized districts. Atypical students appear to do worse on average in unionized districts as a result of the greater standardization of instructional modes and techniques. For example, unionization is associated with decreased achievement for social minority group students who attend schools where they make up a minority of the students, but with increased achievement for minority group students who attend schools where they make up a majority of the students. Despite the overall productivity advantage for unionized schools, other costs associated with unionization, particularly in the form of higher teacher salaries and benefits, more than offset the productivity advantage of unionized schools, so that the cost of a given quality and quantity of instruction is higher in unionized schools, where all other factors are the same. In many countries, but to a lesser extent in the United States, national teacher unions focus on national issues of educational finance and policy, and place less emphasis on local bargaining.

See also: Education Production Functions; Macroeconomics of Educational Time and Learning; Microeconomics of School Production; Teachers as Professionals; Teacher Evaluation

References

Baugh W H, Stone A 1982 Teachers, unions, and wages in the 1970s: Unionism now pays. *Industrial and Labor Relations Review* 35(3): 368–76

Blackmore J, Spaull A 1987 Australian teacher unionism: New directions. In: Boyd W L, Smart D (eds.) 1987 *Educational Policy in Australia and America: Comparative Perspectives*. Falmer Press, New York

J G Chambers 1977 The impact of collective bargaining for teachers on resource allocation in public school districts. *Journal of Urban Economics* 4(3): 324–39

Duclaud-Williams R 1985 Teacher unions and educational policy in France. In: Lawn M (ed.) 1985 *The Politics of Teacher Unionism: International Perspectives* Croom Helm, London

Eberts R W 1984 Union effects on teacher productivity. *Industrial and Labor Relations Review* 37(3): 346–58

Eberts R W, Stone J A 1984 *Unions and Public Schools: The Effect of Collective Bargaining on American Education*. Lexington Books, Lexington, Massachusetts

Eberts R W, Stone J A 1986 Teacher unions and the cost of public education. *Economic Inquiry* 24 (October): 631–43

Eberts R W, Stone J A 1987 The effect of teacher unions and the productivity of public schools.

Freeman R B, Medoff J L 1984 *What Do Unions Do?* Basic Books, New York

Gallagher D G 1979 Teacher negotiations, school district expenditures, and taxation levels. *Educ. Admin. Q.* 15(1): 67–82

Grimes P W, Register C A 1991 Teacher unions and black students' scores on college entrance exams. *Ind. Rel.* 30(3): 492–500

Hall W C, and Carroll N 1975 The effect of teachers'

organizations on salaries and class size. *Ind. Lab. Rel. Rev.* 26(2): 834–41
Hanushek E A 1986 The economics of schooling: Production and efficiency in the public schools *J. Econ. Lit.* 24(3): 1141–77
Hirschman A O 1970 *Exit, Voice, and Loyalty: Responses to decline in Firms, Organizations, and States*. Harvard University Press, Cambridge, Massachusetts
Kasper H 1970 The effect of collective bargaining on public teachers' salaries. *Industrial and Labor Relations Review* 24(1): 52–72
Kleiner M M, Petree D L 1988 Unionism and licensing of public school teachers: Impact on wages and educational output. In: Freeman R B, Ichniowski C (eds.) 1988 *When Public Sector Workers Unionize*. The University of Chicago Press, Chicago, Illinois
Kurth M 1987 Teachers' unions and excellence in education: An analysis of the decline in SAT scores. *J. Lab. Res.* Vol. 8, Fall, pp. 351–67
Lortie D C 1977 *Schoolteacher: A Sociological Study*. University of Chicago Press, Chicago, Illinois
Milkman M I 1989 Teacher unions and high school productivity, unpublished PhD dissertation, University of Oregon, Eugen, Oregon
Pepin L 1990 The defense of teachers' trade union rights. *Int. Lab. Rev.* 129(1): 59–71
Perry C 1979 Teacher bargaining: The experience in nine-systems. *Industrial and Labor Relations Review* 33(1): 3–17
Saltzman G M 1985 Bargaining laws as a cause and consequence of the growth of teacher unionism. *Industrial and Labor Relations Review* 38(3): 335–51

R. W. Eberts; J. A. Stone

Teacher Unions

Organizations of school teachers have existed in most Western countries for many years, but it is only since the late nineteenth century that teachers have belonged to unions that represent their economic as well as their professional interests. This entry focuses on the growth of unions, their relationship to the state and public education authorities, their political and industrial activities (including union militancy), and the way unions serve the complex needs of teachers in both Western and Third World countries.

1. Growth of Teacher Unions

1.1 Forerunners

The first teachers' organizations were either education societies for professors, administrators, and principals, or teacher associations, which were often controlled by the same type of people. Their purpose was to enhance the training, public status, social fellowship, and annuity prospects of teachers. Some teachers' associations, or new separate associations, extended their activities to encompass interests directly related to the material conditions of teaching or protested about the arbitrary control exerted by school boards, superintendents, churches, or the state over teachers' working and social lives. The transformation of these mutual aid groups into associations for protest or resistance marks the embryonic beginnings of teacher unionism (Spaull 1984). Such associations were apparent in the activism among teachers in Paris in the 1830s (Wishnia 1990), in Berlin, Brandenburg, and Düsseldorf in the 1840s (McClelland 1991), and in Melbourne and Sydney in the 1870s, or around Toronto in the 1870s and again in the mid-1880s. Teachers who participated were often suppressed (by dismissal, transfer, or even jailing of leaders) by authorities fearful not only of syndicalist tendencies in teachers but of their potential for involvement in liberal political movements. Other associations collapsed from lack of teacher support after they failed to obtain tangible concessions.

1.2 Emergence of Teacher Unions

The first phase of emergent teacher unionism based on independence from employers and the state and the formation of a central authority for local associations occurred at different sites between 1870 and 1910. For successful teacher union formation to occur, three interrelated variables of growth were required. These were:

(a) changes in the work situation of teachers, including material rewards and increased subordination of teachers to school or system management;

(b) the emergence of a leadership dedicated to promoting teacher unionism;

(c) a favorable sociopolitical climate which provided a sound platform for trade union formation and growth (Spaull 1984).

These factors explain the emergence of teacher unionism in Germany and the United Kingdom in the 1870s and its diffusion from the *Deutscher Lehrerverein* (DLV—German Teachers' Union) to Scandinavia or from Great Britain to the "White" self-governing colonies of Australasia and South Africa in the same period. The National Union of Teachers (NUT), established in 1871, became an organizational model, and its name explains the use of the term "union" (a union of local associations, not a trade union) in the establishment of state teachers' unions in Australian colonies between 1886 and 1896 and in Jamaica (1895), Southern India (1908), Malta (1919), Fiji (1930), and Nigeria (1931).

The absence of a favorable sociopolitical climate, frequently accompanied by the lack of charismatic leadership dedicated to trade union principles, delayed the emergence of teacher unionism in the form of syndicates in Italy, France, and Portugal until the early 1900s. The same absence of a favorable sociopolitical climate had a similar effect in North

America: only in 1898 did women teachers in Chicago form the first teachers' union. This then prompted the creation of city-based unions in New York, Boston, Denver, and San Francisco. In 1916 local unions formed the American Federation of Teachers (AFT) (Urban 1982). In Canada teachers transformed various provincial education associations and formed central unions in the same period (Spaull 1991).

The momentum toward teacher unionism was driven by the relative decline in teachers' salaries and working conditions, increased centralization of schooling, and the consolidation of strong liberal and trade union formations which encouraged public employees, such as teachers, nurses, firefighters and police, to unionize. Similar economic and social forces led to the formation of Japan's first, but short-lived, teacher unions—the *Keimeska* in 1919 and the *Shokyoren* in 1929. A significant new feature of this later phase of teacher union formation was that the American Federation of Teachers and the *Fédération National Syndicats des Instituteurs* in France, established in 1905, affiliated with their national labor movements, as did the older Irish National Teachers' Organization (1869), which affiliated to both the Trade Union Congress and the Irish Labour Party between 1919 and 1945.

Both the DLV in Germany and the NUT in England and Wales maintained as one of their primary objectives "teacher unity," or the attachment of all sectional unions to the central union or federation. However, both remained mainly unions of male teachers, in elementary education, and they were controlled by head teachers. In most Western countries teaching as an occupation had become segmented by gender, level, hierarchy, and site. Teacher unions tended to reflect this segmentation. Central unions such as the DLV and the NUT never succeeded in attracting these other unions; particularism and fragmentation became pervasive characteristics of teacher unionism in Europe, and elsewhere. Teacher unionism in England and Scotland was not as fragmented as in Germany but serious schisms occurred between head teachers and assistants, between men and women, and between teachers in the NUT and secondary and vocational teachers (Ozga and Lawn 1981).

1.3 State Incorporation

The next phase of union growth was characterized by the effect on union growth and behavior of state incorporation of teacher unions and/or teachers. This occurred in many countries in the interwar years as a form of legitimation of teacher unions. It brought state control over teacher activities and union behavior. In its mildest form, in the United Kingdom, the central government bestowed official recognition on some teacher unions to help determine national salary levels through the Burnham scheme established in 1919. In this scheme, the government, through the appropriate minister of state, had the right to nominate the teacher union to the salary panel and in doing so enhanced the industrial status of the NUT while restricting the access of its rivals, the National Association of Schoolmasters and the National Union of Women Teachers. However, the same process impeded the NUT, and especially its more militant branches, from negotiating directly with local employers. Further incorporation of unions occurred in the interwar years when the state relaxed its direct control over teachers by offering them both employment security and a measure of professional autonomy, provided the unions remained outside of laborism and party politics, and refrained from challenging school reform (Lawn 1987).

Other forms of state incorporation occurred in Australia and Canada. Between 1917 and 1925 most Australian state-based teacher unions were granted access to compulsory arbitration by Labor governments. To obtain a place in the arbitration system, teacher unions had to apply for registration and this required teachers to divest multiunionism in favor of a single union in each state. In Canada during the 1930s and 1940s, at the request of struggling unions, provincial governments legislated Teaching Profession Acts that recognized a single province-wide union (except for Ontario and Quebec) which all public schools teachers were mandated to join (Manzer 1969). In both countries teacher unions were expected to conform industrially as a result of this incorporation.

These forms of incorporation encouraged overt industrial agendas in teachers' unions, often against the intentions of the state. Teacher unions had defined these agendas before the First World War and had intensified their concerns both during the war and during the frequent economic downturns in the interwar years. As a result there was a balancing of industrial activities with those concerned with curriculum, teacher training reform, and reorganization of school systems. Widespread prohibitions on bargaining for civil servants and teachers in this period meant that most teacher unions attempted to influence salary levels by organized pressure on public opinion, legislatures, and government. This was apparent in the United States, where the National Education Association (NEA), with its self-imposed prohibition on the right to collective bargaining, shifted its focus of power away from local associations to state and national organizations. In contrast, AFT locals, although committed to bargaining rights, became embroiled in city school politics, but to little effect because of their increasingly left-wing ideological positions.

Extreme forms of incorporation occurred in the Soviet Union, Italy, and Germany, where the totalitarian state gradually absorbed teacher unions into the party apparatus, so that they lost their status as independent organizations.

In contrast to Italy and Germany in this period, France's disparate teacher unions became part of the wider antifascist movement and, as a result of the initial success of the Popular Front in French politics, the two major teacher unions merged into the *Fédération Générale de L'Enseignement* (FGE) and affiliated as before with the *Confédération Générale du Travail*. In August 1940, the Vichy government dissolved the FGE. Like many other French unions, the FGE went underground for the remainder of the war. Earlier in the decade, all teacher unions in Portugal and Spain had been dissolved following the establishment of dictatorships in those countries.

1.4 Consolidation and Maturity

The third major phase of teacher union growth was over the period 1945–70. This phase was characterized by the consolidation of existing and older unions and by the emergence of new teacher union structures in those countries that had suffered different forms of restrictive state control. Examples of the latter were the re-emergence of strong sectional and local unions in France and Germany. In France a new national organization, the *Fédération de l'Education Nationale* (FEN), representing all levels of teaching, was formed at the end of the Second World War. In 1948, following the communist takeover of the major trade union congress, it decided to operate independently of the labor movement. This decision met with some defections; it also ensured intense ideological factionalism and sectionalism within the FEN. Nevertheless, the FEN became powerful but reactive in French education policy, although this was more a product of its place in a highly centralized education system than of its size, teacher coverage, and nonaffiliation with labor (Duclaud-Williams 1985). In West Germany a large federal union, the *Gewerkschaft Erziehung und Wissenschaft* (GEW), was formed in 1949, but it remained affiliated to the trade union federation and supportive of the Social Democratic Party. Despite the factionalism and interunion competition characteristic of these West European unions, they experienced patterns of membership growth similar to those of teacher unions in North America, Japan, and Australia. That growth was derived from the rapid increase in teaching forces that accompanied the expansion and extension of public schooling in the 1950s and 1960s, the increasingly vocal demands by teachers for subtantial improvements in working conditions, the inadequate funding of schools from traditional sources and by the national or federal governments, and the significant growth of teacher union services aimed at meeting the changing professional and consumer needs of teachers. The enhanced industrial orientation of teacher unions was assisted by the establishment or extension of regulated forms of industrial negotiations for teachers in Scandinavia, Australia, Canada, the United Kingdom, and, to a lesser extent, the United States (until the 1960s).

Most teacher unions in these countries operated politically in the education system in some form of partnership with the government (and/or the employer). For the first time (with the exception of Norway where it occurred much earlier), teacher unions were involved in decision-making processes in educational policies and school system management. Consultation and participation were the most common processes, but this involvement ensured that the unions became dependent on government and management. Unions were more proactive in Scandinavia, parts of West Germany, and Australia where, because of their affiliation with the trade union movement, social democratic governments were responsive to union demands. Elsewhere, teacher unions were increasingly recognized by authorities as being indispensable sources of information on teachers and teaching for the efficient administration of the school system (Manzer 1970).

The partnership model in educational policy-making had limitations in particular jurisdictions. For example, "breakaway" teacher unions, such as those for secondary teachers in England and Wales, Scotland, New Zealand, and Victoria, Australia, were often excluded from the established polity on the advice of the larger "parent" unions to government. Japan's *Nikkyoso* (Japan Teachers' Union) provides the best example of a national federation which, although restricted in its involvement in educational decision-making, became a constant challenge to the ministry of education and the ruling conservative government. It became a giant federation with over 600,000 members in its affiliates, and has exerted strident oppositional tactics, not only in education but also on government policies related to trade union control (including denial of industrial rights for teachers), defense, rearmament, and economic affairs. To articulate its positions it has employed mass teacher boycotts, street protests, and illegal strikes, as well as providing sustenance to the socialist party, which added to the authorities' determination to maintain unilateral decision-making in education.

2. Formation of New Unions

The 1970s also witnessed the emergence of new formations, resulting from either the removal of national restrictions on teacher union organization or the establishment of postcolonial national societies. Portugal and Spain illustrate the first trend—a trend that intensified with the collapse of the communist empire in Europe in the late 1980s. Teacher unionism in new independent nations that were former European colonies also underwent restructuring, to give teachers a more effective role in nation-building and new national systems of education. Unfortunately in some African countries, teacher unionism lost much of its independence and positive momentum following the trend toward the one-party state. Elsewhere—in Malaysia, Jamaica, and Papua New Guinea—new organizations emerged and developed to provide a distinctive strand of national trade unionism.

3. Teacher Union Militancy

Since the late 1960s teacher militancy has been a worldwide feature of union behavior. This can be distinguished from earlier periods, such as before and after the First World War, when union militancy was confined to a small number of systems in the United Kingdom, Australia, and North America (Seifert 1987). Teacher militancy finds expression in many forms, but is commonly identified with strikes, demonstrations, boycotts, and, to a lesser extent, union intervention in the electoral process. Union militancy, especially by strike action, first occurred in metropolitan societies, but since the late 1970s it has spread to non-Western countries.

Each jurisdiction has its own explanations for the growth in militancy, but there are a number of general factors that led to its appearance and persistence in metropolitan school systems. These are as follows:

(a) Teacher unions were prepared to take industrial and political action to secure, or modify, collective bargaining, especially where the right to bargain existed for private sector workers. In many jurisdictions, once teachers had secured collective bargaining, the bargaining process encouraged the use of threats or actual industrial action to achieve a satisfactory outcome.

(b) Of greater significance was a shift in teachers' basic loyalties away from the school system to their union. Teaching forces had emerged as part of large bureaucracies, and they felt marginalized in the system. This was particularly true of young teachers who had not been inducted fully into career structures.

(c) Teacher unions began to perceive themselves as trade unions, and therefore rejected the established view that it was inappropriate for teachers to engage in trade union activity. This change was part of a wider process whereby middle-class employees adopted tactics traditionally associated with working-class activism (Spaull 1977).

(d) Teacher unions felt increasingly displaced (or excluded) from the educational partnerships of the 1950s and 1960s. This became apparent as education authorities (under pressure from central governments) were consistently unresponsive to union demands.

(e) School systems became politicized in this period as public education found a strategic place in national and state politics and became a major component of fiscal expenditures. Politicization implied a polarization of views on teachers' conditions, professional development, school reform, and funding. It led to a sustained contestation of government policy and management styles. This contestation required new industrial responses from unions.

(f) The successful industrial action undertaken by teacher unions (particularly in the early 1970s) encouraged a widespread belief in the advantages of militant action. Teacher unions incorporated the notion of a "strike ideology" within their industrial objectives.

It is difficult to discern a pattern of "issues" in the growth of teacher militancy. Obviously unions often employed militant tactics to secure recognition, bargaining rights, or changes in negotiating machinery (Spaull and Hince 1986). Equally, where industrial action occurred during bargaining for new contracts or determinations, the issues were limited to salaries and working conditions as defined by the parameters of collective agreements. Nevertheless, union militancy was also directed to issues such as the control of the school system, the management of the teaching force (supervision, appraisal, and qualifications), or attempts to change schooling and funding priorities. Union militancy has also been associated with issues of teachers' civil and union rights, employer victimization of teachers, and "solidarity actions" with other trade unions over more general government policies. This last issue has been a widespread recent development in Western Europe, Japan, and African countries.

Teacher strikes come in different forms and are of varying duration. Unions have employed other types of stoppages, often to avoid the illegality of the "public employee strike." These have included street demonstrations, mass boycotts and sick leaves, the "long mess break," and, in parts of Asia, hunger strikes. Prolonged strikes (three or more weeks) have occurred in places as different as Quebec, Peru, Spain, and Senegal, but more frequently in individual school districts in North America. Long rolling strikes, which close only sections or sites in a school system, occurred in the United Kingdom and in Australia in the early 1970s and again in the mid-1980s. Elsewhere, strikes of a shorter duration (1–2 days) have been more frequent, with teachers returning to work (Australia) after arbitration or as a result of having achieved the desired effect on public opinion or negotiating authorities.

Less frequently, industrial action is accompanied or followed by electoral intervention, when unions adopt partisanship during elections. This strategy is not widely employed because most unions eschew party affiliations or endorsements. Endorsements are used in the United States at all levels (Berube 1988) and partisan intervention has occurred at times in provincial politics in British Columbia, Quebec, and some Australian states. Intervention raises strategic problems, however: (a) it is not always successful; (b) if used regularly it loses its impact; and (c) if successful, there is no guarantee that new governments will be responsive to teachers' demands.

Teacher militancy has helped to reduce the gulf between teacher unions and the trade union movement. In the United Kingdom and Australia most unions affiliated with trade union federations following the upsurge in industrial action in the 1970s. But the reasons for shifts in attitude can also be attributed to changes in the character of national trade unionism, and the need to extend teachers' political influence in national politics. Teacher militancy can also have undesirable effects on union behavior. Prolonged actions result in a "crisis of faith" in organizations, which can lead to intense struggles over tactics, decline in membership, and occasionally the formation of breakaway unions with antistrike philosophies (as in the United Kingdom and Australia).

Official responses to extended teacher militancy have been predictably hostile and, in some systems, overtly repressive (Pépin 1990). Reactions have included the removal of unions from negotiating processes (British Columbia), dismantling of special machinery for teacher negotiations (the United Kingdom and parts of Australia), and, more widely, suspension of the "checkoff" concession for payment of union fees. Victimization of teacher militants has included mass dismissals (Turkey, The Philippines), jailing of leaders (Quebec, Japan), and even their torture or death (Nepal, Colombia).

Teacher union militancy has not shrunk in the face of neoconservative attacks on public education, school teaching, and teacher unionism. But it has produced changes in strategies and in the exponents of militancy. It has emerged in Spain, Portugal, in the new union formations in Eastern Europe, and in North Africa. In the Western world, teacher strikes and other actions became prominent in the early 1990s. In the United States, for example, teacher strikes were on the increase, especially in NEA locals. Compared with the early 1970s, union militancy in the United States, Western Europe, and Australasia was supported by an aging group of militants of both sexes and in all levels of schooling who were disenchanted with restricted career opportunities, concerned with teacher welfare and pension issues, and suspicious of the restructuring of schooling and teachers' work.

4. Developments and Prospects

During the 1980s questions were raised about the survival of teacher unions as effective voices for school teachers (Adam 1982). Some commentators suggested that unions had outlived their roles in collective bargaining and they should become "professional unions" at the workplace (Kerchner and Mitchell 1988). Such views misunderstand the multifaceted character of modern unions. Western teacher unions have matured into large complex organizations. They are not only self-serving of the wide interests of teachers, but are concerned with the quality of schooling (including teaching) as well as a range of public policy issues unrelated to education. This latter area would once have been regarded as lying outside a union's legitimate domain.

Nevertheless, unions in metropolitan societies (governed by either conservative or liberal administrations) have declined in status and influence because of public constraints on public employment, the social services, and even trade unionism. Unions have been forced onto the defensive and have at times become more compliant in their political negotiations. In France and the United Kingdom membership declined because of this relative ineffectiveness—the unions can no longer claim to be always representative of teacher opinion. But in other systems (New Zealand, British Columbia), where the challenge to unions has been as formidable, membership has increased and the unions have displayed considerable resolve to resist reactionary policies. In these and other systems, teacher unions have confronted challenges by restructuring their organizations. The NEA is a good example, having transformed itself into a classroom teachers union. Elsewhere union energies have been directed toward promoting school-based or regional unionism and special semiautonomous caucuses for rural, vocational, and women teachers.

The issue of union fragmentation also is being addressed. Sweden effected a major merger of the "old" union with one of its rivals in 1991: the Swedish Teachers' Union now has over 180,000 members. Germany has been moving in a similar direction with the impetus arising from the need to incorporate teachers from the former East Germany into national organizations. In the United States the NEA has examined its prohibition on mergers with the AFT, while the major unions both in England and Wales, and in Scotland have also discussed the possibility of merging with their rivals—a complicated task in England and Wales given the degree of fragmentation and different philosophies toward strikes. Australian unions have followed a different path. Two unions representing teachers in the states' public and private sectors obtained federal registration in 1988 possibly as a step to seeking national conditions. The registration process brought the two unions closer and, encouraged by the trade union council's agenda to form single industry-wide unions, the teacher unions have considered some form of federation to cover all school teachers. (Spaull 1992).

These are illustrations of positive responses by unions. The same neoconservative hegemony in public education has created serious schisms in other teacher unions. In Italy the major union faced a revolt of militant rank and file teachers in 1987 who, like other Italian public employees, formed *Comitati di base* for grassroots industrial negotiations, in opposition to the national federation (Bordogna 1989). In 1990 in France the FEN, already experiencing turbulence with teachers quitting the union and the socialist parties, found itself unable to control its more militant constituents. In order to reduce internal conflict and to maintain control over its dissidents, FEN restructured itself into a national central union. The decision intensified the sectional rivalry between militant secondary teachers and primary teacher. In Japan, *Nikkyoso* paid the penalty for compromising with the ruling conservative party. Its decision in 1989 to affiliate with a new trade union federation supportive of the government was unacceptable to some 25 of its left-wing, militant unions. In 1991 they broke from *Nikkyoso* and established *Zenkyo*, which has maintained ties with the socialist movement.

Despite changes in strategies and the internal restructuring of some union movements, most Western unions have expanded their international roles in support of emergent unionism in other countries. Building on the Canadian Teachers' Federation's long-standing involvement in Africa and the Caribbean, other unions now play a constructive part in the professional development of teachers, and in the strengthening of their unions, in Eastern Europe and the Third World.

Much of this work is accomplished by bilateral arrangements and/or arrangements under the auspices of one or more of the four international teachers' federations. Western European unions have provided practical encouragement for the formation and expansion of teacher unions in countries such as Bulgaria and Albania. Western unions have also offered physical support and international solidarity to local union involvement in new political movements in Latin America, the Philippines, and New Caledonia. The international teacher union federation, the World Confederation of Organizations of the Teaching Profession (WCOTP), has campaigned persistently against the persecution of teachers and their unions in Nepal and Turkey, often by taking their claims to the International Labour Organisation. In South Africa a fragmented and fragile African teachers' movement has been transformed into the South African Democratic Teachers' Union. The impetus for reorganization came from local teacher unions, but was carried through with the support of other African teachers and trade unions, WCOTP, and teachers' unions in Sweden and Australia: a national federation was created in October 1990. It aimed to incorporate all South African teachers into a single union, eradicate apartheid, and create a single nonracial education system.

The spirit of internationalism has pervaded the international federations after decades of ideological rivalry. Many teacher unions now see the practical value of a united teachers' voice in international and regional affairs. In January 1993 WCOTP and the International Federation of Free Teachers' Unions merged into a new international body, Education International. Another international organization, the World Federation of Teachers' Unions, which was funded by the Soviet bloc, also faced financial collapse. It seemed as if most of its national members would elect to affiliate with the new body.

5. Conclusion

Teacher unions have played a strategic role in the protection and advancement of school teachers' rights and working conditions and the liberalizing of public education. At times their roles have not been appreciated by authorities, many of whom have resented the influence exerted by unions in their school systems. The historical growth of teacher unionism in many countries has been erratic and divisive, but in most modern eras teacher unions have mobilized against the economic and political challenges of the time.

In these precarious times for public education and school teaching, a new sense of purpose is apparent in many teacher unions, old and new. The 1990s and the new century will test the capacities of unions to represent teachers effectively, especially in those societies with a tradition of robust teacher unionism. Developments may also stimulate the attainment of that most elusive ideal: "strength through teacher unity," not only in individual systems, but in international arenas.

Future research on the roles of teacher unions should continue the "new" social histories of individual unions, extend studies of the organizational character of local associations and sections within unions (e.g., women), and introduce comparative studies, especially of union responses to restructuring of education.

See also: Labor Relations in Education; Teacher Unionization, Economics of

References

Adam R 1982 The future of teachers' unions. *Comp. Educ.* 18(2): 197–204

Berube M R 1988 *Teacher Politics: The Influence of Unions*. Greenwood, New York

Bordogna L 1989 The COBAS fragmentation of trade-union representation and conflict. In: Leonardi R, Corbetta P (eds.) 1989 *Italian Politics: A Review*, Vol. 3. Pinter, New York

Duclaud-Williams R 1985 Teacher unions and educational policy in France. In: Lawn M (ed.) 1985 *The Politics of Teacher Unionism*. Croom Helm, London
Kerchner C T, Mitchell D E 1988 *The Changing Idea of a Teachers Union*. Falmer Press, London
Lawn M A 1987 *Servants of the State: The Contested Control of Teaching 1900–1930*. Falmer Press, London
Manzer R A 1969 Selective inducements and the development of pressure groups: The case of Canadian teachers' associations. *Can. J. Pol. Sci.* 2(1): 103–17
Manzer R A 1970 *Teachers and Politics in England and Wales: The Role of the National Union of Teachers in the Making of National Education Policy Since 1944*. University of Toronto Press, Toronto
McClelland C E 1991 *The German Experience of Professionalization: Modern Learned Professions and their Organisations from the Early Nineteenth Century to the Hitler Era*. Cambridge University Press, Cambridge
Ozga J T, Lawn M A 1981 *Teachers, Professionalism and Class: A Study of Organized Teachers*. Falmer Press, Lewes
Pépin L 1990 The defence of teacher trade union rights. *Int. Lab. Rev.* 129(1): 59–71
Seifert R V 1987 *Teacher Militancy: A History of Teacher Strikes 1986–1987*. Falmer Press, London
Spaull A D 1977 Trends in teacher militancy. In: Spaull A D (ed.) 1977 *Australian: Teacher to Militant Professionals From Colonial Schoolmasters*. Macmillan, Melbourne
Spaull A D 1984 The origins and formation of teacher unions in 19th century Australia. In: Palmer I (ed.) 1984 *Melbourne Studies in Education 1984*. Melbourne University Press, Melbourne
Spaull A D 1991 Fields of disappointment: The writing of teacher union history in Canada. *Historical Studies in Education* 3(1): 21–48
Spaull A D 1992 Federal registration of Australia teacher unions. *Australian Journal of Labour Law* 5(1): 40–51
Spaull A D, Hince K 1986 *Industrial Relations and State Education in Australia*. AE Press, Melbourne
Urban W J 1982 *Why Teachers Organized*. Wayne State University, Detroit, Michigan
Wishnia J 1990 *The Proletarianizing of the Fonctionnaires: Civil Service Workers and the Labour Movement Under the Third Republic*. Louisiana State University, Baton Rouge, Louisiana

Further Reading

Barber M 1992 *Education and the Teacher Unions*. Cassell, London
Blum A A (ed.) 1969 *Teacher Unions and Associations: A Comparative Study*. University of Illinois Press, Urbana, Illinois
Cooper B S (ed.) 1992 *Labor Relations in Education: An International Perspective*. Greenwood Press, Westport, Connecticut
Johnson S M 1984 *Teacher Unions in Schools*. Temple University Press, Philadelphia, Pennsylvania
Lawn M (ed.) 1985 *The Politics of Teacher Unionism: International Perspectives*. Croom Helm, London
Lawn M, Grace G (eds.) 1987 *Teachers: The Culture and Politics of Work*. Falmer Press, London

A. D. Spaull

Teachers and Policy: Implications for Management

During the 1980s and early 1990s, teachers in a number of countries claimed greater authority in determining educational policy and practice. Such changes in the power and responsibilities of teachers have implications for the roles and activities of administrators. This entry discusses the reasons behind these changes, describes some of the forms they take, and identifies implications for future administrative practice.

1. The Origins of Change

Historically, teachers have been expected to transfer knowledge to students. A standardized curriculum, consisting largely of material to be mastered and tested, provided teachers with direction about what to teach and when to teach it. Compliant learning on the part of students was sufficient, given the low level of skills required for employment in most sectors of the economy. Increasingly, however, society requires employees with far more sophisticated skills than was provided by this conventional approach to instruction. Graduates of today's schools must not only master basic content in a variety of subject areas, but also think creatively and critically about that content. Increasingly, there is a demand for teachers who understand the structure of the disciplines they teach, even if the assignment is fourth-grade mathematics. Reformers have further argued that, if students are expected to exercise greater responsibility for their own learning, teachers must also be accorded greater responsibility in determining the substance and methods of teaching and must be given the opportunity to participate meaningfully in school management (OECD 1990).

2. The Regulation of Teachers' Work

In the early 1980s, when the public began to realize that students' school performance had declined, analysts first blamed teachers for the failure. Special commissions in various countries criticized the schools and recommended tightening requirements and improving standards. The most publicized of these studies was the United States report *A Nation at Risk* (United States National Commission on Excellence in Education 1983). In response to evidence of failure, educational authorities introduced an array of regulatory mechanisms designed to exact greater compliance from teachers and to ensure that they would teach the prescribed curriculum successfully. Government officials instituted closer supervision of teachers' work and relied on standardized tests for greater accountability. This approach to school reform, often called the "First Wave" in the United States, did not achieve the results its advocates had hoped. Students' test scores in the United States failed to rise and sometimes actually dropped in response to these measures. Talented teachers who resented the generic standards and external control of their work became disenchanted and left the profession (McNeil 1987). In Australia, where the curriculum had been closely prescribed for years, teachers criticized the practices of inspectors, assigned to supervise their work, and advocated that teachers develop curricula in their schools (Australia, Schools Council 1990).

3. The Empowerment of Teachers

Increasingly, reformers recognized that students would not become creative and critical thinkers if their teachers were bound by regulation. The Carnegie Task Force on Teaching as a Profession (1986) published an influential report which argued that, rather than being the objects of reform, teachers should become its agents. Similarly, OECD analysts concluded: "Teachers lie at the heart of the educational process. The greater the importance attached to education as a whole—whether for cultural transmission, for social cohesion and justice, or for the human resource development so critical in modern, technology-based economies—the higher is the priority that must be accorded to the teachers responsible for that education" (OECD 1990 p. 9).

Since the mid-1980s in many West European countries, the United States, and Australia, teachers have assumed greater responsibility for curriculum, instruction, and testing; they have been granted greater authority to determine policy and practice; they have assumed a wider variety of roles in their schools; and their salaries have changed, both in level and structure. It is worth noting that many of the goals of this movement to professionalize teaching have also been achieved in Japan, where teachers have exercised a high degree of discretion in their work even though the educational system is centralized; where teachers are active in matters of school management; and where they enjoy high levels of status and pay (Stevenson and Stigler 1992).

3.1 Curriculum and Testing

Reformers who advocate expanding teachers' roles in developing curriculum have argued that, if students are to succeed with a more demanding and creative academic program, teachers will have to be involved in its development. They cannot be expected to function simply as agents of transfer in the process. However, intense debate continues about how much curricular control teachers should exercise and how much curricular variation should be encouraged or tolerated. Some reformers, such as Sizer (1992), have contended that the curriculum should be developed school by school to meet local students' needs. Others, such as Smith and O'Day (1991), have argued that teachers' autonomy should be exercised within the structure of state-wide or national curricular frameworks, which set forth "curricular themes, topics, and objectives in sufficiently long-range chunks (e.g., four-year blocks) to allow for a maximum of flexibility and creativity at the local level while still establishing the clear instructional direction and goals for the system as a whole." (p. 248)

In addition to assuming greater roles in curriculum development, teachers have increasingly become active participants in assessing student learning. Teachers in England and Wales have been involved in developing assessment guidelines for the General Certificate of Secondary Education and in conducting the assessments, which were formerly externally administered (OECD 1990). In the United States there has been a growing interest in alternative approaches to assessment, such as reviewing portfolios of students' work, which call for far greater initiative and judgment on the part of teachers. Here, as with curriculum, there has been a debate about whether this move away from reliance on standardized testing should be embedded in a larger system of assessment or whether it should be controlled locally. In either case, it seems clear that teachers will be increasingly involved in its development and implementation.

3.2 Educational Policy-making

Historically, teachers have had little role in policy-making; they granted administrators authority in areas such as hiring, budget, and testing in exchange for retaining autonomy within their classrooms (Johnson 1990). However, changed expectations for schools have led teachers to demand greater authority in setting educational policy.

In a number of school districts in the United States much of this shift has occurred through the process of collective bargaining in which traditional adversaries have formally negotiated school reforms (Rosow and Zager 1989). Such changes have given teachers responsibility for assessing their peers, developing long-range plans, and assigning staff to schools. Teacher employers and teacher unions in Australia have also begun to collaborate closely in the National Project on the Quality of Teaching and Learning. Such cooperative efforts have promoted considerable debate among school administrators about whether teachers should be involved in managerial decisions and what the appropriate relationship between teachers and administrators should be. In general, teacher advocates have responded that administrators and teachers should share equal power and responsibility in such reform structures although many contend that, ultimately, teachers will assume full professional control of schooling.

A second, and often related, effort to redistribute policy-making authority occurs through decentralization, whereby the school, rather than the district or the state, becomes the place where important decisions about curriculum, budget, and staffing are made. Sometimes decentralization results from collective bargaining or from unilateral decisions by management. In other cases, such as in the state of Victoria (Australia) or in Chicago, school-site management is the result of political and legislative action. In Chicago, a school-site council composed of six parents, two community members, two teachers, and a nonvoting principal has extensive authority in decisions about the curriculum, budget, and staffing, including the appointment of the principal. In Miami-Dade County (Florida) where school-site management resulted from collective bargaining, teachers hold a decided majority of the seats on the school-site council.

There is continuing debate about whether decentralization inevitably leads to greater autonomy for schools or greater professional influence for teachers. Some Australian analysts have suggested that decentralization is actually a strategy on the part of educational officials to abdicate responsibility for the schools (Chapman and Dunstan 1990). Teachers in large United States districts, including New York City and Chicago, have found that, although authority may have been redistributed formally, central office administrators have retained many controls over school-site practice. Connors and McMorrow (1990 p. 84) argued that senior systems administrators in Australia managed devolution in order to ensure "their own survival." Similarly, McRae (1990 p. 104) observed that, at the school-site level, some principals who are the strongest advocates of decentralization fail to share responsibility for school governance with their teachers.

3.3 New Roles

Although teachers in some countries such as England and Australia have long held roles as head or lead teachers, teachers' roles in the United States are rarely differentiated in that they spend their days almost exclusively teaching alone in their classrooms. Moreover, they typically have the same responsibilities at the beginning and end of their careers. Since the mid-1980s, there has been increasing effort to differentiate teachers' roles, both by enhancing and enlarging their jobs.

The changes in teachers' roles have frequently come about as a result of redistributing responsibility for curriculum, assessment, and policy-making. If teachers are to become active in redesigning the curriculum, experimenting with new strategies for assessment, or developing the school budget, their roles must change. In some cases, their jobs are simply enlarged; they assume these new responsibilities after school and during vacations. In others, the entire configuration of the job is changed and teachers assume positions as lead or mentor teachers. They are granted time to develop curriculum or to assess their peers and, in some cases, they form management boards to replace principals and run their schools.

These changes in roles, most of which are still experimental, have important implications for principals. If administrators believe that hierarchical authority is an essential aspect of school administration, then there are likely to be struggles between teachers and principals, as was the case in Rochester (New York), when teachers assumed the right to assess their peers. However, evidence suggests that teachers are willing to work cooperatively with principals who share responsibility with them. Teachers' primary interest is centered on the classroom and they rarely wish to assume full responsibility for managing their schools. Fullan and Stiegelbauer (1991) and others have found that collaborative schools, in which teachers exercise meaningful leadership, typically depend on principals to establish and sustain them.

3.4 Salaries

In Japan teachers are paid as much as university professors, "2.4 times the national per capita income, as opposed to only 1.7 times for teachers in the United States" (Stevenson and Stigler 1992 p. 162). Those seeking to attract and retain larger numbers of able and talented teachers in other countries often argue that higher salaries would not only make careers in teaching financially feasible, but would increase the status of the profession. Therefore, many reform initiatives have included higher pay for teachers.

Among the most controversial issues associated with the topic of pay are whether teachers should be offered financial incentives or paid on the basis of merit as evidenced by student test scores or evaluations of classroom practice. An OECD report (1990) noted that "attitudes, within and across countries, differ sharply on this matter" (p. 59). There has been intense debate on this subject in France. An incentive pay plan introduced in the United Kingdom in 1987 still had not been implemented by 1990. In the United States various states and local districts tried to initiate performance-based pay during the 1980s, but these efforts are generally regarded as having failed. In part, their demise was the result of vigorous opposition by teacher unions, but they were also abandoned because they promoted competition rather than cooperation, rested on faulty evaluation practices, and were very expensive to implement.

There seems to be somewhat more support for career ladder plans that would pay teachers on the basis of their rank; for example, as novice, professional, and expert teacher. In some cases, these steps on the career ladder involve expanded professional responsibilities and opportunities, such as becoming a mentor teacher or conducting research in the classroom. In others, the steps simply indicate differences in salary and seniority. It appears that in countries where positions of lead teacher are grounded in past practice, such as Australia and England, there will be greater acceptance of such schemes than in the United States, where egalitarian norms militate against making such distinctions among teachers. Nonetheless, there are districts in the United States that are developing career ladders with differentiated rewards and responsibilities.

School administrators have rarely been involved in determining pay for teachers. Placement on salary scales has been determined largely by objective criteria such as seniority and coursework. However, merit pay and career ladder plans typically depend upon administrators' evaluations and, therefore, those evaluations are likely to be scrutinized more closely when they are used to support such salary judgments. In some instances, a teacher who achieves the highest level on the career ladder may earn more than an administrator, thus calling into question the legitimacy of an administrative hierarchy and the attractiveness of administrative positions.

3.5 Professional Certification

Educational bureaucracies license teachers to practice. However, in most cases, these licenses set forth minimal qualifications rather than advanced standards. Some who would improve schooling by improving the quality of teaching believe that teachers should be encouraged to pursue advanced certification after some years of successful teaching experience. In the United States the National Board for Professional Teaching Standards, established in 1987 and composed of a majority of classroom teachers, will set standards for professional teaching practice in particular fields and will begin to grant advanced credentials by the mid-1990s. Although the Board functions outside the government, it hopes to influence the practice in school districts by identifying very able teachers who can then assume positions of responsibility for writing curriculum, preparing assessments, or assessing peers. These individuals might well be the teachers who occupy the top rungs of career ladders. Thus, Board-certified teachers would potentially be the very kind of teachers that reformers in the mid-1980s claimed were in such short supply.

This change, and a similar one being considered for Advanced Skills Teachers in Australia, would have potential implications for administrators, since it is likely that these teachers would command high salaries and considerable respect for achieving such an accomplishment. If teachers were to assume elevated positions in the schools, it is possible that central office administrators and school principals might well find their jobs, influence, and salaries reduced. Alternatively, administrators' responsibilities might be shifted away from curriculum and instruction and confined to more conventional managerial responsibilities, such as supervising custodial services or ordering supplies.

4. Implications for Administrators

Research during the late 1970s by Edmonds (1979) in the United States and Rutter et al. (1979) in England pointed to the importance of the principal in establishing an effective school. The principal who emerged from the Effective Schools Movement came to be seen as a decisive and confident instructional leader, ready to take a stand and direct teachers' work. Since then a different image of the principal has been emerging. Barth (1990) and Fullan and Stiegelbauer (1991) called for principals to act as collaborative leaders, respect teachers, and engage school staffs in solving problems and improving instruction for children.

There is no question that changes are underway in many countries to enhance the role of teachers and, therefore, the quality of teaching. Although principals originally assumed their titles because they were principal-teachers, there is considerable variation across countries in the extent to which school-site administrators understand instruction and are regarded as competent teachers. It does appear that the need for the principalship endures, that there are important functions of leadership which cannot simply be aggregated from the various efforts of individual teachers. However, there are few clear models of this new administrative role and principals are therefore working to develop them with their staffs. Notably in Japan, where teachers enjoy greater status, higher pay, and considerable autonomy within a centrally determined curriculum, administrators "frame their role in terms of maintaining good relations with the district, buffering teachers from outside influences, and managing the school environment in ways that enable teachers to act in accord with their best professional judgment" (Sato and McLaughlin 1992 p. 361).

Similarly, it seems likely that the roles of central office administrators will change if the involvement of teachers in educational policy continues to increase. If schooling is truly decentralized and decisions about budget and staffing are vested in school-site councils, central administrators will necessarily change, becoming less involved in control and more committed to providing services for the school.

References

Australia, Schools Council 1990 *Australia's Teachers: An Agenda for the Next Decade*. Australian Government Publishing Service, Canberra

Barth R 1990 *Improving Schools From Within: Teachers, Parents, and Principals Can Make the Difference*. Jossey-Bass, San Francisco, California

Carnegie Task Force on Teaching as a Profession 1986 *A*

Nation Prepared: Teachers for the 21st Century: The Report of the Task Force on Teaching as a Profession. Carnegie Forum on Education and the Economy, Hyatsville, Maryland
Chapman J D, Dunstan J F (eds.) 1990 *Democracy and Bureaucracy: Tensions in Public Schooling.* Falmer Press, London
Connors L G, McMorrow J F 1990 Governing Australia's public schools: Community participation, bureaucracy and devolution. In: Chapman J D, Dunstan J F (eds.) 1990 *Democracy and Bureaucracy: Tensions in Public Schooling.* Falmer Press, London
Edmonds R A 1979 Effective schools for the urban poor. *Educ. Leadership* 37(15): 15–24
Fullan M, Stiegelbauer S 1991 *The New Meaning of Educational Change.* 2nd edn. Cassells, London
Johnson S M 1990 *Teachers at Work: Achieving Excellence in Our Schools.* Basic Books, New York
McNeil L M 1987 Exit, voice, and community: Magnet teachers' responses to standardization. *Educ. Policy* 1(1): 93–113
McRae D 1990 Exploring trails in school management. In: Chapman J D, Dunstan J F (eds.) 1990 *Democracy and Bureaucracy: Tensions in Public Schooling.* Falmer Press, London
Organisation for Economic Co-operation and Development (OECD) 1990 *The Teacher Today: Tasks, Conditions, Policies.* OECD, Paris
Rosow J, Zager R 1989 *Allies in Educational Reform: How Teachers, Unions, and Administrators Can Join Forces for Better Schools.* Jossey-Bass, San Francisco, California
Rutter M, Maughan B, Mortimore P, Outston J 1979 *Fifteen Thousand Hours: Secondary Schools and Their Effects on Children.* Harvard University Press, Cambridge, Massachusetts
Sato N, McLaughlin M W 1992 Context matters: Teaching in Japan and in the United States. *Phi Del. Kap.* 73(5): 359–66
Sizer T R 1992 *Horace's School: Redesigning the American High School.* Houghton Mifflin, Boston, Massachusetts
Smith M S, O'Day J 1991 Systemic school reform. In: Fuhrman S H, Malen B (eds.) 1991 *The Politics of Curriculum and Testing.* Falmer Press, New York
Stevenson H W, Stigler J W 1992 *The Learning Gap: Why Our Schools Are Failing and What We Can Learn From Japanese and Chinese Education.* Summit Books, New York
United States National Commission on Excellence in Education/Gardner D P et al. 1983 *A Nation at Risk: The Imperative for Educational Reform.* US Government Printing Office, Washington DC

Further Reading

Chapman J (ed.) 1990 *School-based Decision-making and Management.* Falmer Press, London
Clune W H, Witte J F (eds.) 1990 *Choice and Control in American Education. Vol. 2: The Practice of Choice, Decentralization and School Restructuring.* Falmer Press, London
Darling-Hammond L, Berry B 1988 *The Evolution of Teacher Policy.* The Rand Corporation, Santa Monica, California
United States National Board for Professional Teaching Standards 1989 *Toward High and Rigorous Standards.* National Board for Professional Teaching Standards, Washington, DC

S. M. Johnson

Teachers as Artists

The idea of the teacher as artist is a metaphor. It is not an empirical research topic on which evidence can be amassed and evaluated. It is closely related to debates about appropriate styles of educational research, for if teaching is an art rather than a science, then teaching should be researched by aesthetic critics rather than scientific investigators. This entry examines the pervasiveness of the metaphor of teacher as artist, introduces the concept of indeterminacy, and explores the importance of the metaphor for researchers.

1. The Pervasive Metaphor

Most scholars start their discussion of the teacher as artist with James's *Talks to Teachers on Psychology* (1983), originally published in 1891. James wrote: "Psychology is a science, and teaching is an art: and sciences never generate arts directly out of themselves" (p. 15).

Writing on this topic in the 1980s and early 1990s did not progress beyond James's statement, in that little empirical evidence was gathered on teaching as an art, and little theoretical work was devoted to analyzing what "art" means in this widely used metaphor.

The lack of incisive theorizing and empirical material has not, however, prevented many authors from using the metaphor. For example, a British expert on teaching English as a second or foreign language, Morris (1954), called his book *The Art of Teaching English*, stating that a living language is "a source of aesthetic gratification" (p. 3), a perspective that should be conveyed by the teacher! Over a decade later Colman (1967) argued that all master teachers were also artists. His book sets out 20 different teaching methods, from the Socratic through the Jesuit and the Montessori to "Communist" methods, and ends with a chapter called "Be an Artist." Colman told his readers, who are believed to be teachers in training, that: "Variety remains the spice of life, and the teaching craftsman is never content until he develops a great repertoire of methods, techniques, and procedures for the production of his art" (p. 168).

In the 1970s Travers and Dillon (1975) produced a book centered on: "Teaching as a performing art, and in the performing arts, each player must give his own interpretation of that which he wishes to portray" (p. vii). Their model is Konstantin Stanislavski's approach to the training of actors and the production of plays, which he devised at the Moscow

Art Theater to counteract artificial and overacted performances. Central to Stanislavski's ideal was the actor "becoming" the character, so that if cast as Hedda Gabler the actress must eat, sleep, walk, dress, and bathe as Hedda, not as herself. Travers and Dillon advocated that the student teacher should become as absorbed in the role of teacher as an actress cast as Hedda. Their book essentially presented a set of minidramas in classrooms which would allow students to rehearse their new roles as teachers.

In the 1980s Rubin (1985) again offered the metaphor. He wrote for "those teachers-in-training who believe teaching can be an art, and whose aim is to make themselves Artist Teachers" (p. iii). Early in this volume Rubin suggested there are two routes to being an artist teacher: "Some, blessed with natural gifts, rely principally on instinct. Others, less intuitive, cultivate equally impressive artistry through practice and effort" (p. 15).

All these books, from two continents, written over a 40-year period, invoked the metaphor of the teacher as an artist. None is particularly well-known or widely used. They all deployed the same metaphor, but not in a cumulative way, for none of the authors referred to the earlier volumes in the sequence. These were all prescriptive texts, not reports of research. Among researchers, the metaphor is rarely used.

2. The Metaphor and Research

In the early 1990s the metaphor of the teacher as artist has been associated with Gage (1978) and Eisner (1977), both of whom paid tribute to the evocation of teaching produced by Jackson (1968). Gage's work was more concerned with establishing the scientific base on which the artist can build than with exploring what "artist" means. Eisner was more interested in artistry in educational research and evaluation than in artistry in teaching.

These two leading researchers have not been alone. Scholars doing empirical research on teachers and teaching have not made much use of the metaphor; nor have they tried to pin it down in their investigations. A content analysis of one of the leading journals in the field, *Teaching and Teacher Education*, revealed that in the 32 issues after its foundation in 1984/5, containing 288 articles written by authors based in 20 different countries from Australia to Thailand, only one paper used the metaphor of the teacher as artist (Trumbull 1986). (This paper drew on Rubin 1985.) Not a single paper in *Teaching and Teacher Education* has focused on Eisner's work on aesthetic criticism as an approach to the study of teaching.

Teaching and Teacher Education is a journal predominantly for researchers with a background in the psychology of education. The metaphor of the teacher as artist is equally rare in the sociological literature on teaching. Waller (1932) deployed several metaphors about teachers—especially the teacher as stranger—but not that of the teacher as artist. Similarly, the only time the British sociologist of teaching Hargreaves (1983) has used the phrase "The Art of Teaching" was when he was writing about the teaching of art and aesthetics. The Australian Connell (1985) also evoked many facets of teaching without the metaphor of artistry. One reason that researchers who gather data on teaching have not used the metaphor of teaching as artistry as often as those writing training manuals may be the vagueness of the idea. Moreover, few authors (except Travers and Dillon 1975) have examined the type of artist they are invoking.

3. The Unspecified Artist

The invocation of teaching as artistry is a vague one. Those who use the metaphor rarely specify what kind of artistic performer or creator they have in mind. Is the teacher an actor, a painter, a sculptor, a poet, a ballet dancer, a musician, a composer, a chef, a playwright, a novelist, a film-director, a choreographer, a quiltmaker, a fashion designer, or a singer? Is the teacher a performer of someone else's script, the creator of his or her own, or the director/conductor/choreographer of the children's performance? In general, no particular artistic role has been specified by educational writers. It is not clear whether the teacher should be emulating a reclusive novelist such as J D Salinger, a gregarious country and western star such as Dolly Parton, or a conductor such as Andrew Davies. Authors have left the idea of "artistry" unspecified and, apart from mentioning creativity, unexplored. Indeed the vagueness of the metaphor brings it perilously close to that other old warhorse: the teacher as cultivator. Lacey (1970) was scathing about the "teacher as gardener" metaphor long ago:

> Educationalists and even sociologists frequently use gardening analogies when talking about the process of education, e.g. "cultivating" pupils. The metaphor is totally misleading. I have yet to hear of a gardener being reduced to a nervous wreck by errant plants, but I have not taught or done research in a school where at least one member of staff did not suffer chronic discipline problems. (p. 170)

At its unspecified and rhetorical worst, the metaphor of teacher as artist is just as misleading.

There is, however, a real issue behind the metaphor, and the work of Gage (1978) has addressed it. When Gage examined *The Scientific Basis of the Art of Teaching*, he was exploring the tension between rules and formulae on the technical side and creativity on the artistic. He wrote: "As a practical art, teaching must be recognised as a process that calls for intuition, creativity, improvisation, and expressiveness—a process that leaves room for departures from what is implied by rules, formulas and algorithms" (p. 15). This contrast has been written about extensively in the sociology of the professions: a literature ignored by authors on teachers and teaching. The contrast Gage made between "science" and "art" has elsewhere been described as a contrast between technicity and indeterminacy.

4. *The Indeterminacy of Teaching*

The French sociologists Jamous and Peloille (1970) made an attempt to reorganize sociological thinking about occupations by focusing on each job's location in a two-dimensional space of "indeterminacy" and "technicality." What writers on teaching such as Gage mean by "artist" is someone with what Jamous and Peloille called "indeterminate" skills.

Jamous and Pelolle argued that all occupations involve two contrasting types of skill and knowledge: technical and indeterminate. Technical skills and knowledge are the explicit, rule-governed, codified parts of the job. For example, a London taxi driver has to have a clean driving licence and pass a test on "the knowledge": a detailed examination of factual material on London streets, stations, hotels, taxi routes, and short cuts. A lawyer has to have a knowledge of legal codes and cases in the law books. A police officer has to know how to caution a suspect and what the local laws are. For Gage (1978) a teacher has to have subject-matter knowledge and a grasp of the research on teacher effectiveness—the scientific basis—and that is Jamous and Peloille's technicity.

Indeterminacy is the "hidden curriculum" of the job performance: all the tacit, implicit, unexamined facets of any job. All jobs involve rules of thumb and "judgment calls" that leave space for flair, genius, and unspecifiable virtuosities. For the taxi driver, dealing successfully with drunks, bewildered tourists, the police, other drivers, and hotel doormen involves such indeterminate skills and knowledge. For the lawyer it is dealing with judges, clients, and juries; for the police officer it is knowing when to caution and when to arrest, when to call for back-up and when to go in, how to cope with both criminals and victims and distinguish between them. (For further work on indeterminacy versus technicity see Atkinson et al. 1977, Atkinson 1983, Atkinson and Delamont 1985).

When educational writers say that teachers must be artists, what they actually mean is that the job of teaching has both technical and indeterminate aspects: educational research that loses sight of this is bound to fail. The lack of attention paid to the work of Jamous and Peloille in Anglo-American educational circles has been due to their French location and the fact that they have written about doctors. Educational researchers have been too narrowly focused on teachers to recognize research on other occupations as being central to their dilemmas.

5. *The Lessons for Research on Teaching*

There are two lessons for research on teaching. First, it is vital to do research that challenges the taken-for-granted boundaries of the "educator subculture" (Wolcott 1981). As Wolcott pointed out, it took a colleague from outside educational research "to jolt me into realising that the kinds of data teachers gather 'on' and 'for' each other so admiringly reflect the dominant society and its educator subculture" (p. 253)

Second, it is important to do research on the indeterminate aspects of teaching, not just the technical, even though the latter are easier to measure. Eisner (1985a, 1985b) pioneered the use of aesthetic criticism as a research style in educational inquiry. In the same vein, Lightfoot (1983) invoked the art of portraiture to describe her study of six outstanding American high schools. Both authors were attempting to capture indeterminate aspects of schooling and teaching. Good research on teachers will always have to capture the indeterminate as well as the technical.

See also: Teachers as Professionals; Teachers as Researchers; Teachers' Roles; Teaching, Cognitive Developmental Theories of

References

Atkinson P 1983 The reproduction of professional community. In: Dingwall R, Lewis P (eds.) 1983 *Sociology of the Professions*, Macmillan, London

Atkinson P, Delamont S 1985 Socialisation into teaching: The research which lost its way. *Brit. J. Soc. Educ.* 6(3): 307–22

Atkinson P A, Reid M, Sheldrake P 1977 Medical mystique. *Sociology of Work and Occupations* 4(3): 243–80

Colman J E 1967 *The Master Teachers and the Art of Teaching*. Pitman, New York

Connell R W 1985 *Teachers' Work*. Allen and Unwin, Sydney

Eisner E 1977 On the uses of educational connoisseurship and educational criticism for evaluating classroom life. *Teach. Coll. Rec.* 78(3): 345–58

Eisner E 1985a *The Art of Educational Evaluation: A Personal View*. Falmer Press, London

Eisner E 1985b *The Educational Imagination*, 2nd edn. Macmillan Inc. New York

Gage N L 1978 *The Scientific Basis of the Art of Teaching*. Teachers College Press, New York

Hargreaves D H 1983 The teaching of art and the art of teaching. In: Hammersley M, Hargreaves A (eds.) 1983 *Curriculum Practice*. Falmer Press, Lewer

Jackson P W 1968 *Life in Classrooms*. Holt, Rinehart, and Winston, New York

James W 1983 (1st edn. 1891) *Talks to Teachers on Psychology*. Harvard University Press, Cambridge, Massachusetts

Jamous H, Peloille B 1970 Professions or self-perpetuating

system. In: Jackson J A (ed.) 1970 *Professions and Professionalization*. Cambridge University Press, Cambridge
Lacey C 1970 *Hightown Grammar*, Manchester University Press, Manchester
Lightfoot S L 1983 *The Good High School*. Basic Books, New York
Morris I 1954 *The Art of Teaching English as a Living Language*. Macmillan, London
Rubin L J 1986 *Artistry in Teaching*. Random House, New York
Travers R M W, Dillon J 1975 *The Making of a Teacher*. Macmillan Inc., New York
Trumbull D J 1986 Teacher's envisioning, *Teaching and Teacher Education* 2(2): 139–44
Waller W 1932 *The Sociology of Teaching*. Wiley, New York
Wolcott H F 1981 Confessions of a "trained" observer. In: Popkewitz T S, Tabachnick B R (eds.) 1981 *The Study of Schooling*. Praeger, New York

Further Reading

Eisner E 1991 *The Enlightened Eye*, Macmillan Inc., New York
Gage N L 1989 The paradigm wars and their aftermath. *Teach. Coll. Rec.* 91(2): 135–50
Nespor J, Barber L 1991 The rhetorical construction of "the teacher". *Harv. Educ. Rev.* 61(4): 417–33
Wolcott H F 1990 On seeking—and rejecting—validity in qualitative research. In: Eisner E, Peshkin A (eds.) 1990 *Qualitative Inquiry in Education*. Teachers College Press, New York

S. Delamont

Teachers as Clinicians

Teaching can be conceptualized as a form of problem-solving and decision-making which has many properties in common with the work of physicians. This conceptualization has led to a body of research which has investigated the decision-making of teachers, focusing in particular on the information about pupils that teachers use to make decisions and the way they tailor instruction to individual pupil needs. The resulting research has contributed to knowledge of teachers' planning and interactive thinking.

1. Historical Context

The metaphor of teaching as clinical decision-making initially arose in the 1970s, primarily as a result of three factors: a dissatisfaction with purely behaviorist conceptions of teaching; the development of interest in the cognitive aspects of teachers' work; and the growth of research in medical education concerning the nature and development of physician's decision-making. While much of the research on teaching at this time focused on the classroom behaviors of teachers, such as the types of questions teachers asked (e.g., Rosenshine 1971), it was recognized that an important aspect of effective teaching was the cognitive activity involved, for instance, in asking the appropriate question of the appropriate child at the appropriate time (Shavelson 1973). This recognition highlighted the importance of the decision-making of teachers, an area of enquiry that received particular support in the United States from the 1974 National Institute of Education conference on Studies in Teaching. One of the panels at this conference (panel 6) drew attention to the similarities between the teacher as diagnostician of children's learning and prescriber of fruitful learning activities, and the diagnostic and remediation functions of the physician (NIE 1975). Teachers, like physicians, the panel claimed, face the task of making sense of a diverse range of information, and bringing to bear a range of theories and evidence as well as personal beliefs and expectations on problem situations in order to form judgments and make decisions.

2. Research Focus and Methodology

This field of research has addressed questions concerning the nature of teachers' judgments and decisions, and the factors that influence them. The principal research methods employed have been policy-capturing and stimulated recall. In policy-capturing studies, teachers have been given descriptions of problem situations and have been asked to make judgments or decisions. By systematically varying the nature of the information contained in the descriptions it becomes possible to trace back the factors influencing teachers' judgments. For example, Rohrkemper and Brophy (1983) provided a sample of 98 teachers with 24 vignettes describing problem students in uncooperative classroom situations, to which teachers were asked to say how they would respond. From these data, the researchers were able to identify factors associated with the children and with the classroom situations that influenced teachers' responses. These relationships were also tested for reliability against observational data.

In stimulated recall studies, a teacher's classroom interactions have been videoed, and the video replayed to the teacher shortly afterward with the request that the teacher recall what was going through his or her mind at the time. The resulting data have usually been classified into cognitive acts (whether teachers were making judgments or decisions, or simply expressing an awareness of a feature of classroom activity) and the content of the thinking (e.g., curriculum, children, teaching strategy). Morine-Dershimer (1989), for instance, in a study of 10 teachers, identified qualitatively different types of decision-making among teachers (e.g., reflective as opposed to "in-flight" decision-making) and the proportion of time in a lesson spent thinking of different content. In studies of the thinking and decision-making involved in the planning phase of teaching, teachers have frequently been asked to plan "out loud," verbalizing their normally covert thoughts which are then recorded (e.g., Yinger 1980).

The limitations of the methodology for research on teachers' thinking and decision-making have been discussed at great length in the literature. In particular, attention has been drawn to the importance of the inferences that teachers make in policy-capturing studies and the extent to which teachers' previous experience and existing knowledge is brought to bear in making judgments in problem situations. In the case of stimulated recall studies, researchers' concerns have focused mostly on the status of recalled thoughts, namely their incomplete nature and the extent to which they might represent post hoc rationalizations rather than actual thoughts at the time.

3. Major Findings

The findings emerging from this research have concerned the nature and content of teachers' thinking in both the planning and interactive phases of teaching. They have led to new ways of conceptualizing the cognitive aspects of teachers' work with implications for teacher education and further research.

3.1 Teachers' Planning

Prescriptive models of teachers' planning have tended to depict the planning process as a linear deductive process, beginning with aims and objectives which are translated into content and procedures. Research on the thinking and decision-making of teachers, however, suggests first of all that planning occurs at various levels (yearly, termly, unit, daily, lesson). Furthermore, at the higher levels, its focus is on organization and content, whereas at the lower levels its focus is on the construction of activities and on what teachers and students will do. Rather than involving a linear deductive process, then, planning seems to involve a much more creative problem–finding and problem-solving process. In this process, teachers use their vast knowledge of children, the curriculum, teaching strategies, school facilities, and educational objectives to construct activities which will be manageable within the classroom context (Yinger 1980, McCutcheon 1980).

3.2 Interactive Teaching

Whereas the metaphor of teaching as clinical decision-making has initially presumed that teachers' classroom activity is characterized by diagnostic judgments and remediation decisions, research on teachers' thinking during interactive teaching suggests that teachers actually make few decisions in the classroom. Much of teachers' thinking focuses on the children and the instructional process and is concerned with implementing the planned activity or adjusting the activity to the children and context using well-established instructional routines.

During interactive teaching, teachers seem to be particularly attentive to cues that have strategic significance in indicating how the activity is progressing and whether children in general understand and are able to complete the activity. Lundgren (1972), for example, found that in whole class teaching in secondary science lessons, teachers took particular note of the progress of lower ability students and paced the lesson accordingly. Bromme (1987) also found that after teaching a lesson, secondary mathematics teachers were able to remember and comment on examples of children's understanding and misunderstanding. These examples represented significant moments in the lesson when the teacher found they had to explain, elaborate a point, or move on. However, teachers did not associate these incidents with the abilities or progress of individual children. Teachers, it seems, rarely act as diagnosticians and remediators of individual children's difficulties, but have developed ways of understanding and responding to difficulties which are more specifically adapted to the complex classroom context.

4. New Ways of Conceptualizing Teachers' Cognitions

Research on teaching as clinical decision-making has led researchers to develop further conceptualizations of teaching which recognize the complexity of teachers' knowledge and the interaction between teachers' preactive (i.e., planning) and interactive (i.e., in classroom) thinking. Putnam (1987) suggests that the diagnostic/remediation model does not fit well with the behavior of experienced teachers and suggests an alternative model based on the concepts of curriculum script and agenda. A curriculum script is viewed as an ordered set of goals and actions for teaching a particular topic. When teaching the topic, the script largely determines the teacher's agenda, a dynamic mental plan for the particular lesson. As the lesson is taught, the teacher notes various performance cues which are used to add to, revise, or update the agenda. Experienced teachers are seen as having a vast repertoire of curriculum scripts that provide the foundation for individual lesson agendas.

An alternative conceptualization is offered by Clark and Yinger (1987), who suggest that both planning and interactive teaching contain characteristics of a design process. They propose that Schon's (1983) notion of "reflection-in-action" captures well some of the creative aspects of teaching. When teachers encounter a novel situation, they draw upon their past experience to develop hypotheses about the nature of the problem and possible solutions to it. This reflection-in-action leads teachers to try out certain solution strategies, monitor their effects, and interpret the outcomes to determine future action.

5. Implications for Teacher Education

Research on the differences between experts and novices in the way they plan and think about their work, and research on the processes by which student teachers acquire knowledge related to the task of teaching have led to the consideration of alternative means of training teachers (see Clark 1988). In particular, research has highlighted the complexity of teachers' knowledge and the need to develop means by which the knowledge of the experienced teacher becomes more accessible to the novice (McAlpine et al. 1988). The importance of having opportunities for reflection and analysis in the training period has been emphasized (Clift et al. 1990). The value of case studies of classroom practice in offering opportunities for student teachers to explore how teachers' knowledge and particular contextual features have led to particular decisions and actions has also been acclaimed (Merseth 1991).

6. Implications for Further Research

Research into the thinking and decision-making of teachers has raised several questions about the knowledge that teachers and other professionals possess and use. Several enquiries into the qualitative differences in teachers' knowledge and the processes of knowledge growth have been made. The research has involved a move away from the earlier methods of stimulated recall and policy-capturing to much more fine-grained case studies involving detailed examination of the knowledge, knowledge use, and processes of knowledge growth of teachers (Beyerbach 1988, Calderhead and Robson 1991, John 1991, Clift 1991). It is expected that through such enquiry, clearer models will emerge of how student teachers learn to teach and how they learn to accommodate the individual differences among children in the context of the school curriculum and the complex classroom setting.

See also: Teacher Planning, Approaches to; Teaching: Reflective

References

Beyerbach B A 1988 Developing a technical vocabulary on teacher planning: Preservice teachers' concept maps. *Teaching and Teacher Education* 4(4): 339–47

Bromme R 1987 Teachers' assessments of students' difficulties and progress in understanding in the classroom. In: Calderhead J (ed.) 1987

Calderhead J, Robson M 1991 Images of teaching: Student teachers' early conceptions of classroom practice. *Teaching and Teacher Education* 7(1): 108

Clark C M 1988 Asking the right questions about teacher preparation: Contributions of research on teacher thinking. *Educ. Researcher* 17(2): 5–12

Clark C M, Yinger R J 1987 Teacher planning. In: Calderhead J (ed.) 1987

Clift R T 1991 Learning to teach English – maybe: A study of knowledge development. *J. Teach. Educ.* 42(5): 357–72

Clift R T, Houston W R, Pugach M C 1989 *Encouraging Reflective Practice in Education: An Analysis of Issues and Programs*. Teachers' College Press, New York

John P D 1991 Course, curricular and classroom influences on the development of student teachers' lesson planning perspectives. *Teaching and Teacher Education* 7(4): 359–72

Lundgren U P 1972 *Frame Factors and the Teaching Process: A Contribution to Curriculum Theory and Theory on Teaching*. Almquist and Wiksell, Stockholm

McAlpine A, Brown S, McIntyre D, Hagger H 1988 *Student Teachers Learning from Experienced Teachers*. Scottish Council for Research in Education, Edinburgh

McCutcheon G 1980 How do elementary school teachers plan? The nature of planning and influences on it. *The Elementary School J.* 81(1): 4–23.

Merseth K K 1991 The early history of case-based instruction: Insights for teacher education today. *J. Teach. Educ.* 42(4): 243–49

Morine-Dershimer G 1989 Preservice teachers' conceptions of content and pedagogy: Measuring growth in reflective, pedagogical decision-making. *J. Teach. Educ.* 40(5): 46–52

Gage N (ed.) 1975 *Teaching as Clinical Information Processing: Report of Panel 6 National Conference on Studies in Teaching*. National Institute of Education, Washington, DC

Putnam R T 1987 Structuring and adjusting content for students: A study of live and simulated tutoring of addition. *Am. Educ. Res. J.* 24(1): 13–48

Rohrkemper M M, Brophy J E 1983 Teachers' thinking about problem students. In: Levine J M, Wang M C (eds.) 1983 *Teacher and Student Perceptions: Implications for Learning*. Lawrence Erlbaum Associates, Hillsdale, New Jersey

Rosenshine B 1971 *Teaching Behaviours and Student Achievement*. National Foundation for Educational Research, Slough

Schon D A 1983 *The Reflective Practitioner*. Basic Books, New York

Shavelson R J 1973 What is the basic teaching skill? *J. Teach. Educ.* 24(2): 144–51

Yinger R J 1980 A study of teacher planning: Description and a model of preactive decision-making. *Elem. Sch. J.* 80(3): 107–27

Further Reading

Calderhead J 1987 *Exploring Teachers' Thinking*. Cassell, London

Clark C M, Peterson P L 1986 Teachers' thought processes. In: Wittrock M C (ed.) 1986 *Handbook of Research on Teaching*, 3rd edn. Macmillan, New York

Kagan D M 1988 Teaching as clinical problem solving: A critical examination of the analogy and its implications. *Rev. Educ. Res.* 58(4): 482–505.

J. Calderhead

Teachers as Curriculum-makers

Teachers fulfil manifold functions concerning the creation and implementation of curriculum materials. Whether creating curriculum or using externally prepared materials, teachers always act as "curriculum makers," because curriculum development and use are dependent on teachers' thinking and actions. Connelly and Clandinin (1988) claim that it is "teachers' 'personal knowledge' that determines all matters of significance relative to the planned conduct of classrooms" (p. 4). In this sense all teachers who plan their classrooms' activities are engaged in curriculum making.

One may distinguish between various modes of teachers' curricular activities in different contexts (Ben-Peretz 1990). Teachers act as "choice makers" applying their own educational principles and criteria in order to make decisions about the specific curriculum content they will teach. Teachers may also be viewed as "curriculum adaptors" who change the curriculum materials they use, responding to perceived needs and interests of their students, drawing on their pedagogical content knowledge (Shulman 1986). Teachers may function as "creators of their own curricula," whether through involvement in the process called "teacher-based curriculum development" or as participants in centralized curriculum efforts. Curricular issues constitute a major part of teachers' everyday professional activities at all grade levels.

This entry will deal separately with teachers as curriculum makers in two different contexts: as users and implementors of materials which are developed outside their classrooms, and as creators of curriculum.

1. Teachers as Curriculum Implementors

Teachers encounter curricula in many forms. The most common of these forms are a syllabus, teacher guidelines, and student textbooks. A syllabus consists of lists of specified content which may include the rationale for choices of content items, as well as intended learning outcomes and suggested time allocation to the various topics. Teacher guidelines are often developed by central educational authorities and represent the formal curricular demands and expectations in specific domains of study.

Student textbooks are the dominant form of curricula at all school levels (Goodlad 1984). Fullan (1982) claims that teachers tend to "take and teach the textbook" (p. 118). Yet even in their use of textbooks teachers function as curriculum makers, deciding in what order and what manner to treat the various chapters, and how much time to devote to each.

1.1 Major Concerns About Curriculum

The function of teachers as users of curricular materials developed by agents outside their classrooms, raises the issue of adherence to the given text versus autonomy to introduce changes and modifications. Teachers tend to express a strong desire for professional autonomy and many want to add personal aspects to their curricular responsibilities (Lortie 1975). The sense of professionalism may be reflected in teachers' choices of instructional strategies and time allocations (Ben-Peretz and Silberstein 1982).

Teachers' autonomy and professional expertise is expressed in the generation of instructional representations of subject matter based on teachers' subject-specific pedagogical knowledge (Wilson 1989, Wilson and Wineburg 1988). Teachers' concerns about issues of content in the curriculum are well-documented (Lortie 1975, Goodlad 1984, Wilson et al. 1987). A persistent theme of teachers' curricular concerns relates to content coverage. Teachers are highly sensitive to the coverage of curriculum content that will be tested, and tend to adapt their teaching to the preparation of students for forthcoming examinations (Connelly et al. 1978), aiming at maximum coverage of materials rather than at in-depth teaching of selected issues. Coverage becomes a major factor in curriculum choices made by teachers.

Another major concern of teachers implementing externally prepared materials relates to the adaptability of these materials to divergent student needs in heterogenous classes. Butt et al. (1986) characterize the key issue as "the degree to which prescription, external testing and specific subject matter is perceived to allow for flexible adaptation, in terms of both content and pedagogy, to meet pupils' needs and interests, as well as the teacher's style and beliefs" (p. 316).

1.2 Strategies of Curriculum Adaptation

Teachers may function as curriculum makers, through adaptation of existing materials to their specific educational situations. Through their adaptation they become partners in the process of curriculum development as user–developers (Connelly 1972, Connelly and Ben-Peretz 1980). Several strategies may be utilized by teachers, in their efforts to use curriculum materials wisely, creatively, and appropriately. Key factors in this process are: (a) curriculum analysis and interpretation; (b) identification of possible learning opportunities in the materials; (c) diagnosis of educational needs, priorities, and difficulties in specific situations; and (d) enactment of possible learning opportunities in the classroom according to perceived needs and educational priorities.

Curriculum analysis is guided by questions asked about curriculum materials in order to reveal their characteristics. The explicitly stated rationale of curriculum developers may be the source for questions.

For instance the developers of a curriculum in history may declare their intention to use historical sources so that students may understand their function as evidence in order to gain insights into past events. In such a case teachers may try to analyze the materials asking questions about the frequency of presentation of historical sources, their nature, and treatment in the textbook.

Teachers may also use "external" frames of curriculum analysis which are not related to the developers' rationale but are based on different theoretical frameworks. Questions stemming from external diverse perspectives, such as approaches to scientific inquiry, have the power to illuminate different aspects of the analyzed materials and to provide insights into their nature. Curriculum analysis is one strategy for recovering curriculum meanings. On the basis of uncovering the meaning of curriculum materials, teachers may deal with the possible educational implications of the insights gained. Teachers interpret the various forms of curriculum materials and transform these into a "curriculum in use," into concrete learning experiences. Curriculum materials may be viewed as an embodiment of curriculum potential, of predetermined, as well as unintended curricular uses which may be disclosed through deliberate interpretation efforts, providing teachers with manifold possible modes of enactment (Ben-Peretz 1990).

2. *Teachers as Curriculum Creators*

Teachers may be included in curriculum development committees at different institutional levels. In the process of school-based curriculum development teachers are engaged in localized development efforts. Teachers' participation in central development projects is common practice in different societies, such as the United States, Canada, the United Kingdom, and Israel. This societal level of development is remote from teachers' daily work and constitutes a different mode of involvement.

2.1 Teachers as Makers of School-based Curricula

The movement toward school-based curriculum development (SBCD) is linked with tendencies to emphasize teacher autonomy and professionalism. Skilbeck (1987) suggests four different types of professional autonomy in the curriculum:

(a) decisions about the nature of the school curriculum, that is, its goals and content;

(b) decisions about resources needed to sustain the school curriculum;

(c) decisions about planning of learning experiences for groups of students and for individual students; and

(d) decisions about evaluation of the curriculum.

Skilbeck (1987) states that "it can scarcely be claimed that these types or levels of decision fall exclusively to the teaching staff" (p. 23). He argues that, paradoxically, the British move to establish a national curriculum framework has the potential "to stimulate and to provide much needed guidance for the goals, processes, and outcomes of school-based curriculum development" (p. 26).

The idea of schools developing and teaching their own curricula is highly attractive to many educators. Gordon (1987) analyzes the complex issues pertaining to school-based curriculum development. According to Gordon, three components of autonomy are necessary in order for SBCD to happen. These are the belief component, the ability component, and the desire component. If school personnel believe that they are not free to develop their own curricula, lack the abilities to do so, and do not wish to become involved, school-based development will falter. Marsh et al. (1990) examined the factors affecting SBCD and conclude that motivation of principals and teachers, awareness of innovative approaches, as well as a sense of control and ownership, are vital for SBCD activities. Other important factors are school climate, leadership, time and other resources, and external initiatives and support. Institutional recognition and status are especially important in promoting teacher involvement in curriculum development.

Typical procedures of SBCD are, according to Loucks-Horsley and Hergert (1985): establishing the project, assessment and goal-setting, identifying a solution, preparing for implementation, implementing the project, reviewing progress and problems, and maintenance and institutionalization. Teachers may lack the necessary abilities for carrying out SBCD. Sabar et al. (1982) analyzed the characteristics of coordinators for SBCD and described a training process which will prepare coordinators for their role.

School-based curriculum development may yield highly innovative approaches to curriculum planning. An example of such a new approach is Schonmann's work on "organic curriculum planning" (Schonmann 1990). Organic curriculum planning is based on simultaneous creation and implementation of curricula. The formative process, shared by teachers and students, is the program itself. The curricular text of organic curriculum planning is not a finished and packaged product. It is rather a "performance" that exists as a complete unit as it is being enacted in the classroom setting.

Teachers' involvement in school-based curriculum development allows for better accommodation to situation-specific needs of students and communities, may yield more flexible and relevant materials, and serves to enhance teachers' professional abilities.

2.2 Teachers as Participants in Central Curriculum Development

Teacher participation in curriculum development

outside their classrooms has been supported for a variety of reasons. Young (1989) analyzes the grounds for this support. Teachers have concrete and contextual knowledge of classrooms and are able to assess the usability of materials. Their contribution may make the materials more intelligible to other teachers, and finally, the materials may be more acceptable to their colleagues and peers. Teacher participation depends on their motivation and on their attitudes toward certain kinds of educational decision-making. It seems that teachers tend to prefer curriculum decision-making with immediate application to the classroom (Lortie 1975, Young 1979). Young (1989) identified six major factors related to teacher's readiness to participate in central curriculum development. These factors are: self-assurance, professionalism, pragmatism, opinion of committee work, demands of teaching, and competition with other interests. Participation in central curriculum development may yield positive gains for the individual teacher and for the schools. Young (1985) argues that: "participation in curriculum development outside of the classroom will be attractive to teachers when it counteracts certain negative aspects of teachers' lives in schools, specifically their low position in the educational hierarchy, their isolation from other educators and the paucity of rewards they receive for teaching" (p. 409).

The role of teachers as curriculum makers outside their schools requires that they be assigned a central role in the curriculum process (Schwab 1983). Ben-Peretz (1980) described a development project in which experienced teachers from different schools joined in constructing an innovative unit in environmental studies. The possible tendency of teachers to subordinate their ideas to those of subject matter or curriculum specialists was avoided because these experts were not part of the regular deliberations of the development team. Their advice was sought whenever the teachers needed it.

3. Conceptual Orientations Concerning Teachers as Curriculum-makers

Teachers may be treated as transmitters of curricular ideas originating outside their classrooms. It has been recognized that teachers have considerable influence on the implementation of curricular ideas, because of their major role in realizing and making the curriculum in use. Inservice programs and action research may serve to ensure implementation of new curriculum materials according to the intentions of developers.

A different view of teachers as curriculum makers is based on the notion of curriculum potential. Teachers are viewed as experts who read and study curriculum materials as texts to be analyzed and interpreted (Ben-Peretz 1990). Teachers may discover and create a variety of potential curricular uses in any text and make their own curriculum on the basis of their interpretations and insights.

Connelly and Clandinin (1988) view curriculum as experiences in certain situations. The teacher and the students, books, and processes such as reading, interact in the curricular experiences, connecting the past and the future, as every situation leads to another. "The past shapes the future through the medium of a situation, and the future shapes the past through the stories we tell to account for and explain our situation" (1988 p.9). Claiming that people understand their lives by telling stories about them, Connelly and Clandinin (1988) introduce the notions of "narrative" and "personal practical knowledge" as central to their understanding of planning and curriculum making. Narrative is a way of making meaning of one's life, of reading one's own "text." Personal practical knowledge is seen as embodied in everyone. It "is a moral, affective and aesthetic way of knowing life's educational situations" (p.59). Teachers' curriculum making is part of their narrative, an expression of their personal knowledge.

The role of teachers in the curriculum may be perceived as evolving from an approach which views teachers as "instruments" to be molded by external agents, to increased emphasis on the personal aspects of curriculum making, on teachers as independent curriculum interpreters, expressing their personal practical knowledge.

See also: Curriculum Development at School Level; School-based Management; School Reform and Restructuring

References

Ben-Peretz M 1980 Teachers' role in curriculum development; An alternative approach. *Canadian Journal of Education* 5(2): 52–62

Ben-Peretz M 1990 *The Teacher-Curriculum Encounter: Freeing Teachers from the Tyranny of Texts.* SUNY Press, Albany, New York

Ben-Peretz M, Silberstein M 1982 A curriculum development case study in biology: Two levels of interpretation. *Eur. J. Sci. Educ.* 4(4): 377–89

Butt R, Raymond M D, Ray J 1986 Personal, practical and prescriptive influences on teachers' thoughts and actions. Paper presented at the conference of the International Study Association on Teacher Thinking (ISATT), Leuven

Connelly F M 1972 The functions of curriculum development. *Interchange* 3(2–3): 161–77

Connelly F M, Ben-Peretz M 1980 Teachers' role in the using and doing of research and curriculum development. *J. Curric. Stud.* 12(2): 95–107

Connelly F M, Ben-Peretz M, Enns R J 1978 Assessing the compatability of curriculum policy and school programs with external testing. *Crucible* 9(6): 4–10

Connelly F M, Clandinin D J 1988 *Teachers as Curriculum Planners: Narratives of Experience.* Teachers College Press, New York

Fullan M 1982 *The Meaning of Educational Change.* OISE Press, Toronto

Goodlad J 1984 *A Place Called School*. McGraw Hill, New York
Gordon D 1987 Autonomy is more than just the absence of external constraints. In: Sabar N, Rudduck J, Reid W (eds.) 1987 *Partnership and Autonomy in School-Based Curriculum Development*. USDE Papers in Education 10, University of Sheffield, Sheffield
Lortie D C 1975 *Schoolteacher: A Sociological Study* University of Chicago Press, Chicago, Illinois
Loucks-Horsley S, Hergert LF 1985 *An Action Guide to School Improvement*. ASCD, Alexandria, Virginia
Marsh C, Day C, Hannay L, McCutcheon G 1990 *Reconceptualizing School-Based Curriculum Development*. Falmer Press, London
Sabar N, Silberstein M, Shafriri N 1982 Needed: Curriculum coordinators for teachers developing learning materials: A systematic analysis of coordinators' characteristics for better planned training. *Curric. Inq.* 12(1): 53–67
Schonmann S 1990 Organic curriculum planning: A case study—Drama in education. Doctoral dissertation, University of Haifa,
Schwab J J 1983 The practical 4: Something for curriculum professors to do. *Curric. Inq.* 13(3): 239–65
Shulman L S 1986 Those who understand: Knowledge growth in teaching. *Educ. Researcher*. 15(2): 4–14
Skilbeck M 1987 School-based curriculum development and central policies in England and Wales: A paradox in three acts. In: Sabar N, Rudduck J, Reid W (eds.) 1987 *Partnership and Autonomy in School-Based Curriculum Development*. USDE Papers in Education 10, University of Sheffield, Sheffield
Wilson S M 1989 A case concerning content: Using case studies to teach subject matter. The National Center for Research on Teacher Education, East Lansing, Michigan
Wilson S M, Shulman L S, Richert A 1987 150 different ways of knowing: Representations of knowledge in teaching. In: Calderhead J (ed.) 1987 *Exploring Teachers' Thinking*. Cassell, London
Wilson S M, Wineburg S S 1988 Peering at American history through different lenses: The role of disciplinary knowledge in teaching. *Teach. Coll. Rec.* 89(4): 525–39
Young J H 1979 The curriculum decision-making preferences of school personnel. *Alberta Journal of Educational Research* 25(1): 20–9
Young J H 1985 Participation in curriculum development: An inquiry into the responses of teachers. *Curric. Inq.* 15(4): 387–414
Young J H 1989 Teacher interest in curriculum committees: What factors are involved? *J. Curric. Stud.* 21(4): 363–76

Further Reading

Lewy A 1991 *National and School-based Curriculum Planning*. International Institute for Educational Planning, Paris

M. Ben-Peretz

Teachers as Professionals

The long-standing debate over whether teaching is or is not a profession has been unproductive. "The teaching profession" is a phrase in widespread usage not only among teachers themselves but among laypersons, politicians, and the media. However, the fact that teaching is widely referred to as a "profession" is only a starting point for the analysis of the nature of teaching as an occupation since the term "profession" is a potent metaphor and, at times, an ideological weapon. The debate about "teaching as a profession" and "teachers as professionals" is not primarily a matter of semantics, but raises a number of substantive issues which ultimately relate to the quality of education. The first section of this entry will discuss "profession" and related concepts. The second will outline major criticisms of the way in which the term has been deployed. The third will address a number of central issues, organized for heuristic purposes according to the main criteria attributed to the professions.

1. The Concept of a Profession

Systematic sociological analysis of the distinguishing criteria of professions began only in the early years of the twentieth century. A number of sociologists generated lists of putative criteria which were allegedly fully met by the undisputed professions, but met to a lesser degree by occupations termed "semi" or "quasi" professions. Thus, professions were placed along a hypothetical continum, with teaching usually classified as a "semi-profession." "Emergent professions" were those in the process of meeting the criteria more fully and, hence, moving along the hypothetical continuum, a process usually referred to as "professionalization." The ideology which underpins an occupation's quest for professionalization tends to entail the assumption that, in meeting the criteria to an increased degree, the quality of service provided by the occupation will be enhanced. Although this may normally be the case, it cannot be taken as axiomatic. Thus, in the literature, the term "professionalism" is sometimes used to refer to the rhetorics and strategies used by occupations in their professionalization project, while the term "professionality" refers to the quality of skill and service provided.

A number of criteria have been designated by various writers, and it is often argued by critics that there is a lack of consensus among these lists. In fact, the opposite interpretation is possible and a high correlation has been demonstrated (Hickson and Thomas 1969). Rather than report any one of those lists, or attempt to conflate them, the major criteria can be presented according to the assumption implicit in the functionalist theory of the professions. This theory holds that the professions are those occupations whose members bring a high degree of knowledge and skill to those social functions which were most central to the well-being of society. Hoyle (1980) has summarized the theory and enumerated the criteria it generates:

(a) A profession is an occupation which performs a crucial social function.

(b) The exercise of this function requires a considerable degree of skill.

(c) This skill is exercised in situations which are not wholly routine, but in which new problems have to be handled.

(d) Thus, although knowledge gained through experience is important, this recipe-type knowledge is insufficient to meet professional demands and the practitioner has to draw on a body of systematic knowledge.

(e) The acquisition of this body of knowledge and the development of specific skills requires a lengthy period of higher education.

(f) This period of education and training also involves the process of socialization into professional values.

(g) These values tend to center on the pre-eminence of clients' interests, and to some degree they are made explicit in a code of ethics.

(h) Because knowledge-based skills are exercised in nonroutine situations, it is essential for the professionals to have the freedom to make their own judgments with regard to appropriate practice.

(i) Because professional practice is so specialized, the organized profession should have a strong voice in the shaping of relevant public policy, a large degree of control over the exercise of professional responsibilities, and a high degree of autonomy in relation to the state.

(j) Lengthy training, responsibility, and client-centeredness are necessarily rewarded by high prestige and a high level of remuneration.

Although variations occur between societies, teaching meets some of these criteria but usually not all. Furthermore, those criteria which teaching does meet are not always met in full. These criteria are not only the products of sociological theorizing, but also inform the rhetoric of professional elites as they negotiate with employers and governments on behalf of their members.

2. *Criticisms of Traditional Approaches to the Professions*

Several criticisms have been levelled at the traditional sociological approach to the professions. First, the debate about professions is an Anglo-Saxon phenomenon and has little relevance to, for example, the European context in which professionals are largely state employees. Moreover, professionalism as an ideology is to be viewed as relative to a particular historical period and can be seen as being in decline (Perkin 1989).

Second, the functionalist interpretation is held to be ahistorical. It thereby underestimates the degree to which the current high status of the leading professions can more appropriately be attributed to the acquisition of the power to control the market for its services than to the gratitude of the general public for services provided (Larson 1977). Third, the contention that only a relatively small proportion of the population has the potential to become professionals is an argument for closure and credentialism rather than an accurate portrayal of the pool of ability (Sykes 1987). Fourth, the criteria have been derived from an analysis of the structures of occupations which have already achieved status through controlling a market, and from the rationalizations of their elites rather than from an evaluation of professions at work. Thus, the criteria have only a limited relationship to reality. One example is that practitioner autonomy is, in fact, a form of protection against accountability (Bessant and Spaull 1972).

Finally, the term "profession" is almost invariably used in a rhetorical or ideological manner both by the professional elites and by governments (Ozga and Lawn 1981), and as a strategy of control at the school level (Shanker 1985).

The reification of the concept of "profession" has led to such frustration that it has been suggested that it be abandoned altogether. A less radical suggestion has been that sociologists should focus on what professionals actually do. There have been some excellent studies of professional practice using a variety of approaches which have remained unconstrained by the functionalist perspective. Nevertheless, because issues raised about autonomy, knowledge, responsiveness to client, and the like remain relevant, the concept of "profession" provides at least a heuristic perspective. However, it should be recognized that there are other approaches—notably the labour process view which takes its inspiration from the work of Braverman (1974).

3. *Issues Relating to Teaching as a Profession*

This section outlines some issues relating to the notion of teaching as a profession, organized around five key criteria of a profession: social function, knowledge, practitioner autonomy, collective autonomy, and professional values.

3.1 Social Function

Teaching undoubtedly performs a crucial social function since education is a key social process in both developing and developed societies. The functionalists would argue that teaching lacks the social status of medicine, law, dentistry, and other similar professions, because education is less central to the needs of society. This argument would be extremely difficult to substantiate. Differences in status are much more likely to be due to other factors (e.g., the size of the teaching profession, the characteristics of teachers, relationships with clients, and the work situation of teachers) than the importance of the social function. The importance of education, and hence teaching, to the well-being of society as a whole is sufficiently self-evident.

The significance of education increases as the link with occupation (particularly in terms of credentials) tightens. However, there are a number of factors which militate against public perceptions of the importance of this function. One is related to time-scale. The benefits of education accumulate over time and are the results of the efforts of many teachers. Individual contributions are difficult to identify. Moreover, the fact that children are taught in groups further militates against the identification of a single teacher with individual achievement.

Teaching also differs from the major professions in terms of the consequence of the service provided. Generally, this service is not, in the literal sense, vital. Much of the work of all professionals is routine and, in practice, they vary very little in this respect. However, there are occasions when judgments have profound consequences for the clients of doctors and lawyers in particular, but also those of accountants and architects. These moments rarely occur for teachers. Perhaps the importance of these moments has been overemphasized by the elites of the major professions and reinforced by the media. Nonetheless, the contribution of teaching to the well-being of society as a whole and to the well-being of individuals is difficult to evaluate.

3.2 Knowledge

The knowledge-base of teaching as a profession remains a highly contentious issue. That teachers need knowledge of the subject matter to be transmitted is not in dispute. However, there is considerably more skepticism among outsiders and teachers themselves about the knowledge which can be broadly termed "educational theory" (Jackson 1987). Teachers are thus confronted with a problem. If they criticize the theory to which they have been exposed in their training as irrelevant to practice, they are denying to themselves one of the traditional characteristics of a profession. If teaching is no more than an experience-based skill with a limited set of precepts, the occupation is indistinguishable from the crafts of, say, plumbing or motor mechanics.

However, the problem of the professional knowledge of teachers is complex. Necessary distinctions between different kinds of theoretical knowledge, between—to oversimplify—pedagogical, curricular, and socioeducational theory, are not always made, although they perform different functions. Another difficulty is that the venerable theory–practice debate has been largely conducted on the assumption that pre-existing, systematic, codified knowledge is somehow applied to pupils. However, the pedagogic knowledge-base of "teacher" is being reconceptualized in a way in which it is more readily articulated with practice (Calderhead 1987).

The social dimension of practice, in the past a maligned element of educational theory, is being recognized in relation to medicine, law, architecture, and other professional areas. Teachers would appear to be moving from "restricted" to "extended" professionality (Hoyle 1974), particularly in those countries which have made a substantial commitment to the continuing professional development of teachers. However, there is a paradox here in that the forms which this development is taking are unlikely to enhance status. One must also note the argument that, at least in some systems, the opposite tendency is at work and that the closer control is resulting in the deskilling of teachers (Apple 1987).

3.3 Practitioner Autonomy

Practitioners greatly value their autonomy. However, no practitioner can expect complete autonomy. The debate about autonomy is somewhat complex in that its limits can function at different levels. Autonomy can be limited by the state (e.g., via a national curriculum, or prescribed textbooks), by administrators and principals, by the local community, and by peers. The patterns vary across systems. For example, French teachers have their autonomy limited by the state, but their attitude towards professionality is such that this is not experienced as a restriction. Within this framework, however, French teachers experience a high degree of autonomy in relation to administrators and colleagues. French teachers thus have a narrower view of their professional roles than the teachers in, say, the United Kingdom (Broadfoot and Osborn 1987).

An important issue concerns the limits to teacher autonomy imposed by administrators. A theoretical conflict between bureaucratic constraint and professional autonomy has a long history in sociology. This conflict between the constraints imposed by bureaucracy and the freedom of teachers to work is dependent upon a number of factors which vary over different systems (e.g., whether the role of the principal is seen as that of administrator or leading educational professional, the degree of hierarchy in the school, the nature of teacher evaluation, and the managerial style of the principal).

Although conflict between the principal's authority and the teacher's autonomy is an ever-present possibility and can become acute, in practice actual conflict is constrained partly by the structure of the school and partly by a widely accepted norm. Schools are loosely coupled in that the separate components—units and people—are relatively independent of the center. Teaching is not an activity which is amenable to close control. Thus, there tends to be a balance between control and autonomy underpinned by the acceptance that administrators and teachers have their proper spheres of influence which indeed overlap and generate the need for conflict resolution through negotiation and micro-politics, but which are generally in a state of mutual accommodation (Hanson 1979). However, as teaching becomes more stratified according to administrative roles, the conditions for differential status arise and the relationship between professionalism and bureaucracy becomes less clear. When this occurs, the managerial, rather than the teaching, element of professionalism comes to the fore.

Ironically, the threat to teacher autonomy is inherent not only in bureaucratic but also in collegial patterns of organization in which control by colleagues can be constraining. In many systems, there is a move towards a greater independence of teachers as they collaborate in curriculum development, staff development, organizational development, and schemes of peer appraisal. These may be inimical to individual autonomy and it may be the case that these elements in the conventional model of a profession will decline and a new form—collaborative professionality—might be emerging. It can be argued that some loss in individual autonomy may lead to an enhancement in the quality of provision (Anderson 1987).

3.4 *Collective Autonomy*

Teaching has been less successful than the major professions in achieving self-governing status and independence from the state. In perhaps the majority of countries, teachers are state employees expected to carry out the educational policies laid down by central government. The degree to which the organized profession is consulted in the shaping of these policies varies over countries and over time. In few systems have teachers succeeded in creating self-governing bodies responsible for admitting members and disciplining them, shaping policy, and determining the pattern of its implementation. Teachers are usually organized into unions rather than professional bodies, and this shapes their relationship with the state.

Nevertheless, teachers have, in some countries, enjoyed a great deal of influence over the practice of education which perhaps reached its apotheosis in some Western nations in the 1960s and early 1970s. In the 1990s this movement is being rolled back. This is the era of accountability and of a general backlash against the professional society. Thus, although teaching still aspires to the status of an independent profession, which it has nowhere achieved historically, contemporary social forces are strongly against this status. Indeed, the very professions which teaching has sought to emulate are themselves experiencing demands for greater accountability and attempts to reduce their autonomy.

3.5 *Professional Values*

Although professions are held to be distinguishable by a particular set of values, it is virtually impossible to make generalizations about this aspect in relation to professions in general or the teaching profession in particular. The field itself is inadequately mapped. Perhaps the central professional value is that of "client centeredness," but there are those who claim that profit is as central to the professions as to business. Moreover, insofar as client centeredness exists, it is perhaps exhibited as much by craft workers and members of the service industry as by professionals.

Client centeredness among teachers is difficult to determine, not least because teachers have multiple clientele—including pupils, their parents, and the state—and the balance of sometimes conflicting interests is difficult to establish. In many societies, codes of ethics for teachers have been established, but their provenance varies (e.g., teacher unions, the state, independent commissions). Thus, there are differences in these codes, particularly in the extent to which priority is given to relationships between colleagues and relationships with clients. Despite the attention of a number of philosophers, the ethical basis of the teaching profession needs further development (Langford 1978).

4. *Conclusion*

By general usage, teaching is designated a profession. However, for a variety of reasons, its status is not as high as that of other professions owing to such factors as its size, the characteristics of its members, the nature of relationships with clients, and the teacher's work situation.

It is widely argued that there are likely to remain limits in the degree to which teachers can enhance their status (Bull 1990) and debates center on the quality of provision which teachers, as professionals, provide. Some writers, while retaining the concept of "profession," note that its inherent elitism distracts from the progressive strategy which would enhance service to clients (Burbules and Densmore 1991). On the other hand, there are those who continue to view the enhanced professionalization of teachers as a prerequisite to the enhancement of educational quality (Holmes Group 1986). Since the concept of "profession" remains contested, its usage in any debate must be clarified by the protagonists.

See also: Teaching: Social Status; Teachers as Researchers

References

Anderson L W 1987 The decline of teacher autonomy: Tears or cheers? *Int. Rev. Educ.* 33(3): 357–73

Apple M W 1988 *Teachers and Texts: A Political Economy of Class and Gender Relations in Education*. Routledge and Kegan Paul, New York
Bessant B, Spaull A D 1972 The myth of the teaching profession. In: Bessant B, Spaull A (eds.) 1972 *Teachers in Conflict*. Melbourne University Press, Carlton
Braverman H 1974 *Labor and Monopoly Capital*. Monthly Review Press, New York
Broadfoot P, Osborn M 1987 Teachers' conceptions of their professional responsibilities: Some international comparisons. *Comp. Educ.* 23(3): 287–301
Bull B 1990 The limits of teacher professionalization. In: Goodlad J I, Soder R, Sirotnik K P (ed.) 1990 *The Moral Dimensions of Teaching*. Jossey Bass, San Francisco, California
Burbules N L, Densmore K 1991 The limits of making teaching a profession. *Educational Policy* 5: 44–63
Calderhead T 1987 *Exploring Teachers' Thinking*. Cassell, London
Hanson E 1979 *Educational Administration and Organizational Behavior*. Allyn and Bacon, Boston, Massachusetts
Hickson D J, Thomas M W 1969 Professionalization in Britain: A preliminary measurement. *Sociology* 3(1): 37–53
Holmes Group 1986 *Tomorrow's Teachers: A Report of the Holmes Group*. Holmes Group Inc., East Lansing, Michigan
Hoyle E 1974 Professionality, professionalism and control in teaching. *London Educational Review* 3(2): 13–19
Hoyle E 1980 Professionalization and deprofessionalization in education. In: Hoyle E, Megarry J (eds.) 1980 *World Yearbook of Education, 1980: The Professional Development of Teachers*. Kegan Page, London
Jackson P 1987 Facing our ignorance. *Teach. Coll. Rec.* 88: 384–89
Langford G 1978 *Teaching as a profession*. Manchester University Press, Manchester.
Larson M S 1977 *The Rise of Professionalism: A Sociological Analysis*. University of California Press, Berkeley, California
Ozga J, Lawn M 1981 *Teachers, Professionalism and Class: A Study of Organized Teachers*. Falmer Press, Lewes.
Perkin H 1989 *The Rise of Professional Society: England Since 1880*. Routledge, London
Shanker A 1985 *The Making of a Profession*. American Federation of Teachers, Washington, DC
Sykes G 1987 Reckoning with the spectre. *Educ. Researcher* 16: 19–21.

Further Reading

Friedson E 1986 *Professional Powers*. University of Chicago Press, Chicago, Illinois
Halmos P (ed.) 1973 *Professionalization and Social Change: Sociological Review Monograph 20*. University of Keele, Keele
Leggatt T 1970 Teaching as a profession. In: Jackson J A (ed.) 1970 *Professions and Professionalization*. Cambridge University Press, Cambridge
Lortie D C 1977 *Schoolteacher: A Sociological Study*. University of Chicago Press, Chicago, Illinois

E. Hoyle

Teachers as Researchers

The international movement to recognize, prepare, and learn from teachers as researchers has come of age in the years since Elliott's entry on the topic (1985) in *The International Encyclopedia of Education 1st Edn*. This new entry summarizes the breadth, diversity, and significance of the teacher-as-researcher movement across three interrelated areas: curriculum improvement, professional and structural critique, and societal reform. Since teacher researchers are concerned simultaneously with ways to (a) improve their practice, (b) change the situations in which they work, and (c) understand their practices within the larger society, the organization of this entry is not intended to be linear of hiearchical. The discussion, instead, is framed in terms of different organizing focuses.

1. Curriculum Improvement

Curriculum improvement research is a derivative of what was known as "action research" and which led to the conceptualization of teachers as researchers within a process model (Stenhouse 1983). The work in this area produced both immediate curriculum changes on the part of teachers (first-order research), and observations about teacher research from collaborating academics (second-order research).

1.1 Action Research

The use of experimental social science to investigate various programs of social action was popularized in the United States by social psychologist Kurt Lewin (1946). Corey (1953) adapted the concept to improve school practices. He and his faculty colleagues at Teachers College at Columbia University worked cooperatively with public-school personnel on curriculum projects in action. In the post-Sputnik climate of the late 1950s, however, primary funding went to curriculum projects which followed traditional research, development, and dissemination models. Action research, suspect as "unscientific" in such a climate, became "interactive R & D [research and development]," disseminating research results through inservice teacher training. Much of that federally funded work, however, supported regular seminars in which teachers were encouraged to investigate topics related to their practices. It was the curriculum reform movement in the United Kingdom, however, that first popularized teachers as researchers.

1.2 Teachers as Researchers

Stenhouse (1983) is credited with developing the concept of teachers as researchers at the University of East Anglia. As director of the Schools Council's Humanities Project, Stenhouse came to see teachers' authority and autonomy as a basis for curriculum improvement and innovation. Like Corey, Stenhouse used the scientific method of developing and testing curricular hypotheses, but felt that its use to develop replicable results across classrooms was limited. He also questioned the ethical stance of separating the performance from the performer. Stenhouse thus rejected the "objectives model" of curriculum adoption (Tyler 1949) and asked teachers to engage in a "process model" of curriculum innovation where professional and curricular development became part of the same enterprise.

1.3 Developing the Process Model

Three factors made action research in the process model a viable alternative in the late 1970s and 1980s: the difficulties of disseminating quantitative, experimental methodologies to local educational settings; (b) an increasing acceptance of the concept of curriculum as integrated with human deliberation (Schwab 1973); and (c) a professional and political reaction to post-Sputnik accountability as an approach for improving and changing curriculum. Elliott (1991), a colleague of Stenhouse, emphasized the interpretive-hermeneutic nature of inquiry. He saw action research as a pedagogical paradigm—a form of teaching. He argued that educational research should be modeled after action research: "a moral science paradigm to which teacher researchers would be the main contributors, rather than those in academic disciplines" (McKernan 1991, p. 23).

1.4 The Impact of First- and Second-order Research on Curriculum Improvement

First-order research examines changes in the curriculum made by teachers. Examples of such research are included in reports prepared by public-school teachers (Philadelphia Teachers Learning Collaborative 1984), descriptions of university-level teachers' research on their curricular practices (Lampert 1989), and summaries included in texts detailing the action of teacher researchers and academics (Clandinin et al. in press). Examples of second-order research (that is, discussions about teacher research) can be found in outlines of skills needed by teacher researchers (Hopkins 1985), in discussions of teacher researchers' cognitive development (Oja and Smulyan 1989), in descriptions of teacher networks (Smith et al. 1991), and in understandings gained from teacher–university collectives (Carini 1988).

The cumulative effect of this work has changed the manner in which teachers are perceived as professional curriculum developers. It has also influenced collaborative research models and school restructuring plans which emphasize "teacher empowerment." One of the best examples of curriculum-based teacher research, one which improved practice and then led to theoretical, professional, and structural change, is the Bay Area Writing Project (BAWP). Reports from BAWP extensions across the United States range from first-order summaries (Fecho 1992) to second-order analyses of project participants' ideological differences (Schecter 1992).

2. Professional and Structural Critique

Emerging in the 1980s from the success of curriculum improvement research in the United Kingdom and the United States was an attempt to improve social environments and/or conditions of practice through structural and professional critique.

2.1 Structural Critique

Kemmis and his colleagues at Deakin University in Australia and elsewhere have articulated a model of a critical educational science. Their basic premise is that "new ideas are not enough to generate better education. Educational practices and patterns of school and classroom organization must also be changed to secure improvement" (Kemmis and McTaggert 1988, p. 34).

The critical stance of teachers as researchers, focusing on desired and possible changes in the educational structures, has also been noted within the United Kingdom and other countries. Simons (1992), of the University of Southampton, for example, has argued for collaborative partnerships in the teacher research movement, which take into account the practice-oriented views of the curriculum researcher and the structural views of the critical researcher. She points out that reforming schools from the outside cannot work—neither can simple calls for collaboration. Existing structures privilege privacy, hierarchy, and territory within the institution and across collaborative boundaries; thus, structural and professional relationships must change.

2.2 Critiques of Professionalism and Professionalization

Sockett (1989) has drawn educational scholars' attention to the need for professionalism in teaching as well as the professionalization or socialization process by which one becomes a professional. Teacher research is an important part of both processes. Posch (1992) in Austria also speaks of the importance of teacher research for the profession. He argues that teacher professionalism involves teacher research on student professionalism.

Preparing student teachers and experienced teachers to be critical professionals who challenge and change the workplace conditions (including curriculum) is an important part of a professional and structural critique. Feminists involved in teacher education help teachers to develop radical pedagogies or "styles of teaching which help make visible to pupils the structural social inequities which constrain their lives" (Middleton 1992 p. 18).

2.3 Impact on the Workplace and the Profession

Although the preparation of teachers as critical

inquirers is not yet widespread, structural and professional changes influenced by this work have been widely noted in new policies for school and professional restructuring. In the United States, a California decision to retain and reshape the state-sponsored mentoring project followed teacher research investigations into its possibilities and limitations (see Ashton et al. 1990).

Many of the transformative results from the critical professional and structural stance, however, have been far less public and far more personal. The Boston Women's Teachers' Group (Freedman et al. 1983), for example, met for three years to cope with the isolated struggle of their daily work and to study how their work conditions affected them as teachers. Like other groups who have created similar structures, their professional work was critical rather than curricular. They focused on the creation of conditions under which participants could consider their own interests and develop curriculum innovations.

3. Societal Reform

The focus of teachers as researchers in the societal reform sense is on how schools and teaching are shaped in society and what epistemological views are needed for their transformation. In some countries, the societal focus resulted from an awareness of the increasing gap between the concept of democracy and the reality of domination and oppression. Fueled by the Civil Rights and Women's Movements in the United States, even popular teacher-promoted curricular projects challenging static views of knowledge and societal norms were not free from scrutiny (see, for example, Delpit's (1986) critique of the Bay Area Writing Project). Two broad areas of societal reform are epistemological critique and the problem of gender.

3.1 Epistemological Critique

This view of teachers as researchers developed simultaneously with philosophical critiques of societal positions based on privileged conceptions of knowledge. Bruner (1985), for example, questioned the power ascribed the paradigmatic or "rational" view of knowledge and discussed the power of its antitheses: a narrative view of knowledge. Harding (1991) questioned natural science's position on objectivity as too protective of the power-dominant, White, male society. Belenky et al. (1986) raised questions about alternative ways of knowing which could privilege some women over others. Culturally diverse ways of knowing and representing knowledge, such as those pointed out by Lourde (1984), also critiqued societally accepted knowledge. Finally, many critiques either implicitly or explicitly questioned the separation of hierarchically powered social structures and inquiry methods (Winter 1987).

3.2 The Problem of Gender

Zeichner (1990) challenged the problematic social and epistemological hierarchy by speaking of the importance of teachers as women in the second professional wave of educational reform. Zeichner stressed that "Teaching is not just work; it is gendered work" (p. 366). As he expressed hope for societal reform and emancipation in the press for teacher empowerment, he also offered caution. He pointed out the possibility of curricular reform missions being undermined unless teacher research is incorporated into, instead of added to, teachers' work.

For Hollingsworth (in press), the teacher-as-researcher movement takes on a perspective of feminist praxis. A consciousness of the teacher's personal position within society (i.e., most teachers throughout the world are women), an understanding of research, an appreciation of the teacher's ability to construct and critique knowledge, and the integration of those features in classroom teaching suggests that teaching itself is research. Thus, teachers are the researchers of educational and societal reform—a position Elliott (1991) had endorsed earlier from a curricular stance.

Weiner (1989) contrasts teacher research in the School Council Sex Differentiation Project with mainstream professional development or curricular teacher research. Rather than convince teachers of a need to change their practices, gender researchers in the United Kingdom wish to bring about improvements in the social and economic position of women. Similar research is being conducted in the United States (see McIntosh et al. 1992).

3.3 Impact of Societal Reform

Excellent examples of first-order research from the societal reform stance are currently available (Newman 1990). The publication of such work is indicative of the increasing involvement of teachers in emancipatory work. Further, not only are teacher researchers conducting their own professional meetings, but they are participating at national and international research conferences previously reserved for university researchers. For example, since 1989, the American Educational Research Association has registered a special interest group on teacher research. The National Research Center on Literature Teaching and Learning in the United States sponsored a Teacher Research Institute in 1992. These are but a few examples of how the teacher-as-researcher movement is resulting in societal reform.

The concept of teacher-as-researcher is at the center of international attention to reform in all areas of the educational enterprise: research, teaching, the profession, its moral purpose, and its impact on societies. Some might worry that the political implications of teacher empowerment and societal reform might lead to a new and unknown world with unfamiliar epistemological and social norms. Others might be concerned that the growing popularity of teachers-as-researchers will ensure that it becomes yet another form of power and hierarchy inside schools. If so, the concept may be mandated, measured, and become meaningless to actual improvement of practice. Conversely, it may become a new process for reproducing existing school structures and societal outcomes. The trends found in the literature fail to resolve either of those worries. What is clear is that the movement is part of the larger evolution of society into the postinformation age—and that teachers-as-researchers are no longer marginally involved.

References

Ashton D et al. 1990 *Where Do We Go From Here in the California Mentor Teacher Program?: Recommendations by Seven Mentors*. Stanford/Schools Collaborative, Stanford University, Stanford, California

Belenky M F, Clinchy B M, Goldberger N R, Tarule J M 1986 *Women's Ways of Knowing: The Development of Self, Voice, and Mind*. Basic Books, New York

Bruner J S 1985 Narrative and paradigmatic modes of thought. In: Eisnes E (ed.) 1985 *Learning and Teaching the Ways of Knowing, 84th Yearbook of the National Society for the Study of Education*. University of Chicago Press, Chicago, Illinois

Carini P 1988 Prospect's documentary processes. Unpublished manuscript, Bennington, Vermont

Clandinin D J, Davies A, Hogan P, Kennard B in press *Learning to Teach: Teaching to Learn Stories of Collaboration in Teacher Education*. Teachers' College Press, New York

Corey S 1953 *Action Research to Improve School Practices*. Teachers College Press, New York

Delpit L 1986 Skills and other dilemmas of a progressive Black educator. *Harv. Educ. Rev.* 56(4): 379–85.

Elliott J 1991 *Action Research for Educational Change*. Open University Press, Milton Keynes

Fecho B 1992 The way they talk: An English teacher ponders his role. Paper presented at the Ethnography in Education Research Forum, University of Pennsylvania, Philadelphia

Freedman S, Jackson J, Boles K 1983 Teaching: An imperilled "profession." In: Shulman L S, Sykes G (eds.) 1983 *Handbook of Teaching and Policy*. Longman, New York

Harding S 1991 *Whose Science? Whose Knowledge? Thinking from Women's Lives*. Cornell University Press, Ithaca, New York

Hollingsworth S 1992 Learning to teach literacy through collaborative conversation: A feminist approach. *Am. Educ. Res. J.* 29(2): 373–404.

Hopkins D 1985 *A Teacher's Guide to Classroom Research*. Taylor and Francis, London

Kemmis S, McTaggert R 1988 *The Action Research Planner*, 3rd edn. Deakin University Press, Geelong, Victoria

Lampert M 1989 Research into practice: Arithmetic as problem solving. *Arithmetic Teacher* 36(7): 34–36

Lourde A 1984 *Sister Outsider*. The Crossing Press, Freedom, California

Lewin K 1946 Action research and minority problems *J. Soc. Iss.* 2(4): 24–46.

McIntosh P, Style E, Tsugawa T 1992 *Teacher as Researcher*. National SEED Seeking Educational Equity and Diversity, Wellesley College Center for Research on Women, Wellesley, Massachusetts

McKernan J 1991 *Curriculum Action Research: A Handbook of Methods and Resources for the Reflective Practitioner*. St. Martin's Press, New York

Newman J D (ed.) 1990 *Finding our Own Way: Teachers Exploring their Assumptions*. Heinemann, Portsmouth, New Hampshire

Oja S N, Smulyan L (eds.) 1989 *Collaborative Action Research: A Developmental Process*. Falmer Press, London

Philadelphia Teachers' Learning Cooperative 1984 On becoming teacher experts: Buying time. *Lang. Arts* 61(7): 731–36

Posch P 1992 Teacher research and teacher professionalism. Paper presented at the Int. Conf. Teacher Research, Stanford University, Palo Alto, California

Schecter S R 1992 Ideological divergences in teacher research groups. Paper presented at the Ethnography in Education Research Forum, University of Pennsylvania, Philadelphia

Schwab J 1983 The practical 4: Something for curriculum professors to do. *Curric. Inq.* 13(3): 239–65.

Simons H 1992 Teacher research and teacher professionalism. Paper presented at the Int Conf Teacher Research, Stanford University, Palo Alto, California

Smith H, Wigginton E, Hocking K, Jones R E 1991 Foxfire teacher networks. In: Lieberman A, Miller L (eds.) 1991 *Staff Development for Education in the 1990's: New Demands, New Realities, New Perspectives*, 2nd edn. Teachers College Press, New York

Sockett H 1989 Practical professionalism. In: Cass W (ed.) 1989 *Quality in Teaching*. Falmer Press, New York

Stenhouse L 1983 Research as a basis for teaching. In: Stenhouse L (ed.) 1983 *Authority, Education and Emancipation*. Heinemann, Portsmouth, New Hampshire

Tyler R W 1949 *Basic Principles of Curriculum and Instruction*. University of Chicago Press, Chicago, Illinois

Weiner G 1989 Professional self-knowledge versus social justice: A critical analysis of the teacher- researcher movement. *Brit. Educ. Res. J.* *15*(1): 41–51

Winter R 1987 *Action-research and the Nature of Social Inquiry: Professional Innovation and Educational Work*. Gower, Brookfield, Vermont

Zeichner K M 1990 Contradictions and tensions in the professionalization of teaching and the democratization of schools. *Teach. Col. Rec.* *92*: 363–379

S. Hollingsworth

Teachers' Beliefs and Belief Systems

As developing and developed nations struggle with political, social, economic, and environmental problems, they typically call on their schools to provide solutions. During the late 1980s and early 1990s, these calls have taken the form of school reform or restructuring efforts which have sent educational researchers scurrying to find some magic reform/restructuring "pills."

Many researchers have responded by searching for ways of generating greater *skill* among teachers. A few veterans of past reform/restructuring efforts, though, have responded differently, turning their attention to the generation of greater "will" instead. These researchers (e.g., Sarason 1983) have especially focused their attention on teachers' beliefs and on how these beliefs shape school reform/restructuring attitudes, intentions, and actions.

1. The Nature of Beliefs

Beliefs convey ". . . the information that a person has regarding some attribute of an object . . . the object of a belief may be a person, a group of people, an institution, a behavior, a policy, and event, etc., and the associated attribute may be any object, trait, property, quality, characteristic, outcome or event" (Fishbein and Ajzen 1975 p. 12). In understanding the role of beliefs in the school reform/restructuring process, three things must be remembered. First, beliefs vary in strength depending on just how sure the person is that a particular object does indeed possess a certain attribute. Some teacher beliefs, especially about students and their learning, may be held so strongly that they are difficult, if not impossible, to change. Second, beliefs vary in kind: descriptive beliefs come from personal observation; inferential beliefs come from inferences about these observations; and informational beliefs come from outside sources. Descriptive beliefs, since they are rooted in teacher's school experience, are most resistant to change. Third, beliefs begin to cluster over time around related beliefs and form a system or network. Once such a belief system is formed, change in one teacher belief may be difficult or impossible without change in the system of which the belief is now a part.

2. Teacher's Beliefs

The best-known research on teachers' beliefs has focused largely on teachers' inferential beliefs about student success or failure in classroom achievement settings. Clark and Peterson (1986), for instance, have focused on teacher attributions for the causes of their students' achievement and teacher beliefs about their responsibility for students' success or failure. Considerations of student ability and effort, of the learning task, and of luck influence teacher attributions, and issues of teacher egos influence their responsibility beliefs. Some teachers—ego-servers—believe that they are responsible for their students' successes and not their failures. Other teachers—ego-protectors—believe the reverse.

Teacher beliefs about student ability and effort, and about serving or protecting thier own egos, are central not only to the literature on student achievement but on student motivation to achieve as well (see Stipek 1992). Many teachers apparently believe that ability should predominate over effort in school achievement settings. Indeed, they believe that children enter school with a childish conception of ability, where effort counts, that must be replaced with a more mature conception, where ability and effort have been separated and only ability reigns. Again, these teachers' beliefs about the primacy of ability allow teachers to ego-serve by demonstrating high ability themselves or to ego-protect by not demonstrating low ability (Ames and Ames 1984). In such ability-centered classrooms, teachers can brush aside low-ability students and concentrate on their more able peers.

Most of the literature on teacher beliefs and belief systems suffers from three basic problems. First, it is ethnocentric; much of it comes from Western, developed nations, especially the United States. Second, the literature rarely gets past teachers' inferential beliefs to their descriptive ones; too much of it, to use the language of ethnographers, is outsider or "etic" and not enough is insider or "emic". A third problem is that the literature tends to focus on teacher beliefs and belief systems about a small portion of their job; while issues of the management of student learning and classroom achievement are high on most teachers' daily planning list, issues of the management of learners and classroom discipline often are even higher.

Fortunately, work is beginning to appear that addresses each of these problems. On the ethnocentric front, writing has emerged that supplements the Western, industrialized belief literature. Thomas, for example, has companioned his volume on comparative theories of Western child development (Thomas 1992) with one on theories of eastern child development (Thomas 1988). Such supplementation seems especially important in light of cross-national work beginning to challenge the cross-cultural validity of findings from the central paradigm underlying Western teacher belief and belief systems research, namely, the paradigm of attribution theory. Apparently effort is much more highly valued by teachers in the East than by those in the West (Stevenson and Steigler 1992).

On the etic–emic front, culture of teaching scholars such as Feinman-Nemser and Floden (1986) have turned their attention to teachers' descriptive beliefs. The work of the Israeli scholar Freema Elbaz (1991) in giving voice to teachers' practical knowledge is illustrative. Elbaz has suggested, among other things, that teachers have various categories of practical knowledge involving self, milieu, subject matter, curriculum development, and instruction which they use to understand and structure their classrooms. This information is then organized in a hierarchy with general rules of practice (actions) at the bottom, practical principles (thoughts about actions) in the middle, and images (purposes for actions) at the top. Teachers' descriptive beliefs play a central role in shaping their images and, hence, their practical principles and rules.

Finally, on the job front, teacher education scholars (e.g., Lanier and Little 1986) and especially sociologists of teaching (e.g., Rosenholtz 1991) have begun to build a framework for understanding teacher beliefs more broadly. Working under the assumption that the nature of teacher's work shapes the nature of their beliefs, these scholars have focused on understanding the nature of teaching as an occupation. It is a complex and uncertain occupation, one given to the inculcation of beliefs that promote continuity and discourage change.

3. *Sociology of Teaching and Teacher Beliefs*

The picture that educational sociologists paint, at least of teachers in the United States, differs little in broad respects from that crafted by Waller (1932). Waller captured the basic work of teachers as involving the transmission of core cultural values to students whom the teachers believed were uncouth. Since students were believed inclined to resist these transmissions, the essence of teaching became a form of daily institutional dominance—convincing young wills to bend to older wisdom.

Building on the work of Dreeben (1970) and Lortie (1975), for instance, scholars have attempted to identify some of the core values transmitted by teachers in United States schools and some of the institutional constraints they face as they try to inculcate these values in their charges. Values such as achievement, individualism, universalism, and particularism still are transmitted in classrooms. Moreover, they still are transmitted in a climate where teachers feel internal pressure to get students to learn and external pressure to get them to be compliant (Cusick 1983). Maintaining some semblance of balance between their internal hopes and their external reality generate ego issues of anxiety, self-doubt, and vulnerability (Doyle 1986).

Naturally, many teachers might turn to practices for transmitting these values that help them allay these ego issues. Classroom practices based on the belief that student ability should be the *sine qua non* of classroom life, practices such as competition and tracking (Oakes 1985), would certainly be appealing. High-ability students are believed to pose fewer behavioral and intellectual demands than students of lower ability (Cooper and Tom 1984), so by identifying students of high and low ability and by encouraging the initiations of the former and discouraging those of the latter, teachers could essentially create more ego-protective and, possibly, ego-serving classroom conditions. They also could gain some invulnerability with respect to the more problematic sociorelational aspects of their job, concentrate on its learning aspects, and lay claim to whatever psychic rewards that the learning of their more able students might provide.

Other sociologists have also begun to provide still larger frameworks for the study of teacher beliefs and belief systems. One especially relevant framework generalizes the analysis of scholars such as Lortie, who have compared teaching to other professions, by comparing it to other classes of occupations. In this framework, teachers are looked at as workers, broadly speaking, and scholars focus on the nature of their work and work-related beliefs. Some of these scholars are especially concerned with how teacher work and work-related beliefs shape the nature of their students' work and work-related beliefs. Since teachers are in some sense a student's first boss, the scholars in this framework want to know what kind of boss they are.

Anyon (1981), for instance, has examined the socialization of students by teachers in working-class schools where the majority of working parents were in unskilled and semi-skilled occupations; in middle-class schools where the parents were a mixture of highly skilled blue collar and white collar workers plus public school teachers, social workers, accountants, and middle managers; in an affluent professional school where most parents were highly paid doctors, television or advertising executives, and interior designers; and in an executive elite school where parents were at least vice presidents in multinational corporations or financial firms. Anyon found that students in each school type were socialized to appropriate social class conceptions of ownership of physical and cultural capital, of the structure of authority at work and in society, and of the content and process of one's own work activity. Such findings once again suggest that it makes sense for teachers to believe that their classroom work should be organized along ability lines. Higher-class occupations do seem to make greater demands on student's abilities than do lower-class ones. In emphasizing ability, therefore, the teacher is simply doing his or her cultural transmission job by reproducing the real world of work outside schools and bringing it inside.

Anyon's findings, however, add an important caveat to this sense-making process: the belief in ability alone may prepare students for at best middle-class work. Beliefs in other things—creativity and individualism or effort and social responsibility—are required to build students for professional and elite jobs respectively, so it makes sense to build classrooms on bases other than or in addition to ability.

4. *Educational Researcher and Teachers' Beliefs*

This entry has suggested that researchers are turning their attention to beliefs as one "magic pill" in the search for better school. Some of the frameworks they are using to study teacher beliefs and belief systems were mentioned. Thus far, these frameworks indicate that Western teachers, at least, believe and have reason to believe that their classrooms be organized primarily around student ability. Such classroom organization seems to serve or protect their egos.

Since serious research has begun comparatively recently, the picture drawn of teacher ability-oriented, ego-centered beliefs and belief systems is simplistic. Much remains to be studied regarding the what and why, not only of Western teachers' beliefs and belief systems but other teacher's beliefs and belief systems as well. Much remains to be studied especially from the perspective of the teachers themselves. In both respects, the work of scholars such as Elbaz (1991) who are striving to suggest ways to give teachers worldwide a "voice," especially a critical one, in describing what they do and why they do it in their schools, is welcomed.

It would be remiss, though, to leave researchers with the impression that the matter of better articulating teacher beliefs and belief systems lies solely in their skills at giving practitioners a voice. Researchers need a voice for talking to practitioners. The reason is simple. Teachers' beliefs and belief systems are grounded in their personal experiences and, hence, are highly resistant to change. Typically, though, these experiences are a byproduct of the school context in which they work. If school practitioners are not given outside information about this context that can help them be critical of their past experiences or about new contexts that portend some new experiences entirely, then the risk is that research will actually reify that context rather than reform or restructure it.

This reification-of-context process seems well underway in the early 1990s in the United States as mainstream scholars repeatedly report that teachers' belief systems remain closed especially around issues of student ability and control (Cusick 1983). Other scholars have repeatedly indicted such beliefs as not a solution for, but a cause of, the school reform/restructuring predicament. They have shown beliefs in ability to have constructive learning and motivational consequences for a few students and destructive ones for many. They also have suggested that beliefs in control assuage teachers' egos at the expense of most childrens' egos (Glasser 1990).

These latter scholars need to be heard. Part of a strategy in finding a voice for communicating with teachers must be rhetorical. It has long been known that the beliefs about student ability and control may be flawed. However researchers have avoided sharing that knowledge with teachers in ways that they can understand and appreciate. Floden (1985) has suggested some useful initial ideas for better shaping researchers' rhetoric so that their voices can and will be heard.

However, the larger part of a strategy in changing teacher beliefs and belief systems about student ability and control must be substantive. Rhetoric must be used to help conjure up alternative conceptions of schooling where factors other than ability, like effort, really count. Central to such conceptions will be systematic, informational belief work to examine and, where necessary, challenge teachers' descriptive and inferential beliefs about students and their learning and motivation to learn.

5. *Conclusion*

While Arthur Foshay (1973) was perhaps the first veteran United States school reformer to recognize that implicit beliefs and belief systems about the child and his or her learning power, it was his colleague, Benjamin Bloom (1976) who perhaps first reminded researchers that they have their implicit beliefs and belief systems about the child and his or her learning power.

Bloom summarized some of these beliefs and belief systems in the preface to his landmark volume *Human Characteristics and School Learning* as follows:

> When I first entered the field of educational research and measurement, the prevailing construct was:
>
> **1. There are good learners and there are poor learners.**
>
> This was considered to be a relatively permanent attribute of the individual. It was also the prevailing view that individuals possessed it in different amounts and that a quantitative index of it could be made by the use of an appropriate intelligence, aptitude, or achievement test. Furthermore, it was believed that good learners could learn the more complex and abstract ideas, while poor learners could learn only the simplest and most concrete ideas. School systems throughout the world have been organized on the basis of this construct and the selection systems, grading systems, and even the curriculum has been built on the basis of it.
>
> During the early 1960s, some of us became interested in the Caroll Model of School Learning, which was built on the construct:
>
> **2. There are faster learners and there are slower learners.**
>
> While we were not entirely clear whether or not rate of learning was a permanent trait of individuals, we dedicated ourselves to finding ways by which the slower learners could be given the extra **time and help** they needed to attain some criterion of achievement. In this research, in both educational laboratories as well as classrooms in different nations, it became evident that a large proportion of slower learners may learn as well as faster learners. When the slower learners do succeed in attaining the same criterion of achievement as faster learners, they appear to be able to learn equally complex and abstract ideas, they can apply these ideas to new problems, and they can retain the ideas equally well—in spite of the fact that they learned with more time and help than was given to others. Furthermore, their interests and attitudes toward the school subjects in which they attain the achievement criterion are as posi-

tive as those of faster learners.

During the past decade, my students and I have done research which has led us to the view that:

3. Most students become very similar with regard to learning ability, rate of learning, and motivation for further learning—when provided with favorable learning conditions.

This research questions the first two constructs, especially about the permanence of good–poor learning ability or fast–slow learning characteristics. However, the research does demonstrate that when students are provided with unfavorable learning conditions, they become even more dissimilar with regard to learning ability, rate of learning, and motivation for further learning . . . It is this research which we believe has profound consequences for the prevailing views about human nature, human characteristics, and school learning. (Bloom 1976 pp. ix–x)

As Bloom's quote suggests, beliefs about students and their individual differences, especially their differences in ability, once dominated the thinking of educational researchers. In the early 1990s, beliefs about students and their individual sameness, especially their sameness in ability and in motivation to learn, are beginning to be recognized.

Education researchers can play a role in coaxing these beliefs from the sidelines of thinking about school reform and restructuring worldwide to center stage. After all, beliefs in the potential of virtually all students to learn as well as the best students do offers schooling possibilities for the many students that were once reserved for only the few. Attention to the many rather than the few makes moral sense.

See also: Mastery Learning; Teacher Evaluating Behavior; Culture, Cognition, and Education, Perspectives on

References

Anyon J 1981 Social class and school knowledge. *Curric. Inq.* 11: 1–42

Ames C, Ames R 1984 Systems of student and teacher motivation: Toward a qualitative definition. *J. Educ. Psychol.* 76(4): 535–56

Bloom B S 1976 *Human Characteristics and School Learning*. McGraw-Hill, New York

Clark C M, Peterson P L 1986 Teachers' thought processes. In: Wittrock M C (ed.) 1986 *Handbook of Research on Teaching*, 3rd edn. Macmillan, New York

Cooper H M, Tom D Y H 1984 Teacher expectation research: A review with implications for classroom instruction. *Elem. Sch. J.* 85: 77–104

Cusick P 1983 *The Egalitarian Ideal and the American High School. Studies of Three Schools*. Longman, New York

Doyle W 1986 Classroom organization and management. In: Wittrock M C (ed.) 1986 *Handbook of Research on Teaching*, 3rd edn. Macmillan, New York

Dreeben R 1970 *The Nature of Teaching, Schools and the Work of Teachers*. Scott-Foresman, Glenview, Illinois

Elbaz F 1991 Research on teachers' knowledge: The evolution of a discourse. *J. Curric. Stud.* 23: 1–19

Feinman-Nemser S, Floden R E 1986 The cultures of teaching. In: Wittrock M C (ed.) 1986 *Handbook of Research on Teaching*, 3rd edn. Macmillan, New York

Fishbein M, Ajzen I 1975 *Belief, Attitude, Intention, and Behavior*. Addison-Wesley, Reading, Massachusetts

Floden R E 1985 The role of rhetoric in changing teachers' beliefs. *Teaching and Teacher Education* 1: 19–32

Foshay A W 1973 Sources of school practice. In: Goodlad J I, Shane H G (eds.) 1973 *The Elementary School in the United States, The 72nd Yearbook of the National Society for the Study of Education*. University of Chicago Press, Chicago, Illinois

Glasser W 1990 *The Quality School. Managing Students Without Coercion*. Harper and Row, New York

Lanier J E, Little J W 1986 Research on teacher education. In: Wittrock M C (ed.) 1986 *Handbook of Research on Teaching*, 3rd edn. Macmillan, New York

Lortie D C 1975 *Schoolteacher. A Sociological Study*. University of Chicago Press, Chicago, Illinois

Oakes J 1985 *Keeping Track. How Schools Structure Inequality*. Yale University Press, New Haven, Connecticut

Rosenholtz S J 1991 *Teachers' Workplace*. Teachers College Press, New York

Sarason S B 1983 *Schooling in America: Scapegoat and Salvation*. Free Press, New York

Stevenson H, Steigler J 1992 *The Learning Gap*. Summit Books, New York

Stipek D 1992 *Motivation to Learn*, 2nd edn. Prentice-Hall, Englewood Cliffs, New Jersey

Thomas R M 1992 *Comparing Theories of Child Development*, 3rd edn. Wadsworth, Belmont, California

Thomas R M (ed.) 1988 *Oriental Theories of Human Development*. Peter Lang Publishers, New York

Waller W 1932 *The Sociology of Teaching*. John Wiley and Sons, New York

J. H. Block; K. Hazelip

Teachers, Characteristics of Prospective

The future of educational systems throughout the world depends to a large extent on the number and quality of prospective teachers. Who are these prospective teachers? How many are there and do their numbers meet the expected future demand for teachers? What do we know about prospective teachers in terms of academic ability and affective characteristics? What changes in the characteristics of prospective teachers need to be made to ensure their effectiveness in the classroom? These questions will be addressed in this entry.

1. Number of Prospective Teachers

Prospective teachers include those in traditional teacher education programs, those who have graduated from traditional teacher education programs but who are not currently teaching, degree recipients who did not major in education fields but who meet the requirements for licensure or certification in teaching, and those who are interested in becoming teachers but who lack the official prerequisites for entry into teaching. While there may be a tendency to limit any conception of the current teaching pool to those in traditional teacher education programs and those who have graduated from such programs, it must be pointed out that more than 30 percent of the teachers hired during the mid-1980s in the United States majored in fields other than education (Stern and Chandler 1987). Furthermore, the teaching pool includes those who have "stopped out" of teaching for some period of time, but who intend to return to teaching in the future.

Thanks to their variety, it is difficult to obtain an accurate figure for the number of prospective teachers, let alone describe them. In this regard, Murnane and his colleagues (1991) stated that it is impossible to provide a truly accurate impression of the corps of prospective teachers in the United States as there are no national data on trends in the number of prospective teachers or the characteristics of new licensees. This lack of valid and complete data also exists in other countries, particularly in those undergoing modernization or social upheaval (Leavitt 1991).

To complicate matters further, there is an important difference between prospective and beginning teachers. Not all of those who are licensed to teach seek or obtain employment in schools. In the People's Republic of China, for example, almost 60 percent of those who completed teacher training programs were unwilling to enter the teaching force in 1989 (Chang and Paine 1992). Similarly, in the United States, the Carnegie Foundation for the Advancement of Teaching (CFAT) reported that only 60 percent of all holders of a bachelor's degree who gained licensure or certification for teaching in 1980 were actually teaching in the early 1980s (CFAT 1986, 1987).

Problems of decreased teacher supply and increased teacher demand are worldwide. Between 1990 and 2000, United States schools will require more than 2 million new teachers (Murnane et al. 1991) and less than 65 percent of this demand will be met by new teacher graduates (CFAT 1986, 1987). The Arab Gulf States, Australia, China, Egypt, Malawi, and the Commonwealth of Independent States all cite the recruitment into and retention of academically able individuals in teaching as a critical issue (Leavitt 1992). In the former Soviet Union, low pay and poor living conditions have dissuaded many from choosing a teaching career (Leavitt 1991). In order to meet teacher shortages in Spain, the ministry of education mandated an elimination of any admission requirements for teacher education (Benejam and Espinet 1992).

2. *Portrait of a Prospective Teacher*

Although it is difficult to delineate clearly the prospective teaching population, a well-known portrait of the teacher, particularly in the United States, has emerged. Virtually every descriptive study conducted in the United States notes the propensity of the teaching population to be White, lower to middle class, and female (McDiarmid 1990, Ross and Smith 1992, Zimpher 1989). Women outnumber men by more than four to one, with a higher percentage of women at the elementary level than at the secondary and postsecondary levels. This profile also applies to prospective teachers, at least those enrolled in teacher education programs (Brookhart and Freeman 1992).

It should be noted that most of these reviews have been subjected to harsh criticism. Lanier and Little (1986), for example, argued that the data are often inadequately analyzed and synthesized, thus perpetuating stereotypes, misinformation, and misunderstandings. Brookhart and Freeman (1992) questioned the design of the research suggesting that researchers tend to lack a theoretical framework to guide their interpretations, rely on a single method of data collection and/or on a sample from a single institution, and make an "inadequate distinction among subpopulations" (p. 53).

3. *Cognitive Characteristics of Prospective Teachers*

Spurred on by criticism of the United States educational system, numerous studies of the academic abilities of prospective teachers have been conducted (Vance and Schlecty 1982). The results of these studies are similar. Prospective teachers were over represented among the lowest scorers on standardized aptitude tests, and underrepresented among the highest scorers. Only four fields recorded lower scores than intended education majors. Furthermore, the gap between the mean scores of prospective teachers and those of all other fields combined widened from approximately 60 to 80 points from the mid-1970s to the mid-1980s (CFAT 1986).

Similar results have been obtained in other countries. In Nigeria, for example, disproportionate numbers of undergraduates in education come the lowest 10 percent of university students; 50 percent of those who applied for admission to education had been rejected from their favored programs of study (Avoseh 1992).

These findings have led to the conclusion that to improve the quality of education more academically able prospective teachers must be recruited. This conclusion has not been without its critics, however. As Darling-Hammond (1990) pointed out:

> Test scores are not clear evidence of quality or lack of quality. What we mean by teacher quality should be more influenced by what teacher candidates learn after they enter college than by the entrance examination scores they presented at matriculation. (pp. 272–73)

Furthermore, the desire to enlist students with the highest grade average and test scores can be questioned on several grounds. First, a "positive relationship between a single attribute, academic ability, and quality teaching has not been forthcoming" (Otis-Wilborn et al. 1988 p. 108). Second, despite the vociferous criticism leveled at the teaching field, a consensus has yet to emerge as to the vital academic, personal, and professional qualifications of prospective teachers, particularly in light of the number of new teachers needed (Darling-Hammond 1990).

4. Affective Characteristics of Prospective Teachers

Like the data on academic ability, the available data on affective characteristics of prospective teachers are disappointing. As Lanier and Little (1986) pointed out:

> The research evidence suggests that both prospective and practicing teachers maintain low expectations for the professional knowledge aspects of their education. The desire for serious and continued learning for improvement purposes is also understandably low in light of growing declines in extrinsic and intrinsic rewards for the occupation of teaching itself. (p. 542)

Furthermore, the belief that teaching is a low-status profession may hurt the self-esteem of prospective teachers (Murnane et al. 1991).

At the same time, however, prospective teachers have a stronger orientation to human welfare than their college peers and place greater emphasis on personal relationships. They also "place less emphasis on economic success and what is seen by other groups as efficient or practical" (Coulter 1987 p. 591). Overall, the students majoring in education "have values that differ from those in other fields and, in fact, seem to be somewhat more traditional in their outlook" (CFAT 1986 p. 29).

Brookhart and Freeman (1992) reviewed 44 studies of beginning education students and offered the following synthesis. Candidates for teaching are motivated by a concern for others, possess confidence in their teaching abilities, express greater concern for mastering content than for managing interpersonal relationships, perceive the nurturing aspects of teaching as more important than academic requirements, and interpret the teaching act as one of dispensing information.

Finally, whereas professionals in other fields expect difficult access, hard work, a continuous work history, and enter with a keen appreciation for their academic preparation, preservice teachers express attitudes about teaching that reflect the contrary. They expect easy access, light work, and a discontinuous work life. They also express the opinion that their academic preparation is irrelevant (Lanier and Little 1986).

Research on affective characteristics of prospective teachers has been criticized for its reliance on descriptive studies, many of which are narrowly bounded and framed, and for the lack of attention to socialization issues. For example, folk wisdom dictates that a relationship exists between attitudes of prospective teachers and their teaching effectiveness. However, early research "revealed little evidence of relationships of any strength, consistency, or consequence between student teacher effectiveness and their values, attitudes, or interests" (Coulter 1987 p. 593). Levis (1987) also noted the "limited usefulness of knowledge gained from such research" (p. 587). In the early 1990s researchers called for a different type of research to explore this possible relationship in greater depth. This research would be field-based and qualitative and would include detailed interviews and observations (Brookhart and Freeman 1992).

5. Changing the Characteristics of Prospective Teachers

Most preservice teachers complete their teacher preparation programs without an examination of their deepest values and beliefs, even on such vital issues as pedagogy, teacher roles and responsibilities, curriculum, and the cultural diversity of students (McDiarmid 1990). In addition to examining these issues, changes in the values, attitudes, and beliefs of prospective teachers as they relate to these issues may be necessary.

Concerning the cultural diversity of students, for example, Larke et al. (1990) asserted that teacher attitudes regarding minority students shape educational outcomes. Thus, understanding and reshaping stereotypical attitudes are imperative. However, little research on attitude change has been conducted in the context of preservice teaching. Multicultural education efforts to change attitudes has not been assessed empirically (Grottkau and Nickolai-Mays 1989). In at least some instances little change is expected because the efforts lack strength and direction (Ross and Smith 1992).

As the demographics of the student population change, examining and, when necessary, altering teachers' views on racial minorities become critically important. In the United States, for example, approximately 40 percent of all children enrolled in public schools will be members of minority ethnic groups by the year 2000 (Graham 1987). This figure is substantially higher in the largest cities of the United States. In the 15 largest cities, between 70 and 96 percent of children will be members of minority groups, while less than 5 percent of the teachers of these children will represent minority groups (Ross and Smith 1992).

Particularly troubling in this regard is the finding that prospective teachers prefer to work in a school environment that mirrors their own experiences, thus maintaining their cultural insularity (Ross and Smith 1992, Zimpher 1989). Only 20 percent of prospective teachers in one United States study indicated a preference to work with students from diverse racial and cultural backgrounds (Larke 1990). This problem is compounded by a shrinking number of minority teachers (Murnane et al. 1991), the constantly changing realities of a pluralistic society (Grottkau and Nickolai-Mays 1989), and the lack of awareness of cultural differences that will serve as obstacles to the academic success of minority students (Larke 1990).

6. Conclusion

Information about prospective teachers is limited. Because of the various categories of prospective teachers, the number of prospective teachers in the United States population is uncertain. What is known about prospective teachers is not necessarily flattering. Prospective teachers tend to have lower academic ability than their contemporaries pursuing other professional careers. They also tend to subscribe to more traditional values than their peers. They generally regard the job of teaching as relatively easy and have confidence in their teaching abilities. They are motivated more by humanistic interests than economic concerns. Perhaps because of these other perceptions, they tend to view the academic side of their teacher preparation as difficult and irrelevant.

During the 1980s, serious attention was paid for the first time to answering a variety of questions concerning the characteristics of prospective teachers. The future will determine if the right questions have been asked.

See also: Teacher Recruitment and Induction; Teachers, Professional Socialization of

References

Avoseh O 1992 Nigeria. In: Leavitt H B (ed.) 1992

Benejam P, Espinet M 1992 Spain. In: Leavitt H B (ed.) 1992

Brookhart S M, Freeman D J 1992 Characteristics of entering teacher candidates. *Rev. Educ. Res.* 62(1): 37–60

Carnegie Foundation for the Advancement of Teaching (CFAT) 1986 Future teachers: Will there be enough good ones? *Change* 18(5): 27–30

Carnegie Foundation for the Advancement of Teaching (CFAT) 1987 Prospective teachers: Career choices. *Change* 19(2): 31–35

Chang M C, Paine L 1992 China. In: Leavitt H B (ed.) 1992

Coulter F 1987 Affective characteristics of student teachers. In: Dunkin M J (ed.) 1987 *International Encyclopedia of Teaching and Teacher Education*. Pergamon Press, Oxford

Darling-Hammond L 1990 Teachers and teaching: Signs of a changing profession. In: Houston N R (ed.) 1990 *Handbook of Research on Teacher Education*. Macmillan Inc., New York

Graham P A 1987 Black teachers: A drastically scarce resource. *Phi Del. Kap.* 69(8): 598–605

Grottkau B J, Nickolai-Mays S 1989 An empirical analysis of a multi-cultural education paradigm for preservice teachers. *Educ. Res. Q.* 13(4): 27–33

Lanier J E, Little J W 1986 Research on teacher education: Studying the students of teaching. In: Wittrock M C (ed.) 1986 *Handbook of Research on Teaching*, 3rd edn. Macmillan Inc., New York

Larke P J 1990 Cultural diversity awareness inventory: Assessing the sensitivity of preservice teachers. *Action in Teacher Education* 12(3): 23–30

Larke P J, Wiseman D, Bradley C 1990 The minority mentorship project: Changing attitudes of preservice teachers for diverse classrooms. *Action in Teacher Education* 12(3): 5–11

Leavitt H B 1991 Worldwide issues and problems in teacher education. *J. Teach. Educ.* 42(5): 323–31

Leavitt H B (ed.) 1992 *Issues and Problems in Teacher Education: An International Handbook*. Greenwood, New York

Levis D S 1987 Teachers' personality. In: Dunkin M J (ed.) 1987 *International Encyclopedia of Teaching and Teacher Education*. Pergamon Press, Oxford

McDiarmid G W 1990 Challenging prospective teachers' beliefs during early field experience: A quixotic undertaking? *J. Teach. Educ.* 41(3): 12–20

Murnane R J, Singer J D, Willett J B, Kemple J J, Olsen R J 1991 *Who will Teach? Policies that Matter*. Harvard University Press, Cambridge, Massachusetts

Otis-Wilborn A K, Marshall J D, Sears J T 1988 Commitment: A reflection of the quality of preservice teachers. *Peabody Journal of Education* 65(2): 107–29

Ross D D, Smith W 1992 Understanding preservice teachers' perspectives on diversity. *J. Teach. Educ.* 43(2): 94–103

Stern J P, Chandler M O (eds.) 1987 *The Condition of Education: A Statistical Report*. United States Department of Education, Center for Education Statistics, Washington, DC

Vance V S, Schlechty P S 1982 The distribution of academic ability in the teaching force: Policy implications. *Phi Del. Kap.* 64(1): 22–27

Zimpher N C 1989 The RATE Project: A profile of teacher education students. *J. Teach. Educ.* 40(6): 27–30

J. Neururer

Teachers' Expectations

In the 1960s, an experiment conducted in the United States by Rosenthal and Jacobson (1968) resulted in one of the most exciting and controversial reports in the history of educational research. These investigators presented data suggesting that teachers' experimentally induced expectations for student performance were associated with student performance. That is, students whom teachers expected to achieve at higher levels did in fact achieve at higher levels, even though there was no real basis for these expectations. The study was criticized on several methodological grounds. For example, no observations were conducted in the teachers' classrooms, so there was no basis on which to determine whether teachers interacted differently with the students based on their expectations.

This entry focuses on research on teachers' expectations that has been conducted since the publication of the Rosenthal and Jacobson study. It begins with a definition of teachers' expectations, discusses the major types of research on those expectations and the conceptual frameworks underlying this research, and examines ways in which different expectations are communicated to students, and the perceptions students have of these different teacher behaviors. The entry concludes with a discussion of possible directions for research on teachers' expectations.

1. Defining Teachers' Expectations

Teachers' expectations are inferences that teachers make about the future behavior or academic achievement of their students, based on what they currently know about these students. Teachers' expectations affect student outcomes because of actions that teachers take in response to their expectations. Expectations are an inescapable and important part of daily life (Jussim 1990a), influencing many social issues. Research on expectancies has examined such topics as gender role socialization, affirmative action, political person perception, and equality of educational opportunity. (For discussions of research on the role of expectancies in diverse social areas see Jussim 1990a, 1990b, Oyserman and Markus 1990.)

Cooper and Good (1983) noted that researchers have examined two types of teacher expectation effects. The first is the self-fulfilling prophecy effect, in which an originally erroneous expectation leads to behavior that causes the expectation to become true. The Rosenthal and Jacobson (1968) study deals with this type of expectation effect. In contrast, the sustaining expectation effect occurs when teachers expect students to sustain previously developed behavior patterns to the point that teachers take these patterns for granted and fail to see and capitalize on changes in student potential. Self-fulfilling prophecy effects are more powerful than sustaining expectation effects because they introduce significant change in student behavior (and thinking) instead of merely sustaining established patterns. Self-fulfilling effects can be powerful when they occur, but the more subtle sustaining expectation effects occur more often.

2. Two Types of Research on Teachers' Expectations

To understand the research on teacher expectation effects, two types of studies must be distinguished. The first involves experimental attempts to induce teacher expectations by providing teachers with fictitious information about students. The second type of study uses the expectations that teachers form naturally on the basis of whatever information they have available (e.g., test scores).

Numerous studies have induced expectations in teachers and have explored the consequent effects on student learning (Good and Brophy 1990). Some studies did not produce changes in student outcomes, apparently because the teachers did not acquire the expectations the experimenters were trying to induce. Induced-expectation experiments have produced clear-cut positive results often enough, however, to demonstrate that teacher expectations can have self-fulfilling prophecy effects on student achievement. Such demonstrations are important, because studies of teachers' naturally formed expectations cannot establish cause-and-effect relationships. These experimental studies in classrooms have been enriched by laboratory research in social psychology that has focused on the formation, communication, and interpretation of expectancies (see Jones 1990, Jussim 1990b for reviews).

However, studies linking teachers' naturally formed expectations to their classroom interactions with students are also needed, because they provide information about how teachers' expectations can become self-fulfilling. As Good and Brophy (1990) noted, most studies of teachers' naturally formed expectations have related such expectations to teacher–student interaction rather than to student outcomes. These studies typically demonstrate that many teachers interact differently with students for whom they hold high expectations than they do with students for whom they hold low expectations. They also suggest the mechanisms that mediate sustaining expectation effects.

3. The Brophy–Good Model

In their early research on teacher expectation effects on individual students, Brophy and Good (1970) suggested the following model of the process by which teachers' expectations become self-fulfilling prophecies.

(a) Early in the year, the teacher forms differential expectations for student behavior and achievement.

(b) Consistent with these differential expectations, the teacher behaves differently toward various students.

(c) This treatment tells students how they are expected to behave in the classroom and to perform on academic tasks.

(d) If the teacher's treatment is consistent over time, and if students do not actively resist or change it, it will likely affect their self-concepts, achievement motivation, levels of aspiration, classroom conduct, and interactions with the teacher.

(e) These effects generally will compliment and reinforce the teacher's expectations, so that students will conform to these expectations more than they might otherwise have done.

(f) Ultimately this reciprocal process will affect student achievement and other outcomes. High-expectation students will achieve at or near their potential, but low-expectation students will not gain as much as they could have if taught differently.

The model begins with the assumption that teachers form differential achievement expectations for various students at the beginning of the school year. Teachers use many cues for forming expectations, including track or group placement, classroom conduct, physical appearance, race, socioeconomic status, ethnicity, gender, speech characteristics, and various diagnostic labels (e.g., see Baron et al. 1985, Jussim 1989).

Self-fulfilling prophecy effects of teacher expectations can occur only when all elements in the model are present (Good and Brophy 1990). Often, however, one or more elements is missing. The teacher may not have clear-cut expectations about every student, or those expectations may change continually. Even when expectations are consistent, the teacher may not necessarily communicate them through consistent behavior. Finally, students might prevent expectations from becoming self-fulfilling by counteracting their effects or resisting them.

4. Communicating Differential Expectations

Given that teachers form differential expectations, how do they express those expectations to students in ways that might influence students' behavior? On the basis of several literature reviews, Good and Brophy (1990) suggested that the following behaviors sometimes indicate differential teacher treatment of high and low achievers: (a) waiting less time for "lows" to answer questions before giving the answer or calling on someone else; (b) giving lows answers or calling on someone else rather than trying to improve their responses by giving clues or repeating or rephrasing questions; (c) providing inappropriate reinforcement (e.g., rewarding inappropriate behavior or incorrect answers by lows); (d) criticizing lows more often for failure; (e) praising lows less often for success; (e) failing to give feedback to the public responses of lows; (f) paying less attention to lows or interacting with them less frequently; (g) calling on lows less often to respond to questions, or asking them only easier, nonanalytical questions; (h) seating lows further from the teacher; (i) demanding less from lows (e.g., teaching them less content; accepting lower quality or even incorrect responses from lows; providing excessive sympathy or unneeded help); (j) interacting with lows more privately than publicly, and monitoring and structuring their activities more closely; (k) grading tests or assignments differently (e.g., highs but not lows are given the benefit of the doubt in borderline cases), (l) engaging in less friendly interaction with lows, including less smiling and fewer other nonverbal indicators of support; (m) providing briefer and less informative feedback to questions of lows; (n) using less eye contact and other nonverbal communication of attention and responsiveness (forward lean, positive head nodding) in interactions with lows; (o) using less effective and time-consuming instructional methods with lows when time is limited; (p) accepting and using lows' ideas less often; and (q) exposing lows to an impoverished curriculum (e.g. limited and repetitive information, emphasis on factual recitation).

Three points should be noted when considering these forms of differential treatment. First, these teacher behaviors do not occur in all classrooms. Some teachers do not communicate low expectations; some provide appropriate expectations for all or most students. Second, some of the differences are due to students rather than to the teacher. For example, if lows volunteer less often, it is difficult for teachers to be sure that lows get as many response opportunities as highs. Third, some forms of differential treatment are necessary at times and may even represent appropriate individualizing of instruction rather than inappropriate projection of negative expectations. Low-achieving students in elementary schools appear to require more private structuring of their activities and closer monitoring of their work than do their peers.

When several of these differential communication patterns are observed in a classroom, however, and if the differentiation is significant, the teacher may be communicating inappropriately low expectations to some students. This is especially the case if the differential treatment directly affects students' opportunity to learn. For example, if lows receive less new information and feedback about their performance, they are almost certain to make less progress than highs, regardless of whether lows are aware of such differential treatment.

While research has focused on inappropriately low expectations, teachers can hold too high or too "narrow" expectations so that some students are pushed to do more but not allowed to take time to understand or enjoy academic work. The key is to challenge and guide students in appropriate ways to do more than they are at that time able to achieve (Vygotsky 1978).

5. The Importance of Teachers' Expectations

The effects of teachers' expectations on student learning have often been exaggerated. Indeed, in the popular press the effects have sometimes been touted as almost magical. For example, Good and Brophy (1977) lampooned an advertisement that appeared in *Reader's Digest*: "Just make a wish. Read about how it can come True." Although there is no clear way to predict with certainty the effects of teachers' expectancies on student learning, there is growing consensus among experts that expectancy effects are usually modest (e.g., Jussim 1990b estimates an average effect size of 0.2 to 0.3 standard deviations), but important (Brophy 1983). Even an effect size of 0.2 suggests that 10 percent of students who receive high expectations will show notable improvement, and that 10 percent of students exposed to low expectations will exhibit a significant decline in performance (Jussim 1990b).

There is no doubt that expectancies are common. Rosenthal and Rubin (1978) reported that some type of teacher expectancy effect occurred in about two-thirds of the 345 studies they reviewed. Although the potential importance of expectancies is shown by such reviews (and expectancy effects may compound over time), most students do not receive "average effects"; students are likely to be in classrooms where effects are very high, moderate, or nonexistent.

6. Students' Perceptions of Teachers' Differential Behavior

Unfortunately, many studies that have assessed the effects of teacher expectancies on student performance have not included process or interview data to determine students' perceptions of differential teacher behavior. In addition to expectation effects that occur directly through differences in exposure to content, indirect effects may occur as a result of teacher behavior that affects students' self-concepts, performance expectations, or motivation. Although numerous studies have examined students' achievement motivation and aspirations in classrooms, little of this research has studied these affective variables in relation to teacher behavior. Thus, little is known about how students interpret teacher behaviors and how those behaviors influence students' motivation and effort.

Studies that have been conducted suggest that students are aware of differences in teachers' patterns of interaction with students. Interview and questionnaire data indicate that elementary students see their teachers as projecting higher achievement expectations and offering increased opportunity and choice to high achievers, while structuring the activities of low achievers more closely and providing them with additional help and with more negative feedback about their academic work and classroom conduct (Cooper and Good 1983).

Furthermore, students are more aware of such differentiation in classes in which it occurs frequently (Weinstein et al. 1987). Brattesani et al. (1984) compared classrooms where the students described the teachers as differentiating considerably in their treatment of high and low achievers with classrooms in which students reported little such differentiation. They found that including teacher-expectation measures added from 9 to 18 percent to the variance in year-end achievement beyond what could have been predicted from prior achievement in the high-differentiation classes, but added only 1 to 5 percent in the low-differentiation classes.

7. Good's Passivity Model

Some students receive low expectations so consistently that they appear to internalize these expectations. Studies of expectations have increasingly emphasized how students internalize teachers' expectations, and models have been developed for exploring mediation effects (e.g., Cooper 1985). Good's (1981) passivity model suggested that certain forms of teacher treatment induce passivity in low-achieving students. Over time, differences in the ways teachers treat low achievers (e.g., in the third grade a student is praised or finds teacher acceptance for virtually any verbalization, but in the fourth grade the same student is seldom praised and is criticized frequently) may reduce the efforts of lows and contribute to a passive learning style. Other teacher behaviors may compound this problem. Low-achieving students who are called on frequently one year but infrequently the following year may find it confusing to adjust to different role definitions. Ironically, those students who have the least capacity to adapt may be asked to make the most adjustments as they move from classroom to classroom.

Greater variation among teachers in their interaction with low achievers may occur because teachers agree less about how to respond to students who do not learn readily. Teachers may treat lows inconsistently over the course of the school year as they try one approach after another in an attempt to find something that works.

When teachers provide fewer chances for lower achievers to participate in public discussion, wait less time for them to respond when they are called on (even though these students may need more time to think and form an answer), or criticize lows more per incorrect answer and praise them less per correct answer, the implications are similar. It seems that a good strategy for students who face such conditions would be not to volunteer or not to respond when called on. Students are discouraged from taking risks under such an instructional system (Good 1981). To the extent that students are motivated to reduce risk and ambiguity—and many argue that students are strongly motivated to do so (Doyle 1983)—students would likely become more passive in order to reduce the risk of critical teacher feedback.

Good et al. (1987) found that low achievers were just as likely to ask questions as other students in kindergarten classes, but that lows asked significantly fewer questions than their classmates in upper-elementary and secondary classes. Similarly, in a study involving grades two, four, and six, Newman and Goldin (1990) found that among sixth-graders, the lowest achievers had both the greatest perceived need for help and the greatest resistance to asking for help. Students' ambivalence about asking questions or getting help from teachers becomes especially acute during adolescence, when they are both more concerned about how they are perceived by peers and more sensitive to the costs as well as the benefits of seeking help.

8. *Variation in Teachers' Expectations Over Time*

Relatively little research has focused on students' classroom experiences over consecutive years, and no study examined students' reactions to differential teacher expectations over consecutive years prior to the work of Midgley et al. (1989). Midgley et al. conducted a longitudinal study in the United States of 1,329 elementary and junior high students, examining their self- and task-related beliefs in mathematics as a function of teachers' efficacy beliefs. They found that students who moved from high- to low-efficacy mathematics teachers during the transition from elementary to junior high school ended the junior high year with the lowest expectancies in perceived performance (even lower than students who had low-efficacy teachers both years) and the highest perceptions of task difficulty. Furthermore, the differences in pre- and post-transitional teachers' views of their efficacy had more of an effect on low-achieving than on high-achieving students' beliefs about mathematics.

9. *Increasing Expectations*

There is growing evidence that when (a) low achievers are allowed to enroll in more challenging courses or (b) course content is altered to include more challenging material that is traditionally not available to low-performing students, student performance improves. The decision to allow students to engage in more challenging academic work (e.g., move to a higher reading group) is potentially a powerful strategy for increasing teacher and student performance expectations.

Mason et al. (1992) described a study in which 34 average-achieving eighth-grade mathematics students in an urban junior high were assigned to prealgebra classes rather than placed in traditional general mathematics classes. Results showed that students placed in prealgebra classes benefited from advanced placement in comparison to average-achieving eighth-graders from the previous year who took general mathematics (the cohort comparison group). Specifically, prealgebra students outperformed the comparison cohort group on a concepts subtest while maintaining equivalent performance on the problem-solving and computation subtests of the Comprehensive Assessment Program Achievement Series Test. Particularly important was that prealgebra students, in comparison with the cohort of general mathematics students, subsequently enrolled in more advanced mathematics classes during high school and obtained higher grades in these classes. Moreover, the presence of average achievers in prealgebra classes did not lower the performance of higher-achieving students in these classes.

Mason et al. qualified their findings. For example, the school in which the study took place was implementing a comprehensive school-improvement plan (higher expectations, active mathematics teaching). Hence, it was impossible to determine what instructional, curriculum, or peer effects were most influential in improving student performance. Further, the authors were aware of potential selection and history effects that can occur in a cross-sectional cohort design. Other investigators, however, have obtained similar results. Peterson (1989) found that remedial students who were placed in a prealgebra program for accelerated students achieved significantly higher results on all three mathematics subtests of the California Test of Basic Skills than did comparable students who were assigned to remedial and general mathematics classes. Such results strongly argue the need for educators to assess carefully the standards they use for assigning students to courses, since current standards may limit unnecessarily many students' access to mathematical knowledge, and potentially their access to future careers and advanced study.

Efforts to change low expectations for student performance can go beyond altering the practices of one teacher or a few teachers to include an entire school. For example, Weinstein et al. (1991) reported positive findings from a comprehensive intervention program designed to raise expectations for student achievement. This quasi-experimental field study involved collaboration between university researchers and teachers and administrators at an urban high school. The cooperating teachers attended university classes that focused on ways in which teachers can inadvertently maintain low expectations, and on the special motivational problems of low-achieving students. Teachers and researchers collaborated to develop a program for preventing and remediating low expectations.

The eight areas of the intervention program are: (a) task and curriculum (minimize tasks that heighten ability comparisons, give low achievers frequent opportunities to work on higher-order thinking and application of knowledge); (b) grouping (minimize ability grouping, make use of heterogeneous grouping and cooperative learning activities); (c) evaluation (emphasize qualitative evaluation, provide private feedback that stresses continuous progress achieved through a combination of ability and effort); (d) motivational climate (minimize competition, stress intrinsic rewards in addition to extrinsic rewards); (e) student role in learning (provide opportunities for students to make choices and to assume increasing responsibility for managing their own learning); (f) class relationships (develop a sense of community among the students that includes valuing diversity); (g) parent–teacher communication (emphasize students' positive attributes and progress rather than their deficiencies or problems); and (h) school-level supports (with cooperation from school administrators, establish increased and varied opportunities for low achievers to participate in school activities and get recognition for their achievements in and out of the classroom). The research procedures and organizational issues associated with this complex and innovative intervention cannot be presented here. However, both a rich description of the project (Weinstein et al. 1991) and an extensive analysis of the program (Weinstein 1991) are available.

The program has had some notable positive effects. For example, teachers were able to implement procedures designed to increase communication of positive expectations to low achievers. Project teachers' expectations for students, as well as their attitudes toward their colleagues, became more positive. Project teachers also expanded their roles and worked to change school tracking practices. Positive changes were also evident for the 158 project students. In contrast to 154 comparison students, project students had improved grades, fewer disciplinary referrals, and increased retention in school one year later. Weinstein et al. (1991) noted, however, that progress was not uniform. Students' absences rose and their improved academic performance was not maintained over the 9-month period of the study. According to the researchers, the limited length and breadth of the intervention and evaluation (students' performance was evaluated only in English and history), although sufficient to retain students, may have been insufficient to affect students' attendance and performance. Moreover, some teachers left the project because of excessive time requirements and lack of administrative support.

10. Directions for Research

Expectations research can be expanded in many ways to enhance understanding of classroom teaching and learning. Two of the most promising research areas are teachers' decisions about content assignments and teachers' knowledge of subject matter.

10.1 Selection of Curriculum Content

Many educators have contended that textbooks define the curriculum, although some research challenges this simplistic view and suggests that teachers act as decision-makers, modifying the curriculum in relation to factors such as teachers' beliefs about students' aptitude, their instructional intentions, and their subject-matter knowledge. If teachers influence the curriculum, then their decisions about curriculum partially determine performance expectations for students, just as teacher behaviors and activity structures do.

According to Freeman and Porter (1989), teachers make many decisions that influence how much content students receive. For example, teachers decide how much time to spend on mathematics on a certain day, what topics should be taught, how much time should be allocated for each topic, whether all students are taught the same topics, and in what order topics should be presented. The time spent on instruction and the focus of instruction (e.g., concepts, skills, applications) seem prime ways in which expectations might be communicated. Subsequent research could profitably attempt to integrate teachers' decisions about how much and what type of content to present with teachers' expectations for students (e.g., how students are likely to learn).

10.2 Teachers' Subject-matter Knowledge

Teachers' subject-matter knowledge is likely an important factor affecting the performance expectations they communicate to students. Because some teachers know more about some subjects or concepts than others, teachers' beliefs about subject matter and how to present it to students would probably affect whether or not they set appropriate performance expectations for students. Carlsen (1991) documented the effects of four novice biology teachers' subject-matter knowledge on discourse in their classrooms as they taught eight science lessons. The findings imply that choice of instructional activity affects students' participation in classroom discussion. Teachers used lectures and laboratory activities, which are characterized by high rates of student questioning, with topics about which they were knowledgeable. They tended to use classroom activities that involved few student questions when they were unfamiliar with the subject matter.

Carlsen's results are especially intriguing in that they illustrate that, because all teachers, and especially novice teachers, have inadequate knowledge in some areas, teachers must develop strategies for teaching content that they are still learning themselves. These strategies might include using sources additional to the textbook, bringing in guest teachers who are more knowledgeable, telling students that this is an area about which they are still learning, and presenting to students the questions that the teachers are using to structure the unit (and their own learning).

Research that examines teachers' performance expectations for individual students along with teachers' subject-matter knowledge would be profitable. When teachers instruct students in topics about which teachers have little knowledge, they may exaggerate differential treatment (i.e., avoid unpredictable questions by low achievers; overly depend on students believed to be more capable). Furthermore, the accountability systems and task structures that teachers select may be a function of their subject-matter knowledge.

11. Conclusion

Research on teacher expectancies in the classroom was a rich and exciting area in the 1970s and 1980s and many useful constructs have been derived from this work. Although the importance of teacher expectation effects have sometimes been overstated, it is clear that they are important, especially when considered with other teaching abilities and other general variables (e.g., home–school correspondence). In the 1980s there has been growing interest in the active role that students play in interpreting, internalizing, or rejecting expectations that are conveyed through teacher behavior or classroom structures. In the 1990s and beyond researchers need to study teacher expectancies and student mediation simultaneously. Such work will be enriched if researchers are also willing to explore how curriculum content and teachers' and students' knowledge of content mediate both the communication and interpretation of performance expectations.

See also: Teaching and Learning, Demonstration Methods of; Teaching, Synthesizing Research on

References

Baron R, Tom D, Cooper H 1985 Social class, race and teacher expectations. In: Dusek J (ed.) 1985 *Teacher Expectancies*. Erlbaum, Hillsdale, New Jersey

Brattesani K, Weinstein R, Marshall H 1984 Student perceptions of differential teacher treatment as moderators of teacher expectation effects. *J. Educ. Psychol.* 76(2): 236–47

Brophy J 1983 Research on the self-fulfilling prophecy and teacher expectations. *J. Educ. Psychol.* 75: 631–61

Brophy J, Good T 1970 The Brophy–Good System (dyadic teacher-child interaction). In: Simon A, Boyer E (eds.) 1970 *Mirrors for Behavior: An Anthology of Observation Instruments Continued, 1970 Supplement*, Vols. A and B. Research for Better Schools, Inc., Philadelphia, Pennsylvania

Carlsen W 1991 Subject-matter knowledge and science teaching: A pragmatic perspective. In: Brophy J (ed.) 1991 *Advances in Research on Teaching*, Vol. 2. JAI Press, Greenwich, Connecticut

Cooper H 1985 Models of teacher expectation communication. In: Dusek J (ed.) 1985 *Teacher Expectancies*. Erlbaum, Hillsdale, New Jersey

Cooper H, Good T 1983 *Pygmalion Grows Up: Studies in the Expectation Communication Process*. Longman, New York

Doyle W 1983 Academic work. *Rev. Educ. Res.* 53(2): 159–200

Freeman D, Porter A 1989 Do textbooks dictate the content of mathematics instruction in elementary schools? *Am. Educ. Res. J.* 26(3): 403–21

Good T 1981 Teacher expectations and student perceptions: A decade of research. *Educ. Leadership* 38(5): 415–23

Good T, Brophy J 1977 *Educational Psychology: A Realistic Approach*. Holt, New York

Good T, Brophy J 1990 *Looking in Classrooms*, 5th edn. Harper and Collins, New York

Good T, Slavings R, Harel K, Emerson H 1987 Student passivity: A study of student question-asking in K-12 classrooms. *Sociol. Educ.* 60(4): 181–99

Jones E 1990 *Interpersonal Perception*. Freeman, New York

Jussim L 1989 Teacher expectations: Self-fulfilling prophecies, perceptual biases, and accuracy. *J. Pers. Soc. Psychol.* 57(3): 469–80

Jussim L 1990a Expectancies and social issues: Introduction. *J. Soc. Issues* 46(2): 1–8

Jussim L 1990b Social reality and social problems: The role of expectancies. *J. Soc. Issues* 46(2): 9–34

Mason D, Schroeter D, Combs R, Washington K 1992 Assigning average-achieving eighth graders to advance mathematics classes in an urban junior high. *Elem. Sch. J.* 92(5): 587–99

Midgley C, Feldlaufer H, Eccles J 1989 Change in teacher efficacy and students' self- and task-related beliefs in mathematics during the transition to junior high school. *J. Educ. Psychol.* 81(2): 247–58

Newman R, Goldin L 1990 Children's reluctance to seek help with school work. *J. Educ. Psychol.* 82: 92–100

Oyserman D, Markus H 1990 Possible selves in balance: Implications for delinquency. *J. Soc. Issues* 46(2) 141–58

Peterson J 1989 Remediation is no remedy. *Educ. Leadership* 46(6): 24–25

Rosenthal R, Jacobson L 1968 *Pygmalion in the Classroom: Teacher Expectation and Pupil's Intellectual Development*. Holt, Rinehart, and Winston, New York

Rosenthal R, Rubin D 1978 Interpersonal expectancy effects: The first 345 studies. *The Behavioral and Brain Sciences* 1(3): 377–86

Vygotsky L 1978 *Mind in Society: The Development of Higher Psychological Processes*. Harvard University Press, Cambridge, Massachusetts

Weinstein R 1991 Caught between paradigms: Obstacle or opportunity—a comment on the commentaries. *American Journal of Community Psychology* 19(3): 395–404

Weinstein R, Marshall H, Sharp L, Botkin M 1987 Pygmalion and the student: Age and classroom differences in children's awareness of teacher expectations. *Child Dev.* 58(4): 1079–93

Weinstein R et al. 1991 Expectations and high school change: Teacher–researcher collaboration to prevent school failure. *American Journal of Community Psychology* 19(3): 333–64

T. L. Good

Teachers' Guide

1. Role of Teachers' Guides

Teachers' guides are written specifically for teachers. They differ from syllabuses and textbooks inasmuch as they are support documents directed to the teaching act. Advisory in nature, they generally suggest rather than prescribe as they seek to help the teacher solve practical problems encountered in transmitting subject matter to learners.

Teachers' guides are developed in relationship to changes in subject areas. Commercially a new edition of a textbook provides a new teachers' guide to assist the user in maximizing the benefits of the new product. In the textbook trade, teaching guides are viewed as necessary support materials for textbooks by publishers if they are to be competitive in the public school marketplace. Where teaching is engaging the student in direct experience, and a teacher is central to setting up the experience, guides are very detailed, as can be seen in the extensive teacher's guides prepared for early childhood teachers (New York City Schools 1984). As the instructional practices assume a greater emphasis on verbal learning the character and nature of the guides change to provide more advice on managing the interaction of the learners and subject matter.

Historically teachers have been coached in the act of teaching and many trade secrets have been passed from teacher to teacher as evidenced in the ancient Egyptian saying carved in a pyramid: "A scholar's ear is on his back; beat him and he listens." Motivating learners and getting them to attend to and master a subject have always been critical ingredients in guides for teachers, and as the art and science of instruction have developed the length and emphases of teachers' guides reflect these changes. Thus when guides are examined in historical periods they will reflect the dominant trends in learning theory and development, especially where the process of teaching the subject becomes an integral part of the product of learning. If memorization is synonymous with learning, mnemonic devices are featured in the advice of guides. When instruction in science moved from the memorization of labels and names, to hands-on experience, the teacher's guide promoted the changes through suggested aids to teachers on setting up science centers and conducting field trips to observe and collect specimens in natural settings (Baker et al. 1990). The increased understanding of the process–product relationship in teaching has brought an increased interest in the teaching act and its significance for influencing learner outcomes (Shulman 1986). The gains in achievement are thought by some to be as closely allied to the teaching process of the content as to the content itself (McEwan and Bull 1991).

Many theoretical issues remain unresolved about whether there is a pedagogic content knowledge that is distinct from the subject matter. Some instructional theorists believe the limited capabilities of the more immature and inexperienced learner place demands on the teacher for expertise in pedagogic content knowledge if subject matter is to be efficiently taught and mastered. However, the epistemological problem embedded in the pedagogic content knowledge argument is not given major attention in the practical world of the teachers' guide, where concern for the immediate demands of classroom management hold sway. The teacher who faces a classroom of students wants an answer to a more direct programmatic issue: what keeps students interested and promotes their learning of the syllabus content for which the teacher is held accountable in the prescribed curriculum? A teaching guide that advises and assists a teacher in answering this question commands a ready audience. Where a specific instructional strategy is advocated as being focal to the learning outcome, (e.g., cooperative goal structuring [Johnson 1984]), the testing of the teachers' guide in the classroom and its ability to produce learner-verified results have been recommended by one consumer advocate organization as promoting integrity in claims for outcomes in instructional materials (Komoski 1987). Teachers' guides have undergone major changes as they respond to new fashions and evidence in instructional research. Consequently they are more highly developed and specialized than at any other period in the history of instruction.

2. Content

Teachers' guides are curriculum instruments and their contents are primarily concerned with the provisioning of curriculum in the five dimensions of curriculum components: (a) a framework of assumptions about the learner and the society; (b) aims and objectives of instruction; (c) content or subject matter with its selection, that is, scope (amount and type of content to be covered) and sequence (the order and hierarchy of content relationships); (d) modes of transaction (i.e., teaching strategies and the setting of learning environments); and (e) evaluation and testing. Not all guides give attention to these five components. An examination of guides found that most attention was given to provisioning of transaction modes, particularly recommended teaching strategies. The more specific a commitment to an institutional approach, the more detailed and prescriptive the guide. An example of a guide with a particular instructional bias in competency-based education (CBE) states:

> Competency-based education is a flexible, systematic approach to instruction where students work toward clearly outlined learning objectives. The seven essential elements of competency-based education are:
>
> 1. Program competencies are defined, and they are verified through on-the-job practitioners, program graduates, employers, and advisory committees.

2. Program competencies are assigned to courses. Competency areas within the specific course are identified.
3. Course syllabi containing specific competency statements are given to students. These competency statements clearly state what the student is to learn, as well as how the student will be tested and under what conditions.
4. Learning objectives and activities that teach each of the competencies stated are then designed.
5. Criterion referenced teacher-made tests are constructed and administered to determine the level of student knowledge and/or performance. Criterion reference tests simply test, under the conditions previously specified, the competencies stated in the course syllabus.
6. Remediation and/or acceleration/enrichment is provided for students. CBE requires that students attain an acceptable level of performance. But it also can provide a variable time frame in order to attain that level.
7. The program content and the method of delivery are assessed. They should be reevaluated regularly to determine the effectiveness of instruction. (Seitz 1986).

The guide then outlines each area of instruction objectives consistent with these elements and specific program outcomes. This is a much more prescriptive stance than is found in the customary guide for teachers in higher education and is directed to meeting the needs of community college students who are completing two-year courses of study as occupational preparation.

Teachers' guides advise teachers on alternative representations to make content more accessible to students. Where the content is related more to direct experience, guides suggest the organization of learning environments for more direct experiential learning. In theory the guides focus on either development of subject matter learnings or growth of subject matter in individual minds. In the latter construction there is no separation between subject matter content and subject matter as a manifestation of individual experience. Where the guide emphasizes the subject content the construction is focused more on prescribing assignments, testing, and reteaching than establishing an open-ended learning environment.

3. Typology

A typology of teachers' guides is possible if a classification employing the functional purpose for creation of the guides is used. Because of their practical emphases guides are generic to a certain level and, as subject specialization defines the curriculum, to a certain subject. They give attention to three major components of a teaching situation: (a) teaching strategies and the instructional act, (b) the learner and his/her needs or entering behavior, and (c) the teaching setting and resources. The heaviest emphasis is given to teaching strategies and the instructional act by all levels of guides, with the exception of those which deal with very young learners. An important genre of guides which have been developed more recently are guides for college teaching. College teaching has been more oriented to verbal learning and a heavy reliance on teacher lectures. Nevertheless, many colleges and universities have felt impelled to give attention to the improvement of teaching through the production of teaching guides. These guides, while heavy on instructional design and teaching methodology, do deal with other facets of college teaching and the role of a faculty member. Table 1 presents four guides from large universities which were analyzed on seven components. These guides all give major attention to the practical aspects of classroom teaching in a university: organizing a presentation, making assignments, presenting a lesson, testing, and evaluating.

Over time and with revision they tend to expand their domains of concern to include the role of a faculty member, obligations to a department and a university, potential problems of student misbehavior, and faculty–student relationships. They have also extended their suggestions for alternative approaches to instruction and reducing the excessive reliance on the lecture; however, they have been slow to incorporate instructional research with adult learners into their suggestions (Elshout-Mohr et al. 1988). In their admonishment of the graduate teaching assistant they construe the teaching act as a branch of pedagogic knowledge separate from the subject content and acting on this debatable assumption set forth a guide with one set of teaching tips presumably generalizable across all academic disciplines.

Guides can be classified along the lines of their approach to the teaching act and their advice to help the teacher fulfill the roles. An 1880 teachers' guide for high-school history contained mainly hints on improving the recitation of a lesson to increase the mastery of the historical narrative. This could best be done through the utilization of the principle of association: relating facts to ideas, geography to history, major events to minor events in chronological order, and use of frequent review for linkage of all facts and ideas (Stone 1880). A 1990s social studies guide presents in several hundred pages a management system "to help the teacher make the most of limited preparation time." In contrast to the 1880 edition's three pages of hints to aid the teaching of history, there are unit organizers which present in detail a content outline, teaching schedule, tie-ins (relating the content), worksheets for students, workbook pages, and further activity ideas. The management system lists some 60 skills classified within a scope and sequence chart, under headings of graph skills, thinking skills, research skills, and so on that are taught and cites where the content provides opportunity for skills emphasis. In their competitive search for preserving the teacher's limited prep-

Table 1
University Teacher Guides

	Arizona 1988	Georgia 1987	Stanford 1985	Wisconsin 1985
Teaching environment and tips	X	X	X	X
Evaluation and testing	X	X	X	X
Teaching resources	X	X	X	X
Academic honesty, cheating and plagiarism		X	X	X
Student characteristics		X	X	X
Departmental and university obligations		X	X	X
Evaluating one's own teaching	X	X	X	X

aration time, bulletin board posters are even provided. These management systems give attention to newer instructional findings through their inclusion of criterion-referenced tests, mapping of concepts, and newer conceptualizations of subject areas and their purpose in the curriculum. Because the subject matter has expanded and demands on students and teachers have increased over the past 30 years, the teacher guides that have been produced since 1960 have expanded and developed the management system to assist the teacher in meeting the increased demands.

Teachers have long been dependent upon textbooks as their principle instructional tools. In turn, textbooks, whatever their weaknesses, have provided for commonality in curriculum in a nation's schools. The new teachers' guides have become part of a more complete instructional package, one that a teacher can use without excessive time commitment to the development of resources beyond the text. The designs of these instructional packages within subject areas show a high degree of similarity, primarily because textbook producers tend to stay within a limited range of innovation (i.e., they avoid extreme positions on content or instructional design). Consequently, textbooks published over the same period of time will, upon inspection of the instructional design and its components, closely resemble one another. Major changes have occurred in teachers' guides, but competition among major textbook series orchestrates these changes and brings them in as a whole over a short period of time. The differences among textbook packages are marginal and much as the stylistic differences are separate from the mechanical commonalities of mass-produced cars, the management systems bring similar assistance, advice, and imposed requirements to the classroom teacher.

4. *Differences Among Teachers' Guides*

4.1 Across Subjects

An examination of teachers' guides across the subjects of English, social studies, science, and mathematics finds their designs to be similar, with only minor variations in the provisioning. The differences are lodged essentially in the nature of the subject matter, for example, the sciences use laboratory lessons for hands-on activities, while English classes do not have an exact parallel.

Nevertheless, in the instructional design advice for these areas, similar principles are followed. Whether it be writing a composition or dissecting a crustacean, teachers will need to specify objectives for the class, observe some time parameters in selecting among these objectives, relate the specific lesson to a larger body of instruction, and evaluate student learnings. Provisioning of the components of instructional design has followed advances in instructional research, though very slowly. Thus teachers' guides that accompany instructional packages will respect the school organization and schedule, if they wish to be successfully marketed.

The most profound difference among guides can be seen when contrasting those designed to teach reading with other subject guides. Teaching guides for elementary reading are, in terms of design, the most highly developed of all teachers' guides. Their complexity in development can be traced by contrasting a teaching guide of the 1950s with one of the 1990s. The 1950s teachers' guide lists seven principles which were used in constructing the text of the teachers' guide and utilizes a standardized outline for each story to assist the teacher. In the guide the teacher is provided with (a) a summary of the story to be read; (b) suggestions for preparing the student for reading the selected story; (c) questions for soliciting student interpretation of the story; and (d) questions and activities for evaluating student word analysis, word meaning skills, and various ideational qualities of the story. By contrast the 1990s teachers' guide lists 36 principles. The teacher is provided with a chart of the 26 instructional components and 112 reading skills which are contained in these components. In the instructional components the teacher operates a management system that details the group's instruction in a specific lesson (providing questions to be asked), individual student tutorial aids, an array of tests (for placement, diagnosis, and level of achievement), and a series of form letters to be used in communicating with parents. The teacher, in short, manages a delivery system of prepackaged instruction. The teachers' guide to this instructional system is several hundred pages long and one is provided for each grade, one through eight. A microcomputer management system is available. In 40 years the design of the teachers' guide has moved the reading teachers' role to one of implementing a packaged program of materials and doing little in the way of designing a reading program. Other subject fields are moving toward these prepackaged courses, but none has advanced as far as elementary reading.

4.2 Across Learner Levels

Teachers' guides as a genre give attention to sensitizing the user to the learners, whether they be preschoolers or young adults in college. As the population being taught has shown greater diversity in backgrounds and learning styles, teachers' guides have given more attention to describing the learner's characteristics which have a bearing on the instruction. This may involve describing the characteristics of learning specific to an age level; for example, children at age 5 are eager to learn about their immediate environment. Similarly, teachers' guides are giving more attention to the needs of people with handicaps and how these needs can be met in a regular classroom. Managing the classroom environment therefore becomes as salient as managing subject content, and Teacher's guides have more recently given attention to a broader definition of teaching that moves beyond the teacher's direct verbal interaction with students, though this seems to be the most persistent of teacher behaviors. The thrust of the guides as the grade level advances is to move from attention to the learners and their special characteristics to greater attention to how to communicate the subject matter more efficiently.

4.3 Across Teacher Specialization Levels

Differences across specializations of teachers reflect the differences in subject matter; that is, sciences have more concern about laboratory safety than social science. However, in instructional design teacher's guides show many similarities. A 1990 mathematics guide has the following design components: overview of objectives, scope and sequence, planning chart, management guide which lists objectives and lesson assignments, test items, supplementary materials, and student activities. In addition the teacher is supplied a sheet for recording student progress by objective, a record book for test results, and forms for reporting student progress to parents. These design components would have equal applicability to other content areas. Some specializations will provide greater detail on provisioning and some of the most detailed guides are in vocational education where competency-based education holds sway (Seitz 1986).

5. Factors Influencing Guide Use and Effectiveness

Teachers' guides are expensive to produce as they aspire to assist teachers through instructional packages, upgrade content, and incorporate newer instructional research into classroom teaching. Guides in all subject areas are being written more to generally accepted conventions such as behaviorally oriented objectives and use of criterion-reference testing to foster greater mastery of skills. As subject content becomes more demanding of students' abilities and receives an earlier introduction into the curriculum, the teachers' guide as the chief support for teachers becomes more crucial. However, the conventions of instruction as understood by the professional preparing the guide and the act of instruction of the classroom teacher may not mesh (Harris 1983). The life of the classroom does not mirror the technology of instructional design. Student abilities, motivations, and teacher intentions are not captured by the prepackaged instructional design. This incongruence may explain why, despite rigorous development and close attention to instructional theory, teachers' guides may be ignored by classroom teachers (Evans 1989). For the classroom teacher the key to instruction is not logic but experience. If instructional packages, augmented with the sagest of teachers' guides, do not intersect with this experience, they are likely to be cast aside as unwieldy and unworkable. Work with teachers on evaluating instructional materials showed that instruction suffered because teachers did not apprehend the instructional design built into their materials (Harris 1983). In many cases the teachers had not studied the design in sufficient depth to understand its complexity. In others they needed further instruction on subject content (Dawson 1987). In these cases they felt overburdened with the record keeping and confused by the multiplicity of the components.

Students spend most of their classroom time—estimated to be as much as 90 percent—working with instructional materials (Eash 1974). Teachers' guides that are designed to be supportive in enhancing the teacher's efforts to work more effectively with students take on new significance. Prominent though they are in the educational landscape, their role in influencing educational achievement is largely unstudied.

See also: Schools for Laboratory and Professional Development; Teaching: Behavioral Theories; Teaching: Heuristic Models; Teaching, Cognitive Developmental Theories of; Teaching: Implicit Theories; Teaching: Informational Processing Theories

References

Alberta Department of Education 1990 *Social Studies 16: Teachers Resource Manual* Alberta Department of Education, Edmonton (ERIC Document ED 217447)

Baker C D et al. 1990 *Guidelines for Setting Up an Extended Field Trip to Florida and the Florida Keys*. ERIC Document ED 327394, National Institute of Education, Educational Resources Information Center, Washington, DC
Dawson G G 1987 *Ideas for Teaching Economics in Grades Five and Six* New York State Council on Economic Education, Albany, New York (ERIC Document ED 308120)
Eash M 1974 Instructional materials. In: Walberg H J (ed.) 1974 *Evaluating Educational Performance*. McCutchan, Berkeley, California, pp 125–52
Elshout-Mohr M, Van Daalen-Kapteiins M, Spranges M 1988 The topic-comment technique to study expository text. *J. Exp. Educ.* 56(2): 83–90
Evans R H 1989 *Profiling Elementary Science Teacher's Manuals from Different Perspectives*. ERIC Document ED 306088, National Institute of Education, Educational Resources Information Center, Washington, DC.
Harris I B 1983 Forms of discourse and their possibilities for guiding practice: towards an effective rhetoric. *J. Curric. St.* 15(1): 27–42
Jonson R, Johnson D (eds.) 1984 Teaching Guidebook: *Introduction To Some Basics* Interaction Books, Minneapolis, Minnesota
Komoski P K 1987 *Educational Technology: The Closing-in or the Opening-out of Curriculum and Instruction*. ERIC Document ED 295676, National Institute of Education, Educational Resources Information Center, Washington, DC
Manual for Teaching Assistants 1985 College of Letters and Science, University of Wisconsin, Madison, Wisconsin (ERIC Document ED 285494)
McEwan H, Bull B 1991 The pedagogic nature of subject matter knowledge. *Am. Educ. Res. J.* 28(2): 316–34
New York City Board of Education *Now We Are Six: A Guide to Teaching First Grade*. Division of Curriculum and Instruction, New York Board of Education, Brooklyn, New York, (ERIC Document ED 277484)
Schulman, L 1986 Paradigms and research programs in the study of teaching: a contemporary perspective. In: Wittrock M C (ed.) 1986 *Handbook of Research on Teaching* (3rd ed.) MacMillan, New York
Seitz F 1986 *The Right Angle for Learning*. Beauford Technical College, Center for Staff and Curriculum Development, Beauford, South Carolina (ERIC Document ED 277444)
Stone A P 1880 Hints on the method of teaching history. In: Goodrich C A *History of the United States of America*. Merrill, New York

Further Reading

Bertoletti M C, Dahlet P 1984 Manuels et matériels scolaires pour l'apprentissage du FLE ebauehe d'une grille d'analyse. *Francais-dans-le-monde* 186(6): 55–63
Blake V M, Dinham S M 1988 *Teaching Guidebook: An Introduction to Some Basics*. Arizona University Teaching Center, Tucson, Arizona (ERIC Document 301106)
Chilucos P E 1987 *Perspectives: Readings on Contemporary American Government. Teachers Guide*. Close-up Foundation, Arlington, Virginia (ERIC Document ED 308119)
Fisher M (ed.) 1985 *Teaching at Stanford: An Introductory Handbook*. Center for Teaching and Learning, Stanford University, Stanford, California (ERIC Document ED 281415)
National Council for the Social Studies, Science and Society Committee 1990 *Guidelines for the Twenty-first Century*. CIJ National Council for the Social Studies, Washington, DC
Olsen J K 1983 Guide writing as advice giving: Learning the classroom language. *J. Curric. St.* 15(1): 17–25
Ryan M P, Mertens G B 1989 *Planning a College Course: a Guidebook for the Graduate Teaching Assistant*. National Center for Research to Improve Postsecondary Teaching and Learning, Ann Arbor, Michigan (ERIC Document ED 314998)
Simpson R et al. 1987 *Handbook for Graduate Teaching Assistants* University of Georgia, Athens, Georgia (ERIC Document ED 289426)
1987 *Teaching Tips for TAs: A Sourcebook of Suggestions and Guidelines for Teaching Assistants* University of California, Los Angeles, California (ERIC Document ED(289439)

M. J. Eash

Teachers' Knowledge

While researchers have long been interested in issues related to teachers' knowledge, research in this area has proliferated in the decade from 1983 through 1992. As research on teaching moved from investigations of teacher behavior to considerations of the thinking and decision-making that accompany action, questions concerning the knowledge and beliefs that inform teachers' decision-making quickly arose. Issues related to what teachers know, how they acquire and store that knowledge, and how knowledge informs classroom practice are central to the work of all concerned with the initial preparation and continuing professional development of teachers.

The renewed interest in teachers' knowledge also parallels the movement within several countries to transform teaching into a recognized profession. Evidence of a specialized knowledge base necessary for the work of professionals is one hallmark of a profession. The interest in teacher knowledge since the early 1980s is motivated by practical, political, and academic concerns. Teachers' knowledge has been examined in terms of its domains, its forms or structures, and its relation to classroom practice. This entry will address these areas separately, although many of the issues are interrelated.

1. Domains of Teacher Knowledge

A number of researchers have proposed frameworks for domains of teacher knowledge (Carter 1990, Leinhardt and Smith 1985, Wilson et al. 1987). Although represented as discrete domains in these frameworks, the knowledge domains are usually regarded as interwoven in practice. One possible typology of teacher knowledge includes six domains: (a) knowledge of content, (b) knowledge of learners and learning, (c) knowledge of general pedagogy, (d) knowledge of curriculum, (e) knowledge of context, and (f) knowledge of self.

Content knowledge includes both subject matter

knowledge and more explicitly pedagogical knowledge of the subject matter, termed "pedagogical content knowledge." Knowledge of learners and learning includes knowledge of learning theories; the physical, social, psychological, and cognitive development of students; motivational theory and practice; and ethnic, socioeconomic, and gender diversity among students. Knowledge of general pedagogy includes knowledge of classroom organization and management, and general methods of teaching. Curricular knowledge includes knowledge both of the processes of curriculum development and of the school curriculum within and across grade levels.

Knowledge of context includes knowledge of the multiple and embedded situations and settings within which teachers work, including the school, district, or area, and state or region. Knowledge of context also includes teachers' knowledge of their students and their families, as well as the local community. It can also include knowledge of the historical, philosophical, and cultural foundations of education within a particular country. Finally, knowledge of self includes teachers' knowledge of their personal values, dispositions, strengths, and weaknesses, and their educational philosophy, goals for students, and purposes for teaching.

While all of these domains are important to the work of teachers, research has concentrated on content knowledge, general pedagogical knowledge, and knowledge of self. For example, while much research within educational psychology has focused on topics related to learners and learning, relatively few studies have looked directly at what teachers know or believe in this area. For this reason, this entry will include discussions of the three domains in which the most research exists.

1.1 Knowledge of Content

While subject matter knowledge seems intuitively important for good teaching, early correlational research did not find a relationship between teachers' knowledge and student achievement. Later researchers critiqued the lack of conceptual frameworks to guide this early work and turned their attention to the relationships between teachers' subject matter knowledge and the processes of planning and instruction (Leinhardt and Smith 1985, Shulman 1987). This line of predominantly qualitative research suggests that teachers' knowledge of the content they teach affects both what teachers teach and how they teach it.

In developing curriculum for students, teachers are likely to emphasize those areas in which they are more knowledgeable and to avoid or de-emphasize the areas in which they have relatively less content knowledge (Carlsen 1991, Smith and Neale 1991). Teachers' content knowledge may also influence how they exploit the curriculum potential of a subject (Ben-Peretz 1975, Gudmundsdottir 1990, Wilson and Wineburg 1988). For example, studies of secondary-school social studies teachers have demonstrated how teachers' own disciplinary backgrounds affect how they adapt a given curriculum to match their own disciplinary knowledge (Wilson and Wineburg 1988).

Teachers' content knowledge also influences their interactive teaching. Teachers' knowledge of subject matter affects how they represent the nature of knowing within a content area to their students. Ball (1991), for example, demonstrated that teachers with relatively weak conceptual understanding of mathematics are likely to represent the nature of mathematical knowing as arbitrary and rule bound. Teachers' content knowledge also influences their ability to construct new explanations or activities for students (Leinhardt and Smith 1985, Smith and Neale 1991), as well as the kinds of questions they ask students (Carlsen 1991, Hashweh 1987). For example, in a study of beginning science teachers, Carlsen (1991) found that teachers were more likely to ask cognitively lower level questions in areas in which they were less knowledgeable and higher level questions in those areas where they felt themselves to be knowledgeable.

Studies of teachers' subject matter knowledge also revealed that teachers possess pedagogical knowledge of the content they teach, termed "pedagogical content knowledge" (Shulman 1987). Research on pedagogical content knowledge has examined teachers' beliefs and conceptions regarding purposes for teaching subject matter, their knowledge of students' understandings and misunderstandings of particular topics within a subject matter, and their curricular and instructional knowledge related to specific content. Research in this area suggests that teachers' pedagogical content knowledge is related to teachers' planning and to classroom instruction. Most researchers found a great deal of congruence between teachers' own conceptions of the purposes for teaching a subject and their instructional practice, especially in the case of experienced teachers. Work in mathematics also suggests a tentative link between teachers' pedagogical content knowledge and student learning (Peterson et al. 1991).

1.2 Knowledge of General Pedagogy

Knowledge of general pedagogy includes knowledge about classroom organization and management, general knowledge of lesson structure, and general methods of teaching. Researchers in the area of classroom knowledge have focused on teachers' efforts to establish and maintain order in the classroom during the process of instruction. Successful classroom managers are teachers who are more attuned to student signals and conscious of the overall flow and purpose of classroom activity (Carter 1990). In addition, effective teachers swiftly establish routines for classroom activities at the beginning of the school year (Leinhardt et al. 1987).

Related to work on teachers' routines is teachers' general knowledge of lesson structure, which includes the knowledge necessary to plan and teach lessons, to make smooth transitions between different components of a lesson, and to present clear explanations of content (Leinhardt and Smith 1985). While this kind of knowledge has been designated as general, it is possible that knowledge of lesson structure is implicitly tied to the content to be taught.

Finally, work on expertise in teaching suggests that experienced teachers process information about classrooms differently than do novices (Berliner 1986). For example, when shown slides of classroom activities, the experienced teachers were more likely to identify patterns and to make inferences about the activities they observed than were novices, who provided more literal and superficial descriptions of the activities.

Much of this work has focused more on what teachers do in classrooms and how they process information than what they know explicitly or implicitly about classroom organization and management. Some researchers have explored the relationship between classroom management and teachers' implicit metaphors regarding the role of the teacher. These researchers argue that changes in teachers' classroom management must begin with reconsiderations of these underlying metaphors.

Relatively little work has investigated teachers' knowledge of various instructional strategies or methods of teaching. One line of correlational research on teaching has attempted to isolate general teaching strategies used by effective teachers (Brophy and Good 1986). While this research has produced a set of generalizations about the correlations between particular teaching behaviors and student achievement, it did not investigate what teachers knew or believed that led them to adopt such strategies. Studies of teacher planning suggest that teachers organize their planning around the development of classroom activities (Clark and Peterson 1986), but little research has investigated how teachers think specifically about issues of method in teaching.

Some researchers have argued that teachers' knowledge of teaching methods is organized into curriculum scripts for particular topics (Putnam 1987); both the content and method of teaching are included in these scripts. The European tradition of *Didaktik* also emphasizes the integration of curriculum and method in teacher thinking (Hopmann 1992). Knowledge of teaching method may be filtered through teachers' understanding of the particular content to be taught and their own goals for teaching that content, suggesting an overlap between pedagogical content knowledge and this aspect of general pedagogical knowledge.

1.3 Knowledge of Self

In an early study of teacher knowledge, Elbaz (1983) identified knowledge of self as an important facet of teachers' practical knowledge. This knowledge of self includes teachers' awareness of their own values, goals, philosophies, styles, personal characteristics, strengths, and weaknesses as they relate to teaching. Some researchers have described how teachers draw upon and use this personal knowledge to negotiate classroom dilemmas and to reflect upon their practice (Lampert 1985). Others have documented how issues of self and identity are implicated in the process of learning to teach (Britzman 1986) and how teachers' personal values underlie other forms of knowledge such as pedagogical content knowledge (Gudmundsdottir 1990). Work on teachers' metaphors also stresses the importance of teachers' implicit beliefs in understanding how teachers view their own practice (Munby 1986).

Knowledge of self differs in important ways from the knowledge domains discussed above as it represents neither theoretical nor abstract knowledge, but a more personal and inevitably idiosyncratic domain. Work on many domains of teacher knowledge suggests that abstract or theoretical knowledge about teaching is filtered through teachers' own values, goals, and personal philosophies, leading some researchers to argue that all aspects of teacher knowledge are grounded in personal perspectives and experience (Clandinin and Connelly 1987). This line of research suggests the importance of individual biography in the process of teaching and learning to teach.

1.4 Integration of Knowledge Domains and the Creation of New Knowledge

While each knowledge domain has been addressed separately for analytic purposes, in actual use by teachers, these domains are not as clearly distinguishable. For example, lesson structure knowledge, categorized under general pedagogical knowledge, intersects with pedagogical content knowledge in determining particular content to be taught. Curricular knowledge, pedagogical content knowledge, and general pedagogical knowledge all play a role in creating curriculum scripts for particular topics. The need for teachers to draw from and integrate a number of knowledge domains under conditions of uncertainty has important implications for teacher learning. Teaching these knowledge domains in isolation from one another may misrepresent the interconnected quality of knowledge use, posing difficulties for teachers who must integrate these various domains in practice.

Work on teacher knowledge also reveals its dynamic nature. Teachers' knowledge is not static. In the process of teaching and reflecting upon teaching, teachers develop new understandings of the content, of learners, and of themselves. While teachers can acquire knowledge from a wide variety of sources, they also create new knowledge within the crucible of the classroom. Because teaching has lacked a method for capturing and recording such knowledge, both researchers and practitioners have turned their attention to documenting the wisdom of practice of experienced teachers.

2. Forms of Teacher Knowledge and Relation to Classroom Practice

Researchers have argued about the various forms of teachers' knowledge; some researchers argue for the need for generalizable knowledge of principles of teaching and learning, while others contend that teachers' knowledge is inherently situational and personal, stored in the tacit forms of metaphors or images or the more explicit forms of stories or cases. In describing different potential forms for teachers' knowledge, this section uses Bruner's (1986) distinction between paradigmatic and narrative ways of knowing to describe at least two general forms of teacher knowledge.

Paradigmatic ways of knowing emphasize generalizable laws and principles applicable across a wide variety of contexts. Knowledge within the natural sciences has been described as paradigmatic knowledge. In contrast, narrative ways of knowing are more contextualized and situation-specific. Research on teaching has experienced a shift from the search for paradigmatic knowledge to an interest in narrative knowledge, a shift that has affected research on teacher knowledge.

2.1 Paradigmatic Forms of Knowledge

Some researchers on teaching have argued that teachers need to possess scientific principles regarding teaching, knowledge that has proved to be applicable across different contexts and settings (Gage 1978). These researchers stress the power of propositional knowledge about teaching and learning. Such principles might consist of propositions regarding the importance of "wait-time" for encouraging higher-order thinking, for example. These principles could be derived from large-scale research programs on effective teaching (e.g., Brophy and Good 1986) and taught directly to teachers.

Some researchers in this area have argued that research knowledge can directly affect practice by providing teachers with new principles or rules of practice to use in their own teaching. A number of experimental studies have attempted to teach experienced teachers such generalizable principles derived from correlational classroom research. While many of the studies were successful in the short run, there is little evidence that teachers continued to implement these principles of teaching over time.

Alternative ways in which paradigmatic knowledge can inform practice have also been suggested. Some researchers have argued that results of research on teaching can inform teachers' reasoning about classroom actions rather than dictate teachers' instructional practice (Fenstermacher 1986). Knowledge gained from research can influence classroom practice by influencing teachers' beliefs or by introducing new knowledge and beliefs into teachers' reasoning. Theoretical knowledge thus becomes one, but not the sole, source of knowledge that can guide teachers' curricular and instructional decision-making. A number of studies of knowledge use suggest that teachers sift generalizable principles through the filter of their own perspectives and situations; thus, this approach to using research knowledge may show promise for understanding the relationship between propositional knowledge and classroom practice.

2.2 Narrative Forms of Knowledge

Another line of work rejects the idea of generalizable knowledge and argues that teachers' knowledge is inherently personal and organized in terms of stories or narratives (Clandinin and Connelly 1987, Elbaz 1991). These researchers believe that teachers' knowledge can be best understood through their own stories of teaching, which preserve both the teachers' voice and perspective. Researchers in the area of personal practical knowledge argue that much of teachers' knowledge is inherently tacit, contained within the rituals, routines, and cycles that comprise teachers' work, and embedded within particular local contexts.

From this perspective, knowledge is embodied within classroom practice; distinctions between knowledge and classroom practice are not clear-cut. Others acknowledge a distinction between knowledge and practice, but argue that practice informs knowledge as much as knowledge influences practice. Studies of personal practical knowledge are not intended to inform as much as to illuminate classroom practice from teachers' perspectives. While narratives of personal practical knowledge offer a way of making sense of individual teachers' practice, readers can learn from these narratives through reflecting upon similar issues that arise in their own practice.

Another form of narrative knowledge might take the form of case knowledge, knowledge composed of experiences with a number of cases of particular pedagogical situations (Shulman 1991). Like personal practical knowledge, case knowledge is inherently situational and contextual. Researchers who study knowledge acquisition in ill-structured domains such as medicine or teaching believe that knowledge in these areas is organized into networks of concepts and cases. More general concepts are embedded within specific instances from actual practice. Practitioners within these ill-structured domains must integrate multiple knowledge domains in constantly shifting circumstances. From their experiences in classrooms, teachers construct a contextual understanding of classroom situations that allows them to recognize familiar features of new situations. The process of reasoning from case knowledge, then, is likely to be analogical.

Like personal practical knowledge, case knowledge has usually been represented in narrative form. However, most of these case narratives have explicitly pedagogical purposes. Advocates of case-based methods in teacher education stress the usefulness of cases in learning to teach. Cases can inform practice by offering precedents for handling particular pedagogical situations. The use of case methods can also develop pedagogical ways of reasoning, according to advocates. Most researchers in this area stress the importance of using multiple cases of a similar phenomenon to illustrate more accurately the complexity of practice.

3. The Future of Research on Teacher Knowledge

Research on teacher knowledge has clear implications for teacher education and continuing professional development. What teachers need to know and how they can best construct this knowledge are central questions facing policymakers and teacher educators alike. Considerations of the content, form, and sources of teacher knowledge are likely to become increasingly important as efforts to reform teacher education and to create a teaching profession gain momentum.

Future research will need to investigate further all of the domains of teacher knowledge, including the areas of curricular knowledge, knowledge of learners and learning, and knowledge of educational contexts. While work has been done in each of these areas, questions regarding issues such as what teachers know about motivating students, for example, remain unanswered. Documenting teachers' existing knowledge in all of the domains is essential, as teachers' prior knowledge and belief are likely to influence their future acquisition of knowledge.

Future research will also need to study the connections among teacher knowledge, school context, and student learning. Much of the research on teachers' subject matter knowledge, for example, has investigated the relationship between teachers' knowledge of the content and the processes of planning and instruction, but, with a few exceptions, has stopped short of looking for connections to student learning. As research provides increasingly sophisticated approaches to the assessment of student learning, the connection between teachers' and students' understandings may be studied more effectively.

Finally, research on teacher knowledge must continue to be informed by ongoing explorations into the nature of knowledge and cognition. Work in cognitive psychology and anthropology has demonstrated the contextual nature of cognition, a finding that has direct implications for investigations of teacher knowledge. Work on knowledge acquisition in ill-structured domains also holds implications for research on teacher knowledge. Theorists from both critical and feminist theory pose epistemological issues with which future research must grapple. Finally, work on the narrative aspects of cognition is likely to continue to inform research on teacher knowledge.

See also: Teacher Education, Case Methods in; Teachers' Beliefs and Belief Systems; Research in Education: Nature, Needs, and Priorities

References

Ball D L 1991 Research on teaching mathematics: Making subject matter knowledge part of the equation. In: Brophy J. (ed.) 1991

Ben-Peretz M 1975 The concept of curriculum potential. *Curric. Theo.* 5: 151–59

Berliner D C 1986 In pursuit of the expert pedagogue. *Educ. Researcher* 15(7): 5–13

Britzman D P 1986 Cultural myths in the making of a teacher: Biography and social structure in teacher education. *Harv. Educ. Rev.* 56(4): 442–56

Brophy J E, Good T L 1986 Teacher behavior and student achievement. In: Wittrock M (ed.) 1986 *Handbook of Research on Teaching*, 3rd edn. Macmillan, New York

Bruner J 1986 *Actual Minds, Possible Worlds.* Harvard University Press, Cambridge, Massachusetts

Carlsen W S 1991 Subject matter knowledge and science teaching: A pragmatic perspective. In: Brophy J (ed.) 1991

Carter K 1990 Teachers' knowledge and learning to teach. In: Houston W R (ed.) 1990 *Handbook of Research on Teacher Education.* Macmillan, New York

Clandinin D J, Connelly M F 1987 Teachers' personal knowledge: What counts as personal in studies of the personal. *J. Curric. St.* 19(6): 487–500

Clark C M, Peterson P L 1986 Teachers' thought processes. In: Wittrock M (ed.) 1986 *Handbook of Research on Teaching*, 3rd edn. Macmillan, New York

Elbaz F 1983 *Teacher Thinking: A Study of Practical Knowledge.* Croom Helm, London

Elbaz F 1991 Research on teachers' knowledge: The evolution of a discourse. *J. Curric. St.* 23(1): 1–19

Fenstermacher G D 1986 Philosophy of research on teaching: Three aspects. In: Wittrock M (ed.) 1986 *Handbook of Research on Teaching,* 3rd edn. Macmillan, New York

Gage N L 1978 *The Scientific Basis of the Art of Teaching.* Teachers College Press, New York

Gudmundsdottir S 1990 Values in pedagogical content knowledge. *J. Teach. Educ.* 41(3): 44–52

Hashweh M Z 1987 Effects of subject matter knowledge in the teaching of biology and physics. *Teach. Teach. Educ.* 3(2): 109–20

Hopmann S 1992 Starting a dialogue: Roots and issues of the beginning conversation between European didaktik and the American curriculum tradition. Paper presented at the annual meeting of the American Educational Research Association, San Francisco, California

Lampert M 1985 How do teachers manage to teach? Per-

spectives on problems in practice. *Harv. Educ. Rev.* 55(2): 178–94
Leinhardt G, Smith D A 1985 Expertise in mathematics instruction: Subject matter knowledge. *J. Educ. Psychol.* 77(3): 247–71
Leinhardt G, Weidman C, Hammond K M 1987 Introduction and integration of classroom routines by expert teachers. *Curric. Inq.* 17(2): 135–76
Munby H 1986 Metaphor in the thinking of teachers: An exploratory study. *J. Curric. St.* 18(2): 197–209
Peterson P L, Fennema E, Carpenter T P 1991 Teachers' knowledge of students' mathematics problem-solving knowledge. In: Brophy J (ed.) 1991
Putnam R T 1987 Structuring and adjusting content for students: A study of live and simulated tutoring of addition. *Am. Educ. Res. J.* 24(1): 13–48
Shulman L S 1987 Knowledge and teaching: Foundations of the new reform. *Harv. Educ. Rev.* 57(1): 1–22
Shulman L S 1991 Toward a pedagogy of cases. In: Shulman J (ed.) 1991 *Case Methods in Teacher Education*. Teachers College Press, New York
Smith D C, Neale D C 1991 The construction of subject-matter knowledge in primary science teaching. In: Brophy J. (ed.) 1991
Wilson S M, Shulman L S, Richert A E 1987 150 different ways of knowing: Representations of knowledge in teaching. In: Calderhead J (ed.) 1987 *Exploring Teachers' Thinking*. Cassell Education, London
Wilson S M, Wineburg S S 1988 Peering at history through different lenses: The role of disciplinary perspectives in teaching history. *Teach. Coll. Rec.* 89(4): 525–39

Further Reading

Britzman D P 1991 *Practice Makes Practice: A Critical Study of Learning to Teach*. SUNY Press, Albany, New York
Brophy J (ed.) 1991 *Advances in Research on Teaching, Volume 2: Teachers' Knowledge of Subject Matter as it Relates to their Teaching Practice*. JAI Press, Greenwich, Connecticut
Calderhead J (ed.) 1991 *Teachers' Professional Learning*. Falmer Press, London
Grossman P L 1990 *The Making of a Teacher: Teacher Knowledge and Teacher Education*. Teachers College Press, New York
Shulman J (ed.) 1991 *Case Methods in Teacher Education*. Teachers College Press, New York

P. L. Grossman

Teachers, Professional Socialization of

The term "professional socialization of teachers" refers to the process of change by which individuals become members of the teaching profession and then take on progressively more mature roles, usually of higher status, within the profession. It is clear from this description that the particular characteristics of this process depend on the nature and structure of the teaching profession. Hence, the radical changes that affected the education systems of many countries in the 1980s will be seen to have had a clear effect on the professional socialization of teachers.

The term does not refer to a single period of transformation from student to teacher. Rather, it is a progressive, continuous process with options and choices and sometimes with recognizably different career channels. Nevertheless, there are important similarities in this process which make the study of professional socialization of teachers a rewarding field for researchers. Furthermore, the field is also of great interest to an audience of administrators and teachers whose consciousness of international issues and comparisons is constantly on the increase.

This entry is organized into four major sections: definition, descriptions of research models, research findings, and recent educational changes and international comparisons. The account is enriched by weaving in a number of the themes which illustrate conflicts of ideology and purpose. These themes permeate the subject matter of each section, and relate to contemporary social issues and likely future crises. For example, the question arises as to whether teachers should be more like functionaries of the state, namely bureaucrats who merely carry out the designs and purposes of those who control the state, or whether, as professionals, they should be predominantly educators and visionaries in their own right, whose common purpose is guided and modified by their personal philosophy and individual appraisal of the priorities of education for an increasingly uncertain future. This dilemma underlies many of the contemporary conflicts and disputes within education. The different directions in which this contest is moving has produced contrasting outcomes in many countries, both developed and developing.

1. The Definition of Professional Socialization

In an early classical study of medical students, Merton et al. (1957) produced an important definition of socialization: "The process by which people selectively acquire the values and attitudes, the interests, skills and knowledge—in short the culture—current in groups to which they are, or seek to become a member" (p. 287). The process of professional socialization into teaching therefore amounts to far more than just learning to teach. By including values, attitudes, and interests, Merton indicates that becoming a teacher involves more than the simple acquisition of academic knowledge and the skills necessary to conduct lessons.

Despite the undoubted strength and usefulness of Merton's definition, it falls short of modern practice in a number of respects. There is a strong suggestion in the definition that teaching is a single culture, an agreement about the basic values and practices within the profession; in technical terms, a "central value system." Researchers who have adhered to this view have usually also adopted a "functionalist" model of society and their research can often be described as central tendency analysis.

The major weakness of this viewpoint is that it glosses over the variations and disagreements that almost inevitably arise in any profession, but are particularly marked in teaching. Merton's definition refers to selective acquisition of values, but does not give the process much emphasis. Nor does the definition give prominence to the interactive, conflictual, and situational elements in this process of acquisition and practice. All of these elements have been stressed in later studies of the professional socialization of teachers and therefore need to be examined carefully. In fact, substantial and fundamental conflicts do exist; individuals are active in choosing and selecting from this variety of values and practices; and these individuals are often careful about to whom and in what situation they reveal their views and practices.

2. Early Research Models in the Study of Professional Socialization

As mentioned above, early studies of professional socialization were almost entirely based on functionalist models of society and used relatively crude central tendency methods of analysis. The basic assumptions underlying functionalist views of society are best expressed in the analogy of society as an organism. Parts of society are seen as functioning parts of the whole, carrying out essential tasks in harmony with the main purpose of society. In practical terms, adherence to this model implies that experienced and responsible members of society or members of the profession can recognize "good practice" or "good teachers." This assumption of a widely held and recognizable consensus lay at the root of a research tradition established in the 1950s and 1960s which "arose from a practical interest in finding better methods for selecting persons who would make 'good' teachers and in improving the training and assessment of students and practitioners" (Morrison and McIntyre 1969 p. 13).

This research tradition failed because of its theoretical and methodological weakness. It embodied a philosophy of education and a view of professional socialization that was subjected to increasing critical scrutiny in the 1970s. In addition, it failed in a practical sense to predict the best new teachers and improve the quality of training (Morrison and McIntyre 1969).

Nevertheless, this research tradition is always capable of resuscitation and rebirth. Since the 1980s governments have shown a growing tendency to intervene in reshaping education systems. They have also funded and shaped research into education to supply answers to their major concerns, which may be categorized broadly as making teachers more "efficient" and education more relevant to the needs of industry and production. These pressures have had the effect of regenerating functionalist approaches to research.

The transition from student to professional person has often been characterized as dramatic and abrupt. In Western societies the obvious change in dress from casual or eccentric student styles to the neat relatively formal dress required in schools is easily recognized and often regarded as signifying a more profound transformation of the person to accepting more socially conservative values and practices. Early studies of teacher socialization stressed the relative lack of power of initiates to the profession and gave prominence to the differences between the idealistic and radical opinions of students and the realistic and practical orientations they developed as they became teachers. Teaching appeared to produce an even more dramatic transformation than most professions because the conservative influence of senior colleagues was coupled with the chastening experience of unruly classes for those who failed to adopt authoritarian classroom discipline. Functionalist theories coupled with predominantly central tendency questionnaire designs conspired to legitimate and substantiate these findings.

3. Developments in Adult Socialization

Two publications in the early 1960s paved the way for substantial advances in the study of adult socialization. Becker et al. (1961) undertook a detailed participant observation study of medical students. Earlier socialization research had usually been based on questionnaire studies, designed to allow comparisons to be made over time or with some expected outcome. Becker et al. were more concerned with detailed observation of social processes and identifying a set of concepts that accurately portrayed their understanding of a complex process. They established a tradition of research within the study of professional socialization and a set of usefully applied concepts (e.g., culture, latent culture, perspective, and commitment) that could be used in the study of the professional socialization of teachers.

Wrong's (1961) contribution was very different. His seminal essay points to the oversocialized conceptualization of "man" (sic). He portrayed culture as a violation of human nature and as a consequence described socialization as an imperfect or partial process in which essential elements of individuals can, through choice, stay outside. His conceptualization represents an important modification of early functional theories of socialization in which individuals are assumed to conform or fail because of inability or deviance.

These two contributions represented an important stimulus to later research and although Becker et al. still emphasized the power of the socializing institution (through the concept of situational adjustment, in which individuals transform themselves "into the kind of person the situation demands"), the basis for a deeper, more complex understanding of professional socialization had been established.

4. Modern Research Tradition and its Findings

The modern research tradition in professional socialization can be characterized as bringing together a wider range of research methodologies and a richer framework of concepts and theory, including less determinant notions of culture. It has also broadened the scope of relevant factors to be included in major studies. Earlier studies focused on:

(a) the quality of the training or learning experience;

(b) the stresses experienced in the classroom as students or young teachers struggle with the problems of classroom control, pupil learning difficulties, and a heavy workload;

(c) the influence of important "others" (e.g., tutors, fellow students or teachers, head teachers).

The modern tradition has included these factors, often obtaining deeper insights into these processes and their significance through the use of participant observation as well as questionnaire and interview techniques. This tradition has also given greater emphasis to other factors that have enabled new theoretical insights and concepts to be developed. For example:

(a) the process of selection by which students choose training courses or schools in which to start their careers;

(b) the importance of personal agendas, relating to individuals' purposes in teaching, their ideas about career and their values as well as the contribution that individuals make to building institutions and cultures;

(c) the external influences of government or markets that shape the institutions in which teachers teach, and enlarge or constrict their choices in the various areas of teaching.

4.1 Modification of Early Models of Professional Socialization of Teachers

As noted above, the functionalist social theory and questionnaire methodologies established a picture of teacher socialization as a reversion to the conservative practices of the classroom that new teachers experienced as pupils and that they reexperienced as relatively powerless neophyte teachers. This analysis depended on seeing teaching as a relatively monolithic culture heavily constrained by agreements on what constituted "good practice" and classroom situations that were able to deliver substantial punishment to new teachers who failed to conform: the "reality shock."

During the 1960s and 1970s changes took place within education that made these assumptions less valid. Educational provision expanded in almost all industrial and developing countries. Large numbers of pupils experienced levels of education unknown to their parents' generation. Educators searched for new pedagogies and new subject matter to cater to the new cohorts of pupils, and education entered a phase of flux and experimentation.

Some studies failed to take serious account of these changes. Shipman (1967) felt able to explain student "progressivism" as "impressional management" that withered away as soon as the college situation no longer existed and the reality of the staffroom and classroom became relevant. Similarly, Hanson and Herrington (1976) summarized their conclusions from their study of probationary teachers as follows: ". . . the only way apparently open to the probationers was to conform to the conventional wisdom and recipe knowledge of those around them, and this was largely an accumulation of the indigenous traditions and folkways of (the) staffroom" (p. 61).

The modern tradition has not totally negated these findings nor shown that they do not exist. Rather, it has demonstrated their partial nature and their exclusion of many competing processes. The modern picture of professional socialization emerges from the literature as being closer to a struggle in which individuals confront institutions and make their purposes felt. While this struggle often occurs on an individual basis, it can also arise from group action. The results of these studies reveal the complexity of the interactive process in which individuals may change while at the same time maintaining some stable and unchanging element in their practice and purpose. The studies also demonstrate a link between adult socialization and social change through microchanges produced within institutions.

4.2 Process of Selection and Anticipatory Socialization

Professions are frequently differentiated on the basis of status. Prestigious training institutions are able to attract high-flying individuals from social elites who will go on to obtain prominent positions within their professions and therefore ensure the reputation and high standing of the training institution with the next generation of aspirants. Where competition for entry is fierce this hierarchy of institutions, usually backed by real advantages in career and income, can have a marked socializing effect. It is necessary for individuals to prepare themselves quite carefully to become the kind of person that the professional norms demand. This process of preparation, often termed "anticipatory socialization," is most marked in the older, better paid professions. It is less marked in teaching and it is important to understand the reasons for this.

In all modern societies teaching is a large, relatively open profession. It is difficult for it to become or remain socially exclusive. Most children obtain detailed insights into teaching by attending school. It is therefore the obvious profession for aspiring working class or low caste children to enter. Thus, teaching acts as a channel for social mobility in many societies. It is also a profession with a "caring" as well as a "technical" role. Teaching has traditionally attracted a high proportion of women. While it is possible to demonstrate that in most countries women are discriminated against in terms of promotion and senior posts, it is often the case that teaching represents a relatively good career for women. The reverse is the case for men, where the availability of careers in the older, usually more lucrative, professions of medicine, law, and engineering means that teaching represents only one among many alternative careers. While this pattern is changing slowly, particularly in the rich industrialized countries, it remains a general phenomenon.

Teaching is a divided profession in other respects. It is differentiated according to subject discipline, the qualifications and training that the professionals bring to the classroom, the status of the schools in which they teach, the professional associations and unions that represent the profession, and disagreements over the aims, purposes, and philosophy of education. Some of these divisions are particularly important for the process of professional socialization.

Disputes over the aims and purposes of education have always existed. Education prepares young people for entry into society. As differences of opinion have emerged about the nature of society, so their effect has been felt in education and the training of teachers. One recurring dispute concerns a difference of opinion about the very nature of knowledge. Is knowledge easily defined within subject boundaries, authoratively laid down within the curriculum, and properly passed on as a series of skills and facts? Or is knowledge less easily defined, subject to individual interpretation, and best "discovered" by the learner who is assisted by the teacher? In the United Kingdom in the 1960s and 1970s, these and other similar questions gave rise to recognizably different approaches to the training of teachers. Some university courses became recognizably innovative; others remained relatively traditional. In turn these differences were registered by students, who were able to choose a course that suited their philosophy.

In a study of five university departments of education in the United Kingdom, Lacey et al. (1973) were able to demonstrate this process at work. The five courses in the study had been selected along a traditional–innovatory course dimension derived from course descriptions. The reasons for students choosing their courses were examined and coded according to whether they took the educational content or organization of the courses into account.

The results suggested that students clearly used their knowledge of the way in which the courses were taught to obtain the kind of socializing experience they desired. As a consequence, they influenced the student membership in each course and hence attended a course in the company of students who were more like themselves than would have been the case on other courses. This aspect of student choice is often neglected in studies of socialization.

4.3 Social Strategies

The use of participant observation and intensive interviewing within studies of professionalization gave rise to a wealth of data, much of which could not be explained by existing theories or described using existing concepts. In particular, the complex behavior of individuals observed in seminars or classrooms often could not be reconciled with the descriptive statistics derived from questionnaires. In addition, case studies of individuals showed that action in one situation apparently contradicted action in another. It was not until the individual's purpose in and definition of the situation were taken into account that the actions were capable of interpretation.

The concept of social strategy, developed by Blumer (1969) within interactionist theory, was adopted by a large number of researchers (Lacey 1977, Woods 1977, Hargreaves 1977, 1980). This concept suggests that individuals are purposeful beings, choosing between different courses of action which offer (apparent) solutions to the problems they face. Lacey (1977) developed the concept of situational adjustment into three broad strategies that incorporate the innovatory aspect of human action as well as the conforming aspects stressed by functionalists. They are: (a) internalized adjustment, (b) strategic compliance, and (c) strategic redefinition.

In the internalized adjustment strategy, the individual complies with the constraints and believes that the constraints of the situation are for the best.

Strategic compliance is the strategy where the individual complies with the authority figure's definition of the situation and the constraints on his or her action but retains private reservations about them. This latter strategy is exemplified by the student teacher who, in a written response, explained,

> Although I disagreed with my teacher-tutor, the only way to cope was to concur with her when she was present i.e., discipline of children, approach to timetable, artwork, and importance of art and the story in the curriculum. (Lacey 1977 p. 93)

Strategic redefinition is a strategy in which the individual engages in innovating within situations and, in some measure, actually changes the situation.

Strategic redefinition strategies were pursued by individuals who did not possess the formal power to change situations but who nevertheless did succeed in changing them. They achieved this in most cases by causing or enabling those with formal power (tutors or head teachers) to change their interpretation of what was appropriate in any given situation.

Cooper (1990) and Zeichner and Tabachnick (1985) explored the strategies employed by student teachers and new teachers in pursuit of innovatory teaching techniques during practice teaching and early employment. Detailed case studies of a small number of teachers were made. The results suggested that individuals were able to pursue innovatory teaching methods despite substantial difficulty in doing so. Cooper found that when trying to implement investigations within mathematics teaching the main problem was the student teachers' own inexperience with a new and complex methodology. Zeichner and Tabachnick found that, within the closed system of the classroom, teachers had substantial freedoms and were able to maintain subsystems that conflicted with the expectations of the main school.

5. *Educational Change and International Comparisons*

Since the mid-1970s the economic expansion that followed the Second World War has been interrupted by a series of recessions. The optimistic support of educational expansion, accompanied by measures designed to produce greater equality of opportunity, has given way to criticism. Education has sometimes been made the scapegoat for economic failure. Throughout the world, education has been put under pressure to serve the economic needs of society rather than the educational needs of children. While such pressure has been similar in both rich and poor countries, the outcomes have been surprisingly different.

The education systems of the poor, predominantly agricultural countries, have been characterized by very few resources, including a lack of adequately trained teachers who are restricted to didactic, recitative methods of teaching. Teachers' freedom is often strictly circumscribed by bureaucracy, with little autonomy accorded them in shaping the curriculum. Teachers are usually at the bottom of a formidable hierarchy of political and administrative control and have little choice where and whom they teach. This system has been shown to alienate both teachers and pupils and is largely held responsible for the low levels of literacy and educational achievement in many poor countries.

After the World Conference on Education for All was held in Jomtien, Thailand in 1990, a new consensus emerged. The emphasis was now placed heavily on primary education and a drive for literacy and basic numeracy in poor rural and urban areas was instigated. Changes in educational policy, supported by donor organizations, have produced changes in teacher training and professional socialization. In India and Indonesia, for example, large-scale state-wide projects have been set up to provide inservice training for teachers. This training introduces child-centered techniques, group work, discussion, working with materials, and similar activities. The professional socialization of teachers has moved toward the model of teaching developed in the Western industrialized countries in the 1960s and 1970s and could represent a radical change if it proves to be successful.

In contrast, the critique of education in industrialized countries has occasionally centered on the very teaching methods being adopted in these new projects. The United Kingdom government has been most radical in this respect and has attempted to introduce market mechanisms as a source of competition and control. Schools are expected to publish examination results (including results of new tests introduced by the government), the curriculum has been centralized, and the proportion of the nation's resources allocated to schools reduced. The effects on the professional socialization of teachers will be most marked as teachers and schools compete in a market for pupils and resources. The change from a bureaucratic–professional milieu in which educational and social issues were highlighted to a market–competitive milieu in which a premium is placed on examination results and pupil numbers represents one of the most radical experiments ever undertaken in education. It will have important, and as yet unknown, effects on the patterns of teacher socialization. Now that the mechanisms and processes of adult socialization are better understood, much material for discussion and dispute is set to emerge from this field of study in the 1990s.

References

Becker H S, Geer B, Hughes E 1961 *Boys in White: Student Culture in Medical School.* University of Chicago Press, Chicago, Illinois

Blumer H 1969 *Symbolic Interactionism: Perspective and Method.* Prentice-Hall, Englewood Cliffs, New Jersey

Cooper B 1990 PGCE students and investigational approaches in secondary maths. *Research Papers in Education* 5(2): 127–51

Hanson D, Herrington M 1976 *From College to Classroom: The Probationary Year.* Routledge and Kegan Paul, London

Hargreaves A 1977 Progressivism and pupil autonomy. *Sociol. Rev.* 25(3): 585–621

Hargreaves A 1980 Synthesis and the study of strategies: A project for the sociological imagination. In: Woods P (ed.) *Pupil Strategies.* Croom Helm, London

Lacey C 1977 *The Socialization of Teachers.* Methuen, London

Lacey C, Horton M, Hoad P 1973 *Tutorial Schools Research Project: Teacher Socialization, the Post Grad Training Year*, Social Science Research Council, London
Merton R K, Reader G G, Kendall P L (eds.) 1957 *The Student Physician: Introductory Studies in the Sociology of Medical Education*. Harvard University Press, Cambridge, Massachusetts
Morrison A, McIntyre D 1969 *Teachers and Teaching*. Penguin, Harmondsworth.
Shipman M D 1967 Theory and practice in the education of teachers. *Educ. Res.* 9(3): 208–12
Woods P E 1977 Teaching for survival. In: Woods P E, Hammersley M (eds.) 1977 *School Experience*. Croom Helm, London
Wrong D H 1961 The oversocialized conception of man in modern sociology. *Am. Sociol. Rev*. 26(2): 183–93
Zeichner K M, Tabachnick B R 1985 The development of teacher perspectives: Social strategies and institutional control in the socialization of beginning teachers. *Journal of Education for Teaching* 11(1): 1–25

C. Lacey

Teachers' Roles

The phrase "teacher role" appears in hundreds of studies. In addition, chapters on teacher role may be found in both theoretical and hortative works concerned with teaching, its contexts, and its effects. Unfortunately, use of this phrase is also vague, and several different concepts have been intended by authors who have written about teacher roles. Many who have used this phrase have seemed unaware that it has other uses than the one they intended; thus, the first task facing those reading about it is to distinguish among the major concepts to which the phrase has been applied. Three such concepts are distinguished in this entry. In addition, the use of the phrase "teacher role" declined during the 1980s, and alternative vocabularies have since been employed for teacher-role issues. As a consequence, this review stresses broad concerns rather than specific literature from the 1980s and 1990s that might also be interpreted as concerned with the roles of teachers.

1. Concepts of Teacher Role

Technical use of the social role concept appeared in the 1920s and reflected the influence of at least three seminal contributors: Ralph Linton, Jacob Moreno, and George Herbert Mead. These three men represented different disciplines in the social sciences and used the role concept somewhat differently. For simplicity, three separate concepts are distinguished here that may be designated by the phrase "teacher role" (see Biddle 1979).

1.1 Role as Behavior

Some authors use "teacher role" to refer to behaviors that are characteristic of teachers. Most who use "role" in this sense focus their interests on teacher behaviors in the work context (i.e., in the school or classroom). Nevertheless, teachers may also be found in nonwork contexts, and a few authors have discussed the role behaviors of teachers in their homes, the marketplace, or the political arena. Authors using "role" in this first sense presume that teacher behaviors are existential events that can be observed directly. Moreover, teacher roles may also be observed by other actors, hence are assumed to have the potential for affecting, and being affected by, the behaviors of pupils and other persons who interact with teachers.

1.2 Role as Social Position

Other authors use the phrase "teacher role" to refer to the identity or social position that is shared by teachers. In this usage the word "role" refers to the designating term ("teacher") and the set of persons who are designated by that occupational litle. This second usage focuses on static characteristics of teachers—on the recognition of teachers as a separate social position, the composition of the teacher population, the status of the teaching profession, or conditions for entry into or departure from the field. Authors who intend this second meaning often speak of teachers as "occupying" their roles.

1.3 Role as Expectation

A third group of authors use the phrase "teacher role" to refer to expectations that are held for teachers. Some of these expectations are held by teachers themselves, whereas others are held by parents, school administrators, pupils, politicians, and members of the public. Some expectations are normative in mode, but others may represent beliefs, preferences, or other modes of thought. Some may be widely shared, while others may reflect divergent opinions and generate role conflicts for the teacher. Authors who follow this third usage tend to view teachers (and those with whom they interact) as persons capable of rational, reflective thought. Expectations are thought to be learned through experience and, once they are formed, will affect the behaviors of those who hold them in predictable ways.

None of these three concepts for teacher role precludes the others. Each represents a facet of the complexities that embed the teacher, and each is capable of generating information for educators and other social scientists. Each has also generated research literature. Nevertheless, the fact that such different concepts have all been designated by the same phrase poses problems for investigators and consumers alike. One must read each source carefully to establish the concept a given author intended by the phrase "teacher role," and one must be prepared to discount confusion that has been generated because some authors forgot their conceptual definition or misunderstood those of others.

2. The Behavioral Role of the Teacher

The behavioral role of the teacher may be defined as those behaviors that are characteristically performed by teachers. Like persons in other occupations and professions, teachers respond in characteristic ways. Most are regularly found in classrooms during the working day, and most spend much of that day supervising the instruction of pupils. When not in classrooms, teachers are likely to be found in the hallways or offices of the school building, or in the lunchroom or teachers' lounge. During the evening, teachers are likely to be grading papers, preparing lessons, or attending school-related functions. This does not mean that all teachers behave identically, but to learn that a person teaches for a living means that he or she is more likely to do certain things and less likely to do others, and it is the former that constitute the teacher's behavioral role.

Teachers characteristically do a great many things, so studies of the role of the teacher are normally limited in some fashion. Sometimes that limitation is contextual. For example, an investigator may examine the teacher's role in the classroom, the school, or in some other context in which membership of the teacher's social position is recognized and relevant. Sometimes, also, a sectoral limitation may be placed on the definition, in which case the investigator examines that portion of the teacher's role directed toward members of another social position, such as pupils. (Other sectors of the role are directed toward the school's principal, other teachers, or members of the public.) In contrast, if authors choose to discuss the teacher's role in noneducational contexts, usually that discussion focuses on behaviors that are presumed to be unique to teachers, that is, are not exhibited by other comparable actors.

Sometimes, also, functional limitations may be placed on the definition of the teacher's behavioral role. Like other professionals, teachers may accomplish a variety of things, and authors may single out one or more of those things for discussion. For example, many teachers are called upon to disseminate information to pupils, to serve as pupil counselors, and to grade pupils' performances on a regular basis. Each of these tasks requires somewhat different activities on the part of teachers, and simultaneous performance of these different activity sets may be difficult for the teacher to manage. The difficulty with functional analysis of the teacher's role is that no definitive set of functions is prescribed for most teachers, and behaviors characteristic of teachers may contribute to more than one identifiable function. As a result, many different lists of functions have been suggested for the teacher's role, and behavioral evidence concerning these functional distinctions is hard to find.

The issue of evidence raises another question concerning the behavioral role of the teacher. What is the best way to study such roles? Since behaviors are observable events, then surely the best way of studying them is to observe them directly. Up until about 1960 it was difficult to find studies of behavioral roles that were based on observation, but this has since changed (see Dunkin and Biddle 1974 and many subsequent reviews). Literally thousands of studies have appeared in which the classroom behaviors of teachers and pupils were observed, and these provide a wealth of data concerning the role of participants in that context.

It is more difficult to observe teacher behaviors elsewhere in the school, however, and more difficult still to study teacher activities in nonschool contexts. As a result, studies still appear in which the teacher's behavioral role is examined by asking teachers or others to discuss those activities in interviews and questionnaire responses. Technically, the latter forms of data are measures of what respondents think about the teacher's role and are more validly interpreted as measures of their expectations for teachers. To interpret them as measures of teacher role behavior assumes a simple relationship between role expectations and role behaviors, an assumption that is questioned below. Nevertheless, indirect evidence is better than no evidence, and much of what researchers presume to know about the teacher's behavioral role today is based on it.

3. The Social Position of the Teacher

A social position relates to a set of persons who share some characteristic and who are given a recognized label within the society. Teachers are those persons who regularly instruct pupils, thus the social position of the teacher may be defined as membership of the set of persons who regularly instruct pupils and are given such designations as "teacher," "instructor," "master," and the like. Occasionally the concept of teacher is also extended to include persons who teach students in postsecondary education. However, the teaching of adults involves activities quite different from those involved in the teaching of nonadult pupils, and those who teach adults are normally recruited and trained for their occupations in quite different ways than are teachers. Consequently, most persons who write about the social position of the teacher confine their attention to those who teach at the primary and secondary levels.

Several confusions surround the social position concept. As mentioned, some authors use the term "role" to refer to social position, so one may find articles in which "teacher role" is used to designate those who teach rather than the activities of teaching or expectations for the latter. Other authors use the term "status" to refer to social position, which is also confusing because the word "status" has another meaning concerned with the ranking of social positions vis-à-vis one another. (The status-ranking of teachers is discussed below.) Finally, some authors define the social position concept as a "location" or "niche" in a division of labor. Such definitions are confusing because they presume that all social positions are occupations. Whereas "teacher" is a recognized occupation in industrialized societies, teachers are not always paid for their services elsewhere but may still be recognized, even honored, for their activities.

3.1 The Status of Teachers

A number of characteristics of social positions have been studied over the years. One of these is status, which concerns the ranking of social positions in terms of characteristics deemed desirable. As a rule, three criteria for status ranking have dominated the literature: prestige, wealth, and authority. Members of social positions have prestige when they are able to attract deferential behavior from others who are not members of their social position. They have wealth when they are given or are allowed to control commodities. They have authority when they can get others to follow their dictates.

It is widely assumed that prestige, wealth, and authority go together and that social positions which have one of these qualities in abundance will also have the others. Although this is true on average, there are some social positions that are high on one or two of these criteria but not the others (e.g., church dignitaries, Mafiosi). Studies of the status of social positions may either focus on status as a presumed unitary concept or may involve separate investigations of prestige, wealth, and authority.

3.2 The Prestige of Teachers

Relatively few studies of the prestige of teachers have yet appeared, but these tend to place teachers toward the lower end of middle-class occupations and at the bottom of those occupations deemed to be professions. Moreover, this status ranking tends to hold throughout industrialized countries. A number of reasons have been suggested for the relatively low prestige of teachers: prevalence of women in the teaching profession, lack of specificity in the role expected of teachers, the fact that teachers work primarily with the young, devaluation of the knowledge deemed necessary to teach well, the large numbers of persons employed or available for employment as teachers, and so forth.

Lortie (1975) views teachers as having a "special but shadowed" prestige position. On the one hand, teachers' work is seen as having the aura of a "special mission," but on the other, teachers have largely lost whatever autonomy they once had to manage pedagogical theory and their classrooms because they have become functionaries in hierarchical organizations. Whatever may be the reason, teachers clearly do not attract as much deference as do the other, more secure professions: medicine, the law, the ministry. At the same time, however, teachers receive more deference than do most blue-collar occupations.

3.3 The Wealth of Teachers

Like all occupations, teachers are paid for their services. Most teachers in the West are the employees of organizations that receive public funds, so their salaries are a matter of public record. Not surprisingly then, many studies of the wealth of teachers have appeared and continue to appear on a regular basis. These studies suggest that teachers tend to be paid at about the scale appropriate to their prestige position—above the scale paid to blue-collar workers but below the scale paid to most professionnals. In fact, the wages paid to many teachers are probably sufficient to support a single person but insufficient to support a family. Since many married women do not work, this fact presumably explains why many male teachers find it necessary to work at a second job to supplement their teaching incomes.

The economic systems of most Western countries are capitalistic, and the relative wages paid to teachers tend to rise during periods of teacher shortage. Thus probably the major reason why teachers are not paid better wages is that they have never formed cartels to prevent entry of "unqualified" persons into the profession—as is done widely in medicine. Teachers have begun to unionize, however, and teacher wages have sometimes been improved through collective bargaining and industrial action.

3.4 The Authority of Teachers

Studies of the authority of teachers are quite rare, but as a rule that authority is confined to pupils, the school, and curricular matters. Like the hospital, prison, or university, the school is a people-processing organization, and most school systems feature a bureaucratic hierarchy in which the teachers are the "workers." Given this lowly authority-position, teachers must take orders from most of the rest of the personnel: department heads, subject specialists, principals and their assistants, superintendents, and school board members. Teachers have traditionally been assigned considerable power in the classroom, but this has recently been eroded through laws that constrain teacher conduct, administrative control over the curriculum, and pupil violence.

Despite these erosions, the teacher retains an authority in the classroom that is generated through custom, law, the teacher's expert knowledge, and the teacher's control over grades and promotions for pupils. Teachers also have some authority over parental conduct in matters relating to education, although teacher/parent relationships vary considerably among countries. (Within some countries, such as the United Kingdom, parents are often discouraged from "interfering" with the school, whereas in others, such as the United States, they are usually urged to involve themselves in the education of their children.)

4. The Expected Role of the Teacher

The expected role of the teacher may be defined as the set of expectations that are held for teacher behaviors by both teachers and other persons. Like persons in other social positions, teachers are subjected to a number of expectations for their conduct that reflect law, custom, habit, desires, and theories concerning their activities. These expectations form a context in which teacher conduct is interpreted, and role expectations for the teacher are presumably a major motivator for teacher conduct. On the one hand, those who hold expectations for teacher behavior are presumed likely to pressure teachers to conform to those expectations; on the other, teachers presumably want to follow their own expectations.

The concept of expected role is deceptively simple and hides several issues that should be exposed. First, expectations may be expressed in several different forms. Some expectations are expressed verbally, some are written down in news accounts or codes of conduct, and some are presumably held as covert thoughts by participants. Most authors who write about expectations for the teacher have the last form in mind, but covert expectations cannot be perceived directly. One learns about them by listening to respondents talk about teacher conduct or by asking questions about the topic. Consequently, studies of the expected role of the teacher are normally conducted by means of interviews or standardized questionnaires.

Second, at least three different modes of expectation appear in the literature on teacher role. Some investigators study norms for teacher conduct—statements that express what teachers ought to do. Others study preferences, that is, likes and dislikes, for teacher conduct. Still others study beliefs—statements that express subjective probability for the appearance of teacher behavior. Many investigators confuse these three modes or assume that they are interchangeable, but an expression of what teachers ought to do may not be what is preferred or what is thought likely, and evidence has appeared indicating that these three modes of expectation are not interchangeable (Bank et al. 1977).

Third, expectations for teachers may either be held by persons themselves or may be attributed by those persons to other actors. To illustrate, teachers normally hold expectations for their own conduct and attribute expectations for it to the principal of their school. The principal also holds expectations, of course, and usually he or she also attributes expectations to the teachers. These four different types of expectations are sometimes confused by researchers, or researchers may assume that by measuring one of them a good estimate is also obtained of another. Such assumptions are questionable.

Fourth and last, some authors assume that expectations for teachers are largely shared within the school or society, and teachers or other actors in the school may make similar assumptions. Such assumptions are unwise. Whereas some expectations are surely shared for teacher conduct, others are not. Moreover, teachers may be made quite uncomfortable when they are faced with contradictory expectations that are held by two or more persons who have authority over them. Such situations produce what is termed "role conflict" and have been widely studied for teachers and other employees of organizations.

4.1 Shared Expectations for Teachers

Teachers are employed to instruct pupils because of shared values concerning the importance of education and beliefs concerning the efficacy of schools for fulfilling those valued outcomes. Not surprisingly then, various authors have presumed that agreement also appears on functions or tasks that teachers are expected to perform. Several lists of such functions have been proposed, many of them drawn from the insights of Waller (1932) and Parsons (1959). An example of such a list appeared in Kelsall and Kelsall (1969) who argued that teachers are (consensually) expected to emancipate pupils from their home environments, encourage achievement among pupils, sort out and socialize "winners" and "losers" in the achievement game, inculcate societal norms in pupils, teach technical skills, instill interpersonal sensitivity and discipline, and aid pupils in making decisions and training for occupations.

The Kelsalls' list focused on tasks associated with pupils. Other authors have stressed functions generated by structural properties of the school as an organization or values in the wider society. Thus, it is presumed that teachers are also expected to maintain order in their classrooms, accept and promote a common curriculum, follow the orders of supervisors, maintain effective communication with parents, and exhibit "loyalty" for their schools.

Research has also appeared concerning shared expectations for the teacher. Some of this research concerned beliefs or stereotypes about classroom conduct. To illustrate, Mackie (1972) reported that Canadians believe teachers are sympathetic and supportive of pupils, but are also inclined to dominate the classroom. American studies summarized by Biddle (1969) found that teachers were presumed to be nonaggressive, acquiescent, and to sin largely by omission rather than by commission. Other United States studies uncovered shared preferences for fairness in grading, neatness, and willingness to help pupils (Wright and Alley 1977) and shared norms that teachers should not discriminate among pupils, should be thoughtful and friendly, and should maintain order and discipline in the classroom (Biddle et al. 1961). Such expectations may be fairly universal among Western countries, but the evidence so far available is insufficient to test this proposition. Unfortunately, most of these studies were conducted in the 1960s and 1970s, and research on role expectations for teachers seems to have declined since then.

4.2 Role Conflict, Strain, and Resolution

Not all expectations for teachers are shared, of course, and studies have also reported nonconsensual expectations for teachers. Most of these studies also appeared in the 1960s and 1970s, most focused on norms, and most authors interpreted their findings as indications of role conflict. Several forms of role conflict were suggested in this literature.

A common form of finding concerned evidence that persons in various social positions hold differing norms for teacher conduct. Such disparities were reported in both the United Kingdom and the United States among such social positions as teachers, school principals, parents, pupils, teacher trainees, teacher trainers, persons from differing social classes, and persons from rural and urban communities (see Kelsall and Kellsall 1969, Biddle 1979). Most of this research argued that these disparities pose problems for teachers because those who hold differing norms will presumably bring conflicting pressures to bear on teachers for conformity. However, it was not clear from most of these studies that others would actually produce such pressures, that teachers were aware of these disparate norms, or that teachers were actually made uncomfortable by their appearance.

Some teachers know when others hold disparate norms for their conduct, of course, and this awareness was also interpreted by other authors as role conflict. Studies reporting such awareness have appeared in various countries, and a major investigation appeared reporting equivalent findings from Australia, New Zealand, and the United Kingdom, and the United States that were obtained from national samples of teachers (Adams 1970). This investigation found normative disparities in all four countries. Some findings were common in the countries studied; in particular, teachers everywhere were likely to view teachers as being at odds with principals and other school officials over such issues as willing acceptance of non professional duties, and with parents over curricular matters. Other findings were unique to specific countries. Presumed conflict between teachers and school officials was greatest in Australia, while conflicts involving parents were strongest in the United Kingdom.

The fact that teachers perceive normative disparities among differing groups of persons does not mean that these perceptions are accurate . Biddle et al. (1966) provided data indicating that teachers distort the actual views of principals, parents, and other actors concerned with schools in systematic ways. On the other hand, perceived normative disparities have been found associated with indicators of strain among both teachers and members of other occupations (see Biddle 1979).

Other expectational disparities are generated when a teacher also holds membership in alternative social positions whose tasks are at odds with those of teaching. Studies have appeared reporting role conflict between norms associated with teaching and coaching, teaching and counseling, and teaching and administrative responsibilities, but most of the research has concentrated on the conflicting demands of teaching and home making. Most studies of this latter topic have appeared in the United States, where the bulk of teachers are women, and interest in role conflicts involving women has blossomed. Such conflicts have also been found to be associated with strain.

What does the teacher do when confronted by situations of role conflict? When serious and persisting, such experiences may interfere with the teacher's performance or may cause the teacher to leave the profession. However, many teachers manage to resolve role conflicts in one way or another, by choosing to conform to one of the disparate norms in their behavior, or by compromising among the alternatives advocated.

A general theory of role conflict resolution was originally proposed by Gross et al. (1958) and has since been tested in many contexts. Dunkin (1972) examined reported role conflict resolution among Australian teachers and found that he could predict resolution strategies from personality characteristics. "Self-oriented" teachers appeared to be more likely to resolve conflicts in terms of their own needs whereas "other-oriented" teachers apparently paid more attention to the needs and authority of other persons to whom norms were attributed.

4.3 Role Expectations and Behaviors

Role expectations may be studied for themselves, as a major indicator of the subjective culture of persons who are members of social positions. However, most people who study role expectations do so because they presume that expectations predict behavior. Teachers are presumed to conform (or at least to "want" to conform) to expectations for their social position. Furthermore, others who hold expectations for teachers are thought to exert pressures on teachers for compliance.

The interesting thing about these "reasonable" propositions is that so little evidence is available to support them. Although many studies have been reported on both teacher role expectations and teacher role behavior, little of a systematic nature is known about relationships between these two realms of investigation. (See, however, 520025 and 520029).

A fundamental attraction of role theory for educators is that it presumes that persons are capable of thinking rationally about their own and others' conduct and that those rational thoughts will affect their behaviors in predictable ways. Unless there is a willingness to conduct more research on the relationships between role expectations and role behaviors, that attraction will remain based merely on speculation.

See also: Teaching, Realities of; Student Influences on Teaching; Teachers as Professionals; Teacher Development; Teacher Responsibility; Teachers as Artists; Teachers as Clinicians; Teachers as Researchers; Teacher Roles and Teaching Styles: Adult Education; Teachers as Artists; Teachers, Professional Socialization of; Teachers' Work and Political Action

References

Adams R S (ed.) 1970 Symposium on teacher role in four English-speaking countries: Introduction. *Comp. Educ. Rev.* 14(1): 5–64

Bank B J, Biddle B J, Keats D M, Keats J A 1977 Normative, preferential, and belief modes in adolescent prejudice. *Sociol. Q.* 18: 574–88

Biddle B J 1969 Teacher roles In: Ebel R L (ed.) 1969 AERA Encyclopedia of Educational Research, 4th edn. Macmillan Inc., New York

Biddle B J 1979 *Role Theory: Expectations, Identities, and Behaviors*. Academic Press, New York

Biddle B J, Rosencranz H A, Rankin E F Jr. 1961 *Studies in the Role of the Public School Teacher*. University of Missouri Press, Columbia, Missouri

Biddle B J, Rosencranz H A, Tomich E, Twyman J P 1966 Shared inaccuracies in the role of the teacher. In: Biddle B J, Thomas E J (eds.) 1966 *Role Theory: Concepts and Research*. Wiley, New York

Dunkin M J 1972 The nature and resolution of role conflicts among male primary school teachers. *Sociol. Educ.* 45(2): 167–85

Dunkin J, Biddle B J 1974 *The Study of Teaching*. Holt, Rinehalt and Winston, New York

Gross N, Mason W S, McEachern A W 1958 *Explorations in Role Analysis: Studies of the School Superintendency Role*. Wiley, New York

Kelsall R K, Kelsall H M 1969 *The School Teacher in England and the United States: The findings of Empirical Research*. Pergamon Press, Oxford

Lortie D C 1975 *Schoolteacher: A Sociological Study*. University of Chicago Press, Chicago, Illinois

Mackie M 1972 School teachers: The popular image. *Alberta Journal Educational Research*. 18(4): 267–76

Parsons T 1959 The school class as a social system: Some of its functions in American society. *Harv. Educ. Rev.* 29(4): 297–318

Waller W 1932 *Sociology of Teaching*. Wiley, New York

Wright R, Alley R 1977 A profile of the ideal teacher. *Natl. Assoc. Sec. Sch. Princ. Bull.* 61(406): 60–64

B. J. Biddle

Teachers' Work and Political Action

Most research on teachers has focused on the teacher–student relationship or student teachers in training, and has explored teaching techniques and their presumed sources in personality or training. It has addressed ways of improving teachers' responses, usually through better supervision and the reform of technique or changes in teacher education. In this area of research, the industrial and political dimension of teaching has been curiously lacking.

A new perspective on teachers has been emerging from several disparate research traditions: the sociology of the school as an institution, studies of teachers as a social and economic group, and the history of teaching. This new approach has taken research a great deal further and recognizes that teachers are workers engaged in a labor process in classrooms, schools, and school systems—their workplaces. Their work involves them, either consciously or unconsciously, in social and political projects which have effects within and well beyond the walls of the classroom and the lives of each individual.

1. Converging Research Traditions

The classic study of teachers by Waller (1961) offered a sociology of teaching concerned with the impact of teaching on teachers as people. Waller pointed to some distinctive features of teaching as an occupation: its low remuneration and social standing, and the way in which relationships with students press those entering teaching to show reserve, dignity, and an acceptance of routine.

Organizational research on schools, which in the past has tended to be teacher-blind, has led to a concern with schools as workplaces (Dreeben 1973). Similarly, interactionist sociology of the school, which has focused on interactions between teachers and pupils, has turned attention to interactions among teachers. Both approaches address the constraints on teaching, and on teachers' decision-making and coping strategies. This research has highlighted the work context of teaching (Denscombe 1980).

Research concerned with improving schools has taken the view that teachers are constrained by their work contexts. The school effectiveness movement has sought to enhance schools through a top-down reorganization of the conditions of teachers' work. In contrast, the school improvement movement has taken a more bottom-up approach and has emphasized teachers' experience in their efforts to change education. This concern with teachers' experience has fed back into research that uses life-cycle and biographical approaches to explore teachers' careers and the construction of their identities (Goodson and Ball 1985).

Both organizational research and movements seeking to improve schools reflect a view of schools as institutions that must be managed. Critics of this hierarchical view have also become concerned with teachers' work. Drawing on studies of the labor process (e.g., Braverman 1974), they have presented the impact of top-down reforms as "deskilling," an example of the economy-wide dynamic by which paid work is subdivided, information and control are concentrated among managers, and most employees are redirected to the mechanical execution of "detail-work." With such a degradation of teaching, the teachers' craft has been replaced by a battery of technical procedures. Work is intensified as the number of tasks increases and teachers' control of task and time declines. Some critics have described this process as "proletarianization," suggesting that teachers have become more like industrial workers than middle-class professionals; more technicians than technologists (Apple and Teitlebaum 1986).

Research on teachers as a social group, and on the labor markets governing their employment, have also contributed to the picture. Statistical research has highlighted the social composition of the teaching work force. The higher percentage of women, for example, has been described as the "feminization" of teaching, a concept, however, that has been subject to criticism (Danylewycz and Prentice 1986).

The most elaborate picture of teachers' work is found in social and labor histories of teaching (e.g., Grace 1978, Lawn and Ozga 1981, Theobald and Selleck 1990). This approach has highlighted the fact that most teachers are now employees of the state, and has explored their changing work conditions. Union histories have shown struggles around teachers' work as employers and employees have sought to define and redefine their interrelationship (Lawn 1985). Taking a long historical view has shown gradual changes in teachers' work and has revealed the double-edged character of changes in teachers' work organization in the late 20th century. Such ambiguities have encouraged questions about complacent assumptions of teacher "professionalism" and the alarmist cries of teacher "proletarianization."

On the whole, the insights gained from these different research traditions have been isolated from each other. Some attempts at synthesis (e.g., Connell 1985, Apple 1986, and the social and labor histories mentioned above) indicate that a more powerful social analysis of teaching is possible. It can be built upon methodological and theoretical developments in educational inquiry, discussed below.

2. *Trends in Educational Inquiry*

Waller's (1961) study of teaching in 1932 provided a rich description of the world of schools, written from the viewpoint of teachers and based on anthropological techniques, realist fiction, diaries, and life histories. Waller, however, viewed statistics with distrust, noting: "possibly the understanding of human life will be as much advanced by the direct study of social phenomena as by the study of numerical symbols abstracted from those phenomena" (Waller 1961 pp.v–vi). Research after the Second World War favored abstract "scientific" political arithmetic studies. Variables such as social class, achievement, and criteria of professionalism were bracketed from their social context and assessed in a way that left the interaction and processes of schooling as an unstudied "black box" between input and output. Then, from the late 1960s onward, qualitative and ethnographic approaches again prevailed.

Since the 1960s school and classroom ethnographies have revealed the complex relationships and interaction between teachers and students, as well as teachers' part in the active construction of institutional and social life in schools. These observations have been informed by an interactionist perspective, which emphasizes the following points: (a) the meaning things have for people is central to human action; (b) the attribution of meaning is a continuous process of understanding and acting, not a one-off consequence of individual psychology or social structure; and (c) this process is social and localized, being based in specific contexts of interaction. It makes the study of teachers and the teachers' viewpoint important (Woods 1979).

Ethnographies have also revealed teachers' involvement in conflicting realms of interaction and the way in which their strategies and accommodations have obstructed equality of opportunity—the core principle in liberal views of education. Such insights have challenged postwar functionalist notions of education as a means of socialization in a consensual society and the views of teachers as functionaries playing coherent teacher roles. Rather than being institutions offering universal benefit, schools have been seen to favor some over others in an unequal society. The state has not neutrally arbitrated in pluralist politics, but it has systematically favored ruling interests. Instead of assuming that educational development shows a gradualist, evolutionary progress toward enlightenment and teacher professionalism, the process of educational change has seemed contradictory and crisis-ridden. Questions of social justice have become central.

Structuralist research has examined the way conflict and distortion have been systematically patterned and given order by underlying relationships, organizations, and cultural and linguistic codes that are not immediately evident in experience. Marxist structuralism, for example, has analyzed how schools and teachers have contributed to the maintenance and reproduction of unequal class societies that are governed by the pursuit of profit, cyclical crises, and constant problems of control. These characteristics have put contradictory demands on schools which must be resolved within economic (e.g., fiscal) limits. Their resolution has created patterns and trends in social life such as unequal education for different social groups and the proletarianization of teachers. These resolutions are always imperfect, however. Participants have developed class consciousness as they have seen through the ideology of liberal education. They have come to understand that class society is systematically unequal and exploitative, and that political action is the way to change it. However, the structures of class power in the wider society overwhelm the microdynamics of school life. It has been argued that schooling is an arm of the state that serves ruling class interests, and that teachers are its agents. Class struggle is the assumed premise of this perspective and its explanation of change. This view marginalizes teachers as significant political actors, both individually and as an occupational group, but sees them as contradictory class actors whose politics are a consequence of their location within the class structure (Harris 1982).

Liberal, Marxist, and structuralist views of schooling have been challenged by feminist research. Woman's oppression within patriarchal society has meant that she knows herself in two ways: experientially and through dominant social science, which has been developed by men and has established male experience as a universal norm. Mainstream social science is sometimes termed "malestream," to highlight its roots in male experience and the way it has defined women and their experience as deviant, marginal, or simply absent. Consciously recognizing themselves as women, rather than people, has allowed women to recognize their subordination within gender relations. The personal is political because womens' lived experience provides a standpoint, distinct from mens' experience, from which traditional (i.e., patriarchal) understandings of the world can be challenged. Feminists have criticized the separation of the public and private realms of social life because it falsely divorces and privileges employment over family and authority over care. Women's apparent absence from history is shown to be a consequence not of their incapacity to act but of their political subordination (Weiler 1988).

Feminist research methodologies have made women's experience visible (de Lyon and Widdowson 1988). Life histories and personal narratives have allowed teachers to tell of their lived experience in opposition to dominant social science. It is consciously partial, stressing not the study *of* teachers, the majority of whom are women, but research *for* the subordinated (women, people of color, the old and young) which gives them a voice in cultural politics.

New research on teachers' work has drawn on, and moved on from, these methodological and theoretical trends to develop a perspective on teachers' work that attends explicity to the sexual and social division of labor. The integration of statistical, demographic, ethnographic, and life-history data has been guided by theoretical insights arising from the contradictions of interactionism and structuralism, Marxism and feminism, micro and macro sociology, teacher and researcher perspectives. It has placed teachers at the center of research and it has valued their lived experience as a corrective to researchers' outsider assumptions. It has taken work as a useful lens which focuses teachers' active making of schooling as an economy integrated in the sexual and social division of labor and as a realm of cultural products. The perspective on teachers' work has stressed that these productions, which include students, are made within relations of power, and it has presented teachers and their work in a complex and contradictory field of social forces. Whereas much research has emphasized teachers as individuals, the more integrated teachers' work perspective has stressed the way by which teachers and teaching are shaped by social relationships.

The individualist framework has attempted to classify work and people in more or less static (essential) categories. Teaching is characterized as "professional" or "unprofessional," teachers' work as "proletarianized," the teacher labor market as "feminized". These descriptive categories are easy to apply both in research and in polemic debates, but they are often vague, lacking rigorous definition and clear limits. Above all, the sorting into categories makes the things sorted appear obvious and simple. They are taken as the starting point of analysis rather than as things to be questioned and researched. The category "teacher" is a good example. People are categorized as teachers, something so simple it is easy to take for granted. Teacher behavior or attitudes then become the point from which research commences, neglecting the fact that teachers are not born teachers, but become teachers through social processes which exist because of the broader patterns of social relationships existing in a social order.

A focus on these relationships is characteristic of the new, more relational, approach. It has sought to develop an integrated understanding by examining the pattern of social relationships and processes that constitute, shape, and constrain teachers' work. This means that while simple categories are identified (representing particular arrangements, practices, ideologies, occupations, or individuals), they cannot be taken for granted in an ahistorical way. Instead, descriptive categories are seen as more or less transient social phenomena which appear in lived experience because of the way antagonisms, tensions, and contradictions in a given pattern of social relationships have been accommodated at a particular point in history. This becomes clear in the debate over the meaning of "professionalism" for teachers. The notion of professionalism is not fixed. It has changed historically and has been used to different effect by both teachers and the state (Lawn and Ozga 1981). Teachers have used professionalism as an ideology to enhance and defend their workplace autonomy. Holders of state power have sometimes encouraged teacher professionalism, and the devolution of power over curriculum, as a solution to their own dilemmas. In other circumstances there has been a sharp reaction, with moves to reimpose central control of teachers and their work. Attempts to force "creationism" into science and to define a national curriculum indicate shifting control of content. New patterns of control can also be effected through changing forms of schooling; for example, in pressure for curriculum packages, competency-based approaches, and accountability.

Three further aspects of the relational framework are significant. First, teachers' work is determined by intersecting social relations of, at least, class, gender, race, and age. However, this is not a strong determination which mechanistically stamps individuals and institutions with an enduring imprint of gender or class. It is, rather, a softer process by which individuals and institutions are positioned in historically specific ways within lived and large-scale social relations and structures. These relations and structures cut across one another, creating distinctive and changing constellations of social forces which constitute, shape, and constrain individuals and institutions. This positioning and patterning sets limits and possibilities for action which, again, changes over time.

Secondly, the intersection of these social structures and relationships creates a relatively autonomous space within which teachers can negotiate constraints and develop strategies within personal life and within institutional and broader social settings. The concepts of "constraint" and "strategy" are crucial, but their conceptualization is ambiguous (Scarth 1987). Individualists stress individuals' intentional action in pursuit of their interests and commitments. The relational framework sees individuals as constructions, formed within relations of power. Interests and commitments are also constructions produced within the relatively autonomous space between limits and possibilities. Constraints and strategies may therefore be consciously recognized or go unrecognized by the individual actor.

Finally, teachers' work, which involves conscious and unconscious processes and effects, is both shaped within, and in turn shapes, relations of power. Teachers' practice in economic and cultural production creates asymmetries in individuals' and groups' capacities to define and realize their needs. Teachers' work is therefore also political action because, consciously or unconsciously, it serves to confirm or contest the prevailing social order.

The relational teachers' work perspective has opened up the study of teachers and their work. Four major dimensions of research are emerging: (a) teachers as workers and teaching as an occupation; (b) the teaching labor process; (c) the industrial dynamics of schooling; and (d) the culture and politics of teachers' work.

3. *Teachers and their Work*

3.1 Teachers as Workers; Teaching as an Occupation

Seeing the teacher as a worker immediately raises questions about the teacher as an employee and about relations with other groups of workers, employers, and the state. Teachers are workers with distinctive attitudes to students, to teaching, and to education. The relational perspective sees teacher ideologies arising from relationships that make up the life of a group, rather than being individual attitudes and opinions. These ideologies are not only the emanation of groups of teachers, however. Teacher ideologies are also shaped by social relationships in the broader society (Connell 1985).

Labor market research and historical studies of teaching as an occupation have revealed the social structuring of teachers' work. Teachers' work is patterned by salary scales, avenues for promotion, and status hierarchies. These shape a division of labor within teaching. Teacher supply and demand are further organized by the external labor market, governed by a general availability of jobs and opportunities for transferring between occupations (Warren 1989).

The labor market for teachers (both inside education and beyond) is different for men and women. Wider employment opportunities for men have contributed to the overrepresentation of women in teaching. This has been termed "feminization" but the picture is not straightforward because the concentration of women is not uniform. Historically there have been different regional gender patterns. In nineteenth–century Canada and the United States, for example, urban school systems favoured men, whereas rural schools showed larger numbers of women. These patterns arose partly because in a frontier context men could find alternative work, but also because of expectations about womens' work and existing traditions of domestic tuition in which women worked as teachers. Men and women are usually also distributed differently in the internal labour market: infant schools are strongly feminized, but secondary science departments and school management are masculinized. There are many women teachers, but they are most commonly guided, directed, and controlled by men (Danylewycz and Prentice 1986).

This view of teachers as workers reveals that a teacher's career is not just a matter of choices that shape the course of the individual's life. It is the consequence, at an individual level, of labor market dynamics, patterns of incentives (salary structure and promotion), institutional orthodoxies, organizational structures, and alternative employment opportunities. Men and women make career choices, but they are made within socially defined limits and opportunities. Widely held assumptions about womens' capacities, their domestic and family responsibilities, and interpretations of their different ways of working mean that women and men teachers experience quite different "careers."

3.2 The Labor Process of Teaching

The core of teachers' daily work is a practice so familiar it is easily taken for granted. There are more or less standard techniques for classroom control, for expounding what is to be learned, and for testing. The conventional ways of looking at teachers' methods have emphasized individual variations in these techniques; that is, personal "teaching styles." Classroom observation and teachers' accounts have shown considerable variation in the encouragement of student initiative versus class drill, or formal knowledge versus practical application. The relational approach to teachers' work has argued that these variations in the labor process are not idiosyncratic but are systematically produced by the social relationships surrounding the classroom. They arise in the history of interaction of a school's staff with its particular clientele, such as the emphasis on "drill" in teaching working-class students, in the classroom strategies characteristic of science teachers, or in broad divisions within the curriculum, for example in the teaching of "academic" as compared with "practical" subjects.

Around the business of face-to-face instruction is a battery of other tasks necessary to keep schools running, from playground "police" duty to bookkeeping and inservice training. A good deal of this school work is done with other teachers, a fact that counterbalances the much-discussed "isolation" of classroom work.

The core of the teaching enterprise—getting pupils to learn—is a highly complicated process, involving emotional relationships, intellectual interaction, group dynamics, and the exercise of practical judgement in a constantly changing context. It is also difficult to pin down as "work." This is partly because it is a labor process without a clearly defined object (in the sense of the physical product produced in factory work). The teacher's skill often appears as pure intuition, although this appearance underestimates the sophistication with which the skill may be developed (Connell 1985).

For these reasons, teachers' work, in comparison with jobs that have simpler technical parameters (e.g., manufacturing ballistic missiles), is vulnerable both to limitless expansion or intensification. Because the nature of teaching cannot be tightly specified, it is subject to political redefinitions by employers. The lack of clear boundaries in the labor process is often a major source of industrial conflict.

Academic studies of teachers, using time-and-motion techniques, tend to miss what teachers see as the core of their work, in particular its content, the process of learning, and the dilemma of relationships with students which rest on both care and authority (Steedman 1987). The curriculum is central to an analysis of the labor process. It defines the pupils' learning and at the same time it also defines the teachers' task. As an Australian teacher unionist put it, "curriculum is an industrial issue."

This relationship is clear in the debate on "deskilling." While teachers generally gained in skill and control over their work earlier in the twentieth century, it is argued that deskilling of teaching is a feature of the late twentieth century. This has been reflected in attempts to reassert control over curriculum. "Programmed learning" was an early version which displaced teachers from their key position in the processes and relationships of student learning and reoriented them toward administrative tasks. Examples of techniques used in the 1990s include curriculum packages produced by United States educational publishers, "computer-assisted learning" programs, and "basic skills" testing by means of standardized testing systems (Apple 1986).

Some curriculum "innovations" are said to be "teacher proof" because of the part they play in the control of curriculum and teachers. This link is often overlooked. Curriculum and administrative reforms (such as human relations management) are often justified educationally, in terms of their potential contribution to improved "educational outcomes," without making clear the implications for teachers' work. Indeed, teachers are often seen as a "constraint" to reform, and strategies are developed to minimize their effect in implementation.

Some research at the school level has indicated that significant deskilling does follow the introduction of packaged curricula, although some unexpected reskilling in bureaucratic techniques also occurs (Gitlin 1983). It is unclear how far this has taken place among teachers generally. These trends are opposed by both the industrial power of teacher unions, and the emotional complexity and practical judgements required in classroom work.

The programs that result in deskilling reflect a broader "managerial" perspective. This perspective views teaching as a technical activity, in which the results of academic research on learning or on organizational efficiency can be "applied". A succession of curriculum and administrative innovations have been introduced to this end, but found wanting. The long-standing failure to produce a "science" of education that works has fueled arguments that teaching must be seen as a craft rather than as a technical occupation.

There are two issues here. One emphasizes that

teaching is based upon tacit rather than formal knowledge, and is mainly learned by example and by on-the-job experience rather than from codes or principles. The other emphasizes the way craft knowledge is specific to a particular group of workers and is protected by them, for instance against managerial attempts at redefinition or closer control. The "craft" conception captures important aspects of teachers' experience, and gives some insights into why the curriculum is a contested zone. However, this approach suggests an anachronistic picture of the isolated craft worker in a cottage, and plays down the extent to which teachers work collectively, especially outside the classroom.

3.3 The Industrial Dynamics of Schools

Like all other workplaces, schools have internal industrial politics. This point seems obvious, yet much research has missed it. For example, ethnographic or organizational studies of schools have commonly ignored their industrial relations, while work on industrial relations in education usually looks at the system, or union, but not at the school. Pioneering attempts to characterize the school as a workplace (e.g., Dreeben 1973) explored the character of authority, the school's technical features (such as the layout of classrooms and buildings), and the norms or culture of the school as an institution. This research found that top-down or bureaucratic patterns of authority conflicted with the demands of teacher professionalism. For this reason, among others, it was argued that there are chronic tensions around supervision in schools.

During most of the twentieth century there has been a general shift in schools from direct "line" authority to more indirect forms of control. It has defined what constitutes an acceptable "professionalism," giving teachers some autonomy of action, but confining that autonomy within constraints, such as centrally controlled institutions, guidelines, and an ethos of schooling (Grace 1987). However, the scope for autonomy has been far from uniform between different countries or even between different systems within countries. There is some evidence, for instance, that teachers in private schools come under more insistent scrutiny about deportment and dress, religious observance, and private life ("morals") than do teachers in state schools (Connell 1985).

Changes in the organization of schooling in the late twentieth century suggest that there have been moves toward more direct patterns of authority and control. The changing pattern of authority within schools, for example, is affected by the nature of the state, by the way it changes over time, and by its problems of legitimacy. The shift to indirect control and professionalism through much of the twentieth century has been part of a broader trend to develop the state and schooling as an interventionist and ameliorative agency within welfare capitalism. This social organization, based upon a regulatory state, has been challenged by social movements that seek to "roll back the state." They have favored social regulation predominantly through markets, with a small but strong state to ensure law and order. In schools, the trend has meant that authority operates through economic relations which are buttressed by direct control and hierarchical management in an emerging educational marketplace (Ball 1990).

The social organization of gender, especially the subordination of women, has particular implications for the school. Sexism in society at large has created difficulties for women as teachers, particularly in situations such as the maintenance of classroom control in a large mixed high school. Gender inequality has become obvious also in the serious under representation of women in educational administration—a live policy issue in many countries.

The large-scale structures of gender and class, race and generation, the organization of the state, and the international relations between states and economies, form a complex field of forces bearing on the school. Within this field, and very much under its influence, the face-to-face participants in a school (the administrators, staff, students,and sometimes parents) negotiate an internal political order or "regime." This regime—the pattern of power, consent, alliance, and resistance that is temporarily established as the basis of a school's daily functioning—is central to the educational history of a school. Likewise the regimes that predominate in a system's schools are central to its history as a system. There is therefore a social basis for the notorious conservatism of school systems, in school regimes that entrench the influence of groups who have most reason to resist change, notably middle-class, middle-aged, bureaucratically trained men.

Power generates resistance. Teachers, like other workers, are active in confronting, evading, or blunting control over their work. Where the overall policy of unions is strong (e.g., in Australian state schools) workplace unionism is a major form of defense. Teacher unionism, plus the state's historical shift to indirect control, has sometimes opened a space for industrial democracy. Where this is official policy, however symbolic, it can provide a venue for teachers to negotiate issues of control. In many schools, principals must win some kind of endorsement for their policies from the staff. Where unions are weak (as in much of the United States) resistance is more likely to be informal or individual. Yet it is notable that resistance occurs even in schools dominated by packaged curricula, with teachers asserting some control over how the packages work in the classroom (Gitlin 1983).

3.4 The Culture and Politics of Teachers' Work

The social patterning of teachers and their work has effects that are felt both in and beyond the classroom, school, or school system. Teachers contribute to an economics of schooling and to the production of meaning and significance in educational workplaces. They make and remake a culture and organization of work and so fuel political dynamics which cut across personal and institutional life and play a part in the broader social and historical movements of class and gender formation (Lawn and Grace 1987).

Life history research has revealed how teachers experience and adjust to contradictions in their experience; for example, how the experience of being a teacher of working-class origins in an English grammar school (Worpole 1985) or a Maori girl becoming a teacher in postwar New Zealand (Middleton 1987) shapes practice and, in some cases, politicizes it. Living these contradictions can turn a complex lived experience into a conscious understanding of the way one's space for action is shaped by social limits and possibilities which are made and can be remade through political action.

Resistance, conflict, debate, and struggle are central to political action. They also lead to the formation of distinctive cultural products: school organization, policy documents, and groups of people with distinctive ways of seeing and acting in the world. Pressures to redefine teachers' working conditions and employment relations are experienced differently by different teachers. The young and old see new reforming discourse, which advocates, for example, local management of schools, curriculum reform, and contract employment, as offering quite different patterns of constraint and opportunity. Teachers participate in the politics of reform as "Young Turks" or "Diehards," or by conservatively relinquishing public space in burnout, by withdrawing behind the classroom door, or by retiring early (Riseborough and Poppleton 1991). Deskilling and proletarianization are evident, but as heterogenous trends shaped by the division of labor. They affect men and women of different ages in different ways. They are not unidirectional in their "degradation of work," but appear as complex redefinitions of skill with implications for class and gender formation more generally (Ball 1988). These local, personal, and institutional politics form part of broader discursive politics through which different groups struggle to incorporate support for their experience and commitment. These politics are seen most clearly in policy debates over the course of educational reform (Ball 1990).

In all these cultural and political processes the shaping and making of teachers' work can become part of broader social and historical movements with long-term consequences. In South Africa, a colored woman teacher's commitment to educating her students brings her into conflict with the apartheid regime. It leads to conscious political involvement in the struggle against apartheid, and complex changing relations with her family, friends, students, and other teachers (Russell 1989). Economic crisis in the Philippines has been accommodated through a variety of personal austerity measures by Filipino teachers which have had implications on their immediate and longterm family life. It has also encouraged support for teacher action and organization (Del Fierro and Dalman 1987).

In the above cases, individuals' solutions to complex and contradictory circumstances have coalesced by sheer weight of numbers into a social force for remaking the social and educational order. Sometimes this has been consciously organized in collective action and political movements. In these movements the institutional setting is important. Research on nationalist independence movements in Africa has shown that before and after Independence there were quite different organizational and social arrangements which produced changing limits and constraints on teachers' action. Before Independence the space for teachers' work encouraged political mobilization. After Independence political mobilization was discouraged and teachers' energies were channeled into personal security and career advancement (Dove 1979).

4. *Teachers' Work and Political Action*

Teachers' work is a lens that opens up the study of teachers and their work. As the examples above have shown, however, there are significant ambiguities embedded in the concept of "teachers' work." Researchers can study teachers as workers, and their practice in employment and in professional and industrial politics. However, each of these frames is an abstraction and a methodological convenience which should not be seen as adequate in itself.

One set of ambiguities relates to "work." Teachers' work encompasses practices within employment and beyond: in families, communities, and other social movements. Teachers' work is simultaneously industrial and professional. Indeed the polar opposition commonly assumed between these two categories is empirically redundant and a good example of a politically significant cultural production. The social effects of teachers' work go beyond teaching and raise questions about the relationship between work and employment. It also challenges the familiar separation of education and work which suggests that students learn and workers work, and which establishes an association between learning, which is unpaid, and teaching, which is paid. This separation neglects that learning and work always go hand in hand because every workplace is also a learning place.

Another set of ambiguities centers on the "teacher." The teacher cannot be understood just as a teacher, as in individualist research, or just as a worker. The teacher should be seen as a social and historical actor involved in distinctive educative practices, as well as other practices, at the nexus of changing employment, family, and broader social relations and structures. Teachers are not the only agents of this educative practice, which raises questions about the social structures and processes that differentiate between the legitimated "teacher" as a social construction and the great range of other actors who educate, but beyond the classroom.

The Nicaraguan Literacy Crusade can be used to illustrate the complex interplay between economic and cultural production, and between teachers' work and political action (Arnove 1981). The Crusade was a mass movement which lifted Nicaraguan literacy levels. It was also a multilayered cultural product. Through its sheer existence, its materials, and its "teachers" (the *brigadistas*) the Crusade symbolized social justice and the popular democratic commitment of the Sandinista regime. One of its posters read:

Every home a classroom
Every table a desk
Every Nicaraguan a teacher!

For many Nicaraguans—and for those worldwide who press discourses of democracy, equality, and internationalism—this literacy campaign has been a significant resource which has been drawn on, and referred to, in ongoing cultural politics. For researchers of teachers' work it underlines the importance of treating categories with caution and can confirm that teachers' work is political action.

References

Apple M W 1986 *Teacher and Texts: A Political Economy of Class and Gender Relations in Education*. Routledge and Kegan Paul, London

Apple M W, Teitlebaum K 1986 Are teachers losing control of their skills and the curriculum? *J. Curr. Stud.* 18(2): 177–84

Arnove R S 1981 The Nicaraguan National Literacy Crusade of 1980. *Comp. Educ. Rev.* 25(2): 244–60

Ball S J 1988 Staff relations during the teachers' industrial action: Context, conflict, and proletarianisation. *Br. J. Sociol. Educ.* 9(3): 289–306

Ball S J 1990 *Politics and Policy Making in Education: Explorations in Policy Sociology*. Routledge, London

Braverman H 1974 *Labour and Monopoly Capital: The Degradation of Work in the Twentieth Century*. Monthly Review, New York

Connell R W 1985 *Teachers' Work*. Allen and Unwin, Sydney

Danylewycz M, Prentice A 1986 Revising the history of teachers: A Canadian perspective. *Interchange* 17(2): 135–46

del Fierro A C Jr, Dalman V M 1987 Coping mechanisms of elementary school teachers under economic crisis conditions in three southern Philippine regions. *Philippines Sociol. Rev.* 35: 11–25

de Lyon H, Widdowson F (eds.) 1988 *Women Teachers: Issues and Experiences*. Open University, Milton Keynes

Denscombe M 1980 The work context of teaching. *Br. J. Sociol. Educ.* 1: 279–92

Dove L A 1979 Teachers in politics in ex-colonial countries. *Journal of Comparative and Commonwealth Politics* 17: 176–91

Dreeben R 1973 The school as a workplace. In: Travers R M W (ed.) 1973 *The Second Handbook of Research on Teaching*. Rand McNally, Chicago, Illinois

Gitlin A 1983 School structure and teachers' work. In: Apple M W, Wiess L (eds.) 1983 *Ideology and Practice in Schooling*. Temple University Press, Philadelphia, Pennsylvania

Goodson I, Ball S 1985 *Teachers' Lives and Careers*. Falmer Press, London

Grace G 1978 *Teachers, Ideology and Control: A Study in Urban Education*. Routledge and Kegan Paul, London

Grace G 1987 Teachers and the state in Britain: A changing relation. In: Lawn M, Grace G (eds.) 1987 *Teachers: The Culture and Politics of Work*. Falmer Press, London

Harris K 1982 *Teachers and Classes: A Marxist Analysis*. Routledge and Kegan Paul, London

Lawn M 1985 *The Politics of Teacher Unionism: International Perspectives*. Croom Helm, London

Lawn M, Ozga J 1981 The educational worker? A reassessment of teachers. In: Barton L, Walker S (eds.) 1981 *Schools, Teachers and Teaching*. Falmer Press, London

Lawn M, Grace G (eds.)1987 *Teachers: The Culture and Politics of Work*. Falmer Press, London

Middleton S 1987 Schooling and radicalisation: Life histories of New Zealand feminist teachers. *Br. J. Sociol. Educ.* 8(2): 169–89

Riseborough G F, Poppleton P 1991 Veterans versus beginners: A study of teachers at a time of fundamental change in comprehensive schooling. *Educ. Rev.* 43: 307–34

Russell D E H 1989 Life in a police state: A black South African woman who speaks out. *Women's Studies International Forum* 12(2): 157–66

Scarth J 1987 Teacher strategies: A review and critique. *Br. J. Sociol. Educ.* 8(3): 245–62

Steedman C 1987 Prisonhouses. In: Lawn M, Grace G (eds.) 1987 *Teachers: The Culture and Politics of Work*. Falmer Press, London

Theobald M R, Selleck R J W 1990 *Family, School and State in Australian History*. Allen and Unwin, Sydney

Waller W 1961 *The Sociology of Teaching*. Wiley, New York

Warren D 1989 *American Teachers: Histories of a Profession at Work*. Macmillan Inc., New York

Weiler K 1988 *Women Teaching for Change: Gender, Class and Power*. Bergin and Garvey, South Hadley, Massachusetts

Woods P 1979 *The Divided School*. Routledge and Kegan Paul, London

Worpole K 1985 Scholarship boy: The poetry of Tony Harrison. *New Left Review* No. 153: 63–74

Further Reading

Lipsky M 1980 *Street-level Bureauracracy: Dilemmas of the Individual in Public Service*. Sage, New York

Lortie D C 1975 *Schoolteacher: A Sociological Study*. University of Chicago Press, Chicago, Illinois

Thompson P 1989 *The Nature of Work: An Introduction to Debates on the Labour Process*. Macmillan, Basingstoke

Tropp A 1957 *The School Teachers: The Growth of the Teaching Profession in England and Wales from 1800 to Present Day*. Heinemann, London

T. Seddon

Teaching and Learning, Demonstration Methods of

Demonstration methods of teaching are perhaps the oldest and most common of all teaching methods, not only in the school, but also in the home, at play, and in the workplace. Demonstration is employed to teach a variety of skills ranging from tying shoelaces to neurosurgical operations. In these cases, demonstration is used because it is too complicated to provide a verbal description of the skills. However, demonstrations are not limited to the teaching of specific skills; they also are employed to teach analytical processes. As a method of teaching, demonstration is largely ignored by researchers and teacher educators (with the possible exception of the field of physical education).

1. Understanding Demonstration

Demonstration, which may be defined as "teaching by showing," has the advantage of communicating with learners visually and orally at the same time. Through visual presentation, language barriers can be overcome, communication can be enhanced, and rapport between the teacher and the learner can be established. Through oral presentation what is seen by the learners can be introduced, explained, and summarized by the teacher. In many ways demonstration is the "natural" method of teaching. It provides the imitative behavior so important in learning in early childhood before language is sufficiently developed.

Throughout human history, teaching by demonstration has been the primary method of preparation for living and for passing on the cultural heritage. With the development of trades and crafts, demonstration provided the foundation for apprenticeship training in the medieval guilds and was firmly related to the teaching of practical skills. It was not, however, restricted to the teaching of such skills. Art and music, for example, were two areas in which demonstration by the master to the pupil was particularly productive. Similarly, the demonstration of experimental processes has had a central role in science. The successes in these subject areas raise the question of the extent to which demonstrations can be employed in other subjects.

2. Effects of Technology

The rapid development of educational technology has widened the scope for demonstration methods in education and training. Additionally, technology has greatly increased the instructional effectiveness of demonstration. Initially, films were used to great advantage. With the development of television and video-recording, however, new possibilities have emerged. The smallest details can now be seen by all who observe a demonstration or witness a replay of it from a videorecording. Perhaps the most remarkable developments have occurred in surgery, where not only can the surgeon see more clearly the progress of the operation, but all in the operating theater can now see what is taking place. Moreover, the development of the overhead projector to present computer output on a screen and the distribution of televised programs by satellite have the potential to advance teaching by demonstration, because they have the capacity to increase the clarity of what is presented to increasingly large numbers of students.

3. Art of Demonstration

An important element in many learning situations is the relationship between the demonstration given by the teacher and the practice given to the student. The most effective balance between the two depends upon the learning task, the situation provided for practice, and the quality of communication achieved by the teacher. It is necessary, however, to recognize that human learning through demonstration extends beyond imitative behavior to a wide range of intellectual activities. The art of demonstration is to show the process to be learned in such a way that understanding and the building of internalized links are established. Learning to drive a motorcar, or to fly supersonic jet fighter aircraft, involves more than the development of a certain level of manual dexterity. It requires understanding and analytical skills that will enable appropriate actions to be taken in the case of an emergency or unexpected happenings. Thus, although imitation plays its part in such learning, the simultaneous building of understanding and analytical skills, while the manual operations and procedures are being learned to the degree that they become largely automatic, is also required. The art of teaching by demonstration involves the establishment of competence and complete mastery in all envisaged circumstances through the development of the intellectual basis of action.

From this perspective it is possible to specify seven steps which are involved in teaching by demonstration.

(a) The initial step involves the thorough analysis of the skills and competencies involved in the demonstrated operation. The prerequisite skills and competencies, including knowledge and understanding, must first be identified. There is little point demonstrating how to undertake long division to students who cannot add and subtract. These prerequisite skills and competencies must be placed in a logical or temporal sequence for the purposes of instruction.

(b) The second step involves choosing an appropriate situation within which to present the demonstration. The ideal may not be accessible and, therefore, the choice of the best available situation may need to be made. Sometimes a film or a videorecording is more effective than a direct demonstration.

(c) Since demonstration involves both visual and oral presentation (or in some cases visual and written instruction), it is necessary to plan the manner in which the visual and the oral presentations are to be linked in an ordered sequence. It is at this third step that the analysis of the skills and competencies carried out in the first step is used. The emphasis, however, must always be on understanding, and the nature and sequence of presentation should be directed toward this end.

(d) Since emphasis is on understanding, the learner should always be allowed opportunity to ask questions in order to ensure that understanding is developing. However, it must be recognized that understanding is rarely complete at an early stage, since, like performance skills and competencies, it develops over time. Thus, it is important to recognize that the development of understanding also continues through practice.

(e) In the fifth step the learner is provided with the opportunity to repeat the entire operation (or a section of it) under guidance and in circumstances in which questions can be asked of the instructor both to avoid errors and to advance understanding. In addition, the instructor should prompt, check for understanding, correct, and repeat when necessary.

(f) In the sixth step, the learner is permitted to repeat the operation until mastery is achieved. In this case, mastery means achieving a degree of understanding that will permit appropriate action in a novel situation. This step also includes the development of speed and accuracy of performance.

(g) The final step involves evaluation and, when necessary, repeated practice until perfection or near-perfection is achieved.

4. Demonstration in Specific Subject Areas

The art of demonstration, illustrated in the seven steps outlined above, has been applied in several subjects. Its application in physical education, mathematics, and science is discussed in this section.

4.1 Demonstration in Physical Education

Physical education involves teaching a large number of psychomotor skills. Consequently, visual demonstration is one of the most effective ways of fostering such development. Learners must identify with the demonstrator if they are to duplicate the demonstrator's actions. At the same time, while observing an expert often has an entertaining effect, it does not necessarily have an educating effect. If learners feel that they are comparable in age, experience, and physical characteristics to the demonstrator, they are more likely to acquire the demonstrator's skill and facility. Nevertheless, the actions of the demonstrator must be of reasonable quality and provide an appropriate model for duplication (Karlin and Mortimer 1963).

A film or a videorecording can provide an effective form of presentation if practice follows soon after the viewing (Zuckerman 1950). In addition, verbal instruction must be appropriately placed with respect to action in the film. Both film and videorecording have the advantage that they can be slowed down, stopped, or reversed and rerun to show clearly the detail involved in performing the skill. Moreover, the use of videotaping has the further advantage that it can be used to record the practice of the learners, who can then examine objectively their performance with respect to that shown in the demonstration, a most effective form of feedback.

4.2 Demonstration in the Teaching of Mathematics

A substantial portion of elementary mathematics involves learning specific algorithmic procedures. Although electronic calculators have reduced the extent to which some algorithms need to be mastered with speed and accuracy, the understanding of mathematical operations in general is built upon the demonstration of proofs, problem solving procedures, relationships and identities, and the solving of equations. The most common approach to instruction in mathematics is for the teacher to demonstrate the steps to be followed and then ask questions of students and monitor their answers to check for understanding. After a satisfactory level of understanding has been achieved, teachers provide a series of problems or exercises and help students as they work through them by providing prompts and corrections. As students attain a level of proficiency they move to independent practice which is commonly undertaken as homework.

A major part of the instructional process is the initial demonstration during which the students see what to do and listen to the teacher-led discussion of *why* the prescribed steps are followed. Sometimes the teacher reverts to demonstration during guided practice to clarify a step, so that, while practice and formative evaluation are important and necessary, demonstration is clearly the key instruction.

Rosenshine and Stevens (1986), from a review of research, state that from Grades 4 to 8, more effective teachers spend more time on demonstration in mathematics classes than do less effective teachers. More effective teachers give on average 23 minutes of a 50-minute daily period to presentation, that is, to demonstration and discussion, while less effective teachers give 11 minutes, less than half that time. In addition, Rosenshine and Stevens specify four important aspects of good presentation in mathematics classrooms: (a) clarity of goals and main points; (b) step-by-step presentation; (c) specific and concrete procedures; and (d) checking for students' understanding. However, they note that there is little conclusive research on such issues as: (a) how should new material be organized so that it can be learned most effectively? (b) what are the characteristics of an effective demonstration? (c) how many examples and of what kind should a teacher use? (d) is there an effective way for sequencing examples? and (e) how much information should be presented in the instructional steps?

4.3 Demonstration in Science Teaching

Science is based on evidence obtained through the senses from the natural world. In learning science, observation and experimentation are essential ingredients, and demonstration can contribute to both. Thus, a necessary requirement of demonstration in science classrooms is that every step be clearly seen by every member of the class. With this in mind, some schools have science classrooms with a serviced demonstration bench and tiered seating. However, demonstration experiments and observation can be carried out by students working alone or more commonly in small groups. Under these circumstances a laboratory with flexible furniture is more useful, and a preferred setting for science teaching. Nevertheless, much of the science teaching carried out in a laboratory is essentially in the form of a demonstration rather than an investigation, so that the principles of demonstration teaching apply. Teacher demonstration as opposed to student demonstration as a mode of teaching in science is selected for one or more of the following reasons: (a) to show certain manipulative skills and procedures; (b) because the processes involved are costly, dangerous, difficult, or time consuming; and (c) because the force of a logical argument might be lost if the students' attention is concentrated on performing the practical tasks involved.

Particular attention has to be given in demonstrations in science teaching to employing apparatus, such as scales and meters of sufficient size, so that all members of the group can see for themselves. Where this is not possible, authenticity is achieved by using members of the class as assistants to make the observations and relay them to the class. This approach has the further advantage that it frees the teacher to ask questions of the students that will augment understanding, as opposed to focusing on the set lecture with illustrative material.

The teacher should conduct a trial run of a more complex procedure to ensure that the equipment is in good working order. Demonstrations that do not work, while perhaps not uncharacteristic of scientific investigation, disappoint and disillusion science classes, because students have a high level of expectation and interest when being shown a scientific demonstration. Thus an effective demonstration requires attention to the smallest detail and meticulous rehearsal. Judgment must be exercised and decisions made concerning every step (for example, whether anything is lost if reagents are measured out beforehand, or the electrical connections made so that all that is necessary is to turn on a switch). Fumbling to connect wires or groping for a box of matches can be a distraction.

In general, a demonstration should set a high standard in preparation and manipulation. However, above all, attention should be given to logical presentation and the structure of the scientific argument, since science involves not only the learning of content, but also the development of the processes of investigation and inquiry through observation and experimentation. Toward this end, questioning of the students serves to emphasize investigation and can be used for induction, deduction, and the making of general statements to summarize and recapitulate the findings.

5. Collaborative Demonstration

Collaborative demonstration is concerned more with teaching the processes of investigation and inquiry than with the presentation of specific content. In the learning of science and many other subjects, such as problem solving in mathematics, there is need to engage in more open-ended and heuristic activity so that the skills of inquiry may be appreciated and developed. However, this form of demonstration teaching is much less of a set piece and demands a high level of teaching skill for its success. The demonstrator outlines the problem and then invites the class to advance ideas on how to proceed, what questions to ask, how to obtain answers to these questions, how to assess the value of the evidence, and how to draw conclusions. The method demands skill on the part of the teacher in eliminating suggestions that are going to be unproductive, while accepting those that can lead in a profitable direction or that can be submitted to a thorough discussion, without inhibiting responses from the group.

Much of the value of the demonstration lies in the following of false trails, but pursuing every trail is both time consuming and unrewarding, especially as some students and the teacher may have foreknowledge of the result. Therefore, instead of a rehearsed flow of clearly defined stages along a predetermined path, the demonstration consists of a series of improvisations skillfully managed to achieve the double objectives of extending the students' understanding while at the same time developing their powers of investigation. Preparation for such teaching lies in thinking out what kinds of materials and resources might be required and having them readily available, but out of sight, so that the students are not predisposed to follow routes predetermined by the teacher. The demonstration therefore follows a course which is generally in the desired direction, but to which the students' suggestions have substantially contributed after discussion, refinement, and acceptance by the class as a whole.

New opportunities have arisen for this open-ended type of demonstration teaching with the advent of the desktop computer that may be programed for a simulation study in all fields of learning where evidence is available and where hypotheses or models may be postulated and checked against evidence. The value of such a demonstration lies in learning to work as a group, learning the inquiry approach, learning how to confirm or reject, and above all learning that there may not be a single right answer to every question. While a group is not essential for such demonstration teaching, if groups are used they should be of sufficient size to generate ideas, but not so large as to exclude some members from participating. The critical operation comes at a late stage when ideas are submitted to the test, although the results may frequently lead to starting again along another path or set of paths.

Torrence (1986) reports that such methods of teaching are being used with gifted students, but the approach employed in collaborative demonstration methods of teaching is of such importance that studies using this method with ordinary students are clearly required. In this type of demonstration, the emphasis is on process rather than content. The students themselves, their thoughts, and the procedures they advance are the focus of attention, not the task being undertaken.

6. Conclusion

Demonstration methods of teaching have a long tradition and have proved to be very productive. They have dominated science teaching in some countries in continental Europe at the expense of student-based laboratory work. They have led to the building of special theaters, for example at the University of Uppsala centuries ago, for the teaching of medicine. They have a new role to play as television, video recordings, and other technological advances contribute to the advancement of teaching. However, research in this field would appear to be seriously deficient—almost nonexistent. The reasons for the failure to research this field are difficult to identify, and a cost is borne by all, through the use of less effective and less efficient methods of teaching and learning.

See also: Teaching and Learning, Explanation in; Classroom Discussion; Tutoring

References

Karlin L, Mortimer R G 1963 Effect of verbal, visual and auditory augmentary cues on learning a complex motor skill. *J. Exp. Psychol.* 65: 75–79

Rosenshine B, Stevens R 1986 Teaching functions. In: Wittrock M C 1986 *Handbook of Research on Teaching*, 3rd edn. Macmillan, New York

Torrence E P 1986 Teaching creative and gifted learners. In: Wittrock M C 1986 *Handbook of Research on Teaching*, 3rd edn. Macmillan, New York

Zuckerman J V 1950 Effects of variations in commentary upon the learning of perceptual-motor tasks from sound motion pictures. *Am. Psychol.* 5: 363–64

L. C. Comber; J. P. Keeves

Teaching and Learning, Explanation in

Explanation has been explored as a concept, subjected to measurement and studied as a teacher and student competency. Among other things, it is clear that: (a) the term has a variety of usages, (b) scholars have identified different types of explanations, (c) criteria for judging whether an explanation is satisfactory have been formulated, (d) explanations are significant classroom occurrences during receptive learning and productive thinking, (e) explanations are a component of the larger construct "clarity" which is related to pupil learning, (f) teacher explanation is the subject of empirical study, and (g) instruments exist for its measurement.

1. Explanation as a Concept

Explanation means different things to different people. As a concept, explanation can be best understood by considering its functions and types.

1.1 Functions

The literature on explanation can be confusing unless it is understood that the term serves different semantic purposes in everyday language. In one instance, its meaning is to make some concept, procedure, or rule plain and comprehensible. Thus, a teacher might "explain" a concept (global warming), a procedure (how to subtract), or a rule (we raise our hands to be recognized). In this instance, explanation is synonymous with specification. However, such explanations do not account (that is, give reasons) for any of these things.

In a second instance, explanation is used to account for the occurrence of things. In this instance, explanation requires the teacher to present the "why" of global warming, tell students why subtraction is performed in a specified manner, and explain why pupils must raise their hands. Here explanation is synonymous with giving reasons.

Explanations are generally thought of as provided by teachers and directed toward students. However, students often are called upon to explain their observations, learning, answers, or values. In addition to verbal explanations, explanations can be provided in written form (e.g., textbooks, student essays) or through recordings (e.g., films, videotapes).

1.2 Types

Within these two general functions, academics have identified numerous types of explanations. Hudgins (1974), for example, listed four types: (a) causal (e.g., "Objects fall to the ground because of gravity"), (b) normative (e.g., "They no longer prohibit the sale of alcohol in the United States because of the 21st Amendment to the Constitution"), (c) process (e.g., "This is how matters get to the United Nation's Security Council"), and (d) teleological (e.g., "Certain specialized behaviors observed among animals prior to copulation serve to attract the opposite sex").

Similarly, Fairhurst (1981) identified four types of explanation used by teachers in primary schools: descriptive, prescriptive, aesthetic, and analytic. Descriptive explanations are concerned with what is the case. They include word explanations (definitions), interpretive explanations (e.g., the meaning of a proverb or fable), causal explanations (e.g., the freezing point of water), reason-giving explanations (e.g., discussing a generalization that falls short of a causal explanation), structural explanations (e.g., pointing out the structure of the Union Jack), classificatory explanations or making comparisons (e.g., "this is a tree"), teleological explanations (pointing to a purpose or goal), and sequent explanations or telling a sequence of events.

As the name implies, prescriptive explanations are concerned with prescriptions for action. They include social explanations (e.g., pointing out social rules), ethical explanations (e.g., pointing out a principle of conduct, and procedural explanations (i.e., how to do something to achieve some goal).

Aesthetic explanations include value-giving explanations (e.g., the criteria for grading) and aesthetic interpretive explanations (e.g., interpreting a poem). Finally, analytic explanations pertain to procedures and propositions that inform and clarify concepts and rules (e.g., explaining how to solve a mathematical equation).

Dagher (1989) examined teacher explanation in the context of junior high school science teaching. Based on the results of her study, Dagher formed 10 classifications of science teachers' explanations: "how to," metaphysical, purposive/intentional, anthropomorphic, functional, genetic, mechanical, analogical, rational, and tautological. Because of the number and complexity of her types of explanations, Dagher interrelated them as shown in Fig. 1.

MacDonald (1991), drawing on Ennis (1969), suggests three types of explanation: interpretive (which provides the meaning of concepts or terms),

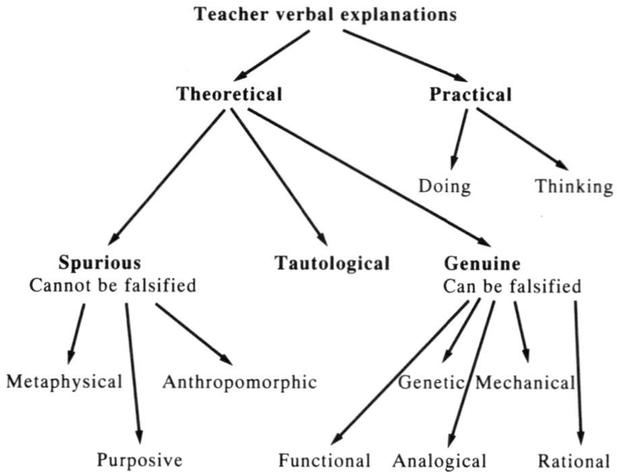

Figure 1
Dagher's Descriptive Framework

Source: The nature of verbal teacher explanations in junior high science classrooms 1989. (Doctoral dissertation, The University of Iowa).

descriptive (which specifies a procedure to be followed), and reason-giving (which clarifies why something is done the way it is or why some event has occurred or is occurring).

Clearly, there are many schools of thought with regard to the meaning of the term "explanation." Based on the results of her study, Dagher (1989) noted that there is little consensus on the functions and forms of explanations. She reiterates Garfinkel's (1981) admonition that an account of the "algebra of explanations" is needed that would serve as a kind of consumer's guide to the use and study of explanation. Table 1 is an initial attempt to integrate the various types of explanations identified by various scholars.

2. Criteria for Judging Explanations

A number of persons speak to the need to identify criteria of a good explanation. Social studies educators seem to be among the most interested. Metcalf (1963) notes the general failure of historians to validate adequately the explanations they make for theses they promote (e.g., Turner's frontier thesis). He also admonishes them for not validating reasons they give for current or past events (e.g., causes of the Gulf War). Since historians fail in this regard, Metcalf argues that pupils should learn how to gauge the logical correctness of historical explanations they receive. "This procedure, highly effective as it is, could not help but make history clearer even to the slowest student, and would reveal in a given case precisely whether an historian knew what he was talking about" (p. 953). Additionally, Metcalf faults social studies textbook writers for confronting pupils with other persons' explanations without providing

Table 1
Types of explanation

Hudgins (1974)	Fairhurst (1981)	Dagher (1989)	MacDonald (1991)
	Aesthetic Value giving, interpretive		
Process Descriptive, illuminating a process	*Prescriptive* Prescribe action	*How to* Prescribe action	*Descriptive* Specifies a procedure
Normative Providing accepted fact	*Descriptive* Describe what is the case	*Anthropomorphic* Attributes human characteristics to non-humans *Genetic* Relates an antecedent sequence of events (not why) *Analogical* Makes use of analogy	*Interpretive* Provides meaning of concepts of terms
	Analytic Procedures and propositions that inform and clarify	*Rational* Evidence is provided for a statement *Tautological* Restatement of a how or why statement without additional information	
Causal Reason giving		*Metaphysical* A supernatural agent is the cause *Functional* Cause that is a function is identified *Mechanical* Causal relationships that are physical in nature	*Reason Giving* Why, causal
Teleological Cause points to some subsequent purpose or goal		*Purpose/Intentional* Cause points to some subsequent purpose or goal	

detail with regard to how or whether they were reached in some valid way.

Swift (1959) suggests that explanations be subjected to analysis using the following criteria: presence of law-like statements, testability of such statements, their truth, and their internal validity, that is, whether the statement describing or naming the event to be explained follows logically from the reasons stated in the major and minor premises.

Swift identified different types of student explanations and categorized them further according to their logical rigor. "Nonrelational explanations" are descriptions or interpretations. For example, the teacher may ask students to explain the separation of powers in government. Students often respond with nonrelational explanations or specifications of what separation of powers is. Rational explanations, on the other hand, are those that explain a phenomenon in terms of some other affair, condition, or situation (Swift 1959 p. 124). Metcalf (1963) concludes that Swift's approach to the analysis of explanation should be made known to preservice and inservice teachers so that, in turn, they may use it to teach students about the importance of valid explanation (p. 961).

Armbruster and Anderson (1984) have been interested in psychological explanations of historical events. A proper textbook explanation in this case should meet each of the following conditions or "frames":

(a) What was the goal of the protagonist(s)? What were the human motives?

(b) What was the plan for attaining the goal?

(c) What action was taken in response to the plan?

(d) What was the outcome(s) of the action taken with respect to the goal?

Additionally, Armbruster and Anderson require that social science textbook responses to the above questions be appropriate for the readers (i.e., within their realm of meaning and understanding, and complete); coherent (i.e., the ideas flow clearly, easily, and in a logical order); and unified (i.e., the information presented is relevant and the amount of text devoted to each question is about right).

Fairhurst (1981) operationally defines an explanation as requiring something to be explained; an explainer or other communication source such as print material; and an explainee who is the recipient of the explanation. She points out that an explanation might be considered satisfactory according to three points of view. From the explainer's point of view, it must meet the conditions of "clarity, orderly presentation and intention to explain." From the explainees' view, the explanation must be a "gap-filler, i.e., it satisfies [their] curiosity or removes a puzzlement [and it is] expressed in terms which are intelligible . . . and related to . . . previous experience" (pp. 206–07). From the detached observer's point of view, the explanation must be a distinct attempt to clarify a point or situation. Additionally, to the observer it must be true, testable, appropriate, adequate, and not circular. Finally, Fairhurst notes that some types of explanation are better in that they meet additional criteria: truth, testability, appropriateness, and noncircularity (pp. 208–12).

MacDonald (1991) prescribes two main requirements of a good explanation. The explanation should be appropriate to the situation and it should be thorough, accurate, and understandable. He provides the following guidelines for presenting logically sound explanations:

(a) Have a clear conception of the purpose of the explanation. Is it to be interpretive, descriptive, reason-giving, or some combination of the three?

(b) Recognize the potential ambiguity of the word "explain" when a student makes an unclear request for information. Does he or she require an interpretive, descriptive, or reason-giving explanation?

(c) When giving an interpretive explanation make sure it is operationally stated, for example a subtrahend is a quantity or number that is subtracted or taken away from another quantity called a minuend. Use of synonyms and examples may be further helpful but should not be substituted for careful analysis of meaning of the term.

(d) Avoid circularity when giving interpretive or reason-giving explanations. Do not define a term using a synonym unless the synonym is understood or it, in turn, is carefully analyzed. Do not use circularity when providing reason-giving explanations, for example, "Communism has failed because it didn't work."

(e) When descriptive explanations are called for, break the procedure to be explained into parts and present the parts in some carefully chosen order. Thus, break down the process of subtraction and present it step-by-step.

(f) Make sure reason-giving explanations are complete or whole (pp. 140–41).

MacDonald (1991) also argues that in addition to explanations being logically sound they must be psychologically appropriate. Among other things, this is accomplished by centering on the learner's frame of reference, providing only enough information that can be assimilated, and using techniques to enhance clarity and emphasis. To center on the learner's frame of reference means to help student rearrange and extend what they already know.

Fairhurst (1981) points out that when giving a proper explanation a primary teacher might use more than one type. She notes: "In explaining the structure of the Union Jack, a teacher would be giving a structural definition, but he might also be showing the class how to draw the flag (a procedural explanation), and whilst he was drawing it he might tell the children how this union of flags came about (a sequent explanation)" (p. 208).

Perceptive teachers recognize that they must be prepared to offer multiple explanations, particularly when teaching mathematical problem-solving and when teaching pupils with divergent learning styles. Relatedly, mathematicians and computer scientists are developing intelligent tutoring systems, for example to teach algebra, "that provide multiple explanations for dynamically generated algebraic word problems" (Schulze 1989–90 p. 236). These systems take into account what individual students know, their current misconceptions, terminology with which they are familiar, and the most effective forms of explanation for them.

3. Explanation in Receptive Learning and Productive Thinking

As one consequence of the United States, effort to develop and promote Smith et al.'s (1969) notion of protocol materials, a catalog of significant pedagogical concepts was written by Hudgins (1974). The concepts Hudgins chose for inclusion fell within the framework of "interactive teaching" defined as "including all the events and transactions that occur in the classroom during the time the teacher and pupils are mutually engaged in implementing the educational program" (p. 8). Explanation appears as a significant pedagogical concept twice, under reception learning (pp. 33–36) and under productive thinking (pp. 45–48).

Reception learning refers to activities whereby pupils receive information (knowledge) and are asked to recall it. Hudgins uses the term "explanation" in the context of reception learning to denote "a pupil statement which provides an account of specified events or conditions in terms of processes, procedures, or cause and effect relationships. The statement represents what the student recalls of an explanation which has been considered previously" (p. 33). Thus, pupils might be asked to recall when the colonization of Australia took place or to recall a teacher or a textbook explanation of why colonization began at that time.

"Indicators" of explanation in reception learning, according to Hudgins, are threefold:

(a) Such explanations result from an effort to clarify.

However, in this case, the explanation provided by the student is not his or her own but one recalled from another source.

(b) Recalled student-given explanations are often partial and require supplementation by teachers.

(c) Explanations, according to Hudgins (and described earlier), are of four types: (i) causal, (ii) normative, (iii) process, and (iv) teleological.

In the context of productive thinking, Hudgins uses the term explanation to denote "the set of cognitive operations and outcomes by which pupil[s] formulate [their] own account of something or apply [their] knowledge of an explanation to a particular instance in which that explanation applies" (p. 45).

"Indicators" here are:

(a) students engaged in clarifying something which they have not explained before;

(b) an explanation which is arrived at independently, although it may not be novel; or

(c) the cognitive process in which the pupils engage, and which is more complex than recounting.

Causal, normative, and process explanations are appropriate for productive thinking.

4. Explanation As a Teacher Competency

That teachers should be competent in explanation seems to be unquestionable. According to Slavin (1991), effective teachers use many explanations and explanatory words (e.g., "because," "in order to," "consequently"). They also frequently use a rule–example–rule pattern when explaining new concepts. This pattern requires that a rule be stated, "Matter may change form but it is never destroyed." An example of the rule is given, "A paper when burned merely combines with oxygen and changes to a gas, mostly carbon dioxide." The rule is then restated, "The matter did not disappear but merely changed form" (p. 273).

There is also strong empirical justification for use of explanation from research on teacher clarity. Students have reported that a teacher's ability to provide thorough, understandable explanations is important in helping them learn the content (Cruickshank and Kennedy 1986, Metcalf and Cruickshank 1991). To be judged clear in this case, teachers must use examples, work examples and explain them, explain unfamiliar words, show similarities and differences between or among things, and explain something and pause to allow students to think.

Scholars in the field of reading and mathematics have studied how effectively teachers explain. Faculty at Michigan State University have looked at the phenomenon of teacher explanation in the context of the teaching of reading. Specifically, they have examined the effects of "explicitness of teacher explanations" on student reading achievement and student reports of what was taught (Duffy et al. 1985). Across studies, Duffy and his colleagues have found that explicit teacher explanations are associated with high pupil awareness of lesson content. However, they are only minimally associated with student achievement (Duffy et al. 1986).

Although mathematicians and mathematics educators believe K-12 pupils should be mostly skilled in problem solving, they are not. This finding seems partly to be the case because K-12 teachers allocate more instructional time to the teaching of computational skill. One possible reason for such time allocation is that "most teachers do not know how to explain cognitive reasoning processes associated with strategies used by successful problem solvers" (Herrmann 1989 p. 1).

5. Methods Used in the Study of Explanation

Instruments have been developed which have been used to study explanation. As a consequence of interest in utilizing logic in the analysis of teaching, two major instruments were developed for use in coding teacher–student linguistic activity. Among other things, both attend to explanation.

5.1 The Illinois Instrument

The Illinois Instrument was developed under the leadership of B O Smith. Smith and Meux (1970) noted two broad types or classes of classroom linguistic activities, "monologues" and "episodes." Monologues follow the common definition, that is, one occurs whenever a single speaker talks for an extended time. Episode is use to describe exchanges between or among speakers.

According to Smith and Meux, episodes typically are initiated by a teacher question, for example, "What causes an eclipse?" Each such question or "entry" has an ideal or more appropriate logical response which would answer the question in the sense it was proposed. The eclipse question above would seem to best call for an explanation. Besides explanation, there are a dozen other concepts used to categorize entries (Dunkin and Biddle 1982 p. 281).

Entries calling for an explanation require that some general rule or set of conditions be given to explain a result or consequence thereof. Explanation is divided into six categories: (a) mechanical (e.g., "How do crickets make sounds?"); (b) causal (e.g., "What makes people lethargic?"); (c) sequential (e.g., "What events led to the Gulf War?"); (d) procedural (e.g., "How do you tack when sailing?"); (e) teleological (e.g., "Why did you teach the lesson as you did?"); or (f) normative (e.g., "Why was South Africa the target of international sanction?").

The Illinois Instrument has been used in studies conducted by Nuthall and Lawrence (1965), Smith and Meux (1970), and Tisher (1970).

Dunkin and Biddle (1982) report that regardless of the subject matter taught and the geographic (national) location of the study, approximately one-fourth of the episodes fall into the "describing" category. "Designating" and "explaining" are also popular. Where teachers ask for explanations that are either of a sequential or procedural kind, students handle them. However, in general, when teachers ask for explanations of a causal, teleological, or normative type, pupils do not generate congruent or logical responses (Nuthall and Lawrence 1965, Tisher 1970). Teachers often responded to student inability to answer the question by attempting to clarify it. Dunkin and Biddle ask, "Could it be that when teachers ask higher level [explaining type] questions, vagueness often enters in and interferes with the communication to pupils?" (p. 293). In this regard, Tisher found that one-fifth of the explanations teachers did accept were logically inappropriate given the question asked.

5.2 The Columbia University Instrument

A second instrument emerged from the work of Bellack et al. (1966) who worked toward identifying and analyzing instruction from a logical perspective. They studied the instructional process and felt it could be described by a series of "moves" or verbal behaviors of teachers and students: structuring, soliciting, responding, and reacting. Thus, whereas the Illinois Instrument categorized only how pupils logically should respond to episode opening entries, mainly questions or solicitations, the Bellack et al. or Columbia University Instrument is capable of classifying everything teachers do, including their monologues or lectures. The Bellack et al. categories are nine in number and not unrelated to Smith and Meux's. Explaining is one category. It is used to refer to: (a) statements of relations between or among objects, events, principles; (b) conditional inference; (c) cause–effect; (d) explicit comparison contrast; and (e) statements of principles, theories, or laws. The other categories are defining–general, defining–denotative, defining–connotative, interpreting, fact stating, opining, justifying, and "logical process not clear." The Columbia University Instrument has been used in studies conducted by Furst (1967), Lundgren (1972), and Power (1971).

With regard to "solicitations," Bellack et al. (1966) found about 80 percent of them were concerned with empirical processes and slightly more of these with "explaining" than with "fact finding." Unlike the findings of investigators using the Illinois Instrument, Columbia University Instrument users found pupil responses to teacher questions to be congruent 85 percent of the time.

While researchers using the Illinois and Columbia University Instruments observed the general use of logic and linguistics during classroom discourse, investigators at Stanford, under the direction of N L Gage, concentrated on the single phenomenon of teachers' ability to explain. Relatedly, Rosenshine (1968) studied lecturing. He found that effective lectures contained more explaining links, that is, "propositions and conjunctions which indicate the cause, result, means, or purpose of an event or idea" (p. 8). Examples include "because," "in order to," "if . . . then," "therefore," and "consequently."

Hiller et al. (1969) also studied lectures using the same data as did Rosenshine. They found in general that vagueness was negatively associated with student achievement. Vagueness is defined as when "a performer . . . does not sufficiently command the facts or the understanding required for maximally effective communication" (p. 670). In other words, what is not known well cannot be explained clearly.

5.3 The Rating Teacher Explanation Instrument

The Rating Teacher Explanation Instrument (Duffy et al. 1985) contains two parts. Part I focuses on the information the teacher presents about the cognitive processes students should follow to do a reading task, and asks observers to rate such information in terms of its clarity, consistency, and explicitness. Part 2 focuses on the means by which the teacher makes clear the information presented. It asks observers to record how the teacher (a) modelled how to do the required cognitive processing, (b) directed attention if students became confused, (c) provided students with independent or guided practice using cognitive processing in a contrived sample (workbook page, ditto sheet, etc.), and (d) helped students apply the cognitive processing when reading basal text stories or in other connected situations.

Mathematics educators have also studied cognitive processing or how students learn. They, too, are interested in how well K-12 teachers communicate successful student learning strategies to their own pupils. Consequently, Herrmann (1989) has used a modification of the Rating Teacher Explanation Instrument to rate teacher explanations given during mathematics instruction in problem-solving.

5.4 Herrmann's Pupil Awareness Rating Form

Herrmann's Pupil Awareness Rating Form (Herrmann 1989) is used to rate pupil responses to three questions asked during a post-teaching interview. The questions are: "What was taught?" "When and how *would* what was taught be used?" and "When and how *could* what was taught be used?". Two other related instruments are presented (Herrmann 1989 pp. 15–17) as well as a sociolinguistic mapping procedure she followed to identify characteristics of more and less explicit units of teacher talk.

6. Need for Further Scholarship and Research

Persons working to understand explanation seem not to be organized. Relatedly, there seems to be no guru or individual who, over time, has engaged in significant related inquiry.

Should the aggregate of researchers in the field be formed into a true group it might argue for scholarship and research such as the following:

(a) a compilation of concepts, definitions, facts, and conditional propositions or "if then" statements that would shed light on precisely what is known about explaining;

(b) the collection and analysis of instruments used for the study of explaining and related concepts;

(c) discussion of perspectives on explaining, its observation and measurement; and

(d) projections of further studies that might include gaining concurrence and consensus of what explaining is, devising further descriptive or qualitative study of it, looking for characteristics of good explainers, determining relationships between explaining and pupil learning and satisfaction, and determining whether teachers can be trained in explanation and the effect of training on student outcomes.

References

Armbruster B B, Anderson T H 1984 Structures of explanations in history textbooks, or so what if Governor Stanford missed the spike and hit the rail? *Curriculum Studies* 16(2): 181–94

Bellack A A, Kliebard H M, Hyman R T, Smith F L 1966 *The Language of the Classroom*. Teachers College, Columbia University, New York

Cruickshank D, Kennedy J 1986 Teacher clarity. *Teaching and Teacher Education* 2(1): 43–67

Dagher Z R 1989 The nature of verbal teacher explanations in junior high science classrooms. (Doctoral dissertation, University of Iowa)

Duffy G G, Roehler L R, Wesselman R 1985 Disentangling the complexities of instructional effectiveness: A line of research in classroom reading instruction. In: Niles J, Lakil R (eds.) 1985 *Issues in Literacy: A Research Perspective. Thirty-fourth Yearbook of the National Reading Conference*. National Reading Conference, Rochester, New York

Duffy G G, Roehler L R, Rackliffe G 1986 How teachers' instructional talk influences students' understanding of lesson content. *Elem. Sch. J.* 87(1): 3–16

Dunkin M, Biddle J 1982 *The Study of Teaching*. University Press of America, Washington, DC

Ennis R H 1969 *Logic in Teaching*. Prentice-Hall, Englewood Cliffs, New Jersey

Fairhurst M A 1981 Satisfactory explanations in the primary school. *J. Phil. Educ.* 15(2): 205–14

Furst N F 1967 The multiple languages of the classroom. (Doctoral dissertation, Temple University)

Garfinkel A 1981 *Forms of Explanations: Rethinking the Questions in Social Theory*. Yale University Press, New Haven, Connecticut

Herrmann B A 1989 Characteristics of explicit and less explicit explanations of mathematical problem solving strategies. *Reading Research and Instruction* 28(3): 1–17

Hiller J, Fisher G, Kaess W 1969 A computer investigation of verbal characteristics of effective classroom lecturing. *Am. Educ. Res. J.* 6(4): 661–75

Hudgins B B 1974 *A Catalogue of Concepts in the Pedagogical Domain of Teacher Education*. Graduate Institute of Education, Washington University, St. Louis, Missouri

Lundgren U P 1972 *Frame Factors and the Teaching Process: A Contribution to Curriculum Theory and Theory on Teaching*. Almqvist and Wiksell, Stockholm

MacDonald R E 1991 *A Handbook of Basic Skills and Strategies for Beginning Teachers*. Longman, White Plains, New York

Metcalf K K, Cruickshank D R 1991 Can teachers be trained to be more clear? *J. Educ. Res.* 85(2): 107–16

Metcalf L E 1963 Research on teaching the social studies. In: Gage N L (ed.) 1963 *Handbook of Research on Teaching*. Rand McNally, Chicago, Illinois

Nuthall G A, Lawrence P J 1965 *Thinking in the Classroom: The Development of a Method of Analysis*. New Zealand Council for Educational Research, Wellington

Power C N 1971 The effects of communication patterns on student sociometric status, attitudes, and achievement in science. (Doctoral dissertation, The University of Queensland)

Rosenshine B 1968 Objectively measured behavioral predictors of effectiveness in explaining. Paper presented at the annual meeting of the American Educational Research Association, Chicago, Illinois

Schulze K G 1989–90 The use of multiple explanations in an open-ended intelligent tutoring system. *Journal of Educational Technology Systems* 18(3): 221–25

Slavin R E 1991 *Educational Psychology. Theory into Practice*. 3rd edn. Prentice-Hall, Englewood Cliffs, New Jersey

Smith B O, Cohen S B, Pearl A 1969 *Teachers for the Real World*. American Association of Colleges for Teacher Education, Washington, DC

Smith B O, Meux M O 1970 *A Study of the Logic of Teaching*. University of Illinois Press, Urbana, Illinois

Swift L F 1959 Explanation as an aspect of critical thinking in secondary school social studies. (Doctoral dissertation, The University of Illinois)

Tisher R P 1970 The nature of verbal discourse in classrooms and association between verbal discourse and pupil understanding in science. In: Campbell W J (ed.) 1970 *Scholars in Context: The Effects of Environment on Learning*. Wiley, Sydney

D. R. Cruickshank; K. K. Metcalf

Teaching and Teacher Education: Comparative and International Studies

Comparative and international research on teaching examines similarities and differences in behavior among teachers from different systems of education from different countries. It also investigates whether influences upon teaching vary from one system or country to another and whether the effects of teaching behaviors and practices also vary from system to system and country to country.

Dunkin (1989) described the different types of research that contribute information of the above types and reviewed relevant research that had been reported up to that time. Most of the studies he discussed had been conducted under the auspices of the International Association for the Evaluation of Educational Achievement (IEA) (see *Educational Achievement: Comparative Studies*). Since then a new generation of IEA studies has been completed and two of them have had their reports published—*The IEA Study of Mathematics* (Robitaille and Garden 1989, Travers and Westbury 1989) and *The IEA Classroom Environment Study* (Anderson et al. 1989). This entry focuses upon those studies.

1. The Second IEA Study of Mathematics

Although this study was essentially of mathematics curricula, it also involved some teacher and teaching variables. The two reports cited above contain material obtained from a total of 20 participating systems of schooling as follows—Belgium (Flemish system), Belgium (French), Canada (British Columbia), Canada (Ontario), England and Wales, Finland, France, Hong Kong, Hungary, Israel, Japan, Luxembourg, the Netherlands, New Zealand, Nigeria, Scotland, Swaziland, Sweden, Thailand, and the United States of America. Two target populations of students were defined, Population A and Population B.

Population A consists of all students in the grade in which the modal number of students has attained the age of 13.0–13.11 years by the middle of the school year. Population B consists of all students who are in the normally accepted terminal grade of the secondary school system, and who are studying mathematics as a substantial part (approximately 5 hours per week) of their academic program (Travers and Westbury 1989 p. 11).

Data for the study were gathered between 1980 and 1982 and included the following teacher variables: age, gender, experience, teaching loads (hours per week), education and qualifications (especially in mathematics, mathematics pedagogy, and general pedagogy), degree of specialization, and teaching practices involving the use of resources, teaching activities, allocation of time, and differentation of instruction, and teachers' perceptions of opportunity to learn mathematics content included in the achievement tests.

Some of the findings for these variables were as follows. The proportion of male teachers ranged for Population A from 20 percent in Hungary to 90 percent in the Netherlands. In Canada (Ontario), Hong Kong, New Zealand, and Scotland, male teachers outnumbered female teachers by between 10 percent and 50 percent, while in Canada (British Columbia), Japan, Luxembourg, the Netherlands, Nigeria, and Sweden, male teachers predominated to a great extent. In three systems—Hungary, Israel, and Thailand—more than 50 percent of the teachers were female. For Population B the balance ranged from 40 percent male in Hungary to 96 percent. In the 15 systems which participated in the study of this population the trend was toward greater proportions of male teachers at this upper level. Robitaille and Garden (1989) commented on these findings as follows: "With such marked gender differences in the composition of the mathematics teaching force in some systems, there is rich ground for investigation of the societal pressures which lead to this situation and of the consequences for mathematics education" (p. 42)

The least experienced Population A teachers came from Swaziland and Thailand, both of which averaged 7 years, and the most experienced came from Japan, averaging 17 years. For Population B the least experienced teachers were from Hong Kong on 9 years and the most experienced from Sweden on 18 years. Teaching loads were measured in terms of number of contact hours per week. These ranged on average from 13 in Belgium (French) to 22 hours in the Netherlands for Population A, and from 14 hours in Japan, Sweden, and Thailand to 21 hours in British Columbia and Scotland for Population B.

In 8 systems more than 10 percent of Population A teachers had not studied any mathematics at postsecondary level and in 6 systems 25 percent of teachers or more had undertaken no study of mathematics pedagogy at postsecondary level. An analysis of the mathematics preparation for Population B teachers produced similar results. In France, Canada (Ontario), Sweden, Hong Kong, and Swaziland large proportions (26%–47%) of Population A teachers had experienced formal training in general pedagogy, while in Sweden, Finland, and Hong Kong over 40 percent had had no such training at the level of Population B. Mathematics teachers of Population A students in Nigeria, Scotland, Japan, Thailand, and Belgium (French) were specialists in between 70 and 96 percent of the cases, while almost none of them were in Canada (Ontario) and Sweden. Specialism at the Population B level was almost exclusively the case in Japan, Scotland, and Thailand but was not common in Sweden, Finland, and Hong Kong.

As regards the study of teaching practices, it was found that the most commonly used resource was the textbook which was used at least "often" by teachers in all systems for Population A. Individualized materials, visual materials, and published tests received very little use in almost all systems.

Resource usage was similar for Population B. For population A, in Belgium (Flemish system) teachers spent a median period of 270 minutes in a typical week on preparation and grading. This ranged down to 60 minutes in Scotland. When marking and grading were expressed in terms of time per student, the greatest time was found in both Belgian systems, Thailand, and France, and the least in New Zealand, Scotland, Finland, Japan, and Sweden. Both preparation time and grading time were higher for Population B students.

Werry (1989) reported the findings for in-class teacher activities as follows:

> In every system and at both levels, most of the time is spent explaining new content, that is, in expository teaching or lecturing. This is especially true for Population B classes. In most systems, between 5 percent and 10 percent of the time in the four categories [of classroom activities] in Population A classes, on average, is spent on administrative matters, with slightly less in Population B classes. A similar amount of time is spent in maintaining order for Population A, but very little with Population B students . . .
> . . . It can be concluded . . . that expository, lecturing styles of teaching are relatively prominent in Belgium (Flemish), Hong Kong, and the United States, but rarer in England and Wales, Israel, Scotland, and Sweden. (p. 56)

The last two teaching activities studied were teachers' allocation of class time and differentiation of instruction. Teachers estimated that in a typical week tests and examinations took up 10 to 15 percent of students' time for both populations in most systems. Highest percentages were reported in France, Luxembourg, the Netherlands, Nigeria, Israel, and the United States, and least in England and Wales, Scotland, and Sweden. Small group work was not common at either level, with the greatest use of it being made with Population B in England and Wales, Israel, and Thailand. Seatwork and listening–discussion groups together accounted for over 70 percent of classroom time for both populations. More than 75 percent of the teachers at both levels claimed that they never or rarely used differentiated tasks for particular groups of students. The highest percentage of usage was in Swaziland and Nigeria, while the lowest was in Luxembourg, Hungary, and France for population A. In general, less use was made of differentiation in Population B where the most common users were Hungary, New Zealand, and Thailand, and those making least use were Finland and Scotland.

Teachers from Hungary and Swaziland reported mean percentages of content coverage across the various subject domains of more than 80 percent for Population A classes. All the others reported mean coverage of between 61 and 80 percent, with the exception of Luxembourg and Sweden, where the mean reported coverage was between 41 and 60 percent. For population B classes, variations in teachers' perceptions of coverage of the items of the achievement tests varied greatly among the systems for the different subject domains. While teachers in all systems reported more than 80 percent coverage in algebra there was great variation, for example, in probability and statistics, for which coverage ranged from 40 percent or less in Hungary to over 80 percent in Finland, Japan, and New Zealand. Unfortunately, the main findings regarding teaching processes from the second IEA study of mathematics were not available at the time of writing this entry.

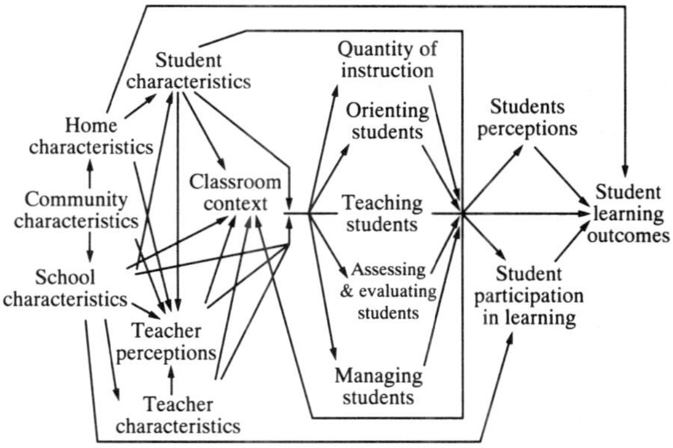

Figure 1
The core model of the classroom environment study
Source: Anderson et al. 1989 p. 23

2. *The IEA Study of Classroom Environments*

The main report on this study is by Anderson et al. (1989), which presented findings from the following participating systems: Australia, Canada (Ontario/English system), Canada (Ontario/French), Canada (Quebec), Hungary, Israel, the Republic of Korea, the Netherlands, Nigeria, and Thailand. Essentially, this was a classroom observational study involving the 15 constructs shown in expected relationship with each other in Fig. 1, which depicts the "core model" of the study. Table 1 lists the specific variables for which data were obtained and analyzed. Table 2 provides an overview of the execution of the research, where it is shown that the grade level of the classes studied ranged from 5 to 8; the subject matter was mathematics in 7 of the systems but physics, science, and history formed the focal points in 3 systems. Sample sizes of schools, classes, and students varied greatly. Most of the data collection occurred from 1981 through to 1983. Teachers' characteristics were summarized as follows:

> The participating countries . . . differed in the predominant sex of the teachers, and their age and years of experience. Within most countries, however, differences among the teachers in age and years of experience also

Table 1
Constructs and variables used in the IEA Classroom Environment Study

Construct/Variables	Construct/Variables
Community characteristics	Oral practice drill
School location	Reading at seats
School characteristics	Written seatwork
Type of school (TYPESC)	Laboratory work
Grade level organization	Direction of verbal interactions
Size of school	Explanation
Time allocated to subject (per year)	Explanation using materials
Teacher characteristics	Demonstration
Sex (SEXT)	Use of examples
Age (AGET)	Structuring cues
Years of experience (YRS)	Directives
Certification	Student questions
Subject area training	Student contributions
Subject contact hours (per week)	Social interactions
Number of additional subjects taught	Silence (absence of verbal interactions)
Total contact hours (per week)	Frequency of extra help
Home characteristics	Number receiving extra help
Father's education	Timing of extra help
Mother's education	Format of extra help
Father's occupation	Type of extra help
Language used in home	Assessing and Evaluating students
Student characteristics	Questioning student
Sex (SEXS)	Questioning group
Age (AGES)	Asks recall questions
Pretest (PRETEST)	Asks higher order questions
Aspirations (ASPIRATION)	Asks opinion questions
Attitude toward school (ATTSCH)	Asks effectiveness questions
Attitude toward subject (PREATTSUBJ)	Amount of questioning
Classroom context	Waits for student(s) response
Typical use of grouping	Student short response
Observed use of grouping	Student recitation
Use of types of materials	Student extended response
Student access to books outside school	Student doesn't answer
Lesson emphasis	Positive acknowledgement
Lesson objective	Says answer wrong
Class size	Repeats answer
Number of adults per classroom	Redirects question
Student attendance	Gives answer
Teacher perceptions	Probes
Teacher autonomy	Probes to student
Relative class ability level	Probes to group
Percent of students needing remediation	Tests for grading purposes
Quantity of instruction	Diagnostic testing
Amount of homework	Managing students
Time for homework	Management and routine administration
Opportunity to learn	Procedural interactions
Allocated time	Transitional interactions
Instructional time	Disciplinary actions
Orienting students	Uninvolved teacher
Specifying objectives	Student perceptions
Reviewing content	Task orientation (TASK)
Teaching students	Structure of lesson (STRUCTURE)
Teacher interacting	Teacher feedback (FEEDBACK)
Teacher monitoring	Student participation
Monitoring individual seatwork	Percent of students engaged in learning (ENGPCT)
Monitoring group work	Student outcomes
Lecture	Student achievement (POSTTEST)
Discourse discussion	Attitude toward subject (POSTATTSUBJ)

Source: Adapted from Anderson et al 1989 pp. 40–43

Table 2
Overview of the execution of the Classroom Environment Study[a]

Country	Grade level	Subject matter	No. of schools	No. of classes	No. of students	Study length (months)	No. of observations
Australia	5	Maths	39	75	1,963	3	8–10
Canada Ontario/English	8	Maths	18	27	751	7	8
Canada Ontario/French	8	Maths	14	18	420	6	8
Canada Quebec	7–8	Maths	9	30	749	6	10
Hungary	5	Physics	40	40	1,180	—	5
Israel	6	History	11	22	671	4	1–5
Korea (ROK)	5	Science	15	45	2,400	2	8
Netherlands	8	Maths	17	50	1,125	7	8
Nigeria	8	Maths	35	35	1,416	—	4
Thailand	5	Maths	77	87	2,572	9	6

Source: Anderson et al. 1989 p. 48
a The number of classes shown in this table represent those classes in which at least one observation was conducted. As a result of various editing procedures and the application of missing data rules, the numbers of classes (and hence the numbers of students) included in each analysis are typically lower than those shown in this table. Finally, in Hungary and Nigeria the study length was not provided by the NRCs.

were notable. The vast majority of teachers included in the study were certified at the elementary school level. Those certified at the secondary school level were exceptions (even for the teachers of seventh and eighth grade students).

Teachers in the various countries also differed in their subject matter training, the number of hours per week spent teaching the subject matter, and the number of additional subjects taught. Fairly large within-country differences in subject matter training also existed. The vast majority of teachers in all countries taught a total of 11 to 30 hours per week. (Anderson et al. 1989 p. 70)

The major findings of the Classroom Environment Study were summarized in two groupings. The first of these were categorized as "descriptive findings," and the second as "associations and influences." Teachers' perceptions of autonomy in decisions about assignments, organization of classrooms, and use of tests, that is, within-classroom matters, were greater than their perceptions of autonomy in determining the curriculum and in holding meetings with parents, that is, outside-classroom matters. Perceptions of autonomy also varied from system to system. Teachers made great use of textbooks but infrequent use of audiovisual and programmed materials. Across the systems, teachers made little use of small group instruction but most use of whole class instruction. Homework assignments were used mainly to identify learning deficiencies and formal tests to assign grades. Less frequent use was made of projects and written reports for those purposes.

Opportunity to learn the content included on the final test varied greatly within systems. Across the systems, teachers were very active in their classrooms, spending most of their time interacting with their students. Communications in the classroom were mostly from teachers to students, with student communications mainly comprised of brief responses to teachers' questions. Apart from Hungary, lectures, seatwork, and management occupied from 50 to 80 percent of all observed activities.

Among the associations and influences reported were the following: differences in specific teaching behaviors observed were unrelated to differences in students' final achievement. Such behaviors were more consistently related to students' academic engagement than to their final achievement. Teachers in larger classes spent less time than other teachers in explaining, structuring, and directing, and more time in classroom management. Teachers who rated their classes as having lower ability spent more time asking the students questions and probing to assess and evaluate them. More experienced teachers spent less time on classroom management. The amount of time students spent engaged in learning was positively related to posttest achievement adjusted for pretest achievement. Student learning was directly affected by the quantity of instruction they received in the form of content coverage and/or homework.

The space constraints of this entry do not permit the presentation of between-country comparisons. Perhaps more important are the implications the authors of the report drew from the findings. These were as follows:

(a) The constraints under which teachers operate impose a sameness on their behavior which makes it difficult for research to test whether variations in teaching affect student learning.

(b) Teachers tend to be occasionally inconsistent, with the result that within-teacher differences are greater than between-teacher differences, again making it difficult for studies such as this present review to identify associations with student learning.

(c) Larger, composite units of teacher behavior which overcome the problem of unreliability of smaller units and result in stronger associations with student learning were identified.

(d) Because student variables, such as their prior knowledge, their perceptions of classrooms and teachers, and their classroom behavior were more closely related to outcome variables than were teacher or teaching variables, classroom research should focus more on students than on teachers.

(e) Studies of teaching should be designed so that classrooms contain students of similar degrees of prior knowledge or ability, variables are conceptually sound and reliably measured, experimental rather than correlational designs are used, differences in opportunity to learn are minimized, and observational instruments are suited to the purposes of the research and the nature of the data required.

(f) Variations in classroom time spent in different subjects—in teacher preparation to teach them and in behaviors exhibited during the teaching of different subjects—suggest that the structure of the subject matter has a strong influence upon classroom teaching.

(g) As teacher classroom behavior appeared to account for only small proportions of the variation in student learning, teacher education should emphasize teacher conceptualizing, theorizing, and decision-making as well as teaching behavior.

3. Conclusion

Anderson and Postlethwaite (1989) reviewed what they described as three generations of IEA studies and arrived at five major generalizations which they thought had emerged about teachers and teaching:

Generalization 1: Greater teacher experience and subject matter knowledge are associated with greater skills in classroom management and higher levels of student achievement. Two main implications were seen to arise from this generalization. The first was that needs for in-service training in such matters as classroom management and instructional strategies are likely to vary for teachers of different levels of experience so that individualization of this training might need to be provided. The second implication was that more attention should be given to teachers' subject-matter knowledge.

Generalization 2: Students who have greater opportunities to learn the knowledge and skills included on the achievement tests are likely to have higher levels of achievement. Two main implications were also seen to arise from this generalization. The first was that differences in opportunity to learn might conceal differences in the effectiveness of teachers and their teaching practices when they are studied in research. The second was that students' opportunity to learn and issues associated with it warrant careful consideration in relation to educational goals, achievement tests, and instruction so that the proper alignments might result.

Generalization 3: The greater amount of time spent on teaching and learning, the greater the achievement of students. This generalization was not seen to warrant simplistic interpretations such as that adding more instructional time in amounts of minutes per day or hours per year would significantly increase achievement. Rather the implications seemed to be more for the careful study of pacing and homework in relation to achievement.

Generalization 4: Differences in the behaviors that teachers exhibit in their classrooms are unrelated to differences in student achievement. Again, two main implications were drawn from this generalization. First, the study of relationships between differences in teacher behavior and differences in student behavior might be more rewarding than the study of the corresponding relationships involving teacher behavior and student achievement. Second, exclusively behaviorist views of teaching are misleading and counterproductive.

Generalization 5: Students' perceptions of what transpires in the classroom are more valid than those of trained observers (and perhaps those of teachers). The implications of this generalization were seen to be that teachers need to monitor students constantly, to provide feedback on their progress, and to assist them in making adjustments where required, and that "teachers should be less egocentric and more sensitive to impact they have (or fail to have) on their students" (Anderson and Postlethwaite 1989 p. 85).

These generalizations yielded by the IEA studies might seem to some observers to be simplistic. Anderson and Postlethwaite (1989 p. 85) responded to such criticism in the following terms:

> We suggest that the strength of the findings of the IEA studies resides not in their insights, but in their grounding in the everyday experiences of school administrators and teachers . . . We contend that the knowledge provided by the IEA studies does, in fact, "ring true." The extent to which the "commonsense" knowledge provided by these studies becomes "commonplace" remains the responsibility of practitioners.

See also: Political Work of Teachers; Teacher Educators, Characteristics of; Mathematics Teacher Education

References

Anderson L W, Postlethwaite T N 1989 What IEA studies say about teachers and teaching. In: Purves A C (ed.) 1989 *International Comparisons and Educational Reform*. Association for Supervision and Curriculum Development, Washington, DC

Anderson L W, Ryan D W, Shapiro B J (eds.) 1989 *The IEA Classroom Environment Study*. Pergamon Press, Oxford

Dunkin M J 1989 Teaching: Comparative studies. In: Husén T, Postlethwaite T N (eds.) 1989 *The International Encyclopedia of Education*, Supplementary Vol. 1. Pergamon Press, Oxford

Robitaille D F, Garden R A (eds.) 1989 *The IEA Study of Mathematics II: Contexts and Outcomes of School Mathematics*. Pergamon Press, Oxford

Travers K J, Westbury I (eds.) 1989 *The IEA Study of Mathematics I: Analysis of Mathematics Curricula*. Pergamon Press, Oxford.

Werry B 1989 The teachers of mathematics. In: Robitaille D F, Garden R A 1989

Further Reading

Anderson L W, Burns R 1990 *Research in Classrooms: The Study of Teachers, Teaching, and Instruction*. Pergamon Press, Oxford

Houston R (ed.) 1990 *Handbook of Research on Teacher Education*. Macmillan, New York

Wittrock M C (ed.) 1986 *Handbook of Research on Teaching*, 3rd edn. Macmillan, New York

M. J. Dunkin

Teaching: Aptitude–Treatment Interaction Model

An aptitude–treatment interaction (ATI) occurs when the characteristics of persons moderate the effects of instructional conditions on those persons. Conversely, ATI implies that the importance of personal characteristics in relation to valued educational outcomes depends on what instructional conditions are administered. The study of aptitude–treatment interactions in education aims at understanding when, how, and why different kinds of persons benefit from different kinds of instruction, so that educational conditions for individual learners can be improved. An adaptive instructional system with respect to individual differences among persons is the goal (see *Individualized Instruction*).

Aptitude–treatment interaction research is a special case of the scientific study of person–environment interaction. The possibility of interactions has long been routinely acknowledged in the physical scientist's qualifier "other things being equal . . . " and in the social scientist's question "Can we generalize to other groups (communities, cultures, etc.)?" Evolutionary biology is basically interactionist. Interactions have been put to practical use in medicine; for example, the physician's choice of antibiotic depends on the patient's answer to the test question: "Have you ever had an allergic reaction to penicillin?"

Cronbach (1957, 1975), recognized that person–environment interaction was both a fundamental concept and a fundamental problem for psychology. Interactional research has accumulated in a variety of fields of psychology (Dance and Neufeld 1988, Endler and Magnusson 1976, Magnusson and Allen 1983, Pervin and Lewis 1978, Snow 1991). Although interactional thinking has been evident in educational philosophies since ancient times, the full implications of aptitude–treatment interaction for education have been systematically addressed only since the 1970s (Cronbach and Snow 1977, Snow 1989).

1. Substantive Definition and Implications for Education

In education, many kinds of individual differences among learners can be observed and measured. When such measures predict individual differences in learning from instruction, they are interpreted as indicators of aptitude, that is, readiness to profit from instruction. When aptitude measures provide differential predictions for learning under different instructional conditions, a conclusion of aptitude–treatment interaction is justified.

Many kinds of aptitude differences among students have been studied, including general and special cognitive abilities, personality and motivational attributes, and cognitive styles. Many kinds of instructional treatments have also been compared. Since ATI findings often occur, there is no doubt that ATI exists in education (Cronbach and Snow 1977). Theoretical and practical understanding of ATI is not, in the early 1990s, sufficient to allow routine use of ATI in educational planning or instructional design.

It is clear, however, that routine use of ATI is both possible and necessary in educational evaluation. Aptitude–treatment interaction methodology is a requisite part of any evaluation study aimed at comparing alternative teaching methods or environments because the evaluation question is never simply which treatment is best on average? It is always which treatment is best for each of the individual learners to be served?

Aptitude–treatment interactions are of interest theoretically because they demonstrate construct validity for aptitude and learning measures in a new way: they show how aptitude–learning relations can be experimentally manipulated and thus understood in a causal rather than only a correlational framework. Neither aptitude constructs nor educational learning processes can be fully understood without reference to one another. Therefore, it is possible that common psychological processes underlie both aptitude and learning differences.

Furthermore, as interactions have appeared ubiquitous in education, they show the need to understand not only persons and situations, but their interface. Learning and aptitude come to be seen as operating in the person–situation union, not just in the heads of persons, thus posing a new theoretical and philosophical problem (Snow 1992).

Practical interest stems from the possibility that ATI can be used to adapt instruction to fit different learners optimally. Many attempts at individualizing instruction have failed to eliminate individual differences in learning outcome because they adapted only to limited aspects of individual performance; for example, by allowing differences in pace. The hope is that research on ATI can provide decision rules that indicate how to vary instructional conditions in ways that mesh with particular learner strengths while avoiding particular learner weaknesses. A related hope is that such research will indicate how best to develop aptitudes directly for persons with different initial aptitude profiles.

Again, the general question for research, and for evaluation studies, is which of the available or conceivable teaching methods, media, or environments is most likely to provide equality of educational opportunity to each individual learner, for his or her aptitude development and educational achievement. The commitment to optimal diversity of educational opportunity (e.g., truly to provide adaptive education as defined by Glaser 1977), demands that educational environments be chosen or invented and evaluated within an ATI perspective (Corno and Snow 1986).

At the same time, however, ATI research has shown that interactions are complex. No simple or general principles for matching students and teachers, teaching methods, or school environments have emerged. Part of the problem stems from the difficulty of conducting ATI research and a widespread lack of understanding of appropriate methods, but part also can be attributed to the multidimensional, dynamic, and often local and even transient character of the person–environment interface. Results to date suggest that work toward instructional theories that seek to optimize instruction for individuals in real school settings will need to be built up from continuous local diagnosis, description, and evaluation activities; local instructional models rather than general educational theory seem to be the more realizable goal (Snow 1991).

2. Statistical Definition and Methodology

Normally, ATI is defined as a statistical interaction: the multiplicative combination of at least one person variable and one treatment variable in affecting one dependent or instructional outcome variable. The interaction exists whenever the regression of an instructional outcome from one treatment upon some personal characteristic of learners differs in slope from the regression of that outcome from another treatment on the same characteristic.

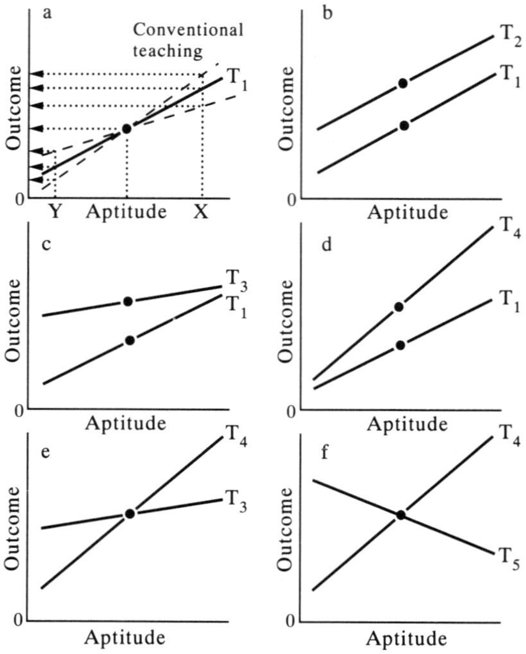

Figure 1
Possible effects of alternative instructional treatments (T) on outcome averages and outcome-on-aptitude regressions

Figure 1 gives the basic patterns of possible relationships. Each graph assumes that student aptitude scores taken before instruction and student outcome scores taken after instruction have been plotted, on the abscissa and ordinate respectively, to form a bivariate distribution for each treatment under investigation. Linear regression slopes have been fitted to each distribution and treatment average effects have been identified (the heavy centered dots). In Fig. 1(a), labeled "conventional teaching," the solid slope (T_1) depicts an aptitude– outcome relationship corresponding to a correlation coefficient of 0.50; the dashed slopes depict variation in this relationship between coefficients of 0.30 and 0.70. These data approximate what has often been found in United States public schools, using general intelligence or prior achievement tests as aptitude measures and cognitive achievement measures to reflect instructional outcomes. Note that a student with aptitude score at X is predicted (dotted arrows) to obtain outcome scores above the mean while a student with aptitude score at Y is predicted to obtain outcome scores below the mean.

An important aim of educational research is to improve upon this state of affairs by finding or devising instructional treatments such as T_2 in Fig. 1(b) that raise the average outcome for everyone over that expected from T_1. When such regression slopes are parallel, as shown here, there is no ATI; T_2 is the better treatment for all students regardless of aptitude. Unfortunately, many educational studies have looked only for such average treatment differences, assuming that aptitude slopes were parallel without investigating them.

The pattern in Fig. 1(c) schematizes the goal of special education and of much research on individualized instruction, where it is hoped that a treatment T_3 can be found to improve achievement of lower aptitude students while maintaining the high achievements of higher aptitude students. However, in searching for generally improved treatments the result shown in Fig. 1 (d) can also be obtained; treatments such as T_4 turn out to be most beneficial for the higher aptitude students rather than for the lower aptitude students. One can think of T_4 as the goal of special programs for the gifted.

The T_3 result has at times been obtained for programmed instruction in comparison to conventional instruction T_1, while the T_4 result has sometimes been obtained in studies of discovery or inductive teaching. This leads to the possibility of combined results such as those in Fig. 1(e). Here, alternative treatments produce improvements for different kinds of students; it is apparent that T_4 should be given to high aptitude students, while T_3 should be given to low aptitude students. In the extreme, if optimal instructional treatments could be found or devised for students like X and Y, the result depicted in Fig. 1(f) might be expected. Negative slopes approximating T_5 do occur at times using cognitive measures, but are more likely when personality or attitudinal characteristics rather than cognitive abilities are used as aptitudes.

Research on ATI seeks to detect nonparallel regression slopes of the sorts shown in Fig. 1 and to understand how instructional treatments can be designed to produce such effects. To the extent that stable interactions like those of Fig. 1(e) and 1(f) can be established, they can be used as suggested above to form decision rules for the assignment of students to optimally different treatments. The regression slopes cross to define the point on the aptitude continuum where persons should be divided to achieve optimal outcome in different instructional treatments. The same regression slope expectations apply to compensatory education programs or to other attempts to develop aptitude directly. The same patterns can be used to interpret evaluation results not aimed at adapting instruction to individual differences. For example, an evaluation that obtained a pattern like that of Fig 1(e) might suggest a revision of T_4 that would improve it specifically for learners below the aptitude mean.

Beyond the simplest cases shown in Fig. 1, there are many technical complications involved in particular study designs and data analyses. Aptitude, treatment, and outcome variables can be multiple; regressions can be nonlinear. Special problems in ATI research attach to the disattenuation of measurements, the evaluation of power of statistical inferences, and the disentangling of regression effects at different levels of aggregation (e.g., individual student, classroom, and school). Since an adaptive instructional system based on ATI would presumably involve periodic aptitude monitoring and reclassification of students, there are also technical issues involved in the sequential assessment of aptitudes and outcomes, and the evaluation of utilities in placement decisions. On these and related topics, see Cronbach and Snow (1977) and Cronbach (1982, 1991).

3. *Examples of Instructional Systems*

An adaptive instructional system such as that envisioned by Glaser (1977, see also Corno and Snow 1986) could be based on ATI. It would contain at least two alternative instructional routes to successful attainment of some criterion achievement level. The route or treatment taken by each learner would depend on an initial diagnosis of aptitude for learning in each available treatment. Also available in such a system would be at least one form of compensatory, direct training of aptitude for learners diagnosed as unready for any of the available instructional treatments.

A variety of alternative instructional treatments have been evaluated using measures of prior ability and generalized achievement as aptitudes. From a summary of that research (Snow 1989), it appears that instructional treatments differ in the information-processing burdens they place on, or remove from, the responsibility of the learner, and the regressions of achievement outcome on scholastic ability become steeper or shallower, respectively, as a result. As learners are required to puzzle things out for themselves, organize their own study, and build their own comprehension, more able learners do well—they can capitalize on their strengths profitably—while less able learners do poorly. However, as instructional treatments relieve learners from difficult reading and inferencing or analyzing of complex concepts on their own, the more such treatments seem to compensate for or circumvent less able learners' weaknesses. Unfortunately, the structured and simplified treatments that seem to help less able learners are suboptimal for able learners, relative to the more burdensome treatments where they excel. The ATI results from a variety of studies of this hypothesis often approximate the pattern shown in Fig. 1(e), and occasionally that in Fig. 1(f).

For some courses of instruction, then, alternative treatment T_4 might be designed to provide relatively unstructured and minimal guidance and to encourage learner self-direction in a discovery-oriented approach. The teacher might guide the inductive process, but instruction would clearly be student centered. In contrast, T_3 might be designed to break down the learning task to give clear step-by-step guidance, feedback, and correction through a series of small units, with frequent summary and review, and simplified demonstrations of the concepts to be learned. Students would be assigned to either T_3 or T_4 on the basis of prior scholastic ability scores taken at the start of instruction. Periodic aptitude and achievement assessments would show the degree to which outcome criterion levels were being achieved for each learner in the particular treatment assigned.

For those students who might not be expected to profit from either alternative, compensatory aptitude training would be assigned. This training might consist of directed work on academic learning or reading skills, study habits, self-management skills, and so on. The aim of this training would be to develop readiness for entry into treatment T_3 as soon as possible.

Student anxiety might also be considered as an aptitude in this adaptive instructional system. It has often been found that more anxious students do relatively poorly under unstructured or student-centered forms of instruction, as compared to teacher-structured conditions. In contrast, less anxious students often appear not to need teacher structure. Furthermore, ability and anxiety appear to combine in higher order interaction in relation to this treatment contrast.

The initial placement decision in the instructional system would thus depend on both prior ability and anxiety indices. Able learners showing little anxiety would be assigned to treatment T_4. The more anxious, able learners and the less able, less anxious learners would receive treatment T_3. The least able and the most anxious students might be given compensatory training adapted to their particular needs: cognitive skills training focused on ability deficits and therapeutic interventions designed to alleviate the effects of anxiety. Periodic monitoring would need to be designed to indicate when particular learners should be switched to alternative treatment assignments.

While these examples provide a hypothetical demonstration, no such system can be properly designed in the abstract. Local conditions must be considered, aptitude measures and alternative treatment designs must be adjusted to these conditions, and periodic evaluation must be relied upon to realize an effective system.

4. Prospects for Research and Development

It is noteworthy that much research in instructional psychology contrasts two treatments without evaluating ATI. Voluminous research on teaching has compared direct teacher-centered instruction with guided discovery. Now research on new instructional technology considers essentially the same contrast in arguments about mastery-oriented computerized tutoring versus discovery learning in computerized microworlds (Glaser and Bassok 1989), again without evaluating ATI. Also, a large number of learning style hypotheses have been developed for use by teachers in adapting classroom instruction to student differences; each such style construct produces an ATI hypothesis, though none have been evaluated as such. Thus, one important prospect for further work is to conduct evaluative research on these developments from an ATI perspective (Cronbach 1982)

A second important line for further research aims at improved analysis of the many different kinds of aptitude constructs and measures that have been used in ATI work (Gustafsson 1989). Several lines of cognitive information processing research have provided analyses of cognitive ability constructs, identifying the underlying component processes and strategies on which individuals may differ (Lohman 1989, Snow 1989, Sternberg 1985a, 1985b).

Another approach has been to examine the differences in learning strategies students engage in during instruction that appear to mediate aptitude–outcome relations. Task analyses of instructional conditions also suggest mediational differences among alternative treatments that may control aptitude–outcome relations. Important new work is investigating prior knowledge differences in relation to cognitive and affective aptitudes for instruction (Schneider and Weinert 1989). There are also important advances in research on conative and affective aptitudes (Heckhausen et al. 1985, Kuhl and Kraska 1989).

Finally, more intensive analysis on outcome measures may help diagnose in detail the particular kinds of cognitive effects that derive from particular aptitude–treatment combinations (Snow and Lohman 1984, 1989). Future research on all these fronts in instructional psychology can be brought together within the ATI framework (Snow and Swanson 1992).

See also: Teaching, Paradigms for Research on; Individualized Instruction

References

Corno L, Snow R E 1986 Adapting teaching to individual differences among learners. In: Wittrock M C (ed.) 1986 *Handbook of Research on Teaching*, 3rd edn. Macmillan, New York

Cronbach L J 1957 The two disciplines of scientific psychology. *Am. Psychol.* 12(11): 671–84

Cronbach L J 1975 Beyond the two disciplines of scientific psychology. *Am. Psychol.* 30(2): 116–27

Cronbach L J 1982 *Designing Evaluations of Educational and Social Programs*. Jossey-Bass, San Francisco, California

Cronbach L J 1991 Emerging views on methodology. In: Wachs T D, Plomin R (eds.) 1991 *Conceptualization and Measurement of Organism–Environment Interaction*. American Psychological Association, Washington, DC

Cronbach L J, Snow R E 1977 *Aptitudes and Instructional Methods: A Handbook for Research on Interactions*. Irvington, New York

Dance K A, Neufeld R W J 1988 Aptitude– treatment interaction research in the clinical setting: A review of attempts to dispel the "patient uniformity" myth. *Psych. Bull.* 104(2): 192–213

Endler N S, Magnusson D (eds.) 1976 *Interactional Psychology and Personality*. Hemisphere, Washington, DC

Glaser R 1977 *Adaptive Education: Individual Diversity and Learning*. Holt, Rinehart, and Winston, New York

Glaser R, Bassok M 1989 Learning theory and the study of instruction. *Ann. Rev. Psychol.* 40: 631–66

Gustafsson J E 1989 Broad and narrow abilities in research on learning and instruction. In: Kanfer R, Ackerman P L, Cudeck R (eds.) 1989 *Abilities, Motivation, and Methodology*. Erlbaum, Hillsdale, New Jersey

Heckhausen H, Schmalt H D, Schneider K 1985 *Achievement Motivation in Perspective*. Academic Press, Orlando, Florida

Kuhl J, Kraska K 1989 Self-regulation and metamotivation: Computational mechanisms development and assessment. In: Kanfer R, Ackerman P L, Cudeck R (eds.) 1989 *Abilities, Motivation, and Methodology: The Minnesota Symposium on Learning and Individual Differences*. Erlbaum, Hillsdale, New Jersey

Lohman D F 1989 Human intelligence: An introduction to advances in theory and research. *Rev. Educ. Res.* 59(4): 333–73

Magnusson D, Allen V L (eds.) 1983 *Human Development: An Interactional Perspective*. Academic Press, New York

Pervin L A, Lewis M (eds.) 1978 *Perspectives in Interactional Psychology*. Plenum Press, New York

Schneider W, Weinert F E (eds.) 1989 *Interactions Among Aptitudes, Strategies, and Knowledge in Cognitive Performance*. Springer-Verlag, New York

Snow R E 1989 Aptitude-treatment interaction as a framework for research on individual differences in learning. In: Ackerman P L, Sternberg R J, Glaser R (eds.) 1989 *Learning and Individual Differences*. Freeman, New York

Snow R E 1991 The concept of aptitude. In: Snow R E, Wiley D E (eds.) 1991 *Improving Inquiry in Social Science*. Erlbaum, Hillsdale, New Jersey

Snow R E 1992 Aptitude theory: Yesterday, today, and tomorrow. *Educ. Psychol.* 27(1): 5–32

Snow R E, Lohman D F 1984 Toward a theory of cognitive aptitude for learning from instruction. *J. Educ. Psychol.* 76(3): 347–76

Snow R E, Lohman D F 1989 Implications of cognitive psychology for educational measurement. In: Linn R L (ed.) 1989 *Educational Measurement*, 3rd edn. Macmillan, New York

Snow R E, Swanson J 1992 Instructional psychology: Aptitude, adaptation, and assessment. *Annu. Rev. Psychol.* 43: 583–626

Sternberg R J 1985a *Beyond IQ: A Triarchic Theory of Human Intelligence*. Cambridge University Press, Cambridge

Sternberg R J 1985b (ed.) *Human Abilities: An Information Processing Approach*. Freeman, New York

Further Reading

Snow R E 1982 Education and intelligence. In: Sternberg R J (ed.) 1982 *Handbook of Human Intelligence*. Cambridge University Press, New York

R. E. Snow

Teaching: Behavioral Theories

Behavioral theories of teaching assume that human behavior is shaped by contextually relevant consequences of behavior. The discipline therefore applies principles derived from experimental analyses of behavior to the enhancement of educational performance. The accomplishment of specific motivational, management, and learning objectives are viewed in relation to their contingent consequences, antecedents, and other contextual factors.

Often preceded by supportive events, behavior followed virtually immediately by sufficient reinforcing consequences is more likely to be repeated. The omission of reinforcers, the substitution of aversive consequences, and/or the presence of unfavorable antecedent events decreases the likelihood that the behavior will be repeated.

An extensive literature documents the effectiveness of the application of behavioral principles in classroom teaching. Proper application of these principles can result in increased levels of academic, motor, social, and professional performance.

1. Behavioral Teaching Theories

Behavioral teaching theories rest on the natural science notion that, like the survival of species through natural selection, a behavioral repertoire evolves within an individual's lifetime as a function of selection by consequences (Catania 1992, Skinner 1981). Influenced by each individual's physical makeup, status, and learning history, behaviors are actions—what people do and say—that impact the environment.

The main thrust of inquiry in behavioral theory is studying how particular antecedents and/or consequential stimuli relate to observable educational performances. These stimuli can differ in their form, timing, scheduling, and quantity. Observable educational performances include students' and staffs' rates of acquiring, sustaining or transferring particular skills or knowledge.

2. Behavioral Principles Especially Applicable to Teaching

Scientific analyses, conducted by examining and/or

modifying the relations between behavior (B), its consequences (C), and its antecedents (A), as set in particular contexts, have yielded many important principles. The application of those principles toward enhancing student and staff performance is the essence of behavioral teaching (see Sulzer-Azaroff and Mayer 1986, 1991). Consequences, antecedents, and other features of the environment may be presented, withheld, removed, or altered in form, intensity, frequency, and in additional ways found to be optimally effective.

Literally thousands of experimentally controlled behavioral studies have been conducted to produce an extensive array of findings that are especially promising for education. Simultaneously, over several decades, strategies for incorporating these principles into educational research and practice have been evolving into an effective and efficient technology of behavioral teaching and program evaluation.

A subset of fundamental principles of behavior that have been found to be especially relevant to education follows.

2.1 The Reinforcement Principle

The probability that a behavior will strengthen is increased through reinforcement; that is, when consequences are reinforcing for the individual under the current circumstances and a sufficient amount of reinforcing consequences are very frequently received immediately following the behavior. For example, if students who like to solve problems correctly (that is, those who are reinforced by being correct) check their answers immediately and find them to be right, they are more likely to solve those and similar problems correctly in the future. Similar results can be achieved when students for whom grades, praise alone, or solving a problem correctly, have no reinforcing value. Instead, along with praise and a good grade, check marks are given that can be exchanged along with other check marks for access to a special activity they do find reinforcing.

2.2 The Chaining Principle

The probability that a behavior will be learned is increased when new behaviors can be constituted from behaviors the individual has already learned. These pre-established behaviors are linked by reinforcing combinations of those components in a process called "chaining." Take, for example, the case of a student who can add, subtract, multiply, and do short division. To then teach long division, reinforcement is delivered as the student connects each element properly to the adjacent sequence.

2.3 The Shaping Principle

The probability that a behavior will be learned is increased when a behavior resembling the learning objective is reinforced. As variation in responding more closely resembling the learning objective occurs, a successive approximation produces reinforcement instead. This shaping process continues until the learning objective is reached. This would be the case in a situation where members of a debating team are trying to learn a specific set of effective debating strategies. Each time improvement is shown, the debater is praised by the coach. Performance continues to improve.

2.4 The Stimulus Control Principle

The probability that a behavior will be learned is increased when a behavior that the person can produce consistently needs to occur sometimes but not at other times (that is, it must be brought under *stimulus control*). When the student detects the circumstances under which the behavior is and is not to occur and acts accordingly, reinforcement follows in a process called "differential reinforcement." Prompting helps to set the occasion for, or evoke, those behaviors already in the repertoire but not yet reliably produced on cue. However, supplemental prompts need to be *faded* if the behavior is or is not to occur under circumstances when prompts are normally absent.

For example, running and shouting in the playground is reinforced; in the library it is not. In the playground, reticent children who are prompted with "It's all right to run and shout here," and are praised when they do, increase their running and shouting there. In a different instance, a trainee who correctly detects all defective parts coming off the assembly line for a week is graduated to a regular job as inspector.

2.5 Principles of Diminishing Behavior

The probability that an unwanted behavior will diminish is increased when: (a) a behavior with which it cannot co-exist is strengthened; (b) it is no longer followed by reinforcement; (c) it is followed immediately and consistently by an event unpleasant or aversive to the student; and (d) preliminary activities impede or help the individual to avoid unwanted responses. Consider the following examples:

(a) rushing through an assignment and missing some critical aspects is found by the student to lead to the teacher requiring that it be re-done, while completing assignments to standards of acceptability consistently produces the immediate recognition and high grades the student loves. The student learns to work more slowly and carefully and errors diminish.

(b) Answers that are shouted out are ignored by the teacher. Raising one's hand and waiting, however, usually leads to being called upon to speak, so students stop shouting out.

(c) Advance preparation of children who are to read

a story in the form of an oral review of the story and its pictures by the teacher leads to children making fewer subsequent trial reading errors (Singh and Singh 1984).

2.6 Transfer of Behavior Principles

The probability that a behavior will transfer (or generalize) to other appropriate situations is increased when (a) reinforcement has been positive rather than aversive; (b) elements common to those new situations are detected and the generalized response is reinforced; (c) the same behavior is learned under many varying conditions; and (d) natural circumstances reinforce and perhaps cue the behavior intermittently (not every time) when and wherever it is to occur. (See Comunidad Los Horcones 1992 for a discussion of this topic.) For example, students receive reinforcement in the form of teacher approval and by seeing evidence of their improved performance when they regularly write down their assignments in each of their classes. Writing down assignments becomes part of their regular routine.

2.7 Principles Pertaining to the Maintenance of Behavior

The probability that a behavior will be maintained over time is increased when: (a) the behavior is fully mastered and expressed fluently, or at a high and steady rate under appropriate but not under inappropriate circumstances; (b) positive reinforcing consequences natural to the setting gradually diminish but continue at low levels; and, (c) any artificial prompts are gradually removed or faded. For example, fewer and fewer prompts are supplied and more and more check marks required of students' for correct problem solutions in order for them to gain access to an enjoyable activity. Over time, checks and special activities are eliminated while praise and immediate good grades continue, but at a diminishing rate.

3. Based on a Technology of Teaching Behavioral Theories

A technology of teaching has evolved because several requirements must be met if behavioral principles are to be applied properly and effectively. The most important requirements are discussed in this section. Instructional objectives must be very clearly specified so that educators know and can arrange to provide specific behaviors or behavioral combinations with appropriate consequences under particular conditions. (Mager 1990). Ongoing behavioral change related to these objectives is assessed by delineating and applying valid, objective measures repeatedly within and across sessions at individual and programmatic levels.

The influence of the application of behavioral principles on accuracy, rate, durability, generality, and other aspects of change is analyzed by using experimental methods designed to eliminate competing explanations for the results (see Johnston and Pennypacker 1993). Such evaluation of performance permits educators to make data-based decisions, rather than choosing methods arbitrarily or on the basis of dogma. In this regard the PLA-check technique (Risley and Cataldo 1973), the repeated probing of the number of students actively engaged in assigned activities within a time block, is a popular way of estimating the proportion of students "on-task" under given circumstances (e.g., Wilczenski et al. 1987). Similarly practitioners of *precision teaching* count the frequency per time unit of skills performed to criteria in a range from basic to higher order subject matters.

Students' repertoires of responding relevant to objectives are thoroughly assessed to identify each person's well-established behaviors, the combination of circumstances and events that reliably function as reinforcers, and what stimuli evoke what responses under what conditions. Thus, educators are able to select curriculum materials, instructional styles, social arrangements, and consequences for current and future use and to avoid using ineffective, unnecessary, or intrusive prompts or reinforcers.

The student's physical and social environment in and out of school should be assessed with respect to performances essential to the learning objectives. Such an *ecobehavioral assessment* permits the identification and perhaps adjustment of supports and impediments to change.

One approach to ecobehavioral assessment involves students, teachers, supervisors, parents, and/or community members in the specification of particular objectives, measures, materials, methods of intervening, and/or consequences, recording progress, and the delivery of consequences. Implementation of these specifications often occurs within a formally negotiated *behavioral contract* (Brooks 1974, see also Sulzer-Azaroff and Reese 1982). One frequently used method is the daily report card (Schumaker et al. 1977) on which teachers check how well the student performs each day or period according to preset standards, such as attending punctually, and parents provide reinforcing consequences based on the report cards.

4. Programs of Behavioral Instruction

About the time that Skinner (1958) wrote the paper in which he elaborated the concept of the teaching machine, behavior principles began to be systematically applied towards educational improvement. Often this application has involved the rearrangement of single or multiple antecedents or consequences, while at other times principles have been combined into instructional, motivational, or management programs or *procedural packages*.

Regardless of the particular form of application, all categories of behavioral education emphasize active student engagement and regularly attained, appropriate consequences. The most demonstrably successful and widely applied models and programs are discussed in this section.

4.1 Token Economies

In token economies neutral symbolic reinforcers, such as objects or check marks, are presented immediately following the desired behavior, behavioral combination, or behavioral approximation. Later, at a more convenient time, those "tokens" are exchanged for items or events of demonstrated reinforcing value for the student. In one such instance (Sulzer et al. 1971), fifth-grade students worked at their own paces in reading and spelling workbooks. On completion of a section, the number of correct answers was tallied and the student was awarded points exchangeable for trinkets or preferred activities in the future. Misbehavior diminished and daily performance increased strikingly, while standardized achievement test scores doubled or tripled in contrast with previous years.

4.2 Peer Proctoring or Tutoring

Properly trained and supervised, peers have been found to serve effectively as tutors of their classmates and they themselves benefit from the experience academically and socially. Peers increase the amount of time in which students engage constructively in academic activities and the reinforcement and feedback the students receive. Peer tutors have increased opportunities for reinforced practice and fluency training while tutoring can also lend social status to the tutor (an immediate, natural reinforcer).

At Juniper Gardens, an extensive educational intervention program for families living in poverty in Kansas City, Kansas, a class-wide peer tutoring program has been formalized and tested to teach a variety of basic tool subjects. The highly successful system has also been replicated for tutoring in spelling across schools, students, teachers, and school years (Greenwood et al. 1987). Peers have also been effectively involved in promoting social effectiveness, play skills, affection, and numerous other skills by demonstrating or modeling the desired behavior and/or reinforcing it when it occurs.

4.3 Group Management Methods

When members of small groups with similar skill levels receive reinforcement for working together or toward a common goal, as in *cooperative learning* (Johnson and Johnson 1983), they tend to assist one another and benefit academically and socially (see *Cooperative Learning*). Similarly, a group management system, the "Good Behavior Game," in which teams disrupting less or behaving appropriately more often receive access to rewarding activities, has demonstrated its ability to improve student conduct very rapidly (Saigh and Umar 1983; Fishbein and Wasik 1981). These systems work especially well because, beyond providing arranged reinforcement, positive social events (such as attention, recognition, and encouragement) are brought naturally into play when peers are acting suitably.

4.4 Social Skills Training

Expressing appreciation, requesting help, refusing or disagreeing inoffensively, entering and participating in play or conversational groups, and other alternatives to socially objectionable behavior have been enhanced through social skills training programs. Specific skills are selected on the basis of observations of the students' deficits and excesses as well as an examination of the environment. Training consists of discussing rationales for the change, cuing, demonstrating, and practicing the skill under simulated or natural conditions, and providing ongoing feedback and reinforcement for progress (see Sulzer-Azaroff and Mayer 1986).

4.5 Programmed Instruction

In programmed instruction, critical information is presented through the media of teaching machines, computers, or workbooks. Students monitor and respond sequentially to small steps of instruction called "frames." Their responses are followed immediately with positive or corrective feedback and sometimes other events such as detailed praise. Depending on the extent to which sufficiently challenging instructional objectives are matched to students' behavioral repertoires, responding accurately and fluently is optimally reinforced. Prompts are precisely selected, applied, and faded to enable correct, fluent responses to be sustained. In this way learning can be rapid, durable, and satisfying.

Programmed instructional programs permit students to progress at varied paces and are capable of widespread use across student populations and subject areas. They mitigate the requirement that teachers be expert in all areas of instructional content and style. Whether the instruction is presented through a machine or a text, however, it is only as effective as the fidelity with which it adheres to fundamental principles of behavior. Insufficiently challenging or interesting material contained in steps too large or small for the student, low success rates, inadequate or inappropriate feedback and reinforcement, too many or too few prompts faded too rapidly or slowly will attenuate the value of any given program within a particular student population. Given the growing sophistication of computer technology, making the necessary adjustments in instructional programs is becoming increasingly feasible.

4.6 Personalized System of Instruction

Primarily applied in higher education to teach a

broad spectrum of subjects, the "Personalized System of Instruction" (PSI) (Keller 1968) closely resembles programmed instruction, but with a few fundamental exceptions. In PSI, the size of the steps tends to be larger (paragraphs or pages in length rather than a few sentences) and feedback is provided by a "proctor" (usually a peer who has already mastered the unit of instruction). Prompts are supplied in the form of study questions that students answer in advance; mastery of the material is assessed via a unit quiz.

Immediately after the quiz the proctor gives the student feedback as to the correctness of the items and, if necessary, details how the student needs to prepare further to display mastery on a different form of the quiz that covers the same content. Once students demonstrate mastery of the material by scoring above a given level (usually 90 percent), they may proceed to the next unit. According to a meta-analysis of over 350 reports (Kulik et al. 1979), PSI has succeeded in significantly enhancing academic performance.

4.7 Precision Teaching

Precision teaching emphasizes fluency building by augmenting the student's rate of response. First, students master a simple or complex fact or skill (for example, correctly spelling a word, applying a mathematical algorithm, giving a list of episodes preceding a historical event, changing a spark plug). This mastery is often accomplished with the assistance of the teacher, programmed material, or formalized, scripted, small group, interactive instruction such as "direct instruction" (Becker and Carnine 1981) (see *Direct Instruction*).

Students continue practicing their skills until they achieve consistently high rates and levels of precision (i.e., fluency) (Bell et al. 1991; Hofmeister et al. 1989)

Often, students monitor their own rates by charting them on logarithmic charts. Used with advanced and delayed learners as well as both children and adults with learning disabilities and economic disadvantages, precision teaching, alone or in combination with direct instruction, peer tutoring, and/or supplementary reinforcement, has been found to multiply academic progress rates by many times. Precision teaching also enhances maintenance and generalization or transfer of learning to other, often more advanced, subject matters and settings.

5. Emerging Trends, Issues, and Future Research

Numerous controlled studies have supported the conclusion that behavioral teaching methods are capable of producing high levels of achievements among students and educators. Although systematically applied and analyzed for over 40 years, the approach is only beginning to be adopted more broadly. Work organizations are starting to use these techniques to teach literacy, numeracy, and job skills. Ecological research on the supports and impediments to the transfer of this technology to school systems is ongoing and will undoubtedly increase. The impact of involving school principals, pupil personnel specialists, school board members and other public servants in the design, implementation and/or assessment of the programs, is also being studied.

Concurrently, new computer technology is stimulating a resurgence of research and development in programmed instruction. Studies of curriculum content, optimal sequencing, prompting and fading strategies, supplemental graphic aids, varied response modes, alternative ways of supplying feedback and reinforcement, and many other aspects of computer-aided instruction are proliferating. Relevant findings from behavioral research on cognitive activity are likely to be increasingly incorporated into instructional design.

Finally, ideal combinations of motivational, management, and instructional packages need to be identified for given individuals and populations. At the same time, the advanced levels of personnel training and labor intensiveness inherent in practical, cost-effective curriculum construction need to be addressed. In these ways, the contributions of behavioral theories of teaching to educational effectiveness should increase.

See also: Teaching, Cognitive Developmental Theories of; Teaching: Linguistic and Sociolinguistic Theories; Teaching: Heuristic Models; Programmed Learning

References

Becker W C, Carnine D W 1981 Direct instruction: A behavior theory model of comprehensive educational intervention with the disadvantaged. In: Bijou S W, Ruiz R (eds.) 1981 *Behavior Modification: Contributions to Education*. Erlbaum, Hillsdale, New Jersey

Bell K E, Young R, Salzberg C L, West R P 1991 High school driver education using peer tutors, direct instruction, and precision teaching. *J. Appl. Behav. Anal.* 24(1): 45–51

Brooks B D 1974 Contingency contracts with truants. *Pers. Guid. J.* 52(5): 316–20

Catania A C 1992 *Learning*. 3rd edn. Prentice Hall, Englewood Cliffs, New Jersey

Comunidad Los Horcones 1991 Natural reinforcement: A way to improve education. *J. Appl. Behav. Anal.* 25(1): 71–5

Fishbein J E, Wasik B H 1981 Effect of the good behavior game on disruptive library behavior. *J. Appl. Behav. Anal.* 14(1): 89–93

Greenwood C R et al. 1987 Field replication of classwide peer tutoring. *J. Appl. Behav. Anal.* 20(2): 151–60

Hofmeister A, Engelmann S, Carnine D 1989 Developing and validating science education videodiscs. *J. Res. Sci. Teach.* 26(8): 665–77

Johnson D W, Johnson R T 1983 Effects of cooperative, competitive, and individualistic learning experience on social development. *Excep. Child.* 49: 323–29

Johnston J M, Pennypacker H 1993 *Strategies and Tactics of Human Behavioral Research*, 2nd edn. Erlbaum, Hillsdale, New Jersey
Keller F S 1968 Goodbye, teacher . . . *J. Appl. Behav. Anal.* 1(1): 79–89
Kulik J A, Kulik C-L C, Cohen P A 1979 A meta-analysis of outcome studies of Keller's personalized system of instruction. *Am. Psychol.* 34: 307–18
Mager R F 1990 *Preparing Instructional Objectives*. Kogan Page, London
Risley T R, Cataldo M F 1973 *Planned Activity Check: Materials for Training Observers*. Center for Applied Behavior Analysis, Lawrence, Kansas
Saigh P A, Umar A M 1983 The effects of a good behavior game on the disruptive behavior of Sudanese elementary school students. *J. Appl. Behav. Anal.* 16(3): 339–44
Schumaker J B, Hovell M F, Sherman J A 1977 An analysis of daily report cards and parent managed privileges in the improvement of adolescents' classroom performance. *J. Appl. Behav. Anal.* 10(3): 449–64
Singh N N, Singh J 1984 Antecedent control of oral reading errors and self-corrections by mentally retarded children. *J. Appl. Behav. Anal.* 17(1): 111–19
Skinner B F 1958 Teaching machines. *Science* 128: 969–77
Skinner B F 1981 Selection by consequences. *Science* 213: 501–4
Sulzer B, Hunt S, Ashby, E Koniarski C, Krams M 1971 Increasing rate and percentage correct in reading and spelling in a 5th grade public school class of slow readers by means of a token system. In: Ramp E A, Hopkins B L (eds.) 1971 *A New Direction for Education*. University of Kansas Follow Through Program, Lawrence, Kansas
Sulzer-Azaroff B, Reese E P 1982 *Applying Behavior Analysis: A Program for Developing Competence*. Holt, Rinehart and Winston, New York
Sulzer-Azaroff B, Mayer G R 1986 *Achieving Educational Excellence Using Behavioral Strategies*. Holt, Rinehart and Winston, New York
Sulzer-Azaroff B, Mayer G R 1991 *Behavior Analysis for Lasting Change*. Holt, Rinehart and Winston, Fort Worth, Texas
Wilczenski F L, Sulzer-Azaroff B, Feldman R S, Fajardo D E 1987 Feedback to teachers on student engagement as a consultation tool. *Professional School Psychology* 2: 261–72

Further Reading

Alberto P A, Troutman A C 1990 *Applied Behavior Analysis for Teachers*, 3rd Edn. Merrill Publishing Company. Columbus, Ohio
Jenson W R, Sloane H N, Young K R 1988 *Applied Behavior Analysis in Education*. Prentice Hall. Englewood Cliffs, New Jersey
Johnson D W, Johnson R T 1975 *Learning Together and Alone: Cooperative, Competitive and Individualistic Learning*. Prentice Hall, Englewood Cliffs, New Jersey
Kazdin A E 1989 *Behavior Modification in Applied Settings*, 4th Edn. Brooks Cole, Pacific Grove, California
Maher C A, Forman S G (eds.) 1987 *A Behavioral Approach to Education of Children and Youth*. Erlbaum, Hillsdale, New Jersey
Markle S 1991 *Designs for Instructional Designers*. Stipes Publishing. Champaign, Illinois
Skinner B F 1968 *Technology of Teaching*. Prentice Hall, Englewood Cliffs, New Jersey.

B. Sulzer-Azaroff

Teaching, Cognitive Developmental Theories of

One of the most perplexing issues in education is the question of how to enhance student learning. On the surface the answer seems simple; present the information the pupil is required to learn in a straightforward manner using a variety of methods, and positive results will follow. The real answer, however, is more problematic.

The United States first recognized psychologist, William James, provides an apt metaphorical account by comparing teaching to warfare.

> In war, all you have to do is work your enemy into a position in which natural obstacles prevent him from escaping . . . then fall on him in numbers superior to his own . . . Just so in teaching; you must simply work your pupil into such a state-of-interest with every other object of attention banished from his mind; then reveal it to him so impressively that he will remember it to his dying day; and finally, fill him with a devouring curiosity to know what the next steps are. (James 1958 p. 106).

The difficulty, as James goes on to say, is that the student, like the opposing general, may be working just as keenly and avidly for a different set of goals. Just what the students think and want may be as difficult for the teacher to discern as the enemy commander.

The cognitive–developmental framework attempts to resolve these difficulties by focusing on both the teacher and the learner. Both contribute to the learning process. Thus, when either is out of phase, learning is reduced.

The rationale for a cognitive–developmental approach to teaching can be found in the original theories of Dewey (1966) and Freire (1981), and in the research of Piaget (1974), Kohlberg (1984), and Vygotsky (1978). Essentially, in this view, teaching is interactive, a dialectic or dialogic between teacher and learner. The student is viewed as an active participant in the process. The teacher's role is to promote the intellectual, interpersonal, and social development of the child. As Dewey noted, "The cause of education . . . is one of development focusing indeed in the growth of students, but to be conceived even in the connection as part of the larger development of society" (1966 p. 69).

Freire (1981), echoing these views, indicated that the aim of education should be fostering critical consciousness, awareness of the political, social, and economic causes of injustice on the part of democratic citizenship: "I was convinced that the Brazilian people could learn social and political responsibility only by experiencing that responsibility through intervention in the destiny of their children's schools (and other agencies) . . . They could be helped to learn democracy through the exercise of democracy" (1981 p. 36).

Simply stated, the educational goals in the cognitive–developmental view of teaching and learning include not only such traditional ideas as literacy broadly defined, but also requisite experiences which will produce an informed citizen ready to guide the process of democratic governance.

1. Traditional Views of Teaching and Learning

The Dewey and Freire views are at odds with teaching practices in most of the world in the 1990s. Reviews of classroom instruction both in the United States and throughout the world reveal a consistent and enduring pattern of rote learning via classroom recitation. Students reciting the fact-based content across the curriculum was first documented in the early part of the twentieth century. Bellack et al. (1966) reported that in the early 1900s students recited rote answers to teachers' questions at the rate of four per minute. Some 70 years later the rate was three per minute. As Goodlad (1984) noted: "In over half the classrooms, the worksheet, recitation rote memory routines were the only method practiced—no films, slides, videos, simulation tapes, teaching machines, or field visits" (p. 241).

Freire (1981) has argued that such a traditional method which he refers to as "banking education," the memorization of bits and pieces of disconnected facts, reinforces all the wrong goals. Students are viewed as inert, empty vessels, to be filled with prescribed knowledge.

Piaget (1974) has noted that to know by heart is not to know. Dewey called this the phonograph method with the teachers inscribing information upon empty phonograph disks, to be replayed later. Vygotsky (1978) referred to this as "ossification." Thus the world over, traditional teaching methods remain entrenched and seemingly resistant to revitalization. The world's classrooms can be summed up in the French phrase, "Plus ça change, plus c'est la même chose"—the more things change, the more they remain the same.

In the United States, there is major concern as a result of national assessments of educational attainment, and with good cause. The results, particularly at the secondary school level, represent an indictment of traditional teaching methods. Of course, such indexes have been available for some time, yet not on such a comprehensive level.

The basic results indicate that elementary age pupils are learning fundamentals, or the three "R's." At the secondary school level, however, comprehension has decreased. This means, for example, that young students learn to break the reading code, add, subtract, and know the capitals of South American countries. By high school, they have less of a grasp of the meaning of what they read, have great difficulty with so-called "word problems" in mathematics (Jones 1988), and exhibit major ignorance of fundamental principles of democratic government (Nickerson 1988).

It is indeed difficult to imagine the traditional method of teaching producing different results. In a classic study Tyler (1933) found a lack of comprehension almost endemic to all of education. The results of Flanagan's (1973) massive study Project TALENT resulted in the same conclusion, as did the more recent study by Goodlad (1984) which was already noted. These studies are summarized in Sprinthall and Sprinthall (1990).

2. Cognitive–Developmental Learning

In cognitive–developmental learning, teaching is to start with the students, particularly, with the understanding that they are not midget-sized adults, empty vessels, or blank phonograph disks. It was Piaget's (1974) pioneering work starting in the 1920s that began to outline the methods of learning that students actually employ when confronted with educational problems to solve. He was able to outline a sequence of stages of conceptual growth: sensory–motor, intuitive, concrete, and formal operational. Each stage represents a qualitatively distinct method of cognitive processing.

Piaget's work, first limited to Europe and then replicated in many other countries, has become the basis for what is called the Attribute Treatment Interaction (ATI) (See *Teaching: Aptitude–Treatment Interaction Model*). According to this conceptual framework, learning is determined by the attributes of the students, including their cognitive stage, interacting with the teaching strategies and content. This reflects the truism that teaching must start where the learner is currently functioning.

The cognitive–developmental view provides a detailed and comprehensive picture of where the learners are. Although the Piaget framework has been continually challenged and modified, the overall framework of stage characteristics and sequence remains intact (Ginsberg and Opper 1988).

A second developmental domain, especially for democratic societies, has been Dewey's notion of educational aims vis-à-vis values and ethics for citizenship. In this regard, the work of Kohlberg (1984) has resulted in a scheme of stages which parallels Piaget's. In the Kohlberg scheme, moral judgment and ethical reasoning proceeds through a sequence from self-centered physical dominance/submission (Stage 1), materialistic hedonism (Stage 2), social conformity (Stage 3), and legal sanctions (Stage 4), to democratic principled thought (either utilitarian consequentialism or deontological universalism). There is also a clear similarity between Kohlberg's stages and nearly all of Freire's stages of consciousness (i.e., Freire's intransitive, semi-intransitive, and naive transitive are the same as Kohlberg's Stages, 1, 2, and 3, and critical consciousness is the same as principled reasoning, Stages 5 and 6). Kohlberg's research began in the United States, and has been expanded to over 50 countries with significant empirical evidence to support both the cross-cultural validity of his work and the gender-neutral component of the sequence of stages. The latter point has been challenged, but meta-analyses by Rest (1986) with 6,000 subjects and by Walker (1986) with 10,000 subjects, find no evidence to support any gender bias.

3. *Cognitive–Developmental Teaching: The Student*

Piaget and Kohlberg both originally assumed that applying these theories to practice was premature, and in fact something that Piaget had warned against (his scathing comments about educational acceleration being "An American Question"). Nonetheless, there have been numerous applications which actually support the Dewey–Freire goals, Vygotsky's aims, and Piaget's and Kohlberg's stages.

Walberg (1986) has shown that the student's Piagetian stage makes a significant contribution to his or her comprehension of intended learning outcomes, particularly in the field of science. For example, if teachers ignore the developmental stage of the student in scientific thought, the students do not understand what they are supposed to learn. Similarly, a series of studies by Renner et al. (1976) has shown the deleterious effects of science teaching that assumes rather than promotes Piagetian development. The work of Feuerstein (1980) with Israeli immigrants also has shown the positive effects of relating pupil developmental stage to instructional methods. Most importantly, his work has shown the applicability of his instructional program across a wide range of academic aptitude.

The research of Barrett (1975), however, has shown the futility of attempting to accelerate development. His work in England demonstrated that trying to teach the meaning of abstract concepts prior to the onset of formal reasoning resulted in no gain in comprehension. While the older students could quickly grasp the concepts after a short review, younger students were unable to grasp them at all. Thus, the teacher who spends a great amount of classroom time trying to teach abstract concepts to concrete learners is destined to be frustrated.

Duckworth (1987) best captures the essence of developmental teaching and learning with her aphorism, "Either we're too late, or they know it already" (p. 31). The implications are two-fold. First, the framework requires an understanding of the current preferred mode of problem-solving, that is, the cognitive–developmental stage of the student. Second, and equally important, is the cognitive–developmental stage of the teacher.

4. *Cognitive–Developmental Teaching: The Teacher*

One of the major changes in the cognitive–developmental framework has been a massive revision in theory. Until the 1970s, the general assumption had been that stages of growth ended somewhere in late adolescence or early adulthood. However, the cognitive–developmental researchers all made the fortuitous mistake of conducting longitudinal research and found a continuation of stage growth during adulthood itself. While Piaget concentrated on early childhood and adolescence, he raised the issue of continuing development in one of his later works (Piaget 1972). Kohlberg (1984) had to revise his earlier views after reviewing his follow-up studies, conducted at five-year intervals. Similar developmental changes have been found in other stage domains (e.g., ego and conceptual development). As a consequence, teachers are now conceptualized as adult learners in a stage and sequence model. What was true for students is now true for teachers.

A major researcher in this area has been Hunt (1974), first in the United States and then later in Canada at the Ontario Institute for Studies in Education. Hunt found that the teacher's ability to understand student cognitive strategies (that is, to start where the learner is), and to modify the curriculum materials and teaching strategies accordingly, depended upon the stage of conceptual development of the teacher. He used the phrase "read and flex" to denote this higher order of ability of teachers (related concepts would include cognitive flexibility and cognitive adaptability).

Hunt was able to show that effective "reading and flexing" produces an effective learning environment, through the use of concrete examples (the rule–example–rule method) for low conceptual stage students and the opposite method (the inductive examples-only model) for higher stage students. Positive outcomes result from effective matching, while negative outcomes follow from employing an inappropriate strategy.

Whether the teacher is capable of appropriate "reading and flexing" is a question of the cognitive complexity of the teacher. In fact, Hunt has used the same system to measure the concept learning capability of both students and teachers. Teachers with higher levels of concept learning capability adapt innovation; view students as teacher–learners (in Freires terms); are comfortable providing detailed highly structured materials for some, and just as comfortable with low-structure inductive teaching for others; and do not follow a single prescriptive approach. In contrast, teachers at lower levels of concept learning capability resist innovation; employ "tried and true" direct methods for all; and are confused by flexible team teaching, learning centers, and cooperative methods. In this regard, Joyce and McKibbin (1980) found that the low developmental stage teachers who attended workshops and were presented with some 100 innovative teaching methods over the course of an entire year used almost none of those methods one year later, while the opposite was true for the higher stage teachers.

A meta-analysis by Miller (1981) of over 200 studies supported the validity of teacher concept learning capability as a predictor of effective teaching. This single finding may explain why so many national attempts to infuse the schools with new and exciting curriculum guides in language, social studies, mathematics, and science have failed so completely. The truism from these multiple failures has been that there is no such thing as a teacher-proof curriculum. The best material in the world will fail unless the teachers themselves are at least at a moderate to a moderately high stage of conceptual development.

A major problem, of course, is that teacher education programs, as presently organized, are themselves no more competent at promoting stage growth than are the schools. Both operate with a seemingly blind eye to the developmental stage of the learner, whether the learner is a student at school or a teacher in training. A review of teacher education programs by a Dutch educator (Veenman 1984) found the framework promising, yet hardly in place. In fact, Hunt (1974) has always claimed that the missing link in teacher education has been the need to view the teacher as a learner within a conceptual stage framework.

In the case of school programs designed to promote moral and ethical reasoning, the same results hold. For example, Oser (1984) in Switzerland and Berkowitz (1985) in the United States have found the effective use of the Socratic approach to moral dilemma discussions to be dependent upon the stage of development of the teachers. Managing student dialogue on controversial dilemmas requires a higher order teaching ability; namely, the ability to clarify and extend student ideas on one hand and to challenge student thinking on the other. In fact, Berkowitz has found that if the teacher is unable to do both, student cognitive growth does not occur.

5. *Goals of Both Teachers and Students: Conceptional and Moral Development*

In a sense, the same teaching and learning rules apply whether this goal is the achievement of conceptual complexity in any of the requisite school disciplines or the promotion of ethical and moral reasoning. The cognitive–developmental model is based on the dialectic of the equilibrium and disequilibrium; of the learner's need to assimilate and accommodate. When the current system of problem-solving is challenged effectively, the equilibrium between "old" learning and "new" learning is upset. Furth (1981) has aptly described this disequilibrium as the dissonance created by a mismatch between current stage process and a knowledge perturbation. Furthermore, Furth asserts that this problem cannot be solved in the current educational system.

Growth depends upon the slow taking-in (accommodation) of new and more complex cognitive processes. In this regard, Furth provides an example of a German youth, a concrete thinker, experiencing the dissonance of seeing a church without a steeple during a Sunday bicycle ride. Whether growth occurs in this example depends upon the dialogue that ensues. Vygotsky (1978) suggests that the learner needs time to gradually give up the old method of perceiving and solving problems for the new. This gradual development of more complex cognitive structures which allow the learner to become more efficient and more effective in the process of critical thinking is referred to as a structuralist approach to learning.

6. *The Cost of Growth*

In the context of the cognitive–developmental framework, the learner (whether student or teacher) must part with the old "tried and true" method of problem-solving. In Piagetian terms, for example, the learner may give up concrete thought for formal operational thought. In Kohlbergian terms the learner would reject social conformity (Stage 3) in ethical decision-making for legal sanctions (Stage 4).

The psychological resistance to such growth has been understated. Most developmental theorists have embraced some version of the "plus one" idea. The learner is attracted to the higher stage because it is a better organization (ensemble or schema) for thought in either the conceptual or the moral domain (Rest 1986). A number of more clinically oriented theorists have suggested that the learner experiences substantial psychological dissonance during the transition phase (Kegan 1982). The learner actually feels less competent and sometimes angry or depressed as the old method reveals itself as inadequate to the problem-solving perturbation at hand. The learner might not in fact excitedly demand to know the next steps in the higher order sequence of problem solving. In James's metaphor of teaching and war, this explains why the student may be working so hard to subvert the teacher.

Kegan suggests exactly this point. New learning creates a period of wary antagonism and initial rejection of the new requirements, as the old method is comfortable to the learner and has produced successful outcomes. These new insights can help to expand the instructional methods particularly during transitions from stage-to-stage (vertical *décalage*) as well as growth within a stage (horizontal *décalage*).

7. Method Characteristics

For students, the most common developmental methods of instruction are aligned with the Dewey and Freire requirements of active learning combined with guided reflection. Ironically, given the continued reliance on banking education through the memorized transmission of culture, there was a major eight-year longitudinal study in the 1930s which provided empirical support for the superiority of the project method (called the activity-based curriculum) over the lectures methods. In this study, teachers used small groups, cooperative learning, research projects, field trips, and role-plays from an interdisciplinary standpoint. The experimental and control samples were large (almost 3,000 pupils participated) and the results on some 18 outcome measures favored the activity approach (Aiken 1942).

A similar, more recent, cross-sectional study of experiential, social role-taking programs (e.g., peer counseling, teaching, and community internships for students) produced similar findings; such programs produce not only an increase in conceptual growth, but also an increase in ethical reasoning (Sprinthall and Collins 1988). Role taking as opposed to role playing requires that students set aside their own self-preoccupations and learn an "iron discipline" of listening. Social perspective taking develops, as does empathy, and both these induce greater moral sensitivity. At the same time the requirement to reflect, read, and analyze such experiences ("praxis" in Freire's terms) promotes cognitive structural growth. Standard or conventional academic courses do not have similar effects (Rest 1986, Hunt 1974).

For teachers, the same framework holds. Teachers usually function at low to modest levels of conceptual and ethical development. Regular academic training during initial student teaching and for inservice programs produces little in the way of development in these domains. The effect of such training on pupils is indirect, yet nevertheless discouraging. Boring routines and passivity among students are common.

Of even greater concern is the impact of these experienced teachers on the student teachers they supervise. One study showed the negative effect of a developmental mismatch: student teachers at higher conceptual and ethical stages than their supervisors (Thies-Sprinthall 1980). The study also demonstrated that higher stage supervising teachers were more effective with a wide range of student teachers.

In general, higher stage teachers tend to be more flexible with their students (Oser 1984). The same holds true for supervisors and indeed for other school personnel such as counselors, principals, and other professionals (Sprinthall and Thies-Sprinthall 1983).

8 Conclusion

The cognitive–developmental framework represents a major shift in thinking about teaching and learning. The basic concepts were developed by Dewey and Freire. In combination, these concepts indicate the importance of viewing the processes of teaching and learning as interactive.

For democratic societies this framework asserts that a direct aim of education is both conceptual and ethical development in order to promote active citizenship throughout the life span. In this regard, Piaget and Kohlberg provide a detailed sequence of stages that can be used to understand the learner's preferred methods of problem-solving.

The dialectic approach implied by the framework involves varying content and method in accord with the learner's stage characteristics. The continuing failure of traditional teaching methods attests to the need for such a change.

The cognitive–developmental framework, however, is not singularly focused on students, but on the teacher as well. There are a number of model programs which demonstrate how the framework can be applied to both learner and teacher.

See also: Teacher Education: Philosophical Issues; Teaching: Implicit Theories; Teaching: Linguistic and Sociolinguistic Theories; Teaching: Heuristic Models; Teaching: Social Psychological Theories

References

Aiken W M 1942 *The Story of the Eight Year Study*. Harper and Row, New York

Barrett B 1975 Training and transfer is combinational problem-solving: The development of formal reasoning during early adolescence. *Dev. Psychol.* 11(8): 700–4

Berkowitz M W 1985 The role of discussion in moral education. In: Berkowitz M W, Oser F (eds.) 1985 *Moral Education: Theory and Application*. Erlbaum, Hillsdale, New Jersey

Bellack A, Kliebard H, Hyman R, Smith F 1966 *Language of the Classroom*. Teachers College Press, New York

Dewey J 1966 *Democracy and Education. An Introduction to the Philosophy of Education*. The Free Press, New York

Duckworth E 1987 *The Having of Wonderful Ideas and Other Essays on Teaching and Learning*. Teachers College Press, New York

Feuerstein R 1980 *Instrumental Enrichment: An intervention Program for Cognitive Modifiability*. University Park Press, Baltimore, Maryland

Flanagan J C 1973 Education: How and for what. *Am. Psychol.* 28: 551–56

Freire P 1981 *Education for Critical Consciousness*. Continuum, New York

Furth H 1981 *Piaget and Knowledge. Theoretical Foundations*. University of Chicago Press, Chicago, Illinois

Goodlad J 1984 *A Place called School*. McGraw-Hill, New York

Ginsberg H, Opper S 1988 *Piaget's Theory of Intellectual Development*, 3rd edn. Prentice Hall, Englewood Cliffs, New Jersey

Hunt D 1974 *Matching Models in Education*. Ontario Institute for Studies in Education, Toronto

James W 1958 *Talks to Teachers*. W. W. Norton, New York
Jones L V 1988 School achievement trends in mathematics and science, and what can be done to improve them. In: Rothkopf E Z (ed.) 1988 *Review of Research in Education*, Vol. 15. American Educational Research Association, Washington, DC
Joyce B, McKibbin M 1980 Psychological states and staff development. *Theory Pract.* 16(4): 248–55
Kegan R 1982 *The Evolving Self: Problems and Process in Human Development*. Harvard University Press, Cambridge, Massachusetts
Kohlberg L 1984 *The Psychology of Moral Development*. Harper and Row, San Francisco
Miller A 1981 Conceptual matching models and interactional research in education. *Rev. Educ. Res.* 51(1): 33–84
Nickerson R S 1988 On improving thinking through instruction. In: Rothkopf E Z (ed.) 1988 *Review of Research in Education*, Vol. 15. American Educational Research Association, Washington. DC
Oser F 1984 Cognitive stages of interaction in moral discourse. In: Kurtines W M, Gewirtz G L (eds.) 1984 *Morality, Moral Behavior, and Moral Development*. Wiley, New York
Piaget J 1972 Intellectual evolution from adolescence to adulthood. *Hum. Dev.* 15: 1–12
Piaget J 1974 *Adaptation vitale et psychologie de l'intelligence*. Hermann, Paris
Renner J et al 1976 *Research, Teaching, and Learning with the Piaget Model*. University of Oklahoma Press, Norman, Oklahoma
Rest J 1986 *Moral Development: Advances in Research and Theory*. Praeger, New York
Sprinthall N A, Collins W A 1988 *Adolescent Psychology: A Developmental View*. McGraw-Hill, New York
Sprinthall N A, Thies-Sprinthall L T 1983 The teacher as an adult learner. In: Griffin G (ed.) 1983 *(NSSE Staff Development (82nd Yearbook)*. NSSE, Chicago, Illinois
Sprinthall N A, Sprinthall R C 1990 *Educational Psychology: A Developmental Approach*, 5th edn. McGraw-Hill, New York
Thies-Sprinthall L 1980 Supervision: An educative or miseducative process. *J. Teach. Educ.* 31(4): 17–20
Tyler R W 1933 Permanence of learning. *J. Higher Educ.* 4: 203–04
Veenman S A M 1984 *Onderzack van het onderwijzen en do cognitief-structurele ontiockkelmgsbenadering*. Instituit Voor Onderwijskunde, Nijmegen
Vygotsky L 1978 *Mind in Society: The Development of Higher Psychological Processes*. Harvard University Press, Cambridge, Massachusetts
Walberg H 1986 Synthesis of research on teaching. In: Wittrock M C (ed.) 1986 *Handbook of Research on Teaching*, 3rd edn. Macmillan, New York
Walker L 1986 Sex differences in the development of moral reasoning: A rejoinder to Baumrind. *Child Dev.* 57(2): 522–26

N. A. Sprinthall

Teaching: Diagnostic–Prescriptive

The term "diagnostic–prescriptive teaching" (DPT) is used in both a broad and a narrow sense (Colarusso 1987). In a broad sense, it is a general label for instruction based on assessment and diagnostic data (i.e., adapting instruction to the different needs of students). In a narrow sense, the term refers to specific models used in special education for remediating learning difficulties. The first part of this entry focuses on the traditional concept of DPT and some of its basic assumptions. The remainder deals with the relationship between assessment (diagnosis) and instruction (prescription) in a broader context.

1. General Features of Diagnostic–Prescriptive Teaching

Most descriptions of DPT refer to two basic features: (a) an initial assessment or diagnosis with respect to variables related to academic learning or achievement; and (b) the use of these diagnostic data to specify prescriptions about effective instruction or intervention (see, e.g., Arter and Jenkins 1979, Ysseldyke and Salvia 1974).

Assessment in DPT has two main general functions (see Lloyd 1984). The first is determining what to teach (i.e., identifying targets for instruction). These can be learning goals that have not yet been attained as well as deficits in basic abilities that are supposed to cause learning problems. The second function is specifying how to teach. The latter function depends on students' learning styles and how they interact with instructional methods. One possibility in making decisions about how to teach is to observe how students react to instructional methods applied in a preliminary way. Sometimes this is called trial-teaching. It can be regarded as a further characteristic feature of DPT.

1.1 DPT in General Education

In general education, DPT mainly refers to strategies of individualizing instruction. Often it is considered as a general approach that forms the basis of various models of individualization. Examples of models include Individually Prescribed Instruction (IPI), Program for Learning in Accordance with Needs (PLAN), and Individually Guided Education (IGE). These models follow a diagnostic–prescriptive teaching cycle where the teacher's activities consist of: (a) finding out what the pupil knows; (b) providing learning materials that are appropriate for the pupil; (c) assigning learning materials for individual student work and monitoring student work; (d) assessing progress and mastery; and (e) offering additional work in case of a student's failure to reach mastery (Kulik 1982).

Sometimes DPT is considered as a specific method of individualization. Establishing objectives, especially behavioral objectives, is usually a first step. Diagnosis then aims at ascertaining which objectives the student has or has not already reached. Prescription is the process of assigning activities for student learning that are supposed to lead to the objectives. Finally, criterion measurement is used to determine whether the student, after completing prescribed activities, has attained the goals (Charles 1980).

1.2 DPT in Special Education

In special education, DPT refers to the setting up of an Individual Educational Program (IEP) for students who are handicapped or have learning difficulties. In special education, DPT is based on the traditional "medical" or "disease" model, which regards learning or behavioral problems as symptoms of some underlying "defect." According to the medical model, diagnosis aims at a classification based on a particular nosological system which in many cases also suggests proven means of treatment. For academic problems, however, diagnosis based on the medical model does not necessarily lead to effective treatment. As a rule, learning problems cannot be accounted for by a single underlying defect to a satisfactory degree; usually many additional factors are involved. Furthermore, empirically supported relations between specific deficits and effective interventions are lacking. Thus, the link between diagnosis and treatment is usually rather weak (Shapiro 1989). Another problem with classification in special education is that it often leads to the labeling of students which may lead to unfavorable psychosocial consequences.

In special education, DPT has often been equated with the so-called ability training model which considers basic abilities or processes (perceptual, attentional, memory, psycholinguistic) as causes of learning problems. It tries to remedy these causes directly or to circumvent them by special treatment. Empirical support for this model, however, is insufficient. As an alternative, a skill-development model has been proposed, which does not focus on general abilities or processes, but more directly on skills underlying academic competence (Arter and Jenkins 1979, Ysseldyke and Salvia 1974).

2. Assumptions of Diagnostic–Prescriptive Teaching

Basic to DPT is the assumption that diagnosis prescribes instruction (i.e., that initial assessment and diagnosis can be used to specify effective instruction and intervention). The validity of this argument rests on a series of related assumptions. These assumptions can be summarized in a single sentence: learners differ with respect to many characteristics which can be assessed in a reliable and valid manner, and which either (a) are directly related to academic learning and achievement, or (b) interact with instructional methods. Reviews on the ability training model in special education (Arter and Jenkins 1979, Ysseldyke and Salvia 1974) have shown that the validity of these assumptions may be questionable, for several reasons. First, reliability has often proven to be insufficient for individual diagnosis, and validity has been questionable. Second, direct remediation of abilities has often turned out to be unsuccessful and/or improvement of the abilities did not lead to higher achievement. Third, empirical support for stable interactions between abilities and instructional treatments has been weak.

Research on aptitude–treatment interaction (ATI) (Cronbach and Snow 1981) can be considered as the most important conceptual and empirical basis for DPT. Aptitudes comprise general and specific intellectual abilities as well as motivational characteristics and cognitive styles (Corno and Snow 1986). Interactions with instructional treatments are found when achievement is differentially related to aptitudes under different instructional conditions. For example, students with low abilities benefit more from highly structured instruction, while the reverse is true for high-ability students (see Cronbach and Snow 1981).

Although only few ATIs have been confirmed in a strict manner (Cronbach and Snow 1981), some general recommendations seem possible. Research on ATIs suggests that instructional treatments differ with respect to the information-processing and/or behavioral control demands that are placed on learners (Corno and Snow 1986). Teachers can try to adapt instructional methods according to the different information-processing capabilities and/or behavioral control capabilities of learners, thus reducing processing and control burdens for weak learners and placing higher demands on good learners.

Although ATI research represents the conceptual and empirical basis for adaptive instruction, its implications for teaching practice are limited. One reason is that in an actual instructional situation numerous individual factors (such as teacher and student personality), teaching style, and classroom context factors may interact with instructional methods in an unpredictable manner (Christenson and Ysseldyke 1989). In other words, conclusions based on ATI group data may not always be applicable to individual students (Shapiro 1989).

Two approaches to assessing student characteristics have emerged: direct assessment, and an idiographic orientation. As its name implies, direct assessment is focused directly on what is taught and typically includes the assessment of learning behaviors and skills in their natural environment (Shapiro 1989). This approach is in accordance with principles of behavioral assessment, where situational and environmental factors, in addition to personal factors, are taken into account.

An idiographic orientation essentially entails focusing on individual performance, tailoring instructional interventions to the individual case, and examining individual change relative to previous performance instead of making interindividual comparisons (Fuchs and Fuchs 1986). As there are many idiosyncratic factors which may interact in an unpredictable way, interventions based on diagnosis should be conceived as tentative and treated as empirically testable hypotheses. That is, interventions should be monitored and, if necessary, modified. In principle, this is a shift from a diagnostic–prescriptive to a formative approach (Deno 1986).

3. *Integration of Assessment and Instruction*

The key to the success of diagnostic–prescriptive teaching is the integration of assessment and instruction. Both formal and informal assessment are useful in this regard.

3.1 *General Considerations*

The integration of assessment and instruction is a topic that has received new interest in the 1980s and 1990s (Fuchs and Fuchs 1986). A major topic of discussion has been the knowledge base of teachers and how that knowledge base is activated and used for planning, preparing, and realizing instruction (Clark and Peterson 1986). There is now a broad consensus that informal diagnosis, mainly teacher judgment based on classroom observation, plays a crucial role. Formal assessment methods, especially tests, are also important because they yield information that can be directly relevant for instructional decisions.

According to Nitko (1989), four decisions can be distinguished when teachers attempt to adapt instruction to students' characteristics. *Placement* decisions are made at the beginning of a course or a longer instructional sequence. The purpose of these decisions is to place students, according to their prior knowledge or other learning prerequisites, into a sequence of instructional units at an appropriate level. *Diagnostic* decisions determine the objectives that are attained and not attained by the students. Furthermore, they are based on what the reasons for success or failure might be and, as a consequence, represent the basis for remedial work. *Monitoring* decisions are based on data concerning whether instructional activities are efficient, meet plans and goals, pose unexpected difficulties, or should be altered (formative evaluation). Finally, *attainment* decisions relate to a final evaluation of achievement and learning at the end of an instructional period (summative evaluation).

In the case of placement decisions, the usefulness of assessment of students' achievement and prior knowledge has been questioned (Nitko 1989). Formal testing for placement decisions is useful if (a) only little information about students' prior knowledge is available, and (b) the instructional system is indeed capable of adapting teaching to students based on this information.

In contrast to placement tests, diagnostic testing usually takes place after instruction has taken place for some time. Diagnostic testing has two major functions: (a) identifying instructional objectives not yet attained, and (b) discovering possible causes for the failure to attain these objectives. Methods of diagnostic testing include analysis of achievement or trait profiles, learning prerequisites, mastery of behavioral objectives, and identification of errors.

Monitoring decisions refer to students' activities and learning processes during instruction. Students' engagement and time-on-task are important indicators in this context. Monitoring as well as diagnostic testing serve a feedback function (i.e., they can be used for modification of learning and teaching). In regular classroom teaching, monitoring decisions are mostly based on informal teacher observations and judgments.

3.2 *Formal Assessment*

Formal assessment refers to the use of methods (especially tests) which are constructed and applied according to scientific standards. These tests differ with respect to their usefulness for instructional decisions.

Commercial *norm-referenced* tests, which sample a broad range of academic skills within a content area, have often been criticized with respect to their role in instructional decision-making and intervention planning (Shapiro 1989). One reason is that there may be little overlap between the curriculum and the test which may lead to incorrect decisions. Specifically, student failure may be attributed to personal ineptitude rather than to insufficient instruction. Another reason is that broad norm-referenced tests are insensitive to instruction and subtle changes in student achievement.

Criterion-referenced tests examine students' mastery of specific skills; ideally, they are based on objectives derived from the curriculum. Individual achievement is not compared with the distribution of results in a reference group, but with an objective standard. Assessment of students' profiles of strengths and weaknesses with respect to curricular objectives informs the teacher about targets for instruction.

Diagnostic tests, which focus on learning prerequisites and errors, are likely to provide even more specific information for instruction (see Nitko 1989). Standardized and easy-to-apply methods for the analysis of these knowledge structures were unavailable in the early 1990s but have considerable potential, especially if computer-based assessment methods can be used.

3.3 Informal Assessment

Informal teacher judgments are crucial for instructional decision-making. Often, preactive and interactive decisions are distinguished. *Preactive* decisions refer to the planning and preparation of instruction and usually occur outside the actual teaching situation. In contrast, *interactive* decisions occur during teaching. Whereas informal judgments in the preinstructional phases can be seen as analogous to placement tests, teacher judgments during interactive teaching phases serve a monitoring function (Shavelson and Stern 1981). Informal judgments may also serve a diagnostic function, in that observations and questions are used to obtain information about students' actual cognitive processing and learning difficulties.

Empirical support for the role of informal teacher diagnosis for instruction and teaching effectiveness comes from a study by Helmke and Schrader (1987). Teachers' accuracy in judging their students' achievement was considered as an indicator of diagnostic competence. Interestingly, diagnostic competence was not related to growth of achievement. However, there were significant interactions of diagnostic competence with two teaching variables, namely the frequency of teachers' structuring cues and teachers' supervision of individual students during seatwork. Classroom achievement gain was particularly high when both teachers' diagnostic competence and either of the two teaching variables were above average. Thus, it is likely that certain teaching methods are only successful when they are applied by a competent educational diagnostician who can then adapt his or her teaching methods to students' actual achievement levels. Of course, further research is needed to clarify the role of teacher judgment and diagnosis for adaptive teaching.

4. Diagnostic Assessment as Based on a Model of Effectiveness of Instruction

Traditional methods of assessment have almost exclusively focused on stable, trait-like learner characteristics. Furthermore, problems of learning were believed to be located primarily within the learner. In contrast, Christenson and Ysseldyke (1989) presented a comprehensive model in which student performance is influenced by three major groups of factors: student characteristics, school factors, and home factors. Student learning results from an interaction of these three classes of factors. School factors include teaching resources, academic focus, and interstaff collaboration. Home factors refer to variables such as participation, expectations, monitoring, and homework involvement.

This is in accordance with recent models of school learning and of educational productivity that emphasizes the existence of multiple determinants of learning and academic achievement. Advocates of these models believe that models that consider only one group of causes (individual, home, school, peer, media) are necessarily incomplete and biased (Walberg 1990). Both school and home factors influence classroom teaching which, in turn, affects instructional outcomes (see Brophy and Good 1986). The interplay and causal structure of these groups of variables is nicely demonstrated in the IEA *Classroom Environment Study* (Anderson et al. 1989).

From a diagnostic–prescriptive perspective, then, student assessment consists of gathering information as to whether instruction has been appropriate or effective for each individual student. Assessment of the educational environment (e.g., by teacher interview and/or classroom observation) is supplemented by assessing family and home background factors. Intervention aims at altering those variables that are supposed to impact on student learning. When intervention is unsuccessful alterations are made. Within this framework, then, the function of diagnosis is not to find prescriptions that are expected to work automatically, but to yield hypotheses about successful intervention which have to be empirically confirmed during subsequent instruction.

5. Conclusion

The traditional DPT model, with its emphasis on initial diagnosis of stable learner characteristics as a basis of effective instruction and intervention, is questionable. There are serious doubts about whether such initial diagnosis is appropriate for prescribing instruction. Several researchers have attempted to link assessment with instruction. In general, they have arrived at the following conclusions.

First, assessment should directly focus on what is taught, and should include environmental factors as well as student characteristics. Selection of the factors and characteristics to be assessed should depend on their empirically demonstrated relations with student achievement.

Second, further research is needed to establish a stable knowledge base about the relationship between instructional and family factors, on the one hand, and achievement and academic problems, on the other, which can be used for practical work. Research on aptitude-treatment interactions should be part of this endeavor.

Third, educational practice seems to require, in addition to a well-established research base, an idiographic orientation. That is, educators must consider individual achievement profiles, intraindividual comparisons, and individually tailored interventions.

Finally, prescriptions derived from assessment data should be considered as tentative hypotheses.

Accordingly, instructional interventions should be monitored in order to examine whether they were as effective as expected. Modifications should be made, when necessary.

See also: Teaching: Heuristic Models; Teaching: Reflective

References

Anderson L W, Ryan D, Shapiro B J 1989 *The IEA Classroom Environment Study*. Pergamon Press, Oxford

Arter J A, Jenkins J R 1979 Differential diagnosis–prescriptive teaching: A critical appraisal. *Rev. Educ. Res.* 49(4): 517–55

Brophy J, Good T L 1986 Teacher behavior and student achievement. In: Wittrock M C (ed.) 1986 *Handbook of Research on Teaching*, 3rd edn. Macmillan Inc., New York

Charles C M 1980 *Individualizing Instruction*, 2nd edn. Mosby, St Louis, Missouri

Christenson S L, Ysseldyke J E 1989 Assessing student performance: An important change is needed. *Journal of School Psychology* 27(4): 409–25

Clark C M, Peterson P L 1986 Teachers' thought processes. In: Wittrock M C (ed.) 1986 *Handbook of Research on Teaching*, 3rd edn. Macmillan Inc., New York

Colarusso R P 1987 Diagnostic–prescriptive teaching. In: Wang M C, Reynolds M C, Walberg H J (eds.) 1987 *Handbook of Special Education. Research and Practice. Vol. 1: Learner Characteristics and Adaptive Education*. Pergamon Press, Oxford

Corno L, Snow R E 1986 Adapting teaching to individual differences among learners. In: Wittrock M C (ed.) 1986 *Handbook of Research on Teaching*, 3rd edn. Macmillan Inc., New York

Cronbach R J, Snow R E 1981 *Aptitudes and Instructional Methods: A Handbook for Research on Interactions*. Irvington, New York

Deno S L 1986 Formative evaluation of individual student programs: A new role for school psychologists. *School Psychol. Rev.* 15(3): 358–74

Fuchs L S, Fuchs D 1986 Linking assessment to instructional intervention: An overview. *School Psych. Rev.* 15(3): 318–23

Helmke A, Schrader F-W 1987 Interactional effects of instructional quality and teacher judgement accuracy on achievement. *Teaching and Teacher Educ.* 3(2): 91–98

Kulik J A 1982 Individualized systems of instruction. In: Mitzel H E (ed.) 1982 *Encyclopedia of Educational Research*, Vol. 2, 5th edn. Macmillan, New York

Lloyd J W 1984 How shall we individualize instruction—or should we? *Rem. Spec. Educ.* 5(1): 7–15

Nitko A J 1989 Designing tests that are integrated with instruction. In: Linn R L (ed.) 1989 *Educational Measurement*, 3rd edn. Macmillan Inc., New York

Shapiro E S 1989 *Academic Skills Problems: Direct Assessment and Intervention*. Guilford Press, New York

Shavelson R J, Stern P 1981 Research on teachers' pedagogical thoughts, judgments, decisions, and behavior. *Rev. Educ. Res.* 51(4): 455–98

Walberg H J 1990 A theory of educational productivity: Fundamental substance and method. In: Vedder P (ed.) 1990 *Fundamental Studies in Educational Research*. Taylor and Francis, London

Ysseldyke J E, Salvia J 1974 Diagnostic–prescriptive teaching: Two models. *Excep. Child.* 41(3): 181–85

A. Helmke; F.-W. Schrader

Teaching: Heuristic Models

Heuristic models of teaching are those models of teaching in which the primary aim is to provide students with strategies or heuristics for solving problems, thinking effectively, or learning for themselves. The aim of these models is to make students independent thinkers and learners who take responsibility for creating their own understanding and knowledge. Proponents of heuristic models of teaching have argued that in a complex and constantly changing society, in which knowledge and technology are quickly outdated, it is more important for students to learn how to think and create new knowledge and solutions to problems for themselves than it is for them to acquire existing knowledge.

1. Historical Development

Heuristic models of teaching have been proposed within European culture for many centuries. Wittrock (1985) traced their origins to Plato's dialogues, especially Plato's account of Socrates teaching the Pythagorean theorem to a young slave. Plato's dialogues exemplify a style of teaching in which the teacher and student engage in a process of rational argument and careful consideration of the validity of evidence. For Plato, true knowledge lies hidden behind the appearance of things and can be discovered through logical analysis and debate about the evidence obtained through the senses.

In later Roman and early medieval European times, rhetoric or the art of public speaking and persuasion had a central place in the education of the ruling classes. As in other societies in which valued knowledge was not widely available in written or printed form, considerable emphasis was placed on accurate memorization of information. In preliterate societies, survival depended on the ability of selected individuals to memorize the society's store of natural and supernatural wisdom. In these and early European societies, methods of memorization had a central place in education. They employed mnemonic heuristics, which involved the use of imagery, rhythmical and musical chanting, and techniques (such as the method of locuses) to link new information to familiar events or places (Metge 1986).

The rise of publicly funded universal education in European societies in the nineteenth century and other societies in the twentieth century resulted in an emphasis on receptive methods of teaching and a decline of interest in heuristic methods. Teaching children to think for themselves became less important than teaching them to become effective workers and morally decent citizens. However, with the extension of democracy there followed the belief that society depends on a more broadly educated population whose members can make informed decisions for themselves. Thus, there has been a renewed interest in heuristic models of teaching. In the United States, for example, Dewey (1933) argued that the skills of reflective thinking must be the prime concern of education for a democracy. Students, he claimed, must develop the habits of mind of skeptical rationalism.

The models of heuristic teaching that emerged in the late twentieth century owed much to the development of cognitive science and to growing dissatisfaction with behavioral models of teaching. The extensive research of Piaget and Bruner served to focus attention on the active nature of the child's mind. The child's intelligence came to be seen as the product of the ways in which the child comprehended and acted upon the physical and social world. Consequently training the child to interpret and think about reality more effectively could increase the development of intelligence.

Also important were studies of the ways in which experts perceive, think about, and solve problems in their area of expertise. Traditional methods of teaching were seen as paying little attention to the heuristics that experts within each discipline use. It has been argued that students in areas such as science and mathematics will not become proficient in these disciplines unless they are given explicit instruction in the heuristics used by expert scientists and mathematicians (Brown and Campione 1990).

There is now evidence that many students who graduate from high school and even college still hold serious misconceptions about basic scientific and social principles and concepts. Gil-Perez and Carrascosa (1990) argued that a major reason for the persistence of these misconceptions is that they reflect historically primitive ways of understanding the world. Receptive methods of teaching may be good at imparting knowledge, but they fail to teach the important attitude of skepticism and the skills of enquiry that underlie modern scientific thinking.

2. *Modern Models of Heuristic Teaching*

There has been a proliferation of models of teaching whose major purpose is to provide students with heuristics for thinking, problem-solving, understanding, and self-regulated learning. Underlying the design of these models are conceptions of how students' minds work; these have determined both the heuristics that should be taught and the methods of teaching that should be used. To be flexible and effective the teacher also needs to have an understanding of the student's mind. For example, the teacher needs to understand that the student needs to know many different learning and thinking strategies and how and when to use these strategies. The student needs to be reflective and planful, to be free from the fear of failure, and to believe in the efficacy of personal effort. In addition, the student should have a wide background of relevant knowledge and to have experienced reward and support for acting as an effective self-regulated learner and thinker (Borkowski and Muthukrishna 1992, White 1992).

The modern models of heuristic teaching tend to fall into five general types. Each of these will be described below, along with one or two examples of each type.

3. *The Reciprocal and Transactional Strategy Instruction Models*

There is a family of heuristic models of teaching that see the student as engaged in a kind of "cognitive apprenticeship" (Collins et al. 1989). In these models, cognitive processes characteristic of an effective or expert thinker or learner are demonstrated to the student, who is helped to imitate and achieve mastery of the processes through guided practice. The most difficult task for the teacher is to make visible and explicit for the student cognitive processes that normally take place in the head of the expert (Brown and Campione 1990).

Perhaps the best-known of these models is the "reciprocal teaching" model developed by Palincsar and Brown (1984). In this model the teacher demonstrates or models a cognitive process (such as predicting what is going to happen next while reading a narrative text), explaining at the same time what he or she is doing and why he or she is doing it. The students are required to try to imitate the model. As the students try out the process and develop their skill in using it, the teacher ceases to provide the model and takes on the role of coach, providing cues, hints, corrective feedback, and encouragement. Students are then helped to take over control of the process for themselves and to engage in self-evaluation of their performance (Palincsar 1986).

The teacher's role is described as providing "scaffolding," within which the student does as much as he or she can and the teacher does the rest (Cazden 1988). By being sensitive to the level of the student's understanding and progress, the teacher is working within the student's "zone of proximal development" (Vygotsky, 1978). If the teacher's guidance is too far in advance of the student's skill, the instruction is less likely to be effective.

Although this model was initially developed as a way of teaching comprehension skills to poor readers, it has been extended to cover the teaching of mathematics and science. Brown and Campione (1990) described the use of the reciprocal teaching model in mathematics education. Their procedures involved the use of a "reflection board" on which a group of students record their progress toward the solution of a mathematical problem. The students recorded what they knew about the problem (their background knowledge), how they planned to solve the problem, their progress through the solution steps, and their checking of the accuracy and the plausibility of the solution they reached. The important role of the "reflection board" was to provide the students with a record they could use to think about and reflect on their problem-solving processes. They identified the procedures that succeeded or failed and learned to think heuristically about solving mathematics problems.

The model of "transactional strategy instruction" described by Pressley et al. (1992) is similar in many respects to the reciprocal teaching model, but it was developed to teach a wider range of thinking, learning, and comprehending skills in a more open-ended and flexible manner. According to Borkowski and Muthukrishna (1992), the model encourages habitual reflecting and planning by students. Teachers using the model "foster an environment in which such reflection is valued more than the completion of assignments or the production of right answers" (p. 479). Teachers have to be sensitive to the needs of the students and encourage them to "evaluate and manage their own learning" (p. 490).

In their analysis of the most successful transactional strategy instruction programs, Pressley et al. (1992) identified the following characteristics. The teachers introduced one strategy at a time. They took extended time to teach each strategy and engaged in a great deal of direct explanation of each strategy. The teachers modeled each strategy themselves, describing what they were doing, and explaining why the strategy worked and when it should be used. The teachers provided the students with consistent and frequent feedback as they practiced and applied the strategy, and provided further description and explanation whenever any difficulties occurred. Throughout the process the teachers kept the students' motivation high, and encouraged the students to plan their use of the strategy carefully and to reflect constantly on how the strategy was working.

4. *Direct Strategy Instruction*

The transactional strategy instruction model has been contrasted with another family of heuristic models of teaching described as "direct strategy instruction." Although these two models have many features in common, direct strategy instruction is carefully structured and depends on the teacher following a closely prescribed pattern of behaviors. Kline et al. (1992) described eight steps for teaching a cognitive strategy. In the first stage, the students are pretested and a contract is set up between the teacher and the students in which the students make a commitment to learn and use the strategy. In the second and third stages the teacher describes the strategy, models it for the students, and encourages the students to try using it. During the fourth and fifth stages, the students learn to use the strategy, to name and explain the steps involved, and to practice it on increasingly difficult material. In the sixth stage, the students practice the strategy on real problems in and out of school, following an individualized program of work, until they reach mastery. In the seventh stage the students are given a posttest. The teacher and students then review progress, celebrate the students' achievements, and make a commitment to continue using the strategy. In the final stage, the teachers guide the students in practicing the strategy in a variety of situations.

5. *Self-instructional Strategy Training*

A different approach to providing students with the heuristics they need to become self-sufficient learners has been described by Miller and Brewster (1992). Self-sufficient learners are described as those students who know about the parameters that affect their cognition, know how to control their own cognitive endeavors, and believe that cognitive effort results in academic success. Self-instructional strategy training involves training students to talk to themselves as they engage in learning and problem-solving processes. There are five types of cognitive processes for which self-verbalizations are taught: (a) analyzing the task and the goals to be achieved ("What do I have to do?"); (b) formulating a plan of action ("How should I do it?"); (c) evaluating the effectiveness of each of the steps in the plan ("How am I doing?"); (d) giving positive feedback for succeeding with each step ("That's good work."); and (e) dealing with obstacles, employing corrective actions ("That's not quite right." "Keep cool." "I will try again.").

When teaching students to carry out these verbalizations, teachers are encouraged to model and display the steps and the verbalizations, to use real learning situations, and to provide students with information about why the verbalizations are necessary and how effectively they work. Self-verbalization training needs to be undertaken in conjunction with training in self-motivation and self-attribution to ensure that students believe in their ability to take control of their own lives and succeed.

6. *Generative and Interactive Teaching Models*

A different type of heuristic teaching model has been variously described as "generative" and "interactive" teaching. This type of model is based on the premise that all significant learning is a generative or constructive process. While it is true that students can memorize and reproduce the information presented to them by teachers or textbooks, for that information to become part of their thinking and guide the way in which they understand and interact with the world, they have to construct or reconstruct it for themselves. All lasting knowledge is the product of the way in which the student's background knowledge and beliefs interact with new experiences (Wittrock 1991, White 1992).

It follows from this premise that students need to learn how to guide their own knowledge construction processes. They need to be taught to take responsibility for the ways in which they understand and question their own beliefs, the new experiences they encounter, and the match or mismatch that may occur between them.

6.1 Generative Teaching Models

Wittrock based his description of the generative teaching model on an analysis of the way in which the mind comprehends new experience and information. Understanding is a process of identifying and building relations between prior knowledge and new knowledge, and between the component parts of the new knowledge. For example, when reading a text, the student must identify how the content of the text relates to the student's prior knowledge and beliefs, and also identify the relations that exist between words, sentences, phrases, and topics within the text.

The teacher who uses the generative model of teaching must begin by identifying the preconceptions, beliefs, and experiences that the student brings to the learning situation. The teacher must then organize classroom experiences so that the student connects the new information to his or her prior knowledge and constructs a new understanding or model of the phenomenon. The teacher must help the student see his or her role as one of generating understanding by relating concepts presented in class to real-world experience. The student must take "control and responsibility for being active in learning, for generating meaning from teaching and attributing success to this active effortful learning" (Wittrock 1991 p. 175). Thus, students must be taught the metacognitive and self-control strategies they need to direct their own cognitive and affective thought processes. The students need to be taught that success in school begins with belief in themselves, their abilities, and their effort.

6.2 Interactive Teaching Models

Closely related to the generative teaching model is the heuristic teaching model described as "interactive teaching" by Biddulph and Osbourne (1984). As with the generative teaching model, the concern is with students taking responsibility for the extent and the validity of their knowledge. This model has been developed in the context of science education and involves five sequential components.

During the first stage a topic for investigation is selected by the teacher. This may be related to the students' current concerns, interests, or problems. The topic should be relevant to the way the students make sense of everyday events and can be related by the students to things that have practical and social significance in their lives. It should also be an area in which it is possible for students to carry out simple practical investigations. During the second stage the teacher encourages the students to think and talk about the topic. The students may engage in exploratory activities, observing, recording, and finding relevant print materials. During this stage the teacher should make it clear that the students' ideas and beliefs are interesting and important. During the third stage the teacher identifies the questions that the students would like answered about the topic. These questions are developed and clarified so that they can form the basis for serious investigation. The teacher must make sure that the questions are important to the students. During the fourth stage, the students develop their plans for carrying out investigations and gathering information to answer their questions. The teacher guides the students, helping them to reflect on their plans and to consider alternative ways of carrying out their investigations. In the fifth and final stage the teacher and students reflect together on the results of the investigations and on the whole process. The teacher helps them to consider alternative explanations of their results and to plan further investigations. It is important that students come to feel both that their ideas are valued and that they are responsible for developing them.

7. Logical Argument Models

Models of teaching have been proposed that focus on thinking as "logical argument." In these models the skills and forms of argument and analysis that are used to argue a case or to defend a proposition against counterclaims are taught. For example, Kuhn (1992) studied the forms of argument and reasons and evidence that people use when they discuss and defend their views on significant social issues. She suggested that an effective heuristic teaching program needs to engage students in guided practice in using reason and evidence. Argument about significant social issues offers the teacher a way to externalize, discuss, and modify the internal and usually unobserved thinking strategies that students use in their everyday lives. However, as Kuhn noted, teachers are wary of introducing genuine debate about controversial issues into the classroom and consequently students are rarely given the chance to have their beliefs challenged or to experience genuine debate.

Ziedler and Lederman (1992) were also concerned with teaching students the use of reason and evidence. They argued that learning critical thinking skills involves learning how to evaluate evidence and reasons and how to identify and avoid common logical fallacies. For example, students need to learn how to distinguish verifiable facts from value claims, how to determine the credibility of a source of information, how to distinguish relevant from irrelevant information, and so on. They should also be taught to identify common fallacies such as begging the question, *ad hominem* or *ad feminam* argument, and the fallacies that arise from ambiguity of terms and normative reasoning. They suggested that this learning should take place in the context of classroom discussion and debate focused on scientific and social issues of relevance to the students' lives.

8. Major Characteristics of Heuristic Teaching Models

The models described in this entry are very diverse but they have some common characteristics. Most involve the teacher in modeling or making visible the thinking or learning processes that the students are required to learn and use. This may involve using visible or verbal aids, such as flowcharts, diagrams, or checklists of procedures. It may also involve naming strategies and developing and using a language for talking about how, when, and where they are used. Most are concerned with avoiding superficial processing of information or rote memorization of procedures. There is an underlying cognitive model of the student as an active, planful, and reflective learner or thinker. Most are concerned with making the student an independent thinker or learner who has the skills, the motivation, and the beliefs required to take responsibility for his or her own achievement and personal development.

The role of the teacher is usually portrayed as flexible and sensitive to the students' skills and background knowledge and experiences. The teacher's role changes during the course of the program as the students' needs change from providing direct descriptive instruction about strategies, through being an "expert" model, to becoming a supportive colleague or coach, encouraging, guiding, and helping. Students report that they learn to think better when they are stimulated by real cognitive challenges, already have considerable relevant background knowledge, are provided with positive models of the strategies they need, and are working in a classroom environment that offers and encourages autonomy (Collins 1992).

The learning process implied by most of the models is one of "internalization." Students are shown a model that is an externalization of cognitive processes that are normally internal and covert. They are expected, through guided practice, to internalize the model and make it a normal part of their internal cognitive processing. This is what is meant by "cognitive apprenticeship" (Collins et al. 1989).

9. Problems of Training Teachers and Assessing Outcomes

Several writers have noted that it takes considerable time and dedication to train teachers to use heuristic models of teaching effectively. Teachers must become committed to a model and incorporate it into their own philosophy of teaching (El-Dinary et al. 1992). They need strong informal peer support and commitment from the administration to support them during the process of change that is required (Kline et al. 1992). The process of training may take several years and the training should itself be structured according to a heuristic model of teaching.

Heuristic models of teaching are primarily concerned with the ability of students to think and learn independently, and are only secondarily concerned with traditional student achievement. As a consequence, they pose considerable challenges for developing appropriate methods of assessing their effectiveness. As Ziedler et al. (1992) have suggested, the problem is to find effective ways of obtaining and evaluating "performances of thought." Although tests of critical thinking have been available for some time, more general methods of assessing how students use their minds are still in the early stages of development and validation (Wolf et al. 1992).

See also: Teaching: Behavioral Theories; Metacognitive Strategies, Teaching and Testing for; Teaching: Informational Processing Theories

References

Biddulph F, Osbourne R 1984 *Making Sense of Our World: An Interactive Teaching Approach*. University of Waikato Science Education Research Unit, Hamilton

Borkowski J G, Muthukrishna N 1992 Moving metacognition into the classroom: "Working models" and effective strategy teaching. In: Pressley M, Harris K R, Guthrie J T (eds.) 1992

Brown A L, Campione J C 1990 Interactive learning environments and the teaching of science and mathematics. In: Gardner M et al. (eds.) 1990 *Toward a Scientific Practice of Science Education*. Erlbaum, Hillsdale, New Jersey

Cazden C 1988 *Classroom Discourse: The Language of Teaching and Learning*. Heinemann Educational, Portsmouth, New Hampshire

Collins C 1992 Improving reading and thinking: From teaching or not teaching skills to interactive interventions. In: Pressley M, Harris K R, Guthrie J T (eds.) 1992

Collins A, Brown J S, Newman S E 1989 Cognitive apprenticeship: Teaching the craft of reading, writing and mathematics. In: Resnick L (ed.) 1989 *Cognition and Instruction: Issues and Agendas*. Erlbaum, Hillsdale, New Jersey

Dewey J 1933 *How We Think: A Restatement of the Relation of Reflective Thinking to the Educative Process*. Heath, Boston, Massachusetts.

El-Dinary P B, Pressley M, Schuder T 1992 Teachers' first year teaching strategies: Case studies in the Students Achieving Independent Learning (SAIL) strategies instruction program. Paper presented to the American Educational Research Association Conference, San Francisco, California

Gil-Perez D, Carrascosa J 1990 What to do about science "misconceptions". *Sci. Educ.* 74(5): 531–40

Kline F M, Deshler D D, Schumaker J B 1992 Implementing learning strategy instruction in class settings: A research perspective. In: Pressley M, Harris K R, Guthrie J T (eds.) 1992
Kuhn D 1992 Thinking as argument. *Harv. Educ. Rev.* 62(6): 155–78
Metge J 1986 *Learning and Teaching: He Tikanga Maori.* Ministry of Education, Wellington
Miller G E, Brewster M E 1992 Developing self-sufficient learners in reading and mathematics through self-instructional training. In: Pressley M, Harris K R, Guthrie J T (eds.) 1992
Palincsar A S 1986 The role of dialogue in providing scaffolded instruction. *Educ. Psychol.* 21(1–2): 73–98
Palincsar A S, Brown A L 1984 Reciprocal teaching of comprehension-fostering and comprehension-monitoring activities. *Cognition and Instruction*, 1(2): 117–75
Pressley M et al. 1992 Beyond direct explanation: Transactional instruction of reading comprehension strategies. *Elem. Sch. J.* 92(5): 513–55
Vygotsky L S 1978 *Mind in Society: The Development of Higher Psychological Processes*. Harvard University Press, Cambridge, Massachusetts
White R T 1992 Implications of recent research on learning for curriculum and assessment. *J. Curric. St.* 24(2): 153–64
Wittrock M C 1985 Heuristic models of teaching. In: Husén T, Postlethwaite T N (eds.) 1985 *The International Encyclopedia of Education, 1st edn*. Pergamon Press, Oxford
Wittrock M C 1991 Generative teaching of comprehension. *Elem. Sch. J.* 92(2): 169–84
Wolf D, Bixby J, Glenn J, Gardner H 1992 To use their minds well: Investigating new forms of student assessment. In: Grant G (ed.) 1992 *Review of Research Education,* Vol 17. American Educational Research Association, Washington, DC
Ziedler D L, Lederman N G, Taylor S C 1992 Fallacies and student discourse: Conceptualizing the role of critical thinking in science education. *Sci. Educ.* 76(4): 437–50

Further Reading

Fleer M 1992 Identifying teacher–child interaction which scaffolds scientific thinking in young children. *Sci. Educ.* 76(4): 373–97
Gardner M et al. (eds.) 1990 *Toward a Scientific Practice of Science Education*. Erlbaum, Hillsdale, New Jersey
Pressley M, Harris K R, Guthrie J T 1992 *Promoting Academic Competence and Literacy in School*. Academic Press, San Diego, California

G. Nuthall

Teaching: Implicit Theories

The explanations given by teachers for what they do are typically not derived from what they were taught in teacher education programs. Though study in such fields as educational foundations, academic disciplines, and curriculum theory is expected to give rise to knowledge relevant to teaching, such knowledge rarely features in the explanations and justifications offered by teachers for their classroom behaviors. Rather, the classroom actions of teachers are guided by internal frames of reference which are deeply rooted in personal experiences, especially in-school ones, and are based on interpretations of those experiences.

These frames of reference include beliefs about educational goals, learners, and learning; images of good and bad teaching; and conceptions of the roles of teachers and students. They are applied daily by teachers to make sense of, and respond rationally to, classroom events; to identify appropriate courses of action; and to realize worthwhile goals. Collectively, these frames of reference allow teachers to identify important variables in teaching and the interrelationships among these variables. They also endow teachers with some capacity to predict what will work and thus produce desired outcomes. These frames therefore can be said to constitute a type of theory, a theory which shapes action in the classroom and is constructed from interpretations of past actions. For this reason, these frames of reference have been referred to as theories for action or practical theories.

Parts of these theories, however, are tacitly held and cannot be readily articulated. For this reason, practical theories are also referred to as implicit theories. The implicit nature of practical theories is usually attributed to: (a) the roots of teaching behaviors being so deeply embedded in the life histories of teachers that they are simply unaware of them, and (b) reasons for what they do in the classroom being forgotten, as patterns of thoughtful action become routinized. Moreover, teachers have had little need to make their practical knowledge explicit and are provided with few opportunities and little encouragement to be introspective. Teachers' implicit theories of teaching are thus the products of teachers' efforts to make sense of their experiences and to generate a basis for effective action in the classroom.

Implicit theories cannot be regarded as scientific theories because, as Sanders and McCutcheon (1986) point out, "theories that count as 'scientific' theories are expected generally to be conceptually precise, specifically explicated, and able to withstand rigorous logical tests. They also are expected to be subject to public disconfirmation" (p. 57). These are characteristics which teachers' implicit theories mostly lack. Implicit theories are at best rough estimates of what will work because the contexts in which they are applied are so variable, indeterminate, unpredictable and capricious; furthermore, because the contexts are not reproducable, the theories cannot be subjected to rigorous tests.

Implicit theories of teaching do not rate as scientific theories on two other counts. In contrast to scientific theories which are universal and impersonal, implicit theories are both context-specific and intensely personal. Each implicit theory has been individually crafted and reflects the unique personal history of an individual and the interpretations of those experiences by that individual. Though teachers' implicit theories may have some elements in common, each teacher's implicit theory is unique. Moreover, a teacher's implicit theory has been abstracted from experiences in a very restricted set of sites and from the perceptions of one person about events in those sites. Accordingly, there is no expectation that an individual's implicit theory will have generalizability.

There is also a general awareness among teachers that what works in one classroom context will probably not be effective in another. Even where a single class is involved, teachers know well that differences in time of day for a lesson, class moods, and the focuses of preceding lessons can render some approaches inappropriate and ineffective. The implicit theory held by one teacher cannot be used in all the contexts in which that teacher works, but has to be adapted to suit the special circumstances of each context.

1. Importance of Recognizing Teachers' Implicit Theories

Interest in the implicit theories of teachers has sparked reforms in research, teaching, and teacher education, many of which are only beginning to gain momentum in the 1990s. Recognition of the existence of such theories and their influence on classroom practice, learning to teach, and the fate of educational innovations reflect a new appreciation of the value of practical knowledge and the importance of experience in, and reflection on, practice. The new status accorded practical knowledge and implicit theories, a status previously denied them, has resulted in shifts in the focus and conduct of research on teaching. The agenda in research on teaching is no longer dominated by a search for causal links between teaching processes and student outcomes ("process–product" or "black box" research), but by attempts to see into the minds of teachers, to document their thinking and knowledge ("glass box" research). The impact of this shift generally has been to elevate the teacher from a position of potential user of research knowledge to one of source and creator of such knowledge. This shift has required a redefinition of the teacher's role in research from being simply an object of research to being a collaborator or partner. The case for recognizing teaching as a profession could not fail to be strengthened by these developments.

The role of teachers in their own professional development has also undergone some marked changes. Professional development is no longer seen as something done to teachers but as something teachers do to themselves. Hence teachers are now viewed as principal agents in promoting their own professional growth. Consequently, the climate is now more favourable for teachers to take the initiative in professional development matters. A much higher priority is given to teachers sharing knowledge with colleagues, reflecting on practice, and articulating their personal philosophies. Where such activities have occurred, teachers have become aware of their belief systems and how their frames of reference affect their teaching roles. By understanding their own implicit theories, teachers are in a better position to improve the quality of their professional actions.

Another worthwhile development has involved teachers exploring their personal metaphors for teaching. Researchers who sponsored this work have reported teacher disclosure of aspects of their practical knowledge of which they were previously not aware (Munby and Russell 1989). Others (e.g., Tobin 1990) have reported that, by constructing new metaphors to reconceptualize their teaching roles, teachers have been able to effect significant changes in instructional practices and improvements in classroom learning environments. The account of the teacher who developed the metaphor of "self as travel agent" to explore and implement constructivist approaches in a science classroom is an example of this (Ritchie and Russell 1991).

Recognition of the implicit theories of student teachers has significant implications for preservice teacher education as well. Assisting student teachers to become aware of their attitudes and beliefs, and the images they have of themselves as teachers, will help to reveal to them the basis for their actions in the classroom and enable them to identify more readily what is inappropriate or problematic in their implicit theories. Teacher educators also need to have knowledge of how their student teachers think. Insights into the implicit theories of student teachers provide a basis for teacher educators to plan more effective specific and generic teaching strategies to help them learn to teach and to effect changes in their beliefs. Attending to the language that student teachers use to talk about their classroom roles might also provide helpful clues about the causes of problems they face in the classroom.

2. Factors Influencing Development of Teachers' Implicit Theories

Implicit theories of teaching are not held only by those who teach. They are products of the culture and life experiences of individuals and form part of the intellectual property of every person. They probably begin to take shape in infancy during informal learning experiences in family settings, but are then molded by 13 or more years of formal schooling. This long exposure to teachers and school life inevitably informs students about the work of teachers, the classroom roles of teachers and students, the nature of knowledge, and culturally endorsed values, beliefs, and behavior norms—all important elements of implicit theories of teaching. Accounts by student teachers of information gained during this extended "apprenticeship" include frequent references to, on the one hand, model teachers and powerful illuminating learning experiences, and on the other, to deficiencies in schooling and gross insensitivity on the part of teachers to the needs of learners.

Experiences in schools and contacts with teachers have been powerful factors in shaping the implicit theories and classroom practices of those just embarking on a teaching career (Calderhead 1988). The critical role of prior beliefs in learning to teach is widely acknowledged (Hollingsworth 1989). These early perspectives or conceptions of teaching are very durable and resistant to change, so much so that they can neutralize the best efforts of preservice teacher educators to change them. In fact, the irrelevance of preservice teacher education to professional development has long been alleged by teachers.

However, the trend in the literature to be dismissive of the effects of preservice programs on implicit theories has been challenged in research from the late 1980s. Preservice teacher education programs can effect changes in beliefs, help transform subject matter knowledge into a pedagogically relevant form, and provide schemata for critically analyzing and improving schooling (Hollingsworth 1989). Another important factor in the development and refinement by teachers of their implicit theories is possession of metacognitive skills. Changes in implicit theories are more likely to occur if teachers are aware of limitations of their implicit theories and can exercise executive control over cognitive processes to extend and refine them (Calderhead 1988, Hollingsworth 1989).

Whereas opinion is divided as to the impact of on-campus components of preservice programs on implicit theories, there is no such ambivalence about the effects of classroom experience. It is widely asserted that most of a teacher's implicit theory is developed through on-the-job experience (Sanders and McCutcheon 1986). How teachers learn from experience is still somewhat unclear; however, cognitive dissonance, or discomfiture with what is, and a commitment and ability to conduct and learn from "practice-centred inquiry" are cited as key components of experiential learning (Sanders and McCutcheon 1986). The earlier view that learning to teach was simply a matter of learning and applying theory is now largely discredited.

3. Methods of Studying Implicit Theories

Implicit theories cannot be studied until they are first made explicit. Disclosure of implicit theories, however, is not easily achieved. Teachers' minds cannot simply be unzipped to allow close inspection of the contents. What compounds the problem of making the implicit explicit is that the substance and structure of implicit theories are not known completely even to the teachers themselves. Hence, asking teachers to articulate their implicit theories inevitably involves them in a process of discovery—a process in which there are few clues for determining when explanations of implicit theories are complete, accurate, and valid. Finding appropriate and valid ways of making implicit theories explicit is therefore a major methodological challenge.

Research undertaken so far has proceeded on the assumption that implicit theories can be discovered in teachers' discourse about teaching, and in their actions, since actions are overt expressions of implicit theories. Accordingly, techniques have been used which call on teachers to generate self-reports of their knowledge and beliefs about teaching. Teachers have been interviewed using approaches labeled as "clinical", "structured", "unstructured", and "ethnographic", to name but a few. Interview procedures involving the use of records of task performance to stimulate recall of in-task thinking have also been used. Teachers have been invited to keep journals or write biographical sketches and stories about themselves and their thinking, and to react to video records of teaching and written accounts of teaching incidents. Teachers have been asked to allow observers and those who wish to adopt a participant–observer role into their classrooms. The data and insights gleaned by these visitors are then used to infer features of the theories implicitly held by teachers. The repertory grid technique, based on personal construct theory and the view of humans as theory builders, has also been used to study teachers' implicit theories. In most studies, some combination of the methods outlined above has been employed.

The next step involves interpreting the data generated by the above methods and assembling models or representations of teachers' tacitly held theories in symbolic or semantic form. In this process, close collaboration between teachers and those wishing to study their implicit theories is essential to ensure that representations of implicit theories ring true. One threat to the validity of these models is the uncritical use of constructs from codified knowledge. The search for frameworks and constructs which accurately represent the ways implicit theories are held has only just begun.

4. Research in Teachers' Implicit Theories

One of the first indications of research interest in the implicit theories of teachers was given by Gage (1978), who observed that the topic might well become ". . .an additional substantive direction for research on teaching" (p. 80). Almost a decade later, the study of implicit theories of teaching was still being described as "nascent" (Clark and Peterson 1986). Over the intervening years there has been a considerable upsurge of interest in research in this field; however, while implicit theories of tertiary teachers have come under some scrutiny (see, e.g., Hughes 1990), most attention has been focused on the theories of elementary and secondary teachers and the contrasts between theories held by experienced or expert teachers and those held by novices.

In their 1986 review of this inchoate research, Clark and Peterson noted that a variety of terms was being used in studies of implicit theories: "personal perspective," "conceptual system," "principles," "practical knowledge," and "beliefs." Some of these terms have lost currency. Terms which have come into favor include "metaphor," "image," and "pedagogical content knowledge." These have not been adopted on the basis of a whim. On the contrary, their emergence reflects important advances in understanding the nonpropositional nature of teachers' knowledge and ways of conceptualizing the form and substance of teachers' implicit theories.

4.1 Metaphors for Teaching

It has been pointed out that when teachers talk about their work, their discourse is replete with metaphorical language. This, it is argued, is because ". . .the human conceptual system is defined and structured metaphorically, . . . human thought processes are largely metaphorical" (Munby and Russell 1989 p. 3). Hence, internal representations of reality are also constructed in metaphorical terms. Researchers have argued that the metaphorical language used by teachers in talking about their teaching will reveal how they have made sense of classroom realities and how they see the roles of learners and teachers. In short, analysis of the metaphors in teacher talk will disclose much about their implicit theories of teaching.

An amazing number of metaphors used by teachers to explain their approaches to teaching have been documented. The list includes teacher as cook, entertainer, counselor, timekeeper, engineer, preacher, conductor, mother figure, horticulturalist, actor, and ship's captain. Frequently, the language of any one teacher about teaching contains references to a number of metaphors. Teachers tend to live by such metaphors—that is, the metaphors used by teachers to conceptualize their role in the classroom are manifest in and consistent with their behaviors (Tobin 1990).

This consistency can be a blessing or a blight. It is a blight when the metaphor is inappropriate or overused. Research indicates that the transmission metaphor, which represents teaching as a mechanical process of knowledge transfer, might well be in this category. Work with metaphors has gone well beyond the identification stage whereby a teacher's language is analyzed to pinpoint the metaphors that inform their teaching and thinking about teaching. Metaphors have also been used as a heuristic device to assist teachers to generate alternative metaphors to redefine their roles in the classroom and to change and improve their teaching (Tobin 1990).

4.2 Images

The notion of images has emerged as another useful way of representing components of teachers' implicit theories. Clandinin (1986), who has broken new ground in her work with this concept, views an image not just as a snapshot stored in memory of some person or event but as a mental coalescence of private and professional experiences. These coalescences or summaries of experience become an important part of a person's life force and "modus operandi." They may find expression verbally, for example as a metaphor, or practically, in a person's private and professional life. Because life experiences are rich in effect and perceived as good or bad, harmful or helpful, so too do images possess emotional and moral dimensions.

Clandinin's study of the implicit theories of two teachers provides compelling evidence of how images link the present with the past and how images constructed from past experiences can provide explanations for what teachers do in the classroom. Images isolated from the professional discourse of Stephanie, an experienced Grade 1/2 teacher in the Clandinin study, included "classroom as home,""herself as a maker,""teaching as teaching children to be makers,""the high school math experience," and "the policeman." The first of these, "classroom as home," was shown to have its origins in Stephanie's private life, namely in her view of herself as an atypical child and the contrasts she made between her home life experiences, characterized by cooperation and extensive interaction, and those she had in schools and during teacher training. In her formal education, the emphasis was on conformity and compliance.

The "classroom as home" image reflected her judgment that the kind of educational packaging she endured at school was harmful and should not have happened. This judgment gave her image a moral dimension. At the same time, the emotional dimension of her image was conveyed in her talk about the quality of relationships in families and her reactions to the depersonalizing effects of formal educational processes. The view that the classroom environment for lower elementary children should be like a home was firmly held and found expression in a range of activities—cooking, growing seeds, celebrations, displays, and farewells—as well as strenuous efforts to establish a convivial atmosphere in which students would feel comfortable and cared for.

4.3 Pedagogical Content Knowledge

A vigorous new program of research has emerged, based on the proposition that teachers' beliefs about, and understandings of, subject matter have a powerful influence on the instruction they provide. It is also proposed that teachers, through learning how to make subject matter teachable, acquire new understandings of content, how to teach it, and how students learn it. This new form of knowledge, referred to as pedagogical content knowledge, cannot be equated either with the special content knowledge of the academic expert or with the knowledge of generic principles of pedagogy. Rather, pedagogical content knowledge is regarded as a unique blend of teacher brands of subject-matter knowledge, topic-specific pedagogy, and psychology of learners and learning. Though there are cross-study variations in how pedagogical content knowledge is construed, it is generally thought to include ". . . overarching conceptions of what it means to teach a particular subject, knowledge of curriculum materials and curriculum in a particular field, knowledge of students' understanding and potential misunderstandings of a subject area, and knowledge of instructional strategies and representations for teaching particular topics" (Grossman 1989 p. 32).

Studies of the pedagogical content knowledge of experienced teachers confirm that their conceptions of subject matter are different from those held by scholars in the field (Gudmonsdottir 1990, Gudmonsdottir and Shulman 1987). Conceptions of content, however, do not stand alone within pedagogical content knowledge. Instead they are amalgamated with pedagogy to form models which are unique and personal to each teacher and undergird the teaching approach adopted by that teacher. Illustrative of these models is one from Naomi, a secondary teacher of English, who describes her model as a "layered onion" with English literature as the inner core: "Surrounding the core are layers that she (Naomi) peeled off in classroom discussions as she examined the text. The first layer involved understanding the text; the second involved probing for deeper significance and the third focused on multiple orientations" (Gudmonsdottir 1990 p. 47).

Gaps in the pedagogical content knowledge of some teachers have also been identified, as well as substantial disparities between the pedagogical content knowledge of expert and novice teachers in terms of extent, richness, complexity, and flexibility of use (Gudmonsdottir and Shulman 1987). A start has also been made on examining the contribution of specific curriculum studies to the development of pedagogical content knowledge in student teachers, but much more work still needs to be done. What is clear is that pedagogical content knowledge is central to the work of teaching and constitutes an essential part of the professional knowledge base of teachers.

4.4 Other Research

Research into teachers' implicit theories has been proceeding on several other fronts. Studies have investigated the knowledge structures or schemata that teachers use to process the plethora of stimuli that classrooms present. Experienced teachers have been shown to have schemata which enable them, by comparison with novice teachers, to screen out irrelevant classroom data more effectively, to better conserve their information-processing capacities, and to interpret classroom events in more instructionally relevant ways. The greater facility of experienced teachers in anticipating, avoiding, and handling in-class problems (behavioral or conceptual) has been attributed to their possessing better developed schemata.

The beliefs and belief systems of teachers have continued to attract the interest of researchers. The pervasive and critical influence of teacher beliefs in shaping, for example, their task performance, how they learn from experience, the environments they create, and their acceptance or rejection of new curricula has been acknowledged in numerous studies. Progress in this field has been slow, however, impeded by the deep-seated implicitness of beliefs and the intractable problems of articulating, classifying, and assessing them. The development of a theoretically based model of belief systems to facilitate systematic and comparative studies in this area is still some way off.

There have also been attempts to map teachers' implicit theories in their entirety rather than focussing on one element such as beliefs or principles. Representations of teachers' conceptualizations of teaching have included elements such as goals, beliefs, student states which teachers sought to create, strategies and conditions affecting teaching, and the relationships among these elements (Brown and McIntyre 1988, Marland and Osborne 1990). Still other research has focused on the implicit theories teachers hold about student learning, evaluation, and planning. These studies have exposed substantial differences between the theories of practitioners and textbook theories.

5. Conclusion

Though study of implicit theories of teaching is still in its infancy, it has demonstrated the crucial importance of practical knowledge and practical ways of knowing. Some progress in revealing the substance, form, and origins of implicit theories has been made. The vital contributions of this research to delineating the professional knowledge base of teaching and to reforming the content and delivery of preservice and inservice teacher education have been recognized.

See also: Teaching, Realities of; Teaching: Behavioral Theories; Teaching: Social Psychological Theories

References

Brown S, McIntyre D 1988 The professional craft knowl-

edge of teachers. *Scottish Educ. Rev.* Special issue: 39–47
Calderhead J 1988 The development of knowledge structures in learning to teach. In: Calderhead J (ed.) 1988 *Teachers' Professional Learning*. Falmer Press, Lewes
Clandinin D J 1986 *Classroom Practice. Teacher Images in Action*. Falmer Press, Lewes
Clark C M, Peterson P L 1986 Teachers' thought processes. In: Wittrock M C (ed.) 1986 *Handbook of Research on Teaching*, 3rd edn. Macmillan, New York
Gage N L 1978 *The Scientific Basis of the Art of Teaching*. Teachers College Press, Columbia University, New York
Grossman P L 1989 Learning to teach without teacher education. *Teach. Coll. Rec.* 91(2): 191–208
Gudmonsdottir S 1990 Values in pedagogical content knowledge. *J. Teach. Educ.* 31(3): 44–52
Gudmonsdottir S, Shulman L S 1987 Pedagogical content knowledge in social studies. *Scand. J. Educ. Res.* 31(2): 59–70
Hollingworth S 1989 Prior beliefs and cognitive change in learning to teach. *Am. Educ. Res. J.* 26(2): 160–89
Hughes J A 1990 The teaching theories of community college faculty. Paper presented at the annual meeting of the Association for the Study of Higher Education, Portland, Oregon
Marland P, Osborne A 1990 Classroom theory, thinking and action. *Teaching and Teacher Education* 6(1): 93–109
Munby H, Russell T 1989 Metaphor in the study of teachers' professional knowledge. Paper presented at the annual AERA meeting, San Francisco, California
Ritchie S M, Russell B 1991 The construction and use of a metaphor for science teaching. Paper presented at the annual AARE conference, Surfers' Paradise,
Sanders D P, McCutcheon G 1986 The development of practical theories of teaching. *Journal of Curriculum and Supervision* 2(1): 50–67
Tobin K 1990 Changing metaphors and beliefs: A master switch for teaching. *Theory Pract.* 29(2): 122–27

Further Reading

Calderhead J, Robson M 1991 Images of teaching: Student teachers' early conceptions of classroom practice. *Teaching and Teacher Education.* 7(1): 1–8
Johnson S 1990 Understanding curriculum decision-making through teacher images. *J. Curric. St.* 22(5): 463–71
Kagan D M 1990 Ways of evaluating teacher cognition: Inferences concerning the goldilocks principle. *Rev. Educ. Res.* 60(3): 419–69
Leinhardt G 1990 Capturing craft knowledge in teaching. *Educ. Researcher* 19(2): 18–25
Marshall H H 1990 Metaphor as an instructional tool in encouraging student teacher reflection. *Theory Pract.* 29: 128–32
Pinnegar S, Carter K 1989 Comparing theories from text-books and practising teachers. *J. Teach. Educ.* 40(1): 20–27
Provenzo E F, McCloskey O S A, Kottkamp R B, Cohn M M 1989 Metaphor and meaning in the language of teachers. *Teach. Coll. Rec.* 90: 551–73

P. W. Marland

Teaching in Small Groups

When the classroom is subdivided into a number of small groups that serve as the social units in which learning is pursued, the role of the teacher differs considerably from that typical of the traditional classroom. While various cooperative small-group learning methods make somewhat different demands on teachers, the fact that students' attention in all of these methods is to be focused on their group mates with whom they interact and not on the teacher, results in a host of consequences for teachers' instructional behavior. Furthermore, introduction into a classroom of an alternative instructional method that diverges from the teaching patterns generally practiced by most other teachers has many school-wide implications for teachers' instructional behavior: decisions about curriculum, the nature of their relationship with colleagues, and the school's policy and administration (Sarason 1982, 1990, Sharan and Sharan 1991). These changes in instructional behavior and teachers' relationships with colleagues may not be identical for all small-group teaching methods. Nevertheless, the differences in teachers' behavior required by the different group-learning methods are probably more a matter of degree than of essence.

For purposes of discussion, the teacher's role in the Group Investigation method (Sharan and Sharan 1992) will be explored as an example of what teachers must consider when implementing cooperative learning in small groups. A short description of the Group Investigation method precedes the discussion of the teacher's role.

1.1 The Group Investigation Method

Small-group instructional methods most often seek to embody a set of theoretical principles derived from a basic philosophical, psychological, or sociological orientation toward the educational process. They are not merely collections of practical procedures. Group Investigation embodies the principles of Dewey's (1938) view of school learning as an investigatory process conducted in collaboration with one's peers. Students plan together what they will study about problems they have identified that invite genuine inquiry (Miel 1952, Thelen 1954, 1981).

The Group Investigation method can be conceived as a sequence of six stages. First, after the teacher presents a general problem for investigation, the class determines subtopics for study and organizes into research groups. Students probe a variety of sources, propose questions, and sort them into categories that serve as topics of investigation for study groups.

Second, groups plan their investigations cooperatively in terms of what they will study, how they will proceed, where they will seek information, and how they will divide the work among themselves.

In the third stage, groups carry out their inves-

Table 1
Five dimensions of classroom instruction

Dimension	Whole-Class	Group Investigation
Behavior of teachers	Sole determiner of study materials, tasks, pace of instruction, criteria for evaluation	Guide students, respond to their initiatives, involve them in planning and decision-making.
Tasks	Uniform for entire class. Products are predetermined	Students choose subtopics and learning activities. Final products unspecified. Tasks foster cooperation among members of small groups.
Behavior of students	Obey instructions, play passive role in determining study tasks and methods	Ask questions, plan, initiate activities. High involvement in learning. Make decisions about various aspects of classroom life.
Physical setting	Permanent, appropriate for one teaching method only	Flexible structure that changes with the nature of the tasks, methods, students' needs.
Communication	Unilateral or bilateral, subject to teacher's mediation	Multilateral among members of groups or between groups.

tigations. They organize and analyze their findings, exchange and clarify ideas through discussion, reach conclusions, and integrate their work into a group product.

Fourth, groups plan their presentations, avoiding lengthy lectures, and seeking interactive methods of presentation such as exhibitions, role-plays, simulations, experiments, learning stations, dramatizations, and demonstrations. A group's presentation must be coordinated with those of other groups in the classroom.

At the fifth stage, groups make their presentations. The audience not only participates but also evaluates presentations.

Finally, group products and individual learning are evaluated. Evaluations can involve students as well as teachers.

2. *Five Dimensions of Classroom Teaching: Whole-class and Cooperative-learning Classes Compared*

With the emphasis clearly on groups of students and students as both teachers and learners, a key question emerges: What is the role of the teacher in the successful implementation of the Group Investigation method?

One approach to examining the role of the teacher is by viewing classroom instruction as consisting of five dimensions to which teachers must attend in order to implement instruction effectively. These five dimensions and their implications for the behavior of teachers and students in the traditional whole-class and small-group classrooms appear in Table 1. As shown in Table 1, the teacher's behavior in the cooperative small-group classroom conducted with the Group Investigation method differs in many ways from what teachers do in the traditional classroom.

2.1 The Teacher's Control Function

First and foremost, in the Group Investigation method the small groups become the center of learning activity through peer interaction, verbal and nonverbal. The teacher must relinquish center stage and transfer some degree of control to the small groups. This control refers to the interpersonal interaction that occurs in the group (i.e., the discussion and exchange of plans, ideas, suggestions, and observations), as well as the management of the group's work through such techniques as role differentiation within the group (e.g., chairperson, recorder, and resource person) or various forms of division of labor relevant to the content of the group's task. Teacher-centered control is not compatible with free exchange of ideas among students, as is well-known from studies of human organization in general. Indeed, teachers who implement cooperative learning in small groups become less concerned with their control function than those who prefer the traditional whole-class form of instruction (Sharan and Hertz-Lazarowitz 1982).

Furthermore, teachers take their cues, in terms of the pace of learning as well as the identification of specific learning tasks, from the progress of the groups. Teachers counsel the groups and help them overcome problems that crop up during the course of their work, both in respect to the study materials as well as in respect to the students' relationships within the groups. Teachers try to encourage students to pursue avenues of study of which students become aware as they pursue their work, thereby taking advantage of the students' initiative and self-motivation. This role differs markedly from the lock-step pace of instruction typical of whole-class teaching.

2.2 Teachers and Students as Curricular Decision-makers: The Design of the Learning Task

Students must be convinced that the teacher has

in fact empowered them to make a wide range of decisions regarding the selection of learning tasks and the nature of the process of investigation. Since teachers are typically the sole determiners of such decisions, students are unlikely to engage in these activities freely until they have tested the teacher and discovered that they have the legitimate right to make and carry out their decisions.

When students are given a genuine role in determining some aspects of the content of learning tasks, a much wider range of possible topics for study is likely to emerge. Moreover, student choice in selecting or identifying desirable topics of study can evoke a wider range of abilities and talents than might be called upon by learning activities set exclusively by the teacher, even when the teacher determines the general domain of the students' investigation on the basis of the school's curriculum. When student choice is permitted or encouraged, the teacher must plan carefully, particularly in terms of the variety of resources that should be made available to the students (Cohen 1986, Sharan and Sharan 1992).

The curricular and behavioral diversity supported by the small-group approaches to classroom learning implies a distinct departure from the uniformity in curricular content and learning activities inherent in traditional instruction. The expectation that all students in the class must study the same material at the same pace and that they should all reach the same educational outcomes is one of the bedrock assumptions of public education in general and of secondary school education in particular. It is precisely this concern for uniformity that is a major impediment to effective instruction in culturally and ethnically heterogeneous classrooms.

Finally, teachers in the small-group classroom must design the learning task to facilitate cooperation and mutual assistance among members of small groups so they have a common goal and purpose for working together. The task must also invite a variety of perspectives or approaches, and not demand simple informational solutions which are easily available in the textbook. Multifaceted and open-ended tasks of this nature encourage participation by many students who can contribute their unique resources to their group's project. Teachers are asked to become aware of these task-design features that are a necessary prerequisite for group-centered learning (Cohen 1986, Sharan and Sharan 1992). If the task does not enable students to cooperate with one another and to perceive their group as a productive arena for achieving academic goals, the group is likely to disintegrate into a collection of individuals working toward uncoordinated goals.

2.3 Students' Role in Seeking Information

Another fundamental feature of the teacher's role in the small-group classroom is the orientation of students toward an investigatory approach to learning rather than the ingestive mode that prevails in most schooling. Such an orientation can be as foreign to the students as it is to teachers. Seeking information to generate ideas and knowledge is a distinctly different form of learning than being told the information, performing various exercises with the information, and then being tested on it. It cannot be assumed that students will know how to participate effectively in the work of a small group. Teachers are advised to provide students with some experience with interactive skills before asking them to function in task-oriented groups (Cohen, 1986, Graves and Graves 1985, Schmuck and Schmuck 1992).

In traditional instruction, the teacher most often asks the questions that students are expected to answer. In small-group instruction, the students' work is directed by the questions they themselves have asked about the subject in hand. The teacher's role is to encourage students to ask questions that can direct their study, to help groups plan and carry out projects that involve the search for and use of information about academic topics. Thus, the change in the teacher's role can be realized only if a parallel change occurs in the manner in which students are expected to behave during the pursuit of learning.

In sum, then, successful learning in small groups entails basic changes in classroom behavioral norms. Students must come to understand that they are expected to help one another in achieving group and individual goals, and realize that teachers value high-quality group products.

2.4 Classroom Organization to Support Student Interaction

Classroom organization must be adapted to the specific needs of the learning tasks and afford opportunities for effective interaction among students. Therefore, classroom organization may undergo changes even during the course of a single lesson as a function of changes in the students' stage of learning activity. Small-group instruction requires flexibility in organizing seating patterns, setting aside corners of the classroom for holding meetings, and preparing other spaces in or out of the classroom where various activities can be conducted by small groups of students engaged in group investigation projects. In small-group instruction, the teacher assumes the role of classroom organizational manager, a role he or she may not be called upon to perform in the traditional classroom where the structure of the classroom remains uniform throughout the year.

2.5 The Teacher as Manager of Classroom Communication

Finally, teachers must alter their patterns of communication with students if the small groups are to function effectively. Teachers may have to unlearn many skills and habits they acquired as part of their experience with traditional instruction in terms of how they address the class (Hertz-Lazarowitz and Shachar 1990). The verbal expository mode of information transfer and questioning which involves mainly unilateral or bilateral channels of speech must be replaced by group-centered multilateral patterns of communication. When this change is made, students can engage in productive talk and not be inhibited or intimidated by the teacher's dominant role.

Another salient aspect of classroom communication that needs to be revised to fit the needs of small-group instruction is the asking of questions. Stimulating students to ask questions about what and how to study subject matter instead of subjecting them to perpetual interrogation is an important feature of small-group instruction, yet doing so may run counter to much of what teachers are taught during their professional education. Indeed, texts on teaching focus on teachers' questions as one of the primary instruments of instruction. These texts fail to deal extensively with ways in which teachers can stimulate and encourage students to ask most of the questions. This omission is tragic, since it is the students' curiosity that must be engaged if they are truly to learn.

3. *Teachers as Observers*

Most authors of books on small-group instruction urge teachers to stand aside on occasion and observe how the groups in their classroom are functioning. Several texts provide extensive lists of categories teachers can use to direct their observations in order to note if students in fact are cooperating and interacting in a constructive fashion (Cohen 1986, Johnson and Johnson 1987).

Teachers can employ the five-category system presented in Table 1 as an observation schedule to ascertain the extent to which group learning with the Group Investigation method is being implemented appropriately in their classrooms. Do the procedures now in use approximate the descriptions in the "Whole Class" column or the "Group Investigation" column? If they are more similar to the "Whole Class", the probability is that a large number of students find themselves excluded from the process of learning. If the procedures in use are more similar to those appearing in the "Group Investigation" column, the likelihood is that students are interacting with one another in positive ways and are actively involved in the process of learning.

It should be noted that the effective implementation of small-group methods in general and the Group Investigation method in particular requires that all five components set forth in Table 1 be implemented in a coordinated fashion. If one component is omitted or implemented as if the class was being taught with the whole-class approach, the net result will be faulty implementation that can disrupt the learning process and result in frustration for both students and teachers. To be effective, teachers must plan for the appropriate use of all five dimensions simultaneously.

In many classrooms one can observe that the teacher has organized students into small groups sitting around tables, but the lesson is delivered in the typical presentation–recitation format. Similarly, teachers provide small groups with learning tasks directed at individual students that require individual work. The groups have no collective task at all, or the task is so routine that no real group effort is required, such as seeking answers to questions of simple fact (who, what, where, when, and how?). The net result is that the students sitting around the table do not really form a group since there is no constructive interaction between them.

4. *The Teacher, the School, and the Classroom*

Discussions of the teacher's role as a classroom instructor should treat the issue of the teacher's relationship with the school administration and with colleagues on the teaching staff of the school as a whole. The school as an organization, with its instructional policy (explicit or implicit) and its expected patterns of relationships among teachers and administrators, exerts considerable, sometimes decisive, influence on teachers' instructional roles as they are carried out in practice, or portrayed in various public pronouncements. The effects of school-wide factors on individual teacher's classroom instruction is often made particularly palpable when teachers seek to implement alternative teaching methods such as small-group instruction or cooperative learning. Since small-group instruction diverges from traditional patterns of instruction, its implementation requires a multitude of adjustments by teachers both in attitude and instructional practices that may conflict with the normative practices of the school as a whole.

Cooperative small-group instruction often diverges from the school's standard instructional policy, from fundamental attitudes held by teachers, or both. Topics on which cooperative small-group instruction typically diverges from the norms accepted in traditionally organized schools include the following:

(a) All students in the class are expected to master all of the material in given units of study. These expectations relate to uniformity in the pace and scope of learning.

(b) The pace and scope of instruction is often monitored in various ways by school authorities, usually through testing programs to evaluate achievement levels. The tests are standardized and not criterion referenced (that is, not based on what students have studied in specific classrooms).

(c) Implementation of group projects on occasion may entail the extension of class time. Such extensions require coordination of class schedules with other teachers. These projects may also entail students' visits to sites outside the school for purposes of direct observation, conducting interviews with various experts, and the like. School-wide scheduling exerts powerful constraints on a teacher's ability to employ alternative instructional methods in the classroom.

(d) If many teachers in a school continue to employ traditional whole-class forms of instruction, teachers seeking to use cooperative small-group approaches may experience some conflict with colleagues. Teachers become concerned with students' expectations and patterns of behavior as they move through the grades in a given school when the students are exposed to distinctly different instructional methods. In such cases, it becomes necessary to negotiate with colleagues and to determine school policy on the subject of instructional methods across the grades.

Given the fact that learning tasks appropriate for small-group instruction must be designed differently from the kinds of tasks generally provided by the curriculum, teachers interested in implementing cooperative small-group methods are often called upon to prepare portions of the curriculum on their own. Often, teacher preparation time in school is very limited. Also, teachers need the collaboration and assistance of colleagues to generate group-centered curricula that challenge groups of students and arouse their genuine curiosity and interest. Thus, preparation of suitable study materials for small-group teaching must become the concern of the school's administration, and cannot be left to the initiative or responsibility of the individual teacher.

Finally, to effect the successful implementation of significant innovation in instruction, teachers must participate in an ongoing process of problem-solving, negotiation, and decision-making on topics relevant to classroom teaching in all of its manifestations, not just in terms of its immediate implications for a given classroom or subject. Teachers may not be prepared by their professional education and experience to assume responsibility for organizational decision-making. Moreover, this role may not even be perceived as a legitimate component of the teacher's professional duties. There is a growing awareness on the part of educators that a significant change in teachers' professional role is a prerequisite for affecting the practice of instruction in the classroom (Darling-Hammond 1988, Murphy 1991, Sarason 1990).

See also: Cooperative Learning; Teaching: Social Psychological Theories; Classrooms: Grouping of Students

References

Cohen E 1986 *Designing Groupwork*. Teachers College Press, New York

Darling-Hammond L 1988 Policy and professionalism. In: Lieberman A (ed.) *Building a Professional Culture in Schools*. Teachers College Press, New York

Dewey J 1938 *Experience and Education*. Macmillan, New York

Graves N, Graves T 1985 Creating a cooperative learning environment: An ecological approach. In: Slavin S et al. (eds.) 1985 *Learning to Cooperate, Cooperating to Learn*. Plenum Press, New York

Hertz-Lazarowitz R, Shachar H 1990 Teachers' verbal behavior in cooperative and whole class instruction. In: Sharan S (ed.) 1990 *Cooperative Learning: Theory and Research*. Praeger, New York

Johnson D, Johnson R 1987 *Learning Together and Alone*, 2nd edn. Prentice-Hall, Englewood Cliffs, New Jersey

Miel A 1952 *Cooperative Procedures in Learning*. Teachers College Press, New York

Murphy J 1991 *Restructuring Schools*. Teachers College Press, New York

Sarason S 1982 *The Culture of the School and the Problem of Change*, 2nd edn. Allyn and Bacon, Boston, Massachusetts

Sarason S 1990 *The Predictable Failure of Educational Reform*. Jossey-Bass, San Francisco, California

Schmuck R, Schmuck P 1992 *Group Processes in the Classroom*, 6th edn. Brown, Dubuque, Iowa

Sharan S, Hertz-Lazarowitz R 1982 Effects of an instructional change project on teachers' behavior, attitudes and perceptions. *Journal of Applied Behavioral Science* 18: 185–201

Sharan S, Sharan Y 1991 Changing instructional methods and the culture of the school. In: Wyner N (ed.) 1991 *Current Perspectives on School Culture*. Brookline Books, Cambridge, Massachusetts

Sharan Y, Sharan S 1992 *Expanding Cooperative Learning Through Group Investigation*. Teachers College Press, New York

Thelen H 1954 *Dynamics of Groups at Work*. University of Chicago Press, Chicago, Illinois

Thelen H 1981 *The Classroom Society*. Croom-Helm, London

S. Sharan

Teaching: Informational Processing Theories

In simple terms, information processing theories of teaching characterize instruction as a series of repeating cycles. Each cycle involves two phases. First, the teacher selects and arranges elements in the instructional environment so that, as students participate in instruction, they are guided to process particular information cognitively. Second, by performing these cognitive processes, students generate their own cognitive representations of subject matter, as well as cognitive representations of other information about learning strategies, self concept, and the formats and norms for participating in various instructional activities. In judging whether instruction has been effective, information processing theories of teaching consider three kinds of achievements: (a) when students' mental representations of information are accurate, appropriate, and complete; (b) when, if a future task calls for that information, they can remember it; and (c) when students are motivated to use that information in performing tasks that correspond to objectives set by the teacher and the students.

Considered in these terms, a thorough information processing theory of teaching must address two main issues. The first is how students acquire, remember, and apply knowledge. The second is how instruction can guide students to engage in tasks that call for particular forms of cognitive processing, and, once these cognitive processes are underway, how teaching can support students' information processing at successive stages of those tasks.

This entry focuses on research-based theories and models that describe teaching in classrooms, and teaching as conveyed by texts and computer software that students study on their own. It highlights how teachers and their surrogates (e.g., textbooks, computer systems) engage and guide students' cognitive processing of information in order to promote achievements. Detailed illustrations of these approaches are presented in Joyce et al. (1992) and Reigeluth (1987).

1. The Cognitive Mediational Paradigm

Students bring prior knowledge to any instructional setting. Prior knowledge is an aptitude (Snow 1992) that mediates how students perceive the setting, how they are inclined to participate in the instructional activities therein, and what they are able to learn by their participation (Winne 1985).

Information processing theories of teaching catalog types of knowledge—both prior knowledge and knowledge that is to be achieved by participating in instruction. Two principal categories are conceptual knowledge and metacognitive knowledge (see *Student Cognitive Processing and Learning*). Conceptual knowledge is information that comprises academic subject matter—facts, principles and rules, frameworks and schemata, and basic skills. Metacognitive knowledge includes: (a) information about methods for learning (cognitive strategies) and for directing one's efforts to learn (self-regulation) within the instructional situation(s) that the teacher (or surrogate) has created; (b) information about self-preferences and attitudes, strengths and weaknesses, motivation, feelings, and so on; (c) information about tasks, how they are structured, and how they unfold; and (d) information about goals the student holds and plans for reaching those goals. Students' prior knowledge can aid or interfere with information processing and, thus, facilitate or inhibit achievement.

During instruction, the teacher (or surrogate) presents subject-matter information that students are to learn (in explicit models) or makes this information available implicitly in materials and within tasks that students pursue to inquire about a topic (inquiry models). The teacher (or surrogate) also provides information that is intended to cue or guide students' information processing of conceptual and metacognitive information. For example, the title given to an activity or to a textbook chapter reveals something what the instructional session is about. This is subject-matter information. The teacher may also intend the title to engage the student in predicting, a particular cognitive routine that jointly manipulates prior knowledge and information that will arise as the activity progresses. For example, the teacher may expect the title to signal to the student that he or she should predict the main idea of a text and then take notes that confirm, deny, or modify that prediction.

Students interpret the subject matter information that the teacher (or a surrogate) presents to construct a personal representation of it. Students also interpret and choose whether and how to use guidance for cognitively processing information that becomes available as the instructional activity unfolds. Therefore, links between instructional events that the teacher structures and achievements that students gain by participating in instruction are mediated by each student's prior knowledge (Winne and Marx 1987, Snow 1992). Information processing theories of teaching address how students' mediations of instruction can strengthen, weaken, or distort effects predicted by theory (Winne 1987).

In information processing theories of teaching, it is usually assumed that students are attentive and motivated to learn, and that they follow rules for the activity structures that typify the lesson. To the extent that these conditions are not satisfied, the explanatory strength of information processing theories is diminished.

2. Explicit Teaching in Classrooms

Explicit teaching is one of the most long-standing and fundamental models of teaching. In this form of teaching, the major objective is for students to elaborate (i.e., supplement or refine) prior knowledge of subject matter by adding to it facts, concepts, principles, basic skills, and other forms of conceptual knowledge (Alexander et al. 1991, Rosenshine 1987, Gagné et al. 1992). Winne (1985) describes this model as consisting of the following key elements.

A lesson or study session begins with the instructor or surrogate identifying goals to be achieved by students. This goal identification provides information students can use to: (a) monitor their progress during the lesson and (b) guide their information processing by applying means–ends analysis during learning (Frederiksen 1984). There then follows a short review of prerequisite knowledge that is intended to activate the prior knowledge the student will use in assembling more elaborate structures of subject-matter information. These structures fuse prior knowledge with new content presented in the lesson. The review also invites the student to recall learning and self-regulatory strategies for cognitively processing forthcoming information.

New subject matter is then presented in relatively small steps to avoid overloading the limited capacity of the student's working memory. Details, clear explanations, and demonstrations of rules are provided to enrich the student's elaborations of new information by assembling it with prior knowledge. During the presentation, students are invited to respond to questions or work out small exercises. Typically, these are organized so that those questions which call for direct retrieval or straightforward application of information outnumber questions that involve processing information or solving a problem to generate an answer by a factor of about 3:7. The aim of these activities is to engage the student in rehearsing information, assembling it into larger, more meaningful structures termed schemata, and translating newly developed structures of information into analogous representations, images, and personally meaningful metaphors (Winne 1985).

Following the presentation, students work alone or in small groups on exercises that involve retrieving and applying the newly presented information. At first, tasks repeat and straightforwardly extend those presented in the lesson. The teacher or a peer provides guidance and, as necessary, directly assists the student when the student cannot complete the task independently. This support, called "scaffolding," becomes more prominent as tasks are gradually extended into the student's zone of proximal development, that is, the region of performance where a student has the potential to achieve but needs some assistance. Systematic feedback to correct errors in students' work is provided as required. As students assemble schemata (e.g., typical forms for persuasive compositions, classes of algebra word problems) and develop automaticity in applying rules of the subject matter (e.g., monitoring for invalid logic in developing an argument, simplifying algebraic expressions), the teacher and scaffolding are withdrawn. Through further practice, the student's retrieval and use of subject-matter rules and cognitive strategies becomes skilled and self-regulated, and transfer of the lesson's information to different and more complex tasks is approached.

2.1 Sequencing

In explicit teaching, the teacher determines the subject-matter information presented within each lesson and across lessons that comprise larger units of study. In both situations, considerations about sequencing information need to be addressed. Van Patten et al. (1986) distinguished microsequencing, namely concern for sequencing information about an individual concept or rule within a lesson, from macrosequencing, a concern about sequencing multiple units of information both across ideas within a lesson and across lessons.

Regarding microsequencing, generalizable definitions are distinguished from instances (examples or nonexamples) of the generalized form. When the objective of a lesson is that students apply the generalized form of information in tasks that are not very different from those encountered in the lesson—that is, tasks that call for near transfer—research suggests that the teacher should first present the generalized form followed by a series of instances of it. When the objective of instruction is that the student transfer the generalized form to tasks that are considerably different from those studied in the lesson—that is, a situation involving far transfer—the more effective sequence is an inductive one in which multiple instances precede presentation of the generalized form. In both cases, successive instances should be ordered from simple to complex, and the instances should be as different from one another as possible (Van Patten et al. 1986).

Research which investigates macrosequencing in classrooms is uncommon probably because of difficulties of valid implementation of complex instructional treatments in the dynamic social setting of a classroom. Macrosequencing, however, has been examined when information processing theories of teaching have been operationalized in text presentations, and thus will be reviewed in Section 5 below.

3. Reciprocal Teaching

In reciprocal teaching (Palincsar and Brown 1984), the teacher or a surrogate (e.g., a more competent peer, or a computer system) engages the student in a dialogue about learning. The dialogue is designed to reveal essential information about subject matter and to illustrate how to self-regulate information processing that constructs achievements. Although reciprocal teaching was developed to teach young children how to understand narratives, the theory can be extended to most subject areas and to other ages.

Reciprocal teaching begins with the teacher modeling the elements of tasks and showing how information can be used to construct achievements from these tasks. At each stage, the teacher explicitly describes the nature of information processing that builds knowledge. After students have been introduced to information processing tasks, they and the teacher (or they and their peers) alternate between the roles of instructor and learner. In the role of learner, students perform the task, monitor how the instructor's comments guide learning in the task, and elaborate on how they are constructing achievements. In the instructor's role, the student leads and monitors a dialogue that addresses four principal kinds of cognitive engagements with information. These engagements create focused opportunities for students to elaborate their routines for processing information. They are as follows:

(a) Learners generate questions about subject-matter information intrinsic to the task and about means for learning it. By generating questions, they are cognitively engaged in monitoring the instructor's activities to discover the essentials of the subject matter and how participating in the task contributes to learning. They are also alerted and aided in monitoring their comprehension as the task proceeds.

(b) Learners are encouraged to clarify difficulties they have in understanding the subject matter, and problems they encounter in carrying out and regulating their cognitive tactics. Clarifying highlights features of the work where the learner might increase attention or reconfigure information processing. It also helps to prevent an accumulation of cognitive and motivational deficits that might overwhelm the student and lead to disengagement.

(c) At the seams between steps of a task or between exercises, learners predict the next stage. To make such predictions, they must stimulate prior knowledge and assemble with it the relevant information about the subject matter and the task that has developed so far. Not only does prediction increase the likelihood that the next steps toward achievement will have meaning for the learner, but making predictions also activates prior knowledge that might otherwise remain inert. Finally, the learner can use prior knowledge to monitor his or her level of understanding as the next stages in the task unfold.

(d) Also at the seams of a task and between exercises, the learner summarizes what has developed so far. Summarizing involves two main activities. The first is monitoring the subject matter to identify its main ideas, a repetition and refinement of monitoring that has already taken place. The other is assembling relations among these key elements or main ideas to construct a high-level representation of the subject matter. This activity increases the student's power to generalize beyond the particulars of the specific tasks so far encountered. Summaries of the information processing that was used to perform tasks also can be prepared.

4. Inquiry-oriented Instruction

The defining feature of inquiry-oriented instruction is that students are not told explicitly the conceptual or metacognitive information that comprises objectives for instruction. Rather, the teacher creates an intellectual and social environment within which students explore to discover both the essentials of subject matter and the cognitive strategies that are useful in those explorations. The principle underlying this orientation is that, by personally constructing plans to identify and acquire knowledge, the subject matter will be inherently comprehensible, tasks will be intrinsically motivating, and metacognitive knowledge will develop naturally. Through the same process of exploration, students also gain a view of aptitude and knowledge as malleable, and they come to interpret processes for learning as developmental, successively building on and refining earlier methods for learning.

Probably the most well-known approach to inquiry-oriented instruction has been developed by Suchman (see Joyce et al. 1992). The model, although initially developed to teach science, applies to all subjects in which data can be organized according to principles. Instruction begins with the teacher presenting a puzzling situation to students. Optimum puzzles are those that challenge students' views of the world, creating a discrepancy between what they observe in the puzzle and their prior understandings of how the world "really" works. Such puzzles are believed to be intrinsically motivating, drawing students to investigate the discrepancy for its own sake, as opposed to merely carrying out an investigation in order to complete a task set by the teacher.

Following presentation of the puzzle, the teacher explains that students, working individually or in groups, should frame hypotheses and seek data with which to test those hypotheses. Their objective is progressively to develop an overarching principle or theory that can account for the initial discrepancy without contradicting other established facts. Upon concluding the investigative period, which may span a considerable time, the teacher and students jointly re-examine the information processing involved in striving to develop, test, and justify the principle(s) that the students generated. This phase of the model addresses cognitive strategies that are applied in problem-solving and self-regulative processes that guide investigations. Thus, as they move through all the stages of inquiry, students engage in the same kinds of information processing activities as in explicit and reciprocal teaching.

5. Teaching by Text

Because experiments using texts to teach are relatively easier to conduct than studies in classrooms, text-based studies of instruction have often been spawning-grounds for information processing models of classroom instruction. Moreover, because adolescent and adult students engage in reading to learn, as often as, if not more frequently than, they participate in classroom lessons, theories of learning from text are an essential complement to those that address students' information processing in classrooms. In practice, almost all educational settings make extensive use of both modes for teaching.

Authors preparing instructional texts for students to study strive to guide students' information processing in two ways. First, they carefully select conceptual knowledge for the text to ease students' assembly of new information with prior knowledge. Second, through supplements to the text such as headings, graphical adjuncts, and rhetorical devices, authors invite students to engage in information processing during and after reading. In principle, an author's planning parallels that which teachers conduct in preparing for classroom lessons. In both cases, theories of students' information processing guide the instructor in creating an effective setting for students to develop knowledge. A common feature of current research on teaching by text is that students are first taught cognitive tactics that match cognitive processing to cues the author includes in the text. When students learn how to identify cues for cognitively processing textual information and how to apply the cognitive routines that the cues signal, and when they are motivated to spend the cognitive effort required to apply these techniques, achievement improves (Pearson and Fielding 1991).

A central task the student faces in comprehending a text is determining which information is important, that is, the gist, topic, macrostructure, or theme of the text (Dole et al. 1992). Research clearly and repeatedly documents that the students who can identify important information are those who comprehend and learn more of the subject matter. Features of the text, such as italics and headings, can be used to cue students to locate these key ideas.

A second main task in learning thoroughly from a text is to summarize its content and so construct a new, substantively equivalent synthesis of the text's macrostructure. Three distinct operations are involved in summarizing: discriminating important ideas from less central ones, condensing information by introducing superordinate knowledge that subsumes individual ideas, and integrating information to create a coherent structure (Hidi and Anderson 1986). Authors can guide students' construction of summaries by presenting summaries directly (Reder 1985) and/or providing readers with an advance organizer, that is, subject-matter information that is at a higher level of generality or abstraction than information in the body of the text. To involve students in generating summaries, supplemental activities such as making concept maps, preparing to instruct a peer about the information in the text, and, of course, writing summaries, have proven effective (Pearson and Fielding 1991). Figures can also cue students to important information and provide an alternative medium for representing summarized material (Mayer 1989). More effective figures are labeled with important information about the text's topic.

Every text invites the reader to draw inferences, a third central task in textual comprehension (McNamara et al. 1991). In framing inferences, students use prior knowledge to develop and elaborate mental models with which they extend the information that is presented explicitly in the text. One means of inviting inferences is to insert, preferably at the beginning of a text, objectives or questions that explicitly guide students toward making inferences (Hamaker 1986).

Finally, in learning from text, readers need to be actively involved in processing information deeply and monitoring the results of these activities (Pearson and Fielding 1991). Deep processing includes the three preceding activities—identifying key ideas, summarizing, and inferencing—as well as cognitive activities such as generating analogies for information the text presents and analyzing new information in terms of known schemata. Readers' self-questioning and their monitoring of their own comprehension creates a platform for assembling new structures of information and helps to prevent an accumulation of gaps in comprehension that undermine learning (see e.g., Walczyk and Hall 1989).

6. *Instruction by Computer Systems*

Computer systems are, in one sense, merely another medium for instructing. However, because they can receive information from students and process it in order to adapt instruction to the student, computer systems are importantly different from teaching with static texts. Information processing theories of instruction adapted to computer systems blend elements from all the preceding orientations. Two issues within these hybrid theories are active areas of current research: balancing instructional guidance with learner control, and using a model of the student's information processing as a basis for adapting instruction during a lesson.

6.1 *Learner Control*

Instructional computing systems can be programmed to offer the student varying degrees of control over access to information and to instructional guidance. For example, in many systems, students can exit instruction when they judge their achievement to be adequate. Other systems offer students menus of topics and of media, including text, graphics, dynamic animations, video, voice and aural information (e.g., music), simulations of systems, and actions performed by machines and robots.

Research on self-regulation (or learner control) is investigating students' adeptness in making such choices. To date, it appears more effective to guide the learner, based on research-based principles coded in the computing system, than to give control over to the student. This finding is reminiscent of research which shows that learners have considerable difficulty developing conceptual knowledge of a new subject and simultaneously guiding their own learning metacognitively (Dole et al. 1992).

6.2 Student Models

A vital professional skill in teaching is knowing what to attend to and what to ignore in planning instruction and then adapting that plan as the student participates in a lesson. This human talent is a major challenge for instructional computing systems. Their model of a student begins as an incomplete theoretical representation of the student's prior knowledge complemented by an organized set of principles for guiding instruction. As a tutorial unfolds, every interaction a student has with the system is a potential datum that might be used to revise the system's model of the student's cognitive participation in instruction and thereby adapt instruction to the student's progress. This immense quantity of data easily overwhelms theoretical models of students' information processing.

Self (1990) offers several suggestions for addressing this surfeit of data. First, rather than straining the system to infer unobserved qualities of the student's information processing, Self suggests that the system rather be designed to elicit metacognitive knowledge directly from the student. In this way, the student can guide the system by constraining the alternatives it considers about guiding instruction. Second, the computing system should not attempt to guide instruction if theory does not address how to do that. Moreover, rather than adopting a reactive stance based on diagnosing students' mistakes, the system should gather descriptive data that researchers can examine to improve the theoretical models for its use in the future. Finally, to stimulate the student's metacognition and deep processing, the system might display its representations of the student's knowledge and invite the student to analyze these. Together, these principles involve students in self-directed learning, implement some elements of reciprocal teaching models (though over a longer time span than in classroom teaching), and directly reflect issues raised in the cognitive mediational model of learning from instruction (Winne 1992).

7. Conclusion

Students are active inquiring agents who seek to guide their information processing based on instructional cues. Two central factors that guide a student's cognitive participation in instruction are prior knowledge (both conceptual and metacognitive) and elements in the instructional environment. If students lack prior knowledge or if cues about useful forms of information processing are vague or absent, the student will apply metacognitive knowledge to improvise, sometimes ineffectively. Information processing theories of teaching seek to understand how to coordinate the knowledge students are to learn with their prior knowledge, and how to guide students' interactions with knowledge so that the desired results are achieved. While successes based on this research are increasing, there is much knowledge still to be gained.

See also: Student Cognitive Processing and Learning; Tutoring; Direct Instruction; Discovery Learning and Teaching; Cognition and Learning; Cognitive Development: Information-processing Approach

References

Alexander P A, Schallert D L, Hare V C 1991 Coming to terms: How researchers in learning and literacy talk about knowledge. *Rev. Educ. Res.* 61: 315–43

Dole J A, Duffy G G, Roehler L R, Pearson P D 1992 Moving from the old to the new: Research on reading comprehension instruction. *Rev. Educ. Res.* 61: 239–64

Gagné R M, Briggs L J, Wager W W 1992 *Principles of Instructional Design.* Harcourt Brace Jovanovich, Orlando, Florida

Frederiksen N 1984 Implications of cognitive theory for instruction in problem solving. *Rev. Educ. Res.* 54: 363–407

Hamaker C 1986 The effects of adjunct questions on prose learning. *Rev. Educ. Res.* 56: 212–42

Hidi S, Anderson V 1986 Producing written summaries: Task demands, cognitive operations, and implications for instruction. *Rev. Educ. Res.* 56: 473–93

Joyce B R, Weil M, Showers B 1992 *Models of Teaching*, 4th edn. Prentice-Hall, Englewood Cliffs, New Jersey

Mayer R E 1989 Systematic thinking fostered by illustrations in scientific text. *J. Educ. Psychol.* 81(2): 240–46

McNamara T P, Miller D L, Bransford J D 1991 Mental models and reading comprehension. In: Barr R, Kamil M L, Mosenthal P B, Pearson P D (eds.) 1991 *Handbook of Reading Research*, Vol. 2. Longman, New York

Palincsar A S, Brown A L 1984 Reciprocal teaching of comprehension-fostering and comprehension-monitoring activities. *Cognition and Instruction* 1: 117–75

Pearson P D, Fielding L 1991 Comprehension instruction. In: Barr R, Kamil M L, Mosenthal P B, Pearson P D (eds.) 1991 *Handbook of Reading Research*, Vol. 2. Longman, New York

Reder L M 1985 Techniques available to author, teacher, and reader to improve retention of main ideas of a chapter. In: Chipman S F, Segal J W, Glaser R (eds.) 1985 *Thinking and Learning Skills. Vol. 2: Research and Open Questions*. Erlbaum, Hillsdale, New Jersey

Reigeluth C M (ed.) 1987 *Instructional Theories in Action: Lessons Illustrating Selected Theories and Models.* Erlbaum, Hillsdale, New Jersey

Rosenshine B V 1987 Explicit teaching. In: Berliner D C, Rosenshine B V (eds.) 1987 *Talks to Teachers: A Festschrift for N. L. Gage*. Random House, New York

Self J A 1990 Bypassing the intractable problem of student modeling. In: Frasson C, Gauthier G (eds.) 1990 *Intelligent Tutoring Systems: At the Crossroads of Artificial Intelligence and Education*. Ablex, Norwood, New Jersey

Snow R E 1992 Aptitude theory: Yesterday, today, and tomorrow. *Educ. Psychol.* 27: 5–32

Van Patten J, Chao C-I, Reigeluth C M 1986 A review of strategies for sequencing and synthesizing instruction. *Rev. Educ. Res.* 56: 437–71

Walczyk J J, Hall V C 1989 Effects of examples and embedded questions on the accuracy of comprehension self-assessments. *J. Educ. Psychol.* 81: 435–37

Winne P H 1985 Steps toward promoting cognitive achievements. *Elem. Sch. J.* 85: 673–93

Winne P H 1987 Why process–product research can not explain process–product findings and a proposed remedy: The cognitive mediational paradigm. *Teaching Teach. Educ.* 3: 333–56

Winne P H 1992 State-of-the-art instructional computing systems that afford instruction and bootstrap research. In: Jones M, Winne P (eds.) 1992 *Foundations and Frontiers of Adaptive Learning Environments*. Springer-Verlag, Berlin

Winne P H, Marx R W 1987 The best tools teachers have: Their students' thinking. In: Berliner D C, Rosenshine B V (eds.) 1987 *Talks to Teachers: A Festschrift for N L Gage*. Random House, New York

P. H. Winne

Teaching: Linguistic and Sociolinguistic Theories

When teaching is observed, what is actually seen is talking, writing, and other forms of communication that occur between teachers and learners. If one wants to understand what is happening in the classroom, then, it seems reasonable to examine the language being used and to study speech interaction (that is, the social process of language use). Whereas linguistic theories of teaching examine the way in which the linguistic resources of teachers and learners affect the success of teaching, sociolinguistic theories examine the way that interactive speech processes facilitate or inhibit teaching effectiveness.

1. Relationships with Other Theories of Teaching and Learning

Most researchers engaged in the study of language and teaching take the view that linguistic or sociolinguistic theories of teaching are alternatives to behavioral and cognitive theories. Some, however, see all of these theories as complementary. In the complementary view, there is a division among the various theories, as follows:

(a) behavioral theories explain why learning has or has not taken place;

(b) cognitive theories explain the role of logic and the learner's cognitive structure in learning; and

(c) language-based theories explain the role of communication in teaching and learning, as well as the impact of the linguistic encoding of information on the form of what is learned.

When linguistic theories are regarded as alternatives to cognitive theories, explanations in terms of conceptual cognitive structures are replaced by analyses of semantic cognitive structures (Vygotsky 1978). Similarly, behavioral theories of learning as reward-inducing or need-reducing stimulus–response associations are seen as explaining an underlying mechanism of learning, rather than specifying in particular instances what is learned or permitting specification in advance of the causes of learning.

Some behavioral theories define rewarding features of an organism's environment as reinforcers of behavior. This definition has a circular character, because whatever has induced learning tends to be defined as a reinforcer, and it is sometimes difficult to specify reinforcers in advance. In principle, sociolinguistic theories can identify culturally valued aspects of relationships as well as instances of the communicative assignment and recognition of these valued meanings. Sociolinguistic theories, then, explain both why any learning at all will occur and why a certain type of learning will take place. Whatever the final outcome of this theory rivalry, and regardless of whether or not an "alternative" theoretical approach is adopted, it is fairly clear that language-based theories can provide useful information about the nature and antecedents of "higher order" or complex learning.

In any case, the reader of language-based analyses of teaching will be struck by the almost complete absence of reference to, or connection with, classical conditioning theory, operant conditioning theory, or social learning theory. Only cognitive-development or socioconstructivist theories of learning appear in the background of language-based research, and, as stated above, there is a tendency to restate cognitive theories in terms of semantic processing rather than to retain their original language of "conceptual schemata" and "logical structure." The picture is further complicated by the fact that one of the most important forms of learning is language itself, and by the fact that language is the medium for other forms of learning.

2. Overview of Major Language-based Theories of Teaching

The field covered in this entry is quite diverse. Some theories contain well-developed principles of the role of language in learning (Vygotsky 1978), others say very little about either what is going on inside the learner, or in the interaction process between teacher and learner (Bernstein 1975), and still others focus on that interaction process (Edwards and Mercer 1987, Cazden 1988), with or without an auxiliary psycholinguistic theory. The first cluster of theories will be called "psycholinguistic," because despite giving much weight to the social character of language, they lack detailed analysis of the social structures of teacher–learner interaction. The second cluster will be called "structuralist," because they rely mainly on the identification and association of language codes and structures, while not saying a lot about processes. The third cluster will be called "interactionist," because they centre on process-through-time descriptions of communicative interaction, while also containing some reference to both language structures and psychological dimensions of learning. A fourth cluster of theories can also be identified. Characterized by a certain eclecticism, they permit an open approach, in which a diversity of analyses of a single classroom event is brought together. Finally, while it is possible in all of these approaches to inject an evaluative or "critical" dimension, there is also a "critical" approach to the study of language.

3. *Psycholinguistic Theories*

Piaget's pioneering cognitive-evolutionary or genetic theory of learning contained a sceptical view of the efficacy of teaching as a means of promoting cognitive development. Although Piaget identified a form of learning-related speech in children, which he called "egoistic speech," he saw children's development as a general product of innate tendencies and interaction with the material environment rather than with any deliberate process of teaching. Teachers could facilitate this interaction with the environment, but could not otherwise affect it. Where teachers could have an impact was in the less important form of learning which involved adding routine information and skills at a given level of development (Kohlberg 1971, Piaget 1972).

The Russian educator and psychologist, Vygotsky, had a different view. He thought that the internalization by the learner of teacher speech was a key part of the learning process. The process of problem-solving in learning, which Vygotsky saw as a developmental process in a manner only broadly similar to Piaget, is something that at first is directed by adults, such as teachers, and gradually internalized by the learner. The adult's model of reasoning is adopted and imitated by the child. At first this imitation shows in the private speech of preschool children, as they "give instructions" and "reasons" to themselves, *sotto voce*. At approximately 7 years of age, this speech becomes silent, "inner speech." The same sequence is repeated in later life when new material has to be mastered (Vygotsky 1978).

The social role of the teacher is to press the child into the zone where the problem to be solved requires the child to develop a higher level of functioning in order to succeed; the "zone of proximal development." The teacher's task is to provide sufficient cognitive demand to stretch children but sufficient support (called "scaffolding") for them to succeed. However, the details of the linguistic interaction involved in promoting development are not well-developed by this group of theorists. Clearly, these theories provide an account of the link between speech and cognitive change (through internalization). However, the task of analyzing the connection between this process and actual problems of classroom speech remains to be carried out.

4. *Structuralist Theories*

The emphasis in structuralist theories of language and learning is on the degree to which students from different class or cultural backgrounds are equipped to benefit from the linguistic environment of the classroom, or to express themselves in linguistically approved ways in language performances, such as written examinations, in which learner's knowledge of both language and other subject matter is assessed. Perhaps the best known of these theories is that of Bernstein .

Although it is commonly believed that Bernstein argued that "working class" children suffered from a "linguistic deficit," this is not the case. He argued that working class children's facility in a language code not much valued in schools was greater than their facility in the code which schools did value. By "code," Bernstein meant the way the resources of words and structures of a language are used, particularly the degree to which they are dependent or independent of shared contextual knowledge. Bernstein's theory is complex, and the significance of his views is in dispute, but the area of language differences among minorities, social classes, and special groups is still a lively focus of research. Bernstein argued that schools are the site of a set of communicative practices which encode "ideology" in society by privileging certain ways of using language and marginalizing others (Bernstein 1975).

Poststructuralist analyses have returned to themes of the connection between communication practices and ideology. It is argued by some poststructuralists, influenced by the French philosopher Foucault, that schooling is a part of a process of symbolic control in which teachers exercise "pastoral power" in the creation of the kind of identity or "subjectivity" societies demand. Education systems are an important part of the regimes of power and knowledge on which modern societies are based. Classrooms are a site where the form of control characteristic of modern societies is reproduced and only some process of "critical pedagogy" might offer the hope of overcoming this control (Aronowitz and Giroux 1991).

5. *Interactionist Theories*

Interactionist theories of language in teaching and learning are as diverse as theories of language in general. Nevertheless, there are common features. First, there is general agreement about the dominant pattern of classroom speech. Second, there is widespread agreement that speech is best analyzed "from the top down", that is, from the perspective of larger segments of interaction, such as "relationships" through "episodes," to "sequences" and finally, to "utterances,""sentences,""clauses," and "words." All of the above terms appear in quotation marks because each theory tends to have its own, often equivalent, terminology. The point, though, is that words or utterances only make interactive sense, and "learning sense," if they are located in wider structures such as relationships, academic subjects, the teaching year or semester, and lessons or lesson sequences.

Third, there is a common dualism in the analyses, one which is most explicit in Green's distinction between the social text (the social roles and the process of cooperative task completion) and the academic text (the structure of the subject matter as academic content) (see Green et al. 1988). Earlier analyses identified this duality as a problem rather than an opportunity, because the teacher's problem of control (basically, getting cooperation in the playing of the social roles of teacher and learner) tended to lead teachers to favor a form of social text which permitted only a "second best" kind of academic text (called above "the dominant pattern").

Fourth, there has been considerable educational common ground among interactionists. Whether guided by a view of learning in which the child's active construction and reconstruction of schemata is central, or politically informed liberal or democratic educational values in which learner autonomy and capacity for independent critical thought are given prominence, interactionists have agreed on the educational inadequacy of the traditional pattern where classroom speech is not only orchestrated, but functionally dominated by the teacher.

5.1 *The Dominant Pattern*

The dominant pattern of classroom speech is one in which the teacher speaks before and after each learner speaks, the teacher speaks around 70 percent of the words spoken in "official" classroom speech, and the speaking role of the teacher involves either exclusive or dominant rights to many important speech functions such as asking questions, evaluating the speech of others, making long statements (including explanations), giving orders, criticizing previous statements, changing or setting the topic, controlling who will speak at any juncture, and interrupting all other speakers. This pattern has been observed in all its essentials as early as 1912 (Hoetker and Ahlbrand 1969). When it is not found in classrooms, as often as not the reason is that students are doing "seatwork" in which the same communicative relationships between teacher and learner are embodied in the written materials. Only the emergence in the 1980s and 1990s of group work, particularly in elementary school classrooms, has substantially broken down this pattern by permitting a great deal of functionally flexible learner–learner speech. However, even in classrooms where group work is the norm, it is common for the part of official or "on task" talk which is teacher–learner speech to be patterned on the dominant pattern.

5.2 *Top-down Analysis*

A top-down view of this pattern suggests that what is at stake educationally is the way learners relate to authority when they deal with problems or with new information. The relationship between learner and teacher is a dependent, possibly disabling one, since it does not seem to be predicated on helping learners to acquire the skills, dispositions, and knowledge necessary to solve problems for themselves. The dependency of the relationships shows up in the way the task of individual lessons is conceived and in the way the teacher and the learner interact in the subtask structure of lessons.

The smallest interactional unit in the social/academic text is the IRE: initiation, response, evaluation. The initiator is usually the teacher and the initiation is often a question. The responder is usually the learner, while the evaluator is also the teacher. A typical (constructed) example is:

T: (initiation) What is the GNP? (pause)
John? (indicating John who has his hand up)
J: (response) The value of the things produced in a country.
T:(evaluation) Good. The value of all the goods and services produced by a national economy.

From a top-down point of view, the nature of the teacher–learner relationship, the nature of the subject of economics as taught by this teacher, and the general character of the lesson, can all be seen in microcosm in this short exchange. (It should be noted, though, that while this example typifies the dominant pattern it would be hazardous to infer the existence of that pattern from a single instance of an IRE of this type. That would be a bottom-up analysis and to be safe would require a large sample of speech. Top-down analysis requires the correlation of ethnographic background information with particular instances of speech so that the communicative character of particular segments can be reliably identified).

5.3 *The Academic–Social Dualism*

In the academic text of the dominant pattern, the learner is not required to sustain a line of inquiry, since the teacher asks the questions. In a string of such exchanges, which is the most common form in which IREs appear, it is the teacher who follows a line of questioning in them. The learner is not required to evaluate individual statements made in answer to questions (which form the building blocks of any accumulation of knowledge across the course of a sequence of such exchanges), or to evaluate the accumulation of previously accepted statements to see if they form a complete argument.

The social text, the speaking roles, does not permit the learner to employ all the functions of speaking necessary to full participation in common inquiry: criticizing, judging, approving, agreeing, doubting, rejecting, accepting, and explaining. If the learner is an active acquirer of a schemata or theory about the subject matter, there is little opportunity for him or her to meet the needs which arise in assimilating new data or in adapting schemata when the problems faced require more than piecemeal development. The linguistically passive role appears better suited to incremental growth of existing schemata but ill-adapted to stage-transcending learning situations.

5.4 Educational Inadequacy of the Dominant Pattern

The reasons why many teachers still display the dominant pattern despite almost a century of negative comment from researchers are still unknown. It is speculated quite persuasively that it is because it permits teachers a certain economy of effort while achieving a relatively high level of control and at least minimal levels of student achievement. Alternative task structures, which involve a wider variety of modes of learner participation, involve more teacher preparation (a textbook is not enough) and pose problems of surveillance and control as lessons move out of the "whole class" instruction pattern into group work and related complex communication patterns. It may also be difficult for learners to know what is required of them in newer patterns, or to provide a productive task structure for themselves, leading to more frustration and "off task" behavior. However, teachers who are willing to try lesson patterns in which learners' speaking roles are more open may find teaching less stressful and more interesting, providing the task structure for learners is made clear (Green et al. 1988).

In an effort to gain a broader understanding of what is at stake in different participation structures, Green et al.(1988) examined a pair of lessons from several standpoints. The propositional structure of knowledge, the way narrative is constructed, the structure of question sequences, and participation structures are analyzed in relation to one another, revealing something of the enormous complexity of what happens in classrooms. When placed alongside traditional psychological approaches, these perspectives from anthropology, sociology, linguistics, computer science, and philosophy are clearly enriching, with profound consequences for interdisciplinary study and for awareness of the complexity of what is at stake in classroom research. The too easy assumption that multivariate behavioral models would provide a scientifically grounded technology of teaching is rapidly losing its credibility as possibilities of collaborative inquiry open up new understandings of the way societal structure, culture, organizational structure, interactional structure, speech, inner speech, and cognition are interlinked in educational processes.

6. Critical Theories

Critical theories of teaching and learning are both linguistic and sociolinguistic. The theory commonly labelled "critical pedagogy" brings a particular value agenda to the analysis of language and learning. However, its proponents argue that this agenda is neither an afterthought nor an addition to some objective analysis. In general, these theorists argue that both the process of teaching and learning and its study are inherently evaluative in character. As a consequence, the description of such processes in intersubjectively acceptable (objective) ways is only a step in a wider critical process. This assertion marks a paradigm split in the study of pedagogy.

Themes of emancipation from the constraints of social institutions and structures, particularly institutions which are regarded as repressing the existential interests of whole classes of people, are key themes of most critical approaches. Oppression is actualized or realized through structured expectations about the interactional roles of different categories of participants such as men and women. Blacks and Whites, adults and children, authority figures and subordinates. All these come into play within the knowledgeable–ignorant relationships of teachers and learners. In addition, existing languages, dialects, and subcultural codes, as well as the terminology and labels of particular professions, embody sedimentations of past subordination or superordination.

Critical theories could be considered within the framework of any of the other theories mentioned earlier, since each theory could and has been employed in conjunction with certain educational values to examine topics where issues of social justice are at stake. For instance, behavioral sociolinguistic studies of the communicative participation of women and girls have shown both quantitative and qualitative disadvantage in the typical patterns of their participation in teaching/learning talk (Cazden 1988).

Some critical linguists, however, (see, e.g. Young 1992) argue that language is inherently evaluative not only because speech expresses participants' values or interests directly or indirectly, but because languages both as systems of words and rules and as structured communicative expectations, represent the concrete operationalization or realization of those values. Furthermore, the interests and values realized are not the personal interests and values of individuals, which others can readily accept or reject, but are constitutive of a social world in which other people's roles as subordinate and the self's role as superordinate are part of the way meaning itself is constructed.

A variety of adaptations of other, noncritical approaches to language have been employed by critical analysts. Critical theorists have sharply divided into two camps which are nevertheless uneasily seeking a rapprochement: the traditional critical theorists and the postmodern or poststructural theorists (mainly feminists). The traditional critical theorists are to some extent rationalists. The possibility is held out that problems of injustice can be resolved through awareness, reflection, and argumentation, leading to reforms of the offending patterns of interaction.

The poststructural position is less optimistic. While the "deconstruction" of existing discourses can uncover oppression, grounds for optimism concerning the possibility of discourses that are less oppressive are few and far between. Thus, perhaps a reconciliation will not be possible. Poststructuralist analyses of critical theories have attempted to identify latent oppression in them and the question of whether it is possible in some sense to have "ideology-free" or even relatively ideology-free interaction remains unresolved.

7. Conclusion

Linguistic and sociolinguistic theories of teaching will be recognized, even if for no other reason, for their contribution in making an understanding of the complexity of classrooms come closer to reality. In turn, the demands of this complexity are fostering new modes of interdisciplinary inquiry and are forcing theoretical and methodological innovations which are moving educational research away from models of simple linear relationships among a few variables of somewhat doubtful relevance to teaching and learning. Critical appraisal of the educational value of the patterns observed has now begun to move toward the exploration of the conditions under which new, more adequate patterns can be realized. A constructive interplay among openly ideological critical pedagogy, poststructuralist, and feminist approaches, and more traditional scientific modes of inquiry is resulting in a crossfertilization in which empirical researchers are allowing questions of value to guide their choice of topics and analyses of data. Similarly, more radical theorists are alerted to the requirements of empirical demonstration of the practical implications of their theories. If discussion were to be opened up with behavioral, social, and cognitive learning theories, an even more fruitful critical dialogue could ensue, leading to an understanding of teaching in a rounded way for the first time.

See also: Teaching: Implicit Theories; Teaching: Behavioral Theories; Teaching, Cognitive Developmental Theories of; Cognitive Development: Information-processing Approach; Linguistics and Language Learning

References

Aronowitz S, Giroux H 1991 *Postmodern Education: Politics, Culture and Social Criticism*. University of Minnesota Press, Minneapolis, Minnesota

Bernstein B 1975 *Class, Codes and Control*, Vol. 3. Routledge and Kegan Paul, London

Cazden C 1988 *Classroom Discourse: The Language of Teaching and Learning*. Heinemann Educational Books, Portsmouth, New Hampshire

Edwards A D, Mercer N 1987 *Common Knowledge: The Development of Understanding in the Classroom*. Methuen, London

Green J L, Weade R, Graham K 1988 Lesson construction and student participation: A sociolinguistic analysis. In: Green J L, Harker J O (eds.) 1988 *Multiple Perspective Analyses of Classroom Discourse*. Ablex, Norwood, New Jersey

Hoetker J, Ahlbrand W 1969 The persistence of the recitation. *Am. Educ. Research J.* 6: 145–67

Kohlberg L 1971 The concept of developmental psychology is the central guide to education. *Proceedings of the conference in Psychology and the Process of Schooling in the Next Decade: Alternative Conceptions*. University of Minnesota, Minneapolis, Minnesota

Piaget J 1972 Development and learning. In: Lavatelli C S, Stendler F (eds.) 1972 *Readings in Child Behavior and Development*. Harcourt Price, New York

Vygotsky L 1978 *Mind in Society: the Development of Higher Psychological Processes*. Harvard University Press, Cambridge, Massachusetts

Young R E 1992 *Critical Theory and Classroom Talk*. Taylor and Francis, London

Further Reading

Atkinson P 1986 *Language, Structure and Reproduction: An Introduction to the Language of Basil Bernstein*. Methuen, London

Green J L, Wallat C (eds.) 1980 *Ethnography and Language in Educational Settings*. Ablex, Norwood, New Jersey

Lemke J L 1986 *Using Language in the Classroom*. Deakin University Press, Geelong

Masschelein J 1991 *Kommunikatives Handeln und paedagogisches Handeln*. Deutscher Studien Verlag, Weinheim

Perrott C 1988 *Classroom Talk and Pupil Learning: Guidelines for Educators*. Harcourt Brace Jovanovitch, Sydney

R. Young

Teaching Methods for Adults

In the teaching of adults there is a gap between most practice and fashionable theory. Knowles (1975) stressed that adult education should be learner-centered, not teacher-centered; because the teacher was only one resource among many, he or she should be a facilitator and resource; the teacher and learner should be in partnership with the possibility of formal contracts being made; learning methods should be largely self-directed and draw heavily on the learner's experience; and that the curriculum should be based on issues and problems, rather than academic subjects. In reality most adult education is lecture-based and fixed within the area of a discipline. In the early 1990s, resources and expertise do not yet match the more demanding approach to the teaching of adults. The following themes reflect the state of the art (for it remains far from a science). Besides short descriptions of learning theories and various teaching methods, this entry will also deal with issues and trends in the teaching of adults.

1. *Teaching the Adult*

It used to be the belief that mental abilities reach a peak of development and then decline. This idea has increasingly been challenged by research (see *Aging and Adult Development; Lifespan Development*). For example, there is little evidence to support the contention that in adulthood there is a decrease in the potential for new learning. While physical capacity may decline, learning potential should not. And writers like Mackenzie (1991) have noted there are dangers in taking the average. There is a wide range of individual differences. Some older adults will do better than younger men and women, some will perform less well, and some will be the same.

Success encourages further effort in adults. An ability to master learning material is rewarding, while a teacher's praise can shape further learning. There is also a need to recognize what the adult has acquired from his or her previous, often very rich and extensive experience, and to build upon it. New learning can be negated by apparently being in conflict with things previously learned. Similarly, an adult student's prejudices can get in the way of learning. Many adults also have a fear of failure which may make them try to avoid new learning. As in most things, those who enjoy what they are learning are likely to be the most successful.

There are numerous ways of approaching the characteristics of adult learners. The most effective are usually those based on common sense. For example, Pratt (1988) looked at the teaching of adults in terms of the support and direction they may require and came up with four categories. There are learners who need substantial direction and support; those who just need direction; those who are largely self-directing, but need support; and those who are self-directing and need little support. Of course many adults expect to assume responsibility for themselves, and often find being told what to do by a teacher an unfamiliar experience. They are used to dealing with concrete situations and establishing their own goals. The formal learning situation and its unfamiliarity may lead them to underestimate their own abilities and to display a lack of confidence. Unlike the child at school, the adult usually works at his or her own pace and will tend to react negatively to completing tasks within pressured time. However, the adult learner has a different time perspective to the child, with value given to the more immediate rather than the long-term.

Daines and Graham (1988) make much of the adult student's expectations. Among these they list the fact that many adults expect education to be similar to their school experience where they recall being "talked at" and will assume that such rigid methods are still in use in adult education. They therefore may be surprised when asked to take part in group activities, and to offer their own experiences and knowledge. They will assume that the teacher has a good grasp of his or her subject matter, and that there will be a competent use of a number of teaching approaches and aids. Teacher competence will be anticipated, and he or she will be expected to be a model of good practice. Daines and Graham (1988) suggest that adults expect to be made to work and will be disappointed if they do not achieve something as a result of attending a course. They may complain of the effort demanded of them, but they do not expect adult education to be easy. Few adults attend a class for social reasons alone. They also can be offended if their adult status is not recognized. While they can accept constructive criticism of their performance and progress they are, in certain respects, more sensitive than children and will not tolerate being patronized, or being subjected to harsh criticism or humiliation. They may well react against what they see as neglect by the teacher.

2. *Learning Theories Relevant to Choice of Method*

What has frequently happened in the education of adults is that experienced teachers seek out learning theories to help justify teaching techniques which they have found to be effective with their students. This is unsurprising as, despite the contribution of the major theories, understanding of the subject has not yet reached a degree of sophistication where a teacher's decision on which teaching method to use is determined more by information on adult learning than the teacher's rule-of-thumb experience. Such learning theories range from Skinner's (1953) work on operant conditioning to Rogers' (1963, 1983) person-centered, humanistic focus, from Maslow's

(1968) self-actualization to Wildemeersch's (1991) learning from regularity, irregularity, and responsibility.

Work on the major learning theories and associated teaching methods which had emerged by the mid-1970s was summarized by Entwistle and Hounsell (1975). They saw the humanist theories of Rogers and Maslow supporting the use of leaderless discussion groups, cooperative projects, and the exploratory reading programs, while the cognitive theories of for example, Bruner et al. (1962) would relate to individual project work. Pask and Scott's (1971) work provided information processing theories and would be associated with such techniques as computer-managed learning or handouts and guided reading. Similarly, Skinner's (1953) behaviorist approach would underpin programmed learning methods. Each established or new learning theory can be associated with one or more teaching methods.

Since the 1970s there has been an increasing output of research and information and a tendency for a number of rival camps supporting differing learning theories to emerge. Besides the over-familiar debate about whether adult learning should be differentiated from child learning by using the term (first established in Europe) of "androgogy" rather than "pedagogy," there are also such discussions as the behavioral versus the normative paradigm, or the traditional didactic approach versus the communication model. Innumerable other rivalries are to be found within the theories of adult learning and adult teaching methods. While this points to an encouraging richness of intellectual development, there is much new thinking based on an awareness of the limitations of the human capacity to acquire an overall knowledge of the whole truth and to develop an adequate all-pervading plan for aiding human learning. The most lauded of sciences is only partly aware of the interacting variables in what is a very complex world.

The teaching methods favored on a program can be influenced by the adult's reasons for wanting to learn. These will be complex, but may include being attracted by the qualification offered, a wish to acquire a new skill, to seek intellectual or technical stimulation, or to gain new ideas or, to the contrary, to have prejudices confirmed. A student's motivation may include social considerations such as a desire to join old friends in a class or because he or she is lonely. In teaching, the more information the teacher has about the students the more likely he or she can make effective the adult student's learning.

Adults' motivation can be hindered by a number of considerations over which the teacher is likely to have some impact. Adults do not like to be talked down to as if they were young children in a classroom. However, like children they do respond to encouragement and praise. They must be given realistic goals as morale drops when they fail to make progress. They appreciate individual attention and a good atmosphere in the group. A common problem in adult classes which can undermine morale and lead to irritation is a student who dominates. Teachers are often judged by how well they handle such a problem. Similarly, the course must be well-organized and the environment in which the group meets comfortable. Perhaps the most common compliment about effective teachers of adult classes is that they are "enthusiatic" about their subject. With this normally goes deep interest and concern that the students should share that enthusiasm.

3. Teaching Methods

If possible, before a program begins it is important for the teacher and the adult students to discuss and agree the aims and objectives of the course. The aims of the course will be the general intentions (e.g., the imparting of knowledge, ideas, and information, or to encourage a change in behavior, improve skills, or modify attitudes) while the objectives are the various stages leading to the course aims. The teacher will have to know before each meeting with the students what he or she will want the students to be able to achieve by the end of the session. Such objectives should be easy to assess.

3.1 Teaching Techniques

Teaching techniques themselves come into three broad categories: expository methods where a tutor presents the content to an adult learner (such as a lecture or talk, lecture or talk with group participation, or a demonstration); direction methods where teachers organize and structure a program so the adult learner arrives at a set of predetermined objectives (as with most discussion methods, group tasks and activities, brainstorming, skills practice, buzz groups, question and answer sessions, role playing, and visits and field trips); and discovery methods where the learners pursue a process of intellectual exploration (most notably through self-directed learning, but also through some forms of gaming and simulation). The methods favored will be those which can be matched to the learning which is to be achieved. Usually a mixture of techniques will succeed best with adults so that the student's interest is maintained.

3.2 The Lecture

Despite many critics over the years, the lecture, talk, address, or speech is probably used more than any other vehicle for encouraging learning among adults. This can take many forms besides the one-hour lecture, ranging from the uninterrupted talk, to the lecture with group participation, to coaching and showing, to debate. The appeal of the lecture is that it permits the speaker to present it to a small audience or a large one. There is often an assumption that it is a cheap way of teaching. Unfortunately the stimulus to learning can be very limited, particularly if members of the audience have no opportunity to enter into a discussion on the points made. The forms of teacher presentation which revolve around demostration are invariably more effective and include numerous models from those seen in keep-fit classes to the adult education tutorial class with its small membership (rarely more than 15 students), the presentation of a paper by the teacher for discussion by the students, and directed reading and writing by the students outside of the class time.

3.3 The Discussion

Usually more favored by both teachers and students in adult education have been various forms of discussion. Such discussion groups may be teacher-led, teacher-advised, or without a teacher. All three forms were to be found as early as the nineteenth century. At that time tutorless discussion groups often resulted because there was no teacher available, or the services of a teacher could not be afforded. Often in the twentieth century a formal decision has been taken by the adult students not to have a teacher. These tutorless groups were much explored by students who felt that what was important in their learning was not what they learned, but how they learned it. Another school of thought was taken up with using discussion as a way of releasing and understanding feelings and often a teacher was felt to get in the way rather than help the learning process. Discussion groups can be used just for discussion, or for problem-solving, group tasks and activities, negotiation, skills practice, projects, case studies, role playing, gaming, or simulation. There are specific forms of discussion groups such as those for brainstorming or buzz groups, or of distinctive organization like study circles (see *Study Circles*).

Discussion can deteriorate easily into a somewhat aimless activity. The group purpose needs to be well-defined before it is used as a teaching method. Back-up materials (from books to videotapes) need to be available. Whether there is a teacher or not there remains the problem of encouraging the less articulate, curbing the over-talkative, and ensuring that there are opportunities for discussion.

3.4 Self-directed Learning

There is also independent or individual learning, sometimes called "self-education" or "individual transactions," with its methods of reading, individual practice, various tasks and activities, homework, and such techniques as diary keeping (preferably kept with a specific theme in mind). Such writers as Brookfield (1981) have defined independent learning as that which takes place in the natural societal setting and independent of a teacher's direction or institutional accreditation. Tough (1967, 1980) used the term "self-teaching" for an adult who takes major responsibility for planning his or her learning, and making sure motivation is maintained, and that all things necessary for learning success are covered (see *Self-directed Adult Learning*).

3.5 Good Practice

Good practice in all forms of adult education seems generally agreed and international in its acceptance. For example, the learning situation created, whatever it is, should take account of individual differences within the adult students. The adult student's present knowledge and attitudes must be taken into account, and the learner must be motivated to learn. It is best if the learning situation gives scope for practice and for the learning to be reinforced. The adult student should be an active participant in the learning, that is, not just a listener. The learning to be covered should be in paced and digestible amounts. The learning should be meaningful to the adult student. Even for the self-directed learner, coaching and guidance is of value in the acceptance of new theories, ideas, and information.

There is a rich array of other than human learning resources available in the teaching of adults. Written resources range from books and articles to promotional material, catalogs, photocopies, handouts, and newspapers. Many classes need to be enriched by bringing in specimens, samples, and models. A policeman explaining his job to a class studying local crime should enhance an adult learner's understanding and provide that element of variety which helps to avoid a group becoming stale.

Local or national events should also be seen as learning resources available to the adult student. The list is potentially enormous and covers visits, conferences, exhibitions, field trips, sports events, cinemas, theaters, public lectures, social gatherings, and so on. Most areas of interest to the adult learner will have some public function available which can be used to enrich a course.

In his article on "The Psychological Characteristics of Students in Adult Colleges and Universities" in China, Zhao An Xiang (1992) notes that adult students have strong views on all kinds of things, and rarely follow others blindly. They like querying things, and want to know why, as well as what. They appraise teachers according to both their words and actions. They dislike teaching methods which attempt to cram students with information, but like discussion and heuristic (i.e., allowing or assisting to discover) techniques. Adults favor absorbing theoretical knowledge according to their work experience. Such students have well-developed abilities in observation, analysis, and solving problems, and are rich in life experience. The things they meet they think about and compare with what they already know. They observe matters from all sides, sum up while drawing on their experience, and then make a judgment of their own. They usually have strong self-esteem and often dislike answering questions in class, preferring to exchange what they have learned in discussion.

4. Audiovisual Aids

The technology which has become available to adult educators since the 1960s is impressive. As always there is a need to retain those aids which have worked well in the past while taking advantage of new possibilities. Adults are more likely to learn effectively if more than one sense is utilized. While hearing is the sense most used, this dominance needs to be challenged by the adult student having much to see. In some adult classes, smell and taste can also be important in the pursuit of learning.

Where distance education has developed, most findings suggest that a complete reliance upon radio and television broadcasts does not lead to substantial learning. The ideas on correspondence education which first appeared in the nineteenth century have continued to provide the most effective material for distance learners. A majority of schemes use broadcasts as a supplement to the printed material and exercises sent to the student by post. Similarly, effort is made to have local centers to which the distance education student may go for some face-to-face teaching. In an institution such as Japan's University of the Air the broadcasts act as audiovisual aids.

Although television represents a highly sophisticated form of audiovisual aid the teacher of adults is more likely to use other ones to help people learn. Such aids must not get in the way of the adult student's understanding so usually those which are clear and simple are best. Daines and Graham (1988) list writing boards, charts, posters, diagrams, flip charts, display boards, flannel boards, magnetic boards, tape recorders, record players, radios, televisions, video recorders, slide projectors, film projectors, overhead projectors, epidiascopes, and microscopes. These are usually easy to make or readily available. The invention of the overhead projector and its wide dissemination has made the presentation of such things as figures on a transparency much easier and usually less crude than earlier technology such as the chalk board or the flip chart.

For those who teach adults in well-resourced institutions such as universities the range of audiovisual aids available will be much more extensive and will include computer-assisted instruction, developments in programmed learning, and gaming simulation. However, when planning adult learning the choice of audiovisual aids has to be carefully integrated. The use of, say, computer-assisted instruction can become a rival diversion to the adult learners. It is easy to swamp a session with an inept use of audiovisual aids so that the learning objectives are lost.

5. Evaluation and Assessment

A belief that course evaluation is a key element in the planning of any adult education is now common in many countries. Alongside the evaluation of the course there should be an assessment of the adult student's learning and the teacher's teaching. The questions such evaluations and assessments attempt to answer include: have the course aims and objectives been fulfilled? Have the students achieved substantial learning and their needs and wants been met? Was the program well planned, and managed? Did the teacher display good practice? Was there plenty of feedback? Was it time well-spent and resources well-used? Within such evaluation and assessment the choice of teaching methods and their effective use hold a central role.

The use of evaluation and assessment is a teaching method in itself. The adult students should be involved in the process as it provides opportunities for learning of notable importance. While most adults are reluctant to discuss directly the teacher's role they will respond to questions about what they liked on the program, or those aspects which could usefully be changed. Too often requests for direct criticism will lead the adult learner to speak only of the good points. Anonymous reports from members of a group at the end of a course can be helpful. Such questionnaires can invite the adult student to make any comments he or she wishes, or can include responses to a series of carefully worded items of the style: "I found the most useful/least useful part of the course to be . . ."

A final evaluation session can be a helpful way to introduce adult students to unfamiliar teaching methods such as buzz groups (where the group is divided up into subgroups or pairs to discuss briefly a topic, having the great advantage of involving all the students), brainstorming (where the class pools its ideas), or small groups reporting back. Self-evaluation, with carefully agreed questions, can also be a useful exercise for adult learners.

6. Conclusion

When advising on the complex issue of effectively teaching adults there is a need to generalize. Alas, each adult, whether student or teacher, is a unique assemblage of characteristics. This being the case there are no universal methods of teaching adults. Each different technique can be appropriate on the right occasion. Even the often maligned one-hour lecture well-presented at the opportune moment has inspired adults to pursue a lifetime's study of a particular subject. As has already been noted, usually a variety of methods helps to maintain interest and motivation. Used with imagination such teaching methods will let the adult student listen, look, talk, and practice, and thus ensure effective learning.

See also: Group Learning; Teacher Roles and Teaching Styles: Adult Ed; Training of Adult Educators; Adult Education: Overview

References

Brookfield S D 1981 Independent adult learning. *Stud. Adult Educ.* 13(1): 15–27

Bruner J S, Goodnow J T, Austin G A 1962 *A Study of Thinking*. John Wiley, New York

Daines J, Graham T B 1988 *Adult Learning: Adult Teaching*. University of Nottingham, Department of Adult Education, Nottingham

Entwistle N, Hounsell D (eds.) 1975 *How Students Learn*. University of Lancaster, Lancaster

Knowles M 1975 *Self-directed Learning: A Guide for Learners and Teachers*. Associated Press, Chicago, Illinois

Mackenzie A M 1991 *Adult Age Differences in Memory*. University of Nottingham, Department of Adult Education, Nottingham

Maslow A H 1968 *Toward a Psychology of Being*, 2nd edn. Van Nostrand, New York

Pask G, Scott B C E 1971 Learning strategies and individual competence. *Internatioal Journal of Man-Machine Studies* 4(3): 217–53

Pratt D D 1988 Andragogy as a relational construct. *Adult Educ. Q.* 38(3): 160–72

Rogers C R 1963 *Freedom to Learn*. Constable, London

Rogers C R 1983 *Freedom to Learn for the Eighties*, rev. edn. Merrill, Columbus, Ohio

Skinner B F 1953 *Science and Human Behaviour*. Macmillan, New York

Tough A M 1967 *Learning Without a Teacher: A Study of Tasks and Assistance during Adult Self-teaching Projects*. Ontario Institute for Studies in Education, Toronto

Tough A M 1980 *Expand Your Life*. College Entrance Examination Board, New York

Wildemeersch D 1991 Learning from regularity, irregularity and responsibility. *Int. J. Lifelong Educ.* 10(2): 151–58

Zhao A X 1992 The psychological characteristics of students in adult colleges and universities. In: Zhang X D, Stephens M D (eds.) 1992 *Adult Higher Education in China*. Shandong Publishing Company, Jinan

Further Reading

Bornstein M H, Bruner J S (ed.) 1989 *Interaction in Human Development*. Erlbaum, Hillsdale, New Jersey

Engestrom Y 1987 *Learning by Expanding*. Orienta-Konsultit Oy, Helsinki

Gagné R 1985 *The Conditions of Learning and Theory of Instruction*, 4th edn. Holt, Reinhart and Winston, New York

Hiemstra R, Sisco B 1990 *Individualizing Instruction: Making Learning Personal, Empowering and Successful* Jossey-Bass, San Francisco, California

Rogers A 1986 *Teaching Adults*. Open University Press, Milton Keynes

Stephens M D 1991 *Education and the Future of Japan*. The Japan Library, Sandgate

Walkin L 1990 *Teaching & Learning in Further & Adult Education*. Stanley Thornes, London

M. D. Stephens

Teaching, Paradigms for Research on

Thousands of studies have been conducted in an effort to understand teaching and learning in classrooms. The concept of paradigm has played an important role in identifying groups of researchers sharing similar approaches to the study of teaching and learning. Paradigms have come to represent ways of differentiating the diversity of inquiry and substantive focus of these studies. Furthermore, several educators and researchers have used the concept to organize the research literature. This entry examines the concept of paradigm and its treatment in the literature on research on teaching.

1. The Concept of Paradigm

Prior to the publication of Kuhn's *The Structure of Scientific Revolutions* (1962), paradigm was used in psychology to refer to any well-used experimental situation or procedure, drawing upon its natural language sense of a recurring pattern, example, or model. With Kuhn's influential work, the concept took on a more significant meaning.

Briefly, Kuhn's thesis was that "normal science" is periodically marked by crises that change the way scientists conceptualize the world. Unexplained observations lead to these crises, a new theory is constructed to explain them, and a new paradigm replaces the older one. The new paradigm gains acceptance by explaining what the earlier paradigm explained plus the anomalous observations. Thus, the concept of paradigm is central to Kuhn's view on scientific progress.

A Kuhnian paradigm is typically characterized as a shared commitment within a scientific community to the nature of the legitimate problems and theories used to study a particular discipline or field. While this characterization captures some of what Kuhn meant by paradigm, it is incomplete and, in some ways, misleading. Kuhn used the concept of paradigm in two fundamental senses—one sociological, what he called "disciplinary matrix," and the other psychological, what he called "shared exemplars." After Kuhn (1974), the two senses will be labeled paradigm 1 and paradigm 2, respectively.

Paradigm 1, the sociological sense of paradigm, is the one typically implied when the concept of paradigm is used. Kuhn outlined four components of this disciplinary matrix: (a) symbolic generalizations (agreed-upon laws or formal expressions of theoretical relationships); (b) commitments to particular models (models, according to Kuhn, provide permissible analogies and metaphors that help determine acceptable explanations); (c) values about the way to practice science and judge theories; and (d) exemplars, the accepted solutions to the problems that prospective scientists are exposed to in laboratories and textbooks, primarily during their graduate training. This fourth component is identical to the more limited psychological sense of paradigm.

Paradigm 2, shared exemplars, is a psychological concept about how scientists acquire their discipline's knowledge during their training. Kuhn asked a basic question about the education of scientists: How is it that novice scientists learn to apply their knowledge of the theories and laws of a discipline to new situations? His answer was that a student discovers (either unaided or with instruction) "a way to see his problem as *like* a problem he has already encountered" (Kuhn 1970 p. 189). This ability to see new situations as similar to earlier ones is the result of doing exemplary problems; it is this learning process that helps a novice scientist come to see the world in a "time-tested and group-licensed way of seeing" (Kuhn 1970 p. 189).

This conception of paradigm as problem solution suggests that paradigm 2 is first and foremost a learning theory, a theory of how prospective scientists learn to think like scientists. What is learned are the "paradigmatic" achievements and beliefs of the discipline: the theories, models, and values shared by practicing scientists. In learning these achievements and beliefs, novice scientists come to see the world in a particular way, the way those who write textbooks and direct laboratories see the world. Having acquired the current theories and models of the discipline, new scientists use them to order their thinking and observations. Paradigm 2, the individual learning theory, offers an explanation for how paradigm 1, an inherently sociological concept, comes about.

The concept of paradigm was also used by Kuhn to characterize the development of disciplinary science. Kuhn described the initial early transformation for a discipline from a "preparadigmatic" period of science to a paradigmatic one. The preparadigmatic period is characterized by competing schools of thought vying for dominance. If and when a school achieves some major achievement, Kuhn suggested that the remaining schools of thought are eliminated, and the achieving school becomes dominant, setting the stage for a more "mature" and paradigmatic approach to disciplinary science. Kuhn later modified this position and stated that schools of thought also possess paradigms and that it was not the acquisition of a paradigm but the elimination of all but one paradigm that defined a mature science (see Kuhn 1970 pp. 178–79, 1974 pp. 460–61).

This part of Kuhn's theory has generated considerable debate among social scientists since it implies that disciplines without a single dominant paradigm are less advanced and do not practice paradigmatic science. Social scientists have responded in at least two basic ways. One response has been to accept Kuhn and attempt to justify the existence of a paradigm or paradigms within their discipline, arguing that if such paradigms can be shown to exist, then by definition their discipline is "paradigmatic." A second response has been to reject Kuhn, arguing that Kuhn's account of scientific progress does not apply to the social sciences. Shulman (1986), for example, argues that multiple, competing paradigms not only characterize the social sciences, but that such plurality is to be preferred over the hegemony of a single paradigm.

2. *Paradigms for Research on Teaching*

Kuhn's work has drawn an extraordinary amount of attention. In the field of research on teaching, the concept of paradigm has been used to organize the large and diverse body of research making up this field. In this section, five well-referenced discussions of paradigms are reviewed. Because the number of paradigms varies across discussions, and there are some inconsistencies in labels and research literatures defining the paradigms, Fig. 1 provides a chronological map of the paradigms through the five discussions.

2.1 *Gage (1963)*

In 1963 Gage was unaware of Kuhn's work, using the concept of paradigm in the natural language sense of recurring pattern or model. Paradigms, according to Gage, were general ways of considering a phenomenon, where the variables of the phenomenon and their relationships were often represented in schematic form. He used the word "commitment" to characterize a researcher's orientation to a research problem once a paradigm was chosen, the paradigm acting as an implicit "framework" or "sense of the whole" for the more specific study. Gage identified three paradigms for research on teaching: (a) criterion of effectiveness, (b) teaching process, and (c) machine.

The criterion of effectiveness paradigm characterized much of the early, pre-1960 research on teaching. The paradigm is simple: a criterion of teacher effectiveness is defined and possible predictors of this criterion are sought. Hundreds of studies correlated measures from these two classes of variables. To help organize this literature, Barr et al. (1952) conceptualized criteria as falling along an "ultimate–proximate" continuum, where the effects of teachers (e.g., pupil success in life, pupil achievement) were classified as ultimate criteria, and teacher characteristics (e.g., teacher knowledge of subject matter, teacher intelligence) were classified as proximate criteria. Mitzel (1960) expanded this continuum to three classes of criterion variables, distinguished temporally: presage (teacher characteristics), process (teacher and student behavior), and product (pupil change). In an unpublished 1957 paper (discussed extensively in Gage 1963), Mitzel added a fourth class of variables, contingency factors (now called context variables), and conceptually related

Gage (1963)	Doyle (1978)	Gage (1978)	Gage (1985)	Shulman (1986)	This entry
1. Criterion of effectiveness	1. Process–Product	1. Process–Product	1. Process–Product	1. Process–Product	Process–Product
				2. Time and learning 3. Pupil cognition	
2. Teaching process	2. Mediating response	2. Extended process–product	2. Extended process–product	4. Teacher cognition and Decision-Making	Extended process–product
	3. Classroom ecology 3a. Ethnographic 3b. Ecological psychology		3. Ethnographic/ Sociolinguistic	5. Classroom Ecology	Ethnographic Ecological Psychology
			4. Intact teaching Style		Teaching methods; Aptitude–treatment interaction
			5. Behavior modification 6. Interactive educational technology 7. Instructional design	(Psychology of instruction)	Instructional Psychology

Figure 1
A chronology of paradigms

the four classes of variables in one of the first pictorial "models" of teaching.

Gage's second paradigm, the teaching process paradigm, summarized a number of models that described or conceptualized teaching behavior but whose primary concern was not establishing empirical predictor–criterion relationships. Gage characterized these models according to four sequential classes of variables: (a) teacher perceptual and cognitive processes, (b) teacher action, (c) pupil perceptual and cognitive processes, and (d) pupil action. These classes of variables foreshadow a number of future paradigms, including the "mediating process" paradigm of Doyle (1978), the "extended process–product" paradigm of Gage (1978), and the teacher cognition and decision-making paradigm of Shulman (1986).

The machine paradigm, Gage's third and final paradim, used the teaching machine as an analogue for teaching behavior. Although the analogy is dated, his depiction of the "human equivalent" flow diagram (p. 131) and his suggestion that "the programs teachers carry around 'in their heads' need analysis" (p. 132) reflect early information-processing language now popular in instructional psychology and cognitive approaches to instruction.

2.2 Doyle (1978)

The second major paper on paradigms was written by Doyle (1978). Doyle explicitly acknowledges Kuhn and defines a paradigm as an "implicit framework that defines legitimate problems, methods, and solutions for a research community," (p. 164) and as a "shared perception of adequacy" (p. 164) for judging and interpreting research and its findings. Three paradigms were identified by Doyle: (a) process–product, (b) mediating process, and (c) classroom ecology.

The process–product paradigm has been the most dominant paradigm for research on teaching to date. The full model of Dunkin and Biddle (1974) specifies temporal relationships between 13 classes of variables organized into the four categories: presage, context, process, and product. Most attention has been given to relationships between measures of teacher behavior (process) and measures of student learning (product), and consequently, the shorter process–product label has been used.

Dunkin and Biddle described the process–product model as a heuristic to "organize the findings of research on teaching," (p. 36), and captioned their pictorial representation "A Model for the Study of Classroom Teaching" (p. 38). They considered "not what teaching is about theoretically" but looked at "teaching from the viewpoint of those who have studied the actual behaviors of teachers and students" (p. 31). The Dunkin and Biddle model was the logical and formal extension of the criterion of effectiveness paradigm, an atheoretical schematic relating four clusters of variables, the relationships being determined primarily by their self-evident temporality.

Doyle's second paradigm was the mediating process paradigm. Noting the exclusive focus on observable teacher and student behavior in the process–product paradigm, Doyle described a paradigm characterized by attention to student's cognitive processes (mediation) that intervene between teaching behavior and learning outcomes. Doyle presents a diverse body of literature under this paradigm, ranging across research on programmed instruction, audiovisual media, special education, prose learning, paired-associate learning, process–process studies, time and learning, and attentional processes. Rather than representing a Kuhnian community of researchers, then, these literatures share an interest in variables intervening between the stimulus conditions of teaching and the responses of students.

Noting the laboratory nature of these literatures and their lack of representativeness to real classroom settings, Doyle described a third paradigm, the classroom ecology paradigm. This paradigm focuses on the demands of the classroom environment and the cognitive strategies students might employ to meet those demands. Doyle framed the paradigm as one where the classroom was viewed as a complex environment with multiple and competing stimuli and one where students are required to develop perceptual and cognitive strategies to negotiate its complexities. Doyle suggested that the classroom ecology paradigm is in an early stage of development, and he characterized the paradigm as consisting "primarily of a set of tentative propositions derived from a two-stage process: identifying environmental demands, and speculating about the mediational strategies necessary to meet those demands successfully" (p. 176). Doyle reviewed two literatures under this paradigm, ecological psychology and ethnographic studies of classrooms. These two literatures represent two very different groups of researchers.

Ecological psychology developed during the early 1950s with the work of Barker and Wright who discovered that some behavior was more predictable by knowing the setting inhabited than knowing the individual person. The concept of "behavior setting" was invented and the methodology for describing such settings was developed (see Barker 1968). Gump has applied the concept to classrooms as a way of characterizing the action programs of different instructional segments (see Gump 1987).

In sharp contrast to ecological psychology is ethnographic research, the second literature considered by Doyle under the classroom ecology paradigm. Borrowing from anthropology, sociology, and sociolinguistics, ethnographic research on teaching is diverse and eclectic, making it elusive to characterize succinctly. Moreover, because it is often defined methodologically rather than substantively, ascertaining its boundary conditions is often difficult.

A limited sense of this paradigm can be obtained from considering a paper by Bolster (1983). In essence, Bolster argues that research on teaching will have little impact on educational practice until it follows a more effective "model" of research, that is, ethnography. The reason why past research on teaching has not been effective, Bolster contends, is because practitioners and researchers conceptualize teaching in fundamentally different ways and therefore the knowledge constructed by researchers has little to offer to the knowledge teachers develop and use to teach in classrooms.

2.3 Gage (1978)

Gage (1978) provides a third discussion of paradigms for research on teaching. He characterizes paradigms as "overarching approaches and theoretical formulations that determine the major purposes, problems, variables, and methods of research workers" (p. 69).

Gage responds to Doyle's (1978) criticism of the process–product paradigm by suggesting an alternative paradigm, the extended process–product paradigm. As the name implies, Gage's second paradigm is not so much an alternative to the process–product paradigm as it is a way of incorporating the mediating response and classroom ecology paradigms of Doyle within a larger process–product framework. Gage argues that the two additional paradigms of Doyle have not "undermined" the process–product paradigm so much as they have "strengthened it" (p. 69). Conceptually, however, it is important to distinguish the boundary conditions between the two.

Gage does not disagree with the largely perceptual point of view of the classroom ecology paradigm (complex classroom environments present a variety of cues that are differentially responded to by students) nor the cognitive point of view of the mediating response paradigm (there are individual differences in how students process information). Rather, he merely sees the emphasis on classroom environmental cues and student mediation of those cues as intervening between teaching behaviors and student product variables.

2.4 Gage (1985)

Gage (1985) now defines paradigms as an "integrated cluster of *substantive* concepts, variables, and problems attacked with corresponding *methodological* approaches and tools" (p. 42). A paradigm, according to Gage, "gathers unto itself a community of investigators" (p. 42) who owe allegiance to the paradigm, citing each others' work more frequently, attending conferences with each other, and publishing in the same journals with each other.

Later in his discussion of paradigms, there is a hint of the discord that surfaced during the 1980s with respect to "paradigm wars" (Gage 1989). For example, Gage asks " . . . are there strongholds of concepts and methods inside which huddle together mutually supportive groups of investigators who have something less than unbound admiration for outsiders, the adherents of other paradigms?" (p. 44). He answers in the affirmative, and outlines seven paradigms for research on teaching: (a) process–product, (b) extended process–product, (c) ethnographic/sociolinguistic, (d) intact teaching styles, (e) behavior modification, (f) interactive educational technology, and (g) instructional design.

The first three paradigms have already been discussed. The fourth paradigm, what Gage calls "intact teaching styles," has traditionally been labeled "teaching methods" research. The search for the best teaching method has a history nearly as long as that of the teacher-effectiveness literature. Despite what would appear to be closely related subject matter, the two literatures overlap very little. The reason is the way teachers and teaching are conceptualized.

In teacher effectiveness research, individual teachers are the focus of study, where differences in individual teacher behavior are related to variation in student performance. In teaching methods research, interest is on the pattern of teaching prescribed by the teaching method, not single teacher behaviors, and individual teachers are important only insofar as they faithfully implement the teaching method.

Two developments during the 1960s changed the nature of teaching methods research. First, researchers became interested in entire systems of individualized instruction encompassing both teacher behavior and teaching method. Second, largely as a result of the work of Cronbach (1957), the question of what teaching method is most effective was reframed as what teaching method is best for what kind of students. This more refined question led to the systematic search for aptitude–treatment interactions and Cronbach and Snow's (1977) classic examination of the teaching-methods literature.

The final three paradigms identified by Gage—behavior modification, interactive educational technology, and instructional design—are grouped together in Fig. 1. Although each of these fields has made important contributions to educational psychology in general as well as instructional psychology, they have been peripheral to mainstream research on teaching. Much of the work in these three fields has led to the development of technologies that work in specialized settings but have yet to demonstrate widespread applicability to problems of classroom teaching.

2.5 Shulman (1986)

Shulman (1986) has also written on paradigms, defining a paradigm as an "implicit, unvoiced, and pervasive commitment by a community of scholars to a conceptual framework" (p. 4). As mentioned in Sect. 1, he disagrees with Kuhn's characterization of the social sciences as "developmentally disabled" and stuck in "a state of preparadigmatic retardation" (Shulman's phrases) because they possess competing "schools of thought" rather than single dominant paradigms. On the contrary, Shulman sees different schools of thought as legitimate and healthy, and suggests the concept of "research program" (Lakatos 1970) may better characterize the social sciences. Shulman outlines five paradigms (research programs) for research on teaching: (a) process–product, (b) time and learning, (c) pupil cognition and the mediation of teaching, (d) classroom ecology, and (e) teacher cognition and decision-making.

His wide-ranging and complex presentation of paradigms connects research literatures on different levels, but his basic structure of five paradigms closely overlaps the previous four discussions. Shulman explicitly recognizes the close similarities between the first three paradigms, remarking that the "time and learning" and "pupil cognition" paradigms share a "fundamental family membership in the process–product tradition" (p. 18). Indeed, both time and learning and pupil cognition focus on student-intervening variables and thus fit the extended process–product paradigm of Gage (1978). The classroom ecology paradigm of Shulman is similar to that of Doyle (1978) except that Shulman restricts this paradigm to the ethnographic approach.

Shulman's fifth and final paradigm, teacher cognition and decision-making, is a logical addition to the extended process–product paradigm. The subject matter of this paradigm covers teachers' beliefs about students and teaching, their thought processes and decisions while planning instruction, and the kinds of decisions they make during teaching (Clark and Peterson 1986). This paradigm focuses on one of the four classes of variables identified by Gage (1963). By adding this class of variables to the extended process–product paradigm, similar to what Winne and Marx (1977) suggest, then the causal sequence is as follows: teacher cognition→teacher behavior→student cue resources and interpretation→student mediating responses→student behavior.

2.6 Summary of Paradigms for Research on Teaching

Figure 2 organizes the paradigms reviewed into six categories, generated by crossing three content areas (teaching, setting, and instruction) with two orientations (internal and external). The paradigms reviewed vary in terms of their primary content focus: teachers and students (teaching), environment (setting), and method variables (instruction). They also vary in terms of their orientation. Paradigms with an internal orientation focus primarily on the cognitive processes of the participants and the meaning attributed to properties of the immediate environment. In contrast, paradigms with an external orientation focus primarily on the properties of the immediate

		ORIENTATION External	Internal
	Teaching	process–product	Extended process–product
CONTENT	Setting	Ecological psychology	Ethnographic
	Instruction	Teaching methods; Aptitude–Treatment interaction	Instructional psychology

Figure 2
Paradigms for research on teaching

environment and the behavior of the participants in that environment.

These six paradigms are the same as those indicated on the right side of Fig. 1. Together, the two figures represent the evolutionary history and a current conceptual organization of substantive approaches to research on teaching.

The external and internal orientations reflect two fundamental ways with which to view humans: by their actions or by their thoughts. These two orientations might also be loosely described as behavioral and cognitive orientations. It is interesting to note that these two competing points of view are consistent with Kuhn's (1970) observation about paradigm 2 in the social sciences. In contrast to the textbook knowledge learned by students in the natural sciences, Kuhn noted that the student in the social sciences: "is constantly made aware of the immense variety of problems that the members of his future group have, in the course of time, attempted to solve. Even more important, he has constantly before him a number of competing and incommensurable solutions to these problems, solutions that he must ultimately evaluate for himself" (p. 165).

3. Conclusion

In much of the social science literature, the concept of paradigm has been used in a fairly casual manner, inviting confusion. Paradigm 1 and paradigm 2 have not been distinguished, the applicability of the concept to the social sciences has not been well justified, and substantive and methodological issues have become intertwined in discussions of paradigms.

It has become popular, for example, to use the concept of paradigm to distinguish methodological approaches to educational research, the "paradigm wars" described by Gage (1989) being a case in point. Yet there is little in Kuhn to suggest methodology as a basic characteristic for paradigms. Indeed, Kuhn characterized paradigms as theories, models, values, and exemplars, all substantive characteristics, and his examples of paradigm shifts during periods of revolutionary science were all examples of change in theory, not method. Whatever the virtues of distinguishing methodological approaches to research, those who make such distinctions should probably not ground them in Kuhnian paradigms.

In light of what has been said, it might also be prudent to ask whether the concept of paradigm is even appropriate for organizing the field of research on teaching. It may be that the concept provides a convenient but inherently difficult concept to apply that leads to unnecessary polarization among researchers studying teaching. If Kuhn is correct in recognizing that the social sciences are characterized more by points of view than paradigmatic consensus, then it may be time to recognize the insights of each points of view in the attempt to understand teacher and student behavior and cognition in classrooms.

See also: Research Paradigms in Education; Research Methodology: Scientific Methods

References

Barker R 1968 *Ecological Psychology: Concepts and Methods for Studying the Environment of Human Behavior.* Stanford University Press, Stanford, California

Barr A et al. 1952 Report of the committee on the criteria of teacher effectiveness. *Rev. Educ. Res.* 22(3): 238–63

Bolster A 1983 Toward a more effective model of research on teaching. *Harv. Educ. Rev.* 53(3): 294–308

Clark C, Peterson P 1986 Teachers' thought processes. In: Wittrock M (ed.) 1986 *Handbook of Research on Teaching*, 3rd edn. Macmillan, New York

Cronbach L 1957 The two disciplines of scientific psychology. *Am. Psychol.* 12: 671–84

Cronbach L, Snow R 1977 *Aptitudes and Instructional Methods: A Handbook for Research on Interactions.* Irvington, New York

Doyle W 1978 Paradigms for research on teacher effectiveness. *Rev. Res. Educ.* 5: 163–98

Dunkin M, Biddle B 1974 *The Study of Teaching.* Holt, Rinehart and Winston, New York

Gage N 1963 Paradigms for research on teaching. In: Gage N (ed.) 1963 *Handbook of Research on Teaching.* Rand McNally, Chicago, Illinois

Gage N 1978 *The Scientific Basis of the Art of Teaching.* Teachers College Press, New York

Gage N 1985 *Hard Gains in the Soft Sciences: The Case of Pedagogy.* Phi Delta Kappa, Bloomington, Indiana

Gage N 1989 The paradigm wars and their aftermath: A "historical" sketch of research on teaching since 1989. *Educ. Res.* 18(7): 4–10

Gump P 1987 School and classroom environments. In: Stokols D, Altman I (eds.) 1987 *Handbook of Environmental Psychology*, Vol. 1. Wiley, New York

Kuhn T 1962 *The Structure of Scientific Revolutions.* The University of Chicago Press, Chicago, Illinois

Kuhn T 1970 *The Structure of Scientific Revolutions*, 2nd edn. The University of Chicago Press, Chicago, Illinois

Kuhn T 1974 Second thoughts on paradigms. In: Suppe F (ed.) 1974 *The Structure of Scientific Theories.* The University of Illinois Press, Urbana, Illinois

Lakatos I 1970 Falsification and the methodology of scientific research programmes. In: Lakatos I, Musgrave A

(eds.) 1970 *Criticism and the Growth of Knowledge*. Cambridge University Press, Cambridge
Mitzel H 1960 Teacher effectiveness. In: Harris C (ed.) 1960 *Encyclopedia of Educational Research*, 3rd edn. Macmillan, New York
Shulman L 1986 Paradigms and research programs in the study of teaching: A contemporary perspective. In: Wittrock M (ed.) 1986 *Handbook of Research on Teaching* 3rd edn. Macmillan, New York
Winne P, Marx R 1977 Reconceptualizing research on teaching. *J. Educ. Psychol.* 69(6): 668–78

B. Burns

Teaching, Realities of

To speak of the realities of teaching is to address the nature and organization of teaching not in terms of ideals, fantasies, models, or rhetoric, but in terms of the complex actuality of the work, and the day-to-day shape it takes with real teachers, in real-classrooms, in real schools. To speak of the realities of teaching, therefore, is to speak of teaching-descriptively, not prescriptively: of how it is, more than how it should be. It is to see teaching holistically, as complex, interconnected sets of tasks, purposes, requirements, and constraints; rather than as fragmented domains of knowledge, skill, or motivation that can be addressed or improved in isolation. Understanding the realities of teaching and engaging with them effectively, therefore, entails understanding and engaging with what teachers actually do, rather than cajoling or exhorting them to do something better.

1. Change and Practicality

Educational reform and teacher reform in particular are often rather poor at recognizing the realities of teaching. Efforts to improve teaching quality have tended to focus on the characteristics of individuals—on knowledge, skill, and personal qualities—much more than on the patterns of work organization and leadership which limit or liberate teachers in their work. Poor teaching quality, it is commonly argued or assumed, tends to result from an absence of knowledge, skills, or qualities in individuals (for examples, see Department of Education and Science 1983). This implies a deficit model of teaching, where poor quality results from deficiencies in personality, gaps in learning, or weak matching of teachers' competencies to the tasks they are required to perform.

Teachers are not just technical learners, though; they are social learners too. As social learners, teachers actively interpret, make sense of, and adjust to the requirements their conditions of work place upon them. In this view, what some might judge to be "poor" teaching quality often results from reasoned and reasonable responses to occupational demands: from interpretive presences, not cognitive absences; from strategic strength, not personal weakness. "Poor" teaching quality, in this respect, often results from poor work environments. Similarly, enhanced work environments which are more collaborative and incorporate principles of recognition, reward, and risk-taking increase teachers' senses of efficacy (Ashton and Webb 1986) and the degree of positive influence they exert on student achievement (Rosenholtz 1989).

Recognizing that teachers are social learners draws attention not merely to their capacity for change, but also to their desires for change (and indeed for stability) (Louden 1991a). Political and administrative devices for bringing about educational change and improvement usually ignore, misunderstand, or override teachers' own desires. In this respect, the devices and desires of teacher development are often incongruent (Hargreaves 1993b). Change devices usually rely on principles of compulsion, constraint, or contrivance to get teachers to change. They presume that educational standards are low and young people are failing or dropping out because the practice of many teachers is deficient or misdirected. The remedy for these deficits and deficiencies, politicians and administrators believe, needs to be a drastic one, calling for decisive devices of intervention and control to make teachers more skilled, more knowledgeable, and more accountable.

At the heart of the realities of change for most teachers is the issue of whether it is practical. Judging changes by their practicality seems, on the surface, to amount to measuring abstract theories against the tough test of harsh reality, but there is more to it. In the ethic of practicality among teachers is a powerful sense of what works and what does not, not in the abstract, or even as a general rule, but for a particular teacher in a particular context. For teachers, the realities of teaching are the practicalities of teaching. To ask whether a new method is practical is therefore to ask much more than whether it works. It is also to ask whether it fits the context, whether it suits the person, whether it is tune with their purposes, and whether it helps or harms their interests.

2. Commitment and Purpose

Teaching is not just a technical business; it is also a moral one. There are two senses in which teaching is a moral enterprise. First, teachers are among the most important influences on the life and development of young children. They help create the generations of the future. Second, at the heart of teaching, as in many other kinds of professional action, is the making of discretionary judgments in situations of unavoidable uncertainty. Teaching is riddled with practical judgments that are also reflective ones, even if only in the most fleeting sense (Louden 1991b). For these decisions, there are few or no clear rules of thumb that can be applied in a systematic way from one situation to the next.

Because teaching is a moral craft, it has purpose for those who engage in it. There are things that teachers value, that they want to achieve through their teaching. There are also things they do not value, things they fear will not work or may actually do harm to the children in their charge. Teachers' purposes motivate what teachers do and explain why they often resist change which does not address those purposes. Stated somewhat differently, they are committed to these purposes. Nias (1989) describes three kinds of teacher commitment: vocational, professional, and career continuance. These forms of commitment do not describe three kinds of teacher; any one teacher may exhibit elements of each of the different forms. In many teachers, however, one of the forms is often dominant.

2.1 Vocational Commitment

This refers to the missionary character of teaching, to the care for and connectedness to young people which motivates many teachers in their work, especially at the primary or elementary level. What Gilligan (1982) calls the "ethic of care," where actions are motivated by concerns for care and nurturing of others and connectedness to others, is central among teachers of younger children. The primary teachers interviewed in Nias's (1989) study talked extensively about care, affection, and even love for their students. Book and Freeman (1986) note how purposes of care and nurturance are much more common as reasons for entering teaching among elementary than secondary school teachers. In Lortie's (1975) classic study of elementary teachers, the joys and satisfaction of caring for and working with young people were the prime psychic rewards of teaching.

Educational reform, however, is often propelled less by ethics of care than contrary (and arguably more stereotypically masculine) ones of responsibility, which stress professional obligations and improvements to planning and instruction. Ignoring the realities of teachers' purposes and vocational commitments is, in this regard, not only professionally disrespectful but also practically perverse. Neglect of teachers' purposes can lead to lowered teacher motivation and decreased effectiveness. Nias (1991) has described how the detailed demands of the National Curriculum in the United Kingdom have led to profound feelings of loss and bereavement among primary teachers, who no longer have time to care for and connect with their children's individual concerns in the ways they feel are important. Neufeld (1991) records similar responses among a group of Canadian elementary teachers pressed and stressed by the time demands of implementing a program of active learning to the exclusion of meeting their students' personal and emotional needs. Apple and Jungck (1992) in the United States describe how tendencies in teachers' work where teachers are becoming more subjected to the detailed, step-by-step requirements of prescribed programs, also erode their capacity to care for the young in the ways they would like.

Care is at the heart of the emotional and moral working life of many teachers. Reform efforts which do not recognize the centrality of care, fundamentally threaten or demean the emotional and moral character of teaching.

2.2 Professional Commitment

This describes the teacher's commitment to being knowledgeable, competent, and instructionally effective. Professional commitment is about doing a good job. As a source of satisfaction, professional commitment tends to strengthen once the earliest years of teaching have passed, and teachers begin to take pride in their own mastery, the breadth of their repertoires, and their capacity to improvise. Professional commitment as a prime commitment also tends to have more prominence among secondary school teachers than elementary school teachers. In secondary school teaching, professional commitment is mainly invested in subject mastery and subject expertise. Commitment to teaching a subject is the main reason why secondary teachers enter the profession (Book and Freeman 1986). Care for individuals is less important for them, a repeated difficulty that afflicts the capacity of many secondary schools to become more caring communities for their students (Hargreaves 1982).

In secondary school teachers' commitments to their academic subjects can be seen the intimate connection between the teacher's purpose and the teacher as a person. Subjects are not just intellectual communities. They are social and political communities as well. They bestow meaning and identity on those who teach in them. Secondary teachers are socialized into subject identities and commitments as school and university students. The subject department is often a more meaningful and visible community for them than that of the wider school. Subjects and their departments provide the major lines of career development and progression at the secondary school level.

Proposals for curriculum integration which challenge teachers' subjects are therefore construed as much more than rational attempts to reconstruct fields of knowledge and learning in tune with the needs and demands of contemporary times. They are also perceived and deeply experienced as threats to career, security, identity, and fundamental senses of competence. As Hargreaves (1980) points out, competence anxiety, the fear of appearing incompetent in front of one's colleagues, is perhaps the most basic anxiety of all in teaching. Proposals for curriculum integration therefore strike at fundamental and deep-seated realities of professional commitment, subject identities, and desires to retain competence among the teaching force.

2.3 Career-continuance Commitment

Career-continuance commitment is the commitment to remain in teaching for the security and extrinsic rewards it brings. Teachers can become committed *by* teaching, as well as *to* it. Teachers in later career who have put a lot of time and investment into their teaching, and have built up families, dependents, mortgages, and other life investments may feel obligated to stay in teaching even when innovation and change profoundly threaten their purposes and satisfactions.

Teachers who remain in teaching for these reasons are among those most prone to become disenchanted and resistant to change. However, the realities of teaching in mid-to-late career are more complex. Research undertaken by Huberman (1992), based on interviews with 160 secondary school teachers in Switzerland, indicated that most teachers in mid-to-late career were unlikely to embrace innovation with enthusiasm. Two groups, whom Huberman describes as "defensive focuses" and "disenchanted" were deeply cynical about change. They had (accurately) predicted the demise of past innovations, steered well clear of them then and continued to do so now, or they had invested a lot in them only to be "sold out" as resources were withdrawn, the innovation collapsed, and the innovators moved on.

Other teachers, whom Huberman calls "positive focusers," were less dismissive but still tempered in their reactions and enthusiasms. They were pragmatic about school-wide innovations, having seen several come and go before. Feelings of mortality were also becoming stronger, leading to greater wishes to balance work with life and tendencies to become more serene, a discovery and development experienced rather later by men than by women (Krupp 1989). These positive focusers were prepared to change, but in ways which built on, instead of overturning, their past expertise and efforts: adding to their repertoires in their own classes, rather than transforming everything they did. The reality of mid-to-late career teaching is a reality in which modest, gradual, and respectful change may be embraced with willingness, but where radical transformative change will almost certainly not be (Fullan and Stiegelbauer 1991).

3. Career and Life Cycle Influences on Teachers

The issues of midcareer teaching in particular point to more general career and life cycle influences that have important impacts on how all teachers teach. Teachers in early career, especially when this coincides with youth, are typically preoccupied with classroom management and establishing competence. They will devote endless hours to their work and, once initial competence has been established, embrace innovation with all the time, energy, and commitment they can muster. Consequently, they are receptive to innovation, but also prone to burnout (Knowles 1988). At the early stages of career entry, young teachers may also still be in relatively early stages of personal ego development in ways that affect their capacity to work successfully and confidently with others, since teachers with poorly developed ego boundaries or sense of self, fear "invasion" when working with others. Young teachers entering the profession can be especially vulnerable here, since they are entering a profession with complex responsibilities and interpersonal relationships, often long before their own personal growth has matured (Nias 1989).

However, age and experience do not necessarily bring greater wisdom: they may also bring fixed views, outmoded understandings, dogmatism, and bigotry. Stoddart (1991), for instance, in case studies of teachers entering teaching through patterns of alternate certification designed to bring people of greater maturity and experience into the profession, found that:

> These individuals brought to teaching strong commitments and personal attributes which could have formed the basis for the development of outstanding professionals. Unfortunately, these attributes were not enhanced by systematic professional education. Faced with teaching dilemmas, they had limited resources with which to develop flexible responses . . . They developed a modal approach to practice which was shaped by the subject-specific curriculum and their own personal perspectives. They applied and misplaced these pedagogies with little opportunity to reflect on and critically analyze the consequences of their teaching actions. (p. 228)

Whatever the teacher's point in the life cycle, the need to reflect on and reconstruct experiences is demonstrable. This need is especially felt as teachers come to appreciate the profound and pervasive influences that their lives exert upon their work. Long-standing attachments to particular belief systems and ideologies can remain abiding influences on how teachers approach teaching and learning (Louden 1991b). Sometimes these commitments have important religious and spiritual dimensions which also influence their work, through, for instance, solicitous Catholicism (Woods 1981) or charismatic fundamentalism (Stoddart 1991). Ethnocultural attachments and identities can also affect teaching, most visibly where the teachers value more traditional, didactic approaches. Gender identity is also influential, though in varying and complex ways. Families and domestic obligations create an unwelcome triple or quadruple shift for many women (Acker 1990a), but for others they can be sources of strength, stability, support, and identity, personal anchors beyond the vocational vortex of work and career that help retain some sense of balance and perspective.

Intense and dramatic personal problems such as bereavement, divorce, family violence, or substance abuse are among the most obvious ways that teachers' lives intrude upon their work, sometimes impairing their performance. In schools where teachers are involved in collaborative working relationships of trust and support, the intermeshing of personal and professional lives is seen as normal and legitimate. In these schools, allowances are made for teachers who are sick, troubled, or stressed, and support is offered to them. Teachers here can show their vulnerabilities and share them with others.

If the research on teachers' lives has one flaw, it is its tendency to explain the relationship between teachers' lives and work in a one-sided way: with the life affecting the work but not vice versa. At its worst, this bias can lend (unintended) support to deficit-based explanations of teachers' problems which diagnose and treat them as personal and private problems when they may actually have their roots in the conditions and management of the workplace (Ashton and Webb 1986). It is important to remember also that problems in the workplace can have a profound impact on the quality of life outside it. This can happen positively as well as negatively. Indeed an important priority for future research on teachers' lives might well be to identify which patterns of schooling and teachers' work enrich rather than enervate the lives of teachers. In particular, there is a case for forging a bond between research on school improvement on the one hand and teachers' lives on the other; to see whether, in the long term, successful and innovative schools drain their teachers dry until nothing of their personal lives and selves is left, or whether they enrich and energize those lives through the ways they generate personal enjoyment and fulfillment.

4. Coping Strategies

Teaching is at least in part a matter of strategy. Teachers are products of their present and previous work environments. They are creatures of circumstance. The ways they teach evolve as strategies to pursue purposes that are important to them. These strategies develop as ways of adjusting to the particular pressures, contingencies, and expectations of their environment. Where these pressures are extreme, teachers' strategies can become desperate, a matter of sheer survival. Even in the most favorable circumstances, all teaching is in part a constructive trade-off (sometimes calculated, sometimes routine and taken for granted) between ideal purposes and practical realities. These constructive trade-offs, or coping strategies, are a key aspect of teaching.

Coping strategies connect the purpose and the person of teachers to the context in which they work. The connection of strategy to context is complex, for teachers' strategies are mediated by all kinds of other factors, such as the teacher's personal biography, career stage, educational purpose, and the ethos or institutional bias of the school. These complexities explain why attempts to "test" coping strategies theory by trying to establish a clean and clear one-to-one match between teaching strategies and the contexts in which they take place, have not been particularly successful. However, in connection with the other realities of teaching, the context of teachers' work remains extremely important in influencing teachers' actions and helping shape the coping strategies which characterize their work.

5. Context

Three forms of work context help frame the realities of teaching: continuing contexts, changing or contemporary contexts, and contexts of variability or diversity.

5.1 Continuing Contexts

The continuing contexts of teaching are to be seen in what Sarason (1990) calls the fundamental regularities of teaching: the apparently fixed, pervasive, and intractable features of the work that define how it is done and that defy attempts to change it. These seemingly fixed regularities, however, have quite specific and deep historical roots (Cuban 1984). Modern school systems, as educational historians have noted, emerged as factory-like systems of mass education designed to meet the needs of manufacturing and heavy industry. They processed pupils in batches, segregated them into age-graded cohorts called "classes" or "standards," taught them in a standardized course or curriculum, and used teacher-centered methods of lecturing, recitation, question-and-answer, and seatwork. These systems of mass education for an increasingly massified society with large laboring classes were supplemented by more selective systems of state and private secondary education for commercial and social elites, rooted in academic and aristocratic traditions of contemplative study, disengaged from utilitarian concerns, and grounded in defined domains known as subjects that conferred cultural capital on those who successfully acquired them. These social and historical conditions have set the parameters and assumptions within which much of teachers' work takes place and which have come to define "real school" for many people. Punctuated lesson periods, age-segregated classes, the subject-based academic curriculum, and paper-and-pencil testing are therefore highly specific sociohistorical products, yet they have come to define a paradigm of teaching and teachers' work that is hard to break or reconstruct, even as the emerging educational needs of the postindustrial age seems to call for new patterns of teaching and teachers' work organization to meet them (Hargreaves 1993b).

5.2 Contemporary Contexts

Notwithstanding the realities and regularities of the continuing context of teachers' work by the accumulation and expansion of new tasks and responsibilities, this work is also changing in quite fundamental respects as the world outside schools also changes. Based on interviews with elementary teachers, Fullan and Hargreaves (1991) recorded teachers' perceptions of how their work is changing in terms of more "social work" responsibilities; the challenge of dealing with an increased range of abilities and behaviors in their classes (particularly since the move toward integration of special-needs students into ordinary classes); greater cultural and ethnic diversity and the demands this places on more diverse and sensitive programming; increased accountability and form-filling; and escalating amounts of time required to work, communicate, and meet with parents, principals, and other colleagues to meet the increasingly complex and pressing demands with which schools are having to deal. Two of the main explanations for this changing contemporary context are those of professionalization and intensification.

Arguments organized around the principle of professionalization emphasize the struggle for, and in some cases the realization of, greater teacher professionalism through extension of the teacher's role. Teachers, especially those in elementary schools, are portrayed as having more experience of whole-school curriculum development, involvement in collaborative cultures of mutual support and professional growth, experience of teacher leadership, commitment to continuous improvement, and engagement with processes of extensive school-wide change. In these accounts, teaching is becoming more complex and more skilled. What Hoyle (1975) calls "extended teacher professionalism" and Nias (1989) more cautiously terms "bounded professionality" is, in this perspective, both an emerging reality and a point of aspiration.

A second line of argument is broadly derived from Marxist theories of the labor process that look at teaching less as a profession or craft, and more as a kind of work with its own distinctive and changing labor process. This approach highlights major trends towards deprofessionalization in teachers' work. Teachers' work is portrayed as becoming more routinized and deskilled, more and more like the degraded work of manual workers, and less and less like that of autonomous professionals. Teachers are depicted as being increasingly controlled by prescribed programs, mandated curricula, and step-by-step methods of instruction.

In addition, drawing on Larson's (1980) broader analysis of the labor process among professionals or semiprofessionals, it is claimed that teacher's work is becoming increasingly intensified, with teachers expected to respond to greater pressures and comply with multiplying innovations under conditions that are at best stable and at worst deteriorating. Intensification, it is argued, leads to reduced time for relaxation and relief of stress, lack of time to upgrade one's skills, insufficient opportunities to collaborate with one's co-workers, chronic and persistent overload with resulting dependency on outside experts and materials, cutting of corners and reductions in quality, and spreading oneself too thinly. Under this view, extended professionalism is a rhetorical ruse, a strategy for getting teachers to collaborate willingly in their own exploitation as more and more effort is extracted from them in the name of shared leadership and the like.

Hargreaves' (1992) investigation of 28 Canadian elementary teachers and their interpretations of and responses to additional preparation time which had been won by their teacher federations raises some critical questions about the intensification thesis and suggests important modifications to it. First, some teachers resisted additional time because it took them away from their own classes and the care they could offer them (it undermined their purposes). Second, preparation time opportunities for teacher collaboration and enhanced professionalism often became administratively contrived and controlled in ways that undermined that professionalism. Third, shortages of specialist expertise among teachers required to cover classes during preparation time perversely led to program dependency, deskilling, and reduction of quality in some of these classes (reproducing the effects of intensification in a context meant to combat it). Acker's (1990b) study of English primary school teachers and their work raises similar questions about being too ready to interpret the changes in teachers' work as ones that amount to deskilling.

The contemporary changes in teachers' work can neither be encompassed by heroic proclamations of increased professionalism, nor by critical theories of intensification and deskilling derived from neo-Marxist theories of the labor process. Unintended consequences, bureaucratic complexities, and the expanded expectations for teaching that follow in an increasingly postmodern society which is pluralistic, culturally diverse, informationally dense, suffused with uncertainty, and intensely influenced by accelerated change and the compressed character of time and space, all help to shape the contemporary context of teachers' work (Hargreaves 1993a).

6. Contexts of Diversity

As well as the continuing and contemporary contexts of teaching that affect most teachers and frame the realities of their work, there are also contexts of difference and diversity that lead to variations in the realities of teaching according to the settings in which it is performed. In a major study of secondary school work contexts, McLaughlin (1993) has conceptually and empirically delineated a range of such contexts and their impact on teachers' work, including the contexts of the students, the subject department, the school, the community, and the system.

Metz (1990) points out that teachers are in many respects defined by their students: successful, high status students reflect and reinforce the perceptions of status that attach to their teachers; and teachers will sometimes, as a result, seek to avoid contact with students who threaten to undermine these perceptions. This reality of teaching is one reason why many teachers avoid assignments to low-track classes if they can; it also provides a justification for detracking or destreaming to counter such inequities (Oakes 1985).

As mentioned earlier, the secondary school subject department provides a more immediate and meaningful context for many secondary teachers than their overall school. Departments vary in the strength of their culture, leadership, and support in ways that impact on the quality of teaching and on willingness to innovate.

They also vary in terms of their shared beliefs about and practices in the areas of pedagogy, subject matter, assessment, and student grouping. Common innovations like curriculum integration or destreaming have a very different reality depending on the departments in which they are experienced.

The same can be said for the differences between communities in which schools are located. McLaughlin's (1993) study, for instance, indicates that teacher collaboration can take on very different meanings depending on the socioeconomic status of the community in which the school is embedded. In middle-class schools, collaboration tends to focus on program and academics. In working-class schools it is more oriented to dealing with the needs and demands of students.

7. Culture

Teachers' commitments, identities, and strategies are not established alone. They are built up and defined through interaction with others who are significant for them. Among these significant others are their colleagues. Teachers' relations with their colleagues comprise what have come to be called "cultures of teaching."

Hargreaves (1993a) distinguishes between two aspects of the teacher cultures: content and form. The content of teacher cultures consists of the substantive attitudes, values, beliefs, habits, assumptions, and ways of doing things that are shared within a particular teaching group or among the wider teaching community. Many different kinds of teacher cultures can be and have been differentiated by their content (e.g., academic elementary and developmental cultures; subject cultures).

The form of teacher cultures consists of the patterns of relationship among members of these cultures. It is through the forms of the teacher culture that the contents of these cultures are realized, reproduced, and redefined. Changes in beliefs, values, and attitudes among the teaching force, may, in this respect, be contingent upon prior or parallel changes in teachers' relations with their colleagues. Hargreaves identifies four forms of the teacher culture: individualism, balkanization, collaborative culture, and contrived collegiality.

7.1 Individualism

Individualism (also known as isolation or privatism), is characterized by situations in which teachers teach mainly alone in their insulated classroom "boxes," giving and receiving little help, advice, support, or feedback, and engaging in little joint planning or reflective dialogue about practice (Fullan and Stiegelbauer 1991). Individualism continues to be the dominant cultural form for most teachers. Although individualism is sometimes celebrated and justified as professional autonomy, history has created it, architecture and school timetables have reinforced it, and teachers have themselves actively and strategically retained it as a way of fending off the overwhelming constraints of bureaucracy. In addition, some teachers also actively elect to work individualistically to maintain care and contact with their own students and to experience the comfort and creativity of personal solitude against the pressures and cultural restraints of groupthink (Hargreaves 1992). While solitude at certain times for certain individuals seems educationally beneficial, widespread cultures of individualism appear to lead to personal insecurity, lowered levels of risk, and reduced levels of teaching quality (Rosenholtz 1989).

7.2 Balkanization

Balkanization is characterized by the fragmentation of teachers into separate and competing subgroups (such as subject departments) pursuing different self-interests in an environment where common purposes, joint understandings, and multiple group memberships are rare. Hargreaves and Macmillan (1992) argue that balkanization makes it difficult for teachers to establish common school goals, leads to inconsistency and redundancy in program and pedagogy, reinforces invidious political and status differences between different kinds of subjects and different forms of knowledge, and reduces teachers' opportunities to learn from one another across territorial boundaries. In balkanized cultures, the organizational whole is less than the sum of its parts.

7.3 Collaborative Cultures

Collaborative cultures among teachers are those

where collegial relationships express principles of help, support, advice, planning, reflection, and feedback as joint enterprises. Little (1990) has identified four kinds of collegial relations among teachers which form a continuum from scanning and storytelling, to help and assistance, sharing and joint work. Only the latter, she argues, expressed in activities like team teaching, peer coaching, and action research, constitutes a strong form of collaboration. With Rosenholtz (1989), Little recognizes that these stronger forms reduce uncertainty, increase risk-taking, foster commitment to continuous improvement, and thereby raise teachers' senses of efficacy and, with that, the successes they have with their students (Ashton and Webb 1986). While advocacy for collaborative school cultures is increasing, they remain a relatively rare cultural reality of teaching.

7.4 Contrived Collegiality

This describes forms of collaboration that are administratively forced more than facilitated (Grimmett and Crehan 1992). While it can help provide structured frameworks to get collaboration going, more often it captures, contains, and constrains it, subordinating teachers' purposes to those of administrators and engaging teachers in efforts that are superficial, wasteful, or divisive. Contrived collegiality is evidenced in such measures as mandatory peer coaching, compulsory collaborative planning, and scheduled meetings with special education teachers. It is a form of collaboration that does not so much create empowerment, as entrapment, enticement, or enslavement.

8. Conclusion

The rhetorics of teaching quality and teacher development are often dominated by discourses of knowledge, skill, and competence. The realities of teaching quality and teacher development are more ones of commitment, context, culture, and career. Reform efforts are at last beginning to address some of these realities but it would be unrealistic not to acknowledge that there still remains a long way to go.

References

Acker S 1990a Creating careers; Women teachers at work. *Curric. Inq.* 22(2): 141–63

Acker S 1990b Teachers' culture in an English primary school: Continuity and change. *Br. J. Sociol. Educ.*, 11(3): 257–73

Apple M, Jungck S 1992 You don't have to be a teacher to teach in this unit: Teaching, technology, and control in the classroom. In: Hargreaves A, Fullan M (eds.) 1992 *Understanding Teacher Development*. Cassell, London

Ashton P, Webb R 1986 *Making a Difference: Teacher's Sense of Efficacy and Student Achievement*. Longman, New York

Book C, Freeman D 1986 Differences in entry characteristics of elementary and secondary teacher candidates. *J. Teach. Educ.*, 37(2): 47–51

Cuban L 1984 *How Teachers Taught: Constancy and Change in American Classrooms (1890–1980)*. Longman, New York

Department of Education and Science 1983 *Teaching Quality*, Cmnd 8836. HMSO, London

Fullan M, Hargreaves A 1991 *What's Worth Fighting for in Your School?* Open University, Milton Keynes

Fullan M, Stiegelbauer S 1991 *The New Meaning of Educational Change*, 2nd edn. Cassell, London

Gilligan C 1982 *In a Different Voice: Psychological Theory and Women's Development*. Harvard University Press, Cambridge, Massachusetts

Grimmett P, Crehan E 1992 The nature of collegiality in teacher development: The case of clinical supervision. In: Fullan M, Hargreaves A (eds.) 1992 *Teacher Development and Educational Change*. Falmer Press, London

Hargreaves A 1992 Cultures of teaching: A focus on change. In: Hargreaves A, Fullan M (eds.) 1992 *Understanding Teacher Development*. Cassell, London

Hargreaves A 1993a *Changing Teachers; Changing Times: Teachers' Work and Culture in the Postmodern age*. Cassell, London

Hargreaves A 1993b Individualism and individuality: Reinterpreting the teacher culture. *Int. J. Educ. Res.* 19(3): 227–45

Hargreaves A, Macmillan R 1992 Balkanized secondary schools and the malaise of modernity. Paper presented at the annual meeting of the American Educational Research Association, San Francisco, California

Hargreaves D 1980 The occupational culture of teaching. In: Woods P (ed.) 1980 *Teacher Strategies*. Croom Helm, London

Hargreaves D 1982 *The Challenge for the Comprehensive School: Culture, Curriculum and Community*. Routledge and Kegan Paul, London

Hoyle E 1975 The study of schools as organizations. In: Machugh R, Morgan C (eds.) 1975 *Management in Education*. Ward Lock, London

Huberman M 1992 *The Lives of Teachers*. Cassell, London

Knowles J 1988 The failure of a student teacher: Becoming educated about teachers, teaching and self. Paper presented at the annual meeting of the American Educational Research Association, New Orleans, Louisiana

Krupp J 1989 Staff development and the individual. In: Caldwell S (ed.) 1989 *Staff Development: A Handbook of Effective Practices*. National Staff Development Council, Oxford, Ohio

Larson S 1980 Proletarianization and educated labour. *Theory and Society* 9: 131–75

Little J W 1990 The persistence of privacy: Autonomy and initiative in teachers' professional relations. *Teach. Coll. Rec.* 91(4): 509–36

Lortie D 1975 *Schoolteacher*. University of Chicago Press, Chicago, Illinois

Louden W 1991a Collegiality, curriculum and educational change. *Curriculum Journal* 2(3): 361–73

Louden W 1991b *Understanding Teaching*. Cassell, London

McLaughlin M 1993 What matters most in teachers' workplace context? In: Little J W, McLaughlin M (eds.) 1993 *Cultures and Contexts of Teaching*. Teachers College Press, New York

Metz M 1990 How social class differences shape teachers' work. In: McLaughlin M, Talbert J, Basia N (eds.)

1990 *The Contexts of Teaching in Secondary Schools: Teachers' realities*. Teachers College Press, New York
Neufeld J 1991 Curriculum reform and the time of care. *Curriculum Journal* 2(3): 283–300
Nias J 1989 *Primary Teachers Talking*. Routledge and Kegan Paul, London
Nias J 1991 Changing times, changing identities: Grieving for a lost self. In Burgess R (ed.) 1991 *Educational Research and Evaluation: For Policy and Practice?* Falmer Press, London
Oakes J 1985 *Keeping Track: How Schools Structure Inequality*. Yale University Press, New Haven, Connecticut
Rosenholtz S 1989 *Teachers' Workplace: The Social Organization of Schools*. Longman, New York
Sarason S 1990 *The Predictable Failure of School Reform*. Jossey-Bass, San Francisco, California
Stoddart T 1991 Learning to teach English and mathematics in an alternative route to certification. *Curriculum Journal* 2(3): 259–81
Woods P 1981 Strategies, commitment and identity: Making and breaking the teacher role. In: Barton L, Walker S (eds.) 1981 *Schools, Teachers, and Teaching*. Falmer Press, London

A. Hargreaves

Teaching: Reflective

Reflective teaching refers to a process of critical analysis whereby teachers develop logical reasoning skills, thoughtful judgment, and attitudes supportive of reflection. Thus, reflective teaching has both cognitive and affective components. In a larger framework, reflective teaching may be thought of as a construct that emphasizes the need for understanding and resolution of contradictions in order for teachers to develop professionally. A teacher is prompted to engage in reflective teaching when trying to determine the rationality and justification of ideas and actions in order to develop new understanding and appreciation of phenomena.

This entry describes the main characteristics of reflective teaching; interprets the potential value of reflective teaching for teachers; specifies attitudes that are necessary for being reflective; summarizes a process for making teaching reflective; and describes the potential role of reflective teaching for teacher education. The entry closes with a discussion of tactics that can be used to promote reflective teaching. The discussion is limited to teaching which occurs in school classrooms or institutions of teacher education.

1. The Nature of Reflective Teaching

An inquiry into the nature of reflective teaching suggests a degree of commonality in the researchers who conceptualize it. One of the most important writers on reflective teaching, Dewey suggests that reflection is the "active, persistent and careful consideration of any belief or supposed form of knowledge in light of the grounds that support it and further conclusions to which it tends" (1933 p. 9). Thus, reflection moves from a stage of uncertainty, doubt, and perplexity, to a goal of mastering the problematic situation or gaining satisfaction when one finds material that will resolve the dilemma.

Dewey (1933) suggested that the development of reflective teaching implied learned predispositions to respond positively to certain situations or persons. Among the most important of these dispositions were open-mindedness, responsibility, and wholeheartedness.

Open-mindedness is a cognitive component that suggests the predisposition to seek out and construct alternative structures in an educational field of study. Open-minded teachers welcome risk-taking and would not automatically accept or reject a teaching hypothesis or the predefined educational and organizational orthodoxy of a school or classroom. Rather, these teachers would examine it in the light of their experience and compare their ideas with those of students, parents, researchers, and the community. They prefer to view problems as having plural, contextual solutions.

Responsibility is a performance component which engages teachers in the consideration of long-term as well as short-term consequences of action. Responsible teachers take an essentially moral stance, emphasizing a conception of teaching and learning in which attention is paid to the social, political, and economic context of educational decisions. Furthermore, responsible teachers inquire about their actions in the light of ethical considerations.

Wholeheartedness is an effective component. It implies that attitudes are not confined to particular teaching situations or disciplines, but permeate the whole of the teacher's instructional and political life.

In support of Dewey, studies conducted by Schön (1987) have shown that teachers, regardless of their age and the academic discipline they teach, make judgments regarding the adequacy of their responses to situations and problems for which no overt rationale has been declared. According to Schön, reflective teaching involves the development of strategies and techniques to deal with the complex, uncertain, unstable, and unique situations of the teaching practice. Acknowledging the complex characteristics of educational settings is the process that Schön calls "reflection-in-action." Thus, teaching is not a technical, fixed, and planned series of activities, but an artistic process. Also, it is an intuitive, creative, and improvisational action and a moral enterprise which requires critical thinking in order to develop contextually theories of good teaching practice. The opposite of reflective teaching is the mindless following of learning theories or unexamined teaching practices.

Reflective teaching entails knowledge of teachers' critical thinking, self-direction, problem-solving strategies, and creative thinking. It implies personal knowledge, self-awareness, and the awareness of the classroom context (Elliott 1991). Reflective teachers seek reasons, are well-informed, use and cite valid sources, look for alternatives, and consider others' points of view.

2. *The Evaluation of Reflective Teaching*

Reflective teaching evaluation has mirrored the contemporary debates surrounding research methodology in education. The state of reflective teaching evaluation in the early 1990s can be reasonably characterized as lying somewhere on a continuum of research methodology between positivism and naturalism, nomothetic and idiographic, and empirical–analytic and "illuminative." Much of the past research on reflective teaching has fallen at the positivist, nomothetic, and empirical–analytic end of the continuum. Psychometric interests dominated this research in which the aim was to generate technical and rational knowledge, usually in the form of causal explanations. Reflection was defined in terms of a measurable set of phenomena within the teaching–learning process; the criteria for evaluating reflection were reduced to observable dimensions of the interactive teaching act.

The major purpose, according to this view of reflective teaching, was to develop teachers who were capable of executing technical skills of teaching to achieve prespecified goals. This approach, which was dominant in the behavioristic paradigm of teacher education, included operationally stated objectives, criterion tasks, gradually increasing difficulty, active student participation, and feedback as important components of effective teaching.

More recently, the methodological emphasis has been on qualitative, ethnographic, or interpretative studies. This change in methodology has been due in part to the complexities of reflective teaching. Varying subject-matter knowledge, complex political and ethical principles underlying teaching, and problematic education institutions do not readily generate plausible and discrete hypotheses to test. Reflective teaching cannot be evaluated using a fixed set of procedures. Typically, the first data on reflective teaching are collected by observing teachers at work gathering data on site and describing the teachers' practical reasoning through extended interviews. In these interviews, teachers are asked to ascribe meaning and values to specific things (e.g., students behavior, parents' educational roles, or their own classroom performance). Finally, there is the problem of determining the merit of reflective teaching: what constitutes good or bad reflection? (Kagan 1990).

3. *Processes of Reflective Teaching*

Drawing on the theory of Habermas, Van Manen (1977) has suggested that reflection occurs at three different stages. These stages correspond to three forms of knowledge and the associated cognitive interests: technical rationality, practical action, and critical reflection.

Technical rationality. At this empirical–analytic level, reflectivity is concerned with the application of knowledge to the pursuit of some desired goal or end point. The dominant concern of the teacher is efficient and effective application of pedagogical knowledge. This level of reflectivity is central in the tradition of pragmatic modes of thinking.

Practical action. At the hermeneutic–phenomenological level, reflectivity focuses on understanding the interaction of individuals. The teacher becomes concerned with clarifying the predispositions underlying competing educational aims and with evaluating the educational consequences toward which a teaching action leads.

Critical reflection. At the critical–theoretical level, reflectivity employs an emancipatory theory of truth. The teacher incorporates moral and ethical criteria into the discourse about practical actions, and reflects upon the underlying assumptions that constrain or shape the practice.

4. *Reflective Teaching and the Curriculum of Teacher Education*

There are several important features of reflective teaching in the preservice teacher education curriculum. Some of the most important are outlined briefly below.

Critical approaches. The curriculum will emphasize critical approaches to field experiences, seminars, methods courses, and social foundations courses. Programs should strive to prepare students critically to analyze ethical and value-based educational practices and to examine knowledge in the following dimensions: teaching-learning process, disciplines, political and ethical assumptions underlying school and university teaching, and, most broadly, the nature of school and university institutions and society itself.

Skills and attitudes. The curriculum will seek to combine certain skills which are involved in classroom inquiry, practical action, and classroom competence, and attitudes of open-mindedness, responsibility, and wholeheartedness. The interests, ideologies, values, dispositions, role functions, and differentiated responsibilities form the dynamic and tacit course context in which preservice teacher education curriculum decisions will be made.

Process model. The curriculum will stress a process model in which teachers will develop "self-monitoring and self-inquiring" habits and be able to evaluate and revise their own practice reflectively. This cyclical or spiralling process provides the fundamental dynamic of teachers' practical theories; the teacher is viewed as a producer of knowledge. Thus, action research can be used as a powerful vehicle for encouraging teachers to tell their own stories, and it also relates to the more socially progressive strands of the teacher-as-researcher movement.

Curriculum integration. Courses will approach an integration of the curriculum. Educators argue that an interdisciplinary curriculum increases student teachers' motivation, enables the learners to confront problems that are ignored by separate disciplines, and relates educational curriculum and research to the student teacher's own insights, reflections, and judgments. Curriculum integration is developed as an interpersonal process among educators and student teachers. This curriculum approach implies the need for a collaborative and cooperative enterprise.

5. *Field Experiences for the Preparation of Reflective Teachers*

Field experience is essential to the reflective process, since it will either reinforce or modify what schooling and curriculum mean to student teachers. The aims of critical reflection can be accomplished through a defined set of field experiences and concomitant workshops which occur in three phases.

In the first phase, the field experiences and workshops are intended to enable teachers to problematize (i.e., problem posing rather than problem solving) the settings in which they work. Through conversation among themselves working as a group, teachers can problematize dilemmas and issues they want to work on in their own practice.

In the second phase, field experiences and workshops provide an opportunity to observe others teach and to discuss their observations with one another. The sharing of experiences inherent in reflective teaching potentially has three positive outcomes. First, student teachers may come to value their personal and craft knowledge (Grimmett and MacKinnon 1992) instead of viewing it as inferior to the pedagogical knowledge produced by expert teachers. Second, shared experiences may lead to strong collegiality. Third, peer collaboration allows meaning to be constructed jointly by student teachers through the process of collegial dialogue and postobservational supervisory conferences. Questions raised during the peer coaching conversation focus student teachers' attention on their initial problematic thoughts and attitudes during teaching, redefine the contextual interpretations of teaching dilemmas, generate the advantages and disadvantages of various solutions within the particular teaching practice context, and permit the consideration of various approaches to evaluating the results.

In the third phase—exploratory experimentation—student teachers are encouraged to consider issues from different perspectives, to reframe the problematic situation in light of its characteristics, to view all solutions of problems as possible, and to act deliberately to produce an end, monitoring the effects of any solution attempted.

Teacher educators need to develop strategies which will actively encourage student teachers' reflection upon practice. In this regard, teacher educators should:

(a) recognize that it is their responsibility to train student teachers to reflect upon their teaching practice;

(b) expose student teachers to the social context and the real and conflicting world of the classroom;

(c) set valid standards by which students' reflection can be measured and judged; and,

(d) create field experiences that require student teachers to function as conscious moral agents in order to create a just society.

6. *Professional Development of Reflective Practitioners*

The image of teacher research is undergoing reevaluation. Teachers' language and judgments have become the medium of school social life as well as the focus of interpretative inquiry. The interpretation of teachers' thoughts, speech, and actions occurs within a social and educational context. The questions teachers ask, the ways they write, and the schemata they use to frame classroom practices can be powerful in heightening teachers' awareness of their own professional reasoning. Within this framework teachers are neither uninformed participants nor merely collaborative resources. Rather, they are simultaneously researchers, instructors, and analysts. Teachers are guided to reveal and examine their craft knowledge and improvisational performance by engaging in four types of analysis: "analysis of self as a practitioner; analysis of the meaning of one's professional actions; analysis of underlying assumptions; and reconsideration of teaching practices in light of the fruits of analysis" (Lalik et al. 1989).

According to Smyth (1989), teachers should engage in four forms of actions in order to change ideologies and the working conditions that constrain them. These actions are describing, informing, confronting, and reconstructing.

Describing is a stage where a teacher answers the question: "What do I do?" As teachers reflect about their actions, they describe the knowledge, beliefs, and principles that characterize their practice. Teaching is viewed as a text written in the language of teachers; the use of journals or diaries comprises the events and dilemmas that form teachers' tacit knowledge.

Informing is a stage initiated by the guiding question: "What does this mean?" Teachers uncover their short-range, explanatory, or local theories that inform their teaching action. As teachers describe, analyze, and make inferences about classroom events, they are creating their own pedagogical principles. These subjective theories help them make sense of what is going on in the school and society and guide further action.

Confronting is a stage at which the teacher responds to the question: "How did I come to be like this?" Teachers seek out the constructions of their assumptions, ideas, values, and beliefs, and how social and institutional forces have influenced them. They see knowledge as constructed symbolically by the mind through social interaction with others.

Reconstructing is the stage at which teachers answer the question: "How might I do things differently?" The intention of this form of action for teachers is to critique and uncover the tensions that exist between particular teaching practices and the larger cultural and social contexts in which they are embedded. The primary characteristic of this social reconstructionist conception is its commitment to reflection as a communal activity where teachers can support each other's knowledge (Zeichner and Tabachnick 1991).

Despite the efforts to promote reflective teaching courses, this approach remains insufficiently widespread. Sykes (1986) gives five broad explanations for the relative absence of reflection-in-action. They are:

(a) The limitations of human information processing. The assumption is that teachers use basic and limited cognitive processes in their daily school lives.

(b) The nature of teaching as work. Teaching is viewed as an unstable and confused activity which does not warrant systematic reflectivity.

(c) The socialization and training of teachers. Prospective teachers have followed a conventional and traditional curriculum of teacher education based on the technocratic tradition.

(d) The organizational context of teaching. School work does not favor inquiry.

(e) The modal characteristics of teachers. This controversial speculation points out that teachers are selected with certain academic characteristics.

7. *Strategies for Promoting Reflection*

Some authors have restricted the focus of reflection to an examination of means, rather than ends. From this perspective, reflective teaching consists of controlled and thoughtfully designed teacher experiences (Gore 1987). Central to this approach is the need to acquire technical teaching skills, such as systematic classroom observation of others, self-assessment of student teaching, journal writing, and simulated teaching (Freiber and Waxman 1990). Schön (1987) portrays the way in which sensitive dialogue, modeling, and the establishment of challenging practical experiences can produce professional artistry or reflective competence in teaching. In addition, Kottkamp (1990) has developed a catalogue of means or tactics to facilitate reflection among teachers and other professionals. Included in this catalogue are the following items:

(a) writing—writing is used to capture teachers' thought processes and yield a product that can be evaluated and reformulated.

(b) journals—data provided in daily records may be used to search for patterns of meaning;

(c) case records—writing a case record is a structured activity that expands the number of teaching alternatives;

(d) contrived situations—these include simulated teaching situations, like role plays, case studies, simulations, and microteaching;

(e) instrument feedback—scales and inventories can be used to provide teachers with data useful for reflection on their actions;

(f) electronic feedback—videotaping teachers' actions provides records of events, issues, and feelings for reflection-on-action;

(g) metaphors—metaphors can be used to clarify the personal meaning teachers attach to their particular teaching's action:

(h) platforms—these are, according to Schön (1987), teachers' espoused theories, their stated intentions. Writing a platform engages teachers in a reflective process on the congruity or incongruity between espoused theory and theory-in-use.

8. *Future Trends*

In the early 1990s there appears to be a major shift in the way teaching and teacher education are conceptualized. There is a greater interest in teacher cognitions and reflective thinking. Research on reflective teaching is under way at major universities in several countries (Korthagen 1985, Carr and Kemmis 1986, Pollard and Tann 1987). The emerging preservice teacher education curriculum points to the emergence and development of the reflective teaching paradigm. There is a growing need for descriptions of existing models of reflective teaching, each specifying its own problems as well as successful solutions. At the same time, however, knowledge about reflective teaching has increased substantially since the late 1980s.

See also: Teachers as Researchers; Dewey, Pragmatism, and Education; Critical Theory and Education; Teaching, Paradigms for Research on; Curriculum Theory

References

Carr W, Kemmis S 1986 *Becoming Critical: Education, Knowledge and Action Research*. Falmer Press, London

Dewey J 1933 *How We Think*. Heath, Boston, Massachusetts

Elliott J 1991 *Action Research for Educational Change*. Open University Press, Milton Keynes

Freiber H J, Waxman H C 1990 Reflection and the acquisition of technical teaching skills. In: Clift R T, Houston W R, Pugach M C (eds.) 1990 *Encouraging Reflective Practice in Education: An Analysis of Issues and Programs*. Teacher College Press, New York

Gore J M 1987 Reflecting on reflective teaching. *J. Teach Educ.* 38(2): 33–9

Grimmett P P, MacKinnon A M 1992 Craft knowledge and the education of teachers. In: Grant G(ed.) 1992 *Review of Research in Education*, Vol. 18. American Educational Research Association, Washington, DC

Kagan D M 1990 Ways of evaluating teacher cognition: Inferences concerning the Goldilocks principle. *Rev. Educ. Res.* 60(3): 419–69

Korthagen F 1985 Reflective teaching and preservice teacher education in the Netherlands. *J. Teach. Educ.* 36(5): 11–15

Kottkamp R B 1990 Means for facilitating reflection. *Educ. Urban Soc.* 22(2): 182–203

Lalik R V, Niles J A, Murphy S B 1989 Using your head and your heart: A study of a process for promoting reflection among student teachers. Paper presented at the American Educational Research Association, San Francisco, California

Pollard A, Tann S 1987 *Reflective Teaching in the Primary School. A Handbook for the Classroom*. Cassell, London

Schön D A 1987 *Educating the Reflective Practitioner. Toward a New Design for Teaching and Learning in the Professions*. Jossey-Bass, San Francisco, California

Smyth J 1989 Developing and sustaining critical reflection in teacher education. *J. Teach. Educ.* 40(2): 2–9

Sykes G 1986 Teaching as reflective practice. In: Sirotnik K A, Oakes J (eds.) 1986 *Critical Perspectives on the Organization and Improvement of Schooling*. Kluwer, Nijhoff, Boston, Massachusetts

Van Manen M 1977 Linking ways of knowing with ways of being practical. *Curric. Inq.* 6(3): 205–28

Zeichner K M, Tabachnick B R 1991 Reflections on reflective teaching. In: Tabachnick B R, Zeicher K M (eds.) 1991 *Issues and Practices in Inquiry-Oriented Teacher Education*. Falmer Press, London

Further Reading

Gore J M, Zeichner K M 1991 Action research and reflective teaching. *Teaching Teach. Educ.* 7(2): 119–36

Habermas J 1971 *Knowledge and Human Interests*. Beacon Press, Boston, Massachusetts

Smith D 1991 Educating the reflective practitioner in curriculum. *Curric.* 12(2): 115–24

Villar L M 1991 *El profesor como profesional reflexivo: Formacion y desarrollo personal*. ICE y Servicio de Publicaciones de la Universidad, Granada

Zeichner K M, Liston D P 1987 Teaching student teachers to reflect. *Harvard Educ. Rev.* 57(1): 23–48

L. M. Villar

Teaching: Social Psychological Theories

Education is fundamentally an interpersonal process involving teachers and students, aimed at transmitting knowledge, skills, and culture from one generation to the next. Thus social psychology (the study of interpersonal, small-group, and organizational dynamics) is perhaps the most relevant social science for educators. The social nature of education is the first issue described in this article. The application of social psychological knowledge to educational practice is then discussed. The theories and research findings included in this article were chosen on the basis of their relevance to educational practice.

1. The Social Nature of Education

A defining characteristic of the human species is the transference of knowledge and tradition from one generation to the next. The process of transferring accumulated knowledge, skills, and cultures across generations is fundamentally a social process, requiring communication and interaction among people who exchange ideas, skills, attitudes, and feelings. Schools have been developed and have evolved to enhance and systematize this transfer. The transfer is conducted not by computers, teaching machines, textbooks, laboratory equipment, and videotapes; rather it is the direct result of interaction between human beings—between teachers and students, and students themselves. Teachers in the middle grades, for example, typically engage in about 200 interpersonal interchanges per hour (Jackson 1968). How much students learn and how successful teachers are depends on the nature and the quality of these classroom interactions.

2. Educational Social Organizations and Role Theory

The transfer of culture from one generation to the next is organized within schools. Schools are social organizations—a planned set of interpersonal relationships structured to achieve certain goals. The better teachers understand how the school works as a social organization, the more effectively they can teach. All social organizations are based on cooperation among members to achieve goals, maintain effective working relationships, and adapt to change. The success of the school depends on cooperative relationships among its members. Relationships are structured through the assignment of roles and the establishment of norms.

The school, like all social organizations, contains a variety of positions, such as teacher, student, and administrator. For each position there is a "role"—a set of prescribed behaviors that anyone who occupies that position should perform. The roles define how adults, children, and adolescents are to relate to one another in repeated and reliable ways so that the school's goals are achieved. The roles are interdependent and complementary. Roles contain both obligations, which individuals in complementary roles expect from a person, and rights, which individuals in complementary roles will do for a person. A teacher, for example, is obligated to structure instructional situations so that students learn; students in turn have the right to expect the teacher to do so.

People in certain roles are expected to behave in certain ways, both by themselves and by those in other roles. When a person holds positions in two different groups that make contradictory demands, there is "interrole conflict." If a student, for example, is in a science class that requires a major report to be written tonight and is also on the football team and is expected to go to rest for tomorrow's game, then there is a conflict between the roles of student and football player. "Intrarole conflict" occurs when other roles hold incompatible expectations of a particular role. If the history teacher, for example, expects students to complete three hours of homework tonight and the science teacher expects the same students to complete a major report, then students have a role conflict.

"Norms" define general expectations for everyone in the school. "No running in the halls" is an example of a school norm. Norms make explicit what behavior is appropriate or inappropriate within the school, and they have a specific "ought" or "must" quality. Roles and norms influence educators' actions so that a coordinated division of labor results within schools.

Because schools are organizations, all the social psychological knowledge contained within the fields of organizational psychology and group dynamics is relevant to educational practice. The continual effectiveness of schools, furthermore, depends on their ability to change and develop over time. Social psychologists have applied organizational development and change theory to schools (Miles 1964). Based on the research, schools are being encouraged to change to team-based cooperative organizational structures (Johnson and Johnson 1989b).

Organizational and role theories help educators understand a wide variety of dynamics within schools. By redesigning roles the effectiveness of schools may be increased. By identifying and reducing role conflicts the productivity of individual members may be increased. Teachers, for example, may coordinate when tests are given and reports are due so that students are not faced with competing assignments on any one night. By changing individuals' roles their perspectives, attitudes, and behavior can change. When students are given the responsibility of teaching other students, for example, their attitudes toward homework may change.

3. *Interpersonal Expectations and Performance*

Closely related to role theory is expectancy theory. Students have a tendency to live up (or down) to teacher expectations. Expectancy theory predicts that what teachers and classmates expect from students tends to influence how much students actually learn (Rosenthal and Jacobson 1968). A number of studies have confirmed this prediction. In addition, there is evidence that people will believe and do what prestigeful others suggest. In order to maximize achievement, both the teacher and classmates should expect students to achieve realistic but challenging learning goals.

4. *Social Interdependence Theory*

Perhaps the most influential social psychological theory for educational practice is social interdependence theory. For each lesson, teachers must decide whether to structure the learning goals cooperatively, competitively, or individualistically. The first experimental studies on social interdependence were conducted in the 1890s in England, Germany, and the United States. The basic theory, based on Kurt Lewin's (1935) field theory, was formulated by Morton Deutsch (1949). Social interdependence exists when each individual's outcomes are affected by the actions of others. Within any social situation, individuals may join together to achieve mutual goals, compete to see who is best, or act independently on their own.

There are two types of social interdependence: cooperative and competitive. The absence of social interdependence results in individualistic efforts. Cooperation exists when one perceives that one is linked with others in a way so that one cannot succeed unless others succeed (and vice versa), and/or one's work benefits others and others' work benefits one. Competition exists when one perceives that one cannot succeed unless others fail (and vice versa) and/or one's work decreases others' chances for success and others' work decreases one's chances for success. Individualistic efforts exist when one perceives that one's success is unrelated to the success or failure of others.

Over 550 experimental and 100 correlational studies have been conducted on this theory (Johnson and Johnson 1989a). These studies demonstrate that working cooperatively, compared with competitive and individualistic efforts, will result in higher student achievement, more positive relationships among students (including between White and minority students, and nonhandicapped and handicapped students), and greater psychological adjustment, social competencies, and self-esteem. Cooperative learning has such consistent, powerful, and numerous effects on educational outcomes that it should probably be used the majority of the school day. A number of social psychologists have worked with schools in implementing cooperative learning within the classroom and cooperative teaching teams within the school (see Johnson et al 1990). Teachers at all grade levels need to be trained in how to structure lessons cooperatively (See also *Goal Structures*).

5. *Distributive Justice*

Closely related to social interdependence theory are theories of distributive justice (Deutsch 1985). Distributive justice deals with how benefits such as grades are granted to group or organizational members. The equity (or merit or competitive) view is that a person's rewards should be in proportion to his or her contributions to the group's effort. The equality (or cooperative) view is that all group members should benefit equally. The need view is that group members should be rewarded in proportion to their need. Whether teachers utilize an equity, equality, or need system, students have to perceive the system as "just." When rewards are distributed unjustly, the group may be characterized by low morale, high conflict, and low productivity. The evidence indicates that before a task is performed the equity reward system is perceived to be fairest, while after a task is performed the equality system is perceived to be most just. Before starting a project, members of a learning group may wish to be ranked from best to worst and given grades accordingly. After the project is completed, students will wish to have all members receive the same grade, believing that the diverse contributions cannot be "justly" ranked from most to least valuable. With increased experience, students tend to achieve higher under the equality system. When a groupmate suffers a life crisis (such as parents getting a divorce), furthermore, students usually wish to have the teacher take "need" into consideration. In terms of giving grades to students and rewarding educators, an equality system or some combination of the three would probably be most effective.

6. *Conflict Theory*

For instructional effectiveness and classroom order, teachers both create intellectual conflict to improve instruction and teach students how to negotiate and mediate in order to reduce discipline problems and improve the quality of life within schools. Controversy exists when one person's ideas, information, conclusions, theories, or opinions are incompatible with those of another, and the two seek to reach an agreement. When academic controversies are structured in the classroom, students are required to conduct research and prepare a position; rehearse orally the relevant information; advocate a position; teach their knowledge to peers; analyze, critically evaluate, and rebut information; reason both deductively and inductively; and synthesize and integrate information into factual and judgmental conclusions with which all sides can agree (Johnson and Johnson 1989a). Controversy theory is based on developmental theories of Piaget (1950), Berlyne (1965), Hunt (1964), and others, who posit that cognitive and social development as well as learning depend on creating cognitive disequilibrium, conceptual conflict, cognitive uncertainty, and epistemic curiosity. Controversy (compared with individualistic and competitive learning, debate, and concurrence-seeking) creates higher achievement, problem-solving, critical thinking, creativity, motivation to learn, and task involvement. Instead of suppressing intellectual conflict among students by lecturing, competition, and individualistic work, according to this theory teachers should structure and encourage it to promote learning.

There are times when the wants and goals of students conflict and procedures for negotiating integrative agreements are needed (Johnson and Johnson 1991). Social psychology has provided a long history of theorizing and research on negotiating integrative agreements (Deutsch 1973). The traditional family, neighborhood, and community procedures for teaching children how to manage conflicts have broken down. Students come to school with diverse ideas about how conflicts should be managed. Teachers need to teach all students to use the same set of procedures and skills in negotiating wise resolutions to their conflicts. Such training programs consist of two steps: (a) teaching all students a negotiation procedure, and (b) involving students in a peer mediation program where they help their classmates negotiate wise agreements to their conflicts (Johnson and Johnson 1991). Students need to be taught to state what they want and how they feel, provide the reasons underlying their wants, accurately take their opponent's perspective, propose at least three options for an agreement, and reach a mutually satisfying agreement. Teaching students how to resolve their conflicts constructively reduces discipline problems and empowers students to regulate their own behavior rather than rely on adult authorities to do so.

7. *Achievement Motivation Theory*

The instructional methods teachers use affect how motivated students are to achieve. Motivation to achieve is the degree to which individuals commit effort to achieve goals they perceive as meaningful and worthwhile. While humans may be born with a motivation to increase their competencies, how meaningful goals appear to be and how much effort individuals decide to exert are basically determined by internalized past relationships, present relationships, or current interaction patterns within the learning situation (Johnson and Johnson 1989a). The two most important theories of achievement motivation were formulated by Atkinson and Feather (1965) and David McClelland (1965). Atkinson states that achievement motivation is a balance between the tendency to achieve success and the tendency to avoid failure. The tendency to achieve success is assumed to be a function of the general motive to achieve success, the subjective probability of success, and the incentive to succeed. McClelland has demonstrated that, with training, the achievement motivation of adults can be increased. Together, their work provides a basis for educators to ensure that students develop a high level of achievement motivation.

One application of achievement motivation to education is Richard DeCharms' (1976) work with personal causation. Students can see their behavior as originating in themselves (they are an origin) or as being the result of external pressure (they are a pawn). Students treated as origins tend to like school tasks, work hard at them, and be more involved in them than are students treated as pawns. Students, furthermore, want to be the origin of their behavior and constantly struggle against the constraint of external causes. The more students believe they are studying because they freely choose to do so, operate under their own control, and are personally committed to learn, the greater their task motivation.

8. *Attribution Theory*

Causal attributions answer "why" questions, such as "Why did I fail this exam?" "Why" questions are asked more frequently after negative, unexpected, or atypical outcomes. The reasons to which students attribute their failures influence how hard they work on subsequent tasks. Attribution theory is concerned with people's explanations of the causes of (a) their own and other's behavior and (b) events (Graham 1991; Heider 1958). Growing out of the social psychological theories on social perception, attribution theory focuses on whether people attribute the causes of behavior to the situation or the individual, ways in which responsibility for success or failure is determined, and how attributional decisions affect subsequent behavior. Causes can be dispositional (within people) or situational (within environment). Students can claim their success is due to their ability or the amount of effort they exerted (dispositional causes) or because the task was easy or they were lucky (situational causes). In most cases, students should be trained to attribute their success to themselves and their failures to situational causes.

Generally, there are three dispositional causal dimensions: locus, stability, and controllability (Weiner 1986). The locus dimension defines the location of a cause as internal or external to the individual. The stability dimension designates causes as constant or varying over time. The controllability dimension refers to whether a cause is subject to one's own volitional influence. Ability is an internal, stable, and uncontrollable cause. Effort is internal, unstable, and controllable.

Teachers should ensure that students think through why they succeeded or failed, while guiding them toward the conclusion that their failure is caused by a lack of effort or using the wrong strategy. What emotions teachers express toward students seems to affect the attributions students make about the causes of their success or failure. Teacher sympathy for failure tends to be interpreted as indicating low ability, while teacher anger towards failure seems to be interpreted as indicating low effort.

9. *Self-esteem Theory*

Students who are confused as to who they are or who lack confidence in themselves hesitate to attempt difficult and challenging learning tasks. Teachers make their jobs easier in many ways by helping students gain a clear and positive sense of identity and self-esteem. Every student needs to acquire a positive self-identity, a sense of self that remains the same over time no matter what else has changed in one's life and environment (Erikson 1968). A person is not born with a sense of self. It is during the first two or three years that a kind of crude self-awareness develops, such as being able to make distinctions between what is part of his or her body and what is part of something else. It takes many years of maturation before full adult self-awareness comes into being. As people develop self-awareness, they formulate a self-conception and develop processes through which they derive conclusions about their self-worth. Self-esteem and self-identity develop primarily from relationships with other people, including working with others to achieve challenging goals; being known, liked, and respected by others; and knowing others well enough to identify similarities and differences. The more teachers involve students in joint projects that allow personal and supportive relationships to develop, the more positive will be students' self-identity and self-esteem.

Self-esteem may also be approached from a social-learning perspective that emphasizes students' perceived competence and self-efficacy, which influence students' choices of tasks, willingness to invest effort in task accomplishment, and persistence in the face of subsequent failure (Bandura 1986). Perceived competence is heavily influenced by initial encounters with novel tasks or new subjects. Individuals who experience initial success or failure in some new undertaking tend to infer that they possess relatively high or low aptitude/competence in that area. Once formed, these beliefs in one's competence are resistant to change. The implication for teaching is that at the beginning of each new class, students should be given success experiences in ways that lead them to believe they have an aptitude for the subject area.

10. School Culture

There is considerable evidence that the work environment can affect the meaning of work to the worker. Schools are no exception. The way the school is managed and the policies it espouses tend to affect staff and student motivation. Within each school a culture has to be built based on shared perceptions of (a) desired goals worth striving to achieve and (b) how these goals may be attained. Differences in school culture help explain why some schools are better than others. School culture comprises four interdependent dimensions (Maehr and Braskamp 1986): (a) goal structures (for both students and staff, cooperative efforts are more productive than are competitive or individualistic efforts), (b) roles and power relationships (students and staff should see themselves as autonomous and self-reliant individuals who are the "origin" of their efforts to achieve, rather than as passive pawns who are controlled), (c) evaluation and feedback systems (internal, student-centered evaluation creates greater task orientation and intrinsic motivation to achieve than does external, teacher-dominated evaluation), and (d) symbols of identity and purpose (effective schools stand for something—goals, values, and expectations for student behavior are expressed through slogans, posters, songs, and role models). A clear and strong school culture is especially important when students are culturally diverse.

11. Social Psychology Of Education

Almost all social psychological knowledge could contribute to educational practice. In order to help teachers, social psychologists have (a) specifically operationalized social psychological knowledge into teaching and managing practices and (b) implemented organizational change procedures to ensure innovations are adopted by schools.

Education takes place through interpersonal interactions structured through roles and norms to achieve the school's goals. Understanding the nature of social organizations and role theory helps teachers clarify the rights and obligations of themselves and their students. The expectations teachers hold for students not only help define their role but also influence how much students learn. The school by its very organizational nature is a cooperative enterprise, but within any lesson teachers may structure students' learning goals cooperatively, competitively, or individualistically. Related to social interdependence theory are theories of distributive justice that help teachers give rewards in ways that are perceived to be "just," and conflict theory which has relevance for improving instruction (especially higher level reasoning) and decreasing discipline problems within the school. Social psychology has developed several theories of achievement motivation that influence how curriculum is designed and how teaching is conducted. Like all organizations, schools develop cultures around the goals they consider worth achieving and how the goals are to be attained.

Social psychology has much to offer teachers. Both preservice and inservice teacher education should emphasize social psychological knowledge. Social scientists interested in education should both advance social psychological theories through systematic research programs and operationalize their findings into more effective teaching procedures. Each of the theories discussed requires considerably more research to maximize its value to teachers. Key studies are especially needed on the ways a cooperative structure provides the context in which the impact of the other theories is maximized. The major problems facing education, furthermore, are inherently social psychological and provide a fertile field for new social psychological research. Ensuring that diversity among students results in mutual understanding, respect, creativity, and sophistication is an inherently social psychological problem. Reducing destructive antisocial behaviors such as drug abuse, suicide, criminality, sexual promiscuity, and so forth requires the application of social psychological knowledge. Motivating at-risk students, lowering dropout rates, and ensuring that women and minorities become interested in mathematics and science require social psychological interventions. Both in its basic nature and in its need to solve major problems, education relies heavily on social psychological knowledge.

See also: Teaching Behavioral Theories

References

Atkinson J, Feather N (eds.) 1966 *A Theory of Achievement Motivation*. Wiley, New York

Bandura A 1986 *Social Foundations of Thought and Action*. Prentice-Hall, Englewood Cliffs, New Jersey

Berlyne D 1965 Curiosity and education. In: Krumboltz J (ed.) 1965 *Learning and the Educational Process*. Rand-McNally, Chicago, Illinois

DeCharms R 1976 *Enhancing Motivation*. Irvington, New York

Deutsch M 1949 A theory of cooperation and competition. *Human Relations* 2(2): 129–52

Deutsch M 1973 *The Resolution of Conflict*. Yale University Press, New Haven, Connecticut

Deutsch M 1985 *Distributive Justice*. Yale University Press, New Haven, Connecticut

Erikson E 1968 *Identity: Youth and Crisis*. Norton, New York
Graham S 1991 A review of attribution theory in achievement contexts. *Educational Psychology Review* 3(1): 5–39
Heider F 1958 *The Psychology of Interpersonal Relations*. Wiley, New York
Hunt J 1964 Introduction: Revisiting Montessori. In: Montessori M (ed.) 1964 *The Montessori Method*. Schocken Books, New York
Jackson P W 1968 *Life in Classrooms*. Holt, Rinehart and Winston, New York
Johnson D W, Johnson R 1989a *Cooperation and Competition: Theory and Research*. Interaction Book Company, Edina, Minnesota
Johnson D W, Johnson R 1989b *Leading the Cooperative School*. Interaction Book Company, Edina, Minnesota
Johnson D W, Johnson R 1991 *Teaching Students to be Peacemakers*. Interaction Book Company, Edina, Minnesota
Johnson D W, Johnson R, Holubec E 1993 *Circles of Learning*. Interaction Book Company, Edina, Minnesota
Lewin K 1935 *A Dynamic Theory of Personality*. McGraw-Hill, New York
Maehr M, Braskamp L 1986 *The Motivation Factor: A Theory of Personal Investment*. Lexington Press, Lexington, Massachusetts
McClelland D 1965 Toward a Theory of Motive Acquisition. *Am. Psychol.* 20(5): 321–33
Miles M 1964 *Innovation in Education*. Teachers College Press, New York
Piaget J 1950 *The Psychology of Intelligence*. Harcourt, New York
Rosenthal R, Jacobson L 1968 *Pygmalion in the Classroom*. Holt, Rinehart, and Winston, New York
Weiner B 1986 *An Attributional Theory of Motivation and Emotion*. Springer-Verlag, New York

Further Reading

Bar-Tal D, Saxe L (eds.) 1978 *Social Psychology of Education*. Hemisphere, Washington, DC
Feldman R 1986 *The Social Psychology of Education*. Cambridge University Press, Cambridge, Massachusetts
Johnson D W 1970 *The Social Psychology of Education*. Holt, Rinehart and Winston, New York

D. W. Johnson; R. Johnson

Teaching: Social Status

Social status of teaching refers to the relative standing of teaching as an occupation in a hierarchy of all occupations. This entry begins with an exploration of the concepts of occupational status and prestige. Next, the place of teaching within the occupational hierarchies of different societies as indicated by studies of occupational prestige will be described. The final three sections will consider explanations which account for the relative prestige of teaching.

1. Concepts of Status and Prestige

The terms "status," "prestige," and "esteem" are used synonymously in everyday language and very often in the sociological literature. They are also given different connotations by individual sociologists. However, as there are inconsistencies in these various usages the connotations to be used in this entry can be briefly outlined.

The social status of an individual—the degree to which he or she is accorded deference—is determined by a number of factors including wealth, education, gender, ethnicity, and life-style. However, in most developed and developing societies the major determinant of status is held to be occupation. Although a number of personal factors may shape the esteem in which individuals are held in their community—including, for example, how well a teacher is regarded as doing his or her job in school and in making a wider contribution to the community—these factors are less significant than membership in an occupation.

Occupational status is the regard in which an occupation is held in comparison with other occupations. Thus, occupational status turns upon the image of an occupation held by other members of society. To establish the nature of an occupational image, and hence status, is difficult. One can analyse natural speech about an occupation, examine how it is represented in the media, or use a variety of other means. By far the most sophisticated study in methodological terms has been carried out by Coxon and Jones (1978, 1979).

The term "occupational prestige" is widely used to refer to the outcome of studies in which people are asked to rate sets of occupations according to some criterion of "higher" or "lower" and a rank order of occupations is produced. Well over a hundred such studies have been undertaken worldwide. The occupational lists have varied in size and content. The samples undertaking the ranking also have varied as have the instructions given to them.

"Schoolteaching" has appeared on virtually all the studies undertaken within this mode. Sometimes it has appeared as a single occupation, but other studies have subdivided it. One of the earliest studies of occupational prestige, undertaken specifically to determine the prestige of teaching, differentiated between primary and secondary teachers (Counts 1925). Most modern studies include hundreds of occupational titles in rank order—usually extrapolated from smaller samples of personal rankings—and differentiate not only between categories of teacher but also categories of principal. However, this entry, except where indicated, will focus on the general category of teacher.

2. The Occupational Prestige of Teaching

A number of studies have undertaken international comparisons of occupational prestige (e.g., Hodge et al. 1966) and have consistently demonstrated a

Table 1
Twenty selected occupations from the Standard International Occupational Prestige Scale

	Scale score	Rank order
Judge	78	1=
Physician	78	1=
University professor	78	1=
Architect	72	4
Dentist	70	5
Physiotherapist	67	6
Airline pilot	66	7=
Middle-rank civil servant	66	7=
Electrical engineer	65	9
High school teacher	64	10=
Pharmacist	64	10=
Minister of religion	60	12
Surveyor	58	13
Primary school teacher	57	14
Social worker	56	15
Nurse	54	16
Actor	52	17
Preprimary school teacher	49	18=
Real estate agent	49	18=
Police officer	40	20

Source: Derived from Treiman (1977)

high degree of correlation between occupational hierarchies despite variations in geographical location, stage of economic development, and point in time at which the study was undertaken. The most detailed analysis of these studies was carried out by Treiman (1977) who reviewed 85 studies carried out in 53 countries. The median correlation across studies was 0.81. Although the correlation is high, some studies show considerable variation by country, by region, and by characteristics of respondents.

He converted these findings into a single scale: the Standard International Occupational Prestige Score (SIOPS). Table 1 locates several teaching categories on the SIOPS continuum.

Data on the occupational prestige of teaching using SIOPS and other scales permit the following generalizations:

(a) Teaching is high in the range of all occupations.

(b) Teaching is relatively high within the group of public and personal service professions (e.g., nursing, social work, and police).

(c) Teaching is higher than that of skilled manual and white-collar occupations.

(d) Teaching is lower than that of the major professions, (e.g., medicine, law, and architecture).

Within the teaching profession as a whole:

(a) Principals are ranked more highly than classroom teachers.

(b) The rank order of teachers from high to low is: college, secondary school, elementary school, infant, and preschool (Bernbaum et al. 1969).

Variations in occupational prestige ratings require explanations in terms of cultural differences, whereas more general explanations are required in order to account for the relative consistency of the occupational prestige ratings over time and location. Three explanations are offered below, although they are not necessarily independent of one another.

3. The Social Functions of Teaching

The general form of this explanation is that occupational prestige is a reflection of the importance of the contribution to the well-being of society. This explanation is often termed the "functionalist" position. Treiman (1977), who uses the term "structuralist" for the same perspective, wrote that "the relative prestige of the social roles known as occupations is essentially invariant in all complex societies and that this must be so as a consequence of the inherent features of the division of labor as it exists in all societies" (p. 2). The implication is that those who fulfill key functions have knowledge, skill, power, privilege, and prestige.

There are, however, a number of arguments against this position. One alternative view is that the high prestige enjoyed by the professions owes more to their success in creating a market for a scarce resource and using the power thereby achieved to limit entry (Larson 1977) (See also *Teachers as Professionals*). Of course, the high correlations in prestige over time and location behove critics of the structural functionalist position to explain the consistency in the historical emergence of professional power.

The position of teaching below the major professions in the prestige hierarchy requires a critical look at the functionalist argument. There can be little doubt that education is a crucial social function in developed and developing societies. Teaching provides the transmission of the knowledge and skills required to sustain and enhance the quality of life in such societies. On this view, the functionalist argument appears less cogent than the argument that teaching has been unable to generate the power enjoyed by the major professions. There are two related reasons why this lack of power exists: the social characteristics of teachers, and the inherent nature of teaching as a professional activity.

4. The Social Characteristics of Teaching

A major barrier to enhanced status stems from the fact that teaching is by far the largest profession. Because the profession is so large, the total salary bill is high and thus individual salaries are depressed below those obtained in other professions. Moreover, because large numbers of teachers have constantly to be recruited, the status-bestowing characteristics of those recruited tend to be lower than those recruited to the major professions. The most important of these characteristics are social class background, gender, and academic achievement.

4.1 Social Class Background

The social class background of teachers is, on average, lower than that of entrants to the major professions and it is argued that this lower class background has a deleterious influence on status. However, apart from this broad generalization, reliable statements about the social class backgrounds of teachers are difficult to make, particularly as they have changed over time. Relatively few studies exist and they have mostly been undertaken in advanced societies. Moreover, relatively few studies (see Betz and Garland 1974 for an exception) take account of changes in the occupational structure over time. In industrialized societies, for example, there has been a shift from skilled craft occupations to technical service and quasiprofessional occupations.

As a very broad generalization relating to developed countries, one could say that teachers are recruited from the full range of social classes but with an underrepresentation from the highest and lowest social groups and with the modal background of all teachers increasing over time. Furthermore, women teachers come from a slightly higher social class background than men, and teachers in secondary schools come from a slightly higher social class background than those in elementary schools. These last two generalizations would at first seem to be incompatible since elementary schools tend to contain the highest proportion of women. Where detailed data exist, however, they show that the anomaly can be explained by the fact that the higher proportion of women in primary schools is offset by the considerably higher social class origins of both men and women in secondary schools.

Available data would indicate that there has been an increase in the social class background of teachers since the 1940s (Havighurst and Levine 1979, Bassett 1958, 1971). In Britain before the Second World War, for example, there were differences in social class backgrounds of teachers in the elementary schools and those in the highly selective secondary schools. However, in the postwar period, with the creation of secondary education for all, there was a degree of convergence between the social class background of teachers in the increasingly integrated system (Floud and Scott 1961). This trend has continued with the comprehensivization of secondary education.

4.2 Gender

The factor of gender functions relatively independently of social class background in the determination of the occupational prestige of teaching. There is a view that the relatively high proportion of women in teaching is detrimental to its social status because of the patriarchal attitudes which persist in many societies. However, whether or not this view is correct is difficult to demonstrate. One can only note that professions with a relatively low proportion of women (e.g., medicine and law) enjoy a higher occupational prestige than those with a relatively high proportion (e.g., teaching, nursing, and social work).

Because women tend to predominate in teaching in all societies one cannot deploy comparative data to test the proposition. One can note, however, that medicine enjoys a higher social status in the West than in the former Soviet Union where women predominate in the medical profession. As noted above, the prestige of primary school teachers, who are predominantly women, is lower than that for secondary school teachers, who are predominantly men. However, the relationship between gender and prestige is quite complex, involving both cultural and economic factors.

4.3 Academic Achievement

The academic achievements of teachers at all school levels is considerably higher than population averages. Nevertheless, the academic achievements of those who enter teaching is generally lower than those who enter the major professions. In the United Kingdom, for example, those entering Bachelor of Education (BEd) courses in colleges of education and polytechnics have lower school attainments than those entering BA and BS courses in universities. Furthermore, those who enter the one-year teacher training course in universities following their BA and BS degrees tend to have lower achievements (and come from slightly lower social class backgrounds) than those who enter other occupations (see Committee on Higher Education 1963).

5. The Nature of Teaching as an Activity

Class, gender, and academic achievement have been selected to indicate the characteristics of teachers which may help to determine their social status. However, although the data indicate social differences between those who enter teaching and those who enter other professions, these differences are not great and are perhaps diminishing. Moreover, as presented, the data imply a deficit model based on market forces and opportunity. Other determinants of teacher status are perhaps to be found in the nature of teaching as an occupational activity and the contexts in which teaching takes place.

Three factors inherent in teaching as an activity

are related to the status of teaching. These factors are reviewed from the perspective of the lower standing of teaching vis-à-vis that of the major professions.

5.1 Knowledge and Skill

The knowledge and skills needed by teachers are regarded as being of a lower order than those required in the major professions. In this regard it is important to recognize that higher status generally is associated with specialization. This factor may account for the higher status of secondary school teachers relative to elementary and early childhood teachers. Furthermore, the uncertain relationship between educational and pedagogic theory, pedagogic practice, and learning outcomes detracts from its capacity to enhance its status.

5.2 Work Situation

The sustained relationship between teachers and pupils in an organized setting differs from the relatively infrequent contact which most professionals have with their clients in organizational settings or consultancy contexts. Thus, the work situation in which teachers find themselves may militate against the improved status of teaching.

5.3 Clients

Perhaps the most fundamental factor influencing the lower status of teaching vis-à-vis other professions is that teachers' immediate clients are children. In addition, virtually the entire adult population has had a sustained and direct experience of teachers at work. Thus, virtually everyone, to some extent, "accomplishes" schooling and leaves it behind as they leave behind their teachers. As Hoyle (1969) has noted, teachers are thus placed in an intermediate status on a number of dimensions: childhood–adulthood ("A man amongst boys and a boy amongst men"), school–work ("Those who can, do, those who can't, teach"), moral idealism–moral realism (The school as "a museum of virtue," Waller 1965), the dissemination of knowledge–the creation of knowledge (The teacher as one who "spreads other people's butter," Geer 1966).

The fact that all have had the experience of schooling robs teaching of any status-enhancing mystique. Moreover, all have seen teachers constantly seeking to maintain control, a problem which is exacerbated where older pupils are in compulsory and often reluctant attendance. This image is powerful and does not apply to other major professions or "semi-professions" where client control is rarely an issue.

6. Conclusion

The occupational prestige of teachers lies in the upper reaches of all scales. The social background of teachers tends to be clustered around the center, suggesting that teaching represents upward social mobility, to some degree, for many. Teachers' educational qualifications are in the upper reaches of the distribution, as is their remuneration. Insofar as teacher status is regarded as "low," this statement can be made only in comparison with the major professions. In this regard there would seem to be limits to the degree to which teachers might enhance their status. These limits stem ultimately from the size of the profession and images of teachers and their work. Despite the high correlations between teachers' prestige ratings across countries, however, there are intercountry variations to indicate that the status of teaching is not wholly immutable.

See also: Teachers' Work and Political Action

References

Bassett G W, 1958 The occupational background of teachers. *Australian Journal of Education*. 2: 79–90
Bassett G W 1971 The occupational background of teachers: Some recent data. *Australian Journal of Education*. 15: 211–14
Bernbaum G, Noble G, Whiteside T 1969 Intra occupational prestige differentiation in teaching. *Paedag. Eur*. 5: 1–59
Betz M, Garland J 1974 Intergenerational mobility rates of urban school teachers. *Soc. Educ*. 47: 511–22
Committee on Higher Education 1963 *Administrative, Financial and Economic Aspects of Higher Education* (Robbins Report), Appendix 2B. HMSO, London
Counts F A 1925 The social status of occupations. *Sch. Rev*. 33: 20–21
Coxon A P M, Jones C L 1978 *The Images of Occupational Prestige*. Macmillan, London
Coxon A P M, Jones C L 1979 *Class and Hierarchy: The Social Meaning of Occupations*. Macmillan, London
Floud J, Scott W 1961 Recruitment to teaching in England and Wales. In: Halsey A H, Floud J, Anderson C A (eds.) 1961 *Education, Economy and Society: A Reader in the Sociology of Education*. Free Press, New York
Geer, B 1966 Occupational commitment and the teaching profession. *Sch. Rev*. 77(1): 31–47
Havighurst R J, Levine D U 1979 *Society and Education*, 5th edn. Allyn and Bacon, Boston, Massachusetts
Hodge R W, Treiman D J, Rossi P 1966 A comparative study of occupational prestige. In: Bendix R, Lipset S M (eds.) 1966 *Class, Status and Power: Social Stratification in Comparative Perspective*, 2nd edn. Free Press, New York
Hoyle E 1969 *The Role of the Teacher*. Routledge, London
Larson M 1977 *The Rise of Professionalism*. University of California Press, Berkeley, California
Treiman D J 1977 *Occupational Prestige in Comparative Perspective*. Academic Press, New York
Waller W 1965 *The Sociology of Teaching*. Wiley, New York

E. Hoyle

Teaching, Student Evaluation of

Students' evaluations of teaching effectiveness (SETs) are commonly collected in United States and Canadian universities, are widely endorsed by teachers, students, and administrators, and have stimulated thousands of studies. Considered here are the purposes for collecting SETs, SET dimensions, issues of reliability, validity and generalizability, potential biases in SETs, and the use of SETs for improving teaching effectiveness. (For earlier reviews see Marsh 1987, Marsh and Dunkin 1992.)

1. *Purposes for Collecting SETs*

Various SETs are collected to provide: (a) diagnostic feedback to faculty for the improvement of teaching; (b) a measure of teaching effectiveness for personnel decisions; (c) information for students for the selection of courses and instructors; (d) an outcome or a process description for research on teaching. The first purpose is nearly universal, but the next three are not. At many universities, systematic student input is required before faculty are even considered for promotion; at others the inclusion of SETs is optional or not encouraged at all. The results of SETs are sold to students in some university bookstores as an aid to the selection of courses or instructors, whereas at other universities the results are considered to be strictly confidential. Surprisingly, SET research has not been systematically incorporated into broader studies of teaching and learning (see Marsh and Dunkin 1992).

Table 1
Categories of effective teaching[a]

Feldman's categories	SEEQ factors
1) Stimulation of interest	Instructor enthusiasm
2) Enthusiasm	Instructor enthusiasm
3) Subject knowledge	Breadth of coverage
4) Intellectual expansiveness	Breadth of coverage
5) Preparation and organization	Organization/clarity
6) Clarity and understandableness	Organization/clarity
7) Elocutionary skills	None
8) Sensitivity to class progress	None
9) Clarity of objectives	Organization/clarity
10) Value of course materials	Assignments/ readings
11) Supplementary materials	Assignments/ readings
12) Perceived outcome/impact	Learning/value
13) Fairness, impartiality	Examinations/ grading
14) Classroom management	None
15) Feedback to students	Examinations/ grading
16) Class discussion	Group interaction
17) Intellectual challenge	Learning/value
18) Respect for students	Individual rapport
19) Availability/helpfulness	Individual rapport
20) Difficulty/workload	Workload/difficulty

a Adapted From Feldman (1976) and the Students' Evaluations of Educational Quality (SEEQ) and endeavor factors most closely related to each category

2. *Dimensions of SETs*

Because effective teaching is a multidimensional construct (e.g., a teacher may be organized but lack enthusiasm), it is not surprising that SETs are also multidimensional (Marsh 1987, Marsh and Dunkin 1992). Information from SETs depends upon the content of the items. Poorly worded or inappropriate items will not provide useful information. If a survey instrument contains an ill-defined mix of items and SETs are summarized by an average of these items, then there is no basis for knowing what is being measured. Careful attention should be given to the components of teaching effectiveness that are to be measured.

Marsh and Dunkin (1992) noted three overlapping approaches to constructing and evaluating multidimensional SET instruments: (a) empirical approaches such as factor analysis and multitrait–multimethod analysis; (b) logical analyses of the content of effective teaching and the purposes the ratings are intended to serve, supplemented by reviews of previous research and feedback from students and instructors; and (c) a theory of teaching and learning. In practice, most instruments are based on the first two approaches—particularly the second. The literature on SETs contains examples of instruments that have a well-defined factor structure, such as the four instruments presented by Marsh (1987). Factor analyses have identified the factors that each of these instruments is intended to measure, demonstrating that SETs do measure distinct components of teaching effectiveness. The systematic approach used in developing these instruments, and the similarity of the factors they measure, support their construct validity.

The strongest support for the multidimensionality of SETs comes from research based on the nine-factor SEEQ (Students' Evaluations of Educational Quality) instrument (Marsh 1987). The SEEQ factors are: learning/value; instructor enthusiasm; organization/clarity; group interaction; individual rapport; breadth of coverage; examinations/grading; assignments/readings; and workload/difficulty. Developers of the SEEQ relied on four sources of information. First, a large item pool was obtained from a literature review, forms in current usage, and interviews with faculty and students about what they saw as effective teaching. Second, students and faculty were asked to rate the importance of items. Third, faculty were asked to judge the potential usefulness of the items as a basis for feedback. Finally, open-ended student comments were examined to determine if important aspects had been excluded. These criteria, along with psychometric properties, were used to select items and revise subsequent versions, thus supporting the content validity of SEEQ responses. (The SEEQ scales are summarized in Table 1.) Marsh and Dunkin (1992) also demonstrated that the content of SEEQ factors is consistent with general principles of teaching and learning.

Factor analytic support for the SEEQ scales is particularly strong. Marsh and Hocevar (1991b), starting with an archive of 50,000 sets of class-average ratings (reflecting responses to 1 million SEEQ surveys), defined 21 groups of classes that differed in terms of course level (undergraduate/graduate), instructor rank (teaching assistant/regular faculty), and academic discipline. The nine *a priori* SEEQ factors were identifiable in each of 21 separate factor analyses. The average correlation between factor scores based on each separate analysis and factor scores based on the total sample was over 0.99. In other research, instructors evaluated their own teaching effectiveness on the same SEEQ form as completed by their students; factor analyses of their self-evaluations also identified the nine SEEQ factors (see Marsh 1987 p. 295). Six studies conducted in Australia, New Zealand, Spain, and Papua New Guinea (see Marsh and Dunkin 1992) provided support for the applicability of SEEQ factors outside the North American context in which they were developed.

Feldman (1976) logically derived the components of effective teaching by categorizing the characteristics of the superior teacher from the student's point of view. He reviewed research that either asked students to specify these characteristics or inferred them on the basis of correlations with global SETs. In a content analysis of factors identified in well-defined multidimensional SET instruments, Marsh (1987) demonstrated that Feldman's categories tended to be more narrowly defined constructs than the empirical factors. Whereas SEEQ provided a more comprehensive coverage of Feldman's categories than other SET instruments considered, most SEEQ factors represented more than one of Feldman's categories (e.g., Feldman's categories "stimulation of interest" and "enthusiasm" were both included in the SEEQ "instructor enthusiasm" factor).

In summary, the debate about which specific components of teaching effectiveness can and should be measured has not been resolved. At the same time, however, there seems to be consistency in those components that are identified in responses to the most carefully designed instruments such as SEEQ. Such instruments, apparently, are applicable to a wide variety of educational settings.

3. Reliability, Stability, and Generalizability

Careful design is an important element of a sound, useful instrument for measuring SETs. The reliability, stability, and generalizability of the responses made to the instrument by students also form a critical element.

3.1 Reliability

The reliability of SETs is most appropriately determined from studies that assess the error caused by lack of agreement among different students enrolled in the same course (see Gilmore et al. 1978 for further discussion). The correlation between responses made by any two students in the same class (i.e., the single rater reliability) is typically in the 0.20s. However, the reliability of the class-average response depends upon the number of students rating the class: 0.95 for 50 students, 0.90 for 25 students, 0.74 for 10 students, and 0.60 for five students. Given a sufficient number of students, then, the reliability of class-average SETs compares favorably with that of the most objective tests (Marsh 1987).

3.2 Stability

Cross-sectional studies typically report that SETs are negatively related to age and years of teaching experience (Feldman 1983). This effect may vary somewhat with the particular SETs dimension and there is some suggestion that SETs may increase slightly during the first few years of teaching. Cross-sectional studies, however, provide a poor basis for inferring how ratings of the same person will change over time. In a longitudinal study, Marsh and Hocevar (1991a) examined changes in ratings of a diverse sample of 195 teachers who had been evaluated continuously over a 13-year period. They found that the mean ratings for this sample showed almost no systematic changes in any of the SEEQ factors. This result held for teachers with little, intermediate, or substantial amounts of teaching experience.

3.3 Generalizability

Some critics have suggested that students cannot recognize effective teaching until they have been called upon to apply what they have learned in further coursework or after graduation. However, cross-sectional studies show good agreement between responses by current students and alumni (see Marsh 1987, Centra 1979). For example, in a longitudinal study (Marsh 1987) ratings in 100 classes correlated 0.83 with ratings by the same students when they again evaluated the same classes retrospectively several years later.

Researchers have also asked how highly correlated SETs are in different courses taught by the same instructor or in the same course taught by different teachers. The results demonstrate that the results of SETs are primarily due to the instructor who teaches a class and not the particular class being taught. For example, Marsh (1987) reported that for the overall instructor rating, the correlation between ratings of different instructors teaching the same course was virtually zero (−0.05), while correlations for the same instructor in different courses (0.61) and in two different offerings of the same course (0.72) were much larger. These results support the validity of SETs as a measure of teacher effectiveness, but not as a measure of course effectiveness independent of the teacher.

Gilmore et al. (1978), applying generalizability theory to SETs, suggested that ratings for a given instructor should be averaged across different courses to enhance generalizability. If it is likely that an instructor will teach many different classes during his or her subsequent career, then tenure decisions should be based upon as many different courses as possible—Gilmore et al. suggest at least five. These recommendations require that a longitudinal archive of SETs is maintained for personnel decisions. These data would provide the basis for more generalizable summaries, the assessment of changes over time, and the determination of which particular courses are best taught by a specific instructor. It is indeed unfortunate that some universities systematically collect SETs but then fail to keep a longitudinal archive of the results.

3.4 Generalizability of Profiles

Marsh and Bailey (1993) used profile analysis to demonstrate that each teacher has a characteristic profile on the nine SEEQ scores (e.g., consistently high on organization and consistently low on enthusiasm). For each teacher who had been evaluated continuously over a 13-year period a characteristic profile of SEEQ scores was determined by averaging across all his or her ratings. Each instructor's characteristic profile was distinct from the profiles of other instructors, generalized across course offerings over the 13-year period, and generalized across undergraduate- and graduate-level courses. This support for the existence of instructor-specific profiles has important implications for the use of SETs as feedback and for the relation of SETs to other criteria such as student learning. The results also provide further support for the multidimensionality of SETs and their generalizability.

4. Validity

Once the development of the instrument and the reliability of the responses have been examined, attention must turn next to the validity of the responses. There are several ways of investigating and estimating validity.

4.1 The Construct Validation Approach

SETs, as one measure of teaching effectiveness, are difficult to validate since no single criterion of effective teaching is sufficient. Historically, researchers have emphasized a narrow, criterion-related approach to validity in which student learning is the only criterion of effective teaching. This limited framework, however, inhibits a better understanding of what is being measured by SETs, what can be inferred from SETs, and how findings from diverse studies can be understood within a common framework. Instead, Marsh (1987) advocated a construct validation approach in which SETs are posited to be positively related to a wide variety of other indicators of effective teaching. In this approach, specific rating factors are hypothesized to be most highly correlated with variables to which they are most logically and theoretically related. Within this framework, evidence for the long-term stability of SETs, the generalizability of ratings of the same instructor in different courses, and the agreement in ratings of current students and alumni can be interpreted as support for the validity of SETs.

Whereas the most widely accepted criterion of effective teaching is student learning, other criteria include changes in student behaviors, instructor self-evaluations, ratings by colleagues and administrators, the frequency of occurrence of specific behaviors observed by trained observers, and the effects of experimental manipulations. A construct validity approach to the study of SETs now appears to be widely accepted (e.g., Cashin 1988, Howard et al. 1985). A difficulty in this approach is obtaining criterion measures that are reliably measured and validly reflect effective teaching. Generally, criterion measures that lack reliability or validity should not be used as indicators of effective teaching for research, policy formation, feedback to faculty, or personnel decisions.

4.2 The Multisection Validity Study

Student learning inferred from standardized examinations typically cannot be compared across different courses. In the multisection validity paradigm, such a comparison may be possible. An ideal study within this paradigm should include the following characteristics: (a) there should be many sections within a large multisection course; (b) students should be randomly assigned to sections so as to minimize initial differences between sections; (c) there should be pretest measures that correlate substantially with final course performance to serve as covariates;(d) each section should be taught completely by a separate instructor; (e) each section should have the same course outline, textbooks, course objectives, and final examination; (f) the final examination should be constructed to reflect common objectives and, if there is a subjective component, it should be graded by an external person; (g) students in each section should evaluate teaching effectiveness on a standardized evaluation instrument, preferably before they know their final course grade and without knowing how performances in their section compare with those of students in other sections; and (h) section-average SETs should be related to section-average examination performance, after controlling for pretest measures.

Despite methodological problems (Abrami et al. 1990, Marsh and Dunkin 1992), meta-analyses of multisection validity research have supported the validity of the SETs by demonstrating that the sections that evaluate the teaching as most effective near the end of the course are also the sections that perform best on standardized final examinations. Cohen (1987), in his summary of 41 "well-designed" studies, reported that the mean correlations between achievement and different SET components were structure (0.55), interaction (0.52), skill (0.50), overall course (0.49), overall instructor (0.45), learning (0.39), rapport (0.32), evaluation (0.30), feedback (0.28), interest/motivation (0.15), and difficulty (−0.04), in which all but the last two were statistically significant. Feldman (1989b) extended this research by demonstrating that many of Cohen's broad categories were made up of more specific components of SETs that are differentially related to student achievement. Thus, for example, Cohen's broad "skill" category was represented by three dimensions in Feldman's analysis that correlated with achievement 0.34 (instructor subject knowledge), 0.56 (clarity and intelligibility), and 0.30 (sensitivity to class level and progress). Cohen (1987) also reported that correlations were higher when specific SET components were measured with multi-item scales instead of single items.

4.3 Multiple Evaluators

Teaching effectiveness can be evaluated by current students, former students, the instructor himself or herself, colleagues, administrators, or trained external observers. Instructors can be asked to evaluate themselves in a wide variety of educational settings, even using the same instrument used by their students to provide tests of convergent and divergent validity. Despite the apparent appeal of instructor self-evaluation as a criterion of effective teaching, it has had limited application. Feldman's (1989) meta-analysis of correlations between SETs and self-evaluations, based on only 19 studies, reported a mean correlation of 0.29 for overall ratings and mean correlations ranging from 0.15 to 0.42 for specific SET components. Marsh apparently conducted the only two studies in which large numbers of instructors (81 and 329) were asked to evaluate their own teaching on the same multifaceted evaluation instrument that was completed by students (see Marsh 1987 p. 295). In both studies: (a) separate factor analyses of SETs and self-evaluations identified the same SEEQ factors (see Table 1); (b) student–teacher agreement on every dimension was significant (median correlations of 0.49 and 0.45) and typically larger than agreement on overall teaching effectiveness (correlations of 0.32); (c) mean differences between student and faculty responses were small and unsystematic; and (d) multitrait–multimethod analyses provided support for both convergent and discriminant validity of the ratings.

Colleague and administrator ratings not based upon classroom visitation have been sometimes substantially correlated with SETs, but it is likely that peer ratings are based on information from students (Marsh 1987, Marsh and Dunkin 1992). In contrast, colleague and administrator ratings based on classroom visitation do not appear to be very reliable (i.e., ratings by different peers do not even agree with each other) or to correlate substantially with SETs or with any other indicator of effective teaching (see Marsh 1987, Centra 1979). While these findings neither support nor refute the validity of SETs, they suggest that the colleague and administrator ratings based on classroom visitation are not valid indicators of teacher effectiveness (see also Murray 1980).

Murray (1980) concluded that SETs outcomes "can be accurately predicted from external observer reports of specific classroom teaching behaviors" (p. 31). For example, Cranton and Hillgartner (1981) examined relationships between SETs and specific teaching behaviors observed on videotaped lectures in a naturalistic setting. They found that (a) SETs reports on effectiveness of discussion were higher "when professors praised student behavior, asked questions and clarified or elaborated student responses"; and that (b) SETs outcomes on organization were higher "when instructors spent time structuring classes and explaining relationships" (p. 73).

In one of the most ambitious observation studies, Murray (1983) trained observers to estimate the frequency of occurrence of specific teaching behaviors of 54 university instructors who had previously obtained high, medium, or low SETs in other classes. A total of 18 to 24 sets of observer reports were collected for each instructor. The median of single-rater reliabilities (i.e., the correlation between two sets of observational reports) was 0.32, but the median reliability for the average response across the 18–24 reports for each instructor was 0.77. Factor analysis of the observations revealed nine factors, and their content resembled factors in SETs described earlier (e.g., clarity, enthusiasm, interaction, rapport, organization). The observations significantly differentiated among the three criterion groups of instructors.

Unfortunately, Murray only considered SETs on an overall instructor rating item, and these were based upon ratings from a previous course rather than the one that was observed. Hence, multitrait–multimethod analyses could not be used to determine if specific observational factors were most highly correlated with matching student-rating factors. The findings did show, however, that instructors who are rated differently by students do exhibit systematically different observable teaching behaviors.

Howard et al. (1985) compared multiple indicators of teaching effectiveness for 43 teachers who were each evaluated in one course by current students in the course (mean N = 34 per class), former students who had previously taken the same course or one selected by the instructor as being similar (minimum N = 5), one colleague who was knowledgeable of the course content and who attended two class sessions, and eight advanced graduate students specifically trained in judging teaching effectiveness who attended two class sessions. They concluded that "former-students and student ratings evidence substantially greater validity coefficients of teaching effectiveness than do self-report, colleague and trained observer ratings" (p. 195). Whereas self-evaluations were modestly correlated with current SETs (0.34) and former SETs (0.31), colleague and observer ratings were not significantly correlated with each other, current SETs, or self-evaluations (see also Feldman 1989a and the discussion of his review by Marsh and Dunkin 1992).

4.4 Other Criteria

A limited amount of research has related SETs to experimentally manipulated teaching situations. Studies of teacher clarity and teacher expressiveness (see reviews by Marsh 1987, Marsh and Dunkin 1992) demonstrated the important potential of this approach. Both of these variables are amenable to experimental and correlational designs, can be reliably judged by students and by external observers, are judged to be important components of teaching effectiveness by students and by teachers, and are related to student achievement in naturalistic and experimental studies. In experimental settings, scripted lessons which differ on these variables are videotaped and randomly assigned groups of subjects view different lectures, evaluate teaching effectiveness, and complete achievement tests. Manipulations of these variables are significantly related to SETs; specifically, they are more strongly related to matching SETs dimensions than to nonmatching SETs dimensions. These results support the inclusion of clarity and expressiveness on SETs instruments, demonstrate that SETs are sensitive to natural and experimentally manipulated differences in these variables, and support the construct validity of the multidimensional SETs.

Teaching and research are typically seen as the most important products of university faculty. Marsh (1987) contrasted opposing theoretical perspectives positing that indicators of the two activities should be positively correlated, negatively correlated, or uncorrelated. Research (see Centra 1983, Feldman 1987, Marsh 1987) suggests that there is a zero to low-positive correlation between measures of research productivity and SETs or other indicators of effective teaching, although correlations may be somewhat higher for student-rating dimensions that are most logically related to research effectiveness. While these findings seem neither to support nor refute the validity of SETs, they do demonstrate that measures of research productivity cannot be used to infer teaching effectiveness or vice versa.

Marsh (1987) also discusses the validity of SETs in relation to student motivation, affective criteria, subsequent coursework selection, student study strategies, and the quality of student learning. More generally, he argued that it is imperative to expand substantially the range of validity criteria used in SETs research (see also Marsh and Dunkin 1992).

4.5 Implications of Validity Research

Because effective teaching is a hypothetical construct for which there is no adequate single indicator, the validity of SETs or of any other measure of effective teaching must be demonstrated through a construct validation approach. SETs are significantly and consistently related to the ratings of former students, student achievement in multisection validity studies, faculty self-evaluations of their own teaching effectiveness, and, perhaps, the observations of trained observers on specific processes such as teacher clarity. In contrast, colleague and administrator ratings based on classroom visitation, and research productivity are not systematically related to SETs or other indicators of effective teaching, calling into question colleague and administrator ratings as measures of effective teaching.

5. Potential Biases in Students' Evaluations

To the extent that SETs are biased, it is important to understand the nature of the biases and how they can be controlled. However, the voluminous study of potential biases to SETs is frequently atheoretical, methodologically flawed, and not based on a well-articulated definition of what constitutes a bias. Marsh (1987) reviewed several large-scale studies of the multivariate relationship between a comprehensive set of background characteristics and SETs. Depending upon the content of the SET items, between 5 and 25 percent of the variance in SETs could be explained by the background characteristics, perhaps the academic discipline, and perhaps the institution(s) where the study was conducted (see also Centra 1979).

In two comprehensive multivariate studies (see Marsh 1987), a set of 16 background characteristics explained about 13 percent of the variance in the set of SEEQ dimensions. However, the amount of variance explained varied from more than 20 percent in the overall course rating and the learning value dimension, to about 2 percent of the organization and individual rapport dimensions. Four background variables were most important and could account for most of the explained variance. They were higher prior subject interest, higher expected grades, higher levels of workload/difficulty, and a higher percentage of students taking the course for general interest only. Path analyses demonstrated that prior subject interest had the strongest impact on SETs, and that this variable also accounted for about one-third of the relationship between expected grades and SETs.

Even these relatively modest relations, however, apparently do not reflect biases. The workload/difficulty relation is in the opposite direction to that predicted by a bias. Prior subject interest primarily influences ratings of learning/value and overall course ratings; a similar pattern of relations was found with instructor self-evaluations of their own teaching effectiveness. Part of the expected grade relation is apparently spurious and is eliminated when prior subject interest is controlled. Furthermore, part of this relation apparently reflects a positive relation between student learning and SETs (see Marsh 1987, Marsh and Dunkin 1992).

Support for a bias hypothesis, as with the study of validity, must be based on a construct approach such as that proposed by Marsh and Dunkin (1992). If a particular background variable has a similar influence on multiple indicators of teaching effectiveness, then that background variable may reflect a valid influence on teaching effectiveness. Similarly, if the pattern of relations between a particular background variable and the multiple dimensions of SETs match *a priori* predictions, then the results may support the construct validity of the SETs instead of a bias.

For example, the SEEQ factors most logically related to class size are group interaction and individual rapport. Empirical results indicate that class size is moderately correlated with these two SEEQ factors and nearly uncorrelated with other SEEQ factors. A similar pattern is observed in instructor self-evaluations. These results suggest that class size actually does affect group interaction and individual rapport in a manner that is accurately reflected in SETs and instructor self-evaluations. Whereas a comprehensive review of potential biases is beyond the scope of this entry, perhaps the best summary of this area is McKeachie's (1979) conclusion that a wide variety of variables that could potentially influence SETs apparently has little effect.

6. *Utility of Student Ratings*

Using a series of related logical arguments, Braskamp et al. (1985), Marsh (1987), Marsh and Dunkin (1992), Murray (1987), and many others have argued that the introduction of a broad institutionally based, carefully planned program of SETs is likely to lead to the improvement of teaching. In support of his argument, Murray's (1987) summary of surveys from seven universities indicated that about two-thirds of faculty staff said that SETs were useful and about 80 percent indicated that SETs led to improved teaching.

None of these observations, however, provides an empirical demonstration of improvement of teaching effectiveness resulting from SETs. In most studies of the effects of feedback from SETs, teachers have been randomly assigned to experimental (feedback) or one or more control groups; SETs have been collected during the term; ratings of the feedback teachers have been returned to instructors as quickly as possible; and the various groups have been compared at the end of the term according to a second administration of SETs and sometimes on other variables as well. In his classic meta-analysis, Cohen (1980) found that instructors who received midterm feedback were subsequently rated about one-third of a standard deviation higher than controls on the total rating (an overall rating item or the average of multiple items), and even larger differences were observed for ratings of instructor skill, attitude toward subject, and feedback to students. Studies that augmented feedback with consultation produced substantially larger differences, but other methodological variations had little effect (see also L'Hommedieu et al. 1990).

The most robust finding from the feedback research reviewed here is that consultation augments the effects of written summaries of SETs, but insufficient attention has been given to determine the type of consultative feedback that is most effective.

7. *Research in Primary and Secondary Classrooms*

This entry is based almost exclusively on research at tertiary level. Despite the voluminous research on teacher effectiveness at the primary and secondary levels, there is a dearth of appropriate SETs research—with a few notable exceptions. Whereas it is tempting to conclude that secondary and particularly primary students apparently lack the sophistication to evaluate teaching effectiveness appropriately, the results from several research programs suggest that this conclusion is false.

Aubrecht et al. (1986) specifically patterned their research on Marsh's university research to determine whether the findings generalized to the high school level. High school teachers and their students completed the commercially available high school version of the IDEA instrument. Factor analyses of both sets of responses revealed similar factor structures and MTMM analyses provided support for convergent and discriminant validity. Aubrecht et al. (1986) concluded that these results "provide support for the validity of high school student ratings of instruction" (p. 223) and predicted that SETs will find a place in high school merit pay systems and professional development activities as they have at university level.

Similarly, Fox et al. (1983) sought to test the generalizability of university findings to the elementary school level. For two consecutive years, 53 sixth-grade teachers were evaluated by their students and observed by different trained observers on multiple occasions. The class-average SETs were stable over the two years ($r=0.68$) and significantly related to each of the three observation scales (organized, stimulating, understanding) in each year of the study (with correlations ranging from 0.38 to 0.68). Noting the need for further research, Fox et al (1983) concluded that the SETs by sixth-grade students "appear to be reliable, valid, useful measures of teacher behavior" (p. 21) (see also Peck et al 1978).

There is clearly need for more research about SETs at the primary and secondary levels, but research programs summarized here suggest that results based on responses by university students may generalize to responses by younger students. Although not the focus of this entry, a provocative question is: why is there so much relevant SETs research at the tertiary level and so little at the primary and secondary levels?

8. Overview and Implications

Research described in this entry demonstrates that SETs are multidimensional, reliable, and stable, primarily a function of the instructor who teaches a course rather than the course that is taught, relatively valid against a variety of indicators of effective teaching, relatively unaffected by a variety of potential biases, and seen to be useful by faculty, students, and administrators. Researchers should adopt a construct validation approach in which the following points are recognized: that effective teaching and SETs designed to reflect teaching effectiveness are multidimensional; that no single criterion of effective teaching is sufficient; and that tentative interpretations of relations with validity criteria and with potential biases should be evaluated critically in different contexts and in relation to multiple criteria of effective teaching. In contrast to SETs, however, there are few other indicators of teaching effectiveness whose use is systematically supported by research findings. As Cashin noted (1988), "student ratings tend to be statistically reliable, valid, and relatively free from bias, probably more so than any other data used for faculty evaluation" (p. 5).

See also: Teacher Evaluation; Evaluation of Educational Personnel

References

Abrami P C, Cohen P A, d'Apollonia S 1990 Validity of student ratings of instruction: What we know and what we do not. *J. Educ. Psychol.* 82(2): 219–31

Aubrecht J D, Hanna G S, Hoyt D P 1986 A comparison of high school student ratings of teaching effectiveness with teacher self-ratings: Factor analytic and multitrait-multimethod analyses. *Educational and Psychological Measurement* 46(1): 223–31

Braskamp L A, Brandenburg D C, Ory J C 1985 *Evaluating Teaching Effectiveness: A Practical Guide*. Sage, Beverly Hills, California

Cashin W E 1988 Student ratings of teaching: A summary of research. IDEA paper No. 20, Kansas State University, Division of Continuing Education, Manhattan, Kansas ERIC Document Reproduction Service No. ED 302 567

Centra J A 1979 *Determining Faculty Effectiveness*. Jossey-Bass, San Francisco, California

Centra J A 1983 Research productivity and teaching effectiveness. *Res. Higher Educ.* 18(4): 379–89

Cohen P A 1980 Effectiveness of student-rating feedback for improving college instruction: A meta-analysis of findings. *Res. Higher Educ.* 13: 321–41

Cohen P A 1987 A critical analysis and reanalysis of the multisection validity meta-analysis. Paper presented at the 1987 Annual Meeting of the American Educational Research Association, Washington, DC (ERIC Document Reproduction Service No. ED 283 876)

Cranton P A, Hillgarten W 1981 The relationships between student ratings and instructor behavior: Implications for improving teaching. *Can. J. Higher Ed.* 9(1): 73–81

Feldman K A 1976 The superior college teacher from the student's view. *Res. Higher Educ.* 5(3): 243–88

Feldman K A 1983 The seniority and instructional experience of college teachers as related to the evaluations they receive from their students. *Res. Higher Educ.* 18: 3–124

Feldman K A 1987 Research productivity and scholarly accomplishment of college teachers as related to their instructional effectiveness: A review and exploration. *Res. Higher Educ.* 26: 227–98

Feldman K A 1989a Instructional effectiveness of college teachers as judged by teachers themselves, current and former students, colleagues, administrators, and external (neutral) observers. *Res. Higher Educ.* 30(2): 137–94

Feldman K A 1989b Association between student ratings of specific instructional dimensions and student achievement: Refining and extending the synthesis of data from multisection validity studies. *Res. Higher Educ.* 30(6): 583–645

Fox R, Peck R F, Blattstein A, Blattstein D 1983 Student evaluation of teacher as a measure of teacher behavior and teacher impact on students. *J. Educ. Res.* 77(1): 16–21

Gillmore G M, Kane M T, Naccarato R W 1978 The generalizability of student ratings of instruction: Estimates of teacher and course components. *J. Educ. Meas.* 15(1): 1–13

Howard G S, Conway C G, Maxwell S E 1985 Construct validity of measures of college teaching effectiveness. *J. Educ. Psychol.* 77(2): 187–96

L'Hommedieu R, Menges R J, Brinko K T 1990 Methodological explanations for the modest effects of feedback. *J. Educ. Psychol.* 82(2): 232–41

Marsh H W 1987 Students' evaluations of university teaching: Research findings, methodological issues, and directions for future research. *International Journal of Educational Research* 11(3): 253–388

Marsh H W, Bailey M 1993 Multidimensionality of students' evaluations of teaching effectiveness: A profile analysis. *J. Higher Educ* 64(1): 1–18

Marsh H W, Dunkin M J 1992 Students' evaluations of university teaching: A multidimensional perspective. In: Smart J (ed.) 1992 *Higher Education: Handbook of Theory and Research*. Agathon, New York

Marsh H W, Hocevar D 1991a Students' evaluations of teaching effectiveness: The stability of mean ratings of the same teachers over a thirteen-year period. *Teaching and Teacher Education* 7(4): 303–14

Marsh H W, Hocevar D 1991b The multidimensionality of students' evaluations of teaching effectiveness: The generality of factor structures across academic discipline,

instructor level, and course level. *Teaching and Teacher Education* 7(1): 9–18
McKeachie W J 1979 Student ratings of faculty: A reprise. *Academe* 65(6): 384–97
Murray H G 1980 *Evaluating University Teaching: A Review of Research*. Ontario Confederation of University Faculty Associations, Toronto
Murray H G 1983 Low inference classroom teaching behaviors and student ratings of college teaching effectiveness. *J. Educ. Psychol.* 71(1): 856–65
Murray H G 1987 Impact of student instructions ratings on quality of teaching in higher education. Paper presented at the 1987 Annual Meeting of the American Educational Research Association, Washington, DC. ERIC Document Reproduction Service No. ED 284 495
Peck R F, Olsson N G, Green J L The consistency of individual teaching behavior. Paper presented at the 1978 Annual Meeting of the American Educational Research Association, Toronto. ERIC Document Reproduction Service No. ED 189 058

H. W. Marsh

Teaching, Synthesizing Research on

Hundreds of studies of teaching are completed each year. Programs of international conferences abound with papers reporting research on teaching. Dozens of scholarly journals publish articles about research on teaching. Several entire handbooks containing thousands of pages have been devoted exclusively to research on teaching. What does all this research amount to? How do people charged with responsibility for making wise decisions about educational practice glean the best guidance from this great mass of research? How do researchers themselves reach conclusions about what has or has not been established about teaching by the mountain of research that has been reported during the twentieth century? These are the questions which those who attempt to synthesize research on teaching address. During the 1970s, 1980s, and 1990s the synthesis of research on teaching has itself become an important and controversial topic of research. Several different approaches are to be found in the literature, each with its own advocates, critics, strengths, and shortcomings.

1. The Importance of Synthesizing Research on Teaching

The findings of research on any one topic, whether in the "hard" physical sciences or the "soft" social sciences, almost always vary from one study to another. Sometimes results are obtained that support a given hypothesis, while on other occasions the results do not support it. Sometimes the support is strong while at other times it is weak. Sometimes the results of one study actually contradict the findings of another. The reasons for these variations are many.

The social or cultural context in which research is conducted may play a part in the results obtained. For example, in some cultures it is regarded as impolite for children to ask questions of adults such as teachers. It might be expected therefore that research would find that students ask questions in classrooms of that culture much less frequently than in another culture where the etiquette regarding questioning does not exist.

Results of testing a hypothesis or answering a question depend on conceptual and methodological variations in research. For example, teachers often ask rhetorical questions in the classroom. Researchers inquiring into the relationship between teacher questioning and student learning have the problem of deciding whether to count such questions. Their results will depend in part on the decision they make.

The researcher who wants to establish the state of the art in research on teacher questions or on any other aspect of teaching has to be aware of these types of variations and develop procedures for dealing with them in coming to general conclusions. Similarly, educational practitioners seeking guidance from research need to know how to take into account such influences on research results. Erroneous conclusions about the accumulated evidence of a body of research can have disastrous consequences when action based on those conclusions is taken. On the other hand, real progress in the form of significantly improved professional practice can be the consequence of appropriate conclusions emerging from the synthesis of research.

Giaconia and Hedges (1987) claimed that there are three aims of research syntheses, as follows: "(a) to summarize findings across studies; (b) to assess the consistency of findings across studies; and (c) to resolve contradictory findings across studies" (p. 124). Furthermore, they suggested that the "careful execution" of research syntheses is important for two main reasons:

> First, research on teaching effectiveness, as a field of inquiry that purports to have a scientific basis, has as one of its aims the cumulation of knowledge. As such, the field should maintain the same degree of rigor in the methods used to synthesize research studies (cumulate knowledge about a topic) that are required in executing the primary research studies that are to be synthesized. Second, the practical uses made of research syntheses suggest the importance of maintaining high standards in their execution . . . Thus valid ways of combining the evidence across the research studies and resolving the often conflicting findings are important in helping public policy makers arrive at the correct conclusions about the true effects of a treatment or the true degree of relationship between variables. (p. 124)

2. Methods of Research Synthesis

Giaconia and Hedges (1987) described four methods of research synthesis: narrative approaches, vote counting methods, combined significance test methods, and effect magnitude methods. To these must be added qualitative research syntheses discussed by Walberg (1986).

2.1 Narrative Approaches

Narrative approaches "consist of a verbal description of the research studies and particular topic, usually chronologically arranged, in terms of what the investigators of each study did and the results they found" (Giaconia and Hedges 1987 p. 128). Walberg (1986) referred to narrative syntheses as "reviews" as distinct from "research syntheses" since they seldom quantitatively analyze studies. Rather, they usually summarize and evaluate them one at a time. McGaw (1985) referred to narrative integration as "the traditional process" which he saw as "essentially intuitive" and lacking in specification of methods. He cited a case in which different reviewers used the same studies to support contradictory conclusions. To McGaw, the most difficult problem for the narrative approach is coping with the volume of relevant literature, leading often to selectivity on the basis of usually unspecified criteria of methodological quality. In spite of these shortcomings, Giaconia and Hedges saw the following advantages in narrative approaches: (a) "a richness of detail about study characteristics . . . that methods that rely heavily on the reported results" cannot provide; (b) a chronological arrangement of studies indicating evolution of aspects of knowledge about the topic; and (c) the ability to synthesize two or more different areas of research that may have an indirect relationship with each other.

Biddle and Anderson (1986) saw traditional reviews as providing the following advantages for the reader:

> a convenient source of references, a conceptual orientation to the field, a discussion of methodological strengths and weaknesses found in published studies, a summary of major findings and conundrums in the data, suggestions for building explanatory theory, and an invitation to explore primary sources for additional information . . . They may . . . help the neophyte to orient himself or herself to the field and warn readers of weaknesses in the research conducted to date." (p. 235)

However, there are deficiencies in narrative approaches, as Jackson (1980) found when he analyzed 87 review articles and found that few of them specified their procedures for identifying studies. Similar observations were made by Waxman and Walberg (1982) who analyzed 19 reviews of process—product research on teaching.

2.2 Vote Counting Methods

Vote counting methods, sometimes called "box-score" methods, "involve categorizing studies on the basis of the direction and statistical significance of the reported results" (p. 129). According to Light and Smith (1971), in vote counting methods:

> all studies which have data on a dependent variable and a specific independent variable of interest are examined. Three possible outcomes are defined. The relationship between the independent variable and the dependent variable is either significantly positive, significantly negative, or there is no significant relationship in either direction. The number of studies falling into each of these three categories is then simply tallied. If a plurality of studies falls into any one of these three categories, with fewer falling into the other two, the modal category is declared the winner. This modal categorization is then assumed to give the best estimate of the direction of the true relationship between the independent and dependent variable. (p. 433)

Giaconia and Hedges (1987) report that vote counting methods arose from the sheer number of studies conducted on particular topics. They saw advantages in speed and replicability of these methods but argued that they were weak in terms of reliability, and unable to indicate the size of treatment effects, resolve contradictory results, or assess the degree of consistency of findings. To McGaw (1985), vote counting methods give so much weight to results that are greatly influenced by sample size that "trivial findings from large studies will be counted as revealing an effect simply because they achieve statistical significance" (p. 3322). Furthermore, common interpretations of frequency counts could be misleading. On this point, Giaconia and Hedges conclude, "for sample sizes and effect magnitude [sic] that are typical of research on teaching effectiveness, as the number of studies to be combined increases, the probability that vote counting methods will detect a true treatment effect approaches zero!" (p. 131).

2.3 Combined Significance Test Models

Combined significance test models "involve combining either the probabilities (p-values) or common test of significance statistics . . . across several studies addressing the same research question and assessing the statistical significance of this overall value" (Giaconia and Hedges 1987 p. 132). These methods are described in detail by Rosenthal (1978), and include such procedures as adding logs, p's, t's, Z's, and weighted Z's, as well as testing mean p and mean Z. Combined significance test methods alleviate problems of small sample sizes in primary studies by pooling numbers of cases across studies, thereby increasing the likelihood that true treatment effects will be discovered. Giaconia and Hedges (1987) illustrated three of the methods. They also acknowledged that this approach conceals inconsistencies in findings across studies and does not indicate the magnitude of treatment effects or degree of relationships between variables.

2.4 Meta-analysis or Effect Magnitude Methods

The term "meta-analysis" was first used by Glass

(1976) to refer to syntheses of research that use quantitative and statistical approaches. Since then the term has been applied chiefly to methods that involve the calculation of effect magnitude, which Giaconia and Hedges (1987) define as "a standardized numerical index of the strength of the treatment effect or degree of relationship between variables that can be derived for individual studies or independent findings within studies" (p. 133). These indexes can then be combined across studies to produce an overall index of treatment effect or degree of relationship. The indices most commonly used are correlation coefficients and standardized mean differences (effect sizes).

The population values of these indexes have the advantage of being independent of sample size and of the variance of any particular test used to measure the dependent variable. Cohen (1969) offered the following guidelines for assessing the magnitude of the effect represented by the population value of the correlation coefficient:

small effect:	0.1
moderate effect	0.3
large effect:	0.5

and for effect size:

small effect:	0.2
moderate effect:	0.5
large effect:	0.8

Giaconia and Hedges (1987) explained the usefulness of these indices in estimating effect magnitudes in single studies, summarizing results, and resolving contradictory findings across studies. While it would appear that these approaches offer advantages not available in others, they are not without their critics. For example, Biddle and Anderson (1986) pointed to six potential problems in meta-analysis which they summarized as follows:

> Meta-analysis appears attractive if one is focused narrowly on findings and strength of evidence, if one assumes simple relationships among terms, concepts, and methods, if one is uninterested in deviant cases, if one is not particularly worried about theory, and—above all—if one wants to make simple knowledge claims from research. Once one begins to question these assumptions, meta-analysis becomes less appealing. (p. 236)

One of the most assiduous critics of meta-analysis is Slavin (1984) who wrote:

> Meta-analysis imparts, in my judgement, a certain patina of science that somehow makes many readers forget that the meta-analysis is no better than the studies that went into it, and focuses readers on a few unqualified main effects, when often the effects cannot really be understood without considering interactions and conditioning variables submerged in the meta-analytic procedure. (p. 12)

McGaw (1985) drew attention to the problem of the conceptual homogeneity of independent variables used in meta-analyses by observing that "blind aggregation of studies is certainly not justified in any review but it is appropriate to count 'apples' and 'oranges' together as long as the concern is with 'fruit'" (p. 3323). Giaconia and Hedges (1987) argued that many of the criticisms leveled at meta-analysis are equally applicable to other approaches.

2.5 Qualitative Research Syntheses

Miles and Huberman (1984) argued that qualitative researchers needed to develop shared, explicit methods for synthesizing findings. Walberg (1986) observed that some qualitative researchers attempted to generalize on the basis of multiple case studies but cited Green (1982) as the only researcher he knew who had proposed and used an explicit approach to the synthesis of case studies research on teaching. After a brief description of the approach, Walberg commented that Green reported "many insightful and useful observations that appear generalizable across a variety of contexts and investigations" (p. 216).

3. Syntheses of Research on Teaching

Concerted attempts to synthesize the findings of research on teaching using other than narrative approaches probably began with Rosenshine's (1971) work using a vote-counting approach. It was soon followed by other attempts and by the early 1990s dozens had been reported and several books had been published on methods of synthesizing research.

3.1 Comparisons of Different Approaches to Synthesis

One of the most interesting stories in the development of methods of synthesizing research on teaching concerns a body of research on the relationship between teacher indirectness and pupil achievement. Dunkin and Biddle (1974) used a combination of a narrative and a vote-counting procedure in their attempt to synthesize the findings of 29 studies reporting findings on this relationship. Twenty of those studies reported findings regarding linear relationships obtained in correlational field studies. Dunkin and Biddle found that the majority (15) of the 20 studies found no significant relationship, while 10 found a significant positive relationship (five of the studies found both, as a result of using two different measures of indirectness). Gage (1978) used a combined significance test procedure to synthesize the results of 19 of the above studies. He found that, across the studies, there was a statistically significant relationship ($p < 0.001$) between the two variables. Glass et al. (1977) conducted a meta-analysis with the same 19 studies and found that for Grades kindergarten to 6 the combined effect was small ($r = 0.16$) but that for Grades 7 to 12 the effect was moderate ($r = 0.30$). This story indicates that the procedures used to synthesize research findings influence the outcomes of that synthesis. To Giaconia and Hedges (1987) it seemed that Glass's meta-analysis was the most informative of the three approaches because it provided an index of the magnitude of the effect, as well as a finding relating the context of the studies to that effect.

A second application of alternative methods to the same body of research concerned the relationship between cognitive levels of teachers' questions and pupil achievement. First, Winne (1979) combined a narrative approach with a vote counting approach and applied them to 18 experiments. He found that 15 percent of the results were in favor of higher order questions, 25 percent favored fact questions, and 60 percent favored neither. Accordingly, Winne was unable to reach a "sturdy conclusion" about the relationship. Two years later Redfield and Rousseau (1981) reported the results of their meta-analysis of 13 of the original 18 studies and obtained an effect size of 0.73 indicating a moderate to large effect in favor of higher order questions.

A third example of the application of different methods in synthesizing research on teaching involved the effects of open classroom methods upon pupil learning. The syntheses were those by Horwitz (1979), Peterson (1979), and Hedges et al. (1981). Horwitz used vote-counting procedures to summarize the findings of approximately 200 studies, most of which compared open education programs with traditional education programs. He concluded that there were no significant differences between the two methods for academic achievement, self-concept, anxiety and adjustment, and locus of control outcomes, but that in relation to attitude to school, creativity, independence and conformity, curiosity, and cooperation, results favored open education methods.

Peterson (1979) conducted a meta-analysis of 45 of the studies analyzed by Horwitz. She did not include doctoral dissertations or studies that did not allow the calculation of effect sizes that were included in Horwitz's study. Peterson found that for most student outcomes effect sizes were so small as to indicate little or no advantage for either method. For mathematics, reading, and composite achievement they were in favor of traditional methods but were only about 0.1 in size. Similarly effect sizes approaching zero were found for locus of control and anxiety. A very slight advantage of open education methods in the form of effect sizes averaging between 0.1 and 0.2 was found for creativity, attitude to school, and curiosity. Larger effect sizes, averaging between 0.33 and 0.5, were found in favor of open education for independence and attitude to teacher.

Finally, Hedges et al. (1981) used methods of meta-analysis that were refinements of those used by Peterson (1979) and added about 90 doctoral dissertations to the latter's sample. For student adjustment, attitude to school, curiosity, and general mental ability, Hedges et al. found that average effect sizes were about 0.2 and were all in favor of open education. For cooperativeness, creativity, and independence, average effect sizes were between 0.25 and 0.33 and were also in favor of open education. For language, mathematics, and reading achievement, although results favored traditional education, average effect sizes were close to zero.

Giaconia (1987) summarized the results of these three attempts at synthesis as follows:

> First, in general, open education is somewhat more effective than traditional education for nonachievement measures. Traditional education is only slightly more effective than open education for the traditional academic achievement measures. For many student outcomes, there are near zero differences between open and traditional education. Second, these general conclusions . . . must be tempered by the fact that the variability of the effects of open education programs is often quite high. (p. 250)

3.2 Syntheses of Syntheses of Research on Teaching

Books by Brophy (1989, 1991) and by Waxman and Walberg (1991) contain numerous examples of syntheses of research on teaching. In addition, Ball (1991) synthesized research on teaching mathematics with a focus on teachers' subject-matter knowledge, while Smith and Neale (1991) reported on the accumulation of evidence about teachers' subject-matter knowledge in primary science teaching. Indeed, the stage has been reached at which the number of syntheses of initial research on teaching are so numerous that syntheses of those syntheses are becoming common. Giaconia's (1987) work is a good example and there are others. Possibly the most comprehensive is the work by Anderson and Burns (1989).

In the final chapter of their book, Anderson and Burns (1989) described their procedures for "reviewing the research reviews." Faced with the dramatic increase in the volume of research on teaching that had occurred during the 1970s and 1980s, Anderson and Burns decided that they would rely on the syntheses of the research that had been conducted in seven earlier works in order to produce generalizations about teachers, teaching, and instruction. As a result of their efforts, Anderson and Burns derived four generalizations about teachers, four about teaching, and five about instruction. Examples of the generalizations in each set are as follows:

> "There is no universal definition of an excellent, good, or effective teacher" (p. 343);
> "Teacher characteristics do not impact directly on student achievement" (p. 345);
> "Teachers progress through a fairly predictable set of qualitatively distinct stages as they move from novice to expert status" (p. 345);
> "Teachers assume a very central, directive, and active

role in their classrooms" (p. 346);
"Differences in individual teaching behaviors are not reliably associated with differences in student achievement" (p. 348);
"Considering teaching from a functional, rather than behavioral, point of view is more likely to result in a greater understanding of teaching in general and effective teaching in particular" (p. 350);
"The subject matter being taught impacts on some, if not all, of the other components of instruction" (p. 351);
"While lecture, recitation, and seatwork predominate in classrooms, there is little if any evidence that changes in format would result in higher levels of student achievement" (p. 352); and,
"Instructional time, content coverage, and pacing are associated with higher levels of student achievement" (p. 353).

4. Conclusion

It is possibly a matter of considerable disappointment that after many decades of research on teaching so few generalizations may be gleaned. Anderson and Burns (1989) described their list as "fairly conservative" (p. 354) and it is certain that others would not share their conservatism. Wang and Walberg (1991), for example, surveyed the opinions of over 1,000 educationists and arrived at a list of approximately 40 instructional and teaching variables that they considered to be "highly important," while Walberg (1986) described his "selective summary of a decade of educational research" as having arrived at "impressive" results (p. 224). It seems clear, on the basis of such disagreements among experts as to the generalizations that syntheses of research on teaching permit that the procedures employed in such syntheses and in syntheses of syntheses continue to deserve much attention from scholars.

See also: Teaching and Teacher Education: Comparative and International Studies; Teaching: Behavioral Theories; Teaching: Social Psychological Theories

References

Anderson L W, Burns R B 1989 *Research in Classrooms: The Study of Teachers, Teaching, and Instruction*. Pergamon Press, Oxford

Ball D L 1991 Research on teaching mathematics: Making subject-matter knowledge part of the equation. In: Brophy J (ed.) 1991

Biddle B J, Anderson D S 1986 Theory, methods, knowledge, and research on teaching. In: Wittrock M (ed.) 1986 *Handbook of Research on Teaching*, 3rd edn. Macmillan, New York

Brophy J 1989 *Advances in Research on Teaching: A Research Annual*, Vol. 1. JAI Press, Greenwich, Connecticut

Brophy J 1991 *Advances in Research on Teaching: A Research Annual*, Vol. 2. JAI Press, Greenwich, Connecticut

Cohen J 1969 *Statistical Power Analysis for the Behavioral Sciences*. Academic Press, New York

Dunkin M J, Biddle B J 1974 *The Study of Teaching*. Holt, Rinehart, and Winston, New York

Gage N L 1978 *The Scientific Basis of the Art of Teaching*. Teachers College Press, New York

Giaconia R M 1987 Open versus formal methods. In: Dunkin M (ed.) 1987 *The International Encyclopedia of Teaching and Teacher Education: Research and Studies*. Pergamon Press, Oxford

Giaconia R M, Hedges L V 1987 Synthesizing research evidence. In: Dunkin M (ed.) 1987 *The International Encyclopedia of Teaching and Teacher Education: Research and Studies*. Pergamon Press, Oxford

Glass G V 1976 Primary, secondary and meta-analysis of research. *Educ. Researcher* 5(10): 3–8

Glass G V et al.1977 Teacher "indirectness" and pupil achievement: An integration of findings. Unpublished manuscript, University of Colorado, Boulder, Colorado

Green J L 1982 *Research on Teaching as a Linguistic Process: The State of the Art*. University of Delaware, Newark, Delaware

Hedges L V, Giaconia R M, Gage N L 1981 *Meta-analysis of the Effects of Open and Traditional Instruction*. Final Report, Stanford Program on Teaching Effectiveness, Meta-analysis Project, Vol. 2, Stanford, California

Horwitz R A 1979 Psychological effects of the "open classroom." *Rev. Educ. Res.* 49(1): 71–86

Jackson G B 1980 Methods of integrative reviews. *Rev. Educ. Res.* 50(3): 438–60

Light R J, Smith P V 1971 Accumulating evidence: Procedures for resolving contradictions among different studies. *Harv. Educ. Rev.* 41(4): 429–72

McGaw B 1985 Meta-analysis. In: Husén T, Postlethwaite T N (eds.) 1985 *The International Encyclopedia of Education: Research and Studies*, 1st edn. Pergamon Press, Oxford

Miles M B, Huberman A M 1984 Drawing valid meaning from qualitative data: Toward a shared craft. *Educ. Researcher* 13(5): 20–30

Peterson P L 1979 Direct instruction reconsidered. In: Peterson P L, Walberg H J (eds.) 1979 *Research on Teaching: Concepts, Findings, and Implications*. McCutchan, Berkeley, California

Redfield D L, Rousseau E W 1981 A meta-analysis of experimental research on teacher questioning behavior. *Rev. Educ. Res.* 51(2): 237–45

Rosenshine B 1971 *Teaching Behaviors and Student Achievement*. National Foundation for Educational Research, Slough

Rosenthal R 1978 Combining results of independent studies. *Psych. Bull.* 85(1): 185–93

Slavin R E 1984 Meta-analysis in education: How has it been used? *Educ. Res.* 13(8): 6–15

Smith D C, Neale D C 1991 The construction of subject-matter knowledge in primary science teaching. In: Brophy J 1991

Walberg H J 1986 Syntheses of research on teaching. In: Wittrock M (ed.) 1986 *Handbook of Research on Teaching*, 3rd edn. Macmillan, New York

Wang M C, Walberg H J 1991 Teaching and educational effectiveness: Research synthesis and consensus from the field. In: Waxman H C, Walberg H J (eds.) 1991

Waxman H C, Walberg H J 1982 The relation of teaching and learning. *Contemp. Educ. Rev.* 20: 103–20

Waxman H C, Walberg H J (eds.) 1991 *Effective Teaching:*

Current Research. McCutchan Publishing, Berkeley, California

Winne P H 1979 Experiments relating teachers' use of higher cognitive questions to student achievement. *Rev. Educ. Res*. 49(1): 13–49

Further Reading

Cooper H 1982 Scientific guidelines for conducting integrative research reviews. *Rev. Educ. Res*. 52(2): 291–302

Cooper H 1984 *The Integrative Research Review: A Systematic Approach*. Sage Publications, Beverly Hills, California

Hedges L V, Olkin I O 1985 *Statistical Methods for Meta-analysis*. Academic Press, Orlando, Florida

Hunter J E, Schmidt F L 1989 *Methods of Meta-analysis: Correcting Error and Bias in Research Findings*. Sage Publications, Newbury Park, California

Light R J, Pillemer D B 1984 *Summing Up: The Science of Reviewing Research*. Harvard University Press, Cambridge, Massachusetts

M. J. Dunkin

Teaming Arrangements in Special Education

Teaming arrangements refer to various configurations of groups of educators engaged in group decision-making. The purpose of these arrangements is to offer and implement specific plans of action for improving educational programming for certain special education students and students who are at risk for school failure. Several different types of teaming arrangements will be described in this entry. Professional collaboration, which forms the underlying base for the various teaming arrangements, will also be discussed. The entry will also consider how certain teaming arrangements may be used to provide special education service delivery. Finally, an international perspective will be offered, describing a continuum of implementation in countries throughout the world that ranges from a complete lack of teaming arrangements to complete implementation.

1. The Team as an Instructional Alternative

School programs have been observed (West and Idol 1990) that use at least five different teaming arrangements: (a) teacher assistance teams, (b) intervention assistance teams, (c) school-based resource teams, (d) student support teams, and (e) child study teams.

1.1 Teacher Assistance Teams

Teacher assistance teams are problem-solving teams formed by representative classroom teachers who serve as advisors or facilitators for other teachers in the same school. The teacher assistance team model was originally developed by Chalfant et al. (1979), with follow-up data available on 96 teams (Chalfant and Pysh 1989). When first developed, teacher assistance teams were comprised solely of classroom teachers; later, within the context of collaborative problem-solving among classroom teachers and special education support staff, some school districts began to use teacher assistance teams which included additional support staff from the school. A practical example of how one school uses such teams, with annual, rotating membership across the faculty, can be found in Saver and Downes (1991).

1.2 Intervention Assistance Teams

Intervention assistance teams are formed as they are needed for particular problems. Each member has expertise in a particular type of teaching or child management strategy that is relevant to the problem that needs to be solved. Team members may come from either inside or outside an individual building. Intervention assistance teams are not permanent but are constructed on an as-needed basis and then disbanded. For example, an intervention assistance team might be formed to help a student who is in crisis due to personal problems, academic problems, and/or social problems. Such a team could be formed to integrate a certain student into a school program, withdrawing when the targeted problem is solved.

1.3 School-based Resource Teams

School-based resource teams are formed within a building and, like intervention assistance teams, are formed to solve a particular school-related problem. Any type of professional may serve on the team, including classroom teachers, administrators, and support staff. Again, these teams are formed on an as-needed basis, but all members of the team come from within the school.

1.4 Student Support Teams

Student support teams are formed specifically for an individual student, and team members are responsible for the educational program of that student. Such student support teams most often take the form of interdisciplinary teams of educators who are responsible for implementing the Individualized Education Program (IEP) for a special education student.

1.5 Child Study Teams

As with student support teams, child study teams are formed specifically for an individual student. The sole purpose of the child study team is to study the student and the existing problems. Child study teams are often used as placement and review teams in special education. The primary function of child study teams is the assessment of child-related problems. The data gathered by the child study team often form the basis for a special education placement decision.

Each of the above five teaming arrangements

involves educators working together, and making joint decisions about the educational needs of students eligible for special education or at risk for school failure. There are several different types of special education service delivery that require professional teaming. These types are described below.

2. *Teaming Alternatives for Special Education Service Delivery*

Certain types of special education service delivery which can be offered to eligible special education students require some type of teaming arrangement. Decisions about which to use must be made on an individual student basis, and must meet the requirements for the local school division, the state, and, in some countries, the national government. Of course, such services can only be offered if the particular type of service delivery is available and approved by the governing educational agency. In the United States, Australia, and Canada, the state (or province) board of education is the governing agency.

These types of service delivery have been described in the special education literature. For example, Reynolds's (1962) framework shows 10 levels of special education service delivery. Within Reynolds's framework, there are several types of service delivery that require a teaming arrangement: (a) regular education placement plus resource room service, (b) regular classroom with supplementary teaching or treatment, (c) regular classroom with consultation, and (d) most problems handled in the regular classroom.

These types of service delivery are listed in hierarchical order, from most to least restrictive. All four are for students who either spend most of the school day in the general education classroom—option (a); or are educated solely in the general education classroom—options (b), (c), (d).

2.1 Regular Classroom plus Resource Room Service

In the first option, the classroom teacher and the resource room teacher should team up, although in many cases such resource programs have been poorly operationalized. Far too often, little if any coordination and collaboration are required among the professionals involved, resulting in programs that are not well-coordinated. The resource program of instruction is often separate and not supportive of the general education program. Preferred program coordination should involve mutual program planning and evaluation, with careful attention given to determining how to interface the content of the resource program with that of the general education program. If other support personnel are partially responsible for a student's resource program, they too should be members of this instructional team.

2.2 Regular Classroom with Supplementary Teaching or Treatment

In the second option, special education service is provided to the identified student in the general classroom, with special education staff providing supplementary teaching or treatment. This option has been described in the literature as cooperative teaching (Bauwens et al. 1989). With cooperative teaching, the classroom teacher and the special education teacher work together to plan and evaluate instruction. The certified special education teacher provides the specialized teaching or treatment. A constraint on this type of programming is that the special educator can only work in one classroom at a time, resulting in inadequate and poorly balanced service delivery across the various levels and types of classrooms in a school.

2.3 Regular Classroom with Consultation

In the third option, the special education student is taught in the general classroom by the classroom teacher. The special education teacher serves as a consultant to the classroom teacher, providing an indirect form of special education service delivery. Idol (1989) defined *indirect* special education service delivery as consultative service provided to the classroom teacher by certified special education staff. Special education students receiving the indirect services are taught by the classroom teacher. The consultant works indirectly with the targeted students by working directly with the classroom teacher. Within this context, the Collaborative Consultation Model (Idol et al. 1986) was developed for special education service delivery.

2.4 Problems Handled in the Regular Classroom

In the fourth option, all planning and instruction is provided by the classroom teacher. In most schools, this fourth option is not considered a form of special education service delivery. For students at this level, special education services are no longer needed or provided. However, in many schools some type of alternative teaming arrangement is provided to the classroom teacher at this level, outside the realm of special education, as a means of preventing a first or repeated referral to special education. Thus, the teaming arrangement is used to prevent referral to special services, and is a resource for classroom teachers for exploring alternative means of teaching and managing students who are difficult to teach.

A second type of teaming arrangement in this category is the Adaptive Learning Environments Model (ALEM), an alternative service delivery approach for serving students with special needs in general classrooms (Wang and Zollers 1990). Within this model, classroom teachers and specialized professionals work collaboratively to provide coordinated and inclusive instructional support in an integrated education system.

3. Collaborative Consultation as a Base for Teaming Arrangements

Regardless of the type of instructional arrangement, collaborative consultation may appropriately be incorporated as a problem-solving process among the professionals on the team (West and Idol 1990). Collaborative consultation is:

> an interactive process which enables people with diverse expertise to generate creative solutions to mutually defined problems. The outcome is enhanced, altered, and different from the original solutions that any team member would produce independently. The major outcome of collaborative consultation is to provide comprehensive and effective programs for students with special needs within the most appropriate context, thereby enabling them to achieve maximum constructive interactions with their nonhandicapped peers. (Idol et al. 1986 p. 1)

The three major purposes of collaborative consultation are: (a) to prevent behavioral and learning problems, (b) to remediate behavioral and learning problems, and (c) to coordinate instructional programs (West et al. 1988). Thus, any of the various teaming arrangements described in this entry may be structured so that the collaborative consultation process, group decision-making, and interactive and process skills are used by the team members; the result can be the development of a collaborative school (Idol and West 1991).

3.1 Staff Development

This kind of collaborative teaming can be especially effective when the team, as well as the entire school staff of potential referring teachers, is trained to use a systematic problem-solving process, such as that discussed in West et al. (1988). This preservice or inservice staff development curriculum provides professional opportunities for training in the 47 different skills that a national panel of experts agreed are essential to a collaborative consultation process (West and Cannon 1988).

3.2 Collaboration and Teaming

To elaborate further on the relationship between collaboration and teaming, Thousand and Villa (1992) described five basic purposes for which effective collaborative teams should strive:

(a) coordinating work to achieve at least one common, publicly agreed-upon goal;

(b) holding a belief system that all members of the team have unique and needed expertise;

(c) demonstrating parity—the equal valuation of each member's input—by alternatively engaging in the dual roles of teacher and learner, expert and recipient, consultant and consultee;

(d) using a distributed-functions theory of leadership, in which the task and relationship functions of the traditional lone leader are distributed among all members of the group;

(e) employing a collaborative teaming process that involves face-to-face interactions, positive interdependence, monitoring and processing of interpersonal skills, and individual accountability.

4. An International Perspective on Teaming Arrangements and Related Issues

Until the 1990s, advancements toward using teaming arrangements for special education service delivery progressed more rapidly in the United States, Canada, and Italy than in other countries. This trend is primarily due to special education services being perceived in these countries as a service that can be provided within the context of general education instruction.

For example, Italy is recognized as having the most complete school integration in all of Europe (Commission des Communautés Européennes 1980), with approximately 90 percent of all children with disabilities educated in general education classes (Ferro 1990). Class size is reduced to 20 when a child with disabilities is assigned, and support teachers and teacher assistants provide extra assistance. In both the United States and Canada, the programs vary tremendously among the various states and provinces, as well as among the various school districts and schools divisions within the states and provinces. In some of these places, all possible teaming arrangements have been implemented; in others, only certain arrangements are used.

Some other countries have made tremendous progress in developing programs that promote inclusion of students with handicapping conditions in the general education program. In Sweden, 90 percent of all children with disabilities attend their local community schools (Diniz and Kropveld 1983, Gartner et al. 1991), but 85 percent of students with moderate to severe mental retardation and 64 percent of students with multiple handicaps are assigned to self-contained classes, rather than integrated full-time into general education (Grunewald 1986). In Norway (since 1986) all children are assigned to the general elementary school, including those with severe disabilities (Krane 1990). Iceland has passed legislation with a similar intent (Bjarnasson 1990).

In England and France, laws provide support for school integration at an ideological level (Centre for Educational Research and Innovation 1981). In these two countries, as well as in the United States, parents may refer to legislation if they wish to appeal a segregated special education placement.

In many countries, provision of special education services has been somewhat limited and slower to develop. South Korea is a good example of this level of development; special education services there are provided mainly in special schools offering residential or day programs and in self-contained special classes. There are few, if any, teacher-consultants, itinerant teachers, or resource teachers (Seo et al. 1992). Another example is Czechoslovakia, where schools and institutions have specific orientations for students with any of the following difficulties: mental retardation, hearing defects, sight deficiencies, speech disabilities, physical handicaps, sickness and weakness, multiple handicaps, and maladjusted behavior. "This system essentially segregates students with disabilities from other students" (Nevin et al. 1992 p. 3).

A different type of example is Australia, where only 2 to 3 percent of the school population is educated in special education programs. Only students with more severe handicapping conditions are served in special education programs, thus limiting specialized service delivery for those students who might qualify for special education if they lived in the United States or Canada. Even so, a pilot project in Sydney, Australia, is utilizing collaborative consultation and various teaming arrangements for special education students and students at risk for school failure. Other regions of Australia and New Zealand are beginning to explore using collaborative teaming in schools.

4.1 Related Legislative, Social, and Educational Developments

Although use of the various teaming arrangements is just beginning to emerge internationally (as described above), there are other developments, related to legislative, social, and educational issues, which have occurred in many countries and which undoubtedly form the basis for future teaming arrangements in schools worldwide.

Since the 1970s most European countries have made significant advances in developing policies aimed at bringing persons with disabilities into the social mainstream (Murray-Seegert 1992). Such advances are consistent with efforts by the European Community to "combat inequality between its citizens" (Commission of the European Communities 1980 p. 3). These policies were designed to make schools more comprehensive, to abolish labels and categories that promote reliance on separatist service systems, and to recognize the important social and personal development—both for individuals with disabilities and those without—that results from positive sustained contact in integrated settings (Centre for Educational Research and Innovation 1981).

The Scandinavian countries have been international leaders in developing social supports for families (e.g., financial subsidies independent of family income, respite care), helping families to keep children with special needs at home. In 1959 Denmark pioneered the principle of "normalization," incorporating it into a federal act which regulates residential services for persons with handicapping conditions (Scheerenberger 1987). Sweden (in 1986) and Norway (in 1990) have since enacted laws designed to help persons with mental retardation by closing all residential institutions and special hospitals and replacing them with small group homes (fewer than 6 residents) or foster care (Grunewald 1986, Jörgenson 1990). The United Kingdom has also been closing its long-stay mental handicap hospitals, instead combining government and private funds to support increasing numbers of persons with disabilities in private homes (Gartner et al. 1992). In both the United States and Europe, families have been prominent in efforts to create small, more normalized alternatives to large-scale facilities for persons with more severe handicapping conditions (Turnbull et al. 1989).

Concepts described in the United States as the "Complete School" (Biklen 1985), the "Comprehensive Local School," or "Quality Education for All" have long been employed in German model classes (Murray-Seegert 1992). Data from 20 years of research have established the effectiveness of the integrated special education model developed in German schools (Bundesminsisterium für Bildung und Wissenschaft 1982, Preuss-Lausitz 1988). But in general, school integration in Germany is said to be about 20 years behind that in the United States, Italy, and the Scandinavian countries (Feuser 1992, Murray-Seegert 1992, Roebke 1992). This is generally true for most of the more developed countries.

5. Conclusion

Teaming arrangements, used to improve educational programs for special education students and students at risk for school failure, occur as five basic configurations of groups: teacher assistance teams, intervention assistance teams, school-based resource teams, student support teams, and child-study teams. There are also four identified types of special education service delivery (Reynolds 1962) that specifically utilize teaming arrangements. These focus on educating special education students in the general classroom for most or all of the school day. All types of teaming arrangements can be facilitated when members of the teams are trained in collaborative group decision-making, systematic problem-solving, and effective communication and interaction skills. Educators in some countries are exploring how best to use the various teaming arrangements within a collaborative context. In other countries, the initial groundwork for legislative, social, and educational efforts has been laid; in many countries, however, the use of teaming arrangements as a means of educating students with special needs in general education has not yet been explored.

See also: Cooperative Learning; Group Processes in the Classroom; Group Learning

References

Bauwens J, Hourcade J J, Friend M 1989 Cooperative teaching: A model for general and special education integration. *Rem. Spec. Educ.* 10(2): 17–22

Biklen D 1985 *Achieving the Complete School: Effective Strategies for Mainstreaming*. Teacher's College Press, New York

Bjarnasson D 1990 A report on the first formal experiment in integration of a severely disabled child into regular school in Iceland. Paper presented to the International Conference on Integration in School, Leisure, and Transition to Work, Institute for Integration, Stockholm

Bundesminsisterium für Bildung und Wissenschaft 1982 Modellversuche BLK Behinderung: Gemeinsame [sic] Forderung behinderter und nicht-behinderter Kinder und Jugendlicher in Schule und Kindergarten. (Unpublished computerized list of federally subsidized projects, National Ministry of Science and Education, Bonn)

Centre for Educational Research and Innovation 1981 *The Education of the Handicapped Adolescent: Integration in the School*. OECD, Paris

Chalfant J C, Pysh M V 1989 Teacher assistance teams: Five descriptive studies on 96 teams. *Rem. Spec. Educ.* 10(6): 49–58

Chalfant J C, Pysh M V, Moultrie R 1979 Teacher assistance teams: A model for within-building problem solving. *Learning Disability Quarterly* 2(3): 85–95

Commission des communautés Européennes 1980 *Special Education in the European Community*. Office of Publications of the EEC, Luxembourg

Commission of the European Communities 1980 *The European Community and the Handicapped: European File*. Directorate-General for Information, Brussels.

Diniz F, Kropveld P (eds.) 1983 *Teacher Training and Special Education in the Eighties*. Association for Teacher Education in Europe, Brussels

Ferro N 1990 Trends in philosophy and practice. Paper presented to the International Conference on Integration in School, Leisure, and Transition to Work, Institute for Integration, Stockholm

Feuser G 1992 First and second invited reactions to the Murray-Seegert paper. *Spec. Educ.* 13(1): 45–46

Gartner A, Kerzner-Lipsky D, Turnbull A 1990 *Supporting Families with a Child with a Disability: An International Outlook*. Brookes, London

Grunewald K 1986 *The Intellectually Handicapped in Sweden—New Legislation in a Bid for Normalisation*. Svenska Institutet, Stockholm

Idol L 1989 The resource/consulting teacher: An integrated model of service delivery. *Rem. Spec. Educ.* 10(6): 38–48

Idol L, Paolucci-Whitcomb P, Nevin A 1993 *Collaborative Consultation*, 2nd edn. PRO-ED, Austin, Texas

Idol L, West J F 1991 Educational collaboration: A catalyst for effective schooling. *Intervention in School and Clinic* 27(2): 70–78

Jörgenson T O 1990 Learning for integration. Paper presented to the International Conference on Integration in School, Leisure, and Transition to Work, Institute for Integration, Stockholm.

Krane J 1990 Gerechtigkeit und Gleichbehandlung: Zum Stand der "Integration" in Norwegen und den USA. *Gemeinsam Leben* 8: 21–25

Murray-Seegert C 1992 Integration in Germany: Mainstreaming or swimming upstream? *Rem. Spec. Educ.* 13(1): 34–43

Nevin A, McNeil M, Thousand J 1992 Impressions of the Czechoslovakian educational system: Before and after the Velvet Revolution. *Teach. Educ. Spec. Educ.* 15(3): 1–7

Preuss-Lausitz U 1988 Nichtaussondernde Schule—Ein Konzept für die Zukunft. In: Rosenberger M (ed.) 1988 *Ratgeber gegen Aussonderung*. Edition Schindele, Heidelberg

Reynolds M 1962 A framework for considering some issues in special education. *Excep. Child.* 28(7): 368

Roebke C 1992 A response to Murray-Seegert. *Rem. Spec. Educ.* 13(1): 44–45

Saver K, Downes B 1991 PIT (Peer Intervention Team): A model for teacher collaboration in an elementary school. *Intervention in School and Clinic* 27(2): 116–22

Scheerenberger R C 1987 *A History of Mental Retardation: A Quarter Century of Progress*. Brookes, Baltimore, Maryland

Seo G-H, Oakland T, Han H-S, Hu S 1992 Special education in South Korea. *Excep. Child.* 58(3): 213–18

Thousand J, Villa R 1992 Collaborative teams: A powerful tool in school restructuring. In: Villa R, Thousand J, Stainback W, Stainback S (eds.) 1992 *Restructuring for a Caring and Effective Education*. Brookes, Baltimore, Maryland

Turnbull H, Turnbull A, Bronicki G, Summers J A, Roder-Gordon C 1989 *Disability and the Family: A Guide to Decisions for Adulthood*. Brookes, Baltimore, Maryland

Wang M C, Zollers N J 1990 Adaptive instruction: An alternative service delivery approach. *Rem. Spec. Educ.* 11(1): 7–21

West J F, Cannon G 1988 Essential collaborative consultation competencies for regular and special educators. *J. Learn. Disabil.* 21(1): 56–63

West J F, Idol L 1990 Collaborative consultation in the education of mildly handicapped and at-risk students. *Rem. Spec. Educ.* 11(1): 22–31

West J F, Idol L, Cannon G 1988 *Collaboration in the Schools: Communicating, Interactive, and Problem Solving. An Inservice and Preservice Curriculum for Teachers, Support Staff, and Administrators*. PRO-ED, Austin, Texas

Further Reading

Idol L 1990 The scientific art of classroom consultation. *Journal of Educational and Psychological Consultation* 1(1): 3–22

Idol L 1992 *Special Educators' Consultation Handbook*, 2nd edn. PRO-ED, Austin, Texas

Reynolds M C, Wang M C, Walberg H J 1987 The necessary restructuring of special and regular education. *Excep. Child.* 53(5): 391–98

Scott J J, Smith S L 1987 *From Isolation to Collaboration: Improving the Work Environment of Teaching*. North Central Regional Education Laboratory, Elmhurst, Illinois

Smith S C, Scott J J 1990 *The Collaborative School: A Work Environment for Effective Instruction*. ERIC Clearinghouse on Educational Management, University of Oregon, Eugene, Oregon

L. Idol